UKRAINE: A HISTORY

Other books by the author

Domination of Eastern Europe

The Mazepists: Ukrainian Separatism in the 18th Century

The Letters of Ivan Mazepa

Habsburgs and Zaporozhian Cossacks (with L. Wynar)

Orest Subtelny

UKRAINE

A HISTORY

Published by the University of Toronto Press

in association with the

Canadian Institute of Ukrainian Studies

Toronto Buffalo London

© University of Toronto Press 1988
Toronto Buffalo London
Printed in Canada
Reprinted in cloth and paper, 1989

ISBN 0-8020-5809-6 cl
    0-8020-6775-1 pb

Printed on acid-free paper

Canadian Cataloguing in Publication Data

Subtelney, Orest
    Ukraine : a history

    Bibliography: p.
    Includes index.
    ISBN 0-8020-5808-6

    1. Ukraine–History
    I. Canadian Institute of Ukrainian Studies
    II. Title

    DK508.51.S82 1988   947'.71   C88-095064-1

Publication of this book was aided
by the generous support of the
Cosbild Publication Endowment Fund
in commemoration of the Millennium of
Christianity in Ukraine.

To those who had to leave their homeland
but never forgot it

Contents

Part Four   Ukraine under Imperial Rule

Part Five   Twentieth-Century Ukraine

Illustrations follow pages 65, 198, 335, 452, and 572.

Maps

Introduction: The Earliest Times

Part Five Twentieth-Century Ukraine

Preface

Ukraine is the second-largest land in Europe. Its population is close to that of France and its GNP is comparable to Italy's. Yet the political prerogatives of the Ukrainians as a nation – not only in Europe but even in their own well-endowed and highly developed land – are minimal. Today the source of ultimate decision-making power over all aspects of Ukrainians' lives is located, as it has been for centuries, beyond the borders of their country. At a time when even the most impoverished and underdeveloped states in the third world enjoy full sovereignty, Ukraine has practically none. This great discrepancy is a historical puzzle, one that calls for an examination of the often overlooked and even more frequently misunderstood past of Ukraine and the Ukrainians.

In dealing with Ukrainian history, I stress two themes. One of them is statelessness. In most national histories the acquisition and development of the nation-state is a paramount feature, but in the Ukrainian case the opposite is true. The frustration of the Ukrainians' attempts to attain self-government is one of the key aspects of their historical experience. Therefore, the Ukrainian past is largely the history of a nation that has had to survive and evolve without the framework of a full-fledged national state.

Modernization is the other major theme of this work. The transformation of traditional agrarian societies into modern industrial and postindustrial ones is, of course, a global phenomenon. But in this general process there is a multiplicity of national/regional forms and variations. Modernization in Ukraine is striking in several ways. Once a quintessentially agrarian society, Ukraine became an industrialized country in an unusually rapid and traumatic fashion. Even more noteworthy is that modernization in Ukraine occurred largely under the aegis of non-Ukrainians. Thus, to this day a crucial dichotomy still exists between things Ukrainian and modern.

Clearly there is much more to Ukrainian history than can be subsumed under these two major themes. Indeed, there are times and events that stand in contradiction to them. For example, in medieval Kievan Rus', Ukraine formed the core of an impressive political, cultural, and economic conglomerate. In the 17th century the Cossacks were singularly successful in expelling foreign domination from the land. And in the late 17th and early 18th centuries the Ukrainians were the representives of modernity for the Russians, not vice versa, as was the case later. The early 20th century witnessed determined efforts on the part of Ukrainians to gain control of their own political and socioeconomic fate. The two themes of statelessness and modernization also cannot encompass the ancient and eventful past of a land that bears some of the oldest traces of human life in Europe, that was part of the classic Mediterranean civilizations, that attracted countless waves of nomadic invaders from Asia, that served as the cultural border between the East and West, and that witnessed the colonization of a vast frontier. Nonetheless, the condition of statelessness and the non-native predominance in modernization are important focal points and they help to illuminate the unusually broad, colorful, and complex canvas that is the history of Ukraine.

I was most fortunate in studying Ukrainian history, a field in which, until lately, good training has not been readily available. At various stages during these studies my mentors were three outstanding historians of Ukraine – the late Ivan Lysiak Rudnytsky, Oleksander Ohloblyn, and Omeljan Pritsak. To them I owe a great debt of gratitude, a modest expression of which is, I hope, the appearance of this book.

Colleagues in the field have helped me greatly in the preparation of the manuscript. For careful readings of and judicious comments on various chapters I thank Marko Antonovych, Yaroslav Bilinsky, Yuri Boshyk, John-Paul Himka, Wsevolod Isajiw, Miroslav Labunka, George Luckyj, and especially Danylo Husar-Struk. The maps were prepared by Carolyn Gondor, Carol Randall and Janet Allin of the York University Cartographic Office, and Vladimira Luczkiw, Andrew Gregorovich, Iosyp Terelia, Taras and Oksana Zakydalsky, and Daria Darevych furnished some of the illustrations. Various institutions provided financial support for this project. They include the Multiculturalism Directorate of the Secretary of State, York University, the Canadian Institute of Ukrainian Studies, and the Shevchenko Scientific Society in the United States. Special thanks are also due to the editorial staff of the University of Toronto Press. Ron Schoeffel greatly expedited the publication of the book and Lydia Burton and Lorraine Ourom, the copy editors, were models of efficiency and expertise with whom it was a pleasure to work. Finally, I owe the sincerest appreciation to my wife, Maria, whose patience, knowledge, and counsel was for me a great support.

Orest Subtelny
Toronto, July 1988

UKRAINE: A HISTORY

Introduction

The Earliest Times

Ukraine means borderland. It is an appropriate name for a land that lies on the southeastern edge of Europe, on the threshold of Asia, along the fringes of the Mediterranean world, and astride the once important border between sheltering forests and the open steppe. Another crucial geographical feature of the land is its lack of natural borders. Except for the Carpathian Mountains in the west and the small Crimean range in the south, 95% of Ukraine's territory is a plain that gradually slopes from the elevated, wooded plateau of Galicia, Volhynia, and Podilia in the northwest down to the gently rolling forested plains on both sides of the Dnieper River and finally to the huge, flat, open steppe that stretches along the Black Sea coast in the south. Indeed, vast plains dominate the Ukrainian landscape to such an extent that a geographer in the early part of this century wrote that "nine-tenths of Ukrainians have certainly never seen a mountain and do not even know what one looks like."[1] In these rolling plains and steppes Ukraine's famous and remarkably fertile black soil (chernozem) regions are found. They encompass about two-thirds of Ukraine's territory. However, the black soil does not extend to the northern and northwestern parts of the country, where forests (which cover only about one-seventh of the country's territory) and less fertile land predominate. Ukraine is rich in mineral deposits, notably coal and iron ore, which are located in the southeast. On the whole, nature has served the land well. One may even argue that in terms of natural resources it is the richest country in Europe.

Flowing southward into the Black Sea are three major river systems that provide Ukraine with an adequate water supply: the mighty 2285-km-long Dnieper (Dnipro in Ukrainian), which bisects the land, the southern Buh, and the Dnister. The climate, although capable of temperature extremes, is generally moderate. Within its present boundaries, Ukraine encompasses about 600,000 sq. km and extends approximately 1300 km from west to east and 900 km from north to south. After Russia, it is the second-largest country in Eu-

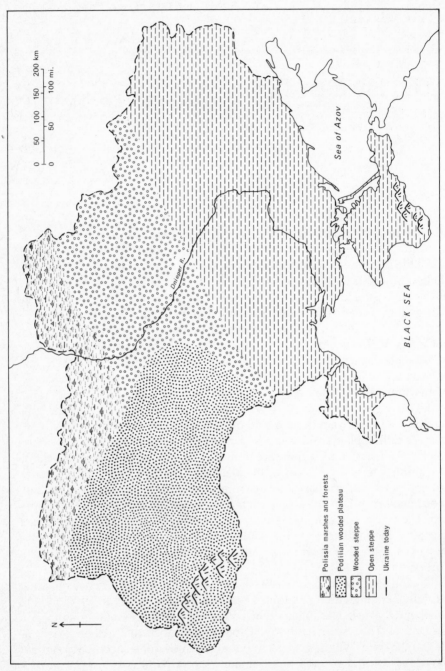

Map 1 Geographic zones

Polissia marshes and forests
Podilian wooded plateau
Wooded steppe
Open steppe
Ukraine today

Dnieper R.

Sea of Azov

BLACK SEA

0   50   100 150 200 km
0   50   100 mi.

N

rope in terms of area. And its current population of about 50 million is close to that of France.

Because science and technology have greatly reduced the dependence of modern people on nature, they often forget the tremendous impact that the physical environment exerted on their ancestors. In Ukraine this fading awareness is doubly suprising because the very name of the land emphasizes the importance of geography. And much of Ukraine's history is a function of its location. Lying astride the main routes between Europe and Asia, Ukraine was repeatedly exposed to various frequently competing cultures. By means of the Black Sea, Ukraine gained access to the invigorating civilization of Greece, both ancient and Byzantine. In contrast, its position on the western fringe of the great Eurasian steppe exposed it to repeated invasions by warring nomads and the bitter struggle against them sapped the country's human and material resources. It also gave rise to the Cossacks, the frontier warriors who became archetypical figures in Ukrainian history and culture.

The vast stretches of chernozem, which are among the largest and most fertile in the world, also had a decisive impact on this region's inhabitants. It was in Ukraine that the earliest agrarian civilizations in Europe developed. And, until very recently, agriculture has been the hallmark of Ukrainian life. The effect that Ukraine's fertile soil has had on its inhabitants is especially striking when compared to the impact of poor soil on the peasants of neighboring Russia. In the Russian north, the barren, sandy soil, the harsh climate, and the shorter growing season – by at least a month compared to Ukraine – forced Russian peasants to pool their resources and to work the land communally. In Ukraine, however, individual farming was much more widespread. Such divergences helped to create important distinctions between the mentalities, cultures, and socioeconomic organization of these two related peoples. These differences became even more profound when, in time, poor agricultural yields forced Russian peasants to seek more promising living conditions in the cities where they were exposed to modernizing influences, while Ukrainian peasants remained in their bucolic but traditionalist villages.

If nature has been generous to Ukraine, history has not. Because of its natural riches and accessibility from ancient past to most recent times, Ukraine, perhaps more than any other country in Europe, has experienced devastating foreign invasions and conquests. Consequently, foreign domination and the struggle against it is a paramount theme in its history. Played out on a vast, open, and richly endowed stage, this history is long, colorful, and unusually turbulent.

ஐ

The Earliest Inhabitants

The earliest traces of human habitation in Ukraine reach back about 150,000 years. Arriving on the shores of the Black Sea by way of the Caucasus and, perhaps, the Balkans, the earliest human inhabitants still possessed the signs of their primitive origins. Their brains were small and they had low foreheads, heavy jaws, and large teeth. But their posture was already upright and their extraordinarily manipulative hands were fully formed. By approximately 40,000 BC, in the midst of the last ice age, the Cro-magnons (or *Homo sapiens*) appeared, the species from which modern man is descended – relatively tall, erect, and with greatly enlarged brain capacity. In response to the cold, unforgiving climate and the difficulties in obtaining food, these hunters and gatherers produced an unprecedented array of technological innovations: flint weapons and tools, fish-hooks, harpoons, and shelters made of animal hides and bones.

After the last of the ice glaciers had retreated by about 10,000 BC and had left behind the landscape that exists in Ukraine today, the tempo of man-made changes began to quicken. Indeed, during the Neolithic period, which lasted in Ukraine from about 6000 to 2000 BC, mankind experienced more profound changes than in the previous two to three million years. Despite its name, the Neolithic, or New Stone Age, had little to do with stone. It is in the radically new ways that humans developed for feeding themselves that the "revolutionary" significance of this age lies. Instead of merely gathering and hunting food, human beings had finally learned to produce it.

In Ukraine, agriculture is thought to have first made its appearance in the southwest, between the Buh and Dnister rivers where the earliest agricultural communities in Eastern Europe evolved about 5000 to 4000 BC. Instead of wandering about in search of game, people settled down in order to be near their fields. Villages came into existence. Because agriculture, unlike hunting and gathering, demanded a relatively large labor force, the population increased rapidly. As it did, primitive forms of political and social organization slowly developed.

The best known of the early agrarian peoples on the territory of present-day Ukraine were associated with the so-called Trypillian culture, which originated along the Dnister, Buh, and Prut rivers and later expanded to the Dnieper.[2] At their high point between 3500 and 2700 BC, they lived in large villages with as many as 600–700 inhabitants. Organized in clans along patriarchal lines, they often lived in long, narrow dwellings in which each nuclear family had its own clay oven and partitioned space. The decorations on their pottery, characterized by flowing designs of ocher, black, and white, reflected a culture rich in magical rituals and supernatural beliefs.

But this culture also had its practical side. The first mechanical device in Ukraine – a drill for boring holes in wood and stone – appeared among the people of the Trypillian culture. Even more important was the introduction of the wooden plow, which definitely made agriculture a more dependable

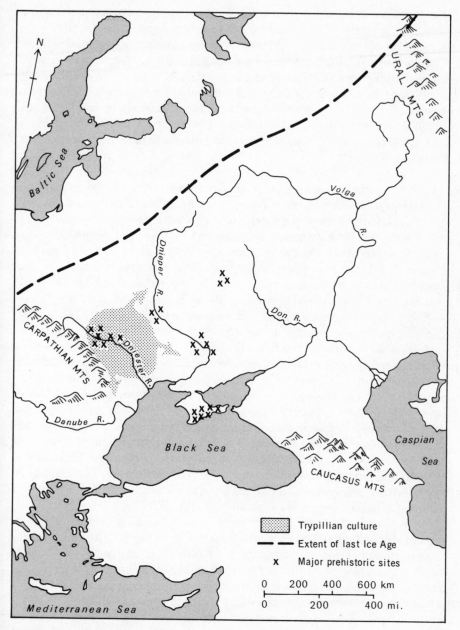

Map 2 Prehistoric cultures and sites

means of obtaining food than hunting. Another innovation, probably imported from Asia, was the use of the first metal – copper.

Little is known about the decline of Trypillian culture. Archaeologists speculate that overpopulation forced many of its people to resettle in new, inhospitable lands. Some of them moved deeper into the steppe, while those who lived along the Dnieper moved northward into heavily forested Polissia and beyond. By 2000 BC, the people of the Trypillian culture had ceased to exist as a distinct cultural entity. Warlike tribes from the steppe probably overwhelmed or assimilated many of them. Others may have taken refuge in the sheltering forests in the north.

The nomads   Stretching from Manchuria to Hungary, the vast Eurasian steppe is the largest expanse of flatland on earth. Although the Tien Shan, the Ural, and the Carpathian mountains intersect it at several points, numerous passes allow for relatively easy access from one end of this approximately 6000-km expanse to the other. On the western edge of this plain, in one of its most temperate and fertile regions, lies Ukraine. This geographic fact has been of inestimable importance for its history because it meant that Ukraine would become a part, and even at times a center, of Eurasian nomadic life.

A distinctive pastoral way of life, based on the maintenance of herds of domesticated animals, emerged in the steppes in about 3000 BC. For roughly two millennia, while raising their herds in the Eurasian steppe, the nomads-to-be also engaged in agriculture and were semisedentary. Sometime around 1000 BC the pastoralists became true nomads and began to roam the steppe in a systematic search for pasture. In the course of this transition, the nomads developed several characteristic features. Most noteworthy was their propensity for warfare. In order to protect their herds and obtain new pastures, fighting skills became an essential requirement of their life-style. Frequent conflicts as well as the need to organize the efficient movement of many people over vast distances encouraged the development of tribal aristocracies. This meant that the relatively peaceful, self-sufficient agriculturalists would be increasingly vulnerable to these aggressive, warlike inhabitants of the steppe.

Pastoralists appeared relatively early in the Ukrainian steppes. The people of the so-called Seredost culture moved in from the east, driving herds of horses (but not yet riding them), in about 3000 BC and occupied the left bank of the Dnieper. They were followed by waves of other pastoralists for many centuries to come. These recurrent migrations, a familiar feature of early Ukrainian history, were apparently caused by overpopulation in the steppes north of the Caspian Sea. As the strongest tribes ejected weaker ones from their pastures, the latter were pushed to the periphery of the Eurasian steppes and beyond. Thus, in a domino effect, waves of pastoralists were sent westward.

The Cimmerians   It was only in about 1500 to 1000 BC that the seemingly simple technique of horseback riding was mastered. And the first nomad horsemen to appear in Ukraine – the Cimmerians – were also its first inhabitants whose name we know. It was Homer who, in the *Odyssey*, mentioned "the land of the Cimmerians" in a passage referring to the northern shore of the Black Sea. This was probably the first literary reference to Ukraine. But, besides noting the name of the people who lived on what was at that time regarded as the murky edge of the world, Homer tells us no more about the Cimmerians. Many scholars hold the view that in about 1500 BC the Cimmerians came to Ukraine from their original homeland on the lower Volga by way of the Caucasian lowlands. Others, however, reject this "migration" theory and argue that the Cimmerians were native to Ukraine. In any case, up to about 700 BC, the Cimmerians inhabited the land between the Don and Dnister rivers. Soon afterward, under pressure from other nomads from the east, the Cimmerians withdrew to Asia Minor.

Exhaustive analysis of the few available sources has led historians to the following conclusions about these "drinkers of mare's milk," as the Greeks called them: (1) the Cimmerians were the first pastoralists in Ukraine to make the transition to the nomadic way of life; (2) they mastered the skill of horseback riding and employed it in warfare; (3) because of their contacts with the skilled metal workers of the Caucasus, the Cimmerians introduced the Iron Age to Ukraine and; (4) the growing importance of mounted warriors led to social changes such as the breakdown of extended family units and the evolution of a military aristocracy.

The Scythians In the early 7th century BC, when the Scythians appeared in the Ukrainian steppe, the more sophisticated societies around the Mediterranean took notice, as these words from the Old Testament attest: "Behold! A people comes from the north. They carry bows and short spears. They are most cruel and merciless. Their voices roar like the sea, they prance about on their horses, moving in unison like one man. They are an ancient people, coming from afar and no one knows their language. Their people devour your crops and bread; they destroy your sons and daughters; and they consume your sheep and cows, your grapes and vineyards. And the cities on which you base your hopes, they destroy with the sword."[3] After ravaging much of the Near East, the Scythians finally settled in the steppes north of the Black Sea where they established the first major political organization based on the territory of Ukraine.

In the 5th century BC, Herodotus, the Greek "father of history," visited Scythia and described its inhabitants. Apparently, they were Indo-Europeans, part of the Iranian-speaking nomads that had dominated the Eurasian steppes for millennia. Herodotus described several types of Scythians. On the right bank of the Dnieper lived the Scythian plowers, an agricultural people who were the aboriginal inhabitants of the land but who probably accepted the

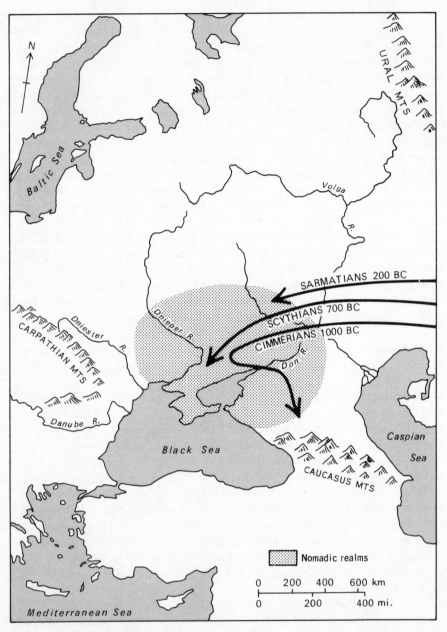

Map 3 Nomadic migrations

name of their nomadic overlords. Some scholars believe that these people were the ancestors of the Slavs. Political power rested in the hands of the nomadic Royal Scythians who considered themselves to be the "most numerous and the best," and who forced other Scythian and non-Scythian tribes of Ukraine to pay them tribute. Their demands were backed by a large, well-armed, and well-disciplined army of horsemen. To develop warlike instincts, Scythian warriors were encouraged to drink the blood of the first enemy they killed, to make gold or silver-mounted chalices out of an enemy's skull, and to take scalps. Fierce and ruthless toward their enemies, these nomads were intensely loyal to their comrades, whose friendship they valued above all else.

Scythian society was very much a man's world. Descent was traced according to the male line, property was divided among sons, and polygamy was the norm. Junior wives were sometimes killed and buried along with their deceased husbands. Judging from the sumptuous burial mounds of the Scythian kings that still dot the Ukrainian steppe, the rich graves of the tribal aristocracy, and the meager burial sites of the commoners, socioeconomic distinctions were quite pronounced among the Royal Scythians. In addition to war booty, trade with the Greek colonies on the Black Sea coast provided the Scythians with most of their wealth. To their trading partners the Scythians offered products for which Ukraine would become famous: grain, wax, honey, furs, and slaves. In return, they obtained wines, fine jewelry and other luxurious goods for which they developed a considerable appetite. This growing interest in the finer things of life was reflected in the highly original decorative style of art that they favored. Characterized by animal motifs, it skillfully rendered dynamic, flowing images of deer, lions, and horses of striking grace and beauty.

Under Scythian rule, Ukraine became an important, albeit distant, part of classical Mediterranean civilization, for through the intermediary of the Greek colonies on the Black Sea, the Scythians came into contact with Greek civilization and learned to value it. But contact with the Mediterranean world also embroiled the Scythians in its conflicts. In 513 BC, the Persian king Darius invaded Ukraine at the head of a vast army. By applying a scorched-earth strategy, however, the Scythians forced him into a humiliating retreat. In the late 5th and early 4th centuries BC, the Scythians expanded westward and overran the Thracians on the Danube. It was a victory they could have done without, for it brought them face to face with Philip of Macedon, the father of Alexander the Great. In 339 BC, the Macedonians inflicted a crushing defeat on the nomads. This marked the beginning of the end for the Scythians. About a century later, the Sarmatians, another powerful nomadic people from the east, overwhelmed and assimilated most of the Scythians, only a remnant of whom managed to find refuge in the Crimea, where their descendants continued to live until the 3rd century AD.

The Sarmatians   For almost 400 hundred years, from the 2nd century BC to the 2nd century AD, the Sarmatians, who emerged from the lower Volga region, dominated the steppes north and east of the Black Sea. Initially, they mingled peacefully with their fellow Iranian speakers, the Scythians, as well as with the Greeks who lived on the northern shore of the Black Sea. However, as enemy tribes began to pressure them from the east, the Sarmatians became more aggressive. Eventually, they overwhelmed the Scythians, absorbing many of the commoners into their own ranks. Like all nomadic rulers of the Ukrainian steppes, the Sarmatians were not a single, homogeneous tribe, but a loose federation of related and frequently feuding tribes, such as the Iazygians, the Roxolanians, and the Alans. Each of these Sarmatian tribes tried to establish its rule over Ukraine. But because their attempts coincided with those prolonged, widespread population shifts commonly called the Great Migration of Peoples and because Ukraine was at the center of these chaotic population movements, Sarmatian control was frequently challenged and disrupted. Finally, in the 2nd century AD, it was completely destroyed by the terrible onslaught of the Huns from the east, the encroachments of the Germanic Goths from the north, and determined Roman resistance in the west.

From the fragmentary information available about the Sarmatians, it is evident that they looked and lived much like the Scythians and other Iranian-speaking nomads. A contemporary wrote about the Alans that "they are tall and handsome, their hair tends to be blond and the ferocity of their glance inspires dread."[4] Their dress consisted of long, billowy trousers, leather jerkins, and soft leather boots and caps. Meat, milk, and cheese constituted the basis of their diet. They lived in tents that were mounted on two- or four-wheeled platforms. A striking Sarmatian peculiarity was the prominent role played by their women. Repeating a legend according to which the Sarmatians were the offspring of a union between the Amazons and the Scythians, Herodotus stated that Sarmatian women followed "the ancient Amazon mode of living, going out on horseback to hunt, joining their husbands in war and wearing the same dress as the men."[5] Archaeological evidence indicates that Sarmatian women were often buried with their weapons and that they frequently performed important religious functions.

When war did not provide them with all their material needs and desires, the Sarmatians engaged in trade. Their caravans ranged far and wide, bringing to Tanais, their capital on the Don River, silks from China, crystal from the Caucasus, and semiprecious stones from Iran and India. In the view of Strabo, a Greek geographer and historian, their contacts with the Greeks and Romans did them more harm than good. "Our mode of life has caused a change for the worse among these people, introducing among them luxury and sensual pleasures and, to satisfy these vices, base artifices that lead to innumerable acts of greed."[6] Other nomadic tribes soon replaced the Sarmatians, but the latter were the last of the Indo-European peoples to come out of the east. After them, the Eurasian steppes would become for almost a millennium the domain of the Turkic peoples.

The Greek Colonies in Ukraine

The sea as well as the steppe brought newcomers to Ukraine. By about 1000 BC, the tiny Greek mainland had become overpopulated by its extraordinarily creative, dynamic, and adventuresome people. Lacking adequate opportunities at home, many Greeks spread out along the Mediterranean, Aegean, and Black Sea coasts in a far-flung colonizing movement. In the words of Plato, from Gibraltar to the Caucasus, the Greeks ringed the seas like "frogs sitting at the edge of a pond." In the late 7th and early 6th centuries BC, they founded a string of colonies on the northern shore of the Black Sea. For the next thousand years, these cities would serve as the outposts of urban civilization in Ukraine.

By the 4th century BC, the Greek cities on the Ukrainian coast were booming. Of these, the richest was Olbia. Situated at the mouth of the Buh River, it became the chief center of the grain trade that developed between the Greek homeland and its Black Sea colonies. Other important centers were Chersonesus and Theodosia on the Crimean coast, and Panticapeum (present-day Kerch), the largest of a cluster of cities located on the Cimmerian Bosphorus in eastern Crimea. For several centuries these cities flourished, but by the 2nd century BC they began to encounter serious difficulties. Social strife increased between the urban elites and the lower strata of the population made up largely of liberated slaves. New nomadic invaders upset the stable relationship that had existed with the Scythians. Cheap Egyptian bread undermined the all-important grain trade. And the rise of Rome upset the political balance that had existed in the Hellenistic world.

For about a century, Panticapeum and its neighboring cities, united in the so-called Bosphoran kingdom under the rule of the Spartocid dynasty, managed to hold their own. But in 63 BC, after the last Spartocid, Mithridates VI, was defeated by the Romans, Rome became master of the Black Sea coast. Roman overlordship returned a measure of economic and political stability to the Greek cities on the Ukrainian coast. However, in the early centuries AD, as barbarian invasions increased and Rome's ability to fend them off declined, it became clear that the cities on the Black Sea were living on borrowed time. In 270 AD, the Gothic invasion dealt them a devastating blow and a century later the Huns destroyed them completely.

æ

If, at the dawn of the 1st century AD, we were to cast a panoramic glance at the evolution of human life in Ukraine, we would discern three distinct

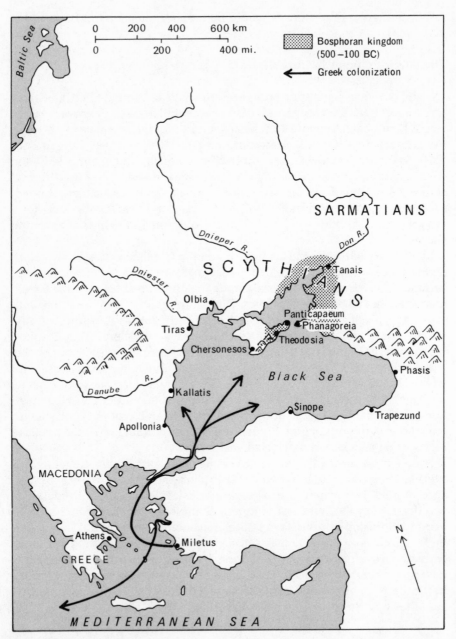

Map 4 Greek colonization

types of societies inhabiting three different geographic zones. In the northern and northwestern wooded plains lived the agriculturalists. Sheltered from invaders by forests and swamps, these oldest inhabitants of the land were politically unorganized, militarily weak, and sluggish from the point of view of cultural development. But, like peasants everywhere, they had tremendous staying power and, while various overlords might have come and gone, they continued to cling tenaciously to the land that fed them.

In the broad middle zone covered by the steppe, the nomads reigned supreme. In their attempts to control ever-greater expanses of territory, these newcomers from the east created the first major political conglomerates in Ukraine. Culturally cosmopolitan, they brought Ukraine into contact with the major centers of civilization. However, the nomads were each other's worst enemies since, in their continual quest for pasture and booty, they repeatedly destroyed the political structures created by other nomads.

Finally, on the thin stretch of the Black Sea coast in the south, the Greeks established their advanced urban civilization. Although these cities, with their commerce, crafts, schools, and far-flung contacts, accelerated the cultural development of the vast Ukrainian hinterland, they remained merely an extension of ancient Greece and not an organic part of the Ukrainian environment.

Part One

Kievan Rus'

The Rise and Decline
of Kievan Rus'

Overshadowed by the spectacular conquests of the nomads and by the sophisticated civilization of the coastal cities, the obscured population of Ukraine's northern forests, meadows, and river banks seemed for ages to be little more than a human backdrop for the fast-moving developments in the south. By the 6th century AD, however, these agrarian peoples began to make their presence felt more forcefully as the focal point of historically significant activity in Ukraine shifted slowly, yet inexorably, from the sea coast and the steppe to the wooded flatlands. As the agriculturalists made their way to the center of the historical stage, their linguistic, ethnic, and cultural features became more discernible to modern historians, who established that these people were Slavs, the direct ancestors of Ukraine's current population.

ᴥ

The East Slavs

The Slavs evolved from the autochthonous Indo-European population of Eastern Europe. Most modern scholars adhere to the view that the original homeland of the Slavs encompassed the northern slopes of the Carpathians, the Vistula valley, and the Prypiat marshlands. From there, the Slavs spread out in all directions, particularly in the early 7th century. In the northeast, they reached deep into Finno-Ugric lands around the Oka and upper Volga rivers; in the west, their settlements extended to the Elbe River in northern Germany. But the greatest flow of Slavic colonization was to the south into the Balkans where fertile land, a warmer climate, and wealthy cities exerted a powerful attraction. Compared with the nomadic invasions, Slavic expansion was a slow movement that radiated out from the core Slavic lands without ever losing touch with them. As a result, it covered a large, contiguous area. A striking feature of this expansion was its relative peacefulness. Except for

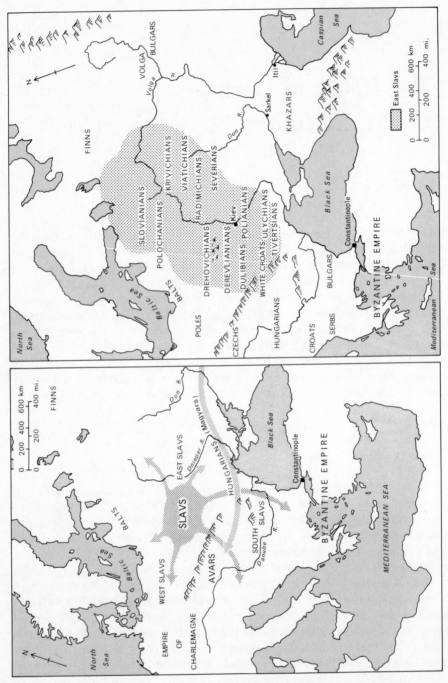

Map 5a Slavic dispersion

Map 5b East Slavic tribes

some fighting along the Byzantine borders, the Slavs generally moved into the new lands as colonists, not as invaders. But as the Slavs spread out, they also became more fragmented. The linguistic analysis of the noted Russian scholar Aleksei Shakhmatov indicates that by the 6th century the common language of the Slavs was evolving into three subgroups: West Slavic, from which such languages as Polish, Czech, and Slovak eventually developed; South Slavic, from which Bulgarian, Macedonian, and Serbo-Croatian arose; and East Slavic, from which Ukrainian, Russian, and Belorussian developed.

In the 7th century, the East Slavs were based on the right bank of the Dnieper River. Soviet scholars, intent on establishing the oldest possible pedigree for the Slavic inhabitants of Ukraine, argue that the East Slavs or their immediate predecessors, the Antes, were native to the region. Western specialists, in contrast, cite the lack of evidence to support this thesis and generally contend that the East Slavs were newcomers to the area. Throughout the 7th and 8th centuries, the East Slavs continued to subdivide and expand. Eventually they consisted of about fourteen large tribal confederations that inhabited parts of Ukraine, Belorussia, and Russia. Of these, the most prominent were the Polianians who lived in central Ukraine, on the banks of the Dnieper. Other East Slav tribes who inhabited Ukraine were the Derevliani-ans who occupied the northwest, the Severians who lived in the northeast, and the Ulychians and Tivertsians in the southwest. Located in the western-most part of the land were the Volhynians and the Dulibians.

The settlements of the East Slavs were numerous but small. Villages, consisting of as few as four and as many as seventy log dwellings, were built one or two miles apart. Thirty or forty miles away, another cluster of villages would be established. At the center of these inhabited areas were fortified strongpoints or *grady* that provided defense and served as tribal meeting places and sites of cult worship. Hundreds of these stockades dotted the East Slavic lands. Hence, the Scandinavian term *Gardariki* – "the country of strongholds" – for this territory. Little is known about the political organization of the East Slavs. Apparently, they had no supreme rulers or centralized authority. Tribes and clans, linked by their worship of common gods and led by patriarchs, most probably reached important decisions by means of communal consensus. Although eventually a class of tribal leaders called *kniazi* did emerge, socioeconomic differentiation did not appear to be great among the tribesmen, who considered land and livestock to be the communal property of extended families. In warfare, the East Slavs were known to be tough, stubborn fighters who could endure extremes of cold and heat and survive with a minimum of provisions. Unsure of themselves in the open plain, they preferred to fight in forests and ravines, where they often employed ambushes to overwhelm their enemies. In both war and peace, persistence and endurance appear to have been their strongest assets.

Trade among the early East Slavs was poorly developed. It received a stimulating impetus in the 8th century, however, when Oriental traders, especially Muslim Arabs, began to penetrate into East Slavic lands. In exchange for precious metals, fine textiles, and jewelry, the East Slavs could offer the traditional products of their land: honey, wax, furs, and a commodity that the Arabs prized most – slaves. In the late 8th century, this trade flourished when the Turkic Khazars, founders of a unique commercial empire on the lower Volga and the Caspian Sea who later converted to Judaism, established contacts with the East Slavs. Some of these, notably the Severians, Viatichians and a part of the Polianians, were even forced to pay tribute to the Khazars. As they became less isolated, the East Slavs entered a new and momentous epoch in their history.

The Normanist Controversy

In the middle of the 9th century, the lands along the Dnieper were still an economic, cultural, and political backwater. About 150 years later, they constituted the core of Kievan Rus', a mighty political conglomerate well on the way to creating one of the most sophisticated societies and flourishing economies in Europe at the time. How was this remarkable transformation achieved? Who were the people who led it? Was it external stimuli or internal developments that made it possible? To deal with these questions, we should first note what the oldest East Slavic chronicle, the "Chronicle of Bygone Years" (*Povest vremennykh let*), has to say about the origins of Kievan Rus':

> In the year 852 ... the land of Rus' was first named ... 859: The Varangians from beyond the sea imposed tribute upon the Chuds, the Slavs, the Merians, the Ves, and the Krivichians. But the Khazars imposed it upon the Polianians, the Severians and the Viatichians, and collected a squirrel-skin and a beaver-skin from each hearth. 860-862: The tributaries of the Varangians drove them back beyond the sea and, refusing them further tribute, set out to govern themselves. There was no law among them, but tribe rose against tribe. Discord thus ensued among them, and they began to war one against the other. They said to themselves, "Let us seek a prince who may rule over us, and judge us according to the law." They accordingly went overseas to the Varangian Russes: these particular Varangians were known as Russes, just as some are called Swedes, and others Normans, Angles and Goths ... The Chuds, the Slavs and the Krivichians then said to the people of Rus': "Our whole land is great and rich, and there is no order in it. Come to rule and reign over us." They thus selected three brothers, with their kinsfolk, who took with them all the Russes and migrated.[1]

In the 18th century, using this passage as evidence, several German scholars in Russian service, such as Gottlieb Bayer, Gerhard Müller, and August-Ludwig Schlözer, developed the so-called Normanist theory. It argued that the foundations of Kievan Rus' were laid by the Varangians, a Germanic-Scandinavian people known in the West as the Vikings or Normans. Angered by this emphasis on Germanic influence and by the implication that Slavs were incapable of organizing their own state, Mikhail Lomonosov, a famous 18th-century Russian scholar, wrote a fiery response that stressed the primary role of the Slavs in the foundation of Kievan Rus'. Lomonosov's statement of what came to be known as the anti-Normanist position ignited a controversy that has continued to this day. In the 19th and early 20th centuries, it seemed that the Normanist view might triumph because most Western and a number of prominent Russian historians accepted it. Two leading Ukrainian historians, Mykola Kostomarov and Mykhailo Hrushevsky, however, remained staunch anti-Normanists. In the 1930s, Soviet scholars began a counteroffensive, declaring that "the Normanist theory is politically harmful because it denies the ability of the Slavic nations to form an independent state." They stressed that Nestor, the monk who compiled the "Chronicle of Bygone Years" in the 11th century, was tendentious, that his tale had many internal contradictions, and that archaeological evidence did not point to a large-scale Scandinavian presence in Kievan Rus'. They insisted, therefore, that the East Slavs created Kievan Rus'.

Much of the ongoing debate is linguistic in nature and centers on the etymology of the word *Rus'*. The Normanists contend that *Rus'* stems from *Ruotsi*, a Finnish word for Swedes that, in turn, derives from the ancient Swedish word *rodr*, "to row." Because the Finns had close and long-standing contacts with both the Swedes and the Slavs, it is assumed that their designation for the former was passed on to the latter. The anti-Normanist explanation associates *Rus'* with the names of the Rus and Rusna rivers in central Ukraine. Another hypothesis raises the possibility that the term is related to Roxolany, a nomadic tribe whose name is derived from the Iranian word *rhos*, meaning "light." Because each of these hypotheses has serious weaknesses, none has won general acceptance. In any case, as far as the use of the term *Rus'* is concerned, it appears that it was first applied to (1) a people, that is, the Varangians/Scandinavians; then to (2) the territory of the Polianians in central Ukraine; and eventually to (3) the political entity that came to be called Kievan Rus'.*

Just as no definite conclusion has been reached about the origin of the term *Rus'*, no consensus has evolved on the broader issue of external Scandinavian influence as opposed to internal Slavic evolution in the rise of Kievan Rus'. Actually, the long and acrimonious debate has produced little in the way of new information. It would appear that this lack of knowledge has gradually induced scholars (Soviets excepted) to seek a compromise solu-

---

* The term "Ukraine" first appeared in the chronicles in 1187. Originally, it was used in a geographical sense to refer to the lands on the periphery of Kiev.

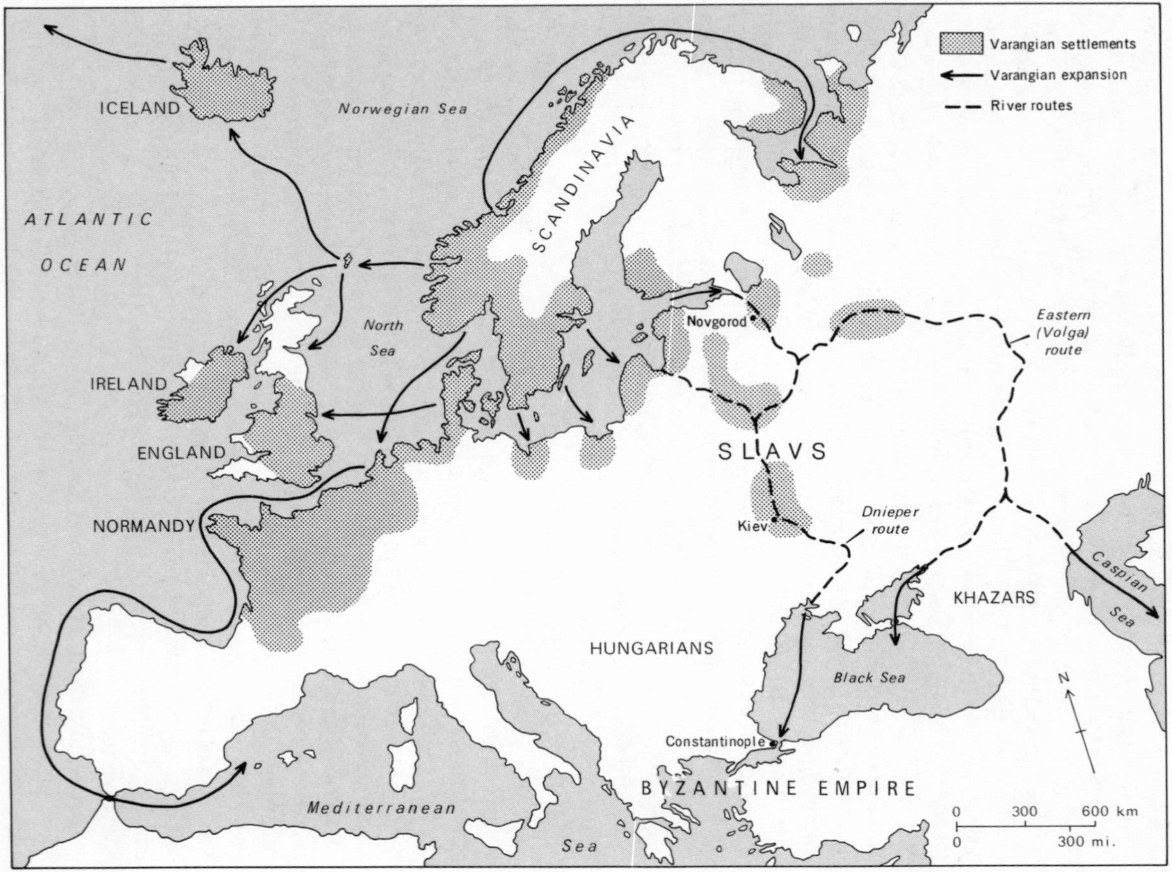

Map 6 Varangian (Viking, Norman) expansion

Legend

- ▨ Varangian settlements
- → Varangian expansion
- --- River routes

Eastern (Volga) route

Dnieper route

KHAZARS

Caspian Sea

Black Sea

BYZANTINE EMPIRE

Constantinople

HUNGARIANS

SLAVS

Kiev

Novgorod

SCANDINAVIA

Norwegian Sea

North Sea

ICELAND

ATLANTIC OCEAN

IRELAND

ENGLAND

NORMANDY

Mediterranean Sea

300   600 km.

300 mi.

0   300

0

tion. There is general agreement now that the Scandinavian impact on East Slav society and culture was minimal. Appearing as small, enterprising bands of warrior-merchants, the Varangians rapidly assimilated the East Slavic language and culture and were probably too few in number to bring about important changes in native ways. However, the participation, if not leadership, of the Varangians in political life is difficult to deny in view of the fact that all the rulers of Kiev up to Sviatoslav had Scandinavian names as did the members of their retinues or *druzhyny*. Either by politically organizing the Slavs over whom they gained control or by posing a threat and forcing the Slavs to organize themselves more effectively, the Varangians acted as catalysts for political development. On certain issues, such as the restriction of Khazar influence, stemming the nomad incursions, or opening and maintaining the Dnieper trade route with Byzantium, East Slav and Varangian interests coincided.

There are, therefore, good reasons to view the rise of Kiev not as the exclusive achievement of one ethnic group or another, but as the result of a complex Slavic/Scandinavian interrelationship. Recently, Omeljan Pritsak has taken this point further and argued that the entire question of the ethnic origins of Rus' is irrelevant.[2] In his view, the original Rus' were a multiethnic and multilingual trading company that tried to control the trade routes between the Baltic and the Mediterranean and in the process established the political entity called Kievan Rus'.

The Rise of Kiev

As in the case of most of the world's great cities, location played a crucial role in propelling Kiev to prominence. Situated midway down the Dnieper, Kiev served as a key transit point for the vast territory encompassed by its headwaters and tributaries. At the same time, it was an excellent springboard for the journey down the Dnieper and across the Black Sea to the rich cities of the Levant. Moreover, its position on the border of two environmental and cultural zones – that of the forests and wooded plains to the north and the open steppe to the south – meant that the city had great strategic importance. It thus became the focal point where two historical processes met and merged.

To one of these processes we have already alluded – the slow amalgamation of the numerous, fragmented East Slav communal units into large, territorially based tribes led by native chieftains and protected by well-fortified stockades. In the forefront of this development were the Polianians, the tribe living in the area in which Kiev would arise. Scholars estimate that as early as the 6th–7th centuries, the Polianians, led by their semilegendary leader, Kyi, formed a strong tribal confederation that lorded over its neighbors and maintained close contacts with Byzantium. According to legend, it was Kyi, together with his brothers, Shchek and Khoriv, and sister, Lebid, who founded

Kiev and gave it its name. Murky though our knowledge of this period is, it can be assumed that the East Slavs in general and the Polianians in particular were well on the way to laying the foundation for the vast political, commercial, and cultural entity that would be called Kievan Rus'.

The other process, which brought the Scandinavians on the scene, was more rapid, far ranging, and decisive. To understand it one must first look to the rocky, barren shores of 8th–9th-century Scandinavia where, for reasons that are still unclear, an unprecedented population boom occurred. Unable to find a livelihood at home, many young, adventurous Norsemen took to their ships and sought their fortunes abroad. They launched devastating raids on Western Europe, where, in time, they settled in the lands they raided, founding kingdoms and principalities in England, Ireland, France, and Sicily. Other Scandinavians crossed the Atlantic and colonized Iceland, Greenland, and, quite possibly, reached the American mainland. Others still, especially those from Sweden and the Island of Gotland who came to be called Varangians, turned to the southeast. Initially they established themselves near the Baltic coast, in Aldeigjuborg on Lake Ladoga and, somewhat later, in Novgorod on Lake Ilmen. The Varangian settlements were not the modest earth and wood stockades of the East Slavs, but substantial fortress towns that housed the Varangian leaders, their retinues, and their families and around which native artisans and traders built their suburbs.

Either by trade or by extortion (when one activity proved fruitless, the other tactic was usually applied), the Varangians obtained furs, honey, wax, and slaves from the natives. But they were after even greater profits than the East Slavs could provide. Using their settlements as a base, they explored the river routes that led south to the great centers of Byzantine and Islamic civilization and wealth. It was not long before they discovered a network of rivers and portages that linked the Baltic with the Caspian by way of the Volga and opened the way to Baghdad, the cosmopolitan capital of the Islamic world. Later an even more important route emerged. Called in the chronicles "the route from the Varangians to the Greeks," it followed the Dnieper down to the Black Sea and across to Constantinople, the great emporium of Levantine trade and the richest city in Christendom.

It was only a matter of time before the enterprising Varangians would move farther south to be closer to Constantinople. According to the "Chronicle of Bygone Years," in approximately 830, two Varangians, Askold and Dir, left the retinue of their lord, Riurik of Novgorod, and sailed down the Dnieper with their followers. Noting Kiev's excellent location high on the river banks, they established control over the settlement and imposed tribute on the Polianians in the vicinity. Apparently they prospered, for in 860 they were in a position to launch a raid against Constantinople together with their Polianian subjects. News of their success soon got back to Novgorod. Although Riurik was no longer alive and his son Ihor (Ingvar in Scandinavian, Igor in Russian) was too young to take command, Oleh (Helgi in Scandinavian, Oleg in Russian), the regent during Ihor's minority, gathered a force of Varangians, Slavs, and Finns and, taking Ihor along, sailed for Kiev. By means of a ruse he lured Askold and Dir outside the city walls, accused them of being usurpers, and killed them. In 862 Oleh established himself in Kiev, declaring that it would become "the mother of all the Rus' cities."

Such is the chronicler Nestor's version of how the Varangians came to Kiev. However, close textual analysis by generations of scholars has revealed numerous internal inconsistencies and weak points in this tale. Modern historians have wondered why the supposedly mighty Riurik is never mentioned in any of the contemporary sources and some question whether he existed at all. Is it likely that such experienced leaders as Askold and Dir would have fallen for Oleh's simple ruse? Was Oleh really associated with Riurik or is the chronicler merely trying to invent for him a more illustrious pedigree? And how can one explain the regent Oleh's extended tenure in power long after Ihor came of age? In short, up to the reign of Oleh, when other sources can be brought to bear on the period, it is difficult to separate fact from fiction in Nestor's account of the origins of Rus'.

The Early Rulers of Kiev

It was not the lofty vision of creating a mighty state (it is highly doubtful whether they were familiar with the concept of statehood) or a flourishing civilization but rather a relentless desire to get at the sources of wealth that primarily motivated the early Kievan princes. For example, Oleh's conquest of Kiev was a successful attempt to unite and control both Kiev and Novgorod, the two main depots on the "Greek" trade route. Indeed, much of the activity of the early Kievan princes represented a combination of commerce and tribute-gathering. Every spring, when the rivers were freed of ice, the tribute that had been collected over the winter from the various East Slavic tribes would be floated down the Dnieper to Kiev. There the princes organized a large armada, loaded with furs and slaves and guarded by their retinue, and dispatched it to Constantinople. It was a difficult and dangerous journey. Below Kiev, the swirling Dnieper rapids (*porohy*) had to be traversed. Because the last one, called Nenasytets (the Insatiable), was virtually impassable, the ships had to be unloaded and dragged around it, leaving the entire trading expedition vulnerable to attack by nomadic marauders who always lurked in the area.

The American historian Richard Pipes has drawn the analogy between the Varangian enterprise based in Kiev and the great early modern commercial enterprises like the East India Company or the Hudson's Bay Company, which were organized for profit but which, in order to extract it most efficiently, were obliged to provide a modicum of administration in areas that had no viable system of government. As Pipes puts it, "the Great Prince was a merchant par excellence, and his realm was essentially a commercial enterprise, composed of loosely affiliated towns whose garrisons collected tribute and maintained, in a rough sort of way, public order."[3] Thus, while pursuing their predatory practices and commercial interests, the early rulers of Kiev transformed it into the center of a large and powerful political conglomerate.

Oleh (d. 912?)   Little is known about this first historically verifiable ruler of Kiev. It is unclear whether he was a member of the Riurik dynasty or an interloper whom the chronicler Nestor, writing several centuries later, associated with that dynasty. What is evident, however, is that Oleh was a gifted and decisive ruler. After conquering Kiev in 882 and establishing control over the Polianians, he forcefully extended his authority (that is, the right to collect tribute) over the surrounding tribes, the most prominent of which were the Derevlianians. This conquest involved him in a war with the Khazars whose ports on the Caspian Sea he plundered. The highlight of his career came in 911 when, at the head of a large army, he attacked and pillaged Constantinople. But the "Chronicle of Bygone Years" probably exaggerated his success when it recounted how he nailed his shield to the main gates of the Greek capital. Nonetheless, the pressure that Oleh exerted on Byzantium must have been considerable because the Greeks were forced to conclude a trade treaty that was quite favorable to the Kievan prince.

Ihor (912–45)   The reign of Ihor was much less successful than that of his predecessor, Oleh. In what became a pattern in the reigns of the early Kievan princes, Ihor spent the initial years of his rule asserting his authority over his rebellious subjects. First the Derevlianians and then the Ulychians rose up against him. It took several years of hard campaigning before Ihor and his *druzhyna* (retinue) could force the rebels to pay tribute again. Only after he reasserted his authority at home could Ihor undertake the large-scale, far-flung part-trading and part-pillaging expeditions that Oleh had conducted. When the peace that Oleh had arranged with Byzantium crumbled in 941, Ihor launched a sea campaign against Constantinople. It was a disaster. With the help of a flammable concoction called "Greek fire," the Byzantines destroyed the Rus' fleet and forced Ihor to beat a hasty retreat. As a result, in 944, he was compelled to sign a highly unfavorable treaty with the Byzantine emperor. That same year, Ihor tried his luck in the east with much better results. A large Rus' force sailed down the Volga, plundered the rich Muslim cities on the Caspian coast, and then managed to return to Kiev with its booty. Ihor's reign ended as it had begun, with a revolt of the Derevlianians. Angered by his repeated tribute-collecting expeditions, the Derevlianians ambushed the prince and killed him and his small entourage.

Olha (945–62)   The compilers of the "Chronicle of Bygone Years" were clearly sympathetic to Olha (Helga in Scandinavian, Olga in Russian), the wife of Ihor and regent during the minority of their son, Sviatoslav. Repeatedly they depict her as being beautiful, vigorous, crafty, and, above all, wise. A male chronicler paid her the ultimate compliment by informing his readers that she was "manly of mind." Her private conversion to Christianity in ca 955 probably explains some of the adulation that the monk-chroniclers lavished upon her. But even without these biased accounts, Olha would have stood out as a remarkable ruler. Vengeance being the moral prerogative of the times, she quickly and effectively avenged herself on the Derevlianians. However, she realized that the arbitrary and haphazard collection of tribute that had been the cause of Ihor's death would have to be altered. Therefore, she introduced the first "reforms" in Kievan Rus', establishing clearly demarcated areas from which specified amounts of tribute were to be collected at regular intervals.

She also saw to it that her subjects were not deprived of all their sustenance to ensure that they would be in a position to pay tribute again. By assigning to the princely treasury exclusive rights to rich fur-bearing areas, she provided it with a steady flow of income. To familiarize herself with her vast domain, Olha made numerous and extensive trips to all its major towns and regions. Her foreign relations were characterized by diplomacy, not war. In 957 she journeyed to Constantinople to negotiate with the Byzantine emperor. Although the chronicles are replete with tales of how she outwitted the emperor, other sources indicate that the talks did not go well. Nonetheless, the very fact that Olha was accepted as a negotiating partner by the mightiest ruler in Christendom was a reflection of Kiev's growing importance.

Sviatoslav (962–72)   Brave, impetuous, simple, and severe, Sviatoslav was a warrior-prince par excellence. Hrushevsky called him "a Cossack on the throne," and his turbulent reign has aptly been described as "the great adventure."[4] Constantly at war, Sviatoslav was enamored of grand and glorious undertakings. His Slavic name, Varangian values, and nomadic life-style reflected a Eurasian synthesis. His reign marked the culmination of the early, heroic period of Kievan Rus'.

In 964, the 22-year-old Sviatoslav launched an ambitious eastern campaign. Its immediate goal was the subjugation of the Viatichians, an East Slavic tribe that lived on the Oka River, the original homeland of modern-day Russians. After this conquest, he sailed down the Volga and crushed the Volga Bulgars. This brought on a climactic confrontation with the mighty Khazars. In a bloody battle, Sviatoslav defeated the Khazar *kagan* and razed his capital at Itil on the Volga. He then swept on to conquer the northern Caucasus. The results of this spectacular campaign were far reaching. With the conquest of the Viatichians, all of the East Slavs now came under Kievan rule and the northeast – the Russia of today – was opened up to Slavic colonization. The defeat

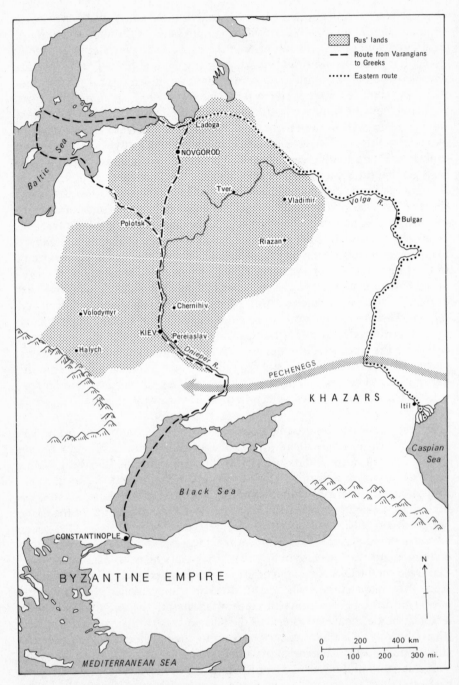

Map 7 Kievan Rus' in the 10th century

of the Khazars removed Kiev's great competitor for hegemony in Eurasia and it placed the great Volga trade route under Rus' control. But the decline of the Khazars also had a drawback: it removed the bulwark that had kept the eastern nomadic hordes, such as the Pechenegs, from penetrating into the Ukrainian steppe.

During the latter part of his reign, Sviatoslav focused his entire attention on the Balkans. In 968 he agreed to help the Byzantines in a war against the powerful and highly developed Bulgarian kingdom. With a huge army he swept into Bulgaria, annihilated his opponents, and captured the rich cities along the Danube, choosing Pereiaslavets as his base. So impressed was he with the wealth of the land that only the threat of a dangerous Pecheneg raid on Kiev could force him to return to his capital. But once the Pecheneg danger passed, Sviatoslav, who now controlled the territory from the Volga to the Danube, declared, "I do not care to remain in Kiev, but should prefer to live in Pereiaslavets on the Danube, since that is the center of my realm; that is where all my riches are concentrated – gold, silks, wine and various fruits from Greece, silver and horses from Hungary and Bohemia, and from Rus', furs, wax, honey and slaves."[5] Therefore, after appointing Iaropolk (his eldest son) to administer Kiev, Oleh (the next oldest) to control the Derevlianians, and Volodymyr (the youngest) to look after Novgorod, Sviatoslav returned once more to Bulgaria.

Worried by this aggressive new neighbor, Byzantium now turned against the Kievan ruler and after a long and brutal campaign, forced him to withdraw. On the way back to Kiev, the decimated Rus' forces were ambushed by the Pechenegs near the Dnieper rapids and Sviatoslav was killed. According to the "Chronicle of Bygone Years," the Pecheneg khan had a chalice made out of his skull. Thus ended Sviatoslav's great adventure.

Kiev at Its Zenith

Amidst these accounts of war and conquest, it is useful to comment on the extent of the power of the Kievan princes. The geographical limits of Kievan Rus' can be established only approximately. They encompassed almost all the territories inhabited by the East Slavic tribes (the lands on the lower Volga, northern Caucasus, and in Bulgaria which had been conquered by Sviatoslav were subsequently lost). But the control that the early Kievan princes exercised over their realm was limited and erratic. Political organization was too primitive, distances too great, and regionalism too strong to allow for the establishment of a unified political entity. Except for their periodic collections of tribute, the early Kievan rulers had very little contact with or impact upon their subjects, especially those who lived beyond the major towns and strongholds. As for the prince's authority to collect tribute, it depended purely on the brute force that the prince's *druzhyna*, originally staffed by Scandinavians, was able to exert. Sharing the risks and profits from their tribute-collecting expeditions, the princes and their retinues maintained a personal, direct, and mutually binding relationship that lay at the heart of the early Kievan political system. Thus, it was in their quest for tribute and for control of far-flung commercial trade routes that, in less than a century, the princes and their retinues created the vast, powerful conglomerate that was Kievan Rus'.

After the death of Sviatoslav, Kievan Rus' experienced the first outbreak of what was to become a chronic, debilitating political malady: internecine struggle among members of the Riurikid dynasty for supreme power in the realm. In a conflict sparked by an argument over tribute-collecting rights, Iaropolk killed his brother, Oleh. Fearing that a similar fate awaited him, the young Volodymyr fled from Novgorod to Sweden. Several years later, he returned at the head of a powerful Scandinavian force and waged a war against Iaropolk in which the latter met his death.

Volodymyr the Great (980–1015)   When Volodymyr (Valdemar in Scandinavian, Vladimir in Russian) mounted the Kievan throne in 980 with complete and unchallenged power in his hands, he initiated a new epoch in the history of Kievan Rus'. No longer would restless Scandinavian princes view Rus' merely as a staging area for their further conquests or as a land that could be exploited with no thought for its welfare. Volodymyr introduced a much more constructive approach to rulership. The focus of his attention rested primarily on the welfare of the realm rather than on the acquisition of territory and tribute, as had been the case with his predecessors. It was during his reign that Rus' began to emerge as an integrated society and polity.

At the outset, however, it did not appear that Volodymyr's reign would be appreciably different from those of his predecessors. He favored his numerous retinue, supported traditional pagan cults, campaigned against the rebellious Viatichians, and extended his control over the Radimichians. Just as his father had done, Volodymyr appointed his sons (he had twelve legitimate ones) to administer the major towns and regions of his realm. In the process, he removed local princes from power and concentrated it exclusively in the hands of his dynasty. When the Varangian retinue demanded an increase in the contributions from Kiev, Volodymyr arranged to have it transferred to Byzantine service.

Instead of launching the traditional long-range expeditions, Volodymyr concentrated on securing his borders. To deal with the threat of the Pechenegs, he built an extensive fortification system, as well as new towns, just south of Kiev. In another break with tradition, he turned his attention to the west, annexing what is Western Ukraine today to his realm and thereby setting the stage for an age-long struggle with the Poles for the region. The Lithuanian Iatvigians were also forced to recognize his overlordship. Volodymyr also established generally friendly relations with the Poles, Hungarians, and Czechs. This new, western orientation was guided by his desire to control the main trade routes to the west and to develop alternate routes to Constantinople. As a result of his conquests, Volodymyr's realm became the largest in Europe, encompassing about 800,000 sq. km.

Undoubtedly, Volodymyr's greatest achievement was the Christianization of his vast realm. Sensing that Kievan Rus' had outlived its traditional animistic, pagan religion, he began to consider more sophisticated ways for his society to express its spiritual, social, and political values. By way of analogy with modern times, his position was that of a rising third-world leader who wishes to push forward the modernization of his country and consequently must adopt one of the two leading ideologies of the world's most advanced societies – capitalism or socialism. In Volodymyr's case, the two highly evolved systems of belief that came into consideration were Christianity and Islam, the religions of the lands with which Rus' had and wanted to maintain the closest commercial and political contacts. Despite the entertaining tales in the "Chronicle of Bygone Years"about how the envoys of Rus' rejected Islam because of its prohibition against alcoholic beverages and supposedly chose Byzantine Christianity because of the awe-inspiring splendor of its religious services, it was concrete political and historical factors that guided Volodymyr's choice.

As Olha's earlier conversion indicated, Christianity had already set down roots in Kiev. The proximity of Rus' to the thoroughly Christianized Bulgarians as well as to the recently converted Poles and Hungarians only hastened this process. However, the immediate reason for accepting Christianity, specifically in its Byzantine variant, was a political one. In 987, as a price for helping the Byzantine co-emperors put down a rebellion, Volodymyr demanded the hand of their sister Anne. Although they were unhappy about diluting the jealously guarded prestige of their imperial dynasty by consenting to a marriage with a "barbarian," the Byzantines tried to make the best of a bad situation by demanding that Volodymyr accept Christianity. But even after Volodymyr converted in 988, they tried to put the marriage off. Pressure in the form of the Rus' conquest of the Byzantine-held Crimean city of Chersonesus (Korsun), however, finally led to the marriage.

Determined to Christianize his subjects as quickly as possible, in 988 Volodymyr ordered a large part of Kiev's population to be herded into the Pochaino River, a tributary of the Dnieper, and baptized it en masse. Despite popular resistance, pagan idols were destroyed and Christian churches built in their place. Not only did the church, whose personnel and organizational structure were imported entirely from Constantinople, receive wide-ranging privileges and autonomy, but 10% of the princely revenues were assigned for its support. As a result of his great innovation, the political prestige of Volodymyr's dynasty, now linked to the highly respected Byzantine ruling house, was greatly enhanced.

As a member of the Christian "family of rulers," Volodymyr's contacts with other European monarchs became much closer. Internally, the conversion also produced positive results. Because the doctrines of the Byzantine church supported a monarch's right to rule, the Kievan princes found in the church's teachings an ideological support they did not have before. Moreover, being a relatively sophisticated organization, the church introduced the rulers of Kiev to organizational patterns from which they had much to learn. And Kievan society was enriched by a dynamic institution that not only provided it with unprecedented spiritual and cultural unity, but that exerted a tremendous influence on its social and economic life as well. In the broader sense, Volodymyr's epochal choice aligned Rus' with the Christian West rather than with the Islamic East, and exposed it to the enormous historical, political, and cultural ramifications that this assocation entailed. The importance of Christianity coming to Kiev from Byzantium and not from Rome cannot be overestimated. Later, when the religious split between these two centers occurred, Kiev would side with Constantinople and reject Roman Catholicism, thereby laying the groundwork for the bitter conflicts that Ukrainians would have with their closest Catholic neighbors, the Poles.

Iaroslav the Wise (1036–54)   The death of Volodymyr in 1015 led to another fratricidal war among the Riurikids. Aided by the Poles, Volodymyr's eldest son, Sviatopolk (often referred to in the chronicles as "the Damned"), turned on his younger brothers, Sviatoslav, Borys, and Hlib, and had them murdered. Young and popular, the latter two were later canonized as saints of the Orthodox church. Following in the footsteps of his father, another brother, Iaroslav of Novgorod, called a large number of Varangians to his aid and defeated Sviatopolk in 1019. This victory did not give him complete control, however. Yet another brother, Mstyslav the Brave, challenged Iaroslav and, in order to avoid further bloodshed, the two agreed to split the realm between them. Remaining in Novgorod, Iaroslav received all the land west of the Dnieper, while Mstyslav, who moved to Chernihiv from Tmutorokan, acquired all the lands east of the river. Because it was too important to grant to one side or the other, Kiev remained unoccupied. Only at Mstyslav's death in 1036 did Iaroslav mount the Kievan throne to become the sole ruler of Rus'.

Iaroslav's long reign is usually considered the high point of the history of Kievan Rus'. Much of what Volodymyr had initiated was expanded and perfected by Iaroslav. Like his father, he continued to extend the boundaries of an already huge realm, winning back the western territories that had been lost to the Poles during the internecine fighting, conquering more Baltic and Finnish tribes, and finally destroying the Pechenegs. As a result of these victories, Iaroslav's authority extended from the Baltic to the Black Sea, and from the Oka River basin to the Carpathians. His military endeavors were marred, however, by an unsuccessful campaign against Constantinople, noteworthy because it was the last attack that Rus' launched against the Byzantines with whom it had had generally friendly relations.

In medieval Europe, a mark of a dynasty's prestige and power was the willingness with which other leading dynasties entered into matrimonial relations with it. Measured by this standard, Iaroslav's prestige must have been great indeed. His wife was a Swedish princess; one of his sisters married a Polish king and another a Byzantine prince; three of his sons acquired European princesses as wives, while three of his daughters were married to the kings of France, Norway, and Hungary respectively. Little wonder that Iaroslav is often dubbed by historians as "the father-in-law of Europe."

It was his achievements at home, however, that assured Iaroslav lasting fame. With his support, the church grew rapidly. Monasteries were established and became centers of learning for an increasingly urban and cultivated population. The construction of churches was of special interest to Iaroslav. During his reign, "golden domed" Kiev was studded with over 400 churches. Its crowning jewel was the Church of St Sophia, modeled on the splendid Hagia Sophia of Constantinople. The prince's concern with ecclesiastical affairs is evident in his nomination in 1051 of the first native metropolitan of Rus' – Ilarion. Some scholars have interpreted this action as Kiev's rejection of the ecclesiastical overlordship of Constantinople. However, most specialists, while acknowledging the impressive growth of the Kievan church, contend that the patriarch of Constantinople still retained his superiority over the Kievan metropolitan.

The achievement with which Iaroslav's name is perhaps most closely linked, and from which he gained his sobriquet "the Wise," was his codification of customary laws that became the basic legal code of the land, the *Ruska pravda* (Rus' Justice). Not only were existing laws systematized, but some were modified, thus reflecting the increasing involvement of the ruler in the lives of his subjects. For example, blood revenge was replaced by monetary payments that were established by the prince or his representatives. It is evident from these and other examples that the wealthy and increasingly urban and sophisticated society of Kievan Rus' had come a long way from the days when the isolated, forest-bound tribes first came into contact with the rough Scandinavian warrior-merchants.

Shortly before his death, Iaroslav attempted to resolve a problem that had bedeviled him and his father, Volodymyr – namely, how to prevent the internecine fighting for control of Kiev that usually broke out among a ruler's sons at his death. His approach was to apply the principle of seniority within the family to the distribution of land and political power. To his eldest son, Iziaslav, Iaroslav assigned Kiev and Novgorod along with their surrounding territories; to the second eldest, Sviatoslav, he gave Chernihiv; to the third, Vsevolod, Pereiaslav; to the fourth, Viacheslav, Smolensk; and to the youngest, Ihor, he gave Volodymyr-in-Volhynia. Whenever a vacancy occurred in any one of these principalities, each brother would, according to Iaroslav's plan, move up a step until each in his turn reached Kiev, which represented the pinnacle of the system. Thus, by providing all his sons with lands and with a chance to rule in Kiev, Iaroslav hoped to avoid the bitter family feuds in which he himself had been embroiled.

Although this system of rotation worked for a time, thanks largely to the co-operation of the three senior sons, Iziaslav, Sviatoslav, and Vsevolod, it soon encountered several obstacles. The most serious of these was the fact that the rotation idea ran counter to another deeply entrenched principle, that of hereditary succession from father to son. It was not long before the sons of some princes demanded to move into their deceased fathers' places rather than stand aside in favor of their uncles. As a result, bitter conflicts between nephews and their uncles became a characteristic feature of the post-Iaroslav era. Moreover, as the number of princes increased, so too did their feuds.

To add to the spreading civil strife, the citizens of Kiev, dissatisfied with the rule of Iziaslav, drove him out and installed his nephew Vseslav in his place in 1068. Although Iziaslav returned and, with Polish aid, put down the rebels, the events of 1068 were noteworthy because they marked the first recorded "revolution" on Ukrainian soil. In addition, an ancient menace from the steppe reappeared on Ukraine's frontiers at this time to afflict Rus'. The nomadic Polovtsians (Cumans), more powerful than the earlier Pechenegs, launched a series of attacks that came perilously close to Kiev and made it difficult to keep the Dnieper trade route open. For some of these incursions, the princes themselves were to blame. Unable to assemble a viable force on their own, many of the younger princes, who had been deprived of their patrimony in the system of rotation (these displaced princes were called *izhoi*) invited the Polovtsians into Rus' as allies in their struggles against their rivals.

Volodymyr Monomakh (1113–25) Despite these troubles, Rus' could still muster the resources to cope. Another outstanding leader, Volodymyr Monomakh, the son of the Grand Prince Vsevolod (Kievan rulers had assumed the title of Grand Prince in the 11th century), emerged and even before he ascended the grand princely throne, he played a prominent role in restoring order in the land. In 1097, he was one of the organizers of a conference of leading princes held in Liubech, near Kiev, that sought to resolve, albeit unsuccessfully, the fratricidal conflicts by proposing a system of hereditary succession in most principalities. However, with regard to Kiev itself, no agreement could be reached and it remained a bone of contention. Volodymyr Monomakh's great fame and popularity stemmed from his inspiring leadership against the Polovtsians. Uniting the princes and mobilizing the populace, Monomakh was said to have conducted eighty-three campaigns against them and to have killed 200 of their chieftains. Especially successful were the campaigns of 1103, 1107, and 1111. They marked Kiev's most glorious hour in its long struggle against the steppe nomads.

An indication of Volodymyr Monomakh's popularity was that when his father died in 1113 and there were other princes in line before him for the Kievan throne, the citizens of the city, erupting in another bout of social unrest, calmed down only after the 60-year-old Monomakh had agreed to become grand prince. By force of his enormous prestige, the new ruler succeeded in uniting most of fragmented Rus'. Never again would the land enjoy the unity and harmony that he was able to impose on it. Monomakh was also concerned with the growing social tensions among his subjects. By restoring order to riot-torn Kiev, he gained the support of the boyars and wealthy merchants. He addressed the grievances of the lower classes – his *ustav* or law code systematized the rights and obligations of freemen and indentured servitors – and his popularity with the masses reached even greater heights. The words of counsel that he left his sons just before his death reflect how seriously Monomakh treated social problems: "Above all, do not forget the poor ... and do not let the mighty oppress the people ... I did not allow the mighty to oppress the most lowly peasant or one poor widow."[6] Volodymyr Monomakh's son Mstyslav still managed to hold the regions of Rus' together and to maintain his authority over the increasingly more numerous princes. But he was the last Kievan ruler to do so. His death in 1132 marked the end of Kiev's role as the dominant center of Rus' and inaugurated the period of political fragmentation.

The Decline of Kiev

Political fragmentation It is not surprising that the territorial conglomerate that the early Kievan rulers had put together began to disintegrate after a relatively short period of time. This same fate befell other medieval empires in Europe, such as that of Charlemagne. These vast but rudimentary political structures simply lacked the technical and institutional means to hold far-flung territories together for extended periods of time. In Rus', the Riurikid dynasty, through its many branches, did provide the land with a semblance of unity, but only so long as the princes agreed among themselves who was the senior and had the right to supreme authority. In the absence of such a consensus, the dynastic, personal bonds among the various principalities loosened dramatically.

But there was yet another dimension to the problem of political fragmentation. As the hereditary (*votchyna*) principle of succession triumphed over Iaroslav's system of seniority or rotation, the princely clans struck still deeper roots in their patrimonial lands and it became increasingly apparent to them that their future was tied to their hereditary holdings and not to Kiev, which was continually being contested. Throughout the 12th century, ten to fifteen such hereditary principalities evolved, the most noteworthy being Halych-Volhynia, Vladimir-Suzdal, Novgorod, Chernihiv, and Smolensk. Each led its own independent political, economic, and even cultural existence. As a result, Kievan Rus' was gradually being transformed into an entity that had multiple centers related by language, common religiocultural bonds, and dynastic ties, but these centers were largely independent and often in competition with each other.

As more and more principalities went their own way, Kiev's wealth, population, and territory shrank until it ranked little higher than other principalities. It was at this stage that the city of Kiev and its surrounding lands became referred to as *Ruskaia zemlia*, the land of Rus', in the narrow sense of the word. Nonetheless, Kiev was still an alluring prize. Whoever acquired it not only enjoyed the prestige of ruling "the mother of Rus' cities," but could also lay claim to being the senior member of the Riurikid dynasty. Because it was the home of the metropolitan and the site of the major churches and monasteries, the city remained the undisputed cultural and religious, if not political, center of all Rus'. Even with the decline in its population and territory, Kiev and its lands were still among the most developed and populous in all of Ukraine.

Kiev's assets were also its liabilities, however. Princely competition for the city continued unabated. The Ukrainian historian Stefan Tomashivsky calculated that between 1146 and 1246, twenty-four princes ruled in Kiev on forty-seven separate occasions. Of these, one ruled seven separate times, five ruled three times each, and eight occupied the throne twice each. Significantly, thirty-five princely tenures lasted for less than a year each.[7] One prince took a rather drastic approach in dealing with the problem of Kiev. In 1169, unsure of his ability to retain control of the city once he had won it and unwilling to have it overshadow his growing domains in the northeast, Andrei Bogoliubsky, the prince of Vladimir-Suzdal and a forerunner of the princes of Moscow, attacked Kiev and savagely sacked it. It never completely recovered from this destructive raid.

Economic stagnation Kiev's political problems were matched by its economic difficulties. As we have seen, the city's location on the great trade route "from the Varangians to the Greeks" had played an important role in its rise to prominence. Beginning with the late 11th century, the importance of this route began to decline. The effect on Kiev's economy was calamitous. Enterprising Italian merchants established direct links between Byzantium, Asia Minor, and the Middle East on the one hand, and Western Europe on the other, thus bypassing Kiev in the process. Moreover, with the Rus' princes absorbed in their feuds, it was difficult to secure the Dnieper route from nomadic attacks.

Another blow to Kievan commerce came in 1204 when the Crusaders pillaged Constantinople. Meanwhile, the once-flourishing Abbasid Caliphate, with its capital at Baghdad, entered a period of steep decline. As a result, Kiev lost two of its biggest trading partners. These economic disasters exacerbated the already tense relations between the rich and poor in the city and led to frequent social upheavals. The once proud center of Rus' was clearly coming apart at its political, economic, and social seams.

The Mongols   Kiev's nemesis was its ancient enemy – the nomads. It was not the Polovtsians, however, who dealt Kiev its death blow, for, after generations of bitter struggle leading to mutual exhaustion, the Rus' principalities had established a stable relationship with these tribes and some of the Rus' princes had even forged matrimonial links with the Polovtsian elite. Rather, it was the Mongols, or Tatars as they are called in the East European sources, who delivered the coup de grâce to Kiev.

Although the origins of the Mongols have not yet been completely clarified, it is known that in the 12th century they were nomads along the northwestern borders of China. Most of their energy and attention was focused on clan or tribal conflicts over scarce pasturage. In the final decades of the 12th century, an unusually gifted leader by the name of Temujin (who in 1206 adopted the august title of Jenghiz Khan or Khan of Khans) emerged among them and achieved the unprecedented: by means of force and political skill he united the warring tribes and compelled them to recognize his absolute authority. Next, he harnessed their tremendous military capacity and aggressiveness against the neighboring sedentary civilizations.

Never very numerous (numbering at most between 120,000 and 140,000 fighting men), but extremely mobile, well organized, and superbly led, the Mongol forces initially conquered China, Central Asia, and Iran. In 1222, a Mongol detachment crossed the Caucasus and attacked the Polovtsians. Koran, the Polovtsian khan, turned to some of the Rus' princes for aid and the latter complied with his request. In 1223, near the Kalka River, a combined Rus'/Polovtsian force met the Mongols and, after a fierce battle, suffered a disastrous defeat. But the Mongols, who had overextended themselves, chose not to follow up this victory and returned to their homeland. The princes of Rus' quickly forgot this catastrophic experience and again plunged into their dynastic feuds. In 1237, however, a powerful Mongol army led by Batu, a grandson of Jenghiz Khan, appeared on the frontiers of Rus'. With fire and sword it overran the towns of the northeast, such as Riazan, Suzdal, and Vladimir. In 1240 it reached Kiev. Although its prince (Mykhailo) fled, the citizens of the city, led by a military commander by the name of Dmytro who had been dispatched by Danylo of Galicia, decided to resist the invaders. A long and bitter siege ensued and even after the Mongols broke through the

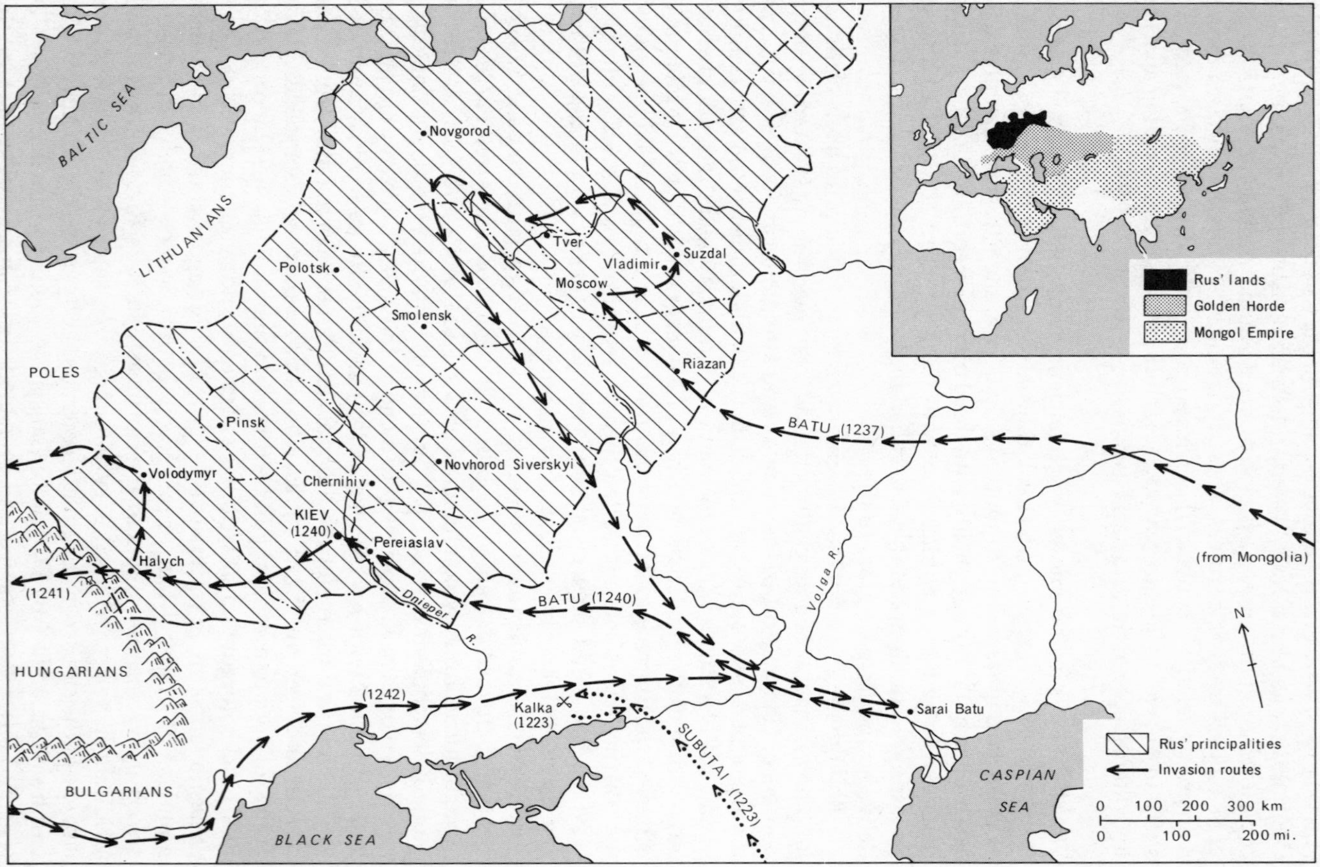

Map 8 Mongol incursions

city walls, fighting ranged from street to street and from house to house. Finally, early in December 1240, the city fell to the Mongols.

ಜಿ

Historians often divide the political history of Kievan Rus' into three phases. Encompassing almost a century, from Oleh's accession to power in Kiev in 882 to the death of Sviatoslav in 972, the initial period was one of rapid expansion. Basing themselves in strategically located Kiev, the Varangian princes gained control of the all-important Dnieper trade artery, "the route from the Varangians to the Greeks," established their control over the East Slavic tribes, and eliminated their major rivals in the region. In the process, they created a vast economic and political conglomerate that was ready and able to challenge the mighty Byzantine Empire.

The reigns of Volodymyr the Great (980–1015) and Iaroslav the Wise (1036–54) encompassed much of the second phase, a time when Kievan Rus' consolidated its gains and reached the height of its political power and stability, economic prosperity, and cultural achievement. In contrast to the expansionism of the preceding period, internal growth and development predominated in this phase. The socioeconomic structure of society became more differentiated. Law and order were better defined. Most important, the introduction of Christianity brought with it a new culture that changed dramatically how the populace of Kievan Rus' viewed its world and expressed itself.

Incessant and destructive princely feuds, increasingly threatening nomadic incursions, and economic stagnation characterize the final phase. Some historians argue that these troubles set in soon after the death of Iaroslav in 1054. Others are inclined to see the onset of decline after the reigns of the last effective rulers of Kiev, Volodymyr Monomakh (1113–25) and his son Mstyslav (1125–32). In any case, when Andrei Bogoliubsky of Suzdal captured and sacked the city in 1169 and then chose to return to the northeast rather than occupy it, it was evident that the political and economic significance of Kiev had already diminished badly. And the total destruction inflicted on the city by the Mongols in 1240 marked the tragic conclusion to the Kievan period in Ukrainian history.

2

The Society and Culture
of Kievan Rus'

In terms of its political organization, it is simpler to establish what Kievan Rus' was not rather than what it was. Kievan Rus' was not a state in the modern sense of the word. To view it as such would be to ascribe to it a much higher degree of political organization than it actually possessed. There was no centralized government, no encompassing specialized bureaucracy. The only contact that existed between rulers and ruled, especially as far as the nonurban population was concerned, was the revenue-collecting process. Personal or dynastic interests motivated princely politics, while institutional or societal concerns were often ignored. Political relationships were loose, fluid, and ill defined. And political problems were often dealt with by means of force. Nonetheless, there was a growing degree of political, social, and economic order and cultural achievement in the society of Kievan Rus' and the goal of this chapter is to survey its major features.

៰

The Political Order

Before the arrival of the Varangians, tribal units constituted the major political entities among the East Slavs. What little is known about this tribal system indicates that extensive authority rested in the hands of clan and tribal leaders who exercised it according to custom and tradition. Meeting in tribal councils to achieve a consensus, these patriarchal figures dominated political activity from the lowest level – that of the commune (*mir, zadruga*) – to the highest – that of the tribal confederation, demonstrated by the Polianians, Severians, and Derevlianians. The centers of political power were located in the numerous tribal stockades situated in forest clearings or on elevated places around which the tribesmen lived.

Upon this East Slavic tribal system, the Varangians imposed their commercially and militarily oriented forms of organization that established a degree of order and unity among the native tribes, thus allowing them to carry out their exploitative operations more efficiently. The major "shareholders" of their commercial enterprises were the members of the Riurikid dynasty and to them went most of the profits and power. But because these princes greatly depended on their retainers or *druzhyna*, they also had to share a significant portion of their gains with them. Indeed, keeping the retinue satisfied so that it would not go off to a rival prince was one of the major concerns of the early Kievan rulers. With the expansion of Varangian control, political power was centered in the cities that sprang up along the major trade routes. The foremost of these was Kiev.

The extent to which the Kievan princes were able to monopolize power varied greatly. Up to the reign of Iaroslav the Wise in the mid 11th century, the most ambitious, talented, and ruthless members of the dynasty managed repeatedly to establish themselves in Kiev and to assert their exclusive authority over their brothers and other rivals. During this period of strongman rule, centrifugal tendencies were contained and cohesion was maintained. In the wake of Iaroslav's reform of the succession system by which each member of the rapidly expanding Riurikid dynasty actually or theoretically gained a share in the realm, decentralization of power set in, with the result that the Grand Prince of Kiev eventually became little more than the titular head of an incessantly feuding, dynastically linked conglomeration of principalities.

Having sketched in broad outline the political development of Kievan Rus', we need next to examine the institutions through which power was exercised. Of these, the most important were the office of prince, the boyar council (*duma*), and the town assembly (*viche*). These institutions were associated with the monarchic, aristocratic, and democratic tendencies that were a part of the Kievan political order. In return for the power and prestige that the prince enjoyed, he was expected to provide justice, order, and protection for his subjects. In performing his military functions, the prince depended first and foremost on his *druzhyna*. When larger military forces were required, town militias or, more rarely, general levies were summoned. The size of these forces was relatively small, averaging about 2000–3000 men or even fewer. As in the case of other pre-state societies, officials such as chamberlains, stewards, and the like, who supervised a prince's personal household, were also used to administer the principality as a whole because distinctions were blurred between the public and private domains. To govern more distant towns and provinces, the princes appointed governors (*posadnyky*), usually chosen from among members of their own families.

On the local level, a prince's will was enforced by the *tysiatsky* (commander) of the local militia and his subordinates. Justice was administered by the prince and his officials according to Iaroslav the Wise's codification of *Ruska pravda*. Clearly, the office of prince was of central importance in Kievan government, but the fact that this single institution had to fulfill military, judicial, and administrative functions is also an indication of how relatively unspecialized and rudimentary the entire system was.

To finance their activities, the princes depended at first on tribute. Later, a more elaborate system of taxation evolved that encompassed each extended household (called a "hearth" or "plow"). Other sources of princely revenue were tariffs on trade, judicial fees, and fines. Fines were an important source of income because Kievan laws called primarily for such payments rather than capital punishment for criminal acts.

For advice and support, the prince depended on the boyar council or *duma*, an institution that had evolved from the senior members of the *druzhyna*, many of whom were descendants of the Varangian warlords or Slavic tribal leaders. Later, the higher clergy also won a place on this council. The functions of the *duma* were never clearly defined nor was the prince obligated to consult it. However, if he failed to do so he risked the possibility that this influential body and its constituency, the boyar elite, would refuse to support his undertakings. Therefore, the princes usually took the views of their boyar council into account.

Representing the democratic aspect of the Kievan political order was the *viche*, or town assembly, which predated the institution of prince and the roots of which probably lay in the tribal councils of the East Slavs. It was called by the prince or the townsmen to consult or express public opinion, as the need arose. Among the issues the assembly discussed were war, the negotiation of treaties, princely succession, appointments to offices, and military organization. While the assembly could criticize or applaud princely policies, it could not formulate its own policies or legislate laws. However, when a new prince ascended the throne, the *viche* did have the right to enter into a formal agreement, or *riad*, with him whereby, in return for its acceptance of his rule, the prince agreed not to overstep the traditional limits of his authority with regard to it. Although heads of households had the right to participate, the urban merchant elite tended to dominate these assemblies, often using them as a forum for factional disputes.

Social Organization

Inhabited by a numerous population – estimates vary greatly and range from 3 to 12 million – and encompassing a vast territory of about 800,000 sq. km (about half of which fell within the boundaries of modern Ukraine), Kievan Rus' was the largest political entity in medieval Europe.[1] It was also a rapidly changing one. Although experiencing a gradual growth of distinctions between commoners and the emerging tribal elite, East Slavic agrarian society in the 9th century was still ethnically and socially relatively homogeneous. But Kiev's rapid expansion brought Varangian trader-warriors, Finnic hunters, Turkic mercenaries, Greek artisans, and Armenian and Jewish merchants into the Slavic midst. Moreover, with the rise of cities, merchants and craftsmen proliferated. Finally, a completely new class – the clergy – appeared with the introduction of Christianity. In short, the inhabitants of Kievan Rus' became culturally more cosmopolitan, ethnically more diverse, and socially more differentiated and stratified.

In the social hierarchy that evolved, the highest place was held by the growing number of members of the various branches of the Riurikid dynasty. The retainers of the princes, senior and junior members of the *druzhyna*, and the local elites formed the boyar, or noble class, also referred to as the *muzhi*. In time, the mostly Scandinavian elite was Slavicized, a process reflected in the transformation of such originally Scandinavian names as Helgi, Helga, Ingvarr, and Valdemar into their respective Slavic equivalents – Oleh, Olha, Ihor, and Volodymyr. As a result of the diminishing opportunities in trade caused by repeated nomadic attacks on the trade routes and by Constantinople's commercial decline, by the 12th century, the early trader-warriors gradually changed into large landowners. Land was not difficult to come by because princes had a surfeit of open, uncultivated territory to give away to their retainers. Unlike in Western Europe where noble landholding was conditional upon service to an overlord, in Rus' the boyars had a hereditary right to their estates (*votchyny*) and retained them even if they left the prince they served for another. Many boyars lived in the cities, renting their lands to peasants in return for a portion of their produce, which they sold on the open market. It was their city orientation, commercial interests, and mobility that differentiated the boyars of Kievan Rus' from the nobility of Western Europe.

Below the boyars were the urban patricians, or *liudy* as they were called, often described as the Kievan middle class. Its foremost members were the great merchants who engaged in foreign trade, intermarried with the boyars, and dominated city politics. Compared with the burghers of Western Europe at the time, the urban elite of Kievan Rus' was much more powerful and numerous, even after the slackening trade brought about a relative decline in its position during the 12th century. Included among the less influential and wealthy urban inhabitants – the *molodshi liudy* or younger men – were the petty merchants, shopkeepers, and skilled craftsmen, such as armorers, masons, glaziers, and goldsmiths, who were organized into trade associations. Lowest on the urban social scale was the *chern* or proletariat, people who owned no property and who hired themselves out as manual laborers.

The vast majority of the population consisted of peasants, or *smerdy*. Because the historical sources focused their attention on the upper classes, little is known about the peasantry. It is generally accepted that throughout the Kievan period, most of the peasants were relatively free. However, as times became more difficult in the 12th–13th centuries, there are indications that peasants became increasingly subject to various forms of bondage. A free peasant had access to a court of law, could move about at will, and his sons could inherit his land (if he had only female heirs, however, the prince had the right to claim his land). The major obligations of the *smerdy* were the payment of taxes (*dan'*) and the performance of military duties in wartime, usually of a supportive nature. An indication of the peasant's low status in society was the penalty imposed by the formulators of the *Ruska pravda* on those responsible for the death of a *smerd*: the blood money was in such cases set at 5 *hryvnia*. By way of comparison, the blood money for killing a merchant or a member of the junior *druzhyna* was 40 *hryvnia*, while that for killing a senior member of the prince's retinue was 80.

If a peasant or member of another social group fell into debt (a frequent occurrence because interest rates ranged from 25 to 50%), or if he simply wanted a cash advance, he could enter into an agreement with his creditor whereby he obligated himself to perform labor for a specified period of time in lieu of monetary payments. These indentured, or half-free, laborers were called *zakupy*. At the very bottom of the social pyramid were the slaves, or *kholopy*. Because slaves were a major commodity of trade between Kiev and Constantinople, it is safe to assume that slavery was commonplace in Rus', especially before the acceptance of Christianity. The ranks of the slaves, many of whom worked on princely estates, were enlarged by prisoners of war, children of slaves, *zakupy* who attempted to flee from their obligations, and other unfortunates. It was possible, however, for slaves to buy their own freedom or to receive it in reward for faithful service to their masters.

The many people who were associated with the church also constituted a separate social group. Parish priests, deacons and their families, monks, and nuns were under the exclusive jurisdiction of the church. In addition, the *izhoi*, a term originally used to designate princes who had lost their patrimony (sometimes referred to as *izhoi*-princes), but later extended to include all individuals who did not fit into a specific social category, were also under the protection of the church. Counted among these were recently freed slaves (the church encouraged the freeing of slaves as a good deed), bankrupt merchants, and priests' sons who were illiterate and therefore excluded from the priesthood.

Historians have long struggled with the question of similarities between the society of Kievan Rus' and that of the medieval West. Specifically, they have been engrossed by the question of whether European feudalism existed everywhere before the age of industrialization. Soviet historians accept it as a matter of fact that Kievan Rus' was a feudal society. This was also the view of such respected non-Marxist scholars as Nikolai Pavlov-Sylvansky, who was impressed by the disintegration of Kievan Rus' in the 12th century into small principalities with an increasingly agrarian-based economy. However, most modern non-Marxist historians disagree with this analysis. They point out that because of the minimal control exercised by princes over their boyars, the institution of vassalage, which was central to feudalism, did not exist in the Riurikid realm. Moreover, the important role played by commerce and the cities in Kievan Rus' and the existence of a largely free peasantry are factors indicating that the situation in the East was quite different from that in the West. Therefore, rather than subsuming Kievan Rus' under the general category of feudal societies, Western historians prefer to consider it a unique and independent social system.

Economic Activity

It is as adventurous, freebooting merchants that the Varangians first appear in the primary sources for the history of Kievan Rus'. From their bases near the Baltic shores, they pushed eastward along the Volga route in the 8th–9th centuries until they reached the Caspian Sea, where they established contacts with the merchants of the Muslim world. By the 9th century, when the focus of trade had shifted to Constantinople in the south, the famous "route from the Varangians to the Greeks" became Kiev's primary commercial thoroughfare. Foreign trade thus came to constitute the basis of the economic system of Kievan Rus'.

It was no accident that the first formal treaty concluded by a Kievan ruler was Oleh's commercial pact with Byzantium (911) that secured exceedingly favorable terms in Constantinople for the merchants of Rus'. When Byzantine trade faltered in the 12th–13th centuries as a result of the Crusaders' attack on Constantinople and the frequent disruptions of the Dnieper trade by the nomads, commercial contacts with the West, extending primarily over the Cracow–Prague–Regensburg route, assumed greater importance for Kiev.

In contrast to the medieval West where the landowning aristocracy eschewed commercial activity, in Kievan Rus' not only was the boyar nobility deeply involved in trade, but so too was the prince. Most of the early Kievan ruler's time was spent in gathering tribute from his scattered subjects, in bringing it down to Kiev, and then in organizing a large flotilla every year for shipment of the slaves, furs, flax, honey, wax, and other raw products down the Dnieper to Constantinople where they were exchanged for luxury goods. Even when the princes and boyars became more settled and acquired large tracts of land, much of the produce from their estates was intended for foreign markets. Opportunities for commerce must have been numerous, for the cities of Rus' supported a substantial merchant class whose most powerful and wealthy members were also active in foreign trade and enjoyed the same legal and political rights as the boyars. But the vast majority of merchants were simply small shopkeepers and petty traders who were involved in the domestic market and who were often exploited by their wealthier colleagues to whom they were frequently in debt.

Modern scholars estimate that 13–15% of the population of Rus' lived in urban centers. The chronicles indicate that there were about 240 towns and cities in the land. However, it is probable that as many as 150 of these were nothing more than fortified settlements inhabited by a semiagrarian population. Of the approximately ninety large towns and cities, Kiev was by far the largest. Before the Mongol invasion, it had a population of approximately 35,000–40,000 (London was only to reach this size a century later). By comparison, such important centers as Chernihiv and Pereiaslav near the Dnieper, Volodymyr-in-Volhynia, and Halych and Lviv in Galicia probably had no more than 4000–5000 inhabitants. Petty merchants and artisans made up most of the population of these towns because handicrafts were highly developed. In Kiev, for example, between forty and sixty different handicrafts were represented, the most important practitioners of which were carpenters, smiths, potters, and leather workers.

Countering those historians who stress the commercial character of the Kievan economy are those who contend that agriculture constituted its basis. Noted Ukrainian scholars such as Mykhailo Hrushevsky, Dmytro Bahalii, and Iaroslav Pasternak, as well as the leading Soviet specialists in the field, are adherents of the latter view. They argue that because the Slavs had traditionally been an agrarian people, it is unlikely that they would have suddenly changed their way of living during the Kievan period. Additional support for this view comes from the frequent references in the chronicles to agricultural activity in Kievan Rus', the agrarian orientation of the ancient Slavic calendar and mythology, and (most convincingly) archaeological evidence.

Recent archaeological excavations have demonstrated that iron plowshares were in use in Ukraine by the 10th century and that the relatively advanced two- or three-field crop rotation system (leaving one-half to one-third of the land fallow) was also used, as it was in western Europe. Wheat, oats, rye, and barley were the favored crops. Livestock breeding was also widespread among the peasants of Rus', providing them not only with meat and milk, but also with leather for clothing and shoes. So too was the raising of horses, swine, sheep, geese, chickens, and pigeons. Oxen made cultivation possible on a larger scale. Although peasants often owned the implements necessary for farming the land on their own, they usually banded together in communes, or *obshchyny* (which consisted of blood relatives from several generations led by a patriarch), to help each other. Communes could also be territorially based and include unrelated neighbors.

If the economy of Rus' was primarily agricultural, how do proponents of this position explain the rise of large urban and commercial centers? The noted Soviet scholar Mikhail Tikhomirov, whose views are shared by many of his Soviet colleagues, has argued that the development and growing sophistication of agriculture encouraged the appearance of numerous handicrafts and where these became concentrated, towns arose.[2] He acknowledges that once towns appeared, commerce played an important role in their expansion, but this trade was primarily between the towns and their agrarian hinterlands rather than large-scale foreign-transit trade.

Confronted by compelling argument on the part of supporters of both the "commercial" and "agricultural" interpretations of the economic history of Kievan Rus', modern historians are inclined to compromise on this question as well. While agreeing that the prince, his retinue, and the richest merchants were primarily interested and involved in a lively and lucrative foreign trade, especially up to the 12th century, they also accept the argument that the overwhelming majority of the people of Kievan Rus' made its living from agriculture.

Kievan Culture

Any discussion of the culture of a medieval society concentrates first and foremost on its religious beliefs and institutions. In the case of Kievan Rus' we have two distinct religious, and therefore cultural, epochs to consider. Prior to 988, animism, based on the deification of the forces of nature and on ancestor worship, was the means by which the early East Slavs sought to satisfy their spiritual needs. The most revered deity in their pagan pantheon was Perun, the god of thunder and lightning, a figure analogous to the Scandinavian Thor, but lacking the elaborate mythology associated with him. Other important deities were Dazhboh and Svaroh, gods of the air and sun, providers of all earthy benefits. As might be expected of an agricultural people, the worship of the gods of fertility, Roh and Rozhdenytsia, was also widespread. In addition, myriad spirits of rivers, woods, and ancestors were also the objects of devotion, which was often expressed by means of animal and occasionally even human sacrifice. The East Slavs did not raise imposing temples to their gods, nor did they have a hierarchically organized priesthood – a fact that helps to explain the relatively weak resistance of their religion to Christianity. Nevertheless, native beliefs did not vanish completely with the coming of the new faith. *Dvoviria* or religious dualism, the practice of originally pagan customs and rites (such as those marking the coming of spring) persisted among the East Slavs for centuries under the guise of Christianity.

With the acceptance of Christianity, Kievan Rus' was introduced to a new, sophisticated, and highly structured religion. In 1037, upon the arrival from Constantinople of the first in a long line of Greek metropolitans (only two non-Greeks would hold the office throughout the entire Kievan period), a metropolitanal diocese was established. Initially, the diocese of Rus' contained eight eparchies or bishoprics, but their number was eventually increased to sixteen. Of these, ten were located in what is Ukraine today. Many of the bishops also came from Byzantium, bringing along with them their entourages of clerks, assistants, and artisans and thereby making their bishoprics centers for the dissemination of Byzantine culture. The clergy was divided into two categories: the "white" clergy, or parish priests who took no vows of celibacy and were usually heads of families chosen from within their communities, and the "black" clergy, who were monks from whose midst high church officials were chosen. Intent on escaping the evils and temptations of this world by living in seclusion, the monks were viewed as the elite of the faithful and their monasteries were centers of Christian devotion and learning. By the 13th century, there were about fifty monasteries in Kievan Rus', seventeen in Kiev alone.

The cultural impact of the institutions of the church on Kievan Rus' was overwhelming. The construction of just one cathedral, the famous St Sophia in Kiev, illustrates graphically how widespread the church's influence was on the arts. Built in 1037 during the reign of Iaroslav the Wise, this splendid stone edifice, which was constructed by Greek artisans and modeled on the Hagia Sophia in Constantinople, had five apses, five naves, and thirteen cupolas. Marble and alabaster columns supported a sumptuously decorated interior. For Kievans who were accustomed to modest wooden structures, this house of the Christian God must have been dazzling. And this was exactly the effect that the cathedral was meant to achieve, for the Greek church realized that the impact of great art on the senses often kindled religious reverence more effectively than did the influence of theology on the mind. To this end, the church supported the introduction of various arts and crafts. For example, the interior of St Sophia was embellished with numerous colorful mosaics and frescoes which recreated the human form with awe-inspiring realism. Another means of inspiring reverence was through the use of icons – religious images painted on specially prepared wooden planks. Icons soon spread from the churches to private homes, where they became the most prized of family heirlooms. All of these new art forms were initially heavily influenced by Greek models. But, in time, the artists of Kievan Rus' learned to incorporate native elements into these artistic genres, creating in the process their own characteristic style. The influence of the Eastern church on some art forms was not always encouraging, however. For instance, because the Byzantines frowned on the use of statues in their churches, sculpture never developed.

Christianity's impact on how the populace of Rus' expressed itself intellectually was equally decisive. A written language, based on an alphabet originally devised by Sts Cyril and Methodius, Greek missionaries to the Slavs, came into use soon after 988. Unlike Rome with its insistence on the use of Latin in liturgical matters, Constantinople acquiesced in the use of native languages among its converts. Thus, Church Slavonic, a literary language based on a south-Slavic dialect and easily understood by all East Slavs, was utilized in church services and other religious observances. Gradually, it became the vehicle for both religious and secular literary expression of an increasing richness and variety.

As might be expected, most of the earliest examples of this written literature were associated with the Christian religion. Thus, excerpts from the Old
and New Testaments, hymns, sermons, and lives of saints abounded. Some
of the more notable of these were the *Paterikon*, a compendium of the lives of
saints prepared by the monks of the Kievan Cave Monastery (Kievo Pecher-
ska Lavra); the sermons and hymns of St Cyril of Turiv; and the writings of
Ilarion, the metropolitan of Kiev in the mid 11th century, probably the most
outstanding intellectual of Kievan Rus'. In his famous work, "On Law and
Grace," a panegyric on Volodymyr the Great that was read in the presence of
Iaroslav the Wise in 1050, Ilarion skillfully counterpoised Christianity against
paganism and described the Christianization of Rus'. His work revealed a sophisticated grasp of Byzantine rhetorics, and also a great familiarity with the
Bible. Yet, despite his indebtedness to Greek culture, Ilarion was not slav-
ishly Greekophile. In "On Law and Grace" he emphasized the importance
and splendor of Rus', downplayed Byzantium's role in its conversion, and
assigned all the credit for this historical event to Volodymyr.

While Greek influence predominated in religious writing, it was less evident in the chronicles. Written for the most part by monks and imbued with
a Christian worldview, the early Kievan chronicles were characterized by realism and richness of detail. They noted both the major issues of the time –
princely conflicts and the struggle against the nomads – as well as details of
specific events. The most important of these works was the "Chronicle of Bygone Years" as it has come to be known in scholarship. Associated with the
names of two Kievan monks, Nestor and Sylvester, it was composed in 1111.
Literary works were also produced by members of the secular elite. Despite
his constant involvement in political affairs, Prince Volodymyr Monomakh
wrote his moving and philosophical "Testament." And there is reason to believe that the anonymous author of the most magnificent poetical work of the
Kievan period, "The Tale of the Host of Ihor" (1185–87), belonged to courtly
circles. While recounting the story of a disastrous campaign by a minor prince
against the nomads, the author infused it with a passionate appeal to all feuding princes of Rus' to unite for the common good. Using rhythmic verse, vivid
imagery, rich language, and a strikingly intimate treatment of nature, the author created a moving literary masterpiece.

But written works, no matter how evocative, were inaccessible to Kiev's
illiterate masses. For them, oral literature – songs, proverbs, riddles, fairy
tales, and especially oral epics or *biliny* – served as the repository of folk
wisdom and creativity. Passed on orally from generation to generation, the
biliny recounted the exploits of such popular heroes as the jovial peasant's
son Ilia Muromets, a kind of Slavic Paul Bunyan; the shrewd priest's son
Alosha Popovych; and the loyal nobleman's son Dobrynia Mykytych – all
members of Prince Volodymyr's mythical retinue. Much like the Knights
of King Arthur's Round Table, these East Slavic paladins sallied forth from

Volodymyr's court to combat the forces of evil. Among their frequent enemies were Tugor Khan of the Polovtsians, who could change himself into the
dragon Tugurin, a character that symbolized in the popular mind the constant
danger from the steppe. Or it could be Zhydovyn, the Jew, whose appearance
in the epics might reflect the survival in popular memory of the long struggle in the past with the Judaic Khazars. Magic and mystery abounded in all
of these tales and Christian values were closely interwoven with survivals of
the pagan past.

There are divided opinions among scholars as to the extent and level of
formal education in Kievan Rus'. Undoubtedly members of the elite were exposed to learning. The chronicles inform us that in 988 Volodymyr ordered
boyar children to be given an education; and his son Iaroslav established a
school in Novgorod for 300 wellborn boys. Again, in Kiev the hub of this activity was St Sophia. By 1037, the cathedral housed on its premises a school
and a library. The nearby Kievan Cave Monastery also had a library and some
of its monks were renowned for their learning, which at that time meant primarily acquiring mastery of religious texts. Respect for learning was also evident among the princes. Iaroslav the Wise was noted for his love of books;
his son Vsevolod is believed to have mastered five languages; and his daughter Anna was literate, an unusual attainment for a woman at the time and
one that set her apart from most French women of the court when she became queen of France. But the question of how widespread education was
among the masses is more difficult to resolve. The discovery in Novgorod of
alphabets written on birch bark for use by schoolboys or of graffitti written
on the walls of St Sophia is viewed by some scholars as an indication that
the lower classes also had access to education. However, many other specialists believe that, by and large, education in general and familiarity with
Byzantine-Christian culture in particular was the domain of the secular and
ecclesiastical elites and thus remained out of reach for the masses.

೩.

Both Ukrainian and Russian historians treat Kievan Rus' as an integral part
of their respective national histories. As might be expected, the question of
who has the greater right to claim its heritage often arises. Traditional Russian
historians, especially those influenced by the 19th-century Juridical School,
argued that because Russians were the only East Slavs to create a state in
modern times (the evolution of statehood was viewed by them as the pinnacle of the historical process), the Muscovite-Russian state's link with the
earliest East Slavic state was the most consistent and significant. By implication, because Ukrainians and Belorussians had no modern state of their
own, their histories had no institutional bonds with the Kievan period. The
influential 19th-century Russian historian Mikhail Pogodin went even further

and claimed that Russian ties with Kiev were not only institutional, but also ethnic.[3] According to his theory, after the Mongol destruction of Kiev in 1240, much of the surviving populace migrated from the south to the northeast, the heartland of modern Russia. Although this theory has long since been discredited, it still enjoys support among many Russian and non-Russian historians.

As the national consciousness of Ukrainians grew in the 19th century, so too did their resentment of Russian monopolization of the "glory that was Kiev." The most forceful argument against the "traditional scheme of Russian history" was advanced in 1906 by Hrushevsky, Ukraine's most eminent historian.[4] Thoroughgoing populist that he was, Hrushevsky questioned the study of history primarily in terms of the state-building process. For him, the accumulated experience of an ethnically related people living on its ancestral lands was the focal point of history. He assumed, and several recent Soviet anthropological studies support his contention, that essentially the same ethnic stock occupied much of Ukraine from the time of the Antes of the 6th century to the 20th century. If people did leave central Ukraine as a result of Mongol attacks – and Hrushevsky downplayed the extent of the devastation and migrations – they returned when relative calm was restored. According to Hrushevsky, who was obviously not a Normanist, Ukrainians are the most direct descendants of the Polianians who played the major role in the development of Kiev and, therefore, this experience looms largest in Ukrainian history.

In Hrushevsky's view, to assign the Kievan period a central place in the Russian past thus not only dilutes the uniqueness of the Poliano-Ukrainian achievement, but also burdens Russian history with an artificial or exaggerated appendage that obstructs the exploration of its true origins. If one does choose to use the state as a vehicle by which the Kievan heritage was passed on to future generations, Hrushevsky argued that it was the principalities of Galicia and Volhynia and, later, the Duchy of Lithuania (with its strong Ukrainian and Belorussian elements) that preserved more of this heritage than did the distant northeastern principalities of Rostov, Suzdal, Vladimir, Tver, and Moscow. What then is the relationship of Russian history to the Kievan period in Hrushevsky's opinion? Just as Gaul, once a Roman province and now modern-day France, borrowed much of its sociopolitical organization, laws, and culture from Rome, so too did Moscow with regard to Kiev. But Moscow was not a continuation, or a second stage in the historical process begun in Kiev. Despite its numerous Kievan borrowings, Moscow's roots, according to Hrushevsky, were embedded in the geographical, political, and ethnic conditions peculiar to the northeast.

Soviet historians take what appears to be a compromise position on the issue of the Kievan legacy. They argue that Kiev was the creation of all three East Slavic peoples – the Ukrainians, Russians, and Belorussians. More precisely, the common ancestors of all three nations – the so-called ancient Rus' people (*drevnerusskii narod*) – constituted the population of Kievan Rus'.5 Soviet scholars continually emphasize how uniform and homogeneous the culture, language, customs, economies, and politics of the "ancient Russians" were. By stressing this point, they hope to make it difficult for "bourgeois nationalist historians" not only to claim a greater share of the Kievan heritage for one or another nation, but even to argue that any regional variations existed in the huge territory of Rus'. This emphasis on the ethnic and cultural uniformity of Kievan Rus' leaves one with the impression that the "ancient Rus'" are a projection onto the past of the homogeneous Soviet nation that is planned for the future.

The view of Soviet historians, which is gradually supplanting the views of traditional Russian historiography on the question, is that because the three East Slavic nations evolved only after the decline of Kiev, there is no point in discussing which of them has the primary claim to its heritage. In explaining why the East Slavs broke up into three separate nations, the major reasons given are the impact of the Mongol invasion and the absorption of the Ukrainians and Belorussians into the Polish-Lithuanian state. This is a rather striking departure from the usual Marxist stress on internal socioeconomic factors to explain the development of nations. Moreover, it implies that were it not for these external factors, no differentiation would have occurred among the "ancient Russians." If anything, the debate over the Kievan heritage only proves once more how closely political, ideological, and scholarly issues are interwoven in the historiography of the Kievan period.

Galicia-Volhynia

The disintegration of vast, hurriedly established political conglomerates, such as Kievan Rus', was a common phenomenon in the medieval period. In the West, prior to the rise of Kiev, Charlemagne's Carolingian empire enjoyed only a brief life span; and in the East, after the fall of Kiev, the huge realm of the Mongols, stretching from the shores of the Pacific to the Carpathians, broke up within a few generations. Given the poor communications, great expanses, and strong particularistic tendencies, political fragmentation was a common phenomenon. Nevertheless, for historians of Kievan Rus' it has been a depressing spectacle to observe. Gone were the grand designs, the broad sweep, and the wide horizons of the early Kievan empire builders. In their place came petty intrigues, local squabbles, limited objectives, and the narrow perspectives of feuding princelings. The imposing cultural achievements that resulted from the concentration of talent in one capital became a thing of the past, unmatched by the frequently admirable but usually isolated efforts of artists and intellectuals dispersed among the many regional centers. In most of the principalities, the boyar elites gradually abandoned their adventurous commercial ventures and turned to the mundane maintenance of their estates. As its political, cultural, and economic life broke down, Kievan Rus' ceased to function as a whole.

≈

Regionalism

One of the reasons why the various principalities pulled away from Kiev was the triumph of the *votchyna* (private property, appanage) concept, formally recognized at a conference of princes held in Liubech in 1097. In order to put an end to the internecine feuding, the princes at this meeting recognized each other's hereditary rights to the lands they currently held. The issue of Kiev, a prize deemed too great for any one princely line to lay claim to, was left unresolved. While some of the senior princes continued to fight for it, others, especially those of junior rank, lost interest in the struggle and in the city itself because they realized that their chances of acquiring the old capital were minimal at best. Instead, they concentrated on expanding and enriching their own hereditary lands, encouraging thereby the growth of a regionalism and particularism that would become the hallmark of the late Kievan period.

These tendencies were reinforced by the boyars' growing involvement in landownership: as a result of their interest in local affairs, their willingness to participate in the princely struggles for distant Kiev or, for that matter, in any all-Rus' cause, diminished. It even became difficult for the Rus' principalities to agree on a common enemy. Novgorod considered the Teutonic Knights to be its greatest threat; for Polotsk it was the Lithuanians; for Rostov and Suzdal, the Volga Bulgars; for Galicia-Volhynia, the Poles and Hungarians; and for Kiev, it was the nomadic Polovtsians. When they were not fighting their enemies, the Rus' princes interacted with them. In fact, some of the princes established closer links with their non-Rus' neighbors than they did with other, more distant regions of Rus'.'

For example, in the north, the ancient city of Novgorod was drawn into the commercial network that a league of north-German cities, later called the Hansa, organized along the Baltic shores. While Kiev's trade declined, Novgorod's boomed and its orientation became increasingly north European. Like many other trading cities, Novgorod developed a republican-like form of government in which the merchant elite, not the prince or boyars, predominated. Another case of regional differentiation evolved in the northeast. In that vast, sparsely populated "land beyond the forest," the heartland of the Great Russians, principalities such as Rostov, Suzdal, Vladimir, and Moscow were founded by junior members of the Riurikid dynasty. Perhaps because these northeastern princes established themselves in these originally Finnic areas before many of the East Slavic colonists arrived, they were in an advantageous position to dictate exacting terms of overlordship to the newcomers. The epitome of the growing absolutist tendency of the northeastern princes was Andrei Bogoliubsky of Suzdal. Dissatisfied with the growing opposition from the local elite in Suzdal, he moved to Vladimir because it had no well-entrenched aristocracy that could thwart him. And, in 1169, he destroyed Kiev so that it would not rival his new capital. This single-minded pursuit of absolute power was inherited by Bogoliubsky's descendants, the rulers of Moscow (originally a minor outpost, Moscow was first mentioned in the chronicles only in 1147), and it helps to explain their future political success.

The Ukrainian Southwest: Galicia-Volhynia

Another extremely important regional development occurred in the Ukrainian southwest, in the principalities of Galicia and Volhynia. If any component of the old Kievan realm could challenge the growing power of the Russian northeast, that is, of Suzdal, Vladimir, and fledgling Moscow, it was the principalities of Galicia and Volhynia in the southwest. Hrushevsky considered these two principalities to be the most direct inheritors of Kiev's political and cultural traditions.[1] Tomashivsky, another eminent Ukrainian historian, called Galicia-Volhynia the first undeniably Ukrainian state because at the height of their power in the 13th century the united principalities encompassed about 90% of the population living within what are today the borders of Ukraine.[2] The principalities were important in other ways as well. Lying on the western periphery of Kievan Rus', they were from the outset the focus of a fierce struggle between Ukrainians and Poles, a conflict that continued unabated until the mid 20th century. The principalities were also a crucial cultural frontier. Depending on one's perspective, they were either the easternmost inroad of the Catholic West or the westernmost outpost of the Orthodox East.

Located along the eastern foothills of the Carpathians at the headwaters of the important Dnister and Prut rivers that flow into the Black Sea, Galicia was originally inhabited by the Dulibian, Tivertsian, and White Croatian tribes. In the east it shared a long border with the rolling, wooded plains of Volhynia, also inhabited by the Dulibians and White Croatians. To the east of Volhynia lay the principality of Kiev. While Galicia had the aggressive Hungarians and Poles to contend with on its western and northern borders, Volhynia's only foreign neighbors were the Lithuanian tribes to the north. Both principalities were fortunate in that they lay beyond the normal range of nomad raiders from the steppe. Volhynia and especially Galicia were well populated and their numerous cities were strategically located on important western trade routes. Moreover, Galicia had great deposits of salt, a commodity upon which all of Rus' depended.

In 980-90, Volodymyr the Great wrested Galicia and Volhynia from Polish control and integrated them into his realm. In Volhynia, he founded the city of Volodymyr, which eventually became the imposing capital of the land. In Galicia, the city of Halych, near the Carpathian salt fields, replaced Peremyshl as the political center of the principality. The Kievan princes were able to assign Galicia and Volhynia to their offspring because these lands were their personal domain. Thus, the Rostyslavychi, the house of a grandson of Iaroslav the Wise, initially ruled in Galicia. Meanwhile, in Volhynia, the house of Mstyslav, a son of Volodymyr Monomakh, came to power.

Although often grouped together in historical studies for the sake of convenience, Galicia and Volhynia were quite different principalities in the 12th and 13th centuries. Perhaps the most striking difference between them was the nature of their respective elites. Undoubtedly, Galicia had the most willful, wealthy, and powerful boyars in all the Rus' lands. So pervasive was the influence of this aristocracy that Galicia is often considered the prime exam-

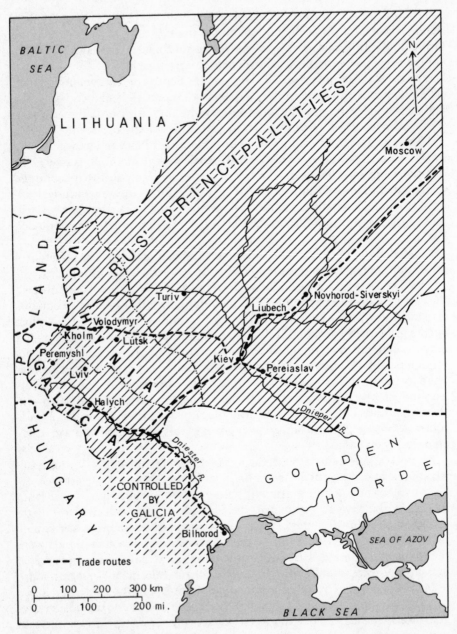

Map 9 Galicia-Volhynia

ple of oligarchic rule in Rus', representing, next to republican Novgorod and absolutist Vladimir-Moscow, the third major variant of the Kievan political system. According to Soviet scholars, the origins of the Galician boyars explain to a large extent their uniquely dominant position.[3] Unlike the boyars of other principalities who usually descended from the princely retinue, the Galician aristocracy apparently emerged primarily from the local tribal elite. And it obtained its estates not from the prince, as was usual, but by usurping open communal lands. When the first Riurikid princes arrived here, they were probably confronted by a well-entrenched aristocracy that was ready to defend its own interests.

Other historians also point out that because the Rostyslavychi provided four generations of relatively stable rule, the boyars had ample time and opportunity to establish themselves. Moreover, many of them participated in the salt trade, which provided them with handsome profits and strengthened their already impressive economic standing. As a result, the wealthiest boyars could afford to maintain their own militias and retinues of lesser landholders. Finally, Galicia's distance from Kiev meant that the Grand Prince could not easily interfere in its affairs, while proximity to Poland and Hungary not only provided models of aristocratic dominance, but also opportunities to summon foreign aid against undesirable princes.

The boyars of Volhynia, in contrast, were cast in a more traditional mold than those of Galicia. Most of them had arrived in the principality in the retinues of their princes, who were frequently appointed and replaced at the will of Kiev, which, because of its proximity, exerted a stronger political influence on the principality than it did on Galicia. The lands these boyars acquired were given in return for services they had rendered their princes. Because the Volhynian elite was dependent on the largesse of its princes, it was relatively loyal and supportive of them. This explains why it was the princes of Volhynia, and not Galicia, who were in the best position to unite the two principalities.

The Rostyslavychi of Galicia   Of all the principalities on the territory of modern Ukraine, Galicia was the first to break away from Kiev. Employing means both fair and foul, the wily Volodymyrko (1123–53) managed to bring the entire land under his control and then successfully withstood the efforts of the Kievan grand princes to dictate the course of events in Galicia. Building on this achievement, his gifted son, Iaroslav Osmomysl (1153–87) – the epithet means one possessed of eight senses – extended the boundaries of his principality south to the mouth of the Dnister River in present-day Moldavia. While maintaining peace and prosperity at home, Iaroslav nurtured cordial relations with the Hungarians and Frederick I Barbarossa of Germany. The fame and prestige that he and his land enjoyed in Rus' was reflected in this laudatory excerpt from "The Tale of the Host of Ihor": "O Iaroslav Osmomysl of Halych! You sit tall on your golden throne, propping up the Hungarian [Carpathian] mountains with your iron regiments, blocking the way to its king, closing the gates of the Danube ... your wrath rolls over the earth."[4] But as Galicia prospered, so did its boyars. In fact, so powerful did they become during Iaroslav's reign that even when he was at the height of his power, they forced him to abandon his second, common-law wife, Anastasia, and later had her burned at the stake.

After Iaroslav's death, chaos ensued. His son Volodymyr (1187–98), the last of the Rostyslavychi, "did not like to take council with his *muzhi* (boyars)," as the chronicle puts it. Before long, the boyars rose up against him and forced him to seek refuge in Hungary. Andrew, the Hungarian king, promised to reinstate him, but when he arrived in Galicia, he claimed the land for himself. As popular uprisings against the foreigners flared up, Volodymyr and the boyars came to an understanding and drove the Hungarians back. What did these years of conflict and destruction lead to? Although Volodymyr finally did regain his throne, he became more dependent on the boyars than ever before. This sorry episode established a pattern that would often be repeated in the next half-century – that of a strong ruler uniting the land, of boyars (fearful of losing their prerogatives) turning on his weaker successors and thereby providing foreign powers with a pretext for intervention, and of chaos ensuing until another strong prince appeared on the scene to master the situation.

The Romanovychi of Volhynia and Galicia   Although the rise of Galicia was a clear indication of the growing importance of the borderlands, its union with Volhynia bore the promise of greater, even epochal consequences for all of Eastern Europe. The man who brought about this union was Roman Mstyslavych (1173–1205) of Volhynia. Immersed in political struggles from early youth, Roman was chosen as prince by the Novgorodians in 1168 to defend their city against Suzdal's aggressive designs in the north, while his father, Mstyslav of Volhynia, competed with Andrei Bogoliubsky of Suzdal for control of Kiev in the south. After his father's death in 1173, Roman took over and reconstituted the fragmented, neglected family holdings in Volhynia. In 1188, the Galician boyars invited him to rule their land, but princely rivals and unfriendly boyar factions prevented him from doing so. Only in 1199 was he able to return to Galicia and unite it with Volhynia, thus creating a new, imposing conglomerate on the political map of Eastern Europe with an energetic, forceful prince of great ability at its head.

In his domestic policies Roman concentrated on expanding his princely power: that is, on undermining the boyars, many of whom he either exiled or executed. "You can't enjoy the honey without killing the bees" was one of his favorite sayings. As was often the case elsewhere in Europe, the prince's allies in the struggle with the oligarchy were the townsmen and minor boyars. However, it was his foreign exploits that added most to Roman's widespread fame. After uniting Galicia and Volhynia, he defeated his Suzdalian rivals and gained control of Kiev in 1203. Thus, all the Ukrainian principalities – Kiev, Pereiaslav, Galicia, and Volhynia (with the exception of Chernihiv) – came under the rule of one prince. It appeared that a renewal of those parts of the old Kievan realm that were on the territory of what is now Ukraine was about to take place. Because Roman came so close to achieving this goal, modern Ukrainian historians have accorded him an exalted place in their histories.

In his efforts to protect the Ukrainian principalities, Roman launched a series of highly successful campaigns against the Polovtsians, while, in the north, he pushed deep into Polish and Lithuanian territory. This desire to extend the boundaries of an already extensive realm proved to be the cause of his undoing. In 1205, while crossing into Polish territory, Roman was killed in an ambush. The territorial conglomerate he had assembled lasted only six years, too short a time for it to crystallize into a stable, permanant political entity. Still, by referring to him as "the Great" and "Autocrat of all Rus'," Roman's contemporaries showed their appreciation for his remarkable achievements.

Soon after Roman's death, the recurrent triumvirate of troubles – boyar intrigues, princely rivalries, and foreign intervention – dismembered the realm he had so assiduously forged. Because his sons, Danylo and Vasylko, were only 4 and 2 years old respectively, the Galician boyars had little difficulty in forcing them and their strong-willed mother, Anna, from the land. In their place, the boyars invited the three Ihorevychi, sons of the hero of "The Tale of the Host of Ihor." For many of the boyars this was a fatal mistake. Unwilling to share power with the oligarchy, the Ihorevychi massacred about 500 of them before eventually being expelled themselves. (Later, the Galician elite returned the favor by capturing and hanging all three of the Ihorevychi.) Next, the boyars attempted the unprecedented: in 1213, they elected their own leader, Vladyslav Kormylchych, as prince. Taking advantage of the general condemnation of this audacious move, the rulers of Hungary and Poland, under the guise of protecting the rights of Danylo and Vasylko, invaded Galicia and divided it between themselves. It was under these conditions that the young Danylo and Vasylko began the process of "gathering together" the lands their father had once ruled.

As might be expected, Danylo first reestablished himself in Volhynia (1221), where both the elite and the general populace remained loyal to his dynasty. But it was not until 1238 that he was able to retake Halych and a part of Galicia. In the following year, Danylo acquired Kiev and sent his military commander, Dmytro, to defend the city against the Mongols. Only in 1245, when Danylo won the decisive battle at Iaroslav, was his hold on all of Galicia secured. It thus took Danylo forty years to reconstitute the realm that his father had created.

Reserving Galicia for himself, Danylo left Volhynia for Vasylko. Despite this division, under the leadership of the older, more forceful Danylo, the two principalities continued to function as a single unit. Like his father, Danylo concentrated in his domestic policies on securing the support of the townsmen and peasants in order to create a counterweight to the boyars. He founded numerous towns – among them Lviv, named after his son Lev, in 1256 – and fortified many others. To populate these new urban centers, Danylo invited artisans and merchants from Germany and Poland, and from other Rus' cities. Large communities of Armenians and Jews, spreading westward as Kiev declined, added to the multiethnic character that was to typify Galician towns into the 20th century. In the countryside, special officials were appointed to protect peasants from boyar exploitation and peasant units were formed in the army.

Danylo's major foreign problem was the Mongols. In 1241, they had passed through Galicia and Volhynia without devastating them as badly as other Rus' principalities. However, the successes of the Romanovychi attracted the Mongols' attention. Soon after his victory at Iaroslav, Danylo received the dreaded summons to appear at the Mongol court. Fearful of antagonizing these dreaded conquerors, he had no choice but to comply. In a certain sense, Danylo's visit 1246 to Batu's capital at Sarai on the Volga was a success. He was well received and, more important, allowed to return alive. But this came at the price of accepting Mongol overlordship. This humiliating fact was underscored by Batu himself who, as he handed Danylo a cup of fermented mare's milk, the favorite Mongol beverage, urged him to get used to it "for you are one of ours now." However, unlike the northeastern principalities that were closer to the Mongols and more exposed to their direct control, Galicia and Volhynia were spared such close supervision. Their major obligation to their new overlords was occasionally to provide auxiliary troops during the Mongol forays into Poland and Lithuania. Mongol influence in Galicia and Volhynia was initially so weak that Danylo was able to conduct a very independent foreign policy, one openly aimed at ridding himself of Mongol overlordship.

After establishing cordial relations with Poland and Hungary, Danylo turned to Pope Innocent IV with a request for aid to organize a Slavic crusade against the Mongols. In return, Danylo expressed to the pope his willingness to place his lands under the ecclesiastical jurisdiction of Rome. Thus, he sounded what would become a major and recurrent theme in Galician history – the relationship of the West Ukrainians to the church of Rome. To encourage the Galician prince, the pope sent him a royal crown and, in 1253, in Dorohochyn on the Buh River, Danylo was crowned king by a papal representative.

Danylo's chief interest, however, was the crusade and other reinforcements from the west. These, despite the pope's assurances, were not forthcoming. Nonetheless, in 1254, Danylo launched a campaign to retrieve Kiev from the

Mongols, whose main forces were far in the east. Despite initial successes, he failed to achieve his objective and he paid dearly for it. In 1259, a strong Mongol force, led by Burundai, moved unexpectedly into Galicia and Volhynia. The Romanovychi were given two options by the Mongols: either raze the walls of all their fortified towns, leaving them vulnerable and dependent on Mongol goodwill, or face immediate annihilation. Dejectedly, Danylo had to oversee the destruction of the walls he had so diligently constructed.

The failure of his Mongol policy did not mean that Danylo's great influence with his western neighbors had declined. In Poland, especially in the principality of Mazowia, Galician authority reached a high point. Therefore, Mendvog, the ruler of Lithuania (which was just beginning its rise to power), was obliged to make territorial concessions there to Danylo. Moreover, as a sign of goodwill, Mendvog was forced to marry two of his offspring to Danylo's son and daughter. More than any other Galician ruler, Danylo became involved in the affairs of central Europe. Using matrimonial links as an instrument of foreign policy, he married his son Roman to Gertrude, the Babenberg heiress, and attempted unsuccessfully to place him on the Austrian ducal throne.

In 1264, after almost sixty years of political activity, Danylo died. In Ukrainian historiography he is considered to be the most outstanding ruler that the two western principalities ever produced. In view of the difficult circumstances under which he had to function, his achievements were remarkable. While rebuilding and expanding his father's domains, Danylo checked Polish and Hungarian expansion. Breaking the power of the boyars, he raised the social, cultural, and economic level of his land until it was among the highest in Eastern Europe. However, not all his plans succeeded. Danylo failed to hold on to Kiev and he did not attain his major objective – to rid himself of the Mongol yoke. Still, he managed to keep Mongol influence to a minimum. In his attempt to stave off the East, Danylo turned to the West, thereby providing West Ukrainians with an example that they would follow for centuries.

For almost a century after Danylo's death, Galicia and Volhynia experienced few apparent changes. The pattern set by Danylo and Vasylko – that of a dynamic, forceful prince in Galicia and a more retiring ruler in Volhynia – was followed to a certain extent by their respective sons, Lev (1264–1301) and Volodymyr (1270–89). The ambitious and restless Lev was constantly involved in political conflicts. After the Arpad dynasty was extinguished in Hungary, he obtained Transcarpathian Rus', thus laying the foundation for future Ukrainian claims to the western slopes of the Carpathians. Lev was most active in Poland, which was embroiled in internecine warfare; and he even aspired to the Polish throne in Cracow. Despite Lev's aggressiveness, both Galicia and Volhynia enjoyed a period of stability during the late 13th and early 14th centuries because their western neighbors were temporarily weakened.

Volodymyr of Volhynia was the antithesis of his Galician cousin and his relations with him were often strained. Unwilling to participate in wars and inactive in diplomacy, he concentrated on such peaceful pursuits as the building of towns, castles, and churches. Described as a "great bibliophile and philosopher" by the Galician-Volhynian chronicle, it seems that his favorite pastime was the reading and copying of books and manuscripts. Volodymyr's death in 1289 saddened not only his subjects, but modern historians as well, for, in what was probably a related development, the Galician-Volhynian chronicle suddenly broke off in that year. As a result, a great gap in the history of the western principalities, stretching from 1289 to 1340, now confronts historians. A few haphazard bits of information are all that are available about what occurred in Galicia and Volhynia in the final phases of their independent existence.

After the death of Lev, his son Iurii, ruled both Galicia and Volhynia. He must have been an effective ruler, for neighboring chroniclers noted that during his peaceful reign his lands "blossomed with riches and fame." Iurii's position was imposing enough for him to title himself "King of Rus'." An even more telling indication of the extent of his authority was an event that occurred in 1303. Dissatisfied with the decision of the metropolitan of Kiev to move his residence to Vladimir in the northeast, Iurii obtained Constantinople's assent to create a separate metropolitanate in Halych. The two last members of the Romanovych dynasty were Iurii's sons, Andrii and Lev, who ruled Galicia-Volhynia together. Worried by the growing power of Lithuania, they forged an alliance with the German knights of the Teutonic Order. In regard to the Mongols they followed an independent, even antagonistic policy and there are some indications that they may have died fighting them.

With the extinction of the native ruling dynasty in 1323, the elite of the two principalities chose Bołeslaw of Mazowia, a Polish cousin of the Romanovychi, as their prince. After changing his name to Iurii and adopting Orthodoxy, the new ruler set about to follow the policies of his predecessors. Despite his Polish background, he fought to regain lands that had in the meantime been lost to the Poles, and he renewed the alliance with the Germans against the Lithuanians. At home, Iurii-Bolesław continued to support the towns and attempted to expand his prerogatives. It was probably this policy that led to a conflict with the boyars who, in 1340, poisoned him under the pretext that he sought to introduce Roman Catholicism and favored foreigners. Thus, by the hand of its own elite, Galicia and Volhynia were deprived of their last prince. Henceforth, the West Ukrainians would have to live under foreign-based sovereigns.

૨▲

For 100 years after the fall of Kiev, Galicia-Volhynia served as the political base of the Ukrainians. In this capacity, the two principalities absorbed much of the Kievan heritage and at the same time prevented the absorption of West Ukrainian lands by Poland. By so doing, they preserved for Ukrainians, or Rusyns as they were then called, a sense of cultural and political distinctiveness at a crucial point in their history. This distinctiveness would be of critical importance to their survival as a separate national entity in the difficult times yet to come.

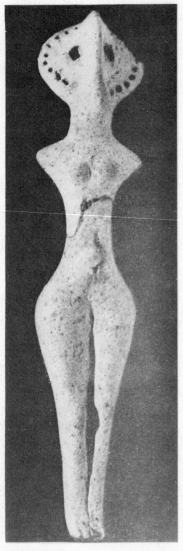

Female statuette made from
mammoth tusk, late Paleolithic period

Trypillian ceramic statuette,
ca. 3000–2500 BC

Gravestones on Polovtsian tombs

Scythians in combat

Scythian binding his comrade's wound

East Slavic pagan idol, ca AD 10th century

A reconstruction of Kiev in 10–13th centuries

ши красотоу црко вноую . и пѣнья . не слоубы . а
архиепискы . и престоялъ едѣ тисонъ . сказоую
ще слоуженне веатсвоѥ . и ниже вси гоумѣнии
бывше . иоудивиша . и похвалиша слоубоу и :

И призвавшая црь . василии . и костантинъ . рѣша
имъ . идѣте въ землю свою . и отпоустиша съ дары
велми . и чтью . они же пришедоша въ землю . и созва
црь боляры своя . и старци . и реⷡ володимеⷬ . се прншла пола
ни нам илоу . да слышиⷨ ꙗ бывшеѥ . и реша ꙗ кꙑ
те премоудроу ѿкꙑною .

OPPOSITE

Christianization of Kievan Rus' from "Chronicle of Bygone Years" (15th-century Radziwill version)

A reconstruction of St Sophia cathedral in 11th century

Mosaic from interior of St Sophia

Mosaic from interior of St Sophia

Dancing couple from 12th-century Chernihiv cup

Part Two

The Polish-Lithuanian Period

4

Under Polish and Lithuanian Rule

For millennia Ukraine had been the crucible of mighty political conglomerates such as the Scythian, Sarmatian, and Kievan realms. Its inhabitants controlled their own destinies and influenced, sometimes decisively, those of their neighbors. The civilizations that were based in Ukraine stood in the forefront of the cultural and socioeconomic developments in all of Eastern Europe. But after the decline of Galicia-Volhynia, an epochal transformation occurred. Henceforth, Ukrainian lands would no longer form the core of important political entities and, except for a few brief moments of self-assertion, the fate of Ukraine's inhabitants would be decided in far-off capitals such as Warsaw, Moscow, or Vienna.*

In cultural and economic terms as well, the status of Ukraine would decline to that of an important but peripheral province whose elites identified with foreign cultures and political systems. No longer dominant but dominated, the natives of Ukraine would have to struggle not only for their political self-determination but also for their existence as a separate ethnic and national entity. This effort became – and remains to this day – one of the major themes of Ukrainian history.

ﷺ

Lithuanian Expansion into Ukraine

The flow and timing of events worked to Ukraine's disadvantage in the 14th century. Precisely at the time when it was sinking to a political, economic, and cultural low point, Ukraine's neighbors – Lithuania, Poland, and Mus-

---

* During the Polish-Lithuanian period, Ukrainians called themselves Ruthenians (*Rusyny*), a name derived from Rus'. Belorussians were also called by this name. At this time, Russians were generally called Muscovites.

covy – were on the rise. Naturally these expanding societies were drawn to the power vacuum that existed in the south. There, ancient Kiev was but a shadow of its former self. Abandoned in 1300 by the Orthodox metropolitan, who moved to the thriving cities of the Russian northeast and eventually settled in Moscow, Kiev also lost many of its boyars and leading merchants. For extended periods of time it did not even have a resident prince. And with the extinction of the native dynasty in Galicia and Volhynia, the West Ukrainian lands were also left leaderless and vulnerable. For about eighty years the titular overlords of the Ukrainian lands were the Mongols. But endemic internal conflicts within the Golden Horde prevented it, even during its relatively brief period of overlordship, from exerting extensive control in Ukraine. Consequently, the land lay ripe for the taking.

Among the first to take advantage of the opportunities that beckoned were the Lithuanians. In the mid 13th century, their relatively primitive, pagan and warlike tribes were united by Prince Mindaugas (Mendvog) in order to withstand the pressure of the Teutonic Order of the German crusader-colonizers that established itself on the Baltic shores. From this struggle the Lithuanians emerged stronger and more united than ever. In the early decades of the 14th century, under the leadership of Grand Prince Gediminas (Gedymin) they moved into Belorussia. And in the 1340s, during the reign of his son Algirdas (Olgerd), who flatly proclaimed, "All Rus' simply must belong to the Lithuanians," they pushed into Ukraine.[1]

By the 1350s, Algirdas extended his sovereignty over the petty principalities on the left bank of the Dnieper and in 1362 his troops occupied Kiev. After inflicting a crushing defeat on the Golden Horde in 1363, the Lithuanians moved into Podilia. At this point, with much of Belorussia and Ukraine under its control (roughly half of old Kievan Rus'), the Grand Principality of Lithuania constituted the largest political entity in Europe. Its creation was a remarkable organizational feat, especially in view of the fact that it was accomplished in less than 150 years.

One ought not imagine the Lithuanian takeover of Ukrainian lands in terms of a violent invasion by hordes of fierce foreigners. Actually penetration, co-option, and annexation are more appropirate descriptions of the manner in which the goal-oriented Lithuanian dynasty extended its hold over the Slavic principalities. Frequently, Algirdas's forces, which consisted largely of his Ukrainian subjects or allies, were welcomed as they advanced into Ukraine. When fighting did occur, it was usually directed against the Golden Horde. Unfortunately, because of the dearth of sources from this period, historians have been unable to establish the details of the Lithuanian expansion. Nonetheless, there is general agreement on the major reasons for the rapid and easy successes.

First and foremost, for the Ukrainians, especially those in the Dnieper region, the overlordship of the Lithuanians was preferable to the pitiless, ex-

Map 10 Polish and Lithuanian expansion

ploitive rule of the Golden Horde. Secondly, because they were too few to control their vast acquisitions – most of the Grand Principality of Lithuania consisted of Ukrainian lands – the Lithuanians co-opted local Ukrainian nobles and allowed them to rise to the highest levels of government. This policy greatly encouraged the Ukrainian elite to join the Lithuanian "bandwagon." Finally, unlike the Tatars of the Golden Horde, the Lithuanians were not perceived as being completely alien. Still pagan and culturally underdeveloped when they expanded into Belorussia and Ukraine, their elite quickly fell under the cultural influence of their Slavic subjects. Numerous princes of Gediminas's dynasty adopted Orthodoxy. Ruthenian (Ukrainian/Belorussian), the language of the great majority of the principality's population, became the official language of government. Always careful to respect local customs, the Lithuanians often proclaimed: "We do not change the old, nor do we bring in the new."[2]

So thoroughly did the Lithuanian rulers adapt to the local conditions in Belorussia and Ukraine that within a generation or two they looked, spoke, and acted much like their Riurikid predecessors. Indeed, they came to view their expansion as a mission "to gather the lands of Rus'" and used this rationale long before Moscow, their emerging competitor for the Kievan heritage, also adopted it. It was for this reason that the Ukrainian historian Hrushevsky argued that the Kievan traditions were more completely preserved in the Grand Principality of Lithuania than in Muscovy.[3] Other Ukrainian historians even claimed that the Grand Principality of Lithuania was actually a reconstituted Rus' state rather than a foreign entity that engulfed Ukraine.[4]

Polish Expansion into Ukraine

Despite the Lithuanians' impressive gains in Ukraine, it was Polish expansion that would exert the more lasting and extensive impact on the Ukrainians. The man who initiated it was Casimir the Great (1310–70), the restorer of the medieval Polish monarchy. In expanding eastward, the king had support from three sources: the magnates of southeastern Poland, who expected to extend their landholdings into the neighboring Belorussian and Ukrainian lands; the Catholic church, which was eager to acquire new converts; and the rich burghers of Cracow who hoped to gain control of the important Galician trade routes. Only nine days after the death of Bołeslaw (the principality's last independent ruler) in April 1340, the Polish king moved into Galicia. He did so under the pretext of protecting the Catholics of the land, who were mostly German burghers. But it was obvious that Casimir had been planning the move for some time, for in 1339 he signed a treaty with Louis of Hungary which stipulated that the two kings would cooperate in the conquest of Ukraine.

The aggrandizement of Ukrainian lands did not proceed as smoothly for the Poles as it did for the Lithuanians, however. No sooner had Casimir returned to Poland than the willful Galician boyars, led by Dmytro Detko, asserted their rule over the land. Unable at the time to launch another incursion, Casimir was forced to recognize Detko as the effective ruler of Galicia. In return, the latter recognized, in a perfunctory and limited fashion, the Polish king as his overlord. An even greater threat to Polish aspirations in Galicia and Volhynia were the Lithuanians. Because Lubart, the son of Gediminas, was the son-in-law of the deceased Galician ruler, Bolesław, the Volhynian boyars recognized the young Lithuanian prince as their sovereign in 1340. Thus, when Detko died in 1344, the stage was set for a confrontation between the Poles and Lithuanians for control over Volhynia and Galicia.

For more than two decades, the Poles, aided by the Hungarians, fought the Lithuanians, with whom most of the Ukrainians sided, for control over Galicia and Volhynia. Unlike the interprincely conflicts that were familiar to the inhabitants of the old Rus' lands, this one had a new and disturbing dimension. Proclaiming themselves to be "the buffer of Christianity," the Poles, partly from conviction and partly in order to gain papal support, represented their push to the east as a crusade against the heathen Lithuanians and the schismatic Orthodox Ukrainians. This view of their non-Catholic enemies as being morally and culturally inferior boded ill for future relations between the Poles and Ukrainians.

In 1349, after a particularly successful campaign, Casimir gained control of Galicia and part of Volhynia. Finally, in 1366, the war ended with the Poles occupying all of Galicia and a small part of Volhynia. The rest of Volhynia remained in Lithuanian hands. But even at this point the Polish grip on their huge Ukrainian acquisitions – consisting of about 200,000 people and approximately 52,000 sq. km, an increase of close to 50% in the holdings of the Polish crown – was not secure. In the above mentioned pact with Louis of Hungary, Casimir had agreed that if he should die without a male heir, the crown of Poland and the Ukrainian lands would revert to Louis. In 1370, Casimir died, leaving four daughters but no son. Now the Hungarians moved into Galicia. Louis appointed Władysław Opalinski, a trusted vassal, as his viceroy and installed Hungarian officials thoughout Galicia. However, what the Poles lost through dynastic arrangements, they regained in the same way. In 1387, two years after she became the queen of Poland, Jadwiga, the daughter of Louis of Hungary, finally and definitely annexed Galicia to the holdings of the Polish crown.

Initially, the Poles were careful about introducing changes among their new subjects. Casimir referred to Galicia as "the kingdom of Rus'," just as its last native rulers had done. Ruthenian was used alongside Latin and the land preserved its own currency. But there were indications that the days of the old ways were numbered. As early as 1341 Casimir had requested Pope Benedict XII to free him of his commitment to the "Orthodox schismatics," to preserve their ancient rights, privileges, and traditions. The pope was happy to oblige. Indeed, the Catholic church (which because of royal generosity soon became the largest landowner in Galicia) stood in the forefront of attempts to undermine the old Orthodox order.

In 1375, a Catholic archdiocese was founded in Lviv. Meanwhile, monasteries, especially those of the Franciscan and Dominican orders, proliferated throughout the land. They served a rapidly growing Catholic population that consisted of Polish, German, Czech, and Hungarian noblemen who received land grants in Galicia and of German townsmen that the Polish monarchs had invited to help to develop the cities. Many of the Galician boyars adopted the faith of their Polish peers, especially after 1431, when they received equal status with the Polish nobles. By the mid 15th century, when Galicia was reorganized into the Ruthenian (Rus') *wojewódstwo* or province of the Polish kingdom and Latin became the official language of the land, there were few remainders left of the once proud Rus' principality of Galicia.

The Polish acquisition of Ukrainian lands and subjects was a crucial turning point in the history of both peoples. For the Poles, it meant a commitment to an eastern rather than the previously dominant western orientation, a shift that carried with it far-reaching political, cultural, and socioeconomic ramifications. For Ukrainians, the impact went far beyond the replacement of native rulers by foreigners: it led to the subordination of Ukrainians to another people of a different religion and culture. Despite certain positive effects produced by this symbiosis, eventually it evolved into a bitter religious, social, and ethnic conflict that lasted for about 600 years and permeated all aspects of life in Ukraine.

The Union of Poland and Lithuania

Once the issue of Galicia was settled, the political leaders of Poland and Lithuania realized that they shared important common interests. Both countries were threatened by the aggressive designs of the Teutonic Order, which controlled the Baltic coast. Especially Lithuania, strained to the limit by its expansion to the east, was in no position to confront the Germans in the north. To make matters worse, Moscow, growing rapidly in power and prestige, posed a threat in the east. Meanwhile, the Poles, dissatisfied with their dynastic connections with Hungary and eager to gain access to the other Ukrainian lands, were looking for new options. At this point the magnates of southeastern Poland proposed a striking idea: a union of Poland and Lithuania to be concluded by means of a marriage between their Queen Jadwiga and Jagiełło (Jogailo in Lithuanian), the new Grand Prince of Lithuania.

In 1385, in a small Belorussian town, the two sides concluded the Union of Krevo. In return for the hand of Jadwiga and, perhaps more appealing, the title of king of Poland, Jagiełło agreed, among other conditions, to the acceptance of Catholicism for himself and the Lithuanians and to attach "for all eternity" his Lithuanian and Ukrainian lands to the crown of Poland.

It seemed, from the formal point of view at least, that in return for the Polish crown, Jagiełło had agreed to liquidate the Grand Principality. But no matter what the Polish magnates and Jagiełło agreed upon, the Grand Principality was too big and vibrant, its elite too self-confident to allow itself to be absorbed by Poland. Lithuanian and Ukrainian opposition to Polish influence galvanized around Jagiełło's talented and ambitious cousin, Vytautas (Vitovt), who, in 1392, forced the king to recognize his de facto control of the Grand Principality. Although Poland and Lithuania remained linked by the person of Jagiełło, under Vytautas the Grand Principality retained its separate and independent identity. In fact, on several occasions, Vytautas attempted to sever all links with Poland and to obtain a royal title for himself. Although these attempts failed, they demonstrated very forcefully that the Ukrainian and Lithuanian elite of the Grand Principality was still very much its own master.

For the Ukrainian nobles – the masses hardly mattered politically – the preservation of the autonomy of the Grand Principality was a matter of great importance because unlike the Poles, the Lithuanians treated them as equals. Moreover, Vytautas followed two policies that warmed the hearts of his Ukrainian subjects. By renewing Algirdas's drive to the east, he continued the "gathering of Rus'" lands. And he pushed southward with the avowed purpose of subjugating the fragmented remnants of the Golden Horde, building in the process a system of fortifications to protect his subjects from the nomads. But the strong-willed Vytautas also instituted measures that were much less pleasing to the Ukrainians. To appreciate their significance, a few general remarks about the political structure of the Grand Principality are in order.

The political policies of the Lithuanian grand princes In a certain sense, the Grand Principality was similar to Kievan Rus'. It was a hodgepodge of semi-independent principalities, ruled by members of Gediminas's dynasty and clustered around a core area of which Vilnius was the capital and the seat of the grand prince. There was, however, a crucial difference, especially evident during the reign of Vytautas, that allowed Lithuania to avoid the fragmentation that Kievan Rus' experienced: the Lithuanian grand princes were clearly supreme rulers, not merely first among the equal members of the dynasty. By introducing a series of reforms in the 1390s, Vytautas saw to it that this did not change. The problem, as he perceived it, was that many Ukrainized princes of the Gediminas dynasty had sprung such deep roots in their principalities that they were more committed to local interests than to those of the Grand Principality as a whole. Some were even suspected of separatist tendencies.

To remedy the situation, Vytautas systematically reshuffled the princely holdings so as to remove the princes from their local bases of support. For example, Fedir Liubartovych was deprived, piece by piece, of his rich Volhynian lands. In exchange he was offered (but did not even bother to accept) the much less attractive Novhorod-Siversk principality, which was taken from Volodymyr Algirdovych, who, in turn, received a lesser holding. If a prince resisted, as did Fedir Koriatovych of Podilia, he was accused of disobedience, attacked by Vytautas's army, and driven into exile. In place of the semi-independent princes, Vytautas appointed his own servitors, who were often untitled boyars and who held their lands "at the Grand Prince's pleasure." Even petty boyars were exposed to change. In order to retain their lands, they were obligated to perform military service for the Grand Prince. Thus, the Ukrainian elite experienced strong, centralized rule of the type it had never known before.

While these policies caused widespread dissatisfaction among the Ukrainians, even more unsettling developments followed. In 1413, at Horodlo, Jagiełło and Vytautus agreed to grant the Catholic boyars of Lithuania the same far-ranging rights the Polish nobles had recently won. To speed up the implementation of this decision, forty-seven Polish noble families invited the same number of Lithuanian boyar clans to share their coats of arms. But as the Polish and Lithuanian nobles drew closer, the gap between the Lithuanian and Ukrainian elites grew deeper. The Catholic/Orthodox split that appeared in the Grand Principality as a result of the Union of Krevo in 1385 was now exacerbated by the social and political distinctions that favored the Catholics. The resentment that this circumstance engendered among the Orthodox came to the fore when Vytautus died in 1430.

That year the Ukrainians, backed by some Lithuanian magnates that disapproved of close ties with Poland, elected as grand prince Jagiełło's youngest brother, Svidrigaillo, who was prince of Siversk in eastern Ukraine. Although a Catholic, this adventurous, politically rather inept prince had always cultivated close ties with the Ukrainian Orthodox and soon after his election he made it clear that he intended to limit or even break off ties with Poland. Fearful of losing their access to the vast eastern lands, the Poles resorted to force and invaded Podilia and Volhynia. They also sought to undermine Svidrigaillo internally by organizing a pro-Polish party among the Lithuanians. This faction declared the election of Svidrigaillo as grand prince to be illegal and proceeded to elect Sigismund of Starodub, the younger brother of Vytautas, to the office. Consequently, in 1432, the Grand Principality split into two enemy camps: the ethnic Lithuanian areas sided with Sigismund while the Ukrainians backed Svidrigaillo.

The issues that separated these two camps were of crucial importance. Would the union of Poland and Lithuania continue to exist? Would the Ukrainians, by retaining Svidrigaillo on the throne, attain dominance in the Grand Principality? Or would the Poles gain access to the Grand Principality's vast, open Ukrainian lands? After some desultory fighting, negotiations ensued in which Sigismund and the pro-Polish side gained the advantage. By granting the Orthodox nobles the same rights that the Catholics enjoyed, Sigismund won over many of Svidrigaillo's Ukrainian followers. When Svidrigaillo employed terror tactics, such as the burning alive of Herasym, the metropolitan of Smolensk, he only encouraged more defections, which eventually led to his defeat. As a result of this conflict, another Ukrainian land, Podilia, came under Polish control. However, Volhynia, whose populace fiercely resisted the Polish invaders, remained a part of the Grand Principality. In any case, it was obvious that Polish influence and pressure had severely disturbed the previously placid relations between the Lithuanians and Ukrainians of the principality.

In the mid 15th century, relations between the Lithuanian and Ukrainian elites took a turn for the worse, especially after the new Grand Prince, Casimir Jagiełło, instituted another series of centralizing reforms. In 1452 Volhynia, occupied by a Lithuanian army, was transformed, in accordance with Polish models, into a common province, which was governed by an official of the Grand Prince. In 1471, Kiev and its surrounding territories experienced a similar fate. Despite the fruitless protests of Ukrainians to the effect that prestigious Kiev should rule itself or, at least, be governed by a prince rather than an untitled official, it was evident that the last institutional remainders of Kievan Rus' and of Ukrainian self-rule were quickly disappearing.

The rise of Moscow　While the Lithuanian grand princes cared little about retaining the goodwill of their Ukrainian subjects, the grand princes of Moscow cultivated it. And they were now a power to be reckoned with. By ingratiating themselves for generations with their overlords, the khans of the Golden Horde, the princes of Moscow rose to a position of prominence among the Russian principalities of the northeast. In time they transformed their predominance into control: in 1463, the principality of Iaroslav; in 1474, Rostov; in 1478, rich and vast Novgorod; and in 1485, the last serious Russian rival, the principality of Tver, succumbed to Moscow. With almost all the northeast under its aegis, Moscow cast off, rather anticlimactically, the centuries-old Mongol yoke in 1480. Along with Moscow's expanding power came the need to rationalize it. Therefore, the so-called Third Rome doctrine was formulated. It proclaimed that Moscow, after the fall of Rome and Constantinople, was destined to be the third – and permanent – holy and universal empire. Meanwhile, Ivan III of Moscow began to title himself "sovereign (*gosudar*) of all Rus'" and to claim that all the lands that were once a part of Kievan Rus' should now belong to Moscow.

For Lithuania, Moscow's actions as well as its words were deeply disturbing. In the 1490s, when Muscovite forces approached a number of Lithuanian principalities in the Chernihiv region of eastern Ukraine, their Orthodox princes voluntarily accepted Muscovite sovereignty. There were other signs of the attraction that Moscow was beginning to exercise on the Ukrainian elite of Lithuania. Earlier, in 1481, Prince Fedir Belsky, a Ukrainized great-grandson of Algirdas, together with several other Orthodox princes, had planned to assassinate Casimir IV, the current Grand Prince of Lithuania and King of Poland, and then place the Ukrainian lands under Muscovite over-lordship. However, the plot was discovered and while Belsky managed to escape to Moscow, his colleagues were captured and beheaded.

An even more dangerous outburst of the Ukrainian elite's discontent oc-curred in 1508 when Mykhailo Hlynsky, an influential and talented mag-nate of Tatar origin and West European education, organized an uprising of Ukrainian princes and nobles against Grand Prince Sigismund. In his exhor-tations to his followers, he spoke of the need to defend the "Greek" faith and of the renewal of the Kievan princedom. However, before the rebellion could spread, a powerful Polish-Lithuanian army forced Hlynsky and his support-ers to flee to Moscow. The uprising of 1508 was noteworthy not only because it reflected the dissatisfaction of Ukrainians in the Grand Principality but also because it was the last time that their elite would be able to muster the self-confidence to defend its rights by force.

The Crimean Khanate   Lithuania's already acute problems were compounded by the appearance in the south of yet another threat. During the Golden Horde's slow decline, its nomadic Tatar vassals who lived along the Black Sea coast broke away and formed the Crimean Khanate under the leadership of the Girei dynasty. Although the Crimean khans and their Nogai tribesmen lorded over the vast steppes that stretched from the Kuban to the Dnister rivers, they were unable to subjugate the rich Genoese and Greek trading cities situated on the Crimean coast. Therefore, they sought aid from their fellow Muslims and recent conquerors of Constantinople, the Ottomans. In 1475, an Ottoman invasion force captured Kaffa and most of the other coastal cities. The mighty and rapidly growing Ottoman Empire now had a foothold in Ukraine that it expanded in 1478 by forcing Khan Mengli Girei to accept the overlordship of the Ottoman sultan. However, the Crimean khans pre-served a large measure of autonomy, often following those policies that best suited their interests. One of their primary undertakings was the organiza-tion of large and frequent raids into the neighboring Ukrainian lands for the purpose of capturing slaves (*iasyr*), which were then sold in the markets of Kaffa and Constantinople. Once again the steppe became a menace to the sedentary peoples who lived on its fringes.

The Union of Lublin (1569)

By the early 16th century, it was evident that the Grand Principality of Lithua-nia was in a state of decline. In 1522, it lost Chernihiv and Starodub in northeastern Ukraine to Moscow. And in 1549 and 1552 it was unable to fend off two major Tatar incursions. The mounting crisis reached a high point during 1562–70 when Lithuania became involved in another protracted war with Moscow. Burdened by the tremendous costs of the conflict and confronted by the threat of a Muscovite invasion, the Lithuanians turned to Poland for aid. The Poles were ready to provide it – for a price. Their main condition was that Poland and Lithuania, whose links at this point consisted basically of possessing a common monarch, now unite into a single political entity.

Fearful of losing their dominant positions to Polish rivals and worried by increased Catholic influence, the Lithuanian and Ukrainian magnates balked at the idea of complete union with Poland. But the middle and petty nobility of the Grand Principality, resentful of the magnates' prominence and hoping to gain the broad prerogatives their Polish colleagues enjoyed, supported the Polish position.

Drama and bitterness marked the common deliberations that King Sigismund Augustus called in Lublin in 1569. Unhappy with the course of the negotiations, the magnates of the Grand Principality, led by the Lithuanian Protestant Krzysztof Radziwiłł and the Ukrainian Orthodox Konstantyn Ostrozky, walked out. In response, the Poles, backed by the petty nobles from the provinces of Volhynia, Pidlasia, and Kiev, proclaimed the annexation of these lands to Poland. This forced the recalcitrant magnates back to the bargaining table and on 1 July 1569 the Union of Lublin was concluded.

As a result of the union, a commonwealth (Rzeczpospolita) was formed that was to have a common, elected king, a common parliament (*sejm*), and common currency, tolls, and foreign policy. But the Grand Principality retained a measure of autonomy and preserved its own local administration, army, treasury, and legal system. However, all the Ukrainian lands that it possessed now became a part of the lands attached to the Polish crown.

For the Ukrainians, the Union of Lublin of 1569 was an event of tremendous import. Despite its shortcomings, for two centuries the Grand Principality of Lithuania had provided them with a hospitable environment in which to live. Although they were not independent, the Ukrainian princes did possess extensive control over their social, economic, religious, and cultural affairs. However, as the fate of Galicia (which had come under Polish rule earlier) indicated, once the Ukrainian lands and populace were transferred from Lithuania to Poland, their continued existence as distinctive societies would be put in question.

ટે

Between the 14th and 16th centuries the powers that would decide the fate of Ukraine for subsequent centuries came to the fore. Lithuania scored the most impressive initial gains in Ukraine and its rule was the most acceptable to its inhabitants. But the more numerous and aggressive nobility of Poland gradually pushed the Lithuanians from Ukraine by means of military pressure and negotiated settlements, and staked out the land as its primary area of expansion. In the background loomed the other important powers that would affect Ukraine: the rapidly expanding tsardom of Moscow and the Crimean Khanate, which was linked to the all-powerful Ottoman Empire. Under the circumstances, the prospects for Ukrainian self-rule were clearly not promising.

There were, however, a few notable attempts by Ukraine's regional elites to stand up for local interests. Most noteworthy was Dmytro Detko's aggrandizement of power in the 1340s in Galicia after the native dynasty died out, the Ukrainian support for Svidrigaillo in the 1430s, and Hlinsky's anti-Lithuanian uprising of 1508. But foreign, especially Polish, dominance introduced a new phenomenon – assimilation of the Ukrainian elites into the culture of the ruling powers. As they gradually identified with the culture of the dominant Poles, the Ukrainian nobles lost their readiness to defend local interests.

Social Structure and Economic Change

The ramifications of the Union of Lublin and the absorption of Ukrainian lands into Poland were not only political in nature; they also had a great impact on the way of life of the Ukrainians. Even before the union, a whole new socioeconomic order, very different from that of Kievan Rus', was evolving in Ukraine. The Ukrainians' exposure to the Poles, and through them, to Western Europe, had a crucial influence on the form and direction this socioeconomic development took. Because of it, society was organized along Western lines. Ukraine's economic links with the West became stronger than ever before. Indeed, rarely in Ukrainian history would the impact of the West on Ukraine as a whole be as great – and as evident in the everyday functioning of society – as it was under the overlordship of the Lithuanians and Poles.

ᴥ

Ukrainians in the Polish-Lithuanian Commonwealth

In terms of both territory and population, the Ukrainian lands in the Polish-Lithuanian Commonwealth formed a major part of what was the largest state in Europe. It is estimated – and one should bear in mind that statistics from this period are only rough estimations – that about 28% or about 2 million people of the Commonwealth's population of 7.5 million were Ukrainians. Poles, who inhabited only 180,000 sq. km of the 815,000 sq. km encompassed by the Commonwealth, made up about 50% of its population. Other ethnic groups in the state were, of course, Lithuanians, Belorussians, Jews, Germans, and Armenians.

After 1569, when the last administrative traces of the old Rus' principalities disappeared, the Ukrainian lands in the Commonwealth were divided into six provinces (*wojewódstwa*). Based on the incomplete data collected by the Polish historian Aleksander Jabłonowski, the size and population of these Ukrainian provinces is shown in table 1.[1]

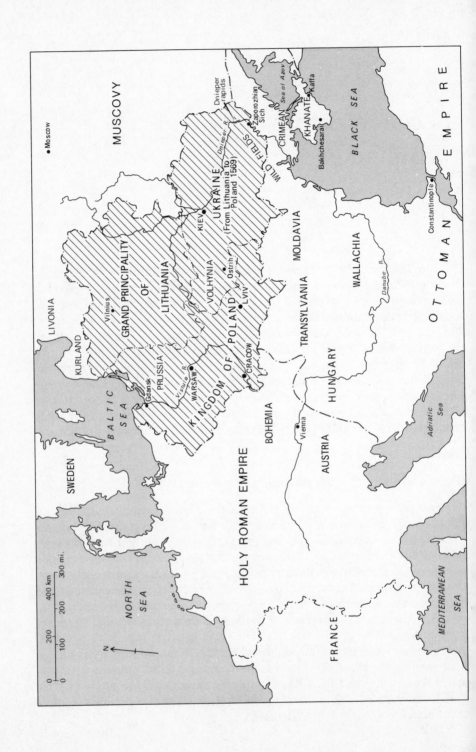

TABLE 1

Size and population of the Ukrainian provinces in the 16th century

Province	Square kilometers	Population (est.)	Population density per sq. km
Galicia	45,000	446,000	10
Volhynia	42,000	294,000	7
Podilia	19,000	98,000	5
Bratslav	35,000	311,000	9
Kiev	117,000	234,000	2
Belz (two regions)			
Kholm	19,000	133,000	7
Pidliassia	10,000	233,000	24

Foreigners who traveled through Ukraine often remarked on its low density of population. While Polish lands, on the average, contained about twenty-two inhabitants per square kilometer, Ukrainian territories (with the exception of Pidliassia which lay closest to Poland) averaged about seven persons per square kilometer. Kiev, the largest Ukrainian province, was practically empty. This had not been the case at the outset of the Lithuanian period. In the early 1400s, when Grand Prince Vytautas's expansionary drive reached the Black Sea, long lines of fortifications were built in the steppe to protect settlements that extended further south than in the times of Kievan Rus'. But as the Crimean Khanate grew stronger and Tatar raids increased, the sedentary population retreated northward until, in the late 1400s, the lower third of Ukraine was empty of sedentary settlements.

The Estate System in Ukraine

As the medieval period drew to a close, the estate system of organizing society, unknown in Kievan Rus', penetrated into Ukraine from the West by way of Poland. Unlike classes that reflect a social group's economic status, estates were based on the legally established rights, privileges, and obligations that each social group possessed. Initially, legal distinctions between the nobles, clergy, burghers, and peasants were fluid and it was possible for individuals to move from one estate to another. However, in time, boundaries between the estates, especially between the nobility and the other estates, became hereditary and well-nigh impenetrable. Indeed, in the early modern period, the estate to which one belonged was at least as important a category of self-definition as was one's religion or nationality.

The nobility   Foremost of the estates that emerged in the 14th–15th centuries was the nobility, whose high position stemmed, at least in theory, from the "blood spilled" in the military service of the king or grand prince. Various socioeconomic groups went into the making of this estate. In Ukraine, while it was still a part of the Grand Principality, the most important component of the nobility were the twenty to thirty princely or magnate families that traced their descent from the once-sovereign princes of the Riurikid or Gediminas dynasties. Most of these princely clans were concentrated in Volhynia, the bastion of Ukraine's aristocracy. The wealthiest among them, the Ostrozky family, had vast holdings that included about 30% of all the land in Volhynia (14,000 sq. km) on which there were 100 towns and over 1300 villages. Other rich and illustrious families were the Sanhusko, Chartorysky, Zbarazky, Vyshnevetsky, Zaslavsky, and Chetvertynsky. These families dominated most of the high offices in the Grand Principality and traces of their former sovereign rights survived in their right to lead their own troops under their personal banners or to be judged only by the grand prince, not by local officials.

The vast majority of the nobility, later called by the Polish term *szlachta*, consisted of those whose privileges derived primarily from military service.[2] The upper stratum of the *szlachta*, numbering several hundred families in Ukraine, some of whom descended from the boyars of Kievan times, owned estates of ten to fifteen villages and monopolized the local administration. Most numerous were the lowest levels of the nobility. Thousands of families, some recently emerged from peasant or burgher backgrounds, obtained noble status by serving as cavalrymen in campaigns, castle or frontier guards, or armed servitors of the magnates. Often they had just enough land to support themselves, and their life-style differed little from that of peasants. Especially in Galicia, whole villages were inhabited by poor noblemen with names like Kulchytsky, Iavorsky, Chaikovsky, and Vytvytsky.

Despite the great socioeconomic differences and tensions that existed within the nobility, the fact that these men of the sword received grants of privileges in common in 1387, 1413, 1430, and 1434 helped to develop among them a consciousness of belonging to a common estate. In Poland, where the nobility was best organized and most powerful, it constituted about 8–10% of the population (the European average was about 1–2%). In the Ukrainian lands of the Grand Principality, the nobles gained special status more slowly and probably did not make up more than 5% of the general population.

The burghers   The inhabitants of the cities in Ukraine, about 10–15% of the population, also evolved into a separate corporate entity. As they grew in size and self-confidence, major towns acquired the highly prized Magdeburg Law from Polish kings and Lithuanian grand princes. Modelled on the administration of the German city of Magdeburg and brought to Ukraine by way of Poland, the law was designed to provide a town with self-government. In 1356 Lviv, in 1374 Kamianets in Podilia, in 1432 Lutsk in Volhynia, and in 1494 Kiev obtained Magdeburg Law, thereby freeing themselves from the interference of royal or princely officials.

Despite the theoretical equality of all citizens subject to Magdeburg Law, sharp socioeconomic distinctions existed among a town's inhabitants. Rich, patrician families, such as the forty or fifty who formed the elite in Lviv, totally dominated town government. Small merchants and tradesmen formed the middle stratum. The urban laborers, who were usually deprived of rights because they owned no property in the town and often lived beyond its walls, made up most of its population. As always, the town dwellers were the most ethnically variegated social group: among them one could find Ukrainians who were descended from the original inhabitants of the towns and, in ever-increasing numbers, newly arrived Polish noblemen and officials, German craftsmen, and Jewish and Armenian merchants.

The peasants While special rights defined the above-mentioned estates, obligations characterized the approximately 80% of Ukraine's population who were peasants. For the right to use land, a peasant owed the landowning nobleman duties, which usually took the form of providing free labor or paying rents in kind. As long as a peasant fulfilled these obligations, and in the 14th century they were relatively light, rarely totaling more than fourteen days of free labor a year, he could not be removed from his plot of land. In fact, a peasant could sell or bequeath the use of his plot to others.

At a time when land was plentiful but people were not, peasants managed to win relatively extensive rights. They were free men – under the pressure of the church and economic constraints, the limited slavery that had existed in Kievan times had died out – who could challenge nobles in law courts and, under certain circumstances, leave their lord's estate to seek better conditions elsewhere. In certain areas of Ukraine there were peasants who were completely independent of nobles. For example, in the Carpathian highlands, where animal husbandry was prevalent, many villages possessed the "Moldavian Law," which provided them with complete autonomy in return for regular payments (usually in the form of sheep) to noble landlords. A similar arrangement existed under the "German Law," whereby an enterprising peasant (*soltys*), in return for a contractually established payment to a noble, obtained the right to establish and administer a village on the noble's land. Along the steppe frontier in central and eastern Ukraine, many peasants were freed from their obligations to their landlords in return for service as frontier guards.

The Lithuanian Statute The numerous grants of rights and privileges to various social groups in the Grand Principality created a need for a codified set of laws. Especially the middle and lower *szlachta*, anxious to convert its privileged status into an article of law, pressed for a legal code. As a result, in 1529, the first edition of the Lithuanian Statute appeared. In addition to confirming noble rights, it incorporated elements of customary law that reached as far back as Kievan times. Simultaneously, it introduced new legal concepts that originated in Germany. In 1568 and 1588 two more editions of the Lithuanian Statute appeared, inspired by the need to adjust to the changes brought on by the Union of Lublin.

It is difficult to exaggerate the importance of the Lithuanian Statute in Ukrainian legal history. Besides institutionalizing the important socioeconomic changes that occurred in 15th–16th century Ukraine, it also formed the basis of the legal system that developed later in Cossack Ukraine. In fact, as late as the 19th century, laws in parts of eastern Ukraine were still based on the statute. There is yet another aspect of the role in Ukraine of the Lithuanian Statute in particular and of the estate system in general that needs to be emphasized. Both of these elements were exceedingly influential in developing a familiarity with and appreciation of such concepts as legally defined and guaranteed rights among Ukrainians. And this consciousness served to link Ukrainians with Western legal and political thought. In contrast, Muscovy, the other outgrowth of Kievan Rus', as a result of centuries of Mongol rule, had little opportunity to familiarize itself with the principles of Western legality.

The Traditional Economy

Prior to the mid 16th century, a landowner produced food mainly to satisfy his household needs, to feed his livestock, and to provide seed for the next harvest. Time-consuming military duties, as well as lack of markets and cash, discouraged noblemen from engaging in commercial activities. Except for the portion of their estates that they reserved for their households, noblemen usually parceled out the rest of their lands to peasants. For the peasants this was a golden age. Noblemen did not interfere in their affairs, colonization increased the amount of available land, and improved agricultural implements raised productivity. While peasants' obligations and rents to their lords remained steady, their income increased.

It was not uncommon for a well-off peasant, of which there were many, to work a twenty-to-thirty-acre plot, own one or two horses or oxen, two or three cows, some pigs, and dozens of chickens and geese. An average Ukrainian's daily diet consisted of about 0.6 kilogram of bread and 2.5 liters of beer. Other common foods were kasha, cheese, eggs, and, when in season, fruits. Meat was eaten only rarely, usually during major holidays. The diet of the average nobleman was much the same except that his family consumed more meat, and sometimes such delicacies as imported spices, raisins, and figs appeared on his table. Sweets were rare and even wealthy noblemen could afford wine only on festive occasions. Even in the best of times, many of the poorer peasants and urban laborers went hungry. Because of poor hygienic conditions, the infant mortality rate was high and the median age was still only about 25–30 years.

For the towns, the 14th–15th centuries were also a time of well-being. Because they were a good source of income and potential allies against the nobility, Polish and Lithuanian rulers founded new towns and expanded existing ones. In order to generate income, rulers often imposed stringent regulations on the towns, such as high tolls, strictly regulated trade routes, and the granting of permission only to certain towns to sell imported goods. However, as noted earlier, they also granted them a great degree of autonomy and this encouraged urban growth.

In the early 15th century, Lviv, with approximately 10,000 inhabitants, was the largest city in Ukraine (Kiev, exposed to Tatar attacks and bypassed by shifting trade routes, had only 3000 inhabitants). Lviv's large population supported thirty-six different professions, grouped in fourteen guilds. Introduced in Ukraine by German immigrants, the guilds were craftsmens' organizations that protected the interests of their members and controlled the quality and quantity of the wares they produced. In Lviv alone, there were over 500 master craftsmen enrolled in their own or related guilds. Because the towns needed food for their growing populations and the countryside desired finished products, local trade – the mainstay of commerce – was conducted at regularly scheduled trade fairs. Foreign trade also prospered, especially in Western Ukraine, because such towns as Lviv and Kamianets lay astride Europe's main trade routes to Crimea and the East.

Yet, despite their growth, urban centers were still relatively scarce in Ukraine. In relatively populous Volhynia, for example, there was only one town per 300 sq. km. Not only their scarcity but also their ethnic composition limited the role of the towns in the lives of Ukrainians. The numerous foreign immigrants – Germans, Jews, Poles, Armenians, and Greeks – who were brought in by rulers to develop the towns in Ukraine soon formed a majority of the urban population, especially in the larger cities like Lviv. Most numerous were the Germans and Poles, whose religion, Catholicism, soon predominated in the towns. After Poland annexed Galicia and, later, the rest of Ukraine, linguistic and cultural Polonization spread rapidly among the urban populace.

For Ukrainian townsmen this led to severe restrictions. Arguing that the town laws applied only to Catholics, the Polonized urban elite excluded Orthodox Ukrainians from offices and courts. It also limited the number of Ukrainians that could reside in the city. For instance, in Lviv, only thirty Ukrainian households, confined to the small, cramped Ruthenian street (*Ruska ulica*), were allowed within city walls. Even Orthodox religious processions were banned in city streets and Orthodox burghers were forced to pay for the support of Catholic priests. In short, the towns became – and remained for centuries – foreign territory for most Ukrainians.

The great grain boom   During the 16th century, much of Europe was bustling with economic activity. Its population grew by leaps and bounds. And so did the price of food. Between 1500 and 1600, the so-called price revolution, exac-

erbated by the influx of silver and gold from the New World, led to unprecedented increases of 400–500% and, in some areas, even 800–1000% in the price
of food products. As the crowded cities of the West clamored for wheat, the
landowners of Eastern Europe, especially those of the vast Commonwealth,
responded. Ever-increasing shipments of grain flowed from the northern and
central areas of the Commonwealth via the Vistula River to Gdansk on the
Baltic Sea and then to Holland for distribution throughout Western Europe.
Meanwhile, in the southern regions of the Commonwealth, such as Podilia,
out of reach of the Vistula River route, great herds of cattle were raised and
driven to southern Germany and Italy. The great East European food rush, in
which Ukraine was to play a very prominent role, was on.

To produce food more efficiently and in greater quantities, nobles began
to transform their land holdings into commercially oriented food plantations
or estates called *folwarki* (*filvarky* in Ukrainian). It no longer made economic
sense for them to collect slowly increasing rents from small, inefficient, peasant holdings. Instead they tried to gain direct control of the peasants' lands
so as to amalgamate them into their estates and, in place of rents, they demanded ever more free labor from their peasants. Unlike in Poland, where
the estate economy spread quickly and extensively, in Ukraine its expansion
was slower. In order to make the estates feasible, access to markets and plentiful labor was essential. Although such conditions existed in parts of Galicia,
Volhynia, and Podilia and therefore estates soon appeared there, they were
absent in central and eastern Ukraine. There the land had to be colonized
before it could be economically exploited.

To encourage colonization, Polish or Polonized magnates whose connections in court helped them obtain grants of vast, empty Ukrainian lands, invited peasants to occupy these lands. To make their offers more attractive,
the magnates offered the lands as *slobody* (that is, areas that were freed from
all obligations and rents for periods of fifteen to thirty years). Thus, in the
sparsely populated Dnieper River basin the appearance of the *folwark* (estate)
system was postponed. When it did appear, it was greatly modified so as to
fit local conditions.

Noble Ascendancy

Its new-found economic strength helped the nobility of the Commonwealth
expand its already extensive privileges and political influence. At first the
szlachta sought to limit its obligations to its rulers. It cajoled the kings practically to eliminate the taxation of the nobility. Loath to go off on arduous
campaigns when there were fat profits to be made from their estates, the erstwhile warriors-turned-entrepreneurs also tried to limit their kings' right to
make war. In the late 15th and early 16th centuries, the *szlachta* gained control
of the local assemblies (*sejmiki*) and, somewhat later, of the *sejm*, the general
assembly of the Commonwealth, which possessed the highest legislative and

executive authority in the land. The *szlachta* was now in a position to limit the prerogatives of its kings more successfully than any other nobility in Europe. In 1505, the noble-controlled *sejm* passed the Nihil Novi Law which forbade the king to pass any new edict without the consent of the nobles' representatives. And in 1573, after the Jagiellonian dynasty died out, the *szlachta* gained the right to elect its monarchs and to define their prerogatives by means of a contractual arrangement called the *pacta conventa*.

Limiting royal power was only one of the nobility's goals. It also wished to deprive every other group in society of the possibility of threatening its favored position. Although the magnates, who numbered less than 100 families, belonged to the noble estate, their virtual monopoly on high offices, their vast landholdings, and their willingness to exploit their fellow nobles raised the ire of the middle nobility especially. Therefore, in the early 16th century, the *szlachta* managed, if only temporarily, to limit the magnates' access to offices and lands.

The towns were another target of the nobles' aggrandizing tendencies. Viewing them as their commerical rivals, the nobles did their best to undermine them. In 1505, they deprived most of the towns of voting rights in the *sejm*. Hoping to eliminate their role as middlemen in trade, in 1565 the noble-dominated *sejm* forbade native merchants from traveling abroad for goods. This action resulted in foreign merchants dealing directly with the nobles and catering to their wishes. Meanwhile, the *sejm* freed the nobles from import and export duties. Unable to withstand the pressure from the noble-dominated countryside, many townsmen decided to join it. Rich burghers invested their capital in estates and tried to marry their daughters into noble families. Craftsmen, unable to find work in the stagnating towns, moved their shops to the estates of the nobles. In Ukraine and elsewhere in the Commonwealth, the pace of urbanization slowed perceptibly.

This expansion of the nobility's privileges was the work of the Polish *szlachta*. In the Grand Principality prior to 1569, the Ukrainian nobility, especially its lower strata, did not enjoy such great rights as its Polish counterpart. The grand prince could still deprive nobles of their lands with relative ease, and the obligations that they owed their monarch were much greater than in Poland. A major reason why the lower nobility of the Grand Principality supported the union with Poland was that it wished to obtain rights similar to those of the Polish *szlachta*. But this meant that Ukrainian nobles would have to adapt to Polish ways. It involved accepting the *szlachta* system of government, adopting its laws and customs, and eventually using its language. Even a change of religion was encouraged because Polish law stipulated that a nobleman who adopted Catholicism would automatically receive the rights of a Polish nobleman. In short, for Ukrainian noblemen to enjoy equal rights with their Polish colleagues it was necessary that they become more like the Poles.

The Enserfment of the Peasantry

As the nobility's fortunes rose, those of the peasantry declined. From the point of view of the nobility, the role of the peasant was to provide cheap labor. Because nobles controlled the political system, they were in a position to raise their demands on the peasants almost at will. In early 15th-century Galicia, for example, labor duties consisted only of two or three peasants from a peasant commune (*dvoryshche*) working for their landlord about fourteen days a year. However, a century later, every adult member of the commune was obligated to work about two days a week on his landlord's estate. This became an article of law when the Voloky Ustav of 1557 – initially designed to introduce a uniform system of land measurement but gradually used to enforce peasant labor obligations – was introduced in the Grand Principality. Later still, peasants were forced to work three or four days a week and sometimes even more. With so little time to work their own plots, the peasants were not only unable to benefit from the higher food prices but they even failed to maintain their previous standard of living.

To facilitate the exploitation of the peasantry, the nobles systematically deprived them of their traditional forms of self-administration, removing or buying out the village elders with their old "Moldavian" or "German" laws and administering the villages directly, in accordance with Polish laws. This process of noble interference and dominance in village affairs began as early as 1457 when the nobles obtained the right to judge their peasants. Eventually, this circumstance allowed a nobleman to control various aspects of his peasants' private lives. Some noblemen went so far as to charge their peasants a fee for allowing them to marry. They also forced peasants to use the mills and taverns that they owned and frequently leased to Jews. By the time the Voloky Ustav of 1557 was passed, the peasants' right to own land was no longer legally recognized. They could work the land, but only a nobleman could own it.

Faced with steadily worsening conditions, many peasants tried to exercise their traditional right to leave their lord's land and seek better conditions elsewhere. But even this option was gradually eliminated. Initially, peasants were allowed to leave only at certain times in the year, most commonly at Christmas, and only if they paid an exit fee and found a replacement. In 1496, this right was restricted to only one peasant household in a village per year. Finally, in 1505, the *sejm* completely forbade peasants to leave their villages without their lord's permission. Unable to move, deprived of personal rights, exploited at will, the peasant became a serf, little better than a slave of his nobleman landlord.Thus, at a time when the institution of serfdom was dying out in Western Europe, the second edition of serfdom, as Engels called it, reemerged in a particularly oppressive form in Eastern Europe and Ukraine.

But the extent of serfdom in Ukraine varied greatly. In the more populated, western regions like Galicia and Volhynia, where Polish influence was strong, it was quite prevalent and severe. However, in the sparsely populated regions like the Carpathian highlands and, especially, the Dnieper River basin, where labor was scarce and concessions had to be made to peasants, serfdom was practically unknown. Moreover, the Ukrainian peasantry did not give in to serfdom without a struggle. In 1490–92, a series of peasant uprisings, led by a certain Mukha, enveloped Moldavia, Bukovyna, and Galicia. Although the rebels numbered about 10,000 men, they were handicapped by the classical weaknesses of all peasant uprisings: inexperienced leadership, lack of organization, poor military skills, and strictly local concerns. As a result, they were quickly defeated, demonstrating thereby that without the help of a militarily and politically more experienced class, the peasantry alone was incapable of challenging the nobles' monopoly on power and privilege.

≥●

While the inclusion of the Ukrainians in the Polish-Lithuanian Commonwealth exposed them to the invigorating influence of the West, it also laid the foundations for deep-seated problems that would bedevil Ukrainians (and Poles) for centuries. As a result of the grain boom, Ukraine's economy, like that of Poland proper, became extremely imbalanced and one-dimensional because almost all economic activity focused on agriculture. Meanwhile, towns and industry stagnated. This economic disequilibrium was accompanied by a great and growing social imbalance: the nobility of the Commonwealth gained extraordinary privileges, while the peasantry experienced a drastic decline in its condition. Because power, wealth, and privilege in the Commonwealth were increasingly associated with Polishness, resentment grew among those who would not or could not identify with Polish culture.

6

Religion and Culture

The struggle to preserve their cultural identity has long been a central theme in the history of the Ukrainians. Constantly ruled by foreign powers they were repeatedly exposed to attempts to assimilate them into the dominant culture. In the 16th century, as the Orthodox Ukrainians came into ever closer proximity with the Catholic Poles, an intense confrontation developed that flared up into religious/cultural warfare. Formulated primarily in terms of Orthodoxy and Catholicism – religion was the preeminent ideological issue for all Europeans at this time – this confrontation sparked the first major ideological debate in Ukrainian history. Although it focused on purely religious issues such as whether the Orthodox or the Catholic church could best assure the salvation of one's soul, it also posed questions that have become perennial in Ukrainian history – namely, whether the Ukrainian cultural heritage was doomed to extinction or capable of survival.

ta

Ecclesiastical and Cultural Affairs

Just as it was in Kievan times, Orthodoxy remained synonymous with culture in the 15th–16th centuries. Indeed, its role in Ukrainian society grew: with no state of their own, their church served for Ukrainians as the only institutional means of expressing their collective identity. Unfortunately for its adherents the church was mired in a state of deep decline – just at the time when a strong, inspiring Orthodox church was needed. More so than Catholicism and Protestantism, Orthodoxy flourished best when it had the protection and patronage of the political leadership. Such was the case in the days of Kievan Rus' and the Galician-Volhynian principality. But a close relationship between the Orthodox church and the Catholic rulers of Poland-Lithuania was difficult, if not impossible, to maintain. While pampering the Catholic church, the rulers treated the Orthodox institution like a neglected stepchild.

When the Ukrainians first came under Lithuanian rule, there was reason for some optimism as far as their church was concerned. Unwilling to leave their numerous Orthodox subjects under the jurisdiction of the metropolitan of Moscow, the grand princes of Lithuania reestablished a metropolitanate in Kiev in 1458. Consisting of 10 dioceses in Ukraine and Belorussia, the new metropolitan's see broke its ecclesiastical ties with Moscow and returned to the jurisdiction of the patriarch in Constantinople. Following the practice of the times, the grand princes and, later, the kings of Poland acquired the right of patronage; that is, they could appoint Orthodox bishops and even the metropolitan himself. Thus, the crucial issue of the leadership of the Orthodox faithful was left in the hands of secular rulers of another, increasingly antagonistic, church.

The results were disastrous. With lay authorities capable of appointing bishops, the metropolitan's authority was undermined. And with every bishop acting as a law unto himself, the organizational discipline of the Orthodox church deteriorated rapidly. Even more deleterious was the corruption that lay patronage engendered. Recently ordained fortune hunters frequently bribed their way into the bishop's office so that they could plunder the diocese by selling off its icons, jewels, and lands. Eventually, even common noblemen took to auctioning off parishes or monasteries situated on their lands to the highest bidder or assigning them to unqualified relatives. Even the highest clergy behaved in the most unseemly manner. Metropolitan Onysifor Divochka, for example, was accused of bigamy; Bishop Kyrylo Terletsky was taken to court, and acquitted, of manslaughter, rape, and assault; Bishop Ion Borzobohaty charged the faithful a fee to use the church. Following the lead of their superiors, parish priests behaved so badly that contemporaries complained that only "human refuse" was to be found among them and that they were more likely to visit a tavern than a church.

Under the circumstances, Orthodoxy's cultural contributions were limited. Schools, once one of the church's most attractive features, were neglected. Unqualified teachers barely succeeded in familiarizing their pupils with the rudiments of reading, writing, and Holy Scriptures. The curriculum of the schools had changed little since medieval times. The fall of Constantinople to the Ottomans in 1453 added to the intellectual and cultural stagnation by depriving the Orthodox of their most advanced and inspiring model. Lacking both external and internal stimuli, Orthodox culture slipped into ritualism, parochialism, and decay.

The Poles, meanwhile, were enjoying a period of cultural growth and vitality. Benefiting from the West's prodigious outbursts of creative energy, they experienced the Renaissance with its stimulating reorientation of thought. Abandoning the medieval preoccupation with the afterlife, individuals like the astronomer Copernicus, the political theorist Andrzej Frycz-Modrzewski, and the author Jan Kochanowski reflected Humanism's new-found interest in man – his experience in this life, and his social and physical environment. The graduates of the university in Cracow and hundreds of Polish students who had studied in the vibrant universities of Italy and Germany helped to spread the new ideas. By the early 16th century, about twenty printing presses and over 3000 parish schools were functioning in Poland.

The Reformation, whose impact in the Commonwealth became noticeable in the mid 16th century, brought new currents of creative ferment. Calvinism, with its emphasis on the role of the laity in religious affairs, found favor among 25–30% of the nobility. Arianism, a radical offshoot of Calvinism that rejected the notion of the Trinity and preached pacifism, established small but influential congregations thoughout Poland, Lithuania, and even Volhynia. To spread their ideas more effectively, the Protestants founded schools of higher learning, established printing presses, and further developed the use of Polish as a literary language. Despite the intense religious rivalries that evolved in the 16th century, the Commonwealth, unlike most of Europe, remained an oasis of religious tolerance. To a large extent, this factor was a function of the nobility's tremendous influence, for, since a noble's rights were inviolable, his religious views, no matter how different, also had to be respected.

When the Catholic reaction to Protestantism gained momentum in the late 16th to early 17th centuries, it achieved some of its greatest successes in Poland. Much of the credit for this achievement belongs to the Jesuits, the shock troops of the Counter-Reformation, who arrived in Poland in 1564. With intensely committed, well-educated, and sophisticated members in its ranks, this highly disciplined religious order was able to entice many of its church's wayward sheep back into the fold. Establishing a network of excellent colleges throughout the Commonwealth, the Jesuits not only educated Poles in a militantly Catholic spirit but also attracted talented Protestant and Orthodox youths into their sphere of influence. Slowly, under the impact of the Counter-Reformation, the former religious tolerance of the Commonwealth began to give way to Catholic fanaticism.

The Polonization of the Ukrainian Nobility

The attractive Polish model of the privileged nobleman exerted a powerful assimilatory influence on the Ukrainian nobility. And the obvious superiority of its culture intensified the appeal of all things Polish. The Jesuits, sure of their victory over Protestantism, now focused their attention on the "schismatics," as they called the Orthodox. Soon after 1569, they moved into Ukraine, establishing collegiums in Iaroslav, Lviv, Kamianets, Bar, Lutsk, Vinnytsia, and Kiev. Their best polemicists, most notably the brilliant Piotr Skarga, castigated the alleged doctrinal fallacies and the cultural backwardness of the Orthodox in sermons and open debates. In his famous work "The Unity of God's Church," Skarga argued that the state of Orthodoxy was so hopeless that its adherents' only alternative was union with Rome. "The Greeks fooled you, O Ruthenian people," Skarga wrote, "for in giving you the Holy Faith, they did not give you the Greek language, forcing you to use the Slavonic tongue so that you could never attain true understanding and learning ... for one can never attain learning by means of the Slavonic language."[1]

For status conscious Ukrainian noblemen – and nobles are by definition status conscious – their association with a religion and culture that was considered to be inferior was extremely galling. As a result, they abandoned the faith of their forefathers in droves and embraced Catholicism along with the Polish language and culture. In 1612, in a mournful work entitled "Trenos or the Lament of the Holy Eastern Church," a leading Orthodox churchman, Meletii Smotrytsky, bemoaned the loss to Rus' and Orthodoxy of its leading families: "Where are the priceless jewels of [Orthodoxy's] crown, such famous families of Ruthenian princes as the Slutsky, Zaslavsky, Zbarazky, Vyshnevetsky, Sangushsky, Chartorysky, Pronsky, Ruzhynsky, Solomyretsky, Holovchynsky, Koropynsky, Masalsky, Horsky, Sokolynsky, Lukomsky, Ruzyna, and others without number? Where are those who surrounded them ... the wellborn, glorious, brave, strong, and ancient houses of the Ruthenian nation who were renowned thoughout the world for their high repute, power, and bravery?"[2] The question was obviously rhetorical, for it was common knowledge that all of these illustrious magnate families had joined the Catholic-Polish camp.

An insight into one of the ways in which the process of assimilation worked was provided by the Polish archbishop of Lviv, Prucznicki, himself a descendant of a Ukrainian family: "When it happened that a wealthy young lady or a rich widow became available then the Polish kings would dispatch their Polish noblemen to Rus' and helped them [to arrange a good marriage] by means of their influence; as these nobles married, they inundated Rus' and introduced the proper, Roman Catholic faith. Conscientious priests saw to the rest, for soon even the magnates in Rus' abandoned the Greek Schism and joined the Roman church."[3] Of the remaining Ukrainian Orthodox magnates, only a few, notably those who began their careers before 1569, when the Ukrainians were still a potent political and cultural force in the Grand Principality, remained true to the old faith. Traditional ways still survived among pockets of poor gentry, which lived in isolated areas, far from the centers of Polish culture. However, they were politically, socially, and economically too weak to stem the process of Polonization.

One cannot exaggerate the profound implications that the loss of their elite had for the Ukrainians. In the hierarchically structured societies of early modern Europe, for a people to be without a nobility was tantamount to being a body without a head. It meant that Ukrainians were left without the class that normally provided political leadership and purpose, patronized culture and education, supported the church, and endowed a society with a sense of ethnopolitical identity. With the spread of Polonization among much of the Ukrainian nobility, Orthodoxy, as well as the Ukrainian language and customs, became associated primarily with the lower classes. As such they became the objects of scorn in the eyes of the Polish establishment in the Commonwealth. Henceforth, ambitious, talented Ukrainian youths would constantly be forced to choose between loyalty to their own people and traditions and assimilation into the dominant culture and society. Usually they opted for the latter. Consequently, the problem of a Ukrainian elite, or rather, the lack of one, now emerged as yet another of the central and recurrent themes in Ukrainian history.

The Orthodox Revival

Despite its weaknesses, Orthodoxy was able to mount a response to the Polish Catholic challenge. Fighting fire with fire, the few Ukrainian magnates who remained committed to their traditional faith established Orthodox schools and printing presses on their estates. In 1568, Hryhorii Khodkevych provided Ivan Fedorov, a printer who had been hounded out of Moscow because of his attempts to employ the "blashphemous" new printing techniques, with a refuge in his residence in Zabludniv in Belorussia and encouraged him in his work. There are indications that in the 1570s Prince Iurii Slutsky founded a school and printing press on his estate. Support was also forthcoming from the energetic Prince Andrei Kurbsky, a Muscovite defector who settled in Volhynia in the 1570s and devoted himself to the defense of Orthodoxy. But the most widely recognized and important patron of the Orthodox church was the "uncrowned king of Ukraine," Prince Konstantyn Ostrozky, one of the richest and most powerful magnates in the Commonwealth.

Konstantyn Ostrozky and the Ostrih Academy Sparing no cost, in 1578 Ostrozky established a printing press, run by the peripatetic Ivan Fedorov, on his estate at Ostrih in Volhynia. Its most famous publication, the scrupulously edited Ostrih Bible, appeared in 1581. It was the first printed Bible to appear in a Slavic language. Ostrozky also founded schools in Turiv and Volodymyr, and, in 1580, he opened the so-called Ostrih Academy. Initially, it was staffed by learned Greeks whom the prince had invited. Later, their most talented Ukrainian pupils, such as Meletii Smotrytsky, also joined the faculty. The curriculum matched that of the best Jesuit schools. It consisted of Greek, Latin, and Church Slavonic and the seven "liberal arts," which were divided into the *trivium* consisting of grammar, rhetoric, and dialectics and the *quadrivium* composed of arithmetic, geometry, music, and astronomy.

Soon the Ostrih center of learning attracted such intellectuals as the nobleman Herasym Smotrytsky (who served as its rector), the priest Damian Nalyvaiko, the monk Vasyl Surazsky (who was a graduate of Italian universities), and the anonymous Ostrih Cleric. Among the foreigners who were associated with the academy were the noted author Krzysztof Bronski, the professor of astronomy from Cracow Jan Latos, and the learned Kyril Lukaris, who later became the patriarch of Constantinople. Inspired by the impact of this cultural center, an Orthodox contemporary wrote: "Our Orthodox faith has begun to shine like the sun again; learned men have returned to God's church and printed books have multiplied." Yet, despite the fact that the Ostrih Academy demonstrated that Ukrainians were capable of impressive intellectual endeavors, its base of support was weak. All depended on Prince Konstantyn Ostrozky. And when he died in 1608, his fanatically Catholic granddaughter, Anna, wasted no time in turning the academy over to the Jesuits.

The brotherhoods (bratstva)   Luckily for the Orthodox, individual magnates of the old school were not the only patrons of Orthodox high culture. Even without its elite, Ukrainian society was too large and too deeply imbued with tradition not to generate other defenders of its religiocultural identity. It was in the towns where Ukrainians were frequently a hard-pressed but tightly knit minority that the new champions of Orthodoxy appeared. In contrast to the lone, aristocratic Ostrozky, they were groups of townsmen who banded together in organizations called brotherhoods (*bratstva*).

Historians speculate that these brotherhoods originated in medieval times for the purpose of maintaining churches, supplying them with candles, icons, and books. Probably influenced by guilds, they adopted an organizational pattern that included annual elections of officers, mandatory monthly meetings, payment of dues, and communal courts. They gained popularity and respect by engaging in such activities as caring for the widows and orphans of deceased members, supporting hospitals, and providing members with interest-free loans. By the 16th century, the most important and influential brotherhood was the one associated with the Dormition (Uspensky) Cathedral in Lviv. It provided the model for other brotherhoods, which appeared in Halych, Rohatyn, Stryi, Komarno, Iaroslav, Kholm, Lutsk, and Kiev.

In terms of social composition, the brotherhoods generally consisted of common merchants and craftsmen. As their influence grew, rich merchants – in Lviv they usually made their fortune in the cattle trade – also enrolled. However, in some brotherhoods other social groups predominated. For example, in Lutsk the nobles seemed to be in the majority, while in Kiev it was the clergy. In a highly stratified society such as that of the Commonwealth, it is noteworthy that the brotherhoods accepted Orthodox members from all social strata. But their membership was never large. In Lviv there were no more than thirty members because that was the number of Ukrainian-owned houses that were allowed in the city. Meanwhile, in Lutsk the membership of the brotherhood was probably no more than fifteen. Nonetheless, these small, cohesive organizations proved to be remarkably effective in their endeavors.

One of their major concerns was education. In the late 16th century, the Lviv brotherhood founded its own school and, except for the learned Greek Arsenii, all of the teachers who taught there – and these included Zyzanii Tustanovsky, Kyrylo Stavrohretsky, and the future metropolitan, Ivan Boretsky – were locally recruited. The exacting, if somewhat unrealistic, standards that these idealistic youths – members of the older generation did not participate in this work – applied to their efforts is evident from the text of the school regulation (*shkilnyi poriadok*): a teacher was to be "pious, wise, modest, mild and not a drunkard, reveler, bribe-taker, and money-lover. Nor should he be easily angered, jealous, a clown, a gossip, a magician, a story-teller, or an adherent of heresies."[4] Emphasizing the great responsibilities that teachers bore, the regulations admonished them "to teach well and to punish the disobedient not tyrannically but so as to teach them a lesson." So successful was the school in Lviv that other brotherhoods approached it with requests for advice and teachers; by the early 17th century, numerous brotherhood schools existed throughout Ukraine.

Another important aspect of the Lviv brotherhood's activity, initiated even before the expansion of its school, was printing. When Ivan Fedorov arrived in Lviv, the brotherhood helped him establish a printing press. In 1574, his first book, "The Apostol," appeared. It was a momentous occasion for it marked the beginning of printing in Ukraine. Fedorov returned to Lviv again in 1582, where he died the following year in great poverty. When foreign creditors threatened to take possession of his press, the Lviv brotherhood bought it and used it to make their city a center of Orthodox book publishing.

The proliferating schools and publications roused the previously passive and conservative Ukrainians. As hundreds of graduates, steeped in native traditions and also acquainted with Western learning, moved into towns and villages in search of a living as itinerant teachers, they carried with them, in addition to the modern knowledge, a new sense of self-confidence and militancy. Rather than succumb to the attractions of Polish Catholicism, Ukrainians became increasingly willing to defend the religious traditions that set them apart from the Poles. An example of these new attitudes was the strong and successful resistance that the Orthodox, led by the Lviv brotherhood, mounted in the late 1580s against Polish Catholic attempts to impose the Gregorian calendar upon them.

Clearly much of the credit for these changes belonged to the brotherhoods. Yet they also had their defects. Lack of funds was always a problem. Despite their proliferation, the brotherhoods never formed an umbrella organization and their links with each other were sporadic. Their levels of activity were erratic because even the work of the leading Lviv brotherhood depended on a few committed individuals. When the latter grew disillusioned, tired, or (as in the case of teachers) moved away to a materially more secure and rewarding position, the activity of the brotherhood often ceased for extended periods of time. Even more serious were the problems arising over the question of the brotherhoods' right to interfere in church affairs. As might be expected, constant conflicts raged between them and the bishops over such issues as control over the resources of a rich monastery (an example was a fierce, protracted struggle between Bishop Balaban of Lviv and the local brotherhood) or a disagreement between the bishop and the townsmen over the interpretation of the Bible. The upshot of the matter was that the brotherhoods, instead of helping to rehabilitate the Orthodox church, often added to the anarchy within it.

The Union of Brest (1596)

Ever since they split in 1054, the Catholic and Orthodox churches had considered the idea of reunion. In Ukraine, attempts to unite the churches dated as far back as the 13th century and, after the Council of Florence in 1439, the idea almost came to fruition. However, in opposition to the inherently attractive concept of Christian unity lay centuries of ill will and mutual suspicion. Especially the Orthodox were fearful that the more powerful Catholic church might try to dominate them if they entered into a union. Their fears were not misplaced, for during the 16th century the Polish Catholics, confident of their superiority, pressed for a union in the belief that this would inevitably lead to the assimilation of the Ukrainian Orthodox and the expansion of Polish Catholic influence. In 1577, Piotr Skarga's persuasively argued work "The Unity of God's Church" had a widespread impact. Meanwhile, Jesuits worked systematically to persuade leading Ukrainian magnates to support the idea of a union. Even Prince Ostrozky declared his support for the concept in principle. And King Sigismund III, a devout Catholic, used all his influence to help the matter along. In addition to religious fervor, the king had political reasons for backing a union because it would bind Ukraine and Belorussia closer to the Commonwealth and remove them from the dangerous influence of neighboring Orthodox Muscovy.

Surprisingly, it was from the Orthodox side that the immediate impetus for arranging a union emerged. In 1590, Gedeon Balaban, the Orthodox bishop of Lviv, infuriated by his endless disputes with the brotherhood and even more by the tactless interference of the patriarch of Constantinople, broached the idea of a union with Rome at a secret meeting of Orthodox bishops in Belz. In addition to Balaban, three bishops – Kyrylo Terletsky of Lutsk, Dionisii Zbyriusky of Kholm, and Leontii Pelchytsky of Turiv – agreed to investigate the matter further. Later, the conspirators were joined by Ipatii Potii of Volodymyr. This energetic, recently ordained nobleman and former Calvinist, together with Terletsky, became the leader of the pro-union coterie of bishops.

A mixture of self-interest and sincere concern for their church motivated the bishops. They believed that the prestigious, well-organized Catholic church would impose much-needed order and discipline among the Orthodox. That this result would raise the bishops' authority over the clergy and laity was also a consideration. By becoming a part of the Catholic church, the bishops hoped to achieve full equality for the Orthodox in the Commonwealth. No longer, they claimed, would Ukrainian burghers be mistreated in the towns or Orthodox noblemen passed over in appointments to office because of their religion. Moreover, the bishops would also benefit because if they received equal status with the Catholic hierarchy, they would gain membership in the prestigious and influential Senate. Egged on by these alluring prospects and following a series of surreptitious meetings with royal officials, Catholic bishops, and the papal nuncio, in June 1595, the four Orthodox bishops agreed to bring their church into a union with Rome. In return for the guarantee that the traditional Orthodox liturgy and rites, as well as such practices as the right of priests to marry, would be respected, they accepted the supreme authority of the pope in all matters of faith and dogma. At the end of 1595, Terletsky and Potii traveled to Rome, where Pope Clement VIII formally recognized the union.

When news about what had occurred spread, the Orthodox community broke into an uproar. Its leader, Prince Ostrozky, was infuriated not by the idea of the union itself but by the manner in which it had been handled. In a widely distributed open letter, he denounced the bishops as "wolves in sheeps' clothing" who betrayed their flock. And he called on the faithful to protest. In addition to lodging a formal complaint with the king – which was ignored – Ostrozky entered into an anti-Catholic compact with the Protestants and threatened to lead an armed uprising. Meanwhile, in all the Ukrainian and Belorussian lands, Orthodox noblemen vociferously denounced the union in their local assemblies. Frightened by the outcry, the initiators of the affair, Bishops Balaban and Kopystensky, deserted their colleagues and formally declared their opposition to the union.

To resolve the matter, a church council (*sobor*) was called in Brest in 1596. Never had Ukraine and Belorussia seen such a multitudinous church gathering. The antiunion forces included the two above-mentioned bishops, Orthodox dignitaries from abroad, dozens of elected noble representatives, over 200 clergy, and numerous lay supporters. To ensure their safety, Ostrozky brought along part of his private army. In contrast, the pro-union camp mustered but a handful of Catholic hierarchs, royal officials, and four Orthodox bishops. It was immediately apparent that the two sides could not find common ground. Realizing that negotiations were pointless, the pro-union or Uniate side publicly reiterated its intention to enter into the union.

Despite protests and threats, the Orthodox could not force them to retreat from their position or to have the king remove them from office. Thus, Ukrainian society split in two: on the one hand were the Orthodox magnates, the majority of the clergy, and the masses, while on the other, backed by the king, was the former hierarchy and a handful of followers. Consequently, a situation existed in which there was a hierarchy without faithful, and faithful without a hierarchy. What had begun as an attempt to unite the Christian churches ended in their further fragmentation, for now instead of two there were three churches: the Catholic, Orthodox, and Uniate (or Greek Catholic as it was later called).

Religious polemics   The controversy surrounding the Union of Brest evoked an unprecedented outburst of polemical writing. Not unexpectedly, the indefatigable Jesuit Skarga fired the first shot in this bitter war of words with his "Union of Brest and Its Defense" (1597). From the centers of Orthodox learning came a quick response. In Ostrih, a nobleman, Martyn Bronevsky, writing under the pseudonym of Khristofor Filalet, published that same year in Polish (and in 1598, in Ukrainian) his *Apokrisis*. It contained a compilation of documents revealing the Greek Catholic bishops' machinations, as well as arguments defending the legitimacy of the Orthodox council held at Brest. With a typical nobleman's distrust of authority and an admixture of Protestant ideas, Bronevsky rejected the bishops' claim to exclusive decision-making rights in the church.

Another member of the Ostrih circle, the unidentified Ostrih Cleric, applied biting satire in the pamphlets he wrote against the Greek Catholics. Somewhat later, in1605, Lviv's contribution to the Orthodox polemical barrage appeared. Entitled "Warning," this unsigned work focused on the selfish motives that allegedly guided the Greek Catholic bishops. On the Greek Catholic side there was only one noteworthy writer – Ipatii Potii. Using well-developed Jesuit models, he published in 1599, in Ukrainian, his *Anti-Apokrisis*, a temperamental reponse to Bronevsky's polemic.

Perhaps the most powerful Orthodox writer of the period was Ivan Vyshensky. A Galician who spent most of his life – he lived sometime between 1550 and 1620 – as a reclusive monk on Mount Athos in Greece, Vyshensky was a fanatical defender of Orthodox traditions. Writing in simple but powerful prose, he mercilessly castigated the Greek Catholics in such works as "A Letter to the Bishops Who Abandoned Orthodoxy" and "A Short Response to Piotr Skarga." But he also criticized the Orthodox, emphasizing the egoism, self-indulgence, and corruption of their nobility, wealthy burghers, and clergy as being responsible for the sorry state of their church. Very much a man of the people, Vyshensky was unique in bemoaning the enserfment of the peasants and fearless in denouncing their exploiters. For all the defects of Ukrainian society, he saw only one solution: a complete rejection of all innovations, including such "pagan tricks as grammar, rhetoric, dialectics, and other infamous temptations," and a return to the simple Orthodox beliefs of old.

The literary output of the polemical writers was not voluminous. All the feuding parties together probably did not produce more than twenty to thirty works during several decades of debate. But as these works circulated around the country, they were carefully read and heatedly discussed at the courts of the few remaining Orthodox magnates, on the isolated estates of noblemen, and in the cramped quarters of the brotherhoods. By involving Ukrainian society in its first full-fledged ideological controversy, they helped it reach a higher state of consciousness about itself and the world around it.

೩⋅

The religious controversies of the late 16th and early 17th century highlighted several pregnant issues in Ukrainian society. They placed the growing tensions with the Catholic Poles on an ideological and highly emotional level. Indeed, Catholic Poland now emerged as the antithesis of Ukrainian society. But the cultural confrontation between the Ukrainians and the Poles cost the former dearly: it forced Ukrainian nobles to choose between their own stagnant, impoverished cultural heritage and the vibrant, attractive Catholic/Polish culture. Not suprisingly, the vast majority opted for Catholicism and the Polonization that invariably followed. Consequently, the Ukrainians lost their noble elite. And this development was of epochal importance for their subsequent history.

Another far-reaching by-product of the Orthodox/Catholic confrontation, specifically of the Union of Brest, was that it divided Ukrainians into Orthodox and Greek Catholics, thereby laying the foundation for the many sharp distinctions that eventually developed between East and West Ukrainians. But the period was not merely one of setbacks for Ukrainian society: the religious controversies sparked a cultural upsurge within it and the confrontation with the Poles led to a sharper definition of a Ukrainian identity.

Part Three

The Cossack Era

The Formative Phase

Since the fall of Kiev in 1240, the western lands of Galicia and Volhynia had served as the stage for major developments in Ukrainian history. However, by the end of the 16th century, the focus of events shifted back to the east, to the lands of the Dnieper basin that had long been partially depopulated. In that vast frontier, which at that time was specifically referred to as *Ukraina* – the land on the periphery of the civilized world – the age-old struggle of the sedentary population against the nomads flared up with renewed intensity, fueled by the bitter confrontation between Christianity and Islam. The oppressive conditions that obtained in the settled western areas provided numerous recruits who preferred the dangers of frontier life to serfdom. As a result, a new class of Cossack-frontiersmen emerged. Initially, the Cossacks concentrated on pushing back the Tatars, thereby opening up the frontier to colonization.

But as they honed their military and organizational skills and won ever more impressive victories against the Tatars and their Ottoman Turkish overlords, Ukrainian society came to perceive the Cossacks not only as champions against the Muslim threat, but also as defenders against the religionational and socioeconomic oppression of the Polish *szlachta*. Gradually, moving to the forefront of Ukrainian society, the Cossacks became heavily involved in the resolution of these central issues in Ukrainian life and, for the next several centuries, provided Ukrainian society with the leadership it had lost as a result of the Polonization of the Ukrainian nobility.

૨૦

Frontier Society

For ages, the sedentary population of Ukraine had attempted to colonize the fertile steppe regions. During the Kievan period, a network of fortifications was built below Kiev to keep out the nomads and encourage settlement. The Mongol invasion, however, swept these strong points away. Later, under the Lithuanian grand princes, a more successful colonizing drive culminated in the establishment of several fortresses on the Black Sea near the mouth of the Dnister. But, with the rise of the Crimean Khanate in the late 15th century, these settlements were destroyed and the forts on the Black Sea fell to the Ottoman Turks. By the mid 16th century, the limits of Ukrainian habitation were pushed back to a line of strongholds that stretched along the northern fringe of the steppe and included Kamianets, Bar, Vinnytsia, Bila Tserkva, Cherkasy, Kaniv, and Kiev. Below this line lay the so-called wild field (*dyke pole*).

The Tatars   What made the "wild field" so forbidding were the Tatars. Year after year, their swift raiding parties swept down on the towns and villages to pillage, kill the old and frail, and drive away thousands of captives to be sold as slaves in the Crimean port of Kaffa, a city often referred to by Ukrainians as "the vampire that drinks the blood of Rus'." For the Tatars these raids were an economic necessity because their relatively primitive pastoral economy could not satisfy all their needs. Only in exchange for slaves could the Tatars obtain from the Ottoman Empire the finished products and luxury goods that they desired. This was hardly a consolation for the Ukrainians whose folk songs frequently reflected the numbing impact of these raids:

> This night at midnight, before the cocks had crowed
> The Tatars flew like the wind into our village
> This night at midnight, an evil came to pass
> When the wild Turkic band plundered all our land.[1]

The Tatar raids, usually directed against the provinces of Kiev and Bratslav (although Galicia, Volhynia, and Podilia were also not spared), were particularly devastating in the late 16th and early 17th centuries. For example, from 1450 to 1586, eighty-six raids were recorded, and from 1600 to 1647, seventy. Although estimates of the number of captives taken in a single raid reached as high as 30,000, the average figure was closer to 3000. In any case, the losses to Ukrainians were serious. In Podilia alone, about one-third of all the villages were devastated or abandoned between 1578 and 1583.

Colonization   Tatars notwithstanding, the lure of rich, open lands was too powerful to resist. As the grain trade expanded, Polish and Polonized magnates, taking advantage of their contacts at court, obtained vast tracts of territory in the east. To colonize these lands, they coaxed peasants away from their previous owners by offering them the use of land, free from obligations, for periods of ten, twenty, and even thirty years (*slobody*). Many peasants also simply ran away from their oppressive masters in Galicia and Volhynia to seek their fortunes in the east. After a generation or two, these peasants in the newly colonized regions developed into a different breed from those in the more settled western provinces they had left behind. Simply by making the risky move to the frontier, they demonstrated that they were bolder and more self-reliant. Because they often had to plow their lands with their muskets at their sides in case of Tatar attack, they possessed military skills that their western compatriots did not. Their children, who had never known serfdom, grew up believing that they were free men who owed no obligations to anyone. This impression survived even when the terms of a *sloboda* ran out, for it was customary for peasants in the frontier regions to pay dues to magnates in cash or in kind, rather than in the form of demanding and demeaning labor. With more land available, the colonists tended to be better off, many owning as much as a *lan* (ca forty acres) of land, which was more than many noblemen owned in the West.

Another characteristic of the newly colonized (actually recolonized) provinces of Kiev and Bratslav in particular was the rapid growth of towns. In the early 1600s, over 200 new towns appeared in the province of Kiev alone, giving it a total of 348, roughly one-third of all urban centers in Ukraine. By the middle of the century, once semideserted Bratslav province had one town per 218 sq. km. Although about 60% of the frontier population lived in towns by the mid 17th century, these were not urban centres in the real sense of the word. They were actually little more than frontier forts with rarely more than 100 households living within their wooden stockades. Many inhabitants were peasants who worked the land nearby but lived in the fortified town for protection. The vast majority of these towns did not have self-rule, but were owned by the magnates who built them and provided troops for their defense.

With most of the frontier lands in the hands of magnates, there was little left for the middle and poorer nobles. Those Polish noblemen who did arrive in the Dnieper basin did not, at least at the outset, come as landowners, but rather as administrators, officers, or servitors on the estates of magnates. Only gradually did they acquire relatively modest holdings. Another reason for the middle and lower nobility's low profile on the frontier was their small numbers. In Kiev province in the mid 17th century, there were only 2000–2500 nobles for a population of 350,000–400,000, that is, less than 1%, whereas in the rest of the Commonwealth, nobles constituted, on the average, 8–10% of the population. But while the magnates' rapid accumulation of the frontier lands impeded the influx of the lower nobility, it encouraged the immigration of Jews to central and eastern Ukraine. Because many magnates preferred to spend their time in Cracow, Warsaw, or Lviv, they frequently employed Jews as administrators of their lands in their absence. Most of the Jews who settled in the burgeoning towns, however, were craftsmen, merchants, and moneylenders whose skills were much in demand. There were already about 120,000 Jews in all of Ukraine in the early 17th century.[2]

At the highest level of frontier society, far above all other elements, was a small coterie of fabulously wealthy magnates. Foremost among them were such Polonized Ukrainian families as the Vyshnevetsky (later Wiśniowiecki), Ostrozky, Zbarazky, and Koretsky families, and Polish newcomers such as the Zamoyski, Koniecpolski, Kalinowski, Ossolinski, and Potocki. By the early 17th century, their huge latifundia dominated the frontier. In the province of Bratslav, 60,000 of a total of 65,000 households belonged to eighteen magnate families. The richest of the magnates, the recently Polonized Jeremi Wiśniowiecki, owned 7500 estates in Kiev province alone and, in addition, controlled almost the entire Poltava region. It has been estimated that over 230,000 peasants lived on his estates. The size of these landholdings was unmatched anywhere in the Commonwealth or, indeed, anywhere else in Europe. Because these magnates controlled more territory and population than many West European princes at the time, they were often referred to as "kinglets."

The epithet was appropriate: many of these arrogant lords behaved like sovereign rulers, building magnificent mansions decorated with Dutch paintings and Oriental carpets, maintaining lavish courts and large private armies. They scoffed at their king's wishes and frequently broke the law of the land. One magnate by the name of Laszcz, notorious for his cruelty to peasants, also mistreated lesser nobles to such an extent that he was sentenced to exile 236 times. The backing of other powerful magnates prevented these sentences from ever being carried out and the brazen Laszcz even dared to have a suit of clothes fashioned out of the writs and to wear it to the royal court. Although representing an extreme example, the case of Laszcz is indicative of the growing strength and arrogance of the magnates on the one hand and the weakness of the royal government on the other.

The Cossacks

Epitomizing the new society that had evolved on the plains of the Dnieper basin was the emergence of a new class that could have evolved only on the frontier – that of the Cossacks. Of Turkic origin, the word Cossack originally referred to the free, masterless men who lacked a well-defined place in society and who lived on its unsettled periphery. Slavic Cossacks first appeared in the 1480s, but it was not until the development of serfdom in the mid 16th century that their numbers increased significantly. Originally the bulk of Cossacks were runaway peasants, although they also included burghers, defrocked priests, and impecunious or adventure-seeking noblemen. Although Poles, Belorussians, Russians, Moldavians, and even Tatars joined the ranks of the Cossacks, the overwhelming majority of those who lived in the Dnieper basin were Ukrainians. A Russian variant of Cossackdom evolved farther to the east, along the Don River.

Early organization   To avoid the authorities, the Ukrainian Cossacks pushed farther south along the Dnieper and its lower tributaries and beyond the small frontier outposts of Kaniv and Cherkasy. In this bounteous but dangerous terrain they engaged in *ukhody*, that is, hunting and fishing expeditions, and in the grazing of cattle and horses. It was during these extended seasonal forays into the steppe that the first signs of organization appeared among them. As they ventured into the "wild field," they chose the most experienced, brave, and resourceful men from among themselves as their leaders or *otamany*, and formed tightly knit groups (*vatahy*) to better fend off marauding Tatars as well as to cooperate in hunting and fishing ventures. Eventually, permanent fortified camps (*sich*) with small, year-round garrisons were established in the steppe and, for many, Cossackdom became a full-time, year-round occupation.

For royal officials (*starosty*) on the frontier, the sight of increasing numbers of armed, independent Cossacks who often flaunted their disrespect for established authority was worrisome. Yet, as members of magnate families, these *starosty* also benefited from the situation, profiting handsomely through the imposition of heavy (often unsanctioned) duties on the fish, animal pelts, etc. that the Cossacks tried to sell in the towns. More important, they found that the Cossacks were ideally suited for defending the frontier from Tatar raids, an onerous and important responsibility of the *starosty*. Thus, in 1520, Senko Polozovych, *starosta* of Cherkasy, recruited a unit of Cossacks as border guards. In the following decades, other *starosty*, such as Ostafii Dashkevych, Predslav Lantskoronsky, and Bernard Pretvych, became active in mobilizing Cossacks not only for defensive service, but also for offensive campaigns against the Tatars.

The magnates who initially began to organize the Cossacks were still Orthodox, not yet Polonized Ukrainians. Most famous among them was Dmytro "Baida" Vyshnevetsky, *starosta* of Kaniv. The kaleidoscopic nature of his career and his legendary fame often make it difficult to separate fact from fiction. However, it is incontestable that in 1553–54, Vyshnevetsky gathered together scattered groups of Cossacks and on the remote, strategically located island of Mala Khortytsia below the Dnieper rapids (*za porohamy*) built a fort designed to obstruct Tatar raids into Ukraine. In so doing, he laid the foundations for the Zaporozhian Sich, generally regarded as the cradle of Ukrainian Cossackdom. Soon afterwards, he launched a series of attacks with his Cossacks against the Crimea and even had the temerity to attack the Ottoman Turks themselves. When the Commonwealth refused to support him in his anti-Muslim crusade, Vyshnevetsky moved to Muscovy, from where he continued his attacks on Crimea. Before long, he grew dissatisfied there and, after returning to Ukraine, became involved in Moldavian affairs. This proved to be his undoing, for the Moldavians treacherously handed him over to the Ottomans, who executed him in Constantinople in 1563. Numerous Ukrainian folk songs, some of them surviving to this day, have preserved the memory of "Baida's" exploits.

The Zaporozhian Sich   Located far beyond the reach of government authorities, the Zaporozhian Sich continued to flourish even after the death of its founder. Any Christian male, irrespective of his social background, was free to come to this island fortress, with its rough wood-and-thatch barracks, and to join the Cossack brotherhood. He was also free to leave at will. Women and children, regarded as a hindrance in the steppe, were barred from entry. Refusing to recognize the authority of any ruler, the Zaporozhians governed themselves according to traditions and customs that evolved over the generations. All had equal rights and could participate in the frequent, boisterous councils (*rady*) in which the side that shouted loudest usually carried the day.

These volatile gatherings elected and, with equal ease, deposed the Cossack leadership, which consisted of a *hetman* or *otaman* who had overall command, adjutants (*osavuly*), a chancellor (*pysar*), a quartermaster (*obozny*), and a judge (*suddia*). Each *kurin*, a term that referred to the Sich barracks and, by extension, to the military unit that lived in them, elected a similar subordinate group of officers, or *starshyna*. During campaigns, the authority of these officers was absolute, including the right to impose the death penalty. But in peacetime their power was limited. Generally, the Zaporozhians numbered about 5000–6000 men of whom about 10% served on a rotating basis as the garrison of the Sich, while the rest were engaged in campaigns or in peacetime occupations. The economy of the Sich consisted mainly of hunting, fishing, beekeeping, and salt making at the mouth of the Dnieper. Because the Sich lay on the trade route between the Commonwealth and the Black Sea, trade also played an important role. Despite the ethos of brotherhood and equality that the Zaporozhians espoused, socioeconomic distinctions and tensions gradually developed between the wealthier Cossack officers (*starshyna*) and the rank and file (*chern*) and caused recurrent upheavals at the Sich.

The town and registered Cossacks   Many Cossacks also lived in the frontier towns. In 1600, for example, the population of Kaniv consisted of 960 people classed as burghers and over 1300 Cossacks and their families. Like their compatriots at the Sich, the town Cossacks ignored the government authorities and recognized only their own elected officers. But although the Polish government realized that it was futile to attempt to control the remote, rebellious Sich, it did have hopes of harnessing the town Cossacks, or at least a selected portion of them, into its service. In 1572, King Sigismund August authorized the formation of a salaried 300-man Cossack unit, led by a Polish nobleman by the name of Badowski, which was formally removed from the jurisdiction of local government officials. Although the unit was soon dissolved, important precedents were set: it was the first time that the Polish government recognized the Cossacks, or at least 300 of them, as a distinct social class that, like the other estates in the land, had the right of self-administration.

Another, more successful attempt to form a government-sanctioned Cossack unit occurred in 1578 during the reign of King Stefan Batory. In return for pay and assignment of the town of Terekhtymyriv, which was to serve as an arsenal and place of convalescence for their wounded, 500 Cossacks agreed to accept nobles as their officers and to refrain from the "self-willed" attacks against the Tatars that often complicated the Commonwealth's foreign relations. Duly inscribed into a register, the functions of these "registered" Cossacks were to serve as a border militia and, equally important, to control the nonregistered Cossacks. By 1589, there were 3000 registered Cossacks. In general, they came from the ranks of the town dwellers – established Cossacks who had families and who often owned considerable property. For example, according to his will, the property of a registered Cossack by the name of Tyshko Volovych included a house in Chyhyryn, two estates with fish ponds, woodlands and pastures, 120 beehives, and 3000 pieces of gold (1000 of which he lent out at high interest).

The relative wealth of these registered Cossacks contrasted sharply with the poverty of their nonregistered counterparts, who owned little more than did peasants. Consequently, tensions between the 3000 registered and the approximately 40,000–50,000 nonregistered Cossacks often ran high. This distinction did not prevent the sons of wealthier Cossacks from going down to the Sich to seek their fortunes, or other Cossacks who had managed to accumulate wealth from entering the ranks of the registered. Thus, by the early 17th century, there were essentially three overlapping categories of Cossacks: the well-established registered Cossacks who had been co-opted into government service; the Zaporozhians who lived beyond the pale of the Commonwealth; and the vast majority of Cossacks who lived in the frontier towns and led a Cossack way of life, but who had no officially recognized status.

The struggle against the Turks and Tatars   In the early phase of their development, the nonregistered Cossacks, and particularly the Zaporozhians, were regarded not only by the magnates and royal officials but also by much of Ukrainian society as little more than brigands and social outcasts. By the late 16th century, this negative image of the Cossack had changed, at least in the eyes of the lower strata of Ukrainian society, largely as a result of the increased frequency, scope, and audacity of Cossack attacks on the Tatars and their powerful overlords, the Ottoman Turks. Ukrainians were not the only ones who suffered at the hands of the Muslim Turks. All of 16th-century Europe shuddered at the very thought of invasion by the Ottomans who, in 1529, had devastated Hungary and had almost captured Vienna; a large part of Eastern Europe remained directly exposed to Tatar raids. Therefore, anyone who dared challenge the *bisurmany*, as the Muslims were referred to in Ukraine, was sure to win sympathy at home and renown abroad.

Although they certainly reveled in the fame that their raids against the Turks brought them, the Zaporozhians also had pragmatic reasons for launching raids: they pushed the Tatars away from their settlements and the rich booty they captured from the Ottoman towns was a handsome supplement to their incomes. Most raids were carried out by sea. For this purpose, the Cossacks constructed flotillas of forty to eighty long, narrow, and shallow galleys called *chaiky*, each of which could hold about sixty men. Slipping past the Ottoman forts at the mouth of the Dnieper, they attacked the Crimean and Turkish strong points along the Black Sea coast. The earliest record of such raids dates back to 1538, before the founding of the Sich, when a Cossack flotilla partially destroyed the Ottoman fortress of Ochakiv. In subsequent years, the Cossacks launched increasing numbers of these raids, gaining great renown thereby, for the Ottoman Empire was at the time the most powerful state in the world. By 1595, the Habsburgs of Austria, enemies of the Ottomans, dispatched an envoy to the Sich, by the name of Erich von Lasotta, to conclude a pact for a coordinated attack against Ottoman forces in Moldavia. The pope also established contact with the Zaporozhians. Indeed, the Sich behaved as though it were a sovereign power, engaging in campaigns and conducting its own foreign relations.

Cossack raids against the Ottomans reached a high point between 1600 and 1620. In 1606, the Cossacks gutted Varna, the strongest Ottoman fortress on the Black Sea; in 1608, Perekop fell to them; in 1609, they sacked Kilia, Ismail, and Akkerman; in 1614, previously untouched Trabizond in Asia Minor was attacked; and in 1615 they dealt a most audacious blow when, within view of the sultan and a garrison of 30,000, about eighty Cossack *chaiky* managed to slip into Constantinople harbor, burn it, and make their escape. In 1620, they repeated the same feat. Meanwhile, in 1616, Kaffa, the emporium of the slave trade in the Crimea, was taken and thousands of slaves freed. In describing these Cossack forays, Naima, a 17th-century Ottoman historian, noted: "One can state with certainty that there are no people on earth who care less about life and have less fear of death than they ... Military experts claim that this rabble, because of its bravery and skill, is unmatched in sea-warfare by anyone in the world."[3]

Equally impressive were the Cossack exploits on land. Infuriated by the Poles' inability to control the Cossacks, Sultan Osman II assembled a huge army of 160,000, together with thousands of Crimean auxiliaries, and moved against the Commonwealth. In 1620, the Poles suffered a disastrous defeat at Cecora. But a year later at Khotyn a Polish force of 35,000 that had tried to hold off the Ottomans was saved from certain annihilation by the timely arrival of 40,000 Cossacks led by Hetman Sahaidachny.

As a result of these successes, Cossack self-confidence grew. In their often acrimonious negotiations with the Poles, the Cossacks began to refer to themselves as defenders of the faith, as a brotherhood of knights, and as paladins fighting for the public good. This rhetoric was partly meant to serve the Cossacks' narrow class interests by convincing the government that they were entitled to the rights and privileges normally accorded fighting men. Yet, to a large extent, the Cossacks took this exalted image of themselves as the defenders of Christendom and of their countrymen seriously. This new sense of mission in turn induced them to confront the burning internal issues of their society.

The Early Insurrections

The Polish government and nobility reacted with confusion and ambivalence to the rapid expansion of Cossackdom. It was difficult for the *szlachta* to understand that the Cossacks – still regarded by many merely as fugitive serfs – had become a distinct, organized social entity. Despite their inherent antagonism to the Cossacks, the nobles of the Commonwealth were not averse to utilizing them when it suited their purposes. The same officials who in peacetime called for the merciless extirpation of the "self-willed rabble" eagerly expanded the register to include more Cossacks and offered them rights, privileges, and pay when they required their services in the wars against Muscovy or the Ottomans. But when peace was restored, these officials often reneged on their promises and again denounced the Cossacks. These inconsistencies were exacerbated by the differences in approach between the local magnates and border officials on the one hand, who were daily at odds with the Cossacks, and the kings on the other, who saw in them a source of experienced, relatively cheap fighting power and a potential counterbalance to the growing power of the eastern magnates. It was only a matter of time before these tensions would come to a head.

The first Cossack uprising occurred in 1591. That year, Krystof Kosynsky, a Ukrainian nobleman and leader of the registered Cossacks, received a land grant from the king for his services to the crown. Before he was able to take possession of it, Janusz Ostrozky, *starosta* of Bila Tserkva and the Polonized scion of the illustrious Ostrozky family, arrogated the land for himself. Realizing that to invoke legal sanctions against a powerful grandee would be useless, Kosynsky took vengeance by leading his Cossacks in a series of raids on the Ostrozky estates. Soon peasants, Cossacks, and even disgruntled military servitors in Volhynia, Bratslav, and Kiev were fighting their own vendettas against their lords. When the shocked nobles finally mobilized their forces, it was the old patriarch of the Ostrozky family, Konstantyn Konstantynovych, who led them to a victory over Kosynsky's force of about 2000 near Piatka River. The punishment of the rebels was unusually light. While the registered Cossacks who joined the uprising were required to swear loyalty to the king, Kosynsky was forced to bow down three times before the assembled Ostrozky clan, and to beg their pardon. Soon afterwards, he was killed in a minor incident under unclear circumstances.

No sooner had the reverberations from one rebellion faded than another insurrection flared up, this time more widespread. Its leader, Severyn Nalyvaiko, was, according to a Polish report, "a man of pleasant countenance, exceptional ability and an excellent cannoneer to boot."[4] The son of a Galician tailor who died after being beaten by a magnate, Severyn, in his youth, found refuge together with his brother, Damian, at the Ostrozky estate in Ostrih. While his brother went on to become a priest and noted author, Severyn chose "to earn his bread the Cossack way." In 1595, after leading about 2500 men on a successful raid against the Ottomans in Moldavia, Nalyvaiko returned to Bratslav province and soon came into conflict with the local nobility. Again the Cossacks proclaimed a rebellion against the hated *szlachta* and again the peasants rushed to join them. More important, the Zaporozhians also came to Nalyvaiko's aid. Among the rebels' vaguely articulated goals was the call to establish a region in Ukraine governed solely by Cossacks.

While the Zaporozhians, led by Hryhorii Loboda and Matvii Shaulo, operated in the Kiev and Bratslav regions, Nalyvaiko marched through Galicia, Volhynia, and Belorussia, urging peasants to revolt and spreading havoc among the *szlachta*. Realizing, however, that the Poles were stronger, the rebels united their forces in the spring of 1596 and began to retreat eastward in hopes of finding refuge in Muscovy. By May they had fought off the Poles, but as hunger and disease spread and casualties mounted, internal dissension broke out. Loboda, who favored negotiation, was accused of having secret contacts with the enemy and was murdered. Thereupon, his supporters, who were mostly officers and well-to-do Cossacks, surreptitiously surrendered Nalyvaiko to the Poles and persuaded the rebels to lay down their arms. In the confusion, the Poles entered the camp and massacred most of the unarmed rebels. Nalyvaiko himself was taken to Warsaw and executed.

The search for accommodation   It seemed to the Poles that after their victory, the Cossack problem had been solved, especially because internal conflicts were becoming increasingly more pronounced among the Cossacks. The well-established, town-based registered Cossacks generally favored negotiation and cooperation with the Commonwealth, hoping that this harmony would secure their status and provide them with the peace they needed to develop their properties, which were often sizable. However, for the majority of Cossacks, consisting of propertyless Zaporozhians and nonregistered Cossacks who were in constant danger of being pushed back into the ranks of the serfs, it seemed that only radical actions could gain for them a better place in society. With tensions between the two factions often expressed by open conflict, it was frequently possible for the Poles to play the two sides off against each other.

Events took a favorable turn for the Cossacks at this critical juncture. Because the Commonwealth became involved in an almost continuous series of wars in the early 17th century, it again turned to the Cossacks as a source of experienced fighters. In 1601, a unit of 2000 Ukrainians participated in the difficult Polish campaign in Livonia, and in 1604 and 1609 the Zaporozhians took part in the Polish intervention in Muscovy's Time of Troubles. Hardly a meeting of the Polish parliament took place in the early 17th century without a Polish statesman producing a resolution or project that sought to utilize the military usefulness of the Cossacks, while not giving in to their demands for an enlarged register and self-determination. During this time of complex political maneuvering, the Cossacks were fortunate to have a leader who could rise to the occasion.

Hetman Petro Konashevych-Sahaidachny   Historians generally agree that, prior to Bohdan Khmelnytsky, Petro Konashevych-Sahaidachny was the most outstanding Cossack leader. An impoverished nobleman from Sambir in Galicia, he studied in the Ostrih Academy and then made his way to the Zaporozhian Sich where, after making a name for himself as a commander of the famous sea raid against Kaffa in 1616, he was elected hetman. Convinced that the Cossacks were not yet a match for the forces of the Commonwealth, he made conciliation with the Poles the keystone of his policy. He mobilized and led the large Cossack armies that fought for the Poles in the continuous wars against Moscow and the Ottomans. A strict disciplinarian who "generously spilled the blood of those who disobeyed him," Sahaidachny liquidated roving bands of undisciplined Cossacks and forced them to recognize his authority. To avoid conflict with the Poles, he agreed in 1619 to lower the register to 3000, forbade unauthorized sea raids, and accepted the king's right to confirm Cossack officers.

Yet Sahaidachny's most outstanding achievement was that he perceived the Cossacks in terms not only of their specific class interests, but also as a potential leading force in Ukrainian society as a whole. It was he who allied the rough, militarily potent Cossacks with the politically weak Ukrainian religiocultural elite. The link was forged in dramatic fashion: in 1620, Sahaidachny enrolled himself and the entire Zaporozhian Host in the Kievan brotherhood. This step was meant to demonstrate that henceforth the Zaporozhians intended to uphold Ukrainian religious and cultural demands.

In that same year, Sahaidachny, together with the Orthodox clergy, invited the patriarch of Jerusalem, Teofan, to visit Kiev in order to consecrate a new

Orthodox hierarchy. Since the Poles had threatened to arrest Teofan as a spy, the hetman guaranteed his safety. After the new metropolitan and bishops were installed, Sahaidachny escorted the patriarch to the Ottoman border at the head of a force of 3000 Cossacks. So great was the prestige of this Cossack hetman that when he died in 1622, the populace of Kiev turned out for his funeral en masse. Kassian Sakovych, the rector of the Kievan brotherhood school, delivered an eloquent eulogy to this wise leader and dedicated patron of Orthodoxy in which he associated Sahaidachny with the traditions of the Kievan princes. It was evident that Cossackdom had now entered the mainstream of Ukrainian society.

More rebellions   After Sahaidachny's death, conflict again dominated Cossack/Polish relations. It had appeared initially that it might be avoided because the deceased hetman's immediate successors, Olifer Holub and Mykhailo Doroshenko, were his close associates and shared his conciliatory views. But Cossack dissatisfaction, especially among the nonregistered, became intense after the Khotyn campaign of 1621, when over 40,000 battle-hardened Cossacks returned to Ukraine with no intention of accepting the serf status the government demanded and yet with no hope of being entered in the register. Some congregated at the Zaporozhian Sich while most returned to their towns and villages. Disgruntled and restless, they were only waiting for an opportunity to vent their frustration. Doroshenko attempted to redirect their animosity and, in the mid 1620s, organized a series of sea raids against the Ottomans, informing the startled Muslims that "the [Polish] king may have made peace with you, but we did not."[5] And for the first time the Cossacks became involved in the factional strife of the Crimea by supporting an anti-Ottoman candidate for the position of khan.

   For the Poles, the Cossack notion of themselves as a state within a state was most irritating. The king complained in parliament that "domestic anarchy is again coming to the fore [in Ukraine], creating difficulties for us and involving us in conflicts with our powerful neighbors. Ignoring the obligations of servitude and the precepts of loyalty, they [the Cossacks] have established their own order, threatening the life and property of innocent people. And, what is more, all Ukraine obeys them."[6] After deciding to adopt a hard line toward the Cossacks, the government chose Stanisław Koniecpolski, a tough and experienced commander with vast estates in Ukraine, to enforce it.

   In 1625, Koniecpolski moved in Ukraine with about 8000 men. A force of about 6000 Cossacks, led by Marko Zhmailo, set out from the Zaporozhian Sich to meet him. After a series of unsuccessful encounters with the Poles, the Zaporozhian officers again reinstated the moderate Doroshenko as hetman and negotiations ensued, ending in a compromise. The register was raised to 6000, something which pleased the wealthier ("more deserving") Cossacks who were included in it, but the majority of the rank and file was expected to return to bondage.

When the register was completed, Doroshenko proceeded to rationalize the organization of the 6000 "legal" Cossacks. They were divided into six regiments (*polky*) based in Kiev, Kaniv, Korsun, Bila Tserkva, Pereiaslav, and Cherkasy. Each regiment was then divided into companies (*sotni*), which were based in the smaller towns on regimental territory. Cossack officers had both civil and military authority over all the Cossacks in their area, while the hetman and his staff, elected by the Cossacks but confirmed by the king, had overall command. Thus, despite close Polish supervision, the registered Cossacks perfected their self-administration. The Zaporozhian Sich, in contrast, the bastion of the most militant and "illegal" Cossacks, although formally subject to the hetman, maintained de facto autonomy.

In agreeing to the expanded register, the Poles hoped that "their" registered Cossacks would control the others. When the ostensibly pro-Polish Hrytsko Chorny was elected hetman in 1629, it seemed that the Commonwealth had found the perfect man for the job. But, in his efforts to please the government authorities, Chorny infuriated many Cossacks, and, early in 1630, a group of Zaporozhians abducted him to the Sich where he was tried and executed. The Zaporozhians and nonregistered Cossacks now elected the daring Taras Fedorovych (nicknamed Triasylo) as their new hetman, and he led a strong force of rebels back into the settled areas. Again Koniecpolski, leading an army of royal troops and registered Cossacks, had a difficult campaign to fight. This time he was less successful than he had been before, and, in a treaty concluded at Pereiaslav in August 1630, the rebellious Cossacks won surprisingly liberal terms: the register was enlarged to 8000; Triasylo went unpunished; and the rebels were granted amnesty. The nagging problem of the thousands of nonregistered Cossacks that lay at the root of the rebellion remained unresolved, however.

In 1635, the Commonwealth applied a new method for dealing with unruly Cossacks, On the Dnieper just above the Sich, the Poles constructed the impressive fortress of Kodak in the hope of checking the Zaporozhians. But, within months of its completion, Ivan Sulyma and a detachment of Cossacks destroyed the fortress and wiped out its garrison. Unfortunately for Sulyma, a group of registered Cossacks, anxious to curry favor with the Poles, handed him over to the royal authorities to be executed. Soon afterwards, in August 1637, yet another rebellious Cossack army, led by Pavlo Pavliuk, took the field against the Poles. As Pavliuk's forces moved northward from the Sich, peasants from the Right Bank and, for the first time, from the newly colonized Left Bank joined the rebellion in large numbers. But once again the rebels were outmaneuvered on the open field and, in December 1637, were decisively beaten by the Polish army at Kumeiki near Chyhyryn. This loss, however, did not signal the end of the rebellion, for it continued on the Left Bank under the leadership of Iakiv Ostrianyn and Dmytro Hunia until it was finally quashed in the summer of 1638.

Victorious and eager to avenge themselves, the Poles were not in a mood to bargain. Instead, they dictated their terms. According to the *ordynacija* or regulations formulated by the parliament, the register was lowered to 6000 and even the registered Cossacks lost their right of self-administration. The office of hetman was abolished and replaced by that of a Polish commissioner appointed by the king. Cossack colonels and adjutants were to be selected from among the *szlachta*. Strict limits were established on areas where Cossacks were allowed to settle and anyone trying to make his way to the Sich without permission was to receive the death sentence. The many thousands of Cossacks who were not included in the register were classified as serfs. In addition to these draconian measures, the magnates, especially Jeremi Wiśniowiecki (Vyshnevetsky), the Polonized grandnephew of the famous Baida Vyshnevetsky and the largest landowner in Ukraine, instituted a reign of terror in the land, indiscriminately torturing and killing anyone even vaguely suspected of disobedience. Cynical Polish noblemen rationalized this brutal approach in the following way, at the same time offering a revealing insight into the *szlachta* perception of the Cossack problem: "The Cossacks are the fingernails of our body politic. They tend to grow too long, and need frequent clipping." And, indeed, during the ensuing decade – a period of unprecedented calm and stability often referred to by Polish historians as the Golden Peace – it seemed that in dealing with the Cossacks, the repressive approach was the most effective.

It is useful to examine the reasons why the five major Cossack/peasant revolts that occurred in Ukraine during the forty-five-year period under consideration were all unsuccessful. To a great extent, failures resulted from the fact that, despite the leading role played by the Cossacks in the revolts, many of the rebels were peasants and, therefore, the uprisings possessed some of the weaknesses inherent in all peasant revolts. Usually spontaneous, these revolts lacked detailed planning and long-term goals. Besides redressing their immediate grievances, both Cossacks and peasants had little idea of what they wanted to achieve. Although endowed with a surfeit of bravery, the rebels were often limited and erratic in their military undertakings because peasants were reluctant to fight beyond the bounds of their own localities or during the planting and harvesting seasons. Socioeconomic differences among the Cossacks added to the problem of inconsistency of action: the rank and file, with little to lose, usually rushed into rebellion, while the well-established *starshyna* generally opted for negotiations, compromise, or capitulation. Yet, despite the setbacks, each successive uprising reflected the growing strength and military sophistication of the rebels. Their numbers grew, their tactics improved, and Cossack identification with the plight of the peasantry and the defense of Orthodoxy deepened. The decade-long Golden Peace merely masked a problem that was waiting to explode again.

Ecclesiastical and Cultural Developments

As in the case of politics and socioeconomic development, the focus of ecclesiastical and cultural activity in Ukraine also shifted eastward in the early 17th century. In Galicia and Volhynia, the proximity to Poland, where the Catholic Counter-Reformation reached a high point, exposed the Ukrainian Orthodox centers there to constant and debilitating pressure. Thus, in 1608, when that stalwart of Orthodoxy Prince Konstantyn Konstantynovych Ostrozky died, his granddaughter, Anna Khodkevych, a recent and fanatical convert to Catholicism, turned the Ostrih Academy over to the Jesuits. The brotherhood school in Lviv also began to falter because the Ukrainian burghers, increasingly discriminated against by the Catholic church and the Polish government, could no longer support it. Meanwhile, the booming eastern provinces were far removed from Catholic Polish pressure. And Kiev, which was steadily growing more populous and more wealthy, again emerged as the center of Ukrainian Orthodoxy.

Initially, the ancient Kievan Cave Monastery served as the catalyst for the Orthodox revival in the newly colonized lands. During the 1620s, its archimandrite, Elisei Pletenetsky, a Galician nobleman by background, assembled a group of learned churchmen, mostly Galicians, such as Iob Boretsky, Kassian Sakovych, Zakhariah Kopystensky, Pamba Berynda, and Lavrentii Zyzanii. After purchasing a printing press, Pletenetsky launched an ambitious publishing program that, within the span of fifteen years, produced about thirty books, mostly of a religious nature. This output was more than the combined total of all the other printing presses in Ukraine. In 1615, inspired by this example and financed from a bequest from Ielyzaveta Hulevych, a wealthy Orthodox noblewoman, the noblemen, burghers, and clerics of Kiev organized a brotherhood associated with the Bohoiavlensky Church.

A unique feature of this brotherhood was its close links with the Zaporozhians. Apparently, these contacts were first established through the intermediary of Iosyf Kurtsevych, the abbot of the monastery in Terekhtemyriv, the site of the Cossacks' hospital, arsenal, and treasury. By 1610, these ties had become so strong that the Cossacks publicly announced: "We stand behind Orthodoxy and the clergy that has not betrayed our ancient faith." Under Sahaidachny's leadership, the Zaporozhians joined the Kiev brotherhood in 1620 and, more important, provided the support needed to consecrate a new Orthodox hierarchy. The latter event was of the utmost importance. Since the Union of Brest in 1596, at which time most of their bishops had joined the Union, the Orthodox had been leaderless. When Teofan, the patriarch of Jerusalem, ordained several bishops and consecrated Iob Boretsky as metropolitan of Kiev, the Orthodox of Ukraine once again had an ecclesiastical leadership. As expected, Catholics and Greek Catholics were infuriated by what they considered to be an illegal act. But, because the Polish government needed Cossack support for the wars, it did not intervene and the legitimacy of the new Orthodox hierarchy was eventually recognized.

The events of 1620 greatly exacerbated the Orthodox/Greek Catholic feud. In addition to differences over dogma and ecclesiastical procedures, the two competitors became embroiled in a bitter conflict over church properties. So violent were the quarrels over who owned the churches, monasteries, and lands attached to them that hundreds of clerics on both sides died in confrontations that often took the form of pitched battles. The most famous of these incidents was the assassination in 1623 of Iosafat Kuntsevych, the Greek Catholic archbishop of Polotsk, by an Orthodox mob that had become enraged by the archbishop's attempt to confiscate two Orthodox churches. Distressed by the fratricidal struggle, several Orthodox churchmen – most notably the archbishop of Polotsk, Meletii Smotrytsky, and the rector of the Kiev brotherhood school, Kassian Sakovych – attempted to arrange a compromise that would "bring together one Rus' with the other." Although several common councils were held in Kiev and Lviv in 1628, these attempts at reconciliation failed.

Frustrated and disillusioned with their recalcitrant Orthodox compatriots, both Smotrytsky and Sakovych eventually went over to the Greek Catholics. Meanwhile, other Orthodox churchmen turned to the tsar of Muscovy for aid. This was not an unprecedented step. Already in the 1570s, the Lviv brotherhood had been in touch with the Orthodox Muscovites, and early in the 17th century numerous Ukrainian Orthodox monks had moved to Muscovy to escape Catholic persecution. In 1625, Metropolitan Boretsky, convinced that the future of the Orthodox under Polish rule was hopeless, petitioned the tsar to accept Ukraine under his overlordship. Moscow, however, was cautious. Fearful of irritating the Poles, it sent funds and words of encouragement to the Ukrainians, but remained noncommittal about standing up for their rights.

So unsettling and destructive was the struggle between the Orthodox and Greek Catholics that finally, in 1632, the Polish government stepped in and imposed a compromise. The Orthodox hierarchy was officially recognized and the disputed properties were divided between the two churches. One of the main architects of this compromise was the newly elected metropolitan of Kiev, Petro Mohyla, often regarded as the leading Orthodox churchman of 17th-century Ukraine. A scion of a leading Moldavian family, Mohyla, like many of his countrymen, received his early education in the Lviv brotherhood school. After completing his university studies in Paris, he returned to Ukraine to pursue an ecclesiastical career. In 1627, at the age of 31, he became the archimandrite of the Kievan Cave Monastery and five years later was appointed metropolitan of Kiev.

Taking advantage of the relative calm that ensued after 1632, Mohyla introduced badly needed reforms in the Orthodox church and its cultural and educational institutions. With the aid of a group of learned theologians and writers, sometimes called the Mohyla Atheneum, he systematized Orthodox dogma and ritual and prepared the first Orthodox catechism for publication. By uniting a school he founded in the Kievan Cave Monastery with the Kiev brotherhood school, Mohyla laid the foundation for the so-called Mohyla Collegium, which was destined to become one of the most important Orthodox educational institutions among the Slavs. Using Jesuit schools as a model, the college emphasized the study of the classics and especially of Latin and Polish. Greek, once favored by the brotherhood schools, was deemphasized. The curriculum of Mohyla's school reflected his general tendency to combine Orthodox-Slavic traditions with those of the Latin-Catholic West. However, in their enthusiasm for the cultural products of the West, Mohyla and his circle sometimes failed to realize that although Latin philosophical tracts, histories of the world, or poetic works were appealing to a small, sophisticated group of scholastics, they did not have a broader appeal for Ukrainian society as a whole. Therefore, a cultural gap gradually developed between the elitist Kiev scholastics and the rest of Ukrainian society.

Ukrainian high culture, that is, the culture of the small, educated elite, continued to be dominated by religious themes. Most books, such as Zakhariah Kopestensky's *Palinodiia* or Kyril Stavrovetsky's "Mirror of Theology," sought to demonstrate the correctness of Orthodox views and to prove that Orthodoxy represented the one and only way for man to attain salvation. Even the "best-sellers" of the times, which were destined for popular consumption, dealt with such topics as the lives of saints or catalogued miracles that occurred in the Kievan Cave Monastery. For the most part, these works were written in the difficult Church Slavonic that still served as the literary language of Ukraine. However, there were signs that the simpler Ukrainian vernacular was also gaining ground among the literati. Pamba Berynda, for example, spent thirty years compiling his *Lexikon*, which provided Ukrainian equivalents for Church Slavonic words. Another innovation in Ukrainian literature during this period was the growing popularity of poetry, especially panegyrics. Among the best-known example of this genre was Sakovych's presentation on the occasion of Sahaidachny's funeral and the poems dedicated to Mohyla by the students of his college. Dramas, often composed and staged in schools, were also popular and frequently incorporated elements of folklore. As the schools produced hundreds of students and over twenty printing presses appeared in Ukraine, literacy became relatively widespread in the land.

While religious issues and Western models stimulated the Kievan cultural elite, the culture of the masses continued to reflect the impact of the agricultural life-style and conditions of the frontier. Folk songs, many of ancient origin, expressed the peasants' concern with nature, their work in the fields and their personal relationships. They praised such simple virtues as hard work and honesty, while deriding immoral or selfish behavior. The epitome of folk creativity during the 16th and 17th centuries was the *duma* or folk epic. *Dumy* were recited to the accompaniment of the *bandura* (a lutelike instrument) by wandering minstrels during market days or religious holidays, in Cossack encampments or village squares. By and large, these lengthy versified tales concentrated on the two major conflicts confronting Ukrainian frontier society: the struggle with the Turks and Tatars and the resistance against the oppression of the *szlachta*.

ᴥ

Frontiersmen were not uncommon in early modern Eastern Europe. Cossackdom developed along the Don River in Russia as well as along the Dnieper in Ukraine. Roughly analogous social groups evolved in Hungary, Croatia, and other Christian land on the unsettled frontier with the Ottoman Empire. But nowhere did these "peripheral" classes come to play such a central role in their respective societies as did the Cossacks in Ukraine. Of course, one could expect frontiersmen to be all-important in a frontier society like Ukraine. And the Polonization of the Ukrainian elite drew the Ukrainian Cossacks into a role that was fulfilled elsewhere by the nobles. Consequently, the Cossack became a key figure not only in the history of Ukraine but also in Ukrainian national consciousness. Today the image of the Cossack is to Ukrainians what the cowboy is to Americans or the Viking to the Scandinavians.

The growing importance of the Cossacks was accompanied by renewed vigor in Ukrainian religious and cultural life. Once more Kiev became a major center of Orthodoxy. For the city's religous/cultural elite, much of which was associated with the Mohyla Academy, it was, as Ihor Ševčenko put it, "a time when spirits were uplifted and minds were expanding." On the one hand, the Orthodox revival helped to stem the tide of Polonization. On the other hand it infused Ukrainian culture with the Western elements that slowed Russification in a later period. Thus, after coming perilously close to assimilation into the dominant Polish culture and society, in the early modern period Ukrainians produced more of the distinctive features that distinguished them from their neighbors.

8

The Great Revolt

The great uprising of 1648 was one of the most cataclysmic events in Ukrainian history. Indeed, it is difficult to find a similar revolt of such magnitude, intensity, and impact in the early modern history of all of Europe. But why Ukraine? What features did it possess that predisposed it to such a tremendous outburst? The recently colonized eastern provinces of Kiev, Bratslav, and Chernihiv that provided the stage for the revolt were unique not only in the Commonwealth, but in all of Europe. They were the domain, on the one hand, of some of Europe's most powerful and wealthy magnates and, on the other, of a population that was willing and able to fight effectively for its interests. In other words, in newly colonized Ukraine, some of Europe's most exploitive feudal lords confronted some of its most defiant masses.

This situation was largely an outgrowth of Ukraine's role as a frontier. It was the presence of the "wild field" that had made the emergence of Cossackdom possible and had allowed the magnates to amass their huge landholdings. The weak, decentralized nature of the Polish government added to the explosiveness of the situation. Unable to protect the frontier itself, it granted vast stretches of territory to the magnates on the condition that they protect them. For the same reason, it acquiesced, albeit in a limited way, in the growth of Cossackdom. However, as both these phenomena mushroomed, the royal government lost control and did nothing to resolve the threatening contradictions that were evolving on the Ukrainian frontier.

❧

On the Eve of the Great Revolt

Although the magnates did much to encourage the colonization or, as 19th-century Polish historians liked to put it, the "civilization" of Ukraine, they were also responsible for the instability and tension that had become endemic in that society. Acting on the principle that might makes right, they regularly resorted to violence in conflicts with their underlings and with each other. These self-centered, anarchistic tendencies and the weakness of royal authority on the frontier led Poles to observe ruefully that "Ukraine is ruled by the lack of rule." The magnates' penchant for coercion was most evident in their treatment of the peasantry. After attracting the peasants to their vast latifundia by means of the obligation-free *slobody*, they clamped down on them as soon as the time limits on them expired. Their demands grew increasingly greater, especially after what seemed to be the final defeat of the Cossack and peasant rebels in 1638.

Formerly unburdened peasants were suddenly forced to provide their lords with three or four days of labor a week. In addition, they had to furnish noblemen landowners with assorted personal services, while at the same time continuing to pay a tax on their homes and farm animals to the royal treasury. To make matters worse, the magnates in Ukraine frequently resorted to the hated practice of *arenda*, or leasing, in which the leaseholder (*arendar*) agreed that anything he could squeeze out of the peasants above a set figure was his profit. Forbidden to own land, but allowed to lease it, Jews often became leaseholders. Thus, on the vast lands of the Ostrorog family, for example, there were about 4000 Jewish leaseholders, and in 1616, over half the crown lands in Ukraine were leased out to Jewish entrepreneurs. Because they had to make good their investment in a relatively short period of two or three years, they exploited the properties and peasants mercilessly, without regard for future consequences. It was not uncommon for a leaseholder to demand six or seven days of labor from the peasants and, with the help of the magnates' minions, to drive them into the fields.

Another form of leaseholding was the leasing out of an estate's monopoly on the production and sale of alcohol and tobacco to a leaseholder, who then charged the peasants whatever price he wished for these prized commodities. Needless to say, such practices did not make Jews popular with the Ukrainian population. As the English historian Norman Davies puts it, Jewish participation in the oppressive practices of the noble/Jewish alliance "provided the most important single cause of the terrible retribution which would descend on them on several occasions in the future."[1]

Among other segments of Ukrainian frontier society, discontent also ran high. The specific nature of the frontier made many of the small, recently established towns vulnerable to magnate pressure. In Kiev and Bratslav provinces, about 50% of the population lived in towns, proportionately three times more than anywhere else in the Commonwealth. Although they possessed town status and, in some cases, even Magdeburg Law, most of the new towns were little more than forts built to protect their inhabitants (many of whom were engaged in agriculture) from the Tatars. This semi-agrarian nature of the towns, plus the fact that many were on magnate-owned territory, provided the oligarchs with a pretext to question the status of the burghers and to demand from them onerous obligations and dues. Even the petty nobility, most of whom were still Orthodox, were liable to mistreatment and expropriation by the magnates. But as frustration and resentment mounted, the usual outlets that had helped alleviate them were being shut off. With the progress of colonization, it became more and more difficult for peasants to find empty lands to run away to, while, after 1638, Cossackdom, which had traditionally attracted the most discontented elements, was severely repressed.

Unlike peasants in other parts of the Commonwealth and even in Western Ukraine, the inhabitants of the Dnieper basin were not only unaccustomed to the burdens of serfdom, but also unwilling to accept them. Regardless of what the magnates contended, many considered themselves to be freemen. Among the Cossacks, for example, it was an article of faith, if not of fact, that in 1582 King Batory had granted Cossacks privileges that made them almost equal to noblemen. For their part, the numerous townsmen argued that, by definition, they were self-governing and free. And after decades on a *sloboda*, it was difficult to convince a frontier peasant that he was not his own master. It was irrelevant how legally justifiable these perceptions were. The point was that most of the inhabitants of the frontier believed that freeman status was rightfully theirs and this belief greatly increased their willingness to resist the *Liakhy*, as they called the Poles. The Polish Catholic persecution of Orthodoxy only heightened Ukrainian recalcitrance.

Combined with the frontier-Ukrainians' inclination to revolt was their general aptitude for fighting. Mass uprisings in early modern Europe were usually characterized by a lack of organization and military expertise. In this regard, the Ukrainian case was different. Foreign travelers frequently noted that life on the dangerous frontier forced even common peasants and townsmen to become proficient in the use of firearms. Moreover, the Cossacks provided the discontented with a core of well-organized, highly skilled fighting men. Even their recent defeats provided Ukrainian Cossacks with experience in fighting regular armies and pitched battles. Thus, as the magnates intensified their exploitation, Ukrainian frontier society increased its willingness and ability to withstand it. Only a spark was needed to set off a vast conflagration.

Bohdan Khmelnytsky

Rarely do individuals dominate epochal developments as completely as did Bohdan Khmelnytsky the great Ukrainian uprising of 1648. Because of his great personal impact on events that changed the course of Ukrainian and East European history, scholars consider him to be Ukraine's greatest military and political leader. Yet, his debut as a major actor on the historical stage occurred late in life and was almost accidental. Born in about 1595, Khmelnytsky was the son of a minor Ukrainian nobleman named Mykhailo, who was the servitor of a Polish magnate. For his services, Mykhailo obtained an estate in Subotiv; he sent Bohdan to a Jesuit school in Iaroslav where he received a good education by the standards of the time, mastering Polish and Latin. In 1620, tragedy struck. In the great Turkish victory over the Poles at Cecora, the elder Khmelnytsky was killed and Bohdan was taken captive. After two years in captivity, Khmelnytsky returned to Subotiv, entered the ranks of the registered Cossacks, married, and concentrated on expanding his estate. Cautious and well established, he avoided involvement in the uprisings of 1625 and 1638. His good standing with the government led to a brief tenure in 1638 as chancellor of the Zaporozhian Host and to his participation in a Cossack delegation to the Polish king, Władysław IV, in 1646. By the time Khmelnytsky, now a captain in the Chyhyryn Cossack regiment, had reached the age of 50, it appeared that the bulk of a moderately successful career was already behind him.

But a typical case of magnate acquisitiveness and arrogance completely altered Khmelnytsky's life and with it the course of his country's history. In 1646, during his absence from Subotiv, Daniel Czaplinski, a Polish nobleman backed by the local magnates, laid claim to Khmelnytsky's estate, raided it, killed his youngest son, and abducted the woman that the recently widowed Cossack captain intended to marry. When numerous appeals to the court brought no satisfaction, the infuriated Khmelnytsky resolved to lead a revolt against the Poles. This rapid transformation from a respected member of the establishment to a raging rebel was not completely out of character. In later years, observers often remarked about the Cossack leader's split personality. Swarthy and stocky, "Khmel," as he was popularly called, was usually reserved, unpretentious, courteous, and even somewhat phlegmatic. But he could unexpectedly explode in a torrent of passion, energy, and charismatic appeal. In such moments, his speech became mesmerizing, his ideas at once fascinating and frightening, and his will to have his way unshakable.

The mesmerizing influence Khmelnytsky could exert on the masses became evident when, hounded by the Poles who had caught wind of his plans, he fled to the Zaporozhian Sich with a handful of followers in January 1648. In short order he persuaded the Zaporozhians to support him, expelled the Polish garrison from the Sich, and managed to have himself elected hetman. At first, the gathering rebellion had all the features of the previous, unsuccessful uprisings: a vengeful Cossack officer, wronged by magnates, making his way to the Sich and persuading the Zaporozhians to stand up for their (and his) rights. But, in Khmelnytsky's case, his exceptional talents as an organizer, military leader, and politician made the crucial difference.

For more than a year before arriving at the Sich, he had plotted an uprising and established a network of supporters. Realizing that the Cossacks' great weakness in fighting the Poles was a lack of cavalry, Khmelnytsky found an audacious solution to the problem: he approached the Crimean Tatars, the Cossacks' traditional enemies, with a proposal for an alliance against the Poles. His timing was perfect. At precisely the time that his envoys arrived in Crimea, the khan's relations with the Poles had become extremely strained and he sent Tuhai-Bey, a noted commander, with 4000 Tatars to the Cossacks' aid. In the spring of 1648, forewarned of Khmelnytsky's actions, the Poles moved their army to the south to nip the rebellion in the bud.

The early victories In mid April 1648, at Zhovti Vody, not far from the Sich, a confident Polish advance guard of 6000 men confronted the combined Cossack/Tatar force of about 9000. On 6 May, after prolonged fighting, which resulted in the desertion to the rebels of several thousand registered Cossacks who had been sent to aid the Poles, the Polish advance guard was annihilated. Astounded by the news and convinced by a Cossack prisoner (planted expressly for the purpose) that the rebels greatly outnumbered them, Marcin Kalinowski and Mikołaj Potocki, the two commanders of the 20,000-man main army, abandoned their strong positions near Korsun and retreated through difficult terrain, led by a guide who was a secret agent of the hetman. Not far from Korsun, on 26 May, the Poles were ambushed by the Cossacks (whose forces had grown to 15,000 not including Tatar cavalry) and, once again, were completely crushed. Both Polish commanders, 80 important noblemen, 127 officers, 8520 soldiers, and forty-one cannons fell into Khmelnytsky's hands. To add to the Poles' misfortunes, only six days before the Battle of Korsun, King Władysław IV died. Just as hordes of rebels were gathering in the south, the Commonwealth had suddenly lost its king, its commanders, and its army.

While Khmelnytsky's victories stunned the Poles, they electrified the Ukrainians. First on the Right Bank and then on the Left Bank, Cossacks, peasants, and burghers rushed to form regiments and either joined the hetman or, led by numerous local leaders, staged mini-rebellions of their own. Many peasants and Cossacks used the opportunity to vent pent-up hatred against their oppressors. The so-called "Eye Witness Chronicle" paints a frightful picture of these events: "Wherever they found the *szlachta*, royal officials or Jews, they killed them all, sparing neither women nor children. They pillaged the estates of the Jews and nobles, burned [Catholic] churches and killed their priests, leaving nothing whole. It was a rare individual in those days who had not soaked his hands in blood and participated in the pillage."[2] Within a few months, almost all Polish nobles, officials, and priests had been wiped out or driven from Ukraine. Jewish losses were especially heavy because they were the most numerous and accessible representatives of the *szlachta* regime. Between 1648 and 1656, tens of thousands of Jews – given the lack of reliable data, it is impossible to establish more accurate figures – were killed by the rebels, and to this day the Khmelnytsky uprising is considered by Jews to be one of the most traumatic events in their history.[3]

Whenever they had the opportunity, the Polish magnates and nobles responded to the massacres in kind. The most notorious practitioner of *szlachta* terror tactics was Jeremi Wiśniowiecki, the wealthiest magnate in the land. When the rebellion caught him on his estates on the Left Bank, Wiśniowiecki mustered his well-trained private army of 6000, gathered together as many of the terrified nobles, priests, and Jews as he could, and set off on an epic, roundabout retreat to the west. Everywhere his forces moved, they tortured and killed Cossacks, peasants, women, and children, leaving behind them a grisly trail of corpses. Although Wiśniowiecki's feats won him adulation in Poland, they so infuriated the Ukrainian masses that they would brook no talk of compromise and vowed to fight him to the death.

During the summer, Khmelnytsky, who was based near Bila Tserkva, concentrated on molding his numerous followers into a disciplined, well-organized army. Its core was made up of sixteen regiments of battle-tested Cossacks led by such proven and respected colonels as Filon Dzhalali, Maksym Nestorenko, and Ivan Hyria. However, experienced and gifted Ukrainian noblemen like Danylo Nechai, Ivan Bohun, and Mykhailo Krychevsky, and townsmen like Martyn Nebaba and Vasyl Zolotarenko, were also awarded colonels' maces. A large auxiliary force of light cavalry was led by Wiśniowiecki's bitter rival, Maksym Kryvonis, one of the most popular rebel leaders. As volunteers continued to pour in, new units were created; by the end of the summer, the Ukrainian forces numbered between 80,000 and 100,000. Of these, only about 40,000 were regular Cossack troops.

The Poles also made good use of their time. In order to hold off the rebels, they engaged Khmelnytsky in desultory negotiations and, at the same time, mobilized 32,000 noblemen and 8000 German mercenaries. As their forces, outfitted in the glittering finery that the *szlachta* so loved, gathered near Lviv, an observer remarked that the Poles were going to war not with iron but with gold and silver. The new Polish army was led by three magnates: the indolent, luxury-loving Dominik Zasławski, the erudite Latinist Mikołaj Ostroróg, and the 19-year-old Aleksander Koniecpolski. Khmelnytsky sarcastically referred to them as *peryna* (the feather-down bed), *latyna* (the Latinist), and *dytyna* (the child). On 23 September, the opposing armies met at Pyliavtsi. During the battle, the Polish commanders lost their nerve and fled and, as the news spread, the rest of the army followed suit. Within hours, this once splendid force was completely decimated by the Cossacks and their Tatar allies.

After Pyliavtsi, there was nothing to stand in Khmelnytsky's way. As he advanced into the West Ukrainian lands of Volhynia and Galicia, the peasants welcomed him and joined the uprising. Even in southern Poland, downtrodden peasants were heard to utter, "If God were only so kind as to give us a

Khmelnytsky also then we would teach those nobles what they get for op-
pressing peasants."⁴ In early October, the Cossack/peasant armies besieged
Lviv and were about to take it when a huge ransom and Khmelnytsky's reluctance to destroy the beautiful city saved it. A month later, while preparing
to besiege the Polish fortress at Zamość, news arrived that the man Khmelnytsky preferred to see on the throne, Jan Casimir, had been elected king and
had offered the hetman an armistice.

It has always been a puzzle to historians why Khmelnytsky, who at this
point was in a position to destroy the Commonwealth, chose to accept the offer and to return to the Dnieper. Apparently, he still hoped to modify the political system of the Commonwealth so that it would accommodate the Cossacks. Moreover, famine and plague were taking their toll of his troops and of
the Ukrainian populace as a whole. And the hetman's Tatar allies were eager
to return home. Under these conditions, it seems that he did not wish to conduct a winter campaign. Early in January 1649, at the head of a triumphant
army, Khmelnytsky returned to Kiev, where he received a tumultuous welcome and was hailed by the assembled Orthodox hierarchy as "the second
Moses" who had "liberated his people from Polish slavery."

Rising complications   Even after Khmelnytsky's dramatic victories, the relationship between Poles and Ukrainians remained unclarified. While the hetman had not yet decided to break off all ties with the Commonwealth, he
knew that his followers were determined not to return to the pre-1648 conditions. For their part, the Poles were willing to make minor concessions to
the Cossacks, but they still insisted that Ukraine return to *szlachta* rule. The
impasse produced a recurrent pattern: year after year, the two sides would
go to war, but because they were unable to defeat each other decisively, they
would conclude their exhausting campaigns with negotiated, unsatisfying
settlements, after which they would return home to prepare militarily and
diplomatically for yet another war.

In the spring of 1649, it was the Poles who went on the offensive. As their
main force of 25,000, led by King Jan Casimir himself, advanced from Volhynia, another force of 15,000, commanded by the notorious Jeremi Wiśniowiecki, moved through Galicia. Responding with his usual deceptiveness and
speed, Khmelnytsky and his Tatar ally, Khan Islam Girei, blockaded
Wiśniowiecki in the Zbarazh fortress with a force of 80,000. When the Polish king hastened to Wiśniowiecki's aid, Khmelnytsky, in a surprise maneuver, attacked and surrounded Jan Casimir's army near Zboriv. But, just at the
point when the Poles were about to go down in defeat at both Zbarazh and
Zboriv, the Tatar khan betrayed the hetman. Bribed by the Poles and worried
by the growing strength of the Ukrainians, Islam Girei withdrew his forces
and demanded that Khmelnytsky reach a negotiated settlement with the Polish king. Under the circumstances, the hetman had no choice but to comply.

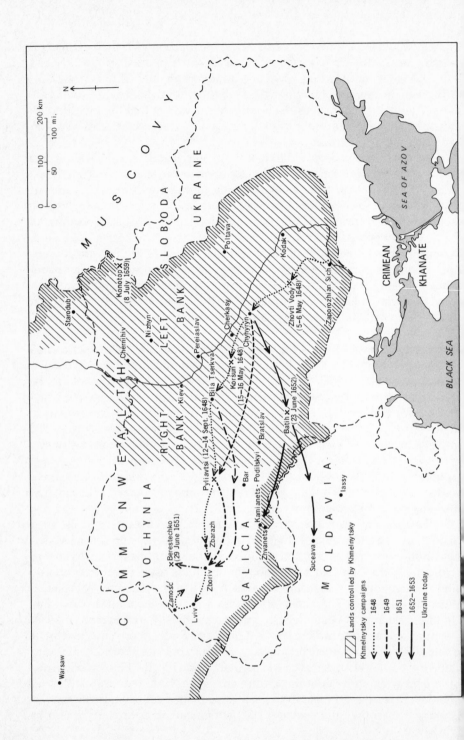

Warsaw

MUSCOVY

SLOBODA UKRAINE

COMMONWEALTH

LEFT BANK

RIGHT BANK

VOLHYNIA

GALICIA

MOLDAVIA

SEA OF AZOV

CRIMEAN KHANATE

BLACK SEA

Starodub

Konotop X
(8 July 1659)

Chernihiv

Nizhyn

Kiev

Pereiaslav

Poltava

Kodak

Chyhyryn

Zhovti Vody
(5–6 May 1648)

Zaporozhian Sich

Cherkasy

Korsun X
(15–16 May 1648)

Bila Tserkva

Pyliavtsi (12–14 Sept. 1648)

Bar

Bratslav

Batih X
(23 June 1652)

Kamianets - Podilskyi

Zvanets

Suceava

Iassy

Zbarazh

Berestechko
(29 June 1651)

Zboriv

Lviv

Zamość

Khmelnytsky campaigns

Lands controlled by Khmelnytsky

1648
1649
1651
1652–1653
Ukraine today

On 18 August 1649, the Zboriv treaty was concluded. It set the register at 40,000, banned the Polish army and Jews from the provinces of Kiev, Bratslav, and Chernihiv where only the Cossack *starshyna* and Orthodox noblemen were allowed to hold public office, and promised the Orthodox metropolitan a seat in the Polish senate. Although amnesty was granted to all who had participated in the uprising, most peasants were required to return to servitude. Polish noblemen, in contrast, were allowed to reclaim their estates. Only Tatar pressure had forced Khmelnytsky to sign this unfavorable agreement, which caused great discontent throughout Ukraine. But as the Poles believed that they had given up too much and the Cossacks were convinced that they had received too little, the treaty was never fully implemented.

The Zboriv agreement highlighted an internal and an external problem that Khmelnytsky would have to face. The fact that peasant interests had practically been ignored at Zboriv was no oversight. Although Khmelnytsky, most of his commanders, and many of the registered Cossacks wished to improve the lot of the peasants, they had no intention of liquidating serfdom altogether. For the Cossack elite, Khmelnytsky included, such an act would have meant undermining the socioeconomic system in which it had a considerable stake. Thus, already at Zboriv, a conflict of interests arose between the Cossack *starshyna* elite and the *chern*, or rank and file. In time, it would prove to be the fatal weakness of the Cossack order that was emerging in Ukraine.

The relationship with the Tatars was the other major problem. Realizing their importance in his recent victories and in the continuing conflict with the Poles, Khmelnytsky wished to maintain his alliance with them at all costs. Among the Ukrainian masses, however, the alliance was most unpopular because, as a price for Tatar aid, the hetman had to allow his allies to take *iasyr*, or captives. While Khmelnytsky hoped to satisfy the Tatars with Polish prisoners, the Crimeans often took what was at hand and this meant that many thousands of Ukrainian peasants were driven off into slavery. Moreover, Tatar policy was not to let any Christian power grow too strong. Therefore, although they backed Khmelnytsky against the Poles, the Tatars would not allow him to defeat them completely. Having used Khmelnytsky to weaken Poland, the Crimean khan also planned to utilize the Ukrainian Cossacks in similar fashion against Moscow. But because Khmelnytsky had great hopes of obtaining aid from the Muscovites, he diverted the Crimean plans to launch a joint Tatar/Cossack attack against Moscow by proposing instead a joint campaign in 1650 against Moldavia, which was rich, more vulnerable, and more accessible. For the next few years, Khmelnytsky became intensely involved in Moldavian affairs and even hoped to make his son, Tymish, ruler of the land, thereby drawing it into close alliance with Ukraine. However, in 1653, Tymish's death during the defense of Suceava brought the costly Moldavian venture to an unsuccessful end.

Meanwhile, in 1651, another round in the Polish-Ukrainian War had begun.

Again it was the Poles, led by Jan Casimir, who went on the offensive and again it was in Volhynia, near the town of Berestechko, that the two armies clashed. By the standards of the time, the size of the opposing forces was huge: the Polish army numbered around 150,000 men, including 20,000 experienced German mercenaries, while the Ukrainians mustered over 100,000 men plus about 50,000 Tatar cavalry. On 18 June, an almost two week-long battle began that ended in a crushing defeat for Khmelnytsky's forces. A deciding factor in the defeat was the actions of the Tatars who, at a crucial juncture, withdrew from the battle. To make matters worse, when Khmelnytsky entreated them to return to the fighting, they abducted him. He was released only after the battle. Under difficult circumstances, the Cossacks, ably led by Filon Dzhalali, managed to extricate some of the Ukrainian forces from Polish encirclement, but at a decisive moment panic broke out and a part of the Cossack army, numbering an estimated 30,000 men, perished under the Polish onslaught. The massive battle was also costly to the victorious Poles and near Bila Tserkva they initiated negotiations.

As might be expected, the Bila Tserkva agreement, signed on 28 September 1651, was much less generous to the Cossacks than the Zboriv treaty had been. The Cossack register was reduced to 20,000; the hetman's authority was limited only to Kiev province; and he was forbidden to maintain foreign contacts, especially with the Tatars. This time, with the Cossacks in disarray and Khmelnytsky unprepared to offer resistance, it appeared that the conditions of the treaty would be implemented. Backed by Polish troops, the Polish nobility began to return to Ukraine. Except for the relative few who were included in the register, most of the peasants and Cossacks again faced serfdom. In order to avoid their inevitable fate, thousands fled across the border into Muscovite territory, where they were well received and allowed to establish the Cossack system, thus laying the foundation for what came to be called Sloboda Ukraine, with its locus in the present-day Kharkiv region.

Despite appearances to the contrary, Khmelnytsky had no intention of accepting these humiliating conditions and, in April 1652, a secret meeting of the major Cossack leaders was held at his residence in Chyhyryn where it was decided to assemble new forces and to renew hostilities against the Poles. Within weeks, Khmelnytsky's forces attacked a 30,000-man Polish army stationed at Batih on the border of Podilia and Moldavia, and on 1 May completely demolished it. As revenge for the defeat at Berestechko, the Cossacks killed all their Polish prisoners.

As news of the victory spread, uprisings against the Polish nobility again flared up and Cossack troops occupied much of the territory they had held before Berestechko. However, by now it was evident that the years of tremendous bloodletting and destruction were taking their toll. Both Poles and Ukrainians were less eager to fight and campaigns dragged on inconclusively as the two sides circled each other like exhausted boxers, unable to administer the decisive blow.

Foreign relations Khmelnytsky realized that if his uprising was to succeed, it needed foreign support. Therefore, he turned his attention more and more to foreign relations. He scored his first diplomatic victory by drawing the Crimean Tatars into an alliance with the Cossacks. But the Tatar alliance proved to be unreliable and transitory. Moreover, it did not resolve Khmelnytsky's key problem of defining Ukraine's relationship to the Commonwealth. At first, the hetman was not ready for a complete break. His goal in dealing with the Commonwealth, ably represented by the leading Orthodox magnate Adam Kysil, had been to obtain autonomy for the Cossacks in Ukraine by making it a separate and equal component of the Commonwealth. But the stubborn refusal of the *szlachta* to accept their former subordinates as political equals precluded the possibility of his ever achieving that goal.

To the modern mind, which views national sovereignty as a natural condition (although the concept did not gain wide currency until after the French Revolution of 1789), the question arises of why Khmelnytsky did not declare independence for Ukraine. During the uprising there were, in fact, rumors to the effect that he wished to reestablish the "old Rus' principality," and even that he planned to form a separate "Cossack principality." Although such ideas may have been considered, it would have been impossible under the circumstances to realize them. As the interminable wars demonstrated, the Cossacks, although able to administer severe defeats to the Poles, were incapable of permanently preventing the *szlachta* from launching repeated efforts to regain Ukraine. To assure themselves of a lasting victory over the Poles, Khmelnytsky needed the continuing and reliable support of a major foreign power. The usual price of such aid was acceptance of the overlordship of the ruler who provided it. In the view of the masses, the main thrust of the uprising was to redress socioeconomic ills, and to many in Ukraine the question of whether these problems were to be resolved under their own or under foreign rule was of secondary importance. Finally, in 17th-century Eastern Europe, sovereignty rested not in the people, but in the person of a legitimate (that is, generally recognized) monarch. Because Khmelnytsky, despite his popularity and power, did not possess such legitimacy, he had to find for Ukraine an overlord who did. At issue was not self-rule for Ukraine, for Ukrainians already had gained it. Their goal was to find a monarch who could provide their newly formed autonomous society with legitimacy and protection.

In Khmelnytsky's opinion, a good candidate for the role of Ukraine's patron and protector in the international arena was the Ottoman sultan. He was powerful enough to discourage Poles from attacking Ukraine and distant enough not to interfere overly much in its internal affairs. Thus, in 1651, after an exchange of embassies, the Ottoman Porte formally accepted the hetman and the Zaporozhian Host as its vassals on the similar loose conditions of overlordship that obtained with regard to Crimea, Moldavia, and Wallachia. However, widespread animosity in Ukraine toward an "infidel" overlord, and internal changes in the Ottoman Porte, prevented this arrangement from ever taking effect.

A much more popular candidate for the role of Ukraine's protector was the Orthodox tsar of Moscow. From the start of the uprising, Khmelnytsky had entreated the tsar, in the name of their shared Orthodox faith, to come to his aid. But Moscow's response had been extremely cautious. Badly mauled in a recent war with Poland, the Muscovites preferred to wait for the Cossacks and Poles to exhaust each other and then to take appropriate action. However, by 1653, with the Ukrainians threatening to choose the Ottoman option, the Muscovites could not put off a decision any longer. Tsar Aleksei Mikhailovich called a general assembly, which decided that, "for the sake of the Orthodox Faith and God's Holy Church, the *Gosudar* [monarch] should accept them under His High Hand." In reaching their decision, the Muscovites also expected to regain some of the lands they had lost to Poland, to utilize Ukraine as a buffer zone against the Ottomans, and, in general, to expand their influence.

The Pereiaslav Agreement

In the final days of 1653, a Muscovite embassy, led by the boyar Vasilii Buturlin, met with the hetman, colonels, and general staff of the Zaporozhian Host in the town of Pereiaslav, near Kiev. On 18 January 1654, Khmelnytsky called a meeting of the Cossack elite and the final decision was taken to accept the tsar's overlordship of Ukraine. On that day, drummers summoned the populace to the town square where the hetman spoke about Ukraine's need for an overlord, presented the four potential candidates for such a position – the Polish king, the Tatar khan, the Ottoman sultan, and the Muscovite tsar – and declared that the Orthodox tsar was best suited for the role. Pleased that the choice had fallen on an Orthodox ruler, the crowd responded favorably to the hetman's speech. Buturlin, Khmelnytsky, and the assembled Cossack dignitaries then proceeded to the town church to seal the decision with a mutual oath.

At this point, an unexpected development created a tense impasse. Under the influence of Polish practice, Khmelnytsky expected the oath to be bilateral, with the Ukrainians swearing loyalty to the tsar and the latter promising to protect them from the Poles and to respect their rights and privileges. But Buturlin refused to swear in the name of his monarch, arguing that the tsar, unlike the Polish king, was an absolute ruler and that it was below his dignity to take an oath to his subjects. Upset by Buturlin's refusal, Khmelnytsky stalked out of the church and threatened to cancel the entire agreement. Nonetheless, Buturlin steadfastly held his ground. Finally, Khmelnytsky and his colleagues, fearful of losing the tsar's aid because of what appeared to be a mere formality, glumly agreed to take a unilateral oath of loyalty to the tsar.

Shortly thereafter, Muscovite officials were sent to 117 Ukrainian towns, and 127,000 people took a similar oath of loyalty to Tsar Aleksei Mikhailovich and his successors. The significance of the dramatic incident at the Pereiaslav church was that it highlighted the different political values and assumptions with which both parties had entered into the agreement. Yet, these differences notwithstanding, the Pereiaslav Agreement was concluded and it marked a turning point in the history of Ukraine, Russia, and all of Eastern Europe. Previously isolated and backward, Muscovy now took a giant step toward becoming a great power. And, for better or for worse, the fate of Ukraine became inextricably linked with that of Russia.

Because of the conflicts that later developed between Russians and Ukrainians, the interpretation of the treaty that brought their two countries together has been the subject of frequent debate among scholars. The issue is complicated by the fact that the original documents were lost and only inaccurate copies and translations have survived. Moreover, the Russian archivist Petr Shafranov has argued that even these copies were falsified by the tsar's scribes. In general, five major interpretations of the Pereiaslav Agreement have been proposed. (1) According to the Russian legal historian Vasilii Sergeevich (d. 1910), the 1654 agreement was a *personal union* between Muscovy and Ukraine, whereby the two parties shared the same sovereign but retained separate governments. (2) Another specialist in Russian law, Nikolai Diakonov (d. 1919), argued that by accepting "personal subjugation" to the tsar, the Ukrainians unconditionally agreed to the incorporation of their land into the Muscovite state and the agreement was therefore a *real union*. (3) Historians, such as the Russian Venedikt Miakotin and the Ukrainian Mykhailo Hrushevsky, believed that the Pereiaslav Agreement was a form of *vassalage* in which the more powerful party (the tsar) agreed to protect the weaker party (the Ukrainians) on condition that he not interfere in their internal affairs and that the Ukrainians provide him with tribute, military assistance, as well as other considerations. (4) Another Ukrainian historian, Viacheslav Lypynsky, proposed that the 1654 agreement was nothing more than a temporary *military alliance* between Moscow and the Ukrainians.[5]

The fifth interpretation of the Pereiaslav Agreement belongs in a class by itself. In 1954, during the elaborate celebrations of the 300th anniversary of the Ukrainian-Russian union in the USSR, it was announced – not by scholars but by the Communist Party of the Soviet Union – that the Pereiaslav Agreement was the natural culmination of the age-old desire of Ukrainians and Russians to be united and that the union of the two peoples had been the prime goal of the 1648 uprising. In the official Soviet interpretation, Khmelnytsky's greatness lay in the fact that he understood that "The salvation of the Ukrainian people lay only in unity with the great Russian people."[6] Although at least one Soviet scholar – Mykhailo Braichevsky – challenged this view in the mid 1960s (with catastrophic consequences for his career), adherence to the Party's interpretation of the agreement remains mandatory for all Soviet scholars.[7]

The Final Phase of the Great Revolt

One of the immediate results of the Pereiaslav Agreement was a radical restructuring of the political alliances in the region. In response to Khmelnytsky's treaty with the tsar, the Poles and Tatars combined forces and a new, expanded phase of the conflict ensued. In the spring of 1654, a Muscovite army, led by the tsar and aided by a Cossack force of 20,000 men, commanded by Vasyl Zolotarenko, pushed into Belorussia and wrested much of it from the Poles. Later, in the fall, the fighting shifted to southwestern Ukraine. The Tatars, now unrestrained by any commitments to the Ukrainians, devastated the region mercilessly. A report by the Polish commander graphically describes the scene: "I estimate that the number of infants alone who were found dead along the roads and in the castles reached 10,000. I ordered them to be buried in the fields and one grave alone contained over 270 bodies ... All the infants were less than a year old since the older ones were driven off into captivity. The surviving peasants wander about in groups, bewailing their misfortune."[8]

During the campaign, an incident occurred that typified the intensity of the conflict. In October 1654, an overwhelming Polish force besieged the Cossack fortress at Busha, killed most of its garrison, and was about to overrun the castle. At this point, the wife of the slain Cossack commander, Zavisny, refused to surrender and instead, ignited the munitions dump, blowing up herself, the surviving garrison, and many of the attacking Poles. As a result of the savage campaigns that were fought on the Right Bank, the most highly developed of the recently colonized lands were left despoiled and practically depopulated.

Misfortune and devastation enveloped Poland as well. In the summer of 1655, the Swedes, taking advantage of the Poles' involvement in the south and east, attacked from the north and occupied much of Poland. Overrun by the Swedes, Russians, and Ukrainians, the Commonwealth seemed to be on the verge of collapse. Polish historians often refer to this period as "the Deluge." For Khmelnytsky, however, the Swedish involvement in the conflict was a godsend, for it provided him with new diplomatic and military options.

Swedish and Ukrainian diplomats were soon discussing combined operations against the Poles, with the Swedes promising Khmelnytsky help in the creation of a Kievan principality. Sensing the imminent demise of the Commonwealth, another neighbor, Gyorgy II Rakoczi of Transylvania, also approached the hetman in 1656. Together they launched a combined operation into Poland with the goal of partitioning the land. With such powerful new backing, Khmelnytsky took a more uncompromising stand toward the

Poles and insisted that all Ukrainian lands, including Galicia and Volhynia, come under his rule.

The Swedes, however, created complications for the hetman as well as opportunities. Eager to settle old scores, they also initiated a war with the Muscovites. With his overlord fighting his new ally, Khmelnytsky found himself in an awkward position. Tensions between Ukrainians and Muscovites began to surface. The stationing of a Muscovite garrison in Kiev and other Ukrainian towns and the interference of tsarist officials in Ukrainian financial affairs alarmed the Cossacks. Bitterness between the allies also grew in recently conquered Belorussia, where the population frequently preferred the Cossack system of government to the Muscovite and swore allegiance to the hetman instead of to the tsar. The competition of "one Rus' [Ukrainians] with another [Muscovites] for control of a third [Belorussians]" nearly led to open warfare and it was some time before the Muscovites could force the Cossacks from the land.

But what infuriated the Ukrainian leadership most was the tsar's conclusion of a peace with Poland in Vilnius in 1656 without consulting it, indeed, without even allowing a specially dispatched Ukrainian delegation to get near the negotiations. Fearful that the Muscovites might sacrifice Ukrainian interests, the hetman and Cossack colonels openly accused the tsar of treason for breaking the terms of the Pereiaslav Agreement. In an irate letter to the tsar, Khmelnytsky compared Muscovite behavior to that of the Swedes: "The Swedes are an honest people; when they pledge friendship and alliance, they honor their word. However, the Tsar, in establishing an armistice with the Poles and in wishing to return us into their hands, has behaved most heartlessly with us."[9] On the heels of this disillusionment came others. The combined Ukrainian-Transylvanian expedition into Poland failed disastrously and disgruntled Cossacks, blaming the hetman for the setback, revolted. Crushed by the news and already ailing, Khmelnytsky died in Chyhyryn on 4 September 1657.

&

It is difficult to overestimate Khmelnytsky's impact on the course of Ukrainian history. Ukrainian, Polish, and Russian historians have compared his achievements to those of such giants of 17th-century history as Cromwell of England or Wallenstein of Bohemia. Studies of the hetman and his age frequently stress his ability to create so much from so little. Where a Ukrainian political entity had long since ceased to exist, he established a new one; out of hordes of unruly peasants and Cossacks he molded powerful, wellorganized armies; from among a people abandoned by their traditional elite he found and united around him new, dynamic leaders. Most important, in a society bereft of self-confidence and a clear sense of identity, he instilled pride in itself and a will to defend its interests. An example of the momentous change in Ukrainian attitudes brought about by Khmelnytsky is provided by the words of a simple Cossack captain addressed to a high Polish official: "In regard to Your Grace's recent letter stating that we, the common people, should not dare to address such high officials as a [Polish] *wojewoda*, it should be known that we are now, thanks be to God, no longer common people but knights of the Zaporozhian Host ... and, may God grant Lord Bohdan Khmelnytsky health, we are now ruled by our colonels and not by your *wojewody*, by our captains and not by your *starosty*, and by our *otamany* and not by your judges."[10]

Clearly, Khmelnytsky had his share of setbacks, mistakes, and miscalculations. There was Berestechko, the disastrous Moldavian venture, the failure of the combined Cossack/Transylvanian campaign into Poland, and, finally, the inability to ensure that both Ukraine's enemies and allies would recognize its integrity. For these failings historians and writers have been quick to take Khmelnytsky to task. In the mid 19th century, Mykola Kostomarov, the father of modern Ukrainian historiography, praised Khmelnytsky for establishing the link with Russia and chided him for his "underhanded" dealings with the Ottomans.

In contrast, Ukraine's greatest poet, Taras Shevchenko, was critical of the hetman for bringing Ukraine into the Russian sphere. Even more extreme in his criticism was Panteleimon Kulish, another leading 19th-century Ukrainian intellectual, who blamed Khmelnytsky for initiating an era of death, destruction, anarchy, and cultural regression in Ukraine. In the 20th century, Hrushevsky raised doubts about Khmelnytsky's consciousness of well-defined goals and argued that it was events that controlled the hetman rather than vice versa. Yet the majority of prominent Ukrainian historians, led by Viacheslav Lypynsky, concluded that the hetman consciously and systematically attempted to build the basis for Ukrainian statehood and that without his efforts, the modern rebirth of a Ukrainian state would have been impossible. Soviet historians are unanimous in their praise of Khmelnytsky, but for different reasons. They emphasize his role in leading an uprising of the oppressed masses and especially his unification (or rather "reunification," as they put it) of Ukraine with Muscovy.

But the fine points of scholarly evaluation have had little effect on the Ukrainian people's instinctive, unbounded admiration for "Batko (father) Bohdan." For the vast majority of Ukrainians, both in his day and up to the present, Khmelnytsky has towered as the great liberator, as the heroic figure who by the force of his personality and intellect roused Ukrainians from a centuries-long miasma of passivity and hopelessness and propelled them toward national and socioeconomic emancipation.

9

The Ruin

The great Ukrainian uprising of 1648 succeeded where most mass uprisings in early modern Europe had failed: it expelled a magnate-elite from most of the land and replaced it with a regime based on a native model. But while this epochal event brought about a great many changes, much remained unresolved. Sharp differences arose among the Cossack leaders as to whether Ukraine should remain under Moscow or seek the overlordship of another neighboring power. Pressing socioeconomic issues also came to the fore. Was Ukraine to become a unique society of free Cossack farmers, as envisaged by the peasants and Cossack rank and file, or would the Cossack *starshyna* simply take the place of the expelled nobles and thereby cause the destabilized social order to revert to the elite-dominated models typical for the period?

In the decades following Khmelnytsky's death, bitter conflicts over these issues pitted Ukrainians against each other. Civil strife, foreign intervention, and further devastation of an already despoiled land ensued. In Ukrainian historiography, the tragic spectacle of Ukrainians dissipating the tremendous energy and resolve that had been generated by the 1648 uprising in seemingly endless, self-destructive conflicts is often called the Ruin (*Ruina*). Twenty years after Khmelnytsky's death, the successes that had been scored against a common foe were cancelled out by the woeful inability of Ukrainians to unite towards a common goal. Their failure resulted in the loss of the promising opportunity created by the Khmelnytsky uprising to attain political self-determination.

จ

The New Order

At the time of Khmelnytsky's death, the Cossacks controlled most of the Right and Left banks of the Dnieper (the former provinces of Kiev, Bratslav, and

Chernihiv), while the West Ukrainian lands of Galicia and Volhynia remained in Polish hands. About 1.2 to 1.5 million people lived in the roughly 250,000 sq. km that were held by the Cossacks. In the first decades after the uprising, about 50% of the land – formerly owned by the Polish crown – became the property of the Zaporozhian Host, which, in return for taxes, allocated most of this land to self-governing peasant villages. The income from a part of these lands, the so-called rank lands, was used to remunerate high-ranking Cossack officers while they were in office. About 33% of the land was owned by Cossacks and Ukrainian nobles. And 17% was confirmed as the property of the Orthodox church.

The Cossacks quickly established their own form of government. The territory they controlled was divided into sixteen military districts (*polky*), corresponding to the regiments in the Cossack army. Colonels who commanded the 3000–5000-man regiments in wartime served as their district's chief administrative and judicial officials in times of peace. Each regimental district was further divided into company subdistricts (*sotni*) in which captains performed military and administrative functions. Both regiments and companies had their headquarters in the major towns in their area and carried their names. At the bottom of this administrative structure were the individual small towns and villages in which Cossack *otamany* held sway. Initially, Cossack officers were elected by the Cossacks in their units. However, in time, these posts became hereditary.

At the pinnacle of this military/administrative system stood the hetman. Theoretically, he was subject to the will of the general Cossack council (*rada*) that had elected him. But the rapid growth in the number of Cossacks during the 1648–56 period made these general councils impractical and, consequently, hetmans called them infrequently. Khmelnytsky and his successors preferred to consult the increasingly influential council of officers instead. In practice, however, hetmans were free to exercise their wide prerogatives and they were considered to be the de facto rulers of Ukraine. In addition to commanding the Cossack army, they conducted foreign affairs, supervised the administrative and judicial systems, and controlled the Cossack treasury and land fund. The fund consisted of the estates that had been confiscated from the Poles and the hetman's right to distribute them as he saw fit contributed greatly to his political leverage. In addition to the confiscated lands, which were used mainly to support Cossack officeholders, the treasury had an annual income of about 1,000,000 gold pieces from taxation, duties, and tariffs.

Assisting the hetman in the fulfillment of his functions was the *heneralna starshyna*, a combination of general staff and council of ministers. Its most important member was the secretary-general (*heneralny pysar*) or chancellor, who established the agenda of the council meetings, formulated key government documents, and supervised the day-to-day conduct of foreign affairs.

Another key member of the staff was the quartermaster-general (*heneralny obozny*), a position analogous to minister of war, who was responsible for the military preparedness of 40,000–60,000 Cossack regulars, including artillery. The judge-general (*heneralny suddia*) looked after judicial affairs and the two adjutants-general (*heneralny osavul*) as well as the standardbearer-general (*heneralny khorunzhy*) were used for special assignments by the hetman. Although Khmelnytsky and his successors always considered Kiev to be Ukraine's major city, the headquarters of the administration was based in the small Cossack town of Chyhyryn and, in the 18th century, in Baturyn and Hlukhiv. The formal designation for the Cossack order and the lands it controlled was the Zaporozhian Host. The Muscovites, however, usually referred to it as Malorossiia (Little Russia), although the Poles continued to call it Ukraine.

Changes in the Social System

From the very beginning of the great revolt, two different conceptions of organizing society vied with each other in Ukraine – the egalitarian and the elitist. Initially, the former predominated. Cossacks replaced the Polish nobility as the dominant class and access to Cossack status was, by tradition, open to all. During the tumultuous period of 1648–56, thousands of burghers, peasants, and Orthodox nobles joined Cossack ranks. According to an incomplete Muscovite census taken in 1654, roughly half the adult male population were Cossacks. If a peasant or burgher could render military service at his own cost, it was not difficult to register in a Cossack regiment and claim such privileges as the right to own land, to be excused from taxes, and to vote for or be elected as a Cossack officer. By the same token, a Cossack who could no longer afford to outfit himself for war or who lost his desire for fighting usually reverted back to peasant or burgher status. In any case, in the immediate aftermath of 1648, social boundaries were extremely fluid and a spirit of egalitarianism, unmatched in Eastern Europe, held sway.

For the peasantry who survived the brutal warfare, the uprising brought considerable improvements.With the expulsion of the *szlachta*, peasants regained their personal freedom, the right to dispose of their property and to move when and where they wished. The more ambitious or wealthier among them now had the possibility of raising their status by enrolling as Cossacks. But the peasants were not freed of all their obligations. Because they occupied lands that the Cossacks had confiscated from the Poles, they were required to render to the Zaporozhian Host certain services and payments. Foremost among them was the obligation to provide Cossack armies with transportation, quarters, and provisions. Although the peasants continued to pay taxes in cash and in kind, the hated labor obligations they had owed to their Polish lords were liquidated.

Yet, in time, these gains were threatened by the elitist tendencies of the *starshyna*. Many members of the Cossack leadership, notably the sizable contingent of Ukrainian nobles and registered Cossack officers who had joined Khmelnytsky, had been a part (albeit a minor one) of the pre-1648 establishment. In their view, the uprising was not meant to create an egalitarian society – something unheard of in Eastern Europe – but rather to expel the hated Polish *szlachta* and magnates, replacing them with a native Ukrainian elite. For them a society without an elite was unthinkable and unworkable. Because of their relatively high status, extensive military and political experience, and wealth, many Ukrainian nobles and well- established Cossacks attained positions of leadership in the Zaporozhian Host. And they used these positions to retain and expand their status and wealth. Moreover, they frequently transformed the public lands attached to their offices into their own private property.

Since hetmans frequently emerged from the officer class and greatly relied on its support, they not only failed to prevent its aggrandizement of power and wealth but actively encouraged it with generous land grants and appointments. As this new elite evolved, it pushed for sharper delineation of the classes in Ukrainian society and it increased its demands upon the peasants and common Cossacks. The latter responded to these attempts to deprive them of the gains of 1648 with growing animosity and even open resistance. As a result, a bitter and eventually fatal cleavage developed in the newly formed society of Cossack Ukraine.

The towns had played a relatively minor role in the uprising and their status remained essentially unchanged. About a dozen large towns, such as Kiev, Starodub, Chernihiv, and Poltava, continued to govern themselves through elected magistrates according to Magdeburg Law. Their contacts with the Cossack-dominated countryside were relatively limited. But the vast majority of small, semiagrarian towns came to be dominated by the local *starshyna* who, like the Polish nobles before it, placed its interests above those of the townsmen. An indication of the stranglehold that the *starshyna* and common Cossacks exerted on the towns was the fact that townsmen had to pay tariffs on the items they traded, while Cossacks, often their commercial rivals, did not. Dissatisfied with Cossack rule, many towns looked to the tsar for support and backed him in his conflicts with the *starshyna*.

In contrast to the townsmen, the Orthodox clergy enjoyed friendly relations with the Cossack leadership because the clergy embodied the Orthodoxy that the Cossacks had fought to preserve. Khmelnytsky and his successors were quick to confirm the rights of monasteries to their lands and to the labor obligations of the peasants living on them. In fact, the hetman's generous support of the church was a major factor in undermining the gains of the peasantry. Pleased with the status quo, the hierarchy of the Ukrainian Orthodox church was opposed to closer ties with Moscow, especially in ecclesiastical affairs, for they considered it to be inferior to them in religious and cultural matters. It would take many years of cajolement and gift-giving before the tsars would be able to bring about a change in the attitudes of Ukrainian churchmen.

The Onset of the Ruin

Khmelnytsky's death came at an inopportune time for Ukrainians. Their half-formed society, surrounded by predatory neighbors and rent by internal problems, had willingly accepted his leadership. But Khmelnytsky's successors, lacking his popularity and prestige, found it much more difficult to mobilize widespread support. Even the immediate issue of succession was not resolved without complications. Hoping to establish a dynasty of Ukrainian Cossack rulers, Khmelnytsky had arranged to have his young son, Iurii, succeed him. Yet, it soon became evident to the 16-year-old boy himself (as well as to the *starshyna*) that he was not prepared to rule at such a crucial juncture. Therefore, in 1657, Ivan Vyhovsky, one of Khmelnytsky's most experienced associates and the secretary-general of the Zaporozhian Host, was chosen hetman.

Vyhovsky and the Polish orientation Vyhovsky was one of the most sophisticated and best educated of the Cossack leaders. An Orthodox nobleman from the Kiev region, he had studied at the renowned Mohyla Academy. In 1648, while serving with the Poles, he was captured at Zhovti Vody. Because he valued his education and experience, Khmelnytsky freed him and Vyhovsky joined the Cossacks, quickly rising to the post of secretary-general. The new hetman soon made it clear that he favored the rising *starshyna*. In international relations, his preference was for the establishment of an independent Ukrainian principality. However, Ukraine was too weak for such a step, so Vyhovsky concentrated on finding a counterbalance to Muscovite influence in Ukraine. For this reason, he established closer ties with Poland.

While the Cossack and ecclesiastical elite supported the rapprochement with Poland, the masses, suspicious of any understanding between the Cossack officers and the Polish nobles, vehemently opposed it. Vociferous in their opposition were the Zaporozhians, led by Iakiv Barabash, and the Cossacks of the Poltava regiment whose colonel, Martyn Pushkar, had ambitions to become hetman. Just as Vyhovsky hoped to play the Poles off against the tsar, the Muscovites, quick to observe the social tensions in Ukrainian society, began to agitate the masses against the hetman. By the end of 1657, a large part of the Cossack rank and file rebelled against the hetman and in June 1658, two opposing Cossack armies clashed in a bloody battle near Poltava. Vyhovsky emerged victorious, Pushkar was killed on the battlefield along with 15,000 rebels, while Barabash was later captured and executed. For the hetman, it was a Pyrrhic victory, for the total cost of the fratricidal struggle was about 50,000 Ukrainian lives.

Realizing that a break with Moscow was imminent, Vyhovsky intensified his efforts to come to an understanding with the Poles. He was greatly aided by Iurii Nemyrych, a Ukrainian aristocrat who had studied extensively in Europe and who espoused the idea of a sovereign Ukrainian principality whose independence would be internationally guaranteed like that of Holland or Switzerland. But Vyhovsky, who was preparing for war with Moscow, was in no position to insist that the Poles recognize Ukrainian independence. In 1658, after lengthy debate, the Ukrainian and Polish envoys reached a compromise solution known as the Treaty of Hadiach.

According to the treaty, the provinces of Kiev, Bratslav, and Chernihiv were to form a Ukrainian principality that, together with Poland and Lithuania, would become the third and equal partner in the Commonwealth. The Ukrainian principality was to have far-ranging autonomy. Its hetman was to be responsible only to the king and it was to have its own army, courts, treasury, and mint. Unless invited by the hetman, Polish troops were to be banned from the territory of the principality. Traditional Cossack rights were to be guaranteed and every year, upon the recommendation of the hetman, 100 Cossacks were to be accepted into the nobility. The Poles made important concessions on the religious issue: the Union of Brest was to be abolished in the principality and the Orthodox were to enjoy equality with the Catholics of the Commonwealth. Finally, two universities were projected for Ukraine and as many schools and printing presses "as were necessary" were to be established.

Although the Treaty of Hadiach has fascinated historians because of its potential impact on Ukrainian, Polish, and Russian history, its actual influence was minimal because it was never implemented. Even before it was signed, a huge Muscovite army of about 150,000, led by the able Prince Aleksei Trubetskoi, invaded Ukraine. Hastily gathering his forces and uniting with his Polish and Tatar allies, Vyhovsky moved to the northeast to confront the invaders. On 29 June 1658, near Konotop, the tsar's troops suffered one of their worst defeats ever. The Russian historian Sergei Soloviev described its effect: "The flower of Muscovite cavalry perished in one day and never again would a Muscovite tsar be able to field such a splendid army. Tsar Aleksei Mikhailovich came out to the people dressed in mourning and panic seized Moscow ... There were rumors that the Tsar intended to leave for Iaroslav beyond the Volga and that Vyhovsky was expected to advance directly on Moscow."[1] The hetman, however, could not take advantage of his brilliant victory. The Muscovite garrisons in Ukraine continued to hold out; a Zaporozhian attack on the Crimea forced Vyhovsky's Tatar allies to return home; and unrest broke out again in the Poltava region. The final blow came when several pro-Moscow colonels accused the hetman of "selling Ukraine out to

the Poles" and rebelled. Unable to continue the war against Moscow, Vyhovsky resigned in October 1659 and retired to Poland.

Moscow now had the advantage. Hoping that the appeal of his father's
name might help to heal internal rifts, the *starshyna* elected the 18-year-old
Iurii Khmelnytsky as hetman. Trubetskoi, who returned to Ukraine with another army, insisted that the young hetman come to his camp to renegoti-
ate his father's treaty with the tsar. By acquiescing, Iurii committed the first
in a long series of political blunders. Terrorized by the powerful Russian
army, bullied by Trubetskoi, and confused by a falsified copy of the Pereiaslav
Agreement of 1654, Iurii concluded another, extremely disadvantageous version of it in 1659. The Pereiaslav pact of 1659 stipulated that Russian garrisons
were to be stationed not only in Kiev, but in all major towns. Furthermore,
the Cossacks were forbidden to conduct wars or to maintain foreign relations without the tsar's permission. Nor were hetmans, *heneralna starshyna*, or
colonels to be elected without Moscow's approval. Thus, young Iurii agreed
to concessions that five years earlier would not even have been considered
by his father. For Moscow, the pact was a major step forward in its systematic
attempts to tighten its hold on Ukraine.

In 1660, war broke out again between Moscow and Poland for control of
Ukraine. When the tsar's troops found themselves surrounded by the Poles
near Chudniv in Volhynia, Iurii and the *starshyna* did not hurry to their
aid. Instead, the young hetman began negotiations with the Poles and when
the Russians suffered yet another disastrous defeat at Chudniv, Iurii agreed
to return Ukraine to the Commonwealth. At this point, the already chaotic
political situation became even more confused. On the Right Bank, where
Khmelnytsky's army and the Poles were ensconced, the hetman's authority
remained intact; on the Left Bank, however, where the tsar was still in control, the Cossacks deposed Khmelnytsky and elected Iakiv Somko as acting
hetman. Rent by social strife and political factionalism, occupied by Polish
and Russian armies, Cossack Ukraine was divided into two parts, each with
its own hetman. The period of Ruin was now in full swing.

Depressed by what was in effect a partition of Ukraine and frustrated by
his inability to deal with a rapidly deteriorating situation, in January 1663
a morose Iurii Khmelnytsky surrendered his hetman's mace and entered a
monastery. The authority of his successor, Pavlo Teteria, was limited to Right-
Bank Ukraine. A strong adherent of a pro-Polish policy, the noble-born and
well-educated Teteria had served in a number of important positions under
the elder Khmelnytsky, but unlike his predecessors, he was unwilling to forge
an independent Cossack policy and generally followed the Polish line. Together with the Poles, he invaded the Left Bank and urged King Jan Casimir
to push the offensive as far as Moscow. When the attack failed, Teteria and
the Poles returned to the Right Bank to crush the numerous insurrections that
had broken out against the *szlachta*.

Eager to take vengeance on the region that had fostered the 1648 uprising, the Poles burned, pillaged, and murdered at every turn. Stefan Czarnecki, the Polish commander, even had Bohdan Khmelnytsky's grave opened and its contents scattered to the winds. Because he was perceived as a possible rival, Vyhovsky was arrested at Teteria's behest and executed by the Poles. As for Iurii Khmelnytsky, he was dragged from his monk's cell and interned in a Polish prison. As a result of his generally detested behavior and his Polish allies, the Right-Bank hetman lost the little support that he had had among the Cossacks, resigned his office, and fled to Poland. It had now become abundantly clear that no matter what rationale was used to justify it, cooperation between Ukrainians (especially of the lower classes) and Poles had, practically speaking, become impossible.

The Ottoman alternative: Doroshenko and Iurii Khmelnytsky   With Ukraine divided into Polish and Russian spheres of influence and with rival hetmans who were little more than puppets of their foreign overlords, responsible Cossack leaders lamented the condition of "our poor mother, Ukraine," and called for a return to past glories. Among the most forceful proponents of Cossack regeneration was Petro Doroshenko, the 38-year-old colonel of Cherkasy and the next hetman of Right-Bank Ukraine.

Doroshenko's qualifications for leadership were impressive. The son of a Cossack colonel and grandson of a hetman, he had worked closely with Khmelnytsky and had held high office under Vyhovsky and Teteria. After removing two dangerous rivals, Vasyl Drozdenko and Stefan Opara, Doroshenko became hetman in 1666. He stressed that his goal was to unite Right- and Left-Bank Ukraine under his aegis. To solidify his position, the new hetman instituted several well-considered reforms on the advice of his friend, Metropolitan Iosyp Tukalsky. In the hope of winning over the masses, Doroshenko frequently called general councils where he listened to the opinions of the rank and file. To free himself from overdependence on the *starshyna*, the hetman organized a corps of 20,000 mercenaries (*serdiuky*) who took orders only from him. However, Doroshenko's most far-reaching innovations were in the realm of foreign relations.

At the outset of his hetmancy, Doroshenko, like all Right-Bank hetmans, followed a pro-Polish line. But this policy changed radically when, in January 1667, the Poles and Russians signed the Treaty of Andrusovo. Although most of the treaty dealt with Ukraine, neither power bothered to consult the Ukrainians. In essence, the treaty partitioned Cossack Ukraine: the Poles recognized the tsar's sovereignty over the Left Bank, and the Muscovites agreed to a Polish return to the Right Bank. On the sensitive issue of Kiev, it was decided that the city would remain under Muscovite rule for two more years, after which it would revert to the Poles. Moscow never honored this point, however, retaining Kiev permanently. The vast, virtually empty lands of the

Zaporozhians were placed under dual Polish/Muscovite overlordship and were to act as a buffer against Tatar attacks.

While both parties were pleased with the arrangement, for the Ukrainians it was an unmitigated political disaster. If it had been difficult enough for Khmelnytsky and Vyhovsky, who ruled all of Dnieper Ukraine, to exercise freedom of action; for their successors, who controlled only half the land and were much more constrained by their foreign overlords, an independent policy was impossible. As the *szlachta* returned to the Right Bank and the realization spread that Moscow had grossly violated its 1654 commitment to keep the Poles out, disillusionment and anger enveloped both sides of the Dnieper.

Doroshenko, who reportedly suffered a seizure upon receiving news of the treaty, abandoned his pro-Polish stance and decided to revive one of Bohdan Khmelnytsky's old projects by approaching the Ottoman Porte for aid. His timing was fortunate, for the Porte had been planning a number of ambitious, expansionary wars and it willingly provided the hetman with support. In fall 1667, a combined Ottoman/Cossack army attacked the Polish forces in Galicia and compelled King Jan Casimir to grant Doroshenko wide-ranging autonomy on the Right Bank. But this success was not enough for the hetman. To rid himself completely of the Poles, he placed Ukraine under relatively loose Ottoman overlordship. With the Right Bank seemingly secured, Doroshenko led his army over to the Left Bank and deposed his rival hetman, Ivan Briukhovetsky. In 1668, Doroshenko reached the height of his power when, backed by the Ottomans and with both Right- and Left-Bank Ukraine under his control, he proclaimed himself hetman of all Ukraine.

His success was fleeting, however. Alarmed by his growing power, the hetman's numerous enemies set about to undermine it. To this end, they utilized the old tactic of supporting rivals for the hetmancy. The Tatars attempted to replace Doroshenko with a certain Sukhovienko. No sooner had Doroshenko disposed of this rival than the Poles produced a more dangerous one in the person of Mykhailo Khanenko with whom they invaded the Right Bank. Turning to meet the invaders, Doroshenko appointed Damian Mnohohrishny acting hetman of the Left Bank. Now Moscow, seeing its chance, moved into the Left Bank and forced Mnohohrishny to renounce his ties with Doroshenko and recognize the overlordship of the tsar.

As his base of power crumbled, Doroshenko even found it difficult to maintain his hold on the Right Bank. In 1672, with a force of 12,000, he was forced to aid an Ottoman army of 100,000, which pushed the Poles out of Podilia and turned it into an Ottoman province. With his unpopularity growing because of his contacts with the hated infidels, the hetman's support was dwindling fast. The final blow came in 1675–76 when the Muscovites, aided by Left-Bank Cossacks, engaged the Ottomans in a bloody contest for Chyhyryn fortress and Doroshenko found himself supporting the "infidel" Ottomans against his Orthodox countrymen. Realizing that his position was untenable, he surrendered the regalia of his office to Ivan Samoilovych, the new hetman of the Left Bank. Treating him with relative leniency, the tsar ordered this "last of the true Cossacks" into exile near Moscow.

The Ottomans' replacement for Doroshenko was a surprise. In 1677, hoping to take advantage of his famous name, they appointed Iurii Khmelnytsky hetman of the Right Bank. This enigmatic and probably unbalanced individual already had a chequered career behind him. After entering the monastery, he served as an abbot and was subsequently imprisoned for three years by the Poles. Upon his release, he participated in a campaign against the Tatars, was captured by them, and sent to Constantinople where he spent six more years in prison. Unexpectedly, the Ottomans dragged this tragic figure from his cell, thrust the hetman's mace in his hands, and, to add a measure of dignity to their uninspiring puppet, grandiloquently styled him "Prince of Sarmatia and Ukraine, Lord of the Zaporozhian Host." But this title did him little good, for Iurii proved to be as inept in his second tenure as hetman as he had been in his first.

In 1677–78, he joined the Ottomans in several unsuccessful campaigns against his father's old capital of Chyhyryn. Both Russians and Ottomans deployed huge armies in these battles: the sultan's forces numbered about 200,000, while Moscow committed 70,000 Russians and about 50,000 Left-Bank Cossacks. After the inconclusive completion of the Chyhyryn campaigns, Iurii Khmelnytsky launched an incursion into the Left Bank, failing miserably. Unable to mobilize significant support, he controlled only a small stretch of territory in Podilia that the Ottomans had set aside for him. Even here his rule was so unstable and despotic that his Muslim patrons finally lost patience with him and, in 1681, executed him. That same year, Moscow concluded the Peace of Bakhchesarai with the Ottomans and Crimean Tatars, whereby they recognized each other's possessions in Ukraine. Five years later, Russia signed a similar agreement with Poland. By 1686, all of Ukraine was divided up among the powers that surrounded it.

The Left Bank under Russian Overlordship

Because of its proximity to Russia, the Left Bank remained in Moscow's orbit. During the chaotic 1660s and 1670s, the area experienced fewer of the recurrent Ottoman, Tatar, Polish, and Russians invasions that had plagued the once-flourishing Right Bank. Nonetheless, the Left Bank had its share of destructive upheavals, but these were brought on for the most part not by foreign invaders, but by conflicts between the starshyna-elite and the masses.

These internal struggles flared up soon after Iurii Khmelnytsky's first hetmancy. Iakiv Somko, a member of a wealthy burgher family and an outspoken champion of *starshyna* elitism, united with his erstwhile rival, Vasyl Zolotarenko, the colonel of Nizhyn, to secure the latter's election as hetman and thereby assure the *starshyna* a predominant position. Opposing the Somko/Zolotarenko faction was Ivan Briukhovetsky, a man of lower-class origins whose demagogic skill assured him election as *otaman* of the Zaporozhians. As usual, Moscow played one faction off against the other. In this case, it favored Briukhovetsky, since it suspected the *starshyna* of pro-Polish tendencies. In June 1663, Muscovite officials approvingly looked on at the famous "Black Council" (*chorna rada*), a riotous elective assembly at which the Cossack masses (*chern*), reinforced by peasants and poor burghers, overwhelmed Somko's supporters by force and chose Briukhovetsky as hetman. Later, the new hetman had both Somko and Zolotarenko executed.

Ivan Briukhovetsky (1663–68)   Completely dependent on Moscow's support, Briukhovetsky made one concession after another to the tsarist government. He willingly endorsed the disadvantageous 1659 Pereiaslav Treaty and, in addition, offered to pay for the maintenance of Russian garrisons in Ukraine. In 1665, expressing a desire to "gaze upon the shining eyes of the monarch," he became the first hetman to journey to Moscow, accompanied by an entourage of 500. Flattered by the honors showered upon him by the Muscovites (he was awarded the rank of Muscovite boyar and a high-born Russian wife was found for him), he responded by signing an agreement that limited Ukrainian rights even more. It placed almost all major Ukrainian towns under Russian control; allowed the tsar's officials to collect taxes from Ukrainian peasants and burghers; agreed to have a Russian appointed head of the Ukrainian Orthodox church; and stipulated that the tsar's representatives were henceforth to be present at the elections of hetmans, who were now required to appear in Moscow to obtain confirmation in office.

But before long, Briukhovetsky paid dearly for his neglect of Ukrainian interests. As Muscovite garrisons moved into Ukrainian towns, as the tsar's census-takers pried into the people's personal affairs, and as arrogant tax officials imposed exorbitant duties, dissatisfaction grew with the Muscovites and particularly with the hetman who had invited them into Ukraine. Even members of the ecclesiastical elite, some of whom had previously supported a pro-Moscow line, openly protested against more Muscovite influence. The event that most outraged Ukrainians and decisively turned them against Briukhovetsky and Moscow was the Treaty of Andrusovo of 1667.

Like their compatriots on the Right Bank, Left-Bank Ukrainians were shocked and outraged that the tsar, who had promised to defend all of Ukraine against the Poles, had surrendered half of it to the hated *szlachta*. In 1667–68, a series of uprisings spread throughout the Left Bank against the tsar's garrisons and their Ukrainian supporters. Realizing that he had pushed his pro-Moscow policies too far, Briukhovetsky issued manifestos in which he decried "the ruin of our beloved motherland, Ukraine" and secretly established contacts with Doroshenko for the purpose of forming an anti-Russian alliance. But it was too late. As Doroshenko's regiments crossed over to the Left Bank in spring 1668, an angry crowd of Briukhovetsky's former Left-Bank supporters captured him and beat him to death.

Damian Mnohohrishny (1668–72) Polish pressure had forced Doroshenko to return to the Right Bank and to appoint Damian Mnohohrishny, the colonel of Chernihiv, as acting hetman on the Left Bank. A "simple and unlettered man," Mnohohrishny had a reputation for eliciting obedience, if not loyalty, from his subordinates. As the fortunes of his nominal superior, Doroshenko, sank, Mnohohrishny abandoned all thoughts of breaking away from Moscow and instead renewed the pledge of loyalty to the tsar, for which he was rewarded by Moscow by being recognized as hetman of the Left Bank.

However, his rapprochement with Moscow did not mean that, like Briukhovetsky, he intended to be a puppet of the tsar. In characteristically blunt, forceful fashion, Mnohohrishny informed the Russians of Ukrainian grievances and insisted that Moscow's garrisons be withdrawn from the Left Bank. In a compromise solution, the tsar agreed to limit the garrisons to five of the major towns. On the issue of Kiev, the hetman pointedly reminded Moscow that the tsar had not conquered Kiev or the other Ukrainian towns, but that the Zaporozhian Host had submitted them voluntarily under his rule, and that, therefore, the Russians had no right to surrender Kiev to the Poles. In general, Moscow's responses were conciliatory. Apparently, its statesmen had concluded that they had been too hasty and aggressive during Briukhovetsky's tenure in office. Moscow's astute downplaying of its presence on the Left Bank compared favorably with the political ineptitude of the Poles, whose consistently repressive and vengeful measures on the Right Bank only served to increase the population's hatred of them.

In addition to recouping some of the autonomy that had been lost by his predecessor, Mnohohrishny also made headway in restoring law and order to the Left Bank with the aid of his mercenaries (*kompaniitsi*). Yet the hetman's fatal flaw was his lack of tact and inability to cooperate with the *starshyna*. This led the resentful Cossack elite to conspire against him by sending the tsar a series of denunciations implying that Mnohohrishny was secretly corresponding with Doroshenko and planning to accept Ottoman overlordship. Finally, in 1673, the *starshyna* attained its goal. Seeing that the obstreperous hetman was losing support, the tsar ordered Mnohohrishny to be arrested, tortured, and exiled to Siberia.

Ivan Samoilovych (1672–87) While the election of Briukhovetsky reflected the conflict between the *starshyna* and the masses, the deposition of Mnohohrishny highlighted the inherent tensions between the hetmans and the *starshyna*. Fearful, in principle, of powerful hetmans, the *starshyna* delayed electing a successor to Mnohohrishny for about three months. Meanwhile, it turned to the tsar with proposals to limit the hetmans' prerogatives. For its part, Moscow was only too happy to comply. Thus, when Samoilovych was elected in 1672, it was on condition that he not discipline and judge members of the *starshyna* or carry on foreign relations without consulting the *starshyna* council. Moreover, the new hetman was forced to disband the hired troops that had traditionally been under his direct control. By imposing these conditions, the *starshyna* expanded its already considerable influence, but it did so at the cost of undermining the prerogatives of the hetmans and, with them, Ukrainian autonomy.

The son of a priest, Samoilovych had studied with notable success at the Kiev Academy before enrolling in the Zaporozhian Host. For most of his tenure as hetman, he was careful to maintain good relations with the *starshyna*. He awarded it generous land grants and created the so-called companions of the standard, a corps of junior officers – mostly sons of the *starshyna* – who became part of the hetman's entourage and were given special assignments in preparation for assuming the positions that would be vacated by their fathers. By creating this corps, Samoilovych encouraged the development of a hereditary elite on the Left Bank.

In external affairs, Samoilovych, like all hetmans, attempted to extend his authority over all of Ukraine. He tightened his control over the unruly Zaporozhians and in 1676 valiantly led his regiments, together with the Russian armies, in the fierce struggle to evict the Ottomans and Doroshenko from the Right Bank. Probably the most satisfying moment of Samoilovych's career occurred in 1676 when Doroshenko ceremoniously surrendered his mace to him, whereupon Samoilovych began to title himself "Hetman of both sides of the Dnieper." Within two years, however, the Ottomans forced Samoilovych and his Russian allies to abandon the Right Bank. As he evacuated the region, the hetman organized the exodus of the population of the Right Bank to the Left Bank. As a result, the original homeland of the Cossacks was left practically uninhabited.

Another setback to Samoilovych's hopes of reuniting Ukraine came in 1686 when the Poles and Russians signed the so-called Eternal Peace. It placed Kiev and the Zaporozhian lands permanently under the sovereignty of the tsar. Yet, despite the hetman's remonstrations to Moscow that the Right Bank and Eastern Galicia (the Rus' palatinate) belonged to the Ukrainians and should not be given up, these lands were left under Polish contol. Disgruntled by Moscow's policies, Samoilovych was not very cooperative when the Russians launched a huge campaign against the Tatars in 1687. Although over 100,000 Russians and about 50,000 Cossacks participated in the offensive, poor preparedness and natural calamities turned the campaign into a costly fiasco. Accused by dissident members of the *starshyna* of illegally enriching himself and his family and blamed by Russian commanders for the failure of the campaign, Samoilovych was removed from office in 1687 and exiled to Siberia.

Territorial Fragmentation

For the Ukrainians, a positive aspect of the pre-1648 Commonwealth was that it brought almost all of them together within a single political system. After Russia and Poland partitioned Ukraine during the Ruin, this would not occur again for almost 300 years. Not only would important differences evolve between the Ukrainians in the Russian and the Polish spheres, but distinctions among Ukrainians living within each of these spheres were already becoming marked. The lands inhabited by the roughly 4 million Ukrainians at the end of the 17th century had distinguishable political, administrative, and regional features.

RUSSIAN-CONTROLLED LANDS

The Left Bank (The Hetmanate) Prior to the 1648 uprising, the territory on the left bank of the Dnieper had only recently been colonized and was therefore sparsely populated. Yet, because an autonomous, well-ordered Cossack system of government survived there and because of the massive influx of Right-Bank refugees, the Left Bank (which had an approximate population of 1.2 million in 1700) became the center of Ukrainian political and cultural life. In Ukrainian historiography, this region is often referred to as the Hetmanate (*Hetmanshchyna*). Because of its importance, it will be discussed in greater detail in a separate section.

The Zaporozhian lands As the Cossack system of government spread over much of Ukraine and the hetmans established their authority in the main population centers, the Zaporozhian Sich, once the center of Cossack life, lost its prominence. In the late 17th century, it no longer stood in the forefront of all-Ukrainian political, religious, and social causes. Instead, the Zaporozhians tended to concentrate on their own affairs, that is, those of a relatively small (they rarely numbered more than 10,000), isolated Cossack fraternity based in the vast, empty steppes between the Hetmanate in the north and the Crimean Khanate in the south. The Zaporozhian lands were placed under dual Russian/Polish control in 1667, but from 1686, they came under exclusive Russian overlordship.

While the Left-Bank hetmans always considered the Sich to be subject to their authority, this issue had never been clearly resolved and the Zaporozhians were often at odds not only with hetmans but also with any other power that sought to control them. For much of the late 17th century, they continued to conduct raids against the Tatars and Ottomans, although such actions did not prevent them from sometimes reversing their notoriously erratic political affiliations and joining the Muslims against a hetman, a Polish king, or a Russian tsar. An archetypical leader of the Zaporozhians during this period was Ivan Sirko, who gained a resounding reputation as an intrepid leader of numerous successful raids against the Turks and Tatars. Yet, quite typically, Sirko often ignored or even exacerbated some of the political problems that confronted Ukrainian society during the Ruin.

In socioeconomic terms, the Zaporozhian Sich also underwent major changes. No longer were booty or payments for military service the major source of income among the Zaporozhians. Many of them engaged in fishing, hunting, and beekeeping. They practiced trades such as metalworking and boatmaking, or partook in the extensive north/south trade. Some of the Zaporozhian officers obtained landed estates on the Left Bank or in the vicinity of the Sich, giving rise to the socioeconomic differences and tensions that were to plague the Zaporozhians. Nonetheless, it was at the Sich that the old Cossack customs and the ethos of the "Cossack brotherhood" still survived. And the isolated Sich continued to be a magnet and a refuge for the discontented elements in the north. Because of this role played by the Sich, the Zaporozhians retained widespread popularity among the Ukrainian lower classes

Sloboda Ukraine This vast territory, located east of Poltava and centered around present-day Kharkiv, was technically within the borders of Russia. Because it was largely unpopulated and vulnerable to Tatar attacks, the tsarist government allowed several waves of Ukrainian refugees (who were fleeing the constant strife in their homeland) to settle in this region in the mid 17th century and to establish autonomous, Cossack-style self-government. By the end of the century, the region had a population of about 86,000 Ukrainian males, of whom 22,000 were liable for military service in their Cossack regiments. Like the neighboring Left Bank, Sloboda Ukraine was divided into regimental districts, named after the five major settlements of Kharkiv, Sumy, Okhtyrka, Ostrohsk, and Izum. In contrast to the Left-Bank colonels, those in the *slobody* were elected for life. However, Moscow was careful not to allow the Ukrainian Cossacks on its borderlands to elect a common leader or hetman and thereby to create a strong, united presence, as they had done in the Commonwealth. Instead, the tsar appointed a governor (*voevoda*), stationed in Bilhorod, who carefully monitored Cossack activities and with whom each of the five colonels dealt separately. Thus, while the Sloboda regions contained a significant and growing Ukrainian population, they were not able to play an autonomous political role.

POLISH-CONTROLLED LANDS

The Right Bank The provinces of Kiev, Bratslav, Volhynia, and Podilia on the right bank of the Dnieper suffered most during the great uprising and the repeated Polish, Ottoman, Muscovite, and Tatar incursions that took place during the period of the Ruin. The depopulation of the region after the ruinous Chyhyryn campaigns of the late 1670s and Samoilovych's mass evacuation was almost total. Yet, as soon as the fighting died down in 1681, the Poles wasted little time in encouraging the area's recolonization. Realizing that the most effective means of achieving this goal was to allow the Cossacks to return to their devastated lands, the Commonwealth formally reinstituted Cossackdom (with its traditional forms of self-government) on the Right Bank in 1685. Actually, Cossack settlers had already appeared in the region several years earlier.

The Ukrainian Cossacks and peasants, many returning from the Left Bank, resettled the land with astonishing speed. Cossack colonels, such as Semen Palii, Samuilo Samus, and Zakhar Iskra, organized and led this colonizing movement. Some regimental districts sprang up around such settlements as Fastiv, Bohuslav, Korsun, and Bratslav. As had been the case earlier, the Poles also utilized the Cossacks in their wars. For example, in 1683, King Sobieski engaged about 5000 of them in his famous and victorious battle with the Ottomans at the walls of Vienna. By 1684, a year before a renewed Cossack organization was formally sanctioned by the Polish parliament, there were already about 10,000 Cossacks on the Right Bank. As the land became more settled, the Polish *szlachta* also returned. Thus, the tensions that had led to the 1648 uprising began to simmer again.

The West Ukrainian lands   Galicia and Polissia, formally called the provinces of Rus' and Belz, had long been densely settled and possessed a well-entrenched nobility. Therefore, Cossackdom, a frontier phenomenon, never developed in these regions. With no Cossacks to stand up to the *szlachta*, the peasants in these western lands were especially hard pressed. The cultural influence of nearby Poland was most widespread here and, unlike elsewhere in Ukraine, the Greek Catholic church was well entrenched. A thoroughly Polonized nobility showed no interest in establishing a native Ukrainian political entity. Although the 1648 uprising reached well into Galicia – and Khmelnytsky, as well as other hetmans, claimed lands as far west "as the Ukrainian language is spoken" – the Poles had little trouble in controlling the West Ukrainian lands and often used them as a base of operations for their attacks upon the Cossacks.

The remainder of West Ukrainian lands were ruled by other neighboring powers. From 1672, the Ottomans occupied most of Podilia, relinquishing the region to the Poles only in 1699. Northern Bukovyna, however, remained in Ottoman hands. The Ukrainian population on the western slopes of the Carpathians continued to be ruled, as it had been for centuries, by the Hungarians.

Cultural Activity

Despite the upheaval and devastation brought on by the 1648 revolt and the Ruin, cultural activity in Ukraine continued to develop and to reach broader segments of the population. As the Christian Arab Paul of Aleppo, who traveled through Ukraine on his way to Moscow, wrote in 1655, "Even villagers in Ukraine can read and write ... and village priests consider it their duty to instruct orphans and not let them run in the streets like vagabonds."[2] Teachers, trained in the brotherhood schools and hired by village communes, were numerous, and the wandering graduates of the Kiev Academy (*bakalary*) frequently served as tutors for the well-to-do. Higher education, even in the worst of times, was available in the Kiev Academy or its affiliates in Vinnytsia and, later, Hoshcha in Volhynia. In the forty years since Mohyla's reforms, the academy developed a rigorous twelve-year course of study that emphasized, at various stages, the mastery of Latin, Greek, and Church Slavonic, rhetorical and oratorical skills, and (for the most advanced) philosophy and theology. Astronomy, geography, and mathematics were also taught, reflecting a growing interest in the natural sciences.

Most of the academy's students were the sons of the Cossack *starshyna* or rich burghers, although not infrequently the sons of simple Cossacks and even peasants also gained access. The old practice of sending youths to West European universities also continued, and even under Russian overlordship, Left-Bank Ukrainians maintained close contact with European and particularly with Polish culture. This openness of Ukrainians to foreigners and their ways was also noted by Paul of Aleppo, who stated that the Ukrainians "were all friendly and did not treat us as strangers," while in Russia he felt "as if my heart was padlocked and all my thoughts repressed, for no one is able to feel free and joyous in Muscovy."[3]

The faculty of the Kiev Academy, which included such luminaries as the famous ecclesiastical leader and writer Lazar Baranovych, the German-born polymath Inokentii Gizel, and the fiery polemicist Ianokii Galiatovsky, constituted an impressive cultural elite that was famous throughout the Orthodox world. Many of their works were widely read, notably Gizel's *Synopsis*, which dealt with early Ukrainian and Russian history and was permeated with a protsarist spirit. In the 150 years following its appearance in 1674, the work was published in twenty editions. By and large, the Kievan scholastics, who were all churchmen, still perceived the central issues of life in religious terms. Anti-Catholic and anti-Greek Catholic themes predominated in their works and a favorite political idée-fixe of theirs, reflected in Galiatovsky's "The Swan," was the formation of a union of all Orthodox Slavs, led by the tsar, to combat the hated Muslims.

They wrote in a florid, baroque style and used the artificial Church Slavonic language, which was far removed from the spoken Ukrainian of the day. Among these intellectuals, it was considered bad form to write in the language of the "commoners." In contrast, the works of secular authors tended to use the vernacular and dealt with more concrete topics. For example, the "Eye-Witness Chronicle," which was probably written by the Cossack official Roman Rakushka-Romanovsky, concentrated on the events of the period 1648–57. Books were not lacking in late 17th-century Ukraine. Despite the ravages of war, the land had 13 printing presses, of which 9 were Ukrainian, 3 Polish, and 1 Jewish. The most active Ukrainian presses were in Kiev, Novhorod-Siversky, and Chernihiv. Of the 20 books that the Novhorod-Siversky press put out, 15 were by Ukrainian authors; and in 1679 alone, the press published over 3000 copies of various textbooks for elementary schools.

Ecclesiastical Changes

Initially, the Orthodox church in Ukraine benefited from the 1648 uprising. Khmelnytsky repeatedly stressed that the defense of Orthodoxy was a major goal of the revolt and both he and his successors were quite generous in providing the church with land and privileges. In fact, the grants they bestowed upon it were so great that the church acquired 17% of all the arable land in Ukraine, thereby becoming a major economic force. Its political position, however, suffered a setback.

Under the rule of the early hetmans, the metropolitans of Kiev (such as Sylvester Kosiv and Dionysii Balaban) had almost complete freedom of action. The Cossack leadership did not interfere in ecclesiastical affairs and the clergy and church peasants constituted an almost autonomous segment of Ukrainian society. Even in relations with the tsars and the kings of Poland, where there were still many Orthodox, the Kievan metropolitans pursued their own policies. But eventually the question arose of who should exercise ecclesiastical jurisdiction over the Ukrainian church. It was occasioned by Metropolitan Balaban's decision in 1658 to follow Hetman Vyhovsky over to the Polish side. In the view of Moscow, for the spiritual head of the Ukrainian Orthodox to be based on the territory of its Polish archenemies was unacceptable. Therefore, the tsar appointed Lazar Baranovych, archbishop of Chernihiv, as the "temporary" metropolitan of the Left Bank, thereby splitting the Orthodox hierarchy in two. Furthermore, the Russians applied pressure to have the Ukrainian church removed from the jurisdiction of the patriarch of Contantinople and placed under the patriarch of Moscow.

At first, the Ukrainian clergy on the Left Bank was vehemently opposed to being subordinated to the Muscovite church, which it regarded as being culturally inferior. But by 1686, after decades of careful and tactful persuasion, the Left-Bank clergy capitulated and the newly elected metropolitan, Prince Gedeon Sviatopolk-Chetvertynsky, agreed to place his church under the patriarch of Moscow. Hetman Samoilovych, the Cossack *starshyna*, the lower clergy, and the brotherhoods accepted this decision without protest. Meanwhile, the Orthodox church on the Right Bank was exposed to extreme Polish pressure and – as such important dioceses as Lviv, Peremyshl, and Lutsk went over to the Greek Catholics – it entered into a state of decline.

༄

During the period of the Ruin, the newly established Cossack polity in Ukraine experienced a catastrophic reversal of fortune. A powerful, aggressive force in the days of Khmelnytsky, it became in the twenty years following his death the helpless object of civil strife, foreign incursions, and partitions. Among the underlying causes for the setbacks suffered by Ukrainians during the Ruin were the following: (1) the internal contradictions between the elitist and egalitarian tendencies in Cossack society; (2) the intense external pressure applied on the incompletely formed Cossack society by Muscovy, Poland, and the Ottomans – Eastern Europe's three greatest powers; and (3) the Cossacks' lack of well-defined political goals and of adequate institutions to govern effectively all segments of Ukrainian society. As a result, Cossack Ukraine was able to preserve only a part of the gains it had achieved in 1648.

10

The Hetmanate

After the chaos of the period of Ruin subsided, the Hetmanate on the left bank of the Dnieper emerged as the center of Ukrainian political, cultural, and economic life. The focus of historically significant development in Ukraine now shifted completely from the westernmost lands to the easternmost. The Hetmanate was an autonomous political entity, not an independent one. Nonetheless, it provided Ukrainians with a greater measure of self-government than they had enjoyed since the days of the Galician-Volhynian principalities. As part of the Russian Empire, it existed in what was for many Ukrainians still a relatively new political environment. It was no longer the fractious and failing Commonwealth of the Polish nobles that Ukrainians had to deal with; rather, since the collapse of the Polish and Ottoman options during the Ruin, they now had to contend with the exacting rulers of expanding Russia.

Intent on monopolizing power, the tsars were inherently opposed to the idea of Ukrainian, or any other, self-rule. This attitude was reinforced by the spread of absolutist principles and practices throughout Europe in the 18th century. Such committed proponents of absolutism as Peter I and Catherine II, two of Russia's foremost rulers, believed that centralized government was the most efficient and enlightened. This view, however, ran counter to the form of self-government – based on uniquely Ukrainian institutions and traditions – that existed in the Hetmanate. Thus, the central political issue of Ukrainian life in the 18th century became the struggle, long and drawn out, between imperial Russian centralism and the Ukrainian desire for autonomy.

≥∙

Cossack Government

By the late 17th century, after the Poles regained the Right Bank and the Zaporozhians asserted their autonomy, only about one-third of the territory once controlled by Khmelnytsky (roughly one-sixth of present-day Ukraine) remained under the direct authority of the hetmans. Situated on the Left Bank, this land was called the Hetmanate by Ukrainians, while Russians referred to it as Malorossiia. It included ten regimental districts: Starodub, Chernihiv, Nizhyn, Pryluky, Kiev, Hadiach, Lubny, Pereiaslav, Myrhorod, and Poltava. Early in the 18th century, the town of Baturyn served as the hetman's official residence and the administrative capital of the land. The Hetmanate was a relatively densely settled and well-developed territory. It included 11 major cities, 126 towns, and about 1800 villages. In 1700, it was inhabited by about 1.2 million people, approximately one-quarter of the total Ukrainian population at the time.

The Hetmanate's Cossack system of government had changed little since 1648. The chancellery, however, had grown markedly and its personnel, often recruited from the Kiev Academy, formed a kind of proto-bureaucracy. Because the hetmans did not distinguish between their private funds and those of the Hetmanate, finances were often in disorder. To deal with the problem, two treasurers-general (*heneralni pidskarbii*) were added to the administration. But these adjustments contributed little to solving the key fiscal problem of the Hetmanate, namely, the steady erosion of income resulting from privatization of public lands by Cossack officers. Apparently the hetmans were unwilling or unable to prevent the *starshyna* from expanding their private holdings at the expense of the Hetmanate's rapidly shrinking fund of "rank" or office-related lands.

Although the structure of Cossack government underwent only minor changes, major shifts occurred in the socioeconomic system of the Hetmanate. By the late 17th century, the *starshyna* had virtually excluded the common Cossacks from higher offices and the decision-making process. The decline in the fortunes of the common Cossacks was closely tied to their mounting economic problems. The almost endless wars of the 17th and early 18th centuries financially ruined many Cossacks who had to go to war at their own cost. As might be expected, the decline in the number of battle-ready Cossacks also had a great effect on the armed forces of the Hetmanate: in 1730, these forces numbered only 20,000 men. Moreover, the equipment, military principles, and techniques employed by the Cossacks had increasingly become outdated. Thus, by the 18th century, the Cossack army had become a mere shadow of the potent fighting force it had once been.

Leadership style also changed. While some Cossack leaders of Khmelnytsky's generation had been characterized by political vision and bold and assertive actions, the leaders of the Hetmanate, born in the post-heroic era, adhered to limited and pragmatic goals. They concentrated on adapting to existing political situations rather than attempting to alter them. In general, their aim was twofold: to maintain a satisfactory relationship with the tsar and, as members of a rising Cossack elite, to consolidate their socioeconomic gains vis-à-vis the common Cossacks and peasants.

The Turning Point

From the time Moscow established its sovereignty over Cossack Ukraine, it strove to transform its nominal overlordship into direct control. For their part, the Cossack leaders, who had been disillusioned during the Ruin with the Polish and Ottoman options, no longer questioned the need to maintain links with Moscow. Nevertheless, Cossack hetmans were still committed to preserving what was left of the rights that had been guaranteed them by the Pereiaslav Agreement of 1654. They hoped that, by adopting a loyalist policy, they would convince the tsars of their reliability and thus be allowed to maintain their autonomy.

Ivan Mazepa (1687–1709) A decisive phase in the relationship of the Hetmanate to Moscow occurred during the hetmancy of Ivan Mazepa, one of the most outstanding and controversial of all Ukrainian political leaders. Born on the Right Bank in 1639 into a Ukrainian noble family that was "highly esteemed in the [Zaporozhian] Host," Mazepa received an exceptionally broad education. After studying in the Kiev Academy, he transferred to a Jesuit college in Warsaw and later entered the service of the Polish king as a gentleman-in-waiting. This provided him with opportunities to travel extensively in Western Europe and to serve as a royal emissary to Cossack Ukraine. After returning to the Right Bank in 1669, Mazepa entered the service of Doroshenko, hetman of Right-Bank Ukraine. On his first diplomatic mission, however, he was captured by the Zaporozhians, who handed him over to the Left-Bank hetman, Ivan Samoilovych. The polished Mazepa managed to turn a potentially disastrous situation into a personal triumph. His international experience and impeccable manners convinced Samoilovych to make him his confidant. These same qualities helped Mazepa establish close contacts with highly placed tsarist officials. In 1687, when Samoilovych was deposed, it was Mazepa who, backed by Russian officials, was elected as his successor.

For most of his twenty-one years in office, Mazepa pursued the traditional policies of the Left-Bank hetmans. With unparalleled consistency he issued over 1000 land grants to the *starshyna*, thereby greatly strengthening its position. Nor did he neglect his own interests. Thanks to generous grants from the tsar and his own acquisitive instinct, the hetman managed to accumulate nearly 20,000 estates, thus becoming one of the wealthiest men in Europe. A man of intellect and refinement, Mazepa contributed a significant part of his personal wealth toward the support of religious and cultural institutions. An avid patron of Orthodoxy, he built a series of beautiful churches throughout the Hetmanate in the ornate style that some call the Mazepist or Cossack

Baroque. His support of the Kiev Academy made possible the construction of new buildings and increased enrollment to 2000 during his term in office. In addition, he endowed many other schools and printing presses in order that "Ukrainian youths might be able to indulge in any aptitude they had for learning."[1]

But while Kievan students and churchmen composed effusive panegyrics in his honor, the peasants and common Cossacks had little good to say about Mazepa. His open, systematic support of the *starshyna* led to widespread discontent among the masses and the antielitist Zaporozhians. A potentially explosive situation developed in 1692 when Petro Ivanenko Petryk, a well-connected chancellerist, fled to the Sich where he began organizing an uprising against the hetman. Proclaiming that the time had come to rise up against the "blood-sucking" *starshyna* and to "tear away our fatherland Ukraine from Muscovite rule," Petryk gained Tatar support for the formation of an independent Ukrainian principality.[2] However, when his Tatar allies turned against him and attacked the populace instead, Petryk's popular support dwindled and the revolt petered out.

Relations with Moscow   Mazepa's remarkable rise from prisoner to hetman and his success in controlling the grasping, backbiting *starshyna* while at the same time ushering in an era of great cultural and economic growth were achievements of the first order. Yet, perhaps Mazepa's most impressive political skill was his ability to protect his own and Ukrainian interests while at the same time maintaining good relations with Moscow. When the young and dynamic Peter I came to the throne in 1689, the hetman once more utilized his uncanny ability to charm those in power. He vigorously aided the tsar in his ambitious campaigns against the Ottomans and Tatars that culminated in the capture of Azov, the key Ottoman fortress on the Azov Sea, in 1697. The aging hetman also regularly provided his inexperienced young sovereign with astute advice about the Poles and a close personal friendship developed between them as a result. Cossack colonels wryly noted that "the tsar would sooner disbelieve an angel than Mazepa," while Russian officials declared that "there has never been a hetman so helpful and beneficial to the tsar as Ivan Stepanovych Mazepa."[3]

His close relations with Peter I allowed Mazepa to take advantage of a great Cossack revolt that broke out in 1702 on the Polish-controlled Right Bank. When the region was resettled, the Polish *szlachta* attempted to drive out the Cossacks. Led by a popular colonel by the name of Semen Palii, the Right-Bank Cossacks rose up in revolt and panic-stricken Polish officials reported that Palii intended to "follow in Khmelnytsky's footsteps." The rebel forces already numbered 12,000 when other Cossack leaders, among them Samuilo Samus, Zakhar Iskra, and Andrii Abazyn, joined them. Soon such Polish strongholds as Nemyriv, Berdychiv, and Bila Tserkva fell to the rebels.

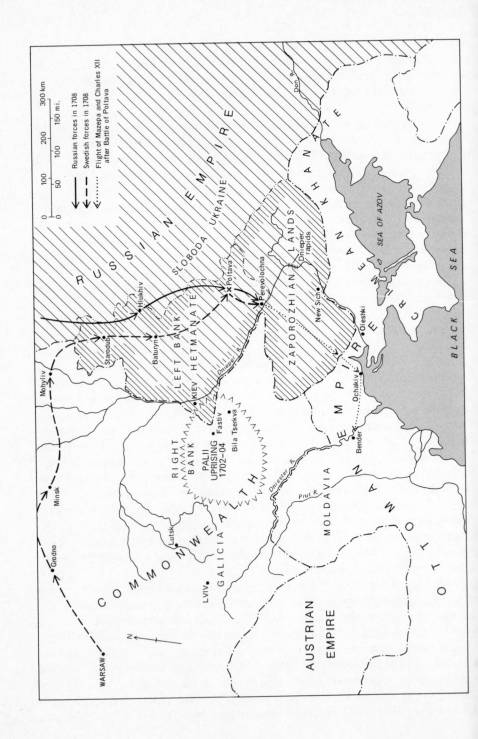

RUSSIAN EMPIRE

UKRAINE

SLOBODA

LEFT BANK HETMANATE

KIEV

ZAPOROZHIAN LANDS

Dnieper rapids

KHANATE

CRIMEAN

SEA OF AZOV

BLACK SEA

Don R.

Hlukhiv
Baturyn
Starodub
Poltava
Perevolochna
New Sich
Oleshki
Ochakiv
Bender

Mohyliv
Minsk
Grodno
WARSAW

RIGHT BANK
PALII UPRISING 1702–04
Fastiv
Bila Tserkva
Lutsk
LVIV
GALICIA
COMMONWEALTH

Dnieper R.
Dniester R.
Prut R.

MOLDAVIA

OTTOMAN EMPIRE

AUSTRIAN EMPIRE

N

0   100   200   300 km
0   50   100   150 mi.

Russian forces in 1708
Swedish forces in 1708
Flight of Mazepa and Charles XII after Battle of Poltava

As the Polish *szlachta* fled westward, it appeared that a lesser version of 1648 was in the making. Yet, in 1703, the Poles managed to regain much of the lost territory and besieged Palii in his "capital" of Fastiv. At this point, Charles XII of Sweden, Peter I's archenemy, invaded Poland. In the confusion, Mazepa convinced the tsar to sanction his occupation of the Right Bank. Once again the two halves of Dnieper Ukraine were united and Mazepa was able to take the credit for it. To ensure that the popular Palii did not pose a threat, the hetman, with Peter I's approval, had him arrested and exiled to Siberia.

Early in the 18th century, however, the mutually beneficial relationship that Mazepa had so skillfully cultivated with the tsar began to show signs of strain. The Great Northern War began in 1700. In this exhausting twenty-one-year-long struggle for control of the Baltic Sea coast, the main opponents were Peter I of Russia and Charles XII, the militarily gifted but politically inept 18-year-old king of Sweden. After suffering a number of disastrous defeats early in the war, Peter I, who was a great admirer of Western ways, resolved to modernize his army, government, and society. All his subjects were exposed to greater centralization, more government controls in all aspects of life, and the elimination of "old-fashioned particularities." In the process, the traditional autonomy of the Hetmanate, which had been guaranteed in 1654, was placed in jeopardy.

Unprecedented demands were made upon the Ukrainians by the tsar during the war. For the first time, Cossacks were expected to fight solely for the tsar's interests. Instead of warding off their traditional Polish, Tatar, and Ottoman enemies close to home, Ukrainians now had to confront modern Swedish armies in far-off Livonia, Lithuania, and central Poland. It became painfully obvious during these campaigns that the Cossacks were no match for the regular European armies. Year after year, their units would return from the north with casualty rates as high as 50%, 60%, and even 70%. Cossack morale worsened when, in 1705, in an effort to coordinate his forces, Peter I assigned Russian and German officers to the Cossack regiments. Contemptuous of what they regarded as inferior troops, these foreign officers often used Cossacks simply as cannon fodder. As rumors spread that Peter I intended to reorganize the Cossack army, the *starshyna*, whose positions were linked to their military rank, began to feel uneasy.

Peasants and townsmen in Ukraine also became disgruntled on account of the war. They protested that Russian troops, quartered in their towns and villages, badly mistreated the local populace. "From everywhere," Mazepa wrote to the tsar, "I received complaints against the willfulness of the Russian troops."[4] Even the hetman himself began to feel insecure as rumors spread that the tsar intended to replace him with a foreign general or a Russian favorite.

The grievance that finally forced Mazepa to seek an alternative to Russian overlordship involved the issue of protection. When Charles XII's Polish ally, Stanisław Leszczyński, threatened to invade Ukraine, Mazepa turned to Peter I for aid. The tsar, facing a Swedish invasion, replied: "I cannot even spare ten men; defend yourself as best you can."5 For the hetman, this was the last straw. When Peter I broke his commitment to defend Ukraine from the hated Poles – a guarantee that constituted the basis of the 1654 treaty – the Ukrainian hetman no longer felt bound to remain loyal to him. On 28 October 1708, when Charles XII diverted his drive on Moscow and moved into Ukraine, Mazepa went over to the Swedes in the hope that his land would be spared from devastation. About 3000 Cossacks and many leading members of the *starshyna* followed him. The terms under which the Ukrainians joined Charles were established in a pact concluded the following spring. In return for military aid and provisions, Charles promised to protect Ukraine and to refrain from making peace with the tsar until it was completely free from Moscow and its former rights restored.

It was with "great wonderment" that Peter I learned of "the deed of the new Judas, Mazepa." Within days of the hetman's defection, Prince Aleksander Menshikov, the Russian commander in Ukraine, attacked the hetman's capital at Baturyn and massacred its entire population of 6000 men, women, and children. As news of the Baturyn massacre spread and as Russian troops in Ukraine began a reign of terror, arresting and executing anyone even vaguely suspected of siding with Mazepa, many would-be supporters of the hetman reconsidered their plans. Meanwhile, Peter I ordered the *starshyna* that had not followed Mazepa to elect a new hetman and, on 11 November 1708, it chose Ivan Skoropadsky.

Frightened by the terrible example set in Baturyn, cowed by the Russian troops in their midst, and put off by the Protestant Swedes, much of the Ukrainian populace refused to join Mazepa. It preferred to wait and see how matters developed. Surprisingly, the one numerically significant segment of the Ukrainian population that did side with the hetman was the Zaporozhians. Although they had often been at odds with him because of his elitism, they regarded Mazepa as a lesser evil than the tsar. But the Zaporozhians were to pay dearly for their decision. In May 1709, a Russian force destroyed their Sich and the tsar issued a standing order for the immediate execution of any Zaporozhian who was captured.

Throughout the fall, winter, and spring of 1708–09, the rival forces maneuvered for strategic positions and competed for popular support in Ukraine. Finally, on 28 June 1709, the Battle of Poltava – one of the most decisive battles in European history – took place and Peter I emerged the victor. As a result, Sweden's attempt to dominate northern Europe ended in failure and Russia, now assured control of the Baltic coast, rose to become one of the great powers of Europe. For the Ukrainians, the battle marked the end of their attempts to break away from Russia. It was now only a matter of time before the Hetmanate would be completely absorbed in the expanding Russian Empire. Indeed, Peter I considered the English subjugation of Ireland to be a fitting model for his plans regarding Ukraine.

Closely pursued by Russian cavalry, Mazepa and Charles XII sought refuge in Ottoman-ruled Moldavia after their defeat. It was here near the town of Bender that a dejected 70-year-old Mazepa died on 21 September 1709.

Pylyp Orlyk (1710–42) About fifty leading members of the *starshyna*, almost 500 Cossacks from the Hetmanate, and over 4000 Zaporozhians had followed Mazepa to Bender. These "Mazepists," as the refugees are sometimes called by historians, constituted the first Ukrainian political emigration. In spring 1710, they elected Pylyp Orlyk, Mazepa's chancellor, as their hetman-in-exile. Anxious to attract potential support, Orlyk drafted the *Pacta et constitutiones*, often referred to as the Bender Constitution, which obligated him to limit the prerogatives of the hetman, to eliminate socioeconomic exploitation, to preserve the Zaporozhians' special status, and to work for the political and ecclesiastical separation of Ukraine from Russia if he were to regain power in Ukraine. With the backing of Charles XII, Orlyk concluded alliances with the Crimean Tatars and the Ottoman Porte and early in 1711 launched a combined Zaporozhian/Tatar attack against the Russians in Ukraine. After some impressive initial successes, the campaign failed. For the next several years, Orlyk and a small group of followers wandered from one European capital to another in search of aid for their cause. Eventually, the hetman-in-exile was interned in the Ottoman Empire. But, he never ceased to bombard French, Polish, Swedish, and Ottoman statesmen with manifestos about Ukraine's plight or to plan with his son, Hryhor, ways of freeing his homeland from the "Muscovite yoke."

The Decline of Ukrainian Autonomy

After the failure of Mazepa's plans, the Ukrainians were put on the defensive. Nonetheless, the absorption of the Hetmanate into the Russian Empire was a long drawn-out process. Not all Russian rulers in the 18th century were such dedicated centralizers as Peter I. Because the tsarist government needed Ukrainian support during its many wars against the Ottomans, it was careful not to antagonize the "Little Russians" (*Malorosy*), as they called the Ukrainians. In general, however, the Russians pushed on with their attempts to limit Ukrainian self-government. In doing so, they applied all the usual techniques of empire builders. A favorite was the divide-and-conquer strategy in which conflicts between the hetman and the *starshyna* were encouraged. Another was to cow the *starshyna* into submission by threatening to support the peasantry. Any failing in the Ukrainian administration or any complaint by commoners against the *starshyna* was used by the central government as an excuse to introduce Russian administrative "improvements." Such changes were invariably accompanied by pious declarations that they were necessitated by the sovereign's concern for the public welfare.

Basically, Russian centralizing policies in Ukraine had three goals: (1) to coerce the Ukrainian elite and general populace into complete obedience; (2) to coordinate Ukrainian government, economy, and culture with those of Russia; and (3) to extract the maximum from Ukraine's human and economic resources. It should be noted that Ukraine was not unique in this respect, for the tsarist government applied the same policies in the other lands bordering the empire and in the Russian heartland as well.

Ivan Skoropadsky (1708–22)   Although Skoropadsky was implicated in Mazepa's plans and committed to Ukrainian autonomy, Peter I agreed to his election because Skoropadsky was old and unaggressive. In fact, Skoropadsky offered little resistance to Peter I's reforms. But, at the same time, there was little he could do. Immediately after his election in 1708, the tsar assigned a resident, A. Izmailov, and two Russian regiments to Skoropadsky's court with secret instructions to arrest him and his officers if they acted suspiciously. At about this time, Peter I confirmed the agreement of 1654, but only in very general terms. When Skoropadsky requested confirmation of specific points, the tsar rebuffed the request with the comment that "Ukrainians already enjoy more freedoms than any other people under the sun."[6] Soon coordinative policies commenced. The hetman's residence was moved from Baturyn to Hlukhiv, closer to the Russian border. The Cossack army received a Russian as its commander-in-chief. Russians and other foreigners were appointed to head the regimental districts. For the first time Russians (most notably the tsar's favorite, Prince Aleksander Menshikov) acquired large landholdings in Ukraine. Even publishing was supervised lest Ukrainian books "disagree with Great Russian publications."[7]

The extraction of Ukrainian resources took various forms. Between 1709 and 1722, Ukrainians had to support ten Russian regiments that were stationed in the land. Meanwhile, tens of thousands of Cossacks were sent to the north to work on the construction of the Ladoga canal and the tsar's new capital of St Petersburg under exceptionally harsh conditions, in which many of them perished. In 1719, Ukrainians were forbidden to export their grain directly to the west. Instead, they had to ship it to the Russian-controlled ports of Riga and Arkhangelsk, where it was sold at a price set by the government. Finally, Russian merchants were given preferential treatment to export their goods to the Hetmanate, while Ukrainians had to pay huge duties on the items they shipped to the north.

But the greatest shock for Ukrainians came in 1722 when the Little Russian Collegium, a Russian governmental body made up of six Russian officers based in Ukraine, was empowered to share power with the hetman. This was too much even for the patient Skoropadsky. He traveled to St Petersburg to request that the tsar relent. Peter I refused and the old hetman died soon after his return to Hlukhiv.

Pavlo Polubotok (1722–24) After Skoropadsky's death, the *starshyna* requested permission from the tsar to elect a new hetman. In the meantime, it chose the respected and self-assertive colonel of Chernihiv, Pavlo Polubotok, as acting hetman. Polubotok took immediate and vigorous steps to thwart the Little Russian Collegium, repeating the requests for the election of a new hetman. Irritated by his persistence, the tsar replied that all hetmans had been traitors and that there would be no election until a trustworthy candidate could be found. Undaunted, Polubotok pushed on. When Peter I was involved in a war in Iran, the acting hetman obtained an order from the imperial senate that forced the collegium to inform him of its plans and to coordinate its activity with the Ukrainian government. Because the collegium was ostensibly created to deal with the complaints of Ukrainians against their government and especially against the corrupt judicial system, Polubotok resolved to address these problems himself rather than have the Russians do it. He reorganized the courts along collegial lines, forbade bribetaking and appointed inspectors to see that his orders were carried out. To reduce peasant complaints, he pressured the *starshyna* to act less blatantly in its exploitation of its subjects.

These changes, initiated by the Ukrainians, greatly irritated the tsar. In the summer of 1723, he summoned the acting hetman and his associates to the capital to explain their obstruction of the collegium's work. Seeing a chance to undermine Polubotok, Veliaminov, who was the chairman of the collegium, persuaded several Ukrainians to lodge complaints against him and to request the introduction of Russian institutions in the Hetmanate. The acting hetman responded by sending an emissary to Ukraine to organize a petition campaign that overwhelmingly supported Ukrainian self-government. Infuriated further by his recalcitrance, Peter I imprisoned Polubotok and all those who had signed the petition. Only the death of the tsar early in 1725 saved them all from exile to Siberia. Most of the *starshyna* returned home, except for Polubotok: a few months before Peter I's death, he had died in his cell in St Petersburg.

Danylo Apostol (1727–34) With Polubotok gone, the collegium had free rein in the Hetmanate. In 1722, to the great dismay of Ukrainians, it introduced direct taxation. By 1724, Veliaminov proudly reported a 600% increase in taxes over what the tsarist government had previously extracted from the Hetmanate. However, Veliaminov's success proved to be his undoing. He demanded that the Russians who owned land on the Left Bank also pay the new tax. Suddenly, Prince Menshikov, the most influential statesman in the empire, who was the owner of vast estates in the Hetmanate and a bitter opponent of Ukrainian autonomy, began to speak up in defense of Ukrainian self-government and strongly criticized the collegium. Other Russian officials also started to take a more benign view of Ukrainian autonomy because in 1726 it appeared that war with the Ottomans was imminent and, under the circumstances, they did not want to alienate the Ukrainians. Therefore, in 1727, Menshikov's influence and strategic considerations led the imperial council to dismantle the first Little Russian Collegium and to decree that "a person who is worthy and loyal should be chosen as hetman in order to satisfy and appease the local populace."[8]

In October 1727, Danylo Apostol, the 70-year-old colonel of Myrhorod, was elected hetman. The general approval with which this event was met was tempered by the fact that the imperial government not only refused to confirm all the articles of the 1654 Pereiaslav Agreement, but imposed further limitations on the hetman. A Russian resident was to supervise all his foreign contacts, a Russian field marshal was to control military affairs, and the tsar had the right to make land grants in the Hetmanate. As a consolation to the Ukrainians, the Hetmanate was removed from the jurisdiction of the imperial senate and returned to that of the foreign ministry. Realizing that any attempt to restore the Hetmanate's political prerogatives was doomed to fail, Apostol concentrated on improving social and economic conditions in it.

He continued with the reform of the judicial system and established an office of the treasury that provided the Hetmanate with its first annual budget. Because the fund of public or "rank lands" had been seriously depleted, between 1729 and 1731 Apostol conducted a thorough survey and restored many of the lost lands. He was especially effective in supporting Ukrainian commercial interests, successfully protecting Ukrainian merchants from unfair Russian competition and reducing the onerous customs duties that had been imposed by imperial officials. He even scored a few political victories. By regaining the right to appoint the general staff and colonels, Apostol greatly reduced the number of Russians and other foreigners in his administration. He also brought Kiev, which had long been under the sway of the Russian governor, under his own jurisdiction. A dramatic indication of the improved conditions in the Hetmanate was the return to Russian sovereignty in the spring of 1734 of the Zaporozhians who had lived in exile on Crimean territory since 1708. Apostol did not live to see this event, for he died in January of that year.

The Governing Council of the Hetman's Office (1734–50)   As tsars changed in St Petersburg, so too did their policies towards Ukraine. Immediately after Apostol's death, the new empress, Anna Ivanovna, again banned the election of a hetman and established yet another a new collegium, called "The Governing Council of the Hetman's Office." It consisted of three Russians and three Ukrainians and was headed by a Russian president, Prince

Shakhovskoi. While creating the impression that his collegium was only a temporary arrangement, Shakhovskoi received secret instructions to spread rumors blaming previous hetmans for the taxes and mismanagement that existed in the Hetmanate. The aim was to persuade Ukrainians that the abolition of the Hetmanate was in their best interests.

The imperial government also ordered Shakhovskoi to discourage the marriage of members of the Ukrainian *starshyna* either with the Polish or Belorussian gentry or with Right-Bank Ukrainians. At the same time, matrimonial ties between Ukrainians and Russians were to be encouraged by all means. Attempts to dilute Ukrainian distinctiveness took other forms as well. In 1734, the new president of the Governing Council, Prince Bariatinsky, arrested the entire city council of Kiev and confiscated their ancient charters of rights so that "in time, these burghers will forget their contents and, lacking documents, will be unable to bring up the issue of their rights."9 In that same year, the imperial senate twice refused to confirm a Ukrainian as mayor of Kiev and acquiesced only after proof had been provided that there was no Russian in the city qualified for the post.

During the reign of Anna Ivanovna and her all-powerful German favorite, Ernst Biron, a mood of fatalism enveloped the Left-Bank elite, resulting in its tendency to avoid public affairs and to concentrate instead on personal matters. The mood was occasioned by the application of such Russian political practices as the infamous *slovo i delo* (Word and Deed Statute), according to which the expression of even the slightest criticism of or opposition to the tsarist regime in either word or deed made one liable to be summoned to the dreaded Secret Chancellory for interrogation, torture, and possible death or exile. Moreover, the *slovo i delo* obligated even one's closest friends and family members to inform the authorities of any suspicious talk or behavior. Thus, fear and mutual suspicion became the order of the day on the Left Bank.

Peasants and Cossacks also suffered greatly during the so-called *Bironovshchina*, or the period of supremacy of Anna's favorite, Biron. The greatest burdens imposed upon them were associated with the Russo-Turkish War of 1735–39, a conflict in which the Left Bank served as the main staging area for the imperial forces. During the course of these four years, tens of thousands of Cossacks and peasants were mobilized to aid in the war effort. Ukrainian fatalities during the war reached 35,000, a huge figure for a population of about 1.2 million. As well, in 1737–38, Ukraine had to maintain at its own expense between fifty and seventy-five Russian regiments. This maintenance cost the Hetmanate about 1.5 million rubles, ten times its annual budget. The demands of the Russo-Turkish War were doubly painful to Ukrainians because they were preceded by a long series of destructive conflicts. Most of the nearly century-long Cossack/Polish/Russian/Ottoman wars had been fought in Ukraine. And by 1740, it had been bled white. Even Russian officers who traversed the land were astounded by the devastation they encountered. For decades to come, the Ukrainian *starshyna* would complain that their land was unable to recover from these losses.

The Governing Council did manage one constructive achievement. Because of the chaotic state of Ukrainian law, most of which was still based on the Lithuanian Statute of the 16th century, a commission was formed in 1728 to codify it. In 1744, after sixteen years of work, the eighteen-man commission finally completed a new codex entitled "The Laws According to which the Little Russians Are Governed."

Kyrylo Rozumovsky (1750–64) While Biron brought Ukrainians little in the way of benefits, the husband of the next empress, Elizabeth, was more helpful. When she came to power in 1741, Elizabeth's consort was Oleksii Rozumovsky, a simple, personable Cossack from the Hetmanate who had caught the fancy of the future empress when he had been a singer in the imperial choir. Although Oleksii avoided politics, he did have a great affection for his homeland. Apparently, some of this attitude rubbed off on his wife, especially after she had been received with great enthusiasm on a visit to Kiev in 1744. On that occasion, the Ukrainian *starshyna* approached Elizabeth with yet another request for a new hetman. The empress responded positively. However, she put the matter off because the candidate she had in mind, Kyrylo, the younger brother of Oleksii, was only sixteen and needed experience before he could take the post. Young Kyrylo was sent off to study in the universities of Western Europe. In the meantime, Russian troops were removed from the Hetmanate and the Governing Council was gradually dismantled. Upon his return from Europe, Kyrylo was appointed president of the Imperial Academy of Sciences. In 1750, in Hlukhiv, amid great pomp, he was inaugurated as the new hetman at the age of twenty-two.

Under Rozumovsky, the Hetmanate experienced the golden autumn of its autonomy. Although he spent much of his time in St Petersburg where he was deeply involved in court politics, Rozumovsky maintained close contacts with the Left Bank. Realizing that the society of the Hetmanate had become too complex for the *starshyna* to perform judicial as well as administrative and military functions, Rozumovsky started organizing a separate judiciary. In 1763, after much preparation, the Hetmanate was divided into twenty judicial districts, each of which had courts specializing in criminal matters, boundary claims, and property conflicts. Judges were elected, usually from among the landowning elite. As had been the case previously, townsmen were judged before their own courts.

Rozumovsky also succeeded in extending once again the hetman's authority over Kiev and the Zaporozhians. Moreover, he initiated a somewhat superficial attempt at modernizing the Cossack army by systematizing its drills, providing it with uniforms, and improving its artillery. Plans were drawn up to establish a university in Baturyn, Mazepa's old capital, and to extend primary education to the sons of all Cossacks. However, political developments prevented their implementation. The hetman did succeed in bringing a touch of European sophistication to Hlukhiv by adorning it with gracious palaces, English gardens, and a theatre in which visiting Italian opera companies performed. The town had numerous coffee shops and French fashions became the rage among the elite.

With the hetman frequently away at the imperial capital, the *starshyna* governed the land as it saw fit. It was during Rozumovsky's tenure that the Cossack elite finally came into its own, completing the transformation, begun late in the 17th century, from an officer corps to a typical nobility. It now began to refer to itself as *shliakhta*, the Ukrainian equivalent of the Polish term for the nobility (*szlachta*).

Yet, even the lenient Elizabeth did not respond positively to many of the hetman's initiatives. When he asked for permission to establish diplomatic relations with European courts, the petition was refused. The response was also negative when he tried to have Ukrainian troops exempted from wars not directly related to Ukrainian interests. Even during these favorable times for the Hetmanate's autonomy, some aspects of imperial centralization were pushed through. In 1754, for example, the budget of the Hetmanate was put under Russian control and the customs boundary between Ukraine and Russia was eliminated. When Rozumovsky sought a free hand in distributing lands on the Left Bank, he was informed that only the empress enjoyed this prerogative. It was clear that there were established limits to the extent to which Ukrainians were to be allowed to control their own affairs.

After Catherine II came to power in 1762, Rozumovsky returned to the Hetmanate to concentrate on its affairs. In 1763, the hetman and *starshyna* held an important council at Hlukhiv. Its original purpose was to discuss judicial reforms. But the discussion soon expanded to a consideration of the decline of the Hetmanate's political prerogatives. In the end, the delegates sent a strongly worded petition to the new empress that called for the return of their lost rights and the creation of a parliament of nobles on the Left Bank, modeled after the Polish *sejm*. The Hlukhiv petition was based on the premise that the hetman and *starshyna* considered their land to be a distinct political and economic entity linked to Russia only in the person of the monarch. In the view of Zenon Kohut, the petition "contained some of the most autonomist views publicly expressed since the time of Mazepa."[10] Rozumovsky followed it up with the bold proposal that the empress make the hetmancy hereditary in his family. In other words, what the Ukrainians were asking from Catherine was a permanent commitment to their autonomy.

But the Ukrainian elite had miscalculated. At exactly this time, influenced by a scathing attack on Ukrainian autonomy written by Teplov, Rozumovsky's former tutor, Catherine II decided to abolish this autonomy altogether. She ordered Rozumovsky to the capital and demanded his resignation. After procrastinating and making some attempts at bargaining, Rozumovsky relinquished his office on 10 November 1764.

The liquidation of the Hetmanate   Catherine II finished the work that Peter I had begun in Ukraine. Although herself a German who married into the Romanov dynasty, Catherine was a dedicated proponent of Russification and centralization. Like so many other rulers during the age of enlightened absolutism, she was convinced that a government based on the absolutist principle and devoid of such "feudal relics" as special status for various regions was the most rational and efficient. Hence, her negative attitude toward Ukrainian as well as Livonian and Finnish autonomy. "These provinces," she argued, "should be Russified ... That task will be easy if wise men are chosen as governors. When the hetmans are gone from Little Russia, every effort should be made to eradicate them and their age from memory."[11] And the empress did choose a wise man – Peter Rumiantsev, an outstanding Russian military leader and statesman – to rule the Left Bank as its governor-general.

In carrying out his functions, Rumiantsev was aided by a second Little Russian Collegium, which consisted of four Russian officers and four trusted members of the *starshyna*. In a set of secret instructions, Catherine enjoined Rumiantsev to move carefully "so as not to arouse hatred for the Russians."[12] To prepare the ground for the elimination of Ukrainian autonomy, the governor-general was further advised to stress to the peasants that their worsening plight was primarily a result of the backwardness of "Little Russian ways." Meanwhile, Rumiantsev was to apply a carrot-and-stick approach toward the *starshyna*. While all expressions of autonomist tendencies were to be severely punished, those "who were not infected with the disease of self-willfulness and independence"[13] were to be offered attractive posts in the imperial government. They were also promised that their status would be equalized with that of the Russian nobility and that they would gain greater control over the peasantry.

Rumiantsev fulfilled his mandate well. Initially, he avoided major changes and concentrated on winning goodwill. Numerous Ukrainians were appointed to his staff, a postal service was introduced, and a thorough survey of the socioeconomic conditions of the land was carried out. But not everything went according to plan. Anxious to demonstrate the enlightened nature of her regime, Catherine II established her famous Legislative Commission in 1767. Delegates from all strata of society (with the exception of the peasantry) and from all regions were assembled in Moscow to present their views and desiderata to the empress. To the great chagrin of Catherine and Rumiantsev, a number of Ukrainian delegates, led by Hryhorii Poletyka, used the occasion to reiterate their desire for the renewal of the hetmancy and the restitution of traditional Ukrainian rights. Similar disturbing views were expressed by delegates from the other bordering lands. Using the ensuing war with the Ottomans as a pretext, the empress permanently "postponed" the sessions of the commission.

After the Russo-Ottoman War of 1768–75, Rumiantsev made his decisive moves. The first blow was aimed at the Zaporozhian Sich, which was destroyed in 1775 during a surprise attack by Russian troops. The turn of the Hetmanate itself came in 1781 when, in conjunction with an all-imperial administrative reorganization, the traditional ten regimental districts of the Left Bank were abolished. In their place, three provinces (those of Kiev, Chernihiv, and Novhorod-Siversk) were established. These were similar in size and organization to the thirty other provinces of the empire. Simultaneously, the appropriate branches of the imperial bureaucracy replaced Ukrainian administrative, judicial, and fiscal institutions. The abolition of the famous old Cossack regiments came next. In 1783, they were replaced by regular dragoon regiments to which peasants and non-Ukrainians were recruited for six-year periods. A separate Ukrainian Cossack army thus ceased to exist. Contrary to government propaganda, the extension of the Russian imperial system to the Left Bank exacerbated rather than improved the plight of the Ukrainian peasantry. In 1783, they were deprived of the right to leave their landlords just as Russian peasants had been long ago. In other words, the peasantry of the Left Bank now became formally enserfed.

The Ukrainian elite, in contrast, benefited from these changes. The peasants were finally placed under its complete control and, in 1785, it was exempted from all government and military service by Catherine's "Charter to the Nobility," thus attaining equality with the Russian nobility. For these reasons, the leadership of the former Hetmanate accepted the liquidation of its autonomy with scarcely a complaint. There were only rare cases of protest against the changes, such as that of Vasyl Kapnist, who in 1791 secretly tried to win Prussian support for the restitution of the Hetmanate. These actions were insufficient, however, to prevent the absorption of Cossack Ukraine into the Russian Empire.

Russian Expansion

Russian expansionism has been a dominant fact in the history of Eastern Europe and of Ukraine in particular since the 15th century. From 1462, when the nascent Muscovite state encompassed a mere 24,000 sq. km, until 1914, when the Russian Empire occupied 13,800,000 sq. km, or one-sixth of the land surface of the earth, Russia expanded at an average rate of 80 sq. km per day.[14] In the late 18th century, it concentrated its efforts on a great drive southward. Its goal was the vast Black Sea hinterland (which had been the domain of the Tatars) and the Ottoman-dominated seaways that offered ac-

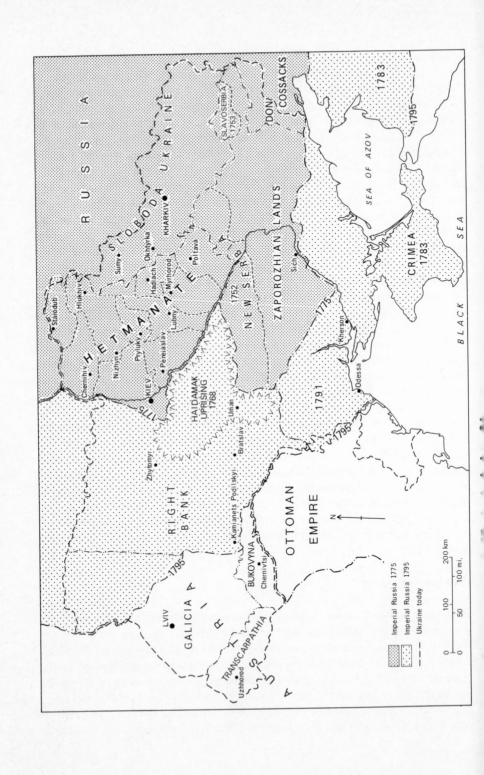

RUSSIA

SLOBODA UKRAINE

HETMANATE

Starodub
Hlukhiv
Chernihiv
Sumy
Okhtyrka
KHARKIV
Hadiach
Myrodod
Poltava
Nizhyn
Lubni
Pryluky
Pereiaslav
KIEV

SLAVOSERBIA
(1753)

DON
COSSACKS

NEW SERBIA

ZAPOROZHIAN LANDS

Sich

1752

1775

Kherson

SEA OF AZOV

CRIMEA
1783

1783

1795

HAIDAMAK
UPRISING
1768

Uman

Bratslav

Zhytomyr

1791

Odessa

1795

RIGHT
BANK

Kamianets Podil'skyi

BUKOVYNA

Chernivtsi

OTTOMAN

EMPIRE

BLACK SEA

N

GALICIA

LVIV

TRANSCARPATHIA

Uzhhorod

Imperial Russia 1775

Imperial Russia 1795

Ukraine today

0   100   200 km

0   50   100 mi.

cess to the Mediterranean and world trade. As long as Ukrainian aid was needed in this southward expansion, the Hetmanate was allowed to exist. But after the Treaty of Kuchuk Kainarji in 1774 that concluded Russia's successful war with the Ottomans and recognized its presence in the Black Sea and its sovereignty over the Crimean Khanate, Ukrainian autonomy was of necessity doomed. A similar fate awaited the other lands that lay between Russia and the Black Sea.

The destruction of the Zaporozhian Sich Upon their return under Russian sovereignty in 1734, the Zaporozhians regained their former lands and built a new Sich close to its previous site. From the viewpoint of the imperial government, this return was a mixed blessing. In the ensuing wars against the Ottomans, the Zaporozhians performed so well that Catherine II showered them with medals and praise. Yet, they also caused her much concern. Because there was no serfdom and much open land on its territory, the Sich became a haven for runaway peasants. Moreover, whenever antinoble uprisings flared up, Zaporozhians were invariably involved. In 1768, for example, they played a key role in the bloody *haidamaky* rebellion on the Right Bank, and when the Russian Cossack Emelian Pugachev staged his huge uprising in southern Russia in 1772, the Zaporozhians offered his men refuge from the wrath of the empress.

Among the Zaporozhians themselves, violence and social upheaval were common. As the Zaporozhian lands became more settled (by 1770, they contained about 200,000 inhabitants, most of whom were not Cossacks), large-scale farming, trading, and livestock raising developed. These activities were largely dominated by Zaporozhian officers. The last Zaporozhian leader (*koshovy*), Petro Kalnyshevsky, for example, owned over 14,000 head of livestock. Most of his fellow officers were as wealthy. As in the Hetmanate, sharp socioeconomic distinctions developed between the Zaporozhian *starshyna* and the propertyless rank and file (*holota*) and conflicts often broke out between the rich and poor at the Sich. In 1768, for instance, an especially violent clash forced the *starshyna* to flee to the nearby Russian garrisons, disguised as monks. Order was restored only after the intervention of imperial troops. The constant unrest at the Sich, coupled with the Zaporozhians' stubborn obstruction of Russian efforts to colonize the Black Sea littoral, convinced Catherine II that the problem called for a radical solution. Therefore, as soon as the 1768–75 war was over and the Tatars no longer posed a threat, she ordered the Sich destroyed a second time.

On 4 June 1775, when most of the Zaporozhians were still at the Turkish front, a returning Russian army commanded by General Tekeli surrounded the Sich and razed it to the ground. Despite the fact that Kalnyshevsky and the *starshyna* had followed a pro-Russian line, they were arrested and eventually exiled to Siberia. The largest segment – about 5000 men – sought refuge

on Ottoman-held territory near the mouth of the Danube. About half the Zaporozhian lands were distributed among Russian grandees and the remainder were assigned to German and Serbian colonists. Catherine II even attempted to obliterate the Zaporozhians from popular memory. When she announced their liquidation, she added that "the use of the word 'Zaporozhian
Cossack' shall be considered by us as an insult to our imperial majesty."[15]

There is a postscript to the Zaporozhian story. The 5000 Zaporozhians who
fled to the Ottoman Empire were allowed to settle at the mouth of the Danube
River. In 1784, to counterbalance their presence, the Russian government settled the remaining ex-Zaporozhians between the Buh and Dnister rivers. In
1792, these Buh Cossacks were renamed the Black Sea Host and transferred
to the Kuban. Under the leadership of Iosyp Hladky, a part of the Danube
Cossacks returned to the Russian Empire in 1828 and eventually joined their
brethren in the Kuban. From 1864 until 1921, they were known as the Kuban
Cossacks.

The absorption of the Crimean Khanate For almost a century after the disastrous campaign of 1687, the Russians had attempted to conquer the Crimea.
Between 1734 and 1739, Russian and Ukrainian troops managed to fight their
way into the peninsula, but lack of provisions and epidemics forced them
back. In 1774, they occupied the entire peninsula and, in the treaty of Kuchuk
Kainarji (1774), forced the Ottomans to renounce their sovereignty over the
khanate. Finally, in 1783, at the same time that the last vestiges of the Hetmanate were being obliterated, Catherine II announced the absorption of the
khanate into the Russian Empire. For Ukrainian history as well as for that of
Eastern Europe as a whole, this was an epochal event. The Turkic nomads,
whose last bastion in Europe had been the Crimean Khanate and whose last
major raid into Ukraine, involving tens of thousands of Tatars, had occurred
in 1769, were finally trammeled. The steppe, which for millennia had been a
source of danger for the sedentary populations that ringed it, had at last been
made accessible to the peasant's plow.

The partitions of Poland-Lithuania Even the Commonwealth, with a population of 11 million and a territory of 733,000 sq. km, was not safe from Russian
expansionism. On account of its vaunted "golden freedoms" that, practically
speaking, provided its nobility with immunity before the law, the land became almost impossible to govern. Near anarchy, encouraged by magnates
and foreign powers who benefited from a weak central government, reigned
for most of the 18th century. Exploiting its role as the patron of the Commonwealth's Orthodox, neighboring Russia was especially effective in foil-
ing the efforts of Poles to reform and revitalize their state. Finally, the Commonwealth's three aggressive neighbors, Russia, Prussia, and Austria, moved
in. As a result of three partitions – those of 1772, 1775, and 1795 – Poland-

Lithuania ceased to exist. Russia received the lion's share, 62% of the former territory of the Commonwealth and 45% of its population; Austria acquired 18% of the land and 32% of its inhabitants; and Prussia obtained 20% and 23% respectively. These radical changes in the political map of Eastern Europe affected Ukrainians directly. In 1772, the Ukrainians of Galicia and Bukovyna came under Austrian rule. By 1795, the entire Right Bank was incorporated into the Russian Empire. Ukrainian history now entered a new phase.

ह

For about a century, the Hetmanate had been the focus of Ukrainian political life. Although Russians controlled its foreign contacts and military campaigns, and constantly interfered in its internal affairs, the administration, courts, finances, army, and socioeconomic policies of the Hetmanate had been created and maintained by Ukrainians. Self-government encouraged the rise of a Ukrainian noble elite that was attached to and proud of its traditions. As late as 1767, the *starshyna* delegates to the Legislative Commission rejected Catherine's reforms and confidently declared: "Our laws are best." It was in the Hetmanate that, prior to the 20th century, the precedent for Ukrainian self-government had been set.

More than a half-century after the Hetmanate was abolished, Taras Shevchenko wrote:

> Once there was a Hetmanate
> It passed beyond recall.
> Once, it was, we ruled ourselves
> But we shall rule no more.
> Yet we shall never forget
> The Cossack fame of yore.[16]

Not only was the Hetmanate not forgotten, but its memories helped to create a new era in Ukrainian history, for it was from among the descendants of the *starshyna* that many of the intellectuals who later formulated modern Ukrainian national consciousness hailed. The history of the Hetmanate became a key component of national history and the nation-building myth. The example of self-rule that it set helped to arouse the desire of modern Ukrainians for their own nation-state.

11

Society, Economics, and Culture

The experiment in Cossack egalitarianism had failed. During the 18th century, the social structure of Left-Bank Ukraine was brought back into line with that of the neighboring East European lands. As an elite of nobles emerged in the Hetmanate, the peasantry again slipped back into serfdom, and the status of Cossacks sank to that of peasants. The Polish *szlachta* reestablished its regime on the Right Bank and the old order returned there. In Russian-ruled Ukraine, social tensions were eased somewhat by the opening up for settlement of the vast fertile Black Sea hinterland, which the imperial government had wrested from the Zaporozhians and the Crimean Tatars. But in the Polish-ruled Right Bank, where socioeconomic oppression was exacerbated by religious discrimination, the Ukrainian peasantry rose up in bloody revolt against the *szlachta* in 1768. The revolt failed, however, and the *szlachta* regained control. It appeared that the socioeconomic order was immutable. In the realm of culture, in contrast, heightened activity marked the early and middle parts of the 18th century in the Hetmanate. Nevertheless, by the end of the century, Ukraine assumed a decidedly provincial character in all regions and on all levels – cultural, social, and economic.

ðð

The Economy

Agriculture remained the basic form of livelihood in the Hetmanate, and commerce and manufacturing, although showing some signs of activity, remained underdeveloped, even in comparison with the Russian north. Like the other absolutist states of Europe, the Russian imperial government made attempts to stimulate economic growth in Ukraine, but only if doing so did not interfere with the development of Russia. In any case, the effects of these policies were limited throughout most of the century.

Agriculture and related occupations The most noteworthy development in Ukrainian agriculture was its expansion into southern Ukraine. Yet despite the increased acreage and the excellent quality of the new land, agricultural yields did not increase significantly because of outdated implements and techniques. The wasteful system of three-field rotation continued to be used and in the new lands, colonists often moved on to virgin soil rather than enriching the lands they had already worked. Typical harvests of wheat were only three to four times greater than the amount of grain sown – a pitifully low yield by European standards. Serfdom encouraged this backwardness. As free labor was abundant, landowning nobles were not constrained to innovate.

Moreover, serfdom, particularly as it was practiced in Ukraine, discouraged occupational diversification. In the Russian north, where the soil was poor, landowners often encouraged peasants to buy off their obligations (*obrok*) by earning money in the fledgling commercial and manufacturing enterprises that were based in the towns. In fertile Ukraine, in contrast, nobles generally demanded labor obligations (*barshchina*) from the peasantry. As a result – and this point deserves to be emphasized – the Ukrainian peasant became more firmly bound to the traditional way of life in the village and in the field than did the Russian peasant.

General sluggishness notwithstanding, some diversification did appear in the rural economy. New crops, such as corn and potatoes, were introduced in the late 18th century. More than ever before, landowners invested in agriculture-related, cash-producing enterprises. Mills were especially favored. Not only did landowners use them to grind their own grain, but they also allowed their peasants to do so for a price. By 1782, there were over 3300 water mills and about 12,000 windmills on the Left Bank alone. However, the most profitable sideline for entrepreneurs among the nobility was the distillation of wheat-based spirits (*horilka*), the sale of which earned many nobles as much as 50% of their cash income. Not surprisingly, in 1750, the regimental districts of the Hetmanate averaged 500 distilleries each. Other landowners branched out into breeding the famous Ukrainian oxen and sheep as well as horses. For example, Kyrylo Rozumovsky had a herd of 5000 horses, 800 of which were thoroughbred. Also, such traditional occupations as beekeeping retained their popularity, with some apiaries on the Right Bank numbering as many as 15,000 hives.

Commerce Although trade in Ukraine was still hampered by poor means of communication, lack of cash, and exhorbitant borrowing rates (ranging from 20% to 50% per annum), it grew markedly. Expanding agricultural production encouraged commerce and the reverse was also true. Because of the difficulty of travel, people would gather in certain towns and villages at regular intervals to buy and sell their wares. Such large commercial fairs, which lasted for weeks and offered a vast array of goods for sale, took place in Nizhyn, Romny, Kiev, Pereiaslav, Poltava, Kharkiv, and other towns. By the 1780s, the Left Bank, which was economically more dynamic than the Right Bank, had close to 400 fairs. Small-scale trade was carried on in the region's 700 local bazaars. Another popular form of small-scale trade, particularly among Cossacks and wealthier peasants, was salt and fish trading. Those who could afford a wagon and a team of oxen banded together in large caravans to make the dangerous journey to the Black Sea coast where they obtained the salt and fish that were distributed throughout Ukraine. Some of these traders, called *chumaky*, gradually accumulated enough capital to invest in large-scale enterprises. Thus, a money economy developed in Ukraine in place of the barter system, or simple exchange of goods and services.

Before the opening of the Black Sea ports in the late 18th century, foreign trade was quiescent. As might be expected, the primary exports were agricultural products. But whereas in earlier times Ukrainian merchants had had extensive contacts with the Baltic ports and Western markets, imperial policies caused this trade to shift to the north. In 1714, Peter I forced these merchants to ship their wheat to such Russian or Russian-dominated ports as Arkhangelsk, Riga, and St Petersburg. In 1719, the export of Ukrainian grain to the West was forbidden and the stringent import duties were imposed at the Polish-Ukrainian border were meant to prevent the import of Western finished products that might compete with Russia's fledgling industries. As we have seen, Russian merchants received preferential treatment in the export of their products to the Left Bank, while Ukrainians paid duties of 10–40% on the finished goods they shipped to the north. Taking advantage of this situation, Russian merchants became heavily involved in Ukrainian trade. By 1754, when trade barriers were lifted between Russia and the Left Bank, Russians were in control of large-scale commerce.

Manufacturing   In comparison with Russia, manufacturing in Ukraine developed more slowly. On the one hand, abundant opportunities in agriculture absorbed the attention and energies of Ukrainians; on the other, imperial policy encouraged industrial development in Russia while treating Ukraine primarily as a source of raw materials. This situation led a number of Soviet economic historians of the pre-Stalin era to describe the economic relationship between Russia and Ukraine as a colonial one. Manufacturing was not totally neglected in Ukraine, however, and although on a small-scale, it was broadly based. The *starshyna* on the Left Bank and the Polish magnates on the Right Bank established a number of iron foundries and glass works that employed about 15–20 workers each. Monasteries were involved in paper manufacturing. In the towns, craftsmen such as smiths, glassmakers, carpenters, painters, tailors, and tanners could often number 400–600 per town. Some villages, especially those in the less fertile northern areas of the Hetmanate, gained their livelihood exclusively from textile production and woodworking. In contrast to the urban-based industrial centers of Western Europe, manufacturing enterprises in Ukraine and Russia were often located in the countryside, the residence of the entrepreneur nobles. Another difference from European practice was the leading role played by the government in encouraging industry. For example, huge textile works employing thousands of workers were established in Sloboda Ukraine by the imperial government, which simply assigned serfs to work in the factories in the same way as they would work for landlords.

Social Change in the Hetmanate

The new elite   By the 18th century, the newly formed elite was already well ensconced at the top of the Hetmanate's social order. The demise of Cossack egalitarianism was almost inevitable because East European societies knew of no other way of ordering their political and socioeconomic life than by allowing a nobility to control the land and the peasantry on it in return for defending and governing this territory. Consequently, as the Left Bank became more settled and stable, it developed social relations similar to those of its noble-dominated neighbors.

The most evident manifestation of the triumph of elitism in the Hetmanate was the Society of Notable Military Fellows (Znachne viiskove tovarystvo). Its rolls contained the names of male adults from *starshyna* families who did not yet hold office, but who were eligible to do so if an opening appeared. By the 1760s, the Military Fellows were ranked according to an elaborate hierarchy that included about 1300 names. In addition, there were roughly 800 individuals who actually held office. Thus, about 2100 adult males, out of a total male population of over one million, constituted the elite in the Hetmanate of the mid 18th century. In 1785, when the imperial government attempted to incorporate the Ukrainian elite into the Russian nobility (*dvorianstvo*), this number increased severalfold. Because St Petersburg was unsure of how to define nobility in the Hetmanate, thousands of Ukrainian petty officers and wealthier Cossacks claimed noble status, many using falsified documents.

With elite status came land. It was granted to the *starshyna* by the hetmans and tsars. In many cases, the officers also illegally privatized their office-related lands. As a result, by 1735, over 35% of the cultivated land in the Hetmanate was the private property of the elite. And their offices gave them control of an additional 11% of the land. Thus, less than 1% of the population controlled close to 50% of the land.

Like everywhere else in Europe, wealth was distributed most unevenly among the elite. A few families, particularly those whose members were hetmans, colonels, or members of the general staff, acquired vast latifundia by virtue of their influence and contacts. Mazepa, for example, owned 19,654 estates; Skoropadsky 19,882; and Apostol 9103. The holdings of the average *starshyna* member, however, were modest, usually consisting of a single estate with about 30 peasants – about one-third of the holdings of an average Russian nobleman. These figures indicate that in the Hetmanate, the elite was relatively more numerous and enserfed peasants fewer than in Russia. But rich or poor, the Cossack *starshyna* (or *shliakhta*, as it styled itself) exploited both peasants and Cossacks alike. From the former it demanded increasingly onerous rents, labor duties, and personal services; from the many impoverished Cossacks, it bought or extorted land and attempted to impose upon them the obligations of peasants.

The social antagonism between the *chern* ("rabble") and the *starshyna* had important political ramifications, for it allowed the tsarist government to play one segment of Ukrainian society off against the other. Thus, in the 17th century, Moscow supported the masses against the Cossack elite when it attempted to throw off the overlordship of the tsars, while in the 18th century, the tsars helped the officers, chastised after the failure of their separatist attempts, to exploit the peasantry, thereby strengthening the dependence of the Ukrainian elite on its Russian sovereigns. Thus, although some members of the *starshyna* were still committed to the Hetmanate and its traditions of self-government, the primary loyalties of many focused, for practical reasons, on the Russian sovereign and the empire.

This imperial orientation came to the fore especially after 1785 when Catherine II, in her Charter to the Nobility, equated the Ukrainian elite with the Russian nobility. Equally enticing, especially to the poorer members of the *starshyna*, were the career opportunities that opened up in the Russian imperial government as a result of its vast new acquisitions. Because of their relatively good education and administrative experience, members of the Ukrainian elite obtained posts not only in the imperial administration of the former Hetmanate, but also in the recently acquired Crimean lands, on the Right Bank, and even in far-off Georgia in the Caucasus.

By the late 18th century, Ukrainians occupied some of the highest positions in the empire. In the 1770s and 1780s, the Bezborodkos, Zavadovskys, Kochubeis, and Troshchynskys provided chancellors and ministers for the empire and helped many fellow Ukrainians obtain influential posts in St Petersburg. The numerous personal opportunities and advantages that imperial service provided explain to a large extent why the resistance of the Ukrainian elite to the abolition of the Hetmanate was so weak. And because advancement in imperial service demanded familiarity with imperial culture, many Ukrainian nobles abandoned their colorful Cossack dress, adopted European fashions, and began to speak Russian and French. Only a few, condescendingly viewed as romantics, bemoaned the passing of the Hetmanate and the glories of the Cossack past.

Cossack decline   The Cossacks had emerged from the uprising of 1648 with extensive privileges. In return for military service, they could own land and were exempted from taxation. They enjoyed self-government, could participate in trade, and had the right (formerly reserved for nobles) to distill alcoholic beverages. Thus, while most Cossack landholdings were scarcely larger than those of the peasantry, their rights were almost as great as those of the expelled Polish nobles. The only privilege denied Cossacks was the right to demand labor obligations from the peasantry, a right reserved for nobles alone. Despite these advantages, a steady deterioration was noticeable in the status of the rank and file Cossacks beginning from the late 17th century.

As a result of the growing influence of the *starshyna*, common Cossacks lost such important political prerogatives as the right to elect their officers and to participate in councils. Even more harmful to their welfare were the Cossacks' economic problems. The crux of these problems lay in the fact that Cossacks were expected to function both as farmers and as soldiers. During the pre-1648 era, this dual role had been feasible because campaigns were brief, booty plentiful, and Polish government subsidies provided extra income. But, under the tsars, military conflicts, such as the twenty-one-year-long Great Northern War, dragged on interminably. And when Cossacks were not fighting, they were often forced by Russian officials to work on construction projects.

Because this protracted, exhausting service had to be borne at the Cossacks' own expense, many fell into debt. As a result, numerous Cossacks sold their lands to their *starshyna*-creditors, often under pressure and invariably at low prices, and continued to live on their former properties as tenants who fulfilled peasant-like obligations. Only a few Cossacks managed to join the rapidly closing ranks of the *starshyna*. Thus, the "downward mobility" of the Cossacks reduced their number from 50,000 in 1650, to 30,000 in 1669, and to 20,000 in 1730.

Worried by the dwindling supply of cheap fighting men, tsarist authorities forbade the sale of Cossack lands in 1723 and again in 1728. But these measures were ineffective because they addressed only the symptoms and not the real cause of the problem. In 1735, the government of the Hetmanate attempted more thoroughgoing reforms. It divided Cossacks into two categories: the wealthier, battle-ready Cossacks, called *vyborni*, and those who were too impoverished to fight, called *pidpomichnyky*. While the former were away at war, the latter were expected to collect and deliver supplies, act as messengers, and even work the land of the fighting men. The *pidpomichnyky* were taxed, but only at half the rate of peasants. In effect, the poorer Cossacks became the servitors of their wealthier colleagues and of the *starshyna*. Despite these changes, the economic condition of all Cossacks continued to deteriorate. In 1764, there were 175,000 *vyborni* Cossacks and 198,000 *pidpomichnyky* on the rolls. But, in reality, only 10,000 of the *vyborni* Cossacks were actually battle-ready. The number of debt-free Cossack farms also continued to decline. By the end of the century, most of the poorer Cossacks had sunk to the level of state-owned peasants. Beset by economic pressures, encroached upon by the *starshyna*, outdated in their military techniques, and redundant in view of the vanishing frontier, Cossackdom, for all practical purposes, ceased to exist in Ukraine.

The reenserfment of the peasantry The condition of the Left Bank peasants (one of Eastern Europe's few free peasantries), like that of the Cossacks, deteriorated steadily from the high point it had reached immediately after 1648. But even the hetmancy of Bohdan Khmelnytsky had presaged the return of the old order, for the hetman had allowed certain Ukrainian monasteries to continue collecting their traditional dues from the peasants who lived on their lands. The major decline in the peasants' status came in the 18th century, when the free, self-governing "military villages" in which the peasants lived were turned over from the land fund of the Hetmanate to individual *starshyna* landlords.

Initially, these landlords collected modest rents and expected additional services from their tenants such as chopping wood or transporting hay. In Mazepa's time, the maximum labor obligation rose to two days a week; although this burden was heavy compared to the period when Left Bank peasants had no obligations at all, it was still only one-half to one-third of what Polish and Russian peasants were forced to provide. Only a generation later, however, the average labor obligation rose to three days a week. In some cases, it reached as many as four or five days per week. In addition, in times of war peasants had to provide food and shelter for the imperial troops and their horses, maintain roads, build bridges, and perform other similar services. When peasants appealed to the Russian monarchs for help, they encountered little sympathy, for the plight of Russian peasants was much worse than theirs. Indeed, the example of the downtrodden Russian serf encouraged greater exploitation of the Ukrainian peasant.

Yet as long as the peasant had the right to depart, he could move to a more lenient landlord, to another village, or to the open steppe. For this reason, the *starshyna*, backed by the Russian government, gradually increased the limitations on peasant mobility. In 1727, a law stipulated that peasants who left their lords forfeited the property they had left behind and, in 1760, peasants were required to obtain written permission from their landlords if they desired to leave them. As they lost their legal right to departure, many peasants in the Hetmanate resorted to illegal flight. A favorite destination for thousands of runaways was the lands of the Zaporozhians, providing one of the reasons for Catherine II's destruction of the Sich. In 1783, Catherine took the final step when she forbade Left Bank peasants from leaving their lords under any circumstances. Thus, 130 years after his liberation in 1648, the Left Bank peasant once again became a serf.

TABLE 2

Social structure of Left-Bank Ukraine (1795)

Social category	Population	Percent
Nobles	36,000	1.6
Clergy	15,000	0.7
Townsmen	92,000	4.0
Cossacks	920,000	40.0
Peasants	1,240,000	53.7
Total	2,300,000	100

The neglected townsmen   In the agrarian, village-based society of the Het-manate, the position of townsmen was decidedly underprivileged. Except for such hetmans as Mazepa and Apostol, the Cossack administration neglected them at best and tried actively to undermine them at worst. Burghers were denied access to any offices outside their own towns. Even within their own towns, their governing and judicial bodies could exercise no authority over the numerous members of the *starshyna*, Cossacks, and peasants who resided there because these were subject to the Cossack administration. Consequently, there were numerous instances in which the majority of a town's population consisted of Cossacks and peasants who were not subject to its laws. In some cases, the *starshyna* simply liquidated the autonomy of small or weak towns and placed their inhabitants under its direct jurisdiction. As a result, the number of towns in the Hetmanate dropped from 200 in 1723 to 122 sixty years later.

Not only were townsmen politically disenfranchised, they were also economically disadvantaged. Because Cossacks were not liable to taxation, they could sell their wares in the towns without paying local duties. Meanwhile, in order to provide their towns' treasuries with funds, burghers were compelled to pay a tax on the products they sold. Townsmen thus often owned fewer shops and stalls in their towns than did Cossacks, soldiers from the Russian garrisons, or even monks. Under the circumstances, the population of most Left Bank towns was modest, averaging between 3000 and 5000 inhabitants. (See also table 2.)

In the midst of this general stagnation, however, there were pockets of prosperity and growth. Because of its role as an administrative, military, commercial, and cultural center, Kiev's population rose from 11,000 in 1723 to approximately 43,000 in the 1780s. Towns like Starodub and Nizhyn, located in the north near the Russian trading centers, also prospered. An insight into the kind of economic activity that took place in these prosperous towns may be gained from the following data on the city of Nizhyn: in 1786, it had 387 outdoor shops, 6 coffee shops, 29 smithies, 73 public houses (*shynky*), 124 taverns, 8 brick-making operations, 2 sugar refineries, and 15 windmills. On the whole, though, economic growth in Ukrainian cities was slow throughout

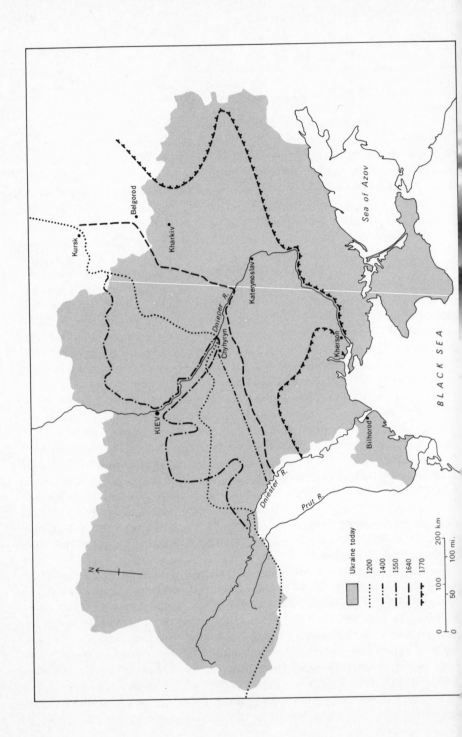

Sea of Azov

BLACK SEA

Belgorod

Kursk

Kharkiv

Katerynoslav

Dnieper R.

Chyhyryn

Kherson

KIEV

Bilhorod

Dniester R.

Prut R.

N

Ukraine today

1200
1400
1550
1640
1770

0   50   100
0   100 km   200 km
       50   100 mi.

the 18th century. This fact made the coming boom in southern Ukraine all the more dramatic.

The Opening of the South

For ages, the primordial drive of the East Slavs to the rich black-earth region in the south and to the Black Sea had been a constant factor in the history of Ukraine. By the end of the 18th century, these goals had finally been attained. It was largely through the efforts of the Russian imperial government that the southern third of Ukraine was opened up to development, an achievement analogous to the opening up of the American west. In the colonization of the south, the interests of Ukrainian society coincided with the aims of Russian imperial expansion.

Even before the destruction of the Sich and the absorption of the Crimean Khanate, the colonization of the Black Sea hinterlands had already been under way. Because of the increasing exploitation of the peasantry in the Hetmanate and the Polish-ruled Right Bank, thousands of runaways raised the population of the Zaporozhian lands from a mere 11,000 males in 1740 to over 100,000 males in 1775. Moreover, the imperial government encouraged colonization by foreigners. In 1752, in spite of the protests of the Zaporozhians, several thousand Orthodox Serbs who were fleeing persecution in the Catholic Habsburg empire were assigned to a western portion of the Cossack lands. The new colony was called New Serbia. A year later, another Serbian colony – Slavo Serbia – was established east of the Sich. During the reign of Catherine II, German settlers also received generous land grants in the area. Meanwhile, the Russian administrative and military presence in the south grew steadily. Zaporozhian resistance to these encroachments only hastened the destruction of the Sich in 1775. With the Zaporozhians gone and the Crimean Khanate dismantled, the great boom in the settlement of the south began in the 1780s.

In order to attract nobles to the new lands, the imperial government offered them attractive inducements. The nobles (mostly Russian officers and civil servants) received grants of 4000 acres each on condition that they settle twenty-five peasant households on them. But although land was plentiful, peasants were not. To attract peasants, nobles were obliged to make concessions to them. Instead of the usual four or five days of labor obligations, newcomers only had to work two days to earn the right to use large, 160-acre plots. Many of the peasants recruited were Ukrainians from the Right Bank. However, numerous Russian Old Believers, Germans, and Moldavians also moved into the province, which, despite repeated reorganizations and name changes, was generally known as Novorossiia (New Russia). By 1796, its population was already an impressive 554,000 males, 80% of whom were Russians and Ukrainians.

Even more rapid than the colonization of the steppe was the growth of cities along the Black Sea coast. Cities named Oleksandrivsk, Kherson, Mykolaiv, and Odessa sprang up on the sites of ancient Greek polises or old Turkish fortresses. They were inhabited by a cosmopolitan population consisting of Russians, Greeks, Armenians, and Jews. Grain was the mainstay of the flourishing trade that developed on the Black Sea. For centuries, Ukraine had produced an abundance of wheat, but it had lacked convenient access to world markets.When the new Black Sea ports finally provided it, both grain producers and merchants were quick to take advantage of the new opportunities this afforded. Between 1778 and 1787, harvests in Novorossiia increased by 500%. Foreign trade in the Black Sea ports, primarily Odessa, leaped by 2200% between 1764 and 1793. Landowners, who once produced primarily for home consumption, now produced for commerce. At long last, Ukraine ceased to be Europe's steppe frontier and now became the granary for the entire continent.

Demographic and Spatial Dimensions

By the end of the 18th century – a period when population growth in Europe increased dramatically – Ukrainians numbered close to 10 million and, following the Russians, inhabited the largest land area in Europe. But lacking a state of their own and governed by foreign states, they were politically imperceptible. For an overview of the regions in the Russian Empire and the Polish-Lithuanian Commonwealth that were largely inhabited by Ukrainians, see table 3.

The population density of the Ukrainian lands was uneven. The most heavily populated region was Eastern Galicia with a population density of 35 per sq. km; on the Left Bank it was 25 per sq. km; on the Right Bank 20 per sq. km; and in the recently acquired steppe region of southern Ukraine, it was a mere 5 per sq. km. By comparison, Western Europe at this time had an average population density of about 50 per sq. km. The ethnic composition of the lands inhabited by Ukrainians also varied greatly from region to region. Ukrainians made up about 95% of the population of the Left Bank; about 90% of the Right Bank; close to 75% of Eastern Galicia; and about 65% of southern Ukraine. Migratory movement was considerable and most of it flowed from the Left Bank to the Right and especially to the south.

The Right Bank under Polish Rule

Despite the gradual loss of its autonomy, the Hetmanate on the Left Bank remained a distinctly Ukrainian political, cultural, and socioeconomic entity governed by its own native elite for over a century. This self-rule was not the case for the approximately 50% of Ukrainians who remained under Polish

TABLE 3

Ukrainian-inhabited lands in the late 18th century

Territory	Land area (sq. km)	Population (approx.)
Left-Bank Hetmanate or Malorossiia (Russian Empire)	92,000	2,300,000
Sloboda Ukraine (Russian Empire)	70,000	1,000,000
Southern Ukraine (Russian Empire)	185,000	1,000,000
Right-Bank Ukraine (Commonwealth)	170,000	3,400,000
Eastern Galicia (Commonwealth)	55,000	1,800,000
Transcarpathia (Habsburg Empire)	13,000	250,000
Bukovyna (Ottoman Empire until 1772)	5,000	150,000
Total	585,000	10,000,000

rule. With their elite largely Polonized and lacking any political institutions, these Ukrainians (the vast majority of whom were peasants) were helpless in the face of extreme socioeconomic and religious oppression. Little remained of the once dynamic cultural centers of Western Ukraine. Especially calamitous was the fate of the Right Bank. This original homeland of the Cossacks and the primary arena for the 1648 uprising had initially seemed destined to become the center for a new Cossack order. But the devastating wars of the period of the Ruin turned it into a depopulated wasteland. Poland regained it in 1667 although it was not until 1713, that the Right Bank again saw the establishment of the Polish *szlachta* order.

Dividing up the land into the four traditional provinces of Volhynia, Podilia, Bratslav, and Kiev (the city itself remained under Russian control), the Poles proceeded to sell or distribute vast stretches of open land to a few magnate families. The most prominent of these were the Lubomirski, Potocki, Czartoryski, Branicki, Sanguszko, and Rzewuski families. By the middle of the 18th century, about forty magnate families, many of whom were the sons or grandsons of the Polish grandees who had been expelled in 1648, owned almost 80% of the Right Bank. Just as they had a century earlier, the magnates enticed peasants into the area by offering them obligation-free leases on the land for fifteen to twenty years. The peasants responded with enthusiasm, pouring in from Galicia, the Left Bank, and even central Poland. Predictably, as the land became more settled and the time limits on these *slobody* ran out, the landlords' demands on the peasantry increased. By the end of the 18th century, the peasants in most of the northwestern lands of the region had become enserfed and forced to work the nobles' estates for four to five days a week. In the less settled areas in the south, conditions were somewhat more favorable because rents rather than labor were the primary form of peasant obligation there.

While the countryside rebounded quickly, the revitalization of the urban centers on the Right Bank was a slower process. In addition to the destruction they had suffered, the towns were bedevilled by their old nemesis: the nobles. Ensconced in their self-sufficient country estates, the nobles undermined the development of the towns in various ways: the numerous craftsmen who worked on the nobles' estates competed with those in the towns; burghers were banned from participating in such lucrative enterprises as milling, textile manufacturing, potash works, and especially the profitable distilleries of the nobles; many towns were towns in name only because they were the private property of magnates, with upwards of 80% of their population consisting of peasants who worked the surrounding lands. Despite these difficulties, some towns, such as Lutsk and Dubno in Volhynia, Kamianets-Podilskyi and Bar in Podilia, and Berdychiv and Uman in the provinces of Kiev and Bratslav, managed to grow perceptibly, thanks mainly to the active role they played in local and international trade. Much of this trade was carried on by Jews who were highly urbanized. The primary exports of the Right Bank were grain and cattle. Traditionally, these had been shipped overland to the West or to Baltic ports; however, as the 18th century came to a close, Polish magnates gradually shifted their orientation to the ports on the Black Sea coast.

Almost all the wealth generated by the Right Bank went into the pockets of the Polish "kinglets" whose holdings and extravagance became legendary. The Lubomirski family alone owned 31 towns and 738 villages, while one member of the Potocki clan had 130,000 serfs and was attended at his court by 400 noblemen. An example of the conspicuous consumption of the magnates is provided by a description of one of their banquets at which 60 oxen, 300 calves, 50 sheep, 150 pigs, and close to 20,000 fowl were washed down with 270 barrels of Hungarian wine, not to mention huge quantities of other beverages. With the costs of such extravaganzas being borne by the Ukrainian peasantry, it was evident that the Polish *szlachta* chose not to draw any lessons from 1648.

Another example of the resurgence of the old habits of the *szlachta* was renewed persecution of the Orthodox on the Right Bank. With the strong backing of the Polish government and army, the Greek Catholic hierarchy conducted a systematic campaign to undermine the Orthodox clergy and convert its parishioners to Catholicism. It was so effective that, by the 1760s, there were only about twenty Orthodox parishes left in the provinces of Kiev and Podilia. Deprived of their churches, the Orthodox came to view their monasteries as the strongholds of their faith. In 1761, Melkhysedek Znachko-

Iavorsky, the young and energetic abbot of the Montronynsky Trinity Monastery and leader of the Orthodox on the Right Bank, began to organize opposition to Catholic and Greek Catholic pressure. His most important act was to ask Catherine II of Russia to come to the aid of the Orthodox of Poland. With the involvement of Orthodox Russia, the religious issue on the Right Bank took on a new and ominous dimension.

The haidamaky Except for the relatively few Cossacks who were hired to serve in the private armies of the Polish magnates, Cossackdom no longer existed on the Right Bank. As a result, in contrast to the situation that had existed in 1648, the oppressed peasantry lacked the leadership that could help it stand up against the *szlachta*. Nonetheless, a widespread, albeit haphazard, form of popular resistance did emerge. Its participants were called *haidamaky*. Like the word "Cossack," the term *haidamak* was also of Turkic origin and meant "vagrant" or "robber." From the early 18th century onward, it was applied by the Poles to those runaway peasants who hid deep in the forests from whence they emerged periodically to plunder isolated nobles' estates. The phenomenon of social outcasts making a living by robbing the rich, often with the support of the masses, was a common one in early modern Europe. In analyzing it, the English historian Eric Hobsbawn coined the term "social banditry." According to him, "social bandits" were motivated by a combination of simple, predatory instincts and semi-altruistic desires to avenge the oppression of their compariots by expropriating the property of the rich.[1] But apart from these vaguely idealistic motivations, "social bandits" had no well-defined ideology or plan to establish an alternate socioeconomic system to the one that already existed. To a large extent, Hobsbawn's concept can be applied to the *haidamaky*.

Appearing initially as a minor irritant, the *haidamaky* gradually became a major threat to the Right Bank *szlachta*. One reason for their growing numbers was the expiration of the fifteen-to-twenty-year exemptions from peasant obligations. After so many years of freedom, many peasants refused suddenly to accept enserfment and preferred instead to join the *haidamaky*. Doing so was made all the easier by the weakness of the Polish army. Because of *szlachta* unwillingness to finance a large army, the forces of the Commonwealth had dwindled to only 18,000 men. Of these, 4000 had been assigned to the Right Bank – too few to ensure order. But perhaps the crucial factor contributing to the growth of the *haidamak* movement was *haidamak* proximity to the Zaporozhian Sich from whence supplies, recruits and, most important of all, experienced leaders could be obtained.

The *haidamaky* were especially dangerous to the *szlachta* at times when the Poles were distracted by international conflicts or crises. Thus, in 1734, when the Russians and two Polish factions were fighting over the election of a new Polish king, an officer in the private army of Prince Jerzy Lubomirski by the

name of Verlan deserted and proclaimed a revolt against the *pany* (lords).
Falsely declaring that he had the support of the Russian empress, Verlan mobilized about 1000 *haidamaky* and peasants into Cossack-style units and embarked on an extended plundering raid through Bratslav, Volhynia, and Galicia. Polish forces finally forced him to seek refuge in Moldavia. Encouraged
by his success, other *haidamak* bands sprang up to emulate Verlan's achievements. The *szlachta*, however, fought fire with fire It bribed a noted *haidamak*
leader, the Zaporozhian Sava Chaly, to hunt down his compatriots. For several years, Chaly performed his task most effectively until he was assassinated by Zaporozhians on Christmas day in 1741. In 1750, *haidamak* outbursts
again increased substantially. In the province of Bratslav alone, 27 towns and
111 villages were plundered. Only the arrival of army reinforcements quelled
what had become a major conflagration.

"Social banditry" was also widespread in Western Ukraine, especially in
the Carpathian highlands. There, bands of outlaws, called *opryshky*, usually
numbered thirty to forty men and frequently attacked noblemen, rich merchants, and Jewish leaseholders. The most famous of the *opryshky* was Oleksa
Dovbush who, in a manner reminiscent of the mythical Robin Hood, distributed among the poor much of the booty he robbed from the rich, thus
gaining great popularity among the Carpathian highlanders. After Dovbush
was murdered in 1741 by the husband of his mistress, other outlaw leaders, such as Vasyl Buiurak and Ivan Boichuk, emerged to take his place. The
second of these, after suffering a setback in Galicia, fled to the Zaporozhian
Sich from where he attempted, unsuccessfully, to lead another band back to
the west. Despite repeated efforts by Polish authorities to repress them, the
opryshky continued to operate in the Carpathians until the region became part
of the Austrian Empire in 1772.

Koliivshchyna   1768 was a year of general unrest. In the Commonwealth, the
szlachta was becoming increasingly irritated by the constant intervention of
Catherine II of Russia in Polish affairs. First she pushed through the election of
her lover, Stanisław Poniatowski, as king of Poland; then she forced the Poles
to guarantee religious freedom to the Orthodox. Infuriated by Russian bullying, the Polish nobles formed the so-called Confederation of Bar in February
1768 and attacked the Russian troops based in their homeland. For the Orthodox of the Commonwealth, these were anxious times. Many were convinced
that the Bar Confederates would turn on them because of the support they
received from the Russians. Others decided to strike at the *szlachta* before it
attacked them.

In May 1768, a band of seventy *haidamaky*, led by Maksym Zalizniak, a Zaporozhian from the Left Bank, set out from the Montronynsky Monastery. As
they moved northward into the settled parts of the Right Bank, Zalizniak's
men urged the peasants to revolt. Their manifestos declared: "The time has

come to liberate ourselves from slavery ... to take vengeance for all the suffering, scorn, and unprecedented oppression that we have suffered at the hands of our masters."[2] Within days, the band was inundated with recruits from the peasantry and roving *haidamaky*. Town after town fell to the rebels: Fastiv, Cherkasy, Korsun, Bohuslav, and Lysianka. By early June, over 2000 *haidamaky* surrounded Uman, a well-fortified town in which thousands of nobles, Catholic and Greek Catholic priests, and Jewish leaseholders had sought refuge. The fate of Uman was sealed when Ivan Honta (Gonta), an officer in Stefan Potocki's guard, went over to the rebels with his entire unit. When the town surrendered shortly thereafter, a merciless massacre ensued in which thousands of men, women, and children were brutally killed.

Late in June, the entire provinces of Kiev and Bratslav and parts of Podilia and Volhynia were in rebel hands. Only the presence of Polish and Russian troops in the other West Ukrainian lands prevented them from joining the revolt. The downfall of the rebellion was brought about unexpectedly by the Russians. Worried that the uprising might spread to the Left Bank, Catherine II ordered her commander, General Mikhail Kretchetnikov, to aid the Poles. On the night of 6 July 1768, Kretchetnikov invited the unsuspecting Zalizniak, Honta, and other *haidamak* leaders to a banquet at which they and their astounded followers were arrested. After surrendering Honta (who was tortured and executed) and 800 of his men to the Poles, the Russians exiled Zalizniak and the rest of the *haidamaky* to Siberia. For the next several years, the Polish commander, Jozef Stępkowski, continued to exact a terrible revenge on the Ukrainian peasants, thousands of whom he tortured to death at his headquarters at Kodnia. Thus the last great uprising of the Ukrainian peasantry against its Polish lords came to an inglorious end.

Cultural Activity

The 18th century was a paradoxical era in the history of Ukrainian culture. It witnessed a remarkable flowering of Ukrainian arts and literature, expressed in the ornate Baroque style. Almost simultaneously, however, it saw the creation of conditions that deprived Ukrainian culture of its distinctive features and forced it to adapt to Russian imperial models.

The church For centuries, the Orthodox church had been the focal point and generator of cultural activity in Ukraine. As a result of its struggle against Polish Catholicism, it came to embody Ukrainian distinctiveness. But this distinctiveness receded once the Russian Empire stepped forward as the champion of all the Orthodox – Ukrainians included. Deprived of its raison d'être, the Ukrainian church lost its driving force. At about the same time, it ceased to exist as a separate entity.

The absorption of the Ukrainian church into the imperial ecclesiastical establishment was a parallel development to the liquidation of the autonomy of the Hetmanate. For a time after it accepted the jurisdiction of the patriarch of Moscow in 1686, the Ukrainian church flourished: its schools were the best in the empire; its well-educated churchmen were eagerly sought out by Russia; and, thanks to Mazepa's patronage, its economic base was sound. Yet there were developments that did not bode well. As early as 1686, the diocese of Chernihiv was detached from the metropolitanate of Kiev and placed under the authority of Moscow. Somewhat later, the same was done with the diocese of Pereiaslav.

The authority of the Kievan metropolitan was curtailed even more between 1690 and 1710, when such old bastions of Ukrainian Orthodoxy as the dioceses of Lviv, Peremyshl, and Lutsk finally succumbed to Polish pressure and went over to the Greek Catholics. The most devastating blow came in 1721 when Peter I abolished the Moscow patriarchate and established the Holy Synod, a bureaucratic body consisting of churchmen and government officials, that supervised church affairs. This in effect made the Orthodox church in both Russia and Ukraine a bureaucratic appendage of the state. Ukrainians were deeply involved in these changes: Teofan Prokopovych, the tsar's closest adviser in ecclesiastical affairs, supported them, while Stefan Iavorsky, the leading Orthodox cleric in the empire, was opposed to them.

It was only a matter of time before bureaucratic centralism undermined the autonomy and distinctiveness of the Ukrainian church. In 1722, Varlaam Voniatovych was appointed by the Holy Synod to head the Ukrainian church rather than elected by his peers, as had been the custom. Because he persistently protested against the reforms, he was exiled to the far north in 1730. Xenophobic Russian churchmen, long suspicious of Ukrainians whom they accused of being "contaminated" with Latin influences, proceeded to mold the Ukrainians in their own image. Under the pretext of rooting out "heretical deviations," the Holy Synod forced Ukrainians to print their books, paint their icons, and build their churches according to Russian models. In 1786 all ecclesiastical lands were secularized and the church became totally dependent on the government for financial support. By the end of the century, most of the hierarchy in Ukraine consisted of Russians or Russified Ukrainians. The Ukrainian Orthodox church, once individualistic and Western-oriented, now became merely a ready medium for the dissemination of imperial Russian culture.

Education   In comparison with Russia, the educational level in the Hetmanate was high. In the 1740s, data from seven out of ten regimental districts revealed that there were 866 primary schools that taught the rudiments of reading and writing in a three-year course. This structure contrasted sharply with the Right Bank, where the Jesuits controlled most of the schools and Polish-run primary education was practically unavailable to Ukrainian peasants. This was one of the reasons why the Right Bank played only a minor role in Ukrainian cultural life of the period.

On the secondary level, the Left Bank could boast several colleges, such as those at Chernihiv, Pereiaslav, and Kharkiv. The principal institution of the educational system was the Kiev Mohyla Academy, which was raised to the status of an academy in 1701. Generously subsidized by Mazepa, it became one of the leading schools in the Orthodox world. In the decade before the Battle of Poltava, it enrolled as many as 2000 students a year. Its faculty included such luminaries as Ioasaf Krokovsky, Stefan Iavorsky, and Teofan Prokopovych. So respected was the academy's rigorous twelve-year course of study that hundreds of its teachers and graduates were eagerly recruited by Russian rulers to fill the highest ecclesiastical and government posts in the empire.

The Kiev Academy's relations with Russian rulers were not always amicable, however. After the Mazepa episode, a tsarist crackdown reduced the academy's student body to less than 200. During the 1740s, under the dedicated leadership of Rafail Zaborovsky, enrollment rose again to over 1000 and the academy experienced one last period of growth. Many of the causes for its ultimate decline were of its own making. Closely bound to the church and staffed by clerics, the academy continued to stress traditional subjects such as philosophy, theology, rhetoric, and logic. Its scholastic pedagogical methods were badly dated and attempts to assimilate the rationalistic, scientific currents emanating from Europe were halfhearted and ineffective. Because of its ecclesiastical orientation and traditionalism, the academy failed to attract students interested in acquiring modern knowledge. By 1790, over 90% of its 426 students were the sons of clerics. Eventually, the famous old institution was transformed into a theological seminary. Meanwhile, those Ukrainians who desired a modern education enrolled in great numbers in the new Russian institutions (such as Moscow University or the Medical Academy) that were established in the 1750s. Aware that their institutions of higher learning were outdated, Hetman Rozumovsky and the *starshyna* requested permission from the imperial government to found a university at Baturyn, but it was denied. By the end of the 18th century, a complete reversal had taken place: it was no longer in Ukraine but in Russia that the leading educational institutions of the empire were to be found.

Cultural achievements   From about the mid 17th to the late 18th centuries, the Baroque style dominated artistic and intellectual expression in Ukraine. Its advent coincided with and helped to mold an impressive cultural epoch in the history of the land. Catering to the tastes of the elite, the Baroque emphasized grandeur, sumptuousness, and decorativeness. It sought to stimulate the senses and thereby sway the mind. It stressed form over content, complexity over simplicity, and synthesis over originality.

But it was perhaps the penchant for synthesis that made the Baroque especially appealing to Ukrainians. Situated between the Orthodox East and the Latin West, they were naturally attracted to a synthesizing style. The Baroque did not bring new ideas to Ukraine; rather, it provided new techniques, such as paradox, exaggeration, allegory, and contrast, all of which helped the cultural elite to define, elaborate, and expound old truths more effectively. Many members of this elite were not "Ukrainian" in the sense of showing interest in local affairs or national causes. Their primary frame of reference was the whole Orthodox world or the empire. For this reason, some modern Ukrainian cultural historians have criticized them for their lack of national roots, their aridness, and their isolation from the life around them. Nonetheless, the Baroque brought to Ukraine a cultural dynamism, a desire to shine, and a thirst for Western contacts. It would be a long time before Ukrainian cultural life would again be as ebullient.

Literature and the arts   Many of these Baroque features were reflected in the works of the so-called migratory birds – Ukrainians who had studied in Polish or West European institutions and had returned to Kiev to teach in the academy. Because of their European sophistication, they were summoned by Peter I to Russia to head its ecclesiastical and educational institutions. Foremost among them were Teofan Prokopovych, Stefan Iavorsky, Dmytro Tuptalo, and Simeon Polotsky. But there were many others. Indeed, between 1700 and 1762, over seventy Ukrainians and Belorussians occupied the highest ecclesiastical posts in the empire. The much more numerous Russians filled only forty seven. Although most of their careers were spent in the north, some of these peripatetic churchmen-scholars made significant cultural contributions when they were still in Kiev. As a professor of poetics at the Kiev Academy, Prokopovych wrote his famous historical drama, *Vladimir*, in 1705 to commemorate the introduction of Orthodoxy to Rus'. Dedicated to Mazepa and Peter I, the play contained strong traces of patriotism, elements of which were also evident in Prokopovych's concept of Kiev as the "second Jerusalem." However, these sentiments did not prevent Prokopovych from becoming the leading ideologist for Peter's secularizing and centralizing reforms. Stefan Iavorsky, a rector of the Kiev Academy, who in 1721 rose to the highest position in the Russian church, was famous for his elegant poems written in Ukrainian, Polish, and Latin. While in Russia, he wrote "The Rock of the Faith," an eloquent attack on Protestantism.

The Kiev Academy also produced another breed of writers. Neither clerics nor professors, they were students who went on to become Cossack officers or chancellorists. In contrast to the theological issues, flowery panegyrics, and learned disputations that absorbed their teachers, these writers were primarily interested in the history of their homeland and composed the so-called Cossack chronicles. The most interesting of these works was written by Samuil Velychko, a chancellorist who completed his "Tale of the Cossack Wars with the Poles" in 1720. In the introduction to his work, this bookish Cossack asked: "Is there anything so pleasant, kind reader, and so satisfying to the curious disposition of man ... as the study of books and the knowledge of past events and human actions?"[3] Velychko then explained how the devastation of Ukraine had kindled his interest in his land's past:

I saw in various places many human bones, dry and bare under the naked sky and I asked myself, "Whose bones are these?" My answer was: "The bones of all those who died in these wastes." My heart and spirits were oppressed, since our beautiful land, Little Russian Ukraine, which before was inundated with the blessings of the world, has now been turned by God's will into a desert, and our own famous forefathers have been forgotten. I have asked many old people why this happened, for what reasons and by whom was this land of ours turned into ruin, but their replies were varied and contradictory. Therefore, I found it impossible to learn from these various explanations the true reason for the downfall and destruction of our country.[4]

Another work of this genre was written by Hryhorii Hrabianka. Entitled "The Most Bitter Wars of Bohdan Khmelnytsky," it proposed to show that "the Ukrainians are the equal of others." In their analyses of the recent past, both Velychko and Hrabianka strongly supported the claims of the *starshyna* to socioeconomic and political dominance in Ukraine. The liquidation of the Hetmanate also sparked a literary response. For example, in 1762, Semen Divovych wrote a long, polemical poem entitled "The Dialogue of Little Russia with Great Russia," in which he defended Ukraine's right to autonomy. The works of Hryhorii Poletyka were written in the same vein. A revealing insight into the mentality of the Cossack elite was provided by the diaries and journals of Mykola Khanenko, Iakiv Markovych, and Pylyp Orlyk.

The arts also reached a high point in the 18th century. Ukrainian artists, most of whom worked in Russia, were especially prominent in music, with composers such as Dmytro Bortniansky, Maksym Berezovsky, and Artem Vedel laying the foundations for the great Ukrainian and Russian choral traditions. Many of their works were influenced by Ukrainian folk melodies. In painting, Dmytro Levytsky, and in architecture, Ivan Hryhorovych Barsky, achieved widespread recognition. Early in the century, Mazepa's financial support led to the construction of a series of churches in the so-called Cossack Baroque style which was more restrained and elegant than its West-European models. Later in the century, such glorious examples of Baroque architecture as the church in the Kievan Cave Monastery and the cathedrals of St Andrew in Kiev and St George in Lviv were erected. In the countryside, meanwhile, folk theatre (*vertep*) proliferated and wandering minstrels or bandurists appeared in great numbers.

Skovoroda (1722–94) Undoubtedly, the most original Ukrainian intellectual of the age was Hryhorii Skovoroda. The son of a poor Left-Bank Cossack, Skovoroda enrolled in the Kiev Mohyla Academy at the age of twelve. His long and varied education included extensive travel in the West and legend has it that he walked through much of central Europe in order to observe the people more closely. He mastered Latin, Greek, Polish, German, and Old Church Slavonic and was thoroughly familiar with the philosophical writings of ancient and modern writers. Between 1751 and 1769, Skovoroda intermittently taught poetics and ethics at the colleges of Pereiaslav and Kharkiv. However, the antagonism of the ecclesiastical hierarchy to his unorthodox views and pedagogical methods led him to abandon formal teaching and to undertake the life of a wandering philosopher.

Often called the "Ukrainian Socrates," Skovoroda traversed his native Left Bank and Sloboda Ukraine on foot, engaging all types of people in markets, roads, and village gardens in probing philosophical discussions. His major concern was the attainment of true happiness for the individual. According to Skovoroda, the key was to "know thyself" and to do in life that for which one was naturally suited. Personal independence had to be maintained at all cost and unnecessary riches and honors avoided. This conviction led Skovoroda to criticize the *starshyna* and clergy openly for their exploitation of the peasantry. His numerous writings included collections of poetry, textbooks on poetics and ethics, and philosophical treatises. Living as he preached, Skovoroda enjoyed great popularity among the common people and many of his views were incorporated into folk songs and *dumy*. It is said that for his gravestone Skovoroda prepared the following epitaph: "The world tried to entrap me, but it did not succeed."

⁊⯭

This vibrant, multifaceted cultural epoch drew to a close at the end of the century. As a result of Peter I's conquests, Russia obtained its long-sought-after "window to the West" in the Baltic – and Ukraine's invigorating role as transmitter of cultural influences became redundant. Imperial borders greatly reduced Ukraine's contacts with the West. Now it was Russia – benefiting from direct access to Europe as well as from the westernizing efforts of its monarchs and from the "brain drain" from Ukraine – that moved to the cultural vanguard. Meanwhile, Ukraine, isolated and defensively traditionalist, sank into provincialism. Having lost its political autonomy, it was now in danger of losing its cultural distinctiveness as well.

Church-fortress in 15th-century Podolia

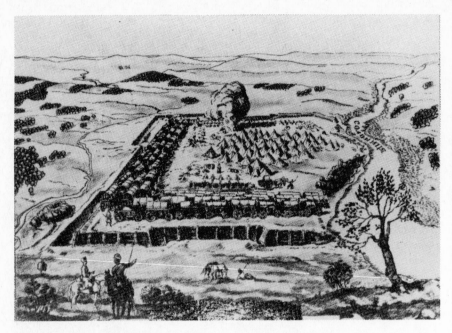

A Cossack camp, based on a contemporary engraving

Zaporozhians dancing by T. Kalynsky, late 18th century

Lviv in early 17th century

Battle of Poltava, 1709

Bohdan Khmelnytsky. Contemporary engraving by Hondius

Zaporozhians Writing a Letter to the Turkish Sultan. Painting by E. Repin (1891)

Students of the Kiev Academy from engraving of late 17th–early 18th century

Title page of Kiev Academy thesis. Engraving by H. Levytsky (1739)

Peasant girl

Peasant

Four inhabitants of Left-Bank Ukraine. Engravings by T. Kalynsky (1778–82)

Noble woman

Cossack colonel

Church on Left-Bank Ukraine, late 18th-century engraving

Part Four

Ukraine under Imperial Rule

Russian and Austrian Imperial Rule in Ukraine

For close to 150 years, from the late 18th to the early 20th centuries, Ukrainians lived in two empires: about 80% of them were subjects of the Russian emperors, and the remainder inhabited the Habsburg empire.* Thus, at the dawn of the modern era, Ukrainians found themselves in political systems that were radically different from those to which they had been accustomed. Like all empires, those of the Russian Romanovs and the Austrian Habsburgs were vast territorial conglomerates containing huge populations of ethnically and culturally diverse peoples. Political power was highly centralized and vested in the person of the emperor, who saw no need to take into account the views or desires of his subjects. Emperors and their officials demanded absolute obedience and loyalty from their subjects, viewing these obligations not only as political duties, but also as moral and religious ones. In return for subservience, empires promised their subjects security, stability, and order. It was an arrangement that many of the empire's subjects found reasonable and even attractive.

In governing their numerous and widely scattered subjects, emperors depended primarily on the army and the bureaucracy. The army defended and, if the opportunity arose, expanded imperial borders. It could also serve to preserve internal order. The bureaucracy extracted taxes (most of which went to support itself and the army) and attempted to arrange society in a manner that best served the interests of the empire. In contrast to the nobles – both Ukrainian *starshyna* and Polish *szlachta* – who dominated Ukrainian society in the 18th century and acted on the principle of the less government, the better, the imperial bureaucrats who governed in the 19th century believed that

---

* In the 18th and 19th centuries the Ukrainians in the Russian Empire were usually called Little Russians (*Malorossy*). Those in the Austrian Empire continued to refer to themselves as Ruthenians (*Rusyny*).

the more rules and regulations they imposed on society, the better off society would be. Although local elites continued to be important, it was increasingly imperial ministers, based in far-off capitals, who made the crucial decisions that affected the lives of Ukrainians.

ॐ

The Russian Empire

The Russian Empire was one of the largest in the world. Apart from its imposing size, it possessed political features that differed markedly from those of other European powers. Nowhere on the continent did rulers have the unlimited power of the tsar-emperors. Nowhere was the bureaucracy as domineering, the police as harsh, or the people as bereft of rights as in Russia. In the 18th century, as a result of the modernizing reforms of Peter I and Catherine II, the empire had come a long way from its rude, semioriental beginnings in the principality of Moscow. It boasted a huge, modern army, a growing European-style bureaucracy, and an increasingly Westernized elite. Yet, despite these changes, autocracy – the central principle of old Muscovite politics that stipulated that the tsars had absolute power over all their subjects and over all aspects of their lives – was not abandoned by Russia's rulers.

At the onset of the 19th century, there were a few ambiguous indications that the young and popular Alexander I might push reforms to their logical conclusion and grant his subjects a constitution, thereby replacing autocracy with the rule of law. But it soon became apparent that the "enlightened" emperor did not treat the idea of a constitution seriously. Nevertheless, he did raise hopes in the tiny liberal segment of the imperial elite, and in December 1825, immediately after his death, a group of nobles attempted a coup for the purpose of establishing constitutional government. Although the Decembrist Revolt, as it was called, failed miserably, the new emperor, Nicholas I, was deeply shaken by this challenge to his authority and resolved to impose greater control over his subjects than ever before.

A military man at heart, Nicholas I attempted to impose the discipline and regimentation of his beloved army on the entire society. To attain his goals, he expanded the bureaucracy, and in 1826, introduced the Third Section of the Imperial Chancellery, Russia's first secret police. He also ordered the formation of the Corps of Gendarmes, or regular police, and greatly increased censorship. Because of such measures, the Russian Empire during the lengthy reign of Nicholas I entered a period that the great Russian historian Vasilii Kliuchevsky called "the most bureaucratic era in our history."[1]

The Russian imperial presence in Ukraine   Adherents of Russian autocracy often cited another argument in its favor. It related to the multiethnic nature of the empire and was formulated most clearly by Prince Oleksander Bezborodko, one of the most illustrious of the many Ukrainians who joined the imperial service and, it should be noted, a man who was known for his love of his native Ukraine: "Russia is an autocratic state. Its size, the variety of its inhabitants and customs, and the many other considerations make it [autocracy] the only natural form of government for Russia. All arguments to the contrary are futile, and the least weakening of the autocratic power would result in the loss of many provinces, the weakening of the state, and countless misfortunes for the people."[2] Attitudes such as this encouraged bureaucrats to administer the empire as if it consisted of a single people – the Russians – and to disregard the different ethnic origins and historical traditions of its many other subjects.

Because Ukrainians were linguistically and culturally closely related to the Russians, the government found it easy to view Ukraine essentially as a Russian land. If one were to ask an imperial official (and very few people ever dreamed of doing so) by what right Russia ruled much of Ukraine, the reply would have been similar to the inscription on a medal struck in honor of Catherine II in 1793, which read: "I have recovered what was torn away." The implication was that Ukraine had always been an integral part of Russia and that it was only as a result of historical accident that it had been temporarily separated from it. The differences that existed between Russians and Ukrainians, an imperial bureaucrat would argue, were simply the result of this temporary separation. Now that they were united once again with the Russians, Ukrainians, or "Little Russians," were expected to lose their distinguishing features and become "true Russians." Until the collapse of the empire, it was government policy to speed this "natural" process along.

A concrete and ubiquitous sign of the imperial presence in Ukraine was the army. Its numerous garrisons and forts dotted the countryside and its commanders demanded onerous obligations from the populace. The most dreaded military burden was conscription, introduced in Ukraine in 1797. For those unfortunates who fell into the hands of recruiting agents, the length of service was twenty-five years. Because of the inhumane discipline and frequent wars, such a term of service was widely regarded as tantamount to a death sentence. Little wonder that recruits were often led away in chains and landlords would punish their most troublesome serfs by having them conscripted.

An outgrowth of the tsar's militaristic approach to government was the establishment of the hated military colonies by Alexander I and his fanatically authoritarian minister, Aleksei Arakcheev, between 1816 and 1821. About 500,000 soldiers were ordered to establish settlements, which were run like military camps and in which every aspect of family life, including permission to marry and the timing of children, was regulated by strict and detailed instructions. There were about twenty of these regiment-sized settlements in

Ukraine. However, the stifling regulations proved to be counterproductive and, by 1857, most of these military colonies were disbanded. Nonetheless, they served as a telling, if extreme, example of the tsarist bureaucracy's efforts to impose military discipline on civilian activities.

The process of imposing imperial administrative structures on Ukrainian lands began as early as the 1770s, but it was not until the 1830s that it assumed its final form. At that time, Ukraine was divided into nine provinces (*gubernii*), which could be subdivided informally into three distinct regions: Left-Bank Ukraine, where Cossack and *starshyna* traditions were strongest, consisted of Chernihiv, Poltava, and Kharkiv provinces; the recently acquired Right Bank, where Polish nobles still exercised socioeconomic domination over the Ukrainian peasantry and where the towns were populated mainly by Jews, consisted of Kiev, Podilia, and Volhynia provinces; and the newly colonized south, once the domain of the Zaporozhians and the Crimean Khanate, was divided into the provinces of Katerynoslav, Kherson, and Tavria (Crimea). Each of these provinces was further subdivided into counties (*povit/uezd*), and these were broken down into townships and villages.

The hierarchy of officials who administered these units was similar throughout the empire. Provinces were headed by governors who were appointed by the tsar. Aiding the governors were an administrative board and various bureaus that dealt with matters such as public order, education, and taxes. The upper levels of the administration were usually made up of professional bureaucrats. However, on the county level and lower, many officials, such as police commandant, marshal of the nobility, and judges, were local nobles elected by nobles. The empire simply did not have enough full-time bureaucrats to fulfill all its needs.

In general, the new administrative structure worked to the disadvantage of Ukraine's oldest cities, most of which had enjoyed autonomy under the ancient Magdeburg Law. In 1835, Kiev was the last city to lose the special status associated this law. Henceforth, most of Ukraine's cities were subordinated to the provincial administration. On the lowest administrative level – that of the village – the maintenance of law and order was the responsibility of local noblemen.

In terms of social background, the people who staffed the administration and were responsible for the day-to-day government of Ukraine in the 19th century tended to be noblemen-turned-bureaucrats. The highest offices, such as governor, usually went to officials who belonged to important aristocratic families, while middle-level offices were generally staffed by average noblemen. Such lowly positions as clerks or scribes were the domain of townsmen or sons of priests. Peasants almost never rose to even the most insignificant posts.

The ethnic composition of the bureaucracy in Ukraine varied according to region. In Left-Bank Ukraine where scions of the old Cossack *starshyna* were recognized as nobles, well-known Ukrainian names, such as Myloradovych, Myklashevsky, Kochubei, Zavadovsky, Kapnist, and Poletyka, could be found among the highest officials. On the Right Bank, Poles and Russians predominated. And in the south where there had been an influx of various peoples from throughout the empire, the backgrounds of officials were exceedingly varied, although again, Russians predominated. It should be noted, however, that once a non-Russian entered the ranks of the bureaucracy, he tended to become Russified, often becoming more "Russian" than the Russians in the process.

The imperial bureaucracy was organized along military lines and was replete with ranks and uniforms. Many of its members were notorious for their proclivity to fawn before their superiors, while simultaneously bullying underlings. With no constitution to protect the rights of individuals, bureaucrats could, and often did, interfere in people's personal lives. Their irritating presence was mitigated somewhat by their relatively small numbers: because the Russian Empire was a comparatively poor country, it could afford to support only about 12 officials per 10,000 inhabitants. By comparison, the ratio in the West was three to four times higher.

The Russian government's inability to pay its officials adequate wages encouraged widespread corruption that was informally tolerated by the government, especially on the local level. As long as its officials supplied the imperial treasury with the assigned amount, it cared little how much they extorted from the populace on their own. While Russians were more accustomed to this burdensome bureaucratism, it was still a new and strange phenomenon for Ukrainians in the early 19th century. Perhaps this explains why it was a Ukrainian, Nikolai Gogol, who satirized the imperial bureaucracy so brilliantly in his famous play *The Inspector General* (1836).

Until the reign of Nicholas I (1825–55), the Russian Empire had only informal, haphazard police supervision and there was no institution that specialized in political repression. But, in 1826, after the shock of the Decembrist Revolt, the tsar's formation of the Third Section produced the empire's first regular secret police. Although its full-time staff was relatively small at first, the Third Section employed numerous informers who frequented fairs, taverns, universities, lectures, and other public gatherings, carefully noting suspicious views and behavior. Censorship as a means of stifling potential opposition had always been practiced in Russia, but during the reign of Nicholas I it was applied more rigorously than ever before, with special committees closely inspecting everything that appeared in print. The tsar's obsession with controlling unsanctioned ideas led Ukraine's greatest poet, Taras Shevchenko, to remark that all the peoples of the empire, "from the Finns in the north, to the Moldavians in the south are silent in every tongue."[3]

Yet despite its repressive features, the empire was by no means a police state. Corrupt, inefficient, and spread over vast territories, its bureaucrats could not or would not fulfill all the instructions that poured forth from the capital. For every martinet there was usually an official who, out of kindness or for the sake of bribes, ignored minor offences or softened prescribed sentences. Moreover, foreign travel was allowed for the few who could afford it, and Western influences spread among the ruling elite, mitigating some of the worst abuses of the regime.

The Little Russian (Maloros) mentality   Impressed with the empire's power and grandeur, attracted by its career opportunities, and placated by acceptance into the Russian imperial nobility, many members of the former Ukrainian *starshyna* needed little urging to become loyal, even devoted, subjects of the tsar-emperor. For them Ukraine became little more than a part, albeit an endearing one, of the imperial whole, and Ukrainians were but a "tribe" of the Russian people. They were indifferent and even antagonistic to any political action based on the notion of Ukrainian separateness. Typical of the "Little Russian mentality" were the words of Viktor Kochubei, a Ukrainian who became the chairman of the imperial council in the 1830s: "Although I was born a *khokhol* [a somewhat derogatory term for Ukrainians], I am more Russian than anyone else ... My position puts me above all sorts of petty considerations. I look at the concerns of your provinces [Ukraine] from the point of view of the common interests of our entire society. Microscopic views are not my concern."[4]

Among 20th-century historians of the nationalist school, the Little Russian mentality has been severely criticized. Viacheslav Lypynsky, the leading proponent of Ukrainian elitism and statehood in the 1920s, commented that it was a typical complex of stateless peoples. He argued that in advocating assimilation into the Russian imperial model, the Little Russians often gave up some of the best features of Ukrainians while adopting many of the worst traits of Russians.[5] Nonetheless, the fact remains that Little Russian attitudes were quite prevalent among the 19th-century Ukrainian elite and Ukrainians themselves were sometimes the greatest opponents of Ukrainian distinctiveness.

Political Developments

It was fortunate for the Russian Empire that it had evolved into a stronger, tighter structure by the early 19th century, for this was the time when the tsarist regime was severely tested.

The Napoleonic invasion   The first shock was the most traumatic. It occurred in 1812, when Napoleon's Grande Armée, numbering 640,000, invaded Russia. As is well known, Russia managed not only to repulse the invaders, but to push them all the way back to Paris – though at great cost and with tremendous effort. The impact of the invasion on Ukraine was relatively minor. A part of Napoleon's forces broke into Volhynia and caused considerable damage there. For the most part, Ukrainians responded willingly to the tsar's call to join the war effort. Several volunteer regiments were quickly organized along Cossack lines on the Left Bank. The widespread support for these units demonstrated not only the readiness of Ukrainians to fight for the empire, but also the popularity of Cossack traditions. However, there were also rumors that several scions of Cossack *starshyna* families were drinking toasts to Napoleon's health and hoping that he would smash the tsarist empire. Recent precedents for such attitudes were not lacking. In 1791, for example, Vasyl Kapnist (a prominent member of the Left Bank nobility) had secretly journeyed to Prussia on a fruitless mission to obtain Prussian aid for a Ukrainian uprising against the tsar. Nonetheless, antitsarist attitudes were the exception and the vast majority of Ukrainians fought loyally and well in defense of the empire.

The Decembrist uprising   During the lengthy Napoleonic wars, many of the tsar's officers who for years had fought in Europe were exposed to and impressed by the political institutions and values of the West. After their victorious return, they expected their seemingly liberal tsar, Alexander I, to introduce Western-style reforms in Russia. But the enigmatic ruler empowered reactionaries such as Arakcheev to rule the land instead. Deeply disillusioned, a small but dedicated group of young army officers, mostly members of Russia's most illustrious families, formed secret societies whose goal was the overthrow of autocratic rule and the establishment of constitutional government.

The first of these societies, the Union of Salvation, was founded in St Petersburg in 1816. About five years later, it broke up into two separate groups. The aristocratic Northern Society, still based in St Petersburg, continued to work for the establishment of a republic. Lacking strong leadership, it accomplished little. However, the Southern Society, based in Tulchyn in southern Ukraine where its leader, Colonel Pavel Pestel, was stationed, was much more effective. Iron-willed and talented, Pestel convinced another secret group, the Society of United Slavs, to join his organization. Among the leaders of the United Slavs were two Ukrainians, the Borisov brothers from Poltava. Pestel also managed to convince a Polish revolutionary group based in Ukraine to cooperate. Thus, by 1825, his original group of about thirty officer/conspirators had grown to approximately 160.

Pestel's program, as formulated in his "Russian Truth" (*Russkaia pravda*), was more radical than that of the northern constitutionalists. It advocated the abolition of all social and political inequalities, economic modernization of the land, leadership by a revolutionary elite, and rigid, centralized gov-

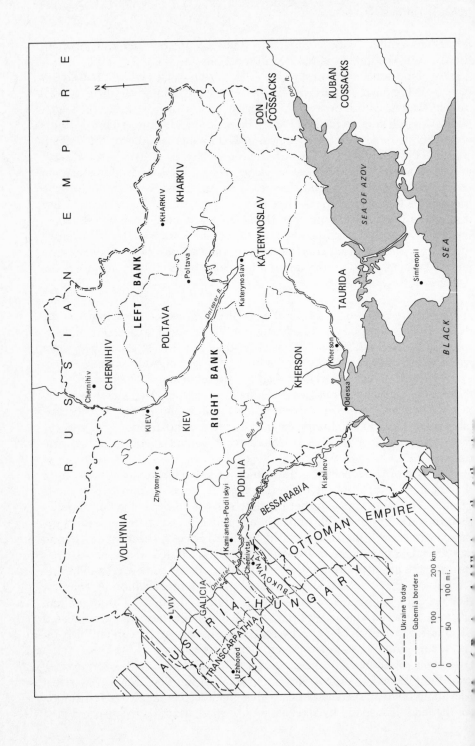

ernment. Although based in Ukraine, Pestel evinced little interest in the non-Russian peoples of the empire. He argued that, except for the Poles who had a highly developed culture of their own, all other minorities should be Russified. As for the Ukrainians in particular, he stated blankly that "Little Russia ... never was and never can be independent ... It must, therefore, surrender its right to be a separate nation."[6] For generations, other Russian revolutionaries would hold similar views on the Ukrainian issue.

Members of the United Slavs did not share Pestel's centralist bias. They favored the reorganization of the empire along federal lines. But, despite the fact that there were Ukrainians in the United Slav leadership, Ukraine was not included among the members of the proposed confederation. There is, however, some evidence that suggests that yet another secret society, not connected with Pestel and consisting of Ukrainian noblemen existed at this time. It was led by Vasyl Lukasevych, the marshal of the nobility of Poltava. Apparently, its platform called for a return of Ukrainian autonomy.

Idealistic but amateurish, the members of both the Northern and Southern societies were caught unprepared by Alexander I's death in December 1825. After much confusion, the leaders of the Northern Society mobilized several thousand troops under their command in St Petersburg and tried to topple the new tsar, Nicholas I. The uprising failed, however, and all the leaders were arrested. In Ukraine, the Southern Society fared only slightly better. Because Pestel was arrested shortly before the uprising in the capital, leadership in Ukraine fell into the irresolute hands of the Bestuzhev-Riumin and Muraviev-Apostol brothers. Although they managed to convince about 1000 of their men to join them in revolt, efforts to gain more support from the soldiers and peasants in Ukraine failed. After a week of aimless wandering in the vicinity of Chernihiv, they were crushed by loyal troops. The Decembrist uprising, the empire's first revolutionary outburst, thus came to a disastrous conclusion.

The Polish uprising of 1830 Ukraine was the scene of yet another uprising. In November 1830, a secret society of young Polish officers, inspired by revolutions that had just occurred in France and Belgium, ignited an uprising against the Russians in Warsaw. After initial successes, however, internal conflicts dissipated Polish energies. In an effort to extend the revolt to Right-Bank Ukraine where the Polish nobility was well entrenched, a Polish force moved into Volhynia in early 1831. Although lack of support and Russian pressure forced it to retreat to Eastern Galicia, about 5000 Polish nobles on the Right Bank nevertheless attempted to continue the struggle.

It was obvious that for the Polish rebels to succeed they would need popular, that is peasant, support. In an effort to gain the backing of anti-tsarist Russians and Ukrainians, the Poles coined their famous slogan, "We fight for our freedom and yours as well." However, more than mere slogans were needed to convince Ukrainian peasants to aid their hated Polish landlords. Some of the Polish rebels suggested freeing the serfs in return for their cooperation, but this idea was rejected by most nobles. As a result, most Ukrainian peasants on the Right Bank adopted a neutral stance, while some took this opportunity to avenge themselves on their Polish lords. Many Polish peasants also refused to back the rebellious nobles in 1830–31, indicating that even among the Poles, national consciousness and solidarity had not yet penetrated to the masses. By the middle of 1831, the uprising was crushed. But for many years thereafter, secret Polish societies continued to conspire against the tsar.

From the point of view of Ukrainian history, it is noteworthy that these conspiracies and uprisings had little to do with Ukrainians as such, although they occurred for the most part on Ukrainian soil. This fact was in itself a telling indication of how vague and emasculated the political significance of Ukraine and the Ukrainians had become in the Russian Empire in the early 19th century.

Russian Imperial Reforms

After the Polish uprising of 1830, the imperial government resolved to amalgamate the so-called western provinces that had once belonged to the Polish Commonwealth – that is, Right-Bank Ukraine, Belorussia, and Lithuania. Just as the Left Bank had been deprived of its distinctive features in the 1780s, so too was the Right Bank to be subjected to a similar process in the 1830s and 1840s. However, in the 19th century, the process of imperial amalgamation was more systematic and thorough than it had been in the 18th century. Not only was administrative uniformity established, but an attempt was made to transform the Right Bank into a culturally "genuinely Russian land." The policy of Russification now emerged in full force.

Although their primary goal was to reduce Polish influence on the Right Bank, Russian policies also had a great impact on the Ukrainian peasantry and the Jewish townsmen of the region. In November 1831, Tsar Nicholas I formed a special commission for the western provinces, based in Kiev. Viktor Kochubei, the commission's chairman, was ordered "to bring these western lands into conformity with the Great Russian provinces in all respects."[7] Within months, all the Polish schools (there were almost no Ukrainian ones) were closed and the school system was reorganized along imperial lines, with Russian as the language of instruction. The famous Polish college at Kremianets was also closed. In its place, a Russian university, named after St Vladimir, was founded in Kiev. As far as the goals of the new university were concerned, Sergei Uvarov, the minister of education, did not mince words in his inaugural address: "The university of St Vladimir is my creation. But I will be the first to repress it if it does not fulfill its assignment ... and this is to disseminate Russian education and Russian nationality in the Polonized lands of western Russia."[8]

The incarnation of the harsh new regime on the Right Bank was General Dmitrii Bibikov, governor-general of Kiev, Podilia, and Volhynia provinces from 1837 to 1852. During the tenure of this martinet, "whose every word was like a blow from a cane," Kiev was transformed into a bastion of Russian culture and a major stronghold of the imperial army.

Backed by powerful military forces, Bibikov carried out his policies unrestrained. On his order, about 60,000 Polish noblemen were deprived of their patents of nobility and demoted to the status of commoners. Many were exiled to the depths of Russia. About 3000 confiscated nobles' estates were transformed into military colonies and Russians were brought in to replace Poles in the bureaucracy. The abolition of the Lithuanian Statute (a law code based on medieval Western models) in 1840, together with the earlier abolition of Kiev's Magdeburg Law, marked the end of what had essentially been Western legal practices in Russian-ruled Ukraine.

Some of Bibikov's measures were aimed at the Ukrainian masses. In 1839, he renewed a campaign (originally launched by Catherine II) to convert – or rather reconvert – the Greek Catholics to Orthodoxy. In the provinces of Volhynia and Podilia, as well as in Belorussia, the Greek Catholic church, which acknowledged the supremacy of Rome, was well established, consisting of over 2 million adherents. By means of mass deportations, bribery, and even executions, Bibikov succeeded in practically eliminating the Greek Catholic church in the empire. Only a small number of Greek Catholics in the region of Kholm managed to retain their adherence to it.

Although it had certainly not been the governor-general's intention, some of his policies had unforeseen advantages for Ukrainians. For example, by supporting St Vladimir University, which had been set up as a counterbalance to Polish cultural influences in Kiev, he helped to develop an institution that would play an extremely important role in the coming Ukrainian cultural resurgence. Similarly, by organizing a commission in 1843 to assemble ancient Ukrainian documents that he hoped would prove that Ukraine had been Russian "from time immemorial," Bibikov inaugurated the first systematic collection of Ukrainian archival materials and gave Ukrainian patriots working on the commission an opportunity to delve into their land's non-Russian past.

His approach to the peasantry also had unexpected results. In 1847, hoping to gain the goodwill of the Ukrainian peasants and to alienate them even more from their Polish landlords, the governor-general introduced the Inventory Regulations. These stipulated exactly the amount of land a peasant had at his disposal and the type of work he owed his landlord. It abolished private taxation by landlords and limited their right to interfere in the peasants' personal affairs. However, in a fashion that was typical of the Russian bureaucracy, Bibikov's successors added so many amendments to the regulations that they became impossible to implement and the nobles carried on as before. Instead of being grateful to the authorities, the confused and frustrated peasants on the Right Bank staged a series of minor revolts against them. These miscarried measures were merely one of the many indications during this highly regimented age that, despite the seemingly unshakable control the imperial regime exercised over society, it could never be sure of the full impact of its policies or of the course of social developments.

The Austrian Empire

Austria, it has been said, was an imperial organization, not a country. In the 19th century, it consisted of a hodgepodge of eleven major nationalities and a number of minor ethnic groups who inhabited much of Eastern Europe and comprised about one-seventh of Europe's population in 1800. Because no nationality represented an absolute majority in the empire, no one culture molded Habsburg imperial society to the extent that Russian culture did in the tsarist empire. And although German, which was the language of the most influential nationality in the Habsburg Empire, predominated in the army and bureaucracy, the Habsburg Empire's most striking characteristic was its ethnic diversity.

In expanding its sovereignty over its subjects, the Habsburg dynasty did not, at least at the outset, tamper with the traditional forms of government in the various kingdoms, duchies, provinces, and cities that it acquired. It was not merely that the Habsburgs did not wish needlessly to arouse opposition, but they lacked the strong, centralized institutions necessary to standardize administration. Therefore, well into the 18th century, their empire was a ramshackle, uncoordinated conglomerate, which was frequently in a state of crisis because of internal discord or external pressure.

In the 1740s, Empress Maria Theresa concluded that for the empire to survive, reforms were necessary. Despite fierce opposition from local nobilities, she pushed through a series of measures that strengthened central ruling institutions and created offices of local government. In order to staff these positions, she expanded the bureaucracy. She also laid the foundations for a large, permanent military establishment. A prudent politician, she did not, however, attempt to impose complete uniformity. In dealing with the recalcitrant Hungarians, for example, she would often choose a compromise solution rather than demand total compliance with her wishes.

An even more ardent reformer was Maria Theresa's son, Joseph II. Committed to current Western ideas of good government, he resolved to make his reign the epitome of enlightened absolutism. In the words of an English historian, "it was enlightened because Joseph II believed that it was a monarch's duty to promote the welfare of his subjects ... and absolute because it was for him alone to say in what that welfare consisted and how it should be achieved."[9]

The emperor made it his goal to improve the lot of the peasants, invigorate the stagnant economy, raise the efficiency of the bureaucracy, and improve educational facilities throughout the empire. True to his absolutist principles, he also intended to eliminate the particularistic rights and privileges that his various lands enjoyed and that greatly impeded the implementation of his reforms. Inevitably, to Joseph II's bitter disillusionment and frustration, only some of these ambitious goals could be realized. Nonetheless, Joseph II's reign marked a high point in the empire's will and ability to invigorate and renovate itself.

The aforementioned reforms were of tremendous relevance for Ukrainians because they came precisely at the time of Galicia's incorporation into the empire. Thus, from their point of view at least, Ukrainians were introduced to the Habsburg imperial system at its best.

Ukrainians under Habsburg Rule

The vast majority of Ukrainians in the Austrian Empire lived in Galicia, a southeastern part of the old Polish Commonwealth, acquired by the Habsburgs after the first partition of Poland in 1772. Two years later, Bukovyna, a small Ukrainian-inhabited area that Vienna snatched away from the faltering Ottoman Empire, was attached to Galicia. Finally, in 1795, after the third and final partition, ethnically Polish lands (including the city of Cracow) were incorporated into the province as well. Thus, while Eastern Galicia (Ukrainian: Halychyna) was inhabited primarily by Ukrainians, Western Galicia was largely Polish. The inclusion of these two peoples in one administrative province would be a future source of tension for all concerned.

There was yet another Ukrainian-inhabited region under indirect Habsburg rule. Transcarpathia, on the western slopes of the Carpathian Mountains, had since medieval times been a part of the kingdom of Hungary. In the 19th century, it remained in the Hungarian part of the Habsburg Empire and was isolated from the other Ukrainian lands.

The peasants   One word summed up conditions in the Ukrainian-inhabited areas of the Habsburg empire: poverty. Hilly terrain and small plots made agriculture difficult, while the exploitive rule of the Polish nobles had left peasants in a permanent state of economic and physical exhaustion. Moreover, the plight of the small, grimy Galician towns worsened when they were cut off from their traditional markets in Russian-dominated Ukraine as a result of the partitions. Little wonder that Galicia had the dubious distinction of being one of the most destitute and backward areas of the empire.

The vast majority of West Ukrainians were enserfed peasants and exploitation was for them a fact of daily life. In return for the use of their meager plots of land, they owed their landlords labor duties that amounted to as many as five to six days of labor per week. In addition, noblemen frequently pressed peasants into domestic service and demanded payment in agricultural products. It has been calculated that roughly one-half to one-third of a peasant's meager income went to his landlord. To make matters worse, estate owners systematically expropriated their serfs' plots and public lands, thereby decreasing the size of peasant holdings. Thus, while in 1819, the average size of a peasant's plot in Eastern Galicia had been 14 acres and a nobleman's estate 1051 acres, by 1848, their respective holdings were 9.6 acres and 1400 acres. Eastern Galicia provided a graphic example of a society in which the rich were getting richer while the poor were becoming progressively poorer.

Under such circumstances, even survival was no simple matter. Isolated in about 3500 nearly inaccessible villages and utilizing primitive farming methods, the peasants of Eastern Galicia managed to attain only about one-third the output of their Czech or Austrian counterparts. Their food intake, which consisted mainly of cabbage and potatoes, was only about one-half that of a West European farmer. When famine struck, as it often did, the already weakened serfs would perish in great numbers. In fact, there were times, such as the period between 1830 and1850, when the death rate in Eastern Galicia exceeded the birth rate. As might be expected, the life expectancy of the West Ukrainian peasant was low, averaging only 30–40 years.

To alleviate the misery of their condition, peasants often took to drink. They were encouraged in this by their Polish landlords, who had a legal monopoly on alcohol production, and by the tavern-keepers, most of whom were Jews. Some landowners even set regular consumption quotas for their serfs, hoping thereby to dispose of the alcohol they produced. The thought of easing or improving the lot of the peasant rarely, if ever, came to the mind of the Galician nobleman. In all probability, most would have wondered at the very need or feasibility of such an idea, for to them the peasant represented a lower form of human life that defied any kind of improvement.

The clergy   Not all West Ukrainians were peasants, however. The Greek Catholic clergy constituted a distinct social group that was the closest thing West Ukrainian society had to an elite. The clergy had gained a position of leadership among the peasantry by default when the native nobility had alienated itself from Ukrainian society in the 16th–17th centuries by becoming Polonized (and hence Catholicized). Because members of the lower clergy, unlike the hierarchy, were allowed to establish families, priestly dynasties evolved that often came to be associated with specific regions for many generations. In the 19th century, there were about 2000–2500 such priestly families in Eastern Galicia. Frequent assemblies, lengthy visits, and intermarriage had made the Greek Catholic clergy a tightly knit, hereditary caste with a strong sense of group solidarity.

Bound to the masses by a common faith, they enjoyed great influence and authority among their peasant parishioners. Yet – especially prior to Habsburg rule – the material and cultural levels of the Ukrainian village priest were scarcely higher than those of the peasant. True, the priestly plots provided by the community were generally larger than those of the peasant, and fees from christenings, weddings, and funerals provided additional income. But the widow and children of deceased parish priests often lived from the same plots as new appointees, while the expense of preparing sons for the priesthood and daughters for suitable marriages bankrupted many a priest.

Because theological training was inadequate, many Greek Catholic priests in Eastern Galicia in the late 18th to early 19th centuries could barely read the Church Slavonic liturgical texts. Consequently, their worldview was not much broader than that of the peasantry. Polish nobles showed the Greek Catholic clergy little respect. For example, it was not uncommon, prior to Habsburg rule, for nobles to force priests to work on their estates. Yet these conditions yielded a positive result, for the Ukrainian clergy developed much closer personal and cultural bonds with the peasantry than did its Polish counterpart. This relationship made it easier for the Greek Catholic clergy to provide the peasantry with leadership and guidance, not only in religious, but in other matters as well. Thus, for much of the 19th century, West Ukrainian society consisted of only two social groups – a mass of peasants and a small priestly caste. As the Poles jokingly phrased it, there were among the Ukrainians only the *khlop* (peasant) and the *pop* (priest).

Because Ukrainians in West Ukraine lacked a nobility and were underrepresented among the townsmen to an even greater extent than Ukrainians in the Russian Empire, some modern historians have described their society as being "sociologically incomplete."[10] As the phrase implies, a "sociologically incomplete" society is severely handicapped; and indeed, in 19th-century Eastern Europe, Ukrainians had little access to political power because of their lack of a nobility. Without townsmen, they were excluded from commerce and industry. That is not to say, of course, that Galicia as a whole lacked a nobility or urban class. In the late 18th century, Polish nobles numbered about 95,000, or 3.4% of the population of the province, and the townsmen, most of whom were poor Jewish artisans and shopkeepers with a sprinkling of wealthy merchants, numbered about 300,000, or 10% of the population. In addition, with the coming of Habsburg rule, a new social group appeared – the bureaucrats. Mostly Germans, or German-speaking Czechs, they were never very numerous. However, tens of thousands of other Germans were also brought into the province by the Habsburg authorities as colonists in the hope that they would provide models of good farming and invigorate the rural economy. Thus, Galician society as a whole was both multiethnic and rigidly stratified, with each of its individual ethnic groups occupying its own distinct and insular social, economic, and cultural sphere.

The Impact of Habsburg Reforms on West Ukrainians

While the Habsburg reforms of the late 18th century applied to the entire empire, their impact was especially great on Galicia, which was in greatest need of improvement. Joseph II developed an especial interest in the province, which he viewed as a kind of laboratory in which he could experiment with various means of restructuring society and, specifically, of improving its productive capacity. At the outset, Vienna's goals in Galicia were twofold: first, to dismantle the old noble-dominated governmental system and to replace it with a disciplined, centralized bureaucracy, and second, to improve the socioeconomic conditions of the non-noble population.

The administrative reorganization of Galicia was accomplished quickly and effectively. By 1786, Austrian laws replaced Polish ones and the nobles' assemblies were abolished. To soften the blow to the old elite and to give it a voice in government, Vienna instituted an Assembly of Estates composed of nobles and clergy. But the assembly had no real decision-making power of its own, for it could only address petitions to the emperor. Real power lay in the hands of the imperial bureaucrats. The entire province was divided into eighteen regions (their number rose to nineteen with the addition of Bukovyna), each of which was headed by an official appointed by Vienna and his German-speaking staff. At the top of the bureaucratic hierarchy was the governor, personally appointed by the emperor. The entire bureaucratic apparatus was based in Lviv, or Lemberg as the Austrians called it, which became the administrative and judicial center of the province.

The reforming emperor   Of Joseph II's many reforms, the most important dealt with the peasantry. In 1781, realizing that he could not improve socioeconomic conditions in Galicia if he did not alleviate the plight of the peasants, the emperor decided on a bold policy that called for the dismantling of serfdom. Among the steps taken towards this goal were the following: a limit of three days per week or 156 days per year was set on the labor that a landlord could demand from his peasants (the poorest peasants owed even less labor); additional services to landlords were strictly limited; the peasant's right to work his plot was legally recognized and the peasants received such individual rights as being able to marry without first obtaining their lord's permission, to move to other plots, and to lodge complaints against their lord in a court of law.

These were momentous changes. No longer was the Galician peasant someone who was ignored and unprotected by the law. He now became an individual with certain legal rights. This is not to say that these reforms made peasants equal to the other classes. In many ways the peasant remained subordinated and dependent upon his landlord. However, his condition improved from being mere chattel to being something like a hereditary tenant whose relationship with the landlord was regulated by law. The bold and progressive nature of these reforms is all the more evident when we realize that at exactly the time they were being implemented, Joseph II's fellow monarch, Catherine II of Russia, was imposing serfdom on the peasantry of Left-Bank Ukraine.

The Greek Catholic church also benefited greatly from the new policies. From the start, Maria Theresa and Joseph II applied the principle of parity in dealing with the Greek and Roman Catholic churches. For the Greek Catholic clergy, which had long been discriminated against under the Polish regime, this principle represented a marked improvement. No longer could Polish landlords interfere in the appointment of parish priests, who now enjoyed equal legal rights with their Roman Catholic counterparts. Moreover, the economic status of the Greek Catholic clergy was elevated by the payment of modest government salaries. The crowning measure was the renewal of the office of metropolitan of Halych in 1808 after a hiatus of about 400 years. Thus, the Greek Catholic church, the one and only institution with which the Ukrainian peasantry could identify, entered the 19th century rejuvenated.

A major reason for the growing confidence of the Greek Catholic clergy was the educational reforms initiated by Maria Theresa. In 1774, the empress founded the Barbareum, a Greek Catholic seminary in Vienna that provided West Ukrainian students not only with systematic theological training, but also with an invigorating exposure to Western culture. In 1783, a larger seminary was founded in Lviv. As usual, Joseph II carried his mother's measures a step further: anxious to obtain more well-trained bureaucrats and priests, he founded a university in Lviv in 1784. It was the first such institution of higher learning on Ukrainian soil. About 250 students, mostly Poles, but also a sizable minority of Ukrainians, enrolled in its four faculties. Because the professors, most of whom were Germans, lectured in German and Latin, which the Ukrainians could not understand, a separate faculty, called the Studium Ruthenum, was organized for the Ukrainian students. Its language of instruction was an artificial and stilted language that combined Church Slavonic and Ukrainian vernacular.

Elementary education was practically nonexistent in Eastern Galicia. The few one-class schools that could be found in the villages were usually the domain of half-literate deacons who did little more than teach their pupils the rudiments of the alphabet and the Holy Scriptures. As early as 1774, to improve this situation, the Austrians introduced a system of three types of schools: parochial, one-class schools, using the native language of the region; three-class schools, using German and Polish; and four-year schools, preparing pupils for further training in the high schools (*gymnazia*) and universities.

The old secondary schools that a number of Catholic monastic orders had maintained for the sons of the nobility were abolished.

Impressive though they appeared, Joseph II's reforms were in reality more an indication of what he attempted rather than what he actually achieved. In Galicia, as elsewhere in the empire, many of the measures encountered insurmountable obstacles. For example, the emperor believed that by improving the lot of the peasants, he could make them and the province more productive. But it soon became apparent that Galicia's economic problems went beyond the peasantry. Unlike Russian-ruled Ukraine, Eastern Galicia had no vast, open lands to colonize or a seacoast to encourage trade. In contrast to Western Europe, where peasants were beginning to move into bustling cities to work in proliferating factories, Eastern Galicia's approximately sixty largest towns were economically stagnant. In short, economic options in the region were extremely limited. Furthermore, Vienna's economic policies only exacerbated the situation. Their goal was to keep the eastern half of the empire agricultural and to encourage industry in western provinces like Austria and Bohemia. Assigned to serve as a source of food and raw products and as a market for finished goods, Galicia in effect functioned as an internal colony of the more developed western provinces of the empire.

The reforms were also hampered by the nobles, who seized every opportunity to subvert them. Angered by the confiscations of its land and the reduction of its role in education, the Roman Catholic church was also slow to cooperate. Finally, opposition to change reached a critical point when the Hungarians, incensed by the centralizing and Germanizing policies of Vienna, threatened to revolt. Frustrated and disillusioned, Joseph II was forced to revoke many of his measures.When he died in 1790, he left behind the bitter epitaph: "Here lies Joseph II who failed in all his endeavors."

In the early 19th century, Habsburg rulers, especially the conservative Francis I, continued to retreat from the position taken by the reforming emperor. Most notably, many of the improvements in the position of the peasantry were revoked and serfdom was reinstituted in effect. However, some of the changes dealing with the church, education, and law remained in force. Without them and the other enlightened precedents set by Joseph II, the liberalization of the empire that was to come in the late 19th century would have been difficult to achieve.

Ruthenianism (Rutenstvo)   Although limited and incomplete, the reforms of Maria Theresa and Joseph II nonetheless improved the conditions in which the West Ukrainians – one of the most downtrodden peoples in the empire – lived; and they affected not only the conditions of their material existence, but their views and attitudes as well. As might be expected, the reforms evoked a deep sense of gratitude among Ukrainians to the Habsburgs in general, and

Joseph II in particular. This loyalty to the dynasty became so deeply rooted that the Ukrainians were called "the Tyrolians of the East."

This deep dependence and even subservience to the Habsburgs had its negative effects. It bred the so-called *rutenstvo*, a set of attitudes that came to prevail among the West Ukrainian elite well into the 1830s. Its proponents – mostly priests – were characterized by an extreme provincialism that identified Ukrainians exclusively with Galicia, Greek Catholicism, and the priestly caste.

The new conservatism that held sway in Vienna reinforced the suspicion of innovation and of new ideas that was inherent to the West Ukrainian clergy-elite. Aping the Polish nobility (even to the point of adopting the Polish language), the *rutentsi* practiced a pseudo-aristocratism that included looking down on the peasants and their "swineherd language." Having had its status elevated by the Habsburgs loosened the clergy's identification with the peasantry among whom it lived. The clergy began to look only toward Vienna, servilely accepting all that the capital deigned to grant it and posing no demands of its own. For generations, this *rutenstvo* mentality helped to maintain West Ukrainian society in its oppressed and backward state and discouraged Ukrainians from taking any initiative to improve it. Thus, in Austrian-ruled Ukraine, just as in Russian-ruled Ukraine, many members of the native elites helped to keep their own countrymen firmly set in the imperial mold.

ða

Imperial rule exposed Ukrainians to much tighter, more extensive, and intrusive forms of political, social, and economic organization than they had ever known before. Through the intermediary of its bureaucrats, the imperial state became a major presence in Ukrainian communities. With this presence came a new feeling that in the splendid if distant imperial capital an all-powerful, all-knowing emperor was ordering, indeed, molding Ukrainian lives. As the image of awesome majesty projected by the empire – be it Russian or Austrian – captivated the Ukrainian elite, its commitment to its homeland faded. Ukrainian lands were, after all, clearly only a part of a greater whole. By the same token, consciousness of a distinct Ukrainian identity – which had been strong in the 17th- and 18th-century Cossack Ukraine – weakened.

Another feature of the imperial age was that it highlighted the existence of two distinct Ukrainian societies, one in the Russian Empire and the other in the Austrian Empire. True, Ukrainians had lived in two very different political systems since 1654, when Moscow extended its overlordship over the Left Bank while most of the Ukrainian lands remained in the Polish-Lithuanian Commonwealth. But the political, cultural, and socioeconomic significance of the West Ukrainians in the latter stages of the Commonwealth's existence reached such a low point that it was almost imperceptible. As we shall see, in the 19th century and under Austrian rule, this position changed dramatically, and West Ukrainians again assumed a prominent role in the history of their people. Consequently, the course of modern Ukrainian history has largely been the tale of two parallel paths, one tread by the West Ukrainians in Austrian Empire and the other by the East Ukrainians in the Russian Empire.

The Growth of
National Consciousness

Rarely has there been a more exciting, varied, and widespread flowering of new ideas than in the 19th century. By that time, the disengagement from the medieval belief that the world could be comprehended only in terms of God's will, begun in the Renaissance, had long since been completed. Educated Europeans were secure in the conviction that the mind of man was fully capable of analyzing and guiding human life. This intellectual confidence led to an unprecedented growth of ideas and ideologies. Indeed, ideology – that is, a system of ideas that claims to explain the past and present world and to serve as a guide for a better life in the future – emerged as a major historical force at this time.

Closely linked to these developments was the rise of intellectuals or intelligentsia, as the roughly analogous social group was called in Eastern Europe. As specialists in the formulation and propagation of ideas and the mobilization of people in behalf of these ideas, the intelligentsia would be in the forefront of political and cultural change in Eastern Europe. And one of the most gripping concepts developed by the intelligentsia during the 19th century was that of nationhood. It was, as we shall see, a wholly new way not only of viewing society, but also of influencing its behavior. In Ukraine, as elsewhere in the world, the rise of the concept of nationhood was an unmistakable indicator of approaching modernity, for with nationhood came ideas and causes that are still with us today.

ૐ

The Modern Idea of Nationhood

Today nationhood is such a pervasive reality that it is difficult to imagine that in early 19th-century Eastern Europe, and indeed, in much of the world, it was only a hazy, slowly unfolding notion. This is not to say that premodern peoples were oblivious to ethnic differences. People always felt a close attachment to their homeland, language, customs, and traditions. But until relatively recently, ethnicity was not considered to be a primary basis for defining group identity. Legal and socioeconomic distinctions embodied in the feudal estate system, that is, distinctions *within* a people, were generally thought to be more significant than differences *between* peoples. In other words, a Ukrainian, Russian, or Polish nobleman believed that he had more in common with noblemen in other countries than with peasants or townsmen in his own land. Only in the 19th century did a new concept of community – one based on common language and culture – begin to emerge. In Ukraine, as elsewhere, the evolution and slow dissemination of the idea of ethnically based nationhood would become one of the major themes of modern history.

It was the French Revolution, which reflected the disintegration of feudal society and the advent of a new, mass-based political and socioeconomic system, that helped this idea gain prominence. In its wake, growing numbers of Europeans accepted the ideas of individual rights and of sovereignty being vested in the people, not in their rulers. The common folk began to come into their own – and their speech, customs, and traditions also gained recognition. In fact, these latter elements became the key integrating factors in the creation of national consciousness.

The most persuasive argument for the importance of native languages and folklore was provided by the German philosopher Johann Herder. Reacting against the "lifelessness" of the impersonal imperial systems and the artificiality of the foreign languages and fashions that dominated royal courts and noble salons, Herder focused his attention on the ethnic culture of the peasantry. The noted historian Hans Kohn wrote: "Herder was the first to insist that human civilization lives not in its general and universal, but in its national and peculiar manifestations; each cultural manifestation must be original, but its originality is that of the national community and the national language. By nature and history men are above all members of the national community: only as such can they be really creative."[1] Among the intelligentsias of Eastern Europe, which was dominated completely by monolithic empires, Herder's ideas found an especially appreciative response; and it was the intellectuals who would take the lead in developing and spreading the modern concept among East Europeans.

While the ways in which national consciousness developed in every society varied considerably, modern scholars have discerned three general and partly overlapping stages in the development of East European national movements.The initial phase, marked by a somewhat nostalgic mood, generally consisted of a small group of scholarly intellectuals collecting historical documents, folklore, and artifacts in the belief that the individuality of their people would soon disappear with the onslaught of imperial culture. The second or cultural phase usually witnessed the unexpected "rebirth" of vernacular languages and their increasing use in literary and educational activities. And the third or political stage was marked by the growth of nationally-based organizations and the formulation of nation-oriented demands that implied, to a greater or lesser extent, the desire for self-rule. As we shall see, the evolution of Ukrainian national consciousness fits well into this general pattern.

The Intelligentsia

One cannot fully appreciate the evolution and dissemination of the new ideas that appeared in Ukraine, as in all of Europe, in the 19th century without taking into account the emergence of the new category of people that produced them. In Eastern Europe these "new people" were called the intelligentsia, a term only roughly equivalent to the West European "intellectual." First introduced in Russia and then throughout Eastern Europe, the term intelligentsia was used in the broad sense to designate the relative few who possessed a higher education. But in the narrower and historically more significant sense, "intelligentsia" referred to those individuals who committed themselves out of ideological conviction to the cultural, social, and political improvement of the masses, that is, the peasantry.

The "newness" of the intelligentsia manifested itself in several ways. The intelligentsia perceived life in terms of ideas and ideologies and not, as was the case previously and with other social groups, in terms of concrete social rights, privileges, and obligations. Instead of viewing society from the narrow perspective of a nobleman, townsman, or peasant, members of the intelligentsia believed that they looked at society as a whole and considered the interests of all. In time, criticism of the status quo became a standard feature of intelligentsia discourse – so much so that in the late 19th century, a part of the intelligentsia even dedicated itself to changing the status quo at any cost and by whatever means necessary.

In the Russian Empire, as in all of Eastern Europe, the appearance of the intelligentsia was a development of great importance. This was especially true for societies, such as that of Ukraine, that had "lost" their noble-elites through assimilation to imperial culture and service. For it would be the intelligentsia that would provide Ukrainians with cultural and, eventually, political leadership throughout the modern period.

As might be expected, the intelligentsia usually appeared in cities, especially those where institutions of higher learning were located. Thus, Kharkiv, where in 1805 the first university in Russian-ruled Ukraine was founded, became an early center of the land's evolving intelligentsia. The circumstances in which this university appeared were noteworthy: they differed greatly from those of the empire's other universities, which were founded at the initiative of the government for the purpose of training servants of the state. Fueled by local patriotism and a desire to raise the cultural level of Ukraine, a group of local gentrymen, led by the indefatigable Vasyl Karazyn, success-fully lobbied Emperor Alexander I for permission and raised the funds neces-sary for the establishment of the university. Only in 1834, when St Vladimir's University was founded in Kiev, did that city displace Kharkiv as the intel-lectual center of Ukraine.

The social milieu from which the first generation of Ukrainian intelligentsia primarily emerged was that of the old Cossack *starshyna*-nobility. However, this group was not that of the wealthy and influential aristocrats whose con-tacts allowed them to obtain easily high ranks in the imperial bureaucracy. It was, instead, the impoverished gentrymen whose shrinking estates forced them to seek other means of livelihood that were most drawn to higher edu-cation. A small fraction of these early intellectuals consisted of sons of priests, townsmen, and Cossacks. Members of the intelligentsia who were of peasant background were extremely rare before 1861.

In Ukraine, as elsewhere in Eastern Europe, the numbers of the intelli-gentsia were quite small. Prior to 1861, Kharkiv University produced a total of 2800 graduates, while the newer and larger university in Kiev had about 1500 alumni. From this tiny pool of well-educated individuals, only a small num-ber evinced an interest in things Ukrainian. Thus, those who were involved in the creation of a new sense of identity in Ukraine were only a minute fraction of its populace.

Members of the intelligentsia generally congregated in "circles" (*kruzhky*) – small discussion groups where ideas, philosophies, and ideologies would be introduced, analyzed, and debated. Another focal point was the journals that provided like-minded intellectuals with a forum for their works. The intelli-gentsia's contacts with other sectors of society, especially the peasants with whom, in theory, they were primarily concerned, were minimal. For much of the 19th century, the Ukrainian intelligentsia, like the Russian, remained a minute sector of society, frequently fragmented by intellectual debates, in-creasingly alienated from the government, isolated from the masses, and im-mersed in activities that were of interest only to itself. Yet when the appro-priate conditions emerged, the impact of these seemingly irrelevant, esoteric activities was much greater than the intelligentsia could ever itself have imag-ined.

The Building Blocks of National Identity

Although the evolving intelligentsia emerged from among educated bureau-crats and nobles, it did not fit in well with the imperial elite, which had little interest in new ideas or independent thinking. Therefore, many among the in-telligentsia gradually developed a sense of estrangement from the empire's establishment. This, in turn, inclined them to show a greater interest in the long-neglected peasant masses.

The impact of Western ideas strengthened this inclination. Herder's notions and their ready acceptance in Eastern Europe were a case in point. In the early 19th century, the German philosopher's adulation of peasant culture dovetailed with the spreading influences of Western Romanticism. In many ways, Romanticism was an intellectual revolt against the Enlightenment of the 18th century. The Enlightenment, which molded the thinking of the Habsburg and Russian empire-builders, stressed rationality, uniformity, universality, and order. In contrast, Romanticism, which captured the imagination of the new East European intelligentsia, glorified emotion, spontaneity, diversity, and nature. And in drawing attention to the unique features of the world's various peoples "in their natural state and habitats," the ideas of Herder and the Romantics gave rise to the concept of national characteristics and provided thereby the means for defining nationhood.

In establishing the elements of national identity, the Ukrainian intelligentsia, like others in Eastern Europe, focused on such unique features of their ethnic group as their history, folklore, language, and literature. Of course, when Ukrainian intellectuals first embarked on their studies of these fields, they did not have a grand, predetermined plan of creating a Ukrainian national identity. If asked why they were drawn to such seemingly esoteric pursuits as the collection of old documents and rare folk songs or the emulation of peasant speech, many intellectuals would probably describe their activities as little more than a hobby encouraged by local patriotism or a nostalgic affection for a disappearing world. Nonetheless, as a result of these early, amateurish labors, a consensus arose among a small clique of the educated as to what were the basic elements of a distinctively Ukrainian culture. Eventually, these conclusions would become the basis of Ukrainian national consciousness.

The road to national consciousness was paved with books. They were the storehouses in which information about Ukrainian culture was collected. Simultaneously they served as the means for the dissemination of this information among literate Ukrainians. Furthermore, in the process of writing these books, the intelligentsia developed and refined the Ukrainian language, the one element that was most effective in creating a feeling of fraternity among all Ukrainians. For this reason literary works loom large in the early history of Ukrainian nation-building.

The re-creation of a national history In the growth of national consciousness throughout the world, the study of national history has always played a crucial role. In achieving a new sense of community, it was necessary for a people to believe that it had shared a common fate. Moreover, this shared historical experience should be perceived as a glorious one that instilled in individuals a sense of pride and encouraged them to identify with their nation. As important as a glorious past was an ancient past. An extended history gave people a sense of continuity, a feeling that the current sad state of their nation was but a passing phase. A glorious and ancient past was also useful in rebutting the arguments of numerous skeptics who claimed that a given nation never existed, that it was a new, artificial creation (hence nationalist writers in Eastern Europe preferred to speak of a national rebirth or renaissance). Because national histories fulfilled these functions, it is not suprising that among Ukrainians, as well as other peoples, it was historians who were in the forefront of the nation-building process.

By the late 18th century, there were signs that interest in history, especially that of the Cossacks, was growing among the gentry-intelligentsia of the Left Bank. This interest was reflected in the work of several scions of old *starshyna* families who, after retiring from imperial service, devoted themselves to compiling and publishing historical materials. For the most part, they were motivated by simple antiquarianism or local patriotism and were completely unaware of the broader ramifications of their work. The most noteworthy of these amateur historians, all of whom wrote in Russian, were Vasyl Ruban ("The Short Chronicle of Little Russia," 1777), Opanas Shafonsky ("Typographical Description," 1786), Oleksander Rigelman ("A Description According to the Chronicles of Little Russia," 1798), and the young, extremely patriotic Iakiv Markovych ("Notes Concerning Little Russia," 1798). Their works were all well received by the Ukrainian gentry.

But the motives of some of these amateurs were not only altruistic. In approximately 1800, the Imperial Heraldic Office began to question the right of the descendants of the *starshyna* to noble status because, in the words of a Russian bureaucrat, "In Little Russia there was never a genuine nobility."[2] As a wave of indignation and protest swept through the Ukrainian elite, some of its members, such as Roman Markovych, Timofei Kalynsky, Vasyl Chernysh, Adrian Chepa, Vasyl Poletyka, and Fedir Tumansky, took to collecting historical documents. And, between 1801 and 1808, they wrote a series of essays attesting to the glorious deeds and high status of their forefathers. After the controversy was resolved in the 1830s in favor of most Ukrainians, some of the Left Bank nobles retained their interest in the history of their land and encouraged further historical studies.

Because the early historians were untrained dilettantes, the need for a more sophisticated, well-researched history of Ukraine soon became apparent. In 1822, Dmytro Bantysh-Kamensky (a Moscow-born and educated son of an archivist and secretary of Prince Repnin, the governor-general of the Left Bank) completed his thoroughly documented and very popular four-volume history, "A History of Little Russia." The appeal of Bantysh-Kamensky's work to the Ukrainian elite lay not only in its professionalism but also in its interpretation of the Ukrainian past. A loyal tsarist bureaucrat, Bantysh-Kamensky argued that Ukrainians, despite their distinctive and heroic history, were nonetheless a branch of the Russian people and their reunion with

Russia was a high point of their history. For many Ukrainian nobles this interpretation was convenient and convincing, for it allowed them to acknowledge their Ukrainian (*Maloros*) distinctiveness while stressing their loyalty to the tsar and adherence to the powerful Russian state and nation.

A very different work from those mentioned above was the *Istoriia Rusov* ("History of the Rus'"). An air of mystery surrounds this extremely influential historical tract. Neither the place nor the date it was written is known. Historians can only deduce that it probably appeared in the first decade of the 19th century, somewhere in the Novhorod-Siverskyi region of the Hetmanate. For decades the *Istoriia Rusov* remained unpublished, circulating widely but surreptitiously among the Left-Bank gentry. Only in 1846 did it apear in print. Even the most painstaking and detailed historical detective work has failed to identify the author conclusively, although specialists have narrowed the circle of possible authors to such members of the gentry-intelligentsia as Hryhor Poletyka and his son Vasyl, as well as Opanas Lobosevych and Oleksander Bezborodko.

Why the mystery? Apparently it is because of the dangerously inflammatory tone of the *Istoriia Rusov*, which was actually more of a political tract than a scholarly history. The work unabashedly glorified and romanticized the Cossack past, and although the author did not advocate outright independence for Ukraine, he did view Ukrainians as a people separate from the Russians and called for some form of self-government. His heroes were Khmelnytsky and, significantly, the recalcitrant Polubutok who stood up to Peter i. He also argued that it was Ukraine and not Russia that had a primary claim to the heritage of Kievan Rus'. Although the author portrayed the Poles as the Ukrainians' worst enemies, a subtle note of anti-Russianism also permeates the work. For example, in contrast to the Ukrainians' love of freedom, the author of the *Istoriia Rusov* claims that "serfdom and slavery in the highest degree reign among the Muscovite people ... it is as if their people were created only that they might become serfs."[3]

But while the *Istoriia Rusov* brims with national pride, it is not based on narrow ethnocentrism. The author contends that truth and justice are the cornerstones of any political system and the defense of life, liberty, and property are the inalienable rights of all individuals. Even more radical is the work's argument that no government can rest on tyranny and serfdom. Thus, on the one hand, the work's colorful (if not always accurate) depiction of the Cossacks heightened interest in the Ukrainian past, and on the other hand, it raised questions about Ukraine's place in the present political order. Consequently, with the appearance of the *Istoriia Rusov* the study of Ukrainian history began to have an ideological and political significance.

The glorification of folklore   Another absorbing and widespread activity among the early Ukrainian gentry-intelligentsia was the study of folklore. This new interest in the customs, traditions, and songs of the peasants was in striking contrast to the past, when educated elites had always insisted on maintaining a gap between their own culture and that of the masses. Again, it was Herder's ideas, which slowly seeped into Ukraine, that sparked the Ukrainian intelligentsia's interest in native culture.

In Herder's view, the chief prerequisite for a vibrant, creative culture was naturalness. Unfortunately, in his estimation, the cultural activity of late 18th-century Europe was dominated by cosmopolitan, imitative courts and nobilities that readily adoped foreign languages, manners, and values, thus creating an atmosphere that stifled the expression of a people's unique cultural characteristics. The solution, Herder argued, was to reject the artificial "high culture" and turn for fresh sources of inspiration and modes of expression to the unspoiled, authentic, and organic culture of the common people. It was not long before the East European intelligentsia began to adopt the view that the folk songs of the people were more beautiful than the most elaborate Baroque music, peasant customs more charming than courtly manners, and ancient proverbs more enlightening than weighty tomes written in foreign languages.

In the early decades of the 19th century, many young intellectuals tramped throught the countryside in order to discover, collect, and, later, to publish these pearls of folk wisdom and creativity. For example, the noted Ukrainian historian Kostomarov recalled how in his youth he "went off on ethnographic expeditions to the villages around Kharkiv ... listened to the tales and discussions, noted down interesting words and phrases, entered into conversations, questioned people about their lives, and asked them to sing their songs."[4]

Because Ukrainians were largely a peasant people, one of their most appealing features was a rich, vibrant folklore. Herder himself was so smitten by the beauty of this folklore that he declared, "Ukraine will become another Greece: the beautiful sky, the gay spirit of the people, their natural musical gifts, and their fertile land will arise one day!"[5] Even Poland's greatest poet, Adam Mickiewicz, acknowledged that Ukrainians were the "most poetical and musical people among the Slavs."[6] It is not surprising, therefore, that ethnographic studies soon became all the rage among the Left-Bank intelligentsia.

Among the early enthusiasts of Ukrainian folklore was Prince Nikolai Tsertelev. Although of Georgian origin and Russian education, Tsertelev grew up in Ukraine and developed a deep attachment to its people. In 1819, he published in St Petersburg his "An Attempt at a Collection of Ancient Little Russian Songs." In the preface, Tsertelev noted that the songs would demonstrate "the genius and spirit of the people, the customs of the times, and, finally, the pure moral quality for which the Little Russians have always been known."[7] A much more comprehensive and systematic study on Ukrainian ethnography entitled "The Little Russian Folk Songs"was completed in 1827 by

Mykhailo Maksymovych, a Ukrainian of Cossack background who became a professor at Moscow University and, in 1834, the first rector of the new university in Kiev. Another Ukrainian professor at Moscow University, Osyp Bodiansky, had devoted his master's dissertation (completed in 1837) to a comparison between Russian and Ukrainian folk songs. With typically Romantic exaggeration, he contrasted the supposedly despondent, submissive tone of the songs of the Russian north with the dramatic, vivacious melodies of the Ukrainian south. "How different is the north from the south," wrote Bodiansky, "and how different are the peoples who live there."[8]

Besides helping to draw distinctions between Ukrainians and their neighbors, the seemingly harmless study of folklore soon affected the intelligentsia in other ways. Observing everyday life in the village, members of the intelligentsia not only saw colorful customs, but also came face to face with the merciless exploitation of the peasantry. Initially they were too absorbed by their idealistic search for universal truths and uniquely Ukrainian characteristics to draw broader conclusions about the socioeconomic plight of the peasantry. However, eventually some of them concluded that they could no longer simply observe the hapless peasants but that something had to be done to help them.

Language: the common link   According to Herder, language is the most important component of nationality: "Has a nationality anything dearer than the speech of its fathers? In its speech resides its whole intellectual domain, its traditions, its history, religion and basis of life, all its heart and soul. To deprive a people of its speech is to deprive it of its one eternal good."[9] But the function of language in the development of national consciousness is even broader than that sketched by the German philosopher. Language establishes most effectively the "natural" limits of a nationality. It distinguishes between native and alien. It binds together various classes and regions. Modern social scientists have argued that not only does a language facilitate communication among its speakers, but – because it constitutes a unique system of perceiving and expressing a particular people's view of the world – it also allows them to understand each other on a deeper, subconscious level.

Given the central importance of language to the nation-building process, it would only be a matter of time before the Ukrainian intelligentsia attempted to transform the vernacular (that is, the spoken language) of the common people into the primary means of self-expression of all Ukrainians. Only by doing so could a common bond be established between the elite and the masses and the basis laid for a shared identity. At the outset, however, this transformation seemed to be an unattainable goal. Compared to prestigious and cultivated languages such as French, German, and, increasingly, Russian, the spoken language of the untutored Ukrainian peasant appeared crude and of limited application. Ukrainian nobles would use the language only to discuss simple and mundane domestic matters with their peasants. Among the educated, the view prevailed that as peasants had little to say of importance and as their way of saying it was crude anyway, it was pointless to raise peasant speech to the level of a literary language. Moreover, because Ukrainian was closely related to Russian, many members of the intelligentsia argued that Ukrainian was not a distinct language but merely a dialect of Russian.

Nevertheless, despite these daunting obstacles, some members of the Ukrainian intelligentsia attempted to refine and uplift the vernacular. But even these pioneers initially had doubts about the viability of their undertaking and they approached the task only as a curious literary experiment. An example was Ivan Kotliarevsky's *Eneida*, the first work ever written in the language of the Ukrainian peasants and townsmen. Its appearance in 1798 marked the advent of Ukrainian as a literary language and of modern Ukrainian literature as well.

Significantly enough, the *Eneida* was a travesty, a burlesque poem. Based on the famous *Aeneid* by the Latin poet Virgil, it portrayed the ancient Greek heroes and Olympian gods as rollicking Cossacks and lusty village maidens who spoke in the pithy and colorful Ukrainian vernacular. Kotliarevsky, a tsarist official and himself the son of a minor Cossack officer, liked to mix with the Ukrainian peasants, note down their customs, and listen to their speech and songs. At first, he did not believe that his linguistic experiment was worthy of publication. Only the urging of his friends persuaded him to publish the *Eneida*, which to his surprise enjoyed instant success among the Left Bank gentry. However, even then Kotliarevsky did not realize that his work represented a linguistic and literary turning point. It merely proved to him that Ukrainian, a language that he loved and in which he continued to write, could be used effectively for comic effect. But he retained his doubts about its usefulness in "serious" literature.

Similarly tentative were the efforts of Oleksii Pavlovsky, who wrote a "Grammar of the Little Russian Dialect" in 1818. The author's attitude toward the Ukrainian language was ambivalent, for although he wished to refine it, he still regarded it as a dialect of Russian. But Pavlovsky's achievement, like that of Ivan Voitsekhovych, who in 1823 compiled a small dictionary of Ukrainian, was significant.

Literature: the enrichment of Ukrainian national culture   The ultimate test of the viability of the Ukrainian language resided in the quality and range of the literature produced in it. Kotliarevsky earned the epithet "father of modern Ukrainian literature" not just because he was the first to write in the Ukrainian vernacular, but also because his *Eneida* was of high literary merit. His success, however, encouraged a host of feeble imitations of his classic, temporarily impeding the development of other genres. For a time, it appeared that written Ukrainian would be used exclusively in jocular, folksy, regionalistic burlesques rather than in "serious" literary productions.

Much of the credit for expanding the range of literary expression in Ukrainian belongs to the Kharkiv Romantics, as they were called. Most of these writers were based in Sloboda Ukraine and were associated with the newly founded Kharkiv University. In the 1820s and 1830s, this easternmost of ethnic Ukrainian lands took its turn in playing the leading role in Ukrainian cultural development.

It was allegedly a wager between Petro Hulak Artemovsky (the son of a priest and rector of Kharkiv University) and Hryhorii Kvitka Osnovianenko (the scion of a prominent Cossack family) that hastened the development of Ukrainian prose. Hulak, who had a strong affinity for Ukrainian and experimented with it in literature, was convinced that its future was dim: "The thought that perhaps the time is near when not only traces of Little Russian customs and antiquity will disappear forever, but also the language itself will merge with the huge river of the mighty, dominant Russian language and will not leave any trace of its existence, plunges me into such melancholy that there are moments when I feel like renouncing all my ambitions and going away to the peaceful refuge of the simple villager in order to catch the last sounds of the native tongue which is dying every day."[10]

Because the Ukrainian nobles were abandoning Ukrainian for Russian and it was only the villagers who spoke it, Hulak argued that the language could not be used to produce serious literature. Kvitka disagreed with him and resolved to prove his point. In 1834, he wrote his "Little Russian Stories by Hrytsko Osnovianenko." These sad, sentimental tales were well received and the astute Osyp Bodiansky quickly proclaimed that they heralded the beginning of Ukrainian prose writing.

Levko Borovykovsky, another Kharkiv writer, further expanded the range of Ukrainian literary genres by composing ballads in Ukrainian. The favorite, indeed almost exclusive, theme of the Kharkiv writers was Cossack Ukraine, which was portrayed in typical Romantic fashion as a sad echo of the glorious past. These mournful ruminations about the past were epitomized by Ambrozii Metlynsky, a professor of Russian literature at Kharkiv University, whose own collections of Ukrainian poetry and translations he characterized as "the work of the last *bandurist* who passes on the song of the past in a dying language."[11]

A myriad of other, minor writers in Kharkiv also contributed to the growth of Ukrainian prose and poetry. Surprisingly, the moving spirit behind much of this literary activity was a Russian – Izmail Sreznevsky – who later became one of Russia's leading philologists. However, the contributions of this fervent convert to things Ukrainian were more on the organizational than on the literary level. Sreznevsky's multivolume anthologies of Ukrainian literature, entitled "Zaporozhian Antiquities" and "Ukrainian Anthology," represented an attempt to address the serious problem of the lack of a suitable forum for Ukrainian writers. The only regularly published journals on the Left Bank, the "Ukrainian Herald" and the "Ukrainian Journal," appeared in Kharkiv in the 1830s, mostly in Russian. Little more than a potpourri of local news, travelogues, ethnographic materials, and some literary works, these journals had a small readership, numbering only several hundred.

To reach a broader and more sophisticated audience, Ukrainian writers often turned to Russian journals published in St Petersburg and Moscow. Many of these, especially the more conservative, were quite willing to publish Ukrainian stories, even those written in Ukrainian. In fact, among Russian Romantic writers of the 1820s and 1830s, there existed something of a vogue for things Ukrainian. To many Russians, the turbulent history and rich folklore of the land evoked fascinating, exotic images, not the least of which was that of Ukraine as a "wild frontier." But although they acknowledged its distinctiveness, they considered Ukraine to be an integral part of Russia and viewed the promotion of Ukrainian "regional" literature merely as an enrichment of general Russian culture. A similar fascination with Ukraine existed among some Polish writers of the time, such as Antoni Malczewski, Bogdan Zaleski, and Seweryn Goszczynski, who formed the so-called Ukrainian School in Polish Romantic literature. They, for their part, viewed Ukraine as part of Poland's historical and cultural heritage.

Thus, despite the progress in Ukrainian literature and scholarship, the intelligentsia of the early 19th century continued to regard Ukraine and Ukrainians in "regionalist" terms. It did not as yet believe that Ukrainian culture could ever develop to the point of displacing Russian cultural dominance in Ukraine. Like their Russian colleagues in St Petersburg and Moscow, Ukrainian literati were convinced that, in cultivating things Ukrainian, they were also enriching the cultural heritage of Russia as a whole. Yet, their work and their efforts would have ramifications that neither Ukrainians nor Russians could foresee. These have been lucidly summarized by George Luckyj: "If one assumes that these early Ukrainian historical and folkloristic researches are the first stirrings of modern Ukrainian consciousness, one must conclude that they provided it with a firm foundation. For what can be more urgent to the needs of an emerging nation than to find its historical origins and its cultural distinctiveness? For the time being, Ukrainians were busy doing just this and discovering thereby their basic identity."[12]

Shevchenko

A peculiar situation evolved among the Ukrainian intelligentsia in the early 19th century. As we have seen, the intellectual currents that permeated much of Eastern Europe and Russia did not bypass Ukraine. The radical, republican ideas of the French Revolution were well represented in Ukraine by the Decembrists and the Ukrainian members of the Union of Slavs, while Herder's philosophical concepts regarding national culture clearly inspired the writings of the Kharkiv Romantics. Yet in Ukraine, political activism and nation-centered cultural activity did not mesh: political radicals remained anational, reserving no place for Ukraine in their political schemes, while the propagators of Ukrainian national culture were apolitical conservatives committed to the tsar and the status quo. This dichotomy, which crippled both ideological tendencies and eventually became a chronic weakness of the Ukrainian intelligentsia, did not seem to trouble the generation of the 1820s. However, for the next generation – that of the 1840s – the synthesis of national culture and political ideology would become a major concern.

The generation of the 1840s, which included individuals such as the historian Kostomarov, the author Kulish, and the poet Shevchenko, was based not in Kharkiv, but in Kiev where a new university had been founded in 1834. Its members hailed from both the Right Bank and the Left Bank and their social origins were more varied than those of their gentry predecessors.

Among the young men of the 1840s, one individual – Taras Shevchenko – towered above the rest. Indeed, it may be argued that Shevchenko's impact on his countrymen was greater than that of any other Ukrainian in modern history. That a poet should have attained such preeminence in a developing nation of 19th-century Eastern Europe is not unusual. Cultural activity was the one arena in which the stateless Slavs could express their individuality, so poets, writers, and scholars often played leading roles as "national awakeners." Nevertheless, it is difficult to find another example of an individual whose poetry and personality so completely embodied a national ethos as did Shevchenko for the Ukrainians.

For his countrymen, Shevchenko's biography symbolized his nation's sad fate. Born in 1814 in Moryntsi, a village on the Right Bank, Shevchenko grew up as an orphaned serf. When his master took him along as a servant to St Petersburg, the youth's talents as a painter attracted the attention of several leading artists who, in 1838, helped him to buy his freedom. Shevchenko then entered the Imperial Academy of the Arts where he obtained a first-rate education. Meanwhile, his growing contacts with the numerous Ukrainian and Russian artists and writers in the capital greatly broadened his intellectual horizons. Soon he was consumed by the need to express himself in poetry. In 1840, his first collection of Ukrainian poems, entitled *Kobzar* ("The Bard"), appeared in print. Based largely on Ukrainian historical themes, these powerful, direct, and melodious poems were quickly hailed as the work of a genius by Ukrainian and Russian critics alike.

The appearance of the *Kobzar*, as George Luckyj notes, was the single most important event in the history of Ukrainian literature because "in his work the Ukrainian language achieved for the first time literary excellence."[13] It transcended the one-dimensional, limited role that Ukrainian literature had fulfilled up until now and disproved the views of those, such as the famous Russian critic Vissarion Belinsky, who believed that the language of the Ukrainian peasant was incapable of expressing cultivated thoughts and feelings. In reply to Belinsky's belittling view of Ukrainian, Shevchenko wrote:

You've given me a sheepskin coat
Alas, it does not fit.
The garment of your own wise speech
Is lined with falsehood's wit.[14]

Shevchenko's success also countered the example set by his contemporary fellow Ukrainian Nikolai Gogol, who believed that if talented Ukrainians wished to attain literary fame and fortune they could do so only within the context of Russian literature.

Shevchenko expanded the flexibility, range, and resources of Ukrainian by synthesizing several Ukrainian dialects, the colloquialisms of peasants and townsmen, and the forms and vocabulary of Church Slavonic. In so doing, he demonstrated to his countrymen that their language could express the fullest range of emotions and ideas with splendid artistry; he thereby proved that Ukrainians did not need to depend on Russian as a vehicle of higher discourse. His poetry became in effect a literary and intellectual declaration of Ukrainian independence.

Shevchenko's concerns and impact radiated far beyond the literary sphere. The former serf never forgot his "unfortunate brothers" and in the thundering tones of a biblical prophet he castigated the exploiters of the enserfed peasantry. Unlike most of his colleagues among the intelligentsia, Shevchenko did not believe in liberal, gradualistic projects of reform. His poems openly advocated radical, revolutionary solutions to injustice in society. In his famous *Zapovit* ("Testament"), Shevchenko called upon his countrymen to bury him on a steep cliff above the Dnieper and then to rise in revolt:

Make my grave there – and arise,
Sundering your chains,
Bless your freedom with blood
of foemen's evil vein!
Then in that great family,
A family new and free,
Do not forget, with good intent
Speak quietly of me.[15]

Inextricably interwoven with Shevchenko's anger about social injustice was his bitterness about national oppression in Ukraine, "this land of ours that is not ours," as he described it. An implacable enemy of tsarist autocracy, he called for Ukrainian self-determination long before his more cautious colleagues espoused the idea. This stand is clearly evident in his treatment of Ukrainian history, his favorite theme. For Shevchenko, Khmelnytsky was a "genial rebel," but also the man responsible for Ukraine's fateful union with Russia that resulted in the loss of Ukrainian self-rule. Cossack leaders who stood up to the tsars, such as Polubotok, earned his sympathy; those who cooperated with Moscow were severely criticized. Shevchenko did not mask his hatred of Peter I whom he called a "tyrant" and "torturer" and Catherine II did not fare better with him. In response to the praise of these monarchs by Aleksander Pushkin, Russia's greatest poet, Shevchenko wrote:

Now I understand
It was the First who
crucified our Ukraine
And the Second finished
off the widowed orphan.
Murderers! Murderers! Cannibals![16]

But Shevchenko's nationalism was not of the narrow, chauvinistic variety. He viewed Ukraine's striving for freedom as part of a universal struggle for justice. As the poems "The Heretic," dedicated to Jan Hus, the famous Czech martyr, and "Caucasus" suggest, he sympathized with downtrodden peoples all over the world.

Shevchenko's poetry, some of it so rebellious that it was not published until 1905, exposed his contemporaries to new and unsettling ideas and emotions. After reading it, the historian Kostomarov wrote that "Shevchenko's muse tore away the shrouds that shielded us from the life of the people and it was terrible, sweet, painful and intoxicating to behold."[17] Shevchenko forced his colleagues to see in the *narod* (the people) not merely colorful customs, but their suffering. In Cossack history he sought not romantic heroes, but lessons that would lead to a better future. For him Ukraine was not just a picturesque region of the Russian Empire, but a land that could and should stand on its own.

The Brotherhood of Sts Cyril and Methodius

On 3 March 1847, Aleksei Petrov, a student at Kiev University, informed the tsarist authorities about a secret society that he had accidentally discovered. The police quickly swooped down on the leading members of the group, brought them to St Petersburg, and subjected them to intense interrogation during which the authorities learned of the existence of the Brotherhood of Sts Cyril and Methodius, the first Ukrainian ideological organization in modern times.

It soon became apparent that the original fears on the part of the authorities about a large, dangerous underground movement were greatly exaggerated. The brotherhood consisted of only about a dozen core members and perhaps several dozen sympathizers. Led by Mykola Kostomarov (the talented historian and university lecturer), Vasyl Bilozersky (a teacher of gentry background), and Mykola Hulak (a minor but well educated bureaucrat), the group consisted of young members of the Ukrainian intelligentsia. Although two other intellectuals – the secondary schoolteacher and writer Panteleimon Kulish and the already well-known poet Taras Shevchenko – were only loosely associated with the brotherhood, they too were arrested. Not only was the membership of the brotherhood small, but its activity was limited. During the approximately fourteen months of its existence, the "brothers" met several times for lengthy philosophical and political discussions (one of which had been overheard by the informant, Petrov) and prepared several statements of their program and goals.

The most important of these statements, formulated by Kostomarov, was entitled "The Law of God" or "The Book of Genesis of the Ukrainian People" (*Zakon bozhyi* or *Knyhy bytiia ukrainskoho narodu*). Written in the Romantic, idealistic spirit of the times, the work (which was permeated with Christian values and Pan-Slavic sentiments and was strongly influenced by Polish models) called for the restructuring of society on the principles of justice, equality, freedom, and fraternity. Specifically, it proposed the liquidation of serfdom, the abolition of legal distinctions among estates, and access to education for the masses. The issue of nationality, which was clearly a major concern for the brotherhood, was placed in a broad Pan-Slavic context: all Slavic peoples should be allowed to develop their cultures freely and, more important, they should form a Slavic federation with democratic institutions "akin to those of the United States." The capital of this federation was to be Kiev.

Ukraine, which Kostomarov and his colleagues considered to be at the same time the most oppressed and the most egalitarian of all Slavic societies because of its alleged lack of an elite, was to lead the way in the creation of the federation. The Christ-like resurrection of the land was described in pseudo-biblical style: "And Ukraine was destroyed. But it only appeared to be so ... because the voice of Ukraine was not stilled. Ukraine will rise from her grave and will call upon her brother Slavs; they will hear her call and all Slavs will arise ... and Ukraine will be a self-governing republic in the Slavic union. Then all the peoples will point to that spot on the map where Ukraine is situated and they will say, 'Behold, the stone which the builders rejected has become the cornerstone.'"[18] This messianic vision of Ukraine's future in the federation, although buttressed by a highly idealized picture of its past, precluded the idea of its complete independence. Apparently, most members of the brotherhood, with the exception of Shevchenko and a few others, had doubts about the ability of their "soft," "poetical" countrymen to stand on their own.

Although they agreed on general principles, the members of the group differed on issues of priority and emphasis. For Kostomarov, Slavic unity and fraternity were most important; Shevchenko was passionate in demanding the social and national emancipation of Ukrainians; and Kulish stressed the development of Ukrainian culture. The majority favored an evolutionary approach, hoping that general education, propaganda, and the setting of "moral examples" to the authorities would be most effective in the attainment of their goals. Shevchenko and Hulak, in contrast, represented the minority view that only revolution could bring about the desired changes. Yet, these differences ought not to be exaggerated. The members of the brotherhood were clearly united by their common values and ideals and, most notably, by their desire to improve the socioeconomic, cultural, and political plight of Ukraine.

Despite the relatively harmless nature of the society, the tsarist authorities resolved to punish its leading members. The punishments varied greatly in severity, however. Kostomarov, Kulish, and the other moderates received comparatively light sentences consisting of banishment to the depths of Russia for periods of a year or less, after which they were allowed to resume their careers. Hulak received a three-year prison sentence. But the severest sentence was reserved for Shevchenko, whom the tsar and his officials regarded as the most dangerous member of the group. He was forcibly conscripted and assigned to a ten-year term in a labor battalion in Siberia. Nicholas I himself added the following note to the sentence: "under the strictest supervision, forbidden to write and sketch."[19] The physical and psychological suffering that resulted from this sentence contributed to Shevchenko's untimely death in 1861.

The Brotherhood of Sts Cyril and Methodius and its liquidation were significant for several reasons. It represented the first, albeit unsuccessful, attempt of the intelligentsia to move from the cultural to the political phase of national development; it alerted the tsarist government (which until this time had tried to play Ukrainophilism off against Polish cultural influences in Ukraine) to the potential dangers of growing Ukrainian national consciousness; it signaled the onset of an anti-Ukrainian policy and marked the beginning of the long, unceasing struggle between the Ukrainian intelligentsia and the imperial Russian authorities.

The Growth of National Consciousness in Western Ukraine

Ukrainian cultural activity was distributed very unevenly. For the most part, it was concentrated on the Left Bank, the territory of the former Hetmanate, and in Sloboda Ukraine. In other areas of Russian-ruled Ukraine, there was little evidence of interest in Ukrainian folk culture. On the Right Bank, a few Polish noblemen – such as Tymko Padura, Michał Czajkowski, and Zorian Dołęga-Chodakowski – developed a highly romanticized vision of Ukraine's Cossack past and dreamed of a time when the Ukrainian peasantry, forgetting its grievances against the *szlachta*, would help to bring the Right Bank into a reconstituted Polish Commonwealth. This tendency made little head way, however, against the Polish cultural hegemony that predominated on the Right Bank. As for the newly colonized Black Sea regions, there were prac tically no signs of Ukrainophilism there.

In Western, or Austrian, Ukraine, evidence of Ukrainian cultural activity in the early 19th century was also very spotty. In such isolated, backward re gions as Romanian-dominated Bukovyna and Hungarian-dominated Trans carpathia, it was almost nonexistent. Only in Eastern Galicia did Ukrain ophilism, even more tentative and narrowly based than on the Left Bank succeed in establishing a foothold.

The West Ukrainian intelligentsia To speak of the West Ukrainian intelli gentsia in the early 19th century is to speak of the clergy. Indeed, because the clergy was the only social group that could avail itself of the opportuni ties for higher learning provided by the Austrian Empire, higher education in Western Ukraine became practically synonymous with the study of theology Thus, in the early 1840s, of the approximately 400 Ukrainian students at Lviv University and other institutions, 295 studied theology while almost all the rest were enrolled in philosophy courses, which were a prerequisite for the ology. Another example of this clerical preponderance is the fact that of the forty-three Ukrainian-language books that appeared between 1837 and 1850 forty were written by priests.

Only in the latter part of the 19th century would a secular intelligentsia composed of teachers, lawyers, scholars, writers, and bureaucrats, become a significant factor in Western Ukraine. Conversely, one should not assume that every priest was an intellectual. The vast majority of the clergy were poor and isolated village priests, whose education and intellectual horizons were only marginally broader than those of the peasants to whom they ministered. It was only a small minority based in cities such as Lviv and Peremyshl (which were centers of ecclesiastical administration and had institutions of higher learning, libraries, and printing presses) that had an opportunity to engage in cultural activities.

Even where such opportunities existed, the inbred conservatism of the clergy and its slavish loyalty to the Habsburgs discouraged intellectual growth. Provincial and conservative, the thin, educated stratum of Western Ukraine looked with extreme suspicion on new ideas and preferred to ex pend its limited intellectual resources on secondary (but furiously debated issues such as those dealing with alphabets, calendars, and church proce dures. For the few who sought to explore more radical Western ideas or to become involved in revolutionary activity, the only avenue open was in the Polish context. As a result, in the 1830s, a small number of young Ukrainian seminarians joined Polish revolutionary groups that were striving to rebuild the Polish Commonwealth and who viewed Ukrainians as nothing more than a confused and backward branch of the Polish nation.

The attractions of the prestigious Polish culture, even to the most traditionalist members of the clergy-intelligentsia, were so great that – as the legal, educational, and material standing of the West Ukrainian elite improved – they began to emulate Polish ways. Upward mobility had linguistic ramifications and the more a Ukrainian improved his social status, the more embarrassed he became about using the language of the peasantry.

As a result, the use of Polish gradually became more widespread among the clergy and intelligentsia, and Ukrainian was confined more and more to communication with the peasants. A telling example of the decline in the use of Ukrainian (that is, of the artificial and unwieldy mixture of the vernacular, Church Slavonic, and Latin, Polish, and German words that passed for literary Ukrainian at this time) by the educated, was the dismantling of the Ukrainian-language Studium Ruthenum at Lviv University in 1809. Paradoxically, it was brought about not by the Poles or Austrians, but by Ukrainians themselves. Because all other courses at the university were taught in German, the Ukrainian students at the Studium Ruthenum considered it discriminatory that they too were not taught in that language and they readily agreed to have it replace Ukrainian.

But if higher education highlighted the inadequacies of the Ukrainian language, it also produced its defenders. While pursuing their studies in Lviv or Vienna, some Ukrainians could not help but hear about the ideas of Herder concerning the importance of one's native language. Often they came into contact with Polish or especially Czech intellectuals who were far ahead of other Slavs in the Habsburg empire in terms of national consciousness and cultural development. Inspired by the successes of their neighbors, a small but growing number of West Ukrainian members of the intelligentsia, despite the discouraging milieu in which they lived, began to develop an appreciation of the new idea of Ukrainian nationhood.

The "national awakeners" in Western Ukraine   The first signs of growing interest in the cultural aspects of nationhood appeared in the early 19th century in the ancient city of Peremyshl, the seat of a Greek Catholic eparchy, site of a lyceum and rich libraries, and the home of some of the most sophisticated members of the Ukrainian clergy. For several decades, this westernmost city on Ukrainian-speaking territory would perform for Austria's Ukrainians a role in the development of national consciousness that was analogous to the role played by Kharkiv, on Ukraine's easternmost fringe, for Russia's Ukrainians at approximately the same time. However, it ought to be stressed that it was from the Kharkiv Romantics that the Peremyshl clerics, with their more limited literary and creative talents, took their cue.

Among the members of the Peremyshl circle, Ivan Mohylnytsky, a highly placed churchman and superintendent of primary education in the eparchy, was the most prominent. In 1816, with the support of his superior, Bishop Mykhailo Levytsky, Mohylnytsky organized a group of clergymen into a Clerical Society, the purpose of which was to prepare and distribute simple religious texts, written in Ukrainian, to the peasantry. Considering the Polonophile attitudes that were predominant at the time, this act was viewed as an unorthodox undertaking. Mohylnytsky and his colleagues were apparently not motivated solely by Herder's ideas or East Ukrainian examples, an important realization was that if Polish-language materials alone became available to the peasants, they might turn to Roman Catholicism.

Although the results of the society's efforts, which consisted of the publication of several prayer books and primers, were modest and the group soon disbanded, its appearance was noteworthy: it was the first attempt of the Ukrainian intelligentsia, both in the west and in the east, to organize itself; and more important, it focused attention on the language issue that would remain for decades a key concern of the West Ukrainian intelligentsia. However, in his attempts to "improve" the vernacular, Mohylnytsky insisted on using it with many Church Slavonic admixtures. The resulting artificial linguistic hybrid did little to dispel questions about the appropriateness of Ukrainian for literary use.

In addition to the Peremyshl circle, in the 1820s a few isolated Western Ukrainian scholars appeared who, in the spirit of collectors and antiquarians, gathered materials about the history of Eastern Galicia and its native folklore. Some of the members of this small group were the historians Mykhailo Harasevych and Denys Zubrytsky, as well as such grammarians and ethnographers as Iosyf Levytsky and Iosyf Lozynsky. But, because their works were written in Latin, German, or Polish, their impact was limited.

The Ruthenian Triad   In the 1830s, the center of national consciousness-raising activity shifted to Lviv, where young, idealistic seminarians, captivated by Herder's ideas, came to the fore. Their leader was Markian Shashkevych, a 21-year-old youth endowed with poetical talent and an inspiring personality. Together with his two close associates, the scholarly Ivan Vahylevych and the energetic Iakiv Holovatsky, they formed what is commonly referred to as the Ruthenian Triad. In 1832, they organized a group of students that set for itself the ambitious goal of raising the Ukrainian vernacular, free of Church Slavonic and other foreign "refinements," to the level of a literary language. Only this, they believed, would give the peasants access to the knowledge that might improve their lot and allow Ukrainians to express their long-suppressed cultural individuality.

To the Greek Catholic authorities, the idea of writing in the plain, unmodified language of the peasantry in a simplified Cyrillic script seemed outlandish. In no uncertain terms they let Shashkevych and his associates know that they could expect no support from the church for their undertaking. But encouragement did come from Russian-ruled Ukraine, where the Ruthenian Triad established contacts with such Ukrainophiles as Izmail Sreznevsky, Mykhailo Maksymovych, and Osyp Bodiansky. And from the west came the inspiring example of the flourishing Czech national movement. With the help of Karel Zap, a Czech intellectual serving in the administration of Galicia, the threesome, especially Holovatsky, developed a lively correspondence with such experienced "national awakeners" and avid Slavophiles as the Slovaks Ján Kollár and Pavel Šafarik, the Slovene Bartholomeus Kopitar, and the Czech Karel Havliček.

To set their plans in motion, the Ruthenian Triad resolved to publish an almanac, entitled *Rusalka Dnistrovaia* ("The Nymph of the Dnister"), which would contain folk songs, poems, and historical articles written in the vernacular. When news of the almanac reached the Greek Catholic hierarchy, they condemned it as being "undignified, indecent, and possibly subversive."[20] Meanwhile, the German police chief of Lviv noted: "We already have enough trouble with one nationality [the Poles], and these madmen want to resurrect the dead-and-buried Ruthenian nation."[21] The local censor, Venedikt Levytsky, a Greek Catholic clergyman, blocked publication of the almanac in Lviv, so Shashkevych and his colleagues were forced to publish it in far-off Budapest in 1837. Of the 900 copies that were transported to Lviv, almost all were confiscated by the police. Only a handful found their way into the hands of a skeptical public. Disillusioned by this response and hounded by church authorities, Markian Shashkevych died a young man; Vahylevych eventually joined the Polish camp; Holovatsky alone, carefully but stubbornly, continued to work for the attainment of the Ruthenian Triad's original goals.

Although the publication of the *Rusalka Dnistrovaia* initially appeared to be a fiasco, it set an important precedent, demonstrating in Western Ukraine that the language of the Ukrainian peasant could in fact be used as a literary language. Moreover, it focused attention on the common people and their "unspoiled" culture. Under the influence of the *Rusalka Dnistrovaia*, a new generation of Western Ukrainian intelligentsia would begin the slow, yet irreversible, process of shifting its orientation to the Ukrainian masses from among whom it would draw most of its members.

৯৪

The spread of the idea of nationhood in Ukraine was, as we have seen, a laborious and halting process. At the mid 19th century, it had not progressed far beyond the point of small groups of Ukrainian intelligentsia defining for themselves the essential ingredients of a Ukrainian cultural identity. Hurdles to progress beyond this cultural phase were numerous and daunting. Except for the intelligentsia, there were no social groups in Ukraine – an agrarian, traditionalist, and provincial society – that were receptive to new ideas. Moreover, the view that Ukrainians were a separate nationality and that their language and culture were worth cultivating found numerous skeptics and detractors among Ukrainians themselves. The pull of the prestigious, more highly developed cultures of the Poles and Russians was difficult to withstand. Yet, inspired by Western examples and convinced that they were responding to the needs of the idealized "*narod*," the "national awakeners" persevered.

From the outset, there were important differences in the spread of national consciousness in Eastern and Western Ukraine. On the Left Bank, where Cossack traditions and the memory of self-government were still strong and the intelligentsia more numerous and sophisticated, national consciousness-raising activity got off to a promising start. However, the harsh treatment of the Brotherhood of Sts Cyril and Methodius revealed that once the Ukrainian movement in the Russian Empire transcended certain limits, it faced an implacable and overwhelming enemy in the tsarist government. In Eastern Galicia, progress was more modest and much of the resistance was due to the conservatism of the Greek Catholic establishment. Nonetheless, there were no dramatic setbacks there and the growth of national consciousness, although sluggish, was perceptible. Finally, the parallel, if differing, development had another important consequence: after centuries of limited contact, East and West Ukrainians began to evince a growing interest in each other. The process of national integration had begun.

Imperial Reforms

Conservatism reigned supreme in all of Europe in the middle of the 19th century but nowhere was it more evident than in Austria and Russia, the two empires inhabited by Ukrainians. For them, as for the other subjects, their lives and minds were dominated by the principles of authoritarianism, obedience, social order, and traditionalism. Change, in every form, was looked upon with great suspicion. Nevertheless, the new ideas, social forces, and economic relationships that were permeating Europe also seeped into the Austrian and Russian domains, despite strenuous efforts to restrain them. As internal and external pressures mounted, the Habsburg and Romanov emperors realized that the old order could no longer remain impervious to change. This realization, born of crisis, generated an era of great reforms – first in Austria and then in Russia. These reforms had an especially great impact on the Ukrainians because they were among the most disadvantaged subjects of both empires.

ॐ

Change in the Austrian Empire

At the beginning of 1848, the Habsburg ruling elite was confident about the future of the empire. One reason for its confidence was the recent Habsburg success in dealing with such trouble-spots as Galicia, where small groups of Polish nobles and intelligentsia had conspired for decades to restore the old Commonwealth. Convinced that they stood for general political freedom, the Poles had always assumed that all inhabitants of the dismembered Commonwealth, regardless of their social or ethnic status, supported their goals. This attitude was reinforced in the 1830s when a group of Ukrainian seminarians joined the Polish conspiratorial cells. However, when their Polish colleagues refused to recognize them as a separate nationality, the Ukrainians withdrew.

In 1846, Polish assumptions about widespread support suffered an even more devastating blow. Upon learning that Polish nobles were planning an uprising, Austrian officials convinced the peasants of Western Galicia that their lords intended to continue their unlimited exploitation of them as of old. Infuriated, Polish peasants turned on their own nobles, massacring great numbers of them and thereby undermining the abortive revolt.

The revolution of 1848 in Galicia   The series of revolts that engulfed much of Europe in spring 1848 signaled a dramatic change in Habsburg fortunes. These revolts, brought on not just by demands for political and socioeconomic reform, but also, in central and Eastern Europe in particular, by the awakening desire for national sovereignty, hit hard at the conservative, multinational empire. During this "spring of nations," when nationhood emerged as the paramount political issue, the Habsburgs' German and Italian subjects rose up to demand unification with their brethren outside the empire. Simultaneously, the Hungarians commenced a war of national independence, and the Poles once again agitated for the restoration of their lost statehood. Influenced by these events, other peoples of the empire also proceeded to formulate their national demands. As chaos ensued, the empire appeared to be on the verge of collapse.

When news of the riots in Vienna, of the resignation of the hated Prince Metternich, and of the promises of the badly shaken Emperor Ferdinand to implement political liberalization and social reform reached Lviv on 19 March 1848, the Poles immediately sprang into action. They sent off a petition to the emperor calling for even more liberalization and greater political rights for Poles in Galicia, but they totally ignored any mention of the Ukrainian presence in the province. To mobilize support for these demands, a Polish National Council was organized in Lviv on 13 April. Soon afterwards, a network of local councils and a newspaper were founded. To the great surprise and disappointment of the Poles, the Ukrainians – whom the Poles did not consider a separate nationality – rejected invitations to join in these efforts. Instead, they formed their own representative body, the Supreme Ruthenian Council (Holovna Ruska Rada), along with a system of local branches and a newspaper. Fortunately for the Habsburgs, they had an unusually intelligent and enterprising defender of their interests in Galicia in the person of Count Franz Stadion, the recently appointed governor of the province. In the tense situation that developed in Galicia, he was able to manipulate skillfully the key issues and play the Ukrainians and Poles off against each other in a generally successful attempt to retain Habsburg control over the province.

From the Ukrainian point of view, there were two main and closely intertwined issues that predominated in 1848. One was socioeconomic in nature and dealt with the traditional problem of the peasantry, particularly its crushing feudal obligations to the landlords. The other was concerned with the new concept of nationality and, specifically, how two peoples – the Poles and Ukrainians – who had until recently always viewed themselves simply as peasants or noblemen, Greek Catholics or Roman Catholics, but who were now beginning to define themselves as separate and distinct ethno-cultural communities or nations (with competing national aspirations) were to coexist in a single province.

The peasant problem   Already for many years prior to 1848, it was clear to open-minded bureaucrats, liberal intelligentsia, and even some noblemen that the feudal rights the landlord nobility exercised over the peasants who worked on its estates were badly outdated. As early as the 1780s, during the reign of Joseph II, major changes were introduced in the landlord/peasant relationship. The most important of these was that the peasants obtained the right to defend their interests in court. Another reform distinguished the landlord's lands from those lands set aside for the use of peasants. However, a major feature of the feudal lord/peasant relationship, namely corvée (*pan-hchyna* in Ukrainian), remained – especially in the less advanced areas of the empire, such as Galicia. Corvée was the obligation of peasants to work on the lands of their lord, usually two or three days per week, in return for the use of their plots. It was this hated obligation that was the cause of most dissatisfaction and bitterness among the Galician peasantry.

The revolution of 1848, and particularly the tense situation it engendered in Galicia, finally created the conditions for the abolition of this last vestige of serfdom. Having learned their lesson in 1846, Polish patriots – mostly nobles – now eagerly sought the goodwill of the peasantry in an effort to strengthen their position in Galicia. To this end, they urged their fellow Polish noblemen to abolish the hated corvée voluntarily. The nobility's response was generally negative, however. Nevertheless, Polish tactics were so worrisome to Stadion that he desperately urged Vienna to take the lead in freeing the peasants of their obligations. He argued that this would not only check Polish designs, but it would also win the gratitude of the peasants for the monarchy at a most critical moment. Persuaded by these arguments, Emperor Ferdinand issued the historic manifesto abolishing the corvée in Galicia on 23 April 1848. It preceded a similar patent banning the corvée in the rest of the empire by about five months.

Stadion's plan succeeded. Ukrainian peasants in particular greeted the announcement with enthusiasm and pledged their loyalty to the Habsburgs (although it was clear that the patent left many questions unanswered). To mollify the nobles, the Viennese government announced that it would pay them for the lost labor. (Later it shifted about two-thirds of the cost of this indemnity onto the peasantry itself.) Furthermore, although the peasants received 70% of the cultivated lands and the landlords 30%, the crucial question of who owned the forests and pastures – lands previously held in common – was not

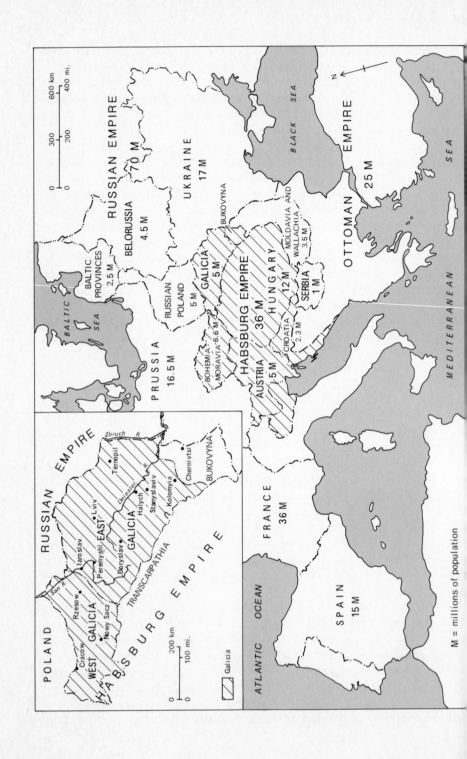

M = millions of population

esolved. In time, landlords would obtain ownership of these common lands ind peasants would become dependent on them for the all-important fire- vood and grazing land. Finally, the size of peasant allotments was pitifully mall: over 70% of these were less than fourteen acres, an area that at best arely allowed for the subsistence of an average family.

This is not to say, however, that the impact of the abolition of the corvée panshchyna) on the peasant was slight; on the contrary, it cut the last formal ond between him and his lord (pan) and made the peasant outright owner if his own land. By making the Galician peasant master of his own fate, it wakened in him an interest in political, educational, and even cultural issues hat he had never before evinced. From this time onward, the West Ukrainian easant would become a political factor that could no longer be ignored.

he nationality issue The revolution of 1848 provided the small, educated egment of West Ukrainian society (which consisted chiefly of members of he clergy and intelligentsia) with the impetus and the opportunity to define hemselves formally as a distinct nationality and to establish their own na- ional institutions. The timid West Ukrainian elite was strongly encouraged nd supported by the Habsburg governor, Stadion, who openly favored the Jkrainians throughout 1848 in hopes of using them as a counterweight to he more aggressive Poles. Because of Stadion's policies, the Poles would or many years accuse the Habsburgs of "inventing the Ruthenians" (i.e., Jkrainians), implying thereby that the Ukrainians were merely a by-product if Austrian machinations and not a genuine nationality. Nonetheless, flat- ered by government attention and resentful of Polish attitudes, the Ukraini- ns resolved for the first time in the modern era to enter the political arena.

On 19 April, at the instigation of Stadion, a group of Greek Catholic cler- ymen, associated with St George's cathedral in Lviv and led by Bishop Hry- orii Iakhymovych, addressed a petition to the emperor. Unlike the earlier 'olish appeal, it was a timid, loyalist document. Its introduction consisted if a historical survey stressing the national distinctiveness of the Ukrainians if Eastern Galicia, the past glories of the medieval principality of Halych, s subsequent subjugation and exploitation by the Poles, and the fact that he populace "belonged to the great Ruthenian [Ukrainian] nation, whose 15 illion members, of whom 2.5 live in Galicia, all speak the same language."[1]

The petition itself requested the introduction of the Ukrainian language n the schools and administration of Eastern Galicia, access to government ositions for Ukrainians, and the genuine equalization of the Greek and Ro- nan Catholic clergy. Two weeks later, on 2 May 1848, the Supreme Ruthenian ouncil, the first modern Ukrainian political organization, was established n Lviv. Led by Bishop Iakhymovych, it consisted of sixty-six members, al- nost half of whom consisted of clergy and theology students and the other alf of the secular intelligentsia. In the weeks that followed, fifty local and hirteen regional branches of the Supreme Ruthenian Council were estab-

lished throughout Eastern Galicia by priests who acted as the chief organiz
ers. Another unprecedented event was the publication of the first Ukrainia
weekly, *Zoria Halytska*, on 15 May. Meanwhile, contacts with the Ukrainian
of Bukovyna and Transcarpathia were also established.

The rise of Ukrainian political activism in Eastern Galicia necessarily led t
the growth of Ukrainian/Polish antagonism. Because the Poles considere
Galicia to be the cornerstone of their plan to restore Polish statehood, the
regarded the emergence of a Ukrainian movement that was pro-Vienna as
grave threat. Therefore, they attempted to neutralize the Supreme Ruthenia
Council by forming a rival "Ukrainian" organization that was pro-Polish
On 23 May, a handful of thoroughly Polonized nobles and intelligentsia c
Ukrainian origin of the type who usually referred to themselves as "Ruthen
ans of the Polish nation" (*gente Rutheni natione Poloni*) met in Lviv to form th
Ruthenian Council (Ruskyi Sobor). A Ukrainian newspaper, *Ruskyi Dnevny*
published in Latin script, was also established. The Poles scored a cou
of sorts when they enticed Ivan Vahylevych, a member of the Ruthenia
Triad, to become its editor. But this was their only success. Almost univer
sally shunned by Ukrainians, the Ruthenian Council and its newspaper ha
a brief, ephemeral existence. Moreover, the entire episode only soured Po
ish/Ukrainian relations.

The Prague congress Poles and Ukrainians soon clashed head on. Ironicall
the confrontation occurred in early June at the Slav Congress organized i
Prague by Czechs specifically to celebrate Slavic solidarity and common ir
terests. Delegates were sent to Prague by the Supreme Ruthenian Council, th
Polish National Council (Rada Narodowa), and the Ruthenian Council. 1
the great consternation of the Czechs, the Poles and Ukrainians immediatel
commenced a heated, protracted debate about who should represent Gal
cia and what the relationship between its two peoples should be. The mo
controversial issue, however, emerged somewhat later, when the Ukrainiar
demanded that Galicia be divided into separate Polish and Ukrainian admir
istrations, an idea the Poles adamantly opposed.

Because the fierce Polish/Ukrainian rivalry was impeding the genera
progress of the congress, the Czechs intervened and helped effect a compro
mise between the two delegations. If the Ukrainians would drop their de
mands for the partition of Galicia, the Poles would agree to recognize ther
as a separate nationality with equal linguistic rights and equal occupation
opportunities, especially in the administration. This agreement was never in
plemented, however, for only days after it was reached, Austrian troops bon
barded Prague, forcing the congress to disband and rendering its decisior
meaningless. The modern debut of Ukrainians on the international politica
stage was thus cut short.

Ukrainians in the imperial parliament While the Prague congress was still in session, elections commenced in Galicia to the Reichstag, or lower house, of the newly founded imperial parliament. For the Ukrainians, and the peasants in particular, these elections were a new and confusing experience. The Poles, in contrast, being politically much more sophisticated, enjoyed a distinct advantage, and they succeeded by means of rumors and threats in keeping many Ukrainian peasants away from the polls. Those who did vote often supported fellow peasants, many of whom were illiterate, rather than the priests and members of the city-bred intelligentsia recommended by the Supreme Ruthenian Council. As a result, the Ukrainians won only 25 of the 100 seats allotted to Galicia. Of these, 15 were held by peasants, 8 by priests, and 2 by members of the intelligentsia.

In the parliamentary debates that took place in the latter part of 1848, first in Vienna and then in Kromeriž, the Ukrainians concentrated on two issues: the question of compensation to landlords for the abolition of corvée and, once again, the proposal for administrative division of Galicia. The Ukrainian peasant delegates vehemently rejected any form of compensation. In the first speech ever made by a Ukrainian in parliament, Ivan Kapushchak, a simple peasant, emotionally denounced the centuries-old exploitation of the peasantry by the nobles, concluding with these words: "Should we pay an indemnity for this mistreatment and abuse? I think not. Let the whips and knouts that lashed our tired bodies be our indemnity payment. Let them satisfy the landlords!"[2]

Although this memorable speech was greeted with enthusiastic applause, the indemnity proposal nevertheless passed by a narrow margin. Disillusioned, the peasant members lost interest in all further discussions. The non-peasant members of the Ukrainian delegation, for their part, considered the administrative division of Galicia into separate Ukrainian and Polish parts as "a matter of life and death for our people." To back their proposals, they produced a list of about 15,000 signatures, which later swelled to 200,000. But after months of acrimonious debate, they too failed in their attempt to convince the majority of parliament. Meanwhile, the imperial government was slowly regaining control of the situation. In December, soon after the new emperor, the 18-year-old Franz Joseph, ascended the throne, parliament was disbanded.

Ukrainian activity in Eastern Galicia Ukrainian achievements on the local level were more concrete. Taking as their model the Czech cultural institution, Matica, they established the Halytsko-Ruska Matytsia in Lviv in July 1848. The goal of this organization was to publish inexpensive books for the general reader on religion, customs, crafts, agriculture, and pedagogy. It also strove to encourage the use of Ukrainian in the schools. On 19 October, the Supreme Ruthenian Council convened a congress of Ukrainian scholars to assess general Ukrainian cultural needs and to discuss the standardization of the Ukrainian language. Of the approximately 100 participants, over two-thirds were members of the clergy, while the remainder belonged to the intelligentsia. Not surprisingly, they concluded that Ukrainian culture in Galicia was in a sad state. About two-thirds of educated Ukrainians were Polonized and the majority of peasants were illiterate. The problem was exacerbated by the lack of standardization in the Ukrainian language. After lengthy debates, the congress unanimously recommended the use of the Cyrillic rather than the Latin alphabet. It also reached the consensus that the spoken language should serve as the basis for the literary language, but this motion was accepted only after much opposition and many qualifications.

During this period, Ukrainians began the construction of a National Home in Lviv, which was to include a museum, a library, and printing facilities. They also successfully lobbied for the establishment of a chair of Ukrainian language and literature at the university. Its first holder was Iakiv Holovatsky. Finally, late in 1848, because of their reluctance to join the Polish-controlled Galician National Guard and as a sign of their loyalty to the Habsburgs, they received Vienna's approval to form Ukrainian military units. The 1400-man Ruthenian Riflemen were not trained in time, however, to fight on the Habsburg side against the Hungarian rebels.

Bukovyna and Transcarpathia   In the other West Ukrainian lands, 1848 also sparked a flurry of activity, but on a much smaller scale than in Galicia. Only a few events of note occurred in tiny Bukovyna: several peasant uprisings led by the bold Lukiian Kobylytsia took place against Romanian landlords; five Ukrainian delegates were elected to parliament; and in 1849 the area was separated from Galicia and formed into a separate crown land.

In Hungarian-dominated Transcarpathia, there was a minor upsurge of political activism associated mostly with the talented and energetic Adolf Dobriansky. When the Hungarians revolted against the Habsburgs, they hoped, as the Poles had in Galicia, to gain the support of the non-Hungarians whom they had long oppressed. However, Dobriansky, acting like a one-man Supreme Ruthenian Council, persuaded his countrymen to reject Hungarian blandishments and to pledge loyalty to Vienna. Convinced that the Slavic populace of Transcarpathia belonged to the same ethnic stock as the Ukrainians of Galicia, he also urged the Supreme Ruthenian Council in Lviv to make the union of Transcarpathia with Galicia one of its goals. These views did not prevent Dobriansky and his small circle of associates from having pro-Russian sympathies which were strengthened by the sight of Russian armies advancing through Transcarpathia on their way to crush the hated Hungarians. These Russophile tendencies would later contribute to the confusion regarding national identity that characterized this most isolated of Ukrainian lands.

The significance of 1848   In the West Ukrainian lands, the revolutionary events of 1848 were packed into a mere 227 days. During this remarkably eventful period, the Ukrainians were presented with the opportunity to express themselves as a nation for the first time in their modern history. The experience, however, produced mixed results. For the Ukrainians, the greatest achievements of 1848 were undoubtedly the abolition of the corvée (*panshchyna*) and the introduction of constitutional government. But these gains were not peculiar to the Ukrainians, for they were scored by other peoples of the empire as well, at the expense of the momentarily faltering Habsburg regime. Of the uniquely Ukrainian achievements during this period, foremost was the activity of the Supreme Ruthenian Council. Considering the total lack of experience on the part of Ukrainians in political affairs, the performance of the Supreme Ruthenian Council, which effectively organized previously passive Ukrainians in the pursuit of well-defined goals, was impressive. By establishing institutions that would systematically promote cultural growth, the Supreme Ruthenian Council took the first crucial steps toward making Eastern Galicia an organizational bastion of Ukrainianism.

But 1848 also highlighted West Ukrainian limitations, the most serious of which was the problem of leadership. Because it monopolized positions of leadership, the clergy put its own indelible stamp on West Ukrainian politics. Seeing the Habsburgs as their greatest benefactors, the churchmen of the Supreme Ruthenian Council committed Ukrainian society wholly and unconditionally to the support of the dynasty. As a result, throughout 1848, Ukrainians found themselves supporting absolutism against Polish and Hungarian insurgents who, by and large, espoused liberal, democratic views (while continuing their association with the landowning nobility). Thus, because of the clergy's political and social conservatism and because the anti-Habsburg forces were identified with the hated landowners, Ukrainians often functioned merely as tools of the Habsburgs. Moreover, instead of trying to wring greater concessions from the government for their services, the priests of the Supreme Ruthenian Council did no more than meekly hope for imperial favors. Such an approach brought disappointing results.

Yet taken as a whole, 1848 clearly marked a turning point in the history of the West Ukrainians. It broke their age-old inertia, passivity, and isolation, and launched them on the long and bitter struggle for national and social emancipation.

Change in the Russian Empire

In the mid 19th century, the imperial system of Russia, like that of the Austrian Empire, experienced an unsettling shock that raised questions about its effectiveness and durability. The event that severely tested the regime that had been zealously maintained by Nicholas I during his thirty-year reign was the Crimean War of 1854–55. It began as a typical great-power conflict that pitted Russia against the alliance of England, France, Sardinia, and the Ottoman Empire. This alliance was determined to halt the age-old Russian attempt to expand into the Balkans to gain control of the Straits of Bosphorus and the Mediterranean trade routes, a particularly important goal in view of the expanding wheat trade of the Black Sea ports at this time.

Crimea became the main theater of the war after it was invaded by the allied powers and the impact of the conflict on neighboring Ukraine was greater than on any other area of the empire. The Ukrainian provinces functioned as the primary source of supplies for the imperial armies and their inhabitants were recruited in large numbers to serve either as frontline troops or border guards, wagoners, and fortification workers. An example of the kinds of strains that began to be felt in Ukraine itself was the so-called Kievan Cossack movement of 1855. When the tsarist government announced in that year the formation of a volunteer militia, Ukrainian peasants, construing it to mean a renewal of Cossackdom that, to their minds, was synonymous with freedom from serf obligations, rushed by the thousands to form "Cossack" units and refused to serve their landlords. The situation became critical in Kiev province, where over 180,000 peasants from more than 400 villages identified themselves as Cossacks and demanded an end to serfdom. With the arrival of troops, order was restored, but the incident clearly revealed one of the internal weaknesses that plagued the empire.

These weaknesses were even more apparent on the Crimean battlefront where, despite the heroic defense of Sevastopol, the Russian troops suffered ultimate defeat. Aside from badly undermining Russian prestige, the defeat demonstrated dramatically how far Russia had fallen behind the modernized, industrializing Western countries. Russian backwardness was evident at every turn: their rifles had only half the range of English and French weapons; their supplies and communications networks were less effective than those of the West Europeans, despite the fact that the latter were thousands of miles from their home bases; the Russian command structure, notable exceptions notwithstanding, proved to be incompetent; and tsarist soldiers, most of whom were serfs, although not lacking in bravery, were wanting in both technical skill and initiative. Crushed by the defeat, Nicholas I died in 1855. His son Alexander II came to the throne fully cognizant of the empire's desperate need for reform.

The emancipation of the serfs   During a speech to the nobles of Moscow in 1855, the new tsar declared: "It is preferable to abolish serfdom from above than to wait until the serfs abolish it from below."[3] Even Nicholas I, the arch-conservative father of the new tsar, had let it be known that serfdom would have to be dismantled sooner or later. Radical and liberal members of the gentry-intelligentsia had for decades demanded an end to the "hateful institution." But when Alexander II made his memorable comment, it became clear that he had reached the historic decision to launch a series of reforms aimed primarily at the abolition of serfdom.

As with any historic turning point, the decision to reform sparked a debate among historians about its causes. Some Western scholars are convinced that economic factors were decisive in bringing about the reforms. They argue that the opening of the Black Sea ports and the growing participation of Russia's landowners in world trade made them aware of the drawbacks of serf labor. They point out that the level of productivity of the Russian serf in 1860 was equivalent to that of the English farmer in 1750 and to the central European peasant in 1800. In short, although serf labor was cheap, it was of such low quality as to be uneconomical. Moreover, unprecedented competition and their own mismanagement had forced many landowners into debt. In 1848, over two-thirds of the landowners in Ukraine were indebted to the extent that they could no longer provide seed or food for their peasants, let alone improve their methods of raising cash crops. As a result, serfdom was already in decline well before the reforms were instituted. This is borne out by the fact that although about 58% of the peasants in the Russian Empire were enserfed in 1811, by 1860 the percentage had dropped to 44%.

There are also scholars who contend that although economic factors were important, other considerations were equally, if not more, significant. Soviet historians are adamant in insisting that peasant unrest created a "revolutionary situation" that frightened the tsar and nobles into making concessions.[4] According to their statistics, between 1856 and 1860, there were 276 disturbances involving about 160,000 peasants in Ukraine alone. The American historian Alfred Rieber has argued that the desire to modernize the imperial army was primarily responsible for the reforms.[5] Meanwhile, the Englishman Bernard Pares claimed that it was Russia's anxiety about falling behind the West.[6] Other historians prefer to emphasize the role of the liberal intelligentsia, which, by means of moving novels, polemics, and poems (such as Shevchenko's), made serfdom appear morally reprehensible. There is, however, agreement on one point: the crushing blow of Russian defeat in the Crimean War was the precipitating factor that shocked the imperial establishment into recognizing the need for immediate reform.

Aware of how potentially explosive the emancipation of the serfs could be, Alexander II proceeded carefully. In 1857, he appointed a secret committee (later renamed the Main Committee) composed of leading bureaucrats and public figures of both liberal and conservative tendencies to discuss emancipation and to formulate concrete proposals for its implementation. Ukrainians were prominent in the Main Committee, which was based in St Petersburg. One of these was Hryhorii Galagan, a dedicated abolitionist who was a personal friend of Shevchenko. But another, M.P. Pozen, a wealthy, influential, but unscrupulous landowner from Poltava province, did his best to thwart any progress. To get a sampling of local opinion, the government also established committees of nobles in each of the provinces. In Ukraine, a total of 323 nobles participated in these local committees and represented the differing interests of such regions as Sloboda Ukraine, the Left and Right banks, and southern Ukraine. The peasants were not consulted.

Although many nobles were less than enthusiastic about emancipation, they realized that it was inevitable. Therefore, from the outset, the key questions were the terms of the reform and the manner in which it would be carried out. To calm their anxieties, the tsarist government made it clear that, first and foremost, the interests of the nobility, still considered to be the chief pillar of the regime, would be safeguarded. As for the emancipation of the serfs, the two aspects that had to be considered were the serfs' personal status and their relationship to the land. Although it was assumed that serfs would be declared free men, the question arose whether this freedom would be complete or whether it should be limited in some way. The prospect of millions of peasants suddenly set loose to go where they pleased and do what they wished filled many a noble and bureaucrat with consternation. There was also the complex question of landownership. Was the serf to be freed with or without land? And if he was to be freed with land, on what terms would it be granted to him?

Given the differing landholding patterns that prevailed in various parts of the empire, it is no wonder that nobles were divided on the issue of land allotments to the peasantry. In the less fertile northern lands of Russia, the main source of the serf-owner's income had been *obrok*, or payments in cash. Instead of having the peasants work the unproductive soil, nobles there had encouraged them to find work in towns and cities in order to pay their obligations off in cash. As land was not their only source of income in this region, Russian serf-owners were thus willing to provide serfs with generous allotments of land. However, they demanded compensation in cash for the revenues that would be lost to them as a result of emancipation. In the rich southern black-earth (chernozem) region of Ukraine, however, a very different attitude prevailed. The landlords here had always demanded corvée or labor duties from their serfs because landlords' incomes derived mainly from crop production. Predictably, they were unwilling to provide peasants with land under any conditions. Slight regional variations of this "southern" attitude prevailed in other parts of Ukraine as well. On the Left Bank, especially in Poltava province, landowners were willing to provide peasants only with garden plots. In recently colonized southern Ukraine, where labor was scarce, the owners of large latifundia wanted to see serfdom prolonged by about ten years. And on the Right Bank, the Polish magnates did not want to let the peasants have any land at all. Yet despite the difficulties and obstruction that it encountered, the Main Committee pushed on at the urging of the tsar.

On 19 February 1861, Alexander II issued a manifesto abolishing serfdom. Although a document of epochal significance, it was in effect a clumsy and confusing statement that gave peasants the impression that their long-awaited emancipation would be neither quick nor fully satisfactory.

The act of emancipation did free serfs from the personal authority of their landowners. But, while it transformed former serfs into citizens, it did not entail full equality. Unlike other segments of society, emancipated serfs were still obliged to pay the head tax. They fell under the jurisdiction of special courts that had the right to impose corporal punishment for minor offenses. Although the reform mandated self-government for peasant communities, government officials, who were usually appointed from among the local nobility, retained a supervisory function. Peasants had to obtain passports from their village leadership if they wanted to leave their village. And if they did not meet their financial obligations to the state, village elders were empowered to reorganize their personal affairs to enable them to do so.

The qualifications and complexities associated with the issue of landownership were even more disheartening to the peasants. Basically, the reform allowed landowners to keep about one-half of their estates for personal use, while the other half was to be redistributed among their former serfs. The crucial stipulation was that peasants would have to pay for their allotments. Because peasants had little or no money, the arrangement was that the government would pay the landlords 80% of the cost of the land they sold in the form of treasury bonds, and the peasants would, in turn, be obligated to repay this amount with interest to the government over a period of forty-nine years. The remaining 20% of the cost of the allotments would be paid directly to the landlord by the peasants, either in cash or, what was more likely, in the form of negotiated labor obligations.

For those who could not shoulder the financial burdens of the settlement, an alternative called a "pauper's allotment" was provided in the form of an outright grant of a tiny plot, about 2.5 acres in size. Less fortunate were the serfs who worked as servants in the homes of landlords – in Ukraine they numbered about 440,000 – for emancipation brought them freedom, but no land.

In the allocation of land, the reform took regional variations into account. Cultivated land was divided into three categories: black earth, non-black earth, and steppe land. In general, peasant allotments in the latter two categories, which represented land of poorer quality, were larger, while those in black earth regions, such as Ukraine, were smaller.

Generally speaking, peasants emerged from the reforms with less land at their disposal than they had had prior to 1861. In the Russian north, peasants lost about 10% of their former plots. In the Left Bank and in southern Ukraine their holdings were reduced by almost 30%. Thus, whereas the average size of peasant holdings in the empire was about 27 acres per family, in the Left Bank and in southern Ukraine it was only 18 acres per family.

Landlords in Ukraine appear to have fared especially well in the bargain. Through the use of various tactics during the period of negotiation and redistribution of land, they appropriated forests, meadows, and ponds that had previously been considered common property. Invariably, they kept the most fertile areas for themselves and sold inferior land at inflated prices. In the course of redistribution, they often forced peasants to move, thereby imposing additional expense upon the poor. To be sure, these practices were common throughout the empire, but, in Ukraine, where competition for land was keenest, they were especially widespread. As a result, the peasants of the Left Bank and southern Ukraine fared much worse than their Russian neighbors.

The Right Bank was an exception to this rule. Because the government had serious doubts about the loyalty of the Polish nobles in the region (the Polish uprising of 1863 confirmed their misgivings), it sought to win over the Ukrainian peasantry of the region to its side by making allotments that were about 18% larger than those that had been held by the peasants prior to 1861. But what the former serfs gained in allotment size, they lost in the highly inflated prices they had to pay for their lands at this time.

Another particularity of the reforms in Ukraine involved the forms of landownership. In Russia, where over 95% of the peasants lived in communes (*obshchiny*), deeds to the newly acquired land were held collectively and payment for the land was a communal responsibility. But in Ukraine, communal ownership was rare. Over 85% of the peasants on the Right Bank and almost 70% on the Left Bank worked individual homesteads. Therefore, most Ukrainian peasant families took individual title to their land and personally shouldered the responsibility for the debt on it. This arrangement served to strengthen the already well-developed attachment to private property that distinguished Ukrainian peasants from their Russian counterparts.

We must remember that not all peasants were serfs. Roughly half were state-peasants, of whom there were at least thirty different categories, including about 1 million former Cossacks in Ukraine. They were usually better off than privately owned serfs, for although they paid a higher head tax to the state, which was in effect their landlord, they could leave their villages without permission, had more land at their disposal and there were no petty, exploitative landlords to contend with (but corrupt bureaucrats were a frequent nuisance). The reform of 1861 and the law of 1866, in particular, emancipated the state-peasants more quickly and on terms that were more favorable than those accorded serfs. Along with their freedom, they received larger plots and paid proportionately less for them than did serfs. On the Right Bank, however, the condition of the state-peasants showed very little improvement.

Generally speaking, the peasants, and especially former serfs, were disappointed by the reform. They expected it to bring them immediate and outright ownership of their plots; instead, they found the size of their plots reduced and crushing financial burdens imposed upon them. A wave of unrest rolled through the countryside, but its intensity varied from region to region. On the Left Bank and in southern Ukraine, there were relatively few disturbances. However, on the Right Bank, memories of the *haidamak* uprisings were still strong; religioethnic as well as socioeconomic differences fueled animosities between the Ukrainian Orthodox peasantry and the Polish Catholic nobility; and minor clashes were widespread. But order was always quickly restored and the peasants resumed their struggle for their daily bread, albeit under markedly different circumstances.

Other reforms   The abolition of serfdom entailed other reforms. One aspect of imperial society urgently needing improvement was the local administration. As society changed, and especially after serfs acquired rights of citizenship, demand for local services increased. However, the imperial government had neither the personnel nor the money to meet these demands. Therefore, in 1864, it allowed communities to elect their own representatives on the county and provincial levels to oversee such matters as education, medical care, postal services, road maintenance, food reserves in case of famine, and collection of statistics. To finance these services, the local committees, or *zemstva* (singular: *zemstvo*), were given the right to impose local taxes.

In a radical departure from the usual tsarist practice of appointing all government officials, members of the *zemstvo* were elected from an electorate divided into three separate categories: large landowners, townsmen, and peasants. The impact of voters was proportional to the amount of land they owned. As might be expected, the great majority of *zemstvo* members were noblemen. In Ukraine, they usually made up over 75% of *zemstvo* membership, with peasants rarely constituting more than 10%. But although they were not truly representative, the *zemstva* performed a very important function. Besides helping to raise the general standard of living in the countryside, they introduced local populations to a limited measure of self-government.

In Ukraine, a network of *zemstva* was established on the Left Bank and in the south. However, because the recent rebellion of Polish nobles, *zemstva* were not instituted on the Right Bank until 1911. Because they represented local interests, the *zemstva* tended to be much more sensitive to Ukrainian cultural aspirations than was the imperial bureaucracy. The Poltava *zemstva* in particular became associated with Ukrainophile tendencies in the latter part of the century, and it served as a training ground for many leaders of the Ukrainian movement.

In even greater need of improvement was the legal system. Much of the problem lay in the Russians' poorly developed sense of legality. Imperial bureaucrats, who were responsible for many legal decisions, considered justice to be a department of the state and, in their view, courts existed to decide what was in the interests of the state. Individual rights were irrelevant or, at best, of secondary importance. Thus, trials were held in secret, judges were often corrupt, and their frequently arbitrary decisions were based on class distinctions – with harsher punishments meted out to the lower classes and lighter sentences going to the nobles. The legal reform of 1864 improved this situation considerably: it made the judiciary an independent branch of government, free from bureaucratic interference. Henceforth, trials were held openly, with contending sides arguing their respective cases. One of the ramifications of this change was that it gave the impetus for the rise of a new occupational group – the lawyers.

Important changes were also introduced in other areas of imperial society. The educational reforms of the 1860s provided the lower classes with greater access to all levels of education, universities included. They also improved the curricula and granted universities greater autonomy. At the same time, censorship regulations were loosened, although it still remained unclear to what extent one could advocate "subversive" ideas. In 1874, the harsh terms of militairy service were amended to require all classes, not just the lower strata of society, to render military service. The length of service was also reduced from twenty-five years to six and an array of exemptions was made available.

Significance of the reforms   Although the "great reforms" did not revolutionize the conditions of life for Ukrainians and other subjects of the Russian Empire, they did introduce basic changes. Western scholars often emphasize the personal freedom that they brought the serfs, the development of the *zemstvo*-led local government, and the new appreciation for legality that they introduced. For their part, Soviet historians believe that the reforms ushered in the epochal transition from feudalism to a bourgeois, capitalist society in Russia. It is clear that the reforms had serious shortcomings, but there is general agreement that the subsequent socioeconomic modernization of the empire would have been impossible without them.

In Ukraine, where the percentage of the population who were serfs was roughly 42%, compared to an imperial average of about 35%, the impact of emancipation was that much greater. As education improved, legal protection became more widespread, and local government more entrenched, national particularities and local interests had a greater opportunity for self-expression. Certainly, various ideologies, including that of Ukrainian nationhood, would now find it easier to reach a broader constituency.

જ઼

The changes and reforms introduced by the Austrian and Russian Empires in 1848 and in the 1860s, respectively, had important similarities. Although forced upon both empires, particulary on the Austrian, the reforms were nonetheless implemented "from the top" by regimes that still retained political control. Fundamental, but not revolutionary, they left much of the old regimes intact. Yet they clearly hastened the coming of a new era, one in which the masses and their representatives would exert a growing influence on political, socioeconomic, and cultural activity. Thus, in both the Austrian and Russian empires, the changes of the mid 19th century were a giant step toward modernity.

In terms of understanding the impact of this era on the Ukrainians, the differences between the Austrian and Russian reforms were as significant as were the similarities. The revolutionary year of 1848 brought two main issues to the fore among the Ukrainians of the Austrian Empire: the socioeconomic plight of the peasantry and the national aspirations of the clergy-intelligentsia. Of crucial importance was the fact that in Western Ukraine these issues were interrelated, since the Poles who opposed Ukrainian national goals were often the self-same noblemen who exploited the peasants. Thus, for West Ukrainians, nationality was from the outset associated with such bread-and-butter issues as education, local government, and social legislation. In time, this linkage would endow nationhood with a relevance among the peasants that it had already attained among the intelligentsia. Naturally, Habsburg acquiescence in the establishment of a constitutional government that – despite its limitations and imperfections – allowed West Ukrainians to express and defend their national and socioeconomic interests in parliament, also increased peasant involvement. Thus, the socioeconomically disadvantaged West Ukrainians who inhabited the most backward lands of the Austrian Empire were presented with opportunities for political, organizational, and cultural activity that Ukrainians in Russia did not have.

For the Ukrainians of the Russian Empire, the profound changes of the 1860s had little impact on the development of their national movement. The nationality question in Russia could not share the limelight with socioeconomic problems as it did in Austria for a variety of reasons – including the cultural and demographic preponderance of Russians in the empire; the inherent tsarist distrust of pluralism; the tsar's refusal even to consider a constitution that might create the means for national and regional self-expression; the weakness of communal organizations; and the government's harsh, repressive policies toward the national movements among the non-Russians of the empire. As a result, the crucial linkage between the peasantry's socioeconomic condition and the national aspirations of the intelligentsia was absent. This circumstance severely stunted the growth of national consciousness among the Ukrainians of the Russian Empire.

Socioeconomic Change

New ideas, political upheavals, and social reforms captured the attention of Europeans, Ukrainians included, during much of the 19th century. Yet at this same time, a less noticeable but far more fundamental process of change was under way, namely, the Industrial Revolution. Not since man mastered agriculture in the Stone Age would such profound changes occur in all aspects of human life as those associated with the coming of the machine. In Ukraine, however, industrialization came slowly at first, and the overwhelming majority of Ukrainians remained what they had been for millennia – an agrarian people. But when industrialization finally did develop in the late 19th century in certain limited areas of Ukraine, it did so rapidly and on a large scale. As a result, two radically different systems of production, of social organization, and of values suddenly confronted each other – one associated with the modernizing city, the proletariat, and the machine and the other with the traditionalist village, the peasant, and manual labor. The strains, contradictions, and dilemmas that arose from this confrontation would mold Ukrainian history well into the 20th century.

ॐ

The Troubled Countryside

Although the Emancipation of 1861 freed the peasants of the Russian Empire from their landlords, it did not improve their economic condition. In fact, any discussion of the condition of the peasant in the postemancipation era reads like an endless and depressing litany of troubles. Some of these problems stemmed directly from errors in judgment by the architects of the reforms. Their most grievous mistake was to place too great a financial burden on the peasantry, while at the same time providing it with too little land. Thus, in addition to onerous redemption payments, peasants had to pay a head tax and were also indirectly taxed when they bought such goods as sugar, tea, tobacco, cotton, iron implements, and, most important, vodka. Late in the 19th century, when a government commission investigated the matter of financial overload, it reported that – if redemption payments were included – peasants payed ten times more taxes than did the nobles. Even after the government abolished the head tax in 1886 and redemption payments in 1905, indirect taxes soaked up most of the peasants' meager amounts of cash.

To meet their financial obligations, some peasants would borrow money either from other peasants who were better off or, on the Right Bank in particular, from Jews who specialized in moneylending. But with interest rates often exceeding 150%, the peasants would usually only sink deeper into debt. Others attempted to sell what little surplus produce they had, but customers were few, markets too distant, and prices too low to make small-scale business profitable. Finally, the poorest peasants would often hire themselves out to former landlords or rich peasants at extremely low wages.

Obviously, the chronic lack of cash among 90% of Ukraine's population had serious economic ramifications. Most peasants could not afford to buy either additional land to enlarge their plots or modern implements (not to speak of machines) to improve their productivity. Indeed, on the Left and Right banks, about 50% of the peasants possessed neither horses nor good steel implements. The sight of a peasant harnessed to a dull, wooden plow was common in the Ukrainian countryside. Lack of cash also spelled weakness in Ukraine's domestic market, impeding the growth of commerce, industry, and cities and making it an economic backwater of the empire.

From the peasant's point of view, however, the main reason for his woes was not lack of money but lack of arable land. It was, after all, possible to live without money, but how, he would argue, could one survive without land? The tiny land allotments of 1861, smaller in Ukraine than anywhere else in the empire, could hardly satisfy their holders' already exceedingly modest needs. And natural causes compounded these problems to calamitous proportions. In the latter part of the 19th century, the Russian Empire, like most of Europe, experienced tremendous population growth. Between 1861 and 1897 the population of the empire grew from 73 million to 125 million. By 1917, it had reached 170 million. In Ukraine, the population jumped by 72% in less than forty years.

Because most of the Ukrainians lived in the countryside, it was here that demographic pressures became most evident. In 1890 there were almost twice as many inhabitants per acre of arable land on the Left and Right banks as there had been in 1860. This made the region one of the most densely inhabited in Europe, with twice as many inhabitants per arable acre as in England. Why this sudden jump in population? Paradoxically, improved medical care, brought to the countryside by the zemstva, sharply reduced the infant mortality rate and thereby greatly contributed to population growth. Yet it should be noted that despite these improvements in medical care, the death rate per thousand in the Russian Empire was still twice as high on the average as that in Western Europe.

The consequences of the twin dilemmas of overpopulation and land short-age soon manifested themselves in the Ukrainian countryside in the form of soaring prices for land. In some regions, most notably the southern steppe, they were three to four times higher in 1900 than they had been in 1861, thus making it even more difficult for peasants to obtain the additional land they so desperately needed. Another consequence of rural overpopulation was unemployment. It has been calculated that in the 1890s Ukraine had an avail-able labor force of almost 10.7 million people. Of these, agriculture required 2.3 million and other sectors of the economy utilized 1.1 million. The remain-ing 7.3 million, or 68% of the labor force, constituted a surplus that was largely unemployed or underemployed and that virtually led a hand-to-mouth exis-tence. Little wonder that the living standard of Ukrainians fell far behind that of the West. For example, in 1900 an average Dane consumed 2166 pounds of bread annually, a German 1119, and a Hungarian 1264 pounds. In Ukraine, however, where bread was a larger component of the diet than in the West, the average annual consumption was only 867 pounds – and that in a land that was referred to as the breadbasket of Europe.

Emigration to the east   Desperate for land, peasants were willing to go to any lengths to get more of it. One way was to work a large strip of land for a landlord for free in return for the use of a smaller strip. Although such ar-rangements were disturbingly reminiscent of serfdom, many villagers had no choice but to accept them. A more drastic option was to emigrate. But unlike West Ukrainians who had to travel overseas in search of land and employ-ment, East Ukrainians did not have to leave the boundaries of the Russian Empire. They could travel overland (often for distances as great as that be-tween Eastern Europe and America) to the open areas of the Russian east, particularly the Amur basin near the Pacific coast.

Between 1896 and 1906, after the construction of the trans-Siberian rail-road, about 1.6 million Ukrainians migrated eastward. Discouraged by diffi-cult conditions, many of these migrants returned to their homes. Even so, by 1914 about 2 million Ukrainians lived permanently in the Far East. Moreover, proportionately almost twice as many Ukrainians as Russians moved east-ward in the search for land. Thus, at exactly the same time West Ukrainians from the Habsburg empire were colonizing the prairies of western Canada, their East Ukrainian counterparts were bringing the plow to Russia's Pacific coast. This was a telling indication of the lengths to which the Ukrainian peas-ant was willing to go in order to obtain land.

Differentiation of the peasantry   Despite the generally dismal condition of the peasantry, some, as usual, did better than others. Consequently, in the post-emancipation era, economic distinctions among the peasantry became more marked. Essentially, the socioeconomic structure of the Ukrainian (as well as Russian) village reflected Aldous Huxley's famous dictum that humans tend to be divided into the high, the middle, and the low. The Ukrainian peasantry came to consist of the relatively rich, called *kulaks* (Ukrainian: *kurkuli*); those of average means, called *seredniaky*; and poor peasants or *bidniaky*.

A combination of hard work, initiative, luck, and, quite often, exploitation of their fellows – hence the negative connotations of kulak meaning a grasping, tightfisted person – allowed about 15–20% of peasants to enlarge their plots and accumulate wealth, while others sank deeper into poverty. Intermarriage among the kulaks helped them to further expand and retain their holdings for generations. On the average, this stratum of villagers possessed between sixty-five and seventy-five acres, several horses, and farming machinery. Often they hired labor and engaged in commercial farming. Following the lead of Lenin, Soviet scholars have been particularly harsh in their condemnation of these successful peasants, viewing them as a rural bourgeoisie and an exploitive class. However, many Western scholars argue that the socioeconomic distinctions between kulaks and other peasants should not be exaggerated. Although it is true that the kulaks often took advantage of poorer peasants and the latter were frequently resentful and envious of the former, the kulaks considered themselves and were still perceived by others as peasants, not related in any way to city people or nobles. Indeed, the dream of poor peasants was not to eliminate kulaks, but to become one of them.

The middle stratum of the peasantry was relatively large, constituting about 30% of the village population. Usually, *seredniaky* owned eight to twenty-five acres, which was enough to feed a family. In addition, they often possessed several horses and some livestock. Only very rarely could they afford any type of farm machinery. This solid, hardworking village "middle-class" – whose neat, whitewashed cottages bespoke pride of ownership and self-sufficiency – was particularly widespread on the Left Bank.

Most numerous by far were the *bidniaky*. Making up about 50% of the peasantry, they either had no land at all or only a few acres that were insufficient to provide a living. To survive, the *bidniaky* hired themselves out to richer peasants and nobles or they left the village in search of seasonal work. A family could slip into poverty in a variety of ways. Often, misfortunes such as sickness, death, or natural calamity would force peasants to sell some or all of their land, thereby depriving themselves of a secure economic base. At times, they would deplete their resources through imprudent farming techniques. Not infrequently, laziness and heavy drinking would push a family to the brink of disaster. In any case, as the already high percentage of poorest peasants increased, an undercurrent of tension and disaffection began to

permeate the seemingly peaceful countryside. Thus, for many observers, i
seemed that if revolution was to come to the Russian Empire, it would hav
to begin in the village.

Decline of the nobility   Despite the generous land settlement, financial sup
port from the government, and a variety of social advantages and privileges
the nobility also experienced a sharp decline in the post-1861 period. It wa
a result mostly of the fact that nobles were incapable, by and large, of run
ning their estates efficiently as profitable commercial ventures. Rather tha
investing capital in machinery, they wasted it on ostentatious living; accus
tomed to the free labor of the serfs, they could not adjust to hiring help; an
the discipline, initiative, and hard work required to run a profitable busines
were foreign to many nobles.

To solve their financial problems, they borrowed. By 1877 about 75% o
them were heavily mortgaged. Consequently, many sold their land, usuall
to the ambitious and industrious kulaks, with the result that between 186
and 1914 noble ownership of land in Ukraine declined by 53%. But not o
the Right Bank, however, for there the extremely wealthy Polish landowner
found it easier to weather their difficulties and retain their vast holdings.

The plight of the nobility indicated that the traditional elite in Ukraine an
the empire as a whole was gradually moving into oblivion. After they sol
their lands, nobles usually moved into cities where they became bureaucrats
officers, or members of the intelligentsia. True, they still enjoyed great socia
advantages, and as late as 1917 most of the arable land was still in their hand
But as a class, deprived of its dominance over the peasantry and graduall
losing its control of the land, the nobility was living on borrowed time.

Commercial agriculture   Paradoxically, although the Ukrainian countrysid
was haunted by stagnation and decline, its role as the "granary of Eu
rope" continued to grow. This circumstance occurred because a small seg
ment of the nobility, along with entrepreneurs from other classes, had suc
ceeded – contrary to the general trend – in transforming their estates int
large, bustling agribusinesses that supplied imperial and foreign markets
The anomaly of the situation was caught by Vyshnegradsky, the imperial min
ister of finance, who remarked that "We may go hungry, but we will export."

The export of food had, however, a limited and regional character. Onl
certain parts of Ukraine and a relatively small percentage of the populatio
were involved in it. It was the steppe region, with its open land and easy ac
cess to the Black Sea ports, that became the center of commercial wheat an
bread production early in the 19th century. Even before emancipation, estat
owners in the region were busily expanding the acreage under cultivatior
investing in machinery, and using hired labor. After 1861, when labor be
came mobile and plentiful in the south and transportation improved, Ukrain

in general and the steppe region in particular expanded its food production more rapidly than the rest of the empire. Thus, in the early 20th century, as much as 90% of the empire's main export – wheat – came from Ukraine. Even on the global scale Ukraine's food production was impressive: it accounted for 43% of the world's barley crop, 20% of its wheat, and 10% of its corn.

Wheat, however, was not Ukraine's primary cash crop. This distinction belonged to beets, which were the main source of sugar for the empire and much of Europe. In all of Europe there was no area as well suited for large-scale production of sugar beets as the Right Bank. Consequently, by the 1840s sugar-beet production was well established in the region. As might be expected, it was Polish families, such as the Branicki and Potocki, who owned the largest sugar enterprises. But Russians like the Bobrinsky family; Ukrainians like the Tereshchenkos, Symyrenkos, and Iakhnenkos; and Jews like the Brodskys and Halperins also belonged to the "sugar barons" of the Right Bank. Meanwhile, on the Left Bank, the most important cash crop was tobacco, which accounted for over 50% of total imperial production. On both sides of the Dnieper, the distillation of alcohol was a widespread and profitable industry. With the crucial contribution it made to the economy of the empire, it is little wonder that Ukraine was regarded as an indispensable and an inseparable part of it.

Industrialization

With the liquidation of serfdom, the way was finally cleared for the modernization and industrialization of the empire. This process had already been embarked upon by many countries of Western Europe and America, but the experience of the Russian Empire was unique in a number of important respects. First, the state assumed a much greater role in initiating and guiding industrialization in Russia and Ukraine than it did in the West. The Russian Empire's internal market was too weak; the bourgeoisie, which usually provided capitalist entrepreneurs, was practically nonexistent; and private capital was too scarce to spark the rise of large-scale industry without government support. Second, once the empire did start to industrialize with the aid of capital and expertise, the rate of growth was remarkably rapid, particularly in Ukraine in the 1890s, with industries springing up full-blown in a matter of a few years. Finally, the economic modernization of the empire was most uneven. At the turn of the century in Ukraine, it was not uncommon to see some of the biggest, most modern factories, mines, and steel mills in all Europe amidst villages where peasants still harnessed themselves to the plow and eked out a living from the land as they had for centuries.

As everywhere, one of the first harbingers of economic modernization was the railroad. For military reasons (a major cause of the Russian defeat in the Crimean War had been lack of adequate transport), as well as economic ones,

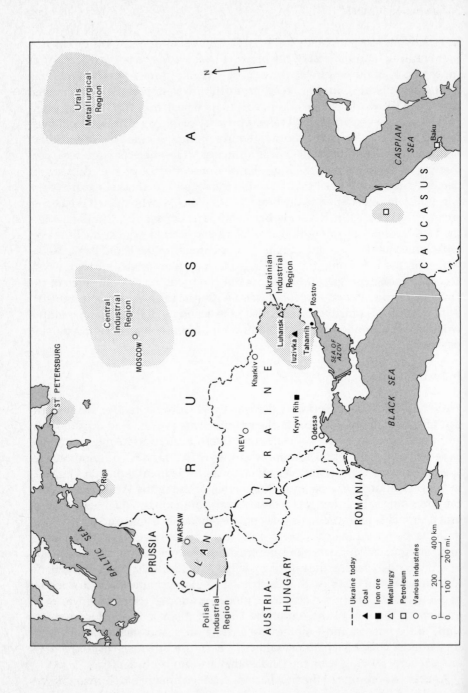

Urals
Metallurgical
Region

R U S S I A

CASPIAN
SEA

Baku

C A U C A S U S

Central
Industrial
Region

MOSCOW○

ST PETERSBURG
○

Ukrainian
Industrial
Region

Luhansk △   Rostov ●
Iuzivka ▲
Tahanrih ■

SEA OF
AZOV

Kharkiv○

○ Riga

KIEV○

Kryvi Rih ■

Odessa
○

BLACK SEA

BALTIC SEA

PRUSSIA

WARSAW
○

P O L A N D

U K R A I N E

ROMANIA

Polish
Industrial
Region

AUSTRIA-
HUNGARY

- - - Ukraine today
▲ Coal
■ Iron ore
△ Metallurgy
□ Petroleum
○ Various industries

0   200   400 km
0   100   200 mi.

the imperial government rushed to create a network of railroads. In Russian-ruled Ukraine the first railroad tracks were laid in 1866–71 between Odessa and Balta to expedite grain exports. By the 1870s – the high point of railroad construction in Ukraine – railroads connected all the major Ukrainian cities with each other. And, most important, they linked Ukraine with Moscow, the center of imperial markets. As Ukrainian food and raw materials moved northward in exchange for an unprecedented flow of Russian finished products to the south, Ukraine's economy, which had heretofore been relatively distinct and self-sustaining, began to be integrated into the imperial system. Furthermore, the rapid growth of railroad construction created a pressing need for coal and iron. Suddenly, the coal and iron reserves that were known to exist in southeastern Ukraine in large quantities, particularly in the basin of the Donets River, became not only valuable, but also accessible.

Between 1870 and 1900, and especially during the frenetic 1890s, two areas in southeastern Ukraine – the Donets basin and Kryvyi Rih – became the fastest growing industrial regions in the empire and, quite possibly, in the world. The combination of factors making this growth possible were the generous government support for industrial development (so that these undertakings were practically risk-free); the continued rise in domestic demand for coal and iron; and abundant Western capital (confronted with shrinking profits in highly developed Europe) that rushed to take advantage of the alluring opportunities in Ukraine.

Signs of the coming boom first appeared in the coal-mining industry of the Donets basin. Between 1870 and 1900, when coal production jumped by over 1000%, the region produced close to 70% of the empire's coal. As the number of mines in the Donets basin increased, so too did the work force: in 1885, it numbered 32,000; in 1900, 82,000; and in 1913, 168,000. The industry was controlled by about twenty joint stock companies and by 1900 about 94% of their stock belonged to French and Belgian investors, who had poured millions of rubles into the development of the mines. These companies formed syndicates that gained a virtual monopoly on the production and sale of coal. Thus, when capitalism finally came to Ukraine, it came fully developed.

In the 1880s, about a decade after the coal boom, came the large-scale development of iron ore production. Concentrated in the Kryvyi Rih region, the growth of the metallurgical industry was even more spectacular than that of coal mining. The stage was set in 1885 when a railroad was built linking Kryvyi Rih with the coal mines of the Donets basin. The government offered entrepreneurs in the budding metallurgical industry an incentive that few could ignore, guaranteeing to buy many of their products at greatly inflated prices. Western investors, again led by the French, responded enthusiastically. By 1914 they had put up more than 180 million rubles for the construction of some of the largest, most technologically advanced foundries in the world. Some of these enterprises grew so fast that they became bustling cities. Iuzivka, for example, named after the Welshman John Hughes, who established a metallurgical plant at the site, became the important industrial city of Donetsk. As late as the 1870s, the Kryvyi Rih region had only 13,000 workers, but by 1917 the number had increased more than ten times to 137,000. Even more striking is the comparison of the growth rate of the metals industry in Ukraine with that of Russia's old metal-producing centers in the Urals: while the antiquated plants of the Urals only managed to raise their production of iron ore fourfold between 1870 and 1900, those of Ukraine had increased by 158 times.

But while the basic, extractive (raw-material-producing) industries of Ukraine burgeoned, other types did not. This underdevelopment was especially evident in the production of finished goods. At the turn of the century, the only industries in Ukraine that showed a marked improvement in the production of finished products were, not surprisingly, factories specializing in farm machinery and, to a lesser degree, locomotive works. For the vast majority of its finished products, Ukraine depended on Russia. In 1913, for example, Ukraine was responsible for 70% of the empire's extractive industry, but had only 15% of its capacity to produce finished goods. Therefore, the economic relationship that developed between the two lands was based on the exchange of Ukrainian raw materials for Russian finished goods. Thus, while the sudden, vast outburst of industrial activity in Ukraine was indeed impressive, it tended to obscure the one-dimensional, imbalanced nature of this growth.

The question of colonial exploitation   The question often raised in the evaluation of the remarkable industrialization of southern Ukraine is the degree to which it benefited Ukraine as a whole. Contemporary Soviet scholars argue that, on balance, the impact was positive. As a result of the growth of transportation and the quantum leap in the transfer of goods and materials between north and south, the economies of Russia and Ukraine finally and irrevocably became integrated. This led to the creation of a larger, more productive and more efficient economic unit – a vast all-Russian market, as they call it – from which both lands benefited greatly. In fact, Soviet economic historians like Ivan Hurzhyi imply that, in the new economic context, Ukraine performed even better than Russia: not only did it gain access to a huge market but, because of its faster industrialization, it consistently enlarged its share of this market.[2] Any suggestion that the Russian heartland derived greater economic advantage from linkage with the Ukrainian periphery is angrily rejected by the Soviets. To buttress their argument, they point out that it was a Russian imperial government that stimulated the faster growth rate in Ukraine.

But Soviet scholars did not always view the issue in this manner. In the 1920s, before the imposition of Stalinist orthodoxy, the leading Soviet historians, such as Mikhail Pokrovsky in Russia and Matvii Iavorsky in Ukraine, unequivocally reiterated that despite industrialization, Ukraine was exploited by Russia.[3] Lenin himself declared in a speech in Switzerland in 1914 (which is not included in the Soviet editions of his works) that "it [Ukraine] has become for Russia what Ireland was for England: exploited in the extreme and receiving nothing in return."[4]

How was the alleged exploitation of Ukraine to be reconciled with its industrial growth? In 1928, Mykhailo Volobuev, a Russian Communist economist in Ukraine, provided an explanation. He stated that Ukraine was not an "Asian" type of colony – poor, nonindustrialized, with its resources simply carried off by an exploitive empire; rather it belonged to the "European" type of colony, that is, an industrially well-developed land that was deprived not so much of its resources as of its capital and potential profits. The main culprit, in his view, was Russia, not Western capitalists.[5] The mechanism by which this capital was syphoned from Ukraine was relatively simple: imperial price-fixing insured that the costs of Russian finished goods would be exceedingly high, while the price of Ukrainian raw materials remained low. As a result, Russian manufacturers made greater profits than Ukraine's producers of coal and iron ore and capital accumulated in the Russian north, not the Ukrainian south. In this manner, the economy of Ukraine (which, Volobuev stressed, was a distinct autonomous entity) was deprived of potential benefits and made to serve the interests of the Russian core of the empire.

Urban development   The 19th century also brought major changes to the cities and towns of Ukraine. However, the tempo and focus of these transformations varied considerably. Prior to 1861, except for the rapidly growing Black Sea ports like Odessa, urban growth was sluggish. In the small- to medium-sized towns of the Left Bank, like Poltava, Romny, Sumy, and Kharkiv, numerous trade fairs (*iarmarky*) – which the region hosted and for which it was famous – slightly increased the population. On the Right Bank, urban growth was somewhat greater because of the influx of Jews to such centers of trade and handicrafts as Bila Tserkva, Berdychiv, and Zhytomyr. The vast majority of Ukraine's urban population (which accounted for 10% of the total) lived in towns with less than 20,000 inhabitants. Only Odessa had a population higher than 100,000.

Radical changes occurred in the latter part of the century, especially between 1870 and 1900, when the rate of urban growth jumped sharply, particularly in the large cities. By 1900, four large urban centers dominated Ukraine: Odessa, a thriving commercial and manufacturing city whose population jumped to over 400,000; Kiev, a focal point of domestic trade, machine building, administration, and cultural activity, which had 250,000 inhabitants; Kharkiv, a city of 175,000, which controlled the trade and industry of the Left Bank; and Katerynoslav, the booming industrial center of the south, which experienced a rise in population from 19,000 to 115,000 in a few decades.

The greater mobility of the peasants after 1861, the expansion of industry and trade, and especially the construction of railroads, which allowed the concentration of economic activity in a few strategically located centers, accounted for much of this growth. As the big cities grew, the towns began to stagnate and by the turn of the century most urban dwellers lived in large cities. Yet these developments did not mean that Ukraine was rapidly urbanizing. Far from it. While the population of the cities multiplied, so did that of the countryside. In 1900 only 13% of Ukraine's total population was urban – less than Russia's 15% and nowhere near West European countries like England, for example, where 72% of the population lived in towns and cities.

The emergence of the proletariat   With accelerated economic development came equally rapid social changes. Of these, the most important was the appearance of a new and as yet relatively small class – the proletariat. Unlike peasants, the proletarians (or industrial workers) did not own the means of production. They sold their labor rather than their produce. And they worked with machines. Because they worked in large, complex enterprises, industrial workers tended to be more knowledgeable and sophisticated than peasants. Because they labored in huge factories with thousands of their fellows, they were quicker to develop a sense of group consciousness and solidarity. And, most important, the highly structured and interdependent nature of their work meant that they were more amenable to organization than were peasants.

Unlike Russia, where enserfed peasants had been assigned to work in factories since the 18th century, industrial workers appeared in appreciable numbers in Ukraine only in the mid 19th century. Initially, most of them were engaged in food production, specifically in the huge sugar refineries of the Right Bank. But the vast majority of the sugar workers were not proletarians in the true sense because their work was seasonal and in the off-season they returned to their villages to work their plots. The half-peasant, half-proletarian character of these workers was typical for most of the empire, but it was especially so among Ukraine's sugar workers.

It was the workers in heavy industry – the coal miners of the Donbas and the iron-ore producers of Kryvyi Rih – who were true proletarians. One could find among them the largest percentage of full-time workers whose fathers and grandfathers had also worked in industry. Yet even among them, there were many who still maintained ties to their villages. In 1897 the total number of industrial workers in Ukraine was about 425,000, with close to half concentrated in the heavy industries of Katerynoslav province. Since 1863 their number had increased by 400%. Yet industrial workers still constituted only 7% of the labor force, and the proletariat remained a small minority in the sea of peasants.

Industrial working conditions in Ukraine, as in the rest of the Russian Empire, were deplorable by European standards. Even after the government legislated improvements in the 1890s, shifts of ten, twelve, or fifteen hours were common. Safety precautions and medical care were practically nonexistent. And the pay (almost all of which went for food and squalid quarters) of the average worker in Ukraine was only a fraction of that earned by his European counterpart. Little wonder that strikes and other confrontations between workers and employers became increasingly frequent.

Other social changes Major modifications also occurred in the intelligentsia, the other newly formed class. Industrial development, social change, modernization of legal institutions, and the growth of the *zemstva* created an increased demand for educated people. The government responded by establishing more professional and technical schools. In Ukraine the number of students rose from 1200 in 1865 to over 4000 in the mid 1890s. By 1897 there were about 24,000 individuals with some form of higher education. The social origins of the intelligentsia also changed. At the beginning of the century, the vast majority of its members were of gentry origin. But by 1900 only 20–25% came from the nobility and the very rich; the remainder were mostly sons of burghers, clerics, and professionals. Peasants and workers, however, were still rare in the universities, mainly because of the lack of adequate academic preparation. With the establishment of higher schools for women, these too began to enter the intelligentsia in increasing numbers. New occupational groups such as engineers, physicians, lawyers, and teachers grew rapidly. No longer composed primarily of socially isolated and alienated sons of the nobility, the more broadly based intelligentsia now moved to the forefront of modernization.

Compared to the societies of Western Europe, the Russian Empire in general, and Ukraine in particular, was marked by a sociological anomaly: its bourgeoisie was so small and underdeveloped as to be insignificant. In Ukraine there was simply too little money to give rise to a bourgeoisie. Government policies drained away capital to the north; domestic trade (especially the fairs) was largely in the hands of Russian merchants; and industry, as we have seen, was owned almost totally by foreigners. Naturally, there were extremely wealthy people in Ukraine, over 100,000 by some estimates. But most of them derived their income not from factories and commercial enterprises but from their estates. Ukrainians even lacked a petite bourgeoisie, that is, artisans and shopkeepers. Business, both large and small, was in the hands of Russians and Jews.

Modernization and the missing Ukrainians Modernization in Ukraine created several paradoxes. As Ukraine's importance as the granary of Europe grew, poverty increased in its countryside. And although its industrial boom was one of the largest in Europe, Ukraine still remained basically an agrarian society. Perhaps most striking was the fact that although Ukrainians constituted the vast majority of the population, they hardly participated in these transformations. Statistics best underscore this point. Among the most experienced workers in the heavy industry of the south, only 25% of coal miners and 30% of metallurgical workers were Ukrainians. It was Russians who constituted the majority in these occupations. Even in the sugar refineries of the Right Bank there were almost as many Russian as Ukrainian workers.

Turning to the intelligentsia, one encounters a similar phenomenon. In 1897, Ukrainians made up only 16% of lawyers, 25% of teachers, and less than 10% of writers and artists in Ukraine. Of 127,000 individuals involved in "mental work" only one-third were Ukrainian. And in 1917 only 11% of the students in Kiev University were of Ukrainian origin. The lack of Ukrainians in the cities was striking. At the turn of the century, they made up less than one-third of all urban dwellers; Russians and Jews accounted for the remainder. As a rule, the bigger the city, the smaller was the number of Ukrainians living in it. In 1897, only 5.6% of Odessa's population was Ukrainian and in 1920 the percentage sank to 2.9%. In Kiev in 1874, those who considered Ukrainian to be their native language constituted 60% of the population; by 1897 the percentage had sunk to 22% and in 1917 to 16%. Clearly, modernization was bypassing the Ukrainians.

Why was the number of non-Ukrainians so great in those areas that were modernizing? In explaining the heavy preponderance of Russians in the proletariat, of utmost importance was the fact that, unlike in Ukraine, industry had existed in Russia since the 18th century. When the sudden boom occurred in the Donbas and Kryvyi Rih, creating an urgent demand for experienced workers, Russians were welcomed with open arms. A contributing reason for this massive influx of workers from the north was the fact that Russian industries were stagnating at the time whereas wages in the booming Ukrainian mines and foundries averaged about 50% more than in Russia.

In the cities, the Russian presence had been growing since Ukrainian lands had been incorporated into the empire. Because many of the towns and cities functioned as administrative and military centers, they attracted Russian bureaucrats and soldiers. As trade and industry grew, so too did the number of non-Ukrainians in the urban centers. Thus, as early as 1832, about 50% of the merchants and 45% of the factory owners in Ukraine were Russians. For reasons mentioned earlier, they had more capital to invest than Ukrainians. As well, many Russian peasants were forced by the infertility of their soil to seek alternate ways of making a living in the cities. Peasant newcomers from the north often became successful merchants in Ukraine, especially on the Left Bank and in the south, where they found numerous opportunities and little competition from the native populace.

The other major non-Ukrainian element in the cities and towns of Ukraine was the Jews. As the focus of economic activity shifted from country estates to cities, and as emancipation loosened the regulations that restricted Jewish mobility, great numbers of Jews moved into urban centers. As a result, the towns of the Right Bank, where most of the Jews in the Russian Empire lived, became preponderantly Jewish. By the late 19th century, the Jewish presence in the large cities also expanded rapidly. In Odessa more than half the population was Jewish, and the city was one of the largest Jewish centers in the world. In 1863 Kiev had 3000 Jewish inhabitants; by 1910 the number had risen to 50,000. Because most of the educated Jews tended to speak Russian, they added to the Russian character of Ukraine's cities.

Cities were also centers of education and culture, and so were home to the majority of the intelligentsia. Non-Ukrainian urban dwellers had easiest access to education and occupational opportunities and, therefore, predominated among the intelligentsia of Ukraine. For the most part, Ukrainian members of the intelligentsia were located in the countryside and small towns where many worked in the *zemstva* as physicians, agronomists, statisticians, and village teachers. Few Ukrainians belonged to the intellectual elite that dominated the universities and press in the large cities.

But why were the Ukrainians so reluctant to enter the urban environment and participate in the modernizing process? Most students of the problem have concentrated on its psychological dimensions. Those with Ukrainophile tendencies argued that the Ukrainian peasant's deeply rooted love for the soil prevented him from giving up agriculture; those less sympathetic to Ukrainians emphasized their alleged sluggishness and conservatism. But historical antecedents lend little support for these arguments. In Kievan times, an inordinately large part of the population of Ukraine lived in cities and engaged in trade. Even as late as the 17th century, as much as 20% of the Ukrainian population lived in an urban environment. And in the early 18th century, it was Ukrainians (not Russians) who predominated among the intellectual elite of the empire.

The political and socioeconomic conditions that obtained in Ukraine in the 18th–19th centuries help explain the relative absence of Ukrainians in the process of urbanization and modernization there. Because the cities and towns were the centers of imperial administration, Russians and their language and culture tended to dominate in them. Meanwhile, the original Ukrainian inhabitants either became assimilated or, in some cases, were forced out. As has been pointed out by Bohdan Krawchenko, the reason for the absence of a Ukrainian peasant migration to the cities was the prevalence of the *panshchyna* (corvée) in the preemancipation era.[6] Unlike Russian peasants, who were encouraged by their masters to seek additional employment and income in the cities, Ukrainian peasants were forced to continue working on the land so as to take advantage of its fertility. This not only made them less mobile but also left them with little opportunity to develop the skills and crafts that allowed Russians and Jews to make the easy transition to an urban environment. Therefore, when the industrial boom and urbanization began, Ukrainians were not prepared to participate in it. Hence, while Russians moved hundreds of miles to the factories of the south, Ukrainian peasants, even those living within sight of a factory, preferred to migrate thousands of miles to the east in search of land. It would not be long before the weighty social, cultural, and political consequences of this phenomenon would make their impact felt on the course of events in Ukraine.

National Minorities in Ukraine

Another important feature of the socioeconomic modernization of Ukraine was the great changes that it brought about in the ethnic composition of its population. As long as the economy of the land was almost exclusively agrarian, its population remained overwhelmingly Ukrainian. Thus, in 1800, Ukrainians constituted about 90% of the inhabitants of Ukraine, with the percentage on the Left Bank reaching as high as 95%. But in the course of the 19th century, a marked change occurred: the Ukrainian component of the population sank to about 80%, while that of the Russians, Jews, and other minorities rose dramatically. To a great extent, this change was the result of the increased tempo of commercial and industrial growth with which the non-Ukrainian minorities were largely associated.

The Russians   Since the union with Moscow in 1654, Russians were a common sight in Ukraine, but they had never been very numerous. Throughout the 18th and 19th centuries, the most numerous category of Russians in Ukraine was the soldiers on garrison duty. In fact, the word *moskal* (Muscovite) by which Ukrainians designated Russians was synonymous with "soldier." Smaller subgroups of Russians included nobles who had been granted estates in the south, tsarist bureaucrats, and, on the Left Bank especially, merchants. In the late 18th to early 19th centuries, when land became available in the south, a steady although by no means massive, stream of Russian settlers, mostly religious dissenters such as the Old Believers, moved into the new territories. Only in the late 19th century, in connection with the industrial boom, did Russians come to Ukraine in great numbers, particularly to the industrial and commercial centers of the south. Voluntary Russification, especially widespread among the Ukrainian gentry, also enlarged the number of Russians. As noted earlier, by 1897 they constituted 11.7% of the land's population.
    Convinced that Ukraine was essentially a Russian land and that theirs was a superior culture, Russians generally made no effort to master the Ukrainian language and showed little respect for or interest in Ukrainian customs and traditions. They insisted on the Russification of all aspects of Ukrain-

ian life and, in the large cities at least, they attained their goal. By and large, the attitude of the Ukrainian peasantry toward the Russians was not sharply antagonistic. Because Russian newcomers were concentrated in the cities and factories, contacts between them and the Ukrainian countryside were limited. Furthermore, Ukrainian peasants realized that Russian peasants and workers were exploited as mercilessly as they were. Finally, a common Orthodox religion and the similarity of languages made the gap between the two peoples easier to bridge. This is not to say that Ukrainian peasants were not keenly aware of the distinctions between themselves and the northerners. They frequently referred to Russians, many of whom wore beards, by the derogatory *katsap* (like a billygoat), while Russians returned the compliment by referring to Ukrainians with the equally contemptuous *khokhol* (a lock of hair on a Cossack's shaven head). It was, however, among the Ukrainian intelligentsia that the resentment against Russian cultural hegemony was most keenly felt.

The Poles Poles had lived in Ukraine much longer than the Russians. In the 16th and 17th centuries they participated in the colonization of the Ukrainian frontier and although the uprising of 1648 drove them from the Left Bank, they managed to retain control of the Right Bank. They viewed this region as an integral part of Poland – even after the integration of the area into the Russian Empire in 1795. Their great influence on the Right Bank certainly did not depend on their large numbers: in the mid 19th century they totaled only about 500,000 and their share of Ukraine's population dropped from 10% in 1795 to 6.4% in 1909. It was their wealthy and influential elite that accounted for the Polish preeminence on the Right Bank. In 1850, about 5000 Polish landowners held 90% of the land and 1.2 million serfs in the region. With 60% of all of Ukraine's nobles concentrated there, the Right Bank remained a bastion of the old order.

Even the emancipation failed to shake the hold of such fabulously wealthy Polish magnates as the Potocki, Czartoryski, Branicki, and Zaslawski families, each of which owned lands totaling hundreds of thousands of acres. With vast capital at their disposal, they easily switched to hired labor and mechanized farming when the need arose. But the great majority of Polish nobles found the transition to commercial farming difficult. By the late 19th century, many of them had sold their estates and moved into towns and cities where they became bureaucrats, merchants, and members of the liberal professions. Nonetheless, in 1904, over 46% of the private landholdings and 54% of the industrial output on the Right Bank were still in Polish hands.

Tensions between Polish landowners and Ukrainian peasants had always been great. The emancipation ameliorated the situation somewhat. Later, when the Poles rebelled against the Russians in 1863, some of them made an effort to win the Ukrainian peasants over by issuing the so-called golden decrees whereby the rebels claimed that they, not the tsar, were granting the peasants land and freedom. In general, the results of these efforts were minimal. Few Ukrainian peasants joined their Polish lords, and about 300,000 volunteered for police duty against the rebels.

Some Polish nobles had an interest in Ukrainians that was not politically or economically motivated. They and their ancestors had lived in Ukraine for centuries. Consequently, in the mid 19th century, a few nobles developed a predilection for things Ukrainian. For example, Tymko Padura took to writing folk poetry in Ukrainian, and the "Ukrainian school" of Polish writers from the Right Bank, which included the famous Juliusz Słowacki, often wrote on Ukrainian themes. As we shall see later, a few Polish or Polonized nobles played a prominent role in the Ukrainian national movement. Yet the conflict of interests between Polish estate owners and Ukrainian peasants remained, and there were few basic changes in the traditional relationship between the two peoples.

The Jews   Of all the larger minorities in Ukraine, the Jews had lived there the longest. Already present during the Kievan period, they moved into Ukraine in great numbers in the 16th and 17th centuries under the aegis of Polish nobles. But while they were ancient inhabitants of Ukraine, they were relatively new subjects of the tsars. Only in 1795 was the Right Bank, where almost all the Ukrainian Jews lived, incorporated into the Russian Empire. The tsarist government adopted a unique policy towards its large number of new Jewish subjects: in order to prevent them from competing with Russian merchants, it forbade Jews to reside in Russia proper. The Jewish zone of residence, called the Pale of Settlement, was limited to their original homelands in the newly acquired western borderlands of Lithuania, Belorussia, and much of Right-Bank Ukraine. Despite some modifications, the Pale remained in effect until 1917.

Throughout the 19th century, especially in its latter part, the Jews experienced a tremendous rise in population. Between 1820 and 1880, while the general population of the empire rose by 87%, the number of Jews increased by 150%. On the Right Bank, this rise was even more dramatic: between 1844 and 1913 the number of its inhabitants rose by 265% while the Jewish population increased by 844%! Religious sanctions of large families, less exposure to famine, war, and epidemics, and a low mortality rate because of communal self-help and the availability of doctors largely accounted for this extraordinary increase. Of the 5.2 million Jews in the empire at the end of the 19th century, over 2 million lived in Ukraine. The disproportionately large number of Jews living in Ukraine is evident from the fact that although in the empire as a whole they constituted 4% of the population, in Ukraine they were 8% – and on the Right Bank 12.6% – of the population.

Traditionally, the Jews were an urban people. Tsarist restrictions against their movement into the countryside reinforced this condition. Therefore, it is not surprising that over 33% of the urban inhabitants of Ukraine were Jewish, and in the small towns (*shtetls*) of the Right Bank, the percentage reached as high as 70–80%. Tight-knit, insular, traditionalist Jewish *shtetl* communities were a world unto themselves. There, Jewish Orthodox religion, culture, and language (Yiddish) dominated. Rabbis and communal self-governing bodies (*kahals*) were most influential, and contact with the "outside" world was restricted to economic transactions. The poverty and overcrowding of the *shtetls* was proverbial, for the Jewish communities simply had more people than their economies could support. To survive in the teeming provincial towns, which had limited opportunities for earning a living and intense competition, required industry, marketable skills, and quick wits.

About three-quarters of Ukrainian Jews made their livelihood as petty traders and artisans. Although by no means wealthy, these shopkeepers, tavern owners, tailors, shoemakers, and jewelers constituted the Jewish "middle class." The unskilled laborers, many of whom barely subsisted on odd jobs and charity, accounted for only about 20% of their labor force. The elite consisted of two subgroups: on the one hand were the rabbis and other greatly respected "men of the book" who exerted great influence in the community and, on the other, the wealthy capitalists. In 1872 these wealthy Jews owned about 90% of Ukraine's distilleries, 56% of the saw mills, 48% of tobacco production, and 33% of the sugar refineries. As educational opportunites improved, many Jews joined the secular, Russified, intelligentsia, especially in such fields as law and medicine. And as industry developed, great numbers of Jews (38% by some estimates) found work in the factories.

But changes also increased the difficulties that confronted the Jews of the empire. There was a rapid growth of Jewish population and a resultant rise in economic competition with non-Jews. The exploitive actions of some Jewish merchants and moneylenders – and, most important, increasingly anti-Semitic government policies – as well as agitation by reactionary groups all contributed to the rise of antagonism toward Jews in the late 19th century. In 1881 and again in 1903–05 the animosity culminated in a series of pogroms, or mob assaults, on Jewish communities and property, leaving dozens dead and causing millions of rubles in damage. Many of the pogroms were carried out by the ultraright Russian nationalist groups such as the Union of Russian People and the notorious Black Hundreds with the connivance or, at least, non-interference of government officials. Yet perhaps the most far-reaching consequence of the pogroms was that they heightened the already acute sense of insecurity among Jews and encouraged the massive emigration of about 1.2 million Jews from the Russian Empire to the United States by 1914.

In general, the relationship between Ukrainians and Jews was not – nor could it hardly have been – a friendly one. For centuries, the two peoples found themselves in structurally antagonistic (yet mutually dependent) positions. To the Jew, a Ukrainian represented the backward, ignorant village; to a Ukrainian, a Jew epitomized the foreign, exploitative city that bought his produce cheaply and sold him goods dearly. Ukrainian peasants feared Russian officials and hated Polish landlords; Jews, for want of other means of making a living, often acted as their representatives or middlemen. Culturally, the Jews and Ukrainians had little in common, and their religions only widened the gap between them.

The relationship between their respective intelligentsias was hardly better. In terms of national orientation, the Jewish intelligentsia saw only two options: either to assimilate into the dominant Russian culture or to work to develop a separate Jewish identity. Developing closer ties with the Ukrainians, who had little to offer Jews culturally, economically, or politically, seemed hardly worthwhile. The Ukrainian intelligentsia, for its part, resented the tendency of Jews, who had lived among Ukrainians for centuries, to identify with the stronger Russians. Although there were attempts at mutual understanding and even cooperation – such as those made by Mykhailo Drahomanov and Aron Liberman or Symon Petliura and other Ukrainian socialists on the one hand, and the prominent Zionist Vladimir Zhabotinsky on the other – they had little impact. Thus, the two communities continued to live in close proximity but in almost total isolation from each other. Moreover, many of their members were more inclined to harbor old resentments than to cultivate common interests and mutual understanding.

૪ા

Three major features characterized the socioeconomic development of Eastern Ukraine in the late 19th century: economic stagnation in much of the countryside, dramatic industrialization in Kryvyi Rih and the Donets basin, and the growing presence in the land of non-Ukrainians. As we have seen, it was the non-Ukrainians, largely Russians and Jews, who were most closely associated with industrial expansion and urban growth. For their part, the Ukrainians remained in the countryside. Consequently a socioeconomic bipolarity emerged: Ukrainians were identified, even more so than before, with the stagnant, backward village, while non-Ukrainians dominated the dynamic, modernizing sectors of the society. To a considerable extent this crucial division still exists today.

Intelligentsia Activism

At the outset of the 19th century it was the imperial government that held the initiative in producing new ideas and providing society with a sense of direction. However, by the end of the century it was clear that the imperial elite was losing its confidence, sense of purpose, and ability to adapt. Meanwhile, society, and especially the intelligentsia – its self-appointed advocate – was emerging as the source of creativity and dynamism, much of it unfettered by the momentous changes of the 1860s–90s. Confronted by the unresponsiveness and even obstructionism of the government, the intelligentsia gradually moved from simply formulating proposals for change to organizing itself and attempting to mobilize society to implement these proposals by revolutionary means if necessary.

In Russian-ruled Ukraine, the intelligentsia championed both national development and social justice. It was a daunting task. Relatively smaller and more isolated than its counterparts elsewhere in the empire, the Ukrainian intelligentsia experienced great difficulties in establishing contacts with the largely uneducated and disinterested masses it sought to help. Its dual goals engendered doubly great problems and repression. The question whether national or social issues deserved most attention brought about confusion and disagreement among Ukrainians. Nonetheless, despite painful setbacks, the Ukrainian movement continued to grow until, in the early years of the 20th century, it appeared to be ready to spread beyond its traditionally narrow social base.

ða

The Ukrainophiles

The nascent Ukrainian movement, which suffered a sharp setback when the Brotherhood of Sts Cyril and Methodius was crushed in 1847, showed new signs of life after the death of the arch-conservative Nicholas I in 1855. Mykola Kostomarov, Vasyl Bilozersky, and finally Taras Shevchenko were released from exile and gathered in St Petersburg where they joined Panteleimon Kulish. These Ukrainophile veterans, some of whom obtained responsible positions (Kostomarov became a well-known professor of history), attracted about a dozen younger Ukrainians and formed a *hromada* (society) in the imperial capital. Similar groups of Ukrainian intelligentsia would serve as the crucible of the national movement for the remainder of the century.

The prime concern of this group was to improve the lot of Ukrainians, especially the peasantry. Except for Shevchenko, all agreed that *hromada* activity should be apolitical and should focus on the enlightenment of the masses. Kostomarov and Kulish were adamant about restricting their activities to the cultural field and avoiding any radicalism that might arouse the ire of the authorities.

To popularize their ideas, the St Petersburg group obtained, with great difficulty, permission from the authorities and in 1861 established *Osnova*, the first Ukrainian periodical in the Russian Empire. It was funded by two wealthy Ukrainians, Vasyl Tarnavsky and Hryhorii Galagan. During its brief twenty-two-month existence, *Osnova* functioned as a means of communication and arouser of national consciousness among the Ukrainian intelligentsia scattered throughout the empire.

The renewed activity of the Ukrainians was well received by the Russian intelligentsia of the capital. Russian journals accepted articles in Ukrainian and supported Ukrainian cultural development. Shevchenko often appeared at public readings with such titans of Russian literature as Ivan Turgenev and Fedor Dostoevsky. According to some accounts, the Russian public received him more warmly than Dostoevsky. Turgenev translated Marko Vovchok's heartrending tales about serfdom in Ukraine into Russian and their impact on the Russian public was similar to that of Harriet Beecher Stowe's *Uncle Tom's Cabin* on Americans. Generally speaking, the feeling of both Ukrainian and Russian intellectuals alike was that they were working together for the benefit of the people (*narod*).

In Kiev, meanwhile, a new generation of Ukrainian enthusiasts composed mostly of students also formed a *hromada*. Numbering several hundred, the Kievans concentrated on developing a network of Sunday schools for the illiterate peasantry. Between 1859 and 1862 they established several schools, with hundreds of pupils, in the region of Kiev. In the long run, however, the most important feature of the Kiev *hromada* was the new type of adherents that it attracted.

Among the Polish and Polonized nobles of the Right Bank there appeared in the early 1860s a small group of students who, conscious-stricken by the age-old exploitation of the peasantry by their own class, resolved to draw closer to the masses among whom they lived. Adopting Ukrainian speech, dress, and customs, this group, led by Volodymyr Antonovych, was called the *khlopomany* (lovers of the peasantry).

On the eve of the Polish uprising of 1863, the *khlopomany* openly broke with Polish society, declared themselves Ukrainians, joined the Kiev *hromada*, and plunged into the work of enlightening the peasantry. Their sense of obligation to the *narod* was reflected in an open letter they sent to a Moscow newspaper: "As individuals who have benefited from a higher education, we should concentrate all our efforts on providing the people with the opportunity to gain an education, become conscious of their own needs, and obtain the ability to fulfill them. In a word, through their own internal [personal] development, the people should reach a level to which they are legally entitled."[1]

In response to a Polish accusation of betrayal, Antonovych, the scion of an old, Polonized Ukrainian noble family, published his famous "Confession"in *Osnova*. In it he argued that the nobles of the Right Bank had two options: they could either "return" to the Ukrainian people and, by means of dedicated labor on their behalf, attempt to compensate them for centuries of exploitation; or they could choose to remain hated parasites who, sooner or later, would be forced to move to Poland. Choosing the first alternative, Antonovych became a famous historian of Ukraine, a life-long populist, and an outstanding leader of the Ukrainian movement. Several of his colleagues, such as Tadei Rylsky, Pavlo Zhytetsky, Borys Poznansky, and Konstantyn Mykhalchuk, also contributed greatly to the Ukrainian cause.

Inspired by the example of the Kievans, the Ukrainian intelligentsia in Poltava, Chernihiv, Kharkiv, and Odessa also established their *hromady* and expanded the Sunday-school network until there were close to 100 such schools in Ukraine. Members immersed themselves in the traditional study of ethnography, philology, and history. In the style of the *khlopomany*, they adopted the dress of the Ukrainian peasants, observed their customs, ate their food, consorted with them in taverns, sang their songs, and, in the privacy of their homes, spoke Ukrainian. There evolved among them a cult of the Cossack, replete with the wearing of colorful Cossack dress. However, it was not Cossack hetmans and *starshyna* whom they idealized but the freedom-loving Zaporozhians and *haidamaky* who supposedly epitomized the nature and strivings of the Ukrainian masses. In the latter part of the 19th century, this romanticized, apolitical combination of populism, volunteerism, and Ukrainian ethnicity became known as Ukrainophilism.

But even the modest, measured activity of the Ukrainophiles aroused suspicions. In 1863, when the Polish uprising was at its height and suspicion of non-Russians mounted, the government and even the Russian intelligentsia concluded that the Ukrainian movement represented a potentially mortal threat to Russia and they turned against the Ukrainophiles. Tsarist officials argued that the Sunday schools were in reality a sinister plot to disseminate Ukrainian separatist propaganda among the peasantry. The seemingly innocent wearing of embroidered Ukrainian blouses and the singing of folk songs were viewed as subversive activities. The minister of war, Dmitrii Miliutin, went so far as to warn the tsar that the *khlopomany* sought to establish an independent Ukrainian state.

Part of the Russian press, led by such ultrapatriotic newspapers as *Vestnik iugozapadnoi Rossii, Kievlianin,* and *Moskovskii vedomosti,* launched a vicious campaign against the Ukrainophiles and their alleged attempts to undermine the Russian state. Soon much of the Russian intelligentsia, which until only recently had viewed Ukrainophiles with benevolence as enthusiasts of a harmless, colorful regionalism, now began to see them as a genuine threat to the empire. While many Russians believed that the Ukrainian movement was a Polish plot to undermine their hold on the Right Bank, the Poles viewed it as a Russian ploy to weaken their position in the region.

The Ukrainians, for their part, hastened to stress their harmlessness. Antonovych and about twenty members of the Kiev *hromada* published an open letter assuring the Russian public that "our goal is only to educate the people," and that "all talk of separatism is a silly joke since we neither need it nor will we benefit from it."[2] But their remonstrances had little effect. In July 1863, Petr Valuev, the minister of internal affairs, secretly banned the publication in Ukrainian of all scholarly, religious, and especially pedagogical publications. Only belles-lettres were allowed to appear in the "Little Russian dialect." Valuev declared that the Ukrainian language "never existed, does not exist and shall never exist."[3] Soon after, the *hromady* disbanded, *Osnova* ceased publication (for want of subscribers more than because of repression), and a number of Ukrainian activists were banished to distant parts of the empire.

For almost a decade the Ukrainophiles were forced to lie low. Early in the 1870s, as the xenophobia of 1863 dissipated and censorship was relaxed, the Kievans slowly resumed their activities. Antonovych (now a professor at Kiev University) and his colleagues, reinforced by such talented adherents as Mykhailo Drahomanov, Oleksander Rusov, Mykola Ziber, and Serhii Podolynsky, surreptitiously formed the Old Hromada, so named to differentiate its older, experienced members (about seventy in number) from the young *hromady* that were also reappearing and that consisted mostly of students. Again, the Ukrainophiles concentrated on nonpolitical activities.

These activities expanded considerably in 1873 when the Kiev branch of the Imperial Geographical Society was founded. The Ukrainophiles enrolled in this semiofficial institution en masse and gained virtual control of it. Under its auspices they commenced the publication of archival materials and founded a museum and a library that collected Ukrainian materials. In 1875, the Old Hromada acquired the Russian newspaper *Kievskii Telegraf* and used it to provide a Ukrainian prespective on current events.[4]

The ban on Ukrainian publications, however, remained a galling impediment to the development of national culture. To circumvent this restriction, individuals such as Kulish, Konysky, Drahomanov, and others established contacts with Ukrainians in Galicia and used their Ukrainian-language press, especially the newspaper *Pravda*, to express views banned in Russia. In 1873, with the help of the aristocratic Elisaveta Skoropadska-Myloradovych and the wealthy sugar-baron Vasyl Symyrenko, the Ukrainophiles initiated and financed the creation in Lviv of the Shevchenko Literary Society, which, several decades later, developed into an unofficial Ukrainian academy of arts and sciences.

But it would only be a matter of time before the Ukrainophiles again aroused suspicion. As was so often the case, some of the Ukrainians' worst enemies emerged from their own midst. In May 1875 Mikhail Iuzefovych, a wealthy, conservative former member of the Kiev branch, sent a stinging denunciation to St Petersburg in which he accused the Ukrainophiles of turning the branch into a subversive organization, of propagandizing the peasantry, and of working for the independence of Ukraine. As a crowning touch, the informer added that the Ukrainophiles spread anti-Russian propaganda in Galicia and that their movement was an Austrian/German plot. The government reacted in predictable fashion.

The Ems Ukaz of 1876   An imperial commission, appointed by an alarmed Tsar Alexander II and including Iuzefovych, recommended a total ban on the import and publication of Ukrainian books, a prohibition against the use of Ukrainian on the stage (even the lyrics of Ukrainian songs that were sung in the theater were translated into other languages), the closing of the *Kievskii Telegraf*, and a subsidy for *Slovo* – a pro-Russian paper in Galicia. The Ministry of Education was instructed to prohibit the teaching of any subject in Ukrainian in the elementary schools, to remove from school libraries books in Ukrainian or by Ukrainophiles, and to replace Ukrainophile teachers with Russians. Finally, the commission proposed the liquidation of the Kiev branch and the exile of several Ukrainian activists, most notably Drahomanov and Pavlo Chubynsky. In short, this was a more systematic and ruthless attempt than Valuev's had been to paralyze the Ukrainian movement. Alexander II, who was vacationing in the German town of Ems, accepted all the recommendations of the commission and on 18 May 1876 the Ems Ukaz went into effect.

Not only did the Ems Ukaz cripple Ukrainophile activity but it brought into question some of the basic assumptions on which the Ukrainian movement rested. Despite the experience of 1863, the Ukrainophiles continued to believe that if they restricted themselves to moderate views and apolitical, cultural work, they would avoid government repression. Kulish even developed a theory to justify strictly cultural Ukrainianism. According to him, the Russians had unusually well-honed, political state-building skills – while the Ukrainians, as demonstrated by their unfortunate history, did not. Therefore, to Kulish it was natural and even beneficial for the Ukrainians to remain in the Russian Empire and to enjoy the security, power, and prestige it afforded them. But he also believed that the Ukrainians with their splendid folklore were culturally more gifted than the Russians. Thus, it seemed only logical that Ukrainians should leave politics to the Russians and concentrate on culture, their strong point. However, the Ems Ukaz shattered Kulish's hopes for a live-and-let-live relationship between Ukrainian culture and Russian politics, and led him to adopt even more unrealistic views to justify his brand of cultural Ukrainianism.

Kostomarov, another of the "founding fathers" of the Ukrainian movement, became openly defeatist after 1876. Having once written defiantly "Let neither Russians nor Poles believe that they own the land upon which the Ukrainians live," he now advised his colleagues to submit obediently to tsarist policies.[5] Other leading Ukrainophiles, such as Antonovych and Zhytetsky, opted for compromise. While they remained committed to fostering Ukrainian cultural distinctiveness, they emphasized that it should not lead to the separation of the Ukrainians from the salutary impact of Russian culture and empire. Indeed, they believed that it was possible to be committed simultaneously to their "narrower" Ukrainian homeland and to the "broader" all-Russian society, which consisted of Russians, Ukrainians and Belorussians. Others still, such as Borys Hrinchenko and Oleksander Konysky, considered themselves to be exclusively and staunchly Ukrainian and wished to minimize Ukraine's links with Russia. But they had no concrete, realistic program for bringing this circumstance about. Thus, under the threat of tsarist repression, considerable differences about the goals, tactics and even the definition of Ukrainian nationhood emerged among the Ukrainophiles and added to their already daunting difficulties.

Drahomanov and the rise of Ukrainian socialism   The need for fresh ideas was most acutely felt by the younger members of the Kiev *hromada*. One of these Mykhailo Drahomanov, almost single-handedly undertook the task of expanding the intellectual and ideological horizons of his fellow Ukrainians. Despite the fact that his views did not win universal acceptance among the Ukrainian intelligentsia, they inspired many younger members to move beyond the cultural activity of their elders and to address, in a Ukrainian context, the key political, national, and socioeconomic issues of the day.

Born in 1841 in Hadiach, near Poltava, Drahomanov belonged to the petty gentry that traced its roots to the Cossack *starshyna* of the Hetmanate. While native traditions were respected in his family, they were overshadowed by the cosmopolitan liberalism of Drahomanov's father, an unusually enlightened and well-read individual. By the time he entered Kiev University, Drahomanov had become a committed democrat, filled with a strong desire to aid the *narod*. This led him to become a leader in the efforts to establish the first Sunday schools in Russia for illiterate peasants. It was while working with the peasants that Drahomanov, realizing the need for Ukrainian-language educational materials, developed an interest in things Ukrainian and joined the Kiev *hromada*. It was, therefore, not a romanticized image of Ukraine that brought him to the Ukrainian movement, but a desire to aid the downtrodden in a practical way.

Drahomanov's goal for Ukraine was the achievement of a political, socio-economic, and cultural status similar to that of advanced European countries. However, he believed that the achievement of this status was possible only if the Ukrainian movement became more broadly based and appealed to the masses by addressing concrete, bread-and-butter issues. In his view, Ukrainians, who were (in his words) a "plebian nation" of oppressed and toiling masses that lacked a national elite, were ideally suited for political programs combining both national and socioeconomic concerns. Hence his declaration that in Ukraine, a true democrat had to be a Ukrainian patriot and a genuine Ukrainian patriot had to be a democrat.

An avowed federalist, Drahomanov did not advocate Ukrainian separatism from Russia. But because he feared the potential of any powerful, centralized state to restrict the rights of the individual, Drahomanov favored the reorganization of the Russian Empire into a loose confederation of autonomous regions – not necessarily ethnically based – in which decision making rested primarily on the local level. Although he often urged Ukrainians, especially those in Galicia, to acquaint themselves with the best of Russian culture, Drahomanov rejected Pushkin's view that "all Slavic rivers should flow into a Russian sea." In a famous article, "The Lost Epoch," he claimed that on balance Ukrainians lost more than they gained under Russian rule. He stated clearly that the loyalty of Ukrainians should not be to "all Russia" but primarily to Ukraine: "Educated Ukrainians usually work for anything in the world except for Ukraine and its people ... They must take an oath to themselves not to desert the Ukrainian cause. They must realize that every educated man that leaves Ukraine, every cent which is not spent for Ukrainian purposes, every word that is not spoken in Ukrainian, is a waste of the capital of the Ukrainian people, and that with things as they are, anything lost is irreplaceable."[6]

Drahomanov's career was that of a man completely committed to his ideals. During the repression of 1875–76, he refused to renounce his views and chose foreign exile instead. Before leaving Kiev, he reached an agreement with the Old Hromada whereby with its financial support, he promised to publish a journal devoted to the Ukrainian cause. This was the genesis of *Hromada*, the first Ukrainian political journal, which appeared irregularly in the late 1870s and early 1880s in Geneva, the home of a small group of Ukrainian political émigrés who joined Drahomanov. But along with national issues, Drahomanov also increasingly espoused radical socialist views in *Hromada*. As a result, a split occurred between him and the much more conservative Kievan Ukrainophiles in 1885 and this rift led to the demise of the journal.

However, as his links with the Ukrainians of Russia weakened, those with the Galician Ukrainians increased. Drahomanov had already visited Galicia and Transcarpathia in the 1870s, and since that time had worked systematically to familiarize West Ukrainians with their compatriots in the east. In time, Drahomanov's ideas struck root among a small but dedicated segment of Galician youth and would lead eventually to the establishment of the first Ukrainian socialist party.

Drahomanov was not the only Ukrainian activist to be drawn to socialism. His close friends from the Kiev *hromada*, Mykola Ziber (a half-Swiss and half-Ukrainian economist) and Serhii Podolynsky (the son of wealthy landowners), also played an important role in spreading socialist ideas among Ukrainians. Ziber is best known for being one of the very first intellectuals in Russia to disseminate Marx's ideas in 1871. The energetic Podolynsky, who developed contacts with Marx and Engels, worked closely with Drahomanov in Europe and helped to organize socialist circles in Ukraine and Galicia.

The Russian Revolutionary Movement in Ukraine

It became evident during the 1870s that, despite emancipation, the economic plight of the peasant was not improving and that despite other reforms, absolutism showed no signs of retreating. Disillusionment spread through imperial Russian society. Among the intelligentsia it resulted in the rise of radicalism and the willingness to do whatever was necessary to destroy the old order. In short, the stage was set for the appearance of the revolutionary.

By the late 19th century the social composition of the intelligentsia, from which almost all revolutionaries came, had undergone a marked change. The postreform liberalization of education meant that nobles would no longer constitute the overwhelming majority of university students or, by extension, the intelligentsia. Now sons of burghers, priests, petty bureaucrats, Cossacks, and even peasants entered the universities in increasing numbers. In the three universities of Ukraine – Kiev, Kharkiv, and Odessa – they made up about 50% of the student body in 1895. These people of varied backgrounds (*raznochyntsi*) gave the new intelligentsia a déclassé flavor that reduced somewhat its estrangement from the masses.

But despite the growth of universities in the late 19th century, the intelligentsia still remained a tiny fraction of society. In 1895 there were only about 5000 university students in Ukraine. And, of course, revolutionaries were only a small part of the intelligentsia. For example, in 1881 (a high point of revolutionary activity in the empire) there were, out of a population of 100 million, fewer than 1000 cases of antistate activity. Finally, the revolutionary movement was essentially anational. Anxious to mold a strong, unified "all-Russian" force against tsarism, its members initially downplayed nationality issues and, with time, viewed them as a major impediment in their revolutionary struggle.

The narodnyky From the 1860s, the radical youth of the empire were usually referred to by the term *narodnyky*. As the term implies, these were people who were identified with the *narod* (the people), which, under the circumstances, meant the peasantry. This identification with and idealization of the peasantry on the part of the radical intelligentsia cannot be understood in purely rational terms. To a large extent, it arose from a sense of guilt that young, idealistic students developed when they compared their privileged and comfortable position to that of the struggling peasantry. A way of subconciously compensating the peasant for his misery was to idealize him. The intelligentsia made much of the supposed moral purity that resulted from the peasant's hard, honest labor. From its point of view, an especially praiseworthy aspect of peasant society was the commune, which seemed to be proof positive of the peasant's natural unselfishness and inborn tendency toward socialism.

But while the idealization of the peasantry was not peculiar to the *narodnyky* (the Ukrainian *khlopomany* and other segments of the imperial intelligentsia shared it to some extent), they were exceptional in their determined commitment to create a revolution that would introduce a new and just order. The first revolutionary *narodnyk* group was organized by Mikhail Chaikovsky in St Petersburg in 1871; similar groups soon appeared throughout the empire. In Ukraine, Fedir Volhovsky organized one such group of about 100 members in Odessa in 1873. Among its members was Andrii Zheliabov, a Ukrainian student of peasant origin who would become one of the most prominent revolutionaries in the empire. Soon afterward, a small, anarchistically inclined circle called the Kiev Commune cropped up in Kiev; it, too, included individuals who would gain revolutionary renown: Vera Zasulich, Volodymyr Debohory-Mokrievych, and Iakiv Stefanovych.

As the revolutionary groups proliferated, a heated debate developed among them about the most effective methods for the attainment of their goals. One tendency, identified with the famous Russian *narodnyk* Petr Lavrov, favored a gradual approach that would prepare the masses for revolution through education and propaganda. Another, initially less popular view, was associated with the colorful, charismatic Russian anarchist Mikhail Bakunin, who urged the revolutionaries to commit violent, incendiary acts that would ignite a massive, spontaneous revolt of the masses. In 1874 Lavrov's approach seemed to triumph when, following a disastrous famine in the Volga region, about 2500–3000 *narodnyky* throughout the empire abandoned their universities, donned peasant garb, and spread out in the countryside to establish contacts with the *narod* and to prepare it for a great uprising. However, this "going to the people," as it was called, failed miserably. Peasants simply refused to associate with the strange city folk, who unsuccessfully and often comically masqueraded as tillers of the soil. Often peasants themselves helped the police to identify and capture the would-be revolutionaries.

In Ukraine "going to the people" occurred mainly in the Chyhyryn region of Kiev province, an area that was chosen by the *narodnyky* because it had been one of the centers of the bloody *haidamak* uprising a century earlier; they hoped to find the rebellious spirit still smoldering there. Although the movement failed, a noteworthy sequel to the affair took place in the region in 1877, when Stefanovych and his Kiev-based anarchist group attempted to take advantage of the peasants' loyalty to the tsar by fabricating "tsarist manifestos" that ordered peasants to form "secret teams" and rise against local landlords and officials. The plot was uncovered and about 1000 peasants were implicated in the so-called Chyhyryn Conspiracy.

While the great majority of *narodnyky* concentrated on the peasantry, a few began to pay attention to the increasing numbers of workers. In 1875 in Odessa, Evgenii Zaslavsky founded an illegal labor association called the South Russian Workers Union that was one of the first in the empire. A few other workers' circles, modeled on those established in the Russian north, emerged in subsequent years, but their existence was brief and their impact ephemeral.

After the failure of the propaganda approach, some of the most radical *narodnyky* turned to Bakunin's ideas and resolved that only violence and terroristic acts could initiate a revolution. In 1878, Vera Zasulich, an erstwhile member of a Kiev anarchist group, shot and wounded General Trepov, the military commandant of St Petersburg. Soon a splinter group, the notorious Narodnaia Volia (People's Will) emerged and made terrorism its primary means of operation. Tightly organized and strictly conspiratorial, the People's Will (among whose leaders was Zheliabov) launched a campaign of political murder that culminated in the assassination of Alexander II in 1881. But instead of revolution, the death of the tsar engendered a general revulsion against violence, discredited the terrorists, and convinced the government to pursue a reactionary course. It is noteworthy that during the terrorist campaign of 1879–81, the *narodnyky* in Ukraine were especially active. A number of important government officials were killed in Kiev and elsewhere. Some revolutionaries even claimed that political assassinations had been invented by such "southerners" as Zheliabov, Dmytro Lyzohub, and Mykola Kybalchych.

The Russian revolutionaries and the Ukrainian issue   Although the focus of the *narodnyky* was social revolution, they could not (in preparation for it) disregard "local conditions," that is, the national particularities of the various peoples of the empire. Lavrov, the leading ideologist of the *narodnyky*, viewed nationalism as a passing phase in world history and expressed great doubts about its ability to aid human progress. Many revolutionaries of Ukrainian origin supported his position, arguing that, painful though it may be, it would perhaps be better for national distinctions to disappear so that a new, global socialist society could emerge. But, for the present, national particularities had to be taken into account.

A graphic example of the type of problem that national particularities caused the *narodnyky* was the issue of the peasant commune. The revolutionaries considered peasant communal landholding in Russia to be a convincing indication of the fact that Russians had a natural inclination toward socialism. From this they concluded that Russia could skip the capitalist stage of development and arrive at socialism more quickly and directly than Europe. However, conditions in Ukraine did not support this theory. In the Ukrainian village private ownership of land was widespread, and some *narodnyky* spoke despairingly of the Ukrainians' "natural aversion" to the commune. Other revolutionaries in Ukraine, such as M. Starodvorsky of the Kamianets-Podilskyi group, simply admitted that "in Little Russia, matters are different. Our people are bourgeois because they are permeated by the instincts of private ownership." Even worse, according to Starodvorsky, this Ukrainian predilection for private property could mean that "Little Russia might serve as a barrier to the spread of the socialist idea in Russia."[7]

These drawbacks notwithstanding, *narodnyky* and Ukrainophiles, particularly the younger generation, had much in common because of their shared interest in the peasantry. Frequently, young Ukrainophiles gathering ethnographic information in the village established friendly relations with *narodnyky* who were spreading revolutionary propaganda there. Indeed, many individuals combined the two activities. Even on the organizational level there were numerous cases of co-operation between revolutionary groups and the "young" *hromady*. However, the "old" *hromady*, whose members were deeply immersed in compiling a dictionary of the Ukrainian language, disapproved of the activities of their younger colleagues and this circumstance became a source of serious tensions between the two generations of Ukrainophiles.

The revolutionary movement not only led to a split among the Ukrainophiles, but it also greatly depleted the number of its adherents. Because of its dynamism, heroic romanticism, and appealing universalism, the revolutionary movement attracted growing numbers of young Ukrainians. Having joined the ranks of the revolutionaries, they adopted an antinational bias and broke with or never developed ties to the Ukrainian movement. At best, these young Ukrainian recruits to the cause of social radicalism sought to create the revolution first and deal with nationality issues later. Thus, the ability of revolutionary populism to attract increasing numbers of Ukraine's most talented and energetic young people resulted in a critical weakening of the Ukrainian movement.

Marxism Perplexed and frustrated by the peasants' blind faith in the tsar and disillusioned by the realization that the average peasant preferred to be a rich kulak rather than struggle for social equality in his village, many radicals began to have their doubts about the revolutionary potential of the peasantry. Consequently, growing numbers of radicals became receptive to ideas that placed hopes for a revolution on a new class – the proletariat.

The source of these ideas was Marxism. Compared to the fuzzy idealism of the *narodnyky*, Marxism's stress on economics seemed to provide a scientific, verifiable way of analyzing social behavior. It provided a framework for the division of all societies into exploiters and exploited and revealed why class struggle was unavoidable and revolution was inevitable. Moreover, it appeared to be capable of explaining social relations throughout history and everywhere on earth.

Another appealing aspect of Marxism was its contemporary relevance. By contending that the last decisive confrontation was already occurring between the capitalist thesis and the proletarian antithesis, Marx predicted that the world's greatest revolution would take place in the foreseeable future. After a titanic struggle, the proletariat would win and usher in the ultimate synthesis – socialism. He thus not only provided radicals with new optimism, but also encouraged them to believe that they themselves could be instrumental in bringing about these epochal events.

Marxist ideas made an early (albeit abortive) appearance in Ukraine when Ziber – whom Marx held in high regard – first introduced them to his Kievan students and colleagues in 1871. According to Soviet scholars, Ziber's failure to generate interest in them was a result of his focus on Marx's economic theories only and not on his revolutionary message. The fact that, at the time, large-scale industrialization had not yet begun and that the proletariat in Ukraine was exceedingly small also helps to explain this initial unreceptiveness to Marxist ideas.

It is Georgii Plekhanov, a disillusioned Russian *narodnyk* who became familiar with Marx's works during his exile in Switzerland, who is usually credited with having introduced Marxism to the intelligentsia of the Russian Empire. In 1883 he founded the first Russian Marxist group, The Liberation of Labor, in Geneva, where it published the works of Marx in Russian translation and disseminated them illegally in the empire.

In Ukraine the first stable Marxist group, called the Russian Group of Social Democrats, appeared in Kiev in 1893. Its formation was largely the work of Iurii Melnikov, a Russian who established a trade school that served as a conduit for the spread of Marxist ideas. Other Marxist groups appeared in Kharkiv, Odessa, and Katerynoslav. Ethnic Ukrainians were rare among these early Marxists, almost all of whom were Russians with a strong admixture of Jews and some Poles. This composition is understandable because the social democrats focused their attention on the largely non-Ukrainian proletariat to which the peasant-oriented Ukrainian intelligentsia found it difficult to relate.

Even in Russia the growth of social democracy was slow. Most of those who had constituted the membership of the Marxist Social Democratic party in 1898 were arrested; by 1903 a new congress had to be called abroad to rebuild the party. Instead of solidifying the party, however, the congress brought about a split in its ranks that would be of great significance to Russia and Ukraine. The Bolsheviks or "majority," led by Vladimir Ulianov (later known as Lenin), opted for the formation of a disciplined, tightly knit organization of professional revolutionaries who would serve as the "vanguard" of the proletariat. From historical hindsight, the appearance of Lenin and the Bolsheviks was an event of tremendous importance. At the time, however, it went unnoticed by the people of Russia and even by the tsarist police, who were well informed about the activities of the social democrats and believed that any movement based on such obtuse, complicated theories as those of Marx had little chance of success in the empire.

Other non-Ukrainian parties in Ukraine The growth of the social democrats also forced their ideological rivals, the *narodnyk*-populists, to mobilize. In 1901 they formed the Socialist Revolutionary party, whose ideology was a mixture of old populist principles and new Marxist ideas and whose tactics still included the use of political assassination. Radical activism finally forced the liberals – whose goal was the establishment of a constitutional system like that of England or France and who were concentrated in the *zemstva* – to form their own party. In 1904 they established the Union of Liberation, which later became the Constitutional Democratic party or Kadets for short. Alarmed at the rise of illegal, antitsarist parties, the government sought to redress the balance by supporting the organization of ultranationalist, progovernment parties such as the Russian Monarchist party and groups such as the Union of Russian People. These ultrarightist groups, which were strongly supported by the Orthodox clergy, were popularly called the Black Hundreds and they specialized in pogroms of Jewish communities and anti-Ukrainian agitation in Ukraine. The national minorities in Ukraine also established their own political organizations. The Poles were represented by the Polish Socialist party (PPS) and the Jews, who were the most politically active and well-organized people in the empire, were led by the nationalist Zionists and the Marxist Bund.

The Russian parties in Ukraine were by no means composed exclusively of Russians. Large numbers of Russified and even nationally conscious Ukrainians were attracted to the Kadets and the Socialist Revolutionaries, for they saw in them the most effective means of combating tsarism. Even in the ultranationalist, anti-Ukrainian organizations, many "Little Russians" competed with Russians in demonstrating their loyalty to the tsar and their hatred of his enemies.

The attitudes of the Russian and non-Ukrainian parties toward the Ukrainian movement varied. Because they favored decentralization, the Socialist Revolutionaries were understanding, if not supportive, of Ukrainian aspirations. The Polish socialists and especially the Jewish Zionists and the Bund – who shared with the Ukrainians a desire for autonomy and cultural rights –

were often willing to cooperate with certain Ukrainian groups. However, on the few occasions that they addressed the issue, the Marxists, and especially the Bolsheviks, were only partially successful in repressing their antagonism to Ukrainian "separatist" tendencies.

Ukrainian Political Parties

Like the Russians and the other nationalities in the empire, the Ukrainians were also caught up in the political activism that characterized the 1890s and early 1900s. They were motivated, on the one hand, by the general reaction to the repression of the 1880s and, on the other, by the inspiring example of the new dynamism and fresh ideas that appeared among Russian radicals. Another important impetus was the appearance of a new generation of Ukrainian activists who no longer wavered about their national identity but proudly referred to themselves as "nationally conscious Ukrainians" and militantly demanded national rights, political freedom, and social justice for their people.

These "new" Ukrainians were, for the most part, students and it was in the milieu of the *gymnazium* (high school) and the university that these individuals established the personal contacts and developed the ideas that led them actively to oppose tsarism. The career of a Ukrainian activist usually followed a familiar pattern. A youth would first be exposed to "subversive" ideas in a *gymanazium* where a liberal teacher or elder colleagues would introduce him to contraband publications and invite him to secret discussion groups. Once in university, such an individual would then join a Ukrainian student *hromada*, some of which, like those in Kiev and St Petersburg, had hundreds of members. As a member of the *hromada*, the student would be exposed to a variety of ideologies, become acquainted with well-known activists, and often commence illegal activities, such as the publication and distribution of antitsarist literature.

Students were further radicalized by conflicts between them and the government. For example, in 1901 the government forcibly drafted into the army 183 student activists from Kiev University. This called forth a massive sympathy strike throughout Ukraine and led to the expulsion from the universities of numerous students, many of whom concluded that their only option was to become revolutionaries. Of course, many students either never engaged in radical activities or abandoned them upon completing their studies. Nevertheless, few were the Ukrainian political leaders who had not first made a name for themselves as student activists, and many were the student *hromady* that served as the initial building blocks of Ukrainian political organizations.

The first organized appearance of these young "conscious" Ukrainians occurred in 1891 when a group of students, led by Ivan Lypa, Borys Hrinchenko, and Mykola Mikhnovsky, gathered at the grave of Taras Shevchenko to form the Brotherhood of Taras (Bratstvo Tarasivtsiv). Concerned that the best of Ukrainian youth were being lost to Russian revolutionary organizations, the brotherhood resolved to forge the Ukrainian movement as a serious alternative to Russian radicalism and Russian culture in general. It established contacts with student groups in Kiev, Odessa, Poltava, and Chernihiv and began sponsoring lectures, plays, and celebrations honoring Shevchenko. Some members of the groups also joined a publications society of about eighty members, mainly elementary school teachers, whose goal was to disseminate Ukrainian literature among students and peasants. Lypa and his colleagues also urged Ukrainian authors to utilize European models in their work instead of Russian ones.

But the brotherhood's most noteworthy achievement was the publication in 1893 of its famous credo, "The Declaration of Faith of Young Ukrainians," in *Pravda*, a Lviv-based newspaper. This strongly worded document reflected a militant nationalism and contained a stinging critique of the Ukrainophiles for their intellectual dependence on Russian culture. Its authors confidently declared their intention of becoming something the older generation had never been – a genuinely Ukrainian intelligentsia. As a sign of their "uncompromising Ukrainianism" they bound themselves to speak Ukrainian at all times, to raise their children in the "Ukrainian manner," to demand the teaching of Ukrainian in schools, and to defend the Ukrainian cause on every occasion. Their political goal was full recognition for Ukrainians as a separate nation within a democratic, federated Russia. Yet, despite these bold declarations and a flurry of cultural activity, the brotherhood attained few concrete results and was soon assimilated by other Ukrainian political groups.

Rumblings of discontent, the appearance of splinter groups led by younger members, as well as the numerical growth of the *hromady* finally forced the elder statesmen of the Ukrainian movement to act after the long hiatus of the 1880s. In 1897, on the initiative of Antonovych and Konysky, they resolved to form a clandestine organization that would unite all the Ukrainian activists in the empire. The result was the General Ukrainian Organization (GUO), a federation of about twenty *hromady* plus many student groups and individual members that was directed by an executive committee in Kiev. According to secret police estimates, its active membership was around 450, about 100 of whom were based in Kiev. As usual, one of the first acts of the organization was to attempt to get the "Ukrainian message" into the printed media. This goal was reflected in the establishment of a GUO literary publishing venture and a bookstore in Kiev. The organization also sponsored morale-boosting anniversaries of Shevchenko and other noted Ukrainian writers. Especially noteworthy in this regard were the festivities honoring Ivan Kotliarevsky in 1903 and the composor Mykola Lysenko in 1904 in which several thousand members of the Ukrainian intelligentsia participated, including representatives from Western Ukraine. To aid those individuals who were persecuted by the police for Ukrainophile activities, the GUO established a special fund. But although the appearance of the GUO indicated that the older generation of Ukrainians had also become aware of the need to organize, the nature of their activities showed that they were still unwilling to renounce cultural activity for politics. Thus, when the 19th century came to an end, the Ukrainians still did not possess what other minorities, such as the Jews and the Poles, already had – a political party.

The Revolutionary Ukrainian party (RUP)   Again it was in Kharkiv that a group of students, which included L. Matusevych, Iurii Kollard, O. Kovalenko, and the sons of several old Ukrainophiles such as Dmytro Antonovych, Mykhailo Rusov, and D. Poznansky, took the initiative. In January 1900 they founded the Revolutionary Ukrainian party (RUP), a tightly knit, conspiratorial group. The aim of this first East Ukrainian political party was to unite various generations and classes in the struggle for national rights and social revolution. Students in particular responded favorably to the initiative of the Kharkiv group. By 1902, six branches, coordinated by a central committee, functioned in Kiev, Kharkiv, Poltava, Lubny, Pryluky, and Katerynoslav. Many smaller groups of *gymnazium* and university students were also affiliated with the party. To facilitate the obligatory publication program, a foreign bureau was established in Lviv in Galicia and Chernivtsi in Bukovyna. RUP published two periodicals, *Haslo* and *Selianyn*, which were designed to politicize the peasantry, and smuggled them into Russian-ruled Ukraine.

The party soon encountered difficulties, especially when it attempted to formulate its program more precisely. From the outset the problem was whether national or socioeconomic issues deserved greater emphasis from a revolutionary standpoint. Initially, as the party's publication of the pamphlet *Samostiina Ukraina* (by the fiery nationalist Mykola Mikhnovsky) indicated, the national question was of great concern to its members. In time, however, in order to expand beyond its original constituency of "conscious Ukrainians" and reach the peasantry, RUP increasingly focused its attention on socioeconomic matters. Moreover, many of its members became converts to Marxism, thus gradually transforming the party into a social democratic organization.

In the process, tensions developed among RUP members. The majority, led by Mykola Porsh and his colleagues Volodymyr Vynnychenko and Symon Petliura, argued that the organization should be a national party, composed solely of Ukrainians but combining nationalism with Marxism. Others, whose foremost spokesman was Marian Melenevsky, wanted RUP to shed its national character and become an autonomous branch of the Russian Social Democratic party, which would represent all workers in Ukraine, regardless of nationality.

A note about factionalism is now in order. The radical intelligentsia was engaged in a bitter struggle with tsarist autocracy that precluded a climate of tolerance in which differing ideas could be discussed openly and calmly. This struggle also prevented the development of the Western art of compromise and majority rule – and, thus, factionalism became a widespread phenomenon in all segments of the revolutionary movement. If one group of revolutionaries disagreed with another, it usually continued to adhere to its position and fanatically accused its ideological opponents of stupidity, at best, and of reactionary tendencies, at worst. The group would then self-righteously break off from the original organization to form its own faction. Often, its contempt for its erstwhile colleagues would match that of its hatred of the tsarist regime.

That Ukrainians formed no exception to this tendency can be readily seen from the splits that developed in RUP. In 1902 a small segment of the party, influenced by Mikhnovsky's intense nationalism, broke off to form the tiny Ukrainian National party. Two years later, a sizable minority that sided with Melenevsky left the party to join the Russian Social Democrats. The goal of Melenevsky's faction (called Spilka) was to become the leading Marxist party in Ukraine under the sponsorship of the Russian organization. What remained of RUP renamed itself the Ukrainian Social Democratic Workers party and continued its efforts to combine Marxism and nationalism.

A noteworthy aspect of RUP activity was its relations with other non-Ukrainian Marxist parties. In their dealings with the Russian Social Democrats, Ukrainian Marxists found confirmation of something that they had long suspected – namely, that Russian revolutionaries shared with the tsarist government the same predilection for centralism. Time after time, whenever the RUP attempted to establish a cooperative working relationship with the Russian Social Democratic party, discussions would collapse because of the Russians' refusal to grant autonomous status to the Ukrainian organization. In contrast, RUP's relations with the Polish socialist party and especially with the Jewish Marxist Bund were excellent. This attitude was reflected in RUP's strong criticism of restrictions against Jews in the empire and in the Bund's support for Ukrainian efforts to gain autonomy in the Russian Social Democratic party.

The moderates Not only did RUP spawn a number of other parties, but it also forced Ukrainian moderates, united in the GUO (General Ukrainian Organization), to take the step that they had long avoided. In 1904, at the urging of Evhen Chykalenko, the GUO voted to transform itself into a liberal political party whose goals would be the establishment of constitutional government, social reform, and full national rights for the Ukrainians in a federated Russian republic. To a large extent the decision of the moderates to take this step was motivated by the fear that the young socialist radicals would take over the Ukrainian movement and lead it on a path that respectable professors, government officials, and *zemstvo* functionaries would find difficult to follow. Predictably, however, ideological conflicts and factional splits developed and in order to accommodate its left-leaning members, the liberal party renamed itself the Ukrainian Radical Democratic party. Despite the change of name, it remained an essentially liberal party much akin to the Russian Kadets.

Thus, by 1905, the Ukrainian movement had experienced considerable growth. It had developed a variety of parties that offered a range of prescriptions for solving Ukraine's national, political, and socioeconomic problems. But all these parties still consisted mainly of the intelligentsia and they were continually at odds with each other. Moreover, because almost all the Ukrainian intelligentsia were left leaning, the conservative viewpoint was not represented in the Ukrainian political spectrum, forcing Ukrainians of that persuasion to join Russian conservative parties. These drawbacks notwithstanding, it was clear that the Ukrainian movement had finally moved beyond culturalism and had commenced a new, political stage in its development.

The Revolution of 1905

Russia's first revolution began on "Bloody Sunday," 22 January 1905, when police in St Petersburg fired on a large, peaceful demonstration of workers carrying icons and portraits of the tsar and led by a controversial priest from Ukraine, Georgii Gapon. In the melee about 130 people were killed and hundreds more were wounded. As shock and revulsion rolled through the empire, a sudden shift of mood occurred, especially among the previously loyal workers and peasants. The image of the tsar as a well-meaning benefactor was badly tarnished and the gross incompetence of the authorities was clearly demonstrated to all. The general anger at the government was quickly transformed into sympathy for the revolutionaries and into a willingness to protest.

Throughout the following spring and summer, a mounting crescendo of strikes enveloped the country. At its high point in October, close to 2 million workers – 120,000 in Ukraine – staged a mammoth general strike. Meanwhile, in the countryside, widespread disturbances spread rapidly, usually taking the form of pillaging and burning the hated landlords' estates. Even in the armed forces there was unrest and a number of rebellions occurred, the most famous of which was the mutiny on the cruiser *Potemkin* in Odessa harbor. Refusing orders to fire on the strikers on the shore, the crew of the *Potemkin* – which consisted mainly of Ukrainians and was led by Opanas Matiushenko, a native of Kharkiv province – rebelled and took control of the ship. One of the few officers to join the mutineers was O. Kovalenko, a leading member of RUP.

In the face of mounting pressure, Tsar Nicholas II grudgingly agreed to concessions. These culminated in the famous October Manifesto (17 October) that granted his subjects full civil rights and promised the establishment of a parliament or *duma*. It appeared that the empire was about to become a constitutional monarchy.

The impact of the revolution in Ukraine   For the Ukrainian movement, the revolution brought two crucial improvements: it finally broke the government's resolve to enforce the hated 1876 restrictions on the Ukrainian language and allowed Ukrainians to associate freely. The results were immediate and impressive: in November 1905 there had been only one Ukrainian newspaper and by early 1906 there were already seventeen. The number of publishing ventures jumped from two to seventeen, thirteen of which were based in Kiev. In almost every town there appeared *hromady* or Ukrainian clubs, as they were now called. In the countryside, Prosvita, a cultural institution modeled after a society of the same name in Galicia, proliferated. Although the first Prosvita in Eastern Ukraine was founded in Katerynoslav at the end of 1905, by the middle of 1907 there were thirty-five in the major cities of Ukraine, each with numerous branches in the surrounding villages and also among the emigrants in the Far East. However, even at the height of the revolution, the government restricted the growth and coordination of the work of these societies for the following reason, as stated in one of its circulars: "Bearing in mind that the measures through which Prosvitas wished to influence the people are considered very dangerous in the present unrest ... and also having in mind that Little Russia is a part of one great Russian state, and that the awakening of national political consciousness of the Little Russian people, at this time, cannot be permitted ... the administration of the *guberniia* decided to refuse the registration of the Ukrainian society Prosvita."[8]

Cooperatives, usually headed by Ukrainian activists, burgeoned: in Kiev province their numbers grew from 3 in 1904 to 193 in 1907, in Podilia from 18 in 1905 to 200 in 1908, and in Kharkiv province from 2 in 1905 to 50 in 1907. It became abundantly clear that once restrictions were lifted, the Ukrainian movement had much greater potential for growth than commonly had been expected.

Although the Ukrainian parties, like all the parties in the empire, were caught unaware by the revolution, they worked feverishly to take advantage of the upheaval. Most dynamic was Spilka, the Ukrainian component of the Russian Social Democratic party, which favored the Mensheviks. It was especially effective in mobilizing the peasants for strikes and demonstrations and drew many of them into its membership. The Ukrainian Social Democratic Workers' party (USDWP), the successor of RUP, was not as successful in expanding its base of support. Claims by its supporters that its membership reached 3000 during the revolution are probably exaggerated. A noteworthy aspect of its activity, however, was the organization, as a gesture of goodwill to the Jewish Bund, of several units of party members in Poltava and Lubny to maintain order and protect Jewish communities from pogroms. The

Ukrainian liberals (URDP) made few efforts to reach beyond the intelligentsia. However, when elections to the Duma were held in the spring of 1906, their influence increased.

The turning point in the revolution occurred in early 1906 when tsarist concessions led to a split among the revolutionaries. Satisfied with guarantees of constitutional government, the liberals agreed to participate in the elections to the Duma. But the radicals, insisting that a social revolution had not yet taken place, decided on a boycott. As a result, the strongest Ukrainian parties – Spilka and the Ukrainian Social Democrats – did not put candidates forward and only a handful of Ukrainian liberals were elected. However, a considerable number of Ukrainians were elected on the tickets of Russian parties. Of the 497 members of the first Duma, the delegates from Ukraine consisted of 63 Ukrainians, 22 Russians, 5 Poles, 4 Jews, and 1 German. When the Duma convened, the Ukrainians quickly organized a parliamentary club consisting of over forty members to formulate their demands.

First and foremost, the Ukrainians in the Duma insisted on greater autonomy for their country. Somewhat unexpectedly, the Ukrainian peasantry backed these demands wholeheartedly. A more specific and equally popular demand called for the Ukrainization of education, especially at the elementary level. But the government, increasingly more confident, resisted this pressure. Its officials were convinced that granting greater autonomy to the Ukrainians would only whet their appetite for independence. As the minister of interior, Petr Durnovo, informed Tsar Nicholas II: "We should expect that, under the influence of revolutionary propaganda, the peasants of this province [Poltava] will pass a resolution for the separation of Ukraine from Russia based on the principle of autonomy."[9]

So displeasing did Nicholas II find his first exposure to parliamentary government that he exercised his prerogative and dismissed the first Duma after only seventy-two days. Only after imposing voting restrictions, which skewed the electorate in favor of the more conservative, propertied classes, did the tsar obtain, in the third and fourth dumas, the conservative majority that he could tolerate. As was to be expected, the Ukrainian parties, being all leftists, were excluded from the latter dumas and Ukrainian issues were thus almost totally ignored.

The postrevolution reaction   By 1907, the government, backed by a conservative majority in the Duma, was ready to go on the counteroffensive against "revolutionary excesses." A state of emergency was declared and all demonstrations strictly forbidden. Military courts were established throughout the empire and hundreds of revolutionaries and rebellious peasants were sentenced to death. Political parties were driven underground and their best-known leaders, including many of the old RUP activists, fled abroad. One by one, the Ukrainian clubs disbanded. Only the Prosvitas – their activity reduced to staging theatricals – and several scholarly societies were allowed to continue. But Ukrainian periodicals, which had appeared in such profusion in 1905, practically disappeared, and all talk of Ukrainizing education now met with open derision on the part of the authorities.

The anti-Ukrainian policies of the government found strong support among certain sectors of Russian society. Petr Struve, a famous liberal spokesman, wrote a series of articles in 1908 that advocated general support for a "Greater Russia" and sharply criticized the Ukrainian movement for its "lack of patriotism."[10] As Russian nationalism mounted to chauvinistic levels in the years before the First World War, Ukrainian activists were increasingly perceived by many Russians as advocates of "treacherous separatism" or, to use a favorite term of the Ukrainophobes, "Mazepism." Repeated rumors and innuendo implied that leading Ukrainians were secretly in the pay of the Germans and Austrians.

In Ukraine, certain Russian newspapers, such as *Novoe Vremia* and *Kievlianin*, made it a point to alert their readers to the "dangers" of Ukrainianism. In 1908 the Club of Russian Nationalists was founded in Kiev for the express purpose of "waging social and cultural war against the Ukrainian movement and defending the foundations of the Russian state in Ukraine."[11]

But the Ukrainians were not without their supporters. In 1911, at the All-Russian Congress of *zemstva* workers in Moscow, the representatives of the Kharkiv and Poltava *zemstva* came out strongly in support of the introduction of Ukrainian in the elementary schools. In general, backing for cultural Ukrainianism was widespread among the *zemstva* in Ukraine. In the academic world, such well-known Russian scholars as the philologists Aleksei Shakhmatov and Fedor Korsh defended the Ukrainian movement against its maligners, as did the Polish linguist Jan Bedouin de Courtney. An especially strong supporter of Ukrainian demands for autonomy was the fiery, Odessa-born Zionist Vladimir Zhabotinsky. However, these well-wishers were rare exceptions to the general hostility of Russian society and of the tsarist government to the Ukrainian movement in the years before the First World War.

Cultural Development

In the history of Ukrainian culture, the period from 1861 to 1914 was most creative and fruitful. Largely because of the great social, economic, and political changes that occurred during this time, creative forces emerged that produced imposing achievements, despite government repression. But this burst of creative energy was an all-imperial phenomenon. This period is often called the Silver Age of Russian culture and undoubtedly the momentum that originated in St Petersburg and Moscow had a stimulating effect on Ukraine. In scholarship, literature, and the arts what was produced in Russia and Ukraine at this time compared favorably to similar developments in

Western Europe. Yet, as so much in the Russian Empire, cultural growth in Ukraine was a study in contrasts: while a thin stratum of society benefited from an increasingly sophisticated system of higher education and was culturally on a par with Europe, the overwhelming majority of the country's inhabitants remained illiterate and untouched by cultural developments. Thus, the "high" culture of the intelligentsia, where improvement was most dramatic, remained far removed from the folk culture of the masses, where changes were few.

Education   If in the 18th century the level of their general education had been a source of pride to Ukrainians, particularly on the Left Bank, in the 19th century it became one of their greatest shortcomings. The extent of this catastrophic reversal is illustrated by the fact that while in 1768 the three largest counties in Chernihiv province had one elementary school per 746 inhabitants, in 1876 they had only one such school per 6750 inhabitants. The introduction of serfdom and the conviction on the part of the government and the nobles that serfs had no need of education were primarily responsible for this decline. The elementary schools that did exist in the early 19th century were almost all parochial and depended on the contributions of impoverished villagers for their survival.

The situation improved somewhat after the emancipation (1861), especially in the 1870s when the *zemstva* took over responsibility for general education. Frequently staffed by progressive individuals, the *zemstvo* school committees, which provided 85% of the schools' budgets, expanded construction of new schools, improved pedagogical techniques, and introduced subjects such as mathematics, history, and geography in place of the traditional rote learning of religious texts.

The quality of teachers, many of whom were idealistic university students, also improved. Nonetheless, serious problems remained. Because education was not mandatory, about two-thirds of the peasants sent their children to work in the fields rather than to the schools. Despite appeals from the *zemstva*, teachers, and celebrated pedagogues, the government refused to allow the use of Ukrainian in the elementary schools, thereby placing Ukrainian pupils at a distinct disadvantage. Finally, on the Right Bank, where no *zemstva* were allowed until 1911, educational improvements were minimal and the educational level of the region was the lowest in all of European Russia. There was, of course, great variability in the literacy rate in Ukraine: at the turn of the century, while only about 20% of the village population was literate, the rate in cities was about 50% – and among workers in Kiev and Kharkiv it reached as high as 60%.

Secondary education, which consisted mainly of the *gymnazia*, also improved considerably. There were several types of *gymnazia*: Most offered a seven-year course of study, others only a partial four-year course; some were of the classical type that stressed the study of Greek, Latin, and logic; others emphasized modern European languages, sciences, and mathematics. By 1870 women's *gymnazia*, designed for the preparation of teachers, were formally sanctioned. Almost every provincial center, and even many county seats, had a *gymnazium* and by 1890 there were 129 throughout Ukraine. Yet their growth hardly matched the need. In Kiev province, for example, there was only one *gymnazium* per 560,000 inhabitants.

With the establishment of a university in Odessa in 1865, the number of universities in Ukraine rose to three. Their combined enrollment increased from 1200 in 1865 to over 4000 in the 1890s. The social background of the students also underwent considerable change: in 1865 more than 71% were sons of nobles, but by the 1890s over 60% were sons of the clergy, burghers, and merchants. As of 1878, women gained access to the universities. In the final decades of the 19th century, the most important issues at these universities, which enjoyed a reputation for excellence, were as often political as academic. Worried that they served as a breeding ground for radicals, the government severely limited the autonomy of the universities in 1884, and student strikes and protests against these measures kept tensions high. After 1905, Ukrainian students launched a campaign to introduce the teaching of Ukrainian subjects on the university level. By 1908 they attained some success at the universities of Kharkiv and Odessa where not only courses but several chairs in Ukrainian studies were established. However, the faculty of Kiev University, which was noted for its conservatism, staunchly refused to give in to Ukrainian demands. As the postrevolutionary reaction set in throughout the empire, even the few Ukrainian courses in Kharkiv and Odessa were abolished.

Scholarly achievements   Inspired on the one hand by the brilliant scientific discoveries of the early 19th century and reacting against the emotionalism of Romanticism and fuzzy metaphysics of idealism on the other, the intellectuals of the Russian Empire turned in the late 19th century toward positivism, with its promise to provide concrete and verifiable proofs and measurements of physical and social phenomena. This trend was encouraged by the emphasis that Russian universities placed on laboratory training, which stimulated teachers and students to work together in solving scientific problems. It was especially evident in the sciences – chemistry, physics, geology, botany, biology – as well as in mathematics. Another reason for the rising popularity of the sciences (in contrast to the humanities and social studies) was that they were unlikely to result in ideological conflicts with the ever-watchful government.

Some of the scientists of imperial as well as European fame who worked in Ukraine were M. Umov, founder of the school of theoretical physics in Kiev; N. Beketov, an innovative chemist in Kharkiv University; O. Liupanov, a mathematician in Kharkiv; the embroyologist A. Kovalevsky, whose work won the praise of Charles Darwin; and I. Mechnikov who, together with M. Hamaliia, established in Kiev in 1886 the first microbiological laboratory in the empire. Although there were some Ukrainians among the leading scientists in Ukraine, a disproportionately large number of them were Russians. This fact can be explained, in part, by the predominance of Russians in cities where universities were located and their easier access to higher education.

Ukrainians, for their part, were more in evidence in the social sciences. Of the historians, who studied Ukraine's past in and of itself rather than as an adjunct to Russian history, the most famous was the talented, energetic, and ubiquitous Volodymyr Antonovych, one of whose many illustrious students was Mykhailo Hrushevsky. Other Ukrainian historians of note were Oleksander Lazarevsky, Oleksandra Efimenko, and Dmytro Bahalii. Even Russian historians in Ukraine, such as Gennadii Karpov and Mikhail Vladimirsky-Budnov, devoted much attention to the history of the land in which they lived, although (as might be expected) their interpretations differed radically from those of their Ukrainian colleagues. Outstanding Ukrainian scholars in other disciplines were the legal specialist Volodymyr Kistiakovsky, the economists Mykola Bunge and Mykhailo Tuhan-Baranovsky, the orientalist Ahatanhel Krymsky, and the linguist Oleksander Potebnia.

Scholars in Ukraine benefited greatly from the numerous scholarly societies, commissions, journals, as well as libraries and archives, that appeared after 1861. A historical commission, the Provisional Committee, which existed from 1843 to 1917 and was chaired for over a decade by the indefatigable Antonovych, published dozens of volumes of archival documents relating to Ukraine's past. In 1873, a historical society, the Society of Nestor the Chronicler, began to concentrate on Ukraine's history, and in 1882 the Ukrainophiles of the Old Hromada established *Kievskaia starina*, a valuable journal of Ukrainian studies (written in Russian). After the revolution of 1905, the Kiev Scholarly Society, which openly proclaimed its intention to develop and popularize various branches of learning using the Ukrainian language, came into being. Its membership rose rapidly from 54 in 1907, to 98 in 1912, and to 161 in 1916. However, the government still found ways to restrain the appearance of Ukrainian books. As a result, of 5283 books published in Ukraine in 1913, only 176 were in Ukrainian.

Literary development   Remarkably, Ukrainian literature not only survived but flourished, despite – or perhaps as a response to – the cultural repression that marked the period from 1876 to 1905. As the numbers of university graduates grew, the number of authors and the size of their readership also expanded. Moreover, the vibrant Galician press provided ample opportunities for East Ukrainian authors to bypass tsarist censorship. An indication of how far the literary movement had progressed beyond the handful of authors and readers of Ukrainian literature of the early 19th century was the massive and enthusiastic participation of thousands of Ukrainian intelligentsia and dozens of Ukrainian authors from both Eastern and Western Ukraine in the dedication of a monument to Kotliarevsky in Poltava in 1903.

The vibrant growth of Ukrainian literature was also a result of its successful adoption of new literary styles. Romanticism, which had exerted great influence on Ukrainian culture in the early 19th century with its focus on the national uniqueness of a people, its love of folklore, its fascination with history, and its stress on national language, had faded by the latter part of the century. Inspired by the social utopianism of French thinkers such as August Comte, harangued by Russian literary critics such as Nikolai Chernyshevsky, and confronted by the misery in the village and the factory, authors throughout the Russian Empire now concluded that no longer was art for art's sake a justifiable slogan. Impelled to use art for the purpose of exposing the injustices and evils in society in the hope that this would lead to its improvement, they embraced a new literary approach – Realism.

Although it did contain some elements of Romanticism – notably the focus on the village and the peasant – Ukrainian Realism finally went beyond the limits of the ethnographic and began to explore the social and psychological dimensions of life. One of the first realist authors was Ivan Nechui-Levytsky, who concentrated on the changes that had occurred in the Ukrainian village after the emancipation. Nechui-Levytsky's writing often evoked a sense of betrayal, a puzzled questioning of why life, instead of becoming better, became worse. In his *Kaidasheva simia* one of the characters asks why "God's earth is so gay and beautiful and yet the lives of the people are so ugly." For Nechui-Levytsky, it was the extreme inequality between the rich and poor imposed by the alien bureaucratic-military "Muscovite" regime, and especially its school system, that was responsible for the extreme poverty, ignorance, superstition, and moral degeneration that he saw in village life.

An even more penetrating treatment of the life of the peasantry was provided by Panas Myrny (Rudchenko). Unlike Nechui-Levytsky, Myrny did not limit himself to social inequality but probed deeply into the psychological impact of injustice on the individual. In his *Khiba revut voly ...?* ("Do Oxen Bellow ...?"), he examined how evil begets evil. The protagonist, the decent if rebellious peasant Chipka, is so frequently abused, exploited, and cheated that he abandons his traditional values and turns into a violent predator whose moral nihilism bursts forth in the statement: "If I could, I would destroy the whole world ... so that a new and better one would arise in its place." Another representative of the realist trend was Anatol Svydnytsky, whose novel *Liuboratsky* dealt with the impact of foreign culture, specifically Polonization and Russification, on several generations of a Ukrainian clerical family.

The numerous poets of this period are much more difficult to categorize.

Most noteworthy were Stefan Rudansky, an unusually talented writer best known for his witty, biting, aphoristic work *Spivomovnyk*; Leonid Hlibov, author of popular fables; and Pavlo Hrabovsky, whose poems were so critical of the tsarist regime that he was condemned to spend most of his life in Siberia.

As a new generation of authors emerged by the turn of the century, they attempted more and more frequently to go beyond the rigid, utilitarian strictures of Realism, to apply modernistic techniques, and to express individualistic perceptions. This tendency was reflected most impressively in the work of Eastern Ukraine's two leading literary figures of this period – the novelist Mykhailo Kotsiubynsky and the poetess Lesia Ukrainka. In his *Fata Morgana*, Kotsiubynsky focused on the traditional theme of social strife in the village. However, his method of describing it was extremely innovative. Using words like an impressionist uses paint, he created the sense of suspense and tension that arises in individuals in situations of terror, hatred, and panic. His "Shadows of Forgotten Ancestors" reflected both the real and mythical world of the Hutsul village and explored the constant movement between the conscious and subconscious world of the individual.

Laryssa Kosach-Kvitka, whose pen name was Lesia Ukrainka, was born into one of Ukraine's most cultured families. Her mother was the noted author Olena Pchilka; her uncle was the famous Drahomanov; and she was related to the composer Mykola Lysenko and the playwright Mykhailo Starytsky. Although she had the benefit of an excellent education that included travel to Europe and the study of French, Spanish, English, German, Greek, and Latin, as well as Russian and Ukrainian, she was plagued by poor health, which never allowed her a painless, carefree day in her life.

It is remarkable, therefore, that her deep, finely wrought poetry exudes inspiring strength, vigor, and optimism – qualities captured in her poem *Contra Spem Spero* ("To Hope against Hope"). In her early lyrical poems, such as "Wings of Song" and "Thoughts and Dreams," the influence of Shevchenko is still evident. But gradually Ukrainka turned to new motifs that were not strictly Ukrainian and that showed a desire to address universal issues. This new approach became evident in her "exoticism" – which used themes from ancient Greece, Palestine, Egypt, revolutionary France, and medieval Germany – and in her treatment of the varieties of love, the confrontation between power and liberty, and the relationship between the poet and society. Her dramatic poem "Forest Nymph" is a powerful portrayal of the clash between an exalted ideal and base reality.

Another departure from village-oriented Realism was the work of Volodymyr Vynnychenko, perhaps the most popular Ukrainian writer and playwright of the prerevolutionary era. His early naturalistic works, such as "Rabble" and "Beauty and Strength," sketched the lives of provincial townspeople and hired laborers in a world of dying village traditions and crum-

ling morality. More innovative were his treatments of such rare characters
ı Ukrainian literature as the revolutionary confronted by psychologically
omplex (albeit somewhat artificial) situations, as in his novel *Zina*. Vynny-
ʌenko's favorite theme, however, was the personality of the cynical egoist
nost forcefully presented in his "Memoirs of a Pug-Nosed Mephistophe-
ɪs"), who in order to be totally honest with himself, finds himself ready to
ɔmmit any crime so long as his actions are in harmony with his feelings,
ɔnvictions, and will.

If one adds to the above-mentioned authors such West Ukrainian writers
ɪs Vasyl Stefanyk, Olha Kobylianska, and the incomparable Ivan Franko, it
ɪ evident that Ukrainian authors, even when measured by West European
tandards, represented a truly impressive array of talent. Thus, by the turn
ɪf the 19th century, Ukrainian literature, which only a generation earlier had
ɪeen struggling for its right to exist, earned a secure place for itself among
ʌe major Slavic literatures.

ʔhe theater An especially popular and important medium of Ukrainian cul-
ɪre during this period was the theater. Relying heavily on Ukrainian ethnog-
ɪphy at the outset, it offered an attractive combination of acting and singing.
ɪ decisive factor in its development, and one of the few concessions made by
ʌe regime to the Ukrainian movement, was the government's permission in
881 to use Ukrainian on the stage. This made the theater the only medium of
ʔkrainian culture that could develop more or less freely; it therefore quickly
ɪecame the focus of much creative energy and talent. The impact of the the-
ter went beyond the artistic, for many Ukrainians felt their first spark of
ɪational pride and consciousness upon seeing a well-performed play in their
ʔten-denigrated native language.

Almost immediately after the government's decision, the first Ukrainian
ɪrofessional theater was founded in Yelysavethrad (Kirovohrad) in 1881 by
ɪarko Kropyvnytsky. One year later, the troupe numbered over 100 mem-
ɪers. By the 1890s, there were at least five professional troupes that performed
ɪith great success throughout the empire and boasted repertoires of twenty
ɪ thirty plays each. Clearly, the theater had come a long way from the 1860s,
ʌhen it could draw on only a few plays in Ukrainian, such as Kotliarevsky's
ɪatalka Poltavka, Shevchenko's *Nazar Stodola*, and Hulak-Artemovsky's "Za-
ɔrozhian beyond the Danube."

Credit for this rapid development belongs to a handful of talented, ener-
ɪtic, and enterprising individuals, such as Starytsky, Kropyvnytsky, and the
ɪmarkable Tobilevych family, members of which went by the stage names
ɪ Ivan Karpenko-Kary, Mykola Sadovsky, and Panas Saksahansky. Not only
ɪd each of these individuals organize his own troupe, but all were outstand-
ɪg actors, directors, producers, and, in the case of Karpenko-Kary, play-
rights. A leading "star" of the Ukrainian theater was Maria Zankovetska.

Ideologically and culturally, as well as economically and socially, the turn of the 19th century was a period of accelerating change. On all levels the traditional order was beginning to crumble and everywhere there were signs of a search for new ways. This was especially evident in the intelligentsia's growing concern with ideology. In Ukraine, the two main ideological currents that came to the fore were nationalism and socialism. The more firmly these two ideologies took root, the more crucial became the question of their relationship to each other. For many Ukrainian activists it became clear that without a socialist dimension, the national movement had little chance of moving beyond its limited, cultural parameters. By the same token, many Ukrainian socialists realized that, without addressing the national issue, socialism in Ukraine would remain a weakly rooted movement consisting mostly of non-Ukrainians. Efforts to find a satisfactory combination of the two ideologies such as those attempted by RUP, did not produce generally acceptable results and – as the Ukrainians entered the 20th century – the relationship between the two ideologies remained unresolved.

Eastern Galicia:
A Bastion of Ukrainianism

How much benefit can legal reforms bring to a society that is economically impoverished, socially underdeveloped, culturally stagnant, and politically weak? More specifically, what impact did the constitutional reforms of the 19th century have on the Ukrainians under Habsburg rule? By the late 19th century, West Ukrainians benefited greatly from the new opportunities that a constitution can bring.* But they also realized that there were disappointing limitations to what the laws and constitutions could do to ensure socioeconomic and national justice. On balance, however, the impact of the Austrian constitutions of 1848 and especially of 1867 was positive, and it stimulated an unprecedented upsurge within West Ukrainian society of political activism and organizational growth. Indeed, this new activism was so great that it moved the severely handicapped Ukrainians of Galicia to the forefront of the Ukrainian national movement. But if the new constitutional order provided opportunities for communal activity, it was the growing competition with the Poles that served as a major impetus for it. And as both Ukrainian and Polish communities mobilized their forces, the intensity of their confrontation grew.

‹‹

The Socioeconomic Aspect

After 1848, Galicia, as well as Transcarpathia and Bukovyna, continued to be among the poorest regions of Europe, a fact that prompted some historians to refer to them as "a storehouse of economic absurdities."[1] One of

---

* In the late 19th and early 20th century, nationally conscious West Ukrainians began to call themselves "Ukrainians," a national name that had been adopted by the Ukrainian intelligentsia in the east. There were two basic reasons for abandoning the traditional designation, *Rusyn* (Ruthenian): it was felt that *Rusyn* was too similar to *Ruskyi* (Russian) and, by adopting the name used by their compatriots in the Russian Empire, the West Ukrainians wished to stress their unity with them.

the major economic drawbacks of these provinces was their lack of major exports such as the wheat and sugar beets that fueled economic growth in Russian-ruled Ukraine. An insurmountable barrier to the development of industry, even on a modest scale, was the competition from such heavily industrialized provinces as Bohemia, Lower Austria, and Moravia, which easily overwhelmed the few Galician attempts to industrialize. The policies of Vienna only worsened the situation. Not only did the imperial government show little interest in improving conditions in Galicia, but by means of unbalanced tariffs, it clearly favored the western provinces. Even more so than Russian-ruled Ukraine, the lands inhabited by West Ukrainians were the internal colonies of the Austrian Empire.

The landowning elite of the province, moreover, was not eager to introduce economic changes for it feared that development, particularly industrial growth, might deprive it of cheap and plentiful labor. Thus, Galicia, Bukovyna, and Hungarian-dominated Transcarpathia remained agrarian societies, with little capital accumulation, weak internal trade, low urbanization, minimal industry, and the lowest wages and highest labor surplus in the empire. Only in the final decade of the century did faint signs of improvement appear.

Vienna's neglect of Galicia should not leave one with the impression that it was an insignificant part of the empire. As of 1910, the province accounted for 15% of the population of the monarchy. In fact, population was one of the few growth areas in the lands inhabited by the West Ukrainians. In Galicia it jumped from 5.2 million in 1849 to almost 8 million in 1910. But this was a mixed blessing, for the rising population density in the countryside – 32 people per sq. km in 1780 and 102 per sq. km in 1910 – only exacerbated socioeconomic problems.

Major changes also occurred in the ethnic composition of Galicia, although at first glance they appeared to be more dramatic than they were in reality. Whereas in 1849 Ukrainians constituted over 50% of the population in the province, by 1910 over 58% of the population was listed as Polish and only 40% were Ukrainians. Even in Eastern Galicia, the Ukrainian share of the population dropped to 62%. To some extent, the migration of Poles from the western to the eastern part of the province and the Polish assimilation of non-Poles, especially the Germans, accounted for these changes. Yet the main reason was the growing tendency of the Jews, whose share of the province's population doubled from about 6% in 1831 to almost 12% in 1910, to identify themselves as Poles, at least in terms of language.

There were, however, few changes in the occupational profile of the province's nationalities. Ukrainians remained an overwhelmingly agrarian people. In 1900 about 95% of them were engaged in agriculture. Only about 1% were in industry (what little there was of it) and a mere 0.2% in trade. Ukrainian intelligentsia, including the priests, was a small group, probably number ing between 12,000 and 15,000 individuals. (According to the calculations of Volodomyr Navrotsky, in 1876 there were about 5000 Ukrainian intelligentsia, including priests. The Poles had over 38,000, not counting the clergy.)[2] By comparison, their rivals, the Poles, had 80% of their people in agriculture, 6.5% in industry, 2% in trade. In 1914, the Poles had over 300 high government officials in Galicia, while the Ukrainians had only 25. Thus, despite the Habsburg reforms, it was clear that the Ukrainians had been able to make little progress in overcoming the socioeconomic disadvantages that had dogged them for centuries.

The plight of the peasant   As in Russia in 1861, the emancipation of the serfs in the Habsburg empire in 1848, while improving their legal status and political rights, did not improve their economic position. Essentially, the problem was one of rising costs and declining incomes. A major burden on the peasantry was the debt owed on the lands they received in 1848. The Vienna government originally promised to cover the cost of the land transfers itself, but in 1853, after order was restored, it shifted most of the expense upon the peasantry. In addition, the peasants were subjected to direct and indirect taxes including the costs of maintaining schools, roads, etc.

But most infuriating to the peasants was the issue of the so-called servitudes. Under the conditions of the emancipation, the landlords generally retained ownership of the servitudes, that is, forests and pastures to which villagers had previously had access. This meant that the peasant now had to pay whatever price the landlord stipulated in order to obtain firewood and building materials or to feed his livestock. Usually the landowners' price was so high that it seemed to a peasant that he had simply exchanged the legal serfdom of the pre-1848 era for the economic enserfment of the post-1848 period. Anxious to cast off the estate owners' economic stranglehold, peasants by the thousands went to court over the servitudes issue. According to Ivan Franko, of the 32,000 servitudinal court cases between 1848 and 1881, the estate owners won 30,000.[3] The outcome of these cases left little doubt about whom the Habsburg system favored.

As their costs mounted, the amount of land owned by peasants – and, therefore, their income – shrank rapidly. In 1859 the average size of a peasant holding in Eastern Galicia was 12 acres; in 1880 it slipped to 7 acres; and in 1902 to 6 acres. Or, to put it differently, the percentage of peasants who could be classified as being poor, that is, who owned less than 12 acres of land, rose from 66% in 1859 to 80% in 1902. The primary reason for this shrinkage was the subdivision of a peasant's land among his children, the average number of which was three to four per family. As peasant holdings became smaller, the large estates grew even bigger as the wealthy bought up the lands of peasants who could no longer survive on their tiny plots. Thus, Eastern Galicia was a and of about 2400 large landowners who held over 40% of the arable land

and hundreds of thousands of tiny peasant plots, which accounted for about 60% of the total territory under cultivation.

For peasants who sought to supplement their incomes, the prospects were not encouraging. If they hired themselves out as laborers to an estate owner, they could expect to receive the lowest wages in the empire – about one-quarter of wages paid in Austria proper. And if they were so desperate as to borrow from local moneylenders – mostly Jewish tavern-keepers in the villages and shop owners in the towns (for there were no banks) – they courted economic disaster. With interest rates ranging from 150 to 250% annually (another reason why capital stayed in moneylending rather than being invested in industry), a small loan taken out by a peasant to tide him over to the next harvest could in a short time turn into a crushing burden. Large debts were also inadvertently incurred by the naive, uncomprehending peasants: local moneylenders would often encourage them to drink or to buy on credit and, after allowing time for interest to accumulate, would present them with huge bills.When peasants could not pay their debts, their creditors either took over their land or auctioned it off.

Although peasants needed little encouragement to drink, their depressing economic plight certainly contributed to the alarming spread of alcoholism. Inducement also came from the estate owners who had a monopoly on alcohol production and from the tavern keepers who sold it. One way of inducing peasants to drink was the aforementioned extension of credit; another method was paying laborers in chits that could only be cashed in taverns. And then there was the great availability of taverns. In 1900 in Eastern Galicia, there was one tavern for every 220 inhabitants (but only one elementary school per 1500 inhabitants).

Not suprisingly, the health of the West Ukrainians was the most neglected of all the empire's subjects. Whereas, in 1900 there was one hospital per 295 inhabitants in Austria, in Galicia the ratio was 1 per 1200. Over 50% of the children died by age of 5, usually as a result of epidemics or malnutrition. But perhaps most shocking was the fact that about 50,000 deaths a year were attributed to malnutrition, that is, famine. In a famous book, "The Misery of Galicia," the Polish author Stanisław Szczepanowski claimed that the productive capacity of a Galician was one-fourth of an average European while his food consumption was one-half.[4] Little wonder that at the turn of the century the life span of a West Ukrainian male was six years less than that of a Czech and thirteen years less than that of an Englishman.

Being an agrarian, sedentary people, the Ukrainian peasants felt an extremely powerful attachment to their native soil and only the most pressing conditions would force them to leave it. By the late 19th century, it was clear that such conditions were at hand and many peasants were confronted with the heartrending necessity of emigrating. Like their brethren in Russian-ruled Ukraine, the West Ukrainians would have to go halfway around the world in search of more promising opportunities. However, unlike the East Ukrainians who migrated eastward to the shores of the Pacific, the West Ukrainians moved westward across the Atlantic to Brazil, Canada, and, most often, to the United States.

Towns and commerce Only about 10% of Galicia's inhabitants lived in towns and cities. As might be expected, the percentage of Ukrainians in urban centers was quite small: in 1900 over 75% of the province's urban dwellers spoke Polish; only 14% used Ukrainian and the rest communicated in German. Even in Eastern Galicia, Ukrainians formed only 25–30% of the urban population, about the same percentage as Poles. The Jews, however, constituted between 40% and 45% of the town dwellers in the eastern part of the province; in some towns, such as Brody, more than 70% of the population was Jewish. Population growth in the cities was uneven. While the populace of Lviv, the cultural, administrative, and economic center of Eastern Galicia, rose from 70,000 in 1857 to over 200,000 in 1910, most cities and towns experienced much slower growth.

As everywhere, the main economic function of cities and towns was trade and commerce. And to speak of trade in the West Ukrainian lands is to speak of the Jews because they completely dominated this sector of the economy. It was the Jews who acted as the middlemen between the village and the town. Jewish peddlers brought modern products (such as matches and kerosene) to isolated villages and Jewish merchants bought up peasant crops for sale in the towns. In the towns themselves, almost all the shops and stalls in which a peasant could buy finished products, such as cloth, boots, or iron pots (which were produced by Jewish artisans), were owned by Jews. If the peasant lacked cash to buy these products, the Jewish merchant would offer credit. In short, it was the Jews who pulled the peasantry into the money economy centered in the towns.

In exchange for their services, Jewish merchants attempted to extract the highest possible profits. To many non-Jews it appeared that these gains were not only excessive, but illgotten. For example, after studying the economic relationship between Jews and Ukrainians in Transcarpathia, a Hungarian economist of Irish descent, Edmund Egan, reported to the government that while the administration, magistrates, and estate owners contributed to the woeful plight of the peasantry, the main fault lay with the Jews, who as moneylenders, merchants, and tavern-keepers, were "dispossessing the Ruthenians of their money and their property."[5] But although the peasantry resented the exploitative practices of many Jewish merchants, it realized that any type of economic activity was practically impossible without Jewish participation. This view was clearly reflected in a secret Habsburg police report, sent to Vienna in 1890, about the attitude of Ukrainian peasants: "Except for their daily bread, the peasants are dependent on the Jew at every stage of their lives. He serves as their customer, counselor, agent, and factotum, in the full sense of the word. And if we wanted to banish them, the peasants would be the first to demand their return. Although the Jews exploit to the full the advantages accruing from this status and, by granting interest-bearing loans, control not only the peasants but also the clergy, it would be a mistake to speak of a prevalence of anti-Semitism in the sense of racial hatred."[6]

It should be emphasized, however, that most Jews were themselves poverty stricken and had few alternative means of making a living. In the late 19th century, their occupational profile was 15% leaseholders and tavern-keepers, 35% merchants, 30% artisans, and 20% miscellaneous occupations. Most Jewish traders were petty merchants, but a tiny minority was exceedingly wealthy and influential and carried on much of the large-scale trade in Galicia.

Industry Given the competition from the industrialized western provinces, the unfavorable government policies, and the lack of a domestic market, industry obviously had little chance to develop. Moreover, there was a dearth of capital. Until the 1890s, there were no commercial banks, Jewish capital was concentrated in trade and moneylending, and wealthy Poles had their money invested in land. Paradoxically, in Galicia the construction of railroads, which began in 1852, retarded rather than encouraged industrial growth.

Prior to the coming of the railroads, the little industry that did exist, such as glassworks or textile and leather production, was protected from external competition by the province's relative isolation. However, when the railroad brought a flood of western goods, many local industries collapsed. Much of the manufacturing that survived was of the handicraft variety, of which the numerous Jewish tailors and shoemakers were typical representatives. Large-scale enterprises were concentrated mainly in lumbering, encouraged by the presence of vast forests and the great need for building materials in the West, and in alcohol production.

By the 1890s, however, there were signs of improvement. In the preceding decade, three banks were established and they became a source of funding for large industrial projects. Polish magnates, such as Prince Andrzej Lubomirski, lobbied in Vienna for support for industrial development, and in 1901 an association of factory owners was formed. In the 1870s and 1880s, the production of oil in the area of Drohobych and Boryslav, financed mainly by Austrian and English capital, developed rapidly. And prior to the First World War, the Galician oil wells produced close to 5% of the world's oil.

Slowly but steadily, the proletariat grew and by 1902 it numbered about 230,000 full and part-time workers. Of these 18% were Ukrainians, 24% Jews, and the remainder Poles. As in Russian-ruled Ukraine, this very "young" class still had strong ties to the villages and many Ukrainian and Polish workers returned to agriculture after working part of the year in industry. These changes, however, were gradual and relatively modest in scale and the West Ukrainian lands remained far behind other provinces in the empire in terms of economic development.

The New Political Order

After they quelled the uprisings of 1848, the emboldened Habsburgs attempted to undo the revolutionary reforms and to restore the emperor to absolute power. They disbanded parliament, cancelled the constitution, and ushered in a decade of stifling neoabsolutist rule. In Galicia, where the Ukrainian clergy drifted back to ecclesiastical pursuits, the Supreme Ruthenian Council dissolved itself voluntarily in 1851. One of the few general Ukrainian concerns that enlivened the drowsy 1850s in the province was the construction of the Ruthenian National Home in Lviv, a cultural center that had been funded by public contributions. However, despite this event, passivity and inertia generally replaced the dynamism of 1848. One Ukrainian wit quipped: "As our National Home rose higher, our cultural activity sank lower."[7]

But important changes already were afoot, even if they were not yet readily perceptible. In 1849, Count Agenor Gołuchowski, a wealthy Polish landowner and confidant of Emperor Franz Joseph, was appointed viceroy of Galicia. There were two important aspects to this appointment: first, in line with Vienna's autocratic policy, the new viceroy was given broad powers which included supervision of law enforcement, the economy, education, and religion in the province; second, Gołuchowski was a new type of Pole who believed that concentration on small but concrete gains would improve the Polish position more than heroic but failed revolts. For the next twenty-five years, Gołuchowski, who served thrice as viceroy of Galicia and twice as minister in Vienna, would play a decisive role in fashioning the new political order that would emerge in the province.

The growth of Polish influence While the new viceroy demonstratively emphasized his loyalty to the Habsburgs and his intention of dealing fairly with the Ukrainians, behind the scenes, he quietly and systematically expanded Polish influence in the government of the province. On his advice, Vienna dropped plans for the division of Galicia into separate Polish and Ukrainian parts. His exaggerated reports about Ukrainian sympathies for Russia shook the imperial government's confidence in the "Tyrolians of the East." As his influence grew, Gołuchowski became more open in his pro-Polish and anti-Ukrainian policies. Hoping to eliminate the Ukrainian presence at Lviv University, he pressured Holovatsky to resign his professorship of Ukrainian literature. Convinced that Ukrainians ought to be Polonized, he even attempted to impose the Roman calendar on the Greek Catholic church and, in 1859, to introduce the Latin script in Ukrainian publications. In this he went too far. Incensed by Gołuchowski's projects, the Ukrainian intelligentsia awoke from its stupor, engaged the viceroy in a fiercely debated "alphabet war," and forced him to retreat on the alphabet issue. On other fronts, the viceroy pushed on, systematically replacing German bureaucrats with Poles and expanding the use of Polish in the schools. Thus, he laid the groundwork for the dramatic rise of Polish influence in Galicia.

In 1859, the Habsburg empire came to another decisive turning point when it suffered a severe defeat against the French and Sardinians in Italy. Weakened externally, the Habsburgs were forced to make concessions internally. As a result, the neoabsolutist regime was dismantled and constitutional, parliamentary government was restored – this time permanently. A central parliament was created in Vienna and each province received its own diet. Up to 1873, delegates to the former were selected from among the members of the latter.

To win the support of the upper classes, Vienna created an electoral system that would greatly favor them. Members of provincial diets were elected by four categories or curia of voters: the great landlords, chambers of commerce, townsmen, and rural communes, each of which was represented by a specific number of delegates. In Galicia's 150-member diet, the great landlords had 44 delegates, the chambers of commerce had 3, the townsmen had 28, and the rural communes (in which landlords could also be elected) had 74. The extent to which the peasants were underrepresented may be seen from the electoral structure: while it took only 52 voters to elect a deputy in the landlords' curia, a deputy from the rural communes needed 8764 voters. For Ukrainians, primarily a peasant people, this was a tremendous disadvantage. Consequently, in the elections to the Galician diet, Ukrainians were usually limited to less than 15% of the diet's membership. They also had a disproportionately low number of delegates in the parliament in Vienna. Clearly, in Galicia it was the Polish nobles who gained most from the parliamentary system.

But the Poles were about to gain even more. In 1867 a familiar pattern was repeated. Defeated in a war with Prussia, the Habsburgs were forced to make far-ranging concessions to the Hungarians, the strongest nationality in the empire. The result was the Austro-Hungarian Compromise of 1867, which placed about half of the empire, including Transcarpathia, under direct Hungarian rule. The Habsburg empire now became the Austro-Hungarian Empire. Hungarian success encouraged the Poles to demand complete control of Galicia. While Vienna refused to acquiesce formally, it did agree to an informal political compromise: in return for Polish support the Habsburgs promised not to interfere in the Polish conduct of Galicia's affairs. In effect, Galicia was to become a Polish "state within a state."

The sudden surge in Polish influence in Galician affairs went far beyond their guaranteed majority in the diet. Until 1916 only Poles could occupy the office of viceroy. When, in 1871, a minister for Galicia was appointed in the central government, he, too, was always Polish. The bureaucracy was purged of Germans and quickly Polonized. The school commission was almost competely in Polish hands, and, in 1869, Polish became the official language of education and administration in the province. On the socioeconomic and cultural level, the Poles were incomparably stronger than the Ukrainians. Their aristocracy owned much of the land; their intelligentsia was relatively numerous, sophisticated, and diversified; their share of the urban population was growing rapidly; and their cultural achievements, even before 1867, were impressive. Little wonder that the Poles expected to get their way in Galicia.

Polish goals in Galicia   Having attained power, what did the Poles intend to do with it? To comprehend Polish policies in the 1868–1914 period one must consider the Polish perspective on events, as well as their hopes and goals. The Poles, that is to say, their nobility and intelligentsia – for the Polish peasantry was almost as politically naive as the Ukrainians – were a frustrated people. In the late 18th century, they had been robbed of their statehood and when they rose up to regain it in 1830 and in 1863, their revolts failed dismally. To Ukrainians they may have appeared as arrogant, overpowering opponents, but many Poles were obssessed with their own weakness vis-à-vis the Germans and Russians. After the disaster of 1863, a major shift occurred in Polish thinking, and Gołuchowski was a major proponent of it. Rejecting revolutionary activity as counterproductive, Polish leaders propagated a policy of "organic work": concrete (if mundane) activity that would strengthen Polish society by modernizing it. The conditions were exceedingly favorable for implementing such an approach in Galicia, which therefore, came to be viewed as a Piedmont or base from which the regeneration of the Polish nation would begin.

And what of the Ukrainians, the Habsburgs' loyal "Tyrolians of the East"? Vienna's attitude on this issue was reflected in the cynical words of an Austrian statesman: "Whether and to what extent the Ruthenians may exist is left to the discretion of the Galician diet."[8] In other words, the Ukrainians were placed at the mercy of the Poles. Given the plans that Polish patriots (many of whom were quite democratic) had for Galicia, their attitude toward Ukrainian national aspirations was naturally negative. Even more opposed to the Ukrainians were the "Podolians," arch-conservative Polish landlords from Eastern Galicia who opposed the Ukrainians not only on political but also on socioeconomic grounds: for them, the assertion of Ukrainian rights was synonymous with growth of peasant demands. Thus, to the old social tensions between the Polish noble and the Ukrainian peasant was added the new, even-more-explosive conflict of national interests. This combination would make the Polish/Ukrainian confrontation in Galicia particularly bitter.

Initially, the Polish approach toward the Ukrainians (especially evident

among the conservative "Podolians") was to negate the existence of Ukrainians as a separate nation and to argue that they were merely a Polish sub-
group. Hence, the statement of a Polish leader: "There are no Ruthenians;
there is only Poland and Muscovy."9 When the upsurge of Ukrainian activity
in 1848 made it difficult to maintain this position, a new line, formulated by
Gołuchowski, was implemented. It called for discrediting the Ukrainians in
Vienna, obstructing their national and social development by all means and
at every level, and enforcing their Polonization.

The area in which these policies were pursued with special determination
was education. After 1867, Polish replaced German as the language of instruction at Lviv University and in all the technical and vocational institutions. The secondary schools, or *gymnazia*, were also thoroughly Polonized;
by 1914 there were ninety-six Polish and only six Ukrainian *gymnazia* in the
province, that is, one for every 42,000 Poles and every 520,000 Ukrainians. In
elementary schools there were three times as many classes available to Poles
as to Ukrainians.

Discrimination against Ukrainians existed at every level. For example, in
1907 Polish cultural institutions received ten times as much financial support as did Ukrainian ones. When investments were made, they were usually funneled into the western, Polish part, of the province. At every turn,
Ukrainians met not only disinterest but active opposition from the provincial
government. They were forced to carry on a bitter, stubborn struggle for each
institution, each position, each office, indeed, for each word of Ukrainian.

The all-pervasive, often petty, nature of this confrontation was exacerbated
by the deep differences in mentality between Polish and Ukrainian leaders.
While the outlook of the Polish intelligentsia bore the imprint of the gentry
worldview, that of the Ukrainian intelligentsia was clearly plebian. As Ivan
Lysiak Rudnytsky put it: "Every educated Ukrainian was only one or two
generations removed from either a parsonage or a peasant hut." The one common trait in the worldviews of educated Poles and Ukrainians was, to quote
Rudnytsky again, that "both communities viewed their conflict as if it were
similar to the great 17th century wars between the Polish aristocracy and the
Ukrainian Cossacks."10

The Ukrainian Response

If 1848 was a high point for the Ukrainians of Galicia, the 1860s were certainly a low point. Vienna's concessions to the Poles shocked and confounded
Ukrainians. During the revolution of 1848 they had confronted the Poles
as political equals; now they found themselves completely subordinated to
them. For generations they had believed that their unswerving loyalty to the
Habsburgs guaranteed them their backing, but in 1867 they painfully realized
that this had been a false assumption. Taking stock of the new political situa-

tion in Galicia, the Ukrainian clergy-leadership, usually referred to as the Old Ruthenians, faced exceedingly bleak prospects. Not only did Vienna prove to be unreliable, but as a result its recent military and political defeats, its power and prestige had been greatly diminished. The Poles were stronger than ever. And among their own people, the Ukrainian leaders saw only an impoverished, illiterate mass of peasants. With their confidence badly shaken, they looked around for new sources of support.

The Russophiles In the 1860s the interest and hopes of many educated Ukrainians focused on Russia. This was not suprising, for at this time various Slavic peoples, such as the Czechs, Serbs, and Bulgarians, who were hard pressed by Germans or Ottomans, also looked to their fellow Slavs, the Russians, for help. For its own purposes, Russia encouraged these Slavophile tendencies by establishing cultural contacts with and providing subsidies to these "kindred" peoples. One of the first and most avid Russian cultural missionaries was Mikhail Pogodin, a noted conservative historian, who in 1835 visited Lviv and established contacts with the Ukrainian intelligentsia. Although at the time his pro-Russian exhortations had little impact, in the climate of the 1860s, they began to bear fruit.

An early convert to Russophilism in Galicia was Denys Zubrytsky, a historian and one of the few Ukrainian noblemen. His efforts and those of the indefatigable Pogodin helped attract other educated Ukrainians, most notably Iakiv Holovatsky, one of the members of the Ruthenian Triad, to this tendency. However, the crucial breakthrough for Russophilism in Galicia came in the late 1860s, when the so-called St George circle of Greek Catholic dignitaries in Lviv espoused its tenets. Thereafter, Russophilism spread rapidly among most of the clergy. Indeed, until the end of the 19th century, the priests served as its primary social base. With much of the West Ukrainian elite as its adherents, the Russophile tendency came to play a major role in the cultural and political life of Eastern Galicia, Bukovyna, and Transcarpathia.

Russophilism was attractive to the Old Ruthenians, not only because of Slavophile propaganda and disenchantment with the Habsburgs, but also because many of the veterans of 1848 believed that the only way they could withstand the Poles was to rely on Russia. Social psychology also played an important role. Even to the casual observer, it was evident that the Ukrainian clergy-elite suffered from an ethnic and social inferiority complex. Like every elite, it yearned for recognition and prestige. Yet Polish noblemen rarely failed to emphasize their social superiority over the Greek Catholic priests. Certainly the peasant nature of Ukrainian society and culture did not provide prestige and after the setbacks of the 1860s, Ukrainianism became even less appealing. Therefore, the opportunity to identify with the mighty tsar, the numerous Russian people and their flourishing culture addressed some of the clergy's deep-seated needs. There was also a pragmatic consideration:

given Austria's weakness and Russia's power, the possiblity that the Russians would take over Galicia sooner or later seemed realistic and many educated Ukrainians thought it prudent to climb on the Russian "bandwagon" early.

The Russophilism of the Ukrainians differed from that of the Czechs and other Slavs in that it went much further in stressing the similarity, even the identicalness, of Ukrainians and Russians. According to its leading proponents, such as Bohdan Didydtsky, Ivan Naumovych, Mykhailo Kachkovsky, and, in Transcarpathia, Adolf Dobriansky, the Ukrainians were one part of the tripartite Russian nation whose other two components were the Great Russians and Belorussians. The first public statement of this view came in 1866 when *Slovo*, the newspaper of the Old Ruthenian establishment, which was secretly subsidized by the Russian government, stated: "We can no longer separate ourselves by a Chinese wall from our brothers and reject the linguistic, literary, religious, and ethnic ties that bind us with the entire Russian world. We are no longer the Ruthenians of 1848; we are genuine Russians."[11]

By retreating completely from the positions of 1848, the Old Ruthenians showed that they did not believe in their ability to stand on their own culturally and, even more so, politically. A popular saying caught the essence of their position: "If we are to drown," Russophiles frequently stated, "we prefer a Russian sea to a Polish swamp." Another ramification of this attitude was that the Old Ruthenians, in placing all their hopes on Russian support, concluded that it was pointless to mobilize the Ukrainian masses. Their policies, therefore, came to be characterized by passivity and inertia.

But the Old Ruthenians were not so bold as to reject the Habsburgs openly. While stressing their cultural ties with Russia, they were careful to declare, in the same *Slovo* article of 1866: "We are and always have been unwaveringly loyal to our august Austrian monarch and the illustrious Habsburg dynasty."[12] Some of them, notably the higher clergy, hedged even further, arguing that they were neither Russians nor Ukrainians but a separate Galician people. This muddled self-perception, as well as stress on localism, kowtowing to the powers that be, and attempts to identify with the mighty Russian Empire while reserving certain regional distinctions for themselves, was, of course, not a new phenomenon in Ukrainian history. Essentially, it was a West Ukrainian variant of the Little Russian (*maloros*) mentality that was widespread in Eastern Ukraine.

Among Ukrainians the impact of Russophilism was most clearly evident in the area of language. In line with their elitism, the Old Ruthenians adamantly refused to use the vernacular (or, "the tongue of swineherds and shepherds," as they referred to it) as a basis for a Ukrainian literary language. They wanted their language to have a recognized literary tradition and prestige. Therefore, Church Slavonic, the ancient language of the ecclesiastical texts, together with an admixture of Polish, Russian, and Ukrainian words, was used in their publications.

This unwieldy, artificial linguistic amalgam, or *iazychie*, as it was called, may have been prestigious but it was also barely comprehensible, especially to the peasantry. Even educated Ukrainians who wrote in it, each according to his own haphazard rules, rarely spoke it, preferring the use of Polish. When asked why they used Polish, an Old Ruthenian responded that "because Little Russian is the language of the peasants and we do not know Russian, therefore we speak in the civilized language of the Poles."[13] The linguistic detour of the Old Ruthenian Russophiles was a rejection of the literary principles that guided the Ruthenian Triad and of the open espousals of the vernacular that appeared in 1848. So adamant were the Russophiles in their opposition to the vernacular that they even welcomed the ban on Ukrainian publications in Russia in 1876. And it was on this issue of language that the earliest opposition, emanating from among Ukrainian students, developed against the Galician Russophiles.

It was no easy matter for the younger generation to do battle with their well-established elders. The Russophiles dominated almost all the Ukrainian institutions. The National Home, the well-endowed Stauropegian Institute, the publishing house of the Galician-Ruthenian *Matytsia*, as well as much of the press, including the largest newspaper, *Slovo*, were in their hands. In addition, in 1870 the Russophiles founded a political organization, the Ruthenian Council (Ruska Rada), which they claimed was the direct continuator of the Supreme Ruthenian Council of 1848, and they attempted to make it the sole representative of all Ukrainians in Galicia. Thus, even among its own elite, the Ukrainian movement had a determined and powerful opponent.

The Populists (Narodovtsi)   In the pre-1848 period, it was the youth, led by the Ruthenian Triad, that espoused the use of the vernacular and, despite the backtracking of their elders, it was youth again that came to the defense of the spoken language in the 1860s. Like the Old Ruthenian Russophiles, many young West Ukrainians also looked to the east. But, while the older generation adulated the tsar, the youth was inspired by Shevchenko. It not only admired the beauty, vitality, and power that he drew from the language of the people, but it also shared his and many East Ukrainians' orientation to the peasantry (*narod*). Hence, the term *Narodovtsi* was commonly applied to the West Ukrainian Populists.

Besides the generational and ideological differences that separated the Russophiles and the Populists, there were also social distinctions. The former tended to be well-placed ecclesiastical and secular bureaucrats and other "solid citizens"; the latter consisted mostly of students, younger clergy, and the rising secular intelligentsia. Yet, one should not exaggerate the initial differences that separated these two emerging camps within the thin stratum of educated West Ukrainians. At the outset, their disagreements focused almost exclusively on linguistic and literary matters. Otherwise, adherents of both groups shared similar values and backgrounds (frequently clerical) and they viewed their disagreements as a falling out among older and younger members of the same family.

External influences, however, gradually widened the gulf between the two factions. While Russophiles perused the works of conservative Slavophile Russian authors, the Populists avidly read the writings of Shevchenko, Kulish and Kostomarov. This literature drew the latter closer to the Ukrainophiles in Kiev. Especially after the anti-Ukrainian measures of 1863 and 1876, East Ukrainian authors began to publish increasingly in the journals of the Galician Populists. These contacts became even closer when Antonovych, Konysky and Kulish, visited Galicia and, for better or worse, became involved in West Ukrainian politics. Under the impact of the liberal East Ukrainians, the intellectual horizons of the provincial, church-bound West Ukrainians expanded somewhat. In the initial phase of this growing relationship, democratic and secular tendencies even predominated. But there were limits to the intellectual and ideological influence of the East Ukrainians on the Populists. When in the late 1870s the exiled Drahomanov attempted to convert them to his cosmopolitan, socialist and anticlerical thinking, they were repelled by his "godless anarchism." Many of the Populists were young rural clergymen who wanted to broaden their contacts with the village. Therefore, Populists were usually unwilling and unable to go far beyond the mentality of the village priest.

The consensus that emerged among the Populists rested, first and foremost, on the recognition of the Ukrainians as a separate nation that stretched from the Caucasus to the Carpathians and that best expressed itself in its own vernacular. They concluded that the most effective way of emphasizing and developing this national distinctiveness was to cultivate and propagate the use of the Ukrainian language. Therefore, to them the main national issue was the linguistic and literary one. This narrow approach precluded the possibility of addressing social problems, challenging the government, and even engaging in politics. In this respect, the Populists were the West Ukrainian variant of the Ukrainophiles in the Russian Empire. A further similarity was that the Populists, like the Ukrainophiles, had no foreign support, as did the Russophiles. Because they had to rely on their "own people," they were (theoretically) more democratic than their conservative Russophile rivals.

Almost all existing Ukrainian institutions, including the press, were controlled by the Russophiles – and the Populists had little access to them. The only solution was to create new ones. Surreptitiously – the Russophile hierarchy forbade seminarians to join Populist groups or to read their journals – the Populists formed several circles, foremost among them being Moloda Rus' established in Lviv in 1861. The main activity of these circles was the publication of journals, a flurry of which appeared in the 1860s: *Vechornytsi* (1862) popularized Shevchenko and reflected the influence of the St Petersburg *Osnova*; *Meta* (1863–65) proclaimed its goal of educating a secular intelligentsia; *Nyva* (1865) and *Rusalka* concentrated on literature; and *Pravda* (1867–80) was a publication in which East Ukrainians often published their works and which served as an all-Ukrainian forum. Except for *Pravda*, these publications, which were edited by inexperienced young enthusiasts and lacked a broad readership and financial resources, quickly faded.

Meanwhile, a number of Populists worked on Ukrainian grammars and dictionaries. Another form of populist activity was the Ukrainian theater. Established in Lviv in 1864, it became, as in Russian-ruled Ukraine, an especially effective means of spreading national consciousness. In 1868 a group of about sixty Lviv students, led by Anatol Vakhnianyn, founded Prosvita, a society for "learning about and enlightening the people." And in 1873, the aforementioned Shevchenko Literary Society was established in Lviv with the financial and moral support of East Ukrainians.

Despite this outburst of literary and cultural activity, it soon became obvious that the Populists had, in fact, little contact with the people. In addition to this realization, several other factors caused them to rethink their position. After the Ems Ukaz of 1876, contacts with the more experienced East Ukrainians suddenly increased. The political weakness of the Ukrainians in Galicia was dramatically demonstrated in 1879 when, under the leadership of Russophiles, they managed to send only three delegates to the provincial diet. By 1880, a new kind of leadership, consisting of secular intelligentsia, professors, and lawyers such as Iuliian Romanchuk, Oleksander Ohonovsky, and the Barvinsky brothers, had emerged.

Under the impact of these developments, the Populists were willing to listen to at least one of Drahomanov's admonitions: "The Poles have pushed you from the Galician diet; the Russophiles have forced you from your institutions ... we advocate that you give up your policy of compromises and mutual denunciations and go instead to the people and organize."[14] As for the Russophiles, Drahomanov advised against any contacts with them. The Populists took this counsel to heart. Those that belonged to Russophile institutions or student clubs resigned from them. In 1880 they established a mass-oriented newspaper, called *Dilo* (The Deed) in pointed contrast to the Russophiles' *Slovo* (The Word). That same year they called the first mass meeting (*viche*) of Ukrainians to discuss the state and needs of Ukrainian society. About 2000 persons, including many peasants, attended. In 1885 Narodna Rada, a representative body, was founded.

The Radicals   To some observers, even the new activism of the Populists was not enough to assure them a constructive and progressive role in Ukrainian society. As for the Russophiles, they were so hopelessly reactionary as to be beyond criticism. These, at least, were the views of Drahomanov. As a representative of the intellectually more sophisticated East Ukrainian intelligentsia, the Geneva-based émigré was shocked by the low cultural level, the provincialism, and the pettiness of the Galicians. He opposed especially the predominant and, in his view, negative influence that the clergy exercised on Ukrainian life (in Eastern Ukraine, where the clergy was largely Russified, its impact on the Ukrainian movement was minimal). This committed socialist was incensed by the argument, repeated by many Galician priests in their sermons, that the poverty of the peasants was largely the result of their drunkenness and sloth. Convinced that the older generation of West Ukrainians (among which, in the 1870s and 1880s, he included the Populists) was too retrograde to rehabilitate, Drahomanov concentrated on developing contacts with Galician students.

In a series of epistles that appeared in the Galician student journal *Druh*, he urged the youth to reject the views of their elders, to broaden their intellectual horizons by familiarizing themselves with the best of European and Russian culture and science, and to commit themselves to aid the exploited masses with deeds, not merely words. Among a small but important segment of West Ukrainian youth, his message struck home, sparking what might be called an intellectual revolution. It led the members of this group to search for a third and socially more relevant way of defending the interests of the Ukrainians.

Drahomanov's first adherents came from Sich, the Ukrainian student club in Vienna. In the late 1870s, two student groups in Lviv, the Russophile Akademicheskii kruzhok and the Ukrainophile Druzhnyi lykhvar, began to espouse his ideas. Several small groups of *gymnazia* students in the provinces also declared their support. But the most important converts to Drahomanov's views were two gifted, energetic, and committed students of humble, peasant origins – Ivan Franko, who would become one of the finest Ukrainian writers, and Mykhailo Pavlyk. It was they who would lead the intellectual and ideological revolt, advocated by their Geneva-based mentor, against the narrow-minded, conservative thinking of the West-Ukrainian leadership.

In the time-honored tradition of the intelligentsia, the first harbinger of intellectual change was a journal. In 1876, Pavlyk and Franko took over editorial control of a Russophile student publication, *Druh*. They quickly discarded the *iazychie* it had used, adopted the Ukrainian vernacular, and began to attack the Russophiles. Soon afterward, they extended their criticism to the Populists, castigating them for their mediocre literary production and social conservatism. Shocked by the sharp criticism, radical tendencies, and anticlericalism of the editors, Galician Ukrainians began to cancel their subscriptions (readership dropped from about 500 to 260) and Drahomanov had to step in with financial support for the journal. Pavlyk also became involved in aiding socialist revolutionaries. And in 1878, to the glee of the Galician Ukrainian establishment, he and Franko were put on trial for subversive activities.

Although he received only a mild sentence, Franko was ostracized by Ukrainian society and had to turn to Polish socialists for support. Meanwhile, new and younger converts to socialism, such as Viacheslav Budzynovsky, Mykola Hankevych, Stanislav Kozlovsky, and Kyrylo Trylovsky, appeared. As a result, a small but active left wing developed among the West Ukrainians in the 1880s. By 1890 these young activists, together with the "old veterans" Franko and Pavlyk, were ready to organize a political party. It would be the first Ukrainian political party in Western and Eastern Ukraine and its appearance (which preceded the East-Ukrainian RUP by a decade) would be symptomatic of the new and dynamic stage of development upon which the Galician Ukrainians had embarked.

The Organizational Upsurge

In modern times, the Ukrainians of Galicia earned a well-deserved reputation for their organizational skill and social discipline, especially in comparison with their compatriots in the east. One reason the Galician Ukrainians developed these traits was that they had the opportunity to practice them. Despite their disadvantages vis-à-vis the Poles, after 1861 the Ukrainians of Austria lived in a constitutional monarchy that allowed much greater freedom of association and expression than was possible in the Russian Empire.

A variety of other factors, however, also contributed to the organizational upsurge that occurred in Eastern Galicia in the late 19th and early 20th century. The West Ukrainians were directly exposed to such paragons of social discipline as the Germans and the Czechs. More immediate was the impact of the Poles who had embarked on a policy of "organic work," which called for the strengthening of their society by mobilizing and developing its economic and cultural resources. If the West Ukrainians wanted to compete with the Poles, it was obvious that they would have to adopt a similar approach. Hence, the slogan of the Populists: "Rely on your own resources." Finally, a new type of leadership, personified by the community activist, or *hromadskyi diiach*, arose among the Ukrainians in the 1880s. Consisting mostly of pedagogues and especially lawyers, it was both idealistic, committing itself wholeheartedly to the welfare of the people, and pragmatic, in that it understood the demands of modern society and sought to prepare the Ukrainian peasant to cope with them.

Educational and cultural achievements   The harbinger of this new tendency was the Prosvita society, founded by the Populists in 1868. Committed to raising the cultural and educational level of the peasantry and, more specifically, increasing its literacy, the Lviv-based society, aided by village teachers and parish priests, gradually established a network of reading rooms and libraries throughout Eastern Galicia. In these, peasants were encouraged to read the press – often one literate villager would read to a group of his illiterate neighbors – and discuss political and social issues. The popularity of these reading rooms was enhanced when, in time, choirs, theatrical groups, gymnastics societies, and cooperatives were formed in association with them. In fact, by the turn of the century they came to rival the church and the tavern as the hub of village life. As a result, they contributed greatly to the rise of political and national consciousness among the peasantry.

Thanks to the dedicated work of such leaders as Anatol Vakhnianyn and especially Oleksander Ohonovsky, by 1914 the Prosvita society had 77 regional branches, close to 3000 reading rooms and libraries, over 36,000 members in its Lviv branch, and about 200,000 members of the village reading rooms. Efforts were also made to organize the village youth. Using the highly successful Czech organizations as a model, gymnastics and firefighting societies called Sokil and Sich were established in 1894. The Radicals, especially Kyrylo Trylovsky, were especially active in this area.

Besides providing young peasants with an opportunity to take part in parades, these youth groups instilled in them an appreciation for discipline, cooperation, patriotism, and education. By 1914 they numbered 974 local branches with over 33,000 members. Organizational growth such as this demonstrated that the Populists were capable of making the transition from activity in ephemeral journals and the loose student groups of the 1860s to the systematic work and broadly based organizations that characterized the 1890s and the early 1900s. To compete with the Populists, the Russophiles established the Kachkovsky Society in 1874, but its membership was much smaller than that of its rivals.

The Galician leadership realized, somewhat belatedly, that in addition to the cultural needs of the peasantry, it would have to address economic issues as well. Given its social position and mentality, it showed little interest in the revolutionary approach, widespread in the Russian Empire, for alleviating economic inequalities. Instead it favored self-help, that is, the cooperative method of improving the plight of the peasants. An initial attempt to mobilize large numbers of peasants for their own welfare occurred in the 1870s, when the clergy launched a campaign to reduce drunkenness in the villages. The massive rallies and communal oath takings helped to reduce the consumption of alcohol, and the campaign became one of the church's most concrete social achievements.

It was, however, the secular intelligentsia that spearheaded attempts at economic improvement. At first, the Prosvita society sponsored cooperative stores, warehouses, and credit unions. But it could not provide the experienced help and specialized cooperatives that were needed. This need was addressed by Vasyl Nahirny, the pioneer of the West Ukrainian cooperative movement, who had spent a decade studying the well-organized cooperatives of Switzerland. In 1883 he organized the Narodna Torhivlia, a consumers' cooperative whose goal was to buy and sell products in large quantities, eliminate the middlemen, and pass on the savings to the villagers. By means of his organization, Nahirny hoped to accustom Ukrainians to commercial activity.

Other cooperatives followed. In 1899 the Silskyi Hospodar, led by Evhen Olesnytsky, was founded to teach peasants modern methods of farming, and by 1913 it had over 32,000 members. Yet the most numerous cooperatives were the credit unions, some of which were organized as early as 1873. However, only in 1894, with the establishment of the Vira union, were they put on a stable and well-regulated footing. Charging about 10% for loans, these unions, which numbered in the hundreds, soon drove most moneylenders out of business. Another important economic institution emerged in 1895, when Dnister, an insurance company, was established in Lviv. By 1907, it had 213,000 policyholders. The growth of the cooperatives led to the organization, in 1904, of a central association of Ukrainian cooperatives that had about 550 institutional affiliates, mostly credit unions, and 180,000 individual members. On the fortieth anniversary of the founding of Prosvita in 1909, activists of the cooperative movement called a congress attended by 768 delegates – the vast majority of whom were young, secular intelligentsia – to plan for the further development of their nation. Reflecting unaccustomed optimism, many of the delegates voiced the opinion that the Ukrainians were finally gaining control over their own fate.

An important aspect of the cooperative movement as well as the work of the Prosvita society was that it encouraged the development of a close, harmonious relationship between the intelligentsia and the peasantry, something that the intelligentsia in Russian-ruled Ukraine had not been able to achieve. The fact that many members of the growing intelligentsia were themselves either directly from the village or a generation removed aided this process considerably. The success of the Populists in mobilizing the masses also meant that their ultimate victory over the Russophiles, whose cooperative membership was only about one-fifth as large as that of the Ukrainophiles, was assured. Finally, the growth of the cooperatives had serious repercussions for the Jewish community: the boycotts of alcohol, the credit unions, and consumer cooperatives badly hurt the Jewish tavern owners, moneylenders and shopkeepers, heightening tensions between Ukrainians and Jews and encouraging many of the latter to emigrate.

Growth in the urban environment Heartened by its organizational achievements among the peasantry, the intelligentsia also strove to strengthen its position in the more sophisticated urban environment. Education, especially on the secondary and university levels, became the focal point of its concern. As might be expected, Ukrainians were badly underrepresented on all educational levels. In the elementary schools, for example, they had only half as many classrooms and teachers as did the Poles. Disparities were even greater in the city-based *gymnazia* and university, where Poles did everything in their power to prevent the growth of a Ukrainian educated elite. Thus, in 1897, of the 14,000 secondary-school students in the province, 80% were Poles and only 16% were Ukrainians (in 1854, before the Poles took over control of education, the proportions were roughly equal). While thirty *gymnazia* were Polish, only two were Ukrainian. At Lviv University, Ukrainians, concentrated mostly in the faculties of theology and law, constituted about 30% of its 1700 students. In 1911 in a faculty of about eighty, there were only eight Ukrainian professors. It was clear, therefore, that if they wished to raise their cultural level, the Ukrainians would have to gain greater access to higher education.

Because the establishment of each *gymanzium* required government approval, Poles and Ukrainians carried on a fierce political struggle over every school. By 1914 the latter managed to squeeze four more state-supported *gymnazia* from the government. The Poles, meanwhile, obtained several times as many secondary and vocational schools. Realizing that reliance on the government would not satisfy their needs, the Ukrainians turned to their own community and, by means of private contributions, founded eight more *gymnazia*. To help students, especially those from the village, to study in the expensive urban environment, numerous privately funded dormitories were established near the *gymanzia* and the university.

At Lviv University, as we shall see, the Poles were even more determined to maintain the "Polishness" of higher education. At times, however, they were forced to make concessions. Thus, in 1894, they grudgingly agreed, under pressure from Vienna, to create one more Ukrainian professorship (in history) at the university. Little did they know that this one appointment would have the impact of many. Because qualified candidates were lacking in Galicia, Mykhailo Hrushevsky, the 28-year-old student of Antonovych in Kiev, was invited to assume the new post. With the arrival in Lviv of Hrushevsky, a new era began in Ukrainian scholarship.

This greatest of all Ukrainian historians quickly began the publication of his monumental *Istoriia Ukrainy-Rusy* ("History of Ukraine-Rus'") with the express purpose of providing the idea of Ukrainian nationhood with historical legitimacy. Almost single-handedly Hrushevsky reorganized the Shevchenko Society into a de facto academy of sciences. The society soon united almost all the leading East and West Ukrainians and included many famous European scholars in its ranks. By 1913 it published, in addition to numerous other works, 120 volumes of its highly regarded *Zapysky*. Meanwhile, its excellent library and numerous subsections served as a training ground for a new generation of talented scholars.

There were also impressive achievements in literature, associated, first and foremost, with Ivan Franko, one of Ukraine's leading writers. Combining an unwincing, almost photographic perception of reality with an idealistic, optimistic belief in man's better instincts, Franko wrote in an extraordinary variety of genres – novels, narratives, psychological and social sketches, satires, poems – and covered a broad range of subjects. Besides the obligatory tales of peasant misery, in his novels *Boa Constrictor* and *Boryslav Is Laughing*, he re-created the brutality in the lives of oil workers. His precisely drawn pictures of prison life appeared alongside psychologically perceptive and warm stories about children. And his deep understanding of sociology came through in sketches of the declining nobility and rising intelligentsia. Franko was also an excellent scholar, a courageous polemicist, and, as we have seen, a prominent political activist who was often misunderstood and mistreated by his own community.

Other West Ukrainian writers of note were Vasyl Stefanyk and Olha Kobylianska. The former was renowned for his short, powerful, and highly concentrated sketches of human tragedy as it occurred in the context of village life, while the works of the latter reflected a "longing for beauty" and an "aristocracy of the spirit." In the arts, such noted painters as Oleksander Novakivsky and Ivan Trush and their many students received encouragement in their work, and were often sent abroad – thanks to the subsidies provided by the new metropolitan, Andrei Sheptytsky. Meanwhile, the world-famous singer Solomea Krushelnytska thrilled the operatic world with her performances, most notably that of Puccini's *Madame Butterfly* whose success she ensured.

Another indication of the cultural and institutional growth of the Galician Ukrainians was a rapidly proliferating press. Under the able editorship of Oleksander Barvinsky, the Populist *Dilo*, founded in 1880, broke the Russophile dominance of the printed media and became the most influential and widely read Ukrainian newspaper. Not to be outdone, the Radicals and other ideological rivals of the Populists also established their own periodicals as did the various educational societies, professional associations, and religious and youth groups. By 1913 the West Ukrainians boasted eighty periodicals, sixty-six in Galicia and the remainder in Bukovyna and Transcarpathia.

Political parties As ideologies evolved, the organizational infrastructure grew, and the need for coordinated participation in the parliamentary system became more pressing, the stage was set for the rise of political parties that would replace the loose populist and Russophile groupings. Unlike the small, radical, underground parties in Russian-ruled Ukraine, the Galician parties developed openly, legally and – in their attempts to appeal to as many voters as possible – adopted a generally moderate tone. Another difference between East and West Ukrainian political parties hinged on the national issue. While the former agonized over its importance relative to socioeconomic concerns, the latter, even the most socialist among them, clearly stressed their membership in one, large Ukrainian nation, demanded equality with the Poles, and declared that their ultimate goal was independent statehood. The demand for independence was not surprising; other nationalities in the Habsburg empire had long since voiced similar aspirations. With the rising militancy of the West Ukrainians, it was only a matter of time before they would do the same. Thus, in 1896 when the young Radical Iuliian Bachynsky first openly advocated the union of all Ukrainians in an independent state in his book *Ukraina Irredenta*, his message had an electrifying effect on nationally conscious Ukrainians.

As we have seen earlier, it was the Radicals who, in 1890, formally constituted themselves into a political organization and thereby laid claim to being the first Ukrainian political party. Guided by Drahomanov and led by Franko and Pavlyk, they espoused "scientific socialism," adopted a critical stance toward the Greek Catholic clergy because of it social conservatism, and advocated cooperation with the Polish workers and peasants. In 1895 they "nationalized" their program by declaring that socialism could be achieved best, in the long run, in an independent Ukrainian state and, in the short run, in a fully autonomous Ukrainian province in the Austrian Empire. However, the enmity of the clergy, which blocked the Radicals from access to the village, the lack of a Ukrainian proletariat, dependence on Polish socialists, and factionalism prevented this dynamic, innovative party from obtaining a broadly based following in Galician society.

In 1899 a regenerated version of the Populists, led by Evhen Levytsky and Volodymyr Okhrymovych (and joined by Hrushevksy and Franko, who had left the quarreling Radicals), formed the National Democratic party. Formulating their program so as to appeal to disgruntled Radicals and disillusioned Russophiles, the National Democrats also made national independence their long- term goal, while autonomy, together with loyalty to the Habsburgs, was their short-range objective. In other respects, the party espoused a typically liberal platform and avoided controversial social issues. Its moderate stance and the backing of such populist organizations as Prosvita soon made the National Democrats the largest Ukrainian party in Galicia.

Two other parties appeared at opposite ends of the ideological spectrum. In 1899, the Marxists Mykola Hankevych and Semen Vityk founded a Social Democratic party to represent the interests of the Ukrainian workers. That same year, some of the clergy formed the Catholic-Ruthenian Alliance. However, both parties had little success because, in the first case, there were too few Ukrainian workers to provide the Marxists with a social base, and, in the second, most of the young Ukrainophile clergy was more attracted by the outspoken nationalism of the National Democrats than by the stodgy conservatism of the clerical party.

In order to attract peasant support, all the parties resorted to the *viche*, public gatherings called by party activists in the countryside to discuss and debate issues of general concern. Often peasants participated in these gatherings in large numbers. During the election campaign of 1905–06, for example, about 20,000 people came to a National Democratic *viche* – a telling indication of the growing political awareness spreading among the peasantry.

As the organizational and political strength of the Ukrainophiles grew, that of the Russophiles declined. For the younger generation of the Ukrainian intelligentsia and even for the semieducated peasants, the *iazychie* language was too artificial, the identification with the Russians too farfetched, the social conservatism of the Russophiles too reactionary, and their dependence on foreign support too demeaning. Russophile attempts to compete with the Ukrainophiles in organizational terms met with little success: in 1914, their Kachkovsky Society had only 300 reading rooms compared to the Prosvita's nearly 3000; while the Ukrainian cooperative union had over 900 institutional members, the analogous Russophile organization had 106. Matters were no better in politics. In 1913, thirty Ukrainophile delegates were sent to the Galician diet and only one Russophile.

Hoping to stem their decline, in 1900 the younger, more-aggressive generation of the Russophiles adopted a "new course" that called for total identification with Russia. They founded the Russian National party, obtained even greater subsidies from the tsarist government, and agitated for the conversion of Galician Ukrainians to Orthodoxy. In order to sow dissension among the Ukrainians, as well as to encourage conservatism, the Polish aristocrats in Galicia began to back the Russophiles. Consequently, the Russophile camp was preserved from complete disintegration largely because of support from tsarist officials and Polish landowners.

Eastern Galicia: a Ukrainian stronghold In 1907 the noted Polish-Jewish liberal Wilhelm Feldman wrote: "The 20th century has seen many nations rise from the ashes but there are few cases of rebirth so rapid and energetic as that of the Ukrainians of Austria ... their unexpected and vigorous growth is mostly the result of self-help and hard-fought gains."[15] While Feldman did not mean to imply that the West Ukrainians had overcome all their troubles – they were still among the empire's poorest and politically most underrepresented peoples – he did stress that they were gaining momentum and quickly developing into a major force. As their organizations proliferated, the West Ukrainians demonstrated that they were finally taking charge of their own affairs and that their national movement was a broadly based, multifaceted phenomenon. In short, it was clear that if and when an opportunity for independent statehood appeared, the West Ukrainians would be ready to grasp it.

The burgeoning national activity in Galicia also had a major effect on relations between East and West Ukrainians. Actually, it was easterners, such as Antonovych, Konysky, Kulish and later Drahomanov and Hrushevsky, who first realized Galicia's potential for functioning as a Piedmont or base of national growth. As early as the 1860s they cooperated with Galician periodicals and financially supported West Ukrainian cultural institutions. As these publications and institutions grew, so, too, did the easterners' participation in them.

By the early 20th century, East Ukrainians were frequent correspondents and subscribers to the Galician press; scholars and literary figures from both regions often worked together in the Shevchenko Society; students from Russian-ruled Ukraine frequently enrolled in Ukrainian summer courses in Galicia; and, especially after 1905, East Ukrainian émigrés often found refuge and established their headquarters in Lviv. As it observed Ukrainian life in the West, the repressed Ukrainian intelligentsia of the Russian Empire was greatly encouraged to see that what for itself was still a dream was turning into a reality in Galicia. Meanwhile, the Ukrainians of Galicia also benefited from the influx of first-rate intellectuals and from the inspiring feeling that they were not a small, isolated people of only about 4 million, but members of a large nation of 25 million. Thus – because of the rights guaranteed by the Austrian constitution, the pressure to organize in order to compete with the Poles, and the moral and intellectual support of the East Ukrainians – small, impoverished and backward Galicia emerged as a bastion of the Ukrainian national movement.

The Polish/Ukrainian Confrontation

As the political and national development of both Ukrainians and Poles quickened, relations between the two peoples went from bad to worse. On almost every major issue the interests of the two nationalities, at least as interpreted by their leaders, clashed: while the Poles were adamant about preserving the unity of Galicia so that it could serve as the basis of their future state, the Ukrainians demanded its division so that they could create their own base in the eastern part of the province; while in Eastern Galicia the Poles constituted the upper classes, the Ukrainians were identified with the lower. The Ukrainians demanded changes and reforms, while most of the Polish leadership defended the status quo. In short, the Poles were the "haves," the Ukrainians were the "have-nots" who were unwilling to accept their status any longer.

Because of organizational growth within both nations, greater numbers of people were drawn into political activities and conflicts. No longer could the Poles be identified with a coterie of nobles or the Ukrainians with a handful of clerics and intelligentsia, in contrast to circumstances in 1848. By the early 20th century, as both sides mobilized their societies, the Polish/Ukrainian conflict grew from a struggle between two national elites into an increasingly menacing confrontation between two national communities.

There were, to be sure, attempts at compromise. Ukrainian and Polish socialists, such as Ivan Franko and Feliks Daszyński, castigated chauvinism on both sides and urged workers and peasants of all nationalities to cooperate for the sake of their mutual interests. East Ukrainians, like Antonovych and Kulish, fearful that the conflict might jeopardize their haven in Galicia, tried to mediate between the antagonists. At times, Vienna attempted to arrange a settlement, hoping to cool tensions on its sensitive eastern borderland. Of the several attempts to reach a compromise, the most publicized was the so-called new era of political peace that was to begin in 1890. As a result of an agreement arranged between the Populists, led by Iuliian Romanchuk and Oleksander Barvinsky, on the one hand, and the Galician government represented by the governor-general, Casimir Badeni, on the other, the Ukrainians were to receive concessions (primarily in the cultural and educational fields) in return for their recognition of the political status quo. However, when these concessions were limited to a few new *gymnazia*, and the provincial government continued to manipulate the elections, the agreement broke down and both sides returned to political warfare. Later efforts to reach an understanding, such as the one in 1908, ended similarly.

In the decades preceding the First World War, the Polish/Ukrainian confrontation focused on three main issues: the peasant question, the university controversy, and the demands for electoral reforms. Highlighted by the extraordinarily low wages agrarian workers received on large estates, the peasant question was a perennial problem. By 1900, many peasants were no longer willing to consider emigration as the sole solution to their difficulties. In 1902, in the midst of the harvest season, the peasants (urged on by the Radicals and, somewhat belatedly, by the National Democrats – but criticized by the Russophiles), launched a massive boycott involving over 100,000 agricultural workers of the large estates in Eastern Galicia. Numerous local committees helped to coordinate the strike and to maintain discipline and calm among the participants.

Shocked by this unexpectedly effective demonstration of peasant solidarity, landlords called on the government to "restore order." Despite the arrest of hundreds, the strikers persevered. The landlords then turned to Polish public opinion with the argument that the strike was actually a Ukrainian attempt to push Poles from their hereditary lands. Thus, an issue that might have united Ukrainian peasants with similarly exploited Polish ones was used with notable success to heighten the national animosities between them. Eventually, the strike ended with a victory for the peasants. The landlords were forced to raise wages and make other concessions. Its broader significance, however, was that it activated many peasants and drew them into the political struggle.

Even more intense, if less widespread, was the conflict at Lviv University. After 1848, Vienna had planned to make the university bilingual – but when the Poles gained control they quickly moved to Polonize the institution. Gradually, the use of Ukrainian, even by professors, was limited and the "Polishness" of the university repeatedly emphasized. Infuriated, Ukrainian students throughout the 1890s mounted a series of protests aimed at reversing this trend. When their protests were ignored, the students raised the demand for the creation of a separate Ukrainian university. The idea caught the imagination of Ukrainian society, including peasants, and large public gatherings were called to support the student demands. Meanwhile, in the Galician diet and the Viennese parliament, Ukrainian delegates repeatedly and vehemently demanded government action on the issue.

But the Poles persisted with their previous policies and, in the initial decade of the 20th century, the situation at Lviv University turned ugly. Gangs of Ukrainian and Polish students, armed with clubs, fought pitched battles in lecture halls; in 1901 Ukrainian students resigned en masse from the university; in 1907 large demonstrations were organized against university authorities; and in 1910, during a fierce melee, a Ukrainian student, Adam Kotsko, was shot and killed. By now Vienna realized that it had to act, and in 1912 it promised that a separate Ukrainian university would be established within five years. The outbreak of war, however, deprived the Ukrainians of this long-sought-after prize.

Yet it was electoral reform that, in the view of the Ukrainian leadership, seemed to be the issue of greatest importance. For if Ukrainians could win fairer representation in the Galician diet and Viennese parliament, they would be in a much better position to improve their lot. The curial system greatly limited the impact of the Ukrainian vote and the Polish-controlled provincial government was notorious for its heavy-handed manipulation of election results. Manipulation occurred in a variety of ways: voter lists were falsified, the time and place of elections were changed only hours before they were to occur, voting boxes were pilfered (an easy matter because Ukrainians did not have vote-counters), and Ukrainian candidates were often jailed on petty charges to prevent them from campaigning. Electoral abuses reached a high point during the "bloody elections" of 1895 and 1897 that took place during the tenure of Badeni, often called "the iron governor." When Ukrainian peasants protested against the unfair practices, Badeni set the police against them with the tragic result that 10 were bayonetted to death, 30 severely wounded, and over 800 arrested.

But in this area, too, improvements were on the way. At first Vienna and then, in 1907 – after much obstruction and resistance on the part of the Polish leadership – Galicia abolished the curial system and introduced universal suffrage. Although the provincial government still practiced electoral fraud, the number of Ukrainian delegates to both the Viennese parliament and the Galician diet rose steadily thereafter. In 1879 the Ukrainians had three representatives in the former body and after the 1907 election they had twenty-seven; in the Galician diet they had thirteen in 1901 and thirty-two in 1913. Nevertheless, Ukrainians still remained underrepresented, in large part because of the electoral chicaneries of Galician governors.

In protest against these malpractices, Myroslav Sichynsky, a young Ukrainian student, assassinated the governor, Andrżej Potocki, on 12 April 1908. The incident reflected the dangerous point to which Polish/Ukrainian relations had come. There were, however, more deeply rooted reasons for the rising tensions. Among the Poles, an ultranationalist movement, led by the Polish National Democratic party of Roman Dmowski, was rapidly gaining influence. The Polish National Democrats, like the Ukrainian National Democrats, established a network of organizations among the peasantry and gained great popularity among the urban middle classes, intelligentsia, and students. Their major concern was the growing Ukrainian challenge to Polish control in Eastern Galicia, a foreboding that echoed in the words of the noted Polish social historian Franciszek Bujak: "Our outlook in Eastern Galicia is not promising. The fate of the English in Ireland and the Germans in Czech lands ... is a bad prognosis for us."[16] Therefore, a primary concern of the Polish nationalists in Galicia was the retention of the Polish "state of possession" in the eastern part of the province. This meant that it was no longer the "Podolians," a coterie of East Galician nobles, who confronted the Ukrainians but a broadly based Polish movement that stubbornly refused to grant any concessions.

Led by their own National Democrats, the Ukrainians responded with equal militancy. They energetically continued their organizational work, confronted the Poles in parliament and the diet on every occasion, and held frequent rallies to demonstrate their growing strength. On 28 June 1914, during a massive rally in Lviv at which thousands of Sich and Sokil members performed drills and gymnastic exercises before a huge and appreciative audience, a messenger rushed up to the podium full of dignitaries with the momentous news that the Habsburg Archduke Ferdinand had been assassinated in Sarajevo. Europe was about to plunge into a horrendous war of conflicting nationalisms.

Bukovyna and Transcarpathia

While 80% of West Ukrainians lived in Galicia, the remaining 20% inhabited the two small regions of Bukovyna and Transcarpathia. In certain respects, the life of Ukrainians in these two regions was similar to that of their compatriots in Galicia. The Ukrainians of Bukovyna and Transcarpathia were overwhelmingly peasants; the landowning elites consisted of non-Ukrainians – Romanians in Bukovyna and Hungarians in Transcarpathia. Very few Ukrainians lived in the sleepy towns, which were largely the domain of Germans and Jews; and industry was practically nonexistent. Like Galicia, both Bukovyna and Transcarpathia were internal colonies of the Austrian heartland. Yet in other ways the situation differed notably from the one that prevailed in Galicia.

In Bukovyna, which in 1861 had been separated from Galicia and formed into a separate province, the approximately 300,000 Ukrainians – about 40% of the total population – lived in the hilly northern areas. The remainder of the population consisted of Romanians (34%), Jews (13%), Germans (8%), and other minorities. Of all the West Ukrainians, the Bukovynian peasants were the best off in terms of landholdings, mainly because the large Romanian landholders did not have the vast influence in Vienna that Poles or Hungarians had. Since it was the policy of Vienna to use the Ukrainians as a counterbalance to the Romanians, the former did have some political leverage. By the late 19th century, this influence resulted in a well-organized Ukrainian school system, access to the university at Chernivtsi, and relatively favorable political opportunities. But there was also a barrier to national and political development. The Bukovynians, like the Romanians, were Orthodox and the hierarchy of the church was largely in Romanian hands. Therefore, unlike in Galicia, the church could not and did not play a major role in the development of Ukrainian national identity in Bukovyna, and the process of nation-building was quite belated in that region.

When that process actually began in the 1870s and 1880s, it was greatly influenced by the proximity of Galicia and the influx of Galician intelligentsia. In 1869 the Ruthenian Society was established in Chernivtsi to promote native culture. One year later, the Ruthenian Council, a political group, was founded to represent the Ukrainians in elections. Originally Russophiles dominated these groups but they were never very strong in Bukovyna. By the 1880s, Ukrainophiles, such as the Galician Stepan Smal-Stotsky (professor of Ukrainian language and literature at Chernivtsi University) and Baron Mykola Vasylko (a wealthy local landowner), took over the leadership of the Bukovynian Ukrainians. Local branches of the Galician National Democrats, Radicals, and Social Democrats soon appeared in the region. The Ruthenian Society, functioning in a manner similar to Prosvita, attracted about 13,000 members by 1914. Meanwhile, a compromise was reached in 1911 with the other nationalities, whereby the Ukrainians were guaranteed seventeen of the sixty-three seats in the provincial diet. In the Vienna parliament, the Bukovynian Ukrainians usually had a respectable five seats. Thus, because of Vienna's more balanced policies in Bukovyna, political compromise was more feasible and national tensions more muted than in Galicia.

In Transcarpathia, in contrast to Bukovyna, there could be no talk of compromise. The Hungarians totally controlled the region, especially after 1867, and Hungarian aristocrats exploited the peasantry at will, while Hungarian nationalists stifled local patriotism in any manner they saw fit. Thus, in almost every respect, the approximately 400,000 Transcarpathians who constituted about 70% of the total population of the region were the most disadvantaged of all West Ukrainians.

The national development of the Transcarpathians also suffered serious setbacks. Immediately after 1848, under the leadership of Adolf Dobriansky and Aleksander Dukhnovych, they gained some influential administrative positions and schools in their native language. But the rise of Russophilism, engendered by the arrival of Russian armies in Hungary in 1848 to put down the oppressive Hungarians, enveloped the small intelligentsia and the Greek Catholic clergy and created a cultural gap between them and the peasantry. After 1867, when the pressure of Magyarization became intense, much of the educated class – lacking a popular base – quickly gave in and became Hungarians or "magyarones" as they were called. The Greek Catholic church, based in the bishoprics of Prešov and Mukachiv, not only failed to halt this process but encouraged it. And because Transcarpathia was isolated from Galicia by the tightly controlled Hungarian/Austrian boundary as well as by traditionally weak contacts, Ukrainophile tendencies could not evolve as they did in Bukovyna. Thus, in the final decades of the 19th century, one Slavic periodical after another disappeared in the region, the number of schools teaching in the vernacular declined from 479 in 1874 to none in 1907, and the Society of St Basil (devoted to fostering cultural growth) barely survived. Only a handful of young populists, such as Iurii Zhatkovych and Avhustyn Voloshyn, attempted to resist the trend toward Magyarization.

&

When Ukrainians from the Russian Empire visited Galicia in the early years of the 20th century, they were invariably struck by the progress their western compatriots had made. In Kiev it was still forbidden to publish a book in Ukrainian, but in Lviv one found Ukrainian learned societies, schools, headquarters of mass organizations and cooperatives, newspapers, political parties, and parliamentary representatives. In Russian-ruled Ukraine, the Ukrainian intelligentsia still gathered in small, urban-based *hromady* to pursue scholarly, esoteric projects, but the Ukrainian intelligentsia in Galicia and Bukovyna (most of which had emerged only recently from the village) worked closely with the peasantry in Prosvitas, cooperatives, and political parties. Perhaps the most encouraging aspect of the the West Ukrainian experience was that it showed that aspirations and hopes for Ukrainian national development were not simply pipe dreams of idealistic intellectuals but something which could be transformed into reality.

Impressive though it was, the progress of the Ukrainians in Galicia and Bukovyna should not be exaggerated. Despite their efforts, West Ukrainians as a whole were still mired in poverty; illiteracy was widespread; and the national consciousness of many peasants was practically nil. Moreover, within the tiny, educated elite there were sharp differences between Ukrainophiles and Russophiles – and also among liberals, conservatives, and radicals – about which direction their society should take. Nonetheless, on the eve of the First World War, a sense of optimism was palpable among the West Ukrainians.

In Search of Work. M. Kuznetsov (1882)

Village Wedding. I. Izhakevych (1896)

West Ukrainian town dwellers

OPPOSITE

top: Ukrainian peasant women at work, late 19th century

bottom: The proletariat: steel workers in Luhansk, late 19th century

Marketplace in Lviv, St George Cathedral in background, early 19th century

Opera house in Odessa, late 19th century

Ivan Kotliarevsky

Volodymyr Antonovych

Mykhailo Drahomanov

Lesia Ukrainka

Taras Shevchenko, after his return from exile

Part Five

Twentieth-Century Ukraine

18

War and Revolution

The First World War was Europe's first shocking experience with modern mass warfare. Even a few statistics reflect the mind-boggling dimensions of this widespread conflict: the thirty-four countries that eventually participated in the war mobilized 65 million soldiers of whom 10 million died and over 20 million were wounded. Civilian casualties were almost as high. Not only was the war massive, but it was total. Entire societies and their economies were harnessed to support the huge armies at the front. But as the losses mounted, the tremendous pressures they created, both at the battlefront and at home, exposed and aggravated the fatal political and socioeconomic weaknesses of Europe's old imperial order. Consequently, for the German, Ottoman, and Austro-Hungarian empires, which constituted the Central Powers, and for the Russian Empire, which, together with Britain, France, and America was a member of the Entente, the war eventually became an exercise in self-destruction.

The Russian Empire was the first to collapse under the impact of the war. Not unexpectedly, its demise was accompanied by the rapid rise of various Russian parties that had long opposed the tsarist regime and now attempted to impose their models of a new socioeconomic and political order on the disoriented society. But to the surprise of many, the former empire's apparently docile non-Russian nationalities also demanded to arrange their affairs as they saw fit. As a result, the common view of the revolution of 1917 as a titanic class struggle in Russia is inadequate for an understanding of what happened in Ukraine; there, a Ukrainian revolution occurred, and it was national as well as socioeconomic in nature.

ਏਕ

Ukrainians in the First World War

For the Ukrainians, who had to fight for both of the warring sides, the impact of the war was immediate, direct, and devastating. Throughout the struggle Galicia was the scene of the biggest, bloodiest battles fought on the Eastern front. Its populace suffered terribly from the destruction and dislocation that resulted from the fighting, as well as from the brutal wartime administrations of both the Russians and the Austrians.

But along with the physical damage, the war highlighted and exacerbated the plight of peoples, such as the Ukrainians, who had no state of their own to protect their specific interests. Vast numbers of Ukrainians – the Russian army alone had 3.5 million Ukrainian soldiers and 250,000 served in the Austrian forces – fought and died for empires that not only ignored their national interests but, in the case of Russia, actively sought to destroy their national movements. Worse still, as combatants on opposing sides, Ukrainians were forced to kill each other. The only positive aspect of the war was the possibility that it would weaken the warring empires and thus create new political opportunities for their repressed subjects. But at the outset at least, this possibility was too remote to be treated seriously.

The Ukrainians in Austria reacted quickly to the outbreak of hostilities. On 3 August 1914, all their parties formed the General Ukrainian Council (Zahalna Ukraiinska Rada) in Lviv, headed by the respected parliamentarian Kost Levytsky, for the purpose of providing Ukrainians with a single, united representative body. Declaring that "the victory of the Austrian-Hungarian monarchy will be our victory and the greater the defeat of Russia, the sooner will come the hour of Ukrainian liberation," the council called on Ukrainians to fight for constitutional Austria (their best friend) against autocratic Russia (their worst enemy).[1] Shortly after its formation, the council issued a call for volunteers for an all-Ukrainian military unit. Over 28,000 nationally conscious young men responded, many of them members of the Sich, Sokil, and Plast organizations. Worried by the prospect of large Ukrainian military units, influential Poles in Vienna saw to it that only 2500 men were accepted for service in the Ukrainian Legion (later the name was changed to Ukrainian Sich Riflemen – Ukraiinski Sichovi Striltsi), as the new unit was called. This was the first Ukrainian military formation in modern times. The vast majority of the other Ukrainians who served on the Habsburg side were inducted into regular Austrian units.

The socialist émigrés from Russian-ruled Ukraine also formed a political organization in Lviv in order to act as (self-appointed) spokesmen for their compatriots under tsarist rule. An important, even historic, feature of this organization, called the Union for the Liberation of Ukraine (Soiuz Vyzvolennia Ukrainy – svu) and led by Volodymyr Doroshenko, Andrii Zhuk, Marian Melenevsky, Oleksander Skoropys-Ioltukhovsky, and Mykola Zalizniak, was that it was the first group that unequivocally announced that its goal was the formation of an independent Ukrainian state. To achieve its purpose, the svu resolved to cooperate with Germany and Austria against Russia.

But even before these organizations began to function, they were forced to flee to Vienna when the advancing Russian armies broke through Austrian defenses and occupied much of Eastern Galicia by early September. This Austrian setback had terrible repercussions for the Ukrainians of Galicia. Looking for excuses for their defeats, Austrian and Hungarian commanders turned a willing ear to accusations made by the Polish provincial administration that their defeat was due to the "treachery of the Ukrainians," who allegedly secretly sympathized with and aided the Russians. As a result, the retreating Habsburg armies, and most notably the Hungarian troops, unleashed a reign of terror among the Ukrainian populace. Initially, Russophiles (but later Ukrainians in general) were arrested by the hundreds and executed without trial. Thousands more were hauled off to Austria, where they were interned in concentration camps. The most notorious of these was Talerhof, where 30,000 Russophiles and Ukrainophiles were kept in squalid conditions and thousands died of disease until the parliament in Vienna, scandalized by this treatment of Austrian citizens, ordered it and the other camps disbanded in 1917.

The fate of Galician Ukrainians who were subjected to Russian occupation was also unenviable. The tsarist government quickly made it clear that it did not consider Eastern Galicia to be a new or temporary acquisition, but rather referred to it as an "ancient Russian land" that was now "reunited forever with Mother Russia." It then set about to transform the myth of Galicia's "Russianness" into a reality. Count Georgii Bobrinsky, a brother of an influential Russian conservative who had long advocated acquisition of Galicia, was appointed governor-general and immediately began a concerted attack on the Ukrainian movement, or "Mazepism" as it was called by tsarist officials. He was enthusiastically supported by the Russophiles, whose leaders, such as Volodymyr Dudykevych, Semeon Bandasiuk, and Iuliian Iavorsky, had earlier fled to Russia and now returned with the victorious Russian armies. Russophiles identified and denounced Ukrainian activists (just as the latter had denounced the former to the Austrians a few weeks earlier), who were then arrested and deported deep into Russia. Thus, as Russians persecuted Ukrainophiles and Austrians repressed Russophiles, the mutual denunciations of Galicia's ideologically divided Ukrainians exacerbated their already sorry plight.

On the orders of the tsarist administration, all Ukrainian cultural institutions, cooperatives, and periodicals were shut down. Limits were placed on the use of Ukrainian and efforts were made to introduce Russian into the educational system. The Greek Catholic church, a hallmark of West Ukrainian uniqueness, was attacked with special vigor. Hundreds of Greek Catholic priests were exiled to Russia and replaced by their Orthodox counterparts who urged peasants to convert to Orthodoxy. Metropolitan Andrei Sheptytsky, who refused to flee before the Russians, was arrested and exiled to

Map 19 Ukraine in the First World War

Suzdal, north of Moscow. His brave and inspiring behavior throughout the war added greatly to his growing popularity. But before all the Russian plans could be fully implemented, the Austrians counterattacked and by May 1915 recovered most of Eastern Galicia. As the tsarist troops retreated, they took with them as hostages several hundred leading Ukrainians, as well as thousands of evacuees, including many Russophiles whose role in Ukrainian politics now came to an end.

The Russian treatment of Galician Ukrainians, which Pavel Miliukov, the noted Russian statesman, denounced in the Duma as a "European scandal," was consistent with the attitude of the tsarist government toward the Ukrainian movement in the Russian Empire. At the outbreak of war, almost all Ukrainian organizations and newspapers were repressed. When Mykhailo Hrushevsky, the acknowledged leader of the Ukrainians, returned to Kiev in 1916, he was arrested and exiled to the Russian north. With undisguised relish, Sergei Sazonov (the tsar's foreign minister) noted at this time: "Now is exactly the right moment to rid ourselves of the Ukrainian movement once and for all."[2] However, after its disastrous losses in 1915, the tsarist government lost some of its confidence and softened its tone somewhat. Cautiously, Ukrainian cooperatives, bookstores, scholarly societies, and several newspapers in the Russian Empire began to function again. A semisecret Ukrainian political organization, the Society of Ukrainian Progressives (Tovarystvo Ukrainskykh Progresystiv – TUP), resumed its work as the coordinating body of the Ukrainian movement and agitated for constitutional government in the empire and autonomy for Ukraine.

Meanwhile, on the Austrian side of the front, West Ukrainian politicians gathered in Vienna in May 1915 and reestablished their representative body, the General Ukrainian Council. As the war dragged on and Austria-Hungary weakened, the nationalities of the empire, Ukrainians included, grew bolder in their demands. Thus, the General Ukrainian Council announced that its goals were independence for Russian-ruled Ukraine, which it hoped would be conquered by the Austrians, and broad autonomy for Eastern Galicia and Bukovyna. However, when in 1916 Vienna promised the Poles even greater powers in Galicia, the council resigned in protest. Thereafter, the Ukrainian Parliamentary Club in the Vienna parliament, headed by Evhen Petrushevych, represented West Ukrainian interests.

The East Ukrainian émigrés of SVU, supported by German and Austrian funds, also carried on their work in Vienna. Their organization dispatched representatives to many European capitals to propagate the cause of Ukrainian independence. Although producing few concrete results, the work of SVU with hundreds of thousands of Ukrainian prisoners in Austrian and German captivity, about 50,000 of whom were placed in separate camps, not only raised the soldiers' national consciousness but led to the creation of the so-called Greycoat and Bluecoat divisions that would later fight for the Ukrainian cause. Thus, as the war dragged on, it was clear that the Ukrainians, like other nationalities, were becoming steadily more aggressive in pursuing their own interests and less willing to concern themselves with the fate of the empires that had ruled them for centuries.

By 1917 almost all the combatants in the war were on the verge of exhaustion. But tensions were especially acute in Russia, where the strain of total warfare was compounded by the weaknesses and blunders of an inflexible, corrupt, and backward regime led by the ineffectual Nicholas II. Of all the participants in the war, Russia had the highest military casualties, with over 8 million men killed, wounded, or captured. These horrendous losses caused much bitterness because they had often been the result of careless mistakes on the part of inept commanders who had been appointed by the tsar. Meanwhile, the extent of the corruption and inefficiency in the Russian bureaucracy and among Russian industrialists was demonstrated in the fact that hundreds of thousands of soldiers had been sent against the enemy without even guns or ammunition. Even more widespread were the strains that the war and governmental blundering imposed on the society as a whole. With about half of all able-bodied men drafted into military service, the production of food and finished goods declined and prices rose drastically. Hunger became commonplace, especially among workers in the cities, and as strikes multiplied, a sense of disillusionment spread among the people.

The Russian Revolutions

There were two Russian revolutions in 1917. The first, called the February Revolution, was more of a collapse than an uprising. It began innocuously enough when on 8 March, Petrograd workers went on strike to protest food shortages. But when they were ordered to fire on civilians, the tsarist troops went over to the side of the workers. Within days, much of the capital's garrison did the same. Meanwhile, the population of the city poured into the streets in a show of solidarity with the strikers. It became suddenly apparent that the tsarist government was almost entirely bereft of popular support. As demonstrations spread thoughout the empire, Nicholas II abdicated, his ministers and officials dispersed, and the hated police went into hiding. By 12 March, the tsarist regime had crumbled like a house of cards.

Although bringing tsardom down had been surprisingly easy, finding a generally acceptable substitute proved to be incredibly difficult. Two claimants to political authority emerged. One was the Provisional Government, which was formed from liberal members of the Duma and which sought to perform a caretaker role until Russia established some permanent new form of government. With the administration in shambles and the police almost completely dispersed, the Provisional Government had little effective power, despite the fact that it was widely recognized at home and abroad. Moreover, it was saddled with the burden of carrying on the unpopular war. The Provisional Government's rival from the outset was the Petrograd Soviet of Workers' and Soldiers' Deputies. Dominated by socialists, among whom the Bolsheviks were initially only a minority, the Petrograd Soviet (council) was an ad hoc assembly of radical intelligentsia, workers, and soldiers that was quickly duplicated throughout the country. Its goal was to "deepen" the revolution by pushing it into a complete transformation of society along socialist lines. As these two bodies constantly clashed, contradicted, and obstructed each other, confusion spread about who possessed ultimate authority in the former empire.

Indeed, this confusion soon became an all-pervasive fact of life in revolutionary Russia. For many, most notably the soviets, the demand for change, which had been sanctified by the revolution, justified an attack on many previously commonly accepted principles and institutions. For example, on 14 March, the Petrograd Soviet issued the notorious Order Number One (which the Provisonal Government failed to block) whereby military units were authorized to establish democratically elected councils to run their affairs. The authority of officers was limited to battle situations. This order effectively undermined the already shaky discipline of the army and, as a consequence, it began to disintegrate. By the summer, as millions of armed, demoralized, and radicalized soldiers deserted the front and streamed homeward, public order collapsed. As one observes the often lamentably inadequate attempts to establish and maintain political authority in those chaotic times, it ought to be remembered that those who tried to do so faced a dilemma akin to striving to erect a structure while the ground constantly gave way underneath.

The Revolution in Ukraine

News of the tsarist regime's collapse reached Kiev on 13 March 1917. Within days, representatives of the city's major institutions and organizations formed an Executive Committee which was to maintain order and act as an extension of the Provisional Government. Meanwhile, the Kiev Soviet of Workers' and Soldiers' Deputies became the center of the radical left. But, unlike in Petrograd, a third player entered the scene in Kiev: on 17 March the Ukrainians established their own organization, the Central Rada (*rada* means "council" in Ukrainian; the Russian equivalent is *soviet*). It was created by the liberal moderates from TUP, led by Evhen Chykalenko, Serhii Efremov, and Dmytro Doroshenko, together with the Social Democrats headed by Volodymyr Vynnychenko and Symon Petliura. A few weeks later, the new, burgeoning Ukrainian Socialist Revolutionary party, represented by Mykola Kovalevsky, Pavlo Khrystiuk, and Mykyta Shapoval, also joined the Central Rada. The well-known and highly respected Hrushevsky, on his way back from exile, was elected president of the Central Rada. Thus, in contrast to the Russians in Kiev who were split between the moderates of the Executive

Committee and the radicals of the Soviet, Ukrainians of all ideological per-
suasions were united in a single representative body.

To the surprise of many, the Central Rada generated immediate and growing support. In Petrograd and Kiev, Ukrainians staged huge parades to publicize their cause and demonstrate their backing for the Central Rada. On 19
April a Ukrainian National Congress was held in Kiev. Attended by 900 delegates from all over Ukraine, from Ukrainian communities throughout the former empire, and from various economic, educational, military, and welfare
organizations, it formally elected 150 representatives to the Central Rada and
reaffirmed Hrushevsky's leadership. On 18 May, when over 700 delegates of
Ukrainians serving in the army met in Kiev, they instructed their representatives to join the Central Rada. About a month later, close to 1000 delegates at
the Ukrainian Congress of Peasants did likewise. Afterwards, the Congress of
Workers also joined the Central Rada. Elated by this show of confidence, the
Central Rada began to view itself not merely as the representative of the relatively few nationally conscious Ukrainians but as the parliament of Ukraine.

For the most part, the social background of the Central Rada's most avid
supporters was, to use a term favored by Marxists, petit bourgeois: it consisted of intelligentsia and the so-called half-intelligentsia – village teachers,
lower clergy, petty bureaucrats, zemstvo officials, junior officers, and well-to-
do peasants. Based mostly in the countryside, these people were motivated
not only by the Ukrainophile intelligentsia's traditional concerns about preserving and developing Ukrainian culture, but also by the pragmatic belief
that a government closer to home would be more responsive to their needs.
The Ukrainian peasant believed that the Central Rada would be more effective than a government in far-off Petrograd in helping him obtain more land,
while the Ukrainian soldier hoped it would get him out of the war more
quickly than a Russian government could.

There were, however, also social and ethnic groups in Ukraine that wanted
no part of the Central Rada. Russian conservatives and even moderates feared
that the growing Ukrainian political presence might lead to the disintegration
of "one and indivisible Russia." Russian radicals, for their part, suspected that
the Ukrainian national movement might break up the "unity of the working
class." And Jews, many of whom identified with Russian culture and were
active in Russian socialist parties, also looked askance at the Central Rada.
Thus, much of Ukraine's small but strategically located urban minority was
greatly disturbed by the unexpected rise of the Central Rada.

But as the limitations of the Provisional government's power became more
obvious, the Central Rada decided to press its advantage. Intent on gaining recognition as the highest political authority in Ukraine, on 23 June it issued its First Universal (manifesto), which proclaimed: "Let Ukraine be free.
Without separating entirely from Russia, without severing connections with
the Russian state, let the Ukrainian people have the right to order their own

lives in their own land."[3] Shortly thereafter, the Central Rada announced the formation of the General Secretariat, which was to function as the executive branch of government. Headed by Vynnychenko and composed of eight ministries, most of which were held by Social Democrats, the General Secretariat took over responsibility for the administration of Ukraine.

These measures infuriated the Russians in Ukraine and the Provisional Government in Petrograd. In mid July, the latter sent a delegation, led by Aleksander Kerensky, to Kiev to negotiate. But weakened by the disastrous failure of its offensive in Galicia, the Russians were forced, although with strong qualifications, to recognize the General Secretariat as the administration of five Ukrainian provinces (Kiev, Poltava, Podilia, Volhynia, and Chernihiv). This recognition marked the high point of the Central Rada's influence and authority.

On the promise of far-ranging cultural autonomy, Russian and Jewish parties in Ukraine reluctantly agreed to join the Central Rada. At this point, the Central Rada consisted of 822 seats, about one-fourth of which were held by Russian, Jewish, Polish, and other non-Ukrainian parties. Ideologically, it leaned heavily to the left. With an agreement, albeit shaky, reached with both the Provisional Government and the minorities, the Central Rada was now free to take on the task of governing.

The Central Rada, however, was soon found sorely lacking in leadership. When the Provisional Government attempted to back away from its recognition of Ukrainian autonomy, the Central Rada wasted its time in endless debates about the extent of its authority – neglecting in the process such pressing problems as the maintenance of law and order, the provisioning of the cities, and the functioning of the railroads. It also failed to address effectively the burning issue of land redistribution. Consequently, the initial unity that the Ukrainians had exhibited earlier soon broke down and the political and ideological conflicts between the dominant Social Democrats and the numerous Socialist Revolutionaries in the Central Rada became intense. Immersed in futile debates and feuds and rarely venturing into the countryside (where their authority had always been limited to the environs of Kiev and some of the larger cities) Central Rada members lost the contact with the masses that had been established briefly by means of the various congresses. Each locality now took care of its own affairs as best it could.

Equally damaging was the ideological narrowness of the young, inexperienced Ukrainian politicians, most of whom were in their 20s and 30s. Caught up in their own revolutionary rhetoric, they were intent on dissociating themselves from the old order. A case in point was their attitude toward the military. In summer 1917, about 300,000 Ukrainian soldiers spontaneously reorganized themselves into all-Ukrainian units that swore allegiance to the Central Rada. In a controversial case, General Pavlo Skoropadsky placed at the disposal of the Central Rada a Ukrainized corps of 40,000 men that was admirably disciplined and equipped when compared to the demoralized Russian troops. However, his gesture was rejected on two counts: first, the ideologues in the Central Rada argued that the revolution eliminated the need for standing armies, and second, they pointed out that Skoropadsky was a rich landowner and therefore untrustworthy. Their attitude toward bureaucrats was similar: they were regarded as the embodiment of the old, repressive "bourgeois" state and Vynnychenko, the head of government, called them the "worst, most harmful people."[4]

But it soon became apparent that without an army and a bureaucracy, government was impossible. Disorder and anarchy spread through Ukraine. Matters worsened in July when the Russian army in Galicia disintegrated, inundating Ukraine (which had been the immediate hinterland of the huge southwestern and Romanian fronts) with millions of heavily armed, radicalized, rampaging soldiers. Their impact was, in the words of a Central Rada member, "worse than that of the Tatar hordes," and it graphically exposed the impotence of the Central Rada.[5]

The Bolshevik Coup and the Central Rada

If the February Revolution was essentially the result of a collapse of power, the second revolution, called the October Revolution, was brought on by a seizure of power. It was carried out by Lenin and the Bolsheviks, a group that only six months earlier would have been considered as most unlikely candidates to rule Russia.

In early 1917, the Bolshevik party in Russia, consisting mainly of Russian and Jewish intelligentsia and workers, numbered less than 24,000 at a time when other socialist parties had hundreds of thousands of members. But the Bolsheviks possessed features that, in those chaotic times, were much more valuable than large membership. They were a disciplined, tightly centralized party of committed, longtime revolutionaries who had, in the person of Lenin, a leader of genius with an unrivaled mastery of revolutionary tactics. Lenin's confidence and sense of direction, as well as his promises to give the masses "peace, bread and land," made his party increasingly appealing to many. By fall 1917, Bolshevik ranks had swelled to 350,000. After wresting control of the soviets from other socialist parties and raising the slogan "All power to the Soviets" on 7 November (25 October, Julian style) the Bolsheviks overthrew the floundering Provisional Government in Petrograd and claimed authority in the name of the workers' and soldiers' assemblies.

Concentrated mainly in the Russian industrial centers, the Bolsheviks were exceedingly weak in Ukraine, where in 1918 there were, mostly in the Donetsk industrial region, about 4000–5000 of them. Thus, of Ukraine's more than 2 million workers, Bolshevik adherents constituted a miniscule portion. By comparison, Ukrainian Socialist Revolutionaries alone had over 300,000 party members at this time. Moreover, because the Bolshevik message was aimed primarily at the proletariat – in which the Ukrainians were poorly represented – it held little appeal for them. Industrial workers in Ukraine were largely Russian and Jewish, and they formed about 75% of the party. Hence, in the words of the Soviet historian Nikolai Popov: "The Bolsheviks in Ukraine were ... a party of the Russian or Russified proletariat."[6]

Like most Russians in Ukraine, the Bolsheviks were antagonistic to the Ukrainian movement. As Marxists, they feared that it would undermine the unity of the working class; as members of a dominant minority, they felt threatened by the mobilization of a previously quiescent majority; and as city people, they were contemptuous of a movement based on the peasantry. A leading Bolshevik, Khristian Rakovsky, even had difficulty acknowledging the very existence of a Ukrainian nation. That this attitude was quite widespread in the party was confirmed by Mykola Skrypnyk, one of the few prominent Ukrainian Bolsheviks, when he noted: "For the majority of our party members, Ukraine as a national unit did not exist."[7] Georgii Piatakov, one of the most influential Bolshevik leaders in Ukraine, flatly stated that the party "ought to reject completely the slogan of the right of nations to self-determination."[8] On another occasion, he argued: "We must not support the Ukrainians, because their movement is not convenient for the proletariat. Russia cannot exist without the Ukrainian sugar, industry, coal, cereals, etc."[9]

Lenin, however, was too astute a politician to allow such attitudes to mold Bolshevik policies. He realized, somewhat belatedly, that nationalism was a potent force that could be used to the advantage of his party. Therefore, he developed a rather contorted argument to the effect that Bolsheviks should acknowledge and even encourage the rights of suppressed nationalities to cultural development and self-government as long as – and this was an extremely crucial qualification – doing so did not hinder the proletarian revolution. Thus, for example, if Ukrainian nationalism were to lead to the separation of Ukrainian workers from Russian workers, this, according to Lenin, "is bourgeois nationalism against which a merciless struggle is imperative."[10] In other words, Ukrainian national aspirations were recognized in theory but rejected in practice.

The great merit of this approach was that it allowed Bolsheviks to claim that they were sympathetic to Ukrainian aspirations and deserved Ukrainian support without compromising their commitment to the socialist revolution. The influence of Lenin's views on his colleagues in Ukraine became evident in August 1917 when ten Bolshevik representatives even joined the Central Rada.

After the Bolsheviks assumed power in Russia, the question arose as to who should rule in Ukraine. Too weak to crush both the Central Rada and the supporters of the Provisional Government in Kiev who gathered around the Army Staff, the Bolsheviks decided, for the time being, to maintain good relations with the Ukrainians while dealing with the Army Staff. On 10 November fighting broke out in Kiev between the approximately 6000 Bolsheviks and the Army Staff, which had about 10,000 men at its disposal. At a crucial point in the conflict, the Central Rada ordered its 8000 men to aid the Bolsheviks, thus forcing the Army Staff to evacuate Kiev.

But, to the great consternation of the Bolsheviks, the Central Rada announced that it was assuming the highest authority in all nine provinces where Ukrainians were in the majority. This was formally restated in the Third Universal, issued on 22 November, which proclaimed the establishment of an autonomous Ukrainian Republic. Because it was still hesitant about breaking all ties with Russia, the Central Rada declared that one of its goals was to work for the creation of a "federation of free and equal peoples" in the former Russian Empire. Hopeful that the Central Rada might be a stabilizing force amidst the spreading anarchy, Ukrainian and non-Ukrainian parties, most of the soviets, and even the Bolsheviks (the latter only grudgingly and temporarily) acknowledged the authority of the Ukrainian government.

It quickly became apparent, however, that conflict between the Central Rada and the Bolsheviks would be unavoidable. While the Central Rada criticized Lenin's use of violence in taking power in Petrograd, Lenin complained that the Ukrainians were allowing Cossack troops to pass through their territory so that they could gather in the south where a Russian anti-Bolshevik movement was taking shape. Meanwhile, in Ukraine, the Bolsheviks suffered several political setbacks. In the December elections to the All-Russian Constituent Assembly, later disbanded by the Bolsheviks, the Ukrainian parties garnered over 70% of the vote while the Bolsheviks won only 10%. Even more embarrassing was their experience at the All-Ukrainian Congress of Soviets that they organized themselves in Kiev on 17 December and which they fully expected to control. But the Ukrainian parties brought in their supporters from the countryside and swamped the approximately 100 Bolshevik delegates with over 2000 of their own. Furious, the small Bolshevik faction abandoned the congress, moved to Kharkiv, denounced the Central Rada as the "enemy of the people," and proclaimed the creation of the Soviet Ukrainian Republic. At the same time, Bolshevik troops from Russia began the invasion of Ukraine.

The Bolshevik invasion of Ukraine   Led by the talented Vladimir Antonov-Ovseenko and his brutal associate Mikhail Muraviev, the Bolsheviks, numbering about 12,000, advanced from the northeast. To oppose them, Symon Petliura, the Ukrainian minister of war, had a force of about 15,000 widely scattered men, consisting of the "Free Cossack" peasant militia, the Sich Riflemen, a unit of former Galician prisoners of war, a few small frontline units, and hundreds of young *gymnazium* students who were sent to the front directly from their schools in Kiev.

Map 20 German/Austrian invasion in 1918

One may well wonder, at this point, about where the 300,000 soldiers of the Ukrainized units were who had pledged support to the Central Rada in the summer. Most of them had returned to their villages and adopted a "neutral" stance, as did many of those who remained under arms. Some went over to the Bolsheviks. The unreliability of the majority of these Ukrainian soldiers – contrasting sharply with the heroic efforts of the relative few who actually fought in support of the Central Rada – was largely a result of the effectiveness of Bolshevik agitators. As Richard Pipes has noted,"In the early months of the Civil War, the population at large was confused, bewildered and hesitant. A good agitator was worth hundreds of armed men; he could sway enemy troops and thus decide crucial conflicts."[11] Indeed, the Bolsheviks spared neither men nor money to infiltrate Ukrainized units, many of whose peasant soldiers were exceedingly naive politically, and to persuade them either to desist from fighting or to join the Bolsheviks. Consequently, by December the latter's forces in Ukraine grew to about 40,000 men.

Another advantage the Bolsheviks enjoyed in Ukraine was the diversionary uprisings against the Central Rada staged in almost every large city by their adherents. The most dangerous of these revolts occurred in Kiev on 29 January 1918, when Russian workers seized the Arsenal and tied down Ukrainian troops for several days before giving in. At the same time, not far to the east at Kruty, Petliura's men made their last major stand against Muraviev's advancing forces. After several days of intense fighting, the Ukrainians were forced to retreat. In the process, a unit of 300 schoolboys was surrounded, and, after fierce resistance, slaughtered. Their deaths earned for them a place of honor in the Ukrainian national pantheon. Meanwhile, in Kiev, the Central Rada, which was meeting day and night, rushed through a radical land-reform bill that called for the nationalization of large landholdings. It issued its Fourth and last Universal (although dated 22 January this important document was actually produced on the night of 24 to 25 of that month) proclaiming that the Ukrainian National Republic had broken its ties with Bolshevik Russia and that henceforth it was a free and independent state.

The Treaty of Brest-Litovsk With defeat imminent, the Central Rada had only one last hope – foreign aid. In general, its sympathies lay with the Entente and from the outset it worked strenuously to gain recognition, especially by France. But the response of the French, who were committed to restoring "one, indivisible Russia," was ambiguous. However, on 22 December 1917, a completely new set of possibilities emerged when Lenin, claiming to represent all the peoples of the former Russian Empire, began peace negotiations with the Central Powers at Brest-Litovsk. Because the Central Rada was not about to let the Bolsheviks represent Ukraine in the peace negotiations, it sent its own delegation. On 9 February 1918, only hours before news arrived that the Central Rada had abandoned Kiev to Muraviev's men, its representatives at Brest-Litovsk signed a treaty with the Central Powers. Essentially it consisted of a German commitment to provide military aid to the Central Rada in return for its delivery of large quantities of foodstuffs to the Central Powers.

Within days of signing the Brest-Litovsk Treaty, the Germans and Austrians, having divided Ukraine into spheres of influence, marched in with a powerful army of over 450,000. After only three weeks, the Bolsheviks, who boasted that "they brought in Soviet power from the north on the tips of bayonets" and who had instituted a reign of terror during their brief stay in Kiev, were forced to flee.[12] But this did not mean that the Central Rada, which returned with the Germans on 2 March, received a warm welcome.

Almost every segment of Ukraine's population was disillusioned with its policies. Non-Ukrainians were distraught about the severing of bonds between Ukraine and Russia; poor peasants had not gotten the land they expected; rich peasants and estate owners were furious about the nationalization of large properties; and all blamed the Central Rada for bringing the heavy-handed Germans into the land. For their part, the Germans were also losing their patience with the young, inept ideologues who dominated the Central Rada. They soon realized that it had practically no administrative apparatus with which to collect the millions of tons of food that the hungry German and Austrian cities so desperately needed. The interminable squabbles, debates, and crises among the socialist parties in the Central Rada convinced the Germans that the "young Ukrainian utopians" were incapable of governing. Therefore, on 28 April, just as the Central Rada was formulating the constitution of the Ukrainian state, a German unit marched into the hall and disbanded the assembly. A day later the Central Rada fell without a move being made to defend it.

૨ꝏ

During the one year that the Central Rada had been the major political factor in Ukraine, it achieved notable successes and experienced dismal failures. Considering the weak, repressed, and politically inexperienced state of the Ukrainian intelligentsia prior to the revolution, the creation and growth of the Central Rada was a considerable achievement. By its activity, it finally put to rest long-standing and widely held doubts about the very existence of a Ukrainian nationality. Indeed, it transformed the Ukrainian issue into one of the key issues of the revolutionary period. In strictly political terms, the Central Rada more than held its own in dealing with the Provisional Government.

It also out-maneuvered the Bolsheviks of Ukraine, forcing them to turn to Russia for aid. Intent on creating a democratic, parliamentary government, the Central Rada adhered to its goals despite the pressure for arbitary action. A striking example of this commitment was its precedent-setting grant of wide-ranging cultural autonomy to the Jewish minority, despite the fact that its representatives were among the severest critics of the Ukrainian government. But perhaps the Central Rada's most far-reaching achievement was that by its stubborn demand for Ukrainian self-government, it seriously challenged the previously untouchable principle of "one, indivisible Russia" and forced both the Provisional Government and, later, the Bolsheviks to retreat (at least in theory) from this shibboleth of Russian political thinking.

The most obvious fact about the Central Rada was, however, that it failed. Among the basic causes of that failure was that it lacked the two main pillars of statehood, namely an effective army and administrative apparatus. Without the latter, the Central Rada was unable to maintain contact with the provinces and countryside where most of its potential support lay. Equally damaging was the lack of consensus on what policies to follow. This deficiency was painfully evident in the bitter feud between Vynnychenko and Petliura, two of the government's key ministers. Vynnychenko argued that the Central Rada should pursue more socially radical policies so that it could "out-socialize" the Bolsheviks and live up to the expectations of the masses for drastic change. Petliura, meanwhile, believed that more emphasis should be placed on building the institutions of a nation-state. Finally, the immediate cause of the Central Rada's demise was its inability to satisfy German demands.

Yet as John Reshetar has demonstrated, in the final analysis, the failure of the Central Rada lay in the underdevelopment of the Ukrainian national movement.[13] In effect, the Central Rada was forced to begin state-building before the process of nation-building had been completed. Because of the repressive nature of the tsarist regime and the socioeconomic peculiarities of Ukrainian society, most of the educated people in Ukraine were either Russians or Russified. The Ukrainian movement had not yet penetrated the cities and these crucial centers of industry, communications, and skilled personnel functioned as bastions of the Russian and Russified minorities who were often militantly anti-Ukrainian. Hence, there was a critical lack of competent individuals available for organizing and staffing the army and administration of a Ukrainian state. The people who were available were young and inexperienced: Vynnychenko was 38, Petliura was 35, Kovalevsky (leader of the largest Ukrainian party, the Socialist Revolutionaries) was 25, Mykola Shrah (who substituted for Hrushevsky as presiding officer of the Central Rada) was 22. Aware of its lack of human as well as material resources, Serhii Efremov, a member of the Central Rada, urged it to refrain from assuming authority, for, he argued, the masses awaited miracles and a Ukrainian government would be sure to disillusion them. In view of these seemingly insurmountable obstacles, it is understandable why Vynnychenko, referring to the Central Rada's efforts, remarked: "Truly, we were like the gods ... attempting to create a whole new world from nothing."[14]

19

The Ukrainian Revolution

After the Bolshevik coup, the revolution turned into a civil war. Gone were the euphoria, the feeling of solidarity, the massive demonstrations, tumultuous assemblies, and heated debates of 1917. For the next three years numerous claimants for power in Ukraine and throughout the former empire were embroiled in a bitter, merciless military struggle, complete with large-scale terror and atrocities, to decide who and what form of government should replace the old order.

For many Ukrainians, the rise of the Bolsheviks in Russia not only ushered in a new, violent phase of the postrevolutionary period but also brought about a radical change in their political thinking. Repulsed by the dictatorial nature of the Bolshevik regime in the north, many Ukrainian leaders abandoned their traditional preference for an autonomous or federal relationship with Russia. Henceforth, independence became their goal. However, Ukrainians, like other peoples of the former empire, became increasingly divided over their other goals and the ways to achieve them. Moreover, because of Ukraine's abundant natural resources and strategic location, almost every participant in the Civil War sought to gain control of the land. Therefore, after the relatively calm hiatus imposed by the German occupation, Ukraine became the scene of the most chaotic, complex events of the Civil War.

ᕒ

The Hetmanate

By spring 1918, significant sectors of Ukraine's populace had had enough of revolution and chaos. As might be expected, these attitudes were most prevalent among the land's propertied classes, the well-to-do peasants, the petty entrepreneurs and businessmen, the factory owners and large landholders, and the upper levels of bureaucracy who constituted about 20% of

Ukraine's population.[1] As well, the Germans and Austrians in Ukraine were exceedingly anxious to restore order so as to expedite the removal of food-stuffs. Therefore, between 24 and 26 April, the representatives of these groups secretly agreed to replace the Central Rada with a conservative Ukrainian government headed by Hetman Pavlo Skoropadsky (the title "hetman" was meant to evoke the quasi-monarchical traditions associated with the Cossack hetmans).

Skoropadsky, a scion of an old Cossack *starshyna* family and one of Ukraine's largest landowners, had been a well-placed member of the tsarist establishment, having served as Nicholas II's aide-de-camp and as a highly regarded general during the war. However, during the revolution he had Ukrainized his army corps, and – after the Central Rada had rejected his ser-vices – he was elected titular commander of the "Free Cossack" peasant mili-tia. With the rise to power of this Russified "Little Russian" aristocrat who had suddenly recalled his Ukrainian roots, a new phase of the revolution in Ukraine set in, characterized by attempts to restore law and order and to undo some of the Central Rada's "socialist experiments."

On 29 April, at a congress called in Kiev by the League of Landowners, which was attended by about 6500 delegates from all over Ukraine, Sko-ropadsky was enthusiastically proclaimed hetman and called upon "to save the country from chaos and lawlessness." That same day he and his support-ers announced the establishment of the "Ukrainian State" (as opposed to the Central Rada's "Ukrainian National Republic"). The new state rested on an unusual mixture of monarchical, republican, and, most notably, dictatorial features. Its citizens were guaranteed the usual civil rights, with strong em-phasis being placed on the sanctity of private property.

While revoking such innovations of the Central Rada as the nationalization of large estates and personal-cultural autonomy, the hetman introduced a dis-tinct category of citizens – the Cossacks – who were actually well-to-do peas-ants. He hoped they would act as the main social pillar of his regime. Most striking were the vast prerogatives reserved for the hetman: he possessed sole authority to issue all the laws, appoint the cabinet, control foreign affairs and the military, and act as the highest judge in the land. Yet these claims to al-most unlimited authority did not hide the fact that it was the Germans (but not the Austrians) who had ultimate power in Ukraine.

As might be expected, the reaction of Ukrainian activists (most of whom were socialists and had belonged to the Central Rada) to the Hetmanate was sharply negative. Therefore, when some well-known Ukrainians were invited to join the Hetman government, almost all of them refused. This left the het-man with no choice but to turn to individuals not associated with the Ukrain-ian movement to form his cabinet, thereby exposing himself to accusations that his government included no "real" Ukrainians. But although the new cabinet – which was led by the prime minister Fedir Lyzohub (a wealthy landowner) and included only one well-known Ukrainian activist, the foreign minister Dmytro Doroshenko – was short on nationalists, it did include a number of skilled administrators.

In a matter of months, an effective bureaucratic apparatus was reestablished in Ukraine. In the provinces, Central Rada appointees were replaced by experienced administrators called *starosty*, who were drawn mostly from among local landowners and *zemstvo* officials. Posts in the central government went to professionals, mostly Russians or Russified Ukrainians. There were, however, difficulties in creating an effective army, for the Germans discouraged the creation of a large military force that might challenge their overwhelming influence. A police force, which like the army, attracted many former tsarist officers, was soon operating (for better or worse) at full tilt.

While the Central Rada had had formal diplomatic relations only with Germany, Austro-Hungary, and the Ottoman Empire, the Hetmanate exchanged embassies with about a dozen countries. Its main foreign policy concerns were the negotiation of a peace treaty with Soviet Russia, concluded on 12 June 1918, and the fruitless discussion with Austro-Hungary about the possibility of annexing such largely Ukrainian lands as Eastern Galicia and the Kholm region.

The government's achievements in education and in the creation of an infrastructure for scholarly activity were especially impressive. On the elementary school level, several million Ukrainian-language textbooks were prepared and Ukrainian was introduced into most of the schools. About 150 new Ukrainian-language *gymnazia*, many located in rural areas, were founded. In October, two new Ukrainian universities were created in Kiev and Kamianets-Podilskyi. A national archive and a library of over one million volumes were also founded. The high point of this activity was the establishment of the Ukrainian Academy of Sciences on 24 November 1918. Thus, in a matter of months, in the area of culture the Hetmanate had achievements to its credit that the Ukrainian intelligentsia had dreamed of for generations.

But while the Skoropadsky regime could boast of administrative skills and concrete achievements, it was burdened with crushing political handicaps. For the most part, they were an outgrowth of the company the hetman had chosen to keep. First, he was compromised by his dependence on the Germans, whose obvious goal was to exploit Ukraine economically. Second, the hetman was closely associated with the propertied classes, which sought to undo the changes brought about by the revolution. Thus, such extremely unpopular measures as the "punitive expeditions," organized by landlords with the support of German troops to punish peasants for confiscating their lands the previous year, were blamed on Skoropadsky. Third, many Ukrainians considered Skoropadsky to be too supportive of Russians. During his term in office, Ukraine – which was an island of stability compared to Russia – became not only a refuge for vast numbers of the former tsarist elite but also a center for attempts to rebuild "one, indivisible Russia." The bureaucracy was inundated with Russians who made no secret of their antipathy to Ukrainian statehood, and most of the cabinet were members of the Russian Kadet party.

Opposition to Skoropadsky began to crystallize from the outset. In mid May, a series of illegal congresses of Ukrainian parties were held and occupational groups such as railroad workers, telegraph operators, peasants, and workers expressed their disapproval of the new government. A coordinating body called the Ukrainian National State Union and led by Vynnychenko arose to act as a center of opposition. Another influential organization, the All-Ukrainian Union of Zemstva, headed by Petliura, also adopted an anti-hetman line. Initially, these groups negotiated with Skoropadsky about ways of implementing a more liberal and nationalist policy, but later they turned to fomenting a rebellion against him.

Ukrainian peasants needed little encouragement to rebel against a government that confiscated their crops, restored lands to rich estate-owners, and sent "punitive expeditions" into their villages. Soon spontaneous, fierce peasant revolts spread through Ukraine. Led by a local, often anarchistically inclined leader called (in the Cossack tradition) an *otaman* or *batko* and armed with readily available weapons, hordes of peasants fought pitched battles with German troops. The scale of these conflicts was huge: for example, in the Zvenyhorod and Tarashchanka regions of Kiev province, peasant forces numbering 30,000–40,000 men, equipped with two batteries of artillery and 200 machine guns, inflicted 6000 casualties on the Germans. However, not all the uprisings were effective. In early August, when the Bolsheviks of Ukraine tried to lead a general rebellion, it collapsed within two days because of the lack of popular support.

By early fall, it was apparent that the Central Powers were about to lose the war. At this point, the hetman was forced to make concessions. Yet another attempt to attract prominent Ukrainian activists into his cabinet failed in late October. Desperately casting about for support, Skoropadsky took a final gamble: on 14 November 1918 he appointed a new cabinet consisting almost entirely of Russian monarchists and announced the Act of Federation, which committed him to link Ukraine with a future non-Bolshevik Russian state. This controversial step was taken in order to gain the support of anti-Bolshevik Russians and the favor of the victorious Entente. That same day, the Ukrainian opposition formed an insurrectionary government, the Directory, led by the two old rivals Vynnychenko and Petliura, and openly declared a rebellion against the hetman.

The Directory's insurrection grew rapidly. Great numbers of peasant partisans, led by their rambunctious *otamany*, poured into Bila Tserkva, west of Kiev, which served as the headquarters of the anti-Skoropadsky forces. Soon these enthusiastic but poorly disciplined irregulars numbered about 60,000. More important, some of the hetman's best units – the Sich Riflemen, commanded by Evhen Konovalets and his chief of staff, Andrii Melnyk, and the Greycoat Division – went over to the Directory, raising the number of its regular troops to 40,000. By 21 November the insurgents encircled Kiev and, after lengthy negotiations to assure safe passage for the German garrison, on 14 December the Germans evacuated the city, taking Skoropadsky with them. That same day, the Directory's forces triumphantly entered Kiev and announced the reestablishment of the Ukrainian National Republic.

The Hetmanate existed less than eight months during which time real power lay in the hands of the Germans, and its impact was limited. Initially, it was able to attract some support because of its promise to restore law and order, something much of the land's population desired. However, it failed to address adequately the two main issues raised by the revolution in Ukraine: socioeconomic reform and nationalism. Skoropadsky's attempt to restore stability by resurrecting the prerevolutionary socioeconomic order, particularly in the countryside, was his most serious blunder. On the nationality issue, his government was ambiguous: although it had major achievements, such as the Ukrainization of education and culture, to its credit, it nonetheless led Ukrainian nationalists to believe that it was "Ukrainian in form but Muscovite in content."

However, as Viacheslav Lypynsky, the ideologist of modern Ukrainian conservatism, noted, the Hetmanate had a broader significance. It consisted of exposing, and even attracting, some members of the largely Russified socioeconomic elite of Ukraine to the idea of Ukrainian statehood. This, in turn, helped to expand the social base of this idea beyond the thin stratum of Ukrainian intelligentsia to the broader, more reliable, and productive class of the "tillers of the land," that is, the landowning peasants and estate owners. Thus, according to Lypynsky, had Skoropadsky survived, he would have made Ukrainian statehood acceptable to the land's most productive inhabitants rather than having it depend on an "ideological sect," as he called the nationally conscious Ukrainian intelligentsia.[2]

Anarchy

In 1919 total chaos engulfed Ukraine. Indeed, in the modern history of Europe no country experienced such complete anarchy, bitter civil strife, and total collapse of authority as did Ukraine at this time. Six different armies – those of the Ukrainians, the Bolsheviks, the Whites, the Entente, the Poles, and the anarchists – operated on its territory. Kiev changed hands five times in less than a year. Cities and regions were cut off from each other by the numerous fronts. Communications with the outside world broke down almost completely. The starving cities emptied as people moved into the countryside in their search for food. Villages literally barricaded themselves against intruders and strangers. Meanwhile, the various governments that momentarily managed to establish themselves in Kiev devoted most of their attention and energy to fending off the onslaughts of their enemies. Ukraine was a land easy to conquer but almost impossible to rule.

As he observed the collapse of one authority after another from his self-sufficient village, the peasant's attitude was one of wishing a pox on the city people and all their governments. His prime concern was to keep his land and, if possible, to obtain more of it. The peasant was willing to support any government that seemed able to satisfy these desires. But the moment that government was unable to fulfill his expectations or placed demands on his land and harvest, the peasant turned against it and went over to a rival. The peasant knew that he did not want the return of the old order, yet he was uncertain of what he wanted to replace it. This made him a rather unpredictable element throughout the Civil War.

Peasant attitudes were all the more important because for the first time in centuries the peasantry had the will and ability to fight. During the Hetman period, hundreds of *otamany* and partisan bands, imbued with a spirit of neo-Cossack anarchism, arose throughout Ukraine. Some favored the nationalists, others backed the Bolsheviks, many switched sides frequently, and all were most concerned with protecting the interests of their villages and districts. If in the process they had a chance to plunder "class enemies" or vent their age-old resentment against Jews, so much the better. Like Chinese warlords, their *otamany* scoffed at all authority and acted as if they were a law unto themselves.

Two of the most powerful partisan leaders were based in the steppes of the south where the richest, most self-confident peasants lived. One was Matvii Hryhoriiv (Grigoriev), a swashbuckling former tsarist officer who led a force of about 12,000 in the region of Kherson and maintained close links with the radical Ukrainian left. The other was the legendary Nestor Makhno, a Russified Ukrainian peasant and an avowed anarchist. In mid 1919 his forces, based in Huliai Pole, numbered between 35,000 and 50,000 men, and they often held the balance in the struggle for southern Ukraine. Thus, as regular armies fought for control of cities and railroad lines and partisan forces dominated the countryside, the only regime that was recognized throughout Ukraine was the rule of the gun.

The Directory

After the expulsion of Skoropadsky, the Directory began transforming itself from a successful insurrectionary committee into a government of the newly resurrected Ukrainian National Republic (UNR). Temporarily retaining the highest executive prerogatives for itself, it appointed a cabinet of ministers, led by Volodymyr Chekhivsky. The composition of the cabinet clearly indicated that young politicians, not "elder statesmen" such as Hrushevsky, would play the leading role in the new government.

On 26 December 1918 the Directory issued its Declaration or statement of goals, which indicated that an attempt would be made to strike a balance between revolution and order. A preference for the former was quite apparent, however. One of the main features of the Declaration was the promise to expropriate state, church, and large private landholdings for redistribution among the peasants. Another was the government's commitment to act as the representative of the workers, peasants, and "toiling intelligentsia" – and its intention to disenfranchise the landed and industrial bourgoisie. To this end it called for a Congress of Workers that would function as the representative and legislative body of the state.

But the new government was able to attain few of its goals before both internal and external problems overwhelmed it. The key internal issue was the split that developed between and within Ukrainian political parties as to whether the government should be a parliamentary democracy (as the moderate socialists wanted) or a Ukrainian variant of the soviet (council) system (as the radical left desired). Led by Vynnychenko, the radical left argued that Ukrainians must pay as much attention to social transformation as to national liberation and that if they adopted the soviet system, they would steal the Bolsheviks' thunder. The more nationalistic moderates, with whom Petliura sympathized, responded that it was exactly this obsession with socialist experiments and the resulting neglect of the army and other state institutions that brought down the Central Rada and that this mistake should not be repeated. Thus, the old dilemma of the Ukrainian intelligentsia – arguing about whether social revolution or national liberation should have priority – again sowed animosity and confusion in its ranks.

This fractious conflict spilled over into the area of foreign relations. In December 1918 the Entente, primarily the French, landed a force of about 60,000 men in Odessa and other Black Sea ports. This unexpected development was brought on by the victorious Western powers' decision to block the spread of bolshevism. Their intention was to lend direct military support to the anti-Bolshevik White forces that were preparing to launch a campaign from the Don in hopes of restoring "one, indivisible Russia." Meanwhile, in the north, there were growing indications that the Bolsheviks were planning to repeat their invasion of Ukraine. The Directory obviously could not confront both intruders and had to come to an understanding with one of them. As might be expected, Vynnychenko and his colleagues from the radical left favored an alliance with Moscow, while the moderates and the army insisted on an agreement with the Entente. However, the issue was decided by the Bolsheviks when – as their representatives conducted peace negotiations with the Directory – their troops attacked Kharkiv.

The second Bolshevik invasion of Ukraine   As the Bolsheviks advanced, the Directory acted in a manner similar to that of the Central Rada a year earlier. In the last desperate days before the fall of Kiev, the Directory engaged in

several symbolic demonstrations of sovereignty. On 22 January 1919 it celebrated the union of the Ukrainian National Republic with the newly formed
West Ukrainian National Republic (zunr) in Galicia, a union that the Ukrainian intelligentsia, in both the east and west, had dreamed of for generations.
However, with both governments fighting desperately for survival, their future prospects looked bleak. Furthermore, both governments still retained
separate administrations, armies, and policies. Hence, it was a union in name
only.

Militarily, the performance of the Ukrainian government's troops was as
disappointing as it had been a year earlier. Even before the second Bolshevik
invasion, the hordes of peasant soldiers who had participated in the overthrow of the hetman returned to their villages, convinced that they had removed the main threat to their well-being and unconcerned about the fate
of the Directory. Given the strong pro-Soviet tendencies that were evident
in the Ukrainian government itself, Bolshevik agitators were even more successful than before in drawing many of these men to their side. Therefore,
the Directory's army, which had numbered well over 100,000 weeks before,
had dwindled to about 25,000. And a large part of this force still consisted of
otamany and their partisans whom the commander-in-chief, Petliura, could
barely control. As the military situation deteriorated further, on 2 February
the Directory abandoned Kiev and moved west to Vinnytsia. By spring, after
a series of military defeats, it was barely able to hold on to a small stretch of
territory around Kamianets-Podilskyi.

Once again the hopes of the Ukrainian government rested on another foreign power, France, whose seemingly invincible troops were ensconced in
Odessa. In order to appear more acceptable to the French, the Directory
purged itself of the radical, pro-Soviet elements. In mid February Vynnychenko resigned and Chekhivsky's socialist cabinet was replaced by moderates led by Serhii Ostapenko. Petliura now emerged as the most influential
individual in the government. Soon it became evident that the French, influenced by their White Russian allies – who hated Ukrainian "separatists" as
much as Bolsheviks – had no intention of offering aid or recognition to the Directory. By early April the entire issue became moot when the French forces,
pressed by Hryhoriiv, one of Petliura's partisan commanders who had just
gone over to the Bolsheviks, departed from Ukraine as abruptly as they had
arrived.

Under pressure from military defeats and diplomatic disappointments, the
ideological conflict among the Ukrainians came to a head. In the two major
political parties, the Social Democrats and the Socialist Revolutionaries, small
but influential factions on the radical left broke off, constituted themselves as
separate parties, adopted a Soviet platform, and joined the Bolsheviks. They
took along with them such powerful *otamany* as Anhel, Zeleny, Sokolovsky,
Tiutiunnyk, and Hryhoriiv. Among the Social Democrats the secession of the
left occurred in January 1919; the Borotbists, who took their name from their

newspaper, *Borotba* (The Struggle), and numbered about 5000, broke off from the Socialist Revolutionaries at about the same time.

The pogroms   One of the worst aspects of the anarchy that gripped Ukraine in 1919 was the widespread pogroms. During the revolution, among the anti-Bolshevik forces, both Ukrainian and Russian, old animosities towards the Jews were heightened by the widespread impression that Jews were pro-Bolshevik. Actually most Jews were apolitical and those who were Marxists usually favored the Mensheviks. But it is a fact that Jews were also disproportionately prominent among the Bolsheviks, notably in their leadership, among their tax- and grain-gathering officials, and especially in the despised and feared Cheka (secret police). Therefore, in the chaos, Jews became the targets of old resentments and new frustrations.

Historians estimate that in Ukraine between 35,000 and 50,000 Jews were killed in pogroms in 1919–20.[3] Peter Kenez, a specialist on the Civil War in Ukraine and south Russia, notes that

before the advent of Hitler, the greatest modern mass murder of Jews occurred in Ukraine, during the Civil War. All the participants in the conflict were guilty of murdering Jews, even the Bolsheviks. However, the Volunteer Army [the Whites or anti-Bolshevik Russians] had the largest number of victims. Its pogroms differed from mass killings carried out by its competitors; they were the most thorough, they had the most elaborate superstructure, or to put it differently, they were the most modern ... Other pogroms were the work of peasants. The pogroms of the Volunteer Army, on the other hand, had three different participants: the peasant, the Cossack and the Russian officer ... The particularly bloody nature of these massacres can be explained by the fact that these three types of murderers reinforced one another.[4]

Although the White Volunteer Army – which moved into Ukraine from the Don in the summer of 1919 – was primarily responsible for the pogroms, the Directory's forces (especially the *otaman*-led irregulars) also perpetrated a series of pogroms. The most serious occurred in Proskuriv, Zhytomyr, Cherkasy, Rivne, Fastiv, Korosten, and Bakhmach. Of these the most savage was instigated by Otaman Semesenko in Proskuriv in February 1919, when several thousand Jews perished.

In general, the Ukrainian pogroms differed from those of the Whites in two ways: in contrast to the premeditated, systematic undertakings of the Russians, they were spontaneous outbursts of demoralized and often drunken irregulars, and they were committed against the express orders of the high command. Unlike the White Russian generals such as Anton Denikin, the Ukrainian socialists, especially the Social Democratic party to which Petliura belonged, had a long tradition of friendly relations with Jewish political activists. Therefore, the Directory renewed Jewish personal-cultural autonomy, attracted prominent Jews such as Arnold Margolin and Solomon Goldelman into its government, appropriated large amounts of money for pogrom victims, and even negotiated with the famous Zionist leader Vladimir Zhabotinsky about the inclusion of Jewish police units into its army.

But while Petliura's attitudes towards the Jews might have been well intentioned, he was unable to control the *otamany* (the court-martial and subsequent execution of Semesenko and other partisan leaders did not improve the situation), and their dreadful deeds were associated with his government. And because many Jews considered themselves to be Russians, they found it easier to lay all the blame for the pogroms on Petliura and the Ukrainians rather than on Denikin and his Russian generals.[5]

The Bolsheviks

After they were expelled by the Germans in early 1918, Ukraine's scattered and disorganized Bolsheviks had almost a year to prepare for their return. The most pressing issue before them was an organizational one: were they to form a separate Ukrainian Bolshevik party so as to broaden their appeal in Ukraine or should they become a "regional" branch of the Russian party as Lenin insisted and Russian centralist traditions dictated? At a party conclave held in April in Tahanrih, where the Ukrainian Skrypnyk and the so-called Kiev faction (which was more sensitive to the nationality issue) predominated, a vote was taken to form a separate Ukrainian party. But at the congress of Ukraine's Bolsheviks held in July in Moscow to establish formally the Communist Party (Bolshevik) of Ukraine – CP(b)U – the strongly centralist and almost exclusively Russian Katerynoslav faction gained the upper hand. The Tahanrih resolution was rescinded and the CP(b)U was declared to be an integral part of the Russian party based in Moscow.

The fall of the Hetman government, evacuation of the Germans, and rise of the Directory provoked another debate among the Bolsheviks. One faction, led by Dmitrii Manuilsky and Vladimir Zatonsky, considered Bolsheviks in Ukraine to be too weak – in July 1918 they had a mere 4364 members – to attempt a takeover of the land. They argued for negotiating a peace with the Directory in order to gain time to strengthen their organization. But the group led by Piatakov and Antonov-Ovseenko pleaded with Lenin to support an immediate invasion so as not to allow the Directory to consolidate its hold. After much wavering, Moscow sanctioned the formation of another Ukrainian Soviet government on 20 November 1918. Initially, it was led by Piatakov but he was soon replaced by the Russified Bulgarian-Romanian Khristian Rakovsky. Almost all the important posts in the government were held by Russians. In December, the Bolsheviks were ready to launch their second attempt to conquer Ukraine.

At the outset, the Bolshevik forces, commanded by Antonov-Ovseenko, consisted of a few Red Army units and scattered irregulars. However, as they moved into Ukraine, one partisan formation after another abandoned the Directory and joined the invaders. On 3 January 1919, Kharkiv fell to the Bolsheviks and on 5 February they marched into Kiev. At this point, their troops numbered about 25,000. But in the next few weeks they more than doubled, when Ukraine's two most important partisan leaders, Hryhoriiv and Makhno, joined them. With their support, by June the Bolsheviks managed to gain control of much of Ukraine.

The second Ukrainian Soviet government lasted about seven months. During this time, it showed that it was fully capable of making as many critical blunders as the other governments that had tried to govern Ukraine. Composed mostly of Russians, Jews, and other non-Ukrainians, it attempted to apply policies in Ukraine that had been developed in Russia, regardless of whether or not they fitted local circumstances. The Russian orientation was especially evident in the "grain crusade," as Lenin called it. Because in 1919 Russian cities were in dire need of food, about 3000 workers from Moscow and Petrograd were dispatched to Ukraine to forage for grain and, much like the Germans had done a year earlier, to use force if necessary to get it. But the Bolsheviks compounded their error. They began an attack on the "bourgeois" principle of private property by introducing collective farms. As might be expected, these measures infuriated not only the kulaks but the middle peasantry as well.

Rakovsky's government also managed to alienate the Ukrainian leftist intelligentsia, such as the Borotbists, by refusing to use the Ukrainian language in administration and ignoring the need for it in education and cultural activity. When criticism and resistance mounted, the Bolshevik response was to loosen the feared and hated Cheka, led by the Latvian Martin Latsis, to arrest and execute "class enemies" at will. The consequences were predictable: after fighting on the Bolshevik side for only a few months, the peasant partisans, led by the Borotbisty and Ukrainian Social Democrats, turned against the Bolsheviks en masse. Especially crucial was the defection in March of the large forces led by Hryhoriiv and Makhno. By the summer, almost the entire Ukrainian countryside was in revolt against the Bolsheviks.

At this point, another invader moved into Ukraine. In June, the White armies led by General Denikin launched an offensive from the Don and by July captured much of the Left Bank. Meanwhile, Petliura's reorganized army attacked on the Right Bank. As Bolshevik resistance collapsed, Lenin ordered the liquidation of the second Ukrainian Soviet government in mid August 1919, and most of its members returned to Moscow. Referring to this second failure in Ukraine in two years, Manuilsky, a member of the former government, remarked dejectedly: "Each spring we equip a successive troupe for the Ukraine which, after making a tour there, returns to Moscow in the autumn."[6]

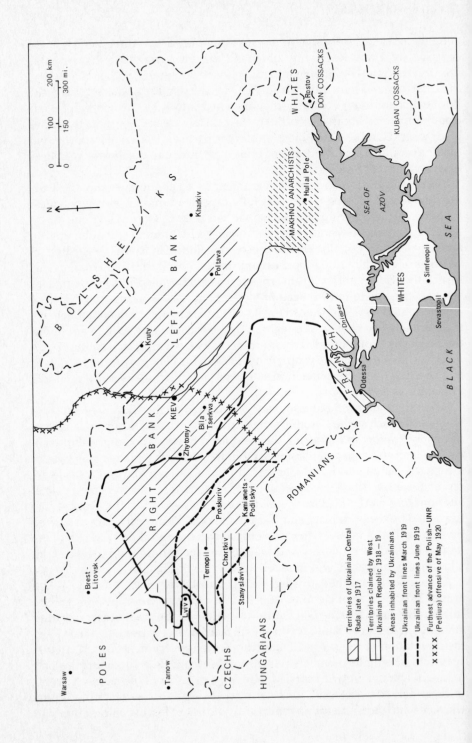

Warsaw

POLES

Brest-
Litovsk

Tarnow

CZECHS

HUNGARIANS

Lviv

Stanyslaviv

Chortkiv

Ternopil

Kamianets-
Podilskyi

Proskuriv

R I G H T   B A N K

Zhytomyr

Bila
Tserkva

KIEV

Kruty

L E F T   B A N K

Poltava

Kharkiv

B O L S H E V I K S

ROMANIANS

Odessa

F R E N C H

Dniester

MAKHNO ANARCHISTS

Hulai Pole

WHITES

DON COSSACKS

Rostov

KUBAN COSSACKS

SEA OF
AZOV

WHITES

Simferopil

Sevastopil

B L A C K   S E A

N

200 km

300 mi.

100

150

0

0

The Struggle in the West

Having suffered a crushing defeat in the war, the Austro-Hungarian Empire began to disintegrate in October 1918, about 20 months after the Russian Empire had collapsed. Even before the Habsburgs acknowledged that the end had come, their subject peoples, the West Ukrainians included, had already made preparations for creating their own independent nation-states. Insofar as the West Ukrainians attempted to establish a Ukrainian state in Eastern Galicia from amidst the ruins of a fallen empire and in the face of fierce opposition, they found themselves in an analogous situation to that of their compatriots in the east. However, in almost every other respect, their efforts at state-building differed radically from those of the East Ukrainians.

As might be expected, the Poles also laid claim to Eastern Galicia. What resulted, therefore, was a conflict of two nations over territory and not, as was the case in the east, a confusing struggle of various governments, parties, and ideologies for the "hearts and minds of men." Perhaps because Austrian constitutionalism had taught the Poles and West Ukrainians to appreciate and participate in government, the fall of the empire did not result in the socio-economic upheaval, chaos, anarchy, and brutality that occurred in the east. For the Ukrainians and the Poles in Eastern Galicia, the issues were clear-cut: national goals were of primary importance and the consideration of socio-economic concerns was postponed until later. The Polish/Ukrainian conflict was fierce but orderly; it was carried on, for the most part, by regular armies, which fought along established fronts and inflicted relatively little damage on the civilian population. In essence, it was a test of strength between the 3.5 million Ukrainians in Eastern Galicia and the 18 million Poles who were simultaneously fighting the Czechs, Germans, and Lithuanians – who also did not want to be included in the Polish state.

As it became evident that Austria was about to fall, on 18 October 1918 the parliamentarians, party leaders, and church hierarchs from Eastern Galicia and Bukovyna formed a Ukrainian National Council to act as a Ukrainian representative body. They also announced their intention to unite all West Ukrainian lands into a single entity that would have an as-yet-unspecified relationship with whatever remained of the Habsburg empire. Meanwhile, the Poles also prepared to take over Lviv and Eastern Galicia. A group of young Ukrainian officers, led by Captain Dmytro Vitovsky of the Sich Riflemen, frustrated by the slow, legalistic approach of the National Council, took matters into their own hands. On the night of 31 October they hastily gathered all the available Ukrainian soldiers serving in the Austrian units in Lviv and vicinity and took control of the city. On 1 November the city's inhabitants awoke to find Ukrainian flags flying from city hall, all major offices in Ukrainian hands, and placards everywhere informing them that they were now citizens of a Ukrainian state. Similar events occurred throughout the rest of Eastern Galicia.

The Ukrainian population greeted the events of 1 November with enthusiasm. The Jews recognized Ukrainian sovereignty or remained neutral. But as soon as they recovered from the shock, the Poles in Lviv turned to active resistance and bitter house-to-house fighting broke out between the Ukrainian troops and the Polish Military Organization. To the northwest, on the border between Eastern Galicia and Poland proper, the key railroad center of Peremyshl fell to the Poles. In Bukovyna, Romanian troops occupied much of the land, while in Transcarpathia the Hungarians remained in power. Nonetheless, much of Eastern Galicia remained in the hands of the Ukrainians and they pressed on with the organization of their state. On 9 November, after all the Ukrainian parties agreed to cooperate in the formation of a government, they appointed a provisional council of ministers or General Secretariat which was headed by the experienced parliamentarian Kost Levytsky. Four days later, the new state was formally constituted as the West Ukrainian National Republic (Zakhidno Ukrainska Narodna Respublyka – ZUNR).

A crushing blow to the fledgling state came on 22 November 1918 when the 1400 Ukrainian soldiers, mostly teenage peasants who were completely disoriented in a city of over 200,000, failed to quell the uprising of the recently reinforced Poles and were forced to abandon Lviv. In January, Stanyslaviv became the new seat of government. It was here that the first systematic efforts were made to establish a functioning government and an effective army.

For most of its eight-month existence, the ZUNR governed a population of about 4 million of whom close to 3 million were Ukrainians. It quickly replaced the temporary authorities with a full-fledged governmental apparatus. On 22–26 November, elections were held in the Ukrainian-controlled lands for a 150-member Ukrainian National Council that was to function as a representative and legislative body. In terms of social composition, the delegates were mostly middle peasants with a large minority of clergy and intelligentsia; ideologically, the vast majority, even the socialists, adopted a liberal-national stance. The ethnic makeup of the council was almost completely Ukrainian, as the Poles boycotted the elections and the Jews and Germans preferred not to participate lest they become embroiled in the Ukrainian/Polish conflict. The chairman of the council, Evhen Petrushevych (a lawyer and former parliamentarian in Vienna), automatically became the president of the republic.

Unlike the East Ukrainian governments, the ZUNR soon had a local administration in place. It was based on old Austrian models – the Galicians did not engage in the radical experiments common in the east – and was staffed by Ukrainians and, quite often, by Polish professionals. Although engaged in a bitter war, the West Ukrainian state succeeded in maintaining stability and order on its territories. Indeed, this remarkably rapid and effective establishment of an administrative apparatus was a feat that few of the new East European states, not to speak of the East Ukrainian governments, could duplicate. To a large extent it was the result of the Galicians' penchant for social organization, honed to a high degree in the decades before the war.

Among the important legislative acts of the National Council were the guarantee of full voting rights to all citizens of the state and broad guarantees of minority rights, including 30% of the seats in a future parliament. These measures were well received by the Jewish populace: having experienced a three-day pogrom that the Poles had staged in Lviv when they retook the city, the Jews tended to side with the Ukrainians. In fact, an all-Jewish unit of about 1000 men was formed in the West Ukrainian army. The all-important land question was treated in straightforward fashion: all large private land-holdings, which were mostly held by Poles, were to be expropriated and the land distributed to peasants with little or no land. From the outset, it was understood that the ZUNR would unite with the East Ukrainian state. On 22 January 1919, the act of unification, which guaranteed the ZUNR complete autonomy, was proclaimed in Kiev.

Probably the most impressive organizational achievement of the West Ukrainian government was the Ukrainian Galician Army. In yet another contrast to the East Ukrainians, the Galicians quickly agreed on the need for a strong, effective regular army. Most Ukrainians in the Austrian army were on the Italian front and had not yet returned home, so there was a lack of trained soldiers. Nonetheless, a general mobilization yielded optimum results and by spring the army had over 100,000 men, of whom 40,000 were battle ready. There were, however, major problems with officers and military materials. Because of their socioeconomic underdevelopment, there were disproportionately few Ukrainian officers in the Austrian army. Thus, only 2 out of 1000 officers were Ukrainians. By comparison, Poles accounted for 27 per 1000. Moreover, the Ukrainian officers were almost all of junior rank. Therefore, the ZUNR turned to East Ukrainians such as General Mykhailo Omelianovych-Pavlenko and several other high officers of the former Russian army to take on the posts of commander and general staff. Many Austrian and German officers, now unemployed, were also used to fill staff positions. But most of the officers were Galicians, and it is noteworthy that, in a time of chaos and social tension, unusually close relations existed between them and their men, probably because both were either peasants or recently emerged from that class. Military equipment was largely acquired from Austrian depots or by disarming the hundreds of thousands of German and Austrian troops from the former occupation army in Ukraine that streamed through Galicia on their way home.

The Polish-Ukrainian War   The conflict can be divided into three stages. During the initial period which ended by February 1919, it was basically a battle between the Ukrainian majority and Polish minority in Eastern Galicia. Because of rapid and effective mobilization, the Ukrainians enjoyed a great numerical advantage and forced the Poles onto the defensive. However, thanks to skillful leadership, effective tactics, and spirited fighting, the Poles held off the slow, unimaginative attacks prepared by the Ukrainian command. In its second stage, during March, April, and May, the war expanded into a conflict between the Galician Ukrainians and the forces of Poland proper. As reinforcements from central Poland moved into Eastern Galicia, the Poles gained a decided numerical advantage. The crucial development at this juncture was the deployment of General Jozef Haller's army against the Ukrainians. Formed in France from Polish prisoners of war, this 60,000-man force was superbly equipped and largely led by French officers. Although the Entente dispatched it to Poland to fight against the Bolsheviks, the Poles redirected the army against the Ukrainians, arguing that all Ukrainians were Bolsheviks or something close to it. In April and May, the Poles broke the Ukrainian encirclement of Lviv and pushed back the demoralized Galician army to the Zbruch River.

A surprising Ukrainian counteroffensive, launched on 8 June by the new commander, General Oleksander Grekov, initiated the final stage of the war. Near the town of Chortkiv, the Galicians summoned up the last of their physical, material, and spiritual resources and hurled themselves against the confident and larger Polish forces. The Ukrainian attack almost reached Lviv. But it was not so much the reinforced Poles as the lack of ammunition that halted the Ukrainian offensive. With five to ten bullets per man and no country willing to supply more ammunition, Grekov's forces were forced to retreat again, thereby ending the Galician army's finest hour. By mid July the Poles had reoccupied almost all of Eastern Galicia and the West Ukrainian army was once more pinned against the Zbruch River.

In this catastrophic situation, the civilian leadership – on 9 June President Petrushevych was appointed dictator by general consent in order to make the government more efficient – argued for accepting internment in Romania. However, the army insisted on continuing the struggle for Ukrainian statehood by crossing over into Eastern Ukraine and joining Petliura in the battle against the Bolsheviks. On 16 July 1919, with Polish artillery hammering at their backs, the Galician army and thousands of West Ukrainian civilians crossed the Zbruch into Eastern Ukraine. The military struggle for Eastern Galicia, which cost the Ukrainians about 15,000 and the Poles over 10,000 lives, was over.

The diplomatic activity of the ZUNR   During the course of the military conflict and even after it was over, the West Ukrainian government placed great hopes on international recognition of its cause. Its optimism rested on the acceptance by the victorious Entente of President Wilson's famous Fourteen Points, one of which guaranteed the right of self-determination to all nations. However, if the Entente's political principles favored the Ukrainian position, the political interests of its leading member, France, favored the Poles. Obsessed with preventing the reemergence of a powerful Germany, the French sought to prevent this possibility by creating a powerful Polish state on Germany's eastern border. And if a powerful Poland demanded the absorption of Eastern Galicia, then so be it.

Although the East and West Ukrainians sent a combined delegation to the Paris Peace Conference – which met in January 1919 to redraw the political map of Europe – in practice the West Ukrainians acted separately in the pursuit of their goals. The West Ukrainians sought the recognition of their statehood and the Entente's help in negotiating a settlement with the Poles. However, both Ukrainian delegations found little sympathy at the Paris conference. Only England, which was not enthusiastic about France's Polish plans and which interested in Galician oil, briefly supported the Ukrainians – but when the government of Lloyd George was defeated in elections, this help evaporated. Meanwhile, the Poles, who developed excellent contacts with the Western powers through the efforts of their fiercely nationalistic (and anti-Ukrainian) leader Roman Dmowski, did their best to discredit the West Ukrainians.

The Poles argued that the Ukrainians were too backward to govern themselves, that their nationality was a German "invention," and that they had Bolshevik tendencies. Because Europeans knew next to nothing about Ukraine and Ukrainians, this Polish propaganda proved to be effective. It was, therefore, not unexpected that on 25 June 1919 the Entente's Council of Ambassadors acknowledged Poland's right to occupy all of Eastern Galicia "in order to protect the civilian population from the dangerous threat of Bolshevik bands."[7] However, the council did not, as yet, agree to Poland's incorporation of Eastern Galicia. It allowed the Poles to govern the land temporarily on the proviso that they respect the rights of the inhabitants and grant them a measure of autonomy. The ultimate fate of Eastern Galicia was to be decided at some point in the future.

Viewed from the historical perspective, the failure of the West Ukrainians to achieve their goals was not surprising. In Eastern Galicia, where the Ukrainians were best organized and most nationally conscious, the problems were basically of a quantitative nature: 3.5 million Galician Ukrainians simply could not stand up to the Poles, who were six times as numerous and far more advanced politically and socioeconomically. When the Galicians began their struggle they counted on aid from two sources: Eastern Ukraine was to provide the military and material aid that would balance the Polish advantage, and the Entente, which loudly proclaimed its commitment to the principle of self-determination, was expected, at least, to recognize Ukrainian aspirations.

As it happened, the West preferred Poland to principles and the East Ukrainians could not maintain their own state, let alone aid the Galicians. Therefore, the Galician Ukrainians, who had clearly demonstrated their ability to govern themselves, failed to achieve statehood for reasons beyond their control. This is not to say that they were without failings: uninspiring leadership, poor strategic planning, and belated contacts with the West certainly undermined their efforts. Nonetheless, were it not for the overwhelming predominance of the Poles, there is little doubt that the West Ukrainian National Republic would have taken its place among the other new nation-states of Eastern Europe.

The Denouement

The retreat of the Galicians into Eastern Ukraine and their link with the forces of the Directory was a momentous occasion in the history of the Ukrainian national movement. For the first time the West and East Ukrainian nationalists, who had for generations emphasized their fraternal bonds, came into contact with each other on a mass scale. Now, as the Ukrainian Revolution entered its final phase, they would have an opportunity to see how well they could cooperate.

Despite their precarious position in the small stretch of Podilian territory that they controlled, there was hope that these two sorely pressed governments and armies would coalesce into a single and effective force. Militarily, the Ukrainians had never been stronger. The Galician army numbered about 50,000 men. Of all the Ukrainian, Bolshevik, and White Russian armies that fought in Ukraine, it was probably the most disciplined and efficient. As a result of its recent reorganization and the addition of several highly talented commanders, the 35,000-man army of the Directory had improved greatly. In addition, about 15,000 partisans, led by *otamany* such as Zeleny and Anhel, coordinated their activities with those of the Directory's forces. Thus, the Ukrainians had a force of about 100,000 battle-tested troops that made them a contender to be reckoned with.

The influx of conscientious Galician officials also had a positive impact on the Directory's administrative apparatus. For the first time, a semblance of law, order, and stability appeared on the Directory's territory. This rise in administrative effectiveness, as well as the peasants' growing disenchantment with the Bolsheviks, led to an increasingly favorable response to the Directory's mobilization efforts on the Right Bank. However, the lack of arms and provisions forced Petliura to send many of the new recruits back to their homes. At this promising juncture in their struggle, two conditions had to be met in order that the Ukrainians could take advantage of the opportunities that glimmered before them. They had to establish a smoothly functioning relationship between the two governments and they needed to convince the Entente to supply them with military supplies.

It quickly became apparent, however, that the differences between the two Ukrainian governments went deeper than their ability to resolve them. First, a highly ambiguous relationship existed between Petliura's Directory and Petrushevych's dictatorship. In theory, the Directory was the all-Ukrainian government and therefore it claimed highest authority; in practice, however, it was the West Ukrainian government that had the stronger army and more efficient administration and so was not predisposed to accept policies with which it disagreed. Second, the two governments were at odds ideologically. The Directory consisted almost exclusively of leftist parties, while the West Ukrainian government had the backing of liberal parties with clearly conservative leanings. As a result, the easterners accused the Galicians of being "reactionaries," and the latter returned the compliment by calling the former "near-Bolsheviks." Highly organized and very nationally conscious, the Galicians reacted to the East Ukrainians' organizational looseness, reliance on improvisation, and social radicalism with scorn. For their part, the East Ukrainians considered the Galicians to be provincial, bureaucratic, and incapable of grasping the broader context of the conflict in Ukraine. In the final analysis, it was clear that the vast cultural, psychological, and political differences that accumulated between East and West Ukrainians during the centuries of living in very dissimilar environments were now coming to the fore.

The impact of these differences became apparent during the combined Ukrainian offensive against the Bolsheviks that was launched in early August 1919. It began successfully and, despite stiff resistance, the Ukrainians captured much of the Right Bank by the end of the month. However, the primary reason for the Bolsheviks' retreat was not the Ukrainian attack but the offensive of the Whites. From Siberia, the forces of Admiral Aleksander Kolchak threatened Moscow; in the Baltic area, General Nikolai Iudenich was preparing to attack Petrograd; and most threatening of all was the onslaught of General Denikin's armies from the Don. In the late summer of 1919, it seemed that the collapse of the Bolshevik regime was imminent.

On 30 August, Galician units marched into Kiev, recently evacuated by the Bolsheviks, and the Directory prepared for a triumphal entry the next day. However, later that day advance units of Denikin's army also moved into the city and confronted the Galicians. Confused about how to react to the Whites – the West Ukrainian government often declared that it had no quarrel with Denikin – the Galicians pulled back, to the great dismay of Petliura and the East Ukrainians, who desperately desired the capture of Kiev for symbolic and political reasons. Days later, when Petliura finally convinced the Galicians to engage the Whites, it was too late to retake the city and the Ukrainian armies retreated westward, embittered with each other and involved in an unwanted conflict with the Whites. In effect, the struggle for Ukrainian statehood ended here. What followed was an extremely confusing and tragic epilogue.

The Whites   Led by reactionary generals who were bent on restoring the old social order and "one, indivisible Russia," the Whites despised the "socialistic adventurer" Petliura and the East Ukrainian "separatist traitors" almost as much as the Bolsheviks. (They had nothing against the Galicians, however, for they considered them to be foreigners.) The Whites' stand on the Ukrainian issue was bluntly stated by Vasilii Shulgin, their leading propagandist, when Denikin's forces captured Kiev: "The Southwest district [Shulgin refused to use the term "Ukraine"] is Russian, Russian, Russian ... we will give it neither to the Ukrainian traitors nor to the Jewish executioners" (a reference to the numerous Jews in the Bolshevik Cheka or political police).[8]

With attitudes like this predominating among the Whites, it is not suprising that the overconfident Denikin refused even to consider several offers by Petliura to cooperate against the Bolsheviks. This response was one of his greatest blunders, for not only did Denikin lose the support of a large Ukrainian army, but by ordering his troops to attack the Ukrainians he created a situation that worked only to the advantage of the Bolsheviks. Such suicidal inflexibility, which was even more evident in the Whites' reactionary social policies, contributed greatly to Denikin's defeat in the fall of 1919. Another way in which the Whites undermined the Directory's efforts was to convince their patrons, the Entente, to reject Ukrainian appeals for recognition at the Paris Peace Conference and, more important, to deny them any material aid.

By fall 1919, the situation of the Ukrainians was truly tragic. The Whites were attacking them from one side, the Bolsheviks were about to strike from another, and in their rear were the aggressive Poles and the hostile Romanians. This constantly shrinking "perimeter of death" became unbearable when, in October, the exhausted, undernourished Ukrainian armies, bereft of supplies and shelter, were struck by a typhoid epidemic. Within a few weeks the vast majority of these troops were dead, dying, or incapacitated by the disease. It was at this point that the once-proud Galician army disintegrated. By the end of October, it reported that it had only 4000 combat-ready men left. Petliura's soldiers numbered only 2000. Those who remained tried to save themselves as best they could.

On 6 November 1919, the Galician commander, General Myron Tarnavsky, placed his men under the command of the Whites on the condition that they would not have to fight against other Ukrainians and that they be given a chance to recuperate. Meanwhile, Petrushevych and his associates made their way to Vienna, where they established a government-in-exile. Petliura and the Directory, for their part, sought refuge in Poland while their troops transformed themselves into partisan units that operated behind Bolshevik lines. Thus, in a depressing finale, remnants of the two Ukrainian governments and armies found themselves in the camps of each other's enemies.

Petliura's alliance with Poland There was, however, a sequel to the protracted defeat of the Ukrainian struggle for independence. On 21 April 1920, Petliura, after renouncing all claims to Eastern Galicia (a move which enraged the Galician Ukrainians), concluded a pact with the Poles for a combined attack against the Bolsheviks in Ukraine. The Polish motive for entering into this unexpected agreement was their desire to create an East Ukrainian buffer state between themselves and Russia. They hoped that once Petliura's reconstituted army appeared in Ukraine, their offensive would gain the support of the land's anti-Bolshevik peasantry. As usual, matters went well at the outset and by 6 May the allied forces, numbering about 65,000 Poles and 15,000 Ukrainians, took Kiev.

The expected ground swell of peasant support did not materialize, however. Apparently Petliura's personal popularity with many peasants was not great enough to overcome their traditional dislike of his Polish "landlord" allies. By June the Bolsheviks launched a counterattack, which eventually led to Polish/Soviet peace talks and the Poles' abandonment of Petliura. The East Ukrainian army, which had grown to about 35,000 men, fought on alone against the Bolsheviks until 10 November 1920, when it was forced to abandon its small stretch of Volhynia and accept internment in Polish-held territory. Except for several unsuccessful partisan operations that were launched into Soviet Ukraine a year later, the war for Ukrainian independence was finally over.

Bolshevik Victory

After their second defeat in Ukraine in the late summer of 1919, the Bolsheviks reevaluated their policies. The Ukrainians in the party, led by Iurii Lapchynsky, were sharply critical of their colleagues' tendency to ignore Ukrainian particularities. They argued that "Ukraine cannot accept as ready-made the forms of life which have been developed in Russia during one and a half years of Soviet construction."[9] The party leadership, if not the rank and file, reluctantly agreed that the Bolsheviks had greatly antagonized the peasants with their grain requisitions and had badly underestimated the strength of nationalism in their previous expeditions into Ukraine. Lenin also played a prominent role in this self-criticism, stating that "to ignore the importance of the national question in Ukraine, of which the Great Russians are very frequently guilty (and probably the Jews are guilty of it only a little less frequently than the Great Russians) means committing a profound and dangerous error ... we must struggle especially energetically against remnants (sometimes subconscious ones) of Great Russian imperialism and chauvinism among the Russian Communists."[10]

Lenin's advice, however, was not to give in to Ukrainian demands for independence – neither the independent statehood that the nationalists wanted nor the organizational independence that many Ukrainian Bolsheviks desired – but to add more Ukrainian "color" to Soviet rule in that country. Therefore, the formation, on 21 December 1919, of the third Ukrainian Soviet government was accompanied with patriotic rhetoric such as "the free and independent Ukrainian Socialist Soviet Republic again arises from the dead."[11] Another manifesto announced that one of the main goals of the Communist Party of Ukraine was to "defend the independence and integrity of the Socialist Soviet Republic of Ukraine."[12] The party's few Ukrainians were given prominent (but not key) positions in the government and instructions went out to party functionaries to use the Ukrainian language whenever possible and to show respect for Ukrainian culture.

To placate the Ukrainian peasantry, the Bolsheviks ceased the collectivization of landholdings, a policy that had met much greater resistance in Ukraine than in Russia. Although they continued to expropriate grain, the Bolsheviks now argued that it was destined for the Ukrainian Soviet army, not for Russia. And greater emphasis than before was placed on tactics that raised tensions among the rich, middle, and poor peasants. Realizing that all attempts to win over the approximately 500,000 kulaks were hopeless, the Bolsheviks concentrated on attracting the middle peasants by assuring them that they could retain their land. The party also expanded its old policy of forming Committees of Poor Peasants (*komnezamy*) in order to neutralize the influence of the kulaks in the village.

Despite these adjustments, it was still the military power of Soviet Russia that assured the ultimate triumph of Bolshevik rule in Ukraine. By fall 1919, the Red Army had 1.5 million men; in spring 1920 it numbered close to 3.5 million, led by about 50,000 former tsarist officers that the Bolsheviks pressed into service. Thus, when the Bolsheviks returned to Ukraine in full force in early December 1919, their victory over their enemies was practically assured. Nonetheless, even when the last of the Ukrainian and White armies were pushed out in November 1920, Bolshevik control of the Ukrainian countryside was far from secure. Large numbers of peasants, especially the kulaks, remained vehemently opposed to communism and they continued a stubborn but uncoordinated guerrilla war against the Bolsheviks.

The anti-Bolshevik partisans, who formed more than 100 major units, numbered over 40,000. In the south, the famous Makhno, benefiting from widespread support, held out until August 1921. In the Kiev region, some of Petliura's *otamany*, such as Iurii Tiutiunnyk, led large, well-armed units of 1000–2000 men and maintained steady contact with the exiled Ukrainian government in Poland. Only after the Bolsheviks committed over 50,000 men, most of whom were members of Cheka, did they manage to break the back of the partisan movement in late 1921. And only then could the Bolsheviks claim not only that they had conquered Ukraine, but that they actually controlled it.

ə•

At a time when empires collapsed and almost all the peoples of Eastern Europe, including such small subject nations of the tsars as the Finns, Estonians, Latvians, and Lithuanians, gained their independence, why was it that the 30 million Ukrainians did not? The question is all the more pertinent because the Ukrainians probably fought longer for independence and paid a higher price in lives than any other East European nation.

In considering the general reasons for the Ukrainian defeat, it is necessary to distinguish between internal and external factors and the East and West Ukrainians' situations. In terms of internal factors, the basic dilemma of the Ukrainians - and this applies mainly to the East Ukrainians - was, to repeat a crucial point, that they were forced to begin the state-building process before they had completed nation-building. The delay and underdevelopment of nation-building was a result of tsarist suppression and of nation-buliding's weak social base. Of all the social groups and classes in Ukraine, the intelligentsia was most prominent in the national movement and the state-building effort. However, the intelligentsia made up only 2–3% of the general population and only a small part of it was involved in the Ukrainian cause. Many of these intellectuals were as deeply steeped in Russian as in Ukrainian culture and it was psychologically difficult suddenly to sever their bonds with Russia. Hence their wavering on independence and their attraction to autonomy and federalism. Finally, even in the course of the revolution and the Civil War, many Ukrainian intelligentsia were still unsure as to which goal was more important: social transformation or national liberation. Therefore, in Eastern Ukraine, the revolution placed idealistic, patriotic but inexperienced intellectuals into positions of leadership and forced them to act before they were sure of what they wanted or how to get it.

In assuming the leadership in the struggle for independence, the Ukrainian intelligentsia counted on peasant support. However, this huge reservoir of potential backers did not live up to its expectations. Uneducated, parochial, and politically immature, the peasant knew what he was against but was not sure of what he stood for. He could understand that he was an exploited toiler. Hence the early success of Bolshevik propaganda. Yet the more complex idea of nationhood was difficult for him to grasp and it was only late in the Civil

War that many of the better-educated peasants definitively began to favor national self-government. But by that time the best opportunities for independence had already passed.

Even when the peasant was willing to support the cause of independence, organizing this support was exceedingly difficult. Unlike the small but compact groups of workers who were concentrated in a few of the largest cities and thus easily accessible to the Bolsheviks, the peasants were scattered in thousands of villages. Convincing them to cooperate was a logistical problem with which the inexperienced intelligentsia found it difficult to deal. If the support that the Ukrainian nationalists had among the intelligentsia and peasants was problematic, the support they lacked in the cities – this applies to Galicia as well – was decisive. Unable to count on the workers, the urban bourgeoisie, and the administrators, officers, and technicians, the Ukrainian armies had great difficulties holding on to cities, which were the centers of communication, transportation, and administration. Thus, the sociological weaknesses of the Ukrainian movement in 1917–20 became strategic disadvantages that had a major impact on the outcome of the struggle.

Although the internal weaknesses of Ukrainian nationalism were considerable, external factors were decisive in its defeat. In the case of the Galician Ukrainians, whose national movement was as strong as those of other East European countries that attained independence, it was clearly not internal weakness but the overwhelming strength of the Poles that was primarily responsible for its failure. In Eastern Ukraine, it was Bolshevik Russia – not the weak Bolsheviks of Ukraine – that blocked the attainment of independence. Late in 1920, Leon Trotsky, the commander of the Red Army, freely admitted that "Soviet power in Ukraine has held its ground up to now (and it has not held it well) chiefly by the authority of Moscow, the Great Russian Communists and the Russian Red Army."[13]

The success of Lenin's party was due not only to its excellent leadership and formidable organization, but also to the fact that it had the vast financial, administrative, industrial, and human resources of Russia at its disposal. The Bolsheviks could count on the support of the Russian and Russified workers in the cities of Ukraine, which allowed them to mobilize adherents when and where it counted most. And the East Ukrainians had another implacable enemy: the Whites. To defeat such enemies would have required greater strength than most emergent national movements could muster.

Confronted with overwhelmingly powerful enemies, both the East and West Ukrainians were unable to gain the recognition and aid of the victorious Entente powers. Among the reasons why the Entente – which was quite forthcoming with military and diplomatic support for the anti-Bolshevik Whites and numerous new East European nation-states – turned its back on the Ukrainians were the following: ignorance of actual conditions in Ukraine, the energetic and effective anti-Ukrainian propaganda of the Poles and Whites, the association of the Central Rada and Hetmanate with the Germans, and the leftist ("Bolshevik") tendencies of the Directory. Finally, the extremely chaotic conditions that existed in Ukraine in 1917–21 greatly impeded the establishment of national self-government.

Yet the Ukrainians emerged from the revolution and Civil War with gains as well as losses. National consciousness, which had been limited to a part of the intelligentsia, spread to all segments of Ukrainian society. On the one hand, the peasant, who had demonstrated his ability to bring down governments and fight for his interests, gained confidence and a sense of self-worth. With this came his desire for greater respect and consideration for his language and culture. On the other hand, the rise of Ukrainian governments taught peasants to identify themselves as "Ukrainians." Therefore, in a mere four years, the nation-building process moved forward tremendously. In this sense, the upheaval of 1917–21 was not only a socioeconomic but also a national revolution.

While the struggle for national self-determination accounted for the distinctive features of the Ukrainian Revolution, the socioeconomic transformation of the land linked it with the all-Russian Revolution. In Ukraine, as elsewhere in the former tsarist empire, the old order disapppeared and the peasants distributed much of the confiscated lands among themselves. Thus, while the dreams of independence were unfulfilled, many Ukrainians had reason to believe that they did not emerge from the upheaval empty-handed. All depended on whether the Soviet government would allow Ukrainians to consolidate and expand on the gains of the revolution.

Soviet Ukraine:
The Innovative Twenties

Almost seven years of war and civil strife had left the Bolshevik-controlled parts of the former Russian Empire in shambles. In Ukraine alone the fighting, executions, and epidemics associated with the upheaval, especially the Civil War, took about 1.5 million lives. Lack of food, heating materials, and employment forced hundreds of thousands to abandon the cities for the villages. The production of goods practically ceased. Completely exhausted, the society was clearly not ready for the radical social transformations that the Bolsheviks envisaged.

Despite their victory, the Bolsheviks – a tiny minority in the midst of a huge and largely antagonistic populace – were in no position to proceed as they wished. Lenin's death in 1924 precipitated a leadership crisis that was exacerbated by a fierce debate in the Communist party about which direction it should take in attempting to create a communist society. Under the circumstances, the party was cautious and pliant in pursuing its goals throughout the 1920s. As long as individuals and groups did not openly challenge the Soviet political system, government interference in their affairs was limited.

Ukrainians profited from Soviet flexibility during this period in two ways: from concessions the government made to the peasantry in general and from Soviet attempts to gain broader support among non-Russians. As a result, during the 1920s, Ukrainian self-confidence and aspirations experienced a surprising resurgence and this period has come to be viewed by many as the golden age for Ukrainians under Soviet rule.

ﾞﾑ

War Communism and NEP

Bolshevik policies during the Civil War had contributed greatly to the economic collapse. Intent on immediately establishing a socialist economic order and at the same time providing food for the Red Army and the starving Russian cities, the Bolsheviks introduced harsh economic policies that went under the name of War Communism. These included the nationalization of large estates and industry, the forced mobilization of labor, the rationing by the government of food and goods, and the most hated measure of all, the expropriation of grain from the peasants.

Backed by armed units, Bolshevik officials descended on villages like locusts and confiscated grain from the peasants for government use. Individual peasants were allowed to keep only about thirty pounds of grain a month for themselves. To aid in these confiscations, the party organized Committees of Poor Peasants (*komnezamy*) whose members received priority in the distribution of land, exemption from taxes, and 10–25% of the "take." Most peasants and workers responded by stopping all production. As the shortfalls in foodstuffs increased, drought hit large parts of southern Russia and Ukraine. The result was the famine of 1921–22 that took hundreds of thousands of lives in Ukraine and even more in the Volga region of Russia.[1] But unlike its behavior a decade later, the Soviet government acknowledged the famine of 1921–22 and organized a massive domestic and international relief effort to aid the hungry.

The catastrophic economic conditions gave rise to a ground swell of dissatisfaction with the Bolsheviks, manifesting itself in military mutinies, violent workers' strikes, and huge peasant uprisings that engulfed Russia and Ukraine in 1921. Although the Red Army and the Cheka ruthlessly suppressed these rebellions, Lenin was forced to admit that War Communism was a failure and that concessions would have to be made, especially to the peasantry.

Once more Lenin's vaunted tactical skill, his willingness to take one step back in order to move socialism forward two steps later – the famous Lenin tango – came into play. On 21 March 1921, at the Tenth Party Congress, he persuaded his reluctant associates to accept the New Economic Policy (NEP) – but only after the dangerous Kronstadt revolt (which occurred at the time of the congress) vividly demonstrated how unpopular current Soviet policies were. This policy was a compromise, a temporary retreat from socialism, a chance for the country to recuperate from the Civil War. The main feature of NEP was the attempt to appease the peasantry and to provide it with incentives for raising food production. Instead of requisitioning grain, the government imposed a moderate tax on the peasantry. After paying the tax, the peasant could sell his surplus grain at whatever price the market would bear. Poor peasants did not have to pay a tax at all. The policy of creating collective farms was also abandoned. In Ukraine most of the lands the Central Rada had nationalized back in 1918 were now redistributed to the poorer peasants.

To invigorate other segments of the economy, NEP removed government controls over internal trade, leased small factories back to their former own-

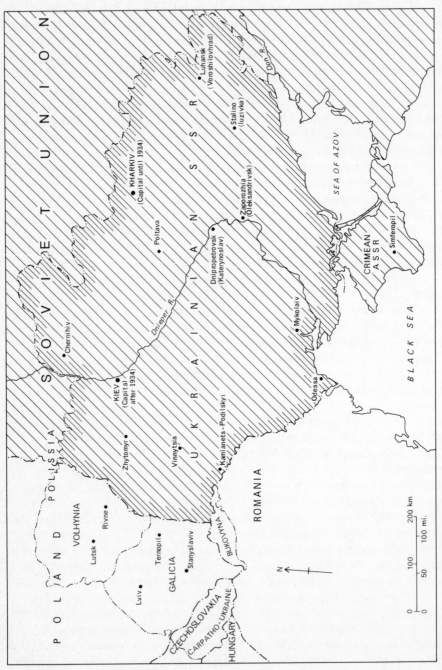

Map 22 Soviet Ukraine during the interwar period

ers, and even encouraged foreign investment. However, although Lenin was willing to compromise with capitalism temporarily, he had no intention of abandoning his dream of creating a socialist economy. Therefore, the government retained control of the "commanding heights" of the economy, such as heavy industry, banking, transportation, and foreign trade.

NEP proved to be a great success. Assured that they could sell their produce to hungry urban dwellers at good prices, Ukraine's 5 million peasant farms quickly raised their productivity. By 1927, there was already 10% more land under cultivation than in 1913. Meanwhile, the consumer-oriented industry, invigorated by the so-called NEP-men or small entrepreneurs who operated with government permission, also reached prewar levels. Only the government-controlled heavy industry lagged behind. As prosperity returned and memories of the nightmarish Civil War years faded, the Ukrainian peasant began to make his peace with the Bolshevik regime that he had previously viewed with such great mistrust.

The Creation of the Soviet Union

Although Lenin and the Bolsheviks had been slow to recognize the importance of nationalism, they treated it with circumspection once they gained power. On the one hand, they came out in favor of national self-determination during the Civil War, "even to the point of separation and formation of independent states." On the other hand, they attempted to crush national movements, arguing that they were led by "bourgeois elements" that would not and could not act in the interests of the working class. But with the defeat of the "bourgeois nationalists," the Bolsheviks (whose hold on the populace was still quite insecure) had to come to terms with the Soviet-led governments of the non-Russian nationalities they had established.

Although the Moscow-based Communist party completely controlled the Ukrainian Soviet government, it was not in a position to dismantle or absorb it. The precedents militating against this move were too great. At Brest-Litovsk, Bolshevik Russia had recognized the Central Rada and its General Secretariat as the sovereign government of an independent state. If they had gone so far as to recognize the sovereignty of a Ukrainian "bourgeois" government, the Bolsheviks could hardly do less for a Ukrainian Soviet government. Therefore, the Ukrainian Soviet government had to be treated, at least in theory, as if it were a sovereign power. Consequently, up to 1923, the Soviet government of Ukraine conducted foreign relations separately from Soviet Russia (concluding forty-eight treaties on its own), carried on foreign trade, and even began to lay the foundations for a separate Ukrainian Soviet army.

Precedents notwithstanding, there were also important groups among the Bolsheviks in Ukraine that agitated for Ukrainian Soviet statehood. They consisted mostly of the Borotbisty and Ukapisty, who had broken away in 1919 from the Ukrainian Socialist Revolutionary and Ukrainian Social Democratic parties, respectively, and had gone over to the Bolsheviks. Of the two, the Borotbisty, led by Oleksander Shumsky, Vasyl Blakytny, and Mykola Shynkar, were by far the more numerous and influential. Because they were an essentially populist party, they had much better ties with the Ukrainian peasantry than did the Bolsheviks. In fact, after the defeat of the second Soviet government in Ukraine in late summer 1919, the Borotbisty even attempted to replace the Bolsheviks as the leaders of the communist revolution in Ukraine. To this end they renamed themselves the Communist Party of Ukraine (Borotbisty) and in early 1920 applied for admission to the Communist International as a separate party. But when the Moscow-controlled Communist International refused their request, the Borotbisty were forced to disband. Because the Bolsheviks sorely needed Ukrainian-speaking members, about 4000 Borotbisty were subsequently accepted into the party and given high posts in the Soviet Ukrainian government. This action allowed many of these nationally conscious leftists to continue the struggle for Ukrainian statehood from within the Soviet regime.

The several hundred Ukapisty underwent a similar experience. They, too, tried to steal the Bolsheviks' thunder by copying them. Calling themselves the Ukrainian Communist party, they attempted, also without success, to gain admittance into the Communist International. In 1925 they were forced to disband and a number of them, including their leaders Mykhailo Tkachenko and Iurii Mazurenko, joined the Bolshevik party for the same reasons as did the Borotbisty: to influence the Ukrainian policies of the party from within.

Unlike these latecomers to the Bolshevik ranks with their divided loyalties, there were a few longtime Ukrainian members of the party who sincerely wanted communism to succeed in Ukraine. They believed that the best way to achieve this goal was to "Ukrainianize" bolshevism in order to make it more appealing to Ukrainians. This meant, first and foremost, that the Soviet government would also have to be a Ukrainian government. Mykola Skrypnyk, a close associate of Lenin and a leading figure in all three Soviet Ukrainian governments, was the most outstanding representative of this group. Finally, there were a number of non-Ukrainian Bolsheviks who had a vested interest in preserving Ukrainian self-government. An example was Khristian Rakovsky, the Russified Romanian-Bulgarian head of the Ukrainian Soviet government, who in 1919 had treated Ukrainian national aspirations with scorn but in 1922 concluded that the more authority a Ukrainian Soviet government had, the more power he personally would wield. Therefore, he, too, became an avowed anticentralist and defender of Ukrainian autonomy.

The above-mentioned views and attitudes were not only widespread among pro-Soviet Ukrainians; they also flourished among the members of the newly formed Soviet governments in the Caucasus and Central Asia. Even Moscow agreed that the ad hoc military alliances and mutual-aid pacts that had formally linked the Soviet republics (the Red Army and the party were the actual forces that held them together) during the Civil War were no longer adequate. Therefore, in the final months of 1922 the party began a major discussion in Moscow on what the permanent form and nature of the relationship between the Russian, Ukrainian, Belorussian, and Transcaucasian Soviet republics should be.

Because he was gravely ill, Lenin's participation in these important debates was limited. This circumstance allowed Josef Stalin, the increasingly powerful commissar for nationalities and general secretary of the party, to play a key role. Although a Georgian by birth, Stalin was an avowed centralist and antinationalist. With the backing of many Russian members of the party, he proposed that the non-Russian republics be absorbed into a single Russian Soviet socialist state. To appease the nationalities, he offered them cultural autonomy within the Russian republic. The proposal caused a furor among the non-Russian Bolsheviks. Skrypnyk and other Ukrainians denounced it as thinly disguised Russian chauvinism. The entire Central Committee of the Georgian Bolshevik party resigned in protest. Sultan Galiev, the spokesman of the Central Asian Bolsheviks, accused the party of sponsoring "Red imperialism."

At this point, Lenin stepped in. He realized that if a Russian Soviet state were to swallow up the other Soviet republics, it not only would erode the very weak support the Bolsheviks had in the non-Russian republics, but also would create a very poor impression of the Soviet system among the colonial peoples of the world. If Russian nationalism and centralism endangered the prospects for global revolution, Lenin declared himself ready "to challenge Great Russian chauvinism to mortal combat."[2] He proposed, therefore, that all the Soviet republics form a "union of equals."

To demonstrate that the union was voluntary, Lenin proposed that every republic have the *right* of secession from the union. And this point was enshrined in the Soviet constitution of 1924. Governmental prerogatives were so arranged that certain affairs remained the exclusive domain of a given republic; other jurisdictions were to be shared by both republican and all-union ministries; still others were to be handled by the all-union government alone. Thus, the Ukrainian Soviet government had, in theory, exclusive jurisdiction in its republic over agriculture, internal affairs, justice, education, health, and social welfare. It was to share authority with the all-union government over matters relating to food, labor, finance, inspections, and national economy. Foreign affairs, the army and navy, transport, foreign trade, and communications were to be the exclusive domain of the all-union government based in Moscow.

But, on Lenin's insistence, a crucial qualification was made to this plan. The all-important right to secede, that ultimate proof of a republic's sovereignty, could be exercised only if the Communist party agreed to it. Because the

Communist party remained a highly centralized and overwhelmingly Russian organization based in Moscow, it was extremely unlikely that any such agreement would be forthcoming. Thus, Lenin's plan allowed for the creation of a federalist structure (or facade, as some have called it) to assuage the non-Russians, while assuring that complete political control remained in the hands of the Moscow-based party.

Although the non-Russians, Ukrainians in particular, had serious reservations about them, Lenin's proposals were clearly preferable to those put forth by Stalin. Therefore, on 30 December 1922, they were endorsed by the representatives of the Russian, Belorussian, Transcaucasian, and Ukrainian Soviet republics and the Union of Soviet Socialist Republics (USSR) came into being.

Upon its entry into the Soviet Union, the Ukrainian republic constituted its second-largest component (the Russian republic being the largest by far). It encompassed a territory of 450,000 sq. km and a population of over 26 million. Kharkiv was selected as the capital of the republic because it was not as closely associated with former national governments as was Kiev. Originally, the republic was divided into 12 *gubernii*; in 1925 an administrative reorganization created 41 *okruhy*; and in 1939 it was reorganized again into 15 *oblasti*. Of the more than 5 million non-Ukrainians in the republic, many inhabited the 12 administrative regions set aside for them.

Various interpretations have been offered to explain why the USSR took on a pseudo-federal form. Some Western scholars argue that this was a clever camouflage for the Russian center's reassertion of control over the non-Russian periphery. Others believe that the federal structure was a concession that the victorious, yet weak, Soviet regime had to make to the nascent national consciousness of the non-Russian nationalities. Soviet authors view their federal system as a successful attempt to create a new and better structure within which various nationalities could coexist harmoniously and develop freely.

But the structure of the USSR did not allow the various nationalities to conduct their affairs as they desired. Ultimate decision-making regarding Ukraine still rested with Moscow, not Kharkiv. Nor had Ukrainians as a whole been consulted about the very formation of the union. Basically, the tiny and predominantly Russian party decided what the relationship between Ukraine and Russia would be.

It would be inaccurate to say, however, that the Ukrainians and other non-Russian nationalities emerged empty-handed from the Soviet federal arrangement. Under the tsars, Ukrainian language, culture, and national identity had been viciously suppressed. The very boundaries of Ukraine had been ill defined and it had been called by such vague terms as "the Southwest" or "Little Russia." Under the Soviets, in contrast, the Ukrainian Soviet Socialist Republic (URSR) became a well-defined national and territorial entity, possessing its own administrative center and apparatus. Thus, the Ukrainians finally obtained a territorial-administrative framework that reflected their national identity. It was something they had not had since the Cossack Hetmanate of the 18th century.

Ukrainization

Despite Bolshevik promises made during the Civil War to respect the principle of national self-determination, and despite the formation of nationally based Soviet republics and the ostensibly federal structure of the Soviet Union, the Communist party still lacked meaningful support among the non-Russians during the early years of its rule. It remained a tiny and overwhelmingly Russian, urban-based organization that perched precariously atop uncertain masses of peasants and non-Russians of dubious loyalty. Ukraine in particular, as Stalin himself openly acknowledged, was "a weak point of Soviet power." Therefore, after appeasing the peasants with NEP, the party initiated an attempt to win acceptance and to broaden its support among the non-Russians.

In 1923, at the Twelfth Party Congress, the party leadership embarked on a policy of indigenization or *korenizatsia* ("taking roots"). It called for a concerted effort to recruit non-Russians into the party and state apparatus, for Soviet officials to learn and use local languages, and for state support of cultural and social development among the nationalities. The Ukrainian version of this policy was called Ukrainization.

Before Ukrainization could be implemented, however, changes had to be made in the party leadership in Ukraine. As it stood, this leadership consisted mostly of Soviet officials sent in from Russia or local Jews. By and large, they showed little understanding for Ukrainization and even less inclination for putting it into effect. Indeed, many of them made a point of espousing Russian superiority over the "locals." For example, one of the highest officials of the Ukrainian party, Dmitrii Lebed, was a Russian who made no effort to conceal his hostility to the Ukrainian language, customs, and Ukrainization in general. He enunciated the "Theory of the Struggle of Two Cultures," which held that because Russian culture in Ukraine was associated with the progressive proletariat and the city – while Ukrainian culture was tied to the backward peasantry and the countryside – Russian culture would inevitably triumph, and it was the duty of Communists to support this "natural process."

Although Lebed's ideas were shared by many of his superiors in Moscow, they were considered untimely, and he and a number of other prominent non-Ukrainian party officials were recalled. Their posts were filled by such loyal and disciplined representatives of Moscow as Lazar Kaganovich, a Ukrainian Jew who took over leadership of the party apparatus in Ukraine and was ready to follow the party's line on Ukrainization, or else by Ukrainians who sincerely wanted Ukrainization to succeed. Among the latter were Vlas Chubar, who replaced Rakovsky as the head of the Ukrainian Soviet government; Oleksander Shumsky, a former Borotbist, who assumed responsibility for the department of agitation and propaganda; and the ubiquitous Old Bolshevik Mykola Skrypnyk, who became commissar of justice. Only after the hard-line "Russian bureaucrats and chauvinists," as Lenin called them, were removed from their posts was the Ukrainian Soviet government ready to implement the new policy.

The first measures introduced under the Ukrainization policy were aimed at expanding the use of Ukrainian, particularly in the party and government. The need for doing so was obvious: in 1922, for every one member of the Ukrainian party who regularly used Ukrainian, seven functioned only in Russian, and in the government the ratio was one to three. In order to deal with this imbalance, government and party officials were instructed in August 1923 to take specially organized Ukrainian-language courses. Those who failed to complete them successfully were threatened with dismissal. By 1925 bureaucrats received instructions to use Ukrainian in all government correspondence and publications. And in 1927 Kaganovich declared that "all party business will be conducted in Ukrainian."[3] Despite the notable lack of enthusiasm among the numerous non-Ukrainians in the government and party, the new policies produced impressive results. Whereas in 1922 only 20% of government business was conducted in Ukrainian, by 1927 the figure rose to 70%.

At the same time, the number of Ukrainians in the political establishment of the republic increased. In 1923 only 35% of government employees and 23% of party members were Ukrainian. By 1926–27 the respective percentages rose to 54% and 52%. Yet, although they had gained a majority in both organizations, as newcomers, Ukrainians were largely concentrated in the lower levels of government and the party. In the late 1920s, their representation in the party's Central Committee was not more than 25%.

The Ukrainization drive penetrated all aspects of life in Soviet Ukraine. Its greatest impact was on education. Unlike the tsarist regime, the Soviets placed a high priority on education, and their achievements in this area were truly impressive. Several factors help to explain the Soviet emphasis on education: from the ideological point of view, Soviet society had to be well educated if it was to serve as a model of the new order; furthermore, an educated populace greatly increased the productive capacity and power of the state; and finally, education provided excellent opportunites for indoctrinating the new generation with Soviet values. Most dramatic were Soviet strides in the elimination of illiteracy. At the time of the revolution, about 40% of the urban populace was literate; ten years later the figure rose to 70%. In the countryside, the literacy rate during this period rose from 15% to over 50%. Because this massive education drive was conducted in Ukrainian, the spread of education meant the spread of Ukrainization among the country's youth.

The driving force behind the Ukrainization of the school system was Skrypnyk, who headed the Commissariat of Education from 1927 to 1933. Working with almost obsessive zeal, he was able to announce in 1929, at the high point of Ukrainization, that over 80% of general-education schools, 55% of vocational schools, and 30% of university-level institutes offered instruction in Ukrainian only. Over 97% of Ukrainian children were taught in their native language. The Russian and Jewish minorities had the opportunity to study in Russian but were expected to take some courses in Ukrainian. Before the revolution, when Ukrainian schools were practically nonexistent, Ukrainophiles could only have dreamt of such conditions; a decade later, Skrypnyk made them a reality.

The success of these measures was all the more imposing in view of the attendant difficulties, particularly the lack of qualified teachers. The Ukrainization program called for 100,000 teachers but only 45,000 were available. In desperation, Skrypnyk attempted to import several thousand teachers from Galicia, but he failed to get Moscow's permission, perhaps because of Soviet fear of the Galicians' highly developed national consciousness. Also, many textbooks were still unavailable. Another problem, evident especially at the university level, was the refusal by many Russians (who constituted the majority of the faculties) to use the "peasant" language for purposes of higher education. Professor Tolstoi in Odessa expressed a typical attitude when he commented, "I consider ... all comrades who have switched to lecturing in the Ukrainian language as renegades."[4] Nevertheless, even in the universities, Ukrainian students soon became the majority. This rapid Ukrainization of the schools gave rise to a general mood of national optimism, which the writer Borys Antonenko-Davydovych captured in his comment: "In the march of millions on their way to the Ukrainian school" he could see "the fire of a great revival."[5]

This same sense of revival was evident in the Ukrainian-language media, which had been harshly repressed by the tsarist regime and treated poorly in the early years of Soviet rule. In 1922 only 27% of the books published in Ukraine appeared in Ukrainian and there were fewer than 10 newspapers and periodicals in that language. By 1927, well over 50% of new books appeared in Ukrainian; and by 1933, of the 426 newspapers in the republic, 373 were in the native language.

Largely as a result of Skrypnyk's complaints that the Red Army acted as an agent of Russification, Ukrainian was introduced into officer-training schools and large reserve units in Ukraine. There were even plans to reorganize the army on a territorial basis. Surprisingly, such well-known non-Ukrainian commanders of the Red Army troops in Ukraine as Mikhail Frunze and Iona Iakir supported these projects.

For Ukrainization to achieve long-lasting results, it had to break the Russian cultural monopoly in the cities. The socioeconomic changes that took place in the 1920s and 1930s encouraged Ukrainizers to believe that such a result was possible. The Soviets' vast industrialization drive, launched in 1928, created a great need for urban workers. Simultaneously, collectivization policies in the countryside forced many peasants from the land. Consequently, masses of Ukrainian peasants poured into the cities, greatly altering the ethnic composition of the proletariat and of the urban population as a whole. Thus, although in 1923 Ukrainians in such important industrial centers as Kharkiv, Luhansk, and Dniepropetrovsk had constituted 38%, 7%, and 16% of their populations, respectively, ten years later these percentages had increased to 50%, 31%, and 48%. By the mid 1930s, Ukrainians were the majority in most of the large cities. And they were encouraged by the Ukrainization programs to retain their native language rather than to adopt Russian, as had been done previously. It seemed, therefore, that in Ukraine, as elsewhere in Eastern Europe, the culture and language of the rural majority was going to overwhelm that of the urban minority.

The success of the policy of Ukrainization, which did not go as far as Skrypnyk and his associates would have wished, was a result, first and foremost, of the fact that it was linked to the general process of modernization. It was not primarily patriotism or traditionalism that caused Ukrainians to retain their native language; rather, it was because, better than any other language, Ukrainian allowed them to obtain an education, to obtain useful information from newspapers and books, to communicate with officials, and to perform their jobs. Because of the Ukrainization programs, Ukrainian language and culture ceased being a romantic, esoteric obsession of a tiny intelligentsia or the hallmark of a backward peasantry. Instead, Ukrainian was well on its way to becoming the primary means of communication and expression of a modernizing, industrializing society.

National Communism

As a result of the variants of communism that have evolved in such countries as China and Yugoslavia, the idea that a nation can pursue "its own road to communism" is well established today. As we have seen, it was the Ukrainian, as well as the Georgian and Turkic, Bolsheviks that had helped bring the Soviet regime to power in 1917–20 and first struck out in this direction, pioneering the phenomenon of national communism. Adherents of this trend were dedicated communists who sincerely believed that Marxism-Leninism was humanity's surest route to salvation. Yet, they also thought that for communism to achieve optimal results, it had to adapt to specific national conditions. This view implied that the Russian way was not the only way and that approaches to communism chosen by other nations were equally valid. In other words, an attempt should be made to harness the forces of nationalism for the building of socialism by providing communism with a "national face."

Given the close ties that the Ukrainian national movement in Eastern Ukraine had long had with socialism, national communist ideas came easily to many Ukrainians in the Bolshevik camp. As early as 1918, two Communists, Vasyl Shakhrai (the first Soviet Ukrainian commissar of foreign affairs) and his colleague Serhii Mazlakh (an Old Bolshevik of Jewish origin), bitterly attacked the party for its hypocritical attitude towards nationalism in general and Ukrainians in particular. With a clear reference to the Russian nationalism that permeated the Bolshevik party, they stressed in their pamphlets, "Revolution in Ukraine" and "On the Current Situation in Ukraine," that "so long as the nationality question is not resolved, so long as one nation rules and another is forced to be subordinate to it, what we have is not socialism."[6]

A year later, national communist views again surfaced in the CP(b)U in the so-called federalist opposition, led by Iurii Lapchynsky. This group called for "the total independence of the Soviet Ukrainian state, which must command its full measure of power, including regional military and economic authority as well as an independent party center in no way subordinate to the Russian Communist party."[7] When Moscow refused to consider these demands, Lapchynsky and his associates caused a furor by resigning from the party.

When the Ukrainization drive began to gain momentum, national communist tendencies in Ukraine, usually identified with the names of their main proponents, again came to the fore.

Khvylovyism   The most direct and emotional call for rejecting the "Russian road" was sounded by Mykola Khvylovy. This remarkable individual, whose real name was Fitilov, grew up in Eastern Ukraine as the son of a petty Russian nobleman. A committed internationalist, he joined the Bolsheviks during the Civil War in hopes of helping to create a truly universal and equitable communist society. After the Civil War, Khvylovy became one of the most popular Soviet Ukrainian writers, an organizer of the avant-garde literary organization Vaplite, and a frequent commentator on Ukrainian/Russian relations, particularly in the area of culture.

An idealistic communist, Khvylovy was bitterly disillusioned by the glaring discrepancies that existed between Bolshevik nationality theory and practice, and also by the Russian chauvinism of party bureaucrats, who, as he put it, masked their bias "behind Marx's beard." To save the revolution from the pernicious impact of Russian nationalism, Khvylovy resolved to expose it. Couching his message in literary terms, he claimed that "passive-pessimistic Russian literature had reached its limits and stopped at the crossroads" and he advised Ukrainians to distance themselves from it: "Insofar as our literature can at last follow its own path of development, the question before us is: toward which of the world's literatures must it chart its course? In no case toward the Russian. This is absolute and unconditional ... The essence of the matter is that Russian literature has weighed us down for centuries. Being the master of the situation, it accustomed our psyche to slavish imitation. For our young art to nourish itself [on Russian literature] would mean stunting its growth. Our orientation is toward the art of Western Europe, toward its style, toward its reception."[8]

To emphasize that Ukrainians were fully capable of creating socialist art on their own, he stated that "the young Ukrainian nation – the Ukrainian proletariat and its Communist intelligentsia – are the bearers of the great revolutionary socialist ideas and they must not orient themselves on the All-Union Philistinism: on its Moscow sirens."[9] Khvylovy's impassioned pleas for Ukrainians to strike out on their own gave rise to the famous slogan: "Away from Moscow!"

While Khvylovy directed his ideas primarily at young writers searching for literary models, his message clearly had political implications. It should be stressed, however, that his anti-Russianism was not so much a product of Ukrainian nationalism as of revolutionary internationalism. Khvylovy was convinced that the global revolution would never succeed if one nation, in this case the Russians, attempted to monopolize it.

Shumskyism   The danger that Khvylovy's views posed to the Soviet regime was heightened by the support that they found not only in Ukrainian literary circles, but also within the Communist party of Ukraine as well, particularly among the former Borotbisty. The leader of the latter was Oleksander Shumsky, the commissar of education, who, despite demands from Moscow loyalists that he condemn Khvylovy refused to do so and came forward with his own criticism of Moscow. The former Borotbisty had their own reasons for believing that the party's approach to the national question was hypocritical. When they first joined the Communist party, Shumsky and his associates were given high government posts so as to provide the Soviet government with a "Ukrainian flavor." But promptly after the Bolshevik victory, almost all of them were demoted or expelled from the party. With the advent of Ukrainization, some of the survivors – most notably Shumsky – were once again raised to high office at Moscow's behest, in order to create the impression that Ukraine was governed by Ukrainians. This time, however, the commissar of education resolved to expose Moscow's machinations.

While he, too, denounced Russian chauvinism, Shumsky's main goal was to attack the sacred Bolshevik principle of centralism. In a letter written to Stalin in early 1926, he pointed to the burgeoning Ukrainian national renaissance and argued that, for the party's own good, such a dynamic, broadly based movement should be controlled by Ukrainian Communists and not by non-Ukrainians. Otherwise, the increasingly nationally conscious Ukrainians, who had never been particularly well disposed to the Bolsheviks, might turn against what they perceived to be a foreign regime and overthrow it. To avoid this possibility, Shumsky proposed that Ukrainian Communists such as Hryhorii Hrynko and Vlas Chubar be appointed to lead the Ukrainian Soviet government and the Communist party of Ukraine and that such non-Ukrainian appointees of Moscow as Emmanuil Kviring (a Latvian) and Lazar Kaganovich (a Russified Jew) be recalled. Presented as a means of ensuring the growth of communism, the proposal called for nothing less than the selection of Ukraine's political leadership in Ukraine, not Moscow.

Shumsky also denounced the Ukrainians who, under the self-serving guise of loyal service to the party, made Moscow's centralism possible. At a meeting of the Ukrainian Communist leadership in May 1927, he declared that 'in the party the Russian Communist governs with suspicion and unfriendliness ... He rules by receiving support from a contemptible Little Russian who, throughout all historical epochs has been basically hypocritical, servilely deceitful and treacherously underhanded. Now he sings his faulty internationalism, defies with his indifferent attitude everything that is Ukrainian and is ever ready to spit at it (sometimes in Ukrainian) if this only would give him the possibility of obtaining a better position."[10]

Shumsky's critique caused an uproar among Communists both within and outside the Soviet Union. Stalin noted that "Comrade Shumsky does not realize that in Ukraine, where the indigenous Communist cadres are weak, such a movement ... may assume in places the character of a struggle ... against Moscow' in general, against the Russians in general, against Russian culture and it greatest achievement, Leninism."[11] While Shumsky's ideas were harshly condemned by party loyalists in Kharkiv and Moscow, they found support in the Galicia-based Communist Party of Western Ukraine (KPZU). The West Ukrainian Communist leader Karlo Maksymovych brought Shumsky's arguments to the forum of the Communist International and used the occasion to attack Moscow's treatment of the Ukrainians. Even some West European socialists showed an interest in the "Shumsky Affair." The German Social Democrat Emil Strauss proclaimed that "European socialism has all the grounds to support morally the struggle of the Ukrainian people for freedom. Since Marx, it has been in the best socialist tradition to struggle against any social and national oppression."[12]

Volobuevism   In early 1928, a new "deviation" appeared among the Ukrainian Communists. Its exponent was a young Ukrainian economist of Russian origin, Mykhailo Volobuev. As did Khvylovy in literature and Shumsky in politics, Volobuev sought to reveal the disparity between Bolshevik theory and practice in the field of economics. In two articles that appeared in *Bilshovyk Ukrainy*, the official theoretical journal of the Ukrainian party, Volobuev argued that, under Soviet rule, Ukraine continued to be an economic colony of Russia just as it had been under the tsars. To buttress his point, he carried out a careful analysis showing how, to the detriment of the Ukrainian periphery, heavy industry continued to be built in the Russian center. In addition, Volobuev claimed that the economy of the USSR was not a uniform, single unit, but a complex of economic components of which Ukraine was but one. Not only was each of these economic components capable of surviving on its own, but each clearly had the capability of becoming a part of the world economy by itself without the intermediary of the Russian economy.

Meanwhile, the Communist party had been ready to make concessions such as Ukrainization. It had even acknowledged some of its failings, such as the prevalence of Russian chauvinism in its ranks. But it could not allow the views of Khvylovy, Shumsky, and Volobuev to spread, for in all probability, this dispersion would lead to a challenge of its control over Ukraine. Even Skrypnyk, the great proponent of Ukrainization, believed that these "nationalist deviations" were a mortal threat to the party, and he led the counterattack against their supporters. Therefore, shortly after each of these "deviations" surfaced, their exponents were put under severe pressure to retract their views and confess to a variety of errors. After expressing varying degrees of defiance, all three complied. By late 1928, Khvylovy returned to strictly literary pursuits; Shumsky was shipped off to a minor party post in Russia; and Volobuev slipped into oblivion. However, during the Stalinist purges in the 1930s, their "sins" would be remembered and would cost these national communists their lives.

Finally, to put these national communist tendencies in proper perspective, they ought to be viewed in conjunction with developments in the party itself. After the death of Lenin in 1924, an intense struggle for power and leadership developed among the Bolshevik elite in Moscow. As a result, party control and discipline loosened, allowing various factions and ideological currents to proliferate. But this period of relative liberalism and pluralism, of an open struggle between conflicting ideas, was about to come to an abrupt end .

The Cultural Upsurge

The 1920s were a time of extraordinary growth, innovation, and ferment in Ukrainian culture. Some writers even refer to it as a period of cultural revolution or renaissance. This multifaceted outburst of creative energy was possible because the Communist party, concerned primarily with maintaining its political hegemony, had not as yet attempted to control cultural development. And the spread of Ukrainian-language education had established a broad basis for Ukrainian culture that had long been lacking in Eastern Ukraine. For the first time, Ukrainian culture could count on state support because important agencies such as the Ministry of Education were controlled by ardent Ukrainians such as Hrynko, Shumsky, and Skrypnyk.

It was, however, the effects of the revolution that provided the major thrust for this renaissance. Although the emigration of a large part of the old inteligentsia was a setback for cultural growth, it was more than offset by the emergence of a vast new pool of creative talents. Some of these young artists were apolitical and believed in the idea of "art for art's sake." Others were ardent revolutionaries who were associated with the Borotbisty and Ukrainian communists. When their hopes for independent statehood were frustrated, many of them saw cultural growth as an alternative means of expressing the national distinctiveness of their people.

The revolution also injected into cultural activity a sense of newness, a feeling that the old world and its restrictions had been swept away. Challenging and stimulating questions arose about the direction Ukrainian cultural development should take, the models it should utilize, and the kind of culture it ought to be. Inspired by a sense of mission and by a growing audience, writers, artists, and scholars plunged enthusiastically into the creation of a whole new cultural universe.

Literature Nowhere was this vibrant new mood so evident as in literature. The Marxist writers espoused the view that in order to fulfill itself, the revolution would have to reach into the cultural as well as social and political realms. That is, the "bourgeois" art of the past would have to be supplanted by a new proletarian art. They were quick to add, however, that "proletarian art can attain international unity only by national paths."[13]

In Russia the attempt to create a proletarian culture led to the formation of a literary organization called Proletcult, which was based on two key principles: that it was possible to create a proletarian culture without regard to the traditions and standards of the past, and that the masses should participate in the creation of this culture. Because Proletcult identified with urban Russian culture, the organization made little headway among Ukrainians. Still, its ideas were influential in the rise of the so-called mass literary organizations in Ukraine.

In 1922, Pluh, the first of the mass literary organizations, emerged in Kharkiv under the leadership of Serhii Pylypenko. Declaring that the masses (which in Ukraine meant primarily the peasants) should produce the kind of literature they wanted, the organization established a network of writing workshops that soon attracted about 200 writers and thousands of aspiring writers. A spokesman for the organization defined its attitude toward art: "The task of our time in the realm of art is to lower it, to bring it down to earth from its pedestal, to make it necessary and intelligible to all."[14] A year later, Vasyl Ellan-Blakytny organized Hart, a literary group that also wished to work for the formation of a proletarian culture in Ukraine. However, the members of Hart were wary of the idea of "massivism," fearing that it might lead to a lowering of standards in the arts.

Alongside these Marxist organizations, small groups of ideologically uncommitted or "nonproletarian" writers and artists also sprang up. Of the

Symbolists, Pavlo Tychyna was the most prominent. The Futurists were led by Mykhailo Semenko. Maksym Rylsky and Mykola Zerov were foremost among the Neoclassicists. By and large, these writers agreed with the view of the Symbolist Iurii Mezhenko that "a creative individual can create only when he holds himself higher than the mass, and when, although independent of it, he still feels a sense of national identity with it."[15] Because the Marxist and non-Marxist groups and organizations published journals that espoused their views and criticized those of dissenting writers, literary debates and controversies abounded.

When Blakytny died in 1925, Hart disintegrated. However, that same year many of its former members – led by Khvylovy and including the playwright Mykola Kulish, the poets Tychyna and Bazhan, and the prose writers Petro Panch, Iurii Ianovsky, and Ivan Senchenko – formed Vaplite (Free Academy of Proletarian Literature), an elitist literary organization. Worried that the pedagogic-enlightenment mentality (*prosvitianstvo*) and "massivism" of Pluh only encouraged Ukrainian provincialism, Khvylovy and his colleagues raised the demand for literary and artistic excellence in Ukrainian literature. They called for its orientation toward Europe and the traditional sources of world literature, and for a declaration of Ukrainian cultural independence from Moscow. Khvylovy's forceful statement of these views sparked an important and far-ranging debate that lasted from 1925 to 1927 and is usually referred to as the "Literary Discussion."

Not only did Pylypenko and other adherents of Pluh disagree with Vaplite, but the members of the Communist leadership in Ukraine also joined in the criticism of Vaplite's "bourgeois-nationalist ideology." Even Stalin pointed out the dangerousness of Khvylovy's ideas. To combat the spread of nationalist ideas in literature, a pro-Soviet organization, VUSPP (the All-Ukrainian Association of Proletarian Writers), was formed in 1927 and the Communist party's surveillance of literary activity increased.

In the midst of this ferment, there appeared literary works of high quality. Pavlo Tychyna and Maksym Rylsky, the two outstanding Ukrainian poets of the period, flourished at this time. Tychyna was immediately acclaimed a poet of genius when his first lyrical collection, *Soniashni kliarnety*, appeared in 1918. In subsequent publications, such as *Zamist sonetiv i oktav* (1920) and *Viter z Ukrainy* (1924), his artistic use of language, ability to evoke the rhythm and melody of folk songs, and lyrical descriptions of the countryside left no doubt that his works represented a milestone in the development of Ukrainian poetry. The son of a prominent 19th-century Ukrainophile, Rylsky presented a striking contrast to Tychyna. Rylsky's poems, which appeared in such collections as *Pid osinnymy zoriamy* (1918), *Synia dalechin* (1922), and *Trynadtsiata vesna* (1926), were reserved, philosophical, and deeply rooted in Western classical traditions. Noteworthy among the many other poets that appeared at this time were Mykola Zerov, Pavlo Fylypovych, Mykhailo Drai-Khmara,

Evhen Pluzhnyk, Volodymyr Sosiura, Mykola Bazhan, and Teofil Osmachka. The predominant themes in the works of the prose writers were the effects of the revolution and Civil War on the individual and society. Written with a refined feeling for the power of words and with a mixture of romanticism and brutal realism, Khvylovy's *Syni Etiudy* (1923) extolled the revolution, while his *Osin* (1924) and *Ia* (1924) reflected its contradictions and a growing sense of disillusionment. Hryhorii Kosynka, of poor peasant origin (as were many of his colleagues), masterfully portrayed the determination of peasants to resist outsiders in works such as *V zhytakh* (1926). In his novel *Misto* (1928), the skeptical, pessimistic Valerian Pidmohylny depicted how a Ukrainian peasant managed to prosper in the foreign city by shedding the best of his peasant values and retaining the worst. Ivan Senchenko, a master of satire, ridiculed the spineless flunkies that the Soviet system encouraged in his *Iz zapysok kholiuia* (1927). Meanwhile, Iurii Ianovsky's novel *Chotyry Shabli* (1930) evoked the spirit of the Zaporozhian Cossacks with its vivid descriptions of peasant partisans. By far the most popular of the prose writers was the humorist Ostap Vyshnia whose irreverent feuilletons were read by millions.

Among the playwrights, Mykola Kulish was the most outstanding. His three most famous plays, *Narodnyi Malakhii* (1928), *Myna Mazailo* (1929), and *Patetychna Sonata* (1930), were sensations because of their modernistic form and tragicomic treatment of the new Soviet reality, Russian chauvinism, the "Little Russian" mentality, anachronistic Ukrainian nationalism, and the spiritual immaturity of doctrinaire communists. The first two plays were staged by Les Kurbas and his famous Berezil troupe. Scandalized party officials, however, banned the showing of *Patetychna Sonata* in Ukraine, although it played in Leningrad and Moscow to enthusiastic audiences. In the new field of filmmaking, Oleksander Dovzhenko achieved world fame with his *Zvenyhora* (1927), *Arsenal* (1929), and *Zemlia* (1930), all of which were based on the impact of the revolution and Soviet rule on Ukraine.

Education and scholarship Experimentation and innovation were also widespread in education. Because its goal was the creation of a new socioeconomic order, the Soviet government encouraged the establishment of new types of schools and approaches to teaching that would hasten the break with the "bourgeois past." Soviet educators argued for the need to link education with the inculcation of communist values and ideology. Consequently, curricula that emphasized the combination of work and study, communal learning, and technical education were introduced into the schools. Meanwhile, the classics and the humanities in general were deemphasized and the study of religion completely banned. The theories of the famous pedagogue Antin Makarenko, stressing the predominance of environment over heredity in the development of children, gained in popularity.

Although the educational value of some of these experiments may have been questionable, the government was clearly successful in making education more accessible than it had ever been. Education in the basic seven-year school, as well as in the specialized vocational and secondary institutions, was free – and children of peasants and workers were encouraged to attend. As a result, between 1923 and 1925 alone, the number of schoolchildren in Ukraine jumped from 1.4 to 2.1 million. Concomitantly, the literacy rate during the 1920s rose from 24% to 57%. Nevertheless, millions of adults still remained illiterate and over 40% of school-aged children received no formal education.

Higher education also underwent major change. The universities were reorganized into numerous institutes (Institutes of Popular Education – INO) that specialized in medicine, physics, engineering, agronomy, or pedagogy. Their goal was the preparation of specialists for the work force. Although most of these institutes charged fees, children of poor workers and peasants (who formed the majority of institute students) were exempted from payment. Of the approximately 30,000–40,000 institute students in Ukraine in the late 1920s, about 53% were Ukrainians, 20% were Russians, and 22% were Jews. In general, Ukrainians were concentrated in such fields as agronomy and teaching, Russians in administrative studies and the sciences, and Jews in medicine and commerce.

Scholarship, and especially Ukrainian studies, enjoyed a renaissance during the 1920s comparable to that in literature. As we have seen, the Ukrainian national governments had been quick to establish scholarly institutions, in part because scholarship in the humanities had played such an important role in the rise of Ukrainian national consciousness throughout the 19th century. Anxious to demonstrate that they stood for progress, the Bolsheviks also encouraged scholarship. In 1919, they not only co-opted the Academy of Sciences in Kiev that had been established by the Skoropadsky government, but they even claimed that it was their creation. During the next several years, the academy and its affiliates – not the universities – were transformed into centers of research. As long as their ideas did not directly challenge the Soviet system, scholars were given relative freedom to pursue their research, present their views, and develop foreign contacts.

Even though almost all the prominent scholars in Ukraine were non-Communists and some even open sympathizers of Ukrainian nationalism, the Soviet government had no choice but to make them the core of the academy. With the implementation of the Ukrainization policies of the mid 1920s, the Ukrainian Communists in control of the Ministry of Education made a concerted effort to induce many leading scholars who had gone abroad during the Civil War to return to their homeland. Consequently, in 1924, the dean of Ukrainian studies (and a political opponent of the Communists), Mykhailo Hrushevsky, returned to Kiev to become a full member of the academy, where he launched the systematic study of Ukrainian history. Numerous other scholars who lived abroad or in Western Ukraine followed Hrushevsky's example. Thus, while the prestige of the academy rose rapidly, it remained a bastion of "bourgeois-nationalist" tendencies.

The first president of the academy was the renowned scientist Volodymyr Vernadsky. However, much of the academy's growth resulted from the tireless efforts of its longtime vice-president Serhii Efremov and secretary Ahatanhel Krymsky. By 1924 the academy had 37 full members and about 400 associates. Its publications rose from 32 in 1923 to 136 in 1929. Of its three sections – the historical/philological, the physical/mathematical, and the socioeconomic – the first, in which Hrushevsky played the dominant role, was the most dynamic and important. It consisted of dozens of chairs, commissions, and committees that systematically studied all aspects of Ukrainian history, literature, and language. The section sponsored the publication of *Ukraina*, the leading journal of Ukrainian studies, and its members published a series of other periodicals as well as hundreds of monographs. Besides Hrushevsky, other important members of the section were the historians Dmytro Bahalii, Mykhailo Slabchenko, Oleksander Ohloblyn, and Osyp Hermaize; the literary specialists Serhii Efremov and Volodomyr Peretts; the ethnographer Andrii Loboda; the art historian Oleksii Novytsky; and the orientalist Krymsky.

In the socioeconomic section, Mykola Vasylenko produced an important work on the history of Ukrainian law, while Konstantyn Vobly pioneered the study of Ukraine's economic geography. Although the science section of the academy was at the outset not as prominent as it became later, it, too, included a number of outstanding scholars, some of whom had international reputations. Among these were the mathematician Dmytro Grave, the physicist Mykola Krylov, and the chemists Lev Pysarzhevsky and Volodymyr Kistiakovsky. But while the academy in Kiev was the major center of scholarship in Ukraine, it was not the only one. Two of its members, the historians Bahalii and Slabchenko, set up research centers in Kharkiv and Odessa, respectively. Many smaller cities, such as Poltava, Chernihiv, and Dniepropetrovsk, also established research institutions.

To counterbalance the influence of the many non-Marxist scholars in the social sciences and humanities, the Soviet government founded the Institute of Marxism in Kharkiv in 1929. Its goal was to prepare specialists in philosophy, economics, and history who would teach their subjects from the Marxist point of view, study the history of the party and the revolution, and act as ideological defenders of the regime. The leading figure in this institute was Matvii Iavorsky, a Galician who attempted to interpret Ukrainian history in Marxist terms and who created a school of Ukrainian Marxist historians.

Ecclesiastical Activity

The Orthodox church in Ukraine had been a pillar of the tsarist regime. After the metropolitan of Kiev was placed under the authority of the patriarch of Moscow in 1686, it adopted Muscovite ecclesiastical usages, reinforced Russification, and preached loyalty to tsar and empire. And although by the end of 19th century, national and social consciousness had begun to spread among the lower clergy and especially among students in the seminaries, the Ukrainian intelligentsia remained generally ambivalent toward the church, viewing it as a bastion of social conservatism and anti-Ukrainianism.

The revolution and the concomitant desire for national self-expression were bound to have an impact upon the church in Ukraine. At the eparchal assemblies and congresses of soldiers and peasants that were held in 1917–18, proposals were raised advocating that the church in Ukraine sever its ties with Moscow and constitute itself as an independent (autocephalous) body. The idea appealed to the lower clergy and the urban intelligentsia in particular. Consequently, in January 1918, an All-Ukrainian Church Council was formed to work toward this goal. However, the left-leaning Central Rada showed little interest in the matter and it was the conservative government of Hetman Skoropadsky, especially his ministers of religion, Vasyl Zinkivsky and Oleksander Lototsky, who unequivocally advocated severing ecclesiastical ties with Moscow. After the fall of Skoropadsky, the Directory also came out in favor of ecclesiastical independence. But because both governments were short-lived, their support did not produce concrete results.

Paradoxically, the drive for an independent Ukrainian Orthodox church reached its high point under Soviet rule. Because the Soviets perceived the Russian Orthodox church, led by the newly chosen Patriarch Tikhon, as their most dangerous religious opponent, they were not averse to the appearance of religious groups that undermined the influence of the established church. Hence their early tolerance of ecclesiastical Ukrainization.

Opposition to this tendency was nonetheless significant. It consisted primarily of Patriarch Tikhon in Moscow and almost all the Orthodox hierarchy in Ukraine. Using the threat of excommunication and anathema, the hierarchy repeatedly blocked all attempts of the All-Ukrainian Church Council to expand its influence. This sharply negative attitude discouraged many priests and members of the laity from casting their lot with the Ukrainizers.

These obstacles notwithstanding, on 21 October 1921, at an assembly attended by about 500 delegates (including 64 priests), the council took a radical step. Disregarding canonical law and ignoring threats by the hierarchy, the council elected one of its members, the priest Vasyl Lypkivsky, as metropolitan; he immediately consecrated an archbishop and four bishops. These, in turn, anointed several hundred priests and deacons. The council then reaffirmed an earlier decision to create the Ukrainian Autocephalous Orthodox church (UAOC).

The new church grew rapidly. By 1924 it boasted 30 bishops, about 1500 priests, over 1100 parishes (out of a total of approximately 9000), and millions of adherents. Many Ukrainian parishes in the United States, Canada, and Europe joined its ranks. In contrast to traditional Orthodoxy, which prided itself on conservatism, the Ukrainian church introduced numerous innovations, such as the use of the Ukrainian language instead of Church Slavonic in church services. It modernized the appearance of its clergy by banning the traditional robes, long hair, and beards. A radical departure from ancient practice was the church's acceptance of married bishops. Reflecting the spirit of the times, the Ukrainian church also adopted a democratic approach to self-administration. It rejected the authoritarianism of the patriarchal system and vested the highest authority in the church in an elected council of bishops, priests, and representatives of the laity. It also extended the elective principle to the selection of bishops and parish priests. Implicit in these reforms was an attempt by the new church to draw closer to the faithful and to involve them in its activity. These efforts to a large extent explained the early success of the UAOC.

Its achievements, however, could not obviate the fundamental weaknesses of the new church. Its radical departure from canonical practice, the repeated declarations by Patriarch Tikhon that it was illegal, and the failure of Orthodox patriarchs outside the USSR to recognize it imposed upon the UAOC an aura of illegitimacy that confused and alienated many early adherents. Furthermore, the UAOC's espousal of elective and democratic principles gave rise to numerous anarchic conflicts between the clergy and laity. Because of its newness, the church had almost no economic base. Even more serious was the problem of personnel. The hurried, haphazard consecration of bishops and priests meant that unsuitable or poorly trained individuals often rose to responsible positions. In time, they proved to be especially vulnerable to government pressures. As these weaknesses surfaced, the UAOC's growth slowed. And although it continued to pose a serious challenge to the Patriarchal or Russian Orthodox church (which was backed by the clergy and especially the monks, the Russian minority, and conservative elements in the Ukrainian population), it retained the loyalty of the vast majority of the Orthodox in Ukraine.

A more menacing set of difficulties arose as a result of government policies. Worried by the unexpected strides made by the Ukrainian church, the Soviet authorities made it a target of their divide-and-rule tactics. They encouraged the rise of dissident church groups in Ukraine that not only undermined the Russian Orthodox church but its Ukrainian rival as well. In the early 1920s, they backed a "progressive" group called the Activist Church of Christ, which was a breakaway faction of the Patriarchal church. When this group failed to make headway in Ukraine, the authorities patronized the newly formed Counciliar-Episcopal church, which emerged in 1925 under the leadership of Teofil Buldovsky. Although this church espoused Ukrainian ecclesiastical independence, which it proposed to attain by canonical means, it adopted an openly progovernment stance.

Despite these tactics, the government failed to destroy or subjugate the UAOC. On the contrary, its weaknesses notwithstanding, the UAOC continued to grow. Therefore, in 1926, the Soviets launched a frontal attack by imposing extremely heavy taxes on the Ukrainian parishes and restricting the activities of their clergy. Soon thereafter, they accused Metropolitan Lypkivsky and a number of his associates of Ukrainian nationalism, had them arrested, and dissolved the All-Ukrainian Church Council. Although the UAOC was allowed to exist for several years more, it was evident that its future, as well as that of religion in general in the USSR, was grim.

৯৯

The relative weakness and restraint that the proponents of communism exhibited in the 1920s assured that nationalism (or at least national consciousness), which spread rapidly among Ukrainians during the revolution and Civil War, would continue to grow. Because the Communist party was intent on achieving a monopoly in the political sphere, Ukrainian national tendencies in this area were limited. However, the fact that the Ukrainians did obtain a semblance of statehood should not be underestimated, for it encouraged among them a feeling that they were a full-fledged nation with all the rights and aspirations that status implied.

The main arena in which the nationalism that had been frustrated from 1917 to 1920 found an outlet was culture. A large number of gifted writers, poets, artists, and scholars transformed Ukrainian culture from being a concern of a small, prerevolutionary intelligentsia to a matter of interest for large segments of the populace. The process of Ukrainization not only disseminated cultural achievements among the people but it identified Ukrainian culture with education, socioeconomic modernization, and even the state. Consequently, it seemed that a creative symbiosis of nationalism and communism was about to emerge that could address the Ukrainians' national as well as socioeconomic needs. But subsequent events would prove that this symbiosis was not to be.

Soviet Ukraine:
The Traumatic Thirties

By the end of the 1920s the Bolsheviks were ready to resume the drive for the creation of a truly communist society. Under the leadership of Stalin, they revoked the concessions made during the NEP period and proceeded to impose socioeconomic and political changes on Soviet society that were so vast and radical that they are often referred to as the "Second Revolution." But along with the massive transformations of the 1930s, there was also a return to certain traditional aspects of Russian politics, in particular rigid centralization and one-man rule. For Ukrainians, this cataclysmic reversal put an end to their efforts to develop their own "road to communism." Once again, as in the days of the tsars, Ukraine would become little more than a part of a larger whole. But, as never before in their history, Ukrainians would be forced to pay a dreadfully high price to attain goals they had not set for themselves.

Stalin and Stalinism

In 1927 Stalin emerged as the victor in the bitter power struggle that had raged among party leaders since Lenin's death. Born in 1879 in Georgia of poor parents, Stalin (his real name was Dzhugashvili) was an early convert to Bolshevism. Prior to the revolution, he had played a relatively minor role in the Bolshevik party. As one of the party's few non-Russians, his assignments had included dealing with the theoretical implications of the nationalities problem – a matter of secondary concern to most Bolsheviks. His expertise in the field, however, would serve him (if not the nationalities) well in later years. An unobtrusive personality – early observers only remember him as a "grey blur" – Stalin lacked the outstanding skills as a writer and orator that characterized many of the leading Bolsheviks. Consequently, he had gravitated toward organizational work during the revolution and, as secretary-general, came to control the recruitment and promotion of party cadres. His control of the party apparatus, as well as his extraordinary cunning, enabled him to eliminate rivals and to become the unchallenged leader of the party – a *vozhd* surrounded by "yes" men.

As Stalin exercised tyrannical dominance of the party, it, in turn, systematically expanded its control over all aspects of society. Open criticism of (let alone resistance to) Stalin became impossible as a powerful and growing secret police methodically terrorized and later liquidated real, imagined, or potential opposition. Some scholars describe this Russian-Marxist combination of personal dictatorship and monolithic organization as totalitarianism. Others simply call it Stalinism. The Soviets view it as a necessary phase in the building of socialism and have long praised Stalin for his leadership, iron will, and realism. But critics have invariably stressed his ruthlessness, incredible disregard for human suffering, and murderous paranoia (which caused him to see enemies and plots everywhere). As Nicholas Riasanovsky remarks about Stalin, there was, as in the case of Ivan the Terrible, whom Stalin admired, madness in his method.[1]

Probably more than other Bolsheviks, Stalin had an exceedingly low opinion of peasants, for he considered them to be incurably conservative and a major barrier to revolutionary change. In the words of his successor, Nikita Khrushchev, "For Stalin, peasants were scum."[2] Although Stalin was not an ethnic Russian, he embraced Russian nationalism as a means of strengthening the Soviet empire. And because Ukrainians were an overwhelmingly peasant people among whom native nationalism was on the rise, they were doubly vulnerable to his designs.

The Great Transformation

A visitor to Soviet Ukraine in the mid 1920s would have been struck by the important changes that had already been brought about by the Soviets. The new ideology, government structure, economic organization, legal order, education, and high culture attested to their far-ranging innovations. But equally striking would have been the realization that much of the old still remained. Ukraine continued to be a land of innumerable villages, of peasants working as before, of the church dominating spiritual life, and of traditional values retaining their hold. In effect, one would have found a society in which two cultures coexisted uneasily. In the cities, Soviet ways seemed to predominate; in the countryside, where the majority of the population lived, changes were relatively few. Perhaps most galling for the Bolshevik revolutionaries was the fact that the peasant showed little inclination for sharing their dreams of a communist utopia. There was, therefore, a real possibility that, despite the revolution, the Soviet Union might remain a backward, predominantly agrarian society. This result would have saddled the party with the frustrating task of trying to establish a dictatorship of the proletariat in a land of peasants.

Stalin perceived the situation as not only depressing, but threatening. Under NEP, the kulaks, bitter enemies of the new regime, had been growing stronger economically. More ominous was the danger of an attack that, Stalin warned, the capitalist countries were planning against the fledgling socialist state. Among party members these perceptions gave rise to a sense of urgency, to a feeling that radical action was needed to preserve the revolution and fulfill its promise.

Despite the fact that he was not a strong theorist, Stalin produced an appealing formula at this critical juncture. Rejecting as unrealistic the appeals of his rival Leon Trotsky for a renewed effort to spread the revolution abroad, Stalin urged the party to build "socialism in one country," in other words, to transform the USSR – as quickly as possible and regardless of the cost – to a modern, industrial, and completely socialist society. If such a rapid transformation were carried out, the Soviet Union would be able to withstand its capitalist enemies and to prove that communism was the most effective road to progress. Because it was unlikely that peasants would support such a program (only 1 of 125 peasants was a Communist), Stalin called for a "revolution from above," that is, one imposed by him, the party, and the government.

The first Five-Year Plan   Adopted by the party in 1928, the initial design for the great transformation was called the first Five-Year Plan (FYP). Its general goal was to "catch up with and bypass the capitalist world" economically. Emphasizing the development of heavy industry, it set stunning objectives for the country: a 250% increase in overall industrial development, with a 330% expansion of heavy industry alone. The other important part of the plan called for the collectivization – the formation of large, communally owned farms – of 20% of all peasant households. It was envisaged that agricultural production would rise by 150%. Eventually, collectivization was to encompass almost all peasant households, thereby removing the "pernicious, bourgeois influence" of private ownership of property.

The plan aimed, in effect, at transforming the entire labor force in the countryside as well as the city into employees of state-controlled enterprises. This structure would not only give the state complete economic control of its citizens but it would also greatly expand its political dominance of the formerly self-sufficient peasants. Stalin expected some resistance to the plan, especially from the peasants who were to be deprived of their lands. But he cynically dismissed it with the famous comment, "You can't make an omelet without breaking eggs."

Industrialization   In terms of industrial development, Ukraine fared well in the first FYP. It received over 20% of the total investment, which meant that of the 1500 new industrial plants built in the USSR, 400 were located in Ukraine. Some of these plants were constructed on a gigantic scale. Completed in 1932 by 10,000 workers, the Dnieper hydroelectric plant was the largest in Europe. The new steel combine in Zaporozhia and the tractor factory in Kharkiv were also among the largest in their categories. In the Donbas–Kryvyi Rih region, so many new plants were being built that the entire area looked like one huge construction site.

In the second and third FYPs, however, the republic received a disproportionately small amount of investment. Arguing that in the event of war, the industrial centers of Ukraine would be too vulnerable to attack, the economic planners in Moscow decided to concentrate on the development of industrial centers in the Urals. Thus, of the 4500 plants built during the second FYP (1932–37), only 1000 were in Ukraine. In the next FYP the drop in Ukraine's share of investment funds was even more marked: it received a mere 600 of the 3000 new plants built. Nevertheless, the construction of thousands of new plants in little more than a decade did turn Ukraine into a major industrial country.

Never before in history had a society attempted such a vast economic transformation in so short a time period. Whereas in the industrial boom of the 19th century, it had taken decades to construct several dozen industrial plants in Ukraine, in the 1930s, the Soviets were building hundreds of plants every year. But achievements like these were possible only if workers were pushed to their limits. It was necessary, therefore, to create an atmosphere of tension, of titanic struggle, of economic war with capitalism in which the outcome depended on the exertions of each and every worker. Stalin set the tone in his famous 1931 speech: "To slow down the tempo [of industrialization] means to lag behind. And those who lag behind are beaten ... We are behind the leading countries by 50–100 years. We must make up this time in ten years. Either we do it or we go under."[3] This appeal to Soviet patriotism (and Russian nationalism) urged Soviet citizens to "show" the world that theirs was the superior system.

Various techniques were used to arouse enthusiasm for this effort. References to economic activity were couched in military terminology: the "breakthrough on the tractor-building front," "the victories of workers' shock brigades," and the "storming of new quotas." Outstanding workers were honored as "heroes of socialist labor." Plants, cities, and even republics competed with each other in the race to fulfill the plan. To a considerable degree, these methods were successful. Among many workers, especially members of the party or Komsomol (Communist Youth League), there was genuine pride in and excitement about what was being achieved and they willingly committed themselves to the challenging tasks set for them by the party. Others who were less enthusiastic were subjected to a battery of coercive measures. Unauthorized lateness, absenteeism, or neglect of duties became a criminal offense that could lead to the loss of food rations (thus raising the prospect of starvation) or housing, and even to imprisonment in Siberian labor camps.

The media's constant exhortations for workers to fulfill their quotas and meet their timetables did not mean that the industrialization drive was conducted in an orderly manner. As early as 1930 it was evident that the frenzied pace of construction was frequently accompanied by astounding confusion, ineptitude, and waste. In some cases, new factories stood empty because the machinery for them was lacking; often machines could not be housed in poorly designed plants. While untrained operators ruined new machines in one factory, experienced workers sat idle in another for lack of the proper equipment. Moreover, the quality of many products was poor.

Ukraine's Communist leadership had its own particular criticisms of the industrialization drive. After the first FYP, its input into the formulation of subsequent FYPS was practically nil and was reflected in the steadily decreasing level of investment in Ukraine. Nor were Ukrainians entirely pleased with the nature of industrial development in their land. Moscow's planners assigned to Ukraine the task of producing raw materials, while Russia's industries monopolized the finished products, especially consumer goods, that were shipped back to Ukrainian markets. Thus, as late as 1932, a few bold Ukrainian economists complained that the "colonial" relationship between Russia and Ukraine that had existed in tsarist days had not altered appreciably. Finally, the geographical distribution of industry in Ukraine was most uneven. While the traditional industrial areas in Donbas and the Dnieper region continued to expand, the heavily populated Right Bank remained economically stagnant.

Despite these drawbacks, the achievements of the first FYPS were impressive. By 1940 Ukraine's industrial capacity was more than seven times greater than in 1913 (Russia's increased ninefold). The productivity of individual workers also increased (but their real earnings generally decreased). Thus, as the USSR as a whole rose from being the world's fifth largest industrial power to the second, Ukraine (with a productive capacity roughly equal to that of France) became one of Europe's most advanced industrial countries.

Urbanization The great growth of industry in the 1930s had an effect not only on the number of Ukrainians who were employed, but also on where and how they lived. For centuries one of the great themes in Ukrainian history had been the confrontation between the Ukrainian village and the non-Ukrainian city. As a result of the FYPS, this relationship began to change as millions of Ukrainians poured into cities to work in industrial enterprises. One might well ask why Ukrainians participated in such great numbers in the industrialization drive of the 1930s, having been conspiciously absent from the initial wave of industrial growth in the 1890s. Because the scale of the Soviet effort was so vast, it created a general labor shortage throughout the USSR. Rus-

TABLE 4
Percentage of Ukrainians in industrial centers, 1923–33

Cities	Percent in 1923	Percent in 1933
Kharkiv	38	50
Zaporozhia	28	56
Dniepropetrovsk	16	48

sian workers no longer came south in search of work in great numbers, so the newly built factories of Ukraine drew on the local work force. As well, conditions in the countryside were calamitous and because the Ukrainian peasant no longer had the option of moving eastward in search of land as he had in the 1890s, he was forced to leave his cherished soil for employment in the city. The irreversible flow from the countryside into the cities which accelerated at this time would bring about momentous changes in the way of life that had defined Ukrainians for millennia.

The expansion of the cities was dramatic. Growing at a rate of about four times that of the population as a whole, the number of urban dwellers in Soviet Ukraine doubled between 1926 and 1939. At the outset of this period, only one in five had lived in an urban environment in Ukraine; before the outbreak of the Second World War, the ratio was one in three. Ethnic Ukrainian participation in the urbanization boom was equally remarkable. In 1920 Ukrainians constituted 32% of the urban population, living mostly in the smaller cities. By 1939, they represented over 58% of urban dwellers and many had moved into large industrial centers. As table 4 indicates, it was in the latter that the influx of Ukrainians was most apparent. The percentage of Ukrainians in the proletariat also rose. Although in 1926 they were a mere 6% of workers, in 1939 almost 30% of all Ukrainians were classified as members of the proletariat.

Most of the expanding industrial centers were located not on the Right and Left banks, where the core of the Ukrainian population lived, but in the Donbas and the south, which had large Russian and Jewish minorities. Later, when the government adopted a policy of Russification, this factor would be of considerable importance. Initially, however, there were simply too many Ukrainians pouring into the cities to be assimilated into Russian culture and it appeared that the traditional Russian hold on the cities was seriously threatened.

The huge influx of new inhabitants created exceedingly difficult living conditions in the cities, especially in regard to housing. Frequently separated from their families, the newcomers were quartered in crowded dormitories, sometimes for years. Those who brought their families along often had no choice but to live in squalid huts on the outskirts of town. Food was scarce and rationed. The only satisfaction that many of these workers could derive from their new situation was that, bad as it was, it was better than what the peasants faced in the villages.

Collectivization   Even more dramatic and sweeping than the changes in the cities was the transformation of the countryside. Here, however, the "Second Revolution" was accompanied by such brutality and horror that it can only be described as a war waged by the regime against the peasantry. In fact, it can safely be said that collectivization, with its devastating consequences, was one of the most traumatic events in Ukrainian history.

The Bolsheviks always argued that collective agriculture eventually had to replace small peasant farming. They were aware of the fact that convincing the peasantry to accept their views would be a lengthy and difficult process, especially after the concessions peasants had won during NEP. Peasant response to the collective and state farms established in the 1920s had not been promising, attracting less than 3% of agricultural workers in the USSR. Therefore, when drafting their first FYP, the Bolsheviks estimated that at best they would be able to collectivize 20% of peasant households (in Ukraine the target was 30%). With its attention focused on industrialization, the Soviet leadership apparently preferred not to take on the massive burdens that would be associated with a radical transformation of agriculture.

It soon became evident, however, that industrialization as the Soviets envisaged it demanded extensive collectivization. Stalin appears to have come to this realization during the grain procurement crisis of 1928. Soviet plans for industrial expansion were based on the assumption that the state would be able to buy grain cheaply from the peasants. Doing so would allow it both to feed the growing work force in the cities and to sell grain abroad at a profit that, in turn, would be used to help finance industrialization. But the prices that the state offered – often as little as one-eighth of the market price – were considered too low by the peasants and they refused to sell their grain. Infuriated by peasant recalcitrance, which he termed "sabotage," Stalin decided that for the FYP to succeed, both political and economic control of the peasantry was essential. Therefore, with practically no advance preparation, he ordered an all-out drive for total collectivization.

Liquidation of the kulaks   Realizing that the wealthier peasants would resist collectivization most bitterly, Stalin called for the "liquidation of the kulaks as a class." This classic divide-and-conquer tactic was calculated to isolate the most successful peasants from the mass of poor peasants. However, defining just who was a kulak (Ukrainian: *kurkul*) was not a simple matter. Officially, kulaks owned more land than the average peasant and hired labor to work it. It was estimated that they made up about 5% of the peasantry. But the government's depiction of kulaks as "blood-sucking usurers" and "exploiters" of their fellow peasants rarely fit reality.

Usually a wealthier peasant owned 10–15 acres, several horses and cows, and some sheep. His net worth measured in current dollars was probably no more than $600–800. Since many of the old kulak families had been destroyed in the Civil War, kulaks were frequently former poor peasants who, by dint of hard work, had prospered during NEP. When it came to deciding who was a kulak – and this was generally done by a *troika* consisting of a secret police representative, the head of the village Soviet (council), and the party secretary – envy, personal grudges, and (very often) opposition to collectivization also played a role. Consequently, many middle and even poor peasants were designated as kulaks or their "helpers."

What did "liquidation as a class" actually mean? Those kulaks who resisted most stubbornly were shot, and a large number were deported to forced labor camps in the Arctic and Siberia. The rest were deprived of all their property (including their homes and personal belongings), barred from the collective farms, and told to fend for themselves. The "dekulakization" process reached its high point in the winter of 1929–30. Its most widespread feature was the deportations. Hundreds of thousands of peasants and their families were dragged from their homes, packed into freight trains, and shipped thousands of miles to the north where they were dumped amidst Arctic wastes, often without food or shelter.[4]

Of the more than 1 million Ukrainian peasants that the Soviet regime expropriated in the early 1930s, about 850,000 were deported to the north where many, especially children, perished. But some of the deportees, notably young men, escaped from exile. Together with those who managed to avoid deportation, they surreptitiously entered the urban labor force (factories were forbidden to hire kulaks). In this way, a large part of Ukraine's most industrious and efficient farmers ceased to exist. "Not one of them was guilty of anything," a Soviet author noted, "but they belonged to a class that was guilty of everything."[5]

To achieve its goals in the countryside, the regime needed assistance, but the number of Communists in the villages was clearly too small to suffice. Initially, the government placed its hopes on the revived Committees of Poor Peasants, assuming that they had little to lose from "dekulakization" and collectivization. But it soon became apparent that being poor did not mean that a peasant was willing to participate in the destruction of his better-off neighbors. Therefore, the government dispatched thousands of urban workers, frequently Russian and Jewish Communists or Komsomol members, to implement its policies in the villages.

In the fall of 1929 about 15,000 workers were sent into the Ukrainian countryside; in January 1930 approximately 47,000 more arrived. At the same time, the "25,000ers" (mostly workers from Russia who were fanatically dedicated to the "building of socialism" regardless of the cost) appeared in Ukraine to lead the local "dekulakization" drives or to act as heads of the newly organized collective farms. The assignment of outsiders, although assuring the implementation of government policies, added to the brutality with which they were carried out.

Restructuring agriculture: phase one   As the kulaks were being crushed, Stalin launched his attack on the peasantry as a whole. Instructions went out to party activists to begin the immediate and total organization of collective farms. Although often hazy on precisely how this massive transformation was to be carried out, Stalin's orders were clear on one point: it must be done rapidly and without regard to protests, difficulties, or costs. Usually the process consisted of party workers descending on a village and calling a meeting during which they browbeat several peasants into agreeing to form a collective. A party activist usually shouted: "Anyone opposed to the collective farm is opposed to the Soviet government. Let's vote. Who is against the collective farm?" And then there was a demand that all the villagers pool their land and surrender their cattle to the collective farm.[6]

These measures produced pandemonium and outrage in the villages. Officials were frequently beaten and shot. Particularly widespread were the so-called *babski bunty* – riots raised by women demanding the return of their property. In several cases, large uprisings of armed peasants forced the regime to send in regular army and OGPU (political police) units to quell them. However, the most widespread form of protest was the slaughter of farm animals. Determined not to let the government have their livestock, peasants preferred to kill their animals and either consume the meat or sell it. The extent to which such acts were committed was staggering: between 1928 and 1932 Ukraine lost about 50% of its livestock. Many peasants fled the collectives and sought work in the cities. To the dismay of Soviet officials, many poor and middle peasants, who had improved their condition during NEP, were often among their most bitter opponents.

To reinforce its officials, the regime sent in the OGPU to arrest the more vociferous protesters and deport them to Siberia. With such coercion, it was only a matter of time before Soviet authorities would impose their will on the peasantry. By March 1930 about 3.2 million peasant households in Ukraine had surrendered to the invaders of their villages and had sullenly entered the collective farms to await their fate.

But the calamitous disruption of the rural economy (not the human cost) worried Stalin. Suddenly, on 3 March 1930, he published an article entitled "Dizziness with Success." In it he claimed that "the fundamental turn toward socialism in the village may be considered already secured." This remark was followed by an astounding assertion: "It is impossible to establish collective farms by force. To do so would be stupid and reactionary."[7] Stalin's intent was clear: first, he wanted to send a message to party activists to ease the pressure for a time, and second, by blaming the lower officials who had obediently followed his directives, Stalin tried to distance himself from the disasters brought on by collectivization.

Interpreting Stalin's statements as a retreat from collectivization, the peasants responded accordingly by abandoning the collective farms in droves. Within three months almost 50% of the collectivized peasants in Ukraine had returned to individual farming. It seemed that the great drive to transform the countryside was an economic and political fiasco.

Restructuring agriculture: phase two   Stalin's retreat helped to stabilize the situation in the villages. It soon became apparent, however, that this was only a temporary maneuver and that the regime intended to continue imposing collectivization, only using different tactics. Its new approach was to make individual farming economically unfeasible. Peasants who left the collective farms were often prevented from taking their farming implements and surviving livestock with them. They received meager plots that were difficult to farm, while the collectivized farmers retained all the best land. Taxes on individual farmers doubled and tripled, while the collectivized farmers were absolved from payment for several years. Furthermore, there was still the possibility that stubborn resisters might be called kulaks and deported. Consequently, many peasants had no choice but to join the collective farms, which by 1932 accounted for about 70% of farming households. By 1940 almost all Ukraine's peasants belonged to its 28,000 collective farms.

Although owned in theory by the peasants, the collective farms were obliged to deliver assigned amounts of produce to the state and were controlled by its officials. Only after a collective farm had fulfilled its obligations to the state were its members allowed to divide what remained among themselves. The less-numerous state farms (*radhospy*) were essentially state-owned agricultural factories in which peasants worked as hired labor, while the Machine Tractor Stations (MTS) provided mechanized aid to the collective farms. The government's monopoly on tractors and other farm machinery also served as a means of coercing the peasants. Indeed, this entire system was designed to give the regime not only economic but also political control over agriculture and those who engaged in it.

Although adept at coercion, Stalin and his cohorts were astoundingly inept when it came to farming. Frequently, the party activists who headed the collective farms would order the planting of inappropriate crops. As was the case in industry, they often succumbed to a mania for the gigantic and created huge, unmanageable agro-enterprises. Because of poor transportation facilities, much of the stockpiled grain spoiled or was eaten by rats. Even more serious was the lack of draught animals, many of which had been slaughtered earlier. Government officials were confident, however, that they could provide enough tractors to replace the missing horses and oxen. But the production of tractors fell badly behind schedule and a very high percentage of those delivered broke down almost immediately. As a result, in 1931, almost one-third of the grain yield was lost during the harvest; by 1932 the total area sown in Ukraine contracted by a fifth. To make matters worse, a drought hit southern Ukraine in 1931.

All these factors contributed to the steadily deteriorating conditions. But the decisive factor was Stalin's ruthless policy of grain procurement. The regime was in desperate need of grain to finance industrialization and continued to impose high grain quotas on the peasants, deteriorating conditions notwithstanding. Because there was not enough grain to meet both government demands and peasant needs, in 1931 Ukrainian Communists beseeched Moscow to lower its quotas. Although Stalin agreed to a small reduction, the new quota he set was still unrealistically high.

To ensure that all the grain required by the regime would be collected, Stalin dispatched two of his closest lieutenants, Viacheslav Molotov and Lazar Kaganovich, to supervise grain procurements in Ukraine. Once again party activists were mobilized and sent into the countryside to confiscate the peasants' grain. Many apparently balked at the task, for about one-third of all those who held reponsible positions in the collective farms had to be purged at this time. To reinforce the activists, Soviet officials used regular troops and the OGPU units, which mercilessly crushed villages that refused to give up their food. Even seed grain needed for sowing next year's crop was expropriated. In spite of these measures, by late 1932, the regime had collected only 70% of its quota. In a speech delivered in January 1933, Stalin ordered the party apparatus to redouble its efforts: "Do not allow your attention to be overshadowed by worries about all sorts of funds and reserves; do not be diverted from the main task; develop the grain procurement campaign ... and speed it up. The first commandment is – fulfill the grain procurements."[8]

The Famine of 1932–33

The famine that occurred in 1932–33 was to be for the Ukrainians what the Holocaust was to the Jews and the Massacres of 1915 for the Armenians. A tragedy of unfathomable proportions, it traumatized the nation, leaving it with deep social, psychological, political, and demographic scars that it carries to this day. And it cast a dark shadow on the methods and achievements of the Soviet system.

The central fact about the famine is that it did not have to happen. Stalin himself proclaimed that "nobody can deny that the total yield of grain in 1932 was larger than in 1931."[9] As Conquest and Krawchenko have pointed out, the harvest of 1932 was only 12% below the 1926–30 average.[10] In other words, food was available. However, the state systematically confiscated most of it for its own use. Despite the pleas and warnings of Ukrainian Communists, Stalin raised Ukraine's grain procurement quotas in 1932 by 44%. His decision, and the regime's brutal fulfillment of his commands, condemned millions to death in what can only be called a man-made famine. The regime's disregard for the human costs of its policies was evident in a series of measures implemented in 1932. In August, party activists received the legal right to confiscate grain from peasant households; that same month the infamous law that carried a death penalty for the theft of "socialist property" was enacted. Any man, woman, or child caught taking even a handful of grain from a government silo or a collective farm field could be, and often was, executed. Under extenuating circumstances, such "crimes against the state" were punished by ten years of hard labor. To prevent peasants from abandoning collective farms in search of food, a system of internal passports was put into effect. In November, Moscow enacted a law stipulating that no grain from a collective farm could be given to the peasants until the government's quota had been met.

In January 1933 Stalin ordered his plenipoteniary, Pavel Postyshev, to castigate the Ukrainian Communists for their "lack of Bolshevik vigilance" and to speed up the collection of grain. Under his leadership, gangs of party activists conducted brutal house-to-house searches, tearing up floors and delving into wells in search of any grain that remained. Even those already swollen from malnutrition were not allowed to keep their grain. In fact, if a person did not appear to be starving, he was suspected of hoarding food. In retrospect, a party activist has described his motivations at that time in the following manner: "We believed Stalin to be a wise leader ... We were deceived because we wanted to be deceived. We believed so strongly in communism that we were ready to accept any crime if it was glossed over with the least little bit of communist phraseology."[11]

Famine, which had been spreading throughout 1932, hit full force in early 1933. It is estimated that at the outset of the year an average peasant family of five had about eighty kilograms of grain to last it until the next harvest. In other words, each member had to survive on about 1.7 kg a month. Lacking bread, peasants ate pets, rats, bark, leaves, and the garbage from the well-provisioned kitchens of party members. There were numerous cases of cannibalism. According to a Soviet author, "The first who died were the men. Later on the children. And last of all, the women. But before they died, people often lost their senses and ceased to be human beings."[12] Even as whole villages died out, party activists continued confiscating grain. One of them, Victor Kravchenko, later wrote: "On the battlefield men die quickly, they fight back, they are sustained by fellowship and a sense of duty. Here I saw people dying in solitude by slow degree, dying hideously, without the excuse of sacrifice for a cause. They had been trapped and left to starve, each in his home, by a political decision made in a far-off capital around conference and banquet tables. There was not even the consolation of inevitability to relieve the horror ... The most terrifying sights were the little children with skeleton limbs dangling from balloon-like abdomens. Starvation wiped every trace of youth from their faces, turning them into tortured gargoyles; only in their eyes still lingered the reminder of childhood."[13]

Of course, Stalin and his associates saw things differently. In 1933, Mendel Khataevich, another of Stalin's lieutenants in Ukraine and the leader of the grain-procurement program, proudly stated: "A ruthless struggle is going on between the peasantry and our regime. It's a struggle to the death. This year was a test of our strength and their endurance. It took a famine to show them who is master here. It has cost millions of lives, but the collective farm system is here to stay. We have won the war!"[14]

Soviet statistics for the period are notoriously unreliable (displeased with the results of the census of 1937 that revealed shockingly high mortality rates, Stalin had the leading census takers shot). And Soviet archival materials dealing with the Stalin era are still generally inaccessible. It is, therefore, difficult to establish conclusively how many died in the famine. Based on demographic extrapolations, estimates usually place the death toll in Ukraine at between 3 and 6 million.[15]

While famine raged in Ukraine, especially its southeastern regions, and in the north Caucasus (where many Ukrainians lived), much of Russia proper barely experienced it. One of the factors that helps to explain this peculiarity is that, according to the first FYP, "Ukraine ... was chosen to serve as a colossal laboratory for new forms of socioeconomic and productive-technical reconstruction of the rural economy for the entire Soviet Union."[16] Ukraine's importance to Soviet economic planners was also proclaimed in a *Pravda* editorial (7 January 1933) entitled "Ukraine – The Deciding Factor in Grain Collection." Consequently, the demands on the republic were inordinately great. As demonstrated by Vsevolod Holubnychy, although Ukraine accounted for 27% of the total all-union grain harvest, it bore 38% of the grain quotas.[17] Krawchenko contends that Ukrainian collective farmers were paid only half of what their Russian counterparts received.[18]

Given their tradition of private ownership of land, Ukrainians tended to resist collectivization more fiercely than did the Russians. Therefore, the regime made a point of pushing its policy – with its horrible consequences – faster and further in Ukraine than elsewhere. As Vasilii Grossman, a Soviet novelist and former party activist, put it: "It was clear that Moscow was basing its hopes on Ukraine. And the upshot of it was that most of the subsequent anger was directed against Ukraine ... We were told that in Ukraine they had an instinct for private property that was stronger than in the Russian republic. And truly, truly, the whole business was much worse in Ukraine than it was with us."[19]

Others argue that the famine was Stalin's way of weakening Ukrainian nationalism. Certainly the relationship between the peasantry and nationalism was not lost on the Soviet leadership. Stalin stated that "after all, the peasant question is the basis, the quintessence of the national question ... In essence, the national question is the peasant question."[20] A leading Communist paper in Ukraine in 1930 carried the equation further when it declared that "collectivization in Ukraine has a special task ... to destroy the social basis of Ukrainian nationalism – individually-owned peasant agriculture."[21] One can conclude therefore that, at best, Stalin viewed the deaths of millions as a necessary cost of industrialization. At worst, he consciously allowed the famine to wipe out resistance in a particularly troublesome region of his empire.

A noteworthy aspect of the famine was the attempts to erase it from public consciousness. Until very recently, the Soviet position was to deny that it occurred at all. If the full extent of the tragedy had become generally known, it would obviously have done serious damage to the progressive image Moscow was attempting to project both at home and abroad. Therefore, the regime has long suppressed open discussion of the famine in the USSR.[22]

Although some newspapers in the West informed the public about the famine, here, too, the realization of its horrendous scope was stifled. Soviet export of grain in the early 1930s and the regime's refusal to accept any foreign aid made it difficult for many Westerners to believe that a famine could be raging in Ukraine. After completing carefully staged tours of the USSR, Western luminaries such as George Bernard Shaw and the former French premier Edouard Herriot returned with glowing accounts of Soviet achievement and of contented, well-fed peasants. To curry Stalin's favor, Walter Duranty, the Moscow-based reporter of the *New York Times*, repeatedly denied the existence of a famine in his articles (while privately estimating that about 10 million people may have starved to death). For the "profundity, impartiality, sound judgment and exceptional clarity" of his dispatches from the USSR, Duranty received the Pulitzer Prize in 1932.

Although Western governments knew about the famine, their attitudes in this regard were similar to the one expressed in a British Foreign Office document: "The truth of the matter is, of course, that we have a certain amount of information about famine conditions in the south of Russia [sic], similar to that which has appeared in the press ... We do not want to make it public, however, because the Soviet government would resent it and our relations with them would be prejudiced."[23] Moreover, during the Great Depression, many Western intellectuals evinced strong pro-Soviet sympathies and vigorously dismissed all criticism of the USSR, especially on the question of the famine. As Conquest notes, "the scandal is not that they justified Soviet actions, but that they refused to hear about them, that they were not prepared to face the evidence."[24]

The Great Terror

Industrialization and collectivization brought with them increased centralization of power in Moscow. In Ukraine this meant that the dreams, illusions, and actual strides toward self-government that characterized the promising 1920s were doomed. Intent on the systematic destruction of almost all aspects of autonomy, Stalin sought to transform the republic into a mere administrative unit of the Soviet Union. And all who stood in his way were marked for liquidation.

In the first phase of Stalin's attack on potential opposition in Ukraine (there was very little actual resistance), the main target was the old Ukrainian intelligentsia, especially those who had been associated with the national governments and non-Bolshevik parties of 1917–20 and who were prominent in areas of culture and scholarship. After fabricating "secret anti-Soviet organizations," the OGPU forced its victims, by means of physical and/or psychological torture, to admit membership in them at highly publicized show trials. In this manner the political police justified the punishment of the accused, discredited all who shared their views, and prepared the way for more arrests.

In Ukraine this tactic was first applied in 1929–30 when forty-five leading scholars, writers, and other intellectuals, including Serhii Efremov, Volodymyr Chekhivsky, Andrii Nikovsky, Osyp Hermaize, Mykhailo Slabchenko, Hryhorii Holoskevych, and Liudmyla Starytska-Cherniakhivska, were accused of belonging to a secret nationalist organization called the Union for the Liberation of Ukraine (Spilka Vyzvolennia Ukrainy – SVU). The goals of the alleged organization were supposedly the separation of Ukraine from the USSR with the aid of foreign powers and émigrés, the organization of peasant resistance to collectivization, and the assassination of Stalin and his associates. Having used the trial to create an atmosphere of suspicion and insecurity, Soviet authorities now launched a broadly based offensive against the intellectual elite.

As might be expected, the All-Ukrainian Academy of Sciences was one of the first institutions to bear the brunt of the attack. After the SVU trial, in which many members of the academy were implicated, the government began to censor the academy's publications, close down its most active sections, and expel "bourgeois nationalists." In 1931 Hrushevsky's history sections were abolished, and he was implicated in yet another secret organization and exiled to Russia, where he died in 1934. Many of his colleagues and almost all of his students were treated much more harshly.

The SVU trial also signaled the destruction of the Ukrainian Autocephalous Orthodox church. Accused of collaborating with that secret organization, the church leadership was forced to call a *sobor* (church council) in January 1930 and to dissolve itself. Soon afterward, the metropolitan (Mykola Boretsky), dozens of bishops, and hundreds of priests were sent to labor camps.

Even before the first wave of repression had run its course, Stalin launched another in 1933. This time it was directed primarily against party members. Purges or "cleansings" were not a new occurrence; in the 1920s they were initiated periodically to "purify" the party by expelling inactive, opportunistic, lax, or otherwise unfit members. But in the 1930s they took on an ominous, terrifying aspect. Party members were purged mostly because of "ideological mistakes and failings," that is, because they disagreed or were perceived to disagree with Stalin. Expulsion from the party usually entailed execution or exile. Consequently, terror became a part of life not only for the masses but even for the Communist elite.

In the Soviet Union as a whole, the high point of the Stalinist purges came in 1937–38, but as Lev Kopelev noted, "In Ukraine 1937 began in 1933."[25] It was probably the threat of national communism on the one hand, and the demor- alization of the Ukrainian Communists by the horrors of collectivization and the famine on the other, that singled out the Ukrainians for special attention. The coming storm was heralded by an ideological shift in Moscow. For years the party had officially reiterated that Russian chauvinism was the primary threat to the Soviet system, while the nationalism of the non-Russians was less dangerous because it was essentially a reaction to the former. However, in 1933 Stalin's spokesmen, arguing that Ukrainian nationalism had greatly increased as a result of kulak support, labeled it as Ukraine's most serious problem. Thus, the way was cleared for the persecution of those Ukrainian Communists who had been closely linked with Ukrainization.

Stalin's dissatisfaction with Ukrainization was not surprising. The Ukrain- ian countryside had never supported the Bolsheviks and as masses of peas- ants poured into the cities – traditionally the bases of Communist support – the possibility that these centers would become breeding grounds for Ukrain- ian nationalism and separatism became real. A more immediate reason for Stalin's intention to "cleanse" the CP(b)U was its supposedly poor perfor- mance during collectivization. Having decided to make Ukraine's Commu- nists the scapegoats for the disasters of 1932–33, Stalin sanctioned the open criticism of Ukrainian Communists. As a result, editorials in *Pravda* and reso- lutions of the All-Union Central Committee condemned the Ukrainian Com- munists for "lack of vigilance" and softness in dealing with kulaks and grain procurements.

The Ukrainian Communists' dilemma was tragic. Confronted by Stalin's demands on the one hand, and the terrible plight of Ukraine's populace on the other, they could neither satisfy the former nor help the latter. Deprived of Moscow's good graces and lacking popular support, the CP(b)U was help- less. The most painful blow came in January 1933 when Stalin appointed Pavel Postyshev to act as his personal representative and, in effect, viceroy of Ukraine. Along with Postyshev came Vsevolod Balitsky, the new head of the OGPU, and thousands of Russian functionaries. It was clear that the days when Ukrainian Communists had "run their own show" in Ukraine were over.

Postyshev's mandate was to complete collectivization regardless of the cost, purge the Ukrainian party, and end Ukrainization. He replaced thousands of local officials in the countryside with his own men. Simultaneously, he launched an attack on the Ukrainizers. Denouncing the emphasis on "national specificity" as a "refusal to submit to all-union interests," he described Ukrainization as a "cultural counter-revolution" whose aim was to fan "national enmity among the proletariat" and "to isolate the Ukrainian workers from the positive influence of Russian culture."[26]

The primary target of these attacks was Skrypnyk, the commissar of education. Rather than retract his support for Ukrainization, Skrypnyk committed suicide on 7 July 1933. Several months earlier, Khvylovy had done the same. The other ideologue of Ukrainian national communism, Shumsky, died in exile. As Postyshev's reign of terror gained momentum, members of the new Soviet intelligentsia that had emerged in the 1920s were executed or exiled by the thousands. According to some estimates, 200 of 240 authors writing at this time in Ukraine disappeared. Of the 85 scholars in the field of linguistics, 62 were liquidated. Philosophers, artists, and editors were denounced as spies or terrorists and arrested. Matvii Iavorsky and his associates at the Ukrainian Institute of Marxism-Leninism who tried to develop a Marxist history of Ukraine were sent to the Siberian camps. Kurbas' experimental Berezil Theater was shut down and he, too, disappeared into a labor camp, as did the playwright Kulish. Dovzhenko's world-famous films were removed from circulation and he was forced to move to Moscow. Several hundred *kobzari* (wandering bards) were invited to a congress, arrested, and reportedly shot. To save themselves, some writers like Bazhan and Tychyna began writing according to the dictates of Moscow.

The destruction of Ukrainian institutions, begun in 1930, now reached its high point. The commissariats of education, agriculture, justice, the Agricultural Academy, the editorial boards of newspapers, literary journals, encyclopedias, and film studios were denounced as "nests of nationalist counter-revolutionaries" and purged. Summing up the results of his work in November 1933, Postyshev boasted that "the discovery of Skrypnyk's nationalist deviation gave us the opportunity to rid ... the structure of Ukrainian socialist culture of all ... nationalist elements. A great job has been done. It is enough to say that we cleaned out 2000 men of the nationalist element, about 300 of them scholars and writers, from the People's Commissariat of Education alone."[27]

But Postyshev's purge was aimed at Ukraine's political elite as well as its cultural activists. Over 15,000 people holding responsible positions were purged on charges of nationalism. In addition to nationalism, party members were accused of "fascism," "Trotskyism," "lack of Bolshevik vigilance," and links with émigrés and foreign powers. Consequently, between January 1933 and January 1934, the CPU lost about 100,000 members. In his report, Postyshev noted that "almost all the people removed were arrested and put before the firing squad or exiled."[28] Even Trotsky admitted that "nowhere do repression, purges, subjugation and all types of bureaucratic hooliganism in general assume such deadly proportions as in Ukraine in the struggle against powerful subterranean strivings among the Ukrainian masses towards greater freedom and independence."[29]

While the waves of repression that rolled across Ukraine in the early 1930s were mainly directed against Ukrainians, the Great Purge of 1937–38 encompassed the entire Soviet Union and all categories of people. Its goal was to sweep away all of Stalin's real and imaginary enemies and to infuse all levels of Soviet society, especially upper echelons, with a sense of insecurity and abject dependence on and obedience to the "Great Leader." In a series of sensational show trials, almost all the "founding fathers" of bolshevism (and the potential rivals of Stalin) were discredited and subsequently executed. The political police, now referred to as the NKVD, repeatedly fabricated plots and terrorist groups to implicate ever broadening circles of people. The usual sentence was summary execution or, at best, lengthy terms in Siberian concentration camps. To assure themselves of an endless supply of "traitors," the NKVD interrogators concentrated on two questions: "Who recruited you?" and "Whom did you recruit?" The "confessions" often doomed casual acquaintances, friends, and even family. Even at a time when the threat of war in Europe was rising, much of the military leadership – the only remaining base of potential opposition – was executed. It was at this point that Stalin's method began to show definite signs of madness.

Again Ukraine was among the worst-hit areas. Unlike the purges of 1933, during which opponents of collectivization and Ukrainizers had been purged, in 1937 Stalin decided to liquidate the entire leadership of the Ukrainian Soviet government and the CPU. The factors that influenced this decision were surprising. Apparently after the famine, Postyshev (the ruthless Russian implementer of the purge of 1933) began to have doubts about Stalin's methods and to identify with Ukraine and Ukrainian interests. More important, both Postyshev and the Ukrainian Communist leadership had refused to carry the purge as far as Stalin wished. Even after the removal of Postyshev and the arrival in Ukraine of Stalin's personal representatives – Viacheslav Molotov, Nikolai Ezhov, and Nikita Khrushchev – in Kiev in August 1937, Ukraine's Communist leadership, consisting of Stanislav Kossior, Hryhorii Petrovsky, and Panas Liubchenko, continued to oppose the purge. As a result, by June 1938 the top seventeen ministers of the Ukrainian Soviet government were arrested and executed. The prime minister, Liubchenko, committed suicide. Almost the entire Central Committee and Politburo of Ukraine perished. An estimated 37% of the Communist party members in Ukraine – about 170,000 people – were purged. In the words of Nikita Khrushchev, Moscow's new viceroy in Kiev, the Ukrainian party "had been purged spotless."

The NKVD slated for extermination entire categories of people, such as kulaks, priests, former members of anti-Bolshevik armies, those who had been abroad or had relatives abroad, and immigrants from Galicia; even average citizens perished in huge numbers. An indication of the vast scope of the Great Purge was the discovery, during the Second World War, in Vinnytsia, of a mass grave containing 10,000 bodies of residents of the region who were shot between 1937 and 1938. Given the lack of complete data, it is difficult for Western scholars to establish the total loss of life brought about by the Stalinist terror. Adam Ulam and others estimate that in the Soviet Union as a whole, about 500,000 were executed in 1937–39 and somewhere between 3 and 12 million were sent to labor camps.[30] One can assume in light of the above-mentioned factors that Ukraine's share of those who were victimized was disproportionately high.

By the late 1930s, the limited self-government that Ukrainians (and other non-Russians) had possessed earlier was almost totally obliterated. Control over all aspects of life was now completely centered in Moscow. Ignoring the prerogatives, wishes, and protests of Ukrainian Communists, Stalin ruled Ukraine by means of his personal emissaries, such as Postyshev and Khrushchev. Despite its economic importance, Ukraine lost all control over the allocation of its resources and investment, the development of industry, and, most important, agricultural policy. In fact, at the height of the famine, the Ukrainian Soviet government could not dispose of one pound of grain without permission from Moscow. Cultural institutions that developed Ukrainian "specificity" were abolished or emasculated. The distinctive features of the republic's system of higher education were removed, and all-union models replaced the school textbooks Skrypnyk had introduced. Indeed, centralization and standardization had gone so far that on several occasions Stalin and his closest associates even discussed abolishing the Soviet Union's republican structure altogether.

Stalin liked to mix crushing policies with minor, propagandistic concessions. Thus, in 1934, in the midst of the centralization drive, the capital of Ukraine was moved from Kharkiv to Kiev, the traditional center. In 1936 Stalin repeated the ploy. On the eve of the Great Purge, he presented the people of the USSR with a new constitution that assured them of all the civil rights enjoyed by citizens of "bourgeois democracies." He declared the Supreme Soviet or parliament, which consisted of a Soviet of the Union and a Soviet of Nationalities, to be the highest organ of state power. He reiterated the right of republics to secede and expanded their number from four to eleven by subdividing the Central Asian and Caucasian regions. A famous example of Stalin's cynicism was his statement, made in the midst of the horrors of the 1930s, that "life has become better, comrades, life has become gayer."

The End of Ukrainization

With centralization came Russification. Initially, in 1933, it took the form of an influx into Ukraine of thousands of Russian functionaries to reinforce the collectivization drive. By the end of the decade, after the purge of the national communists, much of the top party and government leadership in Ukraine, with Nikita Khrushchev at its head, was Russian. Indeed, some scholars have characterized these changes in Ukraine's political elite as "the return of the Russians."

Behind the personnel changes was the decisive shift in Moscow's nationality policy that occurred in 1933 when Stalin declared local nationalism (not Russian chauvinism) the main threat to Soviet unity. This ideological reversal signaled the end of Ukrainization and ushered in a policy of systematic discrimination against Ukrainian culture. The number of Ukrainian-language schools was reduced; the percentage of Ukrainian teachers and researchers declined markedly; outstanding works of Ukrainian scholarship and literature were removed from library bookshelves; hundreds of Ukrainian plays were banned and scores of Ukrainian theaters closed; and museum staffs received orders to stop "idealizing Cossack history." At every opportunity the authorities disparaged "the nationalist theory of the specificity of Ukraine."

Simultaneously, there was a glorification of all aspects of Russian culture and an emphasis on Russia's leading role in the USSR. However, all this was done under the guise of fostering internationalism, proletarian solidarity, and the "friendship of peoples." Thus, in 1936, Stalin argued that the distinctions between Soviet nations were declining: "The characteristics of the peoples of the USSR have been changed at their very roots ... the spirit of distrust among them has disappeared, the spirit of cooperative friendship has developed, and ... in such a manner there has been constructed the present brotherly cooperation of peoples in a system of a single union state."[31]

Not unexpectedly, Soviet ideologists then concluded that the Russian language and culture were best suited for fostering international friendship, cooperation, and progress. In a typical statement, one of them claimed: "The Russian language is studied by the toilers of the whole world. In his time Marx paid tribute to the mighty Russian language, studying it and utilizing in his work primary sources in the Russian language ... In our situation the Russian language is the language of the international community of peoples of the USSR. Knowledge of the Russian language enables the peoples of the USSR to acquire the highest cultural values."[32]

Sullivant notes that not only was their language praised, but also the Russians themselves were idealized for their revolutionary successes and "clothed with the mystical cloak of Marxian superiority over the other peoples in the Soviet Union and throughout the world."[33] An example of this new propaganda line was the following statement: "The Russian people are a great people. They have advanced the movement of all mankind toward the triumph of democracy and socialism. Under the leadership of their working class, the most advanced in the world, the Russian people have been the first in history to be liberated from capitalist oppression and exploitation. The Russian working class has helped to liberate from national, political and economic oppression the whole numerous family of peoples inhabiting former tsarist Russia."[34]

With claims such as these, Soviet ideologists could argue – and they do so to this day – that Stalin's new policy was not a return to traditional Russian chauvinism, but a quicker way to progress, socialism, and internationalism. By implication, they also suggested that the culture of Ukrainians and other non-Russians fostered backwardness and provincialism.

Consequently, in the late 1930s the study of Russian became compulsory in Ukrainian schools; the Ukrainian alphabet, grammar, and vocabulary were drawn closer to the Russian; and the use of Russian in Ukraine generally increased. As early as 1935, Postyshev admitted that "members [of the Communist Party of Ukraine] have begun to de-Ukrainianize themselves and even to stop speaking in Ukrainian."[35] In the printed media there was a similar development: whereas in 1931 about 90% of the newspapers and 85% of the journals had appeared in Ukrainian, by 1940 the respective figures had dropped to 70% and 45%. In literature it became a matter of policy to extol great Russian writers such as Pushkin, Dostoevsky, and Tolstoy, and to emphasize how such Ukrainian authors as Shevchenko had developed under their beneficial influence. In sharp contrast to the late 1920s, when the authorities supported the Ukrainization of the cities, a decade later they energetically worked to expand Russian cultural influences into the countryside.

୧ଈ

Stalin's "revolution from above" introduced staggering changes in the conditions under which Ukrainians and other peoples of the USSR lived. Industry became the main component of the economy. The cities began the remarkable growth that several decades later made them the main abode of the land's inhabitants. Agriculture underwent a radical transformation, one of the key elements of which was the liquidation of private landholding. Such changes, and particularly collectivization in Ukraine, were accomplished through the unprecedented use of coercion and at the cost of tremendous loss of life. Whatever benefits Soviet modernization brought to Ukraine, they will always invite the rejoinder that the costs were needlessly high.

In addition to material changes, Stalin exerted an incalculable impact on the political and cultural life of Ukrainians. The two social bases of Ukrainian nationalism, the intelligentsia and the peasantry, were exactly the groups that bore the greatest losses in Stalin's terror campaigns. As a result, the drive for Ukrainian self-assertion, which appeared to be gathering momentum in the 1920s, lost untold numbers of supporters. This setback was most apparent among two generations of the Ukrainian intelligentsia – those who were active before the revolution and those who came to the forefront in the 1920s. It was these two generations of intelligentsia who had a crucial role to play in nation-building and it was they who were decimated by Stalin. The draining effect of the tremendous demographic losses in the 1930s helps to explain the relative weakness of political will and cultural stagnation that Soviet Ukrainians would evince in the coming years. Finally, Stalin reversed a very important and promising trend in Ukraine. In the 1920s modernization and Ukrainization had merged to a large extent. But when Stalin destroyed the Ukrainian elite in the 1930s and renewed Russification, modernity took on a Russian guise again. Ukrainian culture, meanwhile, was manipulated into focusing once more on its traditional identification with the conservative, backward village.

Western Ukraine between the Wars

A new political order emerged in Eastern Europe after the First World War as nation-states replaced the empires that had, until recently, ruled the region. But although it had won universal acceptance, the principle of national self-determination had been applied unevenly with the result that not all nations obtained statehood. Those that did had large, restive national minorities. Thus, during the interwar period, the nationality question remained unresolved; as tensions between dominant nationalities and disadvantaged minorities increased, it became an explosive issue. And the socioeconomic problems that had plagued the region from the age of the empires only aggravated the situation.

Approximately 7 million West Ukrainians, mostly former subjects of the Habsburg empire, were the only major nationality in Eastern Europe that did not achieve independence at this time. The majority was incorporated into Poland; the rest lived in Romania and Czechoslovakia. As the target of discriminatory policies everywhere, but most of all in Poland and Romania, the West Ukrainians developed an almost obsessive desire for self-rule, which they regarded as the solution to their political, socioeconomic, and cultural problems. Because their aspirations clashed with the assimilationist policies of the states in which they lived, the politics of national confrontation dominated the lives of the West Ukrainians throughout the interwar period.

૨૦

The New Status of the West Ukrainians

Although Poland won the military conflict in Eastern Galicia in 1919, from the points of view of international law and the Entente powers, its right to rule the West Ukrainians remained at issue. Given its formal commitment to the principle of national self-determination, the Entente could not ignore the

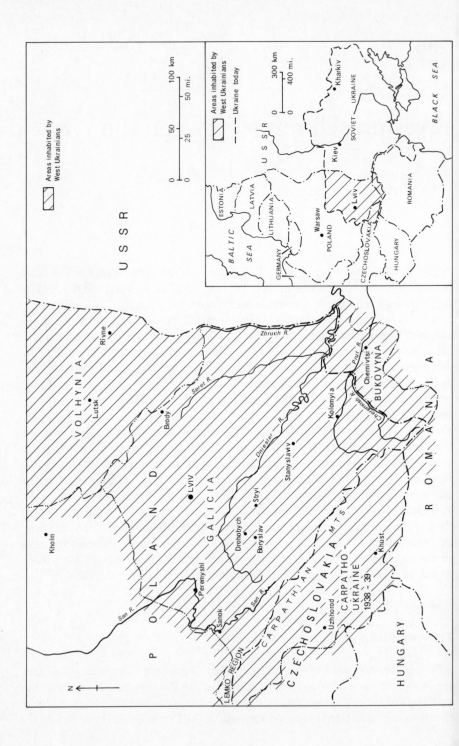

Areas inhabited by
West Ukrainians

0   50   100 km
0   25   50 mi.

Areas inhabited by
West Ukrainians

‒‒‒ Ukraine today

0   300 km
0   400 mi.

U S S R

BLACK
SEA

BALTIC
SEA

ESTONIA

LATVIA

LITHUANIA

GERMANY

Warsaw
POLAND

Kiev

Kharkiv

SOVIET
UKRAINE

LVIV

CZECHOSLOVAKIA

HUNGARY

ROMANIA

U S S R

VOLHYNIA

Rivne

Lutsk

Brody

Kholm

P   O   L   A   N   D

LVIV

G A L I C I A

Peremyshl

San R.

Sanok

LEMKO REGION

San R.

Drohobych

Boryslav

Stryi

Stanyslaviv

Dniester R.

Seret R.

Zbruch R.

Kolomyia

Prut R.

Chernivtsi

BUKOVYNA

Cheremosh R.

C A R P A T H I A N   MTS

CZECHOSLOVAKIA

CARPATHO-
UKRAINE
1938 - 39

Uzhhorod

Khust

HUNGARY

R   O   M   A   N   I   A

protests of the West Ukrainians against the imposition on them of Polish rule. Therefore, until 1923, the Western powers – primarily England and France – continued to deliberate over the permanent status of Eastern Galicia. In the meantime, however, they acquiesced to Poland's administration of the land on the condition that it grant the region autonomous administration and respect Ukrainian national rights.

A phrase that best describes the tense relationship in Eastern Galicia existing between the Ukrainian majority and the new Polish administration during the unsettled period of 1919–23 is "mutual negation." Until the Council of Ambassadors in Versailles reached its decision, the Ukrainians in Galicia refused to recognize the Polish state as their legitimate government. They boycotted the census of 1921 and the elections to the Polish *sejm* (parliament) in 1922. More radical elements among them turned to terror tactics and sabotage against Polish officials and government installations. For its part, the Polish goverment acted as if Eastern Galicia were a completely Polish land, imposing Polish control over the political, cultural, and economic life of the region, and totally ignoring Ukrainian concerns.

For the sake of international opinion, however, the Poles repeatedly proclaimed their readiness to respect the national rights of the Ukrainians and other minorities in their new state. In fact, this commitment was enshrined in their constitution. Consequently, in 1923, after the Polish government once again assured the Western powers that it would grant Eastern Galicia autonomy, allow the use of Ukrainian alongside Polish in administration, and establish a university for the Ukrainians, the Council of Ambassadors recognized Polish sovereignty over Eastern Galicia. The decision was a demoralizing setback for the Galician Ukrainians because, in their view, it placed them at the mercy of their worst enemies.

Its discriminatory policies notwithstanding, Poland was a state based on constitutional principles. While elections to its bicameral parliament were manipulated at times, for the most part they were relatively free. Even after 1926, when Marshal Józef Piłsudski staged a military coup, the rule of law remained in effect (although it was often interpreted in favor of Polish state interests). Consequently, Polish laws provided Ukrainians with the means, albeit limited, of opposing or at least protesting against state policies. This meant that, despite their second-class status, the Ukrainians in Poland were politically better off than their compatriots in the USSR.

The newly formed Polish state contained one of the highest percentages of national minorities in all Europe. In 1921, about one-third of its 27 million inhabitants were Ukrainians, Jews, Belorussians, Germans, and other non-Poles. The Ukrainians were by far the largest national minority, numbering well over 5 million and constituting about 15% of the state's inhabitants (minority statistics were a highly controversial matter in interwar Poland and Polish sources claimed that there were only about 4.5 million Ukrainians, while Ukrainians insisted that they numbered over 6 million). Thus, the numerical preponderance of the Polish majority was not so vast as to allow them to ignore completely and consistently the aspirations of the non-Poles.

Ukrainians in Poland constituted two distinct communities (and the government did everything in its power to emphasize these distinctions). The majority lived in the former Habsburg land of Eastern Galicia or Eastern Little Poland (Małopolska Wschodnia), as it was now called. In 1920 this region was subdivided into the three *wojewódstwa* or provinces of Lviv, Ternopil, and Stanyslaviv. Overwhelmingly Greek Catholic, the more than 3 million Galician Ukrainians were nationally conscious and relatively well organized. The rest of the Ukrainians inhabited western Volhynia, Polissia, and Kholm, areas that Poland had acquired from Russia. They numbered approximately 2 million and were mostly Orthodox; they were also politically, socioeconomically, and culturally underdeveloped.

Poland's Policies toward the Ukrainians

Polish claims to the lands inhabited by the West Ukrainians rested on historical arguments. In the late 18th century, these territories had been part of the Polish Commonwealth and the Poles believed that they should also be part of the Polish state that emerged in 1919. The presence in these lands of substantial and dominant Polish minorities reinforced this view. As for the vast majority of the inhabitants in the eastern borderlands (*kresy*) who were not Polish, the government's intention was to Polonize them. Belief in the efficacy of Polonization rested on two assumptions: that the attractiveness of Polish culture was so great that non-Poles would willingly adopt it and that the national movements among the minorities were too weak to withstand Polish pressure. As it happened, the Poles erred on both counts.

Although generally repressive, Polish policy toward the Ukrainians did have its variations. While the powerful, ultranationalist National Democrats, led by Roman Dmowski and supported by the Polish minority in Eastern Galicia, consistently advocated militantly anti-Ukrainian policies, some highly respected Poles, such as Leon Wasilewski and Tadeusz Hołówko, urged moderation and flexibility in dealing with the minorities. The central authorities in Warsaw from time to time announced concessions to the Ukrainians, but hard-line local administrators, police officials, and army commanders refused to implement them. There were also regional differences. The governor of Volhynia, Henryk Józewski, attempted to entice Ukrainians into supporting the state by granting them limited concessions, while the government's repressive measures in neighboring Galicia reached a high point of brutality. Finally, there was the glaring contradiction between the Polish government's support of the Warsaw-based East Ukrainian government-in-exile (which could be useful in case of war with the

USSR) and its refusal to recognize the political aspirations of West Ukrainians. In the final analysis, however, the Polish government pursued a policy of confrontation in its dealings with the large Ukrainian minority. In 1924 the government passed a law banning the use of Ukrainian in government agencies. That same year, the openly anti-Ukrainian minister of education, Stanisław Grabski, introduced reforms – the notorious *Lex Grabski* – that transformed most Ukrainian-language schools into bilingual institutions in which Polish predominated. Ukrainians were excluded from Lviv University; its Ukrainian chairs were abolished; and the promise to establish a Ukrainian university at government expense was never fulfilled.

An especially galling feature of these early Polish policies for the Ukrainian peasantry was the colonization program. In order to strengthen the Polish presence in the eastern borderlands, in 1920 the government began to bring Polish settlers into Eastern Galicia and Volhynia. Initially, army veterans made up most of the colonists, especially in Volhynia; later, civilian newcomers predominated. Despite the fact that Galicia was one of the most overpopulated agricultural regions in Europe, the Polish settlers received large allotments of the best land as well as generous financial subsidies. Those who chose not to work on the land obtained privileged positions as village policemen, postal and railroad employees, or petty officials. Ukrainian sources claim that by 1938 about 200,000 Poles had moved into the villages of Eastern Galicia and Volhynia and another 100,000 settled in the towns; Polish writers place the total number of colonists at less than 100,000. In any case, while it was too small to alter decisively the ethnic composition of the eastern lands, the influx of Polish newcomers was large enough to arouse fierce Ukrainian resentment.

Although the Piłsudski coup of 1926 ushered in a more authoritarian Polish government, there were initial indications that relations between it and the Ukrainians might improve. The personification of this new approach was Henryk Józewski, who was appointed governor of Volhynia in 1927. He succeeded in winning some goodwill among the Ukrainian peasants by distributing much of the government's parceled lands to the local inhabitants. He also made limited concessions to the political leadership of the Volhynian Ukrainians, while attempting to isolate them from the "destructive influences" of the more nationalistic Galicians. But religious discrimination against the Orthodox Volhynians and the adamant opposition of local officials and Polish nationalists eventually undermined Józewski's efforts.

Ukrainian/Polish relations deteriorated badly during the Great Depression, which struck the Ukrainian-inhabited agricultural areas especially hard. Peasants suffered not so much from the lack of employment as from the disastrous decline in their incomes resulting from a drop in demand for their produce. During these years of economic crisis, the net return per acre on small peasant landholdings dropped by 70–80%. Under the circumstances, the Ukrainian peasants' resentment of the well-subsidized Polish colonists and the wealthy Polish landowners reached new heights. Dissatisfaction among the Ukrainian intelligentsia, and especially among its young (and unemployed) members, also grew because the few government positions that were available invariably went to Poles. Therefore, when the radical Ukrainian nationalists called for active resistance to Polish domination, they found a ready response among Ukrainian youths.

The Pacification   In the summer of 1930 there was a wave of attacks against Polish property in Galicia. These usually took the form of burning the produce on Polish estates. About 2200 such acts of sabotage were recorded. The government's response was massive and brutal. In mid September, large Polish police and cavalry units descended on the Ukrainian countryside and commenced a "pacification" campaign intended to restore order. Employing the principle of collective responsibility, armed units moved into about 800 villages, demolished Ukrainian community centers and libraries, confiscated property and produce, and beat those who protested. Over 2000 Ukrainians, mostly schoolboys, students, and young peasants, were arrested and about one-third of them received lengthy prison sentences. The Ukrainian deputies to the parliament were placed under house arrest to prevent them from participating in the elections that were taking place at this time and their Ukrainian constituents were terrorized into voting for Polish candidates.

Ukrainian protests to the League of Nations made the plight of the Ukrainian minority in Poland in general, and the "pacification" in particular, an international cause célèbre. But while European (and especially British) politicians condemned Polish behavior, a committee of the League of Nations blamed Ukrainian extremists for provoking the "pacification." Although the Polish government soon quelled the disturbances, in the long run its actions only intensified Ukrainian bitterness, encouraged extremists on both sides, and made the search for constructive solutions even more difficult.

While the "pacification" brought a semblance of order to the countryside, it did not break the determination of the young, radical nationalists to resist the Polish regime. The OUN (Orhanizatsiia Ukrainskykh Nationalistiv – Organization of Ukrainian Nationalists) merely changed tactics and in the early 1930s concentrated its efforts on the political assassination of leading Polish politicians and government officials, as well as on attacks on post offices to obtain funds for its activities. The government, for its part, maintained its uncompromising stance toward the Ukrainians. It abolished self-government in the villages and placed them under the administration of Polish officials. In 1934 a concentration camp was established in Bereza Kartuzka for about 2000 political prisoners, most of whom were Ukrainians. Later that year, Poland repudiated the commitment it had made to the League of Nations to safeguard the rights of its national minorities.

These policies of the government reflected the swing to the extreme right taking place in Poland during the 1930s. In 1935 a new constitution concentrated power in the hands of Marshal Piłsudski, curbing the authority of parliament and declaring the interests of the state to be paramount. The electoral process was reorganized to give the government the prerogative of accepting or rejecting candidates for elected office. After the death of Piłsudski in that same year, military cliques played an increasingly dominant role in the conduct of government. Consequently, the Polish state "completed the transition from a democratic-parliamentary framework to a totalitarian one."[1]

Attempts at compromise   There were, however, moderates in both the Polish and Ukrainian camps who grew impatient with the continuing and fruitless Polish/Ukrainian confrontations. On the Ukrainian side, UNDO (Ukrainian National Democratic Union), the largest Ukrainian political party, emerged as a proponent of compromise. Its leaders were clearly disillusioned with OUN violence and the reprisals that it provoked against Ukrainians as a whole. They were also under pressure from the strong Ukrainian cooperative movement (which needed stability to function effectively) to work toward a rapprochment. On the Polish side, there were also indications of a willingness to compromise. In 1933 the government established the *Polish-Ukrainian Bulletin*, a journal that sought to emphasize the positive aspects of Ukrainian/Polish relations. Soon afterwards, the prime minister, Wacław Jędrzejewicz, publicly admitted that mistakes had been made by "both sides." Paradoxically, the OUN's assassination in 1934 of Bronisław Pieracki, the minister of the interior, hastened the rapprochement because, to the government's great satisfaction, both the UNDO and Metropolitan Sheptytsky strongly denounced the act. Thus, in 1935, the stage was set for a limited agreement between the government and UNDO, which came to be known as "normalization."

The arrangement called for the Ukrainians to recognize formally the primacy of Polish state interests and to vote for the new budget. In return, the government allowed UNDO's candidates to stand for election, thus greatly increasing Ukrainian representation in parliament. After the elections, the government made several more concessions. Vasyl Mudry, the leader of UNDO, was chosen vice-marshal (speaker) of the *sejm*. Most of the Ukrainian prisoners in Bereza Kartuzka were freed. And some Ukrainian economic institutions and cooperatives received financial credits. For many members of UNDO it seemed that life under Polish rule could become bearable, especially in view of the horrors that Ukrainians under Soviet rule were experiencing at this time.

But "normalization" was not universally accepted by the Ukrainians. Dissident members of UNDO and other Ukrainian parties attacked the UNDO leadership for "accepting crumbs from the Polish table." Not unexpectedly, the radical nationalists rejected "normalization" and continued their revolutionary activities. Finally, the deep-seated mistrust of Poles in Ukrainian society as a whole fueled widespread skepticism about the success of the rapprochement. Polish attitudes and actions also served to undermine "normalization." Despite the central government's concessions, in the eastern provinces almost every governor, county administrator, and even local police chief adhered to his own, invariably harsh, method of "handling" the Ukrainians. The officials usually had the support of the local Polish minority for this approach. Indeed, when Polish mobs demolished Ukrainian institutions, they often did so in secret collusion with local Polish officials. Polish youths, organized in the armed, paramilitary units of *Strzelcy*, frequently harassed Ukrainians under the guise of helping to maintain law and order. In 1938, the feared border police carried out a "mini-pacification" of areas along the Soviet border inhabited by Ukrainians.

Perhaps the most adamant opponent of "normalization" was the Polish military. As the threat of war increased in the late 1930s, the army leadership came to view the disaffected Ukrainians as a major security problem. To eliminate or reduce this problem, the army applied "divide-and-rule" tactics. In 1938 it launched a campaign to encourage the Ukrainian-speaking Hutsuls, Lemkos, and Boikos of the Carpathian highlands to view themselves as distinct peoples and not as part of the larger Ukrainian nation. Attempts were made to develop the Lemko dialect into a separate language and Lemkos were urged to convert from Greek Catholicism to Orthodoxy in order to create a barrier between them and the Galician Ukrainians. A variant of this approach was the army's efforts to persuade the impoverished or "barefoot" Ukrainian gentry, which, except for its treasured titles of nobility, was identical to the Ukrainian peasantry, that it was both nationally and socially distinct from it.

Meanwhile, in Volhynia, Polish authorities continued their attack on the Orthodox church, the main pillar of Ukrainian identity in the region. Arguing that most of the churches in Volhynia and the Kholm region had once belonged to the Greek Catholics or Roman Catholics, the authorities transferred about 150 Orthodox churches to the latter and destroyed another 190. Thus, of the 389 Orthodox churches in Volhynia in 1914, only 51 survived in 1939. Similar pressures were applied in neighboring Kholm and Polissia regions where armed bands of colonists called *Krakus* terrorized the local inhabitants into converting to Catholicism and where the administration of the Orthodox church, theological training, and even sermons were conducted in Polish.

Socioeconomic Conditions

Despite the vast political transformations experienced by West Ukrainians as a result of the collapse of the Austrian and Russian empires, the struggle for independent statehood, and their inclusion into Poland, the socioeconomic conditions in which they lived remained essentially unchanged. The Ukrainian-inhabited lands, which constituted about 25% of Poland's territory, remained underdeveloped agrarian borderlands or internal colonies that supplied cheap raw resources to the core areas of Poland and bought their high-priced finished products.

Even by Polish standards, the Ukrainians were extremely agrarian: about 80% were peasants compared to the Polish average of 50%, and only 8% were industrial workers compared to the Polish average of 20%. In addition to these structural disadvantages, the Ukrainian populace had to deal with such problems as the wartime devastation; the government's discriminatory economic policies towards them; and the impact of the Great Depression. In short, the socioeconomic plight of the West Ukrainians under Polish rule remained as unsatisfactory as their political status.

As might be expected, the main economic difficulties lay in agriculture, where old problems, such as rural overpopulation and tiny plots, persisted from pre–First World War days. In the Ukrainian-inhabited provinces of Poland, about 1.2 million peasant households owned 60% of the land. The problem was especially acute in Galicia, where the size of over 75% of the peasant plots was less than 10 acres. Meanwhile, about 2000 large estates, owned by Poles and sometimes consisting of 10,000–20,000 acres, controlled close to 25% of the land. In Volhynia, where there were fewer large Polish landowners, the soil was richer and peasant plots were larger, so that conditions in the countryside were somewhat better.

To alleviate the acute shortage of land, the government encouraged the subdivision of large estates in the 1920s. However, the program was of little benefit to Ukrainians in Galicia because most of the subdivided lands went to Polish peasants and newly arrived colonists. Emigration also proved to be less effective than before in alleviating the rural overpopulation because, during the interwar period, the United States and, to a lesser extent, Canada reduced the numbers of immigrants they were willing to receive. As a result, only about 170,000 West Ukrainians emigrated during that time.

Industry continued to offer few options to a Ukrainian peasant anxious to better his lot. The eastern borderlands had a disproportionately small share of Poland's weakly developed industry; it grew even smaller in the 1930s when the government supported industrial growth in central Poland while neglecting the largely non-Polish provinces. Only about 135,000 West Ukrainians were employed as workers, mostly in the forestry and oil industries. Lviv, with a population of about 300,000, most of which was Polish and Jewish, remained the largest urban center in Galicia.

As before the First World War, the intelligentsia continued to provide the political, cultural, and even socioeconomic leadership in West Ukrainian society. But unlike in the 19th century when priests constituted much of this class, during the interwar period the overwhelming majority of the intelligentsia was secular. According to Polish scholars, in the 1930s about 1% of the West Ukrainian working population or about 15,000 individuals belonged to the intelligentsia (among Poles the analogous figure was 5%).[2] A major reason for the comparatively small number of educated Ukrainians was the Polish government's policy of hindering access to higher education for non-Poles. Thus, in Lviv University, Ukrainians constituted less than 10% of the student body.

For the most part, the members of the Ukrainian intelligentsia earned their living as teachers or white-collar workers in the rapidly growing cooperative movement. Some Ukrainians began to enter professions such as law, medicine, pharmacy, and engineering, where Poles and Jews had long held a monopoly. Yet, one of the most common white-collar careers in Eastern Europe – government service – was practically closed to qualified Ukrainians, all such positions being reserved for Poles. A positive aspect of this frustrating situation was that many educated young Ukrainians were forced to abandon their attempts to find employment in the cities and went to work in the countryside, resulting in the impressive cultural and socioeconomic development of the Ukrainian villages. Nonetheless, difficulty in finding appropriate employment, especially during the depression of the 1930s, added greatly to the already precarious material plight of the intelligentsia. It also fueled resentment toward the Polish regime among educated Ukrainians and encouraged in them a conviction that these problems could be solved only if Ukrainians had a state of their own.

The Ukrainian Response

Because it was basically the Polish government that defined the nature of Polish/Ukrainian relations during the interwar years, Ukrainian activity during this period was essentially either a response or a reaction to Polish initiatives. Ukrainians generally remained opposed to the Polish regime and expressed their opposition in one of two ways: either by legal means, which would not jeopardize their already unenviable position, or by violent, revolutionary tactics, which had no regard for the consequences. Of the two, the first approach was by far the most widespread.

Although the "legalists" never abandoned the goal of eventually uniting all Ukrainians in an independent state, they concentrated on preserving the gains that Ukrainians had made under Austrian rule against the discriminatory policies of the Polish state. They participated in the Polish political system by means of legal Ukrainian parties, rebuilt and expanded the cooperative movement, and sought to protect Ukrainian schooling. By developing this "organic sector" of Ukrainian society, the "legalists" hoped that Ukrainians would be better prepared to achieve independence when the next opportunity arose. Such constructive albeit mundane activities attracted mostly the older, more stable elements of Ukrainian society, such as members of the prewar establishment, the clergy, much of the intelligentsia, and the well-to-do peasants.

Political parties An unusually fractious society, Poland had ninety-two registered political parties in 1925 of which thirty-two were represented in parliament. This tendency for political differentiation was also evident among the Ukrainians. Spanning the ideological spectrum from extreme left to extreme right, the Ukrainians had about a dozen political parties, which also reflected the very different political traditions of the "Austrian" Ukrainians of Eastern Galicia as opposed to the "Russian" Ukrainians of Volhynia, Polissia, and Kholm.

There was one party, however, that was larger and more influential than all the others put together – UNDO. It had been formed in 1925 from the merger of the Labor (*Trudova*) party and several smaller groups. Despite the name change, UNDO was actually the direct descendant of the prewar National Democrats, the leading West Ukrainian party prior to and during the Polish-Ukrainian War of 1918–19. Essentially a liberal party, it was committed to constitutional democracy and Ukrainian independence. To prepare Ukrainians for statehood, it supported the policy of "organic development" and agrarian reform. Relatively flexible in its tactics, it initiated the attempt at "normalizing" Ukrainian/Polish relations. But, with Polish repression on the one hand, and Ukrainian nationalist extremists on the other, UNDO found it difficult to maintain its middle-of-the-road policies.

Because most Ukrainian activists, including the vast majority of the intelligentsia and clergy, belonged to UNDO, it was the party of the West Ukrainian establishment. Its members controlled many Ukrainian financial, cooperative, and cultural institutions, including the most influential West Ukrainian newspaper, *Dilo*. During elections, it drew about 600,000 votes and won the vast majority of Ukrainian-held seats to parliament. Some of the party's most important leaders were Dmytro Levytsky, Vasyl Mudry, Stefan Baran, Ostap Lutsky, Milena Rudnytska, and Ivan Kedryn.

Socialist tendencies among the West Ukrainians were strong but fragmented. Their main representative was the Radical party, the oldest of all Ukrainian parties. Its program called for an equitable distribution of land among the peasants, limits on private ownership, and separation of church and state. But it also emphasized that these goals could not be attained until an independent state that united all Ukrainians was established. Therefore, in the 1920s–1930s, the Radicals, who had been strong supporters of the West Ukrainian People's Republic, strongly opposed Poland and the USSR, the main opponents of Ukrainian independence.

In the 1930s the Radicals had about 20,000 members, most of whom were peasants, agricultural workers, and some intelligentsia. In the elections of 1928, the party received about 280,000 votes. Although based in Galicia, the Radicals made a strong effort to expand their influence into Volhynia, Polissia, and Kholm, uniting in 1926 with the smaller Volhynian-based Ukrainian Socialist Revolutionary party to form the Ukrainian Socialist Radical party. Among their best-known leaders were such veterans as Lev Bachynsky and Ivan Makukh. While the Radicals inclined toward nationalism, the other prewar Ukrainian socialist party – the small and weak Social Democrats led by Lev Hankevych – veered toward communism.

During the 1920s, pro-Soviet views spread rapidly in Western Ukraine. To a large extent, this was a reaction to the Western powers' favoritism of the Poles and to Poland's oppression of its minorities. Moreover, the Ukrainization policies in Soviet Ukraine as well as the resurgence of the peasantry under the NEP also appealed to West Ukrainians. To encourage these tendencies, the Soviets appointed Ukrainians as their consuls in Lviv and tried to woo West Ukrainian intellectuals and students, boasting of Soviet Ukrainian achievements, and promising them responsible positions and a warm welcome in Ukraine.

Consequently, a number of leading West Ukrainian intellectuals and scholars, such as Mykhailo Lozynsky, Antin Krushelnytsky, and Stepan Rudnytsky, as well as hundreds of students immigrated to Soviet Ukraine (where almost all of them perished in the purges of the 1930s). Although the Shevchenko Scientific Society in Lviv did not have formal contacts with the Soviet government, it did develop close ties with the Ukrainian Academy of Sciences in Kiev. West Ukrainian cooperatives exchanged expertise and data with their Soviet counterparts. The exiled West Ukrainian government of Ievhen Petrushevych adopted an openly pro-Soviet line after 1923, as did an influential segment of the UNDO leadership. But these pro-Soviet tendencies were short-lived, and in the 1930s, as news about the horrors of collectivization, the famine, and the purges filtered into Western Ukraine, they quickly diminished.

In its ascendancy, however, pro-Soviet feeling gave rise to a number of legal and illegal political organizations. In 1919 a small group of Galicians, most of whom had been prisoners of war in Russia during the revolution, formed the Communist Party of Eastern Galicia. When the Red Army briefly occupied part of Galicia in 1920, these Galician Communists, who consisted of Ukrainians, Poles, and Jews, formed an ephemeral "government." In 1923 the party changed its name to the Communist Party of Western Ukraine (KPZU) and, bowing to pressure from the Communist International, became an autonomous part of the Polish Communist party. Even so, the Ukrainian leaders of this multiethnic party, such as Karol Maksymovych and Roman Kuzma, insisted on maintaining its Ukrainian character and exhibited a surprising degree of independence. They vigorously supported Shumsky and the national communist tendencies in Soviet Ukraine, making an issue of it in the international communist movement. This stance led to the removal of the KPZU's Ukrainian leadership but did not end the fierce factionalism in the party. In 1938 it was dissolved on the orders of Stalin. In the 1930s, the KPZU had over 4000 members, about half of whom were Ukrainians, while the remainder were Poles and Jews who lived in Western Ukraine.

Because it was an illegal, underground party, in 1926 the KPZU encouraged the formation of a legal, broadly based front organization called Ukrainian Workers'-Peasants' Socialist Union (Sel-Rob) for the purpose of gaining greater access to the masses. At the outset it was led by a leftist Russophile, Kyrylo Valnytsky, and by Pavlo Vasylchuk, a Ukrainian socialist from Volhynia. Internal conflicts, similar to those that had wracked the KPZU, soon split the organization into a right faction, which supported Ukrainian national goals, and a left faction, which sided with Moscow. In 1928, at the high point of their influence, Sel-Rob's two wings had about 10,000 members and garnered close to 240,000 votes, most of which came from Volhynia and Kholm and supported the nationally conscious rightists. However, Stalin's policies undermined support for Sel-Rob and when the Polish government dissolved it in 1932, there was little protest.

The remainder of the Ukrainian parties were small, weak, and inclined to cooperate with the Polish government. One of these was Bishop Hryhorii Khomyshyn's Ukrainian Catholic party, which attempted, without success, to mobilize support for a clerical conservatism. The rapidly declining Russophiles established the Russian Peasant and the Russian Agrarian parties, which merged in 1931. This did not, however, prevent many of their rank and file from going over to the Ukrainian parties.

The cooperative movement   "Rely on your own resources!" was the slogan of the activists in the "organic" sector of West Ukrainian society. It implied that since no one – and certainly not the Polish government – would aid Ukrainians in their endeavors, they had to help themselves. Cooperatives were seen by Ukrainians as one of the best ways of achieving such a goal. Before 1914 the cooperatives' main function had been economic development. Under Polish rule, this function was greatly expanded: the cooperative movement came to view itself as a school for self-government and an instrument of economic self-defense. Indeed, one of its slogans proclaimed: "In the cooperatives the people learn to be masters of their own land."

A major factor in the expansion of the cooperatives' role was the thousands of Ukrainian army veterans who joined them. Patriotic, politicized, and frustrated by their defeat, they saw the cooperatives as a means of continuing the struggle for the Ukrainian cause: "By working in the cooperatives we are once again the nation's soldiers." Every cooperative that was organized, every product or service that it provided, and every penny that landed in Ukrainian rather than Polish pockets represented for them a blow against the Polish enemy and a step closer to independence. There was also a practical aspect to involvement in the cooperatives: in many cases the cooperatives provided the only employment opportunities available to the veterans.

The cooperatives quickly established an elaborate organization. Credit unions were united in an association called Tsentrobank; rural consumer and marketing unions formed Tsentrosoiuz; the union of dairy cooperatives was called Maslosoiuz; and Narodna Torhivlia represented the urban retailers. The umbrella organization that united all the cooperatives, audited their accounts, trained their personnel, and provided general guidance was RSUK (Audit Union of Ukrainian Cooperatives). The authority of RSUK was greatly enhanced by the high quality and dedication of some of its leaders, most notably Ostap Lutsky and Iuliian Pavlykovsky.

In the interwar period, rural consumer and marketing cooperatives dominated the movement because they addressed the main problem experienced by the peasants – the low prices they received for their produce and the high prices they had to pay for finished goods – by uniting them into larger, more-effective bargaining units. The dairy cooperatives of Maslosoiuz were most successful in marketing their products and they dominated the West Ukrainian, and even large parts of the Polish, markets.

Statistics testify to the dramatic growth of the cooperatives. In 1921 there were about 580 Ukrainian cooperatives in Eastern Galicia; in 1928 their number jumped to 2500; and by 1939 there were close to 4000. The total membership in the cooperatives on the eve of the Second World War was over 700,000, and they provided employment for over 15,000 Ukrainians. However, close to 90% of the cooperatives were in Eastern Galicia; in Volhynia, Kholm, and Polissia, Ukrainians were forced to join Polish cooperative associations. Nonetheless, Ukrainians had twice as many cooperatives per capita as did Poles, even with the advantage of government support enjoyed by the latter.

But the Ukrainian cooperatives also had serious problems. Alarmed by their growth, Polish government officials made a point of obstructing their further development. Polish tactics included allegations that reports were filled out incorrectly and building or hygienic codes were violated. Although the Ukrainian cooperatives were numerous and well organized, they were far less wealthy than those of the Poles and the lack of capital limited their economic impact. These difficulties notwithstanding, the cooperative movement accelerated social mobilization and national integration among the Ukrainians of Galicia and reflected their desire to take charge of their own affairs.

Education   As might be expected, education was an extremely sensitive and important issue in the Ukrainian/Polish confrontation. Besides providing their children with an education, Ukrainians wanted the schools to raise Ukrainian national consciousness and cultural development. The Poles, for their part, expected the educational system to make non-Poles into loyal citizens of the Polish state. The Poles expanded education on the elementary level, especially in underdeveloped areas such as Volhynia, Polissia, and Kholm; by the 1930s illiteracy had dropped to 28% in the Ukrainian-inhabited areas of the Polish state (although it remained considerably higher in Volhynia). At the same time, however, the Ukrainian-language schools that had been established under Austrian rule were systematically eliminated under the guise of transforming them into bilingual schools. Of the more than 2400 Ukrainian elementary schools existing in Eastern Galicia in 1912, only 352 remained in 1937. In Volhynia the decline during this period was from 440 Ukrainian schools to 8. On the secondary level, the situation was also grim for the Ukrainians: in 1931 there was one Polish *gymnazium* for every 16,000 Poles but only one Ukrainian *gymnazium* per 230,000 Ukrainians.

Anti-Ukrainian discrimination in education was also obvious at the university level. The government never fulfilled its promise to establish a separate university for the Ukrainians and it systematically obstructed Ukrainians from obtaining a university education. Therefore, in 1920, the Ukrainians established a "secret" university in Lviv. Organized without the permission of the authorities, it offered a broad range of improvised courses that were taught in conspiratorial manner in secluded rooms and basements. At its high point, the university had 54 professors, 3 faculties, 15 departments, and about 1500 students. After the government closed down the courses in 1925, many Ukrainian students left to pursue their studies abroad, especially in Czechoslovakia. The net effect of these discriminatory government policies was that many educated Ukrainians became militantly anti-Polish and politically radicalized.

An attempt to meet Ukrainian needs at the secondary-school level was made by Ridna Shkola, an educational society, which by 1938 established about 40 *gymnazia*, lycées, and vocational schools. Dues from its membership, which jumped from 5000 in 1914 to over 100,000 in 1938, and contributions from immigrants in the United States and Canada provided much of the funding for its efforts. General cultural needs remained the domain of the venerable Prosvita society, the "mother" of all West Ukrainian organizations; in 1939 it had over 360,000 members. It supported a vast network of reading rooms, published educational materials, established day-care centers, and conducted a variety of courses.

The Galician penchant for organization carried over into other spheres as well. A variety of prewar youth organizations, such as the village-based Sokil and Luh (the old Sich), continued their activities while new ones, such as Plast, the scouting movement founded in 1911, attracted the children of the urban intelligentsia and groomed them for leadership positions in society.

Convinced that the scouting movement was a hotbed of nationalism, the government banned it in 1930. An important organizational development in the interwar period was the growth of the women's movement. Committed to creating a new, nationally conscious, culturally developed, and socioeconomically progressive woman, the Soiuz Ukrainok, founded in 1920, had over 45,000 members a decade later. Under the able leadership of Milena Rudnytska, a member of parliament, it carried on extensive charitable, educational, and cultural activities. It also had well-developed contacts with international feminist organizations.

The churches   The largest, wealthiest, and most influential West Ukrainian organization was, of course, the Greek Catholic church. But striking changes occurred in the relative importance of this institution in Galician society. Unlike in the 19th century, when the church had been the only institution that the Ukrainians of Galicia had, in the interwar period it was only one, albeit the largest, of many and, therefore, could no longer count on the unquestioning loyalty of all Galician Ukrainians.

In the late 1930s, the church had over 4 million faithful in about 3000 parishes. The church also possessed a network of youth organizations and women's societies, periodicals, and even its own political organization, the Ukrainian Catholic National party. An indication of its ability to mobilize the youth, particularly from the villages, was the massive Youth for Christ rally in 1933, which drew over 50,000 participants. The church also made progress on the educational level. In 1928 it established the only Ukrainian institution of higher learning in Poland, the Theological Academy in Lviv, the rector of which was Josyf Slipy. Three new seminaries were also founded.

The greatest asset of the Greek Catholic church during the interwar period was undoubtedly its leader, Metropolitan Andrei Sheptytsky. Universally respected for his strength of character, breadth of vision, and humanity, the metropolitan was the single-most influential figure in West Ukrainian society. His conviction that the Greek Catholic church was a distinctly Ukrainian institution that should preserve its Eastern ecclesiastical traditions and support the national aspirations of its people added to his popularity. This attitude brought him into conflict with a part of the church hierarchy, led by Bishop Khomyshyn and the Basilian Order, that preferred to stress ties to Roman Catholicism rather than the church's distinctiveness.

The metropolitan also exerted considerable influence on political affairs. In 1930 he energetically protested the "pacification" campaign and five years later he supported the policy of "normalization." While maintaining close relations with the moderates of UNDO, he chastised both nationalist extremists and Communists, constantly appealing for the need for higher values and broader vision.

In Volhynia, Polissia, and Kholm, the Orthodox church included about 2 million Ukrainians. Unlike the Greek Catholic church, it did not have the protection of Rome and was, therefore, more exposed to repressive Polish policies. In 1924, on the insistence of the government, the Orthodox church in Poland broke its ties with the Moscow patriarchate and declared autocephaly (ecclesiastical independence). Although old Russophile sympathies still survived at the upper levels of the church hierarchy, Ukrainian influences increased markedly at the grass-roots level as Ukrainian came to be used in the liturgy, religious publications, and the seminaries. Alarmed by these developments, the Polish government insisted on the use of Polish in church services and began a campaign, accompanied by the widespread destruction of Orthodox churches, to convert the Orthodox to Catholicism. Although Polonization did make some inroads, notably in the liturgy, conversions to Catholicism were rare.

The Revolutionary Movement

The new nationalism   A qualitatively different variety of Ukrainian nationalism emerged in the interwar period. In the 19th century, the nationalism of the largely liberal or socialist Ukrainian intelligentsia was a rather amorphous combination of national consciousness, patriotism, and humanist values. Although the movement became more focused in the 1917–20 period when it accepted national statehood as its goal, it continued to advocate democratic or socialist principles. Indeed, during the war for independence many Ukrainian politicians often wavered when it came to choosing between nationalist or socialist goals. However, in the 1920s there developed among many young Ukrainians, as among many other European peoples, an extreme variety of nationalism often called integral nationalism.

In the Ukrainian case, the genesis of integral nationalism lay primarily in the setbacks of 1917–20. As Alexander Motyl notes: "In essence, Ukrainian nationalism was an attempt to explain why Ukrainian statehood had been lost and how it was to be regained."[3] Convinced that socialist and democratic approaches encouraged the party strife, poor leadership, conflicting purposes, and lack of direction that led to their defeat, young veterans of the war for independence rejected the old ideologies. Instead they called for the creation of a new type of Ukrainian, one who was unconditionally committed to the nation as a whole and to independent statehood. These tendencies were most forcefully articulated by Dmytro Dontsov, an East Ukrainian émigré and former socialist, who became the principal ideologue of Ukrainian integral nationalism.

The ideology   Ukrainian integral nationalism was not based on a closely reasoned system of ideas; rather it rested on several key concepts whose main goal was not to interpret reality but to incite people to action. Dontsov ar-

gued that the nation was an absolute value and that there was no higher purpose than the attainment of independent statehood. Because politics was essentially a Darwinian struggle of nations for survival, conflict was unavoidable. It followed that the end justified the means, that willpower predominated over reason, and that action was preferable to contemplation. To dra-
matize and inculcate these views, integral nationalists mythologized Ukrainian history, emphasizing a cult of struggle, of sacrifice, and of national heroes.
Racism was a relatively minor component of the ideology and although traces
of anti-Semitism could be found in the writings of some proponents, it was
not emphasized.

Integral nationalism espoused collectivism, which placed the nation above
the individual. Nonethless, it also urged its proponents to be "strong individuals" who would stop at nothing to attain their goals. One goal was to have
the nation function as an integrated whole, not as disparate parties, classes,
or regional groups. Hence the all-encompassing scope of the movement, its
stress on *sobornist* (national unity), its rejection of regionalism, and its desire
to control all aspects of Ukrainian society. Integral nationalists were urged
to "force their way into all areas of national life, into all its recesses, into all
its institutions, societies, and groups, into every city and village, into every
family."[4] Along with this need to monopolize all aspects of national life came
intolerance. Convinced that theirs was the only way to attain national goals,
integral nationalists were ready to do battle with all who stood in their path.

Dontsov and other ideologues of the movement were vague about the type
of state and society they wished to have once independence was achieved.
They had little to say about socioeconomic organization, noting only that
it would be basically agrarian and would rest on cooperation between the
state, cooperatives, and private capital. The political system of the future state
would be based on the rule of one nationalist party. A hierarchy of proven
"fighters" or "better people" would form the core of the party and its leadership. At the pinnacle of the movement and the future state was the supreme
leader or *vozhd*, whose authority was unquestionable and unlimited.

Ukrainian integral nationalism clearly contained elements of fascism and
totalitarianism. These tendencies were spreading throughout Europe in the
1920s and their influence, especially that of Italian fascism, was widespread in
Eastern Europe. But, as Ivan Lysiak-Rudnytsky has argued, Western fascism,
which developed in urban, industrialized surroundings, was not the closest
relative of Ukrainian integral nationalism.[5] The latter was far more similar to
the radical rightist movements in agrarian East European societies, such as
the Iron Guard in Romania, the Ustashi in Croatia, the Arrow Cross in Hungary, and related movements in Slovakia and Poland. In the final analysis,
however, Ukrainian integral nationalism was genetically independent, that
is, its primary sources lay within its own society. Confronted with the tragic
plight of Ukrainians under Polish and Soviet rule, having lost faith in tradi-

tional legal methods, and disillusioned with the Western democracies, which had ignored Ukrainian pleas for support and were themselves mired in crisis, Ukrainian integral nationalists believed that they had nothing to gain from the status quo and that they had to use radical means to change it.

The organization Even before the final formulation of their ideology, scattered groups of future integral nationalists had appeared in Galicia and especially among the émigrés in Czechoslovakia. In 1920, a small group of officers in Prague established UVO (Ukrainska Viiskova Orhanizatsiia – Ukrainian Military Organization), an underground organization that sought to continue the armed struggle against Polish occupation. Soon afterward, Colonel Ievhen Konovalets, a Galician who had led the crack Sich Riflemen units in the East Ukrainian armies and a prominent leader in the struggle for independence, was chosen to be UVO's commander. An excellent organizer and a sophisticated politician, Konovalets quickly became the undisputed leader of the integral nationalists during the interwar period.

Initially, UVO was strictly a military organization with a military command structure. It secretly prepared demobilized veterans in Galicia and interned soldiers in Czechoslovakia for a possible anti-Polish uprising, and it carried out operations designed to destabilize the Polish occupation. The most notable of its operations were the attempted assassination of Piłsudski, the Polish head of state, by Stepan Fedak in 1921 and the widespread sabotage campaign of 1922. Consisting of an estimated 2000 men, the organization maintained contacts with both the East and West Ukrainian governments-in-exile and secretly received funding from West Ukrainian political parties.

But in 1923 UVO's position changed drastically. When the Allied recognition of Polish rule in Eastern Galicia raised doubts among many West Ukrainians about the sense of continuing armed resistance, many seasoned members left UVO. The organization, however, refused to modify its demand for militant action against the Poles, thereby alienating the legal parties that now rejected terrorist tactics. Polish police pressure forced Konovalets and much of the leadership to flee Galicia and establish their headquarters abroad.

The ensuing crisis caused a major reorientation in UVO. Konovalets turned to foreign powers, especially Poland's enemies, Germany and Lithuania, for political and financial support. Back in Eastern Galicia, UVO began to recruit *gymnazium* and university students to replenish its dwindling ranks. To propagate its hard-line views in Galicia, the organization smuggled in its journal, *Surma*, from abroad. Most important, UVO established contacts with several student groups, such as Ukrainian Nationalist Youth in Prague, the Legion of Ukrainian Nationalists in Podebrady (Czechoslovakia), and the Association of Ukrainian Nationalist Youth in Lviv, for the purpose of forming an expanded nationalist organization. After several preparatory conferences, the representatives of UVO and the student groups met in Vienna in 1929 and established the Organization of Ukrainian Nationalists (OUN). Most of its cadres were Galician youths, and Konovalets and his associates provided the leadership from abroad.

The role the OUN took upon itself was much broader than that of UVO. Like its predecessor, OUN remained an "underground army." It adhered to military principles of leadership, conspiratorial techniques, and strict discipline and engaged in a campaign of political terror against the Polish state and its representatives. But it also strove to become a broadly based ideological/revolutionary movement, whose objective was the achievement of integral nationalist goals. It made a special effort to popularize its views, especially among the youth, and attempted to dominate all the West Ukrainian social, political, and economic organizations. Those Ukrainians who obstructed the OUN's plans were vulnerable to the same terrorist attacks as Polish officials.

Undoubtedly OUN's greatest success was its ability to attract widespread support among Ukrainian youth. Its stress on revolutionary action, radical solutions, and the creation of a new breed of "super" Ukrainians appealed to youths who felt victimized by the Polish government, frustrated by lack of employment, and disillusioned by the failures of their elders. Initially, OUN attracted a large portion of the university and upper-*gymnazium* students in Eastern Galicia. Almost every secondary school and every university in Poland and abroad where Ukrainians studied had OUN cells. The dormitory (Akademichnyi dim) of the Ukrainian university students in Lviv, who were led by Bohdan Kravtsiv, Stefan Lenkavsky, Stepan Okhrymovych, Ivan Grabrusevych, and Volodymyr Ianiv, became a regular integral nationalist stronghold. When some of these youths returned to their native villages, they spread integral nationalist ideas in the countryside.

In order to expand its influence, OUN also infiltrated various economic, educational, and youth organizations; organized massive patriotic demonstrations, student protests, and boycotts of Polish goods; published numerous newspapers and brochures; and energetically spread its message among the students, peasants, and workers of Galicia and Volhynia. In this work it enlisted the aid of a number of talented young poets, such as Ievhen Malaniuk, Oleh Olzhych-Kandyba, Olena Teliha, and Bohdan Kravtsiv. The major forum for integral nationalist views was the Prague-based journal *Rozbudova Natsii*. With time, however, a series of other publications came under integral nationalist influence.

Although it is exceedingly difficult to establish the size of the OUN's membership, on the eve of the Second World War it is estimated to have had about 20,000 members. The number of sympathizers was many times greater. In any case, the preponderance of youthful, energetic, idealistic, and committed members in its ranks quickly made OUN the most dynamic factor in West Ukrainian political life during the interwar period.

Throughout the 1930s, OUN continued its "war" against the Polish regime, attacking government agencies and post offices in order to obtain funds for its activities, and engaging in sabotage against government property and assassinations. But OUN (and UVO) did not see violence or terror as an end in itself. Its members believed that they were waging a national-liberation struggle by revolutionary means, much like the Irish in the anti-English Sinn Fein and Piłsudski's prewar anti-Russian underground organization. The immediate objectives of such tactics were to persuade Ukrainians that resistance was possible and to keep Ukrainian society in a state of "constant revolutionary ferment." In 1930 an integral nationalist publication elaborated on this concept of "permanent revolution": "By means of individual assassinations and occasional mass actions, we will attract large segments of the population to the idea of liberation and into the revolutionary ranks ... Only with continually repeated actions can we sustain and nurture a permanent spirit of protest against the occupying power and maintain hatred of the enemy and the desire for final retribution. The people dare not get used to their chains, they dare not feel comfortable in an enemy state."[6]

In the early 1930s, besides hundreds of acts of sabotage and dozens of "expropriations" of government funds, OUN members staged over sixty actual or attempted assassinations. Among their most important victims were Tadeusz Hołówko (1931), a well-known Polish proponent of Polish/Ukrainian compromise; Emilian Czechowski (1932), a Polish police commissioner in Lviv; Aleksei Mailov (1933), a Soviet consular official in Lviv who was killed as a response to the famine of 1932–33 in Soviet Ukraine; and Bronisław Pieracki (1934), the Polish minister of the interior, who was held responsible by the OUN for the pacification of 1930. Many assassination attempts were directed against Ukrainians who disagreed with OUN policies. Of these, the most notable was the killing in 1934 of Ivan Babii, a respected Ukrainian pedagogue.

But the policy of violence and confrontation cost OUN dearly. In 1930 Iulian Holovinsky, the leader of its "combat unit," was assassinated by a police agent. A year later, two young workers, Vasyl Bilas and Dmytro Danylyshyn, were hanged for killing an official during an "expropriation." After the assassination of Pieracki in 1934, the Polish police launched a widespread crackdown that netted the entire krai (regional) leadership of OUN in Galicia, including Stepan Bandera and Mykola Lebed, who had organized the attack. After a much publicized series of trials, the youthful leaders received lengthy sentences in the Bereza Kartuzka concentration camp. They were joined by hundreds of OUN rank-and-file members who were rounded up at this time.

These setbacks were only part of OUN's troubles. It soon became evident that the police had infiltrated the organization, a development that was to be expected once OUN began to recruit on a mass scale. Even more demoralizing was the growing criticism that OUN encountered from its fellow Ukrainians. Parents were incensed that the organization exposed their inexperienced teenagers to dangerous activities that often ended tragically. Social, cultural, and youth organizations resented the OUN's attempts to take them over. The legal political parties blamed the integral nationalists for giving the government an excuse to restrict legal Ukrainian activities. And Metropolitan Sheptytsky sharply denounced OUN's "amorality." These accusations and counter-accusations reflected the tensions that had arisen between the generation of fathers in the legal or "organic" sector and that of their children in the revolutionary underground.

Generational tensions emerged in the OUN itself, especially among the leadership. Brought up in the more "civilized" prewar era and tempered by age and experience, the older generation of Konovalets and his associates from the 1917–20 period, such as Dmytro Andrievsky, Omelian Senyk, Mykola Stsiborsky, and Roman Sushko, led the movement from abroad. Although they had their doubts about some OUN tactics, especially the assassinations, they often found it difficult to control their subordinates from a distance. While they did not reject the use of violence, Konovalets and his staff preferred to concentrate on obtaining foreign, especially German, support.

By contrast, the subordinate regional (*krai*) leadership in Galicia, which included Stepan Bandera, Mykola Lebed, Iaroslav Stetsko, Ivan Klymiv, Mykola Klymyshyn, and Roman Shukhevych, was committed to revolutionary action. Mostly in their early twenties, they had not fought in the war for independence and had grown up under the demeaning conditions and frustrations of Polish rule. Their youthfulness and constant exposure to foreign oppression predisposed them to a violent, heroic type of resistance and they were contemptuous of the relative moderation (and more comfortable lifestyle) of their elders abroad. This resentment deepened after 1934, when the entire Galician leadership was incarcerated in the Bereza Kartuzka concentration camp and it was rumored that their capture was the result of the carelessness or even betrayal of some members of the leadership abroad.

Yet the authority, prestige, and diplomatic skills of Konovalets were great enough to prevent the simmering conflict from deepening. It was, therefore, a great setback to the integral nationalist movement when Konovalets was assassinated in 1938 in Rotterdam by a Soviet agent. Thus, on the eve of cataclysmic events, the OUN found itself without an experienced and generally acknowledged *vozhd* (supreme leader). But it is a telling indication of the commitment, dynamism, and discipline of its rank and file that, despite these setbacks, the organization not only avoided disintegration but continued to expand.

Ukrainians under Romanian Rule

Another state that acquired a significant number of Ukrainians during the chaotic 1918–19 period was Romania. According to Romania's statistics, in

1920 there were about 790,000 Ukrainians within its borders, constituting 4.7% of the population. Ukrainians formed three distinct subgroups. One group – about 450,000 Ukrainians – lived in the southeast corner of the country, in the former Russian province of Bessarabia (present-day Moldavia), which bordered on the Black Sea. In 1919, near Khotyn, these poor peasants staged a Bolshevik-led uprising against the Romanian government; but after its failure, they showed little political activity. Another small group of Ukrainians lived in Maramorosh, a former Hungarian territory, and were also politically inactive.

The third group was the most vibrant Ukrainian community: the approximately 310,000 Ukrainians of Bukovyna. Romanian occupation resulted in a drastic political decline for the Bukovynians. Under Austrian rule, Bukovyna had been an autonomous province and Ukrainians, its largest national group, had relatively strong political representation in Vienna, extensive local self-government, and a well-developed system of Ukrainian-language education. All this was lost when the Romanians annexed the region. From being the most favored West Ukrainian community, the Bukovynians became the most oppressed.

Romanian intolerance of its numerous minorities was even greater than that of the Poles. After 1920, when the Western allies formally recognized the Romanian claim to all of Bukovyna, the Romanian government shut down all Ukrainian schools and even refused to recognize the Ukrainians as a distinct nationality. The educational measures of 1924, which Romanized the schools, referred to Ukrainians as "citizens of Romanian origin who had forgotten their native language." By 1927, all traces of Bukovyna's former autonomous administration had been removed and it was treated like any other Romanian province.

There were three distinct phases in the twenty-two years that Ukrainians spent under Romanian rule. During the first phase, which lasted from 1918 to 1928, the Romanian government imposed martial law on the province. For the Bukovynian Ukrainians, who were accustomed to the well-ordered constitutional Austrian system, the brutal liquidation of their rights and the Romanization of their cultural life represented a disorienting shock. They recovered somewhat during the relatively liberal period between 1928 and 1938. But when the military came to power in Romania in 1938, as it did in Poland, a period of harsh, almost totalitarian, rule ensued.

Under the circumstances, it was only during the brief period of 1928–38 that Ukrainian organizational life could be revived, and only modestly at that. Essentially, the members of the small Bukovynian community responded to Romanian rule in a fashion similar to their compatriots in Poland. The older, more-established members opted for legal "organic" work and compromise with the regime. They reestablished cultural societies, choirs, theatrical troupes, student groups, and several publications. In 1927, under the leadership of Volodymyr Zalozetsky, they even formed the Ukrainian National party. However, by 1938, both the party and many Ukrainian organizations had been disbanded. The "revolutionary" or Nationalist camp, led by Orest Zybachynsky, Petro Hryhorovych, and Denys Kvitkovsky, emerged in the mid 1930s. More selective in recruiting its membership than the OUN in Galicia, the organization, while not large numerically, soon dominated the student, youth, and sports societies. Because of its conspiratorial structure, OUN was the only Ukrainian organization in Bukovyna not only to survive government repression but also to expand on account of it.

Ukrainians in Czechoslovakia

In surveying the generally depressing condition of Ukrainians during the interwar period, it is heartening to focus on one, albeit tiny, fragment of this nation – the Ukrainians of Transcarpathia – whose fortunes improved markedly during that time. Isolated from their compatriots by the Carpathian Mountains, the Carpatho-Ukrainians (or Rusyns as they still called themselves) were among the most politically, socioeconomically, and culturally underdeveloped of all Ukrainians. When the fall of Austria-Hungary brought an end to oppressive Hungarian rule, their region was incorporated into Czechoslovakia. In contrast to the forced annexation of other West Ukrainian lands, the Carpatho-Ukrainian association with Czechoslovakia was a voluntary one. As a result of an agreement concluded in Scranton, Pennsylvania, in November 1918 with Czech leaders, emigrants from Transcarpathia accepted incorporation of their homeland into the new Czech state on the condition of Transcarpathian autonomy.

Of all the newly formed states in Eastern Europe, Czechoslovakia was the most democratic. Consequently, it did not follow the openly discriminatory and assimilationist policies toward its minorities that Poland and Romania did. This is not to say that relations between the central government and the populace of Transcarpathia were devoid of conflict. The issue of autonomy, as we shall see, brought about serious tensions between Prague and its easternmost province. Nonetheless, the Czechs allowed the Carpatho-Ukrainians a greater degree of political and cultural self-expression than they had ever had before.

In 1921 there were about 455,000 Carpatho-Ukrainians in Czechoslovakia. Of these, 370,000 lived in the Czech part of the state, and 85,000 inhabited the area of Prešov in the Slovak part of the federation. Committed to modernizing all regions of their new state, the Czechs made an effort to raise the standard of living in Transcarpathia as well. In the 1920s, the large Hungarian-owned estates were broken up and about 35,000 peasant households received additional plots averaging more than two acres each. In sharp contrast to Poland and Romania, the Czech government invested more in its Ukrainian-inhabited areas than it extracted from them. However, the investment was too small to relieve significantly the abject poverty in the region. When the depression of the 1930s set in, the populace of Transcarpathia suffered badly, at times experiencing widespread hunger and even starvation.

In terms of education and culture, Czech policies were a welcome change from the intense Magyarization the Hungarians had practiced. There was, first of all, a dramatic growth in the number of schools. Between 1914 and 1938, the number of elementary schools jumped from 525 to 851 and *gymnazia* increased from 3 to 11. Moreover, the Czech government allowed its population to use the language of its choice in the schools. Such liberalism led to the rapid growth of cultural societies, such as Prosvita and the Russophile Dukhnovych Society. Theatrical troupes and choirs flourished. Writers such as Vasyl Grendzha-Donsky, Andrii Karabelesh, and Aleksander Markush helped to ignite a modest cultural renaissance.

But the cultural life of Transcarpathia was not without its complexities and conflicts. As education became more widespread and the populace was exposed to a democratic political process, the issue of national identity, by this time already resolved in most Ukrainian lands, came to the fore in Transcarpathia. As usual, the resolution of this question became the concern primarily of the budding intelligentsia. And as was generally the norm in the early stages of nation-building, the intelligentsia was divided on this issue.

Nationality issues   Among the older members, who were mostly Greek Catholic clergy, a Russophile tendency evolved in circumstances analogous to those that had obtained earlier in Galicia. Although the Russophiles, who included many leading local inhabitants, established numerous organizations and societies (the most notable of which was the network of reading rooms of the Dukhnovych Society), they suffered from a crucial drawback: try as they might, they could not negate the fact that in terms of language and folk culture they were not Russian. This circumstance led to a growing sterility in their ideology and political orientation and explained why they had difficulty in attracting support among the educated youth.

Another tendency stressed localism, that is, the idea that the Slavic population of Transcarpathia was a distinct Rusyn nationality. Many of its supporters were Magyarized clergymen, who, with the arrival of the Czechs, found it prudent to camouflage their pro-Hungarian attitudes under the cloak of localism. However, the idea of creating a separate nationality out of several hundred thousand people was very tenuous, especially because the Transcarpathians were obviously and closely related to the Ukrainians who lived on the other side of the Carpathians. Consequently, the localist or Rusyn option was the weakest of all.

The Ukrainophile current, which predominated among the new, secular intelligentsia of teachers and students, was clearly the most dynamic. As in 19th-century Galicia, it first began as a populist movement in which the young intelligentsia sought to strengthen its links with the peasantry. As the similarity of language, folk culture, and Eastern Christian traditions between the populace on both sides of the Carpathians began to be felt, and as the Ukrainian national movement in Galicia grew stronger, the populists of Transcarpathia became Ukrainophiles.

Their burgeoning influence was reflected in organizational growth, especially in the 1930s. Led by Avhustyn Voloshyn and Mykhailo and Iulii Brashchaiko, the Ukrainophiles founded the Prosvita educational society, which soon overshadowed the Dukhnovych Society, its Russophile rival. Plast, the 3000-member Ukrainian scouting organization, became especially popular among the young intelligentsia. In 1934 the Ukrainian Teachers' Association counted about 1200 members or two-thirds of all pedagogues in Transcarpathia. University and *gymnazium* students became especially avid supporters of Ukrainianism. Because the Ukrainians of Transcarpathia could express their political and national aspirations openly, the conspiratorial OUN did not have a strong presence in the region for most of the 1930s. While most of the Ukrainophiles became supporters of Ukrainian integral nationalism, a significant segment adopted pro-Soviet positions.

Carpatho-Ukrainian autonomy   Dissension among the Carpatho-Ukrainians suited Czech interests and Prague used it as an excuse to delay granting autonomy to the region. However, in 1938, international developments greatly weakened the Czech government. As a result of the Munich Pact, Nazi Germany obtained a German-inhabited part of Czechoslovakia; with the silent acquiescence of the Western powers, it planned the further dismemberment of the Czech state. Backed by the Germans, the Slovaks obtained autonomy within the Czechoslovak republic. Seeing the Prague government faltering, the leaders of the three Transcarpathian factions united and also demanded autonomy. The Czechs had no choice but to agree. On 11 October 1938, Transcarpathia received its self-government.

Although Russophiles such as Andrei Brodii and Stefan Fentsik led the first autonomous administration, they were quickly discredited when it became known that they were agents of Hungary and Poland. To replace them, Prague appointed a new cabinet, headed by Voloshyn and consisting of Ukrainophiles. The Voloshyn government immediately commenced the work of transforming Transcarpathia, or Carpatho-Ukraine as it was officially called, into an autonomous Ukrainian state. The educational system, publications, and administration were Ukrainized. In February 1939, elections were held for the regional parliament and the Ukrainophiles received the support of 86% of all eligible voters. Meanwhile, a military organization, the Carpathian Sich, was organized and soon had about 5000 men in uniform.

There were pressing reasons for establishing a military force, for as Czechoslovakia slowly disintegrated, neighboring Hungary demanded the return of its former Transcarpathian lands. Indeed, just as the Carpatho-Ukrainian government was being formed, Hungarian troops occupied a southern portion of the region, forcing the Ukrainians to move their capital from Uzhhorod to Khust. Throughout its brief existence, the Carpatho-Ukrainian government continued to face the threat of a Hungarian invasion.

The creation of a Ukrainian government in Transcarpathia had a great impact on the West Ukrainians, especially those in neighboring Galicia. Many saw it as the first step in the imminent creation of an independent, united Ukraine. Eager to protect the first Ukrainian land to gain its freedom, many young integral nationalists from Galicia illegally crossed the border and joined the Carpathian Sich. However, the OUN leadership was divided on what policy to follow. While the young radicals in Galicia demanded immediate and full involvement in Carpatho-Ukraine, their older, foreign-based superiors, aware of German plans, urged restraint.

The reason for the caution of the older integral nationalists soon became apparent. As a result of a secret pact, Hitler agreed to a Hungarian occupation of all of Transcarpathia. And on 14 March 1939, the Hungarian army moved into the region. Hopelessly outnumbered and outgunned, the Carpathian Sich rendered brave but futile resistance. On 15 March, in a symbolic gesture, the Voloshyn government proclaimed the independent Republic of Carpatho-Ukraine. Only hours later it was forced to flee from its homeland.

The Carpatho-Ukrainian experience was paradoxical. Of all the West Ukrainian lands, it was among the least developed in socioeconomic, cultural, and political terms. Yet, it was the only region that achieved a measure of self-government. Brief as it was, the existence of a Ukrainian government in Carpatho-Ukraine had an impact similar to that of the Ukrainian governments in the 1917–20 period: it helped to turn much of the region's population, especially the youth, into nationally conscious Ukrainians. The episode also had important implications for German/Ukrainian relations, for it served as a graphic illustration of how little Ukrainians could depend on the goodwill of Hitler.

❧

National inequalities and socioeconomic difficulties, as well as the imposing growth of Nazi Germany and the USSR, led to a disillusionment with democracy and to the spread of political extremism throughout Eastern Europe during the interwar period. This radicalization increasingly involved not only the intelligentsia, but also the traditionally passive peasantry. Limited though it was, modernization raised the peasants' self-respect and expectations, making them less willing to accept national discrimination and the falling living standards of the 1930s. Moreover, it pushed them, as never before, to political activism, especially of the radical type.

Frustrated in their attempts to gain statehood or self-rule, the West Ukrainians were particularly susceptible to these general trends. Although they put much effort into "organic work," it was clearly the integral nationalism of OUN that became their most dynamic movement, especially among the youth. In sharp contrast to their compatriots in Soviet Ukraine, the West Ukrainians did not experience dramatic socioeconomic changes. Yet, despite their dreary standard of living, it was not communism, which had been discredited by Stalinism, but integral nationalism that captivated them. It was, therefore, in the generation that reached adulthood in the 1930s in Western Ukraine that Ukrainian nationalism reached its high point, eliciting a mixture of fanaticism and idealism.

Mykhailo Hrushevsky

Pavlo Skoropadsky

Evhen Petrushevych

Symon Petliura   Mykola Skrypnyk

Kiev during the proclamation of Ukrainian Independence, 25 January 1918

Ukrainian Greycoat Division

Bolshevik troops enter Odessa, February 1920

Bolshevik officers

Nestor Makhno and his staff

Propagandists on a collective farm, early 1930s

Construction on the Dnieper, early 1930s

Destruction of a church by Red Army men, early 1930s

Dead and dying peasants on the streets of Kharkiv
during the Great Famine, spring 1933

Evhen Konovalets (seated center) at first congress of OUN, Vienna 1929

Metropolitan Andrei Sheptytsky

Peasants on pilgrimage in Transcarpathia in mid 1930s

Ukraine during
the Second World War

It seemed, as Europe moved toward the Second World War, that Ukrainians had little to lose from the radical changes that it promised to bring. Still traumatized by Stalinist excesses and the increasing Polish, Romanian, and Hungarian repression in the western regions, Ukrainians had reason to believe that any change – even that brought on by war – would favorably alter the conditions under which they lived. But those who thought so would be sadly mistaken, for although the war radically transformed the situation of Ukrainians, their plight changed from bad to worse. The collapse of Poland at the outset of the war led to the imposition in Western Ukraine of the even-more-repressive Soviet regime. But when the German invaders swept away the Soviets, they brought with them a Nazi regime that in Ukraine reached the heights of brutality and inhumanity. Caught between the Nazi and Soviet regimes and lacking, for all practical purposes, a state to protect their interests, Ukrainians were especially vulnerable to the devastation of the war and the ruthless policies of its totalitarian protagonists.

ॐ

The War in Ukraine: Phase One

From the Ukrainian point of view, the Second World War took place in two distinct phases. The initial phase began on 1 September 1939 when the Germans attacked Poland and the Soviets occupied its eastern territories soon after. The main feature of this stage, which involved only the West Ukrainians, was the appearance in their lands of new occupying powers, the foremost of these being the Soviets. The second phase, which will be discussed later, commenced with the German invasion of the USSR on 22 June 1941 and lasted until the Soviet expulsion of German troops from Ukraine in the fall of 1944. This phase encompassed all of Ukraine and exposed its inhabitants to the worst horrors of the war.

Among the numerous factors that brought on the war, two diplomatic agreements, both of which had a direct impact on Ukrainians, were of critical importance. With the signing of the Munich Pact on 30 September 1938, the Western powers, led by England, attempted to appease Hitler by allowing him to dismember Czechoslovakia (and Transcarpathia). But rather than satisfying Hitler's demands, this display of Western spinelessness only whetted the Nazi appetite for territorial acquisitions. Even more directly linked with the outbreak of the war was the Nazi-Soviet Pact of 23 August 1939, one of history's most astonishing treaties. Hitler, who made no secret of his loathing for the Soviet system or of his territorial ambitions in the East, needed to neutralize the Soviet Union before launching an attack against his opponents in the West. Stalin, for his part, eagerly desired a nonaggression and neutrality treaty with Hitler, hoping thereby to redirect Nazi aggressiveness against France and England, and thus gain time to build up his own strength while the "capitalists" exhausted themselves in a war. In addition to addressing these immediate needs of the two powers, the Nazi-Soviet Pact also included provisions for the exchange of raw materials and armaments. More important, it contained a secret protocol in which Hitler and Stalin agreed to a divison of Eastern Europe into their respective spheres of influence and occupation. According to this arrangement, almost all the West Ukrainian lands were allotted to the Soviet Union.

Assured of Soviet neutrality, Hitler launched the attack on Poland that began the Second World War. Eager to claim their part of the tottering Polish state, Soviet armies entered eastern Poland on 17 September and occupied almost all of the lands inhabited by the West Ukrainians and Belorussians. Within four weeks, the Polish state ceased to exist.

The Soviet occupation of Western Ukraine   At the outset of their initial, twenty-one-month-long occupation of Western Ukraine, the Soviets went out of their way to win "the hearts and minds" of the populace. They proclaimed that they had arrived as the "flagbearers of high humanitarian principles" and justified their collaboration with the Nazis in the dismemberment of Poland by their desire to aid its oppressed minorities, especially their "brothers," the Ukrainians and Belorussians. A special effort was made to impress West Ukrainians with the new regime's "Ukrainianism." The Soviet troops that entered Galicia were called the Ukrainian Front and were led by Semen Tymoshenko, a general with an obviously Ukrainian name. These symbolic gestures were intended to portray the Soviet invasion as a case of Ukrainians coming to the aid of their fellow Ukrainians.

The new regime also attempted to appear democratic. On 22 October 1939 it organized an election during which the populace was pressured to vote for the single slate of candidates supporting the annexation of Western Ukraine to the Soviet Union. Not suprisingly, about 93% of the voters cast their ballots according to the regime's wishes. In June 1940, the USSR forced Romania to cede Bessarabia and Bukovyna. Thus, over 7 million inhabitants of Western Ukraine were added to the Soviet Ukrainian republic.

Some Soviet policies brought concrete improvements to the West Ukrainians. Much was done to Ukrainianize and enhance the educational system. By mid 1940 the number of elementary schools in Western Ukraine jumped to about 6900, of which 6000 were Ukrainian. Lviv University, long a stronghold of Polish culture, was renamed after Ivan Franko, adopted Ukrainian as the language of instruction, and opened its doors to Ukrainian students and professors. Health care, especially in the villages, improved markedly. The largely Polish- and Jewish-owned industrial and commercial enterprises were nationalized. But perhaps the most popular measure was the Soviet expropriation of the Polish landlords and the promise to redistribute their land among the peasants.

Simultaneously with these reforms, however, the Soviets began to dismantle the political, socioeconomic, and cultural infrastructure that the West Ukrainians had built up. Soon after their arrival, the NKVD arrested West Ukrainian political leaders and deported them to the east. UNDO and the other large Ukrainian political parties were forced to disband. Many cooperatives were eliminated and others were reorganized along Soviet lines. The Prosvita society's reading rooms and libraries had to cease operation. Realizing that they were living on borrowed time, between 20,000 and 30,000 Ukrainian activists fled to German-occupied Poland. With the elimination of the individuals, organizations, and political parties that represented middle-of-the road, liberal tendencies among West Ukrainians, the latter were left with only one viable political organization – the underground network of the OUN.

The conduct of the numerous Soviet officials who poured into Western Ukraine did little to improve the image of the new regime. Accustomed to acting in the "proletarian" style, they often struck the "westerners" as primitive, boorish bullies rather than as representatives of "advanced socialism." The almost universal use of Russian by the representatives of Soviet Ukraine quickly dissipated illusions about its vaunted Ukrainianism.

Support for the Soviets came primarily from local Communists who had emerged from the underground and were now especially useful to the new regime in helping it to "unmask" Ukrainian nationalists. Because Jews were disproportionately numerous among these Communists and because there were also many of them among the officials who arrived from the Soviet Union, anti-Jewish feeling rose among both West Ukrainians and Poles. But soon many local Communists also became disillusioned with the Soviets, especially after Stalin had some of them arrested and executed on suspicion of Trotskyism.

With time, however, the less attractive aspects of the early Soviet reforms became apparent. Lands that had been expropriated from Polish landlords

and "given" to the poorest peasants were declared to be liable to collectivization and about 13% were actually collectivized. When this event occurred,
the vast majority of the peasants, who had been wary of the Soviets from
the outset, turned against the new regime. The intelligentsia, many of whom
were initially pleased with the employment they found in Soviet educational
and cultural institutions, soon realized that they were little more than tightly
controlled functionaries and mouthpieces of the regime and that they faced
arrest and deportation if they did not follow instructions.

Aware of the West Ukrainians' commitment to their church, the new regime
initially treated the Greek Catholic church with caution, imposing only relatively minor restrictions at first. Priests were obliged to carry special passports and the government demanded high rents for the use of churches.
But gradually these restrictions grew more ominous. Soviet authorities removed religious instruction from the schools, confiscated church lands, and
increased antireligious propaganda. Similar policies were applied to the Orthodox church in Volhynia where, moreover, efforts were made to place it
under the patriarch of Moscow.

In spring 1940 the Soviets dropped their democratic guise and repres-
sions began against both Ukrainians and Poles on a massive scale. The most
widespread and feared measure was deportation. Without warning, without
trial, even without formal accusation, thousands of alleged "enemies of the
people" were arrested, packed into cattle cars, and shipped to Siberia and
Kazakhstan to work as slave laborers under horrible conditions. Many of
these deportees, including entire families, perished.

The first waves of deportees consisted of leading Polish, Ukrainian, and
Jewish politicians, industrialists, landowners, merchants, bureaucrats,
judges, lawyers, retired officers, and priests. Later, anyone identified with
Ukrainian nationalism was liable to arrest. In the final stages, in the spring
of 1941, the regime deported people indiscriminately. Those who had relatives abroad or who corresponded with them, those who were visiting friends
when they were arrested, those who were denounced for personal reasons,
or who, by accident, happened to be in the wrong place at the wrong time,
were all deported. "No one, literally no one," wrote an eyewitness to these
events, "was sure that his turn would not come the next night."[1]

According to Metropolitan Andrei Sheptytsky, the Soviets deported about
400,000 Ukrainians from Galicia alone.[2] The Poles, and especially the colonists, suffered even more, for their government-in-exile contended that, during the Soviet occupation of Poland's eastern territories, about 1.2 million
people, the majority of whom were Poles, were deported to the Soviet east.
This catastrophe reflected the dramatic plunge in the political fortunes of
the once-dominant Poles, who, deprived of government backing, suddenly
found themselves transformed from oppressors into the oppressed.

The incorporation of Western Ukraine into the Ukrainian SSR was undoubtedly an event of major historical significance, for it united Ukrainians in a single state structure for the first time in centuries. But, because of its limited duration, this forced unification did not result in deep-rooted changes in either Western or Soviet Ukraine. Nonetheless, it did have an immediate impact: West Ukrainians found their first exposure to the Soviet system to be a generally negative experience and many concluded that "Bolshevik" rule had to be avoided at all costs.

Ukrainians under German occupation   While the vast majority of West Ukrainians came under Soviet rule during the 1939–41 period, some found themselves under German occupation. About 550,000 Ukrainians who lived in the Lemko and Kholm regions on Poland's eastern border were included in the German zone of occupation. Surrounded by Poles and isolated from the centers of Ukrainian activity, the inhabitants of these regions were socioeconomically, culturally, and politically among the most underdeveloped of all Ukrainians. However, between 1939 and 1940 about 20,000–30,000 Ukrainian political refugees from Galicia fled to these areas to escape Soviet persecution. Some settled among their compatriots; others congregated in nearby Cracow, the center of Ukrainian refugee activity, and sparked an upsurge of communal activity in the Lemko and Kholm regions of the General Government (Gouvernement), as this part of German-occupied Poland was called.

The governor-general of the General Government, Hans Frank, was expressly ordered by Hitler to treat the area as a German colony and to grant the inhabitants only a minimum of rights. Although theoretically all power rested in the hands of Frank, who acted on instructions from Hitler, in practice the Gestapo (the Nazi political police) was often as influential as Frank himself in governing the region.

Soon after the Germans arrived, dozens of self-help committees, staffed largely by OUN members or sympathizers who had fled from Galicia, sprang up to look after the basic economic and educational needs of the Ukrainian populace in the General Government. In spring 1940, with the acquiescence of Frank, these committees formed a coordinating body in Cracow called the Ukrainian Central Committee (UCC) and elected Volodymyr Kubijovyč, a well-known geographer, as its head. The UCC was a Ukrainian social-welfare agency whose mandate was to look after the sick, the aged, and homeless children, to care for public health and education, to help prisoners of war, and to represent the interests of the Ukrainian workers from the General Government who were sent to Germany. The Germans made it very clear that the UCC was not to have any political prerogatives whatsoever.

But in fulfilling these functions, the UCC also sought to satisfy its own hidden agenda, which consisted of countering the strong Polonizing influences on its isolated Ukrainian constituents and raising their national consciousness. The Nazis were aware of these objectives and, to a limited extent, encouraged their attainment in hopes that the growth of Ukrainian national consciousness would act as a counterweight to the more numerous Poles. For this reason, the Germans often favored the appointment of Ukrainians to low-level administrative posts or to the police in ethnically mixed communities. When Ukrainians sometimes used their new positions to avenge themselves on Poles for the wrongs they suffered before the war, the Germans were not dismayed by the communal tensions that arose.

Under the able leadership of Kubijovyč and with the help of the refugees from Galicia, the approximately 800 officials of the UCC soon organized Ukrainian schools, cooperatives, and youth groups in almost all localities where there were considerable numbers of Ukrainians. They also established a publishing house in Cracow and greatly expanded the Ukrainian press in the region. Its activities not only helped Ukrainians in these isolated regions to make up for the losses they had suffered during years of Polish repression, but also alleviated some of the heavy burdens that war and German occupation had brought upon them. After the German invasion of the USSR and the incorporation of Galicia into the General Government, the UCC extended its activity into Galicia. Throughout the war, it was the only Ukrainian organization that could, albeit to a very limited extent, defend the socioeconomic interests of Ukrainians in the General Government.

Ukrainians under Hungarian occupation   After the invading Hungarian army brought down the Carpatho-Ukrainian government in March 1939, Transcarpathia was incorporated into Hungary, of which it remained a part for the duration of the war. Because the approximately 550,000 Ukrainian inhabitants of the region had, by and large, bad memories of the centuries-long Hungarian rule that had ended in 1918, they did not welcome the return of the Hungarians. In an attempt to create a favorable initial impression, the Hungarian government promised to grant Transcarpathia autonomy. But all too soon it became apparent that it would not fulfill this commitment and that Transcarpathia's populace would instead be slated for gradual Magyarization.

Almost immediately, the Hungarians launched a concerted attack against the Ukrainophiles. Hundreds were executed, thousands were arrested, and about 30,000 fled to neighboring Galicia (where many were, in turn, deported by the Soviets to Siberia). All Ukrainian publications and organizations, including Prosvita, were banned. But while it was committed to stamping out the growing Ukrainian movement in Transcarpathia, the Hungarian government was not yet ready to introduce total Magyarization (although it steadily increased Hungarian cultural influence, especially in the schools). It chose instead a transitional, or Rusynophile, option, which rested on the premise that the local populace was a distinct Rusyn nationality that for centuries had been organically linked with the Hungarians. Two local politicians and long-time agents of the Budapest government, Andrei Brodii and Stepan Fentsik, became the leading proponents of this approach, and its main social base of support was the heavily Magyarized Greek Catholic clergy.

Hungarian rule was not only politically oppressive, but it also brought about a decline in educational opportunities and a rise in the economic exploitation of the region. The one positive aspect of the six-year-long Hungarian occupation of Transcarpathia was that it spared the region from Nazi rule and, consequently, the devastation that struck much of Ukraine. It did not, however, save the region's more than 100,000 Jews, most of whom perished in the Nazi death camps.

The great rift in the OUN With the outbreak of the war, the tensions that had long been brewing within the OUN surfaced. A sharp division had developed between the older veterans of the 1917–20 struggle, who constituted the foreign-based leadership of the OUN, and the young Galician radicals, who had joined the organization in the 1930s. The latter group had led the bitter struggle against the Polish government on West Ukrainian territory and had often landed in Polish jails. The two camps did not disagree on matters of principle, for both subscribed to the basic tenets of Ukrainian integral nationalism; however, generational differences, personality clashes, and tactical issues did divide them. After the assassination of Konovalets in 1938, his close associate, the gentlemanly and reserved Andrii Melnyk, was nominated as his successor. The young radicals, for their part, argued that their own colleague, the dynamic, strong-willed Stepan Bandera, who had recently been freed from Polish imprisonment, was better qualified to lead the OUN in the critical times that lay ahead.

Even before Bandera and his colleagues emerged from prison, their supporters aimed a barrage of criticism at the OUN leaders abroad. The leaders were condemned for relying too heavily on foreign support, especially that of Germany, while neglecting the development of "organic" ties with the masses in Western Ukraine, for being too slow and passive in dealing with the rapidly changing political scene, and for allowing "political speculators and opportunists" to hold leadership positions. In September 1939, Bandera demanded that the OUN form a military underground force that would be ready to fight against anyone – even Germans if need be – who stood in the way of Ukrainian independence. He insisted that the OUN develop contacts with Western Allies as well as with the Germans. But Melnyk and his associates steadfastly defended their positions, arguing that the emphasis on ties with Germany had to continue because Western powers had shown no interest in supporting Ukrainian aspirations and because the creation of a military underground would only bring German retaliation rather than military or political gains.

But it was the question of who should constitute the new OUN leadership that really enflamed passions. In August 1939, while many of their rivals were still imprisoned, the Melnyk faction called a conference in Rome and formally proclaimed Andrii Melnyk as *vozhd* of OUN. However, on 10 February 1940, Stepan Bandera convened another conference in Cracow, where his faction rejected the decisions of the Rome meeting. Unable to reach a compromise, each group proclaimed itself to be the only legitimate leader of the OUN. Those who sided with Bandera, and these included the youthful majority of the organization, came to be called the OUN-B or OUN-R (revolutionary) or simply Banderites; supporters of Melnyk, who consisted of the more moderate integral nationalists, were referred to as OUN-M or Melnykites.

This schism in the OUN was clearly a great setback for the integral nationalist cause. Antagonism between the two factions reached such heights that they often fought each other as ferociously as they did the enemies of Ukrainian independence. Thus, as Ukrainian integral nationalists prepared to face the great tests set before them by the war, they were badly divided. Moreover, their bitter infighting damaged the Ukrainian integral nationalist movement as a whole, for it lowered its moral authority.

The War in Ukraine: Phase Two

On 22 June 1941, Nazi Germany launched its surprise attack against the USSR. As the two totalitarian systems clashed, a struggle of titanic proportions and unprecedented brutality commenced. Along a 2000-mile front, stretching from the White Sea in the north to the Black Sea in the south, over 3 million German and allied troops stormed Soviet forces numbering over 2 million men. Because of Stalin's great faith in Hitler's commitment to the Nazi-Soviet Pact, the Soviets had disregarded numerous warning signals of the onslaught and were, consequently, caught completely off guard. Moreover, Stalin's generals committed the strategic blunder of stationing too many troops too close to the border. This allowed swift-moving German tank columns to encircle and destroy them in huge pincer movements. As the Soviets suffered one disastrous defeat after another, as panic enveloped the Soviet leadership, including Stalin himself, and as chaos reigned in the government, it appeared that the collapse of the Soviet Union was imminent.

The largest part of the invading force, the German army group South led by Field Marshal Karl von Rundstedt, was assigned to Ukraine. And it was in Ukraine that the Germans scored some of their most impressive early successes, the largest of which was the destruction of a huge Soviet force around Kiev in September 1941 and the capture of over 650,000 prisoners. As a result, about four months after launching their invasion, the Germans occupied almost all of Ukraine. By December 1941 they controlled about 80 million people, or 42% of the Soviet Union's population, and a large part of its economic facilities. They took 3.8 million Soviet military prisoners (of whom an estimated 1.3 million were Ukrainians). The relative ease with which these men were captured was an indication of the indifferent attitude many Red Army men had about fighting in defense of the Soviet system.

Lack of support for the Soviets was even more pronounced among Ukraine's civilian population. In Western Ukraine, where Soviet rule was especially unpopular, Germans were often welcomed as liberators. In Eastern Ukraine the general reaction to the Germans was more guarded, but the feeling was widespread that their coming would lead to improvements over the Stalinist regime. Hence, the frequent photographs that appeared in the German press of cheerful Ukrainians greeting the arriving Germans with the traditional bread and salt.

The Soviets' hurried retreat had tragic consequences for thousands of political prisoners in the jails of Western Ukraine. Unable to evacuate them in time, the NKVD slaughtered their prisoners en masse during the week of 22–29 June 1941, regardless of whether they were incarcerated for major or minor offenses. Major massacres occurred in Lviv, Sambir, and Stanyslaviv in Galicia, where about 10,000 prisoners died, and in Rivne and Lutsk in Volhynia, where another 5000 perished. Coming on the heels of the mass deportations and growing Soviet terror, these executions added greatly to the West Ukrainians' abhorrence of the Soviets.

Overcoming their initial disarray, the Soviet authorities began to organize a more orderly retreat. In traditional Russian fashion, they instituted a "scorched earth" policy, which, in Stalin's words, called for making "life in the rear of the enemy unbearable." As a result, all economic enterprises that might be useful to the Germans were marked for destruction. Kiev, for example, suffered more damage from the retreating Soviets, who blew up many of its major buildings, than from the advancing Germans. In the Donbas, most of the mines were flooded and the huge Dnieper hydroelectric works, as well as all the fifty-four blast furnaces in Ukraine, were destroyed by the Soviets.

A remarkable feature of the Soviet retreat was the massive evacuation of munitions plants, skilled labor, and important intellectuals beyond the Urals and to Soviet Central Asia. In what was perhaps the largest evacuation in history, the Soviets moved about 1500 factories and over 10 million people – more than a third of these from Ukraine – beyond the grasp of the Germans. Ufa, the capital of the Soviet Bashkir republic situated in the Urals, became the wartime seat of the Ukrainian Soviet government. This massive transfer of industrial enterprises and population contributed greatly to the Soviet ability to continue the war.

Particularly active during the course of the evacuation was the NKVD. Suspecting all those who sought to avoid resettlement of disloyalty to the Soviet state, it arrested and executed large numbers of people. Jailed prisoners with sentences over three years were shot so as not to leave behind any anti-Soviet elements who might be of potential use to the Germans. Also, many NKVD

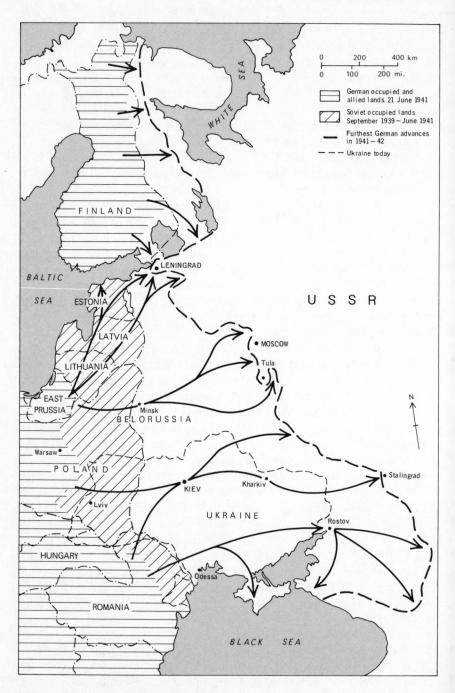

Map 24 The German invasion of 1941

agents were left behind to infiltrate the German administrative apparatus, especially the police, and to observe the behavior of those who had not been evacuated.

The OUN and Nazi Germany

Ukrainian integral nationalists greeted the German attack on the USSR with enthusiasm, viewing it as a promising opportunity to establish an independent Ukrainian state. But although the OUN and Germans shared a common enemy, their goals and interests were far from compatible. In the view of the Germans, the OUN's main usefulness was as a diversionary force that could wreak havoc behind Soviet lines. For their part, the integral nationalists, recently disillusioned by Hitler's treatment of Carpatho-Ukraine, had no intention of serving as the tools of Berlin; their goal was to use the war to spread their own influence throughout Ukraine. Thus, each side sought to use the other for its own, often contradictory, purposes.

The tenuous relationship between the OUN and Nazi Germany had other complications. Among the Germans there were strong differences of opinion regarding the OUN: the *Abwehr* (military intelligence) of Admiral Wilhelm Canaris, which had ties of long duration with the OUN, favored cooperating with the OUN, but the Nazi party apparatus, headed by Martin Bormann, contemptuously refused to treat them as a serious political factor. Moreover, those Germans who wished to deal with the integral nationalists had the problem of deciding which faction to support – the relatively moderate yet weaker Melnyk wing (OUN-M) or the dynamic, more numerous but recalcitrant Bandera supporters (OUN-B). Competition for German support fueled the rivalry between the two factions: each sought to establish itself as the sole representative of the Ukrainian people.

A product of German/OUN collaboration was the creation, shortly before the invasion of the USSR, of a Ukrainian military unit in the German army called the Legion of Ukrainian Nationalists. Composed mainly of pro-Bandera Ukrainians recruited in German-occupied territories, this force consisted of about 600 men divided into two units that bore the code names *Nachtigall* and *Roland*. The Germans planned to use these units for diversionary purposes but the OUN-B hoped that they would become the core of a Ukrainian army, as well as a means of extending the Bandera faction's influence.

Within days of the German entry into Ukraine, the conflict of interests between the integral nationalists and the Germans came to the fore. In an audacious move, which verged on the foolhardy, the OUN-B (supported by members of the *Nachtigall* unit) decided – without consulting the Germans – to proclaim, on 30 June 1941, the establishment of a Ukrainian state in recently conquered Lviv. Bandera's close associate, Iaroslav Stetsko, was chosen to be premier. The OUN-B gambled that the German military commanders would accept this action as an accomplished fact, rather than risk a confrontation with Ukrainians at the outset of the invasion.

The OUN-B not only bypassed the Germans but also attempted, with some initial success, to convince the confused Ukrainian populace that its actions had the support of Berlin. The aged and bedridden Metropolitan Sheptytsky was manipulated into issuing a statement of support for the proclamation. Although the OUN-B had not been far off the mark in its prediction of the indecisive manner in which the German military would react to its bold move, it completely miscalculated the response of the Nazi political leadership. Within days of the proclamation, Bandera and his associates were arrested by the Gestapo and incarcerated. Meanwhile, the OUN-M, which had been careful not to antagonize the Germans, sought to benefit from its rival's misfortune. However, within several months, it too ran afoul of the Nazis.

As part of the strategy to confront the Germans with accomplished facts, both OUN factions – again without German agreement – planned to organize and control the local administration in the newly conquered parts of Ukraine. For this purpose they assembled about 2000 of their members, most of whom belonged to OUN-B, divided them into "expeditionary groups" (pokhidni hrupy), and instructed them to follow the advancing Germans into Ukraine. In each locality these groups were to search out nationally conscious Ukrainians and build a local administration around them. Although this drive to organize Soviet Ukrainians for the integral nationalist cause produced many examples of bravery and enterprise on the part of the young "expeditionary group" members, it also brought out some of the uglier aspects of the struggle between the two OUN factions. The most noteworthy was the assassination, probably by a member of OUN-B, of two leading members of OUN-M – Omelian Senyk and Mykola Stsiborsky – in September 1941 in Zhytomyr. After this episode, assassinations and mutual denunciations to the Germans were not uncommon in the bitter conflict between the two factions of the OUN.

But after the hasty departure of the Soviets, East Ukrainians usually did not need the OUN groups to prod them into action. Because German military authorities were relatively civil in their treatment of the populace during the early months of German occupation, many Ukrainians spontaneously established local administrations. Expecting the Germans to liquidate the hated collective farms and to redistribute the land to individual owners, peasants brought in the harvest under exceedingly difficult conditions. Teachers organized schools and workers often ran factories on their own.

Priests who had somehow managed to survive the 1930s emerged to serve mass and baptize children and young adults en masse. With the religious revival came church politics. The Orthodox church of Volhynia split into two entities – the Autonomous and Autocephalous churches – which then extended their influence into central and eastern Ukraine. The former was more traditionalist and, while not breaking its links with the Moscow patriarchate, supported ecclesiastical autonomy for Ukraine only as long as the patriarchate remained under Soviet rule. The latter revived some of the traditions of the UAOC (Ukrainian Autocephalous Orthodox church) of the 1920s, supported the independence of Ukrainian Orthodoxy, and tended to attract the more nationally conscious Ukrainians into its ranks.

Over 100 non-Communist newspapers appeared throughout Ukraine. In large cities, especially Kiev, Ukrainian literary, scholarly, and social groups sprang up in great numbers. There were even attempts at political organization. In October 1941 in Kiev, members of the OUN-M, who had recently established themselves in the city, took the initiative in forming a Ukrainian National Council, composed largely of East Ukrainians, in hopes that it might become the central governmental body in Ukraine. Civic organizations also appeared in Kharkiv and Dniepropetrovsk. In short, as Soviet rule disintegrated, a spontaneous upsurge of Ukrainian social, cultural, and economic activity occurred, fueled by the expectation that the Germans were about to establish a Ukrainian state.

The Nazis had different plans, however. Annoyed that the integral nationalists had failed to draw the proper conclusions from their liquidation of the OUN-B attempt to establish a government on 30 June 1941 in Lviv, the Nazi political administration, which had arrived to replace the military authorities, resolved to repeat the lesson more forcefully. In September 1941, SS police units arrested and executed many members of the OUN-B "expeditionary groups." About two months later, the Gestapo turned on the OUN-M, concentrating on the influential group in Kiev. Over forty leading members of OUN-M, including the poetess Olena Teliha, were shot, and the popular newspaper, *Ukrainske Slovo*, was shut down. The Kievan press was turned over to pro-Russian groups who obediently followed German instructions. Nazi authorities then executed the Ukrainian mayor of Kiev, Volodymyr Bahazy, and purged outspoken Ukrainians from the administration, police, and press. The Ukrainian integral nationalists went underground; it was clear that their brief honeymoon with the Nazi regime was over.

Nazi Rule in Ukraine

The opinion of Alexander Dallin and other specialists on the Second World War on the eastern front is that "of all the Eastern areas conquered by the Third Reich, the Ukraine was by far the most important. It was the largest Soviet republic which the Germans occupied in full and ... as a provider of food and manpower, it was second to none."[3] In dealing with this valuable prize, the Nazi leadership considered two basic options. The first, usually identified with Alfred Rosenberg, a leading Nazi ideologist, was to gain the support of the Ukrainians against the Kremlin by offering them their own state, which

Map 25 Ukraine under German rule 1941–44

would remain, however, under German tutelage. The other, favored by most of the Nazi hierarchy, was to ignore the interests of the Ukrainians altogether and to exploit them ruthlessly for the benefit of the Nazi empire.

As the only member of the Nazi leadership who had firsthand knowledge of Eastern Europe, Rosenberg initially appeared to be the man who would formulate Nazi policy in the newly conquered lands. His appointment as head of the Ministry for Occupied Eastern Territories strengthened this impression. Rosenberg had an understanding of the aspirations of the region's stateless peoples (which did not preclude their economic exploitation by Germany). His well-known conviction that the most effective way of dealing with Russia, Germany's most dangerous rival, was to break up its multinational empire gave the Ukrainian integral nationalists reason to believe that they could come to an understanding with the Nazis. What the integral nationalists did not realize, however, was that Hitler had a low opinion of Rosenberg's theories in general and of his plans for Ukraine in particular.

Nazi racial doctrines held that all Slavs were subhumans (*Untermenschen*) and that their only role was to serve the German master race. Hitler and most of his party associates viewed Ukraine as the primary area for German colonial expansion (*Lebensraum*) and Ukrainians as the future slaves of the German colonists. His early victories encouraged Hitler in his view that concessions to the Ukrainians were unnecessary. Consequently, when the time came to appoint the Nazi ruler of Ukraine, Hitler chose Erich Koch, a notoriously brutal and bigoted administrator known for his personal contempt for Slavs. Koch's attitude toward his assignment was evident in the speech he delivered to his staff upon his arrival in Ukraine in September 1941: "Gentlemen, I am known as a brutal dog. Because of this reason I was appointed as *Reichskommissar* of Ukraine. Our task is to suck from Ukraine all the goods we can get hold of, without consideration of the feelings or the property of the Ukrainians. Gentlemen, I am expecting from you the utmost severity towards the native population."[4] On another occasion, Koch emphasized his loathing for Ukrainians by remarking: "If I find a Ukrainian who is worthy of sitting at the same table with me, I must have him shot."[5] This was the man who more than any other was instrumental in turning Ukrainians against the Germans.

Nazi attitudes toward the Ukrainians were soon reflected in their policies. In August 1941, completely ignoring Ukrainian national aspirations, Hitler ordered the breakup of Ukraine into separate administrative units. The largest of these, which included the Right Bank and much of the Left Bank, was called Reichskommissariat Ukraine, and was placed in the hands of Koch. Refusing to establish his "capital" in Kiev, the traditional Ukrainian center, Koch chose instead the small provincial Volhynian city of Rivne. In a move that was deeply resented by its Ukrainian inhabitants, Galicia became a district of the General Government of Poland rather than being attached to the rest of Ukraine. Bukovyna and a part of southwest Ukraine, which included Odessa, was given to Germany's ally Romania and called Transnistria. Finally, the easternmost areas in the vicinity of Kharkiv, which were close to the front lines, remained under the jurisdiction of the German army. These actions clearly reflected the view of high Nazi officials that "Ukraine does not exist ... it is merely a geographical concept."[6]

The structure and extent of the German civilian administration in Ukraine left no doubt that the Nazis intended to retain total control. An unusually large number of officials were assigned to Ukraine. But because it was one of the last countries to be conquered, Ukraine received only the dregs of German officialdom. Consequently, German arrogance was often compounded by ineptitude. An inviolable principle of Nazi rule was that all important administrative and economic positions down to the county level should be staffed by Germans. Ukrainians were allowed to hold only the lowest administrative positions, such as village elders, mayors of small towns, and auxiliary policemen.

Early indications of the nature of the Nazi regime were its treatment of Jews and prisoners of war. Because the Soviets had made no special effort to evacuate Ukraine's Jewish population (and remained silent about its persecution), most Jews fell into the hands of the Nazis, who established 50 ghettos and over 180 large concentration camps in Ukraine. Within months of their arrival, the Nazis, and especially the ss execution squads (Einsatzgruppen), killed about 850,000 Jews. In Kiev about 33,000 Jews were executed in Babyn Iar (Babi Yar) in two days alone.

Nazi treatment of Soviet prisoners of war was almost as inhuman. In the first six months of the war, millions of Red Army men had surrendered, many willingly, to the Germans. Confident of victory and anxious to eliminate "surplus" Slavs, Nazi authorities herded the prisoners into open-air camps encircled by barbed wire and allowed them to die of exposure, disease, and hunger. Often they simply executed their captives. Consequently, by the end of the war, of the 5.8 million Soviet prisoners who had fallen into German hands, about 3.3 million had perished. About 1.3 million of these fatalities occurred in Ukraine. This treatment of prisoners was not only inhuman, but also stupid. As news of their comrades' fate filtered back to Red Army men on the other side of the front, their resistance stiffened and German casualties rose.

In August–September 1941, the Germans began to introduce policies that had a profound impact on Ukraine's population as a whole. Disregarding the advice of Rosenberg and his staff, Koch decided that the exploitation of Ukrainian agriculture – his main economic goal – could be conducted most efficiently if the collectives were maintained, albeit under German supervision, in somewhat altered forms, and under different names. The Ukrainian peasantry was thus quickly disabused of its dream that the new regime would abolish the collective farms. At the same time that Koch lowered the peasants' income, he demanded that they work from dawn to dusk. These viciously exploitative measures help to explain why about 85% of the food supplies Nazi Germany obtained from occupied Soviet territories came from Ukraine.

Anti-German feelings increased even more when the Nazis decided to use Ukraine not only as a major supplier of food, but also as their main source of forced labor for the undermanned industries and farms of Germany. Initially, Ukrainians had volunteered to work in the Third Reich in order to escape poor conditions at home or to learn a trade. However, as word spread about the harsh labor discipline, humiliating treatment of *Ostarbeiter* (eastern workers), and ridiculously low wages, people tried to avoid the labor drafts by all means possible. By early 1942, Koch's police had to stage massive manhunts, rounding up young Ukrainians in bazaars or as they emerged from churches or cinemas and shipping them to Germany. The extent to which Ukrainians were "favored" for this type of onerous work is evident from the fact that out of the 2.8 million Soviet *Ostarbeiter* in Germany at the end of the war, 2.3 million were from Ukraine.

The staggering brutality of Nazi rule was also evident in the cities and in the treatment of the intelligentsia. Koch drastically limited the flow of foodstuffs into the cities, arguing that Ukrainian urban centers were basically useless. In the long run, the Nazis intended to transform Ukraine into a totally agrarian country and, in the short run, Germany needed the food that Ukrainian urban dwellers consumed. As a result, starvation became commonplace and many urban dwellers were forced to move to the countryside. Kiev, for example, lost about 60% of its population. Kharkiv, which had a population of 700,000 when the Germans arrived, saw 120,000 of its inhabitants shipped to Germany as laborers; 30,000 were executed and about 80,000 starved to death during the course of the war.

Under the circumstances, the educational opportunities of Reichkommissariat Ukraine's inhabitants were severely limited. Indeed, Heinrich Himmler, the chief of the ss, proposed that "the entire Ukrainian intelligentsia should be decimated."[7] Koch believed that three years of grade school was more than enough education for Ukrainians. He even went so far as to curtail medical services in order to undermine "the biological power of the Ukrainians."[8] German-only shops, restaurants, and sections of trolley cars were established to emphasize the superiority of the Germans and the racial inferiority of the Ukrainian *Untermenschen*.

In order to gain a proper perspective on Nazi rule in Ukraine, it is important to understand that it was in Reichskommissariat Ukraine that the Nazi regime exhibited its most extreme form. Although similar conditions existed in other areas of German-occupied Ukraine, these regions were also marked by appreciable differences in administrative practice. In Galicia, for example, which became a district of the General Government of Poland, German rule was less severe than in the eastern regions. It is true that many of the most hated policies, such as conscription of labor, expropriation of food from the villages, and semi-starvation of the cities, were also implemented there. But Galicians, unlike their compatriots in the east, were allowed to form a representative body in Lviv called the Ukrainian Land Committee. Headed by Kost Pankivsky, it was subordinated to Kubijovyč's Ukrainian Central Committee (UCC) in Cracow in March 1942.

To protect the Ukrainian population from repression, the expanded UCC adopted a policy of avoiding confrontations with the Nazis and concentrated on strengthening the Ukrainian presence in the cities and on developing a modern labor force. However, when the need arose, the UCC vigorously defended Ukrainian interests. For example, when several Ukrainian villages were wiped out in a German operation in February 1943, Kubijovyč, the head of the UCC, boldy protested to the Nazi authorities, remarking to Frank: "One has finished executing Jews and is now beginning to execute Ukrainians."[9] Another advantage that the Ukrainians in the General Government enjoyed was the existence of an extensive elementary, secondary, and vocational system of education. They also were able, on a limited scale, to maintain their cooperatives and to engage in cultural activities. As was customary, the Germans monopolized all the key administrative positions in Galicia. But Ukrainians were generally favored over Poles in appointments to positions in the local administration. This policy exacerbated the already deteriorating relations between the two communities, much to the satisfaction of the Germans.

In the easternmost regions of Ukraine, which remained under military jurisdiction, conditions were similar to those in Reichskommissariat Ukraine except that police terror was less prevalent and some Ukrainian civic organizations, notably the one led by Volodymyr Dolenko in Kharkiv, were allowed to exist. Compared to German occupation, that of the Romanians in southwestern Ukraine (Transnistria) was relatively lax. The Romanians delivered Jews to the Nazis rather than exterminating them themselves, refrained from widespread political terror, and allowed free trade. But they vigorously repressed all manifestations of Ukrainian nationalism, banned Ukrainian publications, and tended to favor pro-Russian groups.

Nazi policies in Ukraine were brutal and irrational. Rarely has an occupying power managed to turn an initially friendly, or at least expectant, populace against it so quickly and completely as did the Nazis in Ukraine. The extent to which the Nazis allowed their theories of racial superiority to cloud their perception of political realities will always remain puzzling. Even some high-ranking officials of the Third Reich seemed to be taken aback by the magnitude of German blunders. For example, as early as 1942, a close associate of Rosenberg, Otto Brautigam, admitted that "the forty million Ukrainians who greeted us joyfully as liberators are today indifferent to us and are already beginning to swing into the enemy camp."[10] But even when they admitted their mistakes, the Nazis did little to correct them. In the view of many modern historians, this Nazi failure to utilize effectively the non-Russian nationalities, and particularly the Ukrainians, against the Soviet regime was one of their greatest political blunders in the war.

Collaboration In dealing with the Nazis, the Ukrainians had two alternatives: to obey or to resist. As throughout all of German-occupied Europe, the vast majority chose obedience. And when obedience went beyond the limits of the passive fulfillment of German commands, it usually became collaboration. In Western Europe, where loyalty to one's state was taken for granted and the Nazis were the one and only enemy, collaboration with the Germans was generally viewed as a form of treason. But in Ukraine, collaboration was a much more complicated issue. It was, first of all, unclear as to how much loyalty Ukrainians owed to Stalin's regime or to the Polish state that had mistreated them. Who was the primary enemy? Was it the Stalinist system, which inflicted such great suffering in the 1930s, or the Nazi regime, which was currently (but perhaps only temporarily) in power? Finally, given the extreme ruthlessness of both regimes in Ukraine, collaboration was often the price of survival for many Ukrainians.

For Ukrainians the war posed the problem of how to make the best of what was essentially a no-win situation. From an average individual's point of view, success generally meant the preservation of one's life. For Ukrainian leaders and their organizations in German-occupied territories the goal – or rather, the puzzle – was how to preserve Ukrainian interests from both the Nazis and the increasingly stronger Soviets. Distasteful as it was, some Ukrainian leaders decided to side with one totalitarian system in order to withstand the other. Because the Soviets appeared to be the greater long-term threat, almost all Ukrainian organizations in the Third Reich collaborated with the Germans at one time or another, but always to a limited degree and for strictly tactical reasons. As a people without a state of their own, Ukrainians operated from a position of weakness. They were unable to formulate policy or influence events. Consequently, Ukrainian collaboration with the Nazis was insignificant compared to that of Germany's allies. Finally, although there were opportunists, anti-Semites, and ideological fanatics among the Ukrainians, there is no evidence indicating that their number was proportionately greater than among other nationalities.

On the individual level, collaboration with the Germans usually took the form of participation in the local administration or the German-supervised auxiliary police. Motives for taking such positions varied. In Western Ukraine, where, before the war, Poles had excluded Ukrainians from even the lowest administrative positions, the desire to have at least a minimum of authority in Ukrainian hands and to turn the tables on hated rivals was often a major motive. The need to find employment or to satisfy personal ambitions was, as always, an important consideration. The most notorious form of collaboration was to act as a concentration camp guard. Invariably, guard positions were held by Soviet prisoners of war, who had the difficult choice of accepting the task or perishing in the camps.

Given the lowly position of Ukrainian collaborators in the Nazi apparatus and the SS monopoly on the actual extermination of Jews, Ukrainian participation in the massacres was neither extensive nor decisive. When it did occur, it usually took the form of auxiliary policemen herding Jews into ghettos. However, there were also many Ukrainians who risked the death penalty by aiding Jews. Metropolitan Sheptytsky was an outstanding example: not only did he shelter hundreds of Jews in monasteries but he also used his sermons to decry the Nazi slaughter of Jews. In 1943 an SS report to Himmler stated that the metropolitan was adamantly opposed to the Nazi anti-Semitic outrages and that he had come to consider nazism to be an even greater evil than communism.[11]

Aside from the abortive interlude between the OUN and the Germans in the early days of the war, the most important case of Ukrainian collaboration with Hitler's regime on the organizational level was the formation of the SS volunteer Galicia Division. In spring 1943, after the stunning German defeat at Stalingrad, Nazi authorities belatedly decided to recruit non-German "easterners" into their forces. Consequently, Otto Wächter, the governor of Galicia, approached the Ukrainian Central Committee (UCC) with a proposal to form a Ukrainian division in the German army. After much debate and despite opposition from the OUN-B, Kubijovyč and his associates agreed. Their immediate reason for the creation of such a division was the hope that it might help to improve German treatment of the Ukrainians. The specter of 1917–20 was also extremely influential in persuading the UCC leadership, for Kubijovyč and his associates (as well as Metropolitan Sheptytsky himself) were convinced that it was the lack of a well-trained army that had prevented Ukrainians from establishing their own state after the First World War. Realizing that the defeat of Germany was probable, they were determined that this time Ukrainians would not be caught in the ensuing chaos without a regular military force.

In the negotiations leading up to the formation of the division, the UCC insisted that the unit fight only against the Soviets. Wächter, on Himmler's instructions, demanded that the entire higher divisional command be German and, in order not to irritate Hitler, that the division be called Galician rather than Ukrainian. When the UCC called for volunteers in June 1943, over 82,000 men responded. Of these, 13,000 eventually became members of the SS Volunteer Galicia Division.

The men of the Galician Division were not the only Ukrainians in Hitler's armies. Scattered among the approximately 1 million former Soviet citizens who wore German uniforms in 1944 were about 220,000 Ukrainians (most of the others were Russians). To put these numbers into perspective, it should be remembered that about 2 million Ukrainians fought on the Soviet side and that large numbers also fought in Polish, Romanian, Hungarian, Czech, American, and Canadian forces. Such was the fate of a stateless people.

Resistance

As elsewhere in occupied Europe, underground resistance to the Germans in Ukraine developed soon after their arrival, primarily in response to Nazi policies. It was aided by the fact that the Germans did not have enough troops to control the vast areas they conquered. Furthermore, there already existed in Ukraine underground networks organized by the OUN, the Soviets, and, in the northwest, the Poles, all of which were capable of putting partisan forces into the field. Recruits for anti-German partisan warfare were not lacking and were drawn from the large numbers of Red Army stragglers, fugitive Ukrainian nationalists, Communist party members, Jews, turncoat policemen, and escapees from forced-labor contingents who took to the forests to escape the Germans. They were joined by those who simply wanted an opportunity to strike a blow against the Nazis. Because much of Ukraine is steppe and, therefore, unsuitable for partisan warfare, most activity was concentrated in the northwestern part of the country, in the forests of Volhynia, the swamps of Polissia, and the Carpathian Mountains.

The UPA (Ukrainian Insurgent Army)   It was in Polissia and Volhynia that the first Ukrainian nationalist partisan units appeared and, surprisingly, at the outset they were not associated with OUN. As soon as the Nazi-Soviet war broke out, Taras Bulba-Borovets, a local Ukrainian activist linked with the UNR-Petliurist government-in-exile in Warsaw, formed an irregular unit called "Polissian Sich," later renamed the UPA (Ukrainska Povstanska Armiia — Ukrainian Insurgent Army), for the purpose of clearing his region of the remnants of the Red Army. When the Germans tried to disband his unit in late 1941, he took his men into "the woods" to fight both the Germans and the Soviets. In 1942, members of both OUN-M and OUN-B, who were fleeing Koch's repression, also established small units in Volhynia.

In late 1942, the OUN-B decided to form a large-scale partisan force and thereby lay the foundation for a regular Ukrainian army, which they believed would be needed when the Nazi-Soviet war came to an end. There were also extremely pressing immediate reasons for such a step: first, as German repression of the local populace increased, the villagers demanded that the OUN take steps to protect them, and, second, as Soviet partisans from Belorussia began to penetrate into northwestern Ukraine by late 1942, it was necessary for the OUN to assume the role of the "people's army" in order to prevent the Soviets from doing so.

In order to unite all the nationalist units, the OUN-B forcibly incorporated the units of Borovets and OUN-M into its own forces for which it now usurped the name UPA. Roman Shukhevych, a member of the OUN-B leadership and the highest-ranking Ukrainian officer in the recently disbanded *Nachtigall* unit was appointed commander-in-chief of the expanded force. Benefiting from the extensive and efficient OUN-B underground network, UPA quickly grew into a large, well-organized partisan army, which took control of large parts of Volhynia, Polissia, and, later, Galicia. Although many Ukrainian émigré sources claim that, at its high point in late 1943 to early 1944, its numbers reached close to 100,000, well-substantiated estimates place the figure at be tween 30,000 and 40,000 fighters.[12] Compared to other underground move ments in Nazi-occupied Europe, the UPA was unique in that it had practically no foreign support. Its growth and strength were, therefore, an indication of the very considerable popular support it enjoyed among the Ukrainians.

The rapid growth of UPA necessitated the broadening of its political base Although the OUN-B provided much of UPA's leadership, it was clear that one integral nationalist faction could not claim to be representative of Ukraini ans as a whole. Therefore, in July 1944, at the initiative of OUN-B, delegates from various prewar West Ukrainian political parties (but not the OUN-M) and spokesmen for the East Ukrainians met secretly near Sambir in Galicia to form the UHVR (Ukrainska Holovna Vyzvolna Rada – Ukrainian Supreme Libera tion Council). The platform of the new organization was noteworthy because it reflected the changes that the war, and especially the contacts with Sovie Ukraine, had exerted on the thinking of the integral nationalists.

Some of these ideological changes were already evident in 1943, when an OUN-B congress declared: "The OUN is fighting against imperialism and agains empires ... for this reason, the OUN is fighting against the USSR and agains Germany's 'New Europe.'"[13] Emphasizing its support for an anti-Nazi and anti-Soviet position, the UHVR also proposed several important amendment to integral nationalist doctrine. It called for greater tolerance of non-integra nationalist ideologies, rejected racial and ethnic exclusivity, and paid much greater attention to socioeconomic issues, which were of greatest interest to Soviet Ukrainians. Furthermore, UHVR urged the non-Russian nationalities of the USSR to unite against Moscow. It soon became evident, however, that no matter what adjustments the integral nationalists made, they would find it extremely difficult to survive in the tightly controlled Soviet system.

The Ukrainian/Polish massacres   Not only did UPA take on both the Nazis and the Soviets, but in the mixed Ukrainian/Polish areas of Volhynia, Polissia and Kholm, it also became involved in an exceedingly brutal conflict with the Poles. Regardless of the outcome of the war, Ukrainian integral nationalist were determined to drive the Poles (many of whom were colonists from the interwar period) out of areas where Ukrainians were a majority. For its part the Polish nationalist underground army, the Armija Krajowa (AK), was jus as determined to retain control of lands that had been part of the Polish state. The result was a murderous struggle – often encouraged by the Germans and provoked by Soviet partisans – between Ukrainian and Polish forces for territory and to settle old scores.

Tragically, it was the civilian population that bore most of the costs. According to Polish sources, in 1943–44 about 60,000–80,000 Polish men, women, and children were massacred in Volhynia by Ukrainians, especially the SB, the security units of the OUN.[14] Ukrainians claim that massacres of their people began earlier, in 1942, when Poles wiped out thousands of Ukrainian villagers in the predominantly Polish areas of Kholm, and that they continued in 1944–45 among the defenseless Ukrainian minority west of the San River. In any case, it is clear that both Ukrainian and Polish armed units engaged in wholesale slaughter, bringing to a bloodly climax the hatred that had been increasing between the two peoples for generations.

Soviet partisans in Ukraine Soon after the German invasion, Communist party officials began to organize underground units behind enemy lines. Throughout the war Soviet partisans were tighly controlled by the Kremlin. Because the Soviet underground developed slowly and achieved few successes in 1941 and early 1942, it was reorganized by the Central Partisan Staff in Moscow in May 1942. A month later the Ukrainian Partisan Command was established, led by Timofei Strokach, a high NKVD official. After the victory at Stalingrad, the numbers and activity of Soviet partisans grew considerably, especially in the desolate, swampy regions of Belorussia.

In Ukraine, however, Soviet partisans never became as significant as they were in Belorussia. Much of the open Ukrainian countryside was unsuited for partisan warfare. And in Western Ukraine, where the OUN was well established, Soviet partisans had no popular base for their activity. Consequently, most of their operations in Ukraine were confined to parts of Volhynia and Polissia.

The goals of the Soviet partisans were to disrupt German communications (they were especially effective in the so-called "railroad war," that is, impeding the flow of German reinforcements to the front); to tie down much-needed German troops; to spread insecurity and disorder behind enemy lines; and to maintain a Soviet presence in occupied territories. A favorite tactic of the Soviet (as well as the UPA) partisans was to launch lengthy raids from the "partisan republics," that is, large, inaccessible areas in Polissia and Volhynia controlled by them. The Soviet partisans often clashed with the UPA, seeking to eliminate its leaders and to undermine its base of support.

Among the major Soviet partisan commanders in Ukraine were Sydir Kovpak, Aleksander Saburov, and Petro Vershyhora. The celebrated Kovpak established himself in Polissia early in 1943. With a staff of well-trained officers and supplies delivered to secret airfields, he built up a force of several thousand men. In the summer of 1943, he launched a lengthy raid into the Carpathians. It did not achieve its main military goal – the destruction of the Carpathian oil fields – and most of the unit was destroyed. But the psychological and political impact of this raid was considerable, for it demonstrated the Germans' inability to secure their hinterland and raised the possibility of a Soviet return.

Soviet authors are quick to note that their underground in Ukraine was a massive internationalist movement, consisting of sixty-two nationalities. But according to Soviet data, Ukrainians were clearly underrepresented in Soviet partisan ranks.[15] Although Ukrainians were close to 80% of the population, they constituted only 46% of the fighters in the five major Soviet partisan units in Ukraine (only one-third of Kovpak's men were Ukrainians). Russians were overrepresented, accounting for more than 37% of the partisans. Some Soviet works claim that the number of Soviet partisans in Ukraine was as high as 250,000 and even 500,000, while others put it at less than 50,000. Western specialists usually accept the last figure.[16] In any case, Soviet depiction of its partisan movement as a massive, patriotic rallying of the Ukrainian masses against the Germans is misleading (as is the nationalist treatment of UPA, which makes similar claims). The vast majority of Ukraine's population during the war remained politically uncommitted and was concerned not so much with resistance as with survival.

The Soviet Return to Ukraine

In 1943 a decisive shift occurred in the Nazi-Soviet war: as the German offensive lost impetus, the Soviets began a huge counteroffensive. The first indication that Hitler's armies had overextended themselves came at the dramatic Soviet victory at Stalingrad on the Volga in January 1943. Marshaling the remainder of their reserves, the Germans made their last great attempt to recapture the initiative in the summer of 1943 at the Battle of Kursk. But here, too, they were defeated. Meanwhile, the Soviets benefited from their vast manpower reserves, improved war production, and a huge influx of Allied war matériel. Immediately after their victory at Kursk, they launched a counterattack whose major goal was to recapture Left-Bank Ukraine.

The Soviet push into Ukraine was massive, involving over 40% of the Red Army's infantry and 80% of its tanks. According to Western historians, the Red Army enjoyed a three-to-one advantage in overall manpower and – thanks to American supplies – an estimated five-to-one advantage in equipment. Soviet sources, however, claim that their numerical advantage was less than two to one and that it was their valor and skill, rather than their overwhelming numbers, that brought them success. In any case, unlike the blitzkrieg of 1941, which had allowed the Germans to overrun Ukraine in four months, the Soviet "bulldozer" moved forward sector by sector, methodically pounding its opponents into exhaustion. In a little more than a year, it had reconquered all of Ukraine.

In late summer and fall of 1943, Soviet forces, led by Ivan Konev, Nikolai Vatutin, and Radion Malinovsky, took the Left Bank and Donbas regions. On 23 August, the Germans lost Kharkiv for the second, and final, time; in September and October, after vicious fighting, the Red Army breached the powerful German defensive line along the Dnieper; and on 6 November, Vatutin entered Kiev. After a brief pause, in January 1944, about 2.3 million Red Army men launched the drive to force the Germans out of the Right Bank and Crimea. An important victory near Korsun-Shevchenko assured them of achieving this goal and, by March, only Western Ukraine remained in German hands.

The third stage in the reconquest of Ukraine began in mid July 1944. Near Brody, the Soviets encircled and destroyed eight German divisions, totaling about 60,000 men. Included among the latter were the 10,000 men of the Galician Division who had the misfortune of receiving their baptism by fire under these catastrophic conditions. About 5000 members of the Galician Division managed to break out of the encirclement, but over 3000 were killed, wounded, or captured. An estimated 2000 eluded captivity and many of them later joined the UPA. After this victory, Soviet forces quickly overran Galicia, capturing Lviv, Peremyshl, and Stanyslaviv on 27 July. In September they crossed the Carpathians and by October 1944 all ethnic Ukrainian territory was in Soviet hands.

Just as the Soviets had done in 1941, the Germans applied a scorched-earth policy during their retreat from Ukraine. In Himmler's orders to his troops, he emphasized: "It is necessary that in retreating from the regions of Ukraine we do not leave behind a single person, head of livestock or measure of grain ... The enemy should find there a completely burned and devastated land."[17] Consequently, in a 200-mile-wide strip along the left bank of the Dnieper, hordes of people were forcibly evacuated from their homes and large parts of Poltava, Dniepropetrovsk, Kremenchuk, and other cities were burned. The right bank of the river was spared the large-scale devastation, although not the massive evacuations.

Stalin's propaganda offensive   Unlike Hitler, Stalin was willing to learn from his mistakes. After seeing how ambivalent Soviet citizens had been toward his regime at the outset of the war, he launched a propaganda campaign. It was designed to encourage Soviet citizens in occupied areas to resist the Germans and to portray his regime in a new light, implying that it would be more tolerable after the war. Because in the fighting against the Germans, nationalism was clearly a stronger motivating force than Marxism, it became the major theme of the campaign. Russian nationalism received the most attention as images of the Russian Empire's glories, of its struggles against foreign invaders in the past, and of its great heroes were repeatedly conjured up. But Stalin also made a strong effort to assure himself of Ukrainian sympathies.

To create the impression that the Ukrainian Soviet Republic was a sovereign state, supplementary Ukrainian ministries of foreign affairs and defense were formed. Like other republics, Ukraine was given the right – but not the opportunity – to engage in foreign relations. Prominent Ukrainians received high government posts. For example, the playwright Oleksander Korniichuk became minister of foreign affairs and the lionized partisan leader Sydir Kovpak was chosen to be minister of defense. There were even indications that Ukraine would have its own military units. Although this possibility never came to pass, the southern sector of the front was renamed the Ukrainian front and a prestigious award for valor was named after Bohdan Khmelnytsky. Control of Ukrainian cultural activity loosened perceptibly and Volodomyr Sosiura's patriotic poem "Love Ukraine" even received the Stalin Prize.

Having noted how quickly and enthusiatically people had turned to religion in the German-occupied regions, Stalin made his peace with the Russian Orthodox church on Soviet territory by eliminating many restrictions on its activities and by disbanding the antireligious propaganda organization, League of Militant Atheists. The Orthodox church returned these favors by encouraging its faithful to fight the Germans and by excommunicating those who cooperated with them.

The Soviet return to Western Ukraine   Because Western Ukraine had been under Soviet rule only briefly, the return of the Red Army had a markedly different effect there than in the Sovietized east. In sharp contrast to their relatively cautious policies of 1939, the Soviets were determined to impose their rule on the nationalistic West Ukrainians quickly and uncompromisingly when they arrived in Western Ukraine in 1944. They mobilized all men between 18 and 50 years of age and sent them – poorly trained and badly armed – into battle. Repression against the Greek Catholic church began immediately. Metropolitan Sheptytsky was put under house arrest when Lviv was occupied and he died several months later. His successor, Josef Slipy, was sent to a Siberian concentration camp. Preparations were also begun for the forced incorporation of the Greek Catholic church into the Moscow-controlled Russian Orthodox church.

Over 30,000 party workers and 3500 specially trained propagandists poured into Western Ukraine to begin once again the process of Sovietizing the region. The intelligentsia was the most nationally conscious segment of the population and Soviet authorities made a concerted effort to alienate it from the peasants and workers. Because Soviet propagandists promised to give "special attention" to those who did not have a Soviet education and who had been brought up in "bourgeois" schools, a large part of the

West Ukrainian intelligentsia fled, together with the retreating Germans, from areas that were not yet occupied by the Red Army.

The arrival of the Red Army in Western Ukraine placed before the leadership of the UPA the difficult question of whether to continue their fight against Stalin's overwhelming forces. Initially the OUN had assumed that, in their struggle for empire, the Nazis and Soviets would bring each other down in a manner similar to 1917–18. When it became clear, however, that the Soviets were going to emerge the victors in the east, the OUN hoped that the defeated Germans and the Western powers would form an alliance to thwart Soviet expansionism. It was this false hope that, to a large extent, convinced the UPA/OUN leadership to continue the struggle against the Soviets.

After the main forces of the Red Army had rolled through Western Ukraine, the UPA staged attacks designed to disrupt mobilization efforts, to prevent deportations of "unreliable elements," and to stem the repression of the Greek Catholic church. Its special targets were the NKVD, Communist party members, and those who collaborated with the Soviets. In spring 1944 in Volhynia, a UPA unit mortally wounded the famous Red Army general Nikolai Vatutin. To eliminate the UPA, Soviet forces staged huge blockades of partisan territories, sent agents to infiltrate UPA units and to assassinate their commanders, and formed special antipartisan battalions. Soviet propagandists also launched an intense campaign to portray the OUN and UPA as the henchmen of the Nazis – a campaign that continues to this day.

Some of the Soviet clashes with the UPA were on a large scale. In April 1944 near Kremianets in Volhynia, for example, about 30,000 Soviet troops participated in an anti-UPA operation. Most clashes, however, were small but frequent. According to Soviet sources, in the fall of 1944 in Volhynia, the UPA carried out 800 raids. In the Stanyslaviv region of Galicia alone it killed about 1500 Soviet activists. During this period, the Soviets claimed to have wiped out thirty-six UPA "bands" totaling 4300 men.[18] As might be expected, the fighting was fierce and no quarter was given by either side. Wounded UPA soldiers frequently committed suicide rather than fall into enemy hands. As the war ended on 9 May 1945, Soviet control of the West Ukrainian countryside was still far from complete.

◆

Even a cursory listing of losses reflects the terrible impact that the Second World War had on Ukraine and its inhabitants. About 5.3 million, or one of six inhabitants of Ukraine, perished in the conflict. An additional 2.3 million had been shipped to Germany to perform forced labor. Over 700 cities and towns and 28,000 villages were totally or partially destroyed, leaving close to 10 million people homeless. A graphic indication of the extremes of Nazi brutality experienced in Ukraine was that for one village that was destroyed and its inhabitants executed in France and Czechoslovakia, 250 villages and their inhabitants suffered such a fate in Ukraine. Because Ukraine suffered more damage in the war than any other European country, the economic losses were staggering. The complete or partial destruction of over 16,000 industrial enterprises and 28,000 collective farms meant that Ukraine lost much of what had been gained at such great cost during the 1930s. Estimates place the total damage to Ukraine's economy at about 40%. Thus, for a second time in little more than a decade, Ukrainians had suffered greatly from the brutal excesses of totalitarian regimes.

Although more nationally conscious than they had been in the 1917–20 period, Ukrainians during the Second World War were caught between the Nazis and Soviets. To the great disillusionment of the integral nationalists, they had practically no opportunity to pursue their own interests. In contrast to the 1917–20 period, Ukrainians were in a position only to react to events in 1939–45 – not to influence them. Yet, despite horrendous losses and setbacks, the final outcome of the war did have some positive features from the Ukrainian point of view. Most noteworthy was the fact that, as a result of the Soviet conquest of Western Ukraine, all Ukrainians were united in a single political entity for the first time in centuries: in the USSR, or more specifically, in the Ukrainian Soviet Socialist Republic (URSR). Moreover, Stalin's temporary concessions to the national aspirations of the non-Russian nationalities gave rise to hopes that after the war "things would be different." Finally, as part of the Soviet Union, Ukraine was included among the victors in the war. For many Soviet Ukrainians the exhilaration of victory gave rise to a feeling of hope, expressed by a Soviet officer in 1945: "The entire atmosphere was charged with the expectation of something new, something magnificent and glorious. None of us doubted in the brightness of the future."[19]

24

Reconstruction and Retrenchment

The impact of the Second World War on Ukraine was not only devastating but unusually far-reaching. In many crucial ways, the Ukraine that emerged from the war was very different from what it had been previously. Its borders had been greatly expanded; its political and economic significance in the USSR grew; the composition of its population changed radically; and, most important, for the first time in centuries all Ukrainians found themselves within the borders of a single state. Both Ukrainian society and the Soviet regime sought to adjust to these changes and their attempts to do so constitute the major theme in the history of postwar Ukraine.

ક

Territorial Settlements and Population Changes

For the Ukrainians the most important territorial settlement brought about by the war was the incorporation of Western Ukraine into the USSR. To the great dismay of the Poles, Stalin persuaded Great Britain and the United States to accept his annexation of lands in which West Ukrainians constituted the majority of the population. Consequently, at the Yalta conference in 1945, the Soviets were able to pressure the newly reestablished Polish state to give up its claims to almost all of Galicia and Volhynia and to draw the border with Soviet Ukraine along the so-called Curzon Line. Especially painful to the Poles was the loss of Lviv, long a bastion of Polish culture and dominance.

Why was Stalin so insistent on annexing Western Ukraine? Formally, his argument was that it was only natural that the oppressed West Ukrainians should be united with their brethren in Soviet Ukraine. But since Stalin's concern for Ukrainian needs was questionable, political self-interest clearly played a role. Because the Poles were in no position to challenge him militarily or otherwise, Stalin simply felt no need to return Galicia and Volhynia to

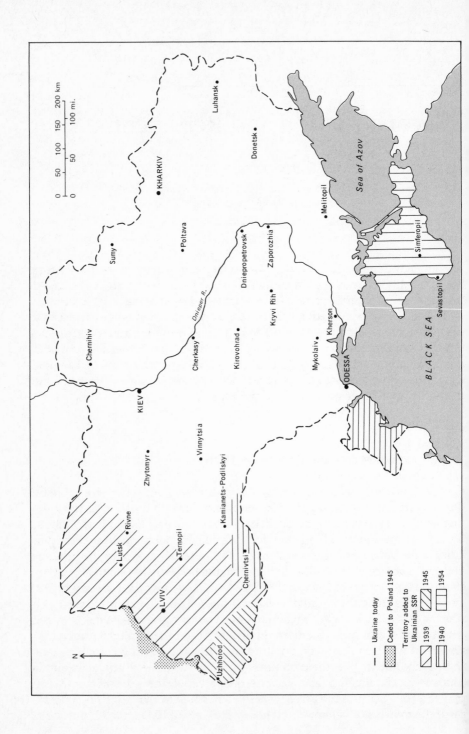

Sea of Azov

BLACK SEA

Sevastopil •

Simferopil •

Melitopil •

Luhansk •

Donetsk •

KHARKIV •

Poltava •

Sumy •

Zaporozhia •

Dniepropetrovsk •

Kryvi Rih •

Kherson •

Kirovohrad •

Mykolaiv •

Chernihiv •

Cherkasy •

KIEV •

ODESSA •

Vinnytsia •

Zhytomyr •

Kamianets-Podilskyi •

Rivne •

Lutsk •

Ternopil •

LVIV •

Chernivtsi •

Uzhhorod •

Dnieper R.

N ←—|

| 0 | 50 | 100 | 150 | 200 km |

| 0 | 50 | 100 mi. |

- - - Ukraine today

Ceded to Poland 1945

Territory added to
Ukrainian SSR

1939   1945

1940   1954

them. Moreover, possession of Western Ukraine gave the Soviets a convenient strategic position with respect to Poland, Hungary, and Czechoslovakia. Finally, Stalin was anxious to destroy Ukrainian nationalism and to do so he needed to control its hotbed in Western Ukraine.

The territorial settlement with the Poles also included provisions for an exchange of populations. Therefore, between 1944 and 1946, the Soviets allowed about 1 million Poles (including a significant number of Jews and Ukrainians masquerading as Poles) to move from Galicia and Volhynia to Poland. In return, close to 520,000 Ukrainians, who had found themselves on the Polish side of the new border, immigrated, voluntarily or under duress, to Soviet Ukraine. This most recent exodus of the Poles concluded their long, drawn-out retreat from Ukraine that had begun back in 1648 when the Polish nobles lost control of the Left Bank. The retreat had continued throughout the 18th and 19th centuries, when these nobles first lost political control of the Right Bank and then their socioeconomic dominance in the area. It concluded after the Second World War, when the Soviets ejected them from Galicia and Volhynia where, 600 years earlier, their advance into Ukraine had begun. With the withdrawal of the Poles, an important, though frequently antagonistic and often invigorating relationship ceased to exist in Ukrainian history – but not before it produced, in 1947, a final and characteristically tragic sequel.

Shortly after the war, Moscow also persuaded Czechoslovakia and Romania to surrender their claims to Transcarpathia and Bukovyna, respectively. Thus, Western Ukraine, with its more than 7 million inhabitants and 110,000 sq. km of territory, was permanently incorporated into the USSR. By late 1945, the territory of Soviet Ukraine expanded to over 580,000 sq. km, inhabited by about 41 million people.

The Poles were not the only ethnic minority whose presence in Ukraine decreased sharply as a result of the war. Prior to 1939 there were about 650,000 Germans in Ukraine, mostly descendants of 18th-century colonists. Fearful lest they join their invading compatriots, Stalin had almost all of them evacuated to Central Asia. A similar fate befell the approximately 200,000 Crimean Tatars whose homeland was later incorporated into the Ukrainian republic. Convinced that they had been overly cooperative with the Germans, Stalin ordered their mass expulsion from the Crimea in 1944. Brutally ejected from their homes in that year, only about one-half of the Tatars survived the journey to Central Asia. But the most tragic fate awaited the Jews of Ukraine. As a result of the Nazi extermination policies, mass evacuations, and population exchanges, of the approximately 2.7 million Jews who had lived among the Ukrainians in the 1930s, only about 800,000 remained.

In sharp contrast to these shrinking minorities, the Russian minority in Ukraine increased dramatically in size. After the war, there was a great shortage of industrial workers, government bureaucrats, and party functionaries in Ukraine, especially in the newly annexed western lands. Encouraged by the Soviet government, hundreds of thousands of Russians moved into Ukraine, particularly into the cities, to fill these positions. Their rapidly rising numbers are evident from the following statistics: in 1939 there were 4 million Russians in Ukraine constituting about 12% of the population; by 1959, the figure had grown to 7 million or 16%. In Western Ukraine, where there had been practically no Russians before the war, by 1959 their number had risen to 330,000, representing 5% of the population.

In the radical restructuring of Ukraine's ethnic composition that took place after the war, peoples such as the Poles, Jews, and Crimean Tatars, who had long played a crucial role in the history of Ukraine, adding greatly to its cultural and ethnic mosaic, faded in importance or practically disappeared. Their places were taken largely by the Russians. Meanwhile, the incorporation of the West Ukrainians did not greatly raise the proportion of Ukrainians in the land because they only made up for the population losses suffered by Ukraine during the war. In this process, Ukraine changed from a multinational into a largely binational society, one in which a demographically stagnant Ukrainian majority existed side by side with a continually growing Russian minority.

Reconstruction

Four years of the most destructive war in history left the Soviet Union with the colossal task of economic reconstruction. Industrial production in Ukraine in 1945, for example, was only 26% of the 1940 level. As might be expected, the Soviet approach to rebuilding its shattered economy began with the formulation of the fourth Five-Year Plan (1946–50). Once again the plan drew on the great advantage of a totalitarian system: the ability to allocate resources without taking the desires or needs of the people into account. Hence its staggering demands: it called on the people to rebuild the ravaged areas, to restore industry and agriculture to prewar levels, and even to surpass those levels – all in less than five years. Stalin proposed a number of grandiose "transformation-of-nature" projects, which in Ukraine included the construction of a huge dam on the Dnieper and the creation of large forested zones in the steppe to control drought. Despite the sacrifices and exhaustion of the war, Soviet workers were expected to work harder than ever because the plan demanded a 36% rise in productivity.

Economic reconstruction   As in the 1930s, the fourth Five-Year Plan produced uneven results. In heavy industry, which received 85% of investment, the reconstruction effort was remarkably successful. By 1950 the industrial output of Ukraine was 15% higher than in 1940. In Western Ukraine, which had practically no heavy industry before the war, progress was especially impressive: by 1950 the industrial output of the region rose by 230%. In the 1950s

Ukraine once again became one of the leading industrial countries of Europe. It produced more pig iron per capita than did Great Britain, West Germany, and France (only West Germany smelted more steel), and it mined almost as much coal as West Germany. But although Ukrainian industry became even stronger than it had been before the war, its share of total Soviet production declined because the new industrial centers that had arisen beyond the Urals grew at an even faster rate.

More and bigger factories, however, did not lead to a significant improvement in the standard of living. The traditional Soviet neglect of consumer goods reached such extremes that the purchase of a pair of shoes, a toothbrush, or even a loaf of bread was fraught with difficulty. By 1950 light industry had reached only 80% of its prewar level. Buying consumer goods became even more difficult because of a currency "reform" in 1947 that devalued the ruble and wiped out personal savings.

Nowhere were the failings of the reconstruction effort more evident than in agriculture, a chronic weak point of the Soviet economy. True, with the loss of most of the livestock and equipment during the war, agriculture was damaged to an even greater degree than industry. But the low priority it was accorded by Soviet planners and the counterproductive agricultural policies applied by Soviet officials greatly impeded improvements in the countryside. To make matters worse, there was a catastrophic drought in 1946 and, for the third time under Soviet rule, Ukrainian peasants experienced famine.

Despite its obvious and chronic problems, Soviet leaders were committed to restoring collectivization and even intensifying it. In 1946 steps were taken to take back from the peasants the land and equipment they had managed to "privatize" during the war. The next year, Nikita Khrushchev first launched in Ukraine, the Soviet Union's agricultural laboratory, an ambitious project to solve agricultural problems. It called for the consolidation of small collective farms into huge "agro-cities" that, in theory, would make most efficient use of the very scarce farm machinery, while providing the approximately 5000 inhabitants with all the amenities of city life. The project also called for the elimination of the private garden plots on which peasants had grown much of their food. Finally, it promised to give the regime even greater control over the rural population. But the proposed elimination of their tiny but crucial plots was too much for the peasants: so widespread were their passive resistance and vocal protests that the government had to drop the "agro-city" scheme. Moreover, the chaos and bitterness that this project engendered only hindered grain production. Thus, by 1950, grain production in Ukraine had reached only about 60% of the 1940 level and food remained a scarce commodity.

Political reconstruction   The Communist Party of Ukraine (CPU) weathered the war suprisingly well, although, at the outset of the conflict, its condition was grim indeed. Much of the onus for the early defeats, mistakes, and staggering losses was laid at the feet of the party, resulting in a drastic decline in its prestige and authority. Mobilization and casualties reduced the number of Ukraine's Communists from over 600,000 in 1940 to less than 200,000 in 1945. Most had been evacuated during the Soviet retreat so that only about 15,000 actually remained in Ukraine during much of the war. However, as Soviet fortunes improved, so also did those of Ukraine's Communists.

A striking characteristic of the party members, especially their leadership, who concentrated on Ukrainian affairs during the war, was the strong sense of solidarity they developed. To a great extent this effect was a result of the camaraderie that flourished in the ranks of the partisan movement that many of them had organized and led. This close-knit coterie of Ukraine's top Communists was often called the "Partisan clan" and many of them later became members of the Ukrainian "mafias" associated with Khrushchev and Brezhnev.

After the war, as Communists returned from military service or evacuation and as new recruits poured in, the party's membership in Ukraine shot up again, and by 1950 it was over 700,000. Still, the number of Communists in Ukraine remained comparatively low: only 20 out of 1000 people belonged to the party, while the all-union average was 30 out of 1000. Significant changes also occurred in the CPU's ethnic composition. Anxious to be part of the victorious Soviet regime, ambitious Ukrainians showed a greater interest than ever in joining the party. Thus, while in 1920 Ukrainians constituted only 19% of the CPU, by 1958 the figure was over 60%. True, Russians were still heavily overrepresented at the uppermost levels, but even there the Ukrainian presence was making itself felt. Another characteristic of the postwar Ukrainian (as well as all-union) party was its tendency to attract an ever-increasing portion of the new Soviet socioeconomic elite. Thus, in the 1950s every fifth doctor and every third engineer was a party member, while only one out of thirty-five workers and one out of every forty-five collective farmers were members. Clearly, the postwar party was assuming the role of a well-entrenched establishment.

The Ukrainian Communists may have been pleased with their quick resurgence after the war, but Stalin expected more of them. Compared to that of other areas of the Soviet Union, Ukraine's industrial reconstruction had progressed slowly; its all-important agricultural sector was in catastrophic condition, and nationalism, especially in Western Ukraine, was far from extinguished. Therefore, in March 1947, Stalin again dispatched his troubleshooter Kaganovich to replace Khrushchev as leader of the CPU. Apparently the unpopular Kaganovich had little success and Nikita Khrushchev, who, although a Russian, exhibited some signs of local patriotism, returned to Kiev once more.

On the governmental level, the most noteworthy effect of the war was the unexpected – although very limited – emergence of Ukraine on the international stage. At Stalin's insistence, in April 1945, Ukraine and Belorussia, along with the USSR, were included among the forty-seven founding states of the United Nations. It is commonly accepted that the main reason for Stalin's position was his desire to obtain extra votes in the UN (originally he had demanded that each of the sixteen Soviet republics have a vote). However, there are indications that the move was also Stalin's way of responding to the Ukrainians' pride in their role in defeating Nazi Germany. In any case, since 1945, a Ukrainian mission has functioned at the UN. According to Soviet sources, by 1950 Ukraine had also become a member of twenty international organizations and concluded sixty-five treaties on its own.[1] However, in the UN as elsewhere, Ukraine has never deviated from positions taken by the USSR. When in 1947, Britain approached Soviet Ukraine about establishing direct diplomatic ties, it never received a response. Western scholars conclude that the function of the Ukrainian foreign ministry is merely "ceremonial, ornamental, and symbolic."

In evaluating the potential significance of Ukraine's international exposure, Yaroslav Bilinsky writes: "The international representation of the Ukrainian SSR, complete with anthem, national flag, and foreign minister undoubtedly belongs to the category of Soviet constitutional trappings ... Should the regime prove successful in emasculating Ukrainian nationalism, no constitutional provisions will be able to reinvigorate it. Should it fail in doing so, such colorful trappings as an international representation will provide food for thought and, under favorable circumstances, may also provide a spark for action."[2]

The Absorption of Western Ukraine

Since 1654, when the tsars began steadily to extend their control over Ukraine, Ukrainians had lived in two distinct worlds: one ruled by the Russians and the other by Poles or Austrians. The contrast between the two Ukrainian societies, as we have had numerous occasions to observe, clearly went far beyond that of political systems and rested on major historical, cultural, socioeconomic, and psychological differences. As a result of the Second World War, the East/West Ukrainian dichotomy, finally ceased to exist, at least on the political level. After the war (the 1939–41 period had been too brief to leave lasting traces), the Soviet regime sought, for better or worse, to bring the West Ukrainians into conformity with the Soviet system and their eastern, Soviet compatriots. This process of amalgamation – of unification of two long-separated branches of the Ukrainian people – was not only a major aspect of the postwar period, but an event of epochal significance in the history of Ukraine.

In achieving their goals, the Soviets had the great advantage of overwhelming military and political might. Nevertheless, their task was still a difficult one, for in Western Ukraine they confronted a society whose major components were antagonistic to them: the Greek Catholic church, the paramount West Ukrainian institution, was clearly incompatible with the new regime; the peasants, who constituted the vast majority of West Ukrainians, were terrified by the prospect of collectivization; and the youth, many of whom were committed to nationalism, saw in the Soviets their greatest enemy.

The liquidation of the Greek Catholic church   Because it was the West Ukrainians' strongest link to the West and because it functioned as the national church par excellence, the Greek Catholic church became an early focus of attack by the Soviet regime. The signal for the anti–Greek Catholic drive was the death, on 1 November 1944, of the immensely popular Metropolitan Sheptytsky. With Sheptytsky out of the way, articles began to appear in the press accusing the church of collaborating with the Nazis and of supporting the Ukrainian underground. Particularly vicious were the writings of the West Ukrainian Communist Iaroslav Galan. The defamation campaign was followed by the arrest and exile to Siberia of the entire Greek Catholic hierarchy, including its new head, Josef Slipy, on a series of patently fabricated charges.

As the hierarchy was being liquidated, a well-known priest, Gabriel Kostelnyk, was persuaded by the Soviets to organize a group of Greek Catholic priests to agitate for the abolition of the union with Rome. Opposition to the group's activities was stifled by a campaign of terror launched by the NKVD among the clergy. On 8 March 1946, the group called a synod – a totally uncanonical act in view of the absence of bishops – to consider its links with Rome. The result was a foregone conclusion: the 216 priests and 19 laity who attended proclaimed the dissolution of the Union of Brest of 1596, a break with Rome, and the "reunion" of the Greek Catholic church with the Russian Orthodox church. Somewhat later, a similar process, accompanied by the seemingly accidental death of Bishop Teodor Romzha, was carried out in Transcarpathia, and by 1951 the Greek Catholic church in that region was also destroyed.

Confused by the disappearance of their hierarchs, cowed by Soviet terror tactics, and fearful about the fate of their families, many priests went over to Orthodoxy. Those who refused were removed from their posts and usually exiled to Siberia. Yet one should not suppose that the Soviets succeeded in simply decreeing the Greek Catholic church out of existence. Many of the priests and laity that supposedly accepted Orthodoxy continued to practice Greek Catholic rites and holidays surreptitiously. Certainly, the continuing flood of Soviet propaganda against the Greek Catholic church indicates that the loyalty of West Ukrainians to their ancient church is far from dead.

The struggle against the UPA   Despite the Soviet occupation of Galicia and Volhynia, the UPA continued to grow. In 1944–45, it had more recruits than it could equip. A major source of manpower was the members of the OUN underground, which continued to exist parallel to the UPA. Many recruits were men and women who had resisted the mass deportations or collectivization. Red Army deserters and those who fled to the forests to avoid mobilization also entered the UPA in great numbers, preferring its ranks to serving as Soviet cannon fodder at the front. Thus, while the victorious Red Army was storming Berlin, in Western Ukraine large, battalion-size units of anti-Soviet partisans gained control of considerable areas where they established an elaborate administrative structure of their own. At this point, the policy of the UPA and of its political superstructure, the UHVR, was to await developments in the West (and to hope for a new war between the Allies and the Soviets). At the same time, it meant to disrupt the establishment of the Soviet system in its homeland. This widespread activity of the UPA was the result of, on the one hand, its popular support and effective organization and, on the other, of the shortage of Soviet troops in Western Ukraine.

After Germany capitulated in May 1945, however, the Soviets were able to mount a systematic and extensive effort to destroy the the the UPA. In 1945–46 their forces – which consisted mostly of MVD and NKVD troops because regular Red Army units contained many Ukrainians who were reluctant to fight against the UPA – blockaded and swept through huge areas of Volhynia and the Carpathian foothills, where the partisans were concentrated. In order to terrorize the West Ukrainian populace and deprive the UPA of popular support, the NKVD utilized a variety of ruthless tactics. It depopulated areas where the UPA had base camps, deporting to Siberia the family of anyone associated with the resistance, and even entire villages. It is estimated that, between 1946 and 1949, about 500,000 West Ukrainians were exiled to the north. Informers were planted in almost every village. In order to discredit the partisans, units of the NKVD, masquerading as UPA soldiers, pillaged, raped, and murdered Ukrainian villagers. The often-ruthless extermination of pro-Soviet elements by the SB, the OUN security police, lent some credibility to these Soviet provocations. Simultaneously, the Soviets showered the partisans, who lived close to starvation in underground bunkers during the winter, with propaganda about the hopelessness of their situation and repeatedly offered them amnesty.

Suffering from heavy losses, the UPA attempted to adjust to the growing Soviet pressure by breaking down its large units into small, maneuverable squads. By 1947–48, when it became obvious that an American-Soviet war would not occur, many of these units disbanded on the orders of the UPA command. Some UPA members joined the OUN civilian underground, but because many of the latter's members had been killed, captured, emigrated or lost their "cover" during the period of open struggle, the OUN's secret network was also no longer as effective or extensive as it had been previously.

Another serious blow to the UPA was the spread of collectivization because, unlike the individual peasant households, the strictly controlled collective farmers could not serve as sources of provisions for the partisans.

In this final stage, the UPA units and the OUN underground, which had in the meantime established loose, sporadic links with the British and American secret services, concentrated on anti-Soviet propaganda and sabotage. They disrupted collectivization, deportations, and the establishment of the Soviet administrative apparatus, and they assassinated NKVD officers, party activists, and those suspected of collaborating with the Soviets. Thus, in 1948, Father Gabriel Kostelnyk was shot, allegedly by OUN members (some accounts implicate the NKVD), for his role in the dissolution of the Greek Catholic church. A year later, the OUN underground killed the noted Soviet propagandist-journalist Iaroslav Galan. But in March 1950, the UPA suffered a decisive setback when its commander, Roman Shukhevych (General Taras Chuprynka), was killed in a skirmish near Lviv. Although some small UPA units continued to operate until the mid 1950s, for all practical purposes UPA and OUN in Ukraine ceased to exist as organizations after Shukhevych's death.

A separate chapter in the history of the UPA was its activity on the Polish side of the border, in the area inhabited by the Ukrainian Lemkos. Between 1944 and 1947, the OUN enjoyed strong support and maintained a powerful presence in the area: thanks to careful studies of the UPA by Polish military historians (which are incomparably more informative than the propagandistic tracts of their Soviet counterparts), we know that its forces included about 2000 UPA soldiers and a network of over 3000 OUN members.[3] Repeated efforts by the Polish military to dislodge the Ukrainian partisans were thwarted with heavy losses to the Poles. In March 1947, when one of its units ambushed and killed Karol Świerczewski, a famous Polish general and vice-minister of defense, the UPA in the region scored one of its greatest successes and at the same time set the stage for its own demise.

Angered by the event, the Polish government resolved to liquidate the "Ukrainian problem." In April 1947, it launched an operation under the code name Wisła which had both a military and a civilian dimension. About 30,000 Polish troops, supported by large numbers of Czech and Soviet forces, surrounded the Ukrainian partisans and, in fierce fighting, killed or captured many of them. Some partisans managed to break through to Soviet Ukraine, and several hundred fought their way through Czechoslovakia and reached the Allied zone in Germany. The fate of the Ukrainian Lemko population that had sheltered the partisans was equally tragic: without warning, almost all the Lemkos, numbering about 150,000, were uprooted from their ancestral villages and resettled throughout Poland in order to prevent the UPA from ever reestablishing itself in the region again. In this manner, the Poles finally rid themselves of the Ukrainian problem that had plagued them for centuries.

Collectivization It was only in 1947–48, after the Soviets had broken the UPA resistance, that collectivization could begin full swing. In general, it followed the pattern set in Soviet Ukraine two decades earlier. Initially, the prosperous peasants (kulaks) were singled out and taxed so heavily that it became impossible for them to retain their farms. As usual, the most recalcitrant were deported to Siberia. Then the mass of the peasantry was harangued by Soviet agitators and pressured during lengthy individual sessions to join the collectives. Political control over the collectives, which was especially tight in Western Ukraine, was exerted by party cells that were established in the Machine Tractor Stations (MTS). Fortunately for the West Ukrainians, the collectivization of their lands was not accompanied by a famine. Another difference between collectivization in Western and Eastern Ukraine was that in the former it was accompanied by the armed struggle of the weakened but nonetheless lethal UPA. In the words of a Soviet source: "The greatest enemies of the working peasant – the kulaks and bourgeois nationalists – bitterly resisted the growing collectivization movement in the western territories, burning down farm buildings on the collectives, killing activists and spreading rumors among peasants designed to raise doubts about the collectives."[4] But resistance was to no avail for by 1951 almost all Western Ukraine's 1.5 million peasant households belonged to collective farms, which numbered about 7000. A major pillar of the Soviet socioeconomic system was thus firmly in place in the newly annexed Ukrainian territories.

As was to be expected, collectivization was accompanied by industrialization. Under Austrian and Polish rule, Galicia had been an impoverished, economically exploited agrarian region, which served as a dumping ground for finished products but which produced few of these itself. Realizing that they could derive great political benefit by improving this situation, the Soviets invested heavily in the industrial development of the region. Old industries such as oil production were expanded and a series of new industries, which included the production of cars, buses, radios, and light machinery, were established. Because the factories were new and often outfitted with machines expropriated from Germany, the West Ukrainian enterprises possessed some of the most modern equipment in the USSR. By 1951 the industrial production of Western Ukraine jumped 230% over the 1945 level and accounted for about 10% of the republic's industrial production, compared to less than 3% in 1940. Rapidly growing Lviv became one of the major industrial centers of the republic.

Along with industrialization came social changes.The initial lack of specialists and experienced workers required to staff the numerous new factories brought a flood of Russians into the region. But a local Ukrainian working class also developed rapidly. In the late 1940s and early 1950s, about 20,000–30,000 new workers were being trained annually in Western Ukraine.

In Lviv the number of industrial workers rose from 43,000 in 1945 to 148,000 in 1958. A stratum of heretofore nonexistent Ukrainian technical experts also appeared. Thus, under the aegis of the Soviets, the long-delayed socioeconomic modernization of Western Ukraine moved rapidly forward.

Perhaps the most popular aspect of Soviet rule was the greatly expanded educational opportunities that it brought. To win the sympathies of West Ukrainians, the new regime expanded and Ukrainized elementary education in 1945 as it had done in 1939. Higher education also expanded rapidly, and in 1950 about 24,000 regular and 9000 corresponding students were enrolled in Western Ukraine's twenty-four institutions of higher learning. However, the rise in educational level also entailed greater Russification. By 1953, instruction in all institutions of higher learning in Western Ukraine was in Russian, a clear indication that the modernization that the Soviets introduced was also meant to encourage Russification.

While education was the feature of the Soviet regime that was most readily accepted, the Communist party was not. Even after the Soviet victory, West Ukrainians showed little interest in joining it. In 1944 there were only 7000 members and candidates to the party in all Western Ukraine, and only several hundred of them were workers. In 1946 the number rose to 31,000 and in 1950, after an intense recruitment campaign, the number grew to 88,000 – still a tiny fraction of the general population. Most of these party members were newcomers from the east. For example, of the 23,000 members of the Lviv party organization in 1950, only 10% were of local origin. In the countryside, Communists were exceedingly few. Thus, although the party organization monopolized political power, it still lacked roots among the West Ukrainian population. Consequently, the latter had the distinct impression that it was living under foreign rule.

Stalinist Retrenchment

Despite the great boost to Soviet morale that victory in the Second World War had brought, Stalin was convinced that the war had inflicted serious ideological damage to Soviet society. In order to raise the fighting spirit of their people during the war, Soviet authorities had encouraged Russian and non-Russian nationalism and loosened restrictions on religion. What was most worrisome for the regime, however, was the fact that about 70 million Soviet people – those who lived in the German-occupied areas, forced laborers, and prisoners of war – had been exposed to the West and Western ways. Soviet annexations had also incorporated into the Soviet Union millions more who were opposed to or at least skeptical about its ideology, political system, and economic order. Therefore, in Stalin's view, the regime needed to tighten its grip on society once again, especially in the ideological realm.

The man to whom Stalin entrusted the task of reestablishing ideological purity was his close aide, Andrei Zhdanov. In summer 1946, Zhdanov launched his offensive against those who longed for a freer cultural climate and admired the achievements of Western civilization. Such an attitude, he claimed, implied criticism of and dissatisfaction with Soviet culture. And this view was unacceptable. "Our job," he announced, "is to ... attack bourgeois culture, which is in a state of miasma and corruption."5 But if their aim was to reject Western culture, Zhdanov and his associates had to provide their people with a more impressive alternative. Hence, the other major thrust of Zhdanov's ideological campaign was the glorification of Russian cultural and scientific achievements. For every invention of the West, Soviet propagandists came up with a Russian who had had the idea earlier; for every major Western author, there was a Russian one who was better; and for every famous Western statesman, there was a Russian counterpart whose achievements were more praiseworthy. The emergence of this new, expanded form of Russian nationalism was not unexpected: already in May 1945 Stalin had foreshadowed it in his famous toast to the Russian people in which he hailed it as "the most outstanding nation ... the leading force in the Soviet Union."6

As so often in the past, Ukrainians found themselves especially vulnerable to Stalin's initiatives. Exposed to Nazi occupation longer than the Russians, it was mostly they who had been taken to Germany as forced labor and it was in Western Ukraine that anti-Sovietism was most virulent. West Ukrainians had been most extensively "tainted" with Western influences. Stalin's remark that he would have deported all Ukrainians to Siberia if there had not been so many of them certainly did not bode well. Indications of the coming crackdown in Ukraine were evident in July 1946, when the Central Committee of the party in Moscow ominously blamed the Ukrainian party for failing "to devote proper attention to the selection of cadres and their ideological-political education in the fields of scholarship, literature and arts where ... hostile bourgeois-nationalist ideology" and "attempts to reinstate Ukrainian nationalist concepts" existed.7 This was the death knell for the modest postwar revival of Ukrainian culture.

A month later, when Ostap Vyshnia, an immensely popular humorist who had been supressed in the 1930s, dared to express the opinion that an artist, in his search for creativity and originality, had the right to make mistakes, a storm of accusations of "ideological laxity" came from Moscow. Taking this event as his cue, Ukraine's Communist party leader Nikita Khrushchev and his deputy in charge of ideology, K.Z. Lytvyn, immediately fired several salvos against the Ukrainian intelligentsia as a whole, accusing it of "bourgeois nationalism." Meanwhile, Lytvyn concentrated on specifics, notably the recently published "History of Ukrainian Literature." According to him, the work had very serious "shortcomings" because it viewed the development of Ukrainian literature in isolation from the class struggle, exaggerated Western influences, and did not go far enough in emphasizing the positive influence of Russian literature. A year later, Lytvyn subjected the new "History of Ukraine" to similar criticism, demanding that it be expurgated of all signs of Hrushevsky's influence.

Scathing attacks were also launched against Ukrainian composers for using traditional Ukrainian themes. The opera *Bohdan Khmelnytsky* was criticized for not giving the Russians a prominent-enough role, and Ukrainian literary journals and encyclopedias were denounced for concentrating on "narrow" Ukrainian topics. The witch-hunt for real or alleged Ukrainian nationalism was particularly severe during the brief stay in Ukraine in 1947 of Kaganovich, who apparently derived perverse pleasure from terrorizing the members of the Ukrainian intelligentsia.

A high point in this ideological tightening of the screws came in 1951 when Sosiura's poem *Liubit Ukrainu!* ("Love Ukraine"), written in the midst of the patriotic fervor of 1944 and awarded the Stalin Prize, was denounced for its "nationalism" and its author was forced to publish a degrading recantation. The search for cases of ideological deviation became even more grotesque – and deadly – as Jews were singled out for persecution. Many leading Jewish authors, scholars, and artists were executed on charges of "rootless cosmopolitanism." The secret police even fabricated a "plot" in which a group of Jewish intellectuals allegedly conspired, with the aid of "international Jewry," to take over the Crimea and break away from the Soviet Union. It was at this time that the ludicrous claim appeared, which has since become a shibboleth of Soviet propaganda, that Ukrainian nationalists and Jewish Zionists were cooperating against Soviet interests.

As indications that Stalin was preparing another murderous purge mounted, panic gripped the intelligentsia of Ukraine. Creative activity practically ceased as intellectuals rushed to admit their mistakes and beg forgiveness. A characteristic example of the demeaning spectacle was the speech of Korniichuk, who together with his Polish wife, Wanda Wasilewska, had written the libretto for the opera *Bohdan Khmelnytsky:*

> We must be more alert since we can never forget that the Imperialists
> and their agents will use every opportunity to harm us. To my regret
> I must admit that during the last several years we in Ukraine have
> been rather lame in our struggle against backsliding into Ukrainian
> bourgeois nationalism in literature and the arts. *Pravda*, the organ of
> the Central Committee of our Party, discovered serious ideological
> regressions and mistakes in the works of certain Ukrainian authors
> ... We authors must take this criticism to heart and draw practical
> conclusions from it. A thousand thanks to our Party for its loving
> and patient guidance to us authors and artists. Thanks to our Party
> which rightfully criticized the libretto of the opera *Bohdan Khmelnytsky*

> and offered instruction on how one should present the history of our people correctly ... Long live the great Party of Lenin and Stalin, long live our beloved leader and teacher, the great comrade Stalin.[8]

It was apparent that the Ukrainian intelligentsia had learned its lessons in the 1930s: namely, that it was better to give in today if one wished to live and write tomorrow. But just as many were bracing themselves for another Stalinist purge, on 5 March 1953, the "Great Leader" died. The sigh of relief in Ukraine was almost audible.

❧

For Ukrainians who had lived under Soviet rule prior to 1939, the aftermath of the war brought a sense of déjà vu. Again they were plunged into vast, exhausting construction projects; again they experienced the depressing transition from a period of relative ideological and cultural flexibility to one of severe reaction and orthodoxy; and again they faced the very real prospect of famine and purge.

For West Ukrainians, however, the postwar years ushered in a new era, exposing them to an entirely different world, one with which they had had only a brief, traumatic encounter in 1939–41. Their incorporation into the USSR meant that they were henceforth separated from the political and cultural values of Europe. It also resulted in the loss of West Ukrainian society's most important asset, its extensive organizational network – of which the Greek Catholic church was the oldest, most-important component and of which OUN/UPA was the most recent – that for generations had been its main defense against foreign rule and the most clear-cut expression of Ukrainian nationhood. But the consequences of Soviet annexation were not all negative: as a result of Stalin's dictates, the Polish/Ukrainian conflict, which had long sapped the energies of both societies, had finally been resolved. Moreover, the Soviets initiated the long-overdue social and industrial modernization of the region. And, of course, it was they who, for better or worse, finally united all Ukrainians in a single state.

The Thaw

Stalin's death introduced a new era in Soviet history. Exhausting, wasteful, and irrational, the dictator's method of ruling by terror and duress could not be maintained indefinitely. Even the Soviet elite yearned for change. The need for a general relaxation of Stalin's rigid controls was obvious and pressing. It was essential that the people of the USSR finally derive appreciable material benefits from the vast political and economic power the Soviet state had amassed. But as the Kremlin cautiously relaxed its grip, issues that had been apparently resolved earlier reemerged and the quest by Stalin's successors for new solutions often created new problems. Although the retreat from Stalinism and the search for fresh approaches to the building of communism were evident in all the republics of the Soviet Union, in Ukraine these changes were especially numerous and noteworthy.

ও

The New Leadership

An early if transitory sign of the coming changes was the "collective leadership" that replaced Stalin's one-man rule. Composed of top party and government functionaries, this rule-by-committee was only a short-lived, transitional phase that allowed a new strongman to establish himself. Initially, it seemed that Lavrentii Beria, the feared chief of the secret police, might triumph. Hoping to broaden his base of support, Beria signaled the non-Russian nationalities, the Georgians and Ukrainians in particular, that he was willing to grant them major concessions. But Beria overreached himself and paid for his failure with his life (it was, however, the last time that an unsuccessful political rival was executed). For a short while, Georgii Malenkov, a spokesman of the government and technocratic bureaucracy and an advocate of economic reforms, moved into the forefront. But the final winner was Nikita Khrushchev, a man whose career was closely linked with Ukraine.

Khrushchev, a Russian, was born in a small village on the Russian-Ukrainian border. A jovial but ruthless party "apparatchik" (functionary), he rose to power thanks to his quick wit, abject subservience to Stalin, and the openings created in the party hierarchy by the purges. As we have seen, in 1938 he was sent to Ukraine to complete the Great Purge and to begin rebuilding the Ukrainian party. A year later he oversaw the incorporation of newly occupied Western Ukraine into the Soviet Union. During the war he helped to organize and lead the Communist partisans in Ukraine. And in the postwar years, Khrushchev supervised the economic reconstruction, the second incorporation of Western Ukraine, and the struggle against the Ukrainian nationalists. Although merciless in fulfilling Stalin's instructions, Khrushchev gained some personal popularity by paying attention to "local color," often appearing in Ukrainian embroidered shirts and demonstrating his affection for Ukrainian songs.

After his transfer to Moscow in 1949, Khrushchev retained his close, mutually beneficial relationship with the Ukrainian party. Consequently, it was the first republican party organization that backed him in the struggle for power and it remained his secure base of support. Khrushchev returned the favor. Only months after Stalin's death, the unpopular Leonid Melnikov, first secretary of the Ukrainian party and a Russian chauvinist, was removed from his post on charges of Russifying higher education in Western Ukraine and discriminating against its local cadres. His replacement was Oleksii Kyrychenko, the first ethnic Ukrainian to hold the post (since then only Ukrainians have held the first secretaryship). Other Ukrainians also received high offices: Demian Korotchenko became head of the republic's government and Nykyfor Kalchenko chaired the council of ministers. The reign of the "three Ks" was reinforced by other appointments that were pleasing to Ukrainians. The maligned playwright Oleksander Korneichuk and Semen Stefanyk, the son of the famous West Ukrainian novelist, received high government positions. In Western Ukraine, Bohdan Dudykevych, an old prewar Communist leader, was placed at the head of the regional party organization.

These personnel changes were accompanied by an upsurge in the numerical strength of the party in Ukraine: in 1952 it had about 770,000 full and candidate members, but by 1959 its membership was close to 1.3 million – of whom 60% were Ukrainians. In sharp contrast to the days of Stalin, when Ukrainians were discriminated against, it was evident from these promotions and their numerical growth that the Ukrainian Communists were being openly wooed by the new leadership in the Kremlin.

Not only did Ukrainian Communists expand their influence in their own republic, but a number of them rapidly rose to prominence on the all-union level. In the military, Rodion Malinovsky, Andrii Grechko, and Kyrylo

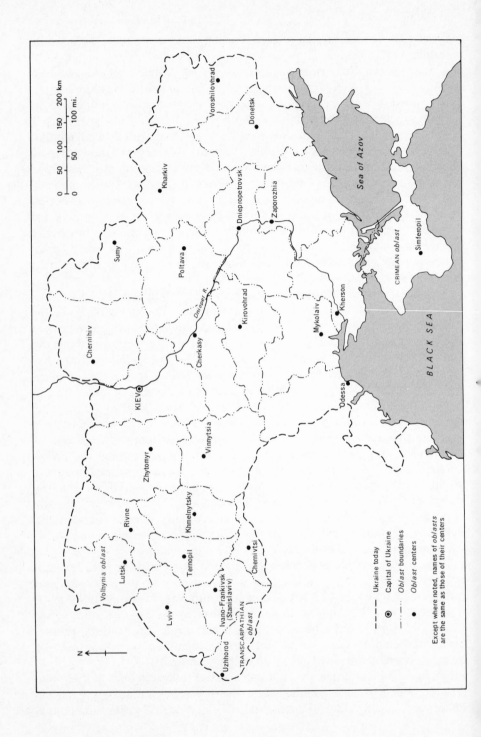

Sea of Azov

Voroshilovhrad

Donetsk

Kharkiv

Dnepropetrovsk

Zaporozhia

Simferopil

CRIMEAN *oblast*

Sumy

Poltava

Dnieper R.

Kirovohrad

Mykolaiv

Kherson

BLACK SEA

Chernihiv

Cherkasy

KIEV

Odessa

Zhytomyr

Vinnytsia

Rivne

Khmelnytsky

Lutsk

Ternopil

Chernivtsi

Volhynia *oblast*

Lviv

Ivano-Frankivsk
(Stanislaviv)

Uzhhorod

TRANSCARPATHIAN
oblast

N

50   100   150   200 km

0

0   50   100 mi.

–·–·–·–   Ukraine today

⊙   Capital of Ukraine

·········   *Oblast* boundaries

•   *Oblast* centers

Except where noted, names of *oblasts*
are the same as those of their centers

Moskalenko attained the exalted rank of marshal of the USSR and the first two also were ministers of defense of the USSR. Volodymyr Semichastny rose to head the all-union secret police; and four Ukrainians – Oleksii Kyrychenko, Mykola Podhorny, Dmytro Poliansky, and Petro Shelest – became members of the eleven-member Politburo, the highest ruling body in the USSR. The main reason for their rise was their close ties with Khrushchev, not the fact that they were Ukrainians. As careerists who sought to rise to the top of the Soviet system, these men generally paid little heed to ethnic loyalties. Nonetheless, their presence at the pinnacles of power attested to the growing importance of Ukrainians and their republic.

Ukraine: Second among Equals

Borys Levytsky aptly described Ukraine's enhanced position in the USSR during the Khrushchev era with the phrase "second among equals."[1] Certainly indications mounted that an implicit understanding had been reached between the Kremlin and Kiev in which the Ukrainians, in return for their support and cooperation, had been offered the role of junior partners – the Russians, of course, were the senior partners – in the running of the Soviet empire. For those Ukrainians who had no confidence in or desire for self-rule, this modern version of the Little Russianism of the 19th century seemed to offer many career opportunities for them as individuals. For the Kremlin, winning the support of the Ukrainians was essential because they were not only the second most numerous nation in the USSR but also the only ones who could seriously challenge Russian hegemony. The close linguistic and cultural ties between the two peoples encouraged and facilitated cooperation.

To celebrate the Russian/Ukrainian partnership, in 1954 the 300th anniversary of the Pereiaslav Treaty was marked throughout the Soviet Union in an unusually grandiose manner. In addition to numerous festivities, myriad publications, and countless speeches, the Central Committee of the all-union party even issued thirteen "theses," which argued the irreversibility of the "everlasting union" of the Ukrainians with the Russians: "The experience of history has shown that the way of fraternal union and alliance chosen by the Russians and Ukrainians was the only true way. The union of two great Slavic peoples multiplied their strength in the common struggle against all external foes, against serf owners and the bourgeoisie, against tsarism and capitalist slavery. The unshakeable friendship of the Russian and Ukrainian peoples has grown and strengthened in this struggle."[2] To emphasize the point that the union with Moscow brought the Ukrainians great benefits, the Pereiaslav anniversary was crowned by the Russian republic's ceding of Crimea to Ukraine "as a token of friendship of the Russian people."

But the "gift" of the Crimea was far less altruistic than it seemed. First, because the peninsula was the historic homeland of the Crimean Tatars whom Stalin had expelled during the Second World War, the Russians did not have the moral right to give it away nor did the Ukrainians have the right to accept it. Second, because of its proximity and economic dependence on Ukraine, the Crimea's links with Ukraine were naturally greater than with Russia. Finally, the annexation of the Crimea saddled Ukraine with economic and political problems. The deportation of the Tatars in 1944 had created economic chaos in the region and it was Kiev's budget that had to make up the losses. More important was the fact that, according to the 1959 census, about 860,000 Russians and only 260,000 Ukrainians lived in the Crimea. Although Kiev attempted to bring more Ukrainians into the region after 1954, the Russians, many of whom were especially adamant in rejecting any form of Ukrainization, remained the overwhelming majority. As a result, the Crimean "gift" increased considerably the number of Russians in the Ukrainian republic. In this regard, it certainly was an appropriate way of marking the Pereiaslav Treaty.

De-Stalinization

The efforts of the new leadership to expand its support among the non-Russians, particularly the Ukrainians, were a part of a much broader plan of reforms. Stalin's approach to modernization – a combination of terror, ideology, and forced industrialization – was an effective but artificial method of pushing Soviet society forward. Khrushchev realized that, in the long run, it was persuasion not coercion, efficiency not stifling control, managerial skills not revolutionary fervor, that would ensure the Soviet Union's continued growth. To make this transition to a new approach it was first necessary to break with the old one.

At the 20th Party Congress held in 1956, Khrushchev delivered one of the most dramatic speeches in Soviet history. To the surprise and consternation of party stalwarts, he launched a lengthy, detailed, and blistering attack on Stalin and his crimes. This "secret speech" signaled the beginning of de-Stalinization. It was followed by a marked change in the atmosphere in the Soviet Union. Ideological orthodoxy was relaxed, leading to a "thaw" in cultural life. The policy of isolation was deemphasized as foreign travel to, and especially tourism within, the USSR was encouraged (but carefully monitored). Among the non-Russian peoples the blatant Russification was toned down. And preparations for introducing major changes in the economy began. This is not to say that the totalitarian features of the regime were dismantled; they remained very much in place. However, the all-encompassing fear and the paralysis of creativity that characterized the Stalin period eased considerably.

Changes in Ukraine   Initially, Ukrainians reacted to these changes with caution, a trait they had learned to cultivate during the Stalin years. But when it was clear that the attack on the Stalin "personality cult" was genuine and widespread, they joined in with a flood of their own complaints and demands. As might be expected, it was in the field of culture, with its many eloquent spokesmen, where the dissatisfaction was the most vocal. An early and oft-repeated recrimination decried the sorry state of the Ukrainian language. Intelligentsia, students, workers, and even party officials repeated the same refrain: acknowledging that Russian deserved special status in the USSR, they stressed that this did not mean that Ukrainian should be discriminated against. Slogans such as "Defend the Ukrainian Language" and "Speak Ukrainian" were heard with increasing frequency throughout the republic, especially among the university students.

The decline in the quality of Ukrainian scholarship was another issue that emerged. Historians – as opposed to the numerous party hacks who called themselves historians – protested that Moscow's tight ideological control over their field had led to "an impoverishment of history." This privation was characterized by provincialism, abject observance of party guidelines, and an exaggeration of the links and similarities with Russia, while downplaying "Ukrainian historical specificity." Literary specialists lodged similar complaints about developments in their own field.

Apparently the Kremlin was listening. In 1957 Ukrainian historians received permission to establish their own journal, the *Ukrainskyi Istorychnyi Zhurnal*. Two years later, the first Soviet Ukrainian encyclopedia began to appear, partially in response to a similar project launched earlier by Ukrainian émigrés in the West. These were followed by impressive, multivolume publications, such as a dictionary of the Ukrainian language, a history of Ukrainian literature, a survey of Ukrainian art, and a detailed survey of Ukrainian towns and villages, which even the Russians did not have.

In its quest to upgrade Ukrainian scholarship and thereby raise the prestige of Ukrainian culture, the intelligentsia not only concentrated on the traditional humanities but also demanded facilities in the republic for the development of modern areas of knowledge such as nuclear research and cybernetics. Thus, in 1957, a computer center was established in Kiev followed by an institute of cybernetics in 1962, which made Ukraine a leader in these fields in the USSR. In the meantime, numerous Ukrainian-language journals in the natural and social sciences appeared. It was evident that the Ukrainian intellectual elite was intent on utilizing the opportunities created by de-Stalinization to introduce modern knowledge in a Ukrainian rather than a Russian guise.

Since Khrushchev acknowledged that many of Stalin's victims were unjustly persecuted, the pressure for their rehabilitation mounted. The first to be considered for a posthumous return to good standing were purged Communists. In Ukraine demands rose for the rehabilitation of such national communists as Skrypnyk, Khvylovy, and the members of the KPZU. Soon such key cultural figures as the playwright Mykola Kulish, the theater director Les Kurbas, the world-famous filmmaker Oleksander Dovzhenko, and the

outstanding 19th-century intellectual Mykhailo Drahomanov – all characterized by their successful efforts to enrich Ukrainian culture and raise it beyond
provincialism – were proposed for rehabilitation. Because the reinstatement
of these individuals touched on such politically sensitive issues as Ukrainian
cultural independence and Ukraine's "own road to communism," the party's
response was cautious and ambiguous. But the fact that the Ukrainian intelligentsia continued to press for rehabilitation of such people indicated that the
ideas of the repressed still exerted a strong appeal.

For the millions of Ukrainians incarcerated in the Siberian forced labor
camps, de-Stalinization brought an unexpected reprieve: many of them were
amnestied and allowed to return to their homes. This partial dismantling of
the huge camp system was hastened by a series of prisoner revolts, such as
those in Vorkuta and Norilsk (1953) and Karaganda (1954), in which many
former members of the OUN and UPA played a leading role. However, the
Kremlin made it clear that it would not tolerate the OUN type of nationalism. In
1954, in the midst of the Pereiaslav celebrations, it announced the execution of
Vasyl Okhrymovych, a prominent émigré OUN leader that the Americans had
parachuted into Ukraine. And in 1956 there were several well-publicized trials of former OUN members that resulted in death sentences. It was clear that
the regime was still ready and willing to repress anyone considered to be too
extreme in defending Ukrainian interests.

Nationality issues   But perhaps the most telling indication of Khrushchev's
determination to adhere to certain basic principles of Soviet nationality policy – even while simultaneously making concessions of secondary importance – was the educational reform of 1958. An exceedingly controversial part
of this vast restructuring of Soviet education dealt with the study of native
languages. Up to 1958, students in the USSR were required to study their native language as well as Russian. Khrushchev's seemingly liberal reform proposed that parents be given the right to choose their children's language of
instruction. In effect, this meant that one could be educated in Ukraine without learning Ukrainian. Given the variety of formal and informal pressures
to learn Russian, it was to be expected that many parents would choose to
have their children study in Russian and not to burden them with a second,
albeit native, language. Despite a storm of protest and indignation in which
even Ukrainian party officials joined, the regime pushed through this blow
to the study of non-Russian languages, indicating that even in times of liberalization it was ready to modify but not abandon completely its policy of
Russification.

The impact of de-Stalinization, however, reached far beyond the politico-
cultural currents and countercurrents that involved the Kremlin politicians
and Kievan intellectuals. The general loosening of ideological controls revealed a new mood emerging among the educated, urban youth. While an

earnest minority was determined to set aright the wrongs of the Stalin period, the vast majority appeared to have little interest in ideological or political issues. Yet, a spirit of defiance against authority and a craving for individualistic approaches to life, so long repressed by Stalinist orthodoxy, were clearly on the rise among the youth. For example, in 1957 the newspaper *Radianska Ukraina* noted with alarm that "during a party conference at Shevchenko University, it was ascertained that there were numerous cases of lack of discipline and amoral behavior among the students and that unhealthy moods are making themselves felt."[3]

Party publications described another university meeting in Kiev as consisting of many "destructive student types," "demagogues," and "loudmouths." Young people bemoaned the monotony of Soviet life, the outdated morality, the old-fashioned dress codes, and the ideology-laden education. To the great consternation of their elders, they developed a liking for Western jazz and "pop" music. Some, the so-called *stiliagi* (stylish ones), even flaunted their predilection for outlandish (by Soviet standards) clothes and "antisocial behavior." A materialist, self-centered "me" generation, already much in evidence in the West – and very different from the previous generation, which had produced such fervent communists and nationalists – was beginning to emerge in Ukraine and throughout the USSR.

Economic Experimentation

Stalin's successors placed great emphasis on improving the economic performance of the Soviet system. Much depended on this success, for if the Soviet Union could outperform the West economically, it could solidify its popular support at home, while proving abroad that communism was truly the superior system. Paradoxically, to prove that communism was superior economically, Khrushchev realized that the party would have to become a less ideological and a more managerial organization.

In the days of the "collective leadership" there were intense debates in the Kremlin about which direction and what form economic reforms should take. But there was general agreement that the chronic weak point of the Soviet economy was agriculture. A simple statistic underlined this fact: between 1949 and 1952 the output of Soviet industry rose by 230% but agricultural production improved by a mere 10%. This statistic was not only an embarrassment to the Soviets but a serious economic, political, and ideological handicap. Poor agricultural productivity meant food shortages, which obviously raised doubts (both at home and abroad) about the superiority of the Soviet system. Therefore, Khrushchev, a self-proclaimed agricultural specialist by virtue of his long years in Ukraine, made a great effort to improve the situation in the countryside. For Ukraine, the breadbasket of the USSR, these changes would be especially important, because, once again, Ukraine would serve as a laboratory for much of the agricultural experimentation.

Agricultural projects   The most ambitious of Khrushchev's experiments was the "virgin-lands" project, which involved bringing about 40 million acres of unused land in Kazakhstan and Siberia under cultivation. The project, initiated in 1954, involved a huge investment of human and material resources, and Ukraine was expected to provide a large share of it. By 1956 thousands of tractors and about 80,000 experienced agricultural workers from Ukraine were transferred to the "virgin lands." Many of these workers settled there permanently. Meanwhile, every spring hundreds of thousands of students from Ukraine "volunteered" for short-term work in the east. While the results of the project were uneven, it clearly siphoned off Ukrainian resources and weakened the republic's agricultural production.

Another experiment involved a sudden switch, involving about 70 million acres throughout the USSR, to raising vast amounts of corn. Following American examples, it was to be used as fodder, which would help to raise the listless livestock production. Several years later, the Kremlin ordered the collective farmers to switch to a new system of crop rotation. As usual, Ukraine bore much of the burden imposed by these complex and costly innovations.

A reform that did have grass-roots support in Ukraine – indeed, in which Ukrainians took the initiative – involved the MTS, the depots providing farm machinery (and political supervision) to the collectives. Because of constant conflicts between the MTS and the collective farms about how the land should be worked, Ukrainians convinced the government to abolish the MTS and to sell their machines to the collectives.

The growing compexity of farming demanded well-educated and technologically proficient people. And these were greatly lacking in the Ukrainian countryside. In 1953, of the 15,000 collective-farm chairmen in Ukraine, less than 500 had a post-secondary education. To improve this situation, experienced technicians from the cities were encouraged to take positions on the collective farms. Those farms that lagged behind were linked with city-based industrial "brother" enterprises, which provided technical aid. As a result, a new and more-sophisticated social group, the "agricultural technocracy," appeared in the countryside. Meanwhile, the government raised the income of the farmers and slowly the earnings gap between the industrial and agricultural workers began to narrow.

Radical changes and grandiose experiments notwithstanding, agricultural production failed to expand as rapidly as expected. The Kremlin still refused to provide the collective farmers with enough incentives to work harder, bureaucrats in far-off Moscow still decided which crops a collective farm should plant and how the planting should be done, and the peasant was penalized for working his own tiny (but exceedingly productive) plot. The disappointing performance of agriculture had major political ramifications for Ukraine's Communists. Khrushchev counted heavily on them in helping to make his agricultural reforms a success. Meanwhile, in Kiev, dissatisfaction mounted with the disproportionately great demands that were placed on Ukraine. The warm relations between Khrushchev and the Ukrainian Communists began to cool.

Changes in industry   Ukraine's industry, like that of the Soviet Union as a whole, had performed very well in the early 1950s. In fact, this was its golden age. But by the late 1950s it began to slow down. Another problem facing the Kremlin leadership was whether to continue emphasizing heavy industry or to invest more heavily in light industry that would benefit the deprived Soviet consumer. Khrushchev opted for heavy industry but, unlike Stalin, he could not totally ignore the consumer, especially since he had promised that the Soviet Union would catch up and bypass the West economically by the 1980s. Consequently, in the early 1960s televisions, vacuum cleaners, refrigerators, and even cars began to appear in the government stores. However, they were exceedingly scarce and of abysmally poor quality.

To deal with the problem of dropping industrial productivity, in 1957 Khrushchev expanded the controversial *sovnarkhoz* (economic council) reform, one of the most radical organizational changes in the Soviet economy since the 1920s. This attempt to shift the center of economic planning and management from the ministries in Moscow to regional bodies, was meant to bypass the bureaucratic bottlenecks and top-heavy bureaucracy. Over 10,000 industrial enterprises were put under the control of the Ukrainian *sovnarkhoz* in Kiev and by the end of 1957, it supervised 97% of the factories in the republic (compared to 34% in 1953). Not surprisingly, Ukrainian economic planners and managers began to emphasize their republics' needs and interests rather than those of the Soviet Union as a whole. By the early 1960s, as the economic autonomy of Ukraine and the other republics reached a high point, Moscow grew alarmed. Charges of "localism," that is, preferring local interests over all-union interests, began to surface. It was evident that here, too, Khrushchev's reforms ran into unexpected complications. As might be expected, Ukraine's fling with economic self-assertiveness would be short-lived.

Although Khrushchev's reforms did not live up to expectations, they did, nevertheless, bring about considerable improvements. In sharp contrast to the days of Stalin, the impressive growth of the Soviet GNP – which outpaced that of the United States until the 1970s – helped to raise the standard of living. In Ukraine, for example, between 1951 and 1958, the income of the average worker rose by 230%. And it was the long-suffering collective farmer who received the proportionately highest raises. Put differently, in the Stalin era personal consumption rose by about 1% a year; during the Khrushchev years the increase was about 4% annually.

Because millions of additional acres of land were put under cultivation, food became more available and varied. At long last, the diet of the average

Soviet family, which was usually based on such staples as bread and potatoes, expanded to include, with some regularity, vegetables and meat. Even
such exotic delicacies as citrus fruits appeared in the shops. Running water,
electricity, and transportation reached remote villages. The daunting task of
the Soviet housewife, who generally held a full-time job, was eased somewhat by the appearance of (relatively) modern appliances. And televisions,
an excellent medium for propaganda as well as entertainment, became a regular household fixture. In the urban centers, housing still remained a major
problem, mainly because about 2.5 million Soviet citizens poured into the
cities every year. But while the standard of living was still far below Western standards, for the Soviet people, whose expectations were low and who
compared their current situation with that of the recent and dreadful past,
these changes were a great step forward. Certainly there was less reason to
complain about the Soviet system in the Khrushchev years than during the
Stalin era.

Intellectual Ferment

In 1961 Khrushchev launched a new wave of de-Stalinization that culminated
in the removal of the dictator's tomb from the Kremlin mausoleum. An attack on Stalin was always good news to the Ukrainians. Other developments
also added to their confidence. Because the republic's harvest was unusually plentiful that year, Ukraine's party leaders were in a good position to
demand further concessions from the Kremlin. Anxious to play down the
tensions that had arisen between him and the Ukrainians over agricultural
production, Khrushchev made a much-publicized pilgrimage to the grave
of Taras Shevchenko in May 1961. Meanwhile, the cultural "thaw" picked
up momentum as Russian authors took some daring steps, such as arranging for the publication abroad of Pasternak's *Dr. Zhivago*, which celebrated
the triumph of human rather than strictly Soviet values, and Solzhenitsyn's
One Day in the Life of Ivan Denisovich, which described in grisly detail the life
of inmates in Stalin's concentration camps. The appearance of these works
seemed to indicate that, despite angry rumblings from the Kremlin, further
liberalization in literature and culture was possible.

In Ukraine, the cultural elite, and most notably the writers, renewed their
efforts to use de-Stalinization as a means of broadening the limits of creative
self-expression. Again they emphasized the great harm that Stalin had inflicted on Ukrainian culture. For example, in 1962 the author Oles Honchar
declared that Stalinism did more than shackle creativity: "Another reason
why the memories of these days weigh heavily on us is that, at the time, some
deep wounds were inflicted on us and our culture by the physical annihilation of a number of gifted artists."[4] Writers of the older generation continued
to press for the rehabilitation of their persecuted colleagues. Thus, Korniichuk
called for the publication of a "Library of the Great 1920s" to popularize the

works of Blakytny, Kulish, Kurbas, and other victims of the purges. Others wished to do the same for the victims of Kaganovich in the late 1940s. All decried the continued advance of Russification.

But most noteworthy was the emergence of a new generation of writers, critics, and poets, such as Vasyl Symonenko, Lina Kostenko, Ievhen Sverstiuk, Ivan Dziuba, Ivan Drach, Mykola Vinhranovsky, and Dmytro Pavlychko, who demanded a correction of the "errors" committed by Stalin in the past and assurances that their nation's cultural development would not be stifled in the future. In their view, these goals could best be achieved by emphasizing a "return to the truth." Impatient with the wavering and inconsistent progress of de-Stalinization, these young writers demanded the end of the party's meddling in art and literature, the right to experiment with various styles, and the recognition of the central role of the Ukrainian language in education and cultural activity of the republic. By the early 1960s members of this new literary generation, which came to be called the "sixtiers," rejected not only the interference of party bureaucrats but denounced the hypocrisy, opportunism, and caution of their older colleagues. Rejection of their elders bristled in Vinhranovsky's short ephithet:

Enough, Enough! I am weary from shame for the apes
who learned to speak, slowly, dully, dumbly, presumptuously
Who speculated with our age's name![5]

The rebelliousness of these talented young people, directed against both party controls and the behavior of their elder colleagues, was clearly pushing far beyond the bounds of liberalization that Khrushchev had established. Moreover, support for this new literary cohort was significant and growing, especially among the young intelligentsia.

The Reaction

The alarming restlessness that spread through Soviet society worried Khrushchev and his associates in the Kremlin. In December 1962 he called in a group of leading Russian writers and warned them not to push liberalization too far. Several months later, several Russian intellectuals were subjected to a vicious attack in the press. It was clear that the regime was about to launch a crackdown against the liberal intelligentsia. Taking their cue from Moscow, party officials in Kiev prepared to rein in the "immature elements" in the Ukrainian literary community.

In spring 1963, Andrii Skaba, the Ukrainian party official responsible for ideological purity, launched the attack by harshly criticizing the work of such literary critics as Sverstiuk, Svitlychny, and especially Dziuba. Soon afterward, the party journal *Komunist Ukrainy* declared that "only a weakening of political vigilance can explain why our literary and artistic criticism did not provide a timely evaluation of these false and ideologically immature works ... Some of our newpapers ... as well as publishing houses and theatres neglected the principles and demands of the party. This also contributed to the propagation in art of works that were of no use to the people."[6]

Valentyn Malanchuk, the ideological watchdog in Western Ukraine, warned against young and inexperienced writers who slipped into the "role of foremost fighters against the [Stalin] personality cult, paid excessive attention to the negative phenomenon of this [Stalin] period and, furthermore, praised the works of Western authors."[7] Besides sounding the obligatory call to struggle against all manifestations of Ukrainian "bourgeois nationalism," he proudly announced his successes in the antireligion campaign – the number of church weddings in his region had decreased – and promised to replace religious feast days with such Soviet "holidays" as the "Day of the Hammer and Sickle" and the "Evenings of Workers' Glory."

Another indication that certain aspects of Stalinism were making a comeback was the appearance of several semiofficial anti-Semitic publications. The most notable of these was the tract by T.K. Kichko, *Judaism without Embellishment*, published in 1964 by the Ukrainian Academy of Science, most likely on instructions from Moscow. As in the final days of Stalin, the propaganda apparatus churned out materials that attempted to show intimate links and close cooperation between Ukrainian nationalists and Zionists. The liberal Ukrainian intelligentsia severely criticized the Kichko book. But in May 1964 its indignation reached a high point when word spread that the library of the Ukrainian Academy of Sciences, which housed thousands of invaluable books and documents dealing with Ukrainian history and culture, had burned down. The self-confessed arsonist who was responsible for this "felony without parallel in the history of world culture" was a psychotic Russophile named Pohruzhalsky, who apparently wanted to destroy the major monuments of Ukrainian cultural identity. Suspicions that the arsonist was linked to the security organs were widespread.

These events were a telling indication of Khrushchev's determination to restore discipline among the intelligentsia. However, the new get-tough policy came too late. A series of foreign and domestic setbacks, which included the Cuban missile debacle, the split with China, the disorganization caused by the reforms, and the disastrous harvest of 1963, fatally weakened the Soviet leader's position. In October 1964 his colleagues lost patience with Khrushchev and forced him to resign. An era of reform, experimentation, and liberalization came to an end.

ঌ

The era of Khrushchev was clearly a transitional phase in Soviet history. Despite the numerous setbacks, disappointments, and unexpected results that his experiments and reforms elicited, they did succeed in transforming Soviet society from one ruled by the terror and draconian measures of Stalin to a more rational, managerial system attuned to an advanced industrial society. This transition was deeply felt in Ukraine, where Stalinism had reached its worst extremes.

What changed and, of equal importance, what did not during the Khrushchev years? Most obvious was the discontinuation of the mass arrests, terror tactics, and purges. The secret police, with its prerogatives limited, now called in "dangerous elements" for a "heart-to-heart" talk, and usually threatened them with the loss of a job or curtailment of educational opportunities for their children. Only if these confrontations did not have the desired effect did arrests (but no executions) follow. Discipline in the workplace became far less rigorous. The standard of living slowly improved. Writers, poets, and other cultural figures obtained, for a time, more leeway in expressing themselves. In Ukraine, in addition to the above-mentioned developments, there was a rise in the self-assertiveness of the republic's Communist leadership and a recognition of Ukraine's economic importance within the USSR. But most striking, especially in view of the terrible losses suffered by the Ukrainian intelligentsia in the 1930s, was the emergence of a new, promising generation of cultural activists.

Many basic features of Soviet life remained unchanged, however. Censorship continued to limit severely what one could read, see, and hear. The Communist party retained an absolute monopoly on political power. Despite the reforms, the economy was still directed by bureaucrats, while everyone worked in government enterprises and institutions and shopped in government stores. Improvements in Ukraine's relative importance in the USSR or the political successes of individual Ukrainians did not alter the fact that Ukrainian interests were completely subordinated to those of the Soviet empire as a whole.

26

Stagnation and Attempts at Reform

During its early decades in power, the Soviet regime was the most radical and innovative in the world. By the 1960s, however, extreme conservatism became a hallmark of its internal policies. Fearful of the unpredictable and undesirable consequences of change, the aging, bureaucratic elite of the USSR opted for maintaining, in a somewhat milder form, the system that Stalin had put into place. For Ukraine this meant that Moscow, not Kiev, continued to make all the major decisions that affected Ukrainians. And the role of Russification in holding the numerous nationalities of the USSR together not only continued but increased.

Yet even the omnipotent and omnipresent Soviet governing apparatus could not exert complete control over society. Dissent, impossible in the Stalin years, emerged among the intelligentsia. More surprising was that the views and policies of the Ukrainian Communist party leadership diverged clearly, if only briefly, from those of the men in the Kremlin. Although the Soviet system remained firmly in place, skepticism about its effectiveness, especially its ability to raise living standards, spread among the populace. By the mid 1980s, the need for change was undeniable and pressing. Consequently, the Soviet oligarchy chose one of its own to usher in reforms – carefully. In Ukraine the impact of these changes was slow in coming and limited in extent. It was enough to reveal, however, that many of the political, cultural, and economic problems the regime claimed to have eliminated in Ukraine were far from resolved.

ã

The Men at the Top

Leonid Brezhnev, like his predecessor Khrushchev, was a Russian whose rise to power was closely associated with Ukraine. Unlike the impetuous and confrontational Khrushchev, the careful Brezhnev exerted influence by building a consensus for his policies within the Soviet oligarchy and by assuring this elite of stability and continuity. Consequently, his eighteen-year tenure was marked by conservative tendencies that, although no longer totalitarian – the noted Sovietologist Merle Fainsod has drolly described the slow Soviet retreat from Stalinism as "the law of diminishing dictators" – were clearly authoritarian. But while the exercise of power was more measured than in the days of Stalin, there was no doubt that it was still concentrated in the party and that it was to be used to expand Soviet might abroad and to exert complete control at home.

Shelest and Shcherbytsky   During the Brezhnev era, Ukraine had two Communist party leaders, Petro Shelest and Volodymyr Shcherbytsky, whose policies, though differing, illustrated the issues confronting Soviet Ukrainian leaders and the context in which Ukrainian, that is, republic-level, politics are played out in the USSR today.

Shelest's tenure as the first secretary of the Ukrainian Communist party lasted from 1963 to 1972 and it featured a resurgence of Ukrainian self-assertiveness. From the skimpy evidence that is available to Western analysts, it appears that this assertiveness was primarily a result of Shelest's attempts to defend Ukrainian interests within the Soviet Union. Shelest was not, however, a crypto-nationalist. Indeed, in many ways he was more of a hard-line Communist than his superiors in Moscow. There are indications that he was adamantly anti-Western, supported the invasion of Czechoslovakia in 1968 lest its reformist tendencies "infect" Ukraine, neglected Western Ukraine, opposed concessions to workers, and preferred to concentrate on heavy industry rather than consumer goods. Apparently even Brezhnev found some of these inflexible positions bothersome.

But there was another aspect to Shelest that concerned the Kremlin even more. It seems the Ukrainian leader took seriously the promise of Ukrainian autonomy enshrined in the Soviet constitution and the principle that all nations within the USSR are equal. Hence, he was loath to acknowledge the Russians' "elder brother" role within the Soviet Union. Probably the status Shelest wanted to attain for Ukraine was similar to that of Poland, Czechoslovakia, or Hungary, that is, of a thoroughly communist society but one whose specific economic and cultural needs were recognized by Moscow.

Ukraine's economic interests were a major concern for Shelest. He demanded more Ukrainian input into the Soviet Union's economic planning process and showed little enthusiasm for the economic development of Siberia, which meant the reduction of investment in Ukraine. When a group of Ukrainian economists provided him with data showing that Ukraine was being shortchanged in its economic relationship with the Soviet Union as a whole, Shelest became a strong proponent of reciprocity, that is, the principle that Ukraine should obtain funds, goods, and services from the USSR that were of equal value to those it contributed to the USSR.

Shelest was even more outspoken in defending Ukrainian linguistic and cultural rights. His speeches contained exhortations to Ukrainians to "treasure" their "beautiful Ukrainian language." In 1965, Iurii Dadenkov, the Ukrainian minister of higher education and a close Shelest associate, called for the expanded use of Ukrainian in the universities and institutes. And in 1970, Shelest's book, *Our Soviet Ukraine*, stressed, directly or by implication, the historical autonomy of Ukraine, the progressive role of the Cossacks, the tsarist exploitation of Ukraine, and the impressive achievements of Soviet Ukraine. Clearly, Shelest's pride in his republic's rapid transition from a backward agrarian land into a modern, industrialized, and technologically advanced society was unusually fierce and evident.

How can one explain such "particularism" in a disciplined, experienced, and apparently sincere Communist – a member of the Politburo, the Soviet Union's highest ruling body? In all probability, Shelest and his many supporters in Ukraine took Soviet pronouncements about national equality within the USSR at face value. They saw no contradiction between the achievement of general Soviet goals, the modernization of Ukraine, and the retention of its national culture. Much like Skrypnyk in the 1920s, Shelest seemed to believe that the satisfaction of Ukrainian economic and cultural needs, not their suppression, was the most effective means of ensuring Soviet success in Ukraine. Shelest may have also concluded that his own personal success in effectively ruling Ukraine depended on the cooperation of the Ukrainian cultural, scientific, and political elite. And this meant paying attention to its specific concerns.

In May 1972 Shelest was removed from his post in Kiev on charges of being "soft" on Ukrainian nationalism and encouraging economic "localism." His successor was Shcherbytsky, an ethnic Ukrainian, a long-time member of Brezhnev's "Dnieper" clan, and a fierce political rival of Shelest. In a fashion reminiscent of the fratricidal political infighting among contestants for the hetman's office in 17th- and 18th-century Ukraine, Shcherbytsky helped to undermine Shelest by repeatedly denouncing him to Moscow for his "local patriotism." Since the fall of his rival, Shcherbytsky has managed to retain the position of the Communist party boss in Ukraine, and his lengthy tenure in this post is a record. What are the reasons for this success? To a large extent they result from a policy of complete subservience to Moscow. So obedient has he been in fulfilling Moscow's instructions, so willing to sacrifice Ukraine's economic interests, and so cooperative in exposing Ukraine to Russification that Shcherbytsky may well go down in history as the Little Russian (*Maloros*) par excellence.

Aided by his watchdog for ideological issues, Valentyn Malanchuk, and the chief of the Ukrainian KGB, V.V. Fedorchuk, Shcherbytsky conducted a relatively mild purge in 1973 that eliminated about 37,000 members from the Communist party ranks, many of whom were probably supporters of Shelest. In sharp contrast to his predecessor, Shcherbytsky has made a point of speaking Russian at official functions and supporting the renewed centralization of the Ukrainian economy and the heavy investment in Siberia. He has also been a proponent of harsh, uncompromising treatment when dealing with dissent.

Yet these efforts did not bring him what he seems to have desired most – elevation to a top position in Moscow, perhaps even nomination as Brezhnev's successor. Therefore, by the early 1980s there were indications that Shcherbytsky was paying more attention to his position in Ukraine by improving relations with its cultural elite and becoming somewhat less assiduous in pushing Moscow's assimilationist policies. With the rise of the reform-minded Mikhail Gorbachev to power in 1985, speculation was rife that Shcherbytsky's days as the Ukrainian party leader were numbered. But to the surprise of many observers, he continued to retain his position, probably because of support from antireformists in the Kremlin.

If one takes the policies of these two important Ukrainian political leaders into account, what conclusions can one draw about their views of Ukraine and its role in the Soviet Union? Clearly, both Shelest and Shcherbytsky envisioned Ukraine's future only in terms of communist ideology and within the context of the Soviet system. Neither was ready even to consider the idea of Ukraine's independence. And each in his own way was an example of the tight control that Moscow exerts over Ukraine's Communist leadership.

Yet the careers of these two men indicate that even in the strictly monitored Soviet political system surprisingly contrasting attitudes and policies toward Ukraine can emerge. As a proponent of equality of nations in the USSR and of a just balance in their economic relations, Shelest wanted Ukraine to be treated as an autonomous state within a genuine Soviet federation. On the one hand, the considerable support Shelest enjoyed not only among the Ukrainian intelligentsia but within the Ukrainian party apparatus reveals that national communism, or at least a territorial or republican patriotism, is deeply rooted in Ukraine. On the other hand, Shelest's downfall is a reminder that such views are still unacceptable to Moscow.

In some ways, the behavior and policies of Shcherbytsky can be likened to those of a Western corporate executive. For such a person, the USSR is probably not unlike a huge Moscow-based corporation. In this context, Ukraine is probably seen as a region of important branch plants, which, if run successfully (that is, according to the wishes of the men in the Kremlin), can catapult its manager to the height of the corporate power structure. Thus, when the interests of the "corporation" have demanded standardization (Russification) in Ukraine, Shcherbytsky has readily complied, arguing that adherence to "local particularities" (national culture) impeded efficiency and progress. When

Ukraine was required to draw on its assets to aid the development of another unit of the "corporation," Shcherbytsky has been forthcoming, thereby demonstrating his ability to "think big." A problem with this branch-plant mentality – which may be considered a modern form of the old Little Russianism – is that those who espouse it often forget that they are dealing not only with administrative and socioeconomic units but with nations.

The Communist Party of Ukraine (cpu)   The influence and importance of Shelest and Shcherbytsky reached far beyond the Ukrainian republic. The former was, and the latter continues to be, a major political player on the all-union level – as a result largely of the growth spurt experienced by the Communist Party of Ukraine after the Second World War, particularly after the death of Stalin. After Khrushchev came into power, membership in the Ukrainian party expanded rapidly. This growth, which was greater in Ukraine than in the other republics, continued throughout the 1960s and early 1970s. Thus, while in 1958 the party in Ukraine had 1.1 million members, by 1971 the number had risen to 2.5 million. The membership also became more evenly distributed throughout the republic. Earlier much of it was concentrated in the heavily Russian Donbas and Dniepropetrovsk areas in the southeast. During the Khrushchev era representation of the largely Ukrainian central and western parts of the republic improved perceptibly in the party membership.

The rise of a new generation of political leaders in Ukraine soon reflected this development. Leadership included more Ukrainians than ever before. Thus, in 1964, out of thirty-three top party officials in the republic, thirty were Ukrainians. The percentage of party members from Ukraine in the Central Committee of the ussr rose to an unprecedented high of 20% in 1961. Given its unusually rapid growth and its close ties with the Kremlin, the cpu earned a reputation as a "model" party in the ussr. But it was exactly this new sense of confidence and importance that led to frustration within the Ukrainian elite with the hypercentralized political and economic policies of the Kremlin. Hence Shelest's autonomist tendencies. That these had the support of the vast majority of the Ukrainian party apparatus is evident: only three of the twenty-five Ukrainian *oblast* (regional) party secretaries voted for his ouster.

The fall of Shelest was also a setback to the Ukrainian party. Its numerical growth slowed and its representation in the Central Committee of the Soviet Union dropped to 15%. Nonetheless, the ability of the hard-liner Shcherbytsky to remain in power in Kiev for so long indicates that the Ukrainian party, which he leads, is still a factor of major importance in the Soviet political system.

Dissent

A remarkable phenomenon surfaced in the Soviet Union in the 1960s and 1970s, when a small but growing number of individuals, commonly called dissidents, began to criticize government policies openly and to demand greater civil, religious, and national rights. After decades of terror and in view of the tight controls and relentless indoctrination the regime has had at its disposal, how could this surprising challenge to it emerge? To a great extent, dissent was an outgrowth of de-Stalinization, of the loosening of the "paralysis of fear" that Khrushchev had initiated. The limited revelations of the horrendous crimes of the Stalin era aroused widespread disenchantment and skepticism about other aspects of the regime. Consequently, when Brezhnev attempted to impose limits on liberalization, he evoked protest and dissent, especially among the intelligentsia.

Dissent in the USSR flowed into three frequently overlapping currents. Because of its access to the Western media, the best known was the Moscow-based civil rights or democratic movement, which consisted mostly of Russian intelligentsia and counted among its leaders such luminaries as the novelist Aleksander Solzhenitsyn and the nuclear physicist Andrei Sakharov. Religious militancy was another form of "deviant" behavior. In Ukraine and other non-Russian regions, dissent crystallized around nationality-oriented as well as civil rights and religious issues.

Initially, the core of the Ukrainian dissidents consisted largely of the "sixtiers," the new and creative literary generation that was just coming into prominence. It included Lina Kostenko, Vasyl Symonenko, Ivan Drach, Ivan Svitlychny, Ievhen Sverstiuk, Mykola Vinhranovsky, Alla Horska, and Ivan Dziuba. Later they were joined by Vasyl Stus, Mykhailo Osadchy, Ihor and Iryna Kalynets, Ivan Hel, and the Horyn brothers. A striking characteristic of this group was that its members were generally model products of the Soviet educational system and well on the way to promising careers. Some were committed communists. Although concentrated mostly in Kiev and Lviv, they stemmed from various parts of Ukraine. While the majority were East Ukrainians, many of them had a West Ukrainian connection, having either studied or worked in the region. Another noteworthy feature was that a large proportion of the dissidents were the first generation in their families to leave the village and to enter the ranks of the urban intelligentsia. Hence the naive idealism and sophisticated argumentation that often characterized their statements. By and large, they were a very loose, unorganized conglomeration of people. There were not more than 1000 active dissidents in Ukraine.[1] However, supporters and sympathizers probably numbered in the many thousands.

What grievances did the Ukrainian dissidents have? And what goals did they want to achieve? As with any group of intellectuals, there was great variety and fluidity in their views. Ivan Dziuba, a literary critic and one of the most prominent of the dissidents, apparently desired civil liberties as much as national rights. His goal was clearly stated: "I propose ... one thing only: *freedom* – freedom for the honest, public discussion of national affairs, freedom of national choice, freedom for national self-knowledge, self-awareness, and self-development. But first and foremost, comes freedom for discussions and disagreement."[2] A national communist, Dziuba was disturbed by the great gap between Soviet theory and reality, especially in the area of nationality rights, and urged the authorities to repair it for the good of the Soviet system as well as the Ukrainian nation. The historian Valentyn Moroz, in contrast, reflected the intellectual traditions of Ukrainian integral nationalism and made no secret of his disgust with the Soviet system and hope for its demise. In general, however, the Ukrainian dissidents called for reforms in the USSR, not revolution or separation. They were against national repression in Ukraine and for civil rights in the USSR.

Among Western analysts of Ukrainian dissent there are divided opinions about the conditions that led people to protest openly. Alexander Motyl has argued that in Ukraine, as in the USSR in general, it was primarily the political policies of the Soviet leadership – specifically Khrushchev's "thaw" and Brezhnev's attempts to reverse it – that led to dissent.[3] Certainly Shelest's openly pro-Ukrainian line provided Ukrainian intellectuals with an added incentive to express their dissatisfaction. Wsevolod Isajiw and Bohdan Krawchenko have stressed that dissent in Ukraine was closely and primarily related to socioeconomic tensions.[4] Given the huge, Moscow-supported influx of Russians into Ukraine, they believe that competition for good jobs grew between privileged Russian newcomers and upwardly mobile Ukrainians, leading many of the latter to join or to support the dissidents' call for greater Ukrainian self-determination. In any case, in its Ukrainian context, dissent was clearly the latest manifestation of the generation-old confrontation between the Ukrainian intelligentsia and the bureaucracy of a Russian-dominated empire.

Manifestations of dissent   The earliest manifestations of Ukrainian dissent appeared in the late 1950s and early 1960s when several small, secret groups in Western Ukraine were organized. The most noteworthy of these was the so-called "Jurists' Group," led by the jurist Levko Lukianenko. It called for Ukraine to use its legal right to secede from the Soviet Union. After discovering these groups, the authorities imposed harsh sentences on their members in a series of closed trials.

But the momentum of de-Stalinization continued to produce unrest among the intelligentsia. In 1963, an official Conference on Culture and Language, held at Kiev University and attended by over 1000 people, turned into an open demonstration against Russification. At about this time, students and intelligentsia began to gather regularly at the statue of Shevchenko in Kiev, ostensibly to hold public readings of the poet's works, but also to criticize the regime's cultural policies. The suspicious fire in 1964 that destroyed the Ukrainian manuscript collection at the Ukrainian Academy of Sciences library elicited a storm of protest by leading literary figures. Fearful that matters were getting out of hand, the Kremlin decided to crack down on dissent throughout the USSR. In Ukraine this policy resulted in the arrest in late 1965 of about two dozen of the most vocal protesters. Hoping to intimidate the dissidents' colleagues, the authorities put the latter on open trial. However, the tactic backfired and led to even greater protest and dissent.

After observing the trials in Lviv, Viacheslav Chornovil, a young journalist and committed Communist, produced his revelatory "Chornovil Papers," a collection of documents that exposed the arbitrary, illegal, and cynical manipulation of the judicial system by the authorities. Dziuba denounced the arrests in a fiery speech before a large audience in Kiev. He also submitted to Shelest and Shcherbytsky his "Internationalism or Russification?" a perceptive, erudite, and damning analysis of the theory and mechanics of Russification in Ukraine. In 1970, after his arrest for anti-Soviet agitation and propaganda, Moroz wrote his "Report from the Beria Reserve," an emotional and powerful denunciation of the cruelty of Soviet officialdom and its degradation of individuals as well as nations. To prevent the authorities from isolating the dissidents from each other and society and to inform the world about the details of Soviet repression, in 1970 the Ukrainian dissidents began the surreptitious distribution of the *Ukrainian Herald*. Although the KGB was able to restrict the circulation of these materials in Ukraine, it could not prevent them from being smuggled to the West. There, with the aid of Ukrainian émigrés, these works were published and publicized, to the consternation and embarrassment of Soviet authorities.

After the fall of Shelest in 1972, Shcherbytsky, in cooperation with the Ukrainian KGB chief Fedorchuk and ideologist Malanchuk, launched a massive "pogrom" of the dissenting intelligentsia that led to hundreds of arrests and far harsher sentences than in 1965–66. Outspoken dissidents and those members of research institutes, editorial staffs, and university faculties who were suspected of "unreliable" views were removed from their positions. This wave of persecution recalled the days of Stalin, traumatized a whole generation of Ukrainian intelligentsia, and led many, including Dziuba, to recant or to give up their dissident activities.

The Ukrainian Helsinki Group   Reduced in number but still determined, dissidents received fresh impetus in 1975 when the USSR signed the Helsinki Accords and formally agreed to respect the civil rights of its people. Taking the Kremlin at its word, dissidents organized open and, in their view, legally sanctioned groups whose task was to monitor the Kremlin's observance of civil rights. The first Helsinki Committee was established in Moscow in May 1976. Soon afterward, in November 1976, a Ukrainian Helsinki Group emerged in Kiev. Similar groups also sprang up in Lithuania, Georgia, and Armenia.

The leader of the Ukrainian Helsinki Group was the writer Mykola Rudenko, a political commissar during the Second World War and a former party official in the literary field. His close associate was Petro Hryhorenko (Grigorenko), a much-decorated and (forcibly) retired general of the Red Army. The group, which numbered thirty-seven people in all, was unusually varied in terms of background. It included dissidents such as Nina Strokata, Vasyl Stus, Levko Lukianenko, Ivan Kandyba, Nadia Svitlychna, and Viacheslav Chornovil, who had already served prison terms; former nationalists (who had survived decades in Stalin's labor camps) such as Sviatoslav Karavansky, Oksana Popovych, Oksana Meshko, Iryna Senyk, Petro Sichko, Danylo Shumuk, and Iurii Shukhevych (the son of the commander of the UPA, Roman Shukhevych); and religious activists, such as the Orthodox priest Vasyl Romaniuk.

Two important features distinguished the Ukrainian Helsinki Group from previous dissidents in Ukraine. One was that the group was an open, civic organization, which, while not controlled by the regime, nonetheless claimed the legal right to exist. This view was unheard of in Eastern Ukraine since the imposition of Soviet rule. The other precedent-setting feature was that the Ukrainian group established contacts with similar groups throughout the USSR, attempting thereby to "internationalize" its concern for civil and national rights.

New thinking was also evident in the group's programmatic statements. They emphasized legality, seeing the solution to society's problems in the rule of law, in general, and in respect for the rights of the individual, in particular. For this reason, the group's members often described their activities as the "movement for the defense of civil rights" (*pravozakhysny rukh*). As Ivan Lysiak-Rudnytsky noted, this emphasis on legality and genuine democracy rather than on ideologies, such as nationalism or Marxism, which had heretofore captivated the Ukrainian intelligentsia, was an important turning point in the history of Ukrainian political thought.[5]

Although some members of the Ukrainian Helsinki Group remained committed, to a greater or lesser degree, to Marxism or to nationalism, an excerpt from the memoirs of Danylo Shumuk, who was both a former communist and nationalist, and who spent close to forty years in Polish, Nazi, and Soviet prisons, probably captures the view of its majority:

Only democracy can save mankind from the dangers of the rightist as well as of the leftist brands of tyranny. Only the unrestricted right, guaranteed by law, for all citizens to express, advertise, and defend their ideas will enable the people to control and direct the policy of the government. Without such a right, there can be no talk of democracy and of democratic elections to a parliament. Where there is no legal opposition, endowed with equal rights in the parliament and among the people, there is no democracy ... I have reached these conclusions after many years of thinking, stocktaking, and analysis, and they have led me ... to adopt a critical attitude to both communists and Dontsovian nationalists.[6]

In sharp contrast to the xenophobia that characterized the OUN brand of nationalism, the ardent patriotism of the Ukrainian dissidents did not imply hostility to other peoples, even the Russians. In 1980 one of their declarations stated: "We understand what it means to live under colonial oppression and therefore proclaim [that] the people who live in our country will be assured the broadest political, economic and social rights. All the rights of national minorities and various religious associations will be guaranteed unconditionally."[7] Given their legalistic views, the members of the Ukrainian Helsinki Group argued that Ukraine's independence could best be achieved by exercising the right, guaranteed by the Soviet constitution, to secede from the USSR. In their view, the most effective manner of "decolonizing" the Soviet Union was to allow its peoples to hold genuinely free elections.

But neither the Helsinki Group's moderation nor the West's insistence that the USSR honor its commitment to the Helsinki Accords prevented Soviet authorities from again decimating the dissidents. By 1980 about three-fourths of the Ukrainian Helsinki Group were imprisoned with sentences ranging from ten to fifteen years. The remainder were exiled from Ukraine or, to appease foreign opinion, allowed to emigrate.

Religious dissent   A distinct type of dissent in Ukraine is based on religion. In theory, freedom of worship is guaranteed by the Soviet constitution. But the regime has used a variety of means to discourage religious beliefs and practices. Such measures include limiting religious publications, forbidding religious education of children and exposing them to atheistic indoctrination, placing its agents within the priesthood and religious hierarchy, closing down places of worship, and imposing social, economic, and educational penalties on those who stand up for their faith. However, the spiritual barrenness of Soviet ideology on the one hand, and resentment against the regime's heavy-handed tactics on the other, have led to a renewed interest in religion, especially in the countryside. With it has come a greater militancy on the part of believers.

The regime's fierce persecution of the Ukrainian Greek Catholic church ("the church in catacombs") failed to obliterate it completely. In recent decades about 300–350 Greek Catholic priests, led by several bishops, have been secretly ministering to the faithful in Western Ukraine. Even hidden monasteries and secret printing presses continue to exist. In 1982, Iosyp Terelia organized the Committee for the Defense of the Ukrainian Catholic Church to demand its legalization. Although the regime has responded by arresting the activists, loyalty to their ancient church is still strong among the Ukrainians of Galicia and Transcarpathia.

The Orthodox church in Ukraine, which is officially called the Russian Orthodox church, is in a more advantageous position because it is tolerated by the Soviet government. But this comes at the price of cooperation with and subservience to the authorities. Consequently, corruption, hypocrisy, and the favoring of state interests over religious concerns are widespread in the Orthodox church, particularly in its hierarchy. This state of affairs has led a few members of the lower clergy, notably the much-persecuted Vasyl Romaniuk, to denounce both their superiors and the Soviet state for manipulating and undermining Orthodoxy.

Probably the most militant and dynamic religious denominations in Ukraine today are the Baptists and other Protestant sects, such as Pentecostals, Adventists, and Jehovah's Witnesses. They practice their faith in autonomous congregations, insist on educating their children according to the dictates of their religions, and often refuse to register with the government, thereby making it difficult for the authorities to control them. Their fundamentalist views, grass-roots organization, and fierce commitment to their faith have attracted numerous converts, particularly in Eastern Ukraine. In recent years they have constituted a disproportionately large part of the "prisoners of conscience" in the USSR. Until his immigration to the United States, Pastor Georgii Vins was the foremost leader of the Baptists.

Suppression of dissent   Although their bravery and idealism were inspiring and the behavior of their persecutors was odious, the dissidents in Ukraine and elsewhere in the USSR failed to attract widespread support. One reason was that, besides denouncing the regime and stressing the need for the rule of law, they did not formulate a coherent political program. Further, the matters they addressed were not bread-and-butter issues of concern to the majority of the population: the workers and collective farmers. Therefore, the social base of the dissidents was narrow, resting almost exculsively on the intelligentsia.

Even more decisive in explaining the failure of the dissident movement was the nature of its opposition. Mustered against the dissidents were all the vast powers of the Soviet system, particularly the all-powerful KGB. Possessing a monopoly on communication, the regime usually prevented information about the dissidents from reaching the public. When information did emerge, it was usually distorted to cast the dissidents in a negative light. With hundreds of thousands of officers, plainclothes agents, and informers at its disposal, the KGB seemed to be everywhere and to know everything, preventing any collective activity from occurring without government supervision. But unlike in the days of Stalin, the secret police was no longer fanatical about physically destroying all real or potential dissidents. In recent times it has sought to isolate the dissidents from society and, by means of escalating pressures, to intimidate them into recanting or remaining silent. Critics of the regime were denied jobs, educational opportunites for their children, and even shelter. Those who persisted were given long prison terms or incarcerated in psychiatric hospitals and given mind-altering drugs. By destroying the few, the KGB successfully intimidated the many.

In Ukraine, the secret police worked under fewer constraints than in Moscow. Isolated from the Moscow-based Western media, the Ukrainian dissidents did not have the relative protection of the "publicity umbrella" that their prominent Russian and Jewish colleagues enjoyed. Moreover, the issue of Ukrainian national rights aroused little interest in the West. Meanwhile, the regime's fear of Ukrainian nationalism led to particularly harsh repression in Ukraine. Hence, the reputation of the Kiev KGB as being the most vicious in the USSR and the disproportionately large number of Ukrainian "prisoners of conscience."

Russification

Viewed from the perspective of the Kremlin, the nationality issue in the USSR is a daunting and complex one. In a society that encompasses about 100 different nationalities – which occupy their own territories and possess sharply variegated histories, cultures, social values, and economic interests – Soviet leaders must find ways to mold a sense of common identity and purpose. To this end Soviet ideologists in the post-Stalin era have produced a number of concepts that are meant to deemphasize the national particularities of their peoples and to stress common Soviet features. Of these concepts, four have been of special importance: *rastsvetanie*, the claim that all nationalities in the USSR have experienced a flowering or development under Soviet rule; *sblizhenie*, the assertion that these nationalities are drawing together because of the creation of common political, economic, and cultural institutions in the USSR; *sliianie*, the fusion of the Soviet nationalities into a single nation; and the emergence of a new type of historical community – the Soviet people (*sovietskii narod*).

Behind the ideological double-talk, which implies that nations can "flower" while losing their identity, is a hidden agenda: Russification. Because Russians are in the majority, because they created the Bolshevik party and the Soviet system, because they occupy most of the top positions, and because their language is the primary means of communication in the USSR, they are seen as the cement that holds the USSR together. Apparently the Soviet leadership believes that the more the other nationalities of the USSR are like the Russians, the greater their feeling of mutual solidarity will be. Hence the view held by many Western scholars and non-Russian dissidents in the USSR that *sblizhenie* (drawing together), *sliianie* (fusion), and *sovietskii narod* (Soviet people) are simply code-words for Russification of the non-Russians.

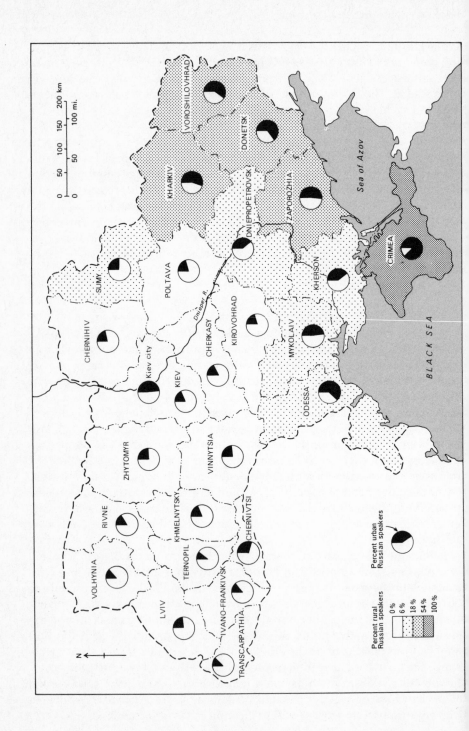

Percent rural
Russian speakers

0 %
6 %
18 %
54 %
100 %

Percent urban
Russian speakers

Russification in Ukraine, as we have seen, was a key grievance of the Ukrainian dissidents. They rejected the claims that the predominance of Russian language and culture is a necessary by-product of the progressive, inspiring task of creating a new type of "brotherly, international community, the Soviet people." In their view, the emphasis on Russian was simply old wine in new bottles. Dziuba argued in his "Internationalism or Russification?" that what was behind Russification was old Russian chauvinism and colonialism packaged in pseudo-Marxist terminology. "Colonialism," he wrote, "can appear not only in the form of open discrimination, but also in the form of 'brotherhood,' and this is very characteristic of Russian colonialism."[8] By extensively quoting Lenin, he tried to show that there was no basis in Marxist-Leninist ideology for the Kremlin's preference for Russian.

In Ukraine assimilatory pressures have been particularly intense in recent decades, partly because of the Ukrainians' linguistic and cultural proximity to the Russians, which makes the former promising targets for Russification. Also, Ukraine's economic importance to the USSR demands that its people do not develop "separatist" tendencies. Because of their relatively large numbers, the Ukrainians have the potential for being a "swing vote" in nationality relations: should they adhere to the Russians, ethnic politics will probably remain stable in the USSR. But if they side with the non-Russians, Russian predominance might be undermined and radical changes could occur in the Soviet political system.

The language issue   In the struggle of the Soviet leadership to create a new Soviet nationality and of the Ukrainians to preserve their national identity, the main battlefront is language. During Brezhnev's years in office, the Kremlin launched a sophisticated, systematic campaign to expand the use of Russian in Ukraine, while discouraging the use of Ukrainian. In pursuing its objectives, the Soviet leadership could count on strong supporters such as the 10 million Russians living in Ukraine and the additional millions of "Little Russians," who are of Ukrainian background but Russian in culture and language. It also had persuasive arguments: Russian is the language of the most numerous and important people in the USSR, it is the only common means of communication among its diverse nationalities, and it is a medium of science and international intercourse.

The authorities have at their disposal a variety of direct and indirect pressures to make people use Russian. Its use in Ukrainian schools has increased rapidly and educational success depends on the mastery of Russian. The same holds true for career opportunities. In Ukraine the most interesting and important publications appear in Russian, while boring, irrelevant subject matter is frequently relegated to Ukrainian periodicals. When the circulation of the latter declines, the authorities have a good excuse to shut down these periodicals. Thus, between 1969 and 1980 the percentage of journals published in Ukrainian decreased from 46% to 19%; between 1958 and 1980 the percentage of books published in Ukrainian dropped from 60% to 24%.

In the cities, social pressure to use Russian is intense and Ukrainian is denigrated as the language of "country bumpkins." The regime has consciously fostered the inferiority complex toward their language and culture that exists among many Ukrainians. And this feeling is reflected in the fact that it is Ukrainians who frequently demand Russian-language education for their children. "What good is Ukrainian? My children need a mastery of Russian to succeed" is a remark one often hears among former (and still socially insecure) Ukrainian peasants who are trying to get ahead in the Russified cities. Some Soviet Ukrainian intellectuals claim, only half-jokingly, that if Ukrainization were imposed today, Jews could be Ukrainized in a year, Russians in Ukraine would accept the policy after about three years, but it would take at least ten years to convince an upwardly mobile Ukrainian *khokhol* to use his native language.

If one persists in using Ukrainian, it may even raise doubts about one's political loyalty. For example, the Soviet police lent great credence to the following statement of a prosecution witness against the dissident poet Vasyl Stus: "I knew right away that Stus was a nationalist because he always spoke Ukrainian."[9]

How effective has linguistic Russification been? In Ukraine between 1959 and 1979 the proportion of Ukrainians who declared Ukrainian to be their native langauge dropped from 93.4% to 89.1%. Today well over 2 million Ukrainians consider Russian to be their mother tongue. Meanwhile, only one in three Russians living in Ukraine has bothered to learn Ukrainian. Does this mean that the demise of the Ukrainian language is only a matter of time? If present trends continue, the future of Ukrainian certainly appears grim. Yet pessimists have predicted the imminent demise of Ukrainian for centuries.

Optimists, though, argue that if, despite the persistent efforts to eradicate it, the language has not died out yet, it never will. They point out that the status of Ukrainian is not as bad as it seems. True, in certain areas, such as the Donetsk industrial belt, in the Kharkiv region, and along the Black Sea coast, the use of Ukrainiar is minimal and declining. However, because of the influx of Ukrainians from the countryside into Kiev in recent years, the use of Ukrainian in the republic's capital has risen slightly. And in Western Ukraine, Ukrainian is much more widespread than before the Second World War. Thus, the language question, which has historically been of crucial importance in Ukraine, is far from being resolved.

Russians in Ukraine   Another major method the regime has used to advance Russification in Ukraine has been to encourage the in-migration of Russians and the out-migration of Ukrainians. Generally this policy has been implemented under the guise of "the fruitful exchanges of personnel" between the republics. Thus, while huge numbers of Russians have been brought into Ukraine to enrich it with their skills, equally large numbers of educated Ukrainians have been directed to jobs in other parts of the USSR (where they often identify with Russians). These huge demographic shifts are meant to intermingle the peoples of the USSR and to encourage the growth of a common identity. Russians, it should be noted, have shown a marked proclivity for leaving their republic. Experts explain this trend by the relative poverty in the Russian countryside and by the widely held belief in the USSR that Russians tend to get the best jobs in non-Russian areas. For Russians, Ukraine in particular is a favorite objective: it has a good climate and a high level of socioeconomic and cultural development, and is culturally and linguistically familiar.

Predictably, these migration processes have led to a dramatic increase in the number of Russians living in Ukraine. In 1926 there were 3 million Russians in the republic; in 1959 their numbers rose to 7 million; and in 1979 the figure was close to 10 million. As always, Russians in Ukraine tend to concentrate in large cities, particularly in the Donbas industrial region and in the south. Today, they constitute about 21% of Ukraine's inhabitants and their influence is far greater than their proportion of the population.

The rapidly increasing number of Russians in Ukraine is not only a result of in-migration, however. Minorities in Ukraine, such as the Jews, Greeks, and Bulgarians, have been assimilating into the Russian nationality. And, as we have seen, so have Ukrainians. This process is reinforced by the high rate of intermarriage between Ukrainians and Russians. In 1970 about 20% of all marriages – 30% in the cities and about 8% in the countryside – were ethnically mixed. By way of comparison, in the early 20th century, when most Ukrainians still lived in isolated villages, only 3% of the marriages in Ukraine were between different ethnic groups.

In view of the rapidly increasing Russian presence in the republic, it is possible to speak, as Roman Szporluk does, of two Ukraines: one heavily Russian and the other still basically Ukrainian.[10] In geographic terms, the "Russified Ukraine" encompasses the industrialized Donbas and the cities of the south, areas that were never a part of historical Ukraine. Meanwhile, in such regions as the Right Bank, parts of the Left Bank, and Western Ukraine, which were always predominantly inhabited by Ukrainians, the language and culture remain predominantly Ukrainian, especially in the countryside. But the line between Russian and Ukrainian languages and cultures in Ukraine can be drawn on a different level as well. The world of the large cities – of the political, economic, and scientific elite, of modernity in general – is basically Russian. The world of the countryside – of collective farmers, of folk customs – is largely Ukrainian. Such was the situation in the days of the tsars. With the aid of more sophisticated tactics, such is the situation that the Soviet leadership encourages today.

But even though the policies of Russification are more insidious and pervasive than ever, they have not stifled the process of Ukrainian nation-building. Two generations ago, most East Ukrainians still called themselves "Little Russians," "*khokhols*," or "locals"; one generation ago, many West Ukrainians defined themselves as Lemkos, Hutsuls, or Rusyns, that is, in terms of their regional cultures. Today their children and grandchildren are self-declared Ukrainians. In short, they are no longer the ethnographic mass they were at the onset of the century. Even non-Ukrainians have become Ukrainians. For example, the Poles who remained in Ukraine have tended to assimilate with Ukrainians. Many Russians who have lived in Ukraine for several generations also have developed a strong sense of territorial patriotism.

Even urbanization can no longer be viewed as a one-way road to denationalization. The Soviet scholar V.V. Pokshishevsky argues that while the city does expose the newcomer to assimilationist (Russifying) currents, it also stimulates a "sharpening of ethnic awareness."[11] Citing the increased Ukrainian presence in Kiev, he states that it is the result of the city's attraction to all Ukrainians and also of "the further consolidation of the Ukrainian nation and a strengthening of ethnic consciousness." Pokshishevky also notes: "It may be supposed that some Kievans, after some hesitation whether to consider themselves Ukrainian, later did so with absolute conviction; more children of mixed marriages have also declared themselves Ukrainian."[12] Thus, as with language, the ultimate success of the Kremlin's homogenizing policies in Ukraine is still open to question.

Social Change

A momentous development occurred in Ukrainian social history in the 1960s: during that decade the percentage of Ukrainians living in cities reached 55%, that is, the majority of them had become city dwellers. And according to Soviet estimates, by the year 2000, over 70% of Ukrainians will be living in urban centers. Of course, rapid urbanization has been a worldwide phenomenon for generations and it was only a matter of time before it would catch up with the Ukrainians. Nonetheless, because Ukraine's inhabitants have always been considered to be agrarians par excellence, and because their culture, mentality, and national consciousness were heavily imbued with the peasant ethos, the evolution of this society of village dwellers into city dwellers can truly be called the Great Transformation.

What has led Ukrainians to leave their villages in such large numbers and to move to the cities? In general, the reasons are similar to those anywhere in the world: better job opportunities, greater access to higher education, an attractive variety of leisure activities, and more convenient conditions for family life. As a result of this influx of Ukrainians into urban centers, the cities of the land, long the bastions of non-Ukrainians, have finally attained Ukrainian majorities. And the traditional dichotomy between the Ukrainian village and the Russian (or Polish/Jewish) city may possibly begin to fade.

There are, however, noteworthy aspects to the process of urbanization in Ukraine. Although rapid, it has still not moved ahead as quickly as in other parts of the USSR. Thus, urbanization in Russia, which in 1970 reached 62%, has proceeded at a rate comparable to that of Japan and Western Europe; in Ukraine, meanwhile, it has advanced at a rate similar to that of Eastern and Southern Europe. Moreover, urbanization in Ukraine is geographically imbalanced, for it is concentrated primarily in the eastern, heavily industrialized (and Russified) areas of Donetsk, Voroshilovhrad, Dniepropetrovsk, and Zaporozhia. Recently, however, there have been indications that the rate of urbanization in the east has slowed while it has been rising in Western Ukraine. The outstanding fact remains that Ukrainians are pouring into cities and the Ukrainian peasant, long the archetypal inhabitant of the land, is now becoming an endangered species.

This development is of immense ideological as well as sociological importance. As the role of the peasant in Ukrainian society has diminished, the populism that was the hallmark of Ukrainian ideologies in the 19th and early 20th centuries has also faded. One can even argue that today the concept of the *narod* - in the traditional sense of the poor, oppressed peasant masses – no longer occupies a central place in the political thinking of Ukrainians.

The economy　Tightly interwoven with that of the Soviet Union as a whole, the economy of Ukraine is highly developed. Ukraine is well endowed with natural resources and has both a very strong agricultural sector and a well-established industrial capacity. How does it compare to the rest of the Soviet Union? As might be expected, it is more oriented to agriculture than the Soviet Union as a whole. The industrial capacity of Ukraine is somewhat less than the Soviet average because of the great imbalance between the highly industrialized provinces and the far less developed western areas.

Ukraine's industry accounts for a major part of the Soviet Union's industrial production (17%). Ukraine is an important industrial area on the global scale as well. Producing about 40% of the Soviet Union's steel, 34% of its coal, and 51% of its pig iron, Ukraine has a GNP comparable to that of Italy. Soviet scholars like to point out that in 1972 Ukraine's industrial production was 176 times higher than in 1922. But, as might be expected, Ukraine's industry has had its ups and downs. In the booming 1950s and early 1960s, when the growth rate was an incredible 10% a year, it performed better than the Soviet average; in the 1970s and 1980s, however, when the growth rate plunged to about 2–3% annually, its industrial growth was even below the average. To a large extent, this slowdown is linked to the the aging and inefficient "smokestack" industries located in Ukraine, a development similar to the one that has occurred in the industrial heartlands of America and Western Europe.

The economic slowdown in Ukraine, and the Soviet Union as a whole, has made the issue of capital investments more acute than ever. While economic planners in Moscow have emphasized huge, new industrial projects in Siberia, Ukraine's industries have been generally neglected. In the days of Shelest, Ukraine's economists were especially vociferous about their republic's declining share of investment funds. Although Shcherbytsky has been reluctant about raising the issue, it has certainly not gone away. There are, however, some bright spots in Ukraine's economic future: greater Soviet emphasis on international trade means that the Black Sea ports will continue to grow rapidly and, because of its proximity to Eastern Europe, Western Ukraine will probably be producing more goods geared for export.

Agriculture   Despite the fact that industry is now the main occupation of Ukrainians, their land has remained the breadbasket of the Soviet Union. It produces as much grain as Canada (only the United States and Russia produce more), more potatoes than West Germany, and more sugar beets than anywhere else in the world. Ukraine has 19% of the Soviet Union's population, but produces more than 23% of its agricultural products. Nonetheless, because of government policies, Ukrainians have to cope with frequent food shortages.

In an effort to raise the already high agricultural productivity in Ukraine, the government has invested heavily in farm machinery and fertilizers in the republic. But the chronic problems that have plagued Soviet agriculture persist. Bureaucratic controls and ill-conceived reorganization schemes often bring more havoc than gain. Even though the wages paid to collective farm workers have increased substantially in recent years, they are still at the bottom of the socioeconomic ladder and their enthusiasm for working on the collective and state farms has not increased. Instead, agricultural workers, particularly those in Ukraine, prefer to concentrate their efforts on their tiny, private one-acre plots. Consequently, in 1970, this private sector of the agricultural economy, which included only 3% of all the land under cultivation, produced 33% of the Soviet Union's meat output, 40% of its dairy products, and 55% of its eggs. In Ukraine, in 1970, for example, private plots provided 36% of total family income (the comparable figure for Russia is 26%).

Another problem is the rapid decline in the rural labor force brought about by urbanization: in 1965 there were 7.2 million agricultural workers in Ukraine, in 1975 the figure sank to 6.4 million, and in 1980 it stood at 5.8 million. Thus, the Ukrainian countryside, where living conditions have improved markedly, continues to lose its young people to the cities. On many collective farms it is the weathered old women who provide the main source of manual labor.

The issue of economic exploitation   A perennial issue in discussions of Ukrainian economic history, the question of whether Ukraine is economically exploited by Moscow is exceedingly complex. On the one hand, it is obvious that Ukraine has experienced tremendous economic growth during Soviet rule. And, on the other, there is strong evidence that it has consistently contributed more to the budget of the USSR than it has received in return. The Soviets refuse to make available statistics that might elucidate this issue.

Soviet spokesmen stress Ukraine's rapid economic progress, arguing that it would have been impossible to achieve without the huge investments, technical expertise, and labor that the "fraternal peoples" of the USSR, most notably the Russians, provided. By implication, they take the position that it is now the turn of Ukrainians to provide economic assistance to other, less-developed regions of the USSR. From the Soviet point of view, there is, therefore, no basis to even raise the issue of economic exploitation.

Some Western economists view the matter very differently. They acknowledge the impressive economic progress that Soviet rule has brought to Ukraine. And they agree that Moscow is intent on developing such relatively poor areas as Central Asia or resource-rich regions as Siberia. But they argue that Ukraine has contributed and continues to contribute more than its share to the economic growth of the USSR. The American economist Holland Hunter states: "The siphoning off of current income from Ukraine for use elsewhere in the USSR is a basic feature of Ukrainian economic history."[13] And the British scholar Peter Wiles estimates that Ukraine regularly contributes 10% more to the Soviet budget than it receives in return.[14] Thus, Volodymyr Bandera and Ivan Koropeckyj argue that while Ukraine continues to make economic progress in absolute terms, relative to Moscow, to other regions of the USSR, and to neighboring countries, it is falling behind economically.[15]

Regardless of the position one takes in the debate over exploitation, the discussion highlights the fundamental question regarding Ukraine's experience under Soviet rule: Who makes the decisions regarding the economic future of Ukraine and whose interests are primarily taken into account when these decisions are made? On this point, at least, the answers are more conclusive: it is clear that the economic fate of Ukraine is decided in Moscow, where Ukraine's economic interests are not a primary consideration.

Demographic conditions   In modern times, the tempo of population growth in Ukraine has changed dramatically. Throughout the late 19th and early 20th centuries, Ukraine's population was among the fastest growing in Europe. Then came two disastrous demographic setbacks: between 3 and 6 million lives were lost in the Famine of 1932–33, purges, and deportations of the 1930s and about 5.3 million inhabitants of Ukraine died during the Second World War. Thus, within little more than a decade, about 25% of Ukraine's population – the mortality rate was especially high among men – perished. Today, the population growth of the country is one of the lowest in the USSR.

In 1983, for example, there was in Ukraine a net increase of 4 per 1000; by comparison, among the rapidly growing populace of Soviet Central Asia, the increases ranged between 25 and 30 per 1000. If these current demographic trends continue, the Ukrainians' share of the Soviet population, indeed that of the Slavs in general, will be drastically reduced.

In part, Ukraine's slow population growth results from demographic disasters: there are simply fewer people to have children. However, the impact of urbanization has also been great. Living in extremely cramped quarters and with the vast majority of women working full-time, urban Ukrainians have opted for small families of one or, at most, two children. In many respects Ukraine's population resembles that of other developed countries: aging and growing slowly, it has a steadily increasing percentage of retirees and a decreasing percentage of full-time workers. But there are also striking demographic particularities in Ukraine and the USSR as a whole. In stark contrast to other industrialized countries, the life span of males has become shorter and infant mortality has risen in recent years . Experts speculate that this is related to widespread alcoholism among both males and females.

Compared to other areas of the USSR, Ukraine is a densely settled land. While in the European parts of the Soviet Union there is an average of 34 inhabitants per square kilometer, in Ukraine the figure is 82 per sq. km. But population is unevenly distributed in the republic. It is dense and growing rapidly in the eastern industrial regions and especially in the Crimea, the "Florida" of the USSR, whose balmy climate is especially appealing to Russians. In Western Ukraine, population growth is about average; but in the Right and Left Bank it is far below average and there are *oblasti* (regions) where the population is decreasing steadily. Nonetheless, taken as a whole, the demographic condition of Ukraine is satisfactory: the republic's population, which in 1987, numbered 50.8 million, is not so small as to hamper economic development and not so large as to stifle it.

Changes in social structure   As we have seen, industrialization, urbanization, and modernization in general have greatly altered the traditional class structure of Ukraine. In 1970, out of a total work force of 16 million people, about two-thirds were classified as industrial workers. From being a distinct minority, blue-collar workers became the overwhelming majority of Ukraine's workers within a single generation. Not only has the proletariat in Ukraine grown rapidly but it has become more Ukrainian in terms of ethnic composition: while in 1959 Ukrainians made up 70% of the industrial work force, in 1970 this figure rose to 74%. Russians are no longer disproportionately numerous among the blue-collar rank and file.

White-collar workers in Ukraine have also greatly increased, especially in recent decades. Between 1960 and 1970, their number doubled, rising from 700,000 to 1.4 million. But here the Russians maintained their disproportionately large presence, accounting for more than one-third of this social group. Thus, while the Soviet educational boom has raised the number of highly trained specialists in Ukraine to levels comparable to and even higher than those in most West European countries, Ukrainians as a nationality have not benefited as much as might be expected. While Ukrainians constitute 74% of the population in their republic, they make up only 60% of the student body in institutions of higher learning.

What are the reasons for this Ukrainian underrepresentation in higher education and among the technical and cultural intelligentsia? Some Western specialists argue that because many Ukrainian youths still obtain their elementary and secondary education in the countryside, where the schools are often of inferior quality, they are handicapped in comparison to city-bred Russians in the fierce competition for places in institutes and universities. Because many Ukrainians have an imperfect command of Russian, they are at a further disadvantage. Finally, since it is government policy to encourage Ukrainian specialists to seek employment outside their republic – and an estimated 25% have done so – the Ukrainian intelligentsia in Ukraine is smaller than it might be. And so is the number of their children who usually obtain a higher education. Meanwhile, those children of the Ukrainian intelligentsia who are educated outside their republic are often Russified.

The standard of living As we have frequently noted, Soviet Ukraine is a major industrial power, richly endowed with natural resources. Yet the living standards of its people are far below those in other industrialized countries. Granted, comparing living standards is exceedingly difficult. What a Soviet Ukrainian may lack in cars, videos, or fashionable clothes, he might have in free higher education and medical care that is unavailable to his American counterpart. Nonetheless, according to a variety of elaborate measurements set up by Western economists, it is evident that the Soviet economic system is unable to satisfy material wants and needs as well as the Western economies do for their people. Thus, in 1970 the per capita consumption in the Soviet Union was about one-half that of the United States. This statistic does not take into account the generally lower quality of goods and services that one receives in the USSR. Put another way, in 1982 a typical weekly shopping basket that cost 18 hours of work in Washington, DC, required approximately 53 hours of work in Kiev. Although rents in the USSR are among the lowest in the world, housing is so difficult to come by that often three generations of one family live in a two-room apartment. The Kremlin's preference for investment in heavy industry and military spending and its habitual neglect of the consumer industry are largely responsible for this state of affairs.

Optimism regarding the Soviet ability to catch up with Western living standards ran high in the 1960s and early 1970s, when the economic productivity of the country was impressive. But when Soviet economic performance plummeted in the 1980s, so did hopes for rapidly raising living standards.

Within the USSR itself, Ukraine occupies fifth place in terms of consumer spending: Russia and the three Baltic republics of Estonia, Latvia, and Lithuania rank higher. Because Ukraine has a surplus of labor, wages in the republic are about 10% lower than the Soviet average. However, prices are also relatively low. In the last two decades, Soviet wage policies have brought noteworthy benefits to many Ukrainians. Intent on reducing the wage differences between rural and urban workers, the government awarded collective farmers a hefty pay increase. Consequently, between 1960 and 1970, farmers' salaries rose by 182%, while those of industrial workers increased by only 38%. Because disproportionately many Ukrainians are farmers, they benefited from this attempt to equalize earnings among Soviet workers. But despite ongoing attempts by the government to improve the plight of Soviet consumers, citizens must still deal with shoddy goods, poor service, and cramped quarters. The living standards of the average Soviet Ukrainian are far below those of West Europeans and North Americans and even lag behind those of Communist Eastern Europe.

Soviet Ukrainian attitudes   What are the views and attitudes of Soviet Ukrainians toward the Soviet political and socioeconomic system? A question such as this is, of course, always difficult to deal with, especially in the case of a society that is only now beginning to publicize the results of public opinion polls dealing with carefully selected issues. Nonetheless, numerous articles and discussions in the Soviet media, interviews with Soviet émigrés, and accounts of travelers to the USSR allow one to establish certain salient features that characterize the mood and thinking of Soviet Ukrainians.

By and large, it seems that most Soviet Ukrainians accept the Soviet regime as their legitimate government and identify with it. Because of the government's monopoly on information and intensive propaganda, they are, at best, only vaguely aware of the hardships that Ukrainians have suffered at Soviet hands in the "ancient" past. Much more influential in shaping their attitudes is the fact that the Soviet system has brought large increases in their income, imposed relative equality among socioeconomic groups, greatly improved social services and access to education, and created numerous opportunities for upward mobility. Many Soviet Ukrainians take pride in the power and prestige of the USSR of which they are an important part.

Intermixed with these generally positive attitudes towards the Soviet system are elements, real and potential, of dissatisfaction. The current economic slowdown has raised such sensitive issues as the economic favoritism of Siberia and Central Asia at the expense of Ukraine. Opportunities for social advancement are less numerous now. Ukrainian party leaders, bureaucrats, and economic managers are increasingly resentful of Moscow's monopoly over decision making. Furthermore, the Ukrainian cultural elite has again begun to protest Russification. According to a 1984 Soviet sociological study, researchers reported that the level of dissatisfaction in Ukraine is higher than in the USSR as a whole. To the question why this is so, the scholars could only reply: "We can give no definite answer."[16]

Especially unsettling for the Soviet leadership is the growing disinterest in Marxist-Leninist ideology throughout Ukraine and the USSR as a whole. Since the 1960s, Western intellectuals have been discussing the "death of ideology" and the coming of a "post-ideological age" in the industrialized West. It appears that a similar ideological waning is now evident in the Soviet Union. Although Soviet authorities are loath to acknowledge this phenomenon, Western analysts have attempted to provide an explanation. Put simply, it argues that the process of modernization, which occurred in Europe during the 19th and early part of the 20th centuries, was accompanied by tumultuous transformations. The resulting insecurity and confusion created the need for ideological analyses, explanations, and guidelines. But, judging by the social climate in industrialized societies, once modernity arrived, it brought with it relative stability. Consequently, the need for an ideology which served to orient adherents in times of rapid change became less pressing.

Be that as it may, it is clear that, despite constant indoctrination, the influence of Marxism-Leninism on the thinking of Soviet Ukrainians is fading. Of course, Ukrainian nationalism, especially of the extreme, integral variety, had been expunged from the Ukrainian worldview decades earlier. Thus, the two main ideological currents in modern Ukrainian history are no longer as influential as they once were.

Because the ideological commitment of its people is a major requirement of the Soviet system, the waning of this commitment has led to a perceptible loss of optimism, purpose, and sense of direction among thoughtful Soviet citizens. To fill the void, the government has redoubled its efforts to instill Soviet patriotism. Hence the recent all-pervasive emphasis on heroic Soviet exploits in the Second World War. But for many, religion has become a more satisfying means of filling the spiritual and ideological void that confronts them in the 1980s.

Among the vast majority, however, there is a growing commitment to what in the West is called middle-class or bourgeois values and consumerism. Instead of building a new society, Soviet surveys indicate that its youth are generally interested in obtaining lucrative, prestigious professional jobs and would like to be engineers (the most popular), factory managers, scientists, and physicians. Few want to be proletarians. Most young people's thoughts and many of their efforts are committed to obtaining high-quality Western consumer goods. Whether this means that the attitudes, values, and goals of Soviet Ukrainian youth are becoming ever more similar to those of their counterparts in the West is still unclear. But it is obvious that they are far from becoming what Lenin wanted them to be.

The Gorbachev Era

The death of Leonid Brezhnev in 1982 ushered in a period of transition in the Soviet leadership. Brezhnev's immediate successor was the sophisticated Iurii Andropov, a former head of the KGB, who appeared ready to introduce radical changes. When he died after less than two years in power, his successor, the aging, ailing Konstantin Chernenko, was a representative of the old regime, who was unwilling to introduce the reforms that the USSR clearly needed. But he, too, died shortly after attaining power. The spectacle of one elderly Soviet leader after another dying in office clearly emphasized the need for younger, more energetic, and innovative leadership. Consequently, in 1985, Mikhail Gorbachev, a protégé of Andropov, was selected by the party leaders to lead the USSR on a new course. With his accession to power, a new breed of party *apparatchiki* (functionaries) came to the fore. Sophisticated and pragmatic, Gorbachev and his associates were the first generation of Soviet leaders whose rise to power did not occur under the aegis of Stalin.

Despite deep-rooted opposition from conservatives in the party and the society as a whole, Gorbachev launched his attempt to make the Soviet system, particularly its stagnant economy, more efficient, stronger, and productive. To achieve his objectives, Gorbachev adopted a new "democratic" style of leadership. He strove to create the impression that his regime was closer, more accessible, to the people and called for more openness (*glasnost*) in the conduct of government and for a restructuring of its economy (*perestroika*).

Chernobyl   Before the impact of Gorbachev's reforms reached Ukraine, however, the country was shaken by a catastrophe of huge proportions and global significance. On 26 April 1986, a reactor at the huge Chernobyl nuclear plant, located about 130 km north of Kiev, exploded. A huge cloud of radiation, incomparably larger than that produced by the bombing of Hiroshima, covered the environs of Chernobyl and then spread over parts of Belorussia, Poland, and Scandinavia. The world was confronted by what it feared most – nuclear disaster.

In traditional fashion, Soviet authorities initially attempted to cover up the catastrophe, which, as was established later, resulted from human error, gross negligence, and the faulty design of the reactor. When the cover-up proved to be impossible, Moscow admitted the scope of the disaster and called for advice and assistance from Western experts. Soviet engineers succeeded in extinguishing the burning reactor by encasing it in concrete and burying it in a gigantic "tomb." According to Soviet sources, the catastrophe resulted in 35 deaths (many Western specialists believe that the number of fatalities was much higher), the hospitalization of hundreds of people, and the exposure to high levels of radiation and increased risk of cancer for hundreds of thousands. About 135,000 people, most of them Ukrainians from the Chernobyl region, were forced to abandon their homes – in many cases, permanently. The ecological damage to the environs of Chernobyl and to areas as far away as Lapland was extreme and long term.

From 1970, when the construction of the plant began, there had been opposition in Ukraine to Moscow's decision to build the huge nuclear plant in the energy-rich republic and in the vicinity of Kiev. Consequently, resentment of the high-handed and irresponsible manner in which Moscow forced the plant on Ukraine was widespread in the republic. In addition, there were indications that the disaster gave rise to tensions between the all-union and the Ukrainian party leaderships, as each strove to blame the other for the accident. Nonetheless, it is evident that Moscow is not about to alter its plans; it still intends to expand the Chernobyl plant and to make Ukraine the center of its growing nuclear industry. This has elicited strong protests from the Ukrainian intelligentsia. Indeed, it appears that environmental issues may become another point of contention between the Kremlin and the Ukrainians.

Gorbachev's "glasnost" and Ukraine In Moscow, evidence of the reforms that Gorbachev has attempted to implement in the face of considerable opposition from hard-liners in the establishment and a skeptical public has been widespread and often dramatic, especially in the realm of culture. Major newspapers now reflect a new mood of openness and self-criticism: the popular magazine *Ogonek*, whose recently appointed editor is the erstwhile Ukrainian poet Vitalii Korotych, has repeatedly attacked the Stalin cult and abuses of power by the police and bureaucracy; Russian poets espousing militantly anti-Soviet views have been published; and Pamiat, a civic organization that propagates a militant and most un-Marxist Russian nationalism and anti-Semitism, has not been suppressed.

By comparision, in Kiev, signs of the "new spirit" have been rare and relatively muted. The reticence of the Ukrainians is understandable. Kiev is the bailiwick of Shcherbytsky, an avowed conservative, who is the last holdover in the Politburo of the old, regressive Brezhnev regime. Moreover, the Ukrainian KGB is reputed to be the most repressive in the USSR. Finally, the Ukrainian intelligentsia remembers all too well how badly it was "burned" when it enthusiastically embraced Khrushchev's reforms in the 1960s.

Despite these inhibitions, some signs of restiveness have surfaced among the Ukrainian intelligentsia. In the fall of 1987, a Ukrainian Culturological Club was established in Kiev. Many of its leading members are former dissidents who wish to test the limits of *glasnost* by openly discussing such politically sensitive issues as the Famine of 1932–33, the millennium of Christianity in Ukraine, and the struggle for independence in 1917–20.

In Lviv, the center of the nationally conscious West Ukrainians, *glasnost* evoked a more dramatic and broadly based response. In June and July 1988 several huge, unsanctioned, and unprecedented public gatherings were held that attracted tens of thousands of participants. Organized by former dissidents such as Chornovil, the Horyn brothers, Ihor and Iryna Kalynets, and a new activist, Ivan Makar, the demonstrations called for the erection of a fitting monument to Shevchenko in Lviv as well as one to the victims of Stalinism. These organizers rejected the party bureaucrats who had chosen themselves to represent Lviv in the upcoming party congress in Moscow. And they gave vent to the numerous national grievances of the Ukrainians. In August the Lviv KGB reacted in typical fashion: it accused the organizers of "anti-Soviet activity" and arrested some of them. It appears that genuine democracy is still a long way off for the Ukrainians.

Somewhat earlier, the representatives of the establishment Writers' Union of Ukraine (which has a vested interest in preventing the decline in the use of Ukrainian) also clashed with the party conservatives grouped around Shcherbytsky over the perennial issues of Russification and the status of the Ukrainian language. In June 1986, a number of well-known Ukrainian writers, including Oles Honchar, Dmytro Pavlychko, Ivan Drach, and S. Plachynda, decried the declining use of Ukrainian in the republic's schools and the Writers' Union formed a committee to maintain contacts with educational institutions. In April 1987, M. Fomenko, the minister of education of the Ukrainian republic, presented a disheartening but not surprising report to the committee about Ukrainian-language education. According to him, there are currently 15,000 Ukrainian-language schools in Ukraine, that is, about 75% of all schools. But the 4500 Russian-language schools, which constitute less than 22% of the total, enroll over 50% of all pupils. In Kiev, the situation is even more abnormal: of 300,000 pupils, only 70,000 study in Ukrainian.

Apparently these statistics are not disturbing to party functionaries. Shcherbytsky's only noteworthy comment on this issue has been an expression of hope that the use of Russian will not decline. In general, it seems that while the party establishment in Ukraine is becoming more receptive to some aspects of Gorbachev's modernization, it has no intention of changing its nationality policy in Ukraine. This position has led to the sharp confrontation between the writers and party functionaries that occurred at the all-Ukrainian conference of teachers held in Kiev in May 1987. Frustrated by the party's reluctance to respond to Ukrainian cultural and linguistic aspirations, while accepting changes in other areas, members of the Writers' Union have become increasingly explicit in expressing their dissatisfaction.

In March 1987, at a meeting of the Writers' Union presidium, Ivan Drach stated that in the schools "Ukrainian language and literature have become the objects of the jokes and insults of an arrogant bourgeoisie with chauvinistic [Russian] tendencies, which hides behind the shield of internationalism and disparages the roots from which it itself emerged."[17] Dmytro Pavlychko demanded that the government of the republic see to it that the study of Ukrainian be enforced in the schools. He added that "if the attitude not only to our language but to all the non-Russian languages does not change ... we will not reach our greatest, most sacred goal – the friendship of nations – for only those nations which retain their own character can enter into a friendship."[18]

ѝ

As the 20th century draws to a close, it is clear that Ukrainians have entered the ranks of the modern, industrialized nations. The historical role of their country as the richly endowed but underdeveloped borderland appears to be over. And the Soviet regime deserves much of the credit for effecting this epochal transformation. It also carries the responsibility for its tragically high costs. By the same token, Ukraine is characterized by what may be called the Great Discrepancy. Despite its large economic role, both in the USSR and in global terms, and its numerous, well-educated population, Ukraine is still unable to decide its own fate. Indeed, the political profile of Soviet Ukraine abroad is so low that many people in the world are still unaware of its distinctiveness. This, too, is largely a result of Moscow's policies.

With the repression of nationalism and the atrophy of communism, the influence of the two great ideologies that for generations molded the thinking of Ukrainians and guided their actions has faded. Meanwhile, changes in the USSR appear to be be in the offing. Under the new conditions that seem to be emerging, questions abound. Where will Ukrainians look for guidelines to their future development? Will they be able to correct the anomalies of their condition? And, most important, do they have the will to do so? There are at the moment very few indicators that might help to clarify the situation. Therefore, as has been true so often in the past, a cloud of uncertainty hangs heavily over Ukraine and the Ukrainians.

27

The Immigrants

During the last century, millions of Ukrainians left their homeland in search of more favorable conditions elsewhere. Most did so for socioeconomic reasons. Vast numbers of East Ukrainians moved, or were moved, to Russia's Asian lands. Because these Ukrainians remained within the confines of the Russian Empire and, later, the Soviet Union, they were not emigrants in the usual sense of the word. By contrast, West Ukrainians headed westward, across the oceans to the New World where they encountered not only unfamiliar lands but radically different political, socioeconomic, and cultural systems. It is they who are generally considered to be Ukrainian emigrants par excellence. Other Ukrainians abandoned their homes primarily for political reasons. Unwilling to accept Soviet rule, they preferred exile. Together these emigrants and political émigrés formed the three distinct waves of Ukrainians that fate has, up to now, brought to foreign shores.

ঈ

The First Wave: The Pre-1914 Immigration

Ukrainians who immigrated to the New World prior to the First World War invariably sought to improve their wretched socioeconomic condition. To do so, they generally chose one of two approaches. Most came to the United States where they found work in the burgeoning factories and mines that were located in or near large cities. Consisting mainly of single, young men, these immigrants initially planned to stay in the United States only until they accumulated enough money to return to their native villages, purchase adequate land, and establish a household. But, in time, prospects in the United States became more appealing and promising than those at home. And as Ukrainian women came to join the men, Ukrainian communities sprang up in many urban centers of the northeastern United States.

The other category of early Ukrainian immigrants was made up of those who left their villages with the intention of continuing an agricultural way of life in countries where land was cheap and available. From the outset, these immigrants – who usually arrived with their families – intended to stay in their new homelands permanently. Because such lands were usually located in unsettled regions, such as remote parts of Brazil and Canada, these immigrants faced a backbreaking, solitary struggle against nature.

Immigration to the United States   Individual Ukrainians found their way to America long before the massive wave of immigration in the late 19th and early 20th centuries. Ukrainian names appear among the founders of the Jamestown colony in Virginia as well as among the combatants in the American Revolution and Civil War. When Russia established colonies in Alaska and California in the early 19th century, Ukrainian Cossacks and civilians were among their inhabitants. However, the man who is commonly recognized as the first nationally conscious Ukrainian in America is Ahapii Honcharenko, an Orthodox priest from the Kiev region, who had been personally acquainted with Taras Shevchenko and had espoused revolutionary ideas. In 1867–72, this original and adventurous individual served as the editor of the *Alaska Herald*, the first American publication that carried some information about Ukraine and its inhabitants. Later, Honcharenko became a prominent figure in California, where he attempted to establish a Ukrainian socialist colony in the early years of the 20th century. Another colorful individual was Nicholas Sudzilovsky-Russel, a physician and revolutionary from Kiev who settled in California in the 1880s and later moved to Hawaii, where he became the president of the Hawaiian senate. He too attempted to attract Ukrainians to his new homeland.

But the first large group of Ukrainian immigrants to the United States was very different from these picturesque forerunners. Composed mostly of hard-working peasants, it originated in Transcarpathia and the Lemko regions, the westernmost and least developed of Ukrainian lands. News about the semi-mythical land far across the sea where one could earn ten to twenty times as much as at home first reached the Lemkos and Transcarpathians from their Slovak, Polish, and Hungarian neighbors. In 1877, an opportunity arose to test the veracity of these tales. That year, a Pennsylvania coal company, confronted by a strike, decided to bring in cheap labor from the poorest areas of the Austro-Hungarian Empire to act as strikebreakers. When its agents offered young Lemkos and Transcarpathians money for the journey – to be deducted later from their earnings – the company found many eager takers. As encouraging news (often exaggerated by agents of the steamship companies) and impressive amounts of money began to arrive in their home villages from the early immigrants, the exodus to America grew rapidly.

Like countless immigrants who preceded and followed them, the young men who made the long, arduous journey to the United States quickly realized that while the country offered many opportunities, it also demanded backbreaking work. From the outset, most of the newcomers were shunted off to the coal mines and steel mills of western Pennsylvania, and the area became the heartland of early Ukrainian immigration. Others found employment in the factories of New York, New Jersey, Connecticut, Ohio, and Illinois.

The early years were difficult: the erstwhile villagers were confronted by a strange land and an incomprehensible language; they were thrust into bustling, confusing cities and towns, where they labored among huge, constantly moving, noisy machines. Prior to the First World War, the average earnings of a factory worker or miner were about $1–2 for a nine-to-ten-hour working day. Usually they lived in crowded company shacks or in boardinghouses. Because the early immigrants intended to return home as soon as they saved several hundred dollars, they were often extremely frugal and spent little money on food, clothing, and other necessities. But many found it difficult to resist the lure of the *korchma* (tavern). The Ukrainian immigrants were generally a self-sufficient and law-abiding group; compared to the other immigrant groups, they had one of the lowest percentages of people on charity (0.04%) or accused of breaking the law (0.02%). In contrast, 4% of the Irish, 1.8% of the German, and 1% of the Polish immigrants were charged with criminal offenses.[1]

The seemingly temporary nature of the early immigrants' stay in the United States greatly influenced their attitude toward American society: they neglected to learn English, to establish contacts with Americans, or to obtain United States citizenship. Few showed any interest in the American political process. Their orientation remained focused very much on their homeland. But as immigration continued and grew, changes set in. More and more of the newcomers decided to stay in the United States. Also, Ukrainian women began to arrive in greater numbers, although as late as 1905, they still made up only 25–30% of the immigrants. Usually they worked as domestic help, often for Ukrainian- or Polish-speaking Jewish families. Later, many of them found employment as seamstresses in clothing factories. As families were established in the United States and wives and children came to join their husbands and fathers, Ukrainian communities and neighborhoods evolved.

To service them, the more enterprising immigrants established small businesses such as boardinghouses, groceries, and butcher stores. Not surprisingly, the most lucrative businesses were taverns, and their owners were often the richest and most influential men in the communities. But generally Ukrainian immigrants were slow to explore ways of making a living except as laborers. Little wonder, for few were prepared to work as anything else. For example, in 1905, a peak year, when 14,500 Ukrainians arrived, only 7 had a higher education (4 of them were priests), 200 were skilled workers or artisans, and the rest were peasants and unskilled laborers. Few went into farming, for this undertaking required a long-term commitment and considerable capital. The only significant group that did so were the Stundists (a Protestant sect) from Russian-ruled Ukraine who arrived in the 1890s and settled in Virginia and North Dakota.

It is difficult to establish how many Ukrainians there were in the United States prior to the First World War. A complicating factor is that some immigrants made multiple trips between their new and old homelands. Because many Ukrainians were uneducated and their national consciousness was low, they were classified by American immigration authorities and census-takers as Hungarians or Austrians, that is, according to the states from which they had come. Some identified themselves with related and more established groups, such as Slovaks. And because the traditional name for West Ukrainians was Rusyns, many were called Russians. In any case, most estimates place the number of Ukrainians in the United States in 1914 at about 250,000–300,000. About half of these were Transcarpathians and Lemkos, who had started to arrive in the 1880s and 1890s, and the other half were mostly Galicians, who came in appreciable numbers about a decade later. They constituted only a tiny fraction of the approximately 25 million immigrants who arrived in the United States between 1861 and 1914.

Immigrant institutions and organizations   In the Ukrainian village, the church was the focus of spiritual and social life. All the major events in a peasant's life – his christening, wedding, and funeral – and most communal festivities were associated with religion. When they arrived in the United States, Ukrainian immigrants sorely missed their churches, without which their lives seemed meaningless, monotonous, and gray. Consequently, the earliest forms of communal organization they set up among themselves were churches and parishes.

In 1884, Ivan Voliansky, an energetic priest from Galicia, arrived in Pennsylvania to minister to his brethren. Within a year he built the first Ukrainian church in America in the town of Shenandoah. He also helped to organize several other parishes in central Pennsylvania. Voliansky was soon joined by a growing number of priests from Galicia and, later, from Transcarpathia. In the final decade of the 19th and the early decades of the 20th century, a wave of church building and parish organizing swept through the evolving immigrant communities. In 1907, the rapidly growing number of Greek Catholic parishes forced the Vatican to establish a Greek Catholic eparchy (diocese) based in Philadelphia and to appoint the Galician monk Soter Ortynsky as its first bishop. By 1913, the Greek Catholic diocese numbered 152 parishes, 154 priests, and about 500,000 parishioners.

But the churches not only served as the focus of communal life, they also became an arena for bitter conflicts engendered by the new American environment. Indeed, for the early immigrants, "church politics" were usually the only politics that mattered. A major problem, which became acute before the appointment of Ortynsky, was the strained relations that developed between the Greek Catholic immigrants and the largely Irish hierarchy of the Roman Catholic church. Ignorant of the particularities of the Greek Catholic rite and contemptuous of all East Europeans, Roman Catholic bishops often made matters difficult for them. For their part, Greek Catholic parishes frequently refused to surrender the deeds to their newly built churches to the "foreign" bishops as was the practice in the Roman Catholic church. Often the results were bitter lawsuits, forced evictions of parishioners by the police, minor riots, and a deepening of ill feeling on both sides.

Greek Catholic priests who came to the United States with their families had additional reasons for being dissatisfied with the Roman Catholic hierarchy. Because Roman Catholic priests, unlike their Greek Catholic colleagues, were not allowed to marry, Roman Catholic bishops refused to recognize married clergymen from Transcarpathia and Galicia as legitimate priests. As the case of Alexis Toth illustrates, the controversial issue of celibacy soon had major repercussions for both Greek and Roman Catholicism in America.

A respected professor of theology in Transcarpathia, a consecrated priest, and a widower, Toth arrived in Minneapolis in 1889 to serve as the pastor of the local Greek Catholic parish. But because he had been married, the Roman Catholic archbishop excommunicated him. Unable to gain redress and convinced that the ancient Byzantine traditions of his rite, which Rome had recognized, were being trampled, Toth and his 365 parishioners made a dramatic decision in 1891 – they went over to Orthodoxy. In the following decades, tens of thousands of Lemko, Transcarpathian, and Galician immigrants, urged on by the well-financed Russian Orthodox Mission in America, opted for membership in the Russian Orthodox church. By 1914 they constituted the overwhelming majority of the Orthodox in the United States, and Alexis Toth was hailed as the "father of Orthodoxy" in that country.

The rush to Orthodoxy had important national/ethnic implications for the Ukrainian-Rusyn immigrants. Because many of them came from the most underdeveloped and isolated Ukrainian regions, such as Transcarpathia, they were generally untouched by the developing sense of Ukrainian national consciousness. Russophilism was also widespread among their clergy, as it had been in the "Old Country." Consequently, when the uneducated Rusyns entered the Russian Orthodox church in the United States, its hierarchy usually succeeded in convincing them that they were ethnic Russians. Today, at a time of heightened consciousness of ethnic origins, the Americanized descendants of these pseudo-Russians are often at a loss to explain why their "Russian roots" lead back to patently Ukrainian lands.

The Galician/Transcarpathian schism Another divisive conflict that developed within the context of the church was the Galician/Transcarpathian schism.

Transcarpathia, which was ruled by Hungarians until 1918, was one of the areas least exposed to the Galicia-based Ukrainian national movement. Initially, the immigrants who arrived from Transcarpathia and, somewhat later, from Galicia established their communities and churches together because they shared a common language, folk customs, the Greek Catholic rite, and their traditional Rusyn identity. But gradually tensions arose between their respective clergies.

Competition for well-established parishes first divided the two factions. Later, the appointment of Ortynsky, a Galician, as bishop infuriated the Transcarpathian clergy, and they launched a vicious campaign against him and all Galicians. In order to alienate their parishioners from Ortynsky, the Transcarpathian clergy exaggerated the differences between Transcarpathians and Galicians. Because their competitors were nationally conscious Ukrainians, the Ukrainian national movement became a major focus of their attacks. Ortynsky and all Galicians were accused of caring more about nationalism than religion. They were denounced as traitors to Rusyn traditions for adopting the modern term Ukrainian. For good measure, the socially conservative and elitist Transcarpathian priests warned their parishioners that the Galician clergy, many of whom were social activists, were godless, socialist radicals.

For their part, the Galician priests denounced their Transcarpathian rivals as Magyarones who were more loyal to Hungarian interests than to those of their own people. In fact, the Transcarpathian clergy generally did speak Hungarian at home and, quite often, even in church. Some continued to receive money from the Budapest government even after they arrived in the United States. Many openly cooperated with the Hungarian government in its efforts to prevent the spread of Ukrainian national consciousness among Transcarpathian immigrants. In the United States, as in the "Old Country," this undermining was usually done by arguing that the Transcarpathian Rusyns constituted a distinct nationality from their Galician compatriots.

Unable to have one of their own appointed bishop, the Transcarpathian clergy demanded that the Vatican create a separate Greek Catholic diocese. In their words, they could not "acquiesce in being ecclesiastically united with the Galician Ukrainians" because "under the guise of the Catholic church, they might be thrown into the slavery of Ukrainianism."[2] Anxious to eliminate the constant feuding, the Vatican gave in. In 1916, it created a separate diocese, based in Pittsburgh, for what came to be called the Byzantine Ruthenian Catholic church. In 1924 it consisted of 155 churches, 129 priests, and about 290,000 parishioners. Meanwhile, the original Philadelphia diocese became the base of the Ukrainian Catholic church, which numbered 144 churches, 129 priests, and about 240,000 parishioners. Thus, the Transcarpathian/Galician split became institutionalized.

In the decades after the split, the Transcarpathian church vacillated over which national orientation it should adopt. Unable to decide, it opted to avoid the issue altogether. Consequently, today it deemphasizes ethnicity and urges its faithful to identify themselves primarily in terms of the Greek Catholic (Byzantine) rite. But the legacy of this bitter Transcarpathian/Galician feud of the late 19th and early 20th centuries remains: although the people in Transcarpathia today consider themselves to be Ukrainians, their distant relatives in the United States still subscribe to the view that they are "anything but Ukrainians."

As a result of these religious and regional controversies, about 20% of the early immigrants from West Ukrainian lands called themselves Orthodox "Russians," another 40% identified themselves as Greek or Byzantine Catholic Ruthenians/Rusyns, and the remaining 40% were Ukrainian Greek Catholics.[3]

Fraternal organizations   Having established their churches, the Ukrainian immigrants next attempted to find communal ways of dealing with their pressing practical needs. Foremost among them was the desire for at least a minimal sense of economic security. Work in the mines and factories was exhausting and dangerous. The hours were long and by American standards, the pay was poor. As might be expected, cases of serious illness, loss of limbs, and fatal accidents were all too frequent. Furthermore, there were no company or government plans to aid those who were incapacitated or their families. In response to the problem, fraternal benefit societies or brotherhoods (*bratstva*) emerged among the various immigrant groups to aid their members.

For a modest monthly payment, these fraternal associations provided insurance in case of illness, incapacitation, or death. Moreover, as their membership and capital grew, they usually sought to address the cultural and educational needs of their members. For the immigrants, the appeal of the fraternal associations was both economic and social: they brought together people of their "own kind" and used their native language. Unlike the churches, the fraternal associations had no roots in the "Old Country"; they were an organic response to the environment encountered by the immigrant in the United States.

In 1885, Reverend Voliansky organized the first Ukrainian fraternal benefit society in America. Consisting of several dozen members, its primary goal was to provide burial costs for deceased colleagues. When Voliansky returned to Galicia, the society disbanded. But others cropped up throughout Pennsylvania. In 1892, the Union of Greek Catholic Russian (Rusyn) Brotherhoods was established and in time grew to considerable size. However, it soon fell under the domination of the pro-Hungarian Transcarpathian clergy and adopted an increasingly hostile attitude toward nationally conscious Ukrainians.

The impetus to found an avowedly Ukrainian fraternal benefit society came from a group of eight young, dynamic, and committed priests who had recently arrived from Galicia and came to be called the "American Circle." Imbued with the activist spirit of the Galician intelligentsia, the group formed the backbone of the Greek Catholic church's drive for ecclesiastical autonomy. Two of its members, Ivan Konstantynovych and Hryhorii Hrushka, became the founders, in 1894, of a fraternal benefit society called the Russkyi Narodnyi Soiuz (Ruthenian National Union), based in Jersey City. In 1915, this organization changed its name to the Ukrainian National Association. Today, with close to 85,000 members, it is the largest and wealthiest Ukrainian secular organization outside the borders of Ukraine.

During the First World War, it became evident that the immigrants had reached a higher level of political sophistication. In 1914, two central organizations, the Federation of Ukrainians in the United States and its rival, the Ukrainian Alliance of America, gathered substantial amounts of money for refugees displaced by the war in their homeland. Later, in 1919, the Ukrainian National Committee worked closely with diplomats from the various Ukrainian national governments in publishing English-language materials about the Ukrainian question. It also made a concerted effort to convince the White House and Congress to recognize Ukrainian independence.

Immigration to Brazil   Initially, Brazil was the most popular destination for West Ukrainians in search of land. In 1895, when agents of Italian shipping companies appeared in Galicia with promises of cheap, fertile land in Brazil, the "Brazilian fever" took hold. Over 15,000 impoverished peasants, who had only the vaguest idea where Brazil was, made their way to that country. But instead of the promised black soil, they received plots of uncleared jungle in the state of Parana, near the town of Prudentopolis.

Left to their own devices, exposed to a debilitating climate, confronted by hostile Indians, and, worst of all, bereft of medical facilities and supplies, many of them perished soon after arrival. Others returned home. The remainder set about making a home in the wilderness. Despite the demoralizing difficulties, the dream of cheap land continued to attract Galicians to Brazil. In the years before the First World War another wave of about 15,000–20,000 Ukrainian immigrants arrived in the Parana region. However, as word of more favorable conditions in the United States and Canada spread, immigration to Brazil shrank. In the interwar period, only 9000 Ukrainians, mainly from Volhynia, went there. After the Second World War, another 7000 joined them. But many of these later left for North America. Today, the Ukrainians in Brazil number an estimated 150,000. Close to 80% of them live in a compact mass in the province of Parana in an area known as "Brazilian Ukraine." The city of Prudentopolis is the center of Ukrainian life in the country. As might be expected, the Ukrainian Catholic church in Brazil, which includes 17 parishes and 52 priests, is by far the strongest Ukrainian institution in the land.

In recent times, a significant and growing minority of Brazil's Ukrainians have become professionals, businessmen, and educators. But the majority of the Ukrainians are still poor farmers, who live much like the early immigrants did. This relative lack of change makes them unique among the Ukrainian communities abroad. Provided with poor land, engaged in unprofitable occupations, and inhabiting underdeveloped and isolated regions, Brazil's Ukrainian farmers are isolated from the modern sectors of Brazil's economy. They continue to live in villages and cottages that look much like those of their ancestors. Although over 90% are Brazilian born, lack of contact with non-Ukrainians has allowed them to retain their language. In many ways, their rural communities are the closest approximation that exists of the 19th-century Galician village.

Immigration to Canada   While Brazil was a disappointment, Canada – in time and after tremendous effort – more than lived up to the expectations of Ukrainian immigrants. Its vast prairies soon became the major destination of the land-seeking peasants from Galicia and Bukovyna. The adventurous Ivan Pylypiw and Vasyl Eleniak are commonly considered to be the first Ukrainian immigrants to Canada. The two set out for western Canada in 1891 and liked what they saw. Upon his return to Galicia, Pylypiw convinced six families from his home village of Nebyliw to move to Canada. Consequently, in 1892, the "Nebyliw Group" established the first permanent Ukrainian settlement in Canada in the locality of Edna-Star, near Edmonton in Alberta.

But the individual who was most responsible for transforming the early trickle of immigrants to Canada into a massive migration was Iosyf Oleskiw. A professor of agriculture and a populist committed to aiding the peasantry, he visited Canada in 1895 to observe conditions firsthand. Impressed by the opportunities the Canadian west offered for agricultural settlement, Oleskiw published a number of widely circulated pamphlets that discouraged immigration to Brazil and advised peasants to go to Canada instead. In his successful efforts to popularize immigration to Canada, Oleskiw received support from Canadian authorities. The minister of the interior, Clifford Sifton, was particularly impressed by the suitability of the hardy Ukrainians for taming the wild prairies: "I think a stalwart peasant in a sheepskin coat, born on the soil, whose forefathers have been farmers for ten generations, with a stout wife and half a dozen children, is good quality."[4] In time, glowing letters from Canada, which often painted conditions in overly rosy colors, and the exhortations of agents for steamship companies served as the major impetus for the growing immigration to the prairies.

Canada clearly had much to offer. The soil of the prairies was rich, although it did require backbreaking work to clear it of thick brush. Water was plentiful. Wood, scarce and highly prized in the "Old Country," was abundantly available for fuel and construction. And the climate was much like at home.

Anxious to populate the uninhabited prairies, the government was practically giving land away at the nominal cost of $10 per 160 acres. Ukrainians were allowed to settle in blocs, so that for miles around they had people of their own kind as neighbors. An added attraction was that Canada's political system was stable and democratic, while its society and economy were modern and expanding.

The opportunities that Canada offered were great, but so was the effort required to take advantage of them. The newcomers arrived in a foreign land with little or no money, unable to speak English and often illiterate. After a long, exhausting journey, they were left to fend for themselves amidst cold, uninhabited plains. Simple survival was the first and most daunting task. To provide shelter against the harsh climate, they built primitive, one-room huts. Lacking money and unable to plant crops until the land was cleared, they faced the threat of constant hunger and even starvation. To earn money for necessities, men crisscrossed the countryside in search of work. Meanwhile, the women were left on their isolated homesteads to improve dwellings or to build new ones, to somehow feed and care for the children, and to begin the backbreaking task of clearing the land. Unable to afford machinery or even draught animals, the immigrants accomplished their work by hand. Usually several years passed before the first crops were ready. And to clear an entire homestead often took fifteen to twenty years of exhausting work.

To make matters worse, the immigrants had to face overt discrimination. Although Sifton and a few government officials recognized the usefulness of Ukrainian immigrants, many Canadians did not. Confronted for the first time by immigrants who were not Anglo-Saxons, the population of western Canada protested against the "dumping of filthy, penniless and ignorant foreigners" in its communities. Many newspapers fulminated against bringing in the "scum of Europe," which would lower the moral and intellectual standards of Canadian society. The fact that the immigrants lived in compact communities, continued to wear traditional clothes, spoke their own language, and worshiped in the Byzantine rite added to their unwelcome foreignness.

Despite these difficulties, the Ukrainian immigrants slowly established themselves. In time they brought millions of acres under cultivation. Their neat, white, thatched cottages and onion-domed churches dotted the broad Canadian plains. When grain prices rose rapidly prior to the First World War, many Ukrainians prospered. As their reputation as hard workers and dedicated farmers grew, public hostility towards them slowly abated. Indeed, Canadians gradually began to recognize the crucial role the hardy Ukrainian immigrant played in transforming the uninhabited prairie into one of the world's most productive grain fields.

By the time the First World War broke out, about 170,000 Ukrainians had come to Canada. Of these, over 85% settled in the prairies. Those Ukrainians who chose to settle in a city usually chose Winnipeg, which became the major center of Ukrainian-Canadian communal life. Because the total population of the Canadian west in 1896 was only about 200,000, it is evident that the newcomers could not but exert a major impact on the region. If the war had not interrupted the flow of Ukrainians to the Canadian prairies, it might well have become a largely Ukrainian region.

Religious issues   As elsewhere, churches were the earliest and strongest institutions established by the immigrants. In Canada, as in the United States, their growth was also accompanied by bitter controversies. Totally lacking Greek Catholic priests, the newcomers turned to their brethren in the United States for help. In 1897, responding to their appeal, Reverend Nestor Dmytriw traveled from Pennsylvania to visit the pioneers on the prairies and to celebrate the first Greek Catholic mass on Canadian soil. In subsequent years, several other Ukrainian priests from Pennsylvania made similar visitations. But these stop-gap measures were clearly incapable of providing stable ecclesiastical leadership and organization for the immigrants.

For its part, the local Roman Catholic hierarchy, which was French Canadian, attempted to impose its jurisdiction over the newcomers. However, in the face of opposition, it retreated. Later, it showed a greater tolerance of Greek Catholics than did the Irish bishops in the United States. Nonetheless, problems remained. Most pressing was the lack of priests. Because a papal edict in 1894 forbade married Greek Catholic priests from serving in North America and because the few celibate priests who emigrated from Galicia usually went to the United States or Brazil, Canada could not depend on the "Old Country" for clergymen. To deal with the dilemma, French and Belgian priests, some of whom accepted the Greek Catholic rite, were assigned to work among the immigrants.

But this measure was unsatisfactory. The immigrants found it difficult to communicate with their non-Ukrainian priests; the celibacy issue was a constant irritant; and the perennial problem of the immigrants' reluctance to deed their churches to Roman Catholic bishops also flared up in Canada. Imbued with the spirit of the New World, many wanted their church to be free of all outside influence.

In 1903, Bishop Serafim, a Russian Orthodox cleric of dubious background, came to Winnipeg from the United States. Backed by a group of radical intelligentsia seeking to create a Ukrainian church that would be independent both of Roman Catholicism and of Russian Orthodoxy, he established the so-called Independent Greek church. His solution for the lack of clergy was straightforward but canonically questionable: he simply ordained about fifty educated and semi-educated community leaders as priests in the new church. These men spread throughout the countryside preaching a brand of Orthodoxy that rejected the authority of any patriarch and accepted trustee ownership of church property. This message obviously appealed to the immigrants, for in two years the new church gained over 60,000 adherents. However, this allegiance was a transitory phenomenon, and within several years Serafim's church disintegrated.

The threat of losing its faithful to a hybrid form of Orthodoxy galvanized the Greek Catholic church. In 1910, Metropolitan Andrei Sheptytsky, the hierarch of the Greek Catholic church in Galicia, toured the Ukrainian-Canadian communities in a morale-boosting and fact-finding mission. Several years later he convinced the Belgian Redemptorist Order to establish a Greek Catholic rite branch in Galicia. Some of its celibate members were then sent as missionaries to Canada's Ukrainian communities. Responding to Sheptytsky's appeals, in 1912 the Vatican appointed Nykyta Budka as the first Greek Catholic bishop in Canada. Unlike Ortynsky in the United States, Budka received far-ranging authority from the outset. Soon, Greek Catholic churches, parishes, and schools multiplied in the prairies. By 1931, the Ukrainian Greek Catholic church encompassed about 58% of Ukrainians in Canada and had 100 priests and 350 parishes. But because about 80% of immigrants had originally been Greek Catholic, it was evident that Budka's church had suffered serious losses.

Many of those who rejected Greek Catholicism entered the Ukrainian Greek Orthodox church, formed in 1918. The base of support for this church was varied. It included the rising Ukrainian-Canadian intelligentsia (mostly bilingual teachers) who espoused the anticlericalism of the Galician Radical party, Orthodox Bukovynians, and the former members of Serafim's defunct church. Because its clergy was Ukrainian and because it was committed to retaining Ukrainian ecclesiastical traditions and practices, the Orthodox church in Canada became closely associated with the growth of Ukrainian national consciousness, which greatly added to its popularity. Thus, while only 15% of the Ukrainians who came to Canada were originally Orthodox, by 1931, over 24% of Ukrainian Canadians belonged to the Ukrainian Greek Orthodox church. The Presbyterian church, which actively proselytized among the Ukrainians, also attracted a considerable number of the immigrants.

Secular organizations Like the churches, the first secular organizations among the immigrants were transplants from the the the "Old Country." As they did in the villages of Galicia and Bukovyna, the Prosvita societies, reading rooms (*chytalni*), and community centers (*narodni domy*) spread throughout the prairies. By 1925, there were about 250 such cultural/educational organizations in Canada.

In terms of formal education, the Ukrainian Canadians briefly enjoyed an advantage that no other Ukrainian immigration possessed. Because their rural communities were totally or overwhelmingly Ukrainian, they were allowed to establish publicly financed bilingual school systems. Approximately 400 such school districts, located mostly in Manitoba, were in existence by

1916. To provide teachers for these schools, the Manitoba government established the Ruthenian Training School in Winnipeg in 1907. Well-versed in both English and Ukrainian, its graduates formed a core of secular, educated community leaders.

But the First World War and a mounting anti-foreigner hysteria brought an end to the bilingual school systems. Nevertheless, the immigrants were determined that their children should receive a Ukrainian-language as well as an English-language education. In part, private Greek Catholic schools founded by the Basilian Order and the Serving Sisters responded to this need. Parish-based *ridni shkoly* also proliferated. However, members of the anticlerical intelligentsia sought other options. In 1916, they founded the Mohyla Ukrainian Institute in Saskatoon. Essentially, the institute was a student residence (*bursa*) whose main function was to provide a Ukrainian environment, including courses in the Ukrainian language, literature, and history, for rural students who had come to the city to complete their education. Similar institutes or *bursy*, usually affiliated with various religious denominations, were also organized in Winnipeg, Edmonton, and Toronto. Members of these institutes also added greatly to the growing ranks of Ukrainian political and cultural activists.

Although prior to the First World War most Ukrainians in Canada had been unsophisticated peasant-farmers, signs of a growing political awareness had emerged among them. One form of political activity reflected the ideological trends spreading in their homeland. In 1907 prominent Ukrainian-Canadian leaders, such as Kyrylo Genyk-Berezovsky, Ivan Bodrug, Ivan Negrych, Myroslav Stechishin, and Taras Ferley (all socialists of the Galician Radical party mold), founded the Ukrainian Socialist Union. Simultaneously, they and others became involved in local Canadian politics. Given their majority in many localities, by 1902 the Ukrainians had already elected their countrymen to municipal office. In 1913, Andrew Shandro won a seat in the Alberta provincial parliament.

Canadian political commentators noted, with some alarm, that "one fact stands out with tremendous clearness – the Ruthenians have become a force ... throughout the prairies."[5] But if Ukrainians assumed that they were fully integrated into the Canadian political system, they were rudely disabused of this notion during the First World War. Because many of the immigrants still held Austrian passports, about 6000 were classified as "enemy aliens" and incarcerated in detention camps for the duration of the war.

The Second Wave: Immigrants and Émigrés of the Interwar Period

During the interwar period Ukrainian immigration to the West continued. However, it was notably different from the pre-1914 phase. A most striking feature was that the number of immigrants declined. Prior to the First World

War, well over 500,000 Ukrainians had immigrated to the West; in the interwar period the number dropped to about 200,000. The Great Depression and the resultant lack of employment in the United States and Canada was primarily responsible for the decline.

There were also considerable differences in the destinations available to the emigrants. Canada remained a favorite goal. But poor economic conditions in the farming regions and more restrictive immigration policies limited the number of new Ukrainian arrivals to 70,000 during the interwar period. Many tended to settle in cities such as Winnipeg, Toronto, and Montreal rather than in the western prairies. A more dramatic change occurred in the United States. There, extremely restrictive measures were taken against immigration during the depression years. Consequently, only about 10,000 Ukrainians entered the country between the wars, a drastic drop from the hundreds of thousands who crowded to its shores before 1914.

Although some countries no longer needed cheap labor, others continued to welcome it. In South America, Argentina opened its doors to immigrants, which it needed both to settle its vast expanses of territory and to work in the factories of its growing cities. About 40,000 Ukrainians immigrated there. Meanwhile, France, which also needed workers for the factories and mines in the north of the country near Metz, also accepted approximately 30,000–40,000 West Ukrainian laborers.

The Ukrainian émigrés Perhaps the most striking feature of the interwar exodus was that it also contained a new type of Ukrainian emigrant – the political émigré. After the defeat of the various Ukrainian governments in 1918–20, tens of thousands of their supporters – soldiers, officers, government functionaries, and, mainly, the nationally conscious intelligenstia and their families – followed them into exile. Initially, they numbered close to 100,000. But in 1923, when the situation in Galicia stabilized, most of the West Ukrainian émigrés returned home. Thereafter, the political emigration, numbering about 40,000–50,000, consisted largely of easterners from Soviet-occupied Ukraine.

These refugees had been forced to flee because of their political convictions. Although many of them were simple soldiers, a large portion were members of the pre-1917 Ukrainian national intelligentsia. Indeed, they included some of its most illustrious representatives. Ideologically committed, frequently idealistic, and obsessed with the mistakes of the recent past, they were often people who had held responsible positions. For many, the desire to help Ukraine achieve independence remained an overriding concern. In order to be close to their homeland, most settled in Poland and Czechoslovakia.

Like all political emigrants, these Ukrainians were prone to extensive fragmentation and infighting. Supporters of the various governments-in-exile often laid more blame on each other for their defeats than on the Bolsheviks.

And they expended much time and effort in attempts to secure for their respective factions the mantle of national leadership. Some became political adventurers and opportunists in the service of foreign governments. Yet, given the many well-educated, talented, and committed individuals in their ranks, they also had noteworthy achievements to their credit. By means of numerous publications and scholarly institutions, they introduced West Europeans to Ukrainian national aspirations. They expressed these aspirations in terms of new, sophisticated ideologies. Their varied cultural activities were often of high quality – an impressive fact because they were carried out amidst dire economic difficulties and political instability.

The majority of the East Ukrainian émigrés left their homeland in the fall of 1920, when the army of the Ukrainian National Republic (UNR) retreated into Poland. About 30,000 were interned in a series of camps. Meanwhile, the Petliura government-in-exile set up its headquarters in Tarnow. But by 1923, when the Poles withdrew their support for Petliura, Poland was no longer a hospitable refuge. Some émigrés remained, especially in Polish-occupied Volhynia; most, however, moved on to Czechoslovakia. Because of the Czechs' humane treatment of refugees in general, and the help it provided young Ukrainians in obtaining a higher education in particular, Prague soon became the major center of Ukrainian political emigration.

With the financial support of the Czech government, institutions such as the Ukrainian Free University in Prague and the Ukrainian Academy of Husbandry and Technology in Podebrady were established. During the interwar period, they produced hundreds of graduates. Meanwhile, Ukrainian scholarly research institutes were founded in Berlin and Warsaw. Numerous newspapers and publishing enterprises also came into being.

The various defeated Ukrainian governments continued a precarious existence in exile. While part of Petliura's UNR government remained in Warsaw, Petliura himself moved to Paris where a UNR diplomatic mission, led by Oleksander Shulhyn, was still active. There, in 1926, he was assassinated by Samuel Shwartzbart, a Jew whom Ukrainian émigrés considered to be a Bolshevik agent. (For their part, Jews praised Schwartzbart as an avenger of the pogroms that had occurred in Ukraine during the Civil War.) Hetman Skoropadsky and the Ukrainian monarchists established themselves in Berlin. After the West Ukrainian government dissolved itself in 1923, Petrushevych also settled in the German capital. Later, Konovalets and the OUN had their headquarters in Berlin for a time. Ukrainian socialists led by Mykyta Shapoval, and liberals such as Dmytro Doroshenko, congregated in Prague. As we have seen, an important contribution of the East Ukrainian émigrés was their elaboration and expansion of Ukrainian ideologies. In Galicia, Dontsov became the ideologue of integral nationalism, while in Vienna, Lypynsky expounded his influential and original views on Ukrainian monarchism and conservatism.

The politicization of Ukrainians abroad   Events in Ukraine in 1917–20 aroused interest in Ukrainian political issues, even among those who had emigrated for socieconomic reasons. This interest was further heightened when new, ideologically committed arrivals joined their communities in the 1920s. A variety of political organizations emerged wherever Ukrainians were concentrated. Soon ideological confrontations began to overshadow religious rivalries as the major bone of contention among the immigrants.

The first to organize were the socialists. As we have seen, already in 1907 a Ukrainian Marxist group was founded in Canada. That same year a socialist club, called the Haidamaks, emerged in New York. Its appeal was that its members addressed, in Ukrainian, concrete issues such as better wages and working conditions for laborers and fairer pricing policies for farmers. The group also provided an organizational base for those who resented the powerful influence that priests wielded in the Ukrainian communities.

After the First World War, impressed by the Ukrainization and modernization process in Soviet Ukraine and disillusioned by the depression in the West, about 1000 Ukrainians entered the Canadian Communist party in which they constituted over one-third of the membership. In 1918, those Ukrainians who were pro-Communist, but preferred to belong to purely Ukrainian organizations, established the Ukrainian Labor Temple Association. For decades, it was the largest pro-Communist ethnic organization in Canada. Dynamic and well organized, the association carried on educational and cultural work as well as ideological indoctrination. By 1939, it boasted over 10,000 committed members. Although the pro-Communists encompassed only about 5% of Ukrainian Canadians, their influence in the Ukrainian-Canadian community was far-reaching.

By the late 1920s, nationalist organizations began to emerge. Consisting largely of post-1920 émigrés, they espoused the cause of Ukrainian independence and were uncompromisingly anti-Communist. Among the first to organize were the supporters of Hetman Skoropadsky. Committed to establishing a Ukrainian monarchy and intent on imbuing Ukrainians with military ("Cossack") virtues, in 1924 they established a network of Sich organizations in the cities of Canada and the United States. Although never numerous, they were well organized. Their smartly uniformed members often participated in military maneuvers. Some branches even owned their own airplanes. The conservative ideology of these Ukrainian monarchists appealed to the Ukrainian Catholic clergy, which lent them its support.

It was, however, the OUN brand of nationalism that exerted the strongest appeal among Ukrainians abroad. At the initiative of Konovalets, pro-OUN organizations, which usually included a mixture of urban-based first- and second-wave immigrants, were created in all major Ukrainian communities in the West. Thus, in the late 1920s and early 1930s, UNO (Ukrainian National Union) was founded in Canada and ODWU (Organization for the Rebirth of

Ukrainian Statehood) in the United States. Similar organizations appeared in France and Argentina. Their numerous members preached ultranationalism, protested against Polish and Soviet mistreatment of their compatriots, and collected funds for the OUN. The vast majority of Ukrainian community activists in the interwar period belonged to or sympathized with one or another of the nationalist organizations.

Assimilation   While some immigrants were deeply immersed in Ukrainian politics, many grew increasingly estranged from things Ukrainian. This was especially so in the United States, where immigrants were systematically urged to assimilate into the American "melting pot." Exposed to intense assimilationist pressures in the schools and repulsed by the constant infighting and bickering in their communities, young Ukrainians often opted to dissociate themselves completely from their ethnic roots. In Canada, where Ukrainians lived in self-contained communities, assimilatory pressures were weaker. But even here, the national consciousness of the early immigrants was weaker than that of recent arrivals. It was evident that wherever Ukrainians settled, assimilation into the dominant culture became, to a greater or lesser degree, an inescapable fact of life.

The Third Wave: The Post–Second World War Displaced Persons

When the Second World War ended, Germany and Austria teemed with over 16 million foreign workers, prisoners of war, and refugees. Of these, about 2.3 million were Ukrainians. The overwhelming majority of them were the *Ostarbeiter*, mostly young boys and girls from Soviet Ukraine who had been forcibly torn from their homes and subjected to years of exhausting and demeaning labor in Germany. As soon as hostilities ceased, the Soviets sent in repatriation missions composed of officers and propagandists to convince Soviet citizens, by all means possible, to return home. During the repatriation process, most of the *Ostarbeiter* returned, either voluntarily or involuntariy, to the USSR. But about 210,000 Ukrainians refused under any circumstances to do so. More than 2.5 million East Europeans also did not go back to their Soviet-dominated homelands. These people came to be called displaced persons (DPS).

To care for the masses of homeless refugees, the United Nations Relief and Rehabilitation Agency (UNRRA) was formed in 1945. Two years later, the International Relief Organization (IRO) took over this role. Basically, these organizations sought to provide the DPS with a modicum of food and shelter until they could be permanently resettled. Often grouped by nationality, the refugees were concentrated in "camps," that is, requisitioned schools, army barracks, and public buildings. Because they were allowed to elect their own leadership to look after administration as well as educational and cultural affairs, these camps, which were located in the American-, British-, and French-occupied zones of Germany, were often referred to as "DP republics." About two-thirds of the Ukrainian refugees lived in the camps, eighty of which were all-Ukrainian. The remainder found private accommodations. Some of the major camps were located in American-occupied Bavaria, specifically in Munich, Mittenwald, Regensburg, Berchtesgaden, and Augsburg. On the average, these large camps had a population of 2000–4000.

The Ukrainian DPS were highly heterogeneous. A minority of about 20% were political refugees par excellence. Consisting largely of members of the intelligentsia, they rejected the Soviet system and fled, often under harrowing circumstances, before the advancing Red Army. The vast majority were workers, who had been forcefully brought to Germany during the war. By refusing the Soviets' insistent repatriation attempts, they, too, became refugees. About two-thirds of the DPS were from Galicia and belonged to the Greek Catholic church, and the remaining third were from Soviet Ukraine and were Orthodox. Other important subgroups among the DPS were émigrés from the 1920s period; Ukrainian students in Germany; former German prisoners of war; and released inmates of the concentration camps. In Italy, there were about 10,000 members of the interned Galicia Division. And in 1947–48, several hundred UPA soldiers, who had fought their way from the Carpathians through Czechoslovakia to Germany, also joined the DPS. Thus, this largest of all Ukrainian political emigrations reflected Ukraine's various regions, religions, social classes, and cultural and political traditions.

Unlike previous emigrations, the DPS had a large pool of well-educated people among them. The numerous professionals included about 1000 teachers, 400 engineers, 350 lawyers, 300 physicians and an equal number of clergy, and close to 200 scholars. There were also more than 2000 university students. Judging by these numbers, it was clear that a large part of the West Ukrainian intelligentsia had chosen not to stay under Soviet rule.

For many of the camp inhabitants, the two to three years they spent there was a unique and not altogether unpleasant experience. The "DP republics" had a surfeit of young, energetic, and educated people. Although simple food and shelter (terribly crowded) were available, jobs in the shattered German economy were practically impossible to find. Therefore, partly in response to pressing needs, partly to express what had been long repressed, and partly to avoid boredom, the DPS generated an extraordinary amount of organizational, cultural, educational, and political activity.

Statistics underscore this point. Despite very limited material resources, the Ukrainian DPS maintained 2 university-level institutions, about 40 gymnazia (high schools), and over 100 elementary schools. They also operated dozens of vocational courses, established 85 parishes, and rebuilt Plast, the scouting organization. Cultural activity was especially great. The camps had 35 libraries, 41 choruses, 13 orchestras, 33 theatrical groups, and 3 profes-

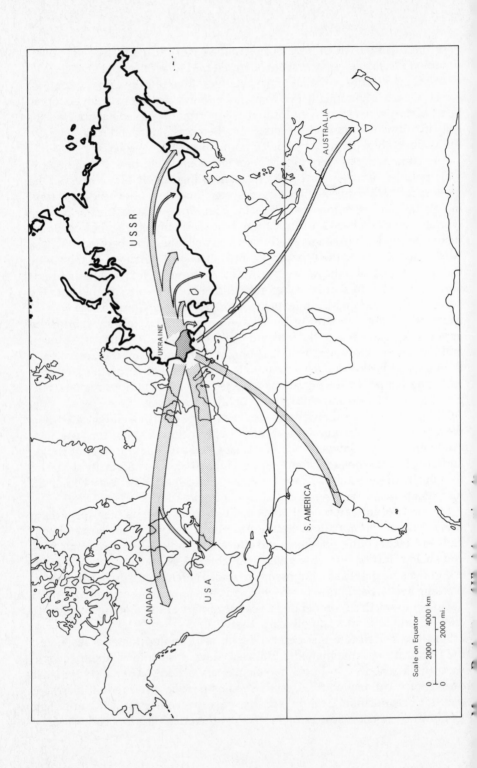

Scale on Equator

| 0 | 2000 | 4000 km |
| 0 | 2000 | 2000 mi. |

sional theatrical troupes. They staged over 1400 plays, 900 concerts, and 350 cultural-commemorative events (*akademii*). A vibrant if qualitatively uneven press produced about 230 periodicals and over 800 books. Young DPS also plunged into other activities. Forced to delay marriages and childbirth by the conditions of war, they established families at a rapid rate.

But the hothouse atmosphere of the camps also brought out negative features among the DPS. Forced to live in close proximity, West and East (Soviet) Ukrainians became painfully aware of the considerable social, cultural, and psychological differences between them. The Catholic/Orthodox split only exacerbated the problem. Most destructive were the feuds that broke out among the numerous political parties that emerged in the camps. Especially bitter, even murderous, was the unabated conflict between the Bandera and Melnyk factions of the OUN. Intent on establishing its political and ideological hegemony over the entire emigration, the numerous Bandera faction was particularly aggressive and domineering. Although the Banderites failed to gain a substantial following among the intelligentsia, they did exert a strong influence among the peasants and workers, who constituted the majority of the refugees. This influence made them a force to be reckoned with among the DPS.

Between 1947 and 1951 the resettlement of the DPS to their permanent homes occurred. The approximate numbers of those who left Germany and Austria for various countries were: United States 80,000; Canada 30,000; Australia 20,000; Great Britain 20,000; Belgium 10,000; France 10,000; Brazil 7000; Argentina 6000. Many of those who went to Britain, France, Belgium, and Latin America eventually settled in North America.

༝

The decision to leave their homeland was one of the most crucial that individual Ukrainians made. Its influence on the socioeconomic, cultural, psychological, and political aspects of their lives was deep and dramatic. Invariably, the question arises of who made the more fortunate choice, those who left or those who stayed behind. Because no empirical studies of this fascinating question have been conducted, one is forced to respond through impressionistic observations.

It would appear that in material terms at least, those who emigrated fared better than those who did not. The emigrants also avoided many of the catastrophes that befell their former homeland in modern times. They enjoyed the priceless advantage of living in free and open societies. But the costs of leaving the homeland were considerable; usually they included gnawing homesickness, psychological insecurity, alienation, and discrimination. For the political émigrés, who had held responsible positions at home, there was often a precipitous drop in social status as a result of their inability to find work in their fields of specialization. Nonetheless, it seems that for those who emigrated, the decision brought a net gain. Ukraine's society, however, probably suffered a net loss. Judging by the emigrants' organizational activity alone, it is evident that Ukraine lost some of its most energetic inhabitants. And in their host countries the contribution of the hard-working Ukrainians has been clearly positive – in Canada, dramatically so.

28

The Ukrainian Diaspora

Today over 2.5 million people of Ukrainian descent live outside the borders of the Soviet Union. In terms of ethnic consciousness, they can be divided roughly into three categories. The largest consists of those whose forefathers left their homeland three, four, and even five generations ago. By and large, they no longer speak Ukrainian, have little or no contact with Ukrainian organizations, and are often only vaguely conscious of their ethnic roots. Another category, usually a generation or two removed from the homeland, is familiar with and even fond of Ukrainian culture but does little to preserve it. The third category is the small but committed minority that still manages to preserve its ethnic heritage. Composed largely of the post–Second World War émigrés and their children, but also including some members of earlier immigrations, it forms the core of the Ukrainian communities in the West.

ᴈ▴

The Ukrainian Americans

As might be expected, the most numerous, best-organized, and dynamic Ukrainian communities abroad are to be found in the United States and Canada. Surveying first the situation in the United States, it is apparent that a strong point of Ukrainian Americans is their relatively large numbers. Most Ukrainians who left their homeland came to the United States, and their immigration was well spaced. The earliest arrivals established the organizational backbone of the community – the churches and fraternal organizations – which were expanded during the interwar period by another wave of immigrants. The post–Second World World War immigrants arrived just in time to replace the "old" immigrants. With many institutions and organizations already in place, they were able to concentrate on forming new ones. Thus the Ukrainians in the United States have been able to maintain a sense of continuity and growth. They are fortunate to live in a society that provides them with numerous opportunities and resources for developing their communal life.

But for those who wished to maintain their ethnic heritage, the United States also had its drawbacks. Economic constraints forced Ukrainians to settle in urban centers where it was difficult to maintain the traditions of a peasant people. Until recently, the educational system was geared to assimilating immigrants into the American melting pot. Although numerous compared to their compatriots elsewhere in the West, Ukrainians are relatively insignificant among the many ethnic groups in the United States. In terms of numbers, they rank twenty-first nationally and ninth in the Middle Atlantic states where they are concentrated. And their political influence is even less than might be expected. The large influx of DPs has had a generally positive impact. It reinvigorated the Ukrainian community and greatly expanded its range of activities. However, the DPs' high degree of politicization, particularly the Melnykite/Banderite feud, has made the Ukrainian-American community the most politically fragmented in the West.

What socioeconomic features distinguish the Ukrainian American from the average American? Traditionally, the Ukrainians have been marked by a relatively low level of education. This circumstance is not surprising because the early and most numerous immigrants arrived from one of the most backward regions in Europe and with an illiteracy rate of about 50%. Consequently, even American-born Ukrainians have long been overrepresented in blue-collar jobs and underrepresented in white-collar occupations. But recent studies indicate that the situation is changing. If current trends among younger Ukrainians continue, it is likely that they will surpass both the white population in the United States and some of the other East European ethnic groups in terms of educational level. The children of the post–Second World War refugees have been particularly successful in attaining managerial and professional status. Thus, it is safe to say that Ukrainians are now solidly ensconced in the American middle class.

On the whole, Ukrainian families are less "modern" than the average American family: they have fewer single-parent families and more of them have parents and other elderly relatives living with them. They marry later, delay childbearing longer, and stay single more often. As befits their generally rural roots, they tend to be conservative in their politics and mores.

Observers have noted that the Ukrainian-American community has a strikingly large number of organizations. Indeed, some argue that it is over organized. The highly developed Galician/Bukovynian tradition of communal organization, the fact that each wave of immigrants established its own organizations, and the attempts of the DPs (many of whom were community activists in Galicia) to reconstruct in America many of the organizations they led at home help to explain this phenomenon.

Today, the strongest Ukrainian institutions in the United States are those that the earliest immigrants established, that is, the churches and the fraternal associations. The Ukrainian Catholic church encompasses about 200 parishes and 285,000 faithful, the various Ukrainian Orthodox churches have about 125,000 members, and the Baptists claim a membership of 50,000. Among the fraternals, the Ukrainian National Association (UNA), with 85,000 members, is by far the largest and richest. It publishes *Svoboda*, the oldest and most widely read Ukrainian daily in the West, and the lively, informative English-language *Ukrainian Weekly*. The Ukrainian Fraternal Association (previously called the Ukrainian Workingmen's Association) has about 25,000 members and publishes *Narodnia Volia* and the well-edited *Forum* magazine. The Providence Association of Ukrainian Catholics has 19,000 members and its press organ is the daily *Ameryka*. The list of other periodicals is too lengthy to enumerate.

Until recently, the Ukrainian Congress Committee of America (UCCA) functioned as the representative and coordinating body for all the Ukrainian organizations in the United States. However, when the Bandera faction and its sympathizers gained control of it in 1980, a counter organization, the Ukrainian American Coordinating Council, was formed. As a result of this split, Ukrainian Americans were deprived of a single, generally recognized body that could legitimately claim to represent them all.

Continuing in the Galician tradition and responding to local needs, the post–Second World War immigrants to the United States have established a growing network of savings and loan associations and credit unions. Together with similar institutions in Canada and elsewhere in the world, they have a membership of about 120,000 and combined assets of close to $1 billion. Another carryover from the "Old Country" is a well-organized women's association, the Ukrainian National Womens League (3700 members and 83 branches in the United States). Of the numerous youth organizations, the strongest are the scouting association Plast and the more nationalistic, pro-Banderite Association of Ukrainian Youth (SUM). Both have a membership of about 4000. Numerous professional societies unite Ukrainian engineers, physicians, professors, teachers, writers, journalists, and businesspeople. Young people are often drawn to the dance ensembles and choruses that are usually found in Ukrainian communities.

Teaching their children the Ukrainian language, history, and culture has always been a major concern of the immigrants. The Ukrainian Catholic school system, which in 1970 consisted of fifty-four parochial schools, six high schools, and two junior colleges, with a total of about 16,000 students, provides varying degrees of ethnic education in addition to its English-language and religious curriculum. The so-called Saturday schools stress exclusively Ukrainian subjects. In 1970 there were about fifty such schools with approximately 3700 students and 200 instructors. On the scholarly level, two institutions, the Shevchenko Scientific Society and the Ukrainian Academy of Arts and Sciences, strive to carry on the traditions of their Lviv- and Kiev-based namesakes. Clearly the most impressive achievement of the Ukrainian American community in terms of preserving its cultural heritage was the endowment in 1970 of three chairs in Ukrainian studies at Harvard University. Subsequently, the Harvard Ukrainian Research Institute was established. The leadership of Omeljan Pritsak of Harvard, as well as the generosity of over 10,000 Ukrainian donors, was largely responsible for the successful completion of this $6 million project.

Another high point in the recent history of the Ukrainian Americans was the raising of a statue of Taras Shevchenko in Washington in 1964, which drew together about 100,000 Ukrainians. In the 1970s, many Ukrainians protested against the Russification of their homeland and demonstrated on behalf of Soviet Ukrainian dissidents. The release and arrival in North America of such dissidents as Valentyn Moroz, Petro Grigorenko, Sviatoslav Karavansky, Nina Strokata-Karavansky, Nadia Svitlychna, Leonid Pliushch (to France), and, most recently, Raisa and Mykola Rudenko greatly buoyed the spirits of the Ukrainian community. But these were deflated in the 1980s when the issue of war crimes during the Second World War, and especially the controversial John Demjanjuk case, raised tensions between the Ukrainian and Jewish communities. In 1983, as they marked the fiftieth anniversary of the Great Famine, Ukrainians succeeded in familiarizing many Americans with this catastrophe. And in 1988 they marshaled their forces to mark the millennium of Christianity in Ukraine.

Clearly the past looms large in the consciousness of Ukrainians in the United States. Some might argue that this orientation on the past exists, in part at least, because their future as a community is not promising. New immigration has practically ceased. Links with their Soviet-controlled homeland are tenuous and fraught with mutual suspicion. Many organizations are obviously on their last legs. And assimilation is moving apace. In 1980, of about 730,000 people of Ukrainian descent in the United States (this number does not include the approximately 500,000 descendants of the Transcarpathian/Ruthenian/Rusyn immigrants) only 123,000 declared Ukrainian to be their primary language. But there are also hopeful signs. Unlike its predecessors, the post–Second World War immigration, thanks to its many youth-oriented organizations, has had notable success in raising a new generation of community activists. Most of them are professionals by occupation and know the American environment well. Meanwhile, a new tolerance for ethnic diversity has emerged in the United States. Finally, many American-born Ukrainians are beginning to discover the psychological and social advantages of belonging to an ethnic in-group. It is, therefore, possible that the century-old Ukrainian community in the United States has more life in it than many pessimists contend.

The Ukrainian Canadians

Of all the Ukrainian communities in the West, the Ukrainian Canadians are in the most advantageous position. Numbering about 750,000 (of whom 530,000 have parents who are both Ukrainians), they are close to their compatriots in the United States in terms of numbers. But their profile and influence in their country are much greater. Because the population of Canada is only one-tenth that of the United States, the Ukrainian Canadians are, in effect, a bigger fish in a smaller pond. Ukrainians in the United States hold the twenty-first position in terms of ethnic group size, but in Canada they rank fifth, constituting 3% of the total population. As the people that settled much of the Canadian prairies, they lay claim to pioneer status. Some Ukrainians even argue that they are one of the "founding nations" of the country. Because they settled in solid blocs, the early immigrants to Canada have withstood assimilation much better than their counterparts in the United States. This homogeneity is reflected in the relatively large number of Ukrainians of the third, fourth, and even fifth generation that still speak the language of their forefathers and participate in Ukrainian community affairs.

Yet foreboding developments also confront Ukrainian Canadians: modernization is threatening their sense of community. The global trend toward urbanization is breaking up the rural bloc settlements in the prairies, the bastions of Ukrainian life in Canada. In 1931 over 80% of Ukrainian Canadians lived in a rural setting; today over 75% are city dwellers. Edmonton, Winnipeg, and especially Toronto, where many DPs settled, are now the centers of Ukrainian life in Canada. Although each of these cities has a large and active community of about 70,000–80,000 Ukrainians and part-Ukrainians, urban life in Canada is clearly not conducive to the retention of Ukrainian ethnic identity. A variety of statistics bear out this assertion. In 1921, over 90% of Ukrainian Canadians declared that their mother tongue was Ukrainian; in 1971, only 49% did so, and the percentage has been dropping rapidly since then. In 1931, over 80% intermarried within their own group; today, less than 50% do so. Even the churches face an uncertain future. In 1931 the Ukrainian Catholic and Orthodox denominations encompassed 82% of Ukrainians; today, the figure is only 52%.

But if Ukrainian Canadians have problems similar to those of their compatriots south of the border, they are better equipped to deal with them. In general, they are more effectively organized than the latter. For example, Ukrainian Canadians have managed to preserve a single, generally recognized umbrella organization – the Ukrainian Canadian Committee (UCC). Moreover, Toronto is the base of the WCFU (World Congress of Free Ukrainians). Many of the organizations that the DPs established in the United States can also be found in Canada. And the ties between them are close. However, in the United States many of the "old-immigrant" organizations – except for the churches and the fraternal associations – have faded, whereas in Canada a considerable number continue to exist. As well, Canada has a strong network of Ukrainian professional and business clubs, which have been able to attract a young, upwardly mobile, professional membership. Especially popular with the grandchildren and great-grandchildren of the early immigrants are the numerous dance ensembles. In western Canada alone, there are over 150 such groups with about 10,000 members. But the organizational strength of the Ukrainians in Canada should not be exaggerated. Only an estimated 10–15% belong to the community organizations. In order to attract new members, some groups are deemphasizing political and nationalist features and concentrating on cultural and social activities.

Unlike their compatriots in the United States, Ukrainian Canadians have developed a cultural tradition of their own. Writers such as Iliia Kiriak have skillfully depicted, in both Ukrainian and English, the experiences of the pioneer generation. The nationally famous painter William Kurelek frequently utilized Ukrainian motifs. The architect Radoslav Zhuk has intertwined traditional and modern elements in the architecture of Ukrainian churches. On the debit side, however, Ukrainians in Canada, particularly those in the west, tend to be more provincial and strictly folklore-oriented in their approach to Ukrainian culture than those in the United States. This may be a result, in part, of the fact that a smaller portion of the Ukrainian intelligentsia that emigrated came to Canada than to the United States.

Like the Ukrainian Americans, the Ukrainian Canadians also have a network of Saturday schools and *ridni shkoly*, which are geared primarily toward the children of DPs. However, it is also possible to study Ukrainian as a subject in public schools in Canada and about 10,000 pupils do so. Recently, bilingual Ukrainian-English schooling was introduced in the prairie provinces. Another contrast lies in the sources of support for Ukrainian studies on the university level. Unlike the privately funded Harvard Ukrainian Research Institute, its counterpart in Canada, the Canadian Institute of Ukrainian Studies (established in 1976 and initially headed by Manoly Lupul), is supported by the government of the province of Alberta. Ukrainian studies at universities in Toronto, Winnipeg, Saskatoon, and elsewhere are also publicly funded to a large extent.

A striking feature of the Ukrainian-Canadian community is the relatively large number of its members that have gained political office on various levels. Ukrainians have been mayors of such large cities as Edmonton and Winnipeg. Close to a 100 Ukrainian Canadians have been elected to provincial legislatures, primarily in the prairie provinces. About thirty have been members of the federal parliament. There have been five Ukrainian senators and dozens of federal and provincial cabinet ministers. Although far from being a major political force in Canada, the Ukrainian Canadians wield more political influence than any other Ukrainian community in the West.

During the Second World War, about 35,000–40,000 Ukrainians, roughly
5% of their total number, volunteered for the Canadian armed forces. Ukrain-
n Canadians still point with pride to this high percentage. But after the
ar, Ukrainian Canadians again turned on each other. In the late 1940s and
rly 1950s, the struggle between the pro-Communists and nationalists flared
p anew. Benefiting from their association with the victorious Soviets, the
krainian pro-Communists were in a strong position. Membership in the
krainian Labor Temple Association was at an all-time high of 13,000 in 1946.
was, therefore, with some confidence that they tried to block the immigra-
on of nationalistic and anti-Soviet Ukrainian DPs to Canada. These efforts
iled, however, and other setbacks followed. As the Cold War and postwar
rosperity set in, communism lost its appeal. Many of the genuine Ukrainian
atriots among the pro-Communists became disillusioned by Russification in
kraine and by the Soviet invasion of Czechoslovakia in 1968. Gradually, the
ore dynamic, articulate DPs became the dominant force in the Ukrainian-
anadian community. Today a handful of aging Ukrainian pro-Communists,
ho are heavily involved in commercial transactions with the USSR, is all that
left of their once-powerful movement.

Another major concern of the Ukrainian-Canadian community was multi-
ılturalism, an issue that emerged in the 1960s. Influenced by the new mil-
ancy of the French in Quebec, ethnic groups that belonged to the so-called
ird element, that is, the non-English and non-French segments of Canadian
ciety, confronted the government with their cultural demands. Ukrainians
ere in the forefront of those who successfully pressured the government to
rmulate a policy of multiculturalism and, in 1987, to enshrine multicultur-
ism in the constitution.

Highlights in the activity of the Ukrainian-Canadian community during
e 1970s and 1980s have been the growth of Ukrainian studies at the univer-
ty level and the publication of the English-language *Encyclopedia of Ukraine*,
major project of the Canadian Institute of Ukrainian Studies which is based
n Volodymyr Kubijovyč's original ten-volume work in Ukrainian. Support
r Soviet Ukrainian dissidents led to the release and arrival in Canada in 1987
f Danylo Shumuk and Iosyp Terelia. In the commemoration of the fiftieth
nniversary of the Great Famine of 1932–33, Ukrainian Canadians produced
widely acclaimed documentary film about the famine. As in the United
ates, in the mid 1980s the war crimes issue aroused passions and raised
nsions between Ukrainians and Jews.

krainian Communities beyond North America

he Ukrainian immigrant communities that exist outside North America may
e divided into two categories. One is characterized by a prevalence of largely
ssimilated "old immigrants," with a small admixture of DPs. It includes the
krainians of Brazil, Argentina, and other Latin American countries. By and

large, these communities are worse off economically than others in the Wes
Even today, a huge proportion of their members are poor farmers. Althoug
their numbers are considerable, they are organizationally weak. In these com
munities, the churches are the main, and often the only, focus of communa
life. Because of the preponderance of pre–Second World War immigrants, th
Ukrainians in France may also be included in this group. However, they di
fer from the aforementioned in that their descendants are mostly employe
in industry and maintain a relatively high West European standard of liv
ing. France has also provided a home for small but important segments c
both the so-called Petliurist and DP emigrations. For example, in the post
Second World War period, Sarcelles, outside of Paris, became a major cente
for DP scholars. There, under the leadership of Volodymyr Kubijovyč, an
with the financial support of Ukrainians throughout the West, the Ukrainiar
language "Encyclopedia of Ukrainian Lore" (*Entsyklopedia ukrainoznavstv*
was produced.

The other category of Ukrainian immigrant communities consists almo:
exclusively of DPs and their children. And the Ukrainians of Germany, Britai
and Australia fall into this group.

Germany   In Germany, the community is composed primarily of the tin
portion of refugees and their descendants who, for a variety of reasons, di
not join the great exodus from the DP camps in the late 1940s. Some were to
old to begin life anew. Others were associated with political parties that re
tained their headquarters in Germany because of its proximity to Ukraine. Fc
Stepan Bandera, the leader of OUN(R), and for another prominent nationalis
Lev Rebet, staying in Germany proved to be fatal. In 1957, Bohdan Stashir
sky, a Soviet agent, stealthily assassinated Rebet; two years later he kille
Bandera.

In Munich, the Ukrainian Free University, an émigré institution that date
back to the 1920s, continues to function. Thus, while Germany has been th
home for a considerable (albeit dwindling) number of political leaders, com
munity activists, and scholars of the DP emigration that were loath to leav
Europe, its Ukrainian community lacks a broad demographic base.

Great Britain   The Ukrainians in Great Britain are, to some extent, in a pos
tion that is the reverse of the German one. Most were members of the Galici
Division that were captured by the British and transported to England afte
the war. While many of their comrades eventually moved to North Americ
a portion of the division's rank and file stayed on to work in British industri
towns, such as Manchester, Coventry, Bradford, and Nottingham. Unlike i
Germany, members of the intelligentsia were relatively scarce among then
Because there was a severe shortage of eligible Ukrainian women, man
Ukrainians in Britain married non-Ukrainians. Nonetheless, militant Ukrair

ian nationalism and the influence of the Banderite OUN are strong among these former members of the Galicia Division.

Italy A small but important center of the Ukrainian diaspora is Rome. After the Soviet government banned the Ukrainian Greek Catholic church in 1946, many of its institutions were transferred to Rome. Monastic orders with links to Ukraine, such as the Basilians, Serving Sisters, and Studites, established their headquarters there. In 1959, the so-called Little Seminary was founded. Largely because of the efforts of Cardinal Slipy, the head of the Ukrainian Catholic church from 1944 to 1984, the Ukrainian Catholic University was established in the late 1960s and the cathedral of St Sophia was completed in 1969. The presence of these institutions in the Eternal City serves as a reminder that Soviet attempts to liquidate the Ukrainian Greek Catholic church have been far from successful. This fact was underscored when, in the summer of 1988, thousands of Ukrainian Catholics from all over the world gathered in Rome to celebrate the millennium of Christianity in Ukraine. It might be added in passing that the Soviet authorities chose to mark this epochal event primarily in Moscow, depriving Kiev of its momentous and rightful anniversary.

Australia Another Ukrainian community that traces its origins to the DPS is the Australian one. Despite its geographic isolation, it is one of the best organized and most active in the diaspora. By 1951, about 10% or roughly 21,000 of the DPS arrived here. Young and energetic, they included almost as many East Ukrainians as West Ukrainians, an unusual feature because the latter generally predominate abroad. Although the majority were laborers, they also included a significant number of members of the intelligentsia. As in Britain, men outnumbered women by a considerable margin. The newcomers generally settled in such large cities as Sydney, Melbourne, and Adelaide. As always, the beginnings were difficult and even the most highly educated immigrants worked as simple laborers. But given Australia's well-developed and expanding economy, the Ukrainian immigrants steadily moved up the socioeconomic ladder. Today their 30,000-member community enjoys a relatively high standard of living and boasts numerous professionals.

Unlike in Canada and the United States, where "old-immigrant" institutions were already in place, in Australia the Ukrainian DPS had to build communal organizations from nothing. Nonetheless, they have achieved notable success in this area. The community's small size and sense of isolation also made cooperation among its various segments a necessity. Consequently, in 1953 the Federation of Ukrainian Organizations was established to represent and coordinate the activity of its seventeen constituent bodies. As usual, the strongest Ukrainian institutions in Australia are the Ukrainian Catholic and Orthodox churches. Other important groups include a women's association (about 700 members), the Plast and SUM youth organizations (about 800 members each), and a variety of professional societies and cultural groups. A system of Saturday schools attempts to provide the youth with some familiarity with the Ukrainian language and cultural heritage. Annual enrollments in the schools have averaged about 1000, although they have been declining of late. Initially, the Shevchenko Scientific Society was the meeting ground for Ukrainian scholars. Following the American and Canadian examples, Ukrainian studies programs were established at Monash and Macquarie universities in the late 1970s.

Despite their achievements, the Ukrainians in Australia confront similar problems to those of their compatriots elsewhere in the West. Among the youth born in Australia, assimilation is increasingly evident. As the older generation passes away and no new immigrants arrive, an uncertain future looms before Australia's Ukrainian community.

The Ukrainians of Eastern Europe

The position of the approximately 450,000 Ukrainians who live in Eastern Europe is quite different from that of their compatriots both in the West and in the USSR. Those in Czechoslovakia and Romania continue to inhabit their ancestral lands, which for a variety of reasons Stalin chose not to annex to Soviet Ukraine. In Poland, as we have seen, the Ukrainians were driven from their homes but continue to live within the borders of that state. And in Yugoslavia, the Ukrainians are early forerunners of the migratory movements of modern times. These will be considered first.

Yugoslavia In the mid 18th century, after the Austrians pushed the Ottomans out of the Bačka and Banat regions of present-day Yugoslavia, they encouraged peasants from Transcarpathia to move into these depopulated lands. Consequently, Ukrainian colonies arose in the Bačka region, especially around such towns as Ruski Krstur and Novi Sad. In the early 20th century, the Ukrainian presence in the region grew, when about 10,000 Ukrainian emigrants from Galicia settled in Bosnia, primarily in the area of Banja Luka. Almost all these Ukrainians, or Rusyns, as some still call themselves, were peasants and lived in self-enclosed village communities. This situation, as well as their Greek Catholic rite, helped the approximately 20,000–30,000 descendants of these immigrants in Yugoslavia to reinforce a strong sense of Rusyn/Ukrainian identity to this day.

Romania The Ukrainians of Romania, numbering an estimated 70,000, are probably the worst off of all Ukrainians in Eastern Europe, both in socioeconomic and in national terms. Scattered in such regions as southern Bukovyna, Dobrudja, Maramarosh, and Banat, they are isolated from each other and from Ukrainians in the USSR and in the West. Most are indigent peasants. Because Romania is one of the poorest East European countries, its Ukrainian inhabitants have limited opportunities to improve their socioeconomic status. The discriminatory policies of the Bucharest government make matters worse. Up to 1947 the government refused to recognize Ukrainians as a distinct nationality. Matters improved somewhat during the relatively liberal 1948–63 period, when Ukrainian-language schools were allowed to function in the villages. About 120 were established with an enrollment of over 10,000 pupils. At the University of Bucharest, a section of Ukrainian language and literature came into being. But in 1964 a reaction set in and the government gradually nullified many gains of the previous years. Today, the cowed Ukrainian minority in the country does not possess a single communal organization.

Czechoslovakia By comparison with their compatriots in Romania, the Ukrainians (or Rusyn/Ukrainians) of Czechoslovakia are much better off. Numbering an estimated 100,000 (official statistics list only 40,000), they inhabit about 300 villages around the town of Prešov in the Carpathian foothills. Although currently the region lies within the borders of the Slovak part of the state, historically it has been closely linked with Transcarpathia, which is now in Soviet Ukraine.

Recent history has not been unkind to the Rusyn/Ukrainians of the Prešov region. The existence of an autonomous Carpatho-Ukraine in prewar Czechoslovakia set a precedent that was difficult to ignore. After the Second World War ended, a newly formed Prešov Region Ukrainian National Council arose to represent the region's populace and to claim autonomy within the Czechoslovak state. Both the Czechs in Prague and the Slovaks in Bratislava refused these political demands. They did, however, make significant cultural and educational concessions.

By 1948, the Rusyn/Ukrainians had their own school system, newspapers, publishing house, youth organization, and theater. Because Russophilism was still prevalent among the region's intelligentsia – isolated Prešov was the last region where this confusing and once-widespread phenomenon still survived – many of the above-mentioned institutions still used Russian. However, by the early 1950s, a program of Ukrainization, introduced by the new Communist government of Czechoslovakia, pushed the Ukrainian literary language and national orientation to the fore. Meanwhile, a new, apolitical organization, the KSUT (Cultural Association of Ukrainian Workers), emerged as the representative body of the Rusyn/Ukrainians.

With the transformation of Czechoslovakia into a communist state in 1948 came collectivization and the replacement of the Greek Catholic church by a Moscow-linked Orthodox church. However, when the Dubček government attempted to "put a human face" on communism in the late 1960s, the Greek

Catholic church was again legalized. But now Slovak influence in the church was greater than before.

As in all of Czechoslovakia, Dubček's innovations sparked an outburst of enthusiasm and activism among the Rusyn/Ukrainians. In spring 1968, plans were made to call a Ukrainian national council. The Ukrainian-language newspapers were filled with calls for political, economic, and cultural autonomy. The literary production of a talented, new generation of Rusyn/Ukrainian intellectuals reached unprecedented heights. And the patriotic Ukrainian tone of Prešov's Ukrainian-language radio programs worried Kiev as well as Bratislava and Prague. But all this came to an abrupt, disillusioning end in August 1968, when about half a million Soviet and satellite troops poured into Czechoslovakia to smash Dubček's promising "revolution."

The harsh repression that engulfed Czechoslovakia in the 1970s and 1980s did not lead to a total dismantling of Rusyn/Ukrainian cultural institutions. The museum in Svidnik, the Ukrainian section at the university in Prešov, the Ukrainian press, and KSUT continue to function. They are, however, closely monitored by the Slovak government. And pressure for Rusyn/Ukrainians to adopt Slovak nationality has increased. Those who wish to stress the positive side of the current situation point out that materially the Rusyn/Ukrainians are better off than before. It is true that in recent decades the government has brought in electrification, new roads, and industry to the once-isolated and backward Prešov region. And today, less than 50% of the area's Ukrainians work in agriculture. Most are employed in industry, the bureaucracy, and the professions. Nonetheless, as of 1968, the average earnings of the Rusyn/Ukrainians were still 40% below the Czechoslovak national average. Thus, in terms of material welfare, as well as national rights, they remain among the underprivileged.

Poland   Of all the Ukrainian communities, that of Poland has suffered the cruelest fate. In 1947 the Polish government forcibly expelled about 170,000 Ukrainians, mostly Lemkos, from their ancestral lands in the Carpathian foothills and dispersed them throughout Poland. Most were resettled in the former German lands that the Poles had acquired. Thus, today, approximately 60,000 Ukrainians live in the Olsztyn region, formerly East Prussia; another 40,000 inhabit the Koszalin region in the northwest; and close to 20,000 are located in the vicinity of Wrocław in the southwest. Because about 20,000 remained in their ancestral lands around Lublin and Peremyshl (Przemyśl) in the southeast, it is evident that the Ukrainians have been neatly dispersed to the four corners of Poland.

Even in their new villages, the government saw to it that the Ukrainians did not form compact communities. Only a few families were assigned to every village. Initially, they received no land and were forced to work for Polish farmers. In the early 1950s, they were allowed to acquire the worst of the former German lands. To make matters worse, the Ukrainian newcomers were exposed to a fierce anti-Ukrainianism, which was especially prevalent among the many Poles who had been expelled from Western Ukraine. For fear of discrimination and insults, Ukrainians were forced to camouflage their nationality, refrain from using their native language, and even conceal their background from their children. In short, the small and vulnerable Ukrainian minority in Poland was made to pay for the centuries of bitter Polish/Ukrainian antagonism.

In 1956, Warsaw granted the Ukrainians some concessions. Perhaps it was because the government realized that they no longer presented a threat to the security of the state. Or perhaps the authorities drew a lesson from the mistakes that the intolerant prewar government had made in its nationalities' policies. In any case, that year a Ukrainian newspaper, *Nashe Slovo*, was allowed to appear. And the USKT (Ukrainian Social Cultural Association) was established. Needless to say, it is closely supervised by the Ministry of the Interior. Nonetheless, both the newspaper and the association receive considerable government subsidies. Today, *Nashe Slovo* has about 8000 subscribers and USKT has approximately 4500 members.

Scrupulously nonpolitical, USKT concerns itself mainly with sponsoring about fifty Ukrainian choirs and dance ensembles. Every year it organizes well-attended festivals of Ukrainian song and music. But the association's efforts to expand Ukrainian educational facilities have had only limited success. In 1970, only about 5% of Ukrainian children in Poland had access to Ukrainian-language education. There is a Ukrainian lycée in Legnica and a pedagogical lycée for teachers of Ukrainian in Bartoszice. However, because of the lack of Ukrainian schools, most of their graduate teachers cannot find employment. At the University of Warsaw, the philology department has a Ukrainian section, as do several such departments in provincial universities. There is a group of well-trained Ukrainian scholars who hold positions in these institutions. As well, several Polish scholars have shown that they can deal with Ukrainian topics dispassionately and well.

Nevertheless, it is evident that the old wounds have not yet healed. While some improvement is noticeable among the members of the Polish intelligentsia, anti-Ukrainianism is still widespread. Books, articles, and films castigating the "barbarism of UPA bandits" (and, by association, all Ukrainians) appear frequently. Successful careers are open to Ukrainians, but it is advisable for them to downplay their national background. Efforts of resettled Ukrainians to return to their ancestral lands are continually blocked.

The position of the Greek Catholic church, to which about 50% of Poland's estimated 200,000–250,000 Ukrainians belong, is an especially sensitive issue today. The premeditated neglect and even wanton destruction of numerous, centuries-old Ukrainian churches in the Lemko region has aroused the ire of Ukrainians in Poland and in the West. Equally disturbing is the reluctance of the Polish Catholic hierarchy to support the appointment of a bishop for the Ukrainian Catholics. However, in fairness to the Poles, it should be noted that they, like the Czechs and Slovaks, are not the only ones who set policy toward their respective Ukrainian minorities. Moscow keeps a close watch on all the Ukrainian communities in Eastern Europe. And it is always ready with forceful advice on how its East European satellites should deal with Ukrainian issues.

 è

A major function of Ukrainian communities abroad, and specifically those in the West, has been to preserve the political and cultural values and traditions of non-Soviet Ukraine. Another has been to speak up for Ukrainian interests, when compatriots in Soviet Ukraine were forced to be silent. Were it not for the efforts of Ukrainians abroad, their homeland would be an almost unknown entity beyond the borders of the USSR. Not surprisingly, the relationship between Soviet Ukraine and the Ukrainian diaspora has been generally an antagonistic one. The early socioeconomic emigrants were bound to their churches, while the DPs were ardent nationalists. Both had grounds to view the Soviets with suspicion at the very least. Meanwhile, propaganda emanating from Soviet Ukraine constantly portrayed Ukrainians as "lackeys of capitalism, fascism, and Rome." Thus, unlike some relationships between homeland and diaspora that have been mutually beneficial – Armenia is a good example – the Ukrainian one has brought neither party much benefit. Soviet Ukrainians have been unable to utilize the Ukrainian communities abroad as a sorely needed window to the West, while the Ukrainian diaspora has been deprived of the cultural and demographic revitalization that it desperately requires.

Despite the fact that most Ukrainians abroad have entered the mainstream of their respective host societies, some still gain psychic as well as concrete benefits from belonging to their ethnic in-groups. But time is not on the side of the Ukrainian diaspora. The growing irrelevance of things Ukrainian for people who have little or no contact with Ukraine is having an effect. Everywhere the specter of assimilation into the culture of the host societies looms large. It is to be hoped that Ukrainians abroad and in Ukraine will be able to develop a fruitful relationship, while there is still time to be of use to each other.

Ukrainians welcoming German troops, June 1941

A church destroyed by retreating Soviets, Kiev, June 1941

Identifying the victims of the retreating NKVD, Lviv, June 1941

Andrii Melnyk

Stepan Bandera

Volodymyr Kubijovyč

Nazis executing OUN members, Stanyslaviv, September 1943

Ukrainian *Ostarbeiter* being sent to Germany for forced labor

Roman Shukhevych (General Taras Chuprynka), UPA commander

UPA unit, 1946

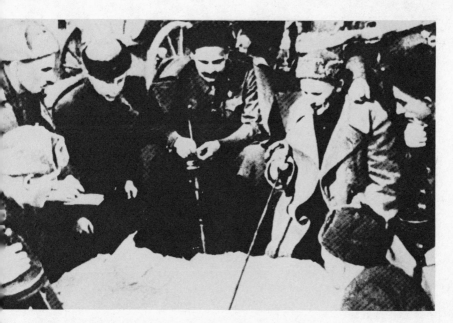

Sydir Kovpak (with pointer), commander of Soviet partisans

Soviet troops retaking Kiev, 1943

Identifying the victims of the retreating Nazis, Kerch, 1943

Kaganovich and Khrushchev in Kiev, 1947

Brezhnev and Shcherbytsky in late 1970s

Aged female collective-farm workers: the backbone of
the agricultural work force

Village schoolgirls, early 1960s

Ukrainian immigrants arriving in Canada in the early 20th century

Members of the banned Ukrainian Greek Catholic church celebrating mass in a forest, summer 1987

A meeting organized in Lviv by Ukrainian activists
in the era of *glasnost*, July 1988

Statue of St Volodymyr overlooking the Dnieper

Notes

Introduction

1 S. Rudnytskyj, *Ukraine: Land und Volk* (Berlin: Soiuz Vyzvolennia Ukrainy, 1916), 27.
2 The term Trypillia derives from the village of the same name in the Kiev region where, in the final decade of the 19th century, V. Khvoiko discovered the archaeological remains of the civilization. See *Arkheologiia Ukrainskoi RSR* (Kiev: Naukova Dumka, 1971) I: 149–205.
3 *Istoriia Ukrainskoi RSR* (Kiev: Naukova Dumka, 1979) I: 126.
4 T. Sulimirski, *The Sarmatians* (London: Thames and Hudson, 1972), 28.
5 G. Rawlinson, ed., *History of Herodotus* (New York: Appleton, 1882) III: 82.
6 Sulimirski, *The Sarmatians*, 32.

Chapter 1

1 S. Cross, ed. and trans., *The Russian Primary Chronicle* (Cambridge: Harvard University Press, 1930), 144–5.
2 O. Pritsak, *The Origin of Rus'* (Cambridge: Harvard Ukrainian Research Institute, 1981), 8–33.
3 See R. Pipes, *Russia under the Old Regime* (New York: Scribner's, 1974), 31.
4 M. Hrushevsky, *Istoriia Ukrainy-Rusy*, new edition (New York: Knyhospilka, 1954) I: 458.
5 Ibid., I: 459.
6 N. Polonska-Vasylenko, *Istoriia Ukrainy* (Munich: Ukrainske Vydavnytstvo, 1972) I: 148.
7 S. Tomashivsky, *Istoriia Ukrainy: Starynni viky i seredni viky* (Munich: UVU, 1948), 72.

Chapter 2

1 G. Vernadsky and M. Karpovich, in their work *Kievan Russia* (New Haven: Yale University Press, 1948) II: 102–5, estimate that the population of Kievan Rus' might have been 7.5 million. However, many Western scholars consider this figure to be too high.

2 M. Tikhomirov, *Drevnerusskie goroda* (Moscow: Vysha Shkola, 1950).

3 M. Pogodin, "Zapiska o drevenem iazike Russkom," *Izvestiia otd. russkogo iazika i slov. Akad. Nauk* (St Petersburg, 1856) V: 70–92.

4 For an English translation of Hrushevsky's famous article see "The Traditional Scheme of 'Russian' History and the Problem of a Rational Organization of the History of the Eastern Slavs," *Annals of the Ukrainian Academy of Arts and Sciences in the United States* (henceforth: *Annals*) 2 (1952): 355–64.

5 V. Mavrodin, *Obrazovanie drevnerusskogo gosudarstva i formirovannie drevnerusskoi narodnosti* (Moscow: Vysha shkola, 1971).

Chapter 3

1 See Hrushevsky, "The Traditional Scheme," 357.

2 Tomashivsky, *Istoriia Ukrainy*, 78.

3 K. Sofronenko, *Obshchestvno-politicheskii stroi Galitsko-Volinskoi Rusi XI–XIII* (Moscow: Akademiia Nauk SSSR, 1955), 36.

4 *The Lay of the Warfare Waged by Igor* (Moscow: Progress Press, 1981), 65.

Chapter 4

1 Hrushevsky, *Istoriia Ukrainy-Rusy*, IV: 98.

2 Ibid., IV: 99.

3 Hrushevsky, "The Traditional Scheme," 358–60. This point is also forcefully argued by the Russian historian M. Liubavsky, *Ocherk istorii litovskogo-russkogo gosudarstva* (Moscow, 1910), 1–3.

4 See D. Doroshenko, *Narys Istorii Ukrainy* (Warsaw: Ukrainskyi Naukovyi Instytut, 1932), 104–5.

Chapter 5

1 See A. Jabłonowski, *Źródła Dziejowe* (Warsaw, 1889) XIX: 73. Soviet Ukrainian historians have challenged these figures as being far too low. They argue that Jabłonowski underestimated the size of the native population in order to make the Polish role in the colonization of the area appear more impressive. See A. Baranovich, "Naselenie predstepnoi Ukrainy v XVII v.," *Istoricheskie zapiski* 32 (1950): 198–232, and O. Kompan, "Do pytannia pro zaselenist Ukrainy v XVII st.," *Ukrainskyi istorychnyi zhurnal* 1 (1960): 65–77.

2 The word *szlachta* derives from the German *Geschlect* (family, lineage).

Chapter 6

1 Hrushevsky, *Istorii Ukrainy-Rusy*, VI: 458.
2 H. Luzhnytsky, *Ukrainska tserkva mizh skhodom i zakhodom* (Philadelphia: Providence Association, 1954), 307.
3 Hrushevsky, *Istoriia Ukrainy-Rusy*, VI: 238.
4 I. Isaevych, *Bratstva ta ikh rol v rozvytku ukrainskoi kultury XVI–XVIII st.* (Kiev: Naukova Dumka, 1966), 153. Also see Polonska-Vasylenko, *Istoriia Ukrainy*, I: 399.

Chapter 7

1 I. Berezovsky, ed., *Istorychni pisni* (Kiev: Naukova Dumka, 1961), 63.
2 See J. Pelenski, "The Cossack Insurrections in Jewish-Ukrainian Relations," in P. Potichnyj and H. Aster, eds., *Ukrainian-Jewish Relations in Historical Perspective* (Edmonton: Canadian Institute of Ukrainian Studies, 1988), 41. Estimates of Jews in the entire Polish-Lithuanian Commonwealth in the 17th century range from 70,000 to 480,000. See B. Weinryb, *The Jews of Poland: A Social and Economic History of the Jewish Community in Poland from 1100 to 1800* (Philadelphia: Jewish Publication Society, 1972), 193–4.
3 Hrushevsky, *Istoriia Ukrainy-Rusy*, VII: 302.
4 Ibid., VII: 218.
5 Ibid., VII: 538.
6 Ibid., VII: 539.

Chapter 8

1 N. Davies, *God's Playground: A History of Poland* (New York: Oxford University Press, 1982) I: 444.
2 I. Dzyra, ed., *Litopys Samovydtsia* ("Eye Witness Chronicle") (Kiev: Naukova Dumka, 1971), 52.
3 Estimates of Jews killed in the uprising have been greatly exaggerated in the historiography of the event. According to B. Weinryb, the total of losses reported in Jewish sources is 2.4 million to 3.3 million deaths, clearly a fantastic figure. Weinryb cites the calculations of S. Ettinger indicating that about 50,000 Jews lived in the area where the uprising occurred. See B. Weinryb, "The Hebrew Chronicles on Bohdan Khmelnytsky and the Cossack-Polish War," *Harvard Ukrainian Studies* 1 (1977): 153–77. While many of them were killed, Jewish losses did not reach the hair-raising figures that are often associated with the uprising. In the words of Weinryb (*The Jews of Poland*, 193–4), "The fragmentary information of the period – and to a great extent information from subsequent years, including reports of recovery – clearly indicate that the catastrophe may not have been as great as has been assumed."

4 Z. Wójcik, *Dzikie Pola w ogniu. O kozaczyznie w dawnej Rzeczpospolitej*, 3rd rev. ed. (Warsaw: Wiedza Powszechna, 1968), 187.
5 The various interpretations of the Pereiaslav Agreement are summarized in J. Basarab, *Pereiaslav 1654: A Historiographical Study* (Edmonton: Canadian Institute of Ukrainian Studies, 1982).
6 Ibid., 180.
7 See M. Braichevskyi, *Annexation or Reunification*, ed. and trans. by G. Kulchycky (Munich: Ukrainisches Institut für Bildungspolitik, 1974).
8 I. Kholmsky [I. Krypiakevych], *Istoriia Ukrainy* (New York–Munich: Shevchenko Scientific Society, 1949), 208.
9 Hrushevsky, *Istoriia Ukrainy-Rusy*, IX (2): 1417.
10 Kholmsky, *Istoriia Ukrainy*, 216.

Chapter 9

1 S. Soloviev, *Istoriia Rossii* (Moscow: Izdatelstvo Sotsialno-Ekonomichnoi Literatury, 1961) VI: 113.
2 Hrushevsky, *Istoriia Ukrainy-Rusy*, IX (2): 977.
3 Ibid., 968.

Chapter 10

1 O. Ohloblyn, *Hetman Ivan Mazepa ta ioho doba* (New York: ODFFU, 1960), 135.
2 Ibid., 176.
3 Letter of Pylyp Orlyk to Stefan Iavorsky in *Osnova* (St Petersburg) 1862 no.11, p. 5. The letter of Mazepa's chancellor, Pylyp Orlyk, is the most informative source available regarding Mazepa's decision to go over to the Swedes. For an English translation of this fascinating document, see O. Subtelny, *The Mazepists: Ukrainian Separatism in the Early 18th Century* (Boulder: East European Monographs, 1981), 178–205.
4 Ohloblyn, *Mazepa*, 261.
5 Orlyk to Iavorsky, *Osnova*, 14.
6 B. Krupnytsky, *Hetman Danylo Apostol i ioho doba* (Augsburg: UVAN, 1948), 28.
7 Ibid., 28.
8 Ibid., 49.
9 Doroshenko, *Narys* , 423.
10 Z. Kohut, "The Abolition of Ukrainian Autonomy (1763–1786): A Case Study in the Integration of a Non-Russian Area into the Empire" (PhD dissertation, University of Pennsylvania, 1975), 85.
11 B. Nolde, "Essays in Russian State Laws," *Annals* 4 (1955): 889–90.
12 Kohut, "Abolition of Ukrainian Autonomy," 111.
13 Ibid., 110.
14 See T. Hunczak, *Russian Imperialism* (New Brunswick: Rutgers University Press, 1974), ix.

15 See V. Golobutsky, *Zaporizka sich v ostanni chasy svoho isnuvannia, 1734–1775* (Kiev: Vydavnytstvo Akademii Nauk URSR, 1961), 410.
16 V. Rich, trans., *Taras Shevchenko: Song out of Darkness* (London: Mitre Press, 1961), 11.

Chapter 11

1 E. Hobsbawn, *Bandits* (New York: Dell, 1969), 16.
2 D. Myshko, "Borotba trudiashchykh mas Pravoberezhnoi Ukrainy na peredodni Koliivshchyny," in *Koliivshchyna* (Kiev: Naukova Dumka, 1970), 47–8.
3 See D. Doroshenko, *A Survey of Ukrainian Historiography*, a special issue of the *Annals* 5–6 (1957): 48.
4 Ibid., 49.

Chapter 12

1 See S. Pushkarev, *The Emergence of Modern Russia* (New York: Holt, Rinehart and Winston, 1963), 21.
2 D. Von Mohrenschildt, *Toward a United States of Russia* (Rutherford: Farleigh Dickinson University Press, 1981), 13.
3 Rich, *Song out of Darkness*, p. 71.
4 See N. Storozhenko, "K istorii malorossiiskikh kozakov v kontse XVIII i v nachale XIX vv.," *Kievskaia starina* 11 (1897): 145.
5 V. Lypynsky, *Lysty do brativ-khliborobiv* (Vienna: Hermann, 1926), 418.
6 M. Slabchenko, *Materiialy do ekonomichno-sotsialnoi istorii Ukrainy XIX st.* (Odessa, 1925–27), 98.
7 F. Iastrebov, *Narysy z istorii Ukrainy* (Kiev: Vydavnytstvo Akademii Nauk URSR, 1939), 106.
8 Ibid., 107.
9 C. Macartney, *The House of Austria* (Edinburgh: Edinburgh University Press, 1978), 1.
10 I.L. Rudnytsky, "Observations on the Problem of 'Historical' and 'Non-Historical' Nations," *HUS* 5 (1981): 358–68.

Chapter 13

1 H. Kohn, *The Idea of Nationalism* (New York: Macmillan, 1961), 429.
2 See D. Miller, "Ocherki iz istorii i iuridicheskogo byta staroi Malorossii: Prevrashchenie malorusskoi starshiny v dvorianstvo," *Kievskaia starina* 1 (1897): 26.
3 O. Ohloblyn, ed., and V. Davydenko, trans., *Istoriia Rusiv* (New York: Visnyk, 1956), 134.

4 N. Kostomarov, *Avtobiografiia: Literaturnoe nasledie* (St Petersburg: Stasiulevich, 1890), 28.

5 J. Herder, "Journal meiner Reise im Jahre 1769," *Herders Sämtliche Werke* (Berlin, 1878) IV: 402.

6 A. Mickiewicz, "Literatura slowian," *Dzieła* (Warsaw, 1955) X: 109.

7 See G. Luckyj, *Between Gogol and Ševčenko* (Munich: Fink Verlag, 1971), 26.

8 Ibid., 33–4.

9 H. Kohn, *Idea of Nationalism* (New York: Macmillan, 1944), 432.

10 Hulak, quoted in Luckyj, *Between Gogol and Ševčenko*, 44.

11 Metlynsky, quoted in ibid., 63.

12 Luckyj, *Between Gogol and Ševčenko*, 36.

13 Ibid., 137.

14 W. Kirkconnell, trans., *The Poetical Works of Taras Shevchenko: The Kobzar* (Toronto: University of Toronto Press, 1964), 62.

15 Rich, *Song out of Darkness*, 85.

16 Ibid., 36.

17 Cited in Luckyj, *Between Gogol and Ševčenko*, 165.

18 G. Luciani, trans. and ed., *Le Livre de la Genèse du Peuple Ukrainien* (Paris: Institut D'Études Slaves, 1956), 140– 2.

19 Luckyj, *Between Gogol and Ševčenko*, 186.

20 J. Kozik, *Ukraiński ruch narodowy w Galicji w latach 1830–1848* (Cracow: Wydawnictwo Literackie, 1973), 103.

21 Ibid., 106.

Chapter 14

1 J. Kozik, *Między Reakcją a Rewolucją: Studia z Dziejów Ukraińskiego Ruchu Narodowego w Galicji w latach 1848–1849* (Warsaw: PWN, 1975), 37.

2 M. Bohachevsky-Chomiak, *The Spring of a Nation: The Ukrainians in Eastern Galicia in 1848* (Philadelphia: Shevchenko Scientific Society, 1967), 44–5.

3 L. Bazylow, *Dzieje Rosji, 1801–1917* (Warsaw: PWN, 1970), 207.

4 See *Revoliutsionnaia sytuatsiia v Rossii v 1859–1861 gg.* (Moscow: Izdatelstovo Akademii Nauk SSR, 1960–72) vols 1–6.

5 A. Rieber, *The Politics of Autocracy: The Letters of Alexander II to Prince A.I. Bariatinskii, 1857–1864* (The Hague: Mouton, 1966), 94–7.

6 B. Pares, *History of Russia*, 3rd ed. (New York: Knopf, 1926), 341–66.

Chapter 15

1 W. Blackwell, *The Beginnings of Russian Industrialization* (Princeton: Princeton University Press, 1968), 26.

2 See I. Hurzhyi, *Ukraina v systemi vserosiiskoho rynku 60–90kh rokiv XIX st.* (Kiev: Naukova Dumka, 1968), 168–78.

3 See M. Iavorsky, *Ukraina v epokhu kapitalizmu* (Kiev: Derzhavne Vydavnytstvo Ukrainy, 1924).

4 R. Serbyn, ed., "Lénine et la question ukrainienne en 1914: le discours 'séparatiste' de Zurich," *Pluriel,* no. 25 (1981): 83.

5 M. Volobuev, "Do problemy ukrainskoi ekonomiky," in *Dokumenty ukrainskoho kommunizmu* (New York: Prolog, 1962), 132–250.

6 B. Krawchenko, *Social Change and National Consciousness in Twentieth Century Ukraine* (New York: St Martin's Press, 1985), 13.

Chapter 16

1 V. Antonovych, "Moia ispoved," *Osnova* 1 (St Petersburg 1862): 85.

2 A. Voloshchenko, *Narysy z istorii suspilno-politychnoho rukhu na Ukraini* (Kiev: Naukova Dumka, 1974), 114–15.

3 See I. Krevetsky, "Ne bylo, net i byt ne mozhet!" *Literaturno-Naukovyi Visnyk* 26 (1906): 138–9. This notorious slogan was originally formulated by Colonel Gribovsky of the Kiev police. See F. Savchenko, *Zaborona Ukrainstva 1876 r.* (Kiev: Derzhavne Vydavnytstvo, 1930), reprinted in Harvard Series in Ukrainian Studies, vol. 14 (1970), 186.

4 For a description of the membership of the Kiev branch see Savchenko, *Zaborona,* 97. Because the membership of the Kiev branch overlapped to a great extent with the Old Hromada, data about the former are a good indicator of who belonged to the latter. The membership of the Kiev branch included, in part, 21 professors, 8 members of scholarly societies, 41 high-level bureaucrats, 3 generals, 21 county and *zemstvo* officials, 10 landowners, 5 physicians, and 24 engineers and lower-level bureaucrats. The vast majority were from Kiev and the Kiev region, although the Poltava, Chernihiv, and Volhynia regions were also well represented.

5 Cited in Iu. Okhrymovych, *Rozvytok Ukrainskoi natsionalno-politychnoi dumky* (Lviv: Novitnia Biblioteka, 1922), 71.

6 I.L. Rudnytsky, ed., *Mykhaylo Drahomanov: A Symposium and Selected Writings* in *Annals* 2 (1952): 115.

7 See V. Zhuchenko, *Sotsialno-ekonomichna prohrama revoliutsiinoho narodnytstva na Ukraini* (Kiev: Vydavnytsvo Kievskoho Universytetu, 1969), 156.

8 *Ridnyi Krai,* no. 37, cited in Y. Boshyk, "The Rise of Ukrainian Political Parties in Russia, 1900–1907" (PhD dissertation, Oxford University, 1981), 366.

9 W. Serczyk, *Historia Ukrainy* (Wrocław: Ossolenium, 1979), 300.

10 In general, the reaction of the Russian intelligentsia to the Ukrainian movement was a combination of surprise, confusion, and hostility. Thus, the noted Russian historian and philosopher G. Fedotov wrote: "The awakening of the Ukraine, and especially the separatist character of the Ukrainian movement, surprised the Russian intelligentsia, and remained incomprehensible to it to the very end. We loved the Ukraine, its land, its people, its songs – and

considered all this our very own" (G. Fedotov, *Novyi grad* [New York: Izd. imeni Chekhova, 1952], 191). In his famous article "Obshcherusskaia kultura i ukrainski partikularizm" (*Russkaia mysl* [January 1912], 85), P. Struve wrote: "Should the intelligentsia's 'Ukrainian idea' ... strike the national soil and set it on fire ... [it will lead to] a gigantic and unprecedented schism of the Russian nation that, I firmly believe, will result in a veritable disaster for the [Russian] state and for the people."

11 V. Doroshenko, *Ukrainstvo v Rossii* (Vienna: SVU, 1917), 91.

Chapter 17

1 V. Budzinovsky, "Ahrarni vidnosyny Halychyny," *Zapysky Naukovoho Tovarystva im. Shevchenka* 4 (1894): 47.

2 I. Vytanovych, *Istoriia ukrainskoho kooperatyvnoho rukhu* (New York: TUK, 1964), 75. According to W. Najdus (*Skice z historii Galiciji* [Warsaw: Książka i Wiedza, 1958] I: 71), in 1900 the Ukrainian intelligentsia in Galicia numbered about 10,000–12,000.

3 Ivan Franko, cited in *Istoriia selianstva* (Kiev: Naukova Dumka, 1967) I: 441.

4 S. Szczepanowski, *Nądza Galicji w cyfrach* ... (Lviv, 1888), 68.

5 Egan quoted in L. Rothkirchen, "Deep-Rooted Yet Alien: Some Aspects of the History of the Jews of Subcarpathian Ruthenia," *Yad Vashem Studies* 12 (Jerusalem, 1977): 163.

6 J. Perenyi, "Iz istorii zakarpatskich ukrajincev," *Studia Historica Academiae Scientiarum Hungariae* 14 (Budapest, 1957): 136.

7 K. Levytsky, *Istoriia politychnoi dumky halytskykh ukraintsiv, 1814–1914* (Lviv, 1926), 71.

8 M. Mykolaievych [M. Stakhiv], *Moskofilstvo. Ioho batky i dity* (Lviv: Hromadskyi Holos, 1936), 45.

9 Levytsky, *Istoriia politychnoi dumky*, 105.

10 I.L. Rudnytsky, "Polish-Ukrainian Relations: The Burden of History," in P. Potichnyj, ed., *Poland and Ukraine: Past and Present* (Edmonton: Canadian Institute of Ukrainian Studies, 1980), 15.

11 Levytsky, *Istoriia politychnoi dumky*, 90.

12 Ibid., 90.

13 Mykolaievych, *Moskofilstvo*, 52.

14 Drahomanov, cited in M. Yaremko, *Galicia* (New York: Shevchenko Scientific Society, 1967), 151.

15 W. Feldman, *Stronnictwa i programy polityczne w Galiciji, 1846–1906* (Cracow: Książka, 1907) II: 316.

16 F. Bujak, *Galicja* (Lviv: Altenberg, 1909–10) I: 94.

Chapter 18

1 Levytsky, *Istoriia politychnoi dumky*, 722.
2 Sazonov, quoted in Serczyk, *Historia Ukrainy*, 319.
3 T. Hunczak, ed., *The Ukraine, 1917–1921: A Study in Revolution* (Cambridge: Harvard Ukrainian Research Institute, 1977), 382. This volume contains translations into English of all four "universals."
4 D. Doroshenko, *Istoriia Ukrainy 1917–1923 rr.* (Uzhhorod 1932; reprinted New York, 1954) I: 127.
5 Ibid., 150.
6 N. Popov, *Ocherki kommunisticheskoi partii (Bolshevikov) Ukrainy,* 5th ed. (Kharkiv, 1933), 13.
7 B. Dmytryshyn, *Moscow and the Ukraine 1918–1953* (New York: Bookman, 1956), 25.
8 Cited in ibid., 42.
9 R. Pipes, *The Formation of the Soviet Union: Communism and Nationalism 1917–1923* (Cambridge: Harvard University Press, 1954), 68.
10 V. Lenin, "Kritichiskie zamitki po natsionalnomu voprosu," *Sochineniia,* 4th ed. (Moscow: Politicheskaia Literatura, 1941–50) XX: 16–17.
11 Pipes, *Formation*, 125.
12 O. Pidhainy, *The Formation of the Ukrainian Republic* (Toronto: New Review Books, 1966), 597.
13 J. Reshetar, *The Ukrainian Revolution, 1917–1920: A Study in Nationalism* (Princeton: Princeton University Press, 1952), 142.
14 V. Vynnychenko, *Vidrodzhennia natsii* (Vienna, 1920) I: 258.

Chapter 19

1 *Istoriia Ukrainskoi RSR, III:* 355.
2 V. Lypynsky, *Lysty do brativ-khliborobiv* (Vienna, 1926), 755–80.
3 According to S. Baron, *The Russian Jews under the Tsars and the Soviets* (New York, 1964), 184, about 50,000 Jews died in the pogroms. J. Pelenski in his "The Cossack Insurrections in Jewish-Ukrainian Relations," in P. Potichnyj and H. Aster, eds, *Ukrainian-Jewish Relations in Historical Perspective* (Edmonton: Canadian Institute of Ukrainian Studies, 1988), 41, citing "reliable Jewish sources," states that the Jewish fatalities numbered about 35,000. Of these, about 27,000 were killed by the Whites. Approximately 6000 Jews died at the hands of the anarchistic and largely Ukrainian partisan forces of Makhno, Zeleny, and Hryhoriiv. And between 1500 and 2000 Jews died in pogroms staged by Ukrainian military units.
4 P. Kenez, *Civil War in South Russia, 1917–1920:* (Berkeley: University of California Press, 1977) II: 166. The Soviet historians I. Rybalka and V. Dovhopol briefly note that during their short stay in Ukraine, the Whites staged 400

pogroms. See their *Istoriia Ukrainskoi RSR: Epokha Sotsializmu* (Kiev: Vyshcha Shkola, 1982), 118.

5 For conflicting views on Petliura's responsibility for the pogroms, see T. Hunczak, "A Reappraisal of Simon Petliura and Jewish-Ukrainian Relations, 1917–1920," and Z. Szajkowski, "A Reappraisal of Simon Petliura and Ukrainian-Jewish Relations, 1917–1920: A Rebuttal," in *Jewish Social Studies* (July 1969): 163–213. B. Wolfe noted that, traditionally, Jews sided with "the Great-Russian culture as against the Ukrainian peasants and the handful of Ukrainian intellectuals who were striving to create a Ukrainian language and literature, and beginning to aspire to autonomy for their culture and their land ... Thus, almost unconsciously most of the Jews in the cities of Poland, Lithuania, and the Ukraine tended to become opponents of the national separation movements that arose during the breakup of the empire." See his *Three Who Made a Revolution* (New York: Dial, 1964), 182–3.

6 Hunczak, *The Ukraine, 1917–1920*, 182–3.

7 M. Lozynsky, *Halychyna v rr. 1918–1920* (Vienna: Institut sociologique ukrainien, 1922), 144.

8 Kenez, *Civil War*, 173.

9 See J. Borys, *The Sovietization of Soviet Ukraine 1917–1923*, rev. ed. (Edmonton: Canadian Institute of Ukrainian Studies, 1980), 249–50.

10 Lenin, quoted in ibid., 254.

11 See Borys, *Sovietization*, 256.

12 Ibid., 257.

13 Trotsky, quoted in ibid., 295.

Chapter 20

1 R. Serbyn argues that although the 1921 famine in Russia was caused by natural calamities, in Ukraine it was caused primarily by Soviet economic and political policies. See his "The Famine of 1921–1923: A Model for 1932–1933?" in R. Serbyn and B. Krawchenko, eds, *Famine in Ukraine, 1932–1933* (Edmonton: Canadian Institute of Ukrainian Studies, 1986), 147–78.

2 Lenin, *Sochineniia*, XXXIII: 335.

3 Kaganovich, quoted in Krawchenko, *Social Change*, 101.

4 Tolstoi, quoted in Krawchenko, *Social Change*, 92.

5 B. Antonenko-Davydovych, *Zemleiu ukrainskoiu* (Lviv, 1942; reprinted Philadelphia, 1955), 148.

6 See Mace, *Communism*, 42–3.

7 G. Lapchynsky, "Gomelskoe soveshchanie (vospominaniia)," *Letopis revoliutsii* (Kharkiv, 1926), 41.

8 See Iu. Lavrinenko, ed., *Rostriliane vidrodzhennia: Antolohiia 1917–1933* (Paris: Instytut Literacki, 1959), 827–8.

9 Ibid., 830–1.

10 See Dmytryshyn, *Moscow and the Ukraine*, 106.
11 Ibid., 104.
12 Ibid., 112.
13 See G. Luckyj, *Literary Politics in the Soviet Ukraine, 1917–1934* (New York: Columbia University Press, 1956), 38.
14 Mace, *Communism*, 130.
15 See Lavrinenko, *Rostriliane vidrodzhennia*, 789.

Chapter 21

1 N. Riasanovsky, *A History of Russia*, 4th ed. (New York: Oxford University Press, 1984), 494.
2 For an analysis of Stalin's views on the peasantry, see M. Lewin, *Russian Peasants and Soviet Power: A Study of Collectivization* (Evanston: Northwestern University Press, 1968).
3 J. Stalin, *Sochineniia* (Moscow: Gosizdat, 1952–55) XIII: 40–1.
4 According to recent statements by semiofficial Soviet sources, during the 1930s about 5 million peasant families were deported to Siberia and a total of 17 million Soviet citizens passed through the gulags. See *Christian Science Monitor*, 16 June 1987.
5 See R. Conquest, *The Harvest of Sorrow: Soviet Collectivization and the Terror-Famine* (New York: Oxford University Press, 1986), 143.
6 For a vivid description by a Communist activist of collectivization in Ukraine, see L. Kopelev, *The Education of a True Believer* (New York: Harper & Row, 1978).
7 *Pravda* 2 March 1930.
8 Stalin, *Sochineniia* XIII: 221.
9 Ibid., 216–17.
10 Conquest, *Harvest of Sorrow*, 221–2.
11 P. Grigorenko, *The Grigorenko Memoirs* (New York: Norton, 1982), 36.
12 See Conquest, *Harvest of Sorrow*, 245.
13 V. Kravchenko, *I Chose Freedom* (New York, 1946), 118.
14 Ibid., 130.
15 M. Maksudov in "Ukraine's Demographic Losses 1927–1938" in *Famine in Ukraine*, 27–44, argues that no less than 4.4 million people perished in Ukraine between 1927 and 1938. According to V. Kozlov, *Nationalnosti SSSR: Etnodemograficheskii obzor* (Moscow, 1975), 249, in the period between 1926 and 1939, the population of Russia rose by 28% and that of Belorussia by 11.3%. During that same period the population of Ukraine dropped by 9.9%.
16 *The Five-Year Plan for Agricultural Construction*, 3rd ed. (Moscow 1930) III: 127.
17 V. Holubnychy, "The Causes of the Famine of 1932–1933," *Meta*, no. 2 (1979): 23.
18 Krawchenko, *Social Change*, 125

19 V. Grossman, *Forever Flowing* (New York, 1972), 148.
20 Stalin, *Collected Works*, VII: 71.
21 *Proletarska Pravda*, 22 January 1930, cited in D. Solovey, "On the Thirtieth An-nivesary of the Great Man–Made Famine in Ukraine," *The Ukrainian Quarterly* 19 (1963): 7.
22 Recently Soviet authorities have begun to admit that the Famine of 1932–33 was largely the result of Stalin's policies. See, for example, the speech of V. Shcherbytsky in *Pravda Ukrainy*, 26 December 1987.
23 M. Carynnyk, L. Luciuk, and B. Kordan, eds, *The Foreign Office and the Famine: British Documents on Ukraine and the Great Famine of 1932–1933* (Kingston: Limestone Press, 1988), 397.
24 Conquest, *Harvest of Sorrow*, 321.
25 Kopelev, *The Education*, 277.
26 Postyshev, cited in Krawchenko, *Social Change*, 131.
27 Postyshev, quoted in Conquest, *Harvest of Sorrow*, 271–2.
28 Postyshev, cited in Krawchenko, *Social Change*, 145.
29 L. Trotsky, *The Writings of Leon Trotsky, 1939–1940* (New York, 1969), 72.
30 A. Ulam, *A History of Soviet Russia* (New York: Praeger, 1976), 130–1.
31 Cited in R. Sullivant, *Soviet Politics and the Ukraine, 1917–1957* (New York: Columbia University Press, 1962), 226.
32 Cited in ibid., 229.
33 Ibid., 229–30.
34 Cited in ibid., 230.
35 Postyshev, cited in Krawchenko, *Social Change*, 147.

Chapter 22

1 J. Tazbir, ed., *Dzieje Polski* (Warsaw: PWN, 1976), 736.
2 M. Drozdowski, *Społeczenstwo, Panstwo, Politycy II Rzeczpospolitej* (Cracow: Wydawnictwo Literackie, 1972), 24.
3 A. Motyl, *The Turn to the Right: The Ideological Origins and Development of Ukrainian Nationalism, 1919–1929* (Boulder: East European Monographs, 1980), 153.
4 Ibid., 144.
5 I.L. Rudnytsky, *Mizh istorieiu i politykoiu* (New York: Suchasnist, 1973), 239.
6 A. Motyl, "Ukrainian Nationalist Political Violence in Inter-War Poland, 1921–1939," *East European Quarterly* 1 (1985): 53.

Chapter 23

1 M. Rudnytska, ed., *Zakhidna Ukraina pid Bolshevykamy* (New York: Shevchenko Scientific Society, 1958), 454.
2 Ibid., 456.

3 A. Dallin, *German Rule in Russia, 1941–1944: A Study in Occupation Policies* (London: Macmillan, 1957), 107.

4 I. Kamenetsky, *Hitler's Occupation of Ukraine, 1941–1944: A Study of Totalitarian Imperialism* (Milwaukee: Marquette University Press, 1956), 35.

5 Dallin, *German Rule*, 67.

6 Ibid., 123.

7 Ibid., 127.

8 Ibid., 141.

9 Quoted in E. Hesse, *Der sowjetrussische Partisanenkrieg 1941 bis 1944 im Spiegel deutscher Kampfanweisungen und Befehle* (Göttingen: Musterschmidt, 1969), 189.

10 Quoted in M. Cooper, *The Phantom War: The German Struggle against Soviet Partisans, 1941–1944* (London: Macdonald and Jane's, 1979), 25–6.

11 J. Armstrong, *Ukrainian Nationalism, 1939–1945* (New York: Columbia University Press, 1955), 172.

12 Ibid., 156.

13 P. Potichnyj and Y. Shtendera, eds, *Political Thought of the Ukrainian Underground 1943–1951* (Edmonton: Canadian Institute of Ukrainian Studies, 1986), 342.

14 A. Szcesniak and W. Szota, *Droga do nikąd* (Warsaw: Wojskowy Instytut Historyczny, 1973), 170.

15 N. Starozhilov, *Partizanskie soedinenniia Ukrainy v Velikoi Otchestvennoi Voine* (Kiev: Vyshcha Shkola, 1983), 67.

16 V. Zamlynsky, "Ukrainska radianska istoriohrafiia pro partyzanskii rukh na Ukraini v roky Velykoi Vitchyznianoi Viiny," *Ukrainskyi Istorychnyi Zhurnal* 1 (1971): 133 argues that previous estimates of 220,000 Soviet partisans in Ukraine were too small and that actually the figure was about 500,000 with 1 million men in reserve. Meanwhile, the authoritative *Sovetskaia istoricheskaia entsiklopediia* (Moscow, 1967) X: 878 states that there were about 62,000 Soviet partisans in Ukraine.

17 Rybalka and Dovhopol, *Istoriia Ukrainskoi RSR*, 366.

18 *Borotba trudiashchykh zakhidnykh oblastei URSR* (Kiev: Naukova Dumka, 1984), 200, and B. Ananiichuk, *Vyzvolennia zakhidnykh oblastei Ukrainy* (Kiev: Vydavnytstvo Kievskoho Universytetu, 1969), 121.

19 P. Pirogov, *Why I Escaped* (New York: Duell Sloan and Pearce, 1950), 232. Cited in Y. Bilinsky, *The Second Soviet Republic: The Ukraine after World War II* (New Brunswick: Rutgers University Press, 1964), 10.

Chapter 24

1 Rybalka and Dovhopol, *Istoriia Ukrainskoi RSR*, 442.

2 Bilinsky, *Second Soviet Republic*, 282.

3 See A. Szcesniak and W. Szota, *Droga do nikąd,* and I. Blum, *Z dziejów Wojska*

Polskiego w latach 1945–1948 (Warsaw: Wydawnictwo Obrony Narodowei, 1960).
4 *Istoriia Ukrainskoi RSR*, VIII: 83.
5 Cited in D. Treadgold, *Twentieth Century Russia*, 4th ed. (Chicago: Rand McNally, 1976), 442.
6 Cited in Bilinsky, *Second Soviet Republic*, 12.
7 See Ukraine: *A Concise Encyclopedia*, I: 896.
8 B. Lewytzkyj, *Die Sowjet Ukraine, 1944–1963* (Cologne: Kiepenheuer & Witsch, 1964), 70.

Chapter 25

1 B. Lewytzkyj, *Politics and Society in Soviet Ukraine, 1953–1980* (Edmonton: Canadian Institute of Ukrainian Studies, 1984), 5.
2 Ibid., 5.
3 *Radianska Ukraina*, 7 December 1957.
4 *Robitnycha Hazeta*, 10 November 1962, quoted in Lewytzkyj, *Politics and Society*, 55.
5 Quoted in ibid., 59.
6 *Komunist Ukrainy*, no. 6 (1963): 53.
7 Lewytzkyj, *Politics and Society*, 65.

Chapter 26

1 Krawchenko, *Social Change*, 251.
2 I. Dzyuba, *Internationalism or Russification* (London: Weidenfeld and Nicolson, 1968), 213.
3 A. Motyl, *Will the Non-Russians Rebel?* (Ithaca-London: Cornell University Press, 1987), 133–4.
4 Krawchenko, *Social Change*, 251–3 and W. Isajiw, "Urban Migration and Social Change in Contemporary Soviet Ukraine," *Canadian Slavonic Papers*, 1 (March 1980): 56–66.
5 I.L. Rudnytsky, "The Political Thought of Soviet Ukrainian Dissent," *Journal of Ukrainian Studies*, no. 6 (1981): 11.
6 D. Shumuk, *Za skhidnim obriem* (Paris-Baltimore: Smoloskyp, 1974), 423–4.
7 Rudnytsky, "The Political Thought," 11.
8 Dziuba, *Internationalism*, 95.
9 Vasyl Stus (b. 1938), one of the most gifted Ukrainian poets of the 20th century, died in a Soviet gulag in 1986.
10 R. Szporluk, "Russians in Ukraine and Problems of Ukrainian Identity in the USSR," in P. Potichnyj, ed., *Ukraine in the Seventies* (Oakville, ON: Mosaic Press, 1975), 212.
11 V. Pokshishevsky, "Urbanization and Ethnographical Processes," *Soviet Geography*, no. 2 (1972): 119.

12 Ibid., 118–19.
13 See I. Koropeckyj, ed., *The Ukraine within the USSR: An Economic Balance Sheet* (New York: Praeger, 1977), 11.
14 Ibid., 311.
15 Ibid., 54 and 263–4.
16 V. Bigulov, et al., "Materialnoe blagosostoianie i sotsialnoe blagopoluchie," *Sotsiologicheskie issledovaniia*, no. 4 (1984): 92, quoted in Motyl, *Non-Russians*, 60.
17 *Literaturna Ukraina*, 12 March 1987.
18 Ibid.

Chapter 27

1 Iu. Bachynsky, *Ukrainska immigratsiia v zedynenykh derzhavakh Ameryku* (Lviv: Balytsky & Harasevych, 1914), 253.
2 P. Magocsi, *Our People: Carpatho-Rusyns and Their Descendants in North America* (Toronto: Multicultural History Society of Ontario, 1984), 32.
3 M. Kuropas, *To Preserve a Heritage: The Story of Ukrainian Immigration in the United States* (New York: Ukrainian Museum, 1984), 9.
4 J. Petryshyn, *Peasants in a Promised Land: Canada and the Ukrainians 1891–1914* (Toronto: Lorimer, 1985), 21.
5 O. Martynowych and N. Kazymyra, "Political Activity in Western Canada 1896–1923," in M. Lupul, ed., *A Heritage in Transition: Essays in the History of Ukrainians in Canada* (Toronto: McClelland and Stewart, 1982), 89.

Abbreviations

DP	Displaced Person
Cheka	Extraordinary Commission for Combating Counter-revolution, Speculation and Delinquency (Soviet political police)
CP(b)U	Communist Party (bolshevik) of Ukraine
CPU	Communist Party of Ukraine
FYP	Five-Year Plan
GUO	General Ukrainian Organization
KGB	Committee of State Security (Soviet political police)
Komsomol	Young Communist League
KPZU	Communist Party of Western Ukraine
MTS	Machine Tractor Station
MVD	Ministry of Internal Affairs
NEP	New Economic Policy
NKVD	People's Commissariat of Internal Affairs (Soviet political police)
OGPU	Unified State Political Administration (Soviet political police)
OUN	Organization of Ukrainian Nationalists
OUN-B	Organization of Ukrainian Nationalists (Bandera faction)
OUN-M	Organization of Ukrainian Nationalists (Melnyk faction)
RUP	Revolutionary Ukrainian party
SVU	Union for the Liberation of Ukraine
UAOC	Ukrainian Autocephalous Orthodox church
UCC	Ukrainian Central Committee
UHVR	Ukrainian Supreme Liberation Council
UNDO	Ukrainian National Democratic Union
UPA	Ukrainian Insurgent Army
UVO	Ukrainian Military Organization
UNR	Ukrainian National Republic
ZUNR	West Ukrainian National Republic

Glossary

boyars	nobles in the Kievan and subsequent periods
chern	term for lower classes, rabble in 16th–18th centuries
chernozem	fertile black-earth soil of Ukraine
druzhyna	retinue of fighting men of a prince during the Kievan period (pl. *druzhyny*)
gymnazium	secondary school, preparatory for university (pl. *gymnazia*)
haidamak	participant in spontaneous, popular uprisings against the Polish nobles in Right-Bank Ukraine in the 18th century (pl. *haidamaky*)
hetman	highest military, administrative, and judicial office among Ukrainian Cossacks
hromada	peasant commune or community; in the late 19th century, associations of Ukrainian intelligentsia
kulak	well-to-do peasant
narod	the people or peasant masses; in modern Ukrainian usage also means nation
narodnyk	populist in late 19th-century Russian Empire (pl. *narodnyky*)
oblast	major administrative unit in Soviet Ukraine
Ostarbeiter	forced laborers from Eastern Europe in Germany during the Second World War
otaman	Cossack leader in the 16th–18th centuries; partisan leader in Ukraine during the 1918–21 period (pl. *otamany*)
rada	council or assembly
sejm	Polish parliament
sloboda	free, uncolonized lands in Ukraine; temporary postponement of obligations for the use of uncolonized lands (pl. *slobody*)
starosta	local Polish official
starshyna	officer elite in Cossack Ukraine
szlachta	nobility of Poland-Lithuania

wojewoda   high Polish administrative and military official
votchyna   hereditary landholdings
vozhd   absolute, unlimited leader
zemstvo   institutions of local administration in late 19th-century
             Russian Empire (pl. *zemstva*)

ILLUSTRATION CREDITS

Sec. 1: Female statuette, Trypillian ceramic, Scythians in combat, Scythian binding, A re-construction, Dancing couple (*Istoriia ukrainskoho mystetstva*, vol. 1 [Kiev, 1966]); Gravestones (Sovfoto); East Slavic idol (Novosti Press Agency); A reconstruction (*Krizviky: Kiev v obrazotvorchomu mystetstvi* [Kiev, 1982]); Christianization (R. Wallace, *Rise of Russia* [New York, 1967]); Mosaic from St Sophia [2] (*Sofiia Kievska* [Kiev, 1971]. Sec. 2: Cossack camp (*Istoriia Ukrainskoi RSR*, vol. 1 [Kiev, 1979]); Church fortress, Khmelnytsky (private collection); Zaporozhians dancing, Four inhabitants (A. Rigelman, *Letopisnoe povestvovanie o Maloi Rossii* [Kiev, 1847]); Lviv in 17th c. (*Istoriia ukrainskoho mystetstva*, vol. 2 [Kiev, 1967]); Battle of Poltava (*Poltavska bytva* [Kiev, 1960]); Zaporozhians writing (*Repin* [Moscow, 1970]); Students of Kiev, Title page (*Krizviky*); Church on Left Bank (*Istoriia ukrainskoho mystetstva*, vol. 3 [Kiev, 1968]). Sec. 3: In search of work, Marketplace in Lviv, Opera house (*Istoriia ukrainskoho mystetstva*, vol. 4 [Kiev, 1969]); Village wedding (*Ukrainske naraodne vesillia* [Kiev, 1970]); West Ukrainian (Forum); Ukrainian peasant women (unavailable); The proletariat (*Ukrainska RSR v period hromadianskoi viiny*, vol 1 [Kiev, 1970]); Ivan Kotliarevsky, Antonovych, Shevchenko (private collection); Drahomanov, Ukrainka (*Encylopedia of Ukraine*, vol. 1 [Toronto, 1984]). Sec. 4: Hrushevsky (*Encyclopedia of Ukraine* vol. 1); Skoropadsky, Petrushevych, Petliura, Metropolitan Andrei, Peasants on pilgrimage (private collection); Skrypnyk, Greycoat Division (*Ukrainska RSR v period hromadianskoi viiny*); Kiev during proclamation (*Encyclopedia of Ukraine* vol. 2); Bolshevik troops (*Ukrainska RSR* vol. 2); Bolshevik officers, Propagandists (not available); Nestor Makhno (M. Palij, *Anarchism of Nestor Makhno* [Seattle, 1976]); Construction on Dnieper, Destruction of a church (J. Carmichael, *An Illustrated History of Russia* [New York, 1960]); Dead and dying peasants (*Famine in the Soviet Ukraine 1932–1933* [Cambridge, MA, 1986]); Evhen Konovalets (V. Martynets, *Vid UVO do OUN* [n.p. 1949]). Sec. 5: Ukrainians welcoming (B. Shub and B. Quint, *Since Stalin* [New York, 1951]); Identifying victims, Andrii Melnyk, Stepan Bandera, V. Kubijovyc, Nazis executing (original source: Bundesarchiv, Koblenz) (Y. Boshyk, ed. *Ukraine During World War II* [Edmonton, 1986]); Ukrainian Ostarbeiter (*Istoriia Ukrainskoi RSR*, vol. 7 [Kiev, 1977]); Roman Shukhevych, UPA unit (*Litopys UPA*); Sydir Kovpak, Soviet troops (*The Great Patriotic War* [Moscow, 1976]); Identifying victims (D. Baltermants, *Izvestiia*); Kaganovich and Khrushchev (not available); Brezhnev and Scherbytsky (*Kiev* [Kiev, 1975]); Aged female, Schoolgirls, Ukrainian immigrants, Members of banned, A meeting, Statue of (private collection).

Selected Readings in English

ABBREVIATIONS OF PERIODICALS

Annals   The Annals of the Ukrainian Academy of Arts and Sciences in the USA
CASS   Canadian American Slavic Studies
CSP   Canadian Slavonic Papers
EEQ   East European Quarterly
HUS   Harvard Ukrainian Studies
JGO   Jahrbücher für Geschichte Osteuropas
JUS   Journal of Ukrainian Studies (formerly Journal of Ukrainian
         Graduate Studies)
NP   Nationalities Papers
PR   Polish Review
RR   Russian Review
SEER   Slavonic and East European Review
SR   Slavic Review
SS   Soviet Studies
SU   Studia Ucrainica
UI   Ukrainskyi Istoryk
UQ   Ukrainian Quarterly
UR   Ukrainian Review

Reference Works

Encyclopedias

Kubijovyč, V., ed. *Ukraine: A Concise Encyclopedia.* 2 vols. Toronto, 1963–71
– *Encyclopedia of Ukraine.* Vols 1–2 (A–K). Toronto, 1984, 1988
Soviet Ukraine. Kiev, 1969

Bibliographies and Other Reference Works

American Bibliography of Russian and East European Studies. Bloomington. Published
annually since 1957
Doroshenko, D., and O. Ohloblyn. *A Survey of Ukrainian Historiography*. Special
issue of *Annals*. New York, 1957
Magocsi, P. *Galicia: A Historical Survey and Bibliographic Guide*. Toronto, 1983
Magocsi, P., and G. Matthews. *Ukraine: A Historical Atlas*. Toronto, 1985
Mirchuk, I., ed. *Ukraine and Its People: A Handbook of Maps, Statistical Tables and
Diagrams*. Munich, 1949
Pelenskyj, E. *Ucrainica: Selected Bibliography on Ukraine in West European Languages*.
Munich, 1948
Weres, R. *The Ukraine: Selected References in the English Language*. Kalamazoo, MI,
1961
Wynar, B. "Doctoral Dissertations on Ukrainian Topics in English." *UI* 6 (1979):
108–27

General Histories

Allen, W. *The Ukraine: A History*. Cambridge, 1940
Chamberlin, W. *The Ukraine: A Submerged Nation*. New York, 1944
Chirovsky, N. *An Introduction to Ukrainian History*. 3 vols. New York, 1981–86
Doroshenko, D. *A Survey of Ukrainian History*. Winnipeg, 1939. Updated by O.
Gerus, 1975
Hrushevsky, M. *A History of Ukraine*. New Haven, 1941
Manning, C. *The Story of the Ukraine*. New York, 1957
Nahayevsky, I. *History of Ukraine*. Philadelphia, 1962
Szporluk, R. *Ukraine: A Brief History*. Detroit, 1979

Collected Essays

Andrijisyn, J., ed. *Millennium of Christianity in Ukraine*. Ottawa, 1987
Potichnyj, P., ed. *Poland and Ukraine: Past and Present*. Edmonton, 1980
Potichnyj, P., and H. Aster., eds. *Ukrainian-Jewish Relations in Historical Perspective*.
Edmonton, 1988
Potichnyj, P., et al. *Ukraine and Russia in Their Historical Encounter*. Edmonton,
forthcoming
Pritsak, O., I. Ševčenko, and J. Labunka, eds. *Essays Commemorating the Millennium
of Christianity in Rus'-Ukraine*. Special issue. *HUS* 12 (1988)
Rudnytsky, I.L. *Rethinking Ukrainian History*. Edmonton, 1981

Readings and Anthologies

Chirovsky, N., ed. *On the Historical Beginnings of Eastern Slavic Europe*. New York,
1976

Gerus, O., ed. *Readings in Ukrainian History, 1687–1984.* Edmonton, forthcoming
Pushkarev, S., comp. *A Source Book for Russian History from Early Times to 1917.* Vol. 1. New Haven and London, 1972
Sichinsky, V., ed. *Ukraine in Foreign Comments and Descriptions from the 6th to the 20th Centuries.* New York, 1953
Subtelny, O., and I.L. Rudnytsky, eds. *Essays in Ukrainian History.* Edmonton, forthcoming

General Works in Related Fields

Chyzhevsky, D. *A History of Ukrainian Literature from the 11th to the End of the 19th Centuries.* Littleton, 1975
Ilarion, Metropolitan. *The Ukrainian Church: Outline of the History of the Ukrainian Orthodox Church.* Winnipeg, 1986
Kononenko, K. *Ukraine and Russia: A History of the Economic Relations between Ukraine and Russia, 1654–1917.* Milwaukee, 1958
Rudnitsky, S. *Ukraine: The Land and Its People: An Introduction to Its Geography.* New York, 1918
Wlasovsky, I. *Outline History of the Ukrainian Orthodox Church.* 3 vols. New York, 1956

From Earliest Times to 1350

Sources

Cross, S., trans. *The Russian Primary Chronicle.* Cambridge, MA, 1930
Heppell, M., trans. *The "Paterik" of the Kievan Caves Monastery.* Cambridge, MA, 1988
Hollingsworth, P., trans. *The Hagiography of Medieval Rus'.* Cambridge, MA, 1988
Nabokov, V., trans. *The Song of Igor's Campaign.* New York, 1960
Perfecky, G., trans. *The Galician-Volhynian Chronicle.* Munich, 1973

Historiography

Chubaty, N. "Kievan Christianity Misinterpreted." *UI* 9 (1972): 100–9
Horak, S. "Periodization and Terminology of the History of the Eastern Slavs: Observations and Analyses." *SR* 31 (1972): 853–62
Miller, D. "The Kievan Principality on the Eve of the Mongol Invasion: An Inquiry into Current Historical Research and Interpretation." *HUS* 10 (1986): 215–40
Polonska-Vasylenko, N. *Two Conceptions of the History of Ukraine and Russia.* London, 1968
Sashkolskii, I. "Recent Developments in the Normanist Controversy." *Varangian*

Problems. Scando-Slavica. Suppl. 1 (Copenhagen, 1970): 21–38

Sulimirski, T. "Late Bronze Age and Earliest Iron Age in the USSR. A Guide to Recent Literature on the Subject." *Bulletin of the Institute of Archaeology in London* 8–9 *(1968–69):* 117–50

Wynar, L. "Michael Hrushevsky's Scheme of Ukrainian History in the Context of the Study of Russian Colonialism and Imperialism." In M. Pap, ed., *Russian Empire,* 19–40. Cleveland, 1985

Studies

Andrusiak, N. "The Kings of Kiev and Galicia." SEER 33 (1954): 342–50

Blum, J. "The Beginnings of Large-Scale Private Landownership in Russia." *Speculum* 28 *(1953):* 776–90

– *Lord and Peasant in Russia: From the Ninth to the Nineteenth Century.* Princeton, 1961

Boba, I. *Nomads, Northmen and Slavs: Eastern Europe in the 9th Century.* Wiesbaden, 1967

Bratzkus, J. "The Khazar Origin of Ancient Kiev." SEER 22 (1944): 108–24

Czekanowski, J. "The Ancient Home of the Slavs." SEER 24 (1946–47): 356–72

Dimnik, M. "The Struggle for Control over Kiev in 1235 and 1236." CSP 21 (1979): 28–44

– *Mikhail, Prince of Chernigov and Grand Prince of Kiev 1224–1246.* Toronto, 1981

Dunlop, D. *The History of the Jewish Khazars.* Princeton, 1954

Dvornik, F. "Byzantine Political Ideas in Kievan Russia." *Dumbarton Oaks Papers* 9–10 *(1956):* 73–121

– *The Slavs in European History and Civilization.* New Brunswick, NJ, 1962

– *Byzantine Missions among the Slavs: Sts. Constantine and Methodius.* New Brunswick, NJ, 1970

Ericson, K. "The Earliest Conversion of the Rus' to Christianity." SR 44 (1966): 98–121

Fedotov, G. *The Russian Religious Mind: Kievan Christianity: The Tenth to Thirteenth Centuries.* Cambridge, 1946

Fennell, J. "The Tatar Invasion of 1223." *Forschungen zur Osteuropaischen Geschichte* 27 (1980): 18–31

Gimbutas, M. *Bronze Age Culture in Central and Eastern Europe.* Paris and London, 1965

Grekov, B. *Culture of Kievan Rus'.* Moscow, 1947

Halpern, C. "The Concept of the *Ruskaia Zemlia* and Medieval National Consciousness from the Tenth to the Fifteenth Centuries." NP 8 (1980): 75–94

– *Russia and the Golden Horde.* London, 1985

Hanak, W. "Some Conflicting Aspects of Byzantine and Varangian Political and Religious Thought in Early Kievan Russia." *Byzantinoslavica* 37 *(1976):* 46–55

Kaiser, D. *The Growth of the Law in Medieval Russia.* Princeton, 1980

Klein, R. *Ice-Age Hunters of the Ukraine*. Chicago, 1973

Knysh, G. "Eastern Slavs and the Christian Millennium of 1988." *SU* 3 (1986): 13–35

Kordysh, N. "Stone Age Dwellings in the Ukraine." *Archeology* 6 (1953): 167–73

– "Settlement Plans of the Trypillian Culture." *Annals* 3 (1953): 535–52

Langer, L. "The Medieval Russian Town." In M. Hamm, ed., *The City in Russian History*, 11–33. Lexington, KY, 1976

Luciw, J. *Sviatoslav the Conqueror*. State College, PA, 1986

Obolensky, D. "Russia's Byzantine Heritage." *Oxford Slavonic Papers* 1 (1950): 37–63

Pasternak, Y. "The Trypillian Culture in Ukraine." *UQ* 6 (1950): 122–33

– "Peremyshl of the Chronicles and the Territory of the White Croats." *Proceedings of the Shevchenko Scientific Society* 2 (1957): 36–9

Paszkiewicz, H. *The Origins of Russia*. New York, 1954

Polonska-Vasylenko, N. *Ukraine-Rus' and Western Europe in the 10–13th Centuries*. London, 1964

Poppe, A. "The Political Background to the Baptism of Rus': Byzantine-Russian Relations between 986–989." *Dumbarton Oaks Papers* 30 (1976): 197–244

– "The Original Status of the Old-Russian Church." *Acta Poloniae Historica* 39 (1979): 5–45

– *The Rise of Christian Russia*. London, 1982

Pritsak, O. "The Invitation to the Varangians." *HUS* 1 (1977): 7–22

– "Oleg the Seer and Oleg the 'Grand Prince of Rus'." In *Festschrift for Oleksander Ohloblyn*, 389–99. New York, 1977

– *The Origin of Rus'*. Cambridge, MA, 1981

– "When and Where Was Olga Baptized?" *HUS* 9 (1985): 5–24

Rice, T. *The Scythians*. London, 1957

Rostovtzeff, M. *Iranians and Greeks in South Russia*. Oxford, 1922

Ševčenko, I. "The Christianization of Kievan Rus'." *PR* 5 (1960): 29–35

– "Byzantium and the Slavs." *HUS* 7 (1984): 289–303

– "The Many Worlds of Petro Mohyla." *HUS* 8 (1984): 9–44

– *Byzantium and the Slavs*. Cambridge, MA, 1988

Stokes, A. "The Balkan Campaign of Svjatoslav Igorevich." *SEER* 40 (1962): 466–96

Sulimirski, T. *The Sarmatians*. London, 1970

Tikhomirov, M. *The Towns of Ancient Rus'*. Moscow, 1959

Vasiliev, V. *The Russian Attack on Constantinople in 860*. Cambridge, 1946

Vernadsky, G. "The Status of the Russian Church during the First Half-Century Following Vladimir's Conversion." *SEER* 20 (1941): 294–314

– *Kievan Russia*. New Haven, 1948

– "The Problem of Early Russian Campaigns in the Black Sea Area." *SR* 8 (1949): 1–9

– "The Royal Serfs (*servi regales*) of the 'Ruthenian Law' and Their Origin." *Speculum* 24 (1951): 255–64

- *The Mongols and Russia.* New Haven, 1953
- *The Origins of Russia.* New Haven, 1959

Voyce, A. *The Art and Architecture of Medieval Russia.* Norman, OK, 1967

Zernov, N. "Vladimir and the Origin of the Russian Church." SEER 28 (1949–50): 123–38, 425–38

Zguta, R. "Kievan Coinage." SEER 53 (1975): 483–92

Zhdan, M. "The Dependence of Halych-Volyn Rus' on the Golden Horde." SEER 35 (1956–57): 505–23

From 1350 to 1800

Sources

Borschak, E. "Pylyp Orlyk's Devolution of Ukraine's Rights." *Annals* 6 (1958): 1296–1312

Hannover, N. *Abyss of Despair. The Famous 17th Century Chronicle Depicting Jewish Life during the Chmielnicki Massacres of 1648–49.* New York, 1950

Levy, A. "The Contribution of the Zaporozhian Cossacks to Ottoman Military Reform: Documents and Notes." HUS 6 (1982): 372–413

Mackiw, T. *English Reports on Mazepa, 1687–1709.* New York, 1983

Perfecky, G. "Mazepa's Speech to His Countrymen." JUS 6 (1981): 66–72

Pernal, A. "Six Unpublished Letters of Bohdan Khmelnytsky, 1656–1657." HUS 6 (1982): 217–32

Struminsky, B. *Psuedo-Meleško: A Ukrainian Apochryphal Parliamentary Speech of 1615–1618.* Cambridge, MA, 1984

- *The Defense of Church Unity in 1617 and Zakhariia Kopystensky's 'Palenodiia.'* Cambridge, MA, 1988

Subtelny, O. *Letters of Ivan Mazepa to Adam Sieniawski, 1704–1708.* New York, 1975

- "The Letter of Pylyp Orlyk to Stefan Iavorsky." In his *The Mazepists: Ukrainian Separatism in the 18th Century,* 178–205. Boulder, CO, 1981

Sysyn, F. "Documents of Bohdan Xmelnyckyj." HUS 2 (1978): 500–24

Wynar, L., and O. Subtelny. *Habsburgs and Zaporozhian Cossacks: The Diary of Erich Lassota von Steblau, 1594.* Boulder, CO, 1975

Historiography

Basarab, J. *Pereiaslav 1654: A Historiographical Study.* Edmonton, 1982

Braichevsky, M. *Annexation or Reunification: Critical Notes on One Conception.* Trans. and ed. by G. Kulchycky. Munich, 1974

Fedenko, P. "Hetman Mazepa in Soviet Historiography." UR 9 (1960): 6–18

Kohut, Z. "Myths Old and New: The *Haidamak* Movement and the *Koliivshchyna* (1768) in Recent Historiography." HUS 1 (1977): 359–78

Krupnytsky, B. "Mazepa and Soviet Historiography." UR 3 (1956): 49–53

Reshetar, J. "The Significance of the Soviet Tercentenary of the Pereyaslav Treaty."
Annals 4 (1954): 981–94

Studies

Andrusyshen, C. "Skovoroda, the Seeker of the Genuine Man." UQ 2 (1946): 317–
30

Babinskii, H. The Mazeppa Legend in European Romanticism. New York, 1974

Backus, O. The Motives of West Russian Nobles in Deserting Lithuania for Moscow,
1377–1514. Lawrence, OK, 1957

– "The Problem of Feudalism in Lithuania, 1506–1548." SR 21 (1962): 635–59

Baran, A. "The Kievan Mohyla-Mazepa Academy and the Zaporozhian Cossacks."
UI 12 (1975): 70–5

– "Shahin Girai of the Crimea and the Zaporozhian Cossacks." In Jubilee Collection
of the Ukrainian Free Academy of Sciences in Canada, 15–35. Winnipeg, 1976

Baran, A., and G. Gajecky. The Cossacks in the Thirty Years War. 2 vols. Rome, 1969–
83

Bartlett, R. Human Capital: The Settlement of Foreigners in Russia, 1762–1804. Cambridge, 1979

Bida, C. "Early Eastern Slavic Primers." SU 1 (1978): 65–74

Borschak, E. "Early Relations between England and Ukraine." SEER 10 (1931–32):
138–60

– "A Little Known French Biography of Yuras' Khmelnytsky." Annals 3 (1953):
509–17

– Hryhor Orlyk, France's Cossack General. Toronto, 1956

Chirovsky, N. "Economic Aspects of the Ukrainian-Muscovite Treaty of 1654." UQ
10 (1954): 85–92

Chubaty (Czubatyj), N. "Mazepa's Champions in the 'Secret du Roi' of Louis XV,
King of France." UQ 5 (1949): 37–51

– "Moscow and the Ukrainian Church after 1654." UQ 10 (1954): 60–70

– "Bohdan Khmelnytsky, Ruler of Ukraine." UQ 13 (1957): 197–211

– Old Ukraine: Its Socio–Economic History Prior to 1781. Madison, 1963

Chynczewska-Hennel, T. "National Consciousness of Ukrainian Nobles and Cossacks from the End of the Sixteenth to the Mid-Seventeenth Century." HUS 10
(1986): 377–92

Chyzhevsky, D. "Ivan Vyshenskyj." Annals 1 (1951): 113–26

Collins, L. "The Military Organization and Tactics of the Crimean Tatars during
the Sixteenth and Seventeenth Centuries." In V. Parry and M. Yapp, eds, War,
Technology and Society in the Middle East. Oxford, 1975

Cracraft, J. "Prokopovyč's Kiev Period Reconsidered." HUS 2 (1978): 158–83

Doroshenko, D. "Ukrainian Chronicles of the 17th and 18th Centuries." Annals 1
(1951): 79–87

Edgerton, W. "Laying a Legend to Rest: The Poet Kapnist and Ukraino-German Intrigue." SR 30 (1971): 551–60

Fisher, A. The Crimean Tatars. Stanford, 1978

Frick, D. "Meletij Smotryckyj and the Ruthenian Question in the Early Seventeenth Century." HUS 8 (1984): 351–75

– "Meletij Smotryckyj and the Ruthenian Language Question." HUS 9 (1985): 25–52

Friedman, P. "The First Millennium of Jewish Settlement in the Ukraine and the Adjacent Areas." Annals 7 (1959): 1483–1516

Gajecky, G. "Cossack General Staff Officers." In Jubilee Collection of the Ukrainian Free Academy of Science, 36–61. Winnipeg, 1976

– The Cossack Administration of the Hetmanate. 2 vols. Cambridge, MA, 1978

Goldblatt, H. "Orthodox Slavic Heritage and National Consciousness: Aspects of East Slavic and South Slavic National Revivals." HUS 10 (1986): 336–54

Gordon, L. Cossack Rebellions: Social Turmoil in Sixteenth-Century Ukraine. Albany, 1983

Grabowicz, G. "Three Perspectives on the Cossack Past: Gogol, Ševčenko and Kuliš." HUS 5 (1981): 179–94

Graham, H. "Peter Mogila – Metropolitan of Kiev." RR 19 (1955): 345–56

– "Theofan Prokopovich and the Ecclesiastical Ordinance." Church History 25 (1956): 127–35

Halecki, O. "Ukraine, Poland and Sweden in the Time of Ivan Mazepa." UQ 15 (1959): 128–32

Horak, S. "The Kiev Academy: A Bridge to Europe in the 17th Century." EEQ 2 (1968): 117–37

Hunczak, T. "The Politics of Religion: The Union of Brest 1596." UI 2–4 (1972): 97–106

Huttenbach, H. "The Ukraine and Muscovite Expansion." In T. Hunczak, ed., Russian Imperialism, 131–66. New Brunswick, NJ, 1974

Ivanytsky, S. "Did the Treaty of Pereiaslav Include a Protectorate?" UQ 10 (1954): 176–82

Kaminski, A. "The Cossack Experiment in Szlachta Democracy in the Polish-Lithuanian Commonwealth: The Hadiach (Hadiacz) Union." HUS 1 (1977): 178–97

Kentrschynskyj, B. "The Political Struggle of Mazepa and Charles XII for Ukrainian Independence." UQ 15 (1959): 241–59

The Kiev Mohyla Academy. Special issue, HUS 8 (1984)

Kohut, Z. "A Gentry Democracy within an Autocracy: The Politics of Hryhorii Poletyka (1723–1784)." HUS 3–4 (1979–80): 507–19

– "The Ukrainian Elite in the 18th Century and Its Integration into the Russian Nobility." In I. Banac and P. Bushkovitch, eds, The Nobility in Russia and Eastern Europe, 65–98. New Haven, 1985

– "The Development of a Little Russian Identity and Ukrainian Nation-building." HUS 10 (1986): 559–76

- *Russian Centralism and Ukrainian Autonomy: Imperial Absorption of the Hetmanate, 1760s–1830s.* Cambridge, MA, 1988
Kortschmaryk, F. *The Kievan Academy and Its Role in the Organization of Education in Russia at the Turn of the Seventeenth Century.* New York, 1976
Krupnytsky, B. "The Mazeppists." *UQ* 4 (1948): 204–14
- "Federalism and the Russian Empire." *Annals* 2 (1952): 239–60
- "The Treaty of Pereiaslav and the Political Orientation of Bohdan Khmelnytsky." *UQ* 10 (1954): 32–40
- "The Swedish-Ukrainian Treaties of Alliance 1708–1709." *UQ* 12 (1956): 45–57
- "The General Characteristics of Pylyp Orlyk." *Annals* 5 (1958): 1247–59
Kulchycky, G. "Three Attempts at Federation in 17th Century Eastern Europe." *NP* 9 (1981): 207–24
Levin, P., and F. Sysyn. "The *Antimaxia* of 1632 and the Polemic over Uniate-Orthodox Relations." *HUS* 9 (1985): 145–65
Levytsky, O. "Socinianism in Poland and South-West Rus'." *Annals* 3 (1953): 485–508
Lewitter, L. "Poland, Ukraine and Russia in the 17th Century." *SEER* 27 (1948): 157–71
Lypynsky, V. "The Ukraine at the Turning Point." *Annals* 3 (1953): 605–19
Mackiw, T. *Prince Mazepa, Hetman of Ukraine.* Chicago, 1967
- "An Imperial Envoy to Hetman Khmelnytsky in 1657." *Annals* 12 (1969–72): 217–27
Manning, C. *Ivan Mazepa, Hetman of Ukraine.* New York, 1957
Medlin, W. "Cultural Crisis in Orthodox Rus' in the Late 16th and Early 17th Centuries as a Problem of Socio-Economic Change." In A. Bland, ed., *The Religious World of Russian Culture,* 173–88. The Hague, 1973
Nadav, M. "The Jewish Community of Nemyriv in 1648." *HUS* 8 (1984): 376–95
O'Brien, C. *Muscovy and Ukraine: From the Pereiaslavl Agreement to the Truce of Andrusovo 1654–1667.* Berkeley, 1963
Ohloblyn, O. "Western Europe and the Ukrainian Baroque." *Annals* 1 (1951): 127–37
- "Where Was the *Istoriia Rusov* Written?" *Annals* 3 (1953): 670–93
- "The Pereyaslav Treaty and Eastern Europe." *UQ* 10 (1954): 41–50
- *The Treaty of Pereyaslav 1654.* Toronto, 1954
- "Ukrainian Autonomists of the 1780s and 1790s and Count P.A. Rumyantsev." *Annals* 6 (1958): 1313–26
Pelenski, J. "The Incorporation of the Ukrainian Lands of Old Rus' into Crown Poland (1569)." In *American Contributions to the Seventh International Congress of Slavists,* 19–52. The Hague, 1973
- "The *Haidamak* Insurrections and the Old Regimes in Eastern Europe." In J. Pelenski, ed., *The American and European Revolutions, 1776–1848: Sociopolitical and Ideological Aspects,* 228–47. Iowa City, 1980
Pernal, A. "The Expenditures of the Crown Treasury for Financing of Diplomacy between Poland and the Ukraine during the Reign of Jan Kazimierz." *HUS* 5 (1981): 102–20

- "The Initial Step Towards the Union of Hadiach." *CSP* 25 (1983): 284–300
Polonska-Vasylenko, N. *The Settlement of Southern Ukraine (1750–1775)*. Special issue, *Annals* 4 (1955)
Pritsak, O. "Kiev and All of Rus': The Fate of a Sacral Idea." *HUS* 10 (1986): 271–8
Prokopovych, V. "The Problem of the Juridical Nature of Ukraine's Union with Muscovy." *Annals* 3 (1955): 917–80
Rosman, M. *The Lords' Jews: Magnates and Jews in the Polish Lithuanian Commonwealth during the 18th Century*. Cambridge, MA, 1988
Scherer, S. "Skovoroda and Society." *UI* 8 (1971): 12–22
- "Beyond Morality: The Moral Teaching and Practice of H.S. Skovoroda, 1722–94." *UI* 18 (1981): 60–73
Senioutovitch-Berezny, V. "The Creation of the Volhynian Nobility and Its Privileges." *Proceedings of the Shevchenko Scientific Society* 2 (1957): 44–6
Serczyk, W. "The Commonwealth and the Cossacks in the First Quarter of the Seventeenth Century." *HUS* 2 (1978): 73–93
Šerech, J. (Shevelov, G.) "Stefan Yavorskyj and the Conflict of Ideologies in the Age of Peter I." *SEER* 30 (1951): 40–62
- "Feofan Prokopovych as Writer and Preacher in His Kievan Period." *Harvard Slavic Studies* 2 (1954): 211–23
Ševčenko, I. "Byzantium and the Eastern Slavs after 1453." *HUS* 2 (1978): 5–25
Subtelny, O. "From the Diary of Pylyp Orlyk." *UI* 6 (1971): 95–104
- "Peter I's Testament: A Reassessment." *SR* 33 (1974): 663–78
- "Great Power Politics in Eastern Europe and the Ukrainian Émigrés, 1709–1742." *CASS* 12 (1978): 136–53
- "Mazepa, Peter I and the Question of Treason." *HUS* 2 (1978): 158–83
- "Russian and the Ukraine: The Difference that Peter I Made." *RR* 39 (1980): 1–17
- *The Mazepists: Ukrainian Separatism in the 18th Century*. Boulder, CO, 1981
- *Domination of Eastern Europe: Native Nobilities and Foreign Absolutism 1500–1715*. Montreal, 1986
Sydorenko, A. *The Kievan Academy in the Seventeenth Century*. Ottawa, 1977
Sysyn, F. "Adam Kysil and the Synods of 1629: An Attempt at Orthodox-Uniate Accommodation in the Reign of Sigismund III." *HUS* 3–4 (1979–80): 826–42
- "Seventeenth Century Views on the Causes of the Khmelnytskyi Uprisings: An Examination of the 'Discourse on the Present Cossack or Peasant War.'" *HUS* 4 (1980): 430–66
- *Between Poland and the Ukraine: The Dilemma of Adam Kysil 1600–1653*. Cambridge, MA, 1985
- "Concepts of Nationhood in Ukrainian Historical Writing, 1620–1690." *HUS* 10 (1986): 393–423
Tazbir, J. "The Political Reversals of Jurij Nemyryč." *HUS* 5 (1981): 306–19
Velychenko, S. "The Origins of the Ukrainian Revolution of 1648." *JUS* 1 (1976): 18–26

- "Bohdan Khmelnytsky and the Rakoczis of Transylvania during the Polish Election of 1648." *JUS* 8 (1983): 3–12
- "The Ukrainian-Rus Lands in Eastern European Politics 1572–1632. Some Preliminary Observations." *EEQ* 19 (1985): 201–8
- "Cossack Ukraine and the Baltic Trade 1600–1648. Observations on an Unresolved Issue." In I. Koropeckyj, ed., *Integration Processes of the Ukrainian Economy: A Historical Perspective.* Cambridge, MA, 1988

Vernadsky, G. *Bohdan, Hetman of Ukraine.* New Haven, 1941

Weinryb, B. "The Hebrew Chronicles on Bohdan Khmelnytskyi and the Cossack-Polish War." *HUS* 1 (1977): 153–77

Williams, G. "Protestants in the Ukraine during the Period of the Polish Lithuanian Commonwealth." *HUS* 2 (1978): 41–72, 184–210

Wójcik, Z. "The Early Period of Pavlo Teterja's Hetmancy in the Right-Bank Ukraine (1661–1663)." *HUS* 3–4 (1979–80): 958–72

Wolff, L. "Vatican Diplomacy and the Uniates of the Ukraine after the First Partition of the Polish-Lithuanian Commonwealth." *HUS* 8 (1984): 396–425

Wynar, L, *The History of Early Ukrainian Printing 1491–1600.* Denver, 1962
- "Ukrainian Cossacks and the Vatican in 1594." *UQ* 21 (1965): 64–78
- "Birth of Democracy on the Dnieper River: The Zaporozhian Kozakdom in the 16th Century." *UQ* 33 (1977): 41–9, 144–56

Yakovliv, A. "*Istoriia Rusov* and Its Author." *Annals* 3 (1953): 620–69
- "Bohdan Khmelnytsky's Treaty with the Tsar of Muscovy in 1654." *Annals* 4 (1955): 904–16

From 1800 to 1914

Sources

Hryhorijiv, N. *The War and Ukrainian Democracy. A Compilation of Documents from the Past and Present.* Toronto, 1945

Kostomarov, M. *Books of Genesis of the Ukrainian People.* New York, 1954

Serbyn, R. "In Defense of an Independent Ukrainian Socialist Movement: Three Letters from Serhii Podolynsky to Valerian Smirnov." *JUS* 7 (1982): 3–32

Historiography

Velychenko, S. "Tsarist Censorship and Ukrainian Historiography, 1828–1904." *CASS*, forthcoming

Studies

Agursky, M. "Ukrainian-Jewish Intermarriages in Rural Areas of the Ukraine in the Nineteenth Century." *HUS* 9 (1985): 139–44

Andrusiak, M. "The Ukrainian National Movement in Galicia." *SEER* 14 (1935): 163–75, 372–9

Bilinsky, Y. "Mykhaylo Drahomanov, Ivan Franko and the Relations between Dnieper Ukraine and Galicia in the Last Quarter of the 19th Century." *Annals* 7 (1959): 1542–66

Bohachevsky-Chomiak, M. *The Spring of a Nation: The Ukrainians in Eastern Galicia in 1848.* Philadelphia, 1967

– "The Ukrainian University in Galicia: A Pervasive Issue." *HUS* 5 (1981): 497–545

– "Feminism in Ukrainian History." *JUS* 7 (1982): 16–30

Brock, P. "Ivan Vahylevych (1811–1866) and the Ukrainian National Movement." *CSP* 14 (1972): 153–90

Chyzhevsky, D. "The Influence of the Philosophy of Schelling (1775–1854) in the Ukraine." *Annals* 5 (1956): 1128–39

Ciuciura, B. "Ukrainian Deputies in the Old Austrian Parliament 1861–1918." *Mitteilungen: Arbeits und Förderungsgemeinschaft der ukrainischen Wissenschaften* 14 (Munich, 1977): 38–56

– "Galicia and Bukovina as Austrian Crown Provinces: Ukrainian Experience in Representative Institutions 1861–1918." *SU* 2 (1984): 175–96

– "Provincial Politics in the Habsburg Empire: The Case of Galicia and Bukovina." *NP* 13 (1985): 247–73

Dmytryshyn, B. "Introduction." In F. Savčenko, *The Suppression of Ukrainian Activities*, v–xxxix. Munich, 1970

Doroshenko, D. "The Uniate Church in Galicia, 1914–1917." *SEER* 12 (1933): 622–7

– "Mykhaylo Drahomanov and the Ukrainian National Movement." *SEER* 16 (1938): 654–66

Elwood, R. *Russian Social Democracy in the Underground: A Study of the RSDRP in the Ukraine, 1907–1914.* Assen, 1974

Flynn, J. "The Affair of Kostomarov's Dissertation: A Case Study of Official Nationalism in Practice." *SEER* 52 (1974): 188–96

Gerus, O. "P.A. Stolypin and the Ukrainian School Question." *UI* 3–4 (1972): 121–6

– "The Ukrainian Question in the Russian Duma, 1906–1917." *SU* 2 (1984): 157–74

Herlihy, P. "Odessa, Staple Trade and Urbanization in New Russia." *JGO* 21 (1974): 121–37

– "The Ethnic Composition of the City of Odessa in the Nineteenth Century." *HUS* 1 (1977): 53–78

– "Death in Odessa: A Study of Population Movements in a Nineteenth-Century City." *Journal of Urban History* 4 (1978): 417–41

– *Odessa, A History 1794–1914.* Cambridge, MA, 1986

Himka, J-P. "Voluntary Artisan Associations and the Ukrainian National Movement in Galicia (the 1870s)." *HUS* 1 (1978): 235–50

– "Priests and Peasants: The Greek Catholic Pastor and the Ukrainian National Movement in Austria, 1867–1900." *CSP* 21 (1979): 1–14

– "Hope in the Tsar: Displaced Naive Monarchism among Ukrainian Peasants of the Habsburg Empire." *Russian History* 7 (1980): 125–38

– "Young Radicals and Independent Statehood: The Idea of a Ukrainian Nation-

State, 1890–1895." *SR* 41 (1982): 219–35
- "The Background to Emigration: Ukrainians of Galicia and Bukovyna, 1848–1914." In M. Lupul, ed., *A Heritage in Transition: Essays in the History of Ukrainians in Canada*, 11–31. Toronto, 1982
- *Socialism in Galicia: The Emergence of Polish Social Democracy and Ukrainian Radicalism, 1860–1890.* Cambridge, MA, 1983
- "Serfdom in Galicia." *JUS* 9 (1984): 3–28
- " The Greek Catholic Church and Nation-Building in Galicia, 1772–1918." *HUS* 8 (1984): 426–52
- *Galician Villagers and the Ukrainian National Movement in the Nineteenth Century.* Edmonton, 1987
Horak, S. "Alexander Herzen, Poles and Ukrainians: A Dilemma in Unity and Conflict." *EEQ* 17 (1983): 185–212
Hryniuk, S. "Peasant Agriculture in East Galicia in the Late Nineteenth Century." *SEER* 63 (1985): 228–43
- "The Peasant and Alcohol in Eastern Galicia in the Late Nineteenth Century: A Note." *JUS* 11 (1986): 75–86
Klier, J. "*Kievlianin* and the Jews: A Decade of Dissillusionment, 1864–1873." *HUS* 5 (1981): 83–101
Kozik, J. *The Ukrainian National Movement in Galicia, 1815–1849.* Edmonton, 1986
Krawchenko, B. "The Social Structure of Ukraine at the Turn of the 20th Century." *EEQ* 16 (1982): 171–81
Luckyj, G. *Between Gogol and Ševčenko: Polarity in Literary Ukraine 1798–1847.* Munich, 1971
- *Panteleimon Kulish: A Sketch of His Life and Times.* Boulder, CO, 1983
Luckyj, G., ed. *Shevchenko and the Critics.* Toronto, 1980
Magocsi, P. "Old Ruthenianism and Russophilism." In P. Debreczeny, ed., *American Contributions to the Ninth Slavic Congress*, vol. II, 305–24. Columbus, OH, 1983
Manning, C. "Gogol and Ukraine." *UQ* 4 (1950): 323–30
Markovits, A., and F. Sysyn, eds. *Nation-building and the Politics of Nationalism: Essays on Austrian Galicia.* Cambridge, MA, 1982
Mirtschuk, J. "The Ukrainian Uniat Church." *SEER* 10 (1931): 377–85
Mishkinsky, M. "The Attitude of the Southern-Russian Workers' Union to the Jews 1880–1881." *HUS* 6 (1982): 191–216
Paneyko, B. "Galicia and the Polish-Ukrainian Problem." *SEER* 9 (1930–31): 567–87
Papazian, P. "N. Kostomarov and the Cyril-Methodian Ideology." *RR* 29 (1970): 59–73
Pipes, R. "Peter Struve and Ukrainian Nationalism." *HUS* 3–4 (1979–80): part 2, 675–83
Pritsak, O. "The Pogroms of 1881." *HUS* 11 (1987): 8–43
Pritsak, O., and J. Reshetar. "The Ukraine and the Dialectics of Nation-Building." In D. Treadgold, ed., *The Development of the USSR*, 236–67. Seattle and London, 1964

Prymak, T. "Herzen on Poland and Ukraine." *JUS* 7 (1982): 31–40
– "Hrushevsky's Constitutional Project of 1905." *NP*, forthcoming
Revutsky, V. "The Act of Ems (1876) and Its Effect on Ukrainian Theatre." *NP* 5 (1977): 67–78
Rudnytsky, I.L. "Mykhaylo Drahomanov as a Political Theorist." *Mykhaylo Drahomanov: A Symposium and Selected Writings*. Special issue, *Annals* 2 (1952): 70–130
– "The Intellectual Origins of Modern Ukraine." *Annals* 6 (1958): 1381–1405
– "The Role of the Ukraine in Modern History." In D. Treadgold, ed., *The Development of the USSR*, 211–28. Seattle and London, 1964
– "The Ukrainians in Galicia under Austrian Rule." *Austrian History Yearbook* 3 (1967): 394–429
– "Mykhailo Drahomanov and the Problem of Ukrainian-Jewish Relations." *CSP* 11 (1969): 182–98
– "The Ukrainian National Movement on the Eve of the First World War." *EEQ* 11 (1977): 141–54
– "Franciszek Duchinski and His Impact on Ukrainian Political Thought." *HUS* 3–4 (1979–80): 690–705
– "Observations on the Problem of 'Historical' and 'Non-historical' Nations." *HUS* 5 (1981): 358–68
– *Essays in Modern Ukrainian History*. Edmonton, 1987
Saunders, D. *The Ukrainian Impact on Russian Culture 1750–1850*. Edmonton, 1985
Serbyn, R. "Ukrainian Writers on the Jewish Question: In the Wake of the *Illustratsiia* Affair of 1858." *NP* 9 (1981): 99–104
Siegelbaum, L. "The Odessa Grain Trade: A Case Study in Urban Growth and Development in Tsarist Russia." *Journal of European Economic History* 9 (1980): 113–51
Sirka, A. *The Nationality Question in Austrian Education: The Case of the Ukrainians in Galicia 1867–1914*. Frankfurt am Main, 1979
Solchanyk, R. "Mykhailo Drahomanov and the Ems Ukase: A Note on the Ukrainian Question at the 1878 International Literary Congress in Paris." *HUS* 1 (1977): 225–9
Theide, R. "Industry and Urbanization in New Russia from 1860 to 1910." In M. Hamm., ed. *The City in Russian History*. Lexington, KY, 1976
Treadgold, D. *The Great Siberian Migration: Government and Peasant in Resettlement from Emancipation to the First World War*. Princeton, 1957
Weinstein, H. "Land Hunger and Nationalism in the Ukraine 1905–1917." *Journal of Economic History* 2 (1942): 24–35
Wilcher, A. "Ivan Franko and Theodor Herzl: To the Genesis of Franko's *Mojsej.*" *HUS* 6 (1982): 233–41
Yaremko, M. *Galicia: From Separation to Unity*. New York, 1967
Yurkevich, M. "A Forerunner of National Communism: Lev Iurkevych 1885–1918." *JUS* 7 (1982): 50–6

20th-Century Ukraine

REVOLUTION AND CIVIL WAR

Sources

Hryhorijiv, N. *The War and Ukrainian Democracy. A Compilation of Documents from the Past and Present.* Toronto, 1945

"The Four 'Universals' of the Central Rada." In T. Hunczak, ed., *The Ukraine, 1917–1921: A Study in Revolution,* 382–95. Cambridge, MA, 1977

Margolin, A. *From a Political Diary: Russia, Ukraine and America 1905–1945.* New York, 1946

Mazlakh, S., and V. Shakhrai. *On the Current Situation in the Ukraine.* P. Potichnyj, ed. Ann Arbor, 1970

Pigido, F., ed. *Material Concerning Ukrainian-Jewish Relations during the Years of the Revolution (1917–1921). Collections of Documents and Testimonies by Prominent Jewish Political Workers.* Munich, 1956

Historiography

Symonenko, R. "The Falsifiers Do Not Let Up: A Soviet Critique of Ukrainian Historiography and Its Studies of the Revolution." *New Review* 8 (1972): 37–50

Studies

Adams, A. "The Bolsheviks and the Ukrainian Front in 1918–1919." SEER 36 (1958): 396–417

– "The Bolshevik Administration in the Ukraine, 1918." *The Review of Politics* 20 (1958): 289–306

– "Awakening of Ukraine." SR 22 (1963): 217–23

– *Bolsheviks in the Ukraine: The Second Campaign, 1918–1919.* New Haven, 1963

Andriewsky, O. "The Triumph of Particularism: The Kuban Cossacks in 1917." JUS 4 (1979): 29–41

Arshinov, P. *History of the Makhnovist Movement 1918–1921.* Detroit, 1974

Borys, J. *The Sovietization of Ukraine 1917–1923.* Edmonton, 1980

Brinkley, G. *The Volunteer Army and the Allied Intervention in South Russia 1917–1921.* Notre Dame, 1966

Chikalenko, L. "Ukrainian-Russian Negotiations in 1920." *Annals* 7 (1959): 1647–55

Chubaty, N. "The National Revolution in Ukraine 1917–1919." UQ 1 (1945): 32–7

Dmytryshyn, B. "German Occupation of the Ukraine 1918: Some New Evidence." *Slavic and East European Studies* 10 (1965–66): 79–92

Dushnyk, W. "The Russian Provisional Government and the Ukrainian Central Rada." UQ 23 (1967): 109–29

Epstein, J. "German-Ukrainian Operations during World War I." UQ 15 (1959): 162–8

Eudin, X. "The German Occupation of the Ukraine in 1918." *RR* 1 (1941): 90–103

Fedyshyn, O. *Germany's Drive to the East and the Ukrainian Revolution 1917–1918.* New Brunswick, NJ, 1971

Gauthier, S. "The Popular Base of Ukrainian Nationalism in 1917." *SR* 38 (1979): 30–47

Gerus, O. "Manifestation of the Cossack Idea in Modern History: The Cossack Legacy and Its Impact." *UI* 19 (1982): 22–39

Holubnychy, V. "The 1917 Agrarian Revolution in Ukraine." In I. Koropeckyj, ed., *Soviet Regional Economics: Selected Works of Vsevolod Holubnychy,* 3–65. Edmonton, 1982

Hunczak, T. "Sir Lewis Namier and the Struggle for Eastern Galicia, *1918–1920.*" *HUS* 1 (1977): 198–210

Hunczak, T., ed. *The Ukraine, 1917–1921: A Study in Revolution.* Cambridge, MA, 1977

Kamenetsky, I. "The Ukrainian Central Rada and the Status of German and Austrian Troops after the Treaty of Brest-Litovsk." *UI* 20 (1983): 119–27

– "Hrushevsky and Ukrainian Foreign Policy 1917–1918." *UI* 21 (1984): 82–102

Kenez, P. *Civil War in South Russia, 1917–1920.* Berkeley, 1977

Liber, G. "Ukrainian Nationalism and the 1918 Law on National-Personal Autonomy." *NP,* 15 (1987): 22–42

Maistrenko, I. *Borotbism: A Chapter in the History of Ukrainian Communism.* New York, 1954

Malet, M. *Nestor Makhno in the Russian Civil War.* London, 1982

Martos, B. "The First Universal of the Ukrainian Central Rada." *UQ* 24 (1968): 22–37

Mazepa, I. "The Ukraine under Bolshevik Rule." *SEER* 12 (1934): 323–46

Meyer, H. "The Germans in the Ukraine 1918." *SR* 9 (1949–50): 105–15

Magosci, P. "The Ruthenian Decision to Unite with Czechoslovakia." *SR* 34 (1975): 360–81

Moskalenko, A. "The Hetmanate in 1918 and Bolshevik Aggression in Ukraine." *UR* 11 (1964): 81–4

Nahayevsky, I. *History of the Modern Ukrainian State 1917–1923.* Munich, 1966

Palij, M. *The Anarchism of Nestor Makhno, 1917–1921: An Aspect of the Ukrainian Revolution.* Seattle, 1976

Paneyko, B. "The Conditions for Ukrainian Independence." *SEER* 2 (1923–24): 336–45

Peters, V. *Nestor Makhno: The Life of an Anarchist.* Winnipeg, 1970

Pidhainy, O. *The Ukrainian-Polish Problem in the Dissolution of the Russian Empire 1914–1917.* Toronto, 1962

– *The Formation of the Ukrainian Republic.* Toronto, 1966

– "The Kiev Bolsheviks and Lenin's April Theses." *Eastern Europe. Historical Essays,* 33–8. Toronto, 1969

Pipes, R. *The Formation of the Soviet Union: Communism and Nationalism, 1917–1923.* Cambridge, MA, 1954

Procyk, A. "Treatment of the Ukrainian Question at the Yassy Conference in November 1918." In *Oleksander Ohloblyn Festschrift,* 400–10. New York, 1977

Prymak, T. "The First All-Ukrainian Congress of Soviets and Its Antecedents." *JUS* 4 (1979): 3–19

– "Mykhailo Hrushevsky: Populist or Statist." *JUS* 5 (1981): 65–78

– *Mykhailo Hrushevsky.* Toronto, 1987

Reshetar, J. *The Ukrainian Revolution, 1917–1920: A Study in Nationalism.* Princeton, 1952

– "Lenin on the Ukraine." *Annals* 9 (1961): 3–11

– "The Ukrainian Revolution in Retrospect." *CSP* 10 (1968): 116–32

Rudnytsky, I.L. "Volodymyr Vynnychenko's Ideas in Light of His Political Writings." *Annals* 16 (1984–85): 251–74

Saunders, D. "Britain and the Ukrainian Question, 1912–1920." *The English Historical Review* 103 (1988): 40–68

Shandruk, P. *Arms of Valor.* New York, 1959

Shulhyn, O. "The Doctrine of Wilson and the Building of the Ukrainian National Republic." *UQ* 12 (1956): 326–31

Sonevytsky, L. "Bukovina in the Diplomatic Negotiation of 1914." *Annals* 7 (1959): 1586–1629

– "The Ukrainian Question in R.H. Lord's Writings on the Paris Peace Conference of 1919." *Annals* 10 (1962–63): 68–84

Stachiw, M. "The System of the Hetman Government in Ukraine in 1918." *Proceedings of the Shevchenko Scientific Society* 2 (1957): 51–3

– *Ukraine and Russia: An Outline of the History of the Political and Military Relations, December 1917–April 1918.* New York, 1967

Stachiw, M., and J. Sztendera. *Western Ukraine at the Turning Point of European History, 1918–1923.* New York, 1971

Voline (Eichenbaum V.). *The Uknown Revolution (Kronstadt 1921, Ukraine 1918–1921).* New York, 1955

UKRAINIAN/JEWISH RELATIONS 1917-1921

Bilinsky, Y. "Ukrainians and Jews: A Review Article." *Annals* 14 (1978–80): 244–57

Bykovsky, L. *Solomon I. Goldelman: A Portrait of a Politician and Educator (1885–1974). A Chapter in Ukrainian Jewish Relations.* New York, 1980

Goldelman, S. "Patterns of Life of an Ethnic Minority." *Annals* 7 (1959): 1567–85

– *Jewish National Autonomy in Ukraine, 1917–1920.* Chicago, 1968

Heifetz, E. *The Slaughter of the Jews in the Ukraine in 1919.* New York, 1921

Hunczak, T. "A Reappraisal of Simon Petliura and Jewish-Ukrainian Relations 1917–1921," and Z. Szajkowski, "A Rebuttal." *Jewish Social Studies* 31 (1969): 163–213

Lichten, J. "A Study of Ukrainian-Jewish Relations." *Annals* 5 (1956): 1160–77
Mintz, M. "The Secretariat of Internationality Affairs (*Sekretariat mizh-natsionalnykh sprav*) of the Ukrainian General Secretariat, 1917–1918." *HUS* 6 (1982): 25–41
Pogroms in the Ukraine 1917–1920 under the Ukrainian Governments. London, 1927
Schechtman, J. "Jewish Community Life in the Ukraine, *1917–1919*" In G. Frumkin, et al., eds, *Russian Jewry, 1917–1967*, 39–57. New York, 1969
Schulman, E. "Pogroms in Ukraine in 1919." *The Jewish Quarterly* 17 (1966): 159–66
Trotsky, I. "Jewish Pogroms in the Ukraine and in Byelorussia." In J. Frumkin, et al., eds, *Russian Jewry 1917–1967*, 72–87. New York, 1969
Ukrainians and Jews: A Symposium. New York, 1966

SOVIET UKRAINE: THE 1920S

Sources

Khvylovy, M. *The Cultural Renaissance in Ukraine: Polemical Pamphlets 1925–1926*. M. Shkandrij, ed. and trans. Edmonton, 1986

Bibliography

Lawrynenko, J. *Ukrainian Communism and Soviet Russian Policy toward the Ukraine: An Annotated Bibliography*. New York, 1953

Studies

Bilinsky, Y. "Mykola Skrypnyk and Petro Shelest." In J. Azreal, ed., *Soviet Nationality Policies and Practices*, 105–43. New York, 1978
Bociurkiw, B. "The Ukrainian Autocephalous Orthodox Church, 1920–1930: A Case Study in Religious Modernization." In D. Dunn, ed., *Religion and Modernization in the Soviet Union*, 105–43. Boulder, CO, 1977
– "Ukrainization Movements within the Russian Orthodox Church and the Ukrainian Autocephalous Orthodox Church." *HUS* 3–4 (1979–80): part I, 92–111
– "The Soviet Destruction of the Ukrainian Orthodox Church 1929–1936." *JUS* 12 (1987): 3–21
Czajkowski, M. "Volodymyr Vynnychenko and His Mission to Moscow and Kharkiv." *JUS* 5 (1978): 6–24
Dmytryshyn, B. "National and Social Composition of the Membership of the Communist Party (Bolshevik) of the Ukraine 1918–1925." *Journal of Central European Affairs* 17 (1957): 243–58
Fedenko, P. "Mykola Skrypnyk: His National Policy, Conviction and Rehabilitation." *UR* 5 (1957): 56–72
Holubnychy, V. "The Views of M. Volobuev and V. Dobrohaiyev and Party Criticism." *UR* 3 (1956): 5–12

- "Outline History of the Communist Party of Ukraine." In I. Koropeckyj, ed., *Soviet Regional Economics: The Selected Works of Vsevolod Holubnychy*, 66–137. Edmonton, 1982

Krawchenko, B. "The Impact of Industrialization on the Social Structure of Ukraine." CSP 22 (1980): 338–57

Liber, G. "Language, Literature and Book Publishing in the Ukrainian SSR, 1923–1928." SR 41 (1982): 673–85

Luckyj, G. *Literary Politics in the Soviet Ukraine 1917–1934*. New York, 1956

Mace, J. *Communism and the Dilemmas of National Liberation: National Communism in Soviet Ukraine 1918–1933*. Cambridge, MA, 1983

- "The *Komitety nezamozhnykh selian* and the Structure of Soviet Rule in the Ukrainian Countryside, 1920–1933." SS 35 (1983): 487–503

Nakai, K. "Soviet Agricultural Policies in the Ukraine and the 1921–1922 Famine." HUS 6 (1982): 43–61

Palij, M. "The First Experiment of National Communism in Ukraine in the 1920s and 1930s." NP 12 (1984): 85–106

Reshetar, J. "Ukrainian Nationalism and the Orthodox Church." SR 10 (1951): 39–49

- "National Deviations in the Soviet Union." SR 12 (1953): 162–74

Serbyn, R. "The Famine of *1921–1923*: A Model for 1932–1933?" In R. Serbyn and B. Krawchenko, eds, *Famine in Ukraine 1932–1933*, 147–78. Edmonton, 1986

Stachiw, M. "Soviet Statehood in Ukraine from a Sociological Aspect." UQ 16 (1959): 38–47

Sullivant, R. *Soviet Politics and the Ukraine 1917–1957*. New York, 1962

Veryha, W. "Famine in Ukraine in 1921–1923 and the Soviet Government's Countermeasures." NP 12 (1984): 265–86

Weinstein, H. "Language and Education in the Soviet Ukraine." SR 1 (1941): 124–48

SOVIET UKRAINE: THE 1930S

Sources

The Black Deeds of the Kremlin: A White Book, vol.1. Toronto, 1953

Studies

Borys, J. "Who Ruled the Soviet Ukraine in Stalin's Time?" CSP 14 (1972): 213–33

Dmytryshyn, B. *Moscow and the Ukraine 1918–1953: A Study of Russian Bolshevik Nationality Policy*. New York, 1956

Dragan, A. *Vinnytsia: A Forgotten Holocaust*. Jersey City, 1986

Kostiuk, H. *Stalinist Rule in the Ukraine.* New York, 1960
Krawchenko, B. "The Impact of Industrialization on the Social Structure of
    Ukraine." CSP 22 (1980): 338–57
– *Social Change and National Consciousness in Twentieth-Century Ukraine.* New York,
    1985
Manning, C. *Ukraine under the Soviets.* New York, 1953
Sullivant, R. "The Agrarian-Industrial Dichotomy in the Ukraine as a Factor in
    Soviet Nationality Policy." *Annals* 9 (1961): 110–25

THE GREAT FAMINE OF 1932–33

Sources

The Black Deeds of the Kremlin: The Great Famine in Ukraine in 1932–1933, vol. 2. De-
    troit, 1955
Carynnyk, M., B. Kordan, and L. Luciuk, eds. *The Foreign Office and the Famine:
    British Documents on Ukraine and the Great Famine of 1932–1933.* Kingston, 1988
Dolot, M. *Execution of Hunger: The Hidden Holocaust.* New York, 1985
The Great Famine in Ukraine: The Unknown Holocaust. Jersey City, 1983
Grigorenko, P. *Memoirs.* London, 1983
Hryshko, W. *The Ukrainian Holocaust of 1933.* Toronto, 1983
Kopelev, L. *The Education of a True Believer.* New York, 1977
Kravchenko, V. *I Chose Freedom.* New York, 1946
Solovey, D., ed. *The Golgotha of Ukraine: Eye Witness Accounts of the Famine in
    Ukraine.* New York, 1953
Woropay, O. *The Ninth Circle.* Cambridge, MA, 1983

Historiography and Bibliography

Brovkin, V. "Robert Conquest's *Harvest of Sorrow:* A Challenge to the Revision-
    ists." HUS 11 (1987): 234–45
Luckyj, G. *Keeping A Record. Literary Purges in Soviet Ukraine (1930s): A Bio-
    Bibliography.* Edmonton-Toronto, 1987
Pidhainy, A. "Bibliography of the Great Famine in Ukraine, 1932–1933." *New Re-
    view* 13 (1973): 32–68
Radziejowski, J. "Collectivization in Ukraine in Light of Soviet Historiography."
    JUS 5 (1980): 3–17

Studies

Ammende, E. *Human Life in Russia.* London, 1936; reprint Cleveland, 1984
Anderson B., and B. Silver. "Demographic Analysis and Population Catastrophes
    in the USSR." SR 44 (1985): 517–36

Carynnyk, M. "The Famine the 'Times' Couldn't Find." *Commentary*, November 1983, 32–40

Conquest, R. *The Harvest of Sorrow: Soviet Collectivization and the Terror-Famine.* New York, 1986

Crowl, J. *Angels in Stalin's Paradise: Western Reporters in Soviet Russia, 1917–1937.* Washington, 1982

Dalrymple, D. "The Soviet Famine of 1932–1934." *SS* 15 (1934): 250–84

– "The Soviet Famine of 1932–1934: Some Further References." *SS* 16 (1965): 471–4

Holubnychy, V. "The Causes of the Famine of 1932–1933." *Meta* (Toronto, 1979): 22–5

Krawchenko, B. "The Man-Made Famine of 1932–1933 in Soviet Ukraine." *Conflict Quarterly* 4 (1984): 29–39

Mace, J. "Politics and History in Soviet Ukraine, 1921–1933." *NP* 10 (1982): 157–79

– "Famine and Nationalism in Soviet Ukraine." *Problems of Communism*, May–June 1984, 37–50

– "The Man-Made Famine of 1933 in Soviet Ukraine: What Happened and Why?" In I. Charny, ed., *Proceedings of the International Conference on the Holocaust and Genocide.* Boulder, CO, 1984

Maksudov, S. "The Geography of the Soviet Famine of 1933." *JUS* 8 (1983): 52–8

Rosefielde, S. "Excess Collectivization Deaths, 1929–1933: New Demographic Evidence." *SR* 43 (1984): 83–8

Serbyn, R., and B. Krawchenko, eds. *Famine in Ukraine, 1932–1933.* Edmonton, 1986

Wheatcroft, S. "New Demographic Evidence on Collectivization Deaths: A Rejoinder to Steven Rosefielde." *SR* 44 (1985): 505–8

WESTERN UKRAINE BETWEEN THE WARS

Bohachevsky-Chomiak, M. *Feminists despite Themselves: Women in Ukrainian Community Life, 1884–1939.* Edmonton, 1988

Budurowycz, B. "The Ukrainian Problem in International Politics, October 1938 to March 1939." *CSP* 3 (1958): 59–75

– "Poland and the Ukrainian Problem, 1921–1939." *CSP* 25 (1983): 473–500

Horak, S. *Poland and Her National Minorities, 1919–1939.* New York, 1961

Magocsi, P. *The Shaping of a National Identity: Subcarpathian Rus', 1848–1948.* Cambridge, MA, 1978

Manning, C. "The Linguistic Question in Carpatho-Ukraine." *UQ* 10 (1954): 247–51

Motyl, A. "The Rural Origins of the Communist and Nationalist Movements in Wolyn Wojewodztwo, 1921–1939." *SR* 37 (1978): 412–20

– *The Turn to the Right: The Ideological Origins and Development of Ukrainian Nationalism 1919–1929.* Boulder, CO, 1980

– "Ukrainian Nationalist Political Violence in Inter-War Poland, 1921–1939." *EEQ*

19 (1985): 45–54
- "Viacheslav Lypynskyi and the Ideology and Politics of Ukrainian Monar-
chism." CSP 27 (1985): 31–48
Orzell, L. "A 'Hotly Disputed' Issue: Eastern Galicia at the Paris Peace Confer-
ence." PR 25 (1980): 49–68
Pelenski, J., ed. *The Political and Social Ideas of Vjačeslav Lypynskyj*. Special issue,
HUS 9 (1985)
Radziejowski. J. *The Communist Party of Western Ukraine, 1919–1929*. Edmonton,
1983
Rudnytsky, I.L. "Carpatho-Ukraine: A People in Search of Their Identity." EEQ 19
(1985): 139–59
Shandor, V. "Carpatho-Ukraine and the International Bargaining of 1918–1939."
UQ 10 (1954): 235–46
Solchanyk, R. "The Foundation of the Communist Movement in Eastern Galicia
1919–1921." SR 30 (1971): 774–94
Sole, A. "The Jews of Subcarpathian Ruthenia, 1918–1938." In *The Jews of Czechoslo-
vakia*, vol. 2, 401–39. Philadelphia–New York, 1968
Stercho, P. *Diplomacy of Double Morality: Europe's Crossroads in Carpatho-Ukraine
1919–1939*. New York, 1971
Wynot, E. "The Ukrainians and the Polish Regime, 1937–1939." UI 7 (1970): 44–60
- "Poland's Christian Minorities 1919–1939." NP 13 (1985): 209–46

UKRAINE IN THE SECOND WORLD WAR

Sources

"Documents relating to Ukrainian Nationalists during the Second World War." In
Y. Boshyk, ed., *Ukraine during World War II: History and Its Aftermath*, 163–246.
Edmonton, 1986
Luciuk, L., and B. Kordan, eds. *Anglo-American Prespectives on the Ukrainian Ques-
tion 1938–1951: A Documentary Collection*. Vestal, NY, 1987
Mirchuk, P. *In the German Mills of Death*. New York, 1975
Potichnyj, P., and Y. Shtendera, eds. *The Political Thought of the Ukrainian Under-
ground 1943–1951*. Edmonton, 1986
Shumuk, D. *Life Sentence: Memoirs of a Ukrainian Political Prisoner*. I. Jaworsky, ed.
I. Jaworsky and H. Kowalska, trans. Edmonton, 1984

Historiography

Veryha, W., "The 'Galicia' Ukrainian Division in Polish and Soviet Literature." UQ
36 (1980): 253–70

Studies

Armstrong, J. *Ukrainian Nationalism, 1939–1945*. New York, 1963; reprint Littleton, CO, 1980

– "Collaborationism in World War II: The Integral Nationalist Variant in Eastern Europe." *Journal of Modern History* 40 (1968): 396–410

Boshyk, Y., ed., *Ukraine during World War II: History and Its Aftermath*. Edmonton, 1986

Dallin, A. *German Rule in Russia 1941–1945: A Study in Occupation Policies*. 2nd ed. Boulder, CO, 1981

Dmytryshyn, V. "The Nazis and the SS Volunteer Division 'Galicia.'" *SR* 15 (1956): 1–10

Elliot, M. *Pawns of Yalta: Soviet Refugees and America's Role in Their Repatriation*. Urbana, 1982

Fireside, H. *Icon and Swastika: The Russian Orthodox Church under Nazi and Soviet Control*. Cambridge, MA, 1971

Friedman, P. "Ukrainian-Jewish Relations during the Nazi Occupation." *YIVO, Annual of Jewish Social Science* 12 (1959): 259–96

Heike, W. *The Ukrainian Division "Galicia," 1943–1945: A Memoir*. Toronto, 1988

Heiman, L. "We Fought For Ukraine – The Story of Jews with the UPA." *UQ* 23 (1964): 33–44

Hunczak, T., ed. *The Second World War in Ukraine*. Forthcoming

Kamenetsky, I. *Hitler's Occupation of Ukraine, 1941–1944: A Study of Totalitarian Imperialism*. Milwaukee, 1956

– *Secret Nazi Plans for Eastern Europe: A Study of Lebensraum Policies*. New York, 1964

– "The National Socialist Policy in Slovenia and Western Ukraine during World War II. " *Annals* 14 (1978–80): 39–67

Kosyk, W. "Ukraine's Losses during the Second World War." *UR* 33 (1985): 9–19

– *The Third Reich and Ukraine*. Forthcoming

Lewin, K. "Metropolitan Andreas Sheptytsky and the Jewish Community in Galicia." *Annals* 7 (1959): 1656–68

Marples, D. "Western Ukraine and Western Belorussia under Soviet Occupation: The Development of Socialist Farming, 1939–1941." *CSP* 27 (1985): 158–77

Possony, S. "The Ukrainian-Jewish Problem: A Historical Retrospective." *UQ* 31 (1975): 139–51

Prociuk, S. "Human Losses in the Ukraine in World War I and II." *Annals* 13 (1973–77): 23–50

Reitlinger, G. *The House Built on Sand: The Conflicts of German Policy in Russia, 1939–1945*. Westport, 1960

Sodol, P. *UPA: A Brief Combat History of the Ukrainian Insurgent Army, 1942–1947*. New York, 1987

Szporluk, R. "War by Other Means." *SR* 44 (1985): 20–6

Tys-Krokhmaliuk, Y. *UPA Warfare in Ukraine: Strategical, Tactical and Organizational Problems of Ukrainian Resistance in World War II*. New York, 1972
The Ukrainian Insurgent Army in the Fight for Freedom. New York, 1954
"Ukrainians in World War II: A Symposium." *NP* 10 (1982): 1–40
Wytwycky, B. *The Other Holocaust: Many Circles of Hell*. Washington, 1980

POST-SECOND WORLD WAR UKRAINE

Historiography

Armstrong, J. "New Prospects for Analyzing the Evolution of Ukrainian Society." *UQ* 29 (1973): 349–57
Bilas, L. "How History Is Written in the Soviet Ukraine." *UR* 5 (1958): 39–47
Horak, S. "Ukrainian Historiography, 1953–1963." *SR* 24 (1965): 258–72
– "Soviet Historiography and the New Nationalities Policy: A Case Study of Ukraine and Belorussia." In J. Shapiro and P. Potichnyj, eds, *Change and Adaptation in Soviet and East European Politics*. 201–16. New York, 1976
Krupnytsky, B. "Trends in Modern Ukrainian Historiography." *UQ* 6 (1950): 337–45
Pelenski, J. "Soviet Ukrainian Historiography after World War II." *JGO* 12 (1964): 375–418
– "Recent Ukrainian Writing." *Survey* 59 (1966): 102–12
Shteppa, K. "The Lesser Evil Formula." In C. Black, ed., *Rewriting Russian History*. 107–19. New York, 1962
Subtelny, O. "The Soviet Ukrainian Historical Journal." *Recenzija* 1 (1972): 38–48
Szporluk, R. "National History as a Political Battleground: The Case of Ukraine and Belorussia." In M. Pap, ed., *Russian Empire*, 131–50. Cleveland, 1985
Tillet, L. *The Great Friendship: Soviet Historians on the Non-Russian Nationalities*. Chapel Hill, 1969
Velychenko, S. "The Origins of the Current Soviet Interpretation of Ukrainian History: A Case Study of Policy Formulation." *Forschungen zur osteuropaische Geschichte* 46 (1990): forthcoming
Wynar, L. "The Ukrainian-Russian Confrontation in Historiography." *UQ* 30 (1974): 13–25
– "The Present State of Ukrainian Historiography: A Brief Overview." *NP* 7 (1979): 1–25

Studies

Bandera, V., and Z. Melnyk, eds. *The Soviet Economy in Regional Prespective*. New York, 1973
Bilinsky, Y. "The Soviet Education Laws of 1958–1959 and Soviet Nationality Policy." *SS* 14 (1962): 138–57

- *The Second Soviet Republic: The Ukraine after World War II.* New Brunswick, NJ, 1964
- "Education of the Non-Russian Peoples of the USSR, 1917–1967." *SR* 28 (1968): 411–43
- "The Incorporation of Western Ukraine and Its Impact on Politics and Society in Soviet Ukraine." In R. Szporluk, ed., *The Influence of East Europe and the Soviet West on the USSR,* 180–228. New York, 1976
- "Shcherbytsky, Ukraine and Kremlin Politics." *Problems of Communism* 32 (1983): 1–20
Clem, R., ed. *The Soviet West: Interplay between Nationality and Social Organization.* New York, 1975
Hodnett, G. "The Views of Petro Shelest." *Annals* 14 (1978–80): 226–34
Hodnett, G., and P. Potichnyj. *The Ukraine and the Czechoslovak Crisis.* Canberra, 1970
Isajiw, W. "Urban Migration and Social Change in Contemporary Soviet Ukraine." *CSP* 26 (1984): 56–66
Kolasky, J. *Education in Soviet Ukraine: A Study in Discrimination and Russification.* Toronto, 1968
- *Two Years in Soviet Ukraine.* Toronto, 1970
Koropeckyj, I., ed. *The Ukraine within the USSR : An Economic Balance Sheet.* New York, 1977
- "A Century of Moscow-Ukraine Economic Relations: An Interpretation." *HUS* 5 (1981): 467–96
- *Integration Processes in the Ukrainian Economy: A Historical Perspective.* Cambridge, MA, 1988
- *Studies in Ukrainian Economics.* Edmonton, 1988
Krawchenko, B., ed. *Ukraine after Shelest.* Edmonton, 1983
Lewytzkyj, B. *Politics and Society in Soviet Ukraine 1953–1980.* Edmonton, 1984
Marples, D. "The Kulak in Post-War USSR: The West Ukrainian Example." *SS* 36 (1984): 560–70
- "The Soviet Collectivization of Western Ukraine." *NP* 13 (1985): 24–44
- *Chernobyl and Nuclear Power in the USSR.* New York, 1986
Motyl, A. "The Foreign Relations of the Ukrainian SSR." *HUS* 6 (1982): 62–78
Pennar, J., I. Bakalo, and G. Bereday. "The Ukrainian and Belorussian Soviet Socialist Republics and Their Schools." In J. Pennar, I. Bakalo, and G. Bereday, eds, *Modernization and Diversity in Soviet Education,* 215–34. New York, 1971
Perfecky, G. "The Status of the Ukrainian Language in the Ukrainian SSR." *EEQ* 21 (1987): 207–30
Potichnyj, P., ed. *Ukraine in the Seventies.* Oakville, 1975
Sawczuk, K. *The Ukraine in the United Nations Organization: A Study of Soviet Foreign Policy 1944–1950.* New York, 1975
Shevelov, G. "The Language Question in Ukraine in the Twentieth Century." *HUS* 10 (1986): 71–170 and 11 (1987): 118–224
Szporluk, R. "Kiev as Ukraine's Primate City." *HUS* 3–4 (1979–80): part 2, 843–9

NATIONALITY ISSUES

Bilinsky, Y. "Assimilation and Ethnic Assertiveness among Ukrainians of the Soviet Union." In E. Goldhagen, ed., *Ethnic Minorities in the Soviet Union*, 147–84. New York, 1968
– "The Concept of the Soviet People and Its Implications for Soviet Nationality Policy." *Annals* 14 (1978–80): 87–133
Birch, J. "The Ukrainian Nationalist Movement in the USSR since 1956." *UR* 17 (1970): 2–47
Farmer, K. *Ukrainian Nationalism in the Post-Stalin Era: Myth, Symbol and Ideology in Soviet Nationalities Policy*. The Hague, 1980
"The Kichko Affair: Additional Documents." *Soviet Jewish Affairs* 1 (1971): 108–13
Motyl, A. *Will the Non-Russians Rebel? State, Ethnicity and Stability in the USSR*. Ithaca and London, 1987
Smal-Stotsky, R. *The Nationality Problem of the Soviet Union and Russian Communist Imperialism*. Milwaukee, 1952
Solchanyk, R. "Molding 'the Soviet People': The Role of Ukraine and Belorussia." *JUS* 8 (1983): 3–18
Szporluk, R. "Nationalities and the Russian Problem in the USSR: An Historical Outline." *Journal of International Affairs* 27 (1973): 22–40
– "The Ukraine and the Ukrainians." In Z. Katz, et al., eds, *Handbook of Major Soviet Nationalities*, 21–48. New York, 1975
– "West Ukraine and West Belorussia: Historical Tradition, Social Communication and Linguistic Assimilation." *SS* 31 (1979): 76–98
– "The Ukraine and Russia." In R. Conquest, ed., *The Last Empire: Nationality and the Soviet Future*. 151–82. Stanford, 1986
Tillet, L. "Ukrainian Nationalism and the Fall of Shelest." *SR* 34 (1975): 752–68
Wexler, P. *Purism and Language: A Study of Modern Ukrainian and Belorussian Nationalism, 1940–1967*. Bloomington, 1974

UKRAINIAN DISSENT

Sources

Browne, M. *Ferment in the Ukraine: Documents by V. Chornovil, I. Kandyba, L. Lukianenko, V. Moroz, and Others*. London, 1971
Chornovil, V. *The Chornovil Papers*. New York, 1968
Dzyuba, I. *Internationalism or Russification: A Study of the Soviet Nationalities Problem*. London, 1968
Moroz, V. *Report From the Beria Reservation*. Ed. and trans. by J. Kolasky. Toronto, 1974
– *Boomerang: The Works of Valentyn Moroz*. Baltimore, 1974
Osadchy, M. *Cataract*. New York, 1976

Plyushch, L. *History's Carnival: A Dissident's Autobiography*. New York and London, 1977

Sverstiuk, I. *Clandestine Essays*. Introduction and trans. by G. Luckyj. Cambridge, MA, 1976

The Ukrainian Herald: Ethnocide of Ukrainians in the USSR. Baltimore, 1976

Verba, L., and B. Yasen, eds. *The Human Rights Movement in Ukraine: Documents of the Ukrainian Helsinki Group*. Baltimore, 1980

Bibliographies

Jones, L., and L. Pendzey. "Dissent in Ukraine: A Bibliography." NP 6 (1978): 64–70

Liber, G., and A. Mostovych. *Nonconformity and Dissent in the Ukrainian SSR, 1955–1975: An Annotated Bibliography*. Cambridge, MA, 1976

Studies

Bilinsky, Y. "Political Aspirations of Dissidents in Ukraine." UI 15 (1978): 30–9

Himka, J-P. "Leonid Plyusch: The Ukrainian Marxist Resurgent." JUS 5 (1980): 61–79

Kamenetsky, I. ed. *Nationalism and Human Rights: Processes of Modernization in the USSR*. Littleton, CO, 1977

Klejner, I. "Ukrainian Dissidents and the Jews." *Soviet Jewish Affairs* 11 (1981): 3–14

Kowalewski, D., and C. Johnson."The Ukrainian Dissident: A Statistical Profile." UQ 40 (1984): 50–65

Krawchenko, B., and J. Carter. "Dissidents in Ukraine before 1972: A Summary Statistical Profile." JUS 8 (1983): 85–8

Luckyj, G. "Polarity in Ukrainian Intellectual Dissent." CSP 14 (1972): 269–79

Potichnyj, P. "The Struggle of the Crimean Tatars." CSP 17 (1975): 302–19

Rudnytsky, I.L. "The Political Thought of Soviet Ukrainian Dissent." JUS 6 (1981): 3–16

Sawczuk, K. "Valentyn Moroz: A Voice of Ukrainian National Renaissance." NP 2 (1973): 1–9

– "Opposition in the Ukraine: Seven versus the Regime." *Survey* 20 (1974): 36–46

THE CHURCH IN SOVIET UKRAINE

Bociurkiw, B. "The Uniate Church in the Soviet Ukraine: A Case Study of Soviet Church Policy." CSP 7 (1965): 83–113

– "The Orthodox Church and the Soviet Regime in the Ukraine, 1953–1971." CSP 14 (1972): 191–211

– "Religion and Nationalism in the Contemporary Ukraine." In G. Simmonds, ed., *Nationalism in the USSR and Eastern Europe in the Era of Brezhnev and Kosygin*, 81–93. Detroit, 1977

- "The Religious Situation in Soviet Ukraine." In W. Dushnyk, ed., *Ukraine in a Changing World*, 173–94. New York, 1977
- "Ukrainization Movements within the Russian Orthodox Church and the Ukrainian Autocephalous Orthodox Church." *HUS* 3–4 (1979–80): 92–111
- "Soviet Religous Policy in Ukraine in Historical Perspective." In M. Pap, ed., *Russian Empire*, 95–112. Cleveland, 1985
Dirscherl, D. "The Soviet Destruction of the Greek Catholic Church." *Journal of Church and State* 12 (1970): 421–39
Dunn, D. "The Disappearance of the Ukrainian Uniate Church: How and Why." *UI* 9 (1972): 57–65
Hvat, I. "The Ukrainian Catholic Church, the Vatican and the Soviet Union during the Pontificate of Pope John Paul II." *Religion in Communist Lands* 11 (1983): 264–79
Markus, V. "Religion and Nationality: The Uniates of the Ukraine." In B. Bociurkiw and J. Strong, eds, *Religion and Atheism in the USSR and Eastern Europe*, 101–22. London, 1975
Moroziuk, R. "Antireligious Propaganda in Ukraine." In M. Pap, ed., *Russian Empire*, 113–30. Cleveland, 1985
Reynarowych, R. "The Catholic Church in Western Ukraine after World War II." *Diakonia* 4 (1970): 372–87
Senyk, S. *Womens' Monasteries in Ukraine and Belorussia to the Period of Suppressions.* Rome, 1983
Sysyn, F. "The Ukrainian Orthodox Question in the USSR." *Religion in Communist Lands* 11 (1983): 251–63

UKRAINIANS ABROAD

Bibliographies

Boshyk, Y., and B. Balan. *Political Refugees and Displaced Persons, 1945–54.* Edmonton, 1982
Boshyk, Y., and W. Kebalo, eds. *Ukrainian DP Publications: A Bibliography of the John Luczkiw Collection at the University of Toronto.* Edmonton, 1988
Momryk, M. *A Guide to the Sources for the Study of Ukrainian Canadians.* Ottawa, 1984
Sokolyshyn, A., and V. Wertsman. *Ukrainians in Canada and the United States: A Guide to Information Sources.* Detroit, 1981

United States

Basarab, S., et al. *The Ukrainians of Maryland.* Baltimore, 1977
Chyz, Y. *The Ukrainian Immigrants in the United States.* Scranton, 1932

Dragan, A. *The Ukrainian National Association: Its Past and Present, 1894–1964.* Jersey City, 1964

Ewanchuk, M. *Hawaiian Ordeal: Ukrainian Contract Workers, 1897–1910.* Winnipeg, 1986

Halich, W., *Ukrainians in the United States.* Chicago, 1937

Isajiw, W., ed. *Ukrainians in American and Canadian Society.* Jersey City, 1976

Isajiw, W., Y. Boshyk, and R. Senkus, eds. *The DP Experience.* Edmonton, forthcoming

Kuropas, M. *The Ukrainians in America.* Minneapolis, 1972

Lushnycky, A., ed. *Ukrainians in Pennsylvania.* Philadelphia, 1976

Magocsi, P. *Our People: Carpatho-Rusyns and Their Descendants in North America.* Toronto, 1980

Magocsi, P., ed. *The Ukrainian Experience in the United States: A Symposium.* Cambridge, MA, 1979

Markus, V. "Ukrainians in the United States." In V. Kubijovyč, ed., *Ukraine: A Concise Encyclopedia,* 1100–51. Toronto, 1971

Pekar, A. "The Historical Background of the Carpatho-Ruthenians in America." *UI* 13 (1976): 87–103 and 14 (1977): 68–84

Procko, B. "Pennsylvania: Focal Point of Ukrainian Immigration." In J. Bodnar, ed., *The Ethnic Experience in Pennsylvania,* 206–32. Lewisburg, 1973

Stefaniuk, M. and F. Dohrs. *Ukrainians in Detroit.* Detroit, 1979

Wolowyna, O., ed. *Ethnicity and National Identity: Demographic and Socioeconomic Characteristics of Persons with Ukrainian Mother Tongue in the United States.* Cambridge, MA, 1986

Canada – Sources

Czumer, W. *Recollections about the Life of the First Ukrainian Settlers in Canada.* Edmonton, 1981

Kolasky, J., ed. *Prophets and Proletarians: Documents on the History of the Rise and Decline of Ukrainian Communism in Canada.* Edmonton, 1988

Kordan, B., and L. Luciuk, eds. *A Delicate and Difficult Question: Documents in the History of Ukrainians in Canada 1899–1962.* Kingston, 1986

Canada – Bibliographies

Boshyk, Y. *Slavs in Canada: A Guide to Archival Resources.* Edmonton, forthcoming

Canada – Studies

Aster, H., and P. Potichnyj. *Jewish Ukrainian Relations: Two Solitudes.* Oakville, 1983

Darcovich, W. *Ukrainians in Canada: The Struggle to Retain Their Identity.* Ottawa, 1967

Gregorovich, A. *Chronology of Ukrainian Canadian History.* Toronto, 1974

Isajiw, W., ed. *Ukrainians in the Canadian City.* Special issue, *Canadian Ethnic Studies* 12 (1980)

Kaye, V. *Early Ukrainian Settlers in Canada, 1895–1900: Dr. J. Oleskiw's Role in the Settlement of the Canadian Northwest.* Toronto, 1964

Kazymyra, B. *The Achievement of Metropolitan Andreas Sheptytsky.* Toronto, 1958

Kolasky, J. *The Shattered Illusion: The History of Ukrainian Pro-Communist Organizations in Canada.* Toronto, 1979

Lupul, M. *Ukrainian Canadians, Multiculturalism and Separatism: An Assessment.* Edmonton, 1978

– *A Heritage in Transition: Essays in the History of Ukrainians in Canada.* Toronto, 1982

Marunchak, M. *The Ukrainian Canadians: A History.* Winnipeg, 1970

Petryshyn, J. *Peasants in a Promised Land: Canada and the Ukrainians, 1891–1914.* Toronto, 1985

Petryshyn, W. *Changing Realities: Social Trends among Ukrainian Canadians.* Edmonton, 1980

Prymak, T. *Maple Leaf and Trident: The Ukrainian Canadians during the Second World War.* Toronto, 1988

Rozumnyj, J., ed. *New Soil – Old Roots: The Ukrainian Experience in Canada.* Winnipeg, 1983

Skwarok, J. *The Ukrainian Settlers in Canada and Their School, 1891–1921.* Toronto, 1929

Swyripa, F. *Ukrainian Canadians: A Survey of Their Portrayal in English-Language Works.* Edmonton, 1978

Swyripa, F., and J. Thompson. *Loyalties in Conflict: Ukrainians in Canada during the Great War.* Edmonton, 1983

Tropper, H., and M. Weinfeld. *Old Wounds: Jews, Ukrainians and the Hunt for Nazi War Criminals in Canada.* Toronto, 1988

Young, C. *The Ukrainian-Canadians: A Study of Assimilation.* Toronto, 1931

Yuzyk, P. *The Ukrainians in Manitoba.* Toronto, 1953

Woycenko, O. *The Annals of Ukrainian Life in Canada.* 4 vols. Winnipeg, 1961–9

Index

For Cileme of course!

And for Appa on his seventy fifth.

DEVELOPMENT AND ETHNOCIDE: COLONIAL PRACTICES IN THE ANDAMAN ISLANDS

by

Sita Venkateswar

Massey University - Palmerston North
Aotearoa/New Zealand

IWGIA
Document No. 111 - Copenhagen 2004

DEVELOPMENT AND ETHNOCIDE:
COLONIAL PRACTICES IN THE ANDAMAN ISLANDS

Author: Sita Venkateswar

Copyright: IWGIA 2004 – All Rights Reserved

Editing: Christian Erni and Sille Stidsen

Cover design, typesetting and maps: Jorge Monrás

Proofreading: Elaine Bolton

Prepress and Print: Eks/Skolens Trykkeri,
Copenhagen, Denmark

ISBN: 87-91563-04-6
ISSN: 0105-4503

Distribution in North America:
Transaction Publishers
390 Campus Drive / Somerset, New Jersey 08873
www.transactionpub.com

INTERNATIONAL WORK GROUP
FOR INDIGENOUS AFFAIRS
Classensgade 11 E, DK 2100 - Copenhagen, Denmark
Tel: (45) 35 27 05 00 - Fax: (45) 35 27 05 07
E-mail: iwgia@iwgia.org - Web: www.iwgia.org

This book has been produced with financial support from the Danish Ministry of Foreign Affairs

CONTENTS

The Islanders in "India": Policies of "Planned" Change

Gender/Power

Strategies of Power: an Analysis of "Jarawa Contact"

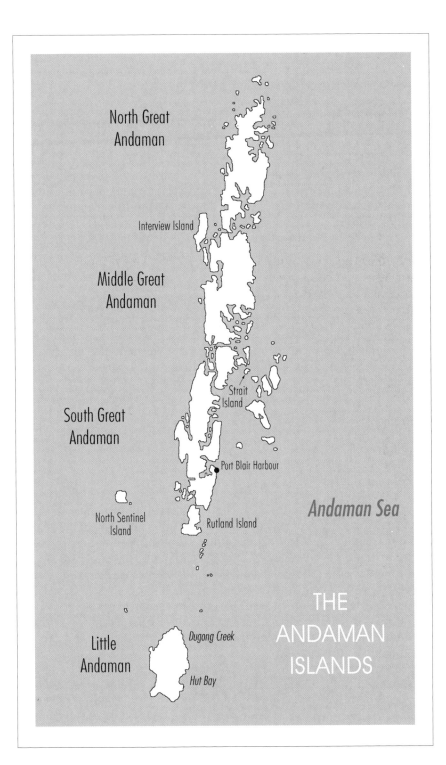

North Great
Andaman

Interview Island

Middle Great
Andaman

Strait
Island

South Great
Andaman

Port Blair Harbour

North Sentinel
Island

Andaman Sea

Rutland Island

THE
ANDAMAN
ISLANDS

Little
Andaman

Dugong Creek

Hut Bay

PREFACE

T his ethnography is a comparative analysis of three groups of Andaman Islanders with very diverse experiences of colonialism, based on my research and experience in the islands from 1989-1992 and, then again, in 2004. The ethnography examines the links between colonialism and 'development', and the many continuities between the policies of the earlier British colonial administration and the ongoing Indian colonization of the Andaman Islands. Within this framework, the situation of the Andamanese, Onge and Jarawa is analysed as integrally intertwined with and affected by shifting agendas of 'development'. The book goes on to analyse how 'development' and the welfare policies of the present Indian administration are a fundamentally gendered process with profound albeit uneven effects on local gendered relations of power. Ethnographic data is explored to explain how impositions of particular masculine identities on the Andamanese and Onge have reconfigured gender relations in these groups, manifested as mundane but protracted struggles over power between genders. Finally, the book considers the location of the anthropologist in both constructing and determining the research process.

The situation of the Andaman Islanders is one that has been experienced by indigenous peoples across the world, brought about by the twin processes of colonialism and capitalism, destroying countless lives in their wake. The accounts of dispossession, disease and death are familiar ones, having been retold over the centuries in line with global patterns of colonialism.

The structure of the narrative to follow juxtaposes ethnographic encounters of the everyday alongside a discussion and analysis of the historical and contemporary administrative interventions in the islanders' lives. I scan the documents compiled by the fascinating figure of Portman, the late nineteenth century administrator-cum-anthropologist, to read between the lines a continuum in the on-the-ground reality as well as to unearth ways in which the islanders may have resisted British interventions. In the light of their earlier experience with indigenous groups elsewhere, I assert that the British colonial administration in the Andaman Islands was complicit in unleashing a process of genocide in the islands.

I repeat the procedure for the contemporary period using the policy document of the tribal welfare agency, which provides a charter for the Indian government's experiment with "planned change". This is a mandate for a process of ethnocide that leads to a different kind of death, one that erases cultural groups and extinguishes lifeways, over-

Looking into a bleak world. Onge couple at the window of their house in Dugong Creek.
Photo: Sita Venkateswar

seen by the Portman-like figure of the current Director of Tribal Welfare, yet another administrator-turned-anthropologist. The discussion then leaps forward to include the compelling turn of events in the final years of the twentieth century and into the next millennium, recounting some of the significant developments that have ensued in the affairs of the islands and its peoples. The judicial interventions by the High Court of Kolkata and the Supreme Court of India, brought about by a coalition of non-governmental organizations and activists taking the Andaman administration to court, has highlighted the significance of forging new coalitions within civil society and the potential for effecting change that lies therein.

Finally, the book includes a section of appendices consisting of a selection of policy documents that have played a crucial role in the unfolding of recent events in the islands. ❏

PROLOGUE: A SENSE OF PLACE

The lush, verdant rainforests of the Andaman Islands are the abode of a small group of people, some of whom practise a way of life that is both threatened and has come under increasing scrutiny[1] over the latter part of the twentieth century as well as into the new millennium. The indigenous people of the Andaman Islands are a part of the dwindling, semi-nomadic, hunter-gatherer, Negrito populations of South and Southeast Asia. They consist of four groups inhabiting different islands of the archipelago. These groups have been separated long enough to have developed substantial linguistic differentiation and are now referred to in the literature as four distinct tribes.[2]

The **Sentinelese**,[3] named after North Sentinel Island, the island they inhabit, are the most isolated or the least known of the islanders, and continue to present a militant front to the outside world, usually thwarting any attempts to approach their island.

The **Jarawa**,[4] who have been steadily pushed to the very margins of their former territory, at present occupy the western borders of Middle and South Andaman Islands. Over the past thirty years, the island administration has initiated "contact" with the Jarawa, and claims to have established some degree of rapport with the people. During the past five years, the Jarawa have been the focus of international attention, largely spearheaded by the efforts of Survival International (an international advocacy group for indigenous rights), as they battled major epidemics of measles, pneumonia and directives to assimilate them into the dominant Indian majority. Currently, their future hangs in the balance awaiting the outcome of a series of judicial interventions.

The **Andamanese**, who are referred to in the literature as the Great Andamanese[5], are the survivors of a former population consisting of ten territorial and linguistic groups spread out across North, Middle and South Andaman Islands. They are reduced to approximately thirty-five[6] people who can claim Andamanese descent. The Andamanese are at present settled on a small island called Strait Island, which has been given over to them, although it remains doubtful as to whether there are any legal documents to that effect. The ravages of the earliest and longest duration of "contact" have been borne by the Andamanese. Their resettlement on Strait Island is perceived by the Andaman government as some measure of reparation for the historical injustices that they have undergone.

The last group is the **Onge**, some coastal populations of whom were *pacified* by M.V Portman in 1886-87 during his tenure as a British ad-

A Jarawa girl on the beach during "contact" Photo: Andaman Administration

ministrator in the islands. Subsequently, coast-dwelling groups in the north of Little Andaman were in the habit of making voyages to Port Blair in their dugout canoes, to obtain tea, sugar[7] and tobacco from the Andamanese. After 1952, with the establishment of a research substation of the Anthropological Survey of India (ASI) in Port Blair, there were Indian research teams frequently visiting Little Andaman. But the Onge were unhindered in their hunting-gathering-fishing way of life until the mid-sixties. A program for the development of Little Andaman was announced and, over the years, the former inhabitants have been sequestered in two permanent settlements at two ends of the island: Dugong Creek, the larger settlement in the north, and South Bay at the southern tip of the island. Their population too has dwindled steadily, and they now number approximately a hundred [8] people.

At present, the islands form a part of the Union Territory of India, which is administered by the central government from New Delhi and does not exist as a separate "state" with an autonomous bureaucratic structure. The four indigenous groups are under the charge of a government-controlled welfare institution known as the Andaman Adim Janjati Vikas Samiti (AAJVS), Committee for the Enlightenment of Primitive Peoples. Both the Andamanese and the Onge currently lead a sedentary life and have rations allotted to them by the AAJVS. But the Onge, more than the Andamanese, continue to hunt, gather and fish. They have coconut plantations planted for them, as part of a program to interest them in cultivation. They are paid wages for keeping the settlement cleared of undergrowth, and for picking coconut. The proceeds from the sale of the coconuts go into a co-operative society that is operated on behalf of the Onge and the Andamanese. There is an ongoing effort to interest the islanders in working for wages, and some talk of dividing the settlement between individual Onge and Andamanese in the future.

The island ecology

The Andaman Islands, comprising of a cluster of 204 small and large islands in the Bay of Bengal, extends over 350 kms in length and 52 kms in breadth, covering a land mass of 8393 sq. kms (Chakraborty 1990). Port Blair is the administrative capital of the Andaman and Nicobar group of islands, situated at a distance of 1200 km to the east of Madras, and 1090 km south-east of Calcutta. The islands are situated much closer to the Burmese than the Indian coastline, about 520 kms due west of Mergui, and 600 km from the northern tip of Sumatra (Majumdar 1975). The islands are an extension of the Burmese Arakan mountain range, and are believed to have been connected to the mainland during the Pleistocene[9]. They are now separated from the Burmese coast by shallow continental waters (Sanctuary Asia-Resources, n.d.).

The Andaman group of islands is divided into a) Great Andaman and b) Little Andaman. Great Andaman is made up of three main islands, North, Middle and South Andaman, and includes Richie's Archipelago, Interview Island, Rutland Island and several adjacent lesser islets. They consist of about four-fifths of the total area of the Andamans. North Sentinel Island lies 18 kms off the west coast of South Andaman (Basu 1990). Great Andaman is covered by a series of hills separated by narrow valleys, carpeted by dense tropical forests. The hills rise to a maximum of 732 metres (Majumdar 1975). The coasts of the Andamans are deeply indented, and have a large number of harbours and tidal creeks, often surrounded by mangrove swamps. Approximately 70 kms south of Great Andaman, and midway between Great Andaman and the Nicobar group of islands, lies Little Andaman. It is a single island, 44 km in length and varying in breadth between 16 to 25 km, with an area of 731 sq. km. Little Andaman is mostly flat, except for a small hilly section in the north. There are no rivers, but a few perennial streams.

The forests of the Andamans are mainly of three types, namely: evergreen, deciduous and mangrove. In both Great and Little Andaman, lumber industries have developed where there are easily accessible forests. The exploitation of timber began with the establishment of a penal settlement in the islands, and a Forest Department was started in 1883 (Majumdar 1975).

Thus forests form the major ecosystem in the islands and developmental activities directly and indirectly affect the forests (Nair 1989). Perhaps 70% of the forests of Andaman Islands are still forested but much of it is degraded, secondary growth. Over the past thirty years, soil, meteorological, land-use and forestry experts have stressed the need to keep the islands under forest cover, despite which large clear-felling and plantation projects are underway (Whitaker1985). Accelerated immigration from mainland India and the growth of a number of forest-based industries have led to extensive settlements and the conversion of forest areas into revenue and agricultural lands (Nair 1989). There have been repeated warnings stressing the islands' incapacity to sustain agriculture. A direct outcome of the growth in population is the problem of encroachment and illegal settlements in areas that have been demarcated as "tribal reserves[10]".

With the improvement in access to and around the islands, economic activities in the Andamans have been integrated with the economy of the mainland, by the cultivation of cash crops, particularly oil palm and rubber. In view of the limited local market, these plantations are primarily aimed at the mainland market (Saldanha 1989).

A series of reports compiled over the past five years document the devastation that has been wreaked on the islands' fragile eco-system and landscape. Over the years, the destructive consequences of sand mining for construction is readily visible in the disappearance of several beaches, with its effects on wildlife in that region, as well as a steadily increasing coastal erosion that even newly installed sea walls are not sufficient to control (Ali and Andrews n.d.). As anticipated, agricultural yields have fallen, the efforts towards regeneration of degraded forests have not proved successful, while accumulating evidence indicates the sharp decrease in mangrove cover, together with the destruction of coral reefs as a consequence of the run-off from land-based activities such as logging, agriculture and unchecked use of pesticides (Sekhsaria 2002).

Tourism has been identified as a potential source of revenue but it is also a cause for concern since the islands cannot sustain it at its current rapidly growing rate unless there is a shift in strategy to a high value, low intensity, environmentally friendly eco-tourism.

Surprisingly, the abundant marine resources remain under-exploited, even though a Department of Fisheries was set up in 1955. The actual utilization of this resource remains far below potential due to the lack of necessary infrastructure required to tap the marine wealth. Since the islands did not have a "non-tribal" population of local fishermen, a "fishermen settlement scheme" was initiated and families of fishermen from the states of Kerala and Andhra Pradesh in India were transported and settled in the Andamans (Saldanha 1989), adding to the jostling mix of ethnicities residing in the islands since the era of the British empire.

This ranges from the numerous and varied descendants of the ex-convicts of the former penal colony; to the descendants of the 200-250 Karen Burmese, primarily nomadic foragers brought in 1925 by the British government with the help of Christian missionaries. They were brought to work in the Forest department and then subsequently provided with land for their own settlements (Sarkar and Pandit 1994); to the mix of refugees from former East Pakistan (now Bangladesh) and the Tamils fleeing the civil war in Sri Lanka; to the numerous tribal groups from the state of Bihar fulfilling the labour needs of both the British and Indian colonial regimes. The continuous inflow of a diverse mix of populations from mainland India has strained the islands' capacities beyond sustainable limits. The current ratio of the remaining groups of Andaman Islanders to the surrounding Indian population stands at approximately 500:500,000, a stark testimony to the scale at which the dominant majority has outnumbered them.

According to Nair (1989), and endorsed by many others over the years (Whitaker (1984, 1985), Sekhsaria (2001,2002, 2003), Ali and An-

Andamanese boy at Strait Island. Photo: Sita Venkateswar

Botale's habitual quizzical expression. An Onge at home at Dugong Creek. Photo: Sita Venkateswar

17

drews n.d.), the Andaman situation is a classic example of an unplanned natural resource exploitation, disregarding basic ecological principles. It is primarily an economy determined by the prerogatives of mainland development. In the process, the indigenous islanders, have succumbed to a "proletarian dependence" on the island administration, "whose commercial transactions and territorial control now determin[e] their daily routine and mode of existence" (Guha and Gadgil 1989:149).

The passage to the field site

There are several alternative routes to arrive at Dugong Creek, the place where the Onge live. My first trip to the Andaman Islands was in 1989 during the national elections in India. In the course of this exploratory voyage to the islands, I became acquainted with the most frequented procedure for travelling to Dugong Creek, where the majority of the Onge lived. I availed myself of the transportation arranged for the election officers who were travelling to the reserved "tribal areas" to ensure that the "tribals" exercised their electoral rights along with the other citizens of India. From Port Blair, the administrative capital of the Andaman Islands, the largest and more comfortable of the ships ferrying passengers between islands, the *Sentinel*, was commissioned for election duty to the southern islands. The *Sentinel* was scheduled to travel from Port Blair to Great Nicobar, the final destination, discharging the appointed election officers at various islands along the way. It would then return from Great Nicobar, collecting the election officers carrying the ballots back to Port Blair. The round trip from Port Blair to Great Nicobar was a week of sea travel.

I procured a ticket for travel to Little Andaman with the assistance of some anthropologists from the Anthropological Survey of India at Port Blair. Before boarding the *Sentinel*, the anthropologists who accompanied me to the docks introduced me to the election officers whose destination was Dugong Creek. The officers were reminded that I was to be included in all the arrangements for travel to Dugong Creek. The first halt at Hut Bay on Little Andaman was an eight-hour journey. It was also my first on board a ship. While the election officers retired to their cabins to doze away the hours, I amused myself identifying the smaller islands en route and following the schools of dolphin that frolicked alongside the ship, until the long, curved outline of Little Andaman filled the horizon.

At Hut Bay, where a breakwater was built to provide a safe harbour for ships, the entire administrative machinery had been harnessed to take charge of the electoral process. A fleet of jeeps and pick-up trucks stood waiting at the jetty. I squeezed into one of the jeeps that would take me to the center of town where the guest houses and marketplace were located. I carried with me several letters of introduction given to me by the Deputy-Director of the Anthropological Survey of India. I was instructed to make my way to the Forest Guest House, and to speak to the Agricultural Officer or the Forest Officer. Obedient to the letter of my instructions, I soon found myself in a very pleasant guest-house set on a small hill, away from the crowded market. After some conferring between the Forest Officer and the *chowkidar* or watchman, I was allotted a room. But I was warned that I would likely have to share the room with any other single females in need of shelter. As it turned out, I had the room to myself for the two days that I was told would be spent at Hut Bay, while the election officers undertook the necessary arrangements for travel to Dugong Creek.

I spent the next two days exploring Hut Bay, and keeping an anxious eye on the movements of the officers on election duty. They were accommodated in a different guesthouse some distance away from where I was housed. Their offhand tone of voice in all conversations with me suggested that I was somewhat a nuisance. The officials conveyed the fact that they had more pressing matters to concern themselves with than remembering some inconsequential female who wished to stay in Dugong Creek for a month. The night before the scheduled departure for Dugong Creek, I received word that I was to be ready by 6 am the following morning.

A jeep was sent for me at the guest house, picking up everybody else along the way to transport us to 22 kms point, where the roadway ended. We disembarked and awaited the group of daily wage laborers who were hired to accompany the officers travelling to Dugong Creek, carrying the provisions and the luggage.

A short stretch on a well-trodden muddy path through the forest led to a creek. A number of country boats, some fitted with outboard motors, were secured to the gnarled roots of rotting tree trunks. The conversation around me, which only partly registered at the time, concerned the timetable of tides and the appropriate time to take the boats down the creek. The significance of that discussion became clearer in later years. I, too, learned to chart the tides in order to wade through streams, and realized the necessity of timing one's journeys according to the movement of tides, to ensure that there was enough sand to walk on along the sea-shore.

The two boats sat low in the water as they were loaded with passengers and provisions. The motor sputtered fitfully as we proceeded down the deep tidewater creek lined with mangrove forests on both shores. Two of the boatmen set to baling the water seeping in from the bottom of boat but, despite their efforts, there was a growing pool of water at our feet. The forty-minute journey down the creek was accomplished without any mishap, allaying my fears of capsizing and being consumed by crocodiles and, therefore, never reaching Dugong Creek. We disembarked at the mouth of the creek before it merged with the sea, marked by swelling breakers crashing ahead of us. Here an Onge awaited us.

Extract from field notes:

November 22nd, 1989
The first Onge I met was Totanange, who was waiting for us by the side of
the creek. He was given the two largest and heaviest sacks containing vege-
tables for the residents of Dugong Creek. Neatly and efficiently, he stripped
a branch from a nearby shrub, peeled off the skin, which formed a strong and
sturdy rope, tied the two sacks together, leaving a loop to go around the fore-
head, and hefted the sacks on his back. With this weight he walked the 11 kms
to Dugong Creek.

Totanange set a steady pace, seemingly unmindful of the humid heat. As the sun moved higher in the sky and the sea receded, exposing more sand to the sun, I became steadily more dehydrated. The frequent swigs I took from my water bottle very quickly depleted my water supply. Moving closer to the shade of the dense forest that skirted the sand meant sinking into deep, dry sand rendering walking more difficult. The damp, packed sand along the sea line was easier to walk on but directly in the path of the sun. A weary group of stragglers finally reached the shores of another creek, *Lebanare*, Dugong Creek, across which lay our destination.

We sat on the sand and waited while Totanange hailed people on the opposite shore. A couple of dug-out canoes made towards us and beached close to where we sat waiting. In turn, four at a time, we climbed aboard the canoes rowed by more Onge, who took us to the opposite shore to the settlement of Dugong Creek. And thus I reached my first field site the very first time that I came to the Andaman Islands, and travelled that same route alone on several subsequent occasions between 1991-92.

On those other occasions, I knew about the public transportation that was available on Little Andaman to take me from the jetty to the town. There were public buses that awaited every arriving ship at Hut Bay, as there were buses between Hut Bay and all the other villages on Little Andaman up to 22 kms. I discovered the tea shops where I would find the owners of the boats that travelled down the creek, known locally as *Bada Nala*. I also learned whose boats were seaworthy enough to brave the churning cauldron of dangerous waves at the mouth of the creek, which had capsized many a boat. Or which boatman's skills could be trusted to gauge the waves and temper the power of his outboard motor to ride them. But no matter how sturdy the boat, or how adept the boatman, every boat with its passengers had, on occasion, overturned. Hence, one of the direct routes to and from Dugong Creek, which could render the journey much less arduous, had its moments of danger when entering or leaving the creek that opened into the sea. I travelled that route on some occasions, but never when I was carrying supplies or my field notes, tapes and film, finding it easier to risk my life if necessary, but never daring to hazard essential resources. To retrace that itinerary, rather than disembarking at the mouth of the creek and walking the rest of the way to Dugong Creek, the boat would continue onwards into the sea.

Some preferred to sit with their backs to the waves. I always chose to face them during the tense moments when the boat first bounced along into the breakers, then becoming sharply vertical as huge wave after wave buffeted the low lying craft, the boatman shouting instructions to his helpers to adjust the baling or the power of the motor. Everyone else would grip the sides of the boat and remain silent, eyes glued ahead. As we reached deep water, the fury of the sea would abate, and the voyage become somewhat smoother. But, no matter what the season, the Andaman Sea is never calm enough to provide an eventless ride, the motion of the sea apparent even in relatively large vessels like the *Sentinel*. The journey does have its enjoyable moments as the boat skims the crests of the waves, fine sea-spray on your face---and the convenience of avoiding the long walk in the dense heat of the scorching sand.

There are other more direct routes from Port Blair, depending on one's importance in the hierarchy of government office. In December 1991, while I was living with the Andamanese at Strait Island, I was invited by the AAJVS to participate in a workshop on Tribal Development in the Andaman Islands. Most of the other participants were anthropologists, scientists and policy-makers from mainland India. The workshop was to be held aboard ship, the *Tarmugli*, the special vessel of the Lieutenant-Governor, while travelling to the "tribal areas," namely, Strait Island, Dugong Creek and the Jarawa areas.

This was to be my most comfortable journey to the settlement at Dugong Creek. From Port Blair, rather than sail towards Hut Bay, the *Tarmugli* headed further north directly towards Dugong Creek. But since it was too large a vessel to enter the shallow creek there, it anchored mid-sea, while the passengers disembarked into a smaller boat that was lowered from the ship, which then traversed the creek. Most dignitaries visiting Dugong Creek travelled this route, enduring the unnerving descent down a ladder into a rocking boat. It added the spice of adventure that was packaged into a visit to the "tribal areas".

When I returned to Dugong Creek at the end of January 1992, I accompanied a group of linguists from the Central Institute of Linguistics in Mysore on mainland India, commissioned to transcribe the Onge language into Devanagiri script. Their scheduled stay at Dugong Creek provided me with yet another vehicle to reach the field site. This time, the AAJVS boat, the *Milale*, a much smaller vessel, more prone to absorbing and transmitting the motions of the sea was requisitioned for these lesser-ranking government officials. After a rough and slow passage, the highest speed of the *Milale* never rising above three knots, a shaky and somewhat sea-sick group staggered off at the jetty at Dugong Creek. As a much smaller vessel, the *Milale* could sail right into the creek at high tide, and deposit its passengers at their door.

The final path to Dugong Creek, the one most often used by the Onge going into town, was through the forest to 22 kms (literally, the point at which the paved road started or ended, depending on the direction of travel). It was not a route that I ever travelled. My ventures into the forest with the Onge had taught me immense respect for their sure-footed navigation through the vines, roots and furrows where boars had rooted for tubers, setting traps for the unwary. Even with my eyes glued to the ground, watching every step forward, I would trip and stumble constantly as I tried to keep up with the unflagging pace set by the Onge who accompanied me. Moreover, every trip that I made into the forest during the dry season was followed by at least five days spent shedding my person, clothes and belongings of ticks. For the Onge couple, removing ticks from each other's bodies was an element of their daily intimacy. But as I single-handedly battled the ticks burrowed in the long hair I had at the time, every determined excursion into the forest meant days of domestic chaos thereafter. And during the monsoons, even the Onge demurred from taking me through the muddy slush of the forest that they so nimbly manoeuvred barefoot, leeches and all.

Yet another factor deterred me from ever taking this route to and from town. The tributaries of the same deep tidewater creek, *Bada Nala*, which I had traversed by boat on my way to Dugong Creek, required crossing on foot as they wound their way through the forest. The Onge had placed logs across the deepest parts. But the thought of balancing my way along a slippery log, across a creek known to be home to crocodiles, was enough to render this particular line of travel the least attractive to me.

Setting up residence

My arrival at Dugong Creek with the linguists provided a number of advantages that was missing during my earlier trip in 1989. For one, in view of their projected extended residence at the settlement, the AAJVS had made arrangements to accommodate the linguists at Dugong Creek. One of the buildings was converted into the official "guest-house". In 1989, it had housed the wireless operator and his family but, since then, there were other quarters allocated for each appointed wireless operator. During my earlier month-long stay in 1989, I stayed with the medical officer and his family. Their hospitality had become strained by the time I left. I was determined that, on resuming fieldwork there, I would organize some means of maintaining separate and independent domestic arrangements. Hence the advent of a "guest-house" at Dugong Creek, with a kitchen attached to it, was a veritable gift from my point of view. The AAJVS had even mustered frames for beds, some mattresses, and equipped the kitchen with basic utensils and other implements. I was delighted at the changes since my last visit.

After some conferring between the three linguists and myself, we decided that they would share one room, and I would take the other. The long veranda in front, facing towards the sea, was converted into a working area with some tables and chairs. We set up a daily mid-morning routine of preparing the meals for each day, which left each of us free to organize the rest of the daylight hours according to our own interests. The three linguists considered me too diminutive and slight to be safe standing on the precarious stool that I used to reach the large utensils placed on the leaping flames of the oven. Instead, I was assigned to chopping or peeling the quantities of vegetables for the daily meals, [11] or cleaning the rice, while they took over the actual cooking of the meals. Every other week, someone from Dugong Creek was sent into town to replenish groceries and the expenses shared equally between us.

But there was one nagging problem that was never quite resolved between us, and which remained an area of tension for all the inhabitants at Dugong Creek (except the Onge, although they too were a part of it). This was the issue of the daily supply of water. There was no piped water at Dugong Creek. Any water for daily use had to be carried from one of the four functioning wells, each one located some distance from the cluster of buildings occupied by the welfare staff and the Onge. Replenishing the water from the well was an arduous chore since there were no conveniently sized buckets available that could be easily carried to and fro. The usual mode was to fill two smaller diesel drums attached by a rope to a bamboo rod, which was then balanced on the shoulder and carried to each dwelling. Despite all my efforts, this was a task that was impossible for me to execute. I even had trouble hauling the full bucket out from the low water-line of the long, deep well, let alone carrying the drums the entire distance between the guest-house and the well.

For all the other welfare staff, an Onge was assigned to come in every day and fill to the brim the large, empty diesel drums found in every quarter. These were the "helpers," whom I discuss in greater detail in a later chapter. In view of the fact that the appointed social worker was responsible for the well-being of all the inhabitants at Dugong Creek, it devolved to him to arrange this daily chore. It was a dependence that the social worker prized, obstructing any efforts to hire a daily wage-labourer for the job. As and when he remembered, he would whimsically assign some Onge to the "guest-house" to fill the drum.

I objected strongly to this arrangement on the grounds that it was not possible to establish a working relationship with the Onge and use them as servants at the same time, regardless of whether they were paid or not. I suggested that we bathe [12] at the well, and, working together in pairs, fill the drum. We contrived something of a routine as we dealt with the chronic shortage of water, and did daily battle with the social worker about employing someone for the task. And thus the linguists and I fell into a pattern of living at Dugong Creek for the next two months, devising a working interaction which was to our mutual benefit. When they left, much to the social worker's consternation, I finally obtained permission from the AAJVS to employ one of the wage-labourers contracted for construction work at the settlement to fill the drum at the guest-house with water every alternate day. For the rest of my stay at Dugong Creek, the water situation eased considerably, although there were periods of crisis when the men I employed took time off to go to town, or visit their families.

Linguistic initiations at Dugong Creek

In the midst of these domestic improvisations, I also commenced my research with the Onge. After the first week spent refamiliarizing myself with faces and names, and renewing the tentative links established during my earlier trip, I settled into a routine that was focused on learning the language. Equipped with my notebook and camera, I would go into the settlement as soon as I awoke in the morning, which became progressively earlier as the heat steadily escalated. I learned to treasure the all too brief, cool respite of daybreak, with the dew still wet on the grass, to plan my activities for the day.

Leading away from the stretch of quarters housing the welfare personnel at Dugong Creek, constructed and segregated according to the hierarchy of office, the winding dirt path reached the Onge "colony". Here the track straightened out, stripped bare of any tree or grass, and was flanked by the two rows of houses, thirteen on each side, accommodating all the Onge residents of Dugong Creek. These asbestos and corrugated sheet roofed, wooden planked, elevated dwellings were constructed on four posts/stilts. They consisted of a single room attached to a veranda reached by a set of stairs. Most of the Onge families had covered the three open sides of the veranda with thatched *pandanus*,[13] thereby converting the space into an additional room. Unlike the predilection for cross-ventilation and open verandas that most Indians share, the Onge preferred sheltered, enclosed spaces. Some families had extended their living area by building an additional thatched space in front of their houses. Breaking the monotony of the line of dark brown houses were two low, upside down, bowl shaped, circular thatched constructions. Some families resided in these during the monsoons, or alternated periodically to get respite from invasions of ticks and fleas.

The interiors of all the Onge dwellings were warm and smoky from the fire that was lit at all times. Platforms made of cane placed at varying heights from the floor spatially organized the room. These served to contain all their objects of everyday use. There was always one placed at a height above the fire for meat to smoke. Strung across a corner of the room were rows of jawbones, trophies of earlier hunts, sometimes painted with red ochre, usually of wild boar, turtle or dugong. Cooking, eating, living and sleeping occurred within the same space in most homes, each one sheltering several human and canine inhabitants. There were some exceptions to this arrangement, notably in the houses of a few of the "helpers," who separated the sleeping area from the cooking and living section. These houses were also less prone to the smoke-filled atmosphere of the others, and were organized according to more conventional norms of order and tidiness.

Entering the Onge part of the settlement meant braving the pack of barking, snarling dogs that sprang into instant activity at the sight of a non-Onge, ready to snap at the ankles at the merest indication of hesitation. Over time, I learned to say "Tchoo" with sufficient authority and venom to disperse the dogs, and to keep handy pieces of stone to fling at them. After negotiating these formalities, which unfailingly shattered the early morning calm, and warned the Onge of the presence of an intruder, I slowly walked down the path noting who was awake, exchanging greetings as I passed, or lingering if anyone seemed inclined to chat. In the ensuing first couple of weeks after my arrival, I was reluctant to encroach upon their privacy so early in the morning.

But as the days went by, I felt they had become more accustomed to my presence. I walked into the houses of those awake, perched myself on a plank of wood or the railing of the veranda with my notebook and pen poised to phonetically record everything that was voiced around me. During my first visit in 1989, I had compiled lists of vocabulary that I cross-checked at this time, attempting tentative phrases constructed after consultation with the rudimentary book on Onge language published a few years earlier. These enlarged steadily as the Onge responded or prompted me with further words that I recorded.

As families gathered around large, simmering cauldrons of black, sweet tea, (regularly diluted with water through the whole day), children waking up and nursing, dogs scratching and being kicked out of the way, adults desultorily eating leftovers from the night before, I sat in a corner quietly, alert to new sounds and phrases. Habituated to the steady stream of anthropologists coming and going over the years, the Onge never questioned my presence there, although I felt compelled to explain. But, as I discovered, I was already assigned a category. I was a *tomolukwa*, one who writes, and a *tineabegi*, a female. Hence, *gulukwenene*, I was reminded frequently, write it down, if I failed to record in my notebook a meaning or a term that was explained to me. *Minyacekamema*, I would respond, I won't forget, *mi koralei tomolukwenene*, I will write it all down when I go back to the "guest-house".

And thus commenced a period of learning and practice of the Onge language, a process to which the presence of the linguists contributed immensely. They rarely ventured into the Onge settlement except in the course of an evening walk to stretch their limbs. But they organized a schedule of regular sessions with individual Onge at the guesthouse, for which the Onge were paid hourly wages.[14] Their method was to elicit from the Onge a large vocabulary, then deduce syntax and eventually the grammar by presenting an array of pictures of objects, activities and sequential processes. The Onge were expected to repeat their responses to these materials several times into a tape-recorder. This was intended to capture the varying pronunciation by and between individuals. Such a systematic procedure was in marked contrast to my own more intuitive method of language acquisition, which followed the needs of the moment and the imperatives of communication.

Every evening for a couple of hours before lights out, [15] liberally anointed with mosquito repellents, with a large fire lit nearby to ward away the other prolific insect life, the linguists and I sat together on the veranda. We pooled the material collected during the day and pored over it. By the end of a month's stay at Dugong Creek, to everyone's surprise – my own, the linguists,' the welfare staff and the Onge – I had made rapid progress in my speech and comprehension of the language. I was constructing sentences independent of the language manual, distinguishing between tenses and could explain the semantic context for the vocabulary accumulated by the linguists. For instance, I could identify how verbs changed depending on the type and location of activity, whether it occurred in the forest or the sea-shore, and when it denoted a return from or an advance towards the particular site.

The linguists quickly took advantage of my progress, and hired me as a "consultant" to obtain culturally significant information and vocabulary for the "primer," [16] the final goal of their project. The next one and a half months sped by during this period of intensive collaboration as the primer took shape. The Onge were mildly interested spectators to our immersion in their language, attending to and correcting constructions and pronunciations, volunteering alternatives and explaining semantic contexts. But the one product of our efforts that was the greatest success with the Onge were the nursery rhymes. These were short rhymes consisting of the primary vocabulary for each chapter of the primer, which I set to the lilting melodies of folk tunes of India. They were appropriated and sung by adults and children alike, just as I hummed the refrains[17] with which the Onge punctuated all their activities.

In the midst of these transactions, all the linguists in turn succumbed to an attack of malaria, which by some strange quirk[18] passed me by. As a result of their illness, they delayed their departure by another two weeks, leaving in the middle of April rather than the end of March as originally planned. Weakened by the intensity of their illness, they all looked forward to their return to more comfortable environs back on mainland India. They entrusted me with a draft of the primer to work with, and the linguists bade me farewell. In the days following their departure, I realized the extent to which their presence and intellectual companionship had buffered me from the trials that accompany the inception of fieldwork in an unfamiliar place. I was finally on my own at Dugong Creek, to make what I could of my time with the Onge. ❑

Notes

1   In anthropology, hunter-gatherers have been the focus of interest since the landmark Man the Hunter (1968) conference. The ongoing interest in hunter-gatherers is affirmed by the four-yearly international conferences that have occurred since 1968. As representatives of the "original affluent society" (Sahlins 1973), with long hours of daily leisure, whose values of sharing (Lee 1968,1994) stand in stark contrast to much that is perceived as lost to modern, Western, capitalist society, they continue to evoke nostalgia. A revisionist trend in hunter-gatherer studies (Schrire 1984, Headland and Reid 1989) has sought to dispel the ahistorical view of hunter-gatherers as a timeless people, living in complete

isolation until "discovered" by the colonial powers, and testimony to a way of life that has survived unchanged for millennia.

2 In India, "tribe" is a legal referent rather than a social category, to designate those groups who are believed to be indigenous or autochthonous to a region. It also serves to distinguish such people socially and economically from the "caste" society characteristic of settled agriculture.

3 In the case of the Sentinelese, their designation is an arbitrary and artificial one derived from the name conferred on the island by the British, and it continues unchanged to this day. We do not know how they refer to themselves or to their island.

4 The term "Jarawa" is derived from the *Aka-bea-da*, one of the linguistically distinct Andamanese groups whom the British first encountered on South Andaman Island, and who ceased to exist before the British left the islands. The *Aka-bea-da* employed the term to refer to any other groups with whom they did not share territorial, affinal or kinship rights and obligations. It is still not completely clear how the *Jarawa* refer to themselves.

5 From the Great Andaman Islands, consisting of North, Middle and South Andaman Islands.

6 Andamanese numbers vary between 25-35 according to the births and deaths of young children.

7 Thus, following Mintz (1985), as sugar production peaked in the Caribbean, the Onge risked their lives in their frail canoes to obtain that valuable commodity from a different outpost of the British empire. And the same holds for tobacco and tea, linking widespread areas of the world as never before.

8 The Onge population teeters between 90-100, varying according to the mortality rates of the very old or the very young. However, in the last few years, there have been a series of inexplicable deaths of young Onge men in circumstances that have not been investigated sufficiently.

9 "The Pleistocene epoch is part of the geologic time scale usually dated as 1.8-1.6 million to 10,000 years before the present, with the end date expressed in radiocarbon years. It covers most of the latest period of repeated glaciation, resulting in temporary sea drops of 100 metres or more." (From Wikipedia, the encyclopedia on the internet).

10 This is particularly noticeable in the areas demarcated as *Jarawa* reserve forests, resulting in poaching and degradation of the islanders' forest resources.

11 The huge quantities of food cooked every day included the meals for the Onge informants as well, who were invited to join us when they stopped by at the guest-house.

12 As it finally resolved, the linguists bathed at the well while I used the small, enclosed space in the guest-house, but washed my clothes at the well. None of the other Indian, female residents at Dugong Creek bathed within public view, and it was inappropriate for me to attempt it. I had to make do with approximately a bucket of water a day to wash in, all the while envying the linguists' freedom to pour several buckets over themselves, twice, sometimes thrice a day as the heat intensified.

13 Pandanus sp. is a tropical plant, also known as screwpine. The fibres from several kinds of Pandanus are used to make rope, baskets, fans etc, as well as flavouring in many south and south east asian cuisines.

14 The payment of wages to the Onge for performing their role as informants was introduced by the linguists, and about which I had mixed feelings. It disrupted my notions of an anthropologist-informant relationship, since I had not envisioned it as a commercial transaction. I regularly brought the Onge gifts – clothes, knives, mosquito nets, bags, umbrellas, the occasional watch, jewellery, toys – everything that they unabashedly demanded of me. Most of my trips to Port Blair were brought about by the growing list of "goods" for the Onge, about which I was reminded whenever they accosted me in the settlement. I distributed these impartially to anyone who asked me to bring something for them, in addition to the wages that I paid them (after this was instituted by the linguists) for formal interview sessions with me. In addition, whenever any Onge stopped by at the guest-house they ate with me.

15 There was no regular supply of electricity at Dugong Creek. At dusk, usually between 5 and 5:30 in the evening, a generator was turned on which ran until 10 pm. Hence evenings were a scramble to finish cooking and eating, keep available a few hours for writing notes, as well as some amount of time to spend with the Onge before darkness enshrouded us all.

16 The "primer" was an elementary pedagogical tool designed primarily for the Onge, both children and adults, and written in Onge. Their oral language was to be transcribed in the Devanagiri script, the same script used to write Hindi, the national language of India. Thus, the primer was intended to provide the Onge with the necessary instruments to read and write in their own language, and thereby guide them towards literacy.

17 One of my most pleasurable memories of Dugong Creek is of the voices of the Onge women and men rising strong and clear, interspersed with sporadic birdcalls, which seemed to provide the perfect foil for the human voices raised in song.

18 Perhaps my "DEET" based insect repellents that I carried with me from the US conferred more efficient protection than the local varieties.

A FRAMEWORK FOR ANAYSIS

*"In this work I sought to formulate some
hypotheses and test them by the simple culture of the Andamans"*

(Radcliffe-Brown 1932, cited in Tomas 1991: 101)

This is an account of three groups of Andaman Islanders, the Onge, Andamanese and Jarawa based on my research and experience with them between the period of 1989 and 1992. The discussion then shifts to the events and processes that accelerated towards the end of the last century and into the present one, propelling the Jarawa along a trajectory that was unimaginable at the time of my research in the islands.

The narrative that follows in the ensuing pages takes a somewhat discrete perspective from the variety of tales[1] that have been recounted over the course of several centuries about the Andaman Islanders. Within a space demarcated as the 'present,' I interrogate the ways in which relations of power have shaped the lives of the Andaman Islanders. By exploring the junctures of sustained interaction between the three aforementioned groups and the majority Indian population who have come to surround the indigenous peoples of these islands, I examine the exercise of power at two different planes. First, as it is deployed in terms of policy, and second, as relationships of power are inscribed in the texture of everyday encounters. Within that broad sweep, I further define shifting fields of power configured across lines of gender, the islanders' and my own, the anthropologist's.

I shift between the institutional and the quotidian contexts in my consideration of power. This foregrounds the ways in which these spheres are intimately intertwined in any analysis of the contemporary situation of the Andaman Islanders. The domain of the institutional impinges upon the lives of the various groups of islanders in the mode of government policies. The interventions that follow from these policy initiatives pervade the circumstances of the daily existence of the Andamanese, Onge and Jarawa. Thus, social relations embedded within networks of power specific to each context, are realigned or "policed" by government interventions, conspicuously so in the case of the Onge and Andamanese. Such administrative strategies recast gender relations, thereby "governing" the terrain of gender which emerges as a contentious site for the constitution of power. The figure of the gendered anthropologist, complicit or contesting according to situation, is located at the margins, but never entirely outside any of these overlapping webs of influence and control.

Envisioning resistance to the mediations of the Indian government has to include a recognition of the sheer inescapability of the Indian presence in the islands. It must also acknowledge the ways in which the islanders have appropriated or internalized social forms and patterns of consumption, (even as they resist some impositions). By transforming subjectivities and aspirations, the very terms of the engagement have been ineluctably altered. To map the possibilities and forms of resistance under the existing circumstances is a parallel but dual endeavor, arbitrarily drawing together the islanders and I in a project that "re-imagines" resistance.

I want to dispel at the outset any notion of homogeneity implied by my inclusion of the three very different situations of the Andamanese, Onge and Jarawa within the frames of a unified discussion of "the islanders." The individual circumstances of each group is the product of a unique constellation of historical and political imperatives. But I link the three groups along a continuum according to the intensity of exposure or propinquity to British and Indian colonial interventions. Such a conjoined and comparative perspective is important for arriving at an understanding of the contemporary situation of the islanders. A singular vision of each in isolation tends to obscure their complex yet precarious position within the boundaries of the Indian, colonial, nation-state.

The three categories "Indian," "colonial," "nation-state," essentially political in their implications, draws attention to the existence of the islanders within larger processes. Many of these occur elsewhere, far removed from the actual locale of daily activities, but impact their lives in unforeseen ways. To juxtapose these terms is intended to convey a series of distinctions. They serve to differentiate the Andamanese, Onge, Jarawa from a dominant majority population who occupy the islands, to stress the nature of the occupation, and, explain the political rationale for such an occurrence. It is also to point to the historical and political trajectories which have marked and altered the tenor of life, of the original inhabitants of a chain of islands in the Bay of Bengal.

Caught within the sweep of "global" events over which they had no control, the Andaman Islanders trod the path of bloodshed, disease and dispossession. Such a route links them with other peoples elsewhere who traversed similar paths. They are connected by the global reach of colonialism and the capitalism that follows in its wake, bringing people in far-flung corners of the world closer together, while simultaneously pushing them out of the larger picture altogether.

In the equation for power which lies at the center of the process, if we follow a chronological derivation in the case of the Andaman Islanders, they were never factored into the calculation. From the British competing with the Danes who had established a mission in nearby Nicobar Islands in the eighteenth century, to securing the Indian Ocean during the wars between the British and the French in the nineteenth. WWII and the Japanese occupation of the islands in the twentieth century. Or the tussle between the newly independent nations of India and Pakistan with Britain for control over these islands during the transfer of power. The thousands of displaced refugees from the harrowing aftermath of Partition, to the war in Bangladesh, or the civil strife in Sri Lanka. People from everywhere hungry for land and stability, all to be accommodated in the Andaman Islands. Wars with Pakistan spawning naval bases in the islands. With each solution to the problematic scenarios listed above, for the islanders it meant more bloodshed, more disease or more dispossession. What was clear was the fact that through a series of historical contingencies, their destinies were integrally intertwined with that of a nation that was constituted as India. And that composed the larger picture of the global reach of world capitalism for the Andaman Islanders, with its episodic moments of colonialism, nationalism, ethnic, religious and civil wars.

Politically marginalized within the existing globalized economy, the Andamanese the Onge, and now the Jarawa, to varying degrees, are enmeshed yet anew within a new global cultural economy of commodities and images. An earlier version of the colonial economy was one that trafficked in the circuit of tobacco, tea, sugar, opium and alcohol, bringing the islanders firmly within the ambit of the British Empire. But the new variant, also colonial in its dimensions as it pertains to the islanders, is more complex in its flow of goods and meanings. The contemporary landscapes of the islanders defy any easy generalizations, challenging the anthropologist to account for and explain the paradoxes that constitute the individuals who have been defined as the "traditional hunter-gatherer-fishers of the Andaman Islands."

What are the cultural frames of reference that can describe Bara Raju, an Onge man, who adroitly navigated the forest as he hunted wild boar, smearing his own face and the muzzles of his dogs with clay to prevent their odours from reaching their prey? Who kept a set of clothes wrapped up on a high branch of a tree on the outskirts of town and changed into polyester "safari suits" Indian "bureaucratese" style when he entered town. Who seriously discussed the prospects of speaking to the Prime Minister of India about building the Onge "pucca" houses like the Bengalis. Demanded that I bring him swiss knives and a walkman radio from the US. And, who was intrigued by the microcassettes and colognes smuggled into Port Blair. Or Tinai, (a female this time), who was disdainful of the gaudy "welfare clothes" given to them by the Indian government. Who clamoured for the kind of outfits that I wore on occasion during fieldwork, a styled "salwar-kameez" that was all the rage across India. But, discarded clothes altogether for three months of mourning when her husband died. And Tai, another male, who angrily stalked a crocodile with his bow and arrow along the banks of a creek, because it grabbed his dog as it swam behind his dugout canoe. Then, went on to discuss the kind of handbag and the appropriate undergarments for his wife that I should select for them. Perhaps, as Hannerz suggests, this kind of involvement with a wider world is merely "a matter of assimilating assorted items into a fundamentally local culture" (Hannerz 1992:238).

But what about Ramu[2] then, another male Onge whose seasonally guided activities and movements had been transposed into a different cycle of travel? As an employee aboard a ferry plying passengers and provisions between islands. Who perceived himself a "cosmopolitan" in comparison to the more "provincial" Onge who had settled into a sedentary lifestyle. Whose "openness towards divergent cultural experiences" (Hannerz 1992:239) rendered him unable to "feel at home" any longer with other Onge. And, who took pride in his attraction for and exploits with women of various cultural traditions, Nicobari, Ranchi tribal, Karen Burmese, even Jarawa.

These brief sketches illustrate the difficulties of conceiving of individuals as "self-evidently linked to particular cultures." (*ibid.*). Additionally, these anecdotal snapshots also imply the varying degrees of "competence" manifested by the Onge, making each of them "cosmopolitans" of different orders, as they made their lives surrounded by various peoples and traditions.

We are confronted with another set of conjunctures in considering the Andamanese. How do we assess the life-history collected from Li-chu, an Andamanese woman, that was modeled on the latest Bollywood films screened in the theaters of Port Blair? What did the weekly variations in her account of herself, changing according to the films playing in Port Blair, reveal to us about her past, her present and her future? Were these fictions, figments of the imagination, or fractured reality itself? And hence, at every turn, in attempting to discuss the provenance of individual lives of the Andaman Islanders we are reminded of similar cultural complexities sweeping across the globe.

What of the "fierce" Jarawa who eluded the grasp of the British colonialists, keeping them at bay with their bows and arrows? They wielded the same weapons, stronger, reinforced with iron arrowheads to defend their territorial boundaries as it was continuously re-mapped by the Indian colonists. Who were lured to remarkably staged encounters by the promise of coconuts, bananas, rice, cloth, plastic buckets, beads, pieces of iron. And who are currently confronting a different set of challenges as the seduction of "goods" and the lure of the globalized economy is poised yet anew, to shatter the Jarawa's fragile life-world, still mostly embedded within the seasonal cycles of the forest and the surrounding seas.

In the face of such contradictory trends, especially as these emerge in the practices of people like the Andaman Islanders, whose descriptions are usually framed by the "traditional," anthropologists are often impelled into a blind search for cultural manifestations that conform to expectations of "authenticity." The documentation of unique cultural forms is a noteworthy project in itself. But, the tendency to focus on those particularities to the exclusion of the more complex medley within which elements of the "authentic" are to be discerned, distorts the ongoing circumstances of the Onge, Andamanese and Jarawa. Or, the concerned anthropologist feels compelled to bemoan the passing of "traditional" ways as the steadily accumulating changes obscure the outlines of a more "pristine" past. Hence, we begin to suspect and "conclude that the [Onge] are no longer themselves" (Geertz 1988:12). Both these strands have inflected my own research and writing, and are likely to surface occasionally despite attempts to check either drift.

Geertz goes on to prescribe that we must "contrive somehow to shift our attention to other pictures" (*ibid.,*). To resolve the dilemma, I have bypassed the realm of the "classic monograph," a genre of anthropological writing that was constituted on the basis of research conducted on peoples like the Andaman Islanders. It legitimated a mode of inquiry "in which a human group is drawn and quartered along the traditional categories of social, economic, religious and other so-called organizations, and everything holds together" (Dumont 1978:12). Instead, I have explored mundane, quotidian contexts, namely the domain of everyday interactions to derive explanations for issues that arose from particular encounters. I have defined the kinds of influences that shape situations of daily contact, and included the ways in which they can be considered significant or suggestive.

Thus, within the context of the ongoing ethnocide of the islanders, I examine the links between colonialism and 'development,' and the many continuities in the policies of the earlier British colonial administration with the Indian colonization of the Andaman Islands. Against this backdrop, I analyze the situation of these groups as affected by shifting agendas of 'development.' The construction of the islanders as 'rare' and 'endangered,' legitimizes interventions by the government to sedenterize the islanders, which in effect deprive them of the forest resource-base formerly under their control.

I go on to examine how 'development' and the welfare policies of the current Indian administration has profound effects on local gendered relations of power. By incorporating ethnographic incidents, I explore how administrative strategies have reconfigured gender relations among the Onge and the Andamanese. They manifest as mundane, quotidian and protracted struggles for and over power between genders.

The discussion then leaps forward to include the compelling turn of events in the final years of the twentieth century and into the next millennium, recounting some of the significant developments that have ensued in the affairs of the islands and its peoples. The judicial interventions by the High Court of Kolkata and the Supreme Court of India, brought about by a coalition of non-governmental organizations and activists taking the Andaman administration to court, has highlighted the transformative potential of forging new coalitions within civil society and the possibility for effecting change that lies therein.

My account of research then, charts both an emotional as well as an intellectual journey. The perspective that I offer, cannot be separated from my own subjectivity as it was constituted during the period of my residence in the islands. Emerging in all its uncertainty, the contours of my personality inflected my perceptions, merging my research and experience with the particularities of my person. Such a process has another productive dimension, whereby, I have countered my inscription of the islanders with an exposure of the limits of my perceptions. Hence, I "police" my prerogative to advance a certain view of the islanders, within the text that I have constructed of my research and experience with them.

Thus, this account offers a "partial" [3] view, located in the historical conjuncture that I define as the "present," tracing how that moment came to be for the Andaman Islanders, and the colonial practices that have governed their lives since their islands were incorporated within the global economy.   ❏

Notes

1   I use the word "tales" here deliberately, to accentuate the constructed qualities of any account, regardless of whether it is a so-called product of scholarly endeavor, or a work of fiction. Hence, the account that follows should be read as one more tale amongst many others that have also been told. This brings to mind James Clifford's (1986b) oft-quoted comment that what anthropologists write are fictions, which, however, does not mean they are fictitious.

2   In 2003, as I revised my account of my research for this monograph, I discovered that Ramu had died in June 2001. Ramu was killed in the forest during a stampede of elephants belonging to the timber industry, and his death in this manner, according to his stepbrother, was one more illustration of Ramu's alienation from the ways of the forest (Pandya 2002).

3   For more discussion on the "partial" and situated perspective see Haraway (1988).

A RECORD OF FIELDWORK

*"Faces daubed with clay or painted in designs – a face mild and
good-humored instantly transforms into something unfamiliar
and mysterious, even somewhat menacing"*

(Extract from field notes, May 6, 1992)

Introduction

In my rendering of research in the islands, along with the "ongoingness"
of daily existence there, I want to convey the fragmentation and uncertainty inherent to the quotidian tasks of fieldwork. To accomplish
this I have interspersed the narration with extracts from entries in my
field journal, and relied on transcriptions of taped interviews. The interviews have been incorporated as recorded, with minor editing where
there are repetitions. I have maintained the dialogic format to impart
the back and forth process of deriving knowledge. The many obscuri-
ties and incomprehensions. The mutual talking at cross-purposes. And
the arbitrary directions of the ground covered during discussions. In
other words, these are open-ended interviews without neat and tidy
answers to questions. But, they do conjure the texture of the interaction with the Onge.

The course of fieldwork was as contingent on the specificities of my
person and personality, and I elaborate on the strategies for acquiring information, i.e. the specific incidents and ethnographic encounters that defined the framework for me to act/react/interact, forging
the basis for my research.

The photographs included in this section intimate the initiation of
research and "discovery," viewed through the lens of a camera. The use
of photographs is deliberate here since the camera performed a dual
function. Both an alibi and a security blanket in the early part of my
research, my camera served to mask my anxiety. It reassured me that
the many reels of exposed film that I was sending away for development were "data," an essential component of anthropological practice.
Moreover, the medium of photography served to maintain a vital continuity to my presence in the islands. The photographs that I carried
on my person during my long stretch of fieldwork starting in 1991
were those from my earlier visit to Dugong Creek and Strait Island in
1989. I distributed these to everyone who requested a copy, while initiating conversation on the events that had occurred in the intervening
period. Births, deaths, marriages, change of welfare personnel, gossip

on the scandals surrounding these changes, and other such ice-breakers. More importantly at the time, my skills with the camera, as evidenced by the copies that I brought back, were summoned to document what the Onge or the Andamanese thought I should record for my research. *"Gitangalenene"* was the crisp imperative from the Onge if I was not as trigger happy as they deemed appropriate, or *"photo khichiyena"* from the Andamanese, mostly the children, who took infinite delight in posing for me.

It should be noted that in the case of the Onge, the images of a lifestyle that I attempted to capture were predominantly of a hunter-gatherer existence. I tried to accommodate my "data" into a mould assembled from everything that I had read previously about hunter-gatherers. The three months that I spent with the Andamanese in Port Blair and Strait Island as soon as I arrived in the Andaman Islands in November 1991 appeared barren because any traces of such a unique lifeway had long vanished. They were like many other marginalized groups of people that I could encounter in the streets of Calcutta. By contrast, when I arrived at Dugong Creek, the Onge offered a veritable panoply of rich "ethnographic" material, which I aspired to scrupulously document. It is in this mode that my research was inflected by the search for the "authentic," whereby everything that did not conform to my expectations of the "traditional lifestyle" was discarded as extraneous or not "truly" ethnographic. As a result, when I first arrived in Dugong Creek in 1989, I noted the incorporation of the Onge into the electoral processes that constituted them as citizens of India. But to foreground that detail diminished my perception of them as "archetypical hunter-gatherers", whose "unique" way of life I sought to record for posterity. This chapter contains the tensions generated by my expectations of the ethnographic and the desire to "exoticize", challenged by the Onge's evasion of the easy slots into which I tried to assign them. Moreover, the day-to-day reality raised other issues that I was forced to reckon with in my research.

The bulk of my dissertation research was conducted with the Onge at Dugong Creek, from the end of January through June of 1992, and then again from September to December of the same year. I left the Andaman Islands in June when the south-west monsoons rendered living conditions extremely difficult. As supplies ran low, replenishment was virtually impossible with the heavy rain and high seas, and transport of supplies between islands became unpredictable.

Reflecting the predominant duration of my research with the Onge, this chapter focuses on my interactions with them. They provided, as it were, 'legitimate' grounds for anthropological enquiry. During the months with the Andamanese, I was hard pressed to justify, even to myself, what I was doing with them. As the entries in my field jour-

Tai preparing a bow. Photo: Sita Venkateswar

Groups of Onge women accompanied by children setting out for the forest in the middle of the day.
Photo: Sita Venkateswar

Entogegi rubbing clay paste on his face after a meal of pork. Photo: Sita Venkateswar

nal mirrored the daily occurrences, noting who was on which binge of drinking, or accusations of who was sleeping with whom, I became doubtful as to whether I could declare any of this as bona fide anthropological "data". In addition, the scepticism with which my claim to be doing research with the Andamanese was treated by those to whom I mentioned it – at the Anthropological Survey of India, administrators at Port Blair etc., – resulted in my tending to silence the Andamanese portion of my research. I have broken that silence as I write about them where these issues can be addressed, but the seed of doubt lingers on.

My four encounters with the Jarawa are dealt with in a separate chapter entitled "Strategies of Power". The first time was as an invited participant at a workshop on tribal development in December 1991. A visit to all the "reserved[1] tribal areas" was presented as a novel agenda on the program. The trip to the Jarawa reserve was the high point of the workshop. The next three visits occurred a year later in December 1992 as I was winding up my research in the islands. As will become clearer later, these encounters produced a decisive finale as I reached the end of my field research with the Andaman Islanders.

Fieldwork among the Onge

April 17, 1992
The linguists and the video team left yesterday. Have been almost continuously occupied with the filming of the primer. Went into the forest with Bara Raju and Oroti. I realize even more intensely now what a mistake the settlement has been, and just how taxing on them. The korale they have built for themselves by the stream – cool, pleasant and pretty. Have never heard Ramesh sing while in the settlement, but his singing could be heard from the distance, ringing through the forest as we advanced towards the korale. The only drawback here are the ticks! Almost all the men have gone into the forest for hunting. Mohan, Entogegi and Langoti brought back tambonuya. Everyone appeared surprised that I actually went to the forest with them, and on successive occasions. They seem pleased, perhaps that denotes a further level of acceptance.

(Extract from field notes)

An extended conversation

The linguists left Dugong Creek in the middle of April 1992 with the onset of the honey collecting season. Many of the Onge families had set up camp in the forest and Dugong Creek was emptied of about half its occupants. I often accompanied them into the forest, on day trips, since the Onge ensured my return to the settlement before dusk. The heat was intense at Dugong Creek but the forest camp, always constructed near a freshwater stream, was surprisingly cool and airy. I thought longingly of the imminent monsoon and consulted with the Onge as to when it was likely to arrive. The Onge obligingly raised their chin towards the south-west, as if their faces were a gauge for the wind, and reassured me that the *Dare* was on its way, it was less than another lunar cycle away. Then Chogegi, smiling mischievously in my direction added, *Dare* would come dancing along, riding on the wind, with *alame* (red clay) mixed with the fat from the *eyuge* (monitor lizard) rubbed on the head.

Preoccupied with their forest-related activities, it was difficult to persuade any of them to engage in interview sessions with me that I could record on tape. When I finally cornered Bara Raju, it proved to be a session that extended over three hours, uninterrupted through lunch and evening tea. We zigzagged through a range of topics but, as the transcription below suggests, Bara Raju kept stern control over the topics discussed and the information that he was willing to divulge.

Extract from field notes:

29 April 1992, at the guest house

Okay, I'm placing the tape here in the middle, so that both our voices can be recorded. I want everything to be in there so that if I forget, or if I haven't written down everything, it will be stored inside.

– During the rains, it becomes very difficult for you?

Yes, everything is wet, or damp, it is very difficult, and people fall sick and die. That's why when it is very wet, it's hard to do anything. A little rain would be good though. Too much rain is not good.

– Nowadays you live in the settlement, so even if you don't hunt there is food for you to eat, jatto jatto, oroti, (rice, chapati). Earlier, what would the Onge do, when they used to live in the forest? There was no ration then, what would they eat? Do you remember, what did your parents do?

During the dry season, they would get jackfruit, *bulundange* and store it. They would fill up big baskets, *tole* with fruit, cover it with leaves, tie it up and hide it in the forest. So when there is a lot of rain there is food. They would also hunt, and bring back pork, and when that finishes they will also eat *bulundange*. There was no tea then, they would only drink water. They would store a lot of dry wood, because once it gets wet it is very difficult to get wood. That's why during *torale*, the dry season, all the wood is obtained and stored. Then before the rain begins, the big *tokabe* (communal hut) is built and during the rains it is very comfortable inside.

– It remains completely dry inside?

Yes. That's how it was. In the past there was no wage work, we had all the time to build our houses, get pork, prawns. In the creeks, in the forest, there is so much fish, we would get fish with the prawns, _ a_a, eat pork rich in fat. Then when kwalokange (the north-east monsoon) starts the boar becomes thin, they have no fat, and they are not tasty. Then they go elsewhere and get pork, and it has a little more fat. They didn't have any utensils, they would make and use clay pots. I have seen those, they were used to cook the pork. They were made like this (gesturing with his hands).

– Who used to make them? (very excited)

Ask Tilai, Tilai knows how to make them.

– Tilai gets the clay and still makes bucu? He goes and gets the clay?

Yes, he mixes different kinds of clay and makes them, he makes *bucu*.

– Small ones?

Small ones and very big ones as well.

– Where are they?

In the forest.

– Take me there, I want to see them.

How can I do that? I don't know, it is Tilai who knows where the particular clay can be found.

– Does he still have any pots with him that I can see?

No, they were taken away.

– Who took them away?

Oh that person from Delhi...

– Who came from Delhi?

There was another woman who came here, and she took away the clay *bucu*.

– Who was this woman?

It was a woman from Delhi. There are always people who keep coming here and taking things away. One goes, another one arrives.

– (laugh) Oh, I'm here to stay.

Okay, but when your work finishes you will leave.

– It won't finish that quickly...

Another will come.

– ...because there is much to be done here. All these entale (government officials) here, they are like ticks, _a_age, getting fat on blood, they take your things and become rich. If anything is to be done about that, then there is much work here. Even if I finish one part of my work now, I will keep returning.
So, Tilai still makes bucu of clay, there is still one person who does that. None of you make them?

No, nobody else, he's the only one, he's one of the old-time Onge.

– In the past, everyone used to make clay bucu?

Yes, different kinds of clays were mixed for that.

– Does Tilai have any left?

Oh he will make more soon, during the dry season.

– So now that he's living in the forest, is he making any now?

How do I know, who will tell me, whenever he feels like it, he will make them.

– Okay, so when Tilai returns from the forest, will you tell him I want to see how they are made? I also want to take photographs. You see, everyone thinks that Onge don't make any clay utensils any more, they have forgotten everything. In the past, they used to make them, but now none of the Onge do. So I want to show people that there is still one person who knows how to make them.

Okay I will tell him to make a small one, and you can take it with you to Port Blair.

– Why don't you learn how to make it?

I'm a lesser Onge, how can I make them?

– Lesser Onge? He's a more important Onge?

He's an important one, he's one of the old-time Onge, that's why he knows how to make them.

– Why don't you learn from him?

It will break if I make one.

– But if you learn properly it won't break? It won't break then. Otherwise, when Tilai dies...bencamebe

Nobody will make them.

– Ekwa totota minyacekame, everybody else would have forgotten. So isn't it important that others learn from him before that happens? And you can also teach your children? And all your knowledge will be passed on. Otherwise everything will be forgotten.

(Agrees). The children will forget.

– Like the warrior Onge of the past, there are none left now. But if there were any now, there wouldn't be any entale who could steal from you, they would cut them up.

(Agrees) Hmm. What can I do? All the old-time Onge are gone, dead, all the big eaters are gone.

– You should teach your children to fight, all of you adults are old, and won't do anything, teach them.

All the Onge of the old times are all gone, are all dead. The Onge of old times didn't know any better, that's why they used to fight.

– What do you mean they didn't know any better?

Killing people, shooting arrows at one another, cutting each other up with knives. That's how we are so little now, this is how we have been so quickly finished off. We used to be so many...

– (interrupting) Accha, you used to be so many...?

...Filling up all the corners of the place.

– What happened?

Everybody was fighting...

– Who was fighting?

One another, the Onge of one *bera* (territorial division) fighting the others, cutting each other up.

– How did you become so little?

That's why. If Onge die one at a time, that's how we can keep increasing. But with arrows large numbers are killed all at once. All the Onge of one *bera* would come, they would go at night, and ambush the Onge of another *bera*, shoot arrows at them in the dark and watch them all try to run in different directions, arrows raining on them all the while.

– Have you seen this?

I know, Tilai told me about this. Everybody would be killed off, then piled up inside the *bera*, and then set on fire. They would cut off a piece of the little finger, or from the wrist and then take these as trophies to show to the women, see how many I've killed. They would string all these hands on a bamboo, and show them to the women, see how many I've shot. Then their kin from another bera would get angry and make preparations, make arrows, more arrows to kill the Onge who shot their kin. They would do all this secretly, so that those Onge would not get any hint of these preparations. The Onge of the olden times were very tricky and secretive. They would let many days go by, making arrows and spears all the while. There was no iron then, we would use the wood from the areca trees....(laughing)

45

– So when did you start using iron? Where would you get it from?

We would get iron from the sea, when it washed ashore. And use the resin from the forest to sharpen it. Otherwise, we would use the wood from the forest. We would make *dange* (dugout canoes) using a different wood, but when it was taken to the water it sank (laughing) so we knew that this wood was no good. So we tried a different wood, took it to the water and saw, yes, it stayed afloat. So that's what we used afterwards. That's how we learned things. In the old days, there was no rope, the fibre used to kill turtles now. We would get into the water and crowd the turtle, we used the incense from the forest, made a torch with *kuendeve* (rattan leaves) and lit it with the incense, as we crowded around the turtle. The light would blind the turtle and that's how we used to catch turtle. We were a lot of Onge then, and that's how we would hem in the turtle. We didn't harpoon the turtle then, we only used arrows to hunt boar.

– How did you hunt dugong, tineabone?

And that's how we caught *dugong* as well. We would wait for low tide and then go to hunt turtle and *dugong* at night. Not when the tide is high, then we would drown. Then when that was done, we would go to the forest again, and get more incense, and light it, and go search for boar.

– You mean you would hunt even at night? I thought you don't venture out at night, you are afraid of Tommanyo?

No, we were a lot of Onge then, we were not afraid of Tommanyo, and we would go into the forest at night. We had no fear then. At that time there were Onge everywhere, many bera all over. There were so many of us then. The boars would go to sleep at night, and that's when we would hunt them. It was so easy then (laughing). We would come back during the day, and go look for the boar we hunted the previous night. Then we would take it back with us, smoke it and cook it. And that's how we lived (swatting a mosquito). Its not that things are difficult now. We get rations, and many other things, so these are also easy times.

– Are these good times, you are such a small group now?

We used to be many more then, but the Onge of the old days killed each other off. I have told you how that happened.

– But now you don't fight one another any more, there aren't any fighting Onge now, why are you still decreasing?

It was the doing of the Onge of old times, they shot arrows and finished each other off. And then we became less and less. Or they sicken, get fever and die.

– Didn't you have any of your own medicines?

We have our own medicines [2] too, medicines from the forest. *Torelulu.*

– Torelulu? What is that?

It is one medicine.

– Is it a leaf?

Yes. The doctors who came from Delhi, took some with them, they took some of the medicines of the forest. They will make it in Delhi they said, and bring it back. But nobody brought back anything.

– So, among you, who is there who knows a lot about such medicines?

Torolulua.

– Yes, besides torolulu...which Onge is best versed about these things?

Shishidangagna is another medicine, *mushinya*; we still get all these in the forest.

– Can you still find these medicines in the forest?

Yes.

– When you go to the forest...

Oh, when we go hunt we can find them.

– Will you bring some back for me? Little by little? See, so much of your forests have been destroyed by outsiders. There are many things that are valuable, like your medicines. So when they clear the forest, they are also destroying your medicines, isn't that so? Not only do all these outsiders hunt your boar, they finish off your medicines. I will take all these medicines to the Lieu-

tenant Governor [3] and say, see, these are all the Onge medicines. If the forests are cleared any more, even these will be gone...

Yes...it is all finishing.

– So, you can take all these medicines to the LG and say these are our medicines. Find out what medicines are contained in these leaves. If they think these are all valuable things, maybe they will stop clearing the forest.

Okay, I will bring them, and I will come with you when you go to Calcutta and take them to the LG. They have cleared so much forest now, the forest they took from us on this side (pointing south) they can keep. But the forest there (pointing west) they should leave alone. The forest south they can clear, make a road, it will make it easier for us to get the things we need. The boars are also gone, all these other people also eat boar now. But the forest west still has everything we need, the medicines, the food we eat, that should remain.

– What will you do if all the forest goes?

What can we do? We will eat fish (sombrely).

– When the first inenele (non-Onge) came to Hut Bay, how big were you?

When Shukla[4] babu came?

– Yes when Shukla came? How big were you?

This big (indicating with his hand). Shukla was also very young.

– Yes, now he is quite old.

Then, when he roamed with us in the forest he was a boy.

– Okay, when you were young, or when your umari (father) was young, there was a white man who came here... his name was Cipriani? Do you remember him? A white man? He also roamed the forest with the Onge? Before Shukla?

Yes, I remember, he roamed the forest with the Onge, and he brought some Burmese with him. He was a white man, I have heard. He roamed all over. When another inene came, a tall one, a bada saab, they first came and brought goods for us, and tobacco, we thought they were bringing all this to make it easier for us to live.

– So at that time, were the warrior Onge still alive?

Yes, they were alive but old men at the time, they didn't fight anymore.

– What did your father think when so many people started coming here?

Oh they would come and take photographs...They would leave all these goods by each *bera,* but also take away things from our *tokabe,* from each *tokabe* they would take things away. They would come in a big ship laden with goods. They came to *Deshenghri* (on the west of Little Andaman) in a big ship, full of goods. The big man was a good man, he brought knives, sugar etc.

– What was the name of that bada saab?

How do I know? Tilai will know... Etonoye, we called that big man Etonoye.[5] He brought many goods for us, tea, sugar, rice, wheat, knives, clothes, matches, he gave all this to everybody. He was a good man, he would hunt his own food. It used to be more difficult earlier, to make rope, to make arrows, he also brought knives. He noticed what we needed and he brought these things. He would take photographs. They anchored the big ship near *Deshenghri* and came ashore on a smaller boat. They told us they would give us many things, bring goods for us and go away to Port Blair. Then they would return with more goods for us. And they would take away things from us. They would load all the goods on the smaller boat and come ashore and call us. They would say, see what we have brought, do you like this? What are the difficulties you have, what do you need? We didn't say anything, a lot of times we didn't understand what they were saying. We would say aha! and walk away. (laughing) Tilai told me all this.

– Your father and others used to go far in the dange, right up to Port Blair...?

Etonoye was angry with us, he stopped bringing goods for us. That's why we started making *dange* that we could take all the way to Aberdeen. We shot one of the *inene* who came with Etonoye. The Onge who shot the *inene* was from *Totibui,* the same *bera* as my wife. That's why Etonoye became so angry, he came quietly in a boat at night. We knew he would come and bring guns with him and start shooting at us with guns from the boats. We lay low on the ground. (laughing) They shot big iron balls into the forest. And we took all this iron and put it to our own use. The Onge from *Totibui* was told to hide in the forest. We knew Etonoye would return and demand to know where he was. Where did he go? Where did he go? Go bring him! That's what Etonoye would say. The Onge would say, no, he died (further laughter). They wouldn't tell him where he was. They would say he died. How did he die, Etonoye would ask angrily, go bring him to me. And he would come with policemen.

– Etonoye would talk in your language, in Onge?

He would come and speak in the language of the white man, and over time, hearing it often enough, we learned to understand the language of the white man. There was one person whom Tilai mentioned who understood the language well.

– Okay, one day we will sit with Tilai and talk about all these things with him. Do your children know all these stories, do you tell your devai and dabai (daughter and son) all these stories?

The *ale* (children) hear all these stories from us and grow up, they hear and hear everything and know it well when they grow up. We don't have to teach them anything, they know by hearing all this. That's how they know. My daughter knows everything. We only teach them how to shoot arrow, how to make *dange*, but we don't have to teach them anything about *totekwata* (the past, days of yore).

– You teach your dabai to make arrows, make dange, what do you teach your devai?

When I was this big (gesturing with his hand), my *umare* would say, don't go there now, you'll have difficulties, don't go too far, play nearby, that's what he would teach me. Don't go near the creek now, *toyge* (crocodile) will get you. Play away from the water. When you are big you can go near the creek. That's how he would teach me. Go bring wood, even the young have to work. That's what he would say.

We didn't have clothes then, we would wear the bark from the forest. The girls would make them with *kuendeve*. Those are some of the things we would do. When we speak with Tilai, you will hear more about us. More about us, much more about us. Yes, it will not finish. He has so much to tell about us. Then you can take all this back with you and everybody who has come before will say, I don't have all this, the Onge have told her everything. That's what they will tell you.

– When I write all this, I will say I talked with Bara Raju. Bara Raju told me all these things, so then I will write all the things you have told me. Then

when I speak with Tilai, I will write, this is what I heard when I talked with Tilai and Bara Raju. Tilai told me all these things. Then I will write all those things down. That's how I will write.

Yes you will get to know a lot, and in all that time, I will also earn a salary.

– Are there any spirits to whom you pray or talk to?

When Onge die of arrow wounds, then they go up and become *Ongegi Onkoboykwo*, but when they sicken and die they go down and become *Tommanyo*. As they go up they are *Tineabogalangle*, when they reach *Benange*, they are *Onkoboykwo. Ongegi gaikwambagi gaikwambanka. Kurangega gaikwambagi bencamemba Tineabogalangle. Onkoboykwo tineabogalangle ikoinene.* They are one and the same, *Onkoboykwo* and *Tineabogalangle*.[6]

– Why are you all afraid of Tommanyo, why do you say don't go there, Tommanyo will get you? Why are you afraid?

We are afraid, *Tommanyo* are evil, they prey on little children, take them down below to eat them. They don't return, *Tommanyo* eats them up.

– What does Tommanyo look like, have any of you seen him?

It was the work of the Onge of olden days, a very long time ago. It was the work of the one that walks in the forest, that's who made humans.

– Eyuge?

You have seen the *eyuge* (monitor lizard) in the forest, it was his work to make Onge.

– How did that happen, how did eyuge make humans? With what were humans made? With mud? Clay?

Not mud, a kind of wood.

– Which kind of wood?

Talaralu is what the *eyuge* used to make Onge. I'll show it to you.

– Okay, bring it for me, or take me there. So how was this done?

It was done by *eyuge* (in tones of 'I've told you already!').

– How was the first Onge made? Why did eyuge make a human?

First there was one Onge who was to live in the forest. Then that Onge went to the forest and brought more *Talaralu*. The Onge made a clearing in the forest, then made a sleeping place and a *kame* (sleeping mat) to sleep on, and then planted the *Talaralu* all around. And the Onge went away to hunt. And *eyuge* said, before you leave say "oohoyi, tu aatbo...".(breaking into laughter)

– Who said that, eyuge? (intent on getting this right)

No, the human, the one human said that. "*Tu aatbo, otapisha.*" And that was what the human did. And then left to hunt. And then when the human returned they all called out and the Onge said in astonished delighted, "Arre, there are so many." They were all very happy and they helped with the boar and they cooked it, and at night it was so much fun with many Onge men and women to enjoy each other's company.

– Wait, wait, I didn't understand. First, eyuge made one human, okay, then built a korale for that human, and where did all the other humans come from?

From the same place, it was the doing of that one human.

– What do you mean, how was it the doing of the human?

(Patiently) By planting *Talaralu,*

– Oh I see, so that human planted the Talaralu and made other human. So eyuge made the first human, and then that human made other humans. What was the name of that human?

That human is Onge.

– So, Onge made other Onge, with Talaralu.

(Relieved that I had finally got it) Yes, with *Talaralu*, then made *kame*, and then cleared the forest, and cleared off all the undergrowth, and then placed the *kame* there, and placed it inside a shelter, and put the *kame* with the *talaralu* within that space. And then went off to hunt. And before going, told all the planted *talaralu*, say this, do this, and I will hear from afar.

– Onge told the talaralu? (in disbelief)[7]

(Simply) Yes, *talaralu* understands everything. And that's how Onge came to live here. It was the work of one human.

– But where did the women come from?

The women too, the talaralu were planted in pairs.

– So, the women are also created from Talaralu? From the same kind of talaralu?

Yes, it was the same kind. And that's how there were Onge and more Onge, who filled all the corners. They made their homes and they married and increased in numbers, and there were Onge everywhere, jaba *jaba* Onge, who went to all the islands.

– I see, that was a incredible piece of work by that human.

(As Bara Raju murmured that Onge increased and increased and were everywhere)

– So eyuge was responsible for creating the Onge, but where did people like me come from, who made the inenle?

That I don't know, it's not for me to know that.

– Who made the Jarawa, the Andamanese, the other people who are like you and live at a distance from you. Who made them?

That's not for me to know either.

– They are different?

Yes they are different, only Onge were made in this way.

– Okay, think of this whole earth, the mud below, the sky above, the trees, who made all that, where did all that come from? The sea..., the food we eat, the frogs, the tamarind trees, the sun, the moon, how were all these things created?

The sun...that was the doing of *Kwalokange, mekange*, it was their doing.

– It was the doing of the spirits?

Yes, they are the people who live with *tonkulu*, the sun.

– Which people?

Onkoboykwo.

– So Onkoboykwo lives with the sun?

Yes.

– So, then, why is it that every day, the sun comes up from that side, (pointing east), and then moves across the sky and goes down? What happens to the sun at night?

Gagyakunuwa, it's like a machine below the ground. And that's how *tonkulu* moves (gesturing the direction of movement), far below the ground, below the sea and much further below, and *Onkoboykwo* moves with it. And when *Onkowboykwo* is angry s/he shuts up the sun.

– Oh, so when Onkoboykwo is angry s/he shuts up the sun and it becomes dark?

Yes, it becomes dark during the day. And when s/he is calm again *Onkoboykwo* lets the sun out.

– What about cileme, the moon, why is it that every so often the moon becomes big and round and then slowly becomes smaller and disappears completely and slowly becomes big again?

When the moon's work is finished, it becomes smaller and smaller and disappears.

– Then where... how does it come back?

Onkoboykwo makes another moon.

– But why does cileme become so small?

After it becomes full, its work is finished so it becomes small and disappears.

– I don't understand.

Why?

– I don't understand why cileme becomes small and then becomes big again, does someone eat it up?

How can anyone eat it? After it is full, its light finishes, so it becomes small, and another one is made. It is the doing of *Onkowboykwo.*

– How about the stars, koyekoyele?

They are all the children of *cileme.* They are all the family of *cileme.* The parents of *cileme* are the big stars, and the children are all the small ones. *Cileme,* brothers, sisters, children.

– Why do we only see them at night? Why don't we see them during the day?

(He laughed). How can that happen? It is only at night.

– So at night, when tonkulu is asleep all the stars come out and play?

Yes, *ekwi cholomba,* they all play. *Cilemega ecelele,* all the children, of the moon, she is the *uteddi,* the mother of the stars.

– Who is the father of the stars?

There is no father.

– So tell me about the tides, why are there high tides and low tides. Why does that happen?

(Hesitating) When there is low tide the fishes go away and with high tide there is a lot of fish.

– Why does that happen?

I've forgotten, I used to know. Tilai knows. There is a hole at the bottom, and the water drains out, that's why the level of water drops. Then all the water comes back. It is the doing of *bulundangle,* the jackfruits. It is the path of the *bulundangle,* that's the path that the water follows. *Ekwacile, bulundangle acile. Wa ingegi uttukeaki, ingele.* Tilai knows all this. There is turtle also below. It is full of turtles below. When the level of water falls, the turtles disappear into the hole, and when the level of water rises the turtles return. Its a huge hole below. But the water does not enter the path of the *bulundangle.* The *narelangle,* turtles, stay there, *belakwebe,* and wait to eat, *ilokwalebe.*

– What do the turtles eat?

Tojye!

– What is Tojye?

Tonoetta, the little fruit that you see at low tide.

– Do you eat it as well?

Yes, we also eat that. And it is to eat these fruits that the turtles come into the water. All these waters have the fruits (gesturing around). Tilai told me all this.

– Tai told me that when they hunt turtles, they pray to Tineabogalangle, because Tineabogalangle lives in the moon, and when the moon becomes full, the narelange come out of the hole and fill the seas. And this is all the doing of Tineabogalangle.

He doesn't know anything, what does he know? I see now that he knows nothing.

– Are there any spirits in the forest? In the seas?

(Hesitating) No there are no spirits in the forest, but there is a spirit of the turtle, that lives in the water, *Ingenamkwe*. When the *dange* overturned and the people were tipped over into the water, *Ingenamkwe* ate them up. *Ingenamkwe* comes out at night. *Onglei, dangegianka, dangegilimeagi ekrive bencame chogegi barime etitokwatemdege. Wa lekriva.* And that's how it ends, *ingenamkwa mame*. *Ingenamkwe* lives with the turtles, dugongs, crocodiles.

– Is that why you all don't go far out in the dange any more?

We used to go in the past. They used a different kind of wood, the Onge whose *dange* overturned. One of the Onge was angry, and he pierced it with a spear, and the water entered the craft and filled and everyone drowned. There were children and women and men, and lots of goods...things to eat...young men and women...

– (abruptly interrupting) How do you refer to fire[8] in Onge?

Nobody will tell you that.

– (surprised) Why?

That is the name of *Tommanyo.*

– What do you mean?

That was the name of Koira's father. All his children will get angry if you mention that name. That's why I can't tell you that.

Okay, that's fine. I don't want to know that.
– Among you, is there one who can talk with the spirits? I have heard that there are Onge who go into the forest and can converse with the spirits? Is that true?

Silence.

– I have heard this from people who have been here earlier, like Shukla etc., that there are some Onge who are exceptionally good people, and they have this power to talk with the spirits. Is this true? Are there still such Onge among you? And I have also heard that such Onge can never have any chil-dren? Is this true?

How did Shukla know all this? Onge don't talk about such things.

– I think he perhaps saw something, he roamed about with you in the forest for so many years.

I can't talk about these things, the spirits will get angry. These are not to be discussed with the *inenle.*

– I understand. You don't have to tell me anything that is not permitted. All I really want to know is, are there still such people among you? I don't want to know any details beyond that.

Tilai told me that I should not reveal the names of those who can hear and talk with the spirits.

– What are such people called, kwa gatiba? I have heard that there are three Onge who can still talk with the spirits.

No, there are no such people any more.

– Yes, I heard, Kwerai, Moroi...

Moroi has become mad that's why he says such things, it's a lie!

– It's a lie?

Yes (vehemently) it is a lie! I went with him and asked him where are the spirits, show me. And he said they will come. And I asked him when will they come, aren't they here as yet? No, he's mad. In the past there were such people, there are none left at present. In the past, when Onge would go into the forest to hunt, the spirits would call them, *chera*, come.

– It doesn't happen anymore?

No, not any more.

– Why? Is Onkoboykwo angry with you? Why don't they call you any more? Isn't it true that it is at present that you most need the spirits since there are so few of you?

Oh, *Onkoboykwo* sees everything from above, but he will not come near us. In the past there were many, that's why *Onkoboykwo* had to hear us. Now *Onkoboykwo* cannot hear us.

– What can you do that Onkoboykwo will hear you?

Onkoboykwo will come with the rain, not during the heat of the summer. *Onkoboykwo* stays far during that season. *Onkoboykwo* comes in a *dange*, I have seen it myself in the sea, the *dane* of *Onkoboykwo*, a big *dange*. It was a long time ago. It only happens during the rain, I will show you if it happens when it rains. Tilai has also seen this.

– (Abrupt change in direction) Where do children come from?

From *Ongega Onkoboykwo*.

– How does your wife know that she is pregnant?

By the bleeding, (or more literally, by the congestion of blood)

– You mean when the bleeding stops?

No, by the bleeding, that's how women know.

– Do you mean there is bleeding when the child is born? But before that hap-pens, when the child is in the abdomen, when for a long time the child sleeps inside, ale omokabe, how does your wife first realise that she is with child? That's when the chenga (blood) stops, doesn't it?

In the beginning the blood comes, and that's where it remains, doesn't go away.

– (Trying a different avenue) Why do adolescent girls start bleeding?

The bleeding stops, all that blood, the child is of blood, it is a child of blood. And it gets bigger in the abdomen. The blood remains in the ab-domen and nourishes the child, and drains off the blood, and becomes human. The eyes are formed first, and slowly the rest of the face and body. And when that is all complete, the child is born, *uttukeba*.

– Why do girls bleed every month? Why is it that boys don't bleed?

Boys are different, for them we have a *tamale*.

– What do you mean?

Tanagirua.[9]

– Oh tanagiru. No, but why is there chenga from girls at every new cileme?

The spirit gives the girls blood.

– Which spirit?

Ongega Onkoboykwo, gives *chenga* as well.

– Why?

There is a big bucket, *ukua tukkotota*, full of blood, and *Onkoboykwo* opens it and the blood pours into the girls, and that's when they bleed. A young girl doesn't bleed, *Onkowboyko* looks to see when they are grown and then opens the blood. It's like a pipe with a tap that opens and the blood pours out. It comes from very far, that's why the blood trickles slowly.

– But how does it get inside the girls?

I don't know how that happens. Tilai would know, he didn't tell me that. He told me it was *Onkoboykwo* who gives the blood. Like a pipe for carrying drinking water, there was a pipe of blood. And when the tap is opened, the blood flows, it comes from very far above. And it stores inside the girl's abdomen. Where does it come from? It comes at night when the girl is sleeping, and it is very warm, and girls don't realise when it starts, and they become very weak and continue to sleep. Others see the *chenga* and exclaim, "Arre, the girl's *chenga* has arrived! Shut her eyes, and her eyes are kept closed. And the girl will keep her eyes closed and hear everything around her. They will tell her to be a good woman, and to not go out, her *chenga* has arrived. To stay in the *korale* and sleep on the *kame*. And after five days (gesturing with his fingers) there will be a ceremony. They will get *batage* (a variety of soft, fleshy leaves) from the forest, and tie it around her crotch, and it will staunch the flow of blood, which will continue to flow for five days and then stop. And the girl will get up. They will get tea for her. In the old days there was no tea...

– So what was given to the girl?

Water, a kind of gruel, and *bulundange*. That's what was given to the girl. *Bulundange ejebo* (literally, the eyes of the jackfruit).

– But bulundange is only available during the dry season, what happens when chenga comes during kwalokange? How will you get bulundange during that season?

We store it.

– Oh you store it and keep some in stock?

When the dry season ends what will we eat during the rains? That's why we store *bulundange* to eat during the day. We will store it in a *uku*, (bamboo container) and it doesn't go bad, it keeps well.

– Okay so you feed the girl with bulundange and then what happens?

We feed her *bulundange* and prawns, _a_a, but no fish or pork, *tambonuya*. Pork is taboo then, and when the *chenga* stops her father goes to hunt. Then he brings back the pork, cuts a little piece and puts a small piece in her mouth. The girl swallows it. Then he takes some fat and rubs it on her (laughing). The girl lies prone on the *kame* and everyone sits around her. Then he tells the others to bring the clay and he rubs it. Then all the women one by one rub the clay on her.

– Which clay, the white or the red?

Decorated with alame (red clay), one of the Onge women during the ceremony to celebrate Cikwegi's tamae angabe, (her first menstruation), thereby becoming "one within whom a spirit as a child can find residence". Photo: Sita Venkateswar

We, the white one, *wega ouebe*. *Ga tullebe omokabe, katita tineage omokabe*, she lies down and remains asleep. And that's how it is done. Then in the evening, the girl gets up, opens her eyes and sits up. She asks them to bring *kuendeve* from the forest to make *nakuinege*.[10] It is very long drawn out...in the past they didn't wear clothes.

– *So, when the chenga comes the girls start to wear the nakuinege? When do they start to wear the nakuinege?*

Small *nakuinege* are made, the *batage* is placed below and the *nakuinege* is fastened on top.

– *Then what happens?*

Omokamokaka, she sleeps for three days (gesturing with his fingers). She eats *bulundange* when there is *chenga*, then when it finishes, when it stops completely, she eats pork. And that's how it is done.

– *What is the meaning of chenga? What does it mean for the girl and for the Onge?*

Tolayu...tolayu.

– *Tolayu?*

Mangagi, yes.

– *What does that mean?*

Matellabege.

– *So, you call or refer to her as tolayu?*

Mangagi, chengaianka, ka beje, yes, when the blood starts to flow..

– *No, what I'm trying to find out is this: amongst us, the inenle, when a girl starts to bleed, she is considered to have become a woman, and if she does marry she can have a child. If she gets married before her chenga starts, then she cannot have a child until it starts.*

First (in the beginning), if she is not married, the *chenga* remains trapped, but after marriage the blood of the child arrives in the abdomen. It is the doing of the spirit for the girls.

– But what is it that you believe, when the chenga starts what does it mean?

There is no *chenga* made for those who are unmarried, the *chenga* is given later. It will not be alive until then. How can it be alive until that happens? Until the *chenga* is given there can be no life, it will die.

– Who will die?

Unnatimbo.

- The girl will die?

Mangagi, yes. *Chenga moba bencame. Chenga ingyna membabe tineage.* The blood is like drinking water for the girls, they cannot remain alive without it. What else?

- They will die without it?

Or else what? It was all the doing of the ancient Onge. If the *chenga* does not come the girl will die, they need the blood. That's why *Onkoboykwo* releases the blood for the girl. We say *jogemaame.*

– Jogemaame?

Jogemaame, it is the name of the blood, *gatibe chenga*. For you also that has happened.

– That's right, its the same for me as well. Okay, why do you have a tanagiru for boys?

Girayewa.

– What's that?

When a boy becomes tall, and he goes to hunt, and if he is afraid... (breaking off) it's going to start for Gulame.

– (very excited) It's going to start?

Yes, shortly, in a while.

– How long?

It will start soon.

– When? when?

It will begin, arre, it will begin soon. I've told them to make the arrows, *cenokwa* for Gulame's *tanagiru*...

– Who is making the cenokwa?

Oh Koirai.

– Cenokwa? Why Koirai?

Koirai will also make it.

– But why Koirai in particular?

Cenokwa!

– Why isn't anyone else making the cenokwa?

Oh the others will also make it. Why should it take everybody to make *cenokwa*? When it finishes, more will be made. The boar will break the arrows, so there will be a need to make more. The arrow head will be tied with a rope to the stem, and when it breaks, more are made. That's how it is. So, the *cenokwa* will be made and kept in the *korale*, and replenished as required.

– So this tanagiru will be for Gulamegi and Prakash[11]?

Yes, it will be for Prakash too. But how can I go to Prakash's ceremony, I have work here in Dugong Creek.

– Yes, he is in South Bay (pondering the problem).

If I go and stay there, how can things function here?

– Talk to Palaiyan.[12]

I can, but he will say, don't go, there is a lot of work here, we need you here. Palaiyan will only get agitated and insist that I not go. There aren't enough people here to manage all the work...(laughing)

– But for a ceremony as important as a tanagiru..?

Yes...(switching track)...the *tanagiru* for Ramesh and Mohan, you couldn't see that!

– I did, I saw the photographs, you want to see them, I have them here in a book?

Yes show it to me. The ceremony for the boys will start. The mother will call the boy and tell him to sit beside her. She will say, there is a girl, will you marry her? And he says, of course I will! When? And the mother will say, she has to grow a little more.

– So, in the case of your daughters, Sakuntala and Lily, how were their marriages arranged? Did Sakuntala come and tell you that she liked Oroti? Or was she too young?

No, she is young. I saw Oroti in South Bay and approved of him and I thought he would be good for my daughter. I asked the old man there...

– Dagule?

Yes, Dagule. I told him, give me this boy for my daughter. And Dagule said alright, in a short while, and then you can take him. Then when the time came Dagule told me take him with you now to Dugong Creek, and marry him to your daughter. And so I took him with me. Oroti's mother told me take my son with you, and marry him to your daughter. And that's why I gave them my daughter, they gave me the boy and I gave them back my daughter.

– You mean your other daughter, Lily? You gave them Lily for Prakash?

Yes, for Prakash. But she is still too young, she needs to grow bigger.

– So then, Lily will go to South Bay?

No, I won't let her go to South Bay. There are no proper medical facilities in South Bay, she will stay here. Who will look after her if she goes there? Conditions are difficult there, and there is a lot of work here. That's why I look after my son-in-law here, I told him to be in charge of taking the children here to school and back. They won't stay in South Bay. My brother is there now, he has been staying and working there for a long time now.

– But South Bay is very beautiful, much more so than Dugong Creek.

Yes, but when the rains come living there becomes difficult. Now during the dry season it is very nice there. It is still very forested there, and you can't see anything until you come up close. During the rains, they stay away from the sea, they move further inland into the forest. There is too much wind from the sea. It will start soon. We will fish during the rains, not hunt, that's why I have made and kept a *dange* ready.

– For fishing?

Yes.

– So, who at Dugong Creek has independently liked someone and decided to marry the person? Is there anyone who went and told their parents, their umeri and kairi, look I like this person, I want to marry this person?

Oh, all that is the doing of the others. My daughters were married differently. Children are too young to know their minds.

– Who do you prefer more, a son or a daughter?

Oh, the youngsters don't know any better. It is up to their mothers to decide. When they grow older they will realise that. We will explain it to them.

– No, what I meant was, when a child is born, do you have any greater preference for a girl or a boy?

It is all the same, we want a daughter and a son. (then returning to the earlier discussion) I decided to marry my daughters to the boys from South Bay, I decided to not marry them to anyone here. I didn't like anybody here.

– Why?

My wife decided that. That's why I went to South Bay and brought them here. I went to South Bay and conferred with the people there, with my wife's brother...

– Botale?

Botale. And he said alright.

– Why didn't you like anybody here? There is Titooi, Rajkumar...? You didn't like them? Santosh?

No, now they won't come near my daughters. Otherwise, they would have taken my daughter to the forest and ...(laughter). Now they are married, so the boys stay away.

– Yes, I know. The children have been telling me stories about all the things they do, playing and fucking...

Enge choloate, they are playing...

– So, you don't have any restrictions about this, that before marriage there should be no ketolo, only after they marry? Do you have any such rules?

Yes, there is. We scold them, but we don't punish them or anything, we only make a row sometimes.

– So you tell them, all you adults tell the children, don't do these things, it is not right?

Yes. The mothers scold the children. She will say, I know what you are up to, I know you are going into the forest for *ketolo*...(laughing) that's what they will say (more laughter). You're only pretending you are going to play...that's how they will say...you are all up to mischief, I know. That's how she scolds them.The children see the others doing all this and they ask their mother, what are those children doing, I don't understand? (laughter). The mothers then scold those other children.

– Does it ever happen that after marriage, one or the other goes away with someone else?

Among the other Onge?

– Yes?

How can I tell you that? Yes of course it happens, but I'm not going to tell you about that.

– Why not?

They will get angry.

– Who will get angry?

It's their business, it is not my concern, all those lesser people do things like this, it's not for me, for more important ones.

– *But it's just these kinds of intrigues between you that has always been ignored by other people who come here. It's the sort of thing that happens everywhere, but everyone pretends it doesn't exist.*

Will you be afraid?

– *Why would I be afraid?*

They won't do anything to you. If I talk about these things the others will get angry and abuse me.

– *How will they know?*

It will all be inside that (pointing to the tape).

– *How will they hear that? My bajagegarena (tape recorder) remains inside my suitcase. And how will anyone else know what I discuss with you? You do this all the time, all the places that I'm really trying to understand, you keep saying you won't tell me. How will I ever understand anything about you if you refuse to tell me the most important things? Okay, I'm turning this off.*

May 10, 1992
Naboralegi's imminent delivery has provided much "food" for discussion. From all the women gathered around, it seems the soul of the child enters the womb through some food that is eaten. When a woman eats some food at someone's house and spits it out or/and throws up, either she is supposed to have conceived at that moment, or the spirit entered the womb through that particular food eaten on an earlier occasion. Therefore, the child is supposed to be the "gotechele" of that food, and the person in whose house the food was eaten becomes the "gutarandi". The denotative term for the child then is, for instance, "tanjai otechele", "titoreve otechele", "tambonuya otechele" etc., according to the specific food associated with it. The relationship between the gutarandi/allankare is that of a parent/child, which suggests that it is a form of godparental relationship.

(Extract from field notes)

October 7, 1992
Quite unexpectedly, Totanange and family trooped into the guest-house, braving the rain. His explanation was simple, the children wanted to come. Then
he settled in for a good, long session, obligingly drawing a map of the differ-

ent routes in the forest, marking out the "bera," and the different kinds of terrain, as they perceive it. There are four, which keep alternating through the territorial divisions:

butu- forest with pathways cleared of undergrowth
tambojoko- dense forest with no paths
totijalo- along the sea shore
Tontebui- alongside the creeks

His response to why they shared their food was "ekwa kotota mijejille,": so how can we eat if somebody else goes hungry?

He says that in the past, Onge fighting was usually over a woman, people from one bera refusing to give a girl in marriage to another bera, so she was kidnapped. Then fights would ensue, with much killing and burning of their tokabe.

(Extract from field notes)

The conversation with Bara Raju came to an end on an irate note. Despite my dissatisfaction with his adamant refusal to be persuaded into divulging what he perceived as best kept away from me, the interview with him proved to be a richly informative blueprint for further research. Later interviews with him and other Onge fleshed out some details, but some areas remained impervious to any negotiations on my part. Aside from the actual content of the discussion, a number of interrelated factors arise from the interview transcribed above, and others that occurred over the months with Bara Raju, Tai, Totanange, Ramesh and Tilai, which I will discuss sequentially below. Foremost among these is the issue of secrecy, and the possible reasons for its existence.

The power of secrecy, the right to withhold

Ehrenreich (1985) remarks on a set of behaviors among the Coaiquer of Ecuador that he defines as a strategy of secrecy and dissembling:

"[T]o project an impenetrable 'false face' image to non-Coaiquer...the intensification of this strategy, long employed by Coaiquer people, is a direct response to the racism and prejudice which has characterized their treatment at the hands of outsiders...Through concealment, manipulation, denial and meticulous efforts at control, Coaiquer create an impression on outsiders which is a carefully constructed sociocultural illusion. They rarely permit outsiders to witness anything but this purposefully misleading and elaborate cultural mirage." (p.300)

He goes on to describe his experience with the Coaiquer as:

> "[N]ever an easy group of people to work among. The essence and core of their culture are in direct conflict, culture encourages silence, secrecy and dissembling from its members as the quintessential responses to inquiries from outsiders." (p.20)

This exposition can very well be transposed to my own fieldwork experience. On the face of it, they were remarkably friendly and obliging, but the moment my inquiries moved beyond the visible, and teetered on the edges of an interior and personal realm, threatening exposure of that world, there was a perceptible withdrawal and silence even though they remained smiling all the while.

Very often, the interactions took on the proportions of a game, hints and cues that were teasingly proffered, but when I eagerly followed in search of more, there was an immediate laughing withdrawal, and I was left to decipher what I could from the glimpses that I had received. On reflection, and by distancing myself from the immediacies of the problems that I encountered at the time, it becomes evident that I probably represented what could conceivably be the worst nightmare of perpetual scrutiny. There I was, this "outsider,"[13] with my notebook, tape-recorder and camera, at any hour of the day or night, perennially questioning, subjecting the Onge to unflagging investigation. There was nothing that they did or thought that did not provide scope for further probing. Moreover, my presence in their midst, my very assumption of admittance, was a declaration of the profound asymmetry of the condition of the Onge with respect to the Indians who surrounded them. I had access to the islanders by virtue of being Indian –the disparity of power that my Indian identity conveyed was an integral feature of their daily lives---and I was engaged in an endeavour "to render all things visible". How else could such a condition be warded off if not by resorting to the strategy of secrecy? As Scheper-Hughes (1987) has so perceptively observed of her own experience of research with the Irish and the Pueblo Indians:

> "Secrecy often serves as an effective form of resistance, especially among peoples whose honesty or hospitality has frequently been violated or abused by outsiders" (p.69).

I fully "appreciate[d] the magic and the power of words, and the mighty right to withhold them" (ibid.:73)(cf. Berreman's (1962) account of the problems that he underwent when conducting research in a Himalayan village in India).

Adrienne Rich's passionate evocation of women's silence enriches Scheper-Hughes' insights into the assertive power of withholding speech:

"Silence can be a plan
rigorously executed

the blueprint to a life

It is a presence
it has a history a form

Do not confuse it
with any kind of absence"
(Rich, cited in Visweswaran 1994: 31).

I want to assert that resorting to secrecy is a strategy that has developed over the years, and is linked with the intensification of the Indian presence in the Onge lives. It has never been mentioned in the accounts of earlier anthropologists, who were explicit about other problems of research in Dugong Creek. Pandya (1993: xxii) admits of his experience of research that *"it should not be assumed that native exegesis [was] ebulliently and effervescently forthcoming"*. But his extended analysis of the very spheres that Bara Raju, Totanange and others were reluctant to discuss with me implies a shift in the attitudes of the Onge since Pandya's stint with them in the early eighties. The weariness that could be inferred from Bara Raju's comment on the comings and goings of anthropologists is suggestive of a realization of the futility of exposing themselves to temporary initiates, who took what they could and then left, rarely to return. The eighties saw the effective entrenchment of the Indian government's welfare efforts, with the Onge steadily incorporated into a cash economy. As the thinly-veiled contempt with which many Indians regard the islanders was grasped by the Onge, there was a simultaneous strengthening of secrecy as the most effective means at hand for keeping the intruders at bay.

This analysis is given support by the events surrounding my efforts to live amidst the Onge. My initial delight in the guest-house had worn thin. I resented the constant back and forth in the scorching sun resulting from the need to coordinate the demands of my own domestic existence with the Onge cycle of daily activities. To my mind, the problem could be solved by actually living with the Onge, in their midst. Being with them all the time, and thereby easily correlating my existence with theirs. One of the houses constructed for the Onge had become empty, the former inhabitants, (Shiela and her children) having moved in with another family since the death of Kanju, her husband.

When I broached the idea to some of the Onge whom I felt I had most access to, the initial response was one of puzzlement as to why I would leave the more comfortable environs of the "guest-house" for the house that I had in mind. The children were astonished that I would want to live alone in that house, especially since the former inhabitant (Kanju) had died – *Tommanyo* was bound to come and get me. I pointed out that I lived by myself[14] at the "guest-house" as well. Kanju had not actually died *in* the house, and I was sure that *Tommanyo* would not bother me. Observing that I was undeterred, the Onge that I talked with smilingly agreed to my proposal, in the same way that they always gave consent to everything that I asked of them.

I had to get approval of my plan from the social worker, Lakra, who was officially responsible for my welfare while I was at Dugong Creek. Lakra registered his disapproval of my idea, and flatly refused to have anything to do with it. He listed every possible inconvenience that I would suffer if I were to foolishly undertake such a course of action. He also prohibited the removal of any furniture from the "guest-house" to set up the house that I had in mind.

I went back to the Onge and informed them of Lakra's displeasure, hoping that would spur them on to back my plan. I then asked if somebody could make me a bed-like structure, something like a raised platform[15] on which I could place my sleeping bag. Again, several people agreed, pointing out the individuals who could make one for me in the coming weeks. I was determined not to let anything come in the way of my plan, and immensely relieved that I would soon be able to pursue my field research "properly". To indicate that I meant business, I set about vigorously cleaning the house.

Every day I went to the house, desultorily cleaned it and made inquiries as to when my bed would be ready. Within the next few weeks it was apparent that there was no bed being made, although everyone, as if on cue, reassured me about its imminent completion. Then Bara Raju, told me that the Onge, on reconsidering, did not think it was a good idea for me to sleep in their settlement. There were many of them who were drunk nightly who would bother me, and not permit me to sleep peacefully. Taken aback by this unexpected withdrawal of support, and seeing my dream of doing fieldwork in the time-honoured fashion of "living with the people" receding into the distance, I tried desperately to salvage some part of the plan.

I agreed that it was probably not such a good idea to stay the night in their settlement under these circumstances. But I could still live in the house through the day – write and cook there, spend time with them. It would be so much easier for me to coordinate going to the forest with them. And then, at night I could go back to sleep at the "guest-house". Bara Raju was at a loss for words. The next day I went to the Onge settlement and, with renewed vigour, tried to sound people out on this new plan of mine. To my surprise, whoever I talked with remained singularly unenthusiastic to the change. Unfazed, I was resolute that I was going to do it, with or without anybody's help.

There was some ongoing construction work at Dugong Creek, and many different kinds of workers hired for the work. For what I had in mind, I required a carpenter – I needed a work-table, a rudimentary bench, and perhaps a shelf. There were large quantities of leftover planks of wood from previous constructions lying around, and it would be very easy to nail some planks together. So, I went to the supervisor in charge of the construction workers and asked if he could spare one of his carpenters to make these few items for me, and I offered to pay the person for his time. The supervisor brushed aside my suggestion of payment, and readily volunteered one of his workers for the task within the next few days. As the days passed by and no bench or table materialized, I made diffident enquiries about the progress of my request. Eventually, the supervisor disclosed that the social worker, Lakra, had told him to disregard any request that I made that would enable me to live in the Onge settlement. I was to receive no encouragement for such a venture.

I finally gave up. I never did get to live with the Onge. Hurt by what I perceived at the time as a rebuff from the Onge, I withdrew from them and decided to leave Dugong Creek for a while. I intended to explore the possibilities of living in the other Onge settlement at South Bay. It was only much later that I started to grasp what was at stake, for the Onge, and for the social worker.

I had understood the implications of the social worker's rejection of the plan at the outset. He did not want anybody like me on the spot who would be witness to his and the other welfare personnel's dealings with the Onge. This was the avenue for the traffic in alcohol, and there was too much at risk for him to permit me the possibility of acquiring direct evidence of its existence. But for the Onge it was an entirely different issue. They did not hide from me these individual pacts that existed between the welfare staff and themselves. It was almost in the nature of a joke that they shared this information with me. For them, however, the settlement was *their* domain, the only one still left to them. Even though they later nominated me as an *ijejille*, one of us, I would remain an outsider to that domain, which they would keep protected in their gentle, inoffensive way from my constant vigilance and interest.

A related aspect of secrecy is Ehrenreich's (1985) discussion of what he terms as "dissembling" behavior, the essence of which is:

"[R]estraint of emotions and concealment of activities, e.g. disguise and

simulation, not lying, deviousness or manipulating, although deceit and manipulation may be involved." (p.28)

Ehrenreich goes on to explain this as:

"[A] behavioral security response employed by individuals and groups in cultural maintenance. Taken together, secrecy and dissembling are defined as mechanisms of sociocultural and political process." (p.29)

This definition provides a framework for understanding the Onge's response to my proposal to live with them. It is by employing a range of dissembling behaviors that the Onge evade the demands of wage-work (or other kinds of labor) that are made on them, and which direct their energies away from the activities that are of greater significance to them. By avoiding direct confrontation and rejecting an outright refusal, the Onge present a smooth, unperturbed front that permits them to maintain untouched those aspects of their lives that sustain their existence.

Gossip and anthropological practice

April 9, 1992

"This evening when the video team had packed up and were leaving the settlement, the kids called me back and indicated that I should sit with them on the sand. They have obtained a square board, on which they have poured sand, and are using it as a "blackboard." Dalda, rather quick and creative, represented Tommanyo, and then erasing it, drew a dange with two people on it, and other roughly constructed dange lying around.

Then, most unexpectedly, Dalda drew the outlines of a vagina, and gestured with her fingers to indicate the act of copulation to explain what it was. She further elaborated by pointing to Shanti, Meena Rani and herself, then me, to show that we are the ones to possess it, meanwhile drawing more vaginas of varying sizes to indicate its enlargement with age. Then, she and all the other children gathered around her explicitly demonstrated how copulation occurs between various couples, both children and adults, embellishing their actions with the appropriate sounds that accompany each couple's activities. All this was within hearing of Choiboi and Bebai, neither of whom hushed the children or appeared embarrassed by the discussion.

The children wanted to know who among all the men presently residing at the "guest-house" I was sleeping with. I had to tell them, regretfully, that my man was far away.

(Extract from field notes)

In his ethnography of Nicaragua during the Sandinistas, Roger Lancaster (1992) unabashedly reveals that gossip was a significant source of his data. Lancaster suggests that, as a form of face-to-face interaction, "gossip established a true collectivism of language. It is all give-and-take. Nothing truly belongs to anyone; it all circulates in the form of information, speculation, between and among us" (1992:71-74). By its essential "tackiness," such that "it sticks to us all," it includes within its reach the anthropologist, who does not stand apart from the quotidian round of gossip that is generated in the field. She, too, is bound "in tangible ways" to the circuitry of gossip as "speaker, spoken to, and spoken about".

By the children's spontaneous disclosure of the ongoing speculation about my sexual activities while residing at Dugong Creek, I became aware of my own inclusion as both participant and subject within the circuitry of gossip. During my stay there, the "guest-house" often housed visiting officials and administrators. Sometimes, the large numbers of people arriving together meant that the two rooms in the "guest-house" had to be organized to accommodate everybody. Maintaining strict gender segregation was not always possible under these circumstances. It struck me that whenever there was a heavy onslaught of visitors to Dugong Creek, I had a stream of Onge suddenly arriving to inspect the "guest-house," and to question me about the existing sleeping arrangements. By the same token, on entering the field of gossip as "gossiped about," I also became privy to information that had been earlier held away from me.

From my discussion above, it is apparent that there is an uneven disjunction between "secrets" and "gossip". There were levels in the flow of information, some of which were permeable to boundaries, while some others remained inflexibly sealed off. Negotiating between these discrepancies is the task of long-term fieldwork. But, whatever the duration of one's relationship to "the people", it must be acknowledged from the outset, with all humility, that one's knowledge is "limited, partial, and one-sided" (ibid.,: 74).

The Andamanese at Strait Island and Port Blair

I made a brief visit to Strait Island in 1989 during my first trip to the Andaman Islands. The island was deserted except for one old couple in residence. The narrative that follows below is a transcription of an interview with Nao (the elder)[16], estimated to be about 80 years of age at the time. Unlike my sessions with the Onge that were to occur later, this was a monologue conducted with minimal prompting on my part. Habituated to being recorded,[17] Nao spoke with practised ease, meandering from one topic to the next, covering all the ground that he inferred to be of interest to me. All conversations with the Andamanese occurred in Hindi.

I am of the Jeru, we (indicating his wife Bowa) are from Mayabunder. All the Andamanese, the different groups, we used to meet at Mayabunder. We didn't always understand each other. The British brought us to Kalapahar. They would send us to the forest to bring things for them, or from the sea. They gave us rations and clothes in return. I was a little boy when the forests of Mayabunder were cleared. After the British won the big battle at Aberdeen, they started cutting down the forest everywhere. We were at least a thousand at the time. We have dwindled to such a small group by eating all kinds of things---alcohol, ganja, opium. The British used to give us many of these things. Before all that, we may have numbered as many as 2000-3000 people. I don't like to think of how little we have become, even we are old. I don't like to think of what will happen afterwards, all my family are dead.

Jirake (the current Raja) and his family, they are Aka-bo, they are from Diglipur. There used to be a different Raja for each group. The Raja was one who was the oldest, who knew the most. He was the wisest, he could advise everybody. Jirake doesn't know anything. He doesn't bother to teach the children anything, their language, their songs, stories. Everyone goes all over the place in search of alcohol. Jirake doesn't do anything to stop it. I am the only one who protests, but no one listens to me anymore. Previously, we had to struggle a lot to get one meal a day. Now we have food, shelter, everything is readily available. But no one works any more. Even when I shout at them and scold – I say, cultivate, look after the cows –I am the only one who tends my plot. Everyone else is only interested in drinking.

We are more comfortable now, we used to fall sick because of the drought and rain. We would treat illnesses with medicinal plants (Tao). We would dry the plant and powder it, then mix it with water and drink it, it was cooling. We used to mix clay with water and apply it all over when you had fever. It would cool the body, and take away the pain. There used to be one among us who knew how to cure all illnesses. He was like a doctor.

The sun, moon and the stars are all made by Biliku, she is a woman, she lives in the east. Tharaye is male, he lives in the west, but Biliku is stronger than him. Dik is the god below Biliku. Dik brought pig for us, and the pig went into the water. He made a small fish and then cut it up, and filled the oceans with fish. Dik has one leg placed in Diglipur and the other in Calcutta. He made the land and stones, previously everything was water. Dik made land, he made mud from his own body, then brought seeds. Dik took a rib and planted it into the soil and made man.

We have a week of fasting during Roja,[18] when we worship Biliku. We used to only drink water, and eat wild roots, or fruits soaked in water. Then at the end of the week we would eat tanten (a tree like the jackfruit). We ate the seeds. It sustains hunger for a long time. We would hunt turtles, fish with arrows and spears. We hunted turtle at night, lit by the phosphorescence and the moonlight.

I have seen the Shaitan,[19] I know what Lau looks like, he looks and speaks like a man. He comes during the day and even in the evening. Your hair stands on end when he comes near. But, I am not scared of him. I don't scare easily.

This is how a marriage took place in the past. The parents selected the couple. The girl and the boy sat together, and the Raja would give them a long talk. He told them what to do, how to live. We made necklaces and bracelets with shells and flowers, there was a great deal of singing and dancing, everyone would come. Two Andamanese boys married Hindustani girls. It didn't last, the girls left. The Raja didn't do anything to advise and prevent the break-up.

(Sighs) I don't like it now, we have become so little. Maybe our girls should marry the Onge boys. The two Rajas should speak to each other about that. Did you know, the Onge used to come by boat and frequently visit us in the past? We have a long relationship.

(Transcription of interview)

Some notes on a distressing field trip

When I returned to the Andaman Islands in 1991 to undertake my long stretch of fieldwork, I met Lichu in Port Blair. She was living at "Adi Basera," the "guest(rest)-house" for the "tribal" peoples, recently renovated by the AAJVS. She was there with her children, and some more Andamanese women. They had all gathered there at the time to be with Surmai, wife of Jirake, who had just delivered twins at the Port Blair General Hospital.

My entry into "Adi Basera" had interrupted something, as I realized from the simmering tension around me. Golat, Lichu's husband had made an unexpected visit to Port Blair that morning. Suddenly, I was in the midst of a domestic brawl, a blur of fists and knives, with choice expletives flying around me. My dismay and discomfort at witnessing such a scene, as I groped for a way to extricate myself and make an unobtrusive exit, was allayed by Lichu's unperturbed insistence that I remain there.

I spent all my waking moments during the next month with Lichu, roaming the streets of Port Blair with her, convinced that I had found my "Nisa". She was going to be the subject of my dissertation. Lichu was articulate and humorous, a streetwise and irreverent urchin, and we hit it off right away. As the weeks went by, while I took copious notes of her "adventures",[20] I realized that Lichu had made a shrewd assessment of just how financially rewarding it was for her to "work" with me. She was going to hold out for the highest bidder. Better yet, Lichu informed me, she would write her life-history herself, with the backing of the Anthropological Survey of India. She would be guaranteed an advance of several thousand rupees from them, she assured me, and that would enable her to live comfortably in Port Blair. Meanwhile, Lichu courteously offered me the use of her house in Strait Island, when I decided to live there with the rest of the Andamanese.

Strait Island is a small island, north-east of South Andaman, a five-hour journey from Port Blair on the bi-weekly ferry service. It is a small, comma-shaped forested island, known for its caves of bird's-nest, and plentiful deer. Unlike the Onge settlement at Dugong Creek, the Andamanese settlement was a pleasant and shady environment, conveniently constructed like a model village in India. Slate-roofed houses, reinforced with concrete, were organized as two large rooms, with a separate kitchen space and a large porched veranda in front. The houses were arranged in a circle, with the Andamanese occupying one half of the semi-circle, and the welfare personnel the other. All around the houses were coconut palms, swaying in the breeze, alternating with tamarind and mango trees.

Availing of Lichu's offer, I actually lived *with* "the people" in this particular field site, surrounded by them on all sides. At night, I shared my room with Lichu's and other children, who were sent to keep me company. Hence evenings and nights erupted into games or quarrels that I was often called upon to adjudicate. But ironically, while I found a way to live with "the people" here, most of the Andamanese themselves were scarce, departing on the bi-weekly ferry to Port Blair, Long Island or Mayabunder, where they had friends among the "Ranchis" [21] and the Karens.

In 1970, when the meagre remnants of the Andamanese population were resettled on Strait Island, it was in tangible ways a rehabilitation, providing the small group with some access to a means for survival that had been appropriated from them. Subsequent to their treatment for various addictions (mostly opium), or other chronic ailments like tuberculosis or syphilis, it was assumed by the Andaman administration that with a stable resource base provided to the Andamanese, they would shortly thereafter revert to their former hunting-gathering-fishing mode of existence.

Generally speaking, three generations can be observed as existing on Strait Island where the Andamanese have been resettled, with striking differences exhibited by each, wrought by their separate historical experiences. The oldest generation, at present comprising four members, distinctly "Andamanese" in their physical appearance, have recollections of another time characterized by a different way of life.

Three generations of Andamanese at "Adi Basera", Port Blair. Photo: Sita Venkateswar

All remember a time in the forests of North Andaman[22] where they lived until they came to Port Blair, and retain habits of work and activity related to a daily procurement of food. These are the people who are never idle, even though at periodic intervals they indulge in binges of drinking. They have survived the ravages of opium addiction, alcoholism, tuberculosis and syphilis, none of which destroyed the core of having to work[23] for their survival, testifying to their strength and resilience. They form the backbone of the community.

The next generation, consisting of about eight individuals, are the ones in flux, bearing the scars and living the consequences of administrative bungling. Cast off and adrift, their lives are a battleground for their changed circumstances of existence. This generation grew up under the auspices of the welfare system and were raised, relatively speaking, in a time of plenty. Assured of a daily supply of food without any individual effort, retaining none of the skills typical of an "Andamanese" or any that would find them a place in mainland society. Habits of work inculcated during childhood were lost because of schooling in Port Blair, which inevitably none of them completed, dropping out within a few years of high school. Now, they are content to be idle, alcohol and affairs with *lau*[24] providing the only diversion for the men and women respectively. Their ambiguity of identity is related to ambiguity in physical appearance. While claiming an "Andamanese" identity, they are uncertain as to what the markers are for such an identity.

The present generation of children ranges in age from a few months to eighteen years. The boys have been introduced to alcohol either by their fathers or the welfare staff, and the girls have only to attain puberty to be seduced (sometimes with their parents' consent), usually by the welfare staff appointed at Strait Island.

Throughout the intervals that I spent in Strait Island, or when I met with them at Port Blair, I was frequently reminded of the imminent ceremony that would be held to mark the coming of age of some of the adolescent Andamanese (a separate one for the boy and girl in question). As time went by, the ceremonies were as regularly postponed to the next season. Meanwhile, Munni became pregnant and underwent an abortion, without any perceptible dent in the proposed grand ceremony for her. All the Andamanese that I spoke to persisted in their promise of an elaborate ritual for me to document before my return to the US.

Invoking a ritual that has ceased to impart any relevance to their ongoing existence seems a pathetic attempt by the Andamanese to assert some semblance of structure and identity to an otherwise meaningless or disconnected lifestyle. Their claim to an Andamanese identity is propped up by reference to a misty past that exists in the memories of only a few surviving members. For those Andamanese as well, their recollections were already divorced from any basis in an ongoing lifeway that could sustain such an identity.

Extract from transcription of discussion with Jirake

December 15, 1991, Strait Island

I have ten children, five girls and five boys. The government tells us to have more children. They tell us we should increase our numbers. We were about 80-90[25] people when I was young. We have dwindled because of various illnesses. We used to stay with the Karens, we learned to take opium from them. I get Rs. 475 and my wife Surmai get Rs. 75 every month from the government. We get free rations. I like it here now, we have lights, electricity, a fan when it's hot. We have become used to living like this, eating food cooked with salt, masaa etc. In the past, we used to heat stone until it was red hot, put leaves on top, then put the meat on top and cover it over with more leaves, add a layer of mud, and that's how we would cook meat. We would dry the meat by placing it on a bamboo platform over the fire, it would keep for several weeks.

I wonder how long the government will continue to help us, nobody is interested in doing anything.

Conclusion

This chapter is an immersion into the "local," focusing narrowly on some key individuals among the Onge and the Andamanese, and the substance of my interactions with them. The context and the content of the encounters between the two groups are radically different. But they are juxtaposed by my insertion into these sites, and the ways in which my expectations, perceptions and, hence, my experience of each was inflected by the other. For instance, as I mentioned earlier, I arrived in the Andaman Islands in search of hunter-gatherers. My disappointment with the Andamanese non-conformity to these expectations led to an over-attribution of "authenticity" to the Onge lifestyle. As demonstrated in my questions in the interviews conducted with the Onge, my field of vision (revealed in the photographs included here) encompassed solely those "unique" characteristics that were affirmative of a hunter-gatherer existence. These photographs, divorced from the contradictory complexities of daily existence, perpetuate a certain representation of the Onge as "Stone Age Tribals" (Mukherjee 1995) living in a "timeless" world (Mason 1994), to which I have been unwittingly complicit. However, neither the Onge nor the Andamanese were easily amenable to the polarities by which I constituted them, and this chapter is riddled with the tensions of my disjunct expectations and experience of each of the two groups of people.

As the interview with Bara Raju and the extracts from my field notes suggest, all my questions were directed towards eliciting information that would render them more "Other". My increasing concern and anger about their situation is also evident, but the predominant leitmotif that runs through my interactions with them is my efforts to capture and synthesize an "exotic" worldview.

But what is also apparent in the response of the Onge is a distinctly pragmatic view of affairs. "What will you do if the forests are gone?" I ask Bara Raju. I hoped for a tragic lamentation of the centrality of forests to their existence. His uncomplicated response was, "We will eat fish." It left me at a loss for words.

Likewise, my queries to Totanange as to why they shared food elicited an answer, equally lucid in its simplicity. "We are all one people," he said, "how can we eat if someone goes hungry?" Bara Raju's response was more practical. "If I don't share my food, how can I get anyone to do work when I want them to?" I was disbelieving of such an obvious explanation, which challenged the basis for the elaborate charts that I had set up to document the distribution of food. Hence, over several months I kept detailed records of who hunted, who apportioned the meat, how many people came to take it, how often, who ate the meat after it was cooked etc. At the end I was forced to conclude that everyone ate everywhere. If anyone was hungry, they just walked over to where there was food. It applied to any kind of edibles, from tobacco and areca nuts to pork and honey.

But food had to be demanded, otherwise the Onge simply concluded that it was unwanted. During my stay at Dugong Creek, I tried to separate myself from the other Indians around, namely the welfare staff, by never asking or taking anything from the Onge, unless it was offered to me. Whenever the Onge returned from a hunt, or with a large catch of fish, crab or shellfish, even before they reached their own houses, the welfare staff waylaid them and demanded a share for themselves. I was scrupulous, I thought, by refraining from following suit, even when I was coping with a very low supply of provisions. I hoped I was making a point that was duly noted by everyone concerned.

One day, after a long trek through the forest, we reached the camp late afternoon, tired and hungry. Ramesh had hunted a large tusked boar, an *olonga*, and the appetizing smell of meat cooking directed us to where the camp was located. Everyone walked up to the cooked meat smoking over the fire, helped themselves to a large chunk, and fell to eating with great gusto. I sat and watched them, getting hungrier by the minute, salivating at the smell, waiting for someone to think of offering me some. I waited in vain.

Finally, unable to bear it any longer, I started a long wail of complaints. I reminded everyone present of all the times that they had stopped by at the "guest-house" and eaten with me. Of how lavish I was in my hospitality, freely offering of my scarce and infrequently replenished supply of food. And here I was sitting beside them, watching them eat, and nobody thought of giving me any. The Onge stopped eating to stare at me in surprise, lips glistening with grease. "We thought you didn't want any," said Oroti. "We thought you don't eat pork cooked the way we eat it," chimed in Entogegi. "You've never asked us for some," added Kokegile, "how do we know you want it unless you ask for it?" "Take it if you want it."

By that time, the meat had been sitting awhile, and the flies and the dogs had started settling on it. I couldn't bring myself to partake of any.

My persistence in attempting to unearth an "authentic and "native" exegesis of all issues was exposed during a discussion with Berogegi. Returning to a question that I had asked of everyone, I wanted to know how he interpreted the decline in their population. What were his views on why their numbers had diminished drastically? Did he, like Bara Raju, lay the blame on the "old-time" Onge, fighting and killing each other off? Berogegi's response was that people started falling sick, getting fevers more frequently and dying. My dissatisfaction was writ large on my face. There was nothing quintessentially "Onge" to this response.

Reading my expression, Berogegi smiled knowingly in my direction. He had surmised what I wanted. "It was *boorage*," he began. "*Boorage* got us. He lives under the ground, this frightful monster. He comes out at night and creeps upon the unwary. He preys on little children and the elderly. Sometimes, when he is very hungry, he even grabs the strong. He is stronger than any Onge, twice as strong as *Tommanyo*. That's how it happened."

Satisfied by my excited scribbling, he turned to leave. "*Boorage* is what you call malaria," was his parting shot. I wrote a note to myself to check for a similar correspondence with other Onge "spirits".

To make such discordances more explicit, and to elucidate the actual process of research, simultaneously fragmentary and uncertain, I have engaged in a variety of writing strategies in this chapter. These are predominantly simulations of dialogue, and a polyphony of voices, including my own, from my field-notes. I have found it a useful strategy to present the very problematics of attempting to engage in dialogue, under conditions that delimit in some instances, or foreclose in others, the possibilities of "open" communication.   ❏

Notes

1 Reserved means off-limits to the general public. A special "tribal permit" is issued by the Andaman administration for a specific duration on provision of sufficient grounds for seeking entry to these areas. The permits are available solely to Indian citizens.

2 A recent report in a journal in India mentions the discovery of a "magic" plant extract used by the Onge, found to be an effective cure against cerebral malaria. The report goes on to discuss the consequences for the Onge of "patent-hungry profiteers jostling their way down there" (Dasgupta 1996:13).

3 The Lieutenant Governor is the highest executive authority in the Andaman Islands.

4 In the early sixties, Janardhan Shukla, a newly trained compounder, decided to live in Little Andaman with the Onge, roaming the forest with them and living as they did for several years. He is now a retired but honorary employee of the AAJVS.

5 It is unclear who Etonoye was, it is possible he is an amalgam of several people. He may have been Portman or Temple who visited Little Andaman in the early part of this century. Cipriani, as Totanange informed me, was referred to as Koshaiangegi.

6 A later discussion with Totanange clarified that while Onkoboywo/Tineabogalangle were one and the same, Tineabogalangle was the form of women's respectful usage when referring to the spirit.

7 The disbelief was a consequence of the incompatibility of this account of Onge origins with the version discussed by Pandya 1993, based on his research with the Onge in 1983-84. Clifford Geertz's prescient comment about such differing renderings of the same people suggests that the situation is integral to anthropological inquiry. "One can go look at the Azande again, but if the complex theory of passion, knowledge, and causation that Evans-Pritchard said he discovered there isn't found, we are more likely to doubt our own powers than we are to doubt his--- or perhaps simply conclude that the Zande are no longer themselves" (1988: 5).

8 The question about fire was brought about by the abrupt change of subject whenever I tried to initiate conversation on the symbolic significance of fire, discussed extensively by Pandya (1993).

9 The rituals surrounding a boy's rite of passage into the world of adult men, marking him as a fearless hunter. These rituals were the focus of Pandya's (1993) research.

10 The tassel of dried cane worn around the crotch by Onge women.

11 Prakash was to be married to Bara Raju's daughter. He was a resident of South Bay, the other Onge settlement at the southern end of Little Andaman. Bara Raju was affinally related to some of the territorial groups of South Bay.

12 Palaiyan was the AAJVS appointed Plantation Officer for South Bay, as well the temporary social worker for Dugong Creek, while the earlier appointee, Lakra was under investigation on charges of financial mismanagement.

13 Abu-Lughod (1991:141) makes a critical point when she notes that the outsider does not simply stand outside, but always in a certain relation "with the Other of the study...within a larger political-historical complex."

14 In the Andamans and in many parts of India, living alone is considered peculiar, the spontaneous question being, "Why would anyone want to be alone?" When I lived with the Andamanese, I always had a few children sent to sleep with me.

15 Due to the danger from snakes and other rather venomous insects, it was a wise precaution to avoid sleeping on the floor.

16 During a recent trip to Port Blair in May 2004, I learned of Nao (Chacha's) death some years earlier.

17 Despite my explanation of who I was, and what I was doing there, Nao was convinced that I was a representative of All India Radio, Port Blair, since they often wanted to record his stories.

18 *Roja* is the period of fasting observed by Muslims during Ramadan.

19 The Hindi word for the devil.

20 After I accompanied Lichu to a few Hindi films playing in Port Blair, I began to suspect that the "stories" that I had eagerly and meticulously taken notes of were, in large measure, scripted from the scenes enacted on screen.

21 The "Ranchis" are "tribal" people from mainland India, from the state of Bihar, one of the largest "tribal" belts in India. They were usually brought to the islands as laborers.

22 The remaining Andamanese trace their origins back to North Andaman groups, mostly *Jeru*. North Andaman is the northern extreme of the Great Andaman group of islands, and the groups of Andamanese who inhabited that island were the last of the various groups of Andamanese to be affected by the consequences of British presence in the islands. By the time the British left the islands in 1947, the Andamanese of Middle and South Andaman were extinct.

23 Here "work", for want of a better word, refers to the subsistence activities that the Andamanese engaged in, prior to receiving monthly rations from the Indian administration. This generation of Andamanese continue to supplement these rations with regular resources from the sea or the forest.

24 *Lau* is how the Andamanese refer to non-Andamanese, formerly also alluding to the "evil" spirits.

25 Jirake is mentioned by Cipriani (1966) when he was in the islands in the early fifties. Jirake was a young boy at the time. This makes Jirake's estimate of their population an exaggeration, since the Andamanese numbered about 23 people at the time.

THE ISLANDERS IN HISTORY [1]

"With lots of winds from all direction all the spirits came down and they had a war (kugebe) with the Ongees [sic]. After the war ended all the Ongees [sic] were made into stones (kuge). Many of the white men followed the rocks formed in the sea due to kugebe and they all came in the big boats to Bomilla Creek"

(Pandya 1993: 7-8)[2]

"Wherever the European has trod death seems to pursue the aboriginal"

(Darwin cited in Arnold 1988:4)

Introduction

This chapter and the next expands the purview of inquiry from the immediately local context of specific interactions, to interrogate how the "locale" (Probyn 1990) has been influenced, articulated and produced through historical interventions. The Onge tale of dispossession, unlike the Andamanese, begins not with the arrival of the "white man" but with the advent of those of a different hue, the "brown man". But the brush with the "white man" did bring about the "pacification"[3] of both the Onge and the Andamanese, marking a cessation in the struggles by the warriors of yore mentioned by Bara Raju to retain control over their land. "What seldom, if ever emerges, are the opinions and feelings of the dispossessed," says Schrire (1995), "[i]t is not that they were silent...[i]t is simply that they went unrecorded" (p.58-59). Hence we are forced to work with the reports of those confrontations as chronicled by the colonists.

> *"Natives had plenty to say, but they were for the most part illiterate... and one price illiterates pay to history is prejudice. Ignorance of the other person's view brings with it a disinterest, a contempt for the history, and even for the sufferings of those who could not write. Where invasion is concerned silence blunts the impact of the newcomers on the lives and spirit of colonized people." (p.3)*

Schrire confronts this void in her book and seeks to redress the silence in "a series of chronicles of colonial contact" (p.9). Given my focus on policy as a site for the deployment of power, I will not attempt to emulate Schrire but leave another interested historian or archaeologist to render for the Andaman Islanders what Schrire has attempted for the *Khoikhoi*[4] – to re-enact the moment of encounter, and reinscribe into the record the missing voice, the voice of the colonised.

The location of the Andaman Islands at the crossroads linking many of the major civilizations of the East (situated, as it was, at the center of a flourishing sea trade between India, east and south-east Asia and Australia) has been crucial in shaping the documented history of the islands. But, in view of its location, it appears curious that the islands should have remained isolated from the booming trade networks that surrounded it on all sides. Cooper (1989) addressed this question and investigated the archives for traces of non-European contact with the Andaman Islands and its people. She was forced to conclude that it was the Nicobar Islands (the group of islands immediately south of Little Andaman) that was drawn into the Arab, Malay, Burmese and Indian trade networks of south-east Asia over the course of the first millennium. Here again, geography was a major factor. As a result of the direction of currents in the Indian Ocean, the Nicobar Islands were directly *en route* to the passage between the east and the west. Ships reached the shores of the Andaman Islands only when they were blown off course by storms, or shipwrecked.

Despite these factors, the Andaman Islands became central to British strategic interests in the region. In view of the Dutch hegemony over the East Indies, and the establishment of a Danish mission in the Nicobar Islands in the early eighteenth century, the extension of British dominion over the Andaman Islands was important in consolidating British presence in the aforementioned commercial traffic.

Aside from the political manoeuvres of the major colonial powers, trade in Andamanese slaves thrived in these parts, many of whom were supplied to the Rajah of Kedah, part of whose tribute to the King of Siam consisted of these slaves. It was acknowledged by the British writers of that era that the reputed ferocity of the islanders was a probable consequence of being taken captive to be sold as slaves. The trade in Andamanese slaves continued long after the British had established a strong presence in the islands.

Although the islands and its inhabitants had long been a subject of European fascination and dread, very little was known of the islanders. But the myth of the Andaman Islands and its fearful inhabitants was kept alive by the various travellers' tales that existed prior to Colebrooke's report of 1795. The view of the islanders that prevailed was that the Andamanese were barbarously cruel cannibals, "the least civilized perhaps in the world, being nearer to a state of nature than any other people" (Colebrooke 1795, cited in Portman 1899:68).[5] Some information of uncertain accuracy was obtained during the first, unsuccessful British settlement in the islands in 1786-94, and additionally from marine survey ships and other subsequent observers. They correspond with early attempts by the British to secure a strategic location and a safe harbour on this major cross-road of south-east Asian trade.

This chapter examines the span of British control over the Andaman Islands, as made known by the records compiled by Portman (1899), who is the main source of information for this chapter. M.V. Portman is best known for establishing contact with the Onge, in the course of which he completed a coastline survey of Little Andaman. His two volume *History of our Relations with the Andamanese*, comprises letters, official reports and orders, as well as his own commentaries on the islands and the people. They document the history of British relations with the Andamanese (here inclusive of all the indigenous groups in the islands), spanning the period from the first British settlement in the islands in 1789 until 1899, and provide the framework for tracing British policy in the islands.

Unlike other major British writers on the Andaman Islanders at the time, notably E.H. Man who preceded him, or Radcliffe-Brown who followed thereafter, Portman is distinct in taking a more self-aware and critical position in terms of British policy in the Andaman Islands. His voice emerges as sometimes sympathetic, more often caustic, all the while mediating between the directives of the Government of India and the reports sent by the local officers and administrators. It is especially interesting to follow the period when he was himself an administrator in the islands, when his procedure of detailing events and documents takes a marked turn such that the chronicle thereafter is as revealing by its omissions as by what Portman actually reports. For example, while he is critical of the repressive measures employed by his predecessors in their dealings with the Andamanese, when it is his own authority that is challenged by particular individuals or groups, Portman's method of teaching those Andamanese "a lesson" is mentioned without any further comment. His passing reference to the Andamanese objection to the clearing of their forests, alongside his own policy for stepped up deforestation as he tracked down the *Jarawas* is another case in point. His narrative also includes the early travellers' accounts, tracing the itinerary of these tales as they reappeared in later writings on the islands and their inhabitants.

The interactions between the British and the islanders followed a familiar trajectory, one that had been repeated earlier in many different parts of the world. Schrire's (1995) inimitable and trenchant prose recapitulates such a trajectory when:

> *"Tasmania was deemed the perfect place to hold the most recalcitrant British convicts. The shock of contact reverberated in bullets, brutality, and disease as the Royal Navy dumped its unsavory load into the*

Aboriginal land. Sterility and death followed fast as reproductive tubes and lungs were strangled with foreign pathogens. Half-crazed European prisoners escaped from the fortresses that were built to protect and contain them and plunged barbarically into the world of so-called savages. It took around seventy-five years for the British authorities to declare the Aboriginal Tasmanians extinct" (p.170-71).

This section traces the development of British colonial policies with respect to the Andaman Islands, particularly as these are interpreted and executed by the administrators who set up and oversaw the settlement and penal colony. Attention to the ways in which British colonial experience elsewhere intersects with their intent in the Andaman Islands exposes the attenuation of their policies in the aftermath of Tasmania,[6] Australia and the Fiji Islands.

I maintain a thematic rather than a strictly chronological consistency, weaving between years to link similar events separated in time. Broad demarcations of intervals are denoted in the form of distinct sections that separate the period of the first settlement from the second. The chapter is divided into two parts. Part one, the bulk of the chapter, deals with the Andamanese, since they were the groups who were primarily exposed to the British presence in the region. Part two includes a discussion on the *Jarawa* and the Onge.

The ten territorial and linguistic subdivisions of the Andamanese were at the time spread out over the main land masses of North, Middle and South Andaman Islands as well as the other outlying islands. Observers at the time (Portman 1899, Man 1884) note that territorial demarcations were maintained between linguistically distinct groups. All the groups opposed the slow British advance north and westwards from their initial site of colonization on South Andaman. North, Middle and South Andaman Islands were referred to comprehensively as Great Andaman. Throughout my account Andamanese refers only to those groups who inhabit Great Andaman and the smaller islands around it. My term "islander" is inclusive of the Andamanese, the Onge, the Jarawa and the Sentinelese).

The Andamanese and the first British settlement: 1789-1796

From the middle of the 18th century, a number of events in the region of the Indian Ocean underscored the strategic importance of the Andaman Islands. With the establishment of a Danish mission on Nicobar Islands and the steady consolidation of Dutch control of the East Indies, a strong British presence in the region became crucial for control of the trade networks. Successive incidents of shipwreck and piracy on the Andaman Sea further emphasized the security of this sea route for British ships. In 1788-89, the Government of Bengal sought to establish a penal[7] colony associated with a harbour of refuge. Lieutenants Colebrooke and Blair were sent to survey and report. The result of their report was that a settlement was established by Lieutenant Blair in September 1789 on the south-east bay of South Andaman, now called Port Blair but then called Port Cornwallis. [8]

The little colony appears to have "flourished" until it was shifted further northwards in 1792, for reasons of superior strategic location. The second settlement, also named Port Cornwallis, proved to be extremely unhealthy, and the high mortality rate resulted in a quick abandonment of the decision to consolidate a settlement on these islands. But the seven years of British and convict presence on the islands, from 1789-1796, is likely to have had a long and insidious impact on the islanders.

Ferguson's (1990) discussion "exploring the multiple interactions between aspects of indigenous culture and the changes wrought by contact" (p.248) offers some means of filling the gaps in the record. As early as 1791, Lieutenant Blair reports that, "the aborigines occasionally visited Chatham Island for the purpose of begging for some scraps of iron or a little food" (Portman 1899:84), suggesting that the process of obtaining "Western goods" was already underway. If later events can be read as a mirror for this period, we can infer the conflicts generated by the "race" to obtain valued metal goods and implements: the fights that erupted, the intensification of prior hostilities between territorially differentiated groups, repeating a pattern described by Ferguson (1990) in Amazonia, North America etc., of the ways in which Western contact transformed the practice of "native" warfare.

The first settlers on the islands were unaware of the several territorial and linguistic divisions of the Andamanese, or of the existence of a further distinction between inland forest-dwelling and coastal populations. From analysis of the vocabulary and material culture collected by Lieutenant Colebrook during this period, it was later surmised that the population inhabiting the region around the first settlement were, in all likelihood, the people referred to as "*Jarawa*"[9] by the *Aka-Bea-da*. As the forest was cleared for the first colony, it is very probable that the *Jarawa* (when their efforts to repel the advances of the white[10] intruders were found to be of no avail) were displaced and forced into the territorial boundaries of the neighbouring group the *Aka-Bea-da*. This, in turn, is likely to have exacerbated any enduring conflicts between the two groups. Portman (1899) writing at the turn of the century acknowledges the possibility of such a scenario:

"Of what took place between 1794 and 1858 we have no knowledge, but when we re-occupied the Andamans in the latter year, the Aka-Bea-

*da were by far the stronger and more numerous tribe (p.704)...it ap-
pears to me quite possible that some disease was introduced among the
Jarawas by the people of Lieutenant Blair's Settlement which reduced
this tribe considerably in numbers, and thus enabled the Aka-Bea-da
to obtain the upper hand."(p.703)*

Extrapolating from the course of events in subsequent years to an
earlier undocumented interval, the three years of British presence in
South Andaman before shifting further north were sufficient for the
transmission of diseases. The probable introduction of "virgin soil"
(Crosby 1988) epidemic diseases, to which native peoples had little or
no resistance, may have initiated the drastic demographic alterations
that were to manifest themselves more acutely in later years in all the
groups brought into contact with the settlement. A consequence of such
changes as noted by Ferguson (1990) for the Amazon tribes (many of
whom were also forest-dwelling foragers) seems plausible in the Andaman case.[11] Raiding to capture women and children to compensate
for the local demographic imbalances, in turn, compounded the hostilities between groups.

Unbeknown to the sincere British officers, efforts to convey their
"goodwill" to the islanders were in all likelihood an important factor
in the transmission of diseases. Some islanders were detained aboard
ships in semi-captivity for a prolonged period when the officers hoped
to impress upon them their "friendly" intentions, and then released
with gifts, comprising:

*"[U]seful articles of peace, such as carpenter's tools, knives, cotton cloth,
cords, axes, metal pots and pans, as well as with beads, looking glasses
and such like objects of savage[12] finery"* (Portman 1899:217).

A memo from the Govt. of India approves of these practices and hopes
that the captives will give "assistance in reclaiming them from the state
of profound and primitive barbarism in which they now exist" (Portman 1899:216). Schrire (1995) captures the essence of these exchanges
when she describes colonialism as:

*"[A] chronicle of betrayals...the exchanges were a mere preamble to the
big takeover, namely the loss of native land, labor, reproductive capacity, and power, in exchange for nothing at all... perhaps not quite nothing. For after all, there was the exchange of pathogens between parties-
-air-borne viruses and semen-borne bacilli, tick-borne fevers, and rat-
borne plagues. The effects on the indigenous populations were striking."* (p.51-52)

The penal colony: 1858-1899

Numerous incidents of shipwrecks on the Andaman Sea, and the "Sepoy Mutiny" on mainland India some sixty years later, reinitiated the significance of maintaining a strategic base in the Andaman Islands. The Sepoy Mutiny also referred to often as "The First Indian War of Independence" was an important turning point in British colonial policies in India. It was only after this event that the British consolidated their holdings in India, becoming an overseas empire.[13] The East India Company was abolished and its administration was decisively taken over by a Court of Directors in London directly under the Queen. R. C. Majumdar (1962) notes that in appreciation of Lord Canning's able handling of the Mutiny, Queen Victoria appointed him as the first Viceroy and Governor-General of India.

A continuous record of the islands and its inhabitants begins when a permanent settlement in the form of a penal colony was established in 1858 on the Andaman Islands, following the Mutiny in mainland India against the British in 1857. The Mutiny brought up the question of accommodating thousands of mutineers sentenced to life imprisonment. Indian historians writing about this period imply that the sole motive for setting up a penal colony in the Andaman Islands was to transport the mutineers to a place where they would pose no political threat to the British. But the documents compiled by Portman indicate otherwise. From 1855 onwards, a rising tide of protests ensued from the increasing incidence of shipwrecks. The subsequent killing of castaways by the islanders, in a region that was considered a part of British dominion, re-opened discussion of the suitability of the Andaman Islands as a safe harbour for ships. Portman comments:

> *I have often heard it asserted that we occupied the Islands after the Mutiny in order to have some distant and safe place across the sea to send our rebels and criminals to, when in the state of the country it would not have been safe to keep them in India; and that the Andamanese have been killed off as a natural result of the occupation, and the country taken from them without their consent and for no fault of their own. But such was not the case. Long before the Mutiny the conduct of the Andamanese[14] had made it imperative that the Islands should be occupied, and friendly relations established with the Aborigines, and this would have been done sooner had the Mutiny not broken out.* (p.186)

The timing of the Mutiny was both coincidental and fortuitous in terms of providing the steady flow of convict labor crucial to the success of the proposed settlement.

British Policies: the ideal and the reality

Much of British policy with respect to the Andaman Islanders was directed towards treating the islanders "with every kindness," as long as they recognized British superiority or did not stand in the way of British interests. It is instructive to note at this point that the earlier genocide and rapid extinction of the Tasmanians was a stark example for the British of the devastation unleashed on small, isolated populations by a penal colony. The Andamanese were repeatedly compared to the Tasmanians whom they appear to have resembled, many theories imputing them to the same race of people. Portman asserts:

> "[T]he English have nothing to reproach themselves with regarding the Andamanese, whatever may have been the case in Tasmania; and, having the unfortunate experiences of that penal colony, and our treatment of the aborigines there, before them, the Government of India adopted a policy towards the aborigines of the Andaman Islands which has made them, above all races of savages, the most carefully tended and petted." [my emphasis] (p 209-210)

Between the years of 1858-70 any strategy, if even faintly reminiscent of Tasmania, was firmly deflected. As Portman contends:

> "[A]nything savouring of cutting off portions of land, or, as formerly proposed... driving the Andamanese out of a portion of the Great Andaman, too closely resembled our treatment of the aborigines of Tasmania to be acceptable to the Government." (p.470)

But yet again British colonial interests in the Andaman Islands stood in the way of directives for "humane" policy, as suggested in the passage cited below:

> "[B]oth the Government of India and the Court of Directors, repeatedly, and in the strongest terms, ordered that the Andamanese were not to be injured, ill-treated, or allowed to suffer in any way from our occupation of their Islands, and when very occasional cases of improper behavior towards the Andamanese occurred, the Government expressed their extreme displeasure with the parties in fault." [my emphasis] (p.186)

Portman then goes on to detail numerous instances of ill-treatment of the Andamanese, directing his disapproval towards the Naval officers, some administrators, the European residents, guards etc. Except when the Andamanese took matters into their own hands, remarkably little punishment was meted out to the perpetrators.

Questions of ownership: looting

Across all the levels of hierarchy within the settlement, there were no exceptions to the practice of taking and carrying away Andamanese goods – implements, weapons, household articles, canoes – whenever the opportunity presented itself. In the early days, "bows, arrows, nets and such of their utensils or weapons as were calculated to throw light on their customs, were taken, their canoes and dwellings were respected, and presents were invariably left" (Portman 1899:231).

But, every visit thereafter to an Andamanese camp meant that the visitors returned "laden with bows, arrows and shells etc.".
Over the years, the officers remarked on the Andamanese habit of hiding their belongings in the forest if they received warning of any intruders.

While there is some recognition of the reasons for this behavior, there is no awareness that the propensity to carry away objects from the huts may be construed as "stealing" by the Andamanese:

> "[S]o many canoes have been taken from them in former times, that they are now afraid to shew them, and draw them up creeks, and hide them in the jungles when they see us coming, and while these fears last our visits must always occasion them inconvenience and anxiety." (p.411)

It was only if the violation was in terms of British notions of property that the identical practice by the "savages" was defined as "plundering" or "looting" of metal implements or tools, and for which they were dealt severe reprisals. According to Man, the founding of the settlement in 1858 met with "serious difficulties... in consequence of the harassing attacks on...working parties by the aborigines, whose cupidity was excited by the iron tools and other implements which in their eyes presented an appearance of adaptability as weapons of the chase". The "Government Gardens" were "likewise freely robbed, until at length stern repressive measures had to be adopted whereby they were instructed for the first time in the laws of private property" (Man 1885: 262). Portman, looking back over the years with a mixture of remorse and censure remarks:

> "People in those days (an indeed even now) never seem to have realised that the Andamanese objected to strangers coming to their villages and taking away their property, quite as much as we should do, and that such conduct on our part could only provoke ill-feeling and hostility on theirs." (p.299)

Questions of justice: rape/murder

An incident that revealed the gap between the ideal of humane policy as posited by the Court of Directors in London and its application by the Andaman administration in the islands occurred in 1862. Naval Brigadesman Pratt was killed by an Andamanese for attempting to rape his wife. The other officers with him at the time lied about the incident, describing it as a "cold-blooded act of treachery" and the Andamanese as "murderers assuming the garb of friendship for the purpose of carrying out their diabolical plans" (p.360-361). Two Andamanese men, "Jumbo" and "Snowball",[15] were imprisoned and kept in irons and fetters for some months before the truth came to light. "Snowball" was released but "Jumbo" languished in prison for some years as punishment for murder. Not surprisingly, a couple of years later when Major Ford became the Officiating Superintendent of Port Blair in 1863 and further investigated the matter, it came to light that it was not "Jumbo" but "*Jacko*" who had killed Pratt.. His report to the Government of India in 1864 reveals that:

> "*When Pratt was killed a prow was here, and the Malay crew were sent over with a promise of reward to catch the Andamanese supposed to be concerned. They went, and in four days brought over eighteen people, from whom were picked two; the original "Jumbo" was of the party, but one Hamilton, Colonel Tytler's orderly, pointed out another man as "Jumbo," who with "Snowball," (since drowned), were made prisoners, and the original "Jumbo" with fifteen more, was released.*"

Portman's comment added in parenthesis states:

> "*This 'original Jumbo' was afterwards known to Mr. Corbyn*[16] *as "Jacko," and was the man who really murdered Pratt for trying to rape his wife.*"(p.471)

All subsequent allusions to the Pratt affair in official correspondence were couched in terms such as "the melancholy tragedy" or "tragedies like Pratt's murder". Portman cites a comment made by Mr. Corbyn, who most often referred to the incident as an "unprovoked tragedy". According to Corbyn:

> "*[T]here will, in the progress of their intercourse with us, be frequent cases in which the aborigines may be unfairly represented, and offences imputed to them of which, if the truth could be divulged, they would be found not to have been guilty.*" (Portman 1899:440)

It was a pity that having grasped the situation so clearly, Reverend Corbyn did not apply it in his later dealings with the Andamanese, of which more details will be discussed below in connection with the "Andaman Homes".

Portman issues a strong condemnation of the manner in which the Pratt affair was handled, then goes on to concede that:

> "[T]he only possible good that the whole affair can have had was that it overawed the Andamanese, showing them that we were the masters, and they the subject race,[17] and that, whatever we might do to them, any unfriendly action on their part would lead to speedy and severe punishment. In this manner, and by our contact with them throughout the affair, they possibly obtained a knowledge of us which smoothed the way for friendly relations afterwards."[my emphasis] (p.369)

It is obvious that, according to British perceptions, there were simply two diametrically opposed behavioral options open to the "savages": "hostile" and "murderous" if they resisted the British presence in the islands, and "friendly" when the demoralized and devastated populations became resigned to their loss. The propensity of every British colonial officer, in turn, to converge the diversity and range of their objectives in any colonial situation within the expression "friendly," and then to go on to also describe their relationship with the colonized populations as "friendly" neatly displaces the burden of consequences that are notably "unfriendly" onto the "subject" populations.

Despite the claims of the administrators at the time with regard to the progress made in establishing a relationship of understanding and mutual tolerance with the Andamanese, the Pratt incident demonstrates the barriers to communication within the designated categories of "subject population" and their "masters". It also problematizes the authoritative ethnological texts that emerged from this period, E. H. Man's and Radcliffe-Brown's for example, all based on information obtained from a "subject" people with whom they claimed they had established a rapport.

Colonial ethnology

It is worthwhile at this stage digressing briefly to consider Man's scholarly research conducted on the Andamanese during this phase of British intervention in the islands. E.H. Man arrived in the Andaman Islands in 1869 as a colonial officer, joining his father Colonel H. Man. In 1858, Colonel Man (Captain Man at the time) was commissioned to reclaim the islands for the British in the name of the East India Company. In 1875 E.H. Man was appointed Officer in Charge of the Andaman Homes.[18] Edwards (1991) suggests that this appointment may have posed a conflict of interests for Man,

> [A]s he enforced the official policy of 'taming' the Andamanese, both morally and physically. The meticulous recording of their traditional culture was perhaps an attempt by Man to come to terms with this insoluble dilemma and his way of accepting the moral responsibility he felt to recompense the Andamanese for their sad fate. (p.109)

During his thirty-year appointment to the Andaman Islands, Man wrote extensively on Andamanese culture, learned the language of the *Aka-bea-da*, and his collection of material artifacts can still be found in many European museums. David Tomas (1987), notes that this mode of anthropological appropriation of the Andamanese was merely an extension of their political appropriation, in both cases established by the existence of the "Andaman Homes".

Man's mode of ethnological enquiry was based on the system developed in *Notes and Queries in Anthropology*,[19] a method of data collection and documentation devised by the British Association for the Advancement of Science in 1874. He gathered his information such that it could be compared, quantified and classified according to the demands of contemporary method. Tomas, citing anonymous sources, describes the published product of Man's research as:

> On the Aboriginal Inhabitants of the Andaman Islands was regarded as "a model for ethnologists," because it followed throughout "the lines laid down in the British Association volume of 'Notes and Queries on Anthropology'...In contrast to the conventional form of narrative or anecdotal accounts, its systematic layout, coupled with Man's extended period of study in the Homes, produced a formidable claim to scientific veracity. The monograph's authority was predicted on its ability to answer the series of "leading questions" posed in the British Association handbook; as one reviewer of Notes and Queries observed in regard to its questionnaire form: "Well asked is half answered. (Tomas 1991: 88)

His ethnological work was restricted to the *Aka-bea-da* and *Pucikwar*[20] groups around the Homes, and hence was contingent on the British presence in the islands. He was inordinately sensitive to criticism of his scholarly interests, as indicated by Portman's comment to E.B. Tylor in 1899:

> Man is very much hurt by the way he thinks I have criticised him...I adhere to my opinion that much of the Notes on their [Andamanese]

Anthropology is incorrect...His work is chiefly written on the information of a few boys of different tribes and two convict Jemadars. This is not my idea of accurate scientific research and the results, though good for 1881 will not do for 1899 (cited in Edwards 1991:113).

Edwards (*ibid.*) offers a compassionate reading of Man, discerning his need for recognition and approval from both the academic and colonial establishment, as well as:

[A] sense of power over, affection and deference from and obligation towards the Andamanese in what was, after all, a lonely station. It was also perhaps a response to the predicament in which he found himself as a primary agent in the orchestrated destruction of a culture about which he felt deeply. (p.113)

It should also be noted that it was Man more than anybody else whose research provided the groundwork for some understanding of Andamanese culture and, thereby, the realization of British policy in the islands.

The local and the metropole

In the Andaman Islands, there were multiple levels of incompatibility between the dispensing of orders and their translation into practice. One such contradiction that emerged right from the outset between those who had to administer the "savages," on the one hand, and their superiors "in the metropole," on the other, is revealed by the following example. In 1858, Captain Man[21] was ordered by the Government of India (in mainland India) to take possession of the Andaman Islands and prepare a Settlement to which the convicts would be sent. He was told that it might be necessary to arm a small number of convicts with muskets "to keep off the savages" (p 209), thus demonstrating that the Government of India was cognizant of "the hindrance and annoyance that the Andamanese would probably cause". But the Court of Directors (in London) did not approve of the proposal to arm the convict sepoys against the aborigines, and ordered that every precaution be taken to protect the Andamanese from "collisions" with the convicts since it "must end in the extermination of the weaker race".

At the level of articulated policy, it is evident that the colonial officers were distressed by the inability of the islanders to appreciate their "benign" intentions. As they "strove" to establish "friendly relations", the British officers vainly hoped that "their advances would at length be met in the spirit in which they were offered" (p. 232).

Even when the servants of the Government of India would appear to have been provoked almost beyond endurance by the implacable hostility and treachery of the Andamanese, the higher authorities in England and India have always insisted on a leniency and consideration being shown to them, which is certainly much in excess of their deserts. But the Government appear to have thought, and rightly, that the Andamanese are more in the position of irresponsible children,[22] than of reasoning enemies, and have treated them accordingly. (Portman 1899:209)

While I am critical of the unfolding of colonial practices, I should not underestimate the magnitude of the task of setting up a penal colony. The state of siege that the officers frequently experienced during the early years of the settlement can be envisioned with some degree of compassion. Surrounded as they were, on one side, by desperate convicts who were "almost maddened by their horror of the Andamans, and the tales of the dreaded savages" (Portman 1899:257), and for whom even capital punishment was not sufficient deterrent to escape. And on the other by "aborigines who appear to be not less hostile to the natives of India than they are to Europeans". In view of this situation, the directives from the Government of India to protect the Andamanese who "were the weaker[23] race from the effects of our occupation of their country" (p.265) were treated with some degree of scepticism. Portman concurs with the officials in Port Blair that it was *they* and *their ships* that required protection from the Andamanese. So great was the fear of the Andamanese at the time that no attempt was made to explore the creeks running off the harbour, and supplies of thatching leaves were obtained all the way from Moulmein, even though they grew in great abundance by the creeks.

These fears, taken together with the rising sickness and mortality from the heavy rains, including malaria from the newly cleared forest, provide some basis for the measures of excessive severity imposed on the convicts, or the scale of revenge exacted on "the savages" for their attacks on the settlement.

For the convicts:

[T]he customs of the Tasmanian discipline were enforced, convicts were handcuffed together in pairs, and these handcuffs were never opened. During working hours the worst[24] characters were taken to the sea beach, and, an iron bar was being passed through the fetters of a number of them, they were thus fastened to the earth, and made to do what work they could in a sitting posture. (Portman 1899:257)

and in the case of the Andamanese:

[A] collision appears to have taken place between the officers and men of the surveying brig Mutlah, and the Andamanese. The quarrel seems to have been commenced by the imprudent conduct of a midshipman, whose promotion was accordingly stopped, and one of the officers of the Mutlah was killed by the Andamanese... forty Andamanese huts were destroyed by the men of the Mutlah in revenge. [my emphasis] (ibid. 265)

It is evident from the response of the Government of India, following orders from the Court of Directors in London, how remote they were from the situation as experienced by their local officers. After coldly calling attention to their policy, which absolutely forbade the use of aggression on the Andamanese, the missive adopted a more conciliatory approach:

The President in Council fully appreciates the difficulties of your position. But the aborigines of the Andamans are apparently unable to conceive the possibility of the two races *co-existing on the islands, except in terms of internecine hostility. This idea is assuredly strengthened by every attack we make upon them, and can only be driven out of their minds by a course of* persistent conciliation and forbearance on our part. [my emphasis] (ibid.272)

The personalities of the administrators who were appointed to the Andamans, particularly the prior experience that they brought with them before taking charge of the settlement, were crucial in determining their attitudes to both the convicts and the Andamanese. One example of such a misfit was Dr. Walker. In 1858, Dr. James Pattison Walker was selected to be the first Superintendent of the Penal Settlement of Port Blair. Dr. Walker had considerable experience as a Jail Superintendent, and bore a high reputation for his excellent management of convicts. Due to various technicalities, Captain Man was unable to make the periodic visits of inspection to the Andamans as was first proposed. It was during Dr. Walker's term of office that many of the more repressive measures described earlier were employed. He tried to implement the same kind of regulated and stern penal discipline that he had been accustomed to in the Agra Jail,[25] never realizing the impossibility of adhering to that code under the frontier conditions that existed in the Andamans. It was only if the administrators had served some years in places like Burma or Malaya, also tropical forests, that they were more successful in adapting to the specific circumstances of the Andaman Islands.

Within the settlement itself the levels of hierarchy that operated, with the concomitant delegation of authority and responsibility, effectively subverted the stated policy of "forbearance" and "conciliation" with respect to the islanders. The Naval Brigademen who formed the principal garrison of the settlement were, for several years, directly involved in the task of initiating and establishing contact with the Andamanese. Portman bluntly characterizes them "as a body, lawless, undisciplined, and quite unsuited to such work as the protection of a penal settlement" (p.259). These men were the principal "looters" of Andamanese goods, and provoked numerous retaliatory attacks from the Andamanese for their misbehavior with Andamanese women, not to mention for the looting itself.

In later years, other Europeans in the settlement posed as much of a danger, bribing the Andamanese with liquor and tobacco in exchange for products from the forest. Portman admits to the mistake of not taking any precautions against misconduct by the guards and others with whom the Andamanese had any contact. He admonishes his predecessors for "not having considered that the Andamanese required to be protected against us, quite as much as we required to be protected against them" (p.481). And, of an historical bent himself, Portman chides his fellow officers for not being better versed in the history of British relations with the Australian and Tasmanian aborigines, or the narratives of travellers in the Pacific Islands. A perusal of these would have shown the inevitable consequences of the mixing of merchant sailors or convicts with "savages".

Civilizing the savage: the "Andaman Homes"

The Andaman Homes played a significant role in assimilating the various groups of Andamanese to British colonial practices, and played a strategic role in reinforcing and extending their sphere of influence within the islands. Similar institutions existed throughout the British Empire to "civilize" the various indigenous groups to the mores of the British, and teach them skills that would be of use to the British in their administration of the islands. Such a role evolved over the years, but in the initial stages, the Homes served as a means to hold the Andamanese hostage during British efforts to "pacify" the various groups whom they encountered.

In 1863, during Colonel Tytler's Superindentship, the "Andaman Homes" were founded, and Mr. Corbyn became the first Officer in charge of them. The Home functioned as the center of "a system of entire pacification", a "foundation stone for civilizing a people hitherto living in a perfectly barbarous state, replete with treachery, murder, and every other savageness". In order to make an example of the hostages and to protect them from "cultural recontamination", Andamanese who were "fresh [in their] ungovernable state of wildness" were prevented access to the Andamanese in the Homes (Tytler cited in Portman 1899: 376-377). According to Pandit (1985:111) the purpose of the Homes was to teach the Andamanese "good manners, to wear clothes, use a fork and knife, practise cultivation and to learn new trades and handicrafts, along with the English language". But, as emerges from the records, there were more immediate and strategic concerns involved in the founding of the Homes than the mere discharge of the "white man's burden". Mr. Corbyn, who was instrumental in setting up the Homes, clearly explains that while the "civilizing" mission was a more distant ideal, the immediate purpose of the Homes was a means to hold some Andamanese hostage since:

> [U]nless we forcibly detain hostages of all the tribes we shall give free licence to a reckless and unreasoning people to damage and destroy wherever their impulse leads them, and to continually provoke bloodshed (Portman 1899:472).

Corbyn goes on describe the fear that the "savages" have of Europeans and of their capacity for destruction, "the widespread havoc we could carry into their homes, the slaughter of their wives and children" (p.396). In a different context (but of equal relevance here), Berkhofer (1978) discusses European representations of the Native American Indians. He draws attention to the use of "counterimages of themselves to describe Indians, and counter-images of the Indians to describe themselves" (p.27), thereby defining European identity and superiority over the worst fears of their own depravity. Corbyn's explanations support Berkhofer's analysis of the colonizer's ascription of the worst attributes of themselves to the colonized, whereas any virtuous traits were acclaimed as a credit to their own influence.

Apart from a meagre sum of money sanctioned by the Government of India for the Homes, the expenses involved in the upkeep of the Homes were borne by the "savages" themselves. The task of "civilizing the savages" was paid for by the collection of forest products or the handicrafts that women and children were coerced into producing for sale. Eventually, "a trade was established for them, weapons, curiosities, etc., being brought in and sold, the proceeds being use to defray the cost of tobacco and other luxuries, by which their hearts were won" (Portman 1899: 470).

While at the Homes, the Andamanese were not permitted to either tattoo or paint themselves as was their wont, since Colonel Tytler, Superintendent of the settlement at the time, "very properly considering this a degrading and barbarous practice, had prohibited it" (Portman 1899:397). They were forced to don clothes as there were "Christian women" at the settlement who would be offended. Another method used to "wean" the Andamanese from their "wild habits" and create "artificial wants to supply, which should involve the necessity of frequent visits to the settlement, and thus form as it were the nucleus of increasing intercourse with a superior race" (Tickell 1864 cited in Portman 1899:169). The islanders were fed "condemned grain" or cargo rice intended for Government elephants, gifts of mouldy biscuits, tobacco and, for a few years, rations of rum.[26] They were also expected to perform a scavenger function for the settlement, by eating the meat of animals dying of disease "or other natural causes" (p.462).

By the early 1880s, the Homes housed "besides a large number of sick and convalescents...a certain quantity of people belonging to different tribes" who were kept "for six months at a time, in order that by their labor in selling the produce of the gardens, diving for lost articles, rowing boats, etc., they may keep up the funds of the department", as well as serving as "hostages for the good behavior of the tribe to which they belong" (Portman 1899: 476). Under the onslaught of the monsoons, the temporary shelters that were constructed for the Andamanese were in ruins, after which they were housed in sties with cattle and pigs. For several years they were forcibly restrained at these "Homes", often chained in irons if they attempted to leave. Having rendered the Andamanese "tractable" and "submissive" by these methods, "reclaimed out of their present state of barbarism" (p.426), Corbyn asserts that they could henceforth be of essential service to the interests of the settlement "by removing the obstacles which are at present opposed to the development of the great natural wealth and advantages of these islands" (p.426).

By the late 1880s, the South Andamanese, in turn, could serve as intermediaries in British attempts to establish "friendly relations" with the Onge of Little Andaman. With these developments, as "the Homes function[ed] to homogenize and transform the indigenous population...[they also] became the generative locale for hybrid intertribal identities, simply because they provided the only stable context for communication and marriage" (Tomas 1991: 81 citing anonymous sources).

The convicts and the savages

Keeping in mind that the context for the events narrated up to this point is a *penal* colony, I have said very little about the convicts, or the interactions between the convicts and the islanders. The situation of the convicts in the Andaman Islands demands a more systematic elaboration (cf. Sen 2000) but is outside the purview of this work. I will touch on them briefly, to the extent their condition impinges on the islanders and the argument here. I have mentioned in passing the "horror" that the Indian convicts experienced when transported to the Andamans. Their dread of the "cannibalistic savages" who inhabited these islands was nurtured through generations of Indian lore. Despite the heavy traffic in human labor during this period, mostly as indentured laborers sent to work in the colonial plantations in the Fiji Islands, Malaysia and the West Indies, according to conventional rhetoric circulating in India, there was no greater punishment for an Indian than to be sent across the "black waters". A person condemned to such a fate was considered lost forever to the families left behind. The initial batches of convicts transported to the Andaman Islands were political prisoners who were involved in the Mutiny of 1857, not ordinary criminals, and whose desperation to escape at any cost was driven by the injustice of a fate that punished them so cruelly.

Portman narrates a series of encounters between the Andamanese and the convicts in 1859 when "the general hostility of the Andamanese towards the settlers was as great as ever, and working parties were continually being attacked by them" (p.276). On one occasion:

> Out of the 446 convicts present, 12 had fetters on, and these the savages selected, and having removed their fetters, carried them off into the jungle, and they have not been seen since. (ibid:277)

And on another:

> [T]he convicts described the savages as showing no disposition to attack any one with a mark of imprisonment (such as the iron ring round the ankle), unless opposed, but as anxious to attack and murder the section gangsmen, the sub-division gangsmen, and the division gangsmen, who do not wear the ring, and are marked by wearing a red turban, badge, and coloured belt...they beckoned to the convicts to come and dance with them, and they from fear complied. Ludicrous groups of savages with a convict on each side, with arms entwined, were engaged in stamping motions which appeared intended for dancing. (ibid:277)

As a consequence, the guards and gangsmen begged to have their distinguishing marks taken off, and to have an axe or a tool in their hands so that they would not be singled out by the Andamanese.

Portman later relates that the Andamanese had objected to the convicts' destruction of the forest. They had noticed that the convicts did not want to work but that the gangsmen made them, and hence they had attacked all the people who were in authority. From the incidents narrated it may be conjectured that the Andamanese had demonstrated a willingness to enter into some kind of alliance with the convicts, whom they appeared to classify separately from the other inhabitants of the settlement. But, as the case of Dudnath Tiwari illustrates, despite the repressive measures instituted by the British who held them prisoners, the convicts perceived themselves as more allied to the British than to the islanders.

Dudhnath Tiwari, Life Convict No. 276, was among the first batch of convicts sentenced to life imprisonment on the Andamans. Within a few weeks of his arrival in 1858, he escaped with a large group of convicts in an attempt to reach Burma and, eventually, make their way back to mainland India.[27] Tiwari was the only survivor from the group.

After living for one year and twenty-four days in the Andaman jungle with the Andamanese, he voluntarily turned himself in to the British authorities, warning them of an impending attack on the convict station at Aberdeen. This was later known as the "Battle of Aberdeen" (14th May, 1859), the most serious and concerted bid by several groups of Andamanese to oust the British from the islands. The event marked a turning point in British relations with the Andamanese, at least the South Andaman groups who, thereafter, realized that the British were too powerful for them to fight and overcome, and that the settlement was to be a permanent feature in their lives.

During the year that he was with the Andamanese, Tiwari lived with the group that had spared his life, learnt their language, wandering about with them and living as they did in the forest. They had even offered him a woman to live with, Lipaia, whom he "left in an interesting condition" (Portman 1899:285) when he returned to the settlement. Tiwari's account of his adventures with the Andamanese was the first accurate picture of their customs, and many of his observations were later corroborated by other more professional studies of the islanders. Despite his year with the Andamanese, it appears Tiwari felt little allegiance to the group he travelled with, exposing them to the British military in an effort to win freedom for himself. As he anticipated, Tiwari was later granted a free pardon for his "good service" to the Government of India.

In later years, the convicts were placed as guards at the "Andaman Homes". Successive administrative officers, in turn, doubted the propriety of any convicts appointed as orderlies or watchman at the Homes since it was here that the convict guards, placed in a position of power over the Andamanese, were often found to ill-treat the "savages".

Disease and the islanders

Predictably, the close contact with the British and the Indian convicts in these efforts to "civilize the savages" led to the spread of a number of infectious diseases, wreaking havoc among all the different groups of the Andamanese. The following observation in the Gazetteer of the Andaman and Nicobar Islands is noteworthy:

> The cause of diminution of the population is infectious and contagious disease, the result of contact with an advanced civilization. Epidemics, all imported, of pneumonia (1868), syphilis (1876), measles (1877) and influenza (1892), together with exposure to the sun and wind in cleared spaces, the excessive use of tobacco and overclothing, have been the chief means of destroying them. Disease has worn down the actual numbers of the tribes and has apparently rendered the union of the sexes infructuous in many cases. (1909:2)

With the onset of the epidemic diseases, issues of "hygiene" and "control" became key terms in British administrative policy. Arnold (1988) contends that "medical intervention impinged directly upon the lives of the people, assuming an unprecedented right (in the name of medical science) over the health and bodies of its subjects" (ibid.: 18). When syphilis was detected at the Homes, precautions were taken to segregate and keep the patients "clean", with a separate hospital built for them. On enquiry, it was found that the Andamanese had been suffering from the disease for three to four years prior to its detection, but were prevented from reporting it by the convicts, who were afraid of being punished. The coercive measures to segregate and restrain the Andamanese at these hospitals often replicated the efforts to "tame" them in the early years of the "Andaman Homes". The futility of these measures is attributed to the ignorance and unhygienic practices of the Andamanese. Portman laments the fact that:

> [T]he Andamanese were too thoughtless and helpless a race to benefit by the precautions...their filthy habits, their custom of sleeping together in a heap, so that the abrasions on the skin of one became inoculated with the syphilitic poison from the open sores of another, and their immorality, all tended to spread the infection. [my emphasis] (p.610)

On the subject of Andamanese morals,[28] General Barwell writes in the Annual Report for 1875-76 that:

"[T]he opinion hitherto prevalent regarding these people, that they are free from any taint of immorality, is entirely unfounded...though they deem chastity a virtue, it is by no means rare for some of them to form improper connections; but in this they assert that they do not differ from the tribes of the other islands." (Portman 1899:604)

Man, during whose tenure many of the major epidemics occurred, took "stringent measures" and "enforc[ed] restrictions" which "the Andamanese, blind to their own interests, resented, and endeavoured to escape from" (p.621). More surprisingly, and apparently subverting his own efforts, Man was also tireless in his exertions to establish "friendly relations" with the Andamanese living in the more distant reaches of North Andaman, and to bring them in contact with the settlement. Portman, who succeeded Man, seemed as blind to the implications of his actions when he took several Andamanese and Onge with him on a tour of Calcutta while there was an outbreak of smallpox in the city. Meanwhile, Portman claims to be astounded by the indifference of the medical authorities, to whose "extraordinary neglect" he attributes the "partial extermination of the race" (p.614). However, despite the attempts to displace responsibility elsewhere, "the connection between the Homes and the spread of infectious disease was acknowledged by administrators" (Tomas 1991: 81). Portman concludes his account of the history of relations with the Andamanese with an explanation for why the Andamanese race was dying out:

"The Andamanese have had no fresh blood for many centuries, and continued in-breeding has weakened their constitutions. The savage, far from being, as people often suppose, a robust man, is generally very delicate...he cannot compare with a European in his endurance of new hardships and altered circumstances. Had the Andamanese been left entirely alone, no doubt they would have continued to exist for many centuries...but when we came amongst them and admitted the air of the outside world, with consequential changes, to suit our necessities, not theirs, they lost their vitality, which was wholly dependent on being untouched, and the end of the race came." (p.875)

Such a rationalization firmly places the burden of consequences back on the Andamanese. In view of the dominant evolutionary currents of the time, the predicament of the Andamanese could be shrugged off as the inevitable consequences of the pressures of natural selection: the "stronger" would prevail over the "weaker" races. Moreover, as Arnold observes:

"As Europe began to free itself from its own epidemiological past, it was forgotten that diseases like cholera, malaria, smallpox and plague,

though increasingly banished to the tropics, were part of Europe's own recent experience. Disease became part of the wider condemnation of African and Asian 'backwardness' just as medicine became a hallmark of the racial pride and technological assurance that underpinned the 'new imperialism' of the nineteenth century. (Arnold 1988: 7)

The subjection of the Andamanese

It is an instructive exercise to note the specific individuals whom Portman finds reasons to single out for special mention in his record of the Andamanese. The individuals marked for attention are those who are perceived as leaders, or "chiefs" of a particular territorial group, distinguished by the influence they appeared to have over other members of their group. Many of these people quickly grasped the situation *vis-à-vis* the British and came to an arrangement mutually beneficial to both. Such an understanding meant the person was relied upon by the British to track escaped convicts, to act as a liaison between the British and other groups who remained distant, and to accept the compact of "friendly relations" with the British officers. In return, the title of "chief" was conferred on these individuals, with an acknowledgment that these were men of "exceptional abilities". Maia Biala, the "chief" of Rutland Island was one such person. Major Ford remarks regarding him:

> *He is very different to any Andamanese I have yet seen. His bearing is so different, so superior to any of them, his demeanour at all times quick and composed. He has a very intelligent countenance, and his gentleness of manner, so different from the somewhat boisterousness of the Andamanese, is as remarkable as it is engaging.* (p.494)

Portman goes on to add that succeeding officers like Man, Protheroe and others were similarly impressed by Maia Biala. His death in the epidemic of measles in 1877 was much regretted. Reading through these descriptions of Maia Biala, "King John" and others recalls Turnbull's remarks about the "highly skilled opportunists" among the Ik, who became "chiefs," or "go-betweens with the administration, thereby benefiting from the resulting hand-outs" (cited in Leacock 1982:163). Some of the other changes that he details in Ik society parallel those that were occurring among the Andamanese brought within the sphere of the Andaman Homes:

> [S]ecret and individual hunting which had become poaching; direct prostitution as well as marriage liaisons with outsiders [in this case

the convicts] that were all but prostitution...spying, thieving,...wage work for the police. (ibid: 163)

Tomas (1991), notes that the surviving Andamanese were assimilated into a number of European roles "in addition to their roles as cultural brokers, interpreters and jungle police" (p.81). These roles, as recorded by Portman, are notably those of domestic servants, gardeners, waiters, navigators, Jinricksha drivers and photographic assistants (Portman 1899:670-71,864).

If "subjection" in its links with power opens up "new avenues of enablement" (Biolsi 1995) then it can be conceived as a process of availing of short-term returns which, in the long-haul, can have detrimental consequences (and which may remain imperceptible at the time). By this argument then, many Andamanese had undergone that process to become "new kinds of individuals with specific practical, recordable, and predictable identities and self-interests" [29] (Biolsi 1995:29).

A summary of events

I have approached Portman's collection of records by extracting from them certain themes for emphasis, commonalities that existed despite the changing circumstances in the islands throughout those years. I have found this a useful method for bridging the lengthy span of time involved in this account. Hence, I have followed a thematic rather than a strictly linear chronological development in my narration of events. During the years encompassed by this account, as the British extended their sphere of control, all the groups of Andamanese were brought within their fold. Thus the effects of "contact" spread across the entire extent of the Great Andaman group of islands and, as we enter the twentieth century, according to one observer, there were no Andamanese found around Port Blair. It was only in the Andaman Homes that any of the local population was visible (Dobson 1874). Portman notes:

> *Twenty years ago the Andamanese resented living in the Homes for long, and preferred the free sporting life in their jungle encampment. Now the only encampments of the Andamanese in the South Andaman are the Homes, which contain nearly 250 Andamanese, against under 100 of 20 years ago.* (Portman 1899: 700)

As early as 1885 Man concedes:

> *It cannot, however, be contended that our attempts to reclaim the Andamanese from their savage state have produced unmixed beneficial re-*

sults, for it is found that in proportion as they gain in intelligence and tractability, the more fat and indolent they become, and having no incentive towards exertion frequently lose in great measure their quondam skill in hunting;– availing themselves of the privileges of free board and quarters, they spend their days together in singing, dancing, and feasting; the spirit of independence becomes thus less conspicuous, as they learn to depend upon others for the supply of their daily requirements, instead of being compelled to make such provision for themselves. (1885: xxiii)

Turn-of-the-century anthropology

It was at this juncture that we have to mark the advent of Radcliffe-Brown in the Andaman Islands in 1906, during a period when:

[E]verybody is agreed that the Nicobars will afford much more invaluable materials than the Andamans where all the natives except the Onge and the Jarawa have become mere hangers-on to the settlement... such Andamanese as were in the neighbourhood... [had] so far left their own mode of life (having lived for years in the Settlement) that they do not remember 'the things of old time'. (Radcliffe-Brown cited in Tomas 1991:95-96)

Despite the "range and magnitude of [his] litany of failures" detailed by Tomas (*ibid.*,), Radcliffe-Brown went on to produce the magisterial work published as *The Andaman Islanders* in 1922, based on his research into the Andamanese between 1906-1908. When he undertook the study, in keeping with the prevailing historical line of enquiry, Radcliffe-Brown attempted an hypothetical reconstruction of the history of the Andaman Islands, and the Negritos in general. In the course of this work, he became convinced that speculative history could not give results of any real importance for the understanding of human life and culture. The influence of the French sociologists, particularly Durkheim, is evident in the radical shift in interest from the origin of institutions to the "structure" and "function" of social "systems," relatively novel terms in anthropology at the time, and containing the gist of Radcliffe-Brown's influential concept of social anthropology. He sought a "function" for various elements of culture "in terms of its role in the maintenance of the present sociocultural system – knowledge that was inaccessible to the native, as it was to the observer intent on hypothetical historical reconstruction" (Stocking 1984: 156). Thus, along these lines, Radcliffe-Brown went on to explain the "meaning" of myths and rituals with reference to their "social function", which was "to maintain and transmit from one generation to another the emotional dispositions on which the society (as it is constituted) depends for its existence" *(ibid.,* 234). He asserts:

> *It therefore seemed to me necessary for ethnology to provide itself with a method of determining meanings as effective and free from 'personal equation' as the methods by which a linguist determines the meanings of words or morphemes in a newly studied language.* (Radcliffe-Brown 1932: ix)

Hence, while "tak[ing] into account the explanations given by the natives themselves", these exegeses were not deemed "scientific explanations", they were simply "data" (ibid.:234-235) to serve as "grist for the functionalist mill" (Tomas 1991:102).

Radcliffe-Brown is represented as very much a British gentleman visiting the colonies. His apparent lack of concern or censor for the "punitive" expeditions that were sent to "quell" the "hostile" Jarawa suggests that he, like Portman and Man who preceded him, was also one who upheld the colonial machinery. His account is a record of the rapidly disappearing Andamanese of North Andaman, and provides a wealth of ethnographic details of groups who, within the decade, would cease to exist. Unlike either Portman or Man, in whose writings emerge the conflicts engendered by the academic and the colonial worlds that they straddled, Radcliffe-Brown does not appear to perceive any contradiction between his scholarly endeavours and the structures of power, of which he was an integral part, that had brought the islanders to the brink of extinction.

Tomas states:

> *In the end, when the Andamanese in the vicinity of the colonial settlement had been almost wiped out or assimilated into the everyday life of a penal colony, the meaning of Andamanese culture could be authoritatively reconstituted, even in the aftermath of a relatively unsuccessful fieldwork sojourn, by a university-trained anthropologist attuned to the latest developments in French social theory. We may even say that while the image of Radcliffe-Brown's "benevolent autocracy" over "the simple Andamanese" remains problematic, there are perhaps grounds for attributing to Radcliffe-Brown – and to the functionalist method he helped promulgate – an epistemological and interpretive authoritarianism, the culmination of a richer and more extensive interrelationship between colonial and ethnographic practices in the Andaman Islands.* (1991: 76-77)

The Jarawa

Posing a contrast to the trajectory of events detailed with respect to the various groups of the Andamanese, a different dynamic of interaction was underway between the British and another group of islanders. At this point I want to switch my attention to an alternate set of people, who provide a case in counter-point to those islanders discussed so far. They are the people known as the *Jarawa*.

Who are the Jarawa?

The query as to who the *Jarawa* are is difficult to answer with any certainty. Through time, the people nominated by the term have served as the mysterious, unknown, hostile "other" for those who have named them as such. *Jarawa* means stranger in the language of the *Aka-bea-da*, the Andamanese with whom the British, over the years since the establishment of the penal settlement, first became acquainted. As mentioned earlier, the British administrators in the Andamans were unaware of the various territorial and linguistic divisions of the Andamanese. Or, of a further distinction between forest-dwelling and coastal populations, namely the *eremtaga* and *ar-yauto* groups.[30] Reflecting on the course of events, Portman (1899) comments:

> *When the present Settlement was first opened we were not aware that there were different tribes of Andamanese speaking different languages, nor did we know of the divisions of the race into Ar-yauto and Eremtaga; Lieutenant Colebrooke's account of the Jàrawas, and his vocabulary, was supposed to apply to all parts of the islands...[w]hen all the Andamanese were equally hostile to us it mattered little whether they quarrelled amongst themselves, and notice was not taken of one Sept more than of another. (p.704)*

From analysis of the vocabulary and comparison of the material culture collected by Lieutenant Colebrooke during this period, it was later surmised that the population residing in the region around the first settlement were, in all likelihood, the people referred to as *Jarawa* by the *Aka-bea-da*. An interesting anomaly resides in the fact that the people whom Lieutenant Colebrooke describes used both canoes and rafts, but those who were later known as the *Jarawa* did not possess canoes. They only constructed rafts to cross streams or travel short distances between islands, a practice characteristic of the *Jarawa* to this day. One possible explanation is that it was the coastal-dwelling *Jarawa* who used canoes but that the technology

112

was unknown to the inland groups. As I have suggested previously, it is probable that some disease was introduced among the coastal groups by Lieutenant Colebrooke and Blair's first settlement in 1789, resulting in a marked reduction of their population. The four years that the British occupied their initial site on the south-east of South Andaman were sufficient to have decimated the coastal populations of the groups referred to as *Jarawa* by the *Aka-bea-da*. It was solely forest-dwelling, raft-using *Jarawas* who were encountered in the interior of South Andaman when the penal colony was established, during the second span of British possession of the islands. Sarkar (1990) suggests that it was the depopulated coastal *Jarawa* who were pushed into the forest by the numerically stronger *Aka-bea-da*, and over the course of half a century of forest existence forgot the craft of canoe-building and use.

It would be instructive at this stage to explore this particular appellation of *Jarawa* by the *Aka-bea-da*, who used it as an inclusive term when referring to the Onge of Little Andaman, as well as the inhabitants of North Sentinel Island. Other groups that the *Aka-bea-da* were unfamiliar with in Middle and North Andaman were never specified as *Jarawa* but by the name by which they designated themselves. Portman's conclusion, which appears to be substantiated by current linguistic research, is that there were two major branches of indigenous people in the Andamans. The Great Andaman branch comprised all the North, Middle and South Andaman groups. The Onge branch included the Onge on Little Andaman, the *Jarawa* on South Andaman and the people on North Sentinel Island.

According to Portman (1899), all the area north of Little Andaman up to the site of Port Blair was, at some time, inhabited by the "Onge Group of Tribes". It was his view that these groups:

> [H]ad passed from one island to another freely; the people on Rutland Island would make excursions in their canoes during the calm weather to the North Sentinel and form a small colony there, as that island has fine, open and easily traversed forest, with plenty of pig, and sheltered lagoons in which fish and turtle could be caught. (p.702)

But these groups came into conflict with the southward movement of the South Andaman Group of Tribes who, over time, occupied all the islands south of Port Blair up to Rutland Island. The Onge, in response, retreated southwards:

> [N]ot often venturing farther north than the Cinque Islands on account of the hostile encounters with the Aka-bea-da they met with...

The Ar-yauto Sept of Onges naturally abandoned the South Andaman,
but the Eremtaga Sept remained in the interior of that Island, and on
Rutland Island, and, not having canoes, only moved by land, or oc-
casionally crossed the creeks on bamboo rafts, as Lieutenant Colebroke
describes, and as I have seen them do now both in the Great and Lit-
tle Andaman. (ibid., p.703)

Portman goes on to suggest that these developments curtailed the
movements of the people on North Sentinel, who no longer dared to
visit Rutland Island, "and the various Septs of the Group thus drifted
apart and became inimical; their bows, altering more or less, but their
languages remaining allied though so altered as to be mutually unintelligible" (*ibid.,*p.703).

Throughout the entire British period, there is much ambiguity as
to who in fact were referred to as *Jarawa*. At various points, canoe-us-
ing *Jarawa* were captured whose language was incomprehensible to
purported raft-using *Jarawa*. In some instances, captured Onge were
sometimes conversant with captured *Jarawa*, and at other times their
languages were found to be mutually unintelligible. Modified ver-
sions of Portman's view were reiterated by subsequent writers on the
Andamans. Radcliffe-Brown (1964) was of the opinion that:

[The Jarawa] are the descendants of emigrants who at some time in the
past made their way across from Little Andaman and thrust themselves
in upon the inhabitants of Rutland Island and the South Andaman
maintaining their footing in the new country by force of arm. (p.13)

On the basis of his observation of the seasonal northward migration of
the Onge located in the northern parts of Little Andaman, the Onge
knowledge of and names for all the islands north of Little Andaman, Cipriani (1966) concludes that the *Jarawa* and the Onge are one
and the same people, some of whom migrated to other islands in the
north as a result of demographic pressure on Little Andaman or tribal warfare.

At present, the only recourse is to designate by geographic location
– the people inhabiting the 700 sq km reserve demarcated in 1920, on
the western margins of Middle and South Andaman being specified as
the *Jarawa*, the islanders on North Sentinel being designated as the Sentinelese. Whether these are the same people who were cited as *Jarawa*
in the past is a matter for conjecture. It is somewhat ironic that to this
day we remain unaware of how the *Jarawa* actually allude to themselves, though some indications from my research suggest that they
too speak of themselves as Onge.

Aggression and hostility

*Today the word Jarawa is synonymous with hostility. And hostile they
are, but defensively hostile. Knowing their history, it is acceptable that
they should have turned to violence with the outside world as a means
of self preservation.* (Whitaker, 1985:66)

In 1931, Bonington of the British government in the Andamans, at the
end of a punitive expedition against the *Jarawa* expostulates: "This expedition did not stop Jarawa raids; like the Bushman of South Africa,
the Jarawa is implacable and will continue to fight to extermination"
(cited in Whitaker 1985:13). In the light of these comments, it may appear surprising that, during the initial era of British occupation of the
Andaman Islands, there was a very different picture painted of the
Jarawa. When Lieutenant Blair first encountered them in the 1790s, he
considered them more timid than hostile, and had less difficulty with
the *Jarawa* than with the "savage" *Aka-bea-da*, with whom friendly overtures were never successful. Moreover, Portman's comments draw attention to the fact that:

*As we became on friendly terms with the Aka-bea-da they prejudiced
us against the Jàrawas whom they described in the blackest terms, and
the latter seeing us allied with the Aka-bea-da against them, resented
or distrusted our friendly overtures, from timidity at first, and finally
from downright hostility.* (Portman 1899:704)

Portman is remarkably perspicuous when he notes:

*"The Jàrawas [sic] seem to be very much what we have made them.
They were much less timid at the time of this [Lt.Colebrooke's] visit
than they are now, and were merely given a bad name by our Andamanese because the latter were at enmity with them, and ignorant regarding them."* (*ibid*: 711)

The first mention of the *Jarawa* as "troublesome aborigines" is made
in 1865 when Major Ford, Superintendent of Port at the time, was engaged in making a road from the settlement in Port Blair south-west
through the forest to Port Mouat on the west coast. Gangs of convicts
employed in clearing the forest around the settlement at Port Blair were
often confronted by the *Jarawa*. The convicts reported to the administrative officers that these people (the *Jarawa*) were not nearly as hostile as the other aborigines but merely took the weapons and utensils
the convicts had and then dismissed them without further harm. During this phase, expeditions were sent out in search of the *Jarawa*, any

dwellings that were found were stripped of all belongings, with "quantities of unsuitable presents" left in their place. Man directed some of the expeditions sent into *Jarawa* territory. In his opinion, such presents would more than compensate the *Jarawa* for the loss of their property. He remarks that "our" Andamanese are afraid of the *Jarawa* and is unable to understand this, as he considered the latter quiet and inoffensive "never molesting or annoying us, and only desirous of keeping away from us, while we were constantly annoying them" (cited in Portman 1899:718). Portman avers:

> "It was unfortunate that, at the outset, the Jàrawas' [sic] huts should have been looted thus, and the presents left, being such things as matches, pipes, tobacco and looking-glasses, the uses of which were unknown to these savages, were useless to them, and by no means compensated them for the articles taken away." (ibid:718)

This state of affairs continued until the 1880s, after which there was an escalation in the extent of forest clearing by the British. It was when Portman was appointed in 1879 that the pace of deforestation in what was already known as *Jarawa* territory was increased, so that:

> "Expeditions in search of Jàrawas [sic] were able to move rapidly along these tracks with rations, etc., and thus I established headquarter stations in the Jàrawa country, and saved much time and toil by not working through the thick jungle." (ibid:726)

As the *Jarawa* steadily retreated in the face of these incursions, the British stepped up their efforts to "know more" about them and "befriend" them. Every time a *Jarawa* camp was discovered in the forest, tracks would be cut from the nearest British clearing to the site, "in order to use it as a headquarter station from which the *Jarawas* could be searched for" (ibid:729). In his Annual Report for 1882-83, Mr. Godwin-Austin acknowledges that:

> "The Jàrawas [sic] have given more trouble during the past year than hitherto, which I am able to account for only in one way. During the past year much has been done in the way of opening out tracks though their country... which they probably took to be a move on our part to hem them in and so capture them on their first appearance." (cited in Portman 1899:735)

Not surprisingly, a beleaguered *Jarawa* response to this kind of harassment changed from retreat to one of outright attacks on anyone encountered in the forest. Exacerbating the situation was the Andamanese encroachment into these parts. Emboldened by the protection conferred on them by the British control of the islands, the Andamanese visited and occupied parts of the forest into which they would never have ventured without risking an encounter with the *Jarawa*. From this point onwards, convicts and Andamanese working or hunting in the forest were regularly attacked and killed by the *Jarawa*. Deploring the state of relations with the *Jarawa*, and the hopelessness of trying to track them in the dense forest, Portman appraises the situation:

> *"At the same time the present state of affairs is not without its advantages, and though I fear that the Jàrawas [sic] will continue for some time to be a source of annoyance to the Settlement, yet they will certainly shoot any runaway convict they may meet, and the knowledge of this acts, I think, as a deterrent to convicts who think of escaping."* (*ibid*:750)

As the *Jarawa* relocated from their former territory further northwards, into the forest previously occupied by groups of the *Aka-bea-da* who had become extinct, expeditions were sent out in their pursuit. If the rationale for such a course of action appears inexplicable, Portman is at pains to elucidate in his Annual Report for 1893-94:

> *"Our only chance of becoming acquainted with the Jàrawas [sic] who at present appear to be hopelessly hostile, is by capturing some of the young men, as was done with the Onges of the Little Andaman, and keeping them apart until they are really friendly. At present any meeting between them and the other Andamanese ends in a fight, and I have, therefore, instructed the latter in the Middle Andaman to capture such Jàrawas as they may meet, if possible without wounding them, and bring them in to me."* (*ibid*:756)

Even at the risk of further transmitting the epidemic of measles, these relentless efforts to bring the *Jarawa* within the British fold did not cease.

> *"I am of the opinion that the only way to catch the Jàrawas [sic] will be by sending out armed parties of Police and convicts, as was done on former occasions when they have been caught, and using our Andamanese merely as trackers, as they are too afraid of the Jarawas to make any real effort to catch them when alone and unsupported with firearms. There are few Andamanese now alive who are acquainted with the Jarawa territory, and those few are old."* (*ibid*:761)[my emphasis]

No dissonance is perceived in acknowledging the dwindling Andamanese population with the efforts to bring yet another group within the domain of British control. Portman's final word on the *Jarawa* is as follows:

> "*In order to tame them, they must be caught, and it is this catching which is so difficult... Once caught, they might be kept with the Officer in charge of the Andamanese until they are to a certain extent tamed, and learn a little Hindustani; they might also be taught to smoke, thus establishing a craving[31] which intercourse with us can alone satisfy;... Possibly, after this treatment, some of them, if returned to their own homes, might be the means of inducing the others to become more friendly. The principal difficulty, after they have been caught, in carrying out the above policy, is, that in captivity, the Jàrawas [sic] sicken and die.*" (ibid:766)

The situation steadily deteriorated with a corresponding increase in the number of mortalities on both sides. At every census operation conducted by the British, (starting from 1901, and repeated at ten-year intervals), large-scale punitive missions were mounted against the *Jarawa*.

Towards the tail end of the British control of the islands, *Jarawa* retaliation took the form of raids and attacks on the settlement itself. The Japanese occupation of the islands (1942-1945), and the death of four Japanese soldiers, prompted indiscriminate bombing and shooting in several parts of the islands, including the *Jarawa* territory, which is believed to have further compounded the situation.

The Onge

There were some important differences in the history of British relations with the Onge. The most significant of these was that there was never any question of occupying Little Andaman since:

> "*[T]here is nothing on it to tempt a settler, and there are no harbours, so beyond visiting the people in order to keep in touch with them, and prevent them from massacring the crew of ship-wrecked vessels, we have no duties there.*" (Portman 1899:844)

Despite their proclaimed disinterest in Little Andaman, it was important to decisively establish British control over *all* the islands, and assure the safety of British ships travelling in these waters. Throughout the 1880s, the several "punitive missions" to Little Andaman subsequent to the deaths of a series of shipwrecked crews in the island re-

The road to take. Onge child deep in thought, perched on a fence cum gate marking the boundaries of the Dugong Creek settlement from the surrounding forest. Photo: Sita Venkateswar

sulted in mortalities on both sides. Portman is finally credited with having successfully "pacified" the Onge and for establishing "friendly relations" with them. The Onge were encouraged to visit Port Blair, and on several occasions were taken on tours of Calcutta to impress upon them that:

> "[W]e are the strongest race, and are to be obeyed. On this point no doubt should be permitted, and obedience must be enforced and all wrong-doing sternly punished, for the Andamanese are a forgetful race." (p.845)

There is ample photographic documentation[32] of the period, aseptic moments captured on film after "pacification" had occurred, devoid of the blood, sweat and tears that marked the violence of those moments.

The Jarawa at North Sentinel Island

The islanders who inhabited North Sentinel island, about whom even less is known, were also referred to as *Jarawa* by the British. Like the *Jarawa* on Great Andaman, they were thought to be similar to the Onge. A number of expeditions were made to North Sentinel Island. There was some talk of converting the whole island into a coconut plantation and much discussion on the "taming" of the inhabitants. Nothing came of the idea, and the Sentinelese (as they are commonly referred to today) remained undisturbed by any large-scale development plans for their island.

Population counts: a table of estimates

The first census operation conducted by the British throughout their sphere of control in the Indian subcontinent was undertaken in 1901. The table below indicates the enumeration of population through the British period, specifying those that are estimates and those that are based on an actual counting of heads. By 1931[33] the number of Andamanese had dwindled to 90. Bonington, Superintendent of Census Operation notes, "This devastating fall in the numbers of the Andamanese in less than 75 years[34] of contact with the administration paralyses comment" (cited in Whitaker 1985:9). The relative isolation of the Onge partly shielded them from the lethal effects of "contact" but they too succumbed to disease. In 1901 the Census estimated their numbers at 672 and in 1931 at 250 (Whitaker 1985).

CENSUS YEARS (*Estimated figures)

ISLANDERS	1901	1911	1921	1931
Andamanese	625	455	209	90
Onge	672*	631*	346*	250*
Jarawa	468*	114*	114*	70*
Sentinelese	117*	117*	117*	70*

Conclusion

There is a marked disjunction between the stated intent of British colonial policies in the Andaman Islands as these pertained to the islanders, and the consequences of their policies as they were implemented in the islands. On the one hand, it was clear right from the outset that unlike Australia, Tasmania or elsewhere, the Andaman Islands were never conceived as a site of permanent European habitation, even convicts of European origin being sent back to be imprisoned elsewhere. Their control of the Andaman Islands was guided by strategic motives, ensuring commercial profits from the extraction of timber[35] etc., and safeguarding it from occupation by other European powers.

On the other hand, the contrast between Tasmania and the Andaman Islands with respect to British interests in the two regions has no correspondence in any differences in the effects of their presence on the two populations. In terms of the consequences to the Andamanese, they differed very little from the Tasmanians. Despite the imputed distinctions between a settler and a tropical dependency, these are merely semantic quibbles, of little or no significance for either the Andamanese or the Tasmanians.

It can be argued that it is *intent* that distinguishes genocide, and there was no large-scale, systematic, planned slaughter of the Andamanese that occurred. Insofar as it was disease that finally wreaked such devastation on the Andamanese population, it can also be claimed that British policies cannot be held culpable for the extinction of the various groups of the Andamanese. But the links between disease and colonial interventions had been, even at the time, too often reiterated, in too many contexts, for explicitly stated intent in the formulation of policies to be the sole criteria for the determination of genocide. In the case of the Tasmanians, it was not the planned shooting of thousands like so many jack rabbits that finished them. It was their final confinement in various squalid settlements, notably on Flinders Island where a series of epidemics "systematically" killed off all the inmates (Schrire 1995). Likewise, the single-minded ardor of Portman, Man and others to convey their "friendly intentions" to the Andamanese by bringing them within the munificent reaches of British control at the "Andaman Homes," can be dismissed as not explicitly genocidal in intent.

But how does one characterize one such as Portman who admonishes his predecessors for not being better versed in history but then exhibits a wilful blindness in taking groups of Onge and Andamanese to Calcutta to demonstrate British power while there was an outbreak of smallpox in the city? Or bringing captive *Jarawa* to the Homes while there was an epidemic of measles raging there? Or one such as Man, meticulously recording arcane details of a dying people even as he strove

121

to bring more of them within the detrimental sphere of his administration? Perhaps they were merely zealous functionaries executing
orders dispensed elsewhere, but the translation of those orders in
the context of their actual implementation was genocidal in its consequences to the Andamanese. Despite their prior experience with
the Tasmanians, the replication of British colonial interventions as
deployed on the Andamanese within almost exactly the same span
of time is too much of an historical congruence to ignore.

In 1876, when Trucanini, "the last Tasmanian" died, several groups
of Andamanese were in the process of extinction. Hence, the tragedies
of history are repeatedly re-enacted in different locales. If British colonial interests in the Andaman Islands are held to be of primary import while human lives are expendable to the consolidation of such an
agenda, then the colonial project has to be designated as genocidal in
my "partial" reading of history.   ❏

Notes

1   Sections of this chapter have been published in *Indigenous Affairs* 2/2002:32-
    38
2   My own discussions with the Onge suggest a more pragmatic view of human
    affairs, placing greater emphasis on human agency and its consequences, rather
    than a perception of hegemonic control of Onge existence by the interventions
    of the spirits who inhabit their universe.
3   "Pacification" is a military term often used during the colonial period to denote
    the silencing of resistance of a conquered people.
4   The Khoikhoi of South Africa and Namibia are popularly referred to as the San
    or the Bushmen.
5   For a view of the Andamanese as inscribed in literature see Arthur Conan
    Doyle's "The Sign of the Four" or Marianne Wiggins' "John Dollar".
6   The case of the Tasmanians has been described as "the swiftest and most
    complete case of genocide in history" (Haydon and Jones 1978). The British first
    colonized Tasmania in 1803 when an estimated population of 4000 inhabited
    the island. By 1830, after a period of the most brutal savagery at the hands of
    convicts and sealers, following an edict to "wipe off every black man on the
    face of the earth" (*ibid.*), with over a million sheep invading prime hunting and
    foraging land, there were less than 100 left in the settled region. These few were
    driven away from the mainland of Tasmania into the smaller outlying islands.
    Finally a handful of frail survivors were confined on Flinders Island where they
    met their death from various diseases.
7   The reason why the settlement should include a penal colony is clearly explained
    in terms of providing a cheap source of labor "which would otherwise be the

chief source of expense, if indeed it could be procured at all on any terms however exorbitant" (Portman 1899:192).

8   The British practice, as that of any other colonial power, of "naming" every place that they "discovered," is to be noted. The implication is, of course, that the place did not exist prior to such an act by the colonizer. These names have continued to the present day. Some later administrators also incorporated the names by which the *Aka-Bea-da* (the Andamanese group first encountered by the British in South Andaman), or the Onge referred to places, notably Portman, but only if they were not already conferred a British name.

9   Jarawa means "stranger" in the language of the *Aka-Bea-da*, the group that most fiercely opposed British occupation during the second settlement in the islands and, bearing the brunt of "contact," the first to become extinct.

10 Here "white" is used quite deliberately to highlight how color was important in constructions of the *human* for the islanders, as it was in representations of the *savage* by the British (cf. Sahlins 1994). The ways in which these differences were construed as revealed by Portman is supported by my research. My research with the Onge and the Andamanese suggests that for them *human* is defined in terms of color, and a lack of color is described by a term that encompasses all of the following meanings: stranger, foreigner, enemy, not-human, devil.

11 This line of reasoning is endorsed by the Onge accounts in which they mention the increased hostilities between groups following on the heels of demographic imbalances.

12 Across the world, the construction of the "savage" as a social evolutionary category hinges on the absence of clothing or permanent structures of habitation, and dependence on wild resources. The more romantic ascription of the "savage" as being in "a state of nature," and hence "wild" and "free" is at the level of rhetoric. All these components also provide the rationale for dispossessing such people of their land, since they are perceived to have forfeited their rights by neglecting to leave permanent and visible marks of their claims to that land.

13 Jenny Sharpe (1994) uses the term colonialism to discuss pre-Mutiny Indo-British relations and imperialism to mark the post-Mutiny era.

14 A series of wrecks of British ships in the Andaman Sea, the *Briton* and *Runnymede*, the *Emily* and the *Flying Fish*, together with the death of the surviving crew at the hands of the islanders, were influential in providing an explicit rationale for a British base in the Andaman Sea.

15 All the names conferred on the Andamanese by the British administrative officers are reminiscent of circus animals. These were individuals of the *Aka-bea-da* whose Andamanese names were Tura and Lokala.

16 The Reverend Henry Corbyn, Chaplain of Port Blair was a zealous functionary of the Crown. He was the first appointed Officer in charge of the "Andaman Homes". The good Rev. Corbyn is commemorated to this day. His name has been bestowed on an exclusive beach resort area in Port Blair known as Corbyn's Cove

17 The racialization of these categories is to be noted.

18 The Andaman Homes were set up to "civilize the savages" and assimilate them to the mores of the British. They are discussed at greater length in a later section of this chapter.

19 "*Notes and Queries* was specifically designed to guide the non-specialist, to legitimate the knowledge-gathering activities of "self-taught" students like Man" (Tomas 1991: 99).

20 Another linguistic and territorial group who became extinct over the course of the British control of the islands. Strait Island, where the current Andamanese population have been resettled was probably included within the *Pucikwar* foraging area. Loka, the former Andamanese *Raja* was of *Pucikwar* descent.

21 Later known as Colonel Man, and in 1869 he was appointed as Superintendent of Port Blair. As mentioned already, he was also the father of E.H. Man. In 1859, when the plans for a penal colony in the Andaman Islands were finalised, Captain Man was the Executive Engineer and Superintendent of Convicts at Moulmein.

22 The prevailing notions about the "primitive" races were that they embodied the childhood of mankind. Such a view reinforced notions of "the white man's burden" and provided the justification for colonial policies as paternalistic responsibilities.

23 At this stage of British occupation, "strength" and "weakness" with respect to the Andamanese were assessed in military terms, and the vulnerability of the islanders to disease was not yet a factor for consideration. Also instrumental to such a definition of the islanders was the perception of "primitive" races as similar to children, and hence "weak".

24 Here, characterizations as "best" and "worst" characters were based on the extent of opposition expressed toward the British.

25 Climate was an important factor here, those unused to the excessive humidity of tropical rainforests wilted under these conditions. The Agra Jail was located in a hot but dry climactic region.

26 The value of alcohol in furthering the cause of "friendly" relations, especially as it applied to the interests of colonialism was well known by this time. The Native American Indians are a case in point.

27 The convicts sent to the Andamans thought there existed a land bridge between the islands and Burma, and that the capital of Burma was within ten days march through the forest.

28 "Man clothes his cosmos in a moral cloak" observes Arnold (1988: 7, citing Paul 1977), "and in every society, present as well as past, disease, especially epidemic disease, takes on wider social, political, and cultural significance." The extent to which endemic yaws was mistaken for sexually-transmitted syphilis is a matter that affords some conjecture here. In later years, the Onge were diagnosed as "constitutionally afflicted with syphilis", subsequently found to be yaws. Arnold goes on to argue that besides pointing to medical misdiagnosis, these statements are also suggestive of presumptions of promiscuity.

29 It is of interest to note here that during World War II when the Japanese occupied these islands, a number of Andamanese worked as spies for British armies who were running an underground guerrilla operation at the time, tracking and reporting on Japanese movements in the islands. One of them is still alive today in Strait Island, Nao (the elder) more often referred to as "Chacha".

30 These terms too are derived from the *Aka-bea-da*.

31 It is not unduly harsh to characterize the British colonial effort as the first of the major drug-trafficking networks to have taken the form that we see today.

32 Man, Portman and Radcliffe-Brown were particularly active in this aspect, and have left large collections in museums in London.

33 1931 was the last census conducted by the British before the outbreak of WWII. The next one was in 1951 after independence from the British.

34 The number of years involved almost exactly parallels the time-frame of extinction in the case of the Tasmanians.

35 Guha and Gadgil (1989) trace the links between the development of British colonial forestry management in mainland India with the boom in the construction of railway coaches and the market for timber. As an area for future inquiry, it would be valuable to search the annals for the history of British forestry operations in the Andamans. The Chatham Saw Mills and the WIMCO match factory are modern-day extensions of British commercial enterprises in the islands.

ISLANDERS IN "INDIA": POLICIES OF "PLANNED" CHANGE[1]

"It is flat, bright and very hot. Like everything that has happened at Dugong Creek. All the trees are gone, the forest is disappearing, everything will become flat and hot. Everything will dry up like death."

(Totanange, commenting on the solar
plant installed at Dugong Creek.)[2]

The "independent" Andaman Islands

In 1947, when the British transferred control[3] of the Andaman Islands to the newly installed Indian government in mainland India, these islands were designated as "Union Territories". As mentioned earlier, "Union Territories" are administered by the central government from New Delhi, and do not exist as a separate "state" with an autonomous bureaucratic structure. The administration within the islands, as in mainland India, maintained the bureaucracy inherited from the British, with minimal alterations to the structure of government.

In the years preceding independence from the British, as the nationalist movement gathered momentum in India, many of the "freedom fighters", i.e. those most radical and active in their opposition to colonial rule, were incarcerated in the Cellular Jail[4] in Port Blair. At independence, the "liberation" of these "heroes" received wide publicity from the press in India, with several months of newsprint devoted to the story of each "hero". The Andaman Islanders themselves did not get much attention from the government headed by Jawaharlal Nehru in New Delhi after independence. However, Nehru travelled extensively to other "tribal"[5] areas in mainland India, to make himself known to the indigenous[6] peoples in these regions, and discuss his plans for assimilating them as citizens of India.

With independence in 1947, the former British colonial territory was partitioned into two nations, India and Pakistan. Pakistan was further divided into an eastern and western bloc, each located across the diagonal extent of India. Many thousands of displaced refugees had to be accommodated in the newly independent country of India. This situation coincided with the emerging plans for a policy of strategic colonization of the Andaman Islands, with the objective of attaining self-sufficiency in terms of food. Displaced Hindu families from East Pakistan (now Bangladesh) were sent to the Andaman Islands and allotted tracts of land on South and Middle Andaman in the vicinity of

Jarawa territory. The large-scale deforestation, as land was cleared for agriculture, villages and roads constructed, with a greater influx of people entering the remaining forest cover for hunting and firewood, led to a marked increase in the frequency of "*Jarawa* incidents"[7] (Pandit 1989, Sarkar 1990).

Post-independence anthropology

During this phase, Lidio Cipriani was commissioned by the Indian government to set up a substation of the Anthropological Survey of India at Port Blair. A sub-regional office of the Anthropological Survey of India (ASI) was established at Port Blair in the early fifties. It included plans for a special unit on Little Andaman, to gain more knowledge of the Onge and "to assist them in any manner desirable and feasible" (Pandit 1989:88). In 1953, on advice from the ASI, a substantial coconut plantation was established at Dugong Creek, a large Onge camp on Little Andaman.

Cipriani was the first anthropologist to conduct fieldwork among the Onge. The English translation of Cipriani's *The Andaman Islanders* was published posthumously in 1966, the material having come into the publisher's hands only after Cipriani's death. The book represents a brief account of his observations during a period of nearly two years between 1952-54 that he spent on Little Andaman with the Onge.

According to Cipriani, he was beckoned by the mystery of the unknown interior of the island, as well as the prevailing lack of information of any kind about the Onge. One of his first tasks was to establish contact with the Onge and survey Little Andaman, marking the routes that the Onge took through the forest, and locating the territorial divisions of the various communal huts dotting the length and breadth of the island. Cipriani admits to a longstanding interest in the question of the origins of the pygmies. He spent some years studying them in Africa, Asia etc. He arrived at the conclusion that the peoples of the Andaman Islands represented the "purest" living example of Negrito stock and culture, having remained in complete isolation until very recently. He makes frequent comparisons with the Semang of Malaya, the Aeta of the Philippines, the Mbuti of Africa, as well as the "Bushmen" of the Kalahari, in terms of their somatic and cultural characteristics.

Based on conclusions derived from his excavations of the kitchen middens in the different islands, Cipriani viewed the islanders as "involuted"rather than primitive, having regressed culturally, physiologically and psychologically. According to Cipriani, because of their prolonged isolation from the outside world, "they now represent the last and decadent expression of a very lengthy stage of biological and cultural development, a point of arrival, and not one of departure" (1966:67), and a process that inevitably led to extinction. As a self-professed humanitarian, Cipriani sought to avert this inevitable decline through "scientific" intervention.

Cipriani set up camp close to the communal huts of every territorial group that he visited on the island. Since the island was teeming with game, wild fruit and edible roots, food was never a problem, and it was even unnecessary for Cipriani to bring with him any provisions. He appears to have partaken of everything that the Onge ate since he is able to vividly describe these culinary experiences. Living so close to the Onge, he was in a position (unlike Radcliffe-Brown, who conducted much of his investigation on the Andamanese who lived close to the civilized center of the colonial administration) to witness intimate details of their everyday activities.

Shocked by "the rampant homosexuality" of the Onge men when they travelled in the forest, he went on to view the Onge as "decadent", and also attempted to ensure that the Onge men who accompanied him brought their wives with them. But their unabashed and unbridled sexual activities with either sex led him to label the Onge as "child-like" with a child's lack of shame, or the absence of any sense of modesty, a complete lack of hygiene, "an infantile vanity," a child's thoughtless cruelty and a child's abandoned pleasure in obscenities. Extending such a view, he believed the Onge had remained virtually unchanged since the Paleolithic.

A number of parallels can be drawn between Man and Cipriani. Man, too, had an obvious affection for the Andamanese, which was both paternalistic and condescending. He viewed the Andamanese as "wayward but attractive children" (Prain 1932:21), conforming to the prevailing ideas about primitive races as embodying the childhood of mankind. But more importantly, both Cipriani and Man played significant political roles, in the ways in which their scholarly work served to endorse official policy. In the period after the departure of the British from the islands, and the transfer of the Andaman Islands to the newly installed Indian government, Cipriani's research with the Onge, together with his appointment as Director of the research sub-station of the Anthropological Survey of India at Port Blair, paved the way for the colonization of Little Andaman and the confinement of the Onge in permanent settlements.

Two decades of policy

The old British tradition of inviting parties of Onge to pay periodic visits to Port Blair and call on the Chief Commissioner was encouraged. In turn, the Onge were given gifts of tobacco, tea, sugar etc. and "offered official hospitality" (Pandit 1989:88). A Chief Commissioner during the fifties, Mr. A.K. Ghosh remarked at the time, "If this continues, they will go the same way as the Andamanese" (cited in Whitaker 1985, p.10).

Of the 23 Andamanese enumerated in the Census of India 1951, the first census operation in independent India, the adult men retained their earlier occupation from British days in the "Bush Police" force, stationed in and around the forest in *Jarawa* territory. The "Bush Police," originally created to protect the British settlement from the *Jarawa*, performed the same function after independence, and remained a potential employment option for male Andamanese.

The sixties and seventies marked a turning point for the islands, with a large influx of settlers from mainland India, comprehensive schemes for the development of the islands and the first enunciation of plans and policies for the islanders. Venkatesan (1990) traces the contours of land allotment on Little Andaman from the late sixties, when the government of India passed a resolution under the Special Area Development Program to resettle refugees[8] on Little Andaman. Almost 30,000 hectares of forest was cleared by the early seventies for settler villages, most of it encroaching on the territories of the remaining Onge groups in the island. Throughout the seventies, intensive clearance and commercial exploitation of the forest was initiated under the supervision of the Andaman and Nicobar Forest and Plantation Development Corporation (ANFP-DC), encouraging private traders to extract timber, with no effort made to control illegal logging. In an attempt to restock the cleared forest, a regeneration project called Red Oil Palm Plantation designated 2400 hectares for regeneration with red oil palm monocrop species. The construction of roads, government offices, private industries, a harbor, a sub-naval base, an agriculture farm and a helipad all added to the large-scale deforestation, pushing the Onge into ever smaller pockets in the northern and southern parts of the island. Bodley (1988) observes that:

> [T]he most intense arenas of conflict between tribals and national governments involve the development of natural resources on tribal lands by outside interests. Tribal populations invariably occupy territories that are but lightly exploited and then only for local, tribal use. National governments... are understandably eager to extract as much wealth as possible from their entire national territory. Thus we see highways, mining operations... lumbering, agri-business, and planned colonization projects, all intruding on tribal territories. (p.135)

The rationale for such a course of events is provided for in the ambiguous status of "tribal" peoples in the Constitution of India. On the one hand, according to Article 46 of the Constitution of India:

"The State shall promote with special care the educational and econom-
ic interests of the weaker section of the people, and in particular of the
Scheduled Castes and Scheduled Tribes,[9] and protect them from social
injustice and all forms of exploitation." (cited in George 1991:22)

But on the other hand, the constitution also maintains that the traditional rights of "tribals" over natural resources and forest lands is a
privilege or a concession granted to them, and can be "terminated at
the will of the Sovereign" (*ibid*:22). Thus, as George (*ibid*.) points out
with some irony, while "India would like to see her tribal people retain their religion, culture, ethos and institutions", the conditions that
would ensure their distinct identity, namely the guarantee of a stable
resource base, is imperilled by the terms of the same constitution. Bodley's survey on "tribal" peoples notes that:

> [T]he most obvious detrimental impacts are caused by a weakening of the
> subsistence base due to resource depletion and/or breakdowns in the so-
> cial organization of subsistence activities. Pressures on natural resourc-
> es may increase immediately as outsiders begin to compete for them or as
> tribal peoples themselves begin to harvest for the market. The territorial
> base may be drastically reduced as official policy restricts tribal access to
> make tribal resources directly available to outsiders. (p.209)

The strategic monopoly over forest lands is clearly a legacy from British days. Guha (1991) notes that a prolonged debate had ensued within
the colonial bureaucracy over a customary use of forests that is based
on "rights" as opposed to "privilege". The debate was settled by an
ingenious use of precedent, by citing the principle that "the right of
conquest is the strongest of all rights---it is a right against which there
is no appeal" (Amery 1876 cited in Guha 1991:38).

This language, formulated in the context of colonial rule, was carried over without any alteration into the constitution of the "independent" India, as it defined the status of the "tribals" within the country. As regards "tribal" access to forests and traditional rights of use,
the policies of the British and the Indian government are formulated
identically---the forest is always perceived as "virgin terrain", available for alternative commercially profitable use. Such sharply opposed
perceptions of the forest was perceptively framed by a colonial officer in mainland India as:

> [T]he struggle for existence between the villagers and the Forest De-
> partment; the former to live, the latter to show a surplus and what the
> department looks on as efficient forest management. (Percy Wyndham
> 1921 cited in Guha 1991)

The special provisions for the protection of the "tribals" were also inherited from the Government of India Act of 1935, Articles 91 and 92. By this Act, "enclaves" were produced, i.e. areas in which the "tribals" were concentrated, outside of ordinary administration, where they would be "insulated" from "exploitation or demoralizing contact with sophisticated outsiders" (Galanter 1984:147). Concurrently, the colonial government maintained rigorous control over the forests customarily available for "tribal" use.

Such a paternalistic framework for the treatment of the "tribals," first drafted during British colonial rule, then further elaborated by the Indian government, lends some salience to a recognition of the situation of "tribals" in India as one of "internal colonialism".[10] Colby and van den Berghe (1969, cited in Whitten 1976:18) distinguish as "internal colonialism", a situation whereby an independent country has, within its boundaries, given special legal status to groups that differ culturally from the dominant group, and created a distinct administrative machinery to handle such groups. Such groups are usually referred to as "tribes"[11] by the state for administrative purposes.

It is not merely coincidental that the plans for the re-population and development of the Andaman Islands was repeatedly alluded to as a program for "colonization" by the Indian government. With their long experience of colonial rule, it is curious (or revealing) that the term should be brought back into administrative currency promptly after shaking off the shackles of colonial dominance. It does suggest that the former colonial subjects have flipped the situation over, and in turn, become the colonizers.

For the Andaman Islanders, it was merely a transfer of power between two colonial regimes, with very little to differentiate the two, except perhaps the colour of the skin. The colonizer changed from the "white man" to the "brown" one after 1947 who, like the former, proceeded to shoulder the "the white man's burden" of undertaking to "uplift" the "backward" "primitives".

The significant factor to be noted here is that, when schemes were proposed on behalf of the islanders, there was concurrently a second agenda implicated: of development plans for the mainland Indian population, which involved the increased clearing of the forest for agriculture, forest-based industries, villages, roads etc. Thus plans for the islanders did not occur in isolation but were mobilized within a larger context that was contingent on reducing the extent of forest available to them. The strategy for colonization of Little Andaman with settlers from mainland India coincided with the program for sedenterization of the Onge.

The situation of the Jarawa

As in the earlier British period, the specific situation of the *Jarawa* presented a set of conjunctures that was not as readily resolved as in case of the Onge or the Andamanese. When the British left the islands, about 765 sq km of South and Middle Andaman were decreed as *Jarawa* Reserve[12] forest. I have noted earlier that when displaced refugees were resettled on South and Middle Andaman, it led to a marked increase in the frequency of "*Jarawa* incidents". According to the Census of India 1961, there were as many as 89 cases of raids between 1946 and 1963 (cited in Sarkar 1990:48).

The 340 km construction of the Andaman Trunk Road through South Andaman, linking Diglipur in North Andaman with Port Blair, brought large numbers of laborers into *Jarawa* territory, and disturbed the area by way of felling of trees, blasting by explosives, the construction of labor camps etc. The entry of large numbers of people into the area also resulted in an increase in the incidence of poaching (Sarkar 1990). The road building was brought to a halt in 1976, when several members of the road-building crew of the Public Works Department died from arrow wounds. The engineers had aligned the road well into the eastern edge of the reserve (Whitaker 1985). The road construction was resumed from a different section, renewing the scale of conflict with the *Jarawa*.

> *In the last 20 years, the Andamans have been increasingly ravaged for resources and used as a dumping ground for the landless; since 1960, the population has expanded from 50,000 to about 180,000, and over 100,000 hectares of forest have been cleared and 600 km of road constructed.* (Whitaker and Whitaker 1984:16)

Whitaker (1985) goes on to assert that the most serious threat to the *Jarawa* in the present is the increasing human pressure on the islands, and the continued encroachment into their territory, which is prime hunting and fishing land. He observes that the *Jarawa* use metal for their arrowheads and undertake considerable risks to obtain it, raiding road-building camps, forest ("bush" police) camps and farms. As the number and scale of "*Jarawa* incidents" indicated, receiving media attention only if there were deaths on the Indian side, the settlers, illegal encroachers and the "Bush" police, without formal government approval, took it upon themselves to launch a mini-war against the *Jarawa*. In this connection, a former Lieutenant Governor was heard to remark that the *Jarawa* "menace" could be ended once and for all by rounding them up and holding them in some place where they would be unable to "cause trouble". Meanwhile, the administration continued to allot land to settlers, or legalize encroachments along the borders of the contested forest tract. For the *Jarawa* too, as Mukerjee (1995) recognized, it was a declaration of war. She reported an incident early in February 1995 when "the tribe attacked a forest outpost, impaling a woman and slaying a calf" (p.20). Dogs and elephants, which were associated with settlers, were regularly killed but "in the process they have protected the pristine forests of their territory, along with its unique wildlife" (p.20).

The "breakthrough"

The following are a series of commentaries made by anthropologists and other observers on the perceived major turning point in the on-going ambivalent relations with the *Jarawa*. The continuity with earlier British policies is remarkable. More astonishing is that these connections are cited as an affirmation of present policy.

> "In 1968, 3 Jarawa boys were captured...and brought to Port Blair, where they were kept[13] for a month under the observation of 2 anthropologists of the Anthropological Survey of India. They were treated well and then set free near their area with a large quantity of gifts." (Pandit 1974 cited in Sarkar 1990:51) "...In fact, the method adopted by Portman 1879-1894 was followed."[my emphasis] (Sarkar 1990:51)

Sarkar (1990) describes the "momentous" occasion when some kind of "connection" seemed to have been made with the *Jarawa*.

> "There was a major breakthrough in February 1974 when a few Jarawa made friendly gestures towards a contact party led by members of the Bush Police, who used to visit the area from time to time. A Jarawa man swam across and came on board the dungi and collected the gifts... Perhaps this had some positive impact and thereafter the Jarawa came forward on their own to greet the Contact Party, as happened in the case of Colebrooke during the first penal settlement." [my emphasis] (Sarkar 1990:51)

Whitaker and Whitaker (1984) are more wary, urging caution in considering the utility of these developments.

> "From 1974 onwards regular contact has been made with the Jarawa at their coastal camp at Chotaling Bang (Middle Andaman). In 1981, another group in South Andaman was contacted using the Chotaling

Bang Jarawa as go-betweens. The latter were taken to Strait Island and shown[15] the Andamanese settlement there." [my emphasis] (*ibid*:13)

A more critical assessment of these policies is drowned in the flood of acclamatory comments on the government's breakthrough efforts. The health hazards of such contact with outsiders is blithely ignored, and the enormity of the risk of taking the *Jarawa* to Strait Island where one or more Andamanese chronically suffer from tuberculosis, is alarming. As Zai Whitaker (1984) urgently points out, "even an influenza virus could prove fatal to people with no immunity to civilization's diseases" (p.70). She goes on to remind those who have become rashly forgetful of the tragic consequences of such imprudent tactics in earlier times:

> "The post-independence policy toward the Jarawa mimics that of the British administration in trying to appease and buy the Jarawa's friend-ship. In a typical display of bureaucratic short-sightedness, we have yet to learn our lessons from the tragedy of the Andamanese extermi-nation. Regular patrols are still sent out with gifts such as cloth, plas-tic buckets and matches; one group of Jarawa has been in contact with these parties for 10 years, and another group has now joined in. These "gift patrols" may spell the end of the Jarawa; the government should take heed and leave them alone. Isolation is apparently the best policy in the delicate Andamans situation until we can be sure our friendship won't kill them...The government's maneuvers look alarmingly like the practice of scattering rice to attract birds to the snare." (ibid.:16)

On the flip side of the "breakthrough in the situation" has been the continuing sequence of "*Jarawa* incidents", when trespassers or poach-ers encountered in *Jarawa* territory were usually attacked and killed. Or the periodic raids that were made on nearby villages every month around full-moon, for metal implements and utensils, bananas, coco-nuts and cooked rice (all of which were customary gift items carried by the "contact" team). Vishwajit Pandya (1992), with some amusement, referred to these incidents as "the bad guys riding into town, to raise hell, and engage in some duty-free shopping".

Some salutary lessons may be drawn from recalling the early days of British contact with the Andamanese, when similar "plundering" by night and acceptance of gifts by day were regular occurrences. Portman cherishes no illusions when he observes, "we must admit the unflattering fact that it is not any particular love of us, but chiefly the greed for [goods and] food which tempts them to the Settlement" (Portman 1899:412).

Caught on the road. A group of Jarawa on the Andaman Trunk Road.
Photo: SANE (Society for Andaman and Nicobar Ecology)

"Retrieval from Precipice"

The following is a close reading from a document entitled "Retrieval from Precipice", published by the Andaman Adim Janjati Vikas Samiti (AAJVS), the Committee for the Enlightenment of Primitive Peoples. The document is a compilation of cumulative reports and the measures adopted for a program of "planned change" that was proposed for the islanders by the Andaman administration in 1976. The "exciting experiment", also named "Retrieval from Precipice", to "retrieve these rare racial groups from the path of extinction down the precipice of death" was conceived as an endeavour that was in keeping with "the noblest tradition of the Indian Civilization".[16] The document gives insight into the strategies followed in the "unique experiment", as well as an explicit rationale for the undertaking.

A committee named "The Andaman Adim Janjati Vikas Samiti" was constituted to monitor the project, with the help of an advisory "Committee on Primitive Tribal Groups" comprising "experts," mainly anthropologists, an eminent geneticist and other government officers. These were heady days for the group, as they responded to the "clarion call" of the former Prime Minister, Indira Gandhi, in her "20-Point Economic Programme", which laid "great emphasis on the weaker section of society". With immense faith in the possibilities offered by the

135

advances in science and medicine, buoyed up by good intentions and the excitement of "experimenting" on human subjects, the committee set about their task.

The preface lays out the framework for the project "for the amelioration of the tribes", the "purest forms" of the "few endangered remnants of the negrito race" who "still survive in their stone age glory" and who are "not cannibals or inhuman" but "weak, hapless" and in need of the Indian government's "magnanimity and protection". The AAJVS is therefore:

> [E]ngaged in a task which shows that they can be befriended, their health and life protected and their living conditions gradually developed into an economic pattern which can, at an appropriate stage, merge with the economic and living patterns of these islands. In the years to come they will survive, develop confidence and a will to live and become useful citizens of India.

In contradiction to the agenda stated here, the former Prime Minister[17] Morarji Desai's message registers a different intent:

> It should therefore be our duty to let these tribes live their lives as they would like to while providing them with such of the amenities of life to which all citizens of our country are entitled. We do not want the tribes to be ethnological exhibits; nor do we want to lose their distinctive personality under pressure. We need imaginative policies rooted in wider sympathetic knowledge of the tribes.

These two mutually contradictory strands alternate in the document with respect to the policies to be followed, i.e. whether to permit the islanders to maintain their distinctive lifestyle or to integrate them with the other populations. Although the former is asserted at the level of political statements, the latter is the program that is in operation.

The strategies to achieve these projected goals required that:

> These remaining specimens of bygone races...be looked after closely, watchfully and carefully in their small population if their survival is to be ensured. Their future can now only be nurtured in a sort of controlled demographic laboratory till they have been regenerated to come once again into their own. (p.31) [my emphasis]

In the case of the Andamanese, described as "all intermixed and indistinguishable in their ethnic identity", the criteria by which their *success* as a population was to be assessed included: literacy, which was "practically absent," work participation rate "as low as 8.3% (13.3% among the males and practically nil among females)" and a dismal reproductive rate as a consequence of "their males having lost their vitality and the females their fertility." (*ibid.:.30*)

The Onge "are a shade better off than the Andamanese" but persist at a "pre-agricultural stage of food gathering in jungles and pig hunting" (*ibid.:31*). In contrast to the Andamanese and the Onge are the Jarawa "who retain their virility and vitality and are of excellent physique" (*ibid.:32*). The future envisaged for the *Jarawa* through the "goodwill" generated by the "plan-of-action" proposed for them: "survi[val] as fully conscious Indian citizens in not too distant a future" (*ibid.:32*). As for the Sentinelese, who "appeared beyond doubt to be fully virile" (p,32), apart from the "occasional dropping of gifts to augment their resources" and to "infuse goodwill", there was little else that was planned.

The program included plans for the appointment of a "suitable, senior and experienced social worker who could exercise his good judgement[,] and a medical officer preferably gynaecologist together with a lady doctor[,] preferably wife of one of the workers" (AAJVS 1978:39).

There were small modifications in the details of the program as it related to the Andamanese and the Onge, based on their separate historical circumstances. In the case of the Andamanese, the primary task at hand was the recuperation of a group of derelicts existing in a state of utter degradation and ill-health. But, after rehabilitation of "these children of nature" and providing the "grown-ups" with a "modest pocket-money allowance" (AAJVS 1978:36), other schemes were proposed to inculcate *useful* work habits. It was resolved that the Andamanese should be engaged in making canoes and ropes. All the necessary tools and materials would be supplied to them free of cost. It was a matter of some excitement for the committee that soon the Andamanese would be "busy in their traditional vocations" (p.45). In addition, a "piggery unit" was set up, and a calf for breeding purposes. Vegetable and fruit seeds were provided free of cost to help raise kitchen gardens.[18] A system of "passes"[19] was instituted, which meant that the Andamanese could leave Strait Island only when they obtained a pass issued for a specific purpose. A report submitted a year after these schemes were underway concludes:

> "The impact of all these welfare activities initiated by the Samiti has been very encouraging. Not only the Andamanese who used to loiter in Port Blair and other places have gone back to their settlement in Strait Island, there are visible signs of their being hopeful to live. A sense of belonging is more dawning on them. No wonder, if the tempo of developmental efforts is further stepped up with more welfare amenities,

the Andamanese may again turn out to be a thriving community as they were a century before." (AAJVS 1978:46)

With the Andamanese satisfactorily re-settled, it was next the turn of the Onge. In 1976, development plans with the professed intention of providing the Onge with "mainstream amenities" were set in motion. The scheme involved the "rehabilitation and resettlement" of the Onge in the north-east corner of Little Andaman known as Dugong Creek.

The "self-contained settlement" that was constructed for the Onge included individual houses for each couple, with asbestos, corrugated roofs constructed by the Public Works Department. The Public Works Department is responsible for government sanctioned constructions in India. They have several categories of "quarters" that are determined according to the official status of the government officers who will live in these houses during the tenure of their appointment. These are classified as Type I, Type II etc. For the Onge, the lowest of these categories was considered appropriate. An interesting additional influence determined the design of the houses intended for the Onge. The Commissioner of the Andamans at the time, who was also the director of the welfare scheme, had returned from an appointment in the remote North-East region of India, in the state of Manipur. In that region, the people lived in raised houses, built on four posts that functioned as stilts. The Commissioner was much taken with this design, and decided to transplant the homes of one group of "tribals" to a different one – after all, there was not much to distinguish one "tribal" from another.

Other "civic amenities like medical care, water, hygiene, general provisions, marketing, recreation etc.," were part of the "Package Scheme" (*ibid*.:39). Here too, "a piggery unit" was established, and "goat rearing" was to be attempted. And, to underscore the sincerity of these intentions, a reward of Rs. 500 was offered to those who acquired a working knowledge of the Onge language.

Food for the islanders

Food aid in the form of rations is distributed to the Onge and the Andamanese every month. Rations[20] were started as an emergency measure after a cyclone in 1976 when the forests of Little Andaman were ravaged by storms, but were continued subsequently as an important element in the administrative strategy for sedenterization.

A striking feature of the ration items is the inherent ethnocentrism with respect to food. It was unthinkable that a people could survive on

Onge woman going about her domenstic chores. Photo: Sita Venkateswar

a diet devoid of rice and wheat staples or spices. These introductions have been extremely deleterious to a people who had subsisted on a predominantly meat/protein diet, and for whom the question of preserving or storing[21] food was never an issue. The introduction of milk powder may have contributed to the unabated infant mortality even after settlement, and the periodic deaths of children from diarrhoea/dysentery.[22] A connection can be made between sedenterization and the introduction of foods without associations or learned rules of consumption. Fischler (1980) suggests the term *gastro-anomie*[23] to describe the characteristic state of normlessness and ignorance about food selection and food use in situations of rapid change. The outcome is illnesses[24] and maldigestion of a kind not previously encountered and hence not treatable in known, traditional ways.

The power of representations

It is obvious from the discussion so far that national discourses that medicalize the islanders as "rare" and "endangered" contribute to the formulation of government policies that seek to either "preserve" an "authentic" *way of life*, or a unique *people*. These discursive formations are problematized by the contradictory policy options that follow from such representations. Since the islanders have been labelled as "rare," the administration is compelled to make available a substantial forest resource base for the islanders' use, to maintain their unique lifeway. But, because the Onge are also designated as "endangered," they are considered in need of administrative protection. This is to be delivered in the form of medical care, aid in food and reproductive incentives. All this is only possible if they are located within a circumscribed area[25] for the efficient functioning of the medical staff appointed to oversee their health. The representations have legitimized the Indian government's attempts to deploy a policy of sedenterization overseen by social and medical welfare providers. Thus, the medicalization of the islanders reinforces the necessity to sedenterize them, eliding the primary fact that these people are endangered only through the encroachment onto their territory.

As past events have demonstrated with the Andamanese, when the British extended their colony across North, Middle and South Andaman and the neighbouring islands, there is a recurrent pattern to these shifting representations of the islanders and the policies that follow thereafter. As soon as plans are finalized for large-scale utilization and a more commercially profitable use of the islanders' territory, government policies are clearly resolved in favor of sedenterization of the islanders. In the years after independence, the forests of Little Andaman became the target for another round of development efforts. And, at present, the same process is visible with the *Jarawa*: the administration periodically proclaiming them a rare people, and espousing the unique way of life of the *Jarawa*, while in the same breath declaring their intention to include the *Jarawa* as "full-fledged citizens of the country". The Sentinelese are assured of a certain degree of security, by occupying a small, isolated island, to which access remains difficult.

Berkhofer (1978) examines how imagery conflates with policy in the case of the Native American Indian, particularly in the context of arguments over rights to land. It mattered little whether the efforts were towards reform of the "deficient" Indian or the taming of the "bloodthirsty savages". Or whether the policies followed were the General Allotment Act or the New Deal for Indians. The ultimate consequence for the Native Indians was the loss of land held collectively by them. Reiterating the justification that what was good for the whites was also good for the Indian, the general perception was that any policy followed had mutually beneficial outcomes.

Likewise, in the Andaman Islands no matter how the policies are framed, for the islanders the consequences are a steady dwindling of territory under their control. This is particularly noticeable in the case of the Onge and *Jarawa*. But the few, remnant Andamanese are the exception to this norm. Barely surviving in the appalling conditions that they were reduced to by the time the British left the islands, the government's plan did result in an improvement in the material conditions of their existence.

An assessment of the welfare system

The "welfare" program was ostensibly designed to benefit the islanders, to arrest their mortality, assure them of health and gently assimilate them into the dominant population. In the intervening years since the program went into operation, these ideals have given way to disillusionment and cynicism. The essential features of the system are presented as I observed its operation between 1989-1992. The general organization of the program is similar for the Onge and the Andamanese but, while the Onge, at the time, appeared mostly unaware of the exploitation they were undergoing, the greater worldliness and sophistication of the Andamanese made them active collaborators in a system that they used and bent according to the situation.

An assessment of the program requires a dismantling of its constituent parts, to permit an analysis of the different levels at which it operates. The first level of appraisal is the primary level at which the program exists, i.e. in the person of the implementers, those who mediate between the islanders and the policy-makers, translating the policies on paper into quotidian practice. These are the welfare personnel who are appointed by the Andaman administration to oversee the scheme to assimilate the islanders into "fully conscious citizens" of the country. The various positions created for this task include a social worker, a teacher, an auxiliary nurse-cum-midwife, a medical attendant, a wireless operator, a generator operator and two guards (a euphemism for "all-purpose functionaries" who are expected to make themselves available for any kind of work). Their term of appointment varies from anywhere between 3 months to 8 years.

The distinctive personalities of individual members of the welfare staff have been significant in determining the ups and downs, swings and shifts in the fortunes of the Onge and the Andamanese, ever since their destinies were placed under the control of the Indian bureaucracy. Most of the welfare staff manage these settlements as if they were their private fiefdoms. Their lowly, ill-paid status in the hierarchy of government office undermines the lofty ideals attributed to their assigned duties. This means that the general attitude of these "government servants" is to appropriate as much as possible during their tenure and "to hell with the *junglees*". Most feel that the islanders are beneficiaries of a largesse that is undeserved and, therefore, it is only just that they direct a share to themselves.

In addition to the welfare staff, there is a medical officer who is a separate appointee of the Directorate of Health Services. At Dugong Creek, the medical officer is the highest paid functionary in the settlement, usually fresh from medical school, and has a term of appointment of 6 months. Every medical officer who has left Dugong Creek at the end of his tenure has made a small fortune from varied means: the medications sent for the Onge, the milk-powder, the rations [26] and the wages that he is responsible for distributing in conjunction with the other welfare staff,[27] the coconuts collected by the Onge and, last but not the least, the ambergris that washes up on the shores of Dugong Creek during the monsoons. At least two former medical officers have been held responsible by Onge elders for introducing alcohol to other Onge as inducements for procuring ambergris for them. In their defense, it is usually conceded that it is the officers' inexperience, together with the loneliness and isolation of the appointment at Dugong Creek that makes the situation difficult to cope with. Hence all succumb to the blandishments of corruption, which is equated with justifying the hardships endured at Dugong Creek. But the situation has proven no different even when senior, more experienced officers are appointed along with their families, so that this particular line of reasoning loses any credibility.

Apart from the long litany of vices of the welfare staff implementing the program, they are as callous in the actual discharge of their duties. Infants continue to die at regular intervals. Most of the Onge and Andamanese are under treatment for tubercular and other respiratory diseases. And every adult and child suffers from anemia and recurring skin infections. Thus, the most conspicuous feature of the welfare system in terms of its execution is that all the personnel are in cahoots with each other in order to prosper from the varied means available for amassing wealth during their appointment.

A government appointment in India is a permanent position, with minimal risk of dismissal. There is no penalty for an unsatisfactory discharge of responsibilities or reprehensible conduct, especially in places as remote as the Andaman Islands. Because of this lack of accountability, and the large sums allocated for "tribal welfare," corruption is an endemic feature of government bureaucracy.

To illustrate these assertions, I will offer some examples of inappropriate conduct by the welfare personnel that came to my attention during the period of my research. The first one occurred at Strait Island where I ascertained the reasons for the odd behavior of Pejeye, one of the Andamanese men. His behavior was the manifestation of symptoms of extreme addiction to a "cocktail" of sedatives, with a shot of methylated spirit for good measure, given to him over several months by the "compounder,"[28] as inducement for procuring "birdsnest" and ambergris for him. This discovery led to the transfer of the "compounder" to a different "tribal" posting in the Nicobar Islands but there was no question of terminating his employment. The explanation offered was that the "compounder" would be coming up for retirement shortly,[29] and it was "unethical" to deprive him of his job at this stage of his employment.

Similarly, the medical attendant at Dugong Creek had a stash of alcohol, regularly replenished during her visits to the nearest town, in exchange for honey, ambergris and incense from the Onge. She too was transferred elsewhere, and this time the justification was the large family she supported. Hence, although her conduct was not to be condoned, it was to be forgiven.

Finally, the medical officer at Dugong Creek assaulted a young, attractive Onge woman, who defended herself with a knife. His behavior was simply laughed away, to the outrage of other Onge. When I queried the Onge as to why they did not take matters into their own hands, they indicated their tenuous control over any situation by confessing their inability to take any strong action against the officer.

This diatribe against the welfare personnel with respect to their dealings with the Onge or the Andamanese has to be juxtaposed against my own personal experience of them during the period of my research in the islands. My memories of the exchanges of hospitalities, small courtesies, the many kindnesses that went a long way towards mitigating the loneliness and hardships of life in these remote outposts, are to be included in my inscription of these people here.These disjunctions problematized day-to-day practices, and the only means out of the impasse was to finally separate (as I did) the sphere of my own interactions with the welfare staff from their conduct with the islanders. It did not make my own daily existence any easier as I negotiated these disjunctions, but such contradictions constituted my experience in the islands and forged the framework for my research there.

It can be argued, as it is by "higher" authorities in the government, that corruption in the lower ranks has deviated the original intent of the program. But the extent of corruption cuts across all levels of the hierarchy as a consequence of the inherent structure of government, and the large profits at stake. Such a situation is typical of government bureaucracies across south and south-east Asia. In my presentation of the contemporary situation of the Andaman Islands, I do not assert that the forms of bureaucracy or scale of corruption is unusual to the islands. It is a feature of nation/states across the world. But that does not make a discussion of such characteristics, or its inclusion here, any less pertinent. The point is to delineate the ways in which the islanders are inextricably linked to larger processes that are globally widespread.

The program, as charted by several anthropologists, the eminent geneticist and some idealistic "top" officials, had very little bearing on the reality of its implementation. But what of the original intent of the program? Can it pass muster without comment? The well-intended policies for the "uplift" of the "primitives" can also be viewed as a charter for the ethnocide of a distinct group of people, albeit, a *benevolent* ethnocide.

The content of policies: ethnocide/benevolent ethnocide

In recent years, the term ethnocide has increasingly come into prominence as a framework for describing the condition of indigenous peoples across the world (Barabas and Bartolemé 1973; Lizot 1976; Whitten, Jr. 1976; Ehrenreich 1985; Escobar 1989; George 1991). As defined by Whitten, Jr. (1976:24):

> [T]he concept of ethnocide is taken from genocide, and refers to the process of exterminating the total lifeway of a people or nation, but in the ethnocidal process many of the peoples themselves are allowed to continue living."

The starting point for this process in contemporary nation/states is very often a situation that I have defined earlier as internal colonialism. By that process, indigenous peoples are deprived of any control over a traditional resource base, are sequestered within "enclaves" where they are rendered dependent on a dominant majority who have taken over their lands, and are left without any alternative means for survival. The dominant majority then proceeds to improve the condition of such "hapless" "primitives" by destroying all the elements of their "backward" lifeway, thus resulting in the ethnocide of a distinct group of people.

Ehrenreich (1985) offers a more nuanced understanding of the ethnocide of contemporary indigenous peoples by associating two apparently irreconcilable terms, namely that of *benevolent ethnocide*. His conceptualization of "benevolent ethnocide" is drawn from his work with the Coaiquer of Ecuador and, in large measure, denotes the condition of indigenous peoples in varied parts of the world. While on the surface policies of "planned change" "are propelled by positive and 'enlightened' humanitarian concerns", Ehrenreich demonstrates how the process is "steeped in racism and basic contempt for indigenous tribal peoples, no matter how well-intended particular proponents in any given case might prove to be" (p.17).

An examination of such policies reveals that they are premised upon the assumption that the lifestyle of indigenous people is inherently inferior, and hence must be supplanted by a different and better one. Moreover, it is also presumed that indigenous peoples are incapable of envisioning or planning their own future, therefore it is "outsiders" who know what is best for them (*ibid.*).

But a careful scrutiny of the entire context in which such policies are formulated reveals that the motives for the amelioration of the condition of the "tribals" is usually suspect. As the example of the Andaman Islanders suggests, the assimilation of the islanders into "the mainstream" benefits primarily the well-intentioned "outsiders". In view of the ambiguous intent underlying policies of "planned change", despite their well-meaning appearance, their ultimate objectives distinguish them as sanctioning a process of ethnocide.

The initiation of ethnocide through policy intersects with a different process, that of "subjection", whereby the islanders become increasingly enmeshed in a trend that effaces their existing way of life. The consequence of such a two-way sequence of events is the destruction of a viable lifeway, and the induction of the islanders into the swelling ranks of other dispossessed marginals of mainland Indian society.

A matrix for subjection: individual autonomy

Biolsi (1995) traces the history among the Lakota of what Foucault (1983) calls "subjection", which Biolsi interprets as the process that constituted the Lakota "as social persons who could fit into the American nation-state and the market system of metropolitan capitalism" (Biolsi 1995:30). The series of administrative techniques deployed to construct these "new individuals" shares a startling resemblance to the welfare program administered by the Indian government, which is also intended to assimilate the Andaman Islanders into the dominant population.

Like the Lakota, the Onge are a particularly individualistic society "in which political power [is] not centralized but tend[s] to cohere around self-made leaders...[b]ut this form of individuality emerged in the context of social relations profoundly different from those of...industrial capitalism" (*ibid*.:29). Individualism[30] as understood in the context of the Onge should be regarded as a marked self-sufficiency. Each individual is autonomous, free to pursue his or her self-interest, and is not subservient to any structure of authority within the community. Therefore the relationship between each individual is that of equality regardless of age or gender.

The Onge's relationships with each other manifests itself on a day-to-day basis in the form of sharing of food, of which the most overt example is the sharing of pork. It is this transaction between individuals that maintains the notion of a "community". Therefore, the atomistic, fissioning tendency as a result of each individual's freedom to pursue his or her self-interest in whichever direction he or she chooses is countered by the strong pull inwards towards the community, which is reinforced everyday by the sharing of food. This is what has maintained the integrity of the community despite the heavy mortality and the disruptions of settlement.

The same characteristic is visible among the Andamanese as well, who can also be described as individuals who are self-sufficient and free to pursue their interests. But in contrast to the Onge, they live in an environment alien to them, a universe that has lost all meaning and significance, and hence there is no possibility of any relationship with and within this universe. Having lost their focal center, and without any basis for transactions between themselves, the Andamanese have splintered into individuals moving outwards and away from each other.

Other reports on the Onge (Basu 1990) have interpreted this quality of individualism as a form of selfishness, where no-one goes to the aid of another person. But as early as 1952, Cipriani comments on the Onge attribute of self-sufficiency as characteristic of other foraging groups as well, while noting the help and generosity extended if a man is injured or his wife is ill. All food is provided and the person relieved of any duties. I concur with Cipriani that it is more accurate to describe the Onge as self-reliant, an attribute that is inculcated at an early age. Children are allowed to play with knives and other implements and become proficient in handling them. Even infants are permitted to clamber about the scaffolding of the *tokabe*, the Onge communal huts, while their fathers are engaged in the construction.

The issue is one of labor. No Onge gives nor expects to receive help in the form of labor, i.e. an activity that can be included within the range of domestic responsibilities, for someone else. In this context, the nuclear family unit is very important in the sharing of labor. It is essential to have a husband or wife and children to complement one's tasks in the quotidian round of activities.

The distribution of domestic tasks is both shared and divided along lines of gender and age. The condition of Nabekutti and Shiela (both recently widowed at the time of my research) is illustrative of the importance of first, a spouse, and next in order of importance, children, to keep the "home fires burning". Nabekutti had lost his wife some years ago and, without any surviving offspring, had abandoned his house in the settlement. He roamed around the forest and the nearby Bengali villages, selling everything that he gathered from the forest for alcohol. During the entire period of my stay in Dugong Creek, even when he occasionally stayed in the settlement, he never cooked in his house but partook of food in other people's homes.

Shiela, on the other hand, with six children to care for, even with the help of her older children, had difficulties organizing her household. She could not count on assistance from her male kin since they were responsible for their own homes. The specific tasks that a husband would have shared with her remained undone, with nobody else who could permanently take over those responsibilities.

It is against such a "matrix of individualism" that the "subjection" of the Onge through the welfare efforts must be assessed. The most significant development that has emerged in recent years is the notion of individual property – objects that are not a product of an Onge's singular effort are now accommodated within the frame of individual ownership: money accumulating in the bank the real value of which is still unintelligible; locks placed on doors and suitcases –this is an impressionistic rendering of a trend that is at odds with other values of sharing, the open give and take, also observable among the Onge. The new attribute of ownership is ascribed by the Onge to objects that they have purchased with money – transistors, tape-recorders, watches that they cannot read etc. But objects that have been given or gifted to them, including their rations of food, as well as things that they have made themselves, still freely circulate between them.

More important, however, are the conflicts over power that have hardened over the years, as a consequence of the individual relationships that have been struck with the welfare staff and other officials of the administration. These in turn, have opened up "avenues for enablement" and privileges not available to everyone else.

Subjection and power

In my discussion of the Andamanese during the period of British control of the islands, I noted the incidence of specific individuals who were singled out by the British officers and conferred certain privileges. Similar observations have been made in the case of the Ik, the !Kung or Native Americans (Turnbull 1972, Wilmsen 1990, Berkhofer 1978 and Biolsi 1995).

I retrace the trajectory of a similar process as it developed in the case of the Onge in my discussion below. Until the breakwater was constructed in the sixties, Little Andaman was surrounded by notoriously rough seas, making landing on the island a risky and difficult undertaking. Dugong Creek was one of the routes to easy access because of the deep, tidewater creek that opened out to sea. Hence the territorial groups of Onge who lived in the Dugong Creek area and its vicinity[31] have historically had more access to outsiders than the groups living in the interior and other coastal parts.

When the settlement at Dugong Creek was constructed, there were a number of different territorial groups of Onge who were accommodated in that area, including all the groups around Dugong Creek itself. Typically, when the welfare program was initiated, Tambolai,[32] an intelligent and personable young man fluent in Hindi, was appointed *Raja*. The other[33] territorial groups around Dugong Creek were allied through affinal relations with Tambolai's group. As a result of their longer duration of "contact", first with the British and then the Indians, members of these groups were more proficient in Hindi than the Onge from the more distant regions of Little Andaman. Young men drawn from these groups were appointed as "helpers"[34] to the welfare staff. Thus, Berogegi, Tai and Totanange were the next rung[35] of Onge with structured links with the Indians. Tambolai was also appointed as member of various executive bodies of the Andaman administration, receiving a large salary, and having to appear for periodic "meetings" in Port Blair. He was flown in as a special guest of the Prime Minister for Republic Day parades in New Delhi and was exempt from all wage-work. The exemption from the tedious grind of wage-work also extended to the other "helpers" who, over the years, have learned to negotiate their duties with the *entale*.[36]

In view of the lack of any permanent, institutionalized structure of authority prior to these events, a three-tiered, hierarchical structure was installed on a purported decentralized, pluralistic and egalitarian[37] people The rumblings of dissent soon became apparent as members of the other[38] territorial groups voiced their claims to the same privileges. Nabekutti from *Deshenghri*, with the support of all his affinal allies, sought to replace Tambolai as *Raja*. But Nabekutti did not have the same presence of personality nor the linguistic abilities of Tambolai. As a gesture of appeasement by the Andaman administration he was made *co-Raja*, but the position did not carry the same weight – he was only a "titular head" in the sense that the welfare personnel referred to him as *Raja* together with Tambolai.

There was yet another basis for the shifting of power over to Tambolai's group. The *torale* or the spirit communicators are purportedly very powerful figures for the Onge, since they alone have the ability to mediate between the human and spirit realms (Pandya 1992). The two extant *torale* were Kwerai of the Chamale group, and Moroi.[39] Moroi was territorially allied with the rival camp, but married to a Chamale woman. Tambolai claimed both as his allies to endorse the position of authority conferred on him by the Andaman administration.

Meanwhile, over the years, another contender to the position of *Raja* had emerged from the rival camp, in the person of Bara Raju. The route that he chose to follow was as a hard-working, reliable recruiter of labor for wage-work. The welfare personnel could always depend on Bara Raju to round up the men required to perform any work in the settlement. Bara Raju had dreams of flying to Delhi for Independence Day or Republic Day parades, attending meetings at Port Blair, and having the ear of the Lieutenant-Governor of the Andamans. The increasing trust placed in him by the authorities in Port Blair enabled him to use it as a lever to negotiate with, and check the excesses of, the welfare personnel at Dugong Creek. Bara Raju was also proficient in Hindi, with an appreciation for the colloquialisms and the flavor of invectives in that language. His claim that he should rightfully displace Tambolai as *Raja* found a growing body of support at Port Blair, since Tambolai, over the years, had also acquired a reputation for drinking. More pertinent, for my purposes, was Bara Raju's agreement to work with me based on his appraisal of the extent to which I could influence the direction of his aspirations, by endorsing his claim to *Rajaship* with the right authorities.

Alongside these power moves, constituted by the entry of the welfare system into Dugong Creek and the incorporation of the Onge within relatively new dimensions of privilege, the "traditional" structure of authority remained invested in the person of Tilai, the last of the "old-time" Onge.[40] [41] He remained distant from the maneuvers of either Tambolai, Nabekutti or Bara Raju, although both Nabekutti and Bara Raju could claim him as a territorial and an affinal ally.

The narrative above clearly illustrates the process of "subjection" that has "seduced" some Onge by offering to them certain privileges that are available by taking the routes to power opened up by the Indian government. The process described here demonstrates the ways in which informal modes of authority have been recast into more permanent, hierarchical structures of power endorsed by the Indian government. The situation exhibits many similarities to Biolsi's work with the Lakota, as they moved into the spaces of power made available by the administration.

But the Andaman administration has met with little success in the other schemes that were also initiated at Dugong Creek, namely the attempts to direct the Onge away from subsistence practices rooted in the forest. "Piggery units", vegetable gardens, dairy cows, goat-rearing projects – have nourished and sustained the welfare personnel. For many years they presented these programs as a great success, until some higher officials came to investigate. The Onge have remained indifferent to these particular efforts to "civilize" and lure them from the forest.

Some observations on anthropology at Dugong Creek

In the early eighties, as the Onge settled into the welfare system, Vishvajit Pandya, a graduate student from the University of Chicago, conducted his dissertation research on the Onge at Dugong Creek. Based on his fieldwork between 1983-84, Pandya's work was published in 1993 as *Above the Forest: A Study of Andamanese Ethnoanemology, Cosmology and the Power of Ritual*. Pandya's study of ritual among the Onge is a densely detailed presentation of the cultural content, cosmological structures and hierarchical system of the Onge. His monograph can be viewed as a model of an earlier era of ethnographic writing in anthropology, with the ethnographer's presence inserted into the preface or introductory chapter, followed by an authoritative exegesis of "native" categories of thought throughout the succeeding chapters.

Using the case of initiation of young males and the role of the spirit communicators, Pandya interprets the belief system of the Onge, examining the changing power relations between humans, animals and the spirits in the transformation of nature and culture. Pandya's success, as Tomas observes in the case of Man's work, is "derived from its power to salvage an authentic image of the 'primitive' from the intense contradictions that existed in an observed reality" (1991: 88). His work also recalls Mintz's (1985) comment that:

"By some strange sleight of hand, one anthropological monograph after another whisks out of sight any signs of the present and how it came to be." (p.xxvii)

The "intact" worldview of the Onge that Pandya presents belies their incorporation into the welfare system and the changes that were already underway in 1983, posing a perplexing conundrum that does not surface in Pandya's smooth account. A couple of paragraphs in the introductory chapter touch upon the current situation of the islanders before moving on to their belief system, recovering[42] and freezing them within an unarticulated present. But these beliefs have to be affected by the conditions of the islanders' existence, which is not visible in his rendition.

His research is strongly influenced by Radcliffe-Brown's work and Pandya admits to bringing that text into this context. The changed context itself is of minimal significance for Pandya as he seeks convergences with Radcliffe-Brown's inscription of the Andamanese, constructing a new text that presents yet again "a closed timeless picture of the integrated organic life of Andamanese culture" (Tomas 1991: 103).

But, as Renato Rosaldo (1989) incisively notes, we all bear witness, since "processes of drastic change are often the enabling condition of ethnographic field research, and herein resides the complicity of the missionary, constabulary officer, and the ethnographer" (p.87). With the intense problematization of ethnographic practice over the past two decades, the fact that a work published in 1993 elides these disjunctions is a curious feature, and one that is itself a problem to be pondered.

Some alternatives?

Tennant and Turpel (1986) point out that the post-war process of decolonization has passed over the claims of indigenous peoples. They stress the fact that the claims of indigenous peoples for sufficient autonomy to ensure their continued existence as culturally-distinct collectivities is a political claim that challenges the territorial sovereignty and nationality of a state. As Maybury-Lewis (1981) notes:

"Land, and the struggle for it, is at the heart of the problem of cultural survival, for the guarantee of their lands is what tribal peoples need most." (p.73)

Since indigenous claims pose a challenge to the state, they have met with little success in resolving their claims domestically, where such claims are both decontextualized and depoliticized into questions of minority rights, language rights etc. International human rights fora, however, provide an environment in which the political aspects of indigenous claims can be discussed. But here too, claims to collective existence as a people cannot be readily accommodated within the existing human rights norms and tend to become fragmented and decontextualized. Falk (1988) suggests that what indigenous peoples can hope to achieve through international human rights norms and procedures is to expand the discussion of their claims, and to underscore the unfinished nature of the decolonization effort.

Arguably such a scenario is not relevant to the existing condition of the islanders, because of their inability to participate to any significant degree in the public institutions of civil society. But the significance of international fora like the United Nations lies in providing the space for developing alternative standards, which can then serve as a point of reference in policy initiatives. The politicization of the islanders, if ever, to avail of such standards and make a bid for an opportunity to define their own rights is a later phase.

Lesser (1968, cited in Ehrenreich 1985:324) argued in the context of the assimilation pressures on the Native American Indian that the "decision to become fully assimilated and to give up Indian identity and community life was not for the nation or the government to make, but the Indians to make for themselves" (1968:591). Such a statement succinctly challenges the patronizing presumptions behind much of the decisions made on behalf of people like the Andaman Islanders. The first step then, as an alternative mode for policy initiatives at the local level, is to acknowledge that the islanders are capable of envisioning their own future, whatever its configuration and trajectory of unfolding.

Conclusion

This chapter traces the development of policies proposed for the assimilation of the islanders after the Andaman Islands became a part of the Republic of India. I argue that the situation of the islanders and other "tribals" in India can be characterized as internal colonialism. The policies of planned change for the "uplift" of "primitives" are initiating a process of ethnocide, erasing a sustaining lifeway as it divests them of their resource base.

The presumed "failure" of the welfare system merits further discussion here. Steeped in the paternalistic, linear, evolutionary and economic rationality characteristic of development interventions everywhere (Escobar 1995), the welfare system has had other "side effects" that should be made "legible" (cf. Ferguson 1990).

I have shown how the medicalization of the islanders is an integral
element of a profoundly political process that divests a people of their

land but is simultaneously depoliticized by the deployment of representations that elides the fact that such a process is underway. Moreover, despite the lamented "failure" of the welfare system, and its deviations from the purported "ideals" as originally formulated, for all the reasons discussed above, it has ensured the incorporation of the Onge and Andamanese into the bureaucratic structures of the state, with the entrenchment of state power into their daily lives.   ❑

Notes

1 A modified version of this chapter has been published in Contemporary Society: Tribal Studies Volume 6, Tribal Situation in India, ed., D. Behera and G. Pfeffer, pp. 17-48. New Delhi: Concept Publishing Company. Sections of this chapter have also been published in Scientific American (1999) May:82-88.

2 The comment was made during a discussion between Totanange, an Onge man with whom I had extensive discussions, Vishvajit Pandya an anthropologist, and myself at Dugong Creek. Totanange was asked about his views on the new solar plant that was being installed at the time.

3 An Indian newspaper article discusses the prolonged negotiations between Britain and the new national governments of India and Pakistan over rights and control over the Andaman and Nicobar Islands (Singh 1995).

4 The Cellular Jail, which grew out of the former penal colony, is a landmark and a major tourist attraction on the Andaman Islands.

5 I have defined "tribal" in an earlier chapter. It is a legal referent, distinguishing such people from "caste" society.

6 Here indigenous is understood as the original inhabitants of their territories. It can be more precisely used in this sense in the Andaman Islands than on mainland India.

7 These are encounters between the "Jarawa" and the Indian population, usually violent, resulting in injury or death to one or both parties

8 The issue of refugees crossing over into India from Bangladesh (formerly East Pakistan) has been a matter of some concern since independence. With the ongoing violence between the Sinhalese and Tamil populations in Sri Lanka, this is another continuous source of refugees. The Andaman Islands is perceived as the last bastion where all such displaced people can be accommodated.

9 Scheduled tribes are defined as those groups who are characterized as "primitive," isolated, and "backward," thus making them deserving of special treatment (Galanter 1984).

10 As discussed by Blauner (1972), the concept of "internal colonialism" or "domestic colonialism" was introduced into political analysis with reference to the situation of Afro-Americans in the United States. He traces the development of its use as it gained currency and respectability. Hechter (1975) applies a Marxist analysis and draws on world-system theory to identify the situation of the Celts as one of internal colonialism. Both Blauner and Hector dwell on racial

differences as a basis for the economic and political dominance of one group of people by another.

11 The propensity for the administrative use of the term "tribe" with reference to indigenous/aboriginal peoples across the world is to be noted.

12 In the absence of any communication with the *"Jarawa"* there is a certain absurdity to declaring a portion as *their* reserve and expecting *"Jarawa"* comprehension of such a demarcation.

13 It should be mentioned that for want of any other alternative accommodation, the captives were housed in the Cellular Jail.

14 *Dungi*, which is a modification of dinghy, is the Andaman word for a boat with an outboard motor.

15 These gestures are reminiscent of Portman's or other British officers' policy of taking the Andamanese and Onge to Port Blair or Calcutta to impress them with the "wonders and pleasures of civilization".

16 This is a part of the congratulatory message sent to the Andaman administration from Charan Singh, the Home Minister at the time, which appeared in the published version of the document "Retrieval from Precipice" 1978.

17 The political situation in India was tense at the time, and there were a number of quick turnovers of the government, headed by the leaders of different political parties.

18 All this is reminiscent of the schemes set up for the Andamanese in the Homes that were created for them by the British. See discussion in chapter 2.

19 The system of "passes" was discontinued some years later and did not exist at the time of my research in the islands.

20 Tobacco was included as one of the ration items and was eliminated recently. However, tobacco, areca nuts and alcohol continue to be used as bribes by the welfare staff and others to obtain forest products from the Onge or as an inducement for extracting labor from the Onge.

21 The tropical climate and the necessity of transporting all ration items by sea hastens the process of spoilage and vermin infestation in the sodden sacks that arrive at the settlement. Moreover, analogous to the earlier British period, the most inferior quality supplies are obtained for the islanders. This is true even in the case of the edible "gifts" carried during *"Jarawa"* contact.

22 Besides the possibility of lactose intolerance, there is also the issue of awareness of the importance of hygienic practices, proper sterilization of milk bottles etc.

23 The situation assumes tragic proportions when such anomie means that potentially harmful substances are offered to children. There is no cognizance of the detrimental effects that alcohol or tobacco can have, and everything that adults like and enjoy is also considered good for children.

24 See Joos (1984) for a discussion on obesity and diabetes among the Florida Seminole Indians, and Fitzgerald (1980) for the effects of dietary change on the Cook Islanders.

25 During the early years of the settlement at Dugong Creek, when their houses were still in the process of construction, the Onge continued to roam about at

will in the forests of Little Andaman. The first few medical officers appointed to the post at Dugong Creek refused to search for the Onge in the forest. They insisted that they could not fulfil their medical responsibilities until it was ensured that the Onge were accessible within a circumscribed area.

26 Many Onge and Andamanese have nowadays taken to selling their rations to obtain cash for the purchase of alcohol.

27 Conflicts between the welfare personnel arise when one or more feel they that they have been left out of their due share of the pickings.

28 The "compounder" is an appointee of the Directorate of Health Services, usually with some pharmaceutical training.

29 Here, "shortly" should be read as a few more years to perform his nefarious activities elsewhere.

30 See Gardner 1991 for a discussion on current theories to account for foragers' individual autonomy.

31 Dugong Creek and its vicinity is referred to as *Lebanare* by the Onge.

32 From the territorially defined group belonging to Dugong Creek.

33 The Tokebui, Chamale and Titaje groups.

34 The term "helper" is a euphemism for a domestic servant for the welfare staff. The appointment has undergone some modifications since it was first conceived by the formulators of the welfare system. These assignments were to enable the Onge to receive training in the specific areas of appointment of the welfare personnel. At present, the duties of a "helper" include the transport and storage of water for daily use, the collection of firewood, scouring of vessels and scrubbing the lodging where the particular staff member is housed.

35 At present there is a back-up crew of other Onge, Ramesh, Chogegi, Kimboi, Kokegile to take over the more disagreeable tasks from this rung of appointees.

36 The Onge word for "officer".

37 Previous reports on the Onge (Portman, Cipriani, Basu etc) especially those prior to their settlement, endorse the egalitarian quality of their social relations.

38 The Tochieddi and the Togalange groups.

39 Bara Raju's vociferous repudiation of Moroi's abilities to communicate with the other world in chapter one should be recalled here. Bara Raju belonged to the same territorial group as Moroi, Togalange, and barely concealed his chagrin when Moroi shifted his allegiance to the affinal allies of his wife's group.

40 Nao's description of the qualities that singled out a person as an informal leader in the 'old days' narrated in chapter one should be recalled here.

41 At the time of revising this manuscript, I was saddened to discover that Tilai, as well as Moroi, the purported *torale*, had both passed away.

42 This is a form of engagement that Clifford (1986) refers to as "salvage ethnography".

GENDER/POWER [1]

"The husband cannot interfere with the decision of women"

(Cipriani 1954 :72)

Introduction

This chapter considers gender relations in the Andaman Islands in the specific forms visible among the Onge and the Andamanese, against the context of the interventions of the Indian government. The chapter is organized into two sections, each one separately addressing the issue of gender *vis-à-vis* first the Onge then the Andamanese. The framework for each section is dissimilar: in the case of the Onge, I interrogate the efforts of the Onge women to maintain a domain autonomous from the infringements of the Indian welfare administration; with the Andamanese, I examine gender relations in terms of their links to the sites of power within the group. In each instance, I appraise the basis of my interpretations, exploring these constructions as a product of my specific positionality to each group.

Gender relations among the Onge

The gendered anthropologist

A significant dimension of my relationship with the Onge was predicated solely on the basis of my gender. In an earlier chapter I detailed the obstacles to physically living with the Onge. I explained the problems I underwent as an aspect of Onge dissembling behaviors related to the maintenance of a domain exclusive to themselves. Such a conclusion is imbricated onto my own efforts at dissimulation, and the reasons for resorting to a measure of secrecy.

After my first, preliminary trip to the Andamans in 1989 to explore the possibilities of undertaking research there, I decided that when I returned I would present myself as a married woman. This seemed to me a practical strategy that would eliminate many of the problems that I had encountered during my initial trip. Hence, when I returned in 1991, I wore on my person some of the signifiers that convey marriage in India. The strategy proved effective by deflecting any unwanted attention from the Indians around me. In the case of the Onge, however, it was another matter. As I realized to my dismay later, my presentation of myself as a married woman was crucial in determining the course of my fieldwork experience.

The Onge found it hard to understand how I could remain there alone, separated from my family, for such a long time. It seemed unthinkable to them that a parent, at least a sibling, if not my husband, was not with me for some part of that time. This was a matter that elicited some comments from the Indians as well but it was shrugged away as "Oh, she's from America" and that was reason enough. I was at pains to explain that I had travelled to America to pursue my graduate studies quite recently, that my family lived in Calcutta, and that I still considered Calcutta *home*. But that made my solitary existence more puzzling, and the only possible reason that could be attributed for the bizarre situation was the "American" connection.

On interrogation by the Onge women as to how long I had been married, I surmised that it was less of a misdeed to be away from one's husband after several years of marriage, and I responded accordingly. But that led me into deeper waters. I was asked how many children I had, and I countered with a none, since I gauged accurately that to have children and not bring them with me was the greatest offence of all. That didn't let me off the hook either. I received a long harangue from more than one woman castigating me for my strange behavior: to be married for as many years as I admitted to being, and not have produced *one* child![2] I weakly promised to do my best as soon as I finished my work with them and returned to my husband. And that was followed by another long rebuke of my errant husband who consented to my living alone, so far from any family. I was frequently reminded that I should send for my husband soon, to ask him to come and take care of me.

The matter did not end there. Well into the months of my stay at Dugong Creek, I realized that, at some level, the Onge women felt a certain alienation from me by my persistence in living alone at Dugong Creek. It was not an issue that I could resolve in terms that would make any sense to them. More frustrating was the behavior of the Onge men, who broke appointment after appointment with me after having assured me that they would meet me at a certain time[3] at the "guest house". Towards the latter part of my fieldwork, when it was almost too late to rectify matters, Bara Raju confided that the men did not show up because they were unwilling to spend long hours alone with me interviewing them at the "guest-house". Such an action on their part would be considered a transgression, and may have given offence to my absent husband. Even though he was so far away, it was necessary that the men show him adequate respect.

I was relieved that I finally had an answer for what had been an inexplicable element of my interaction with them. But, seizing upon an opportunity to berate them about something that I had not yet for-given them for, I shot back that all these problems could have been avoided if I had been permitted to live in the empty house in their settlement. There would always be children and other Onge in and out of my house, and the issue of any man spending time alone with me would never have arisen. This, in turn, revealed to me yet anoth-er tier of protocol that would have been violated had any of the Onge men constructed the furniture that I needed to live in that house. As a married woman, it was a task that was to be undertaken only by my husband, or other male kin. The Onge men were cognizant of the re-spect befitting my husband and family. At that moment, I would have forsworn husbands several lifetimes over if I could have retraced my steps and amended my marital status.

A view of Onge gender relations

In the day-to-day unfolding of Onge gender relations, the Onge's ex-perience of colonization, with its typical sharp exclusion of wom-en from the domain of "official" politics and the more formal deci-sion-making bodies of the administration, has challenged and shaken the basis for Onge women's traditional structure of authority within the community (Cipriani 1954). The loss of Onge territory has simul-taneously corresponded with the fragmentation of their hunting-gath-ering modes of subsistence. These were wedded to patterns of ritu-als that reaffirmed and endorsed the complementary roles of Onge women and men within their conceptual world (Pandya 1993). All of these factors have inflected the conduct of gender roles and relations among the Onge.

Intersecting on these quotidian practices is the Indian administra-tion's penetration of their domestic space, in an attempt to assimilate the Onge into the mores of Indian society. In the aftermath of sed-enterization, with its consequent displacement and marginalization, this is a project in which Onge men are complicit. Sometimes willing, occasionally unwilling, the men's collaboration with the welfare au-thorities is shifting and fluid.

To maintain their independence and autonomy in the face of the many incursions by the Indian administration and the welfare author-ities, the Onge women have resorted to diverse strategies that are dis-cussed below. As Okely (1991) notes, "specific incidents, anecdotes, individual acts or in some cases clusters of women, revealed an aware-ness, albeit fragmented [of the ways in which they were subordinat-ed]" (p.8). I will go on to discuss the particular incidents that mark the Onge women's claim to autonomy, despite the displacement of their sphere to the periphery, away from the site of decision-making as drawn by the welfare authorities.

I argue that with the use of language as well as other prosaic strategies, Onge women assert a separate and autonomous space for themselves. An intriguing offshoot is the developing awareness among Onge men of the contradictions between Onge and Indian perceptions of gender. The assertion of independence by Onge women, purportedly established in Onge traditions (Cipriani 1954, Pandya 1993), appears to have accrued a connotation of diminished masculinity for Onge men. In the throes of intoxication, the behaviors exhibited by Onge men suggest that alcohol is a means to subvert or recast the pattern of gender relations extant in Onge society. Since drinking usually occurs outside the settlement, in the forest or nearby towns where the men often disappear to, through drinking Onge men appropriate a space from which Onge women are excluded. Simultaneously, the men assert a masculinity that attempts to replicate the Indian patterns of gender behaviors.

Language and power

Onge women never speak Hindi but their comprehension of the language is never in doubt, since all communicative events suggest that their knowledge of the language is inclusive of even the colloquialisms. However, a question posed to an Onge woman in Hindi will, in every instance, only bring forth a response in Onge, even when the woman knows that her interlocutor may not follow a word of that language.

Likewise, Onge men also comprehend Hindi, but their speech exhibits different degrees of proficiency, a range of variation that we are not given a chance to detect among the women. A question posed in Hindi to an Onge man may initially bring forth a response in Onge, but on indicating difficulty with that language, an attempt is made to respond in Hindi, however halting. Onge women, on the other hand, insist on a grasp of their language since any communication with them *has* to be always conducted in Onge, thus subtly underscoring their control over the interaction.

A number of interpretations may be given to this behavior. One, Onge men are more obliging and willing to help out when someone has difficulties with their language. Or Onge men perforce had to engage with an outside world within which there was never any possibility of setting the terms of the discourse. Following this line of argument, it is an alternative rendition of the British term *pacification*. Onge men relinquished any semblance of control over their lives after their resounding defeats in battles with the British. But their post-defeat collaboration with the colonial administrations[4] through the medium of Hindi provided entry into the domain of the colonizers. Knowledge of Hindi had the potential for more power/material rewards, since successive colonial administrations have consistently recognized and rewarded linguistic ability. Hence language becomes the primary vehicle for the process of "subjection", as discussed earlier, making available new opportunities and routes to power. This analysis is given support by recalling that the appointment of "chief" or *Raja* (in Hindi) by, first the British and then the Indian administrations, by virtue of which authority and power is vested in an individual, has been determined by linguistic ability.

A third interpretation, often offered by Onge men, is that the women are shy and feel bashful about speaking in Hindi. Though this explanation does give me pause, it is not corroborated by other elements of women's behavior.

In the case of both men and women, there was some modification to their speech when chewing *bebe* (betel leaves) or *cibari* (areca nuts). The excessive salivation produced during this process confers a greater guttural sound to their language. But there was a further marked transformation effected in the speech of Onge women according to whether they were conversing among themselves or they were in mixed company. Speaking with greater rapidity and apparently adding an additional consonant to every syllable, speech among women acquired a coded quality that appeared to be indecipherable even to the men. When summoned to translate, the men's standard response was that the women were conversing among themselves. Further prodding as to what the content of the discussion was produced the same answer, namely, that the women were conversing among themselves. Repeated occurrences of this phenomenon led me to suspect that the men did not completely follow the women's discussion when they spoke to each other. Alternatively, by virtue of the women's marking-off of a private domain, even if the men comprehended the conversation, they were reluctant to divulge the contents.

Such a closing of ranks never occurred with the men, whose language I could follow despite the throaty inflection acquired because of mouths engorged with *bebe* or *cibari* and spittle. The additional option of switching between two languages (Hindi and Onge) provided greater fluidity and ease of conversation with the men. Concurrently, such a practice inserted an additional impediment [5] to my efforts to engage in and maintain a separate interaction with the women.

The obstacles[6] posed by these attenuations to women's conversation meant that I was always "outside" the anthropological invocation of empathy with "the people", within an historical conjuncture that, in this context, linguistically implicated me with the colonizer. Thus, my naive assumption of a facile rapport premised on shared gender was quickly dispelled by the exigencies of fieldwork at Dugong Creek.

Clothes make/(un)make the Onge woman

Conversations with Onge women conveyed their dissatisfaction and resentment with the intrusions into their domains of everyday living. An example that several mentioned was the issue of clothing. Clothes appear to have become a sensitive issue at various levels. Every Onge is given two sets of new garments every year as an item within the welfare system of which they are beneficiaries. During the period that I was at the settlement, everyone received one of these yearly hand-outs. All the Onge women were given identical sets of printed skirts and blouses, and the men shorts and shirts, with some variation between them of color, print and texture.[7] Soon afterwards I noticed that some of the men tried on their new attire, but none of the women were to be seen in theirs. When questioned, some hawked and spat, or others simply shrugged, and in tones of great contempt said *"gibiti ga"*, they're bad, and demanded that I get other outfits for them. Many women made repeated demands for new apparel, like the ones I wore, until finally, in exasperation, I replied that they already had a set of new garments, which the administration had gone to some expense to make for them. Moreover, anything that I obtained for them would be purchased from the limited stocks available at the same stores from where their much maligned clothing had originated.

I was instructed on the niceties of discernment and good taste, perceived as lacking in the welfare administrators. I was told that I could be relied upon to exercise the same discrimination that they showed when selecting outfits for themselves. I would keep in mind their likes and dislikes, their individual personalities, and get items specific for each person, not the uniform trash that the *entale* had given them. Furthermore, they, the womenfolk, should be granted the prerogative of choosing clothes for their families.

A different but related aspect of the vexed subject of apparel is linked to the Indian construction of the "savage". The Onge are often described as *junglee*, which approximates to "forest-dweller", on a par with the other creatures inhabiting the forest. Both the British and the Indian constructions of savagery as a social-evolutionary category were founded on the absence of clothing. Therefore, the first step *en route* to civilization was the donning of cloth.

Onge women were mostly bare-bodied except for a girdle around their hips with a tuft of dried rattan leaves, the *nakuinege*, in front of their genitals. There is a certain delicacy and modesty in the women's comportment such that the genitalia are always concealed. Most women now have some covering of cloth on their bodies, and many continue to wear the *nakuinege* underneath.[8] But the use of external garments has not become completely internalised, as apparent by its elimination when they are completely relaxed and feel their privacy will not be intruded upon. Privacy is, however, something that is hard to establish for the Onge. Friends and family of the welfare staff, government officials of various denominations, arrive to gawk at the *junglees*. They demand that the Onge shed their garments so that the visitors can take back "authentic" photographs of the Onge in their "traditional" attire.

The power of women

One day, late afternoon at Dugong Creek, most of the Onge men were engaged in wage-work. It was around 3:30 pm and the settlement was deserted except for groups of women sitting together and talking. Suddenly, a crowd of militant Onge women, armed with brooms, congregated at the place where the men were working, and set about sweeping vigorously around the area where the men were gathered. Each woman in turn railed and stormed about the lack of *tambonuya* (wild boar), *choge* (fish), that they were "*tambonuya mando ulecebe*" (famished for pork), but all the while the men were engrossed in *totale*[9]. The men broke into smiles and soon put away their implements and made their way back to the settlement, expecting their wives to follow. But the women continued their vigorous cleaning. Each Onge, in turn, went up to his wife and tried to talk her into returning with him. But the women collectively ignored the men and continued their sweeping for at least another hour.

A disconsolate group of men trailed a slow retreat back to the settlement. I followed the men back and found them sitting in front of their houses, calling out as I walked by that they were very hungry. I suggested that they start eating, and they replied that they were waiting for their wives to return, so that they could eat their meal together. The next morning, shortly after daybreak, I arrived at the settlement and found that all the men had left for hunting at dawn. Wage-work at Dugong Creek came to a halt in the ensuing weeks.

During my stay at Dugong Creek, I can recall one incident that exposed the convergence of the various conflicting domains at the settlement. Shiela was a recently widowed woman with several children. One of the children, "Rocky,"[10] had been ailing since birth and had always remained frail. From the beginning of my fieldwork at Dugong Creek he had been ill, and six months after my arrival there he seemed to sink to a point where his death appeared imminent. Meanwhile, the medical officer appointed during this period had chosen to ignore the child's condition until the child's precarious health alerted the medical officer to the possible consequences for himself.

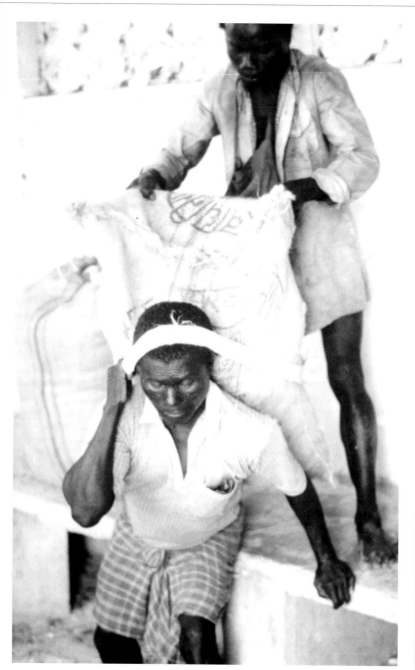

Wage work. Carrying sacks of rations to the settlement store at Dugong Creek.
Photo: Sita Venkateswar

Due to the Andaman Islanders labelling as an "endangered people," every birth of an Onge child is rewarded with a sum of Rs.1,000 to the parents, and every death has to be explained to the highest authorities in the government. The person held accountable for each life is the medical officer, and the possibility that he would be found negligent in the discharge of his duties produced a flurry of panicked responses on his part. He signalled to the Directorate of Health Services at Port Blair that the child was critically ill and had to be removed to Port Blair immediately for more specialised treatment. Then he convinced all the other welfare staff that they too would be held responsible if "Rocky" died. Therefore, they should all help persuade Shiela to take "Rocky" to Port Blair. Only then would they be let off the hook. This was a particularly formidable task since Shiela's husband had earlier been sent to Port Blair for treatment and not returned alive. All the welfare staff in turn coaxed, cajoled and pleaded with Shiela. Shiela and her family were offered every kind of inducement, an advance of money, new clothes for the whole family, any gift that they wanted and a new suitcase to carry everything to Port Blair.

For Timai, Shiela's father and one of the heaviest drinkers among the Onge, this was an opportunity to avail of money that could be spent on alcohol. For Tambole the *Raja*, who, coincidentally, was also the son of Shiela's late husband by a former marriage, the situation was more equivocal. On the one hand he still grieved the loss of his father, and perceived Port Blair as a place of death; on the other, as *Raja* he had to hold his end up and endorse the welfare authorities.

Shiela, troubled by the pressure on all fronts, was reluctant to leave. At a loss for any further excuses that would justify her refusal, and somewhat tempted by all the inducements offered, she appeared to give in.

Meanwhile, the fact that something else was afoot was suggested by the small knots of Onge women who were conferring together. Later that night I asked Shiela about her decision. In a tone that brooked no further argument, she replied that she was not going. All the older women had rebuked her and there was nothing further to be said. Then I went to the welfare staff who told me that everything was arranged. Shiela had agreed to take "Rocky" to Port Blair. The medical officer would accompany them, and the helicopter would arrive early the next morning to take them there.

Next morning, at 6 a.m. the helicopter arrived. It landed with much difficulty, since Dugong Creek is a particularly rough terrain. This is why each such trip costs the administration as much as Rs.50,000. The medical officer, carrying his suitcase, accompanied by the other welfare staff and the helicopter crew, trooped to Shiela's house to get her. Shiela had locked herself inside her house and refused to come out or

Wage work for women at Dugong Creek. Keeping the settlement clear of undergrowth.
Photo: Sita Venkateswar

talk to anyone. Everyone in turn banged on her door, offering blandishments and threats, but Shiela remained mute inside. Finally, the helicopter got ready to leave and the medical officer, enraged and embarrassed, viewing the situation as a personal affront, was told that he would have to send explanations for the debacle.

All the Onge were vastly amused by the spectacle. When charged by the welfare staff with duplicity, they shrugged and replied that the women had decided that it would not be appropriate for Shiela to go to Port Blair, and therefore, there was nothing further to be said about the matter.

Meanwhile, as a result of the medical officer's attempts to ingratiate himself with the Directorate at Port Blair through his assiduous attention to his duties at Dugong Creek, "Rocky" recovered. But the medical officer was transferred shortly afterwards on other charges of misbehavior.

The merriment provoked by the medical officer's discomfiture kept the Onge in good humor for a while. But over time, the occasional jibes and taunts from the welfare staff that they were all dominated by their women, stung. The mood among the men changed to disquiet. The Onge men who seemed most vulnerable to such jeers were the "helpers" assigned to the welfare staff. The dilemma posed by the demand for a simultaneous negotiation between two discordant sets of expectations exposed some of the pressures that these men were under as they dealt with their wives and the *entale*. The several derogatory variations (in Hindi) of a "henpecked husband" tried the customary agreeable dispositions of the men, leading to an increasing stand-off with their wives, as they sought to match an alter image made available with alcohol.

Pleasure as subversion

I have mentioned in passing the growing incidence of drinking among the Onge. Here I want to draw attention to the various registers at which the practice of drinking, with its attendant intoxication, is enmeshed within the Onge social landscape.

The overriding impression that I obtained from talking to the Onge men about drinking was the immense pleasure and fun that they derived from it. The experience of intoxication was described as *tikitikige*, which in Onge means "like a spinning top", and the sensation invited repeated attempts to rediscover it. When recounting their drinking exploits, their manner took on a mischievous air, as if they had indulged in an enjoyable prank. But it was an enjoyment that was cultivated, which they slowly learned to relish. All described their initial experiences with alcohol as disastrous, and it was only over time that the sensations changed and was recognized as pleasurable.

The Onge were aware that their drinking behavior provoked disapproval at all levels of the Andaman administration. I read the traces of subversion in this act of drinking, manifest in their delight at not conforming to the image of the "good",[11] docile Onge (in contrast to the more "wilful" Andamanese) that the authorities would like to promote. Moreover, the pleasure that they derived from the consumption of alcohol, negated the efficacy of any morality constructed around abstinence. Hence the "moralization" of the issue, (Escobar 1984-85) applied or invoked as a form of coercion, was ineffective in this context. And therein lay the tragedy and the perpetuation of the practice.

But, besides its embodiment as pleasure, the itinerary that I have traced for drinking in the context of the ongoing discussion above suggests that it was also intimately intertwined with power as deployed between genders.

The path to collusion

Onge women were vehement about their exclusion from any decisions regarding the supplies stocked in the small shop in the settlement. The designated "helpers" to the welfare staff were frequently consulted about what they wished to buy from the shop but the women were never asked to indicate their preferences. While individually within the domestic space Onge men concurred with their wives' grievances, as a group they tended to keep separate this area of interaction with the welfare personnel. This was the arena of collusion that provided access to alcohol, and with alcohol they could all be "men" together. A dramatic transformation[12] is effected in the behaviors of Onge men once they have consumed alcohol.

The remarkable feature of this change was how closely they mimicked the behavior the Onge had seen displayed by the welfare staff or the drunken exhibitions they had witnessed in the nearby towns. When drinking, Onge men spoke only Hindi, the most halting speaker discovering an amazing facility for the language. In that language, their conversation acquired certain lewdness and the kind of discussion they engaged in was one they shied away from when sober. All tended to gossip about the sexual dalliances of the Onge and a certain pattern emerged from these discussions. In each case, the men who were involved in these extra-marital affairs were married to older women beyond child-bearing age, who had either never borne any children or lost those from earlier marriages. The women who were purportedly indulging in affairs with such men were relatively young, and had several children. How much of this talk had some truth to it and to what extent they were fantasies is debatable. But the element that stood out was that, to a great extent, these accounts mirrored the escapades of the numerous welfare staff that had stayed at the settlement over the years.

For the Onge women, who in other respects tended to keep a firm check on their men, drinking and alcohol became spheres through which the men evaded and eluded them. The deference shown to them by their husbands in their daily lives was erased at a single stroke with alcohol.

A note on generalizations

I want to digress briefly at this stage to qualify the homogeneity implied by the use of generalizations such as "the Onge men" or "the Onge women", since there is substantial variation between individuals, both women and men. Each person's correspondence to the main elements of my representation is a matter of degree, some more, some less.

I have highlighted certain trends, but every single Onge is *not* subsumed by the principle features of my depiction, which exist as a composite. For instance, as I have noted, among the Onge men there are those who have a specified level of propinquity to the welfare authorities, based on their fluency in Hindi. Much of my representation above applies to this group of people. But, here too, there were striking dissimilarities. Tambole, fluent in Hindi, the incumbent *Raja*, a heavy drinker, married to an older woman, but *not* one of those perceived as dominated by his wife, yet was one of the men gossiped about by other Onge. Tambole's explanation for his induction into drinking was, "The 'LG' [13] always has a glass of whisky by him when there are meetings at Port Blair. I'm the *Raja*, I also drink." But Bara Raju, articulate in Hindi, a claimant to the position of *Raja*, never drank, always deferred to his wife, was not vulnerable to any jeers from the welfare staff, nor was there any hint of gossip attached to him.

On the other hand, there was Tai, a "helper," at ease in Hindi, married to Kakeyi, who never conceived again after the death of their child, a sly drinker, and as portrayed by the welfare personnel, always at his wife's beck and call. He was one of those presumed to be in an extramarital relationship. Then there was Berogegi, or Totanange, or Kimboi etc., all of whom had a distinct permutation and combination of the attributes listed above.

In the case of the Onge women, too, there were similar variations in terms of the authority they wielded among other women or with their husbands. Or the extent of resentment expressed towards the welfare staff and their husband's drinking. Botalai, Kamegi, Koilaboi, Kwankitui, Nabimboi, Bagali etc., were all older women, most of who were married to younger husbands, some of whom drank, of whom only Botalai and Bagali had any surviving children, and who comprised the core group of women who influenced Shiela. But the common thread that tied together all the women, without any deviation, was their eschewal of Hindi.

Before concluding my disclaimer on the use of generalizations in this account of the islanders, I want to allude to the tension that exists between the particular and the general. Even Abu-Lughod's (1991) call to an "ethnography of the particular" does not elude the demand for those particulars to make a statement that harks towards the general. Hence, my generalizations are a shortcut, avoiding the necessity of nominating in every instance specific individuals, and a claim to legitimacy.

Towards some explanations

To return to my narrative on the politics of gender among the Onge, is it possible to arrive at some framework that accommodates the incidents described earlier? Are these stray events that have no relevance beyond the telling of a tale?

At the outset, it is clear how the system of welfare that regulates the lives of the Onge, with its attendant concern to assimilate the Onge into a more mainstream "Indian" lifestyle, has penetrated into the "private" domestic existence of the Onge. The disparate positioning of Onge women and men *vis-à-vis* the welfare system and its practitioners gives rise to the complexities that are evident in their everyday actions, and in the contrasting behaviors of women and men. Moreover, their distinct positioning within the welfare system also throws light on the forms of "subjection" (Foucault 1983) and the ways in which Onge women and men are implicated in them. As I have stated earlier, the social classifications conferred on the Onge men, i.e. *Raja*, "helper," etc., in its linkages with nodes of power, "opens up avenues of enablement, that seduces [the Onge to conform] to its rules, and thereby shapes new outlooks and behavior patterns" (Biolsi 1995:30). But there are no new routes to power that are available to the Onge women within such a perspective. In addition, with the dismissal of women from the sphere of "official" politics, and the accompanying lack of awareness of women's influence and participation in decisions that affect the Onge, the "traditional" stature that the women have enjoyed is placed at risk.

The final element that remains unsettled by this argument is the process by which alcohol appears to have reconfigured gender relations among the Onge. An easy response is to dismiss the transformation effected in men's behavior as a release of inhibitions. It may feature as an element of the whole, but I believe drinking has a more complex signification within that totality. Mbembe's (1992) discussion of the *banality* of power offers some resolutions. According to Mbembe, the trappings of power typically involve a conspicuous consumption of food and alcohol, and are inclusive of a demonstration of sexual prowess. For the Onge men, these manifestations have become integral components of their "subjection". In emulating these practices, they can elide the lived reality of colonization and aspire to membership within the larger world of men with power.

A brief note on the Andamanese

It is not insignificant that the last anthropological research conducted on the Andamanese dates back to the seventies, soon after they were re-settled on Strait Island (Chakrabarty 1974). After documenting the standard anthropological categories of kinship, ritual, material culture etc., which permit the compilation of "exotic" details, what is there left to say about 30 odd people whose most prominent attributes are excessive drinking and sexual promiscuity, uncertain health and an astute eye towards material advantages? This is my attempt to take cognizance of the uncomfortable and distressing elements of the lives of the Andamanese, and find a way of articulating and explaining those factors.

Alcohol and the Andamanese

In the Andaman Islands, there exists a culture of drinking among men that cuts across class, regional and the "tribal" mainland divide[14]. All men drink. It is a hobby, a pleasurable activity and a practice that is often enforced among men. To be a man, one must drink. As suggested in the case of Onge men, and perhaps for Andamanese men as well, consuming large quantities of alcohol has become an integral component of their male identities. Andamanese boys are inducted early into the practice of drinking, often by their fathers, or by other older males.

Anthropologists have studied constructions of masculinity in many parts of the world and have tried to analyse the implications of the consumption of alcohol on cultural definitions of male identity. Mac Marshall's (1979) research on drinking among Trukese men revealed that the ostentatious, obnoxious comportment of Trukese young men was inextricably interwoven with basic Trukese beliefs about strength, courage and manhood. Beverly Chiñas'(1992) work on the Zapotec, and David Gilmore's (1990) cross-cultural survey "on the subject of manhood" confirm heavy drinking and sexual aggressiveness as closely linked to notions of male *machismo* in many parts of the world.

An additional strand of complexity in the symbolic power of alcohol emerges in gender relations among the Andamanese. As demonstrated by the married Andamanese men, the consumption of alcohol is also an admission of impotence.[15] It is an expression of awareness that they have been cuckolded, have lost control over their wives and, thereby, the future. Andamanese women seek to have children by non-Andamanese men, often plying their husbands with large quantities of alcohol before going to their current paramours.

Producing more children is a recurrent theme in the community, justifiably so in view of the fact that there are only 35-40 people who can claim some "Andamanese" descent. Except for the children of one couple, all the other children have been fathered either by non-Andamanese men or by "illegitimate unions"[16] from within, but every offspring is listed as "Andamanese," by the community as well as the welfare authorities[18]. Such a course has some immediate monetary returns, since the couple (namely, the "legitimate" couple even if the child is born of an "illegitimate" affair) is "rewarded" by the Andaman administration with Rs.1000 for every birth. The money, in turn, leads to bitter altercations between the registered couple over who has greater rights to it.

Pierre Bourdieu's (1985,1990) discussion of a "generative habitus" provides the guidelines for contextualizing the behaviors of the Andamanese. Through practices guided by a practical logic, in pursuit of objective interests, social formations tend to reproduce themselves. In the interests of reproducing themselves, to exist as a viable community the Andamanese have generated an infinite variety of sexual strategies. Their "feel for the game, for a particular, historically determined game" (p.62) has produced the practical sense of both playing in conformity with the rules and bending those rules. The simultaneous existence of "legitimate" and "illegitimate" unions allows the promise of more offspring, with immediate monetary gains thrown in for good measure. But such a "double strategy" also has its repercussions on social relations among the Andamanese, between genders, across genders, further complicated by the ambiguities of alcohol abuse, whereby battle lines become sharpened between men and women.

They are further exacerbated by the interventions of the welfare authorities in Strait Island and Port Blair, many of whom have intermittently been involved in affairs with the Andamanese women. The "moral" and righteous stance assumed by these men is raucously challenged by the Andamanese women, who then proceed to expose the hollow morality that the lau[15] are incapable of affirming in their practice.

The predicament in which the Andamanese men find themselves is somewhat similar to the Onge men, but the pressures are different in each case. The standards of "good" behavior that they prescribe for their wives are drawn from the norms set by non-Andamanese. By stigmatizing the behaviors of their women, they collaborate in the representations of Andamanese women as women of "bad" character, with "loose" morals. This precipitates the wrath of their wives, in turn leading to violent scenes with them. Concurrently, the men's animosity for the lau, many of whom they know are engaged in affairs with their wives, finds expression when they are intoxicated. Intoxication gives the Andamanese men the license to vent their hostility and aggression towards the women and the lau without penalty. Such behavior, in turn, perpetuates their own stigmatized representations, by the Andamanese women and the lau, as "shiftless alcoholics". Many of the Andamanese men sidestep a sober confrontation with the problematics of these alternatives by adopting a perennially hazy state, from one alcoholic binge to the next, the monotony periodically broken by the scenes with their wives or the lau.

Conclusion

This chapter explored the landscape of gender relations among the Onge and the Andamanese, as manifest in their everyday behaviors and practices, against the backdrop of the interventions of the welfare authorities. I have traced the shifting fields of power deployed between and across genders in quotidian ethnographic contexts. In linking the dynamics of gender to an analysis of subjection, I have demonstrated the imbrication of the administrative strategies of the welfare system with the processes by which the Onge and Andamanese are incorporated within specific structures of power. The differential and multiple articulations of Onge and Andamanese men and women to these linkages inflect the mode of complicity and extent of contestation. The more marginal or excluded from the routes to power, the greater the resentment expressed and opposition to the government initiatives. But of greater significance are the ways in which the terrain of gender has been recast, thereby reconstituting it as a bitterly contentious site for/of power, as acutely evident in the case of the Andamanese. Williams' (1994: 595-600) reformulation of Gramsci's concept of hegemony makes possible an interpretation that is at once more comprehensive and attentive to the ambiguities of power. This leads to an understanding of the ambivalence and contradictions of Onge and Andamanese men's re-forming masculinities, as constituted by structures of power, yet neither totally complicit nor entirely contesting in their articulations with power. ❑

Notes

1 A modified version of this chapter is published in Senri Ethnological Studies (2001)56:207-226. Sections of this chapter have also been published in Crosscurrents, Journal of Gra duate Research in Anthropology (1999)Vol. VIII.

2 I didn't have the heart to point out that there were many among them who had been married for longer but were childless.

3 Time was determined by the position of the sun in the sky.

4 The reference to the colonial administrations here is inclusive of the British and the Indian regimes. As argued earlier, for the islanders the experience of colonization continued after the British left the islands.

5 I have suggested that my solitary existence in Dugong Creek was a factor that led to a certain amount of alienation from the Onge women.

6 While I could engage in banter with the Onge women, or serve as a recipient for complaints about the welfare authorities/system, I was not privy to intimacies that could establish the grounds for an awareness of any woman as a personalized individual.

7 This mode of constructing a gendered homogeneity/heterogeneity in the execution of the welfare system is striking.

8 This led to some problems when, as requested, I purchased a *salwar-kameez* for them, after approximating the sizes that they would wear. They were unable to get into them with their *nakuinege* on. It occasioned much laughter among the women. Finally, they discarded the *nakuinege,* and with their new outfits proudly paraded the length of the settlement.

9 All the work that is performed for non-Onges is referred to as *totale* by the Onges, which translates as "cleaning".However, there is a specific term for every other kind of activity that they perform that is not related to wage-work. The sweeping by the women lends greater weight to their ironic subversion of the men's work.

10 All the names of the children in the settlement have been conferred by the welfare staff after some popular Indian film star, although these names are never used by the Onge among themselves. Forms of appellation are on the basis of kinship categories or some unique characteristic of the individual that distinguishes the person from others. I, too, had a personal nickname conferred on me: *orananjaba,* one with a long nose.

11 Despite the widespread practice of drinking among the Onge, both in Dugong Creek and South Bay, a recent demographic survey of the Andaman Islands published by the Anthropological Survey of India (Pandit and Sarkar 1994) makes the bland assertion that the Onge do not drink, which is a gross misrepresentation of the existing state of affairs.

12 A somewhat similar transformation is noted by Kennedy (1978) among the Tarahumara, although the context in which their altered behavior occurred is very different.

13 The "LG" stands for Lieutenant-Governor, the highest executive authority in the Andaman Islands.

14 The place of origin on mainland India is maintained in the Andaman Islands, so that people are referred to as "the Tamilians," "the Moplahs," "the Bengalis" or "the Ranchi tribals".

15 For some of the men, impotence exists at the level of actuality, as a consequence of addiction to opium in the past or hereditary syphilis.

16 Despite the proscriptions against marriage between particular degrees of relatives, sexual liaisons exist across the board, between generations, between close relatives, within the community. Also contributing to the state of crisis is the inability of the Andamanese to maintain permanent stable relationships with non-Andamanese of the opposite sex.

17 The Indian administration registers these births as the benefits accrued by the Andamanese from the welfare efforts for them.

18 The Andamanese term that refers to non-Andamanese, formerly also alluding to "evil" spirits.

STRATEGIES OF POWER: AN ANALYSIS OF "JARAWA CONTACT" [1]

"They know how to make a fire, which shows they aren't really that backward. Similarly, the way they interacted with us during our trip offered glimpses of the friendly nature that lurks beneath their exterior."

(Chattopadhyay 1992: 5)

Introduction

Maintaining the general theme of power that is foregrounded in my account of the Andaman Islanders, this chapter explores strategies of power as these intersect with race, class and gender. I go on to argue that gender, in some circumstances, becomes an instrument for collusion between men, across race, in maneuvers that are deployed on/over the bodies of women.

This assertion is made within the context of ethnographic encounters with the *Jarawa*. Their historical and contemporary situation presents an intriguing aspect to my comparative vision of the indigenous people of the Andaman Islands. At the time of my research, the *Jarawa* displayed an unpredictable front, despite the concerted efforts made over the previous twenty years by the Indian administration to initiate and maintain "friendly contact".

The politics of "contact"

An integral feature of "*Jarawa* contact" was its connotation of "momentous", "historic", media-grabbing possibilities. What remained hidden was the scrambling and competition involved in ensuring inclusion in the team that was assembled for every "gift-dropping" occasion. To illustrate what this means, I will present the example of the "historic" contact with the Sentinelese early in 1991.

As meagre as the extant knowledge about the *Jarawa* is, the paucity of information about the Sentinelese is of much greater magnitude. Along with the *Jarawa*, the Sentinelese were also the beneficiaries of the "gift-dropping" trips organized by the Andaman administration. For the first time in 1991, a contact party was received without the customary barrage of arrows. In this connection, an interesting piece of information was unearthed[2] offering some explanation for the enigma of why, in January 1991, the Sentinelese came forward to receive coconuts from the "contact team" rather than shower them with arrows. A few years earlier there had been a shipwreck off Sentinel Island. During the fair months of the year, the wreck was salvaged by a scrap-iron dealer and his workers. It was this dealer and his crew who established the "first contact"[3] that, over time, led to the Sentinelese accepting coconuts from the "contact team" organized by the administration. This was of course never made public by the Andaman administration, who did not consider such an "historic" moment worthy of a mere scrap-iron dealer and his crew. Nor did anyone find it curious that the Sentinelese suddenly happened to know the Hindi word for coconut, repeating *narele, narele* while indicating the coconuts.

I will not go into the details of the behind-the-scenes maneuvers that occurred among the anthropologists of the Anthropological Survey of India (ASI), already mentioned in the media attention surrounding the event. Or the efforts to ensure that they were included in subsequent teams, which were immediately sent out to consolidate the momentous "breakthrough" with the Sentinelese. Twenty years of "contact" with the *Jarawa* has not diluted the possibilities of an "historic" moment emerging from the tried routine of a regularly scheduled "gift-dropping trip". Any number of "first–time" occasions was potentially lurking in the wings. As many as 200 *Jarawa* sighted. Or the team invited to feast on pork with the *Jarawa*. The team permitted to stay the night with the *Jarawa* in their huts – the list of possibilities was exciting. The point of this exposition is that the excitement and the romance attached to a *Jarawa* "contact trip" remained as potent as it ever was when "first contact" was made. The romance coloured all interactions between anthropologists and others, as they vied with each other to be included in the team, no matter how many prior trips they may have made when nothing of any "significance" had occurred.

As a graduate student in anthropology from the United States conducting research in the Andaman Islands, it was this setting that I was confronted with when I happened to be in Port Blair. As I shuttled back and forth between Dugong Creek and Strait Island, dividing my time between the Onge and the Andamanese, I was sometimes unwittingly informed of the organization of a *Jarawa* "contact trip". I have been present on four such trips, and on each instance my inclusion led to some discord with other anthropologists of the ASI. I will focus on the third trip during which there were three encounters with the *Jarawa*, and which had "momentous" implications at many registers.

For the duration of my research in the Andaman Islands, I had formally affiliated myself with the Anthropological Survey of India, at Port Blair. When I first arrived in the Andaman Islands in 1989, I did not let it be widely known that I was attached to a university in the

US. Elections were to be held shortly thereafter in the islands, and many rumours of a foreign "hand" in Indian's political instability floating around. Although it seemed rather far-fetched, in view of the prevailing mood in the country, I was warned that I could very easily be perceived as a "foreign agent", up to no "good". On the advice of the former deputy-director of ASI, I did not actually withhold the information, but, by attaching myself to the ASI, I did not have to volunteer the information that I was in a graduate program in the US. As the Indian government's premier research institution on the spot, I could avail of the Survey's unquestioned access to all the reserved tribal areas in the islands, including the resources accumulated over forty years of investigation in the islands.

Vishvajit Pandya, who had conducted his dissertation research with the Onge at Dugong Creek between 1983 and 1984, was also in the Andaman Islands during this period, with funding for a project on the *Jarawa*. On a brief visit that he made to Dugong Creek where we met, he suggested working with him on some part of his project. Collaborating with a senior, male anthropologist, affiliated[4] to an institution in a foreign country, lent me greater credibility in the Andaman Islands. As a lone, Indian, female, without any links to the Andaman bureaucracy, my attempts to gain entry into the closed circle of participants in the *Jarawa* "contact" efforts had met with little success. Given the limited time that I had, awaiting my turn at the ASI was not a sound strategy. The minimal priority given to my inclusion in the "contact trip" became evident whenever I was next on the waiting list. There was always a very good justification offered for someone else (from the ASI) to jump the line.

Pandya's strategy had been to bypass all the lower levels of the bureaucratic hierarchy in the Andamans and go straight to the top. He had directly approached and negotiated a connection with the highest executive authority in the islands, the Lieutenant-Governor. The "LG" was also the director of all the tribal programs, and had the final veto on who could participate in the *Jarawa* contact trips. Through Pandya, I was able to meet the Lieutenant-Governor and, independent of the ASI or the administration, make a bid for an opportunity to participate in the trips. Much to my surprise, since it was accomplished so easily, I was successful. This was rather unpopular with the other anthropologists from the ASI and the lower rungs of the administration. They let it be known that I had out-maneuvered them by directly approaching the "LG". The perception was that these "foreign" anthropologists were given preference over the "in-house", "rightful" claimants to exclusive access to the *Jarawa*.

Pandya's project (or as much as I gathered of it) was designed to consistently build on all prior knowledge of the *Jarawa* language. His plan was to infer relationships and movements between different groups of *Jarawa* inhabiting various parts of Middle and South Andaman. Most importantly, he intended to include Onge as intermediaries and interpreters on these occasions. This was meant to confirm once and for all Portman's long-cited theory of the relationship between the Onge and the *Jarawa* – their purported common origins reflected in their linguistic practice. For all these reasons, the proposed trip to the *Jarawa* area held the promise of a pivotal occasion, with all the ingredients for an "historic" encounter.

The Onge

Hoping to rely on his recollection of the relationships that he had established with the Onge during his fieldwork in Dugong Creek in 1983-84, Pandya tried to ensure the inclusion of those Onge with whom he had worked most closely. His preference was for Totanange or Tambolai, including their families, to participate as interpreters in the Jarawa contact. He had a message sent to that effect by wireless to Dugong Creek, requesting that these Onge travel from Dugong Creek to Hut Bay[5] where we would await them in the *Tarmugli*,[6] the ship commissioned by the administration for this trip to the *Jarawa* area. It remained unclear as to what had transpired at Dugong Creek, or the content of the message that was conveyed to the Onge, but it was Bara Raju and his brother Kokegile, along with their respective families, who boarded the ship at Hut Bay. An earlier attempt to send for Totanange from Dugong Creek, by means of a message transmitted to the social worker at Dugong Creek, had resulted in Chota Raju and his family arriving at Port Blair instead. Thus, we had three Onge families in Port Blair, but not the ones whom Pandya had anticipated working with him as interpreters.

A number of different explanations may account for the substitution of personnel. The welfare staff may have misinformed the Onge about who was required to travel to Port Blair. Substantiating such an inference was the fact that Totanange was the "helper" assigned to the medical officer at Dugong Creek, responsible for replenishing his daily supply of water from the nearby well. Totanange's duties also included the other domestic and sundry tasks that the medical officer deemed beneath his dignity to undertake. It was unlikely that the medical officer would permit Totanange to leave for an indefinite period, even if his departure had the sanction of the "LG's" approval. It was also reported that Totanange was unwilling to travel to Port Blair, hence the welfare staff had tried to send someone else in his stead. This was how Chota Raju happened to arrive at Port Blair.

On the second attempt to involve Totanange in the process, either the same scenario was repeated, or Bara Raju had inserted himself into the proceedings. As explained earlier, Bara Raju has been informally legitimated in his claim to be *Raja* of Dugong Creek by the welfare staff and several administrators at Port Blair. Assessing the situation as one that could work in his favor,[7] it is likely that Bara Raju took advantage of the ensuing confusion[8] at Dugong Creek and volunteered himself and his brother as likely candidates for the trip.

Unable to shake off his preoccupation with notions of the "authentic" even eight years later, and despite the very contrived qualities of the situation as conceived, Pandya envisioned that the meeting between the Onge and the *Jarawa* would follow the lines of a "traditional" reunion between allies. With a view to an exchange of "traditional gifts", the Onge were told to bring with them *alamé*, the red ochre that is used on ritual occasions, and honey, which is always a prized food. Accompanied by a large crowd of Onge who, on the pretext of seeing off Bara Raju and Kokegile could indulge in a rollicking binge of drinking at Hut Bay, and bearing the gifts that had been asked of them, a merry and tipsy throng gathered at the ship at Hut Bay.

The anatomy of "contact"

The following photographs depict some of the phases of "contact" with the *Jarawa*. The years of experience that the captain and the crew of the *Tarmugli* have acquired in the process have made it possible to pinpoint certain areas along the west coast of South and Middle Andaman as likely places where the *Jarawa* can be found. As the ship cruises along these locations, frequently signalling with long blasts on the ship's horn, the contact team lines the deck, intently scanning the shore and the dense forest beyond for the thin spiral of smoke denoting the presence of *Jarawa*. As soon as smoke is spied and suitable anchorage found, preparations are made to load and lower the boats that will transport the team. The gifts of green coconut and banana piled up in one, the stripped[9] down "contact" team with strips of red cloth[10] in another. A third boat with plain-clothe[11] policemen, their weapons hidden in the base of the boat, hovers at a distance from the shore throughout the "contact".

Shortly thereafter, the *Jarawa* are observed emerging from the forest, carrying large nets and baskets, running along the shore following the direction of the boat. As the boat nears the shore, the *Jarawa* wade into the water, scrambling aboard before the boat is beached. Piling their baskets high with coconuts and bananas, snatching the red cloth, a rough and tumble of bodies, pushing and shoving as each individual grabs as much as possible of the "gifts" brought for them.

"Friendly contact"

As the initial excitement of obtaining the bounty offered to them by the "contact team" subsides, the *Jarawa* set about methodically collecting all the goods from the boat. Each individual or family group arranges their share of the "goods" in neat mounds at separate locations along the beach. At this stage in the proceedings, more attention is paid to the people who have offered of this largesse. Usually, members of the team attach themselves to particular *Jarawa*, assisting in the unloading of the boats, dragging the weighty baskets and nets heaped with coconuts and bananas along the sand to the assorted familial piles. Throughout this process, small, mobile enclaves are formed, where other performances are enacted, the nature of which retains elements of the unpredictable and, sometimes, the ominous.

Jayanta Sarkar (1990) and Madhumala Chattopadhyay (1992) wax lyrical about the bond of "trust and friendship" cemented over the years of "contact" with the *Jarawa*. Reporting on his participation as member of the "contact team" in 1988, Sarkar describes the occasion:

> *"While we stayed back ashore, all the adult males and females left the shore for our boat. Leaving their children with us was a clear gesture of faith and trust in us. The children were talking to us, touching us, which was also very heartening."* (p.55)

Going on to describe another instance of "friendly contact", which had followed on the heels of a "Jarawa incident", Sarkar (1990) concludes:

> *"They [the Jarawa] did not equate the members of the Contact Party with other hostile non-Jarawa. They did not misbehave or extract revenge from us. On the contrary, they demonstrated their trust and faith in us. They did not show any signs of hatred or hostility towards the others. They responded to affectionate gestures with affection."* (p.56)

Chattopadhyay (1992), who assigned for herself a kind of Florence Nightingale role during the "contact", carried with her a supply of ointments and bandages to minister to the *Jarawa*. Discussing her experiences, Chattopadhyay narrates:

> *"With time they began to show me their injuries; the men and women kept calm while I applied medicines and ointments on them. The presence of a woman in the "contact" team had apparently worked wonders in disarming the Jarawas: it could well be that these native people*

believed that a woman among the visitors meant that the latter posed no threat to their security." (p.5)

She concludes that:

"[P]opular conceptions of their being hostile are ill-founded. Admittedly, civilization, in the sense that we understand it, has bypassed them: they still rely on bows and arrows to hunt for food just as early man used to. Nevertheless, they possess many of the basic human qualities--love, sympathy, understanding---that we sometimes mistake to be the hallmarks of civilization." (p.5)

Both of these accounts elide the tension coursing through the duration of "contact" or an awareness of the likelihood of something, anything, triggering a violent confrontation with the *Jarawa*. The boat with the policemen hovering nearby serves as a reminder of that possibility. Chattopadhyay (*ibid.*,) touches on it in passing, more to draw attention to her gender in the composition of the "contact team" than to delve into some explanation for the incessant cognizance of danger during the "contact" process:

"On earlier occasions, women members of visiting teams had been attacked by the Jarawas; this had prompted the local administration to prohibit the inclusion of women. Thus it was after a very long time that a woman member – that is, I – had been granted permission to visit the Jarawas." (p.5)

In this context, it should be mentioned that the demographic features of the *Jarawa* who are sighted was an important consideration in determining the extent of precautions or alertness to the unpredictability of the "contact". There was a perceptible sigh of relief when the *Jarawa* group was composed largely of women with children, or adolescent boys. Over the years, veterans of the contact process had identified some adult, male *Jarawa* as potential "troublemakers", i.e. those who indulged in rough-housing, or were aggressive in their interactions with the team. Chattopadhyay posited that "the women kept the men in check, especially if any of them tried to stir up trouble" (p.5). However, other reports obtained from members of the team, as well as my own experience, renders such a statement problematic.

It is worthwhile at this stage examining some aspects of the behavior of the "contact team" that may be significant in delineating the encounter with the *Jarawa*. First, the gender composition of the contact team is usually all-male: women are rarely included. But during the period of my research in the islands, when Chattopadhyay was one of the research staff at the ASI, her participation became more frequent. On such occasions, she was the sole female present, as was the case when I was included in the team. By and large though, it was mostly men who were involved in making "contact" with the *Jarawa*.

The *Jarawa* women and children are inclined to exuberance, and are physically expressive in their approach to the "contact team". Clambering onto people's laps, embracing, taking "piggyback" rides, namely, behaving in a manner that can be construed as demonstrating affection. It should also be noted at this point that the *Jarawa* are naked. Confronting a bevy of unclothed bodies, in easy intimacy with them, can be disturbing to Indians. In general, they tend towards constraint in their expressions between genders. It is also significant that the male members of the "contact team" have assumed an easy familiarity with the *Jarawa* women which, on occasion, veers towards the prurient.

Second, *Jarawa* women and children, in turn, often proffer *their* "gifts" to the team, taking off the ornaments they wear on their person and conferring them on particular members of the team. Such a gesture has, on the occasions when I was present, translated into a forcible appropriation of such items from the *Jarawa* by Indians[12] eager to acquire souvenirs: "tokens" of "friendship" from the *Jarawa*.

Finally, a singular characteristic of the Indian men participating in the "contact" is the marked passivity that underscores their interaction with the *Jarawa* men who are present during the "contact". To the more pugnacious, sometimes physically assaultive actions of the *Jarawa* men, the Indian men on the team present a consistently submissive demeanor. Definitively marking a contrast with the hostile bearing of the Indians whom the *Jarawa* encounter in the forest, or in the nearby villages bordering their territory, while the *Jarawa* men appear to test the limits that will eventuate a belligerent retaliation from the Indians.

The attributes discussed above bear on Chattopadhyay's prior observation that Indian women, if included in the contact team, would be "attacked" by the *Jarawa*. This use of the term "attack" is ambiguous, necessitating a deconstruction of its meaning. A number of different interpretations suggest themselves. One, the physical familiarity displayed by Indian men in terms of their interactions with *Jarawa* women has its counterpart in the behavior of the *Jarawa* men towards Indian women on the team, which is then construed as an "attack". Or, the instances of inappropriate behavior engaged in by Indian men have been noted by the *Jarawa*, who then retrieve an opportunity to retaliate in kind when there are Indian women on the team. Another possibility, suggested by the marked gentleness with which the *Jarawa* responded to the Onge who were present during the "contact" that Pandya engineered, is that the aggressiveness displayed by the *Jarawa* men, to both Indian men and women on the team, is a deliberate ploy to provoke a response from the Indians.

Having sketched an overview of the various elements that comprise "friendly contact" with the *Jarawa*, I want to set up the categories of difference that were constitutive of the encounters in which I was a participant.

Markers for difference: race and culture

The racialization of the indigenous population of the islands by way of the attribution of an innate inferiority of genetic stock has been an integral feature of any discourse involving the Andaman Islanders. The racial construction of the islanders forms the unarticulated but pervasive backdrop against which the situations occurred. In the context of the *Jarawa,* as elsewhere, race connotes difference by virtue of a distinction in physical appearance.Unlike its relevance on mainland India, the dark skin of the *Jarawa* is not usually included in the construction of difference. The Andaman Islands has a large population of people from the south of India with equally dark skin. Hence racial distinctions are seldom posited along lines of color. But the small stature of the *Jarawa*, their distinctive variety of hair type in association with their dark skin, manufactures a separate racial identity for them. All these elements, in turn, converge as signifiers of associative cultural backwardness. The primary marker for their imputed "primitive" condition along the continuum of cultural evolution is the *Jarawa's* unclothed body. This factor comes up repeatedly in any discussion of the *Jarawa*. Interestingly, their nakedness was an issue of some consternation for the Onge as well, who tried to teach the *Jarawa* men to fashion a loin-cloth with the red strips of cloth carried by the "contact team".

Markers of difference: gender and clothing

Gender distinctions are made obvious in the absence of clothing. Within the context of "contact" with the *Jarawa*, the most glaring disparity between the members of the "contact team" and the *Jarawa* is based on the fact that the Indians conceal some part(s) of their bodies, while the *Jarawa* expose all. As mentioned earlier, the Indian men strip down to their bare minimum, while the women remain fully clothed. Most women who participate in the contact wear the long Indian shirt, the *kurta*, and loose trousers, the *salwar*---my standard garb during fieldwork in the islands. However, such a differentiation in attire, as became evident on several occasions, does not denote a separate gen-

Onge loading coconuts harvested at Dugong Creek for transport to Port Blair. The cocnuts are used as gifts during Jarawa " contact". Photo: Sita Venkateswar

Loading baskets with "goods" during Jarawa contact. Photo: Andaman Administration

der identity to the *Jarawa*, even with the insertion of the typical long hair characteristic of most Indian women. Unless the outfit that an Indian woman wears leaves no scope for ambiguity,[13] for all the *Jarawa*---women, men and children---designating gender entails the verification of breasts on the Indian women which, when located, are repeatedly squeezed by everybody present.

To summarize the argument up to this point, the differences in physical appearance based on biology have been expanded to include cultural markers such as clothed/unclothed, with its associative differences in lifestyle. Racial distinctions and cultural attributes become enmeshed and inseparable, with values assigned to these features along a hierarchy of cultural significance.

Constructions of difference:
gender, class and the anthropologist

I have discussed some of the categories constituting the observed differences between the *Jarawa* and the members of the "contact team". Bearing on these considerations is the issue of how the construction of my gendered identity, and my location in terms of class, were instrumental in defining a position for me that separated me from the other members of the "contact team".

In an earlier chapter, I mentioned that in order to deflect attention from Indian men during my fieldwork, I resorted to the strategy of presenting myself as a married woman. Along the same lines and, I suspect, partly influenced by my experience of presenting a "professional" mien in the United States, which involved an obvious suppression of "femininity," my attempt to carve out a "professional" identity for myself in the Andaman Islands also involved playing down my gender. My loose, form-concealing garments, the removal of any kind of adornment from my person, my dismissal of any special privileges that I was offered as a woman, isolated me in a way that I was to be made aware of later, and eliminated some of the protections that I took for granted.

Further marking and separating me was my fluency in three Indian languages, which enabled me to interact with ease and move fluidly between various regional[14] groups in the islands. My delight in the ensuing bewilderment as to which part of India I originally "belonged" to contributed to a "betwixt and between" location for me, by virtue of which nobody could claim me as one of "theirs".

Intersecting with these ambiguities was my class/caste position, according me access to some social groups within the islands but asserting a concurrent distinction between myself and other members of the "contact team". Nita Kumar's (1992) discussion of her upper class position as a determinant of her identity during fieldwork in Banaras was, in some respects, similar to how I was defined during my field research. My reluctance to announce the fact that I was currently based in the US was, to a great extent, founded on my alertness to the class privileges implied by that information. I aspired to maintain a broad, safe, "middle-class" homogeneity which, as I later detected, was subverted by other aspects of the personality that I projected during my research. I was also made aware, for the first time during my fieldwork in the islands, of how easily I could be located in terms of my caste: by my speech, my appearance, etc. Chris Kaplonski's (1994) experience of research in Mongolia, where his appearance (white, male) signified a Russian identity to the Mongolians he met on the streets, thus leaving him open to physical attack, provides another insight into how appearance constructs one's identity during fieldwork.

Fields of power

Imbricated with all the elements that I have identified as relevant to contextualizing the *Jarawa* "contact" situation are shifting fields of power, with conflicting constructions of who, at any moment, exercises that power. On the face of it, the Indian team backed by the police boat with the hidden weapons, has the upper hand. But, as is made explicit through the duration of "contact," it is the *Jarawa* who orchestrate the process, with the Indians thrust into a predicament of inadequacy as they attempt to gauge and adjust to the temper of the interaction with the *Jarawa*.

If the police back-up were truly set up to deploy their weapons, the context would be transformed into a "punitive expedition", reminiscent of turn-of-the-century British relations with the *Jarawa*. Despite the other disjunctions discussed earlier, the Indian administration has attempted to maintain some distance, at least officially, from that particular colonial legacy. Moreover, as became evident on more than one instance, it was the "Bush" police in the boat, even without their *khaki* uniforms, who were fearful of being recognized by the *Jarawa*. Their skittish behavior if the *Jarawa* showed any interest in their boat, bobbing at some distance from the scene of contact, firstly, placed them outside of firing range and, secondly, posed more of a liability for the team than a protection.

I will now recount one of the instances of "contact" in which I participated, which brought to a head all of the elements that I have posited above. Each existed to varying degrees in every "contact" that I was associated with. But it was the one situation I discuss below that

185

exposed the problems inherent in the process and imperiled any hope of evading the problematics of gender as acutely brought to bear during fieldwork.

The *Tarmugli* cruised along the western coast of Middle Andaman, with the ship's captain and crew intermittently scanning the shore for signs of the *Jarawa*. A sudden cry from one of the crew called everyone to attention. The contours of a raft emerged against the blue horizon, with some children perched on top. It was propelled by four swimming *Jarawa*, as they crossed the sea between the islands dotting the western shore of Middle Andaman. Standing at a vantage point on the island, in the direction in which the swimmers were headed, was a *Jarawa* man signalling to the ship with a white object[15] tied to a long stick that he held up as he waved. The ship immediately slowed down, and embarked on the usual routine of dropping anchor, lowering and loading the boats, while the "contact team" made their own preparations to meet with the *Jarawa*.

By what appeared later as a strange coincidence, the policemen who accompanied every "contact team" were not on board at the time but were to rendezvous with the ship later in the day. Thus this "contact team" sallied forth to meet the *Jarawa* without the presumed security of a police back-up. As we approached the shore where the raft had landed, we observed that it was a small group who awaited us, one adult male, two women, the rest infants, children and an adolescent boy. I remained seated in the boat during the usual flurry of activity as the *Jarawa* gathered the "gifts". I observed that the unloading was executed by the two women and children, while the *Jarawa* man sat impassively on one side of the boat in which I waited, along with Pandya and some other crew from the ship. The rest of the team were on shore assisting the women unload the boats.

The *Jarawa* was a middle-aged, well-proportioned man, with a certain commanding presence, made prominent by the conduct of the other *Jarawa* as they deferred to him. His manner, as he made his way along the boat – pushing one of the crew into the water, snatching the camera from another, his eyes roving from one person to the next on the boat – rendered everybody present somewhat uneasy. I was later informed of an encounter between the *Jarawa* man and another member of the team on the second boat, when the *Jarawa* had grabbed his camera, gripping his (the team member's) wrist and bruising him. I missed this particular confrontation as I was coping with the routine examination of my person and verification of gender conducted by the women and children.

Pandya voiced his apprehension by suggesting that we hasten the unloading of the boats and return to the ship. But the other members of the team were out of earshot and were engaged in exploring the is-

Observing the rites of "contact": affirming gender. Photo: Andaman Administration photographer

Anthropologist in the field: playing back a recording during Jarawa "contact".
Photo: Vishvajit Pandya

land. I, too, became increasingly tense as the *Jarawa* eyes settled on me more frequently as he moved progressively closer to where I was seated in the boat. Intending to dispel the growing atmosphere of unease on the boat, I unobtrusively disembarked, and waded ashore to where the others were gathered, somewhat at a loose end, having finished emptying the boat. Meanwhile, the administration photographer who always accompanied the "contact team" was occupied in photographing the various clusters of *Jarawa* and team members that was intermittently forming and dissolving. I noticed that the flash from either the photographer's camera, or from another team member's "aim and shoot" variety, annoyed the *Jarawa* women, who gestured abruptly in the direction of the flash.

Shortly afterwards, I realized that the *Jarawa* man had also proceeded ashore and, duplicating his stratagem on the boat, moved from one small group to the next on shore. Suddenly, he was beside me, holding my wrist and tugging at one end of my *kurta*. Simultaneously, one of the women positioned herself on my other side and pulled at a different end. I struggled to unfasten the grip on my wrist and hold down the *kurta*. He then shifted his grip to the nape of my neck, holding it down firmly as he commenced to rip the back of my *kurta*, separating it from the seams on the shoulder and along one side. The thick, coarse material could not be detached from the other side, snagging at the seam despite the force applied to it by the *Jarawa*. One of the team, who had carried a knife for cutting the green coconuts, helped cut it away. The *Jarawa* woman had not let go of her hold on the front end of the *kurta*, which was now the target of their concerted efforts. The major portion of the front side gave way, leaving a small strip on top to which the gaping sleeves remained attached. The event was brought to a halt when Bakhtawar Singh,[16] an elderly veteran of "*Jarawa* contact", nearly blind, walked into the scene. Literally blundering into the ensuing proceedings, he terminated it by grasping the *Jarawa* and forcing him to release his grip on my neck. The woman, however, continued to pull on the remaining piece but, with my neck free, I was in a position to ward her off.

The tableau occurred in complete silence, the other team members gathered around in a semi-circle, the photographer engaged in not missing a shot, and Pandya and the crew still on the boat some distance away. I made my way back towards the boat in silence, holding down what was left of my *kurta*, and climbed back on board. Pandya handed me his shirt, which I gratefully accepted. The two boats receded from the shore, where the *Jarawa* stood watching as the Indians waved a cheerful farewell to them. It was all in a day's work for the team.

Assembling the elements

It should now be possible to assemble all the different pieces that I have separated in the preceding pages in order to attempt to understand, or offer some interpretations, for what actually transpired during the "contact" that I have described. The first point that I want to assert here is the *Jarawa* domination of the entire encounter with them. They set up the "contact", and orchestrated the entire proceedings from start to finish. This is the case in every encounter but becomes camouflaged, or buried under the flurry of activities that constitute the various sequences of the confrontation with the *Jarawa*. It is *they* who decide if and when to make themselves visible, by announcing their presence with the smoke signal, which then initiates the routine schedule of "friendly contact".

The absence of the police back-up was, I feel, merely coincidental, not altering the situation in any substantial way. Such incidents, perhaps not in the same configuration of events, have erupted in the past and are a perennial feature of any "contact". This is what I meant earlier when I referred to the small enclaves that are formed in the course of contact, which retain within them elements of the unpredictable and the ominous.

In the unlikely event that the policemen revealed their weapons, the possibility of escalating violence, and the exposure of the "contact team" to the risk of death, was enough deterrent to have rendered the policemen redundant as a measure of security. Earlier contexts of "contact" have demonstrated that, at the slightest suspicion of anything untoward, the Jarawa melt within seconds into the surrounding dense gloom of the forest. With the "contact team" sitting ducks for the extended range of the long, lethal Jarawa arrows, the probability of the Jarawa retaining control over any escalating situation remains strong. Thus, it is important to note that the context can only be altered in any substantial way by changing the very terms of the engagement with the *Jarawa*, i.e. by transforming "friendly contact" into an "unfriendly" one. This necessitates the elimination of any "contact team", currently conceived as innocuously offering some of the "goodies" of civilization to the naked *junglees*, whereby "friendly contact" is recast into a "punitive" mission to end the "menace" of the *Jarawa* once and for all.

But in the situation as constituted during the period of my research, whatever the illusions the "contact team" or the Andaman administration may have cherished, it was made explicit that it was the *Jarawa* who held power and wielded it continuously through the entire duration of "contact". This view is given credence by the conduct of the *Jarawa*, which has its antithesis in the behavior of the "contact team": the *Jarawa* challenge the assignment of the bland attribute of "friendly" to the encounter with them at every step.

In terms of the strange immobility of the "contact team" during the incident, it may be that they were too startled by the turn of events to organize a coherent response. But they had enough presence of mind to offer the *dao* to the *Jarawa* to assist in releasing the sides of the *kurta* from the seams. And the photographer was sufficiently alert to the possibilities of a "scoop" to continue photographing the sequence of events. Those photographs, *not* included here, and for which I went to some lengths to obtain all existing copies with their negatives, communicate details that I was not cognizant of at the time. The expressions on the faces of the team as they stood grouped in a semi-circle around me register their awareness of the portions of my unclothed body becoming visible as segments of my garment were hacked away.

Intruding on such a reaction, or lack of it thereby, were the factors that I have enumerated, that were contingent on the personality that I brought to bear during my fieldwork in the Andaman Islands, along with all the ways in which I was positioned in terms of gender and class. By challenging the conventional modes of the "feminine" as defined by the Indians with whom I interacted, I also forfeited many of the protections that are offered to women who conform to the norm. Straying outside of the gender norms effected a greater vulnerability for me in the context of "*Jarawa* contact". As I was intensely made to realize, I could not avail of any of the ordinary shields that I took for granted but which tend to be offered to women who present themselves as in need of protection.

My demeanor subsequent to the incident further estranged me from the norms specified for my gender. I was very composed, and did not succumb to the tears that were expected of me. They would have earned me more sympathy in the circumstances as defined above. Also relevant to my distancing from the other members of the "contact team" is my earlier mention of my class/caste background, enabling me to mingle at ease with the likes of the "LG" at the same time earning the antagonism of my "team-mates".

For the *Jarawa* who met with the "contact team" during the encounter that I have related, and the others[17] that I also participated in, it was quickly evident that I was *with* the team but not really a *part* of the team. In their efforts to find a chink in the docile front presented to them by the Indians, I was an easy target. By their actions, the *Jarawa* clearly signaled who was *puissant*,[18] and explored the limits to which their domination could be extended.

A firm handling of the situation, as manifested in Bakhtawar Singh's[19] effective application of force, could have brought the proceedings to a speedy halt. But for all the Indians grouped around me, this was a moment of collusion with the *Jarawa* to strip me of the strengths that both isolated and sustained me. For all the men gathered

Surveying the scene. The Jarawa man who directed the "contact". Photo: Sita Venkateswar

there, this was an enactment of power, deployed on/over the body of a woman. For the one, it was a testing of the limits to which that power could be exerted. For the other, it was to exact a reprisal for all the ways in which I maintained my independence or refused to submit to the conventional. And in the case of the *Jarawa* woman, whose role belied Chattopadhyay's (1992) contention that the women hold the men in check, hers was an expression of the anger accumulated by the intrusive behavior of the "contact team". Her response revealed the profoundly disjunct contours of power as historically and politically constituted by race and gender. Or the perils of presuming alliances on the basis of one without negotiating the shifting dimensions and ambiguities posed by the inextricable intertwining of both.

A different option can be explored if the removal of my *kurta* is construed as a "social leveler". As the only fully clothed person in the group, by that act I was rendered one with the rest of the team. Hence, the *Jarawas'* actions may be interpreted as a playful gesture, one of curiosity even, to ascertain and establish conclusively that I was, in fact, female. But their facial cast belied such a construction of the scene. As the women's expressions flashed their anger at the incessant and obtrusive photography, the man's roving eyes appropriated the terms of the "gaze". Reversing the direction of the scrutiny that I deployed on the Onge, the prolonged stare of the Jarawa both extended a challenge and unleashed the force of a blow. In the context of "contact", it was the team who flinched and submissively lowered their eyes. Such gestural interplay eliminated any hint of the ludic in the proceedings, making explicit the more ominous underlying dynamic of power that the *Jarawa* appeared willing to push to whatever limit.

The question then arises as to what some of the alternatives would have been had Bakhtawar Singh not walked into the scene, or arrived a little later than he did. It is likely that I would have been divested of my remaining piece of *kurta*, and walked back to the boat bare-breasted until offered Pandya's shirt. It is unlikely that I would have been "dragged off to the forest by the Jarawa and ravished". Despite the later insinuations of the team, as they pondered whether the *Jarawa* (male's) response could have been construed as sexual arousal, the scene was not sexual, at least not where the *Jarawa* were concerned. In view of all the bodily exposure, there was no scope for any doubt on that matter. Moreover, the participation of the *Jarawa* woman suggests otherwise, and clearly leads in the direction of the argument elaborated above. But such a conclusion by the team is in itself revealing, and perhaps intimates their own responses to the scene as it unfolded before them.

A postscript on the Onge

Apart from noting the remarkably gentle *Jarawa* response to the Onge, I have not embarked on any further details of their encounter. Those particulars are not relevant to the argument I make here. Chota Raju and his wife Betibegi were on board the ship when the incident that I have narrated above occurred. He was unwell and did not feel inclined to participate in the "contact". When I related the incident to them, they found my account hilarious and reported it to all the other Onge at Dugong Creek. It was a subject of much merriment for them as well. It remained unclear to me whether it was my matter-of-fact narration of the affair that was funny or if it was the image of my clothes being ripped apart that provoked so much laughter.

Conclusion

The incident that I narrated above and the subsequent laughter of the Onge brought the long emotional journey that I had traveled during the many months of research in the Andaman Islands to a culmination. Unlike my response to the Indians, whom I could easily brush aside, the laughter of the Onge perplexed and hurt me, as I puzzled over its meaning. The barriers to striking a relationship of mutual understanding with "my people" loomed as large at the end of my research as they had when I first arrived at Dugong Creek. Shared laughter is a fundamental moment of empathy, a space of connection that can transcend other disparities. But, at that moment, the laughter of the Onge marked a fundamental expression of irreconcilable differences, one that rendered futile any claims to "rapport" on the eve of my final departure from Dugong Creek.

While I despaired of any resolution, Kwankitui, wife of Moroi the *torale*, nominated me as *ijejille*, "one of us". This was perhaps in response to the reports she had received of my diligent attention to the needs of the Onge during the trip to the *Jarawa* area. Yet again, a comment from one of the Onge challenged the ways in which I construed a situation. It also suggested contrasting views of "connection:" for the Onge it was a recognition of my concern for them, while for me it was the ability to intuitively know them. But, as stated earlier, this *is* a "partial" perspective, and is riven with all the ambiguities inherent to such a view. ❑

Notes

1 A modified version of this paper has been published in Qualitative Inquiry (2001)7(4):448-465.

2 This information was published in the local newspaper by Madhumala Chattopadhyay (1992) but was brought to our attention during an informal discussion with Vishvajit Pandya who, after receiving some inkling of a salvage operation off Sentinel Island, interviewed the scrap-iron dealer and his workers.

3 A perusal of recent reports and articles on the *Jarawa* and Sentinelese emerging from the islands (Chattopadhyay 1992, Pandit 1991, Pandit and Chattopadhyay 1989) suggests that the issue of "first contact", and who was actually present at that moment, is a matter of some concern for the Andaman administration, the anthropologists and others who comprise the "contact team".

4 I too, was affiliated to a foreign institution but, in my case, it did not confer on me any greater importance. On the contrary, for me it created an aura of distance from the realities and immediacies of the Indian situation.

5 Hut Bay is the largest town and harbour in Little Andaman. The original plan was for Pandya and I to travel by ship to Dugong Creek, pick up the Onge from there and return to Port Blair. The rough seas near Dugong Creek rendered it dangerous to send a smaller boat from mid-sea into the settlement, such that Pandya and I were unable to reach Dugong Creek and directly intervene in talking to the Onge.

6   The *Tarmugli* was the "LG's" ship, usually made available only to VIPs visiting the islands. In view of the exciting possibilities offered by the trips that Pandya proposed, the "LG" decided to grace the team with his presence at some point in the proceedings. Ordinarily, the *M.V. Milale* was the ship used for the "contact trips", a more utilitarian and far less comfortable vessel than the *Tarmugli*.

7   All the expenses that the Onge incurred during their stay at Port Blair, and on the trip to the *Jarawa* area, were to be borne by the Andaman administration. Bara Raju would also have the opportunity to directly negotiate his claim with the "LG".

8   Dugong Creek was inundated with wireless messages: from the ship at mid-sea unable to send a boat out to pick up the Onge; from the office of the AAJVS at Port Blair and from the "LG's" office. The welfare personnel at Dugong Creek were hard pressed to understand what had warranted so much wireless time.

9   All the men in the team are usually bare-chested, and disrobe to their under-wear or shorts. Elderly men prefer to keep their trousers on. Any woman present is fully clothed: Indian prudery discourages the exposure of legs or, for that matter, any part of one's body. This is especially the case in small towns or places distant from urban centers.

10 I am not certain how or why the color red was deemed attractive to the *Jarawa* but bolts of red cloth, which are then cut into small strips, are now a regularly purchased gift item. The *Jarawa* use the colored string from the cloth to embel-lish the ornaments they wear about their bodies. Pandya's project incorporated this feature in order to trace the movements of the *Jarawa*: differently patterned and colored cloth would be coded and given to each group that we met at a specific location. On subsequent trips, the specific kind of cloth (or, more pre-cisely, the strings from the strips) found on a *Jarawa* group, would be correlated with the location where the original cloth of that color/pattern was given to the *Jarawa*.

11 The Andaman administration believe that the "Bush" policeman's *khaki* uni-form is easily identified by the *Jarawa*, and liable to provoke aggressive behavior from them.

12 Nowadays, a trip to the *Jarawa* area is offered to VIPs visiting the Andamans: Cabinet Ministers, top government officials and other visiting dignitaries. Such one-time visitors are observed to be typically negligent of the consequences at-tendant on their inappropriate behavior with the *Jarawa*.

13 The potential ambiguity regarding my gender identity was made known to me by the team leader during another "contact" trip, this time through the forest rather than the usual sea-route. Discussing the possibility of meeting some *Jarawa* in the forest, it was joked that an attack by the *Jarawa* could be averted by placing me in front, to draw attention to the presence of a woman in the team. I was then informed that such a strategy would probably fail since I was not immediately recognizable as a woman, and would more likely pass as a boy.

14 As already mentioned elsewhere, regional identity on the basis of place of origin in mainland India is maintained in the Andaman Islands as well.

15 The white object was later identified as a piece of Styrofoam packing material that had obviously washed ashore.

16 Bakhtawar Singh, formerly of the "Bush" police force in the Andamans, is credited with laying the groundwork for, and establishing, "first contact" with the *Jarawa*. Now retired, he is called upon as an "expert" to occasionally accompany the "contact teams". On this occasion, he had wandered away to another side of the island, and was therefore unaware of the occurrence.

17 I have discussed one instance of "contact" in detail since that was the occasion that clarified for me many of the conundrums that had emerged in the course of the other encounters with the *Jarawa*.

18 I use the French synonym here rather than "powerful". To my mind the French word conveys more nuances than the English equivalent.

19 The dynamics of my interaction with the Indian team excluded Bakhtawar Singh. He remained outside of the undercurrents described above and, for the most part, unaware of them.. He was an honoured guest on board, sufficiently secure in his standing with the administration, with enough publicity attending on his role with the *Jarawa* not to be perturbed by my inclusion on the team.

THE END OF FIELDWORK

> *"There are more things on heaven and earth Horatio,*
> *Than are dreamt of in your philosophy"*

> (Hamlet, Act 1, Scene V)

> *"'There must be some way out of here,' said the joker to the thief,*
> *'There's too much confusion, I can't get no relief'"*

> (Bob Dylan, All Along the Watchtower)

M y account of the Andaman Islanders has been inextricably interwoven with my own subjectivity as it was constituted through the process of research in the islands. My multiple positioning during the period of residence in the islands inflected my perceptions, and hence my experience of the various groups whom I encountered and interacted with in the course of research. Such shifting locations are typical of any anthropological research endeavour, and I do not claim that it is unique to my inquiry. But it does engender a partial and fragmentary perspective that does not lend itself to an authoritative exegesis of a "culture".

The issue also becomes one of the extent to which we are willing to bring our subjectivity to the fore, and expose and articulate the contours of our person and personality in all its uncertainty, as it structures our imperfect vision of the world. To establish and engage in an "hermeneutics of vulnerability" (Dwyer 1977), our own as much as for the subjects of our research, is to risk calling into question our authority to speak, and our presumed right to inscribe a certain view of a people (cf. Clifford 1983). Thus, my prerogative to impose a particular perspective of the islanders is countered by my exposure of the ways in which my perceptions were delimited in some instances or foreclosed in others. I have then, "policed" my own power in the text that I have constructed of my experience of/and research in the Andaman Islands.

Relations of power are emphasized in this monograph, and each chapter is constructed around particular dimensions of power as they are constitutive and constituting of ethnographic contexts. Foremost among these are government policies, in the colonial variants of the British and Indian regimes of control over the Andaman Islands. Both historically and in the ongoing Indian jurisdiction of the islands, political power invested as government policies has made significant invasions into the everyday existence of the islanders. This is more pronounced in the case of the Onge and Andamanese but less so where the Jarawa and Sentinelese are concerned only because their very different situations render impossible (as yet) any direct intervention into their quotidian lives. Such an intimate impingement of political power upon the spheres of daily existence has impacted on social relations by articulating them with the structures of government. Through the process of subjection, whereby individuals participate voluntarily in the new opportunities for power made available to them, lines of authority are reconfigured, a process that I refer to, extending its origins in policy, as the "policing" of power.

The same process has profound outcomes in contestations between men and women, as particular forms of masculine identities take root, redefining gender identities and recasting gender relations. The insidious reaches of political power on the terrain of gender leads to my perception of how that site is "governed" by successive administrative strategies, which seek to assimilate the islanders with the dominant Indian population. Gender is also the crucial site of my own disjunct positioning, enabling and disabling according to context but ineluctably constitutive of my experience of research in the islands. As it intersects with class, my gendered location is additionally problematized, and is critically determining of my interactions with various sectors of the Indian population in the islands.

My perception of the islanders has also incorporated a third dimension that exists, at one register, independent of the actual context, and more in my "desire to find a resistant presence" (O'Hanlon 1988), at least in the figure of the Onge women. Resistance remains an "unmarked and unnamed category" (Spivak 1988) that has to be wrested from mundane expressions of opposition to the administrative strategies of the Indian government. Whether as dissembling behaviors or forms of secrecy, expressions of anger and resentment of the welfare system and personnel, reading resistance is a project that exists as much in my own imagination as in the practices in which I search to find it: of discovering a cognizance of and repudiation of colonial control.

The interpenetration of their lives with the Indian administration and population, the ways in which subjectivities have been ineluctably transformed, blurs the possibilities of a clear trajectory of resistance. Moreover, the sheer numbers ranged around them renders the task of negotiating a future separate from the political maneuvers of the Indian nation impossible to envision. "When the *inenle* first came and brought goods for us, and tobacco, we thought they were bringing all this to make it easier for us to live," said Bara Raju. It must be recognized that to a great extent such a view still colours their perception of the Indians, at least, of those with power: that they are available to provide the Onge with "goods" to make life easier for them. The "potlatch" that I held before my final departure from Dugong Creek, to give away to the Onge all of my belongings, which many of them had requisitioned for themselves over the months, was an ironic underscoring of their enmeshment within a world of consumption.

The question then arises as to whether the islanders even want such an existence apart from Indians. Where the Onge or the Andamanese are concerned, the answer can only remain ambiguous. But in the case of the Jarawa or the Sentinelese, their clear stance of challenge, their engagement with the Indian population on no other terms but their own, is an obvious articulation of independence.

The next, and to my mind, the more crucial political-tactical question is, "What is to be done" then? In view of the purported "failures" of the Indian government's policy initiatives, what alternatives can I suggest? I respond as James Ferguson (1994:279) does, that I neither intended to nor presume to prescribe. And like him I agree that the issue is a political one, necessitating a political solution. My articulation of the situation in the ways that I have in this account is the only means I have available of de-naturalizing and re-politicizing the Indian control of the islands and their interventions into the lives of the islanders. I do, however, admit to attempting some alternatives, brought about by the recognition of the significance of political empowerment. It is related to my participation in the project of developing a primer for the Onge.

My interest in anthropology developed from reading Paolo Friere. My desire to work with indigenous peoples derived from the avenues opened up by Freire for participating in altering the conditions of existence of the most marginalized peoples. Developing a primer for the Onge was at the core of Freire's methods for *conscientization*, a process which could only be engendered through the active participation of the Onge in the project. Excited by these possibilities, I communicated that intent to the team of linguists. I thought it essential that they too become involved in working along these lines. I was somewhat chagrined to find that my excitement in the means offered to actively involve the Onge in the project did not find very receptive ears. They pointed out the limited time they had to show a product from their stay in the islands. I read into that response acertain rigidity developed from years of working on government commissioned projects. Despite many attempts, the project could only be executed as per the guidelines laid out by the linguists, developed through their years of experience working with other such people. Including the Onge throughout the process, according to the linguists, would only delay the work. *Conscientization* was not the goal, but a finished primer.

Somewhat disheartened by such a bureaucratic view of things, I nevertheless decided to single-handedly endeavour to follow through

An Onge girl. Photo: Sita Venkateswar

on the project. After all, I was the one who would be around long after the linguists left. And, they depended on *me* to go through the trial phase with the Onge. In the months after the linguists' departure, I struggled to communicate to the Onge the significance of literacy, the importance of learning to read in their own language, and how imperative it was to know how to count. It was the first step to power according to the terms of the world as it existed at present. It was crucial that they too were *tomolukwele*, those who wrote. After many months spent pleading, coaxing and quarreling, all of which I hoped would convey to the Onge what was involved in their active engagement in the process, I decided to give up. It occurred to me, at that crucial moment, that I had my own research to accomplish. I could not stay on at Dugong Creek for ever. *Conscientization* was time-consuming, and I wanted to leave.

What I did not want to acknowledge at the time, as I groped for various justifications for arriving at such a conclusion, was that I was no different from the linguists. In fact, they were more clear-sighted than I was in comprehending the limitations of their time and interests. They had their work cut out, and did not want to meddle with any problematic areas that could hinder the progress of what was expected of them.

Ultimately, I too had to concede the same thing. I was there on a research grant, for certain duration, for which I had to show some concrete output. I had set out to address some defined questions, according to which I had to organize my time and efforts. Anything beyond such a goal was beyond my abilities. Moreover, by that time, I was tired and I wanted to leave. Neither Dugong Creek nor the Andaman Islands ever became an environment that constituted a "home". And so I left.

I end my account of my fieldwork with the Andaman Islanders with Kamala Visweswaran's passionate and eloquent articulation of ethnographic practice. It has been a "process of sundering and reconstitution, of retraction and assertion that I want to foreground as a radical method of feminist ethnography. Of course, I cannot claim total success for this maneuver. Experiments, after all, risk failure" (1994: 15).

Postscript

The questions raised by the encounter with the Jarawa and its aftermath continue to haunt me years after leaving the islands. I am no closer to knowing for certain what really happened on that beach with the *Jarawa* or, more critically for me, why the Onge laughed, apparently not with me but at me. The narration of the incident has become one more instance of what Wiener (1999) described as "the particulars of a certain ethnographic encounter...[as] affected by pre-existing social formations" (pg.99).Yet, it is only in precisely mapping the historical and political terrain in which my fieldwork occurred that one can identify some clues.

For the Andaman Islanders, it has been a continuous history of colonization since the mid-19th century, when the British consolidated a penal settlement on the islands. It may be argued that the prefix *neo* may be added to mark a break from one colonizer to the next (in Anthony Appiah's [1991: 348] sense of a "space-clearing gesture"), when India took control of the islands in 1947. However, it can be argued that the basic form of control has remained no different from the earlier British period, if dispossession, repopulation and external control are identified as some of the commonalities in the two phases of colonization. Some alternatives are suggested by Arnold Krupat's (1994) use of "domestic imperialism" to define the situation of Native Americans because the conditions of Native American groups largely resemble the situation in the Andaman Islands. To maintain some consistency in the context of a discussion of Indian policies, since the Andaman Islanders are classified as "tribal" groups, I will apply the term "internal colonialism" to describe the form of control exerted by India with respect to all "tribal" groups under Indian jurisdiction. But the underlying reality of colonization should be brought to the fore, whatever the particular prefix used to qualify its content.

The question of my location in the context of these historical processes is somewhat more contentious. As an Indian currently residing in the metropolitan West, I can claim the currently fashionable status of a "postcolonial", which serves to redefine my identity in academic circles by reinvesting the privileges of class-based in India into different orders of entitlements. In terms of its relevance to the conduct of anthropological research in the Andaman Islands, identity translates into advantage that grants me access denied to non-Indians. At the same time, my entry into the reserved "tribal areas" of the islands is also an expression of the asymmetric relations of power with respect to the islanders, thus problematizing a transparent view of the anthropologist-research participant relationship in this context. Elsewhere, Henrika Kuklick (1991) has noted that the political conditions created by colonialism directly affect the relationships that anthropologists form with their research participants.

In noting the historical and political conjunctures of my particular and personal location in this context, I also recognize the limits of my purview from these positions. I should, then, view this step as a milestone in a much longer process and muster the courage to return to the Andaman Islands in search of answers. ❑

THE FATE OF THE JARAWA: THE END OF THE ROAD? AN EPILOGUE

"Me titiro whakamuri tatou
Kia mohio ai
Me pehea haere ki mua"[1]

(Mâori saying)

I n April 1996,[2] an adolescent *Jarawa* boy named En Mei was found immobilized and nursing a fractured leg along the edges of the forest close to the village of Kadamtala in Middle Andaman. He was taken by the local authorities to the G. B. Pant Hospital, the main hospital at Port Blair and treated there for his injury. The reasons attributed to the cause of his fracture have been varied,[3] from being hit by a truck on the Andaman Trunk Road (Mynott 2004) or his foot getting caught in an animal trap (Anthropological Survey of India n.d.) to a fall from a tree (Mukhopadhyay 2004).

Six months later in October 1996, En Mei was dropped off near the forest where he had been found, laden with gifts and stories of his time spent at Port Blair. Exactly a year after En Mei returned to the forest, an unprecedented event occurred: a group of *Jarawa* including En Mei in their midst, appeared at a jetty in Middle Andaman during the day, having shed their "hostile" demeanour, and presenting a "friendly" mien instead.

En Mei's injury and the subsequent entry of the *Jarawa* into the settler villages has become the starting point of a new origin story currently in circulation in the Andaman Islands: the story of the sequence of events that led to the *Jarawa's* transformation from a "hostile" people existing in a "state of war" with the neighbouring settler population to a "friendly" one, with the *Jarawa* indicating their willingness to enter into a compact of "peace" with them.

Similar incidents continued to occur in the ensuing months, during which gestures used by the *Jarawa*, pointing towards their bellies, were understood as expressions of hunger and therefore a request for food. Sekhsaria (2003) reports on the decision to airdrop packets of food into the *Jarawa* forest. This was in response to the growing belief by the Andaman administration that the emergence of the *Jarawa* from the forest was a consequence of increasing hunger resulting from food and resource shortages. He goes on to describe an occasion witnessed by him in April 1998 when a large group of *Jarawa*, including women and children, arrived at the same jetty in Middle Andaman. The inability of the local settler community or the administration to respond with sensitivity to such a situation is noted by Sekhsaria. The underlying tension of the encounter as reported by Sekhsaria is similar to my discussion in an earlier chapter, belying the complacent assumption of "friendly relations", and pointing to the fragility of the accord of "peace" as interpreted by the administration and the settlers.

The interpretation of food shortages have been countered by anthropologists at the ASI, who tend to highlight the role played by En Mei in bringing about the transformation of the *Jarawa* from "hostile" to "friendly. But speculation is rife as to what actually transpired between the *Jarawa*, or the discussions that may have ensued amongst them during the lapse of a year since En Mei was released into the forest. In a recent discussion, Mukhopadhyay (2004) is more sceptical. According to him, and purportedly based on conversations that he had with En Mei, the very first instance of the *Jarawa* emerging from their forest cover during the day came about when En Mei was promised food by some of the settlers if he brought other *Jarawa* to the jetty in Middle Andaman. En Mei agreed, went on to comply and the rest is history.

Samir Acharya of the Society for Andaman and Nicobar Ecology (SANE), who became a central figure in the events to come and whom I quote at length below, makes the following scathing critique regarding En Mei's sojourn in Port Blair:

1) *EN-MAI, glorified as Ambassador of Goodwill, was excommunicated from his own community (Tirur). He is known to have killed the suitor of the lady who is now his wife.*

2) *A 'Cargo-cult' has been establishing with En-Mai at the centre. The importance and attention given to him by the authorities, like giving him a separate room in the Hospital, lavish gifts, permitting him a car or jeep to travel in when lesser mortals ride on the back of a truck, etc. This has built up his image among impressionable youngsters and young women.*

3) *In a hunter-gatherer society, the leadership is always with the older people because they are the repository of all knowledge and skills of survival accumulated through experience. Establishing En-Mai as a cult figure has created rifts in the traditional Jarawa Society.*

4) *It is known to all travellers on ATR (Andaman Trunk Road) that the Jarawa encountered on the road are mostly minors with an occasional young woman among them. The able-bodied males and older people are conspicuous by their absence.*

5) *The older people are actually busy in their traditional hunting-foraging activities. The youngsters on the road are losing valuable experience and lessons in survival by their absence from the forest. They would, if they continue in the same path, soon become unfit to survive in the forest.*

6) *The contact parties' only notable success is in making the Jarawa proficient in the choicest Hindi slang. While many years' work of experts and many tens of lakhs [of rupees] later, we are yet to have a Jarawa Primer that would permit us to have a dialogue in their dialect, the Jarawa youngsters on road today puts a veteran sailor or a policeman to shame in a slanging match. So much for acculturation.*

(http://www.andaman.org, The Jarawa case)

Meanwhile, in a bizarre turn of events leading from the perception that the *Jarawa* were suffering from starvation, a local lawyer in the islands filed a legal suit against the Andaman administration. She claimed that, under the Indian constitution, the *Jarawa* had the same right to receive and enjoy "the fruits of civilization" as any other "Indian" but instead had been denied the benefits of civilization by the administration in the islands. She then went on to demand that the *Jarawa* be immediately provided with all modern amenities and rehabilitated like the Andamanese and the Onge. As Sekhsaria (2003:22) comments, this was a "classic example of a move undertaken with the right intentions but seeking the wrong solutions".

In response to the writ petition, an awareness and petition campaign coordinated locally by Samir Acharya of SANE and internationally by Survival International[4] resulted in a flood of outraged and condemnatory letters to the administration from noted anthropologists across the world, drawing attention to the dangers of rendering the *Jarawa* sedentary.

A grimmer and more foreboding set of outcomes was to eventuate from the increased interaction of the *Jarawa* with the local populations. The warnings that had been issued over the years by the Whitakers and others, and which had been consistently ignored by the Andaman administration, finally manifested from July-August of 1999 when a series of illnesses became visible among the *Jarawa*. The intensified "contact" with the *Jarawa*, and the continuing extension of the Andaman Trunk Road right through the heart of *Jarawa* territory with its associated clearing of forests, finally took its toll in outbreaks of epidemics of measles and pneumonia, tuberculosis and conjunctivitis among the *Jarawa* (Ali 1999, Bedi 1999, Sekhsaria 1999). Madhusree Mukerjee (2003), a former journalist with the *Scientific American* who had been conducting research in the islands over the past seven years, notes the bus loads of tourists brought by tour operators up the Andaman Trunk Road to visit the *Jarawa*. She also reports on the increasing incidence of coughs and colds among the *Jarawa* prior to the epidemics, noted in passing by anyone who encountered them.

A Jarawa enjoying a banana. Goods from the Andaman Trunk Road.
Photo: SANE (Society for Andaman and Nicobar Ecology)

The public outcry that followed threw the spotlight on Indian government policies in the islands, and spurred the efforts of the islands' medical establishment to control the spread of the diseases among *Jarawa* populations in the forests. The numbers who remained in the forests and succumbed to the epidemics and other related illnesses remain unknown.

Court cases and committees

The High Court interim order on the case filed by Shyamali Ganguly, the local lawyer, prohibited all entry into *Jarawa* areas and further directed that the *Jarawa* be protected from any encroachments into their reserve, calling for severe penalties for civil servants who failed in their duties. The court directive also required further research to be conducted into why the *Jarawa* were emerging from their forest areas and to ascertain whether they were subject to food shortages. Expert committees were constituted to provide more information to the courts, the second of which was entrusted with the responsibility of researching and formulating a plan of action to deal with the *Jarawa*. Sekhsaria's (2003) recent book, comprising of a compilation of his observations on the islands over the years, details the directives of the High Court and the prevailing mood of optimism that ensued among environmental and indigenous rights activists.

It is instructive at this stage to pay closer attention to the process by which the committees who were responsible for providing more information to the Court were constituted, the chronology of events that led to committees being formed and dissolved and, more significantly, the personnel appointed to serve on the committees.

In May 1999, the High Court appointed Special Officers from *within* the Andaman administration to submit a report on the problems relevant to the *Jarawa*, and to suggest some means for their welfare-cum-rehabilitation. In a surprisingly speedy response, given the slow and protracted process of usual government functioning within the islands, the officers submitted a report within a month. The report was deemed unsatisfactory and was unacceptable to the Court. In February 2000, the entire matter was handed over to an Expert Committee, constituted by the Court itself. Moving its range slightly further than it had in the previous instance, the High Court appointed 6 members, *all* of whom were functionaries of the Government of India, namely the Anthropological Survey of India (ASI) and the Health Services in the islands, with the Chief Judicial Magistrate of the Session Court of Port Blair serving as Member Secretary to the committee. On submission of their report six months later, the Court identified a number of key issues, as detailed below:

"a) Whether the Jarawa should be isolated from the rest of humanity and left to themselves to lead their own way of life as they did a few years back, or

b) Whether the Jarawa should be brought into the mainstream of "civilization", or

c) Whether to ensure their peaceful co-existence as suggested in the Master Plan[5] for the Welfare of the Primitive Tribes of the A&N Islands prepared by Mr. Awaradi, Director of Tribal Welfare" (Expert Committees Report, Government of India)."

These issues were to be settled as a matter of policy by the Government of India after consultation with national and international experts on the subject. In the 60-page judgement that was delivered in April 2001, the Court "ordered that the Ministry of Tribal Affairs, Government of India, should constitute [yet another!] Committee of Experts to spell out in clear terms:

a) Reasons for the sudden change in behaviour of the Jarawa, ie. shedding their hostility, coming out of their forest abode in broad daylight and accepting exogenous items from non-Jarawa and,
b) To suggest remedial measures for the welfare of the Jarawa" (*ibid.*).

Pankaj Sekhsaria (2003) also notes that the report submitted by the ASI based on the studies they had conducted indicated that there was no shortage of food for the *Jarawa* in the forests, but highlighted their vulnerability to various infections, and the scale of illegal poaching that was occurring within the forest and surrounding coast.

Responding to the Court Order, the Ministry of Home Affairs, Government of India, constituted for the third time a "Committee of Experts". The composition of this particular eight-member committee was significant and went on to play a crucial role in the events to come. Yet again, the personnel chosen were various functionaries of the government, some were repeated from the earlier committee but a few surprises were in store in the final report, which was the outcome of their research and deliberations.

While these developments are significant, and are an indication of the efficient functioning of the Indian judiciary, of concern are the terms of reference of the directives. There is no suggestion that the *Jarawa* are offered any agency in the decisions being made about them, nor is their autonomy ever really under consideration. All of the choices listed in terms of future policy require active intervention on the part of the administration, and welfare measures are always on the cards. They also underscore the contradictions inherent in a process whereby the radical potential of the Indian judiciary is countered by other arms of the government executive, determined to maintain an undisturbed status quo. Moreover, the reality on the ground is foreboding and tells a somewhat different story. In an email communication after a visit to the islands in 2002, Mukerjee notes:

> *I learned that a massive team of anthropologists, zoologists, botanists, nutritionists, medical researchers, foresters, social workers and their assorted helpers, a total of sixty to ninety heads, was camped on Jarawa territory. "Its a picnic," reported one policemen. Cooks provided meals at three campsites, while other assistants fetched water, washed up and ran errands. (The Jarawa, if no one else were surely learning about social structures). Trash disposal was into the forest or the sea, and although toilet tents had been set up, most of the men preferred the beach, trusting the tide to cleanse it of their droppings.*

Mukerjee (2003) goes on to observe, "[t]he judges could scarcely have expected their thoughtful verdict to be put in place on such a thoughtless scale"(p. 212).

At the end of her visit Mukerjee despairingly notes:

> *I was told the Jarawa were getting just about every substance. Some of the women would vanish into the jungle with truckers who stopped on the road, for rewards unknown (and taking a generic route for the spread of AIDS), while young Jarawa men routinely begged for sukka, the popular form of chewing tobacco... I heard the aboriginals were getting alcohol and tobacco in exchange for their takings [from the forest], which were discreetly sold back to the public* (p.218).

In a parallel set of developments, Samir Acharya of SANE together with Kalpavriksh, an environmental action group and the Mumbai-based Bombay Natural History Society (BNHS) had filed another public interest case to stop the illegal harvesting of trees in the Onge reserve areas, documenting the deteriorating state of the environment throughout the entire islands. The wide-ranging Supreme Court verdict,[6] communicated to me in a celebratory email message from Sophie Grig of Survival International, delivered a blow to commercial forestry business interests in the Andaman Islands and, according to Mukerjee (2002), made Acharya the most hated man on the islands. Prior to issuing the ruling, the Supreme Court appointed an environmental expert, Professor Shekhar Singh, "to look into the state of the islands' forests and other related matters". At the end of the six weeks allotted to him to submit his report, Singh made extensive recommendations, which included many of Survival's key campaign objectives, namely, "removing the settlers from all the tribal reserves and forests, stopping all logging on the islands and the closing of the Andaman Trunk Road which had been built illegally through the Jarawa's reserve" (Grig 2002).

In an unforeseen move, the Supreme Court endorsed all of Shekhar Singh's recommendations. Sophie Grig conceded that while much had been achieved with the Supreme Court ruling, there were still major obstacles to overcome in terms of the actual implementation of the order, which Survival International would continue to monitor.

But, as Sekhsaria (2002) notes:

> *The court order comes at a significant juncture in the context of the on-going preparation of the National Biodiversity Strategy and Action Plan (NBSAP). Coordinated in the islands by the Andaman and Nicobar Island Environmental Team (ANET), the NBSAP has the potential to create a broad framework in which the future of the islands can be discussed debated and planned... allow[ing] for extensive multi-stakeholder participation... the challenge now is to find a creative way forward (p.4).*

On a more sober note are Sekhsaria's (2003) re-considerations in his epilogue, as the time frame given for the implementation of two of the key directives of the Supreme Court of India has passed without any hint of future implementation by the Andaman administration. Appraising the ongoing situation in the islands, Sekhsaria highlights what is at stake for the *Jarawa* and the future health of the island system in the Andaman administration's non-compliance with the orders. The closure of the Andaman Trunk Road (ATR) in the sections where it transgresses the *Jarawa* reserve, the declaration of the islands as an Inner Line Area with the issue of Islander Identity Cards, are central to protecting the indigenous groups and the fragile island environment, already strained well beyond its capacity.

Of origins and genetics

To add to the already complicated state of matters in the Andaman Islands, at the end of 2002 and early in 2003, a number of papers were published almost simultaneously in the journals *Current Biology* and the *American Journal of Human Genetics*. The articles published brought together various lines of evidence suggesting that the Andaman Islanders were the descendants of the earliest populations of modern humans who migrated out of Africa into Asia approximately sixty thousand years ago, remaining genetically isolated for tens of thousands of years through the cataclysms of the Ice Age and its aftermath. Musing on these developments, Samir Acharya of SANE expostulates:

> *Dr. Erika Hegalberg extracted mitochondrial DNA from the hair roots of some Andamanese hair collected by a British Civilian in the first decade of the last century, and compared it to the mDNA of other negrito people of the world. She found that the Andaman Negrito are closer to the East African bushmen than to the Asian or Australian Negritoes.*

209

Dr. Erika Hagelberg believes that the Andaman Negritoes being one of the earliest migrants from Africa probably hold the key to the very question of human ancestry. She postulates that the Andaman Negritoes had arrived in the Islands at least 40,000 years ago.

The Jarawas and the Sentinelese are the last two tribes that had maintained racial and genetic purity and avoided cultural contamination. They hold the key to the mystery of human evolution. Allowing contamination of their genetic and cultural purity would be like burning the library of Babylon again. Experts today recognise that the New World did not fall to the might of Spanish arms, it fell before the onslaught of European germs. Once again we are exposing a pristine race that is defenceless to our civilised pathogens. Extinction through an epidemic is a reality just a single infection away. The Jarawa has survived the measles epidemic but would they survive if the epidemic was of Syphilis, Hepatitis B or C or AIDS? Continued survival and well being of the Jarawa can only be ensured by banning all contact with the Jarawa, banning attempts like teaching them agriculture, fishing techniques and Hindi(!), evicting all encroachers from within the Jarawa Reserve. Banning construction of any facility near the reserve in the name of " tribal welfare" (http://www.andaman.org The Jar awa Case).

Leaving aside the heated debates that these publications have generated among scholars around the world, we have yet to discern the impact of this information on the existing state of affairs in the islands and on "the last of the planet's first humans" (Mukerjee 2003, p.241). It may provide the final springboard to accelerate the implementation of the Supreme Court order, or in a replay of the scenario described earlier by Mukerjee, bring in its wake scholars of various ilks clamouring for a piece of the action.

Collaborative anthropology: policy initiatives and new coalitions

I did return to the Andaman Islands in May 2004, a decade after I finished my fieldwork there, a trip that was unforeseen, brought about by reasons very different from my earlier visits. At a point in my life when my research in the islands was being archived into my past, while I embraced other issues in different locations, I was catapulted back into active engagement with the islands and its peoples once again.

The narrative of how this came about is located in a different site, in the networks of communication that exist in cyberspace, where scholars, journalists, activists and concerned individuals have shared information and kept abreast of events in the islands. Initiated and moderated by Pankaj Sekhsaria, this cyber forum was to play a crucial role in shaping events over the course of 2004.

To pick up the threads of the narrative from the preceding section, the Committee of Experts constituted by the Ministry of Home Affairs submitted their report in July 2003. The contents of the report were posted by Sekhsaria on a website[7] that included other reports, along with his own articles on the islands over the years. This ensured public and widespread access to a document that was deeply provocative in part, and presented a challenge to the Ministry in its efforts to maintain unchanged its administrative operations in the islands. Sekhsaria's actions countered government efforts to suppress the document, as well as to maintain tight control over and hence restrict the participants involved in the next stage of the High Court directives, namely a seminar convened to formulate policy on the *Jarawa*. According to the Court's directives, as evidenced in the quote below, the seminar(s) were to be convened after widespread public notification and were to include a large cross-section of participants.

For the aforesaid purpose, the Central Government shall arrange seminars and open discussions of the different experts, National and International on the line, Anthropologists, sociologists and others as also individuals and non-governmental organisations having knowledge and experience in the matter inviting them by issuing public notification in widely circulated news papers and sending them letter of invitation and thereafter shall frame the policy decision within the stipulated period after deliberation and discussion on such opinions with the approval of the concerned Ministry. The Central Government shall also publish the papers, discussions and deliberation of such seminar, at its cost, for future reference. The cost for such seminars shall be borne by the Central Government and the cost of travel, boarding and lodging of such experts, organisations and persons and of such research, survey, field work etc. shall also be borne by the Central Government.

It is made clear that for the aforesaid purpose, individuals as also organisation, governmental or non-governmental will be at liberty after issuing of such notification to submit their own opinion, views supported by cogent reasons and materials, in the said seminars also to be considered by the Central Government. (http://www.andaman. org The Jarawa case).

In a typical display of bureaucratic bravado, the Ministry dragged its feet about publicly announcing the dates for the seminar that was to be convened in the city of Kolkata, cancelling the first proposed dates, and leaving sufficient uncertainty about the next ones in an attempt to stall and discourage potential travellers to the venue.

It is at this point that I was inserted into the narrative by an email from Madhusree Mukerjee, alerting me to the significance of the proposed seminar. As an active participant in Sekhsaria's discussion group, Mukherjee had been following the events in the islands since she completed her research there, and had kept me periodically informed about the most important developments. Initially dismissive of any significant outcomes from such a gathering,[8] I quickly changed my mind as I followed the discussions and comprehended the implications of government efforts to muzzle opposing voices by restricting those invited or permitted to speak at the forum. Exploring the possibility of obtaining funding for the travel from the university where I was located in New Zealand, I finalized my plans to attend the seminar and make myself heard at the proceedings.

A core sub-group developed within Sekhsaria's web-based discussion group of those who had taken the time to read the expert committee reports and who were determined, at whatever cost, to storm the seminar if necessary and strategize to ensure that their views would be made known at the proceedings. Coordination with representatives from Survival International meant that they too were apprised of the implications of the forum and could respond accordingly.

It is useful at this stage to pause and examine more closely that part of the report submitted by the Committee of Experts that posed a problem, and the reasons for the consternation it generated within the Ministry and the government bodies whose operations it regulated. The member of the committee who created the stir was Mr. K.D. Saxena, former Secretary in the Ministry of Social Justice and Empowerment. As a retired but respected civil servant with a reputation for his personal integrity, his inclusion within the 8-member committee did not merit any comment. However, the dissenting note that he submitted revealed the lack of consensus within the committee and, more disturbing, the dynamics of power among its members that impacted on its democratic operation. His note with a separate draft policy attached to it, went on to critique the basis for some of the conclusions arrived at by the Health team and proposed a radical overhauling of the tribal welfare organization (AAJVS). He strongly endorsed the closure of the stretch of the ATR that directly traversed the *Jarawa* reserve, and proposed a constitutional amendment to guarantee for perpetuity the rights of the *Jarawa* to their forest base. His dissenting stance enabled another member of the committee from the ASI to finally put in writing his opposition to the ATR and recommend its closure too.

Far-reaching in its sweep and intent, Saxena's note provided the peg to rally together all the opposing voices and give them a blueprint for an alternate and humane policy. The fact that such a policy had emerged from within a committee constituted by the Ministry posed a problem of sufficient magnitude for the government to attempt to suppress the document and limit its dissemination.

The sub-group of 5 that emerged from Sekhsaria's discussion group, of whom I was one, consisted of an interesting mix of academics, activists, journalists and NGOs, located in India and overseas. Brought together by our research and writing about the islands and its peoples, we were energized by our awareness that here was an opportunity to finally make a difference to the lives of the islanders, and one group in particular, the *Jarawa*.

Our presence at the Kolkata seminar, despite attempts to block our entry, completely changed the tenor of the proceedings. We were the only ones present who had actually read the report or were familiar with its content and, as a coordinated pressure group, raised questions and insisted that we be permitted a space to speak to the proceedings. Hence, the challenge provided by Saxena's report could not be hidden from public view. At a gathering that received coverage by the national media, our presence changed the agenda of the conference and ensured that the forum had to take note of the dissenting reports and the alternate policy framework proposed therein. Furthermore, the press conference that we organized for the following day meant that the issues we raised continued to be covered by the media in the ensuing weeks, and reminded the government that we were serious about making ourselves heard.

The conclusions from the Kolkata seminar, which are listed below, fell well short of the recommendations contained in Saxena's draft policy, or those pressed for in Survival International's campaign. Some significant gains had been achieved, particularly in the last two points listed below, but it was clear that the government reserved for itself the right to intervene in the lives of the Jarawa, and would not condone the closure of the ATR. While grudgingly admitting the need for more accountability within all the administrative bodies pertaining to tribal welfare, the framework of welfare itself remained unaltered. Hence, there was much more work yet to be done, and it would have to be accomplished before the next proposed seminar, at which the final policy recommendations were to be hammered out.

1. *Since the Jarawas, numbering only 266, are in an unparalleled situation, they should be perceived and treated as a unique human heritage.*
2. *In the background of the historical experience of dealing with the aboriginal tribes, especially Great Andamanese and the Onges, the approach of maximum autonomy to the Jarawas, and measured interven-*

tion by the Government will be practiced towards the Jarawas. Bringing them to the mainstream and assimilation will not be desirable at this stage of their social development. Rehabilitation of Jarawas in separate islands/locations will not be desirable.

3. A reconstituted AAJVS will advise the Administration regarding the Schemes and measures for the protection and welfare of all aboriginal tribes including the Jarawas.

4. The quality of intervention will be carefully managed through suitably trained and re-oriented personnel, in consultation with and evaluation by anthropologists and experts. The objective will be to avoid dependency syndrome and to ensure their development as a vibrant social group. The personnel working for Jarawas would be provided proper training and sensitized.

5. Periodic health survey of the Jarawa community will be organized through a standing team of health professionals. Only cases needing intensive care may be brought to the hospital but they will be kept in separate enclosures. Appropriate food will be provided instead of the hospital meals. Whenever female Jarawas come or are brought to hospital, female police will be posted invariably.

6. Permanent residence of' Government employees/non tribals in the Jarawa reserve will not be allowed.

7. Provisions of PAT Regulation will be used more effectively. Accountability of officials of different Departments dealing with Jarawa issues may be ensured.

8. Tourists will not be allowed to visit/interact with them so that curious intrusions are avoided.

9. Nutritional and food security survey of the Jarawas will be conducted every year.

10. Codification of the language of the Jarawas may be done with the advice and involvement of ASI. Documentation of their families may also be maintained.

11. Use of Andaman Trunk Road (ATR) will be strictly regulated, thereby limiting the traffic to the essential purposes of supplies and emergency evacuation of patients and persons.

12. Documents about aboriginal tribal policies and events etc. may be properly kept.

13. Periodic review of this policy may be done so that the policy is dynamic and takes into account changing needs and circumstances.

14. A suitable empowered arrangement for enforcements and monitoring the implementation of the policy may be created.

Return to Port Blair

The next seminar, to be convened 6 weeks later, was to be held in Port Blair. And that is how I returned to Port Blair just as the monsoon arrived in the Andaman Islands late in May 2004. But this time with a formal invitation from the Ministry of Tribal Affairs and as a guest of the Andaman administration, along with the others who had stormed the first seminar in a bid to present a united but opposing front there. It meant making a second trip from New Zealand, a point that generated a degree of amazement from the authorities, who also noted the determination to ensure that our views and recommendations be documented and heard.

We were still enthused by an awareness that the situation presented an important opportunity that should not be lost. Thus, the group that crystallized prior to the first seminar continued to work together and in tandem with each other. Madhusree Mukerjee, in consultation with Saxena, drafted an alternate policy framework for the Jarawa and the other islanders, which was to be submitted jointly at the Port Blair gathering. The rest prepared individual submissions that built on the points contained in the alternate framework, and continued to strategize on how best to insert them into the proceedings if we were not allotted individual slots as speakers within the forum.

As the flight skidded to a halt on the runaway at Port Blair, I noted the first point of difference, the runaway had been extended: the hill that had stood at the end of the earlier much shorter one had disappeared. There was no further need to sit nervously at the edge of one's seat wondering whether the brakes would be applied in time before the face of the hill loomed before the nose of the aeroplane. I scanned the streets and buildings trying to reconcile my mental map with the current configuration of the town. Port Blair had been enormously built up over the decade since my departure from its shores, it was virtually unrecognizable. I had 4 days in Port Blair, two of which would be spent at the seminar, and the other two planning strategy with the others of the group, in order to once again ensure that we presented a coordinated and coherent set of interventions at the seminar. I wondered whether I would run into any of the Onge as I walked around Port Blair, perhaps Lichu would still be living somewhere in town.

Lichu, too, was an invited guest at the seminar and I puzzled over the role she would play at the proceedings. She appeared a much sadder and more subdued person, not as voluble as she used to be, wiser perhaps, more resigned, the years had taken their toll. I asked her what her thoughts were about the *Jarawa*, what wouldshe suggest as the best course for them. Her answer shook me: the *Jarawa* should be transported from where they were in Middle and South Andaman and relocated elsewhere, on some other island, just like the Andamanese had been earlier. The Andamanese were none the worse for it, so the *Jarawa* would be fine too. This would solve all the current tensions around the ATR, and put an end to the unending round of conflicts between the settlers and the *Jarawa* once and for all.

My initial stunned silence was followed by a spate of reasoned arguments to demonstrate to her how disastrous such a course would be for the *Jarawa* and then I checked myself. Did I have the time to convince her otherwise in the few minutes I had before the seminar commenced; had she been schooled by the administration, was that why she was invited to the proceedings, to demonstrate to the rest of the world how much at odds the views of one of the "tribals" were with those of the well-meaning proponents of the *Jarawa's* rights to their forest?

I cast worried glances at her from across the room where I was seated, wondering when she would be asked to say her piece. Meanwhile, in a shrewd move calculated as a pre-emptive strike, the organizers had filled the entire morning's agenda with speakers and elected representatives from the settler communities on the islands, everyone of them arguing, vehemently and loudly against the closure of the ATR. If the extent of resistance to that recommendation was to be demonstrated by the volume of sound generated, and the numbers stacked against it, the administration had succeeded very well.

In another surprising move over the course of the rest of the proceedings, the Ministry accepted in its entirety the Alternate Policy Framework drafted by Mukerjee and submitted jointly by us, as well as the draft policy recommendations drawn up earlier by Saxena in his dissenting note. The 3 key concepts of sensitivity, minimality and accountability that had informed the joint submission, and around which the policy recommendations had been constructed, became the administration's new catch phrases for referring to their future plans for the *Jarawa*. Perhaps that should have warned us but the bubble of euphoria that buoyed us along as we savoured our success at the seminar was to evaporate slowly only later, as reality crept in with the other developments in the months to come.

Lichu never spoke at the seminar; she was the token "tribal" present during the proceedings to demonstrate how inclusive the administration was in its list of invitees. In yet another gesture, she was asked to close the proceedings in the couple of minutes she was given, after the lengthy speeches from the stalwart luminaries also present at the concluding session.

The battle ahead

Sekhsaria's cyber forum remains active, keeping abreast of the developments on the islands. Its membership has swelled to about 400, many actively involved in debating and articulating their views. And there is much to debate in the subsequent months, with the government announcing its plans for tourism developments in the islands, followed by a proposal to embark on oil exploration. "It's an all-out assault," despaired Mukerjee in a recent email. The Ministry's strategy of co-opting and silencing the opposition was demonstrated in its announcement of the new board for the tribal welfare agency, which entailed a mere expansion of the existing board with a chosen few who could be relied on to speak the administration piece and not cause too many ripples. The new structure for the overhauled organization proposed in the joint submission and in Saxena's recommendation, which would ensure that it remained accountable and efficient, is never mentioned and has disappeared altogether from the administrations plans. Saxena, who remains grimly watchful of these developments, cautions that the only recourse is to go back to court. Samir Acharya, too, is waiting and biding his time, wary of the shape of things to come.

And what of the *Jarawa*, who remain invisible and distant from the scene of these strategies and maneuvers that, will impact on their lives and determine their futures? While unwilling to tolerate the closure of the ATR, the administration has increased the area allocated to the *Jarawa* by including a section to the right of the ATR, in another typical gesture that looks good on paper but resolves nothing.[10] But what of their day-to-day lives and their futures? Or the Sentinelese, how safe are they in their remote island 'strong-hold'? My brief visit to Port Blair allowed me access to some recent and revealing footage that underscored the continuing vulnerability of both the *Jarawa* and the Sentinelese, despite any decisions that are being taken in the political centre-stage. One showed the ongoing clearing of a section of the denoted forest[11] within the *Jarawa* reserve by a forest officer who, when queried about his actions, responded that he was only following orders from higher authorities within the administration. The other footage, equally gut-wrenching in what it presages, was taken when the former Chief Secretary to the islands commissioned a trip for his visiting family and friends to North Sentinel islands, the sound track recording his voice urging the boatman to go closer ashore where the Sentinelese were lined up, while observing that there was nothing to fear from them any longer, the fierce Sentinelese were harmless.

As matters stand, the Andaman Islanders, and in particular the *Jarawa*, are poised on the threshold of a precarious future that could utterly destroy them. But, if the coalitions that have been forged over the past months can withstand the several battles that lie ahead, the *Jarawa* may yet have another lease of life, perhaps finally on their own terms, as they venture into the new millennium.

I want to end this account of the Andaman Islanders, spread over more than a decade, with a proverb that garners the wisdom of another indigenous people, the Mâori, whose own ongoing battles provide an example of what *can* be achieved:

> *Hutia te rito o te harakeke*
> *Kei hea te k_mako e ko*
> *Ki mai k_ ahau*
> *He aha te mea nui o t_nei ao*
> *Maku e ki atu*
> *He tangata, he tangata, he tangata*

This proverb translates as: *if you pull out the central stalk of the flax plant,* (so that it dies),[12] *where will the bell bird sing?*[13] If you were to ask me, what is the most important thing in this world, I will say to you, it is the people, it is the people, it is the people.

Extrapolating this proverb to the context of the *Jarawa*: if we fail to protect the forest in which the *Jarawa* live, the forest they have kept intact for thousands of years, we destroy not only the forest but also all that which confers beauty on this world in which we live; namely the songs of the birds, as well as the most important *taonga* or treasure we are given in this world: we destroy a people. ❏

Notes

1   The saying translates as: We should look backwards, so we can determine how to go forwards.

2   In the same week that I revelled in successfully defending my PhD thesis, which is narrated in the preceding pages, and went on to celebrate the continued hostility projected by the *Jarawa*, a small act of kindness faraway in the forests of the Andaman Islands was to prove to have profound long-term consequences.

3   Thus, pointing to the continuing lack of clarity in communication with any of the indigenous groups in the islands, despite claims to the contrary.

4   An organization based in London that advocates for the rights of indigenous peoples (http://www.survival-international.org).

5   Mr. Awaradi's Master Plan had been gathering dust within the tribal welfare agency for the past 2 decades. It is interesting that it should be referred to at this time by the High Court as a basis for future policy. It also makes one wonder about the directives emerging from the courts, simultaneously progressive but also limited in their terms of reference where policy pertaining to the *Jarawa* is concerned.

6   See Seksaria (2002) for a more detailed discussion of the various cases brought to court pertaining to forestry in the Andaman islands, and the court rulings on the matter.

7   The informative website is an excellent public source of reports from the various committees.

8   I reminded her of the junket I had participated in during my research and the futility of taking such events seriously. "This one is different," she insisted, "there will be people listening and taking note of what is said."

9   The Andaman and Nicobar Protection of Aboriginal Tribes Regulations of 1956.

10   As noted by Sekhsaria recently in an email communication,, the change merely reinstated the area previously demarcated as *Jarawa* reserve forests.

11   Sekhsaria's presentation at the Port Blair seminar using satellite imagery was a stark illustration of the extent to which the only original and intact forest cover left in the islands was the area demarcated as the Jarawa reserve. Hence, as he demonstrated in his compelling argument, the twin needs of environmental protection and the protection of the Jarawa life-world neatly coincided.

12   The flax is a very important plant for the Maori, it has sacred, medicinal and very practical uses, and many protocols for how the plant is harvested. The leaves that are used are always taken from the sides of the plant, never from the centre, because that is the heart of the plant.

13   The song of the bell bird is one of the most beautiful and haunting sounds of the NZ native bush and forest.

A Final Word From Samir Acharya

Many complain, and not without reason, that the treatment meted out to the Jarawa by our welfare state is not in accordance with the maxims of democracy, equity or the declared principles of a welfare state. 266 people out of a nation of 1,020 million would have no political clout even if they were street-wise, adept in the technique of walking the corridors of power.

The Jarawa are the most misunderstood community in the Andamans. An average Islander considers them to be a race of savage, ferocious, wanton killers. In 2002, we had a long dialogue with En Mey, the Jarawa ambassador of goodwill. We asked him why they used to attack the non-tribals. En Mey told us that the Jarawa believed that we would have killed them otherwise. So, they appear to have killed in self-defence. And when we look at the record of our shooting, electrocuting and setting fire to their huts, we cannot blame them.

The Jarawa do not know that they are the constituents of a thriving democracy. Or that there are special laws to protect them. They do not know how to use our legal system to obtain relief by utilizing an adversarial system of criminal jurisprudence. So, when a Jarawa is injured in a road accident in their own territory by a vehicle that entered the Reserve illegally, he does not get the compensation that all Indian citizens are entitled to. When a Jarawa woman was purportedly raped in a government hospital where she was undergoing treatment, most of the legal provisions were violated. The law demands that an officer of the rank of Deputy Superintendent or above should investigate, she should be paid compensation immediately and should be medically examined. Each of these provisions was flouted. A mere Assistant Inspector "recorded" her statement. The officer could not speak the Jarawa dialect and the victim could speak neither Hindi nor English. The Jarawa do not know that they have an exclusive habitat called the Jarawa Reserve. So, they do not lodge a complaint when someone enters their area illegally. A long list of the victims of Jarawa atrocities is available from the Police. But there is no record of the countless Jarawa killed by the "civilized", as the Jarawa never file a FIR (First Information Report) in the nearest Police Station.

Our welfare state, driven by a guilt complex, makes ever-larger allocations for the welfare of the Jarawa. Money that gets spent buying air-conditioners that do not cool a Jarawa body, computers they do not use, carpets they have never stepped on, cars they do not travel in, ships and boats they have never sailed on board.

In an experiment performed by the Expert Committee appointed by the Calcutta High Court, scientists made a few Jarawa and a few Indian policemen run up and down some steps quickly and recorded the pulse, respiration rate and blood pressure of the subjects before and after the exercise. While the data pertaining to the policemen showed a marked increase, that of the Jarawa hardly varied. I strongly believe that the physical survival of the Jarawa will not be in doubt in their own habitat if we stop infecting them with our 'civilized' germs and allow them to maintain their territorial integrity. We must close the Andaman Trunk Road.

Raising awareness among the Andamanians is of prime importance. People such as Dr. Sita Venkateswar are trying to achieve this. She is one of the few who has studied them over a period of time. We need people like her to come forward and take up the challenge of raising awareness among the Islanders and administrators, and mobilizing public opinion, both national and international.

The Roman Emperor Claudius the God is known to have said, "Wise birds do not foul their own nests, not even nests captured from other birds". The Jarawa had been practising this for millennia before him. A recent study of the Andaman forests by the Forest Survey of India found the Jarawa Reserve to be the best preserved forest in the islands with a high bio-diversity. Claudius the God was also known as Claudius the Fool. Perhaps, that is why we have managed to foul the forests and the territories captured by us from the Andaman Tribes.

The Jarawa have the custom of putting an infant born out of wedlock to death, particularly if sired by a non-Jarawa. We know of at least three such cases during the last four years. Destroying one life in a community of just 266 is alarming. We are so concerned about the high rate of female foeticide in some parts of India, yet a much higher rate of Jarawa infanticide has failed to attract our attention. We know of 5 Jarawa who have become disabled in road traffic accidents, which equates to 2% of their population. And yet, the Andaman Trunk Road (ATR) remains open.

In recent times, certain positive steps have been taken by the Administration, such as enlarging the Jarawa Reserve, removing encroachers, inducting some experts into the AAJVS, etc. But much more needs to be done. The ATR needs to be closed. In order to oversee the overseers, a small group of non-officials with the authority to access records and oversee the officials engaged in Jarawa welfare or administration of the reserve is essential. It is very important for such a group to be totally non-official in order to ensure avoidance of political pressure.

India does not consider the tribes alone to be indigenous. We say that all Indians are indigenous. But in the Andaman & Nicobar Islands, the continued presence of non-tribals has a history of only one hundred and sixty years. In the Islands, the tribes are the only indigenous community. They are the first people. If we fail to protect them, History will not forgive us.

Samir Acharya
SANE (Society for Andaman and Nicobar Ecology)

November 2004

BIBLIOGRAPHY

A. A. J. V. S.
1978 *Retrieval From Precipice*. Andaman Adim Janjati Samiti. Port Blair.

Abu-Lughod, L.
1991 "Writing Against Culture." In *Recapturing Anthropology: Working in the Present*. Richard G. Fox, ed. Pp. 137-162. Santa Fe: School of American Research Press.

Acharya, S.
1997-2004
       In "Appendix N1: The Jarawa Case." From *The Lonely Islands*. Electronic document. http://www.andaman.org

Ali, F.I.
1999 "Official Kiss of death for ancient Andaman tribe." *The New Indian Express*, Sunday, October 17.

Ali, R. and Andrews, H.
n.d.   *Casefile: Andamans Report*. Electronic document. http://www.indianjungles.com/case4801.htm

Anthropological Survey of India
n.d.   *Jarawa Tribes--Confluence of the Present with the Past*. Electronic document. http://www.angelfire.com/az/ausaf/jarawa.html

Appiah, A.
1991 "Is the Post- in Postmodernism the Post- in Postcolonial?". *Critical Inquiry* 17:336-357.

Arnold, David.
1988 *Imperial Medicine and Indigenous Societies*. Manchester: Manchester University Press.

Barabas, A. and Bartholeme, M.
1973 *Hydraulic Development and Ethnocide: The Mazatec and Chinantec People of Oaxaca, Mexico*. Copenhagen: International Work Group for Indigenous Affairs (IWGIA).

Basu, B. K.
1990 *The Onge*. Calcutta: Seagull Books.

Bedi, R.
1999 "Modern world may be death of tribe." *Dominion*, October 11

Berkofer (Jr), R.F.
1978 *The White Man's Indian: Images of the American Indian from Colombus to Present*. New York: Alfred A. Knopf.

Berreman, G.
1962 "Behind Many Masks."*The Society for Applied Anthropology Monograph* 4:1-24.

Biolsi, T.
1995 "The Birth of the Reservation: Making the Modern Individual Among the Lakota." *American Ethnologist* 22(1):28-53.

Blauner, R.
1972 "Internal Colonialism and Ghetto." In *Racial Oppression in America*. Pp. 82-110. New York: Harper Row.

Bodley, J. H. (Ed)
1988 *Tribal Peoples & Development Issues: A Global Overview*. California: Mayfield Publishing Company.

Bourdieu, P.
1977 *Outline of a Theory of Practice*. J. Goody, ed. Cambridge Studies in Social Anthropology. Cambridge: Cambridge University Press.
1990 *In Other Words. Essays Towards a Reflexive Sociology*. Stanford: Stanford University Press.

Chakraborty, D. K.
1974 *Great Andamanese---Study of Persistence of Culture in the Face of Biological Extinction*, Port Blair: Anthropological Survey of India, unpublished MS.
1990 *The Great Andamanese: Struggling for Survival*. Calcutta: Seagull Books.

Chattopadhyay, M.
1992 "My Encounters with the Jarawas." *The Sunday Statesman, Miscellany Section*, November 22: 1-5.

Chiñ_as, B. N.
1992 *The Isthmus Zapotec: A Matrifocal Culture of Mexico*. Fort Worth: Harcourt Brace Jovanovich College Publishers.

Cipriani, L.
1954 "Report on a Survey of Little Andaman 1951-52." *Bulletin of the Department of Anthropology* (Calcutta) 1:61-82.
1961 "Hygiene and Medical Practices Among the Onge (Little Andaman)." *Anthropos* 56:481-500.
1966 *The Andaman Islanders.* New York: Frederic A. Praeger.

Clifford, J.
1983 "On Ethnographic Authority." *Representations* 1((2)):118-146.
1986a "On Ethnographic Allegory." In *Writing Culture: The Poetics and Politics of Ethnography.* J. Clifford and G. E. Marcus, ed. Pp. 1-26. Berkeley: University of California Press.
1986b "Introduction: Partial Truths." In *Writing Culture: The Poetics and Politics of Ethnography.* J. Clifford and G. E. Marcus, ed. Pp. 1-26. Berkeley: University of California Press.

Cooper, Z.
1989 "Analysis of the Nature of Contacts with the Andaman Islands During the Last Two Millenia." *South Asian Studies* 5:133-147.

Crosby, A. W.
1986 *Ecological Imperialism: The Biological Expansion of Europe 900-1100.* Cambridge: Cambridge University Press.

Dasgupta, S.
1996 "No Penny for the Onges?" *Down to Earth,* January 15: 13.

Deleuze, G. and Guattari, F.
1990 "What is Minor Literature." In *Out There: Marginalization and Contemporary Cultures.* M. Gever R. Ferguson, T. Minh-ha and C. West, ed. Pp. 59-70. Cambridge: The MIT Press.

Dobson, G. E.
1874 "On the Andamans and the Andamanese." *Journal of the Anthropological Institute* 4:457-467.

Doyle, A.C., Sir
1977 *The Sign of the Four.* Garden City, N.Y.: Doubleday.

Dumont, J. P.
1978 *The Headman and I.* Austin: University of Texas Press.

Dwyer, K.
1977 "On the Dialogic in Fieldwork." *Dialectical Anthropology* 2:143-151.

1992   "Science Visualized: E. H. Man in the Andaman Islands." In *Anthropology and Photography*. E. Edwards, ed. Pp. 108-121. New Haven: Yale University Press.

Ehrenreich, J. D.
1985   *Contact and Conflict: An Ethnographic Study of the Impact of Acculturation, Racism and Benevolent Ethnocide on the Egalitarian Coaiquer Indians of Ecuador*. Ph.D Dissertation, New York, Dept. of Anthropology, New School of Social Research.

Escobar, A.
1984-85   "Discourse and Power in Development: Michel Foucault and the Relevance of His Work to the Third World." *Alternatives* X (Winter):377-400.
1995   *Encountering Development: The Making and Unmaking of the Third World*. Princeton: Princeton University Press.

Escobar, T.
1989   *Ethnocide: Mission Accomplished?* Copenhagen: International Work Group for Indigenous Affairs (IWGIA).

Falk, R.
1988   *The Rights of Peoples (In Particular Indigenous Peoples)*. Oxford: Clarendon Press.

Ferguson, J.
1994   *The Anti-Politics Machine: Development. 'Depoliticization' and Bureaucratic Power in Lesotho*. Minneapolis: University of Minnesota Press.

Ferguson, R. B.
1990   "Blood of the Leviathan: Western Contact and Warfare in Amazonia." *American Ethnologist* 17(2):237-257.

Fischler, C.
1980   "Food Habits, Social Change and the Nature/Culture Dilemma." *Social Science Information* 19(6):937-953.

Fitzgerald, T. K.
1980   "Dietary Change Among Cook Islanders in New Zealand." *Social Science Information* 19(4/5):805-832.

Foucault, M.

1983 "The Subject and Power." In *Michel Foucault: Beyond Structuralism and Hermeneutics.* H. L. Dreyfus and P. Rabinow, ed. Pp. 208-226. Chicago: University of Chicago Press.

Galanter, M.

1984 *Competing Equalities: Law and the Backward Classes in India.* Delhi: Oxford University Press.

Gardner, P. M.

1991 "Forage's Pursuit of Individual Autonomy." *Current Anthropology* 12(5):543-571.

Geertz, C.

1988 *Works and Lives. The Anthropologist as Author.* Ph.D. dissertation. Stanford: Stanford University Press.

George, R.

1991 *Ethnocide: The Cost of Development.* LL.M Dissertation, Boston, Massachusetts, Harvard Law School.

Gilmore, D. D.

1990 *Manhood in the Making: Cultural Concepts of Masculinity.* New Haven: Yale University Press.

Grig, S.

2002 Personal communication by email.

Guha, R.

1991 *The Unquiet Woods: Ecological Change and Peasant Resistance in the Himalaya.* Delhi: Oxford University Press.

Guha, R. and Gadgil, M.

1989 "State Forestry and Social Conflicts in British India: A Study in Ecological Bases in Agrarian Protest." *Past and Present* 123:141-177.

Hannerz, U.

1992 "Cosmopolitans and Locals in World Culture." In *Global Culture: Nationalism, Globalization and Modernity.* M. Featherstone, ed. pp. 237-252. London: Sage Publications.

Haraway, D.

1988 "Situated Knowledges: The Science Question in Feminism and Privilege of Partial Perspective." *Feminist Studies* 13(3):575-599.

Haydon, T. and Jones, R.
1978 *The Last Tasmanian.* (Video recording). North Sydney: Artis Film Productions.

Headland, T. and Reid, L. A.
1989 "Hunter-Gatherers and Their Neighbours from Prehistory to the Present." *Current Anthropology* 30(1):43-66.

Hechter, M.
1975 *Internal Colonialism: The Celtic Fringe in British National Development, 1536-1966.* Berkeley: University of California Press.

Jameson, F.
1984 "Postmodernism, or The Cultural Logic of Late Capitalism." *New Left Review* 46:53-92.

Joos, S. K.
1984 "Economic, Social and Cultural Factors in the Analysis of Disease: Dietary Change and Diabetes Mellitus Among the Florida Seminole Indians." In *Ethnic and Regional Foodways in the United States: The Performance of Group Identity.* L. K. Brown and K. Mussel, ed. Pp. 217-237. Knoxville: University of Tennessee Press.

Kaplonski, C.
1994 Personal communication.

Kennedy, J. G.
1978 *Tarahumara of the Sierra Madre. Beer, Ecology, and Social Organization.* Arlington Heights: AHM Publishing Corporation.

Krupat, A.
1994 *Native American Autobiography: an anthology. Madison: University of WisconsinPress.*

Kuklick, H.
1991 *The Savage Within: The Social History of British Anthropology, 1985-1945.*Cambridge: Cambridge University Press.

Kumar, N.
1992) *Friends, Brothers and Informants: Fieldwork Memoirs of Banaras.* Berkeley: University of California Press.

Lancaster, R.
1992) *Life is Hard: Machismo, Danger and the Intimacy of Power in Nicaragua*. Berkeley: University of California Press

Leacock, E.
1982 "Relations of Production in Band Society." In *Politics and History in Band Societies*. Cambridge: Cambridge University Press.

Lee, R. B.
1994 "The Hunters: Scarce Resources in the Kalahari." In *Conformity and Conflict: Readings in Cultural Anthropology.* J. P. Spradley and D. W. McCurdy, ed. Pp. 111-125. New York: Harper Collins College Publishers.

Lee, R. B. and DeVore, I. (Eds).
1968 *Man the Hunter.* Chicago: Alden Publishing Company.

Lizot, J.
1976 *The Yanomami in the Face of Ethnocide*. Copenhagen: International Work Group for Indigenous Affairs (IWGIA).

Majumdar, R. C.
1962 *British Paramountcy and Indian Renaissance Part I.* Bombay: Bharatiya Vidya Mandir.
1975 *Penal Settlement in Andaman*. Gazetteers Unit, Dept. of Culture, Ministry of Education and Social Welfare. New Delhi: Government of India Press.

Man, E. H.
1885) "On the Andaman Islands, and Their Inhabitants." *Journal of the Anthropological Institute* 14:253-272.

Marshall, M.
1979 *Weekend Warriors: Alcohol in a Micronesian Culture*. Palo Alto: Mayfield Publishing Company.

Mason, B. S.
1994 "An Archipelago in the Bay of Bengal." *New York Times, Travel*, Sunday, October 30: 6-7.

Maybury-Lewis, D.
1981 "Some Lessons in Cultural Survival." *Odyssey Magazine*. Boston, Publishing Broadcasting Association: 72-73.

Mbembe, A.
1992 "The Banality of Power and the Aesthetics of Vulgarity in the Postcolony." *Public Culture* 4(2):1-30.

Mintz, S. W.
1985 *Sweetness and Power. The Place of Sugar in Modern History*. New York: Penguin Books.

Mouat, F. J.
1863 *Adventures and Researches Among the Andaman Islanders*. New Delhi: Millat Publications.

Mukherjee, M.
1995 "Tribal Struggle. Stone Age Guardians of the Andaman Islands Fight to Survive." *Scientific American* 272(5):17-20.
2002 Personal communication by email
2003 *The Land of the Naked People: Encounters with Stone Age Islanders*. Boston, New York: Houghton Mifflin Company.
2004 Personal communication by email

Mukhopadhyay, K.
2004 Personal communication

Mynott, Adam
2004 *Unique Tribe on Edge of Extinction*. Electronic document. http://news.bbc.co.uk/2/hi/programmes/from_our_own_correspondant/3593989.stm.

Nair, C. T. S.
1989 "Environmental Issues in Forest Land Use in the Andaman Islands." In *Andaman, Nicobar and Lakhsadweep: An Environmental Impact Assessment*. C. J. Saldanha, ed. pp. 94-111. New Delhi: Oxford Publishing Company.

O' Hanlon, R.
1988 "Recovering the Subject: Subaltern Studies and Histories of Resistance in Colonial South Asia." *Modern Asian Studies* 22(1):189-224.

Okely, J.
1991 "Defiant Moments: Gender Resistance and Individuals." *Man* n.s. 26(1):3-22.

Pandit, T. N.

1985 "The Tribal and the Non-Tribal in Andaman Islands: A Historical Perspective." 20:111-131.

1989 "Tribal Policy in the Andaman and Nicobar Islands: The Impact of Nehru's Philosophy." In *Jawarharlal Nehru, Tribes and Tribal Policy*. Pp. 83-92. Calcutta: Anthropological Survey of India.

1991 "Close Encounters with the Stone Age." *Sunday Review. The Sunday Times of India*, April 28: 1-2.

Pandit, T. N. and Chattopadhyay, M.

1989 "Meeting the Sentinel Islanders: The Least Known of the Andaman Hunter-Gatherers." *Journal of the Indian Anthropological Society* 24:169-178.

Pandit, T. N. and Sarkar, B. N. (Eds).

1994 *People of India: Andaman and Nicobar Islands, Volume XII* Anthropological Survey of India. Madras: East-West Affiliated Press.

Pandya, V.

1993 *Above the Forest: A Study of Andamanese Ethnoanemology, Cosmology, and the Power of Ritual*. Delhi: Oxford University Press.

1992 Personal communication

n.d. Deforesting Among Andamanese Children: Political Economy and History of Schooling. pp. 1-18. http://www.vancouver.wsu.edu/fac/hewlett/Pandya.htm. 1/4/2003.

Portman, M. V.

1899 *A History of Our Relations with the Andamanese* Compiled from Histories and Travels and from the Records of the Government of India. New Delhi: Asian Educational Services.

Prain, D.

1932 "Memoir: Edward Horace Man C. I. E. 1846-1929." In *E. H. Man, The Nicobar Islands and Their People*. London: Royal Anthropological Institute (RAI).

Probyn, E.

1990) "Travels in the Postmodern: Making Sense of the Local." In *Feminism/Postmodernism*. L.J. Nicholson., ed. Pp.176-189. New York: Routledge

Radcliffe-Brown, A. R.

1964 *The Andaman Islanders*. New York: Free Press.

Rosado, R.
1989 "Imperialist Nostalgia." In *Culture and Truth: The Remaking of Social Analysis.* Pp. 68-87. Boston: Beacon Press.

Sahlins, M.
1973 *Stone Age Economics.* Chicago: Aldine Atherton, Inc.
1994 "Cosmologies of Capitalism: The Trans-Pacific Sector of "The World System." In *Culture/History/Power.* G. Eley and S. Ortner N. Dirks, ed. Pp. 412-456. Princeton: Princeton University Press.

Saldanha, C. J. (Ed).
1989 *Andaman, Nicobar and Lakshadweep: An Environmental Impact Assessment.* New Delhi: Oxford Publishing Company.

Santuary Asia
n.d. http://www.santuaryasia.com/resources/biogeozones/island.php.

Sarkar, J.
1990 *The Jarawas.* Calcutta: Seagull Books.

Savard, R. J.
1968 *Culture Stress and Alcoholism: A Study of Their Relationship Among Navajo Alcoholic Men.* Ph.D. Dissertation, Department of Mental Health, Minneapolis, University of Minnesota.

Scheper-Hughes, N.
(1987)"The Best of Two Worlds, the Worst of Two Worlds: Reflections on Culture and Field Work Among the Rural Irish and Pueblo Indians." *Comparative Study of History and Society* 26(3):56-75.

Schrire, C.
1984 *Past and Present in Hunter Gatherer Societies.* Orlando: Academic Press.
1995 *Digging Through Darkness: Chronicles of an Archaeologist.* Charlottesville: University Press of Virginia.

Sekhsaria, P.
1999 "Embracing Disease." *Down to Earth,* October 31: 16.
2001) Tribal Africans in India: A History of Alienation. Electronic document.
http://www.raceandhistory.com/historical views/01102001.htm.
2002 "Logging Off, for Now." Electronic document. FrontlineVol. 19(1). http://www.flonnet.com./fl1901/19010650.htm.

2003 *Troubled Islands. Writings on the indigenous peoples and environment of the Andaman and Nicobar Islands.* India: Kalpavriksh and Lead India.

Sen, Satadru
2000 *Disciplining Punishment: Colonialism and Convict Society in the Andaman Islands.* Delhi: Oxford University Press.

Sharpe, J.
1994 "The Unspeakable Limits of Rape: Colonial Violence and Counter Insurgency." In *Colonial Discourse and Post-Colonial Theory.* P. Williams and L. Chrisman, ed. Pp. 221-243. New York: Columbia University Press.

Singh, S.
1995 "The Treasured Islands." *Indian Express,* Sunday December 3.

Spivak, G.
1988 "Can the Subaltern Speak?" In *Selected Subaltern Studies*, R. Guha and G. C. Spivak eds. pp. 3-32. New York: Oxford University Press

Stocking, G. W. Jr.
1984 "Radcliffe-Brown and British Social Anthropology." *History of Anthropology* 2:131-191.

Tennant, C. C. and Turpel, M. E.
1986 "A Case Study of Indigenous Peoples: Genocide, Ethnocide and Self-Determination." *Nordic Journal of International Law* 59(4):287-319.

Tomas, D.
1987 *An Ethnography of the Eye: Authority, Observation and Photography in the Context of British Anthropology 1839-1890.* Ph.D. dissertation, Montreal, Dept. of Anthropology, McGill University, Ph.D thesis.
1991 "Tools of the Trade: The Production of Ethnographic Observations on the Andaman Islands." In *Colonial Situations: Essays on the Contextualization of Ethnographic Knowledge. History of Anthropology* Volume 7. George W. Stock Jr, ed. Pp. 75-108. Madison: University of Wisconsin Press.

Turnbull, C. M.
1972 *The Mountain People.* New York: Simon and Schuster.

Venkatesan, S.
1990 "Ecocide or Genocide." *Cultural Survival Quarterly* 14(4):49-51.

Visweswaran, K.
1994 *Fictions of Feminist Ethnography.* Minneapolis: University of Minnesota Press.

Weber, G.
1997-2004
    The Lonely Islands. http://www.andaman.org

Whitaker, R.
1985 *Endangered Andamans: Managing Tropical Moist Forests: A Case Study of the Andamans.* Environmental Services Group. India: WWF-India and MAB India, Dept. of Environment.

Whitaker, R., and Whitaker
1984 "The Andaman Tribes---Victims of Development." *Cultural Survival Quarterly* 10(2):13-18.

Whitaker, Z.
1985 "A Cry for Survival: The Jarawa Tribals." *The India Magazine,* April: 64-70.

Whitten, J. N. E.
1976 *Ecuadorian Ethnocide and Indigenous Ethnogenesis: Amazonian Resurgence Amidst Andean Colonialism.* Copenhagen: International Work Group for Indigenous Affairs (IWGIA).

Wiener, M.
1999 "Pay No Attention to the Man behind the Curtain": Irreverent Notes on Gender and Ethnography. *Anthropology and Humanism* 24(2):95-108.

Wiggins, M
1989 *John Dollar.* New York: Harper & Row.

Williams, R.
1994 "Selections from Marxism and Literature." In *Culture/History/Power.* G. Eley and S. Ortner N. Dirks, ed. pp. 585-608. Princeton: Princeton University Press.

Wilmsen, E. N.
1989 *Land Filled with Flies: A Political Economy of the Kalahari.* Chicago: University of Chicago Press.

APPENDICES

DRAFT POLICY ON JARAWAS FRAMED BY SHRI K.B. SAXENA, ONE OF THE MEMBERS OF THE EXPERT COMMITTEE ON JARAWAS

With reference to the notings at page 149-150 of the Report of the Expert Committee on Jarawas of Andaman Islands submitted to the Hon'ble High Court of Calcutta, Government of India and Andaman & Nicobar Administration, the draft policy as framed by Shri K.B Saxena one of the Members of the Expert Committee is circulated by placing it in the Andaman & Nicobar Administration's website: www.andaman.nic.in.

(S.A.Awaradi)
Director (TW)
09.10.2003.
F.No. 11-27/AAJVS/2003(PF-III)

1. INTRODUCTION

Andaman Islands have been home to a number of negrito tribal groups of whom four survive in varying strength. Of these four, the Jarawas are inhabiting the western side of South and Middle Andaman. Their mode of subsistence is through hunting and gathering using simple and eco-friendly technology. The Jarawas until recently lived in isolation and displayed 'hostility' to outsiders who made incursions into their territory, exploited their resources or interfered with their way of life. However, since October 1997 they have come out of this isolation and within a short span of more than five years have been thoroughly exposed to the outside world. This happened so suddenly that the Administration had not thought out the likely situations this contact of the Jarawas with larger non-tribal population would produce and, therefore, had not made any prior preparations on how various contingencies arising therefrom could be handled. The intervention of the Honourable High Court in the context of a PIL triggered the process of working out an approach to deal with them. As the situation began to get unfolded, multifaceted adverse impact on the Jarawas and their vulnerability to social and economic exploitation began to emerge. This has caused anxiety about their well being. It has, therefore, become necessary to deal with the problems and predicaments faced by them comprehensively, lest it hurts the tribe irreparably and even threatens their survival. This exercise has produced a policy for protection of the Jarawas, the first ever policy for a hunter and food gatherer tribe.

2. REASONS FOR MAKING A POLICY?

After witnessing the impact which the contact with the outside world has produced on the Jarawas, it was realized that ad-hoe measures for dealing with the problems arising therefrom would neither be sufficient nor effective. It would be necessary to tackle the situation in its entirety. This called for efforts to articulate whole gamut of issues and designing of measures to address them. This exercise in policy making on the Jarawas has been the outcome of this process. There are several reasons why a detailed policy concerning the Jarawas inter-face with the outside world is necessary. These are:

- The Jarawa tribe is coming out from its erstwhile 'hostile' response to outsiders entering into their territory, extracting resources from it or otherwise interfering with their life. This may remove the deterrence to such action that has existed so far.

- The sudden exposure to multi-faceted contact with outside world has created such enormity of adverse and harmful impact on them that they may suffer slow and early extinction if corrective measures are not taken.

- The Jarawa Tribal Reserve has been created for exclusive use of the Jarawa tribe considering their social, organization, mode of subsistence, way of life and cultural values. But this territory is being violated by outsiders for encroaching upon their land, accessing forest produce and fishing in the coastal waters for extracting marine resources. This has threatened the life supporting system and survival base of the Jarawas and, therefore, needs to be stopped.

- Ever since their exposure to the outside world, the Jarawas have been sucked into the vortex of social and economic forces unleashed by the glare of attention, curiosity, commercial interests, tourism, which have already produced damaging consequences for the people of the tribe, their way of life and their future. Measures are necessary to insulate them from these influences.

- A great deal of ecological degradation has been taking place in and around the Jarawa habitat on account of number of factors such as human settlements, encroachment, indiscriminate and unauthorized extraction of forest produce and marine resources, extraction of sand from the beaches, hunting of animal'S for meat, etc. The land use policies and the forestry operations carried out have also had damaging impact on the environment. This affects the Jarawas vitally since the source of their subsistence gets adversely affected. The restoration of ecological balance is required for their sustenance.

- Going by the past experience in relation to other tribes, in particular the Onges, the Jarawa tribe could also become intended or unintended victim of certain policies and programmes undertaken by the Govt. for development of the islands and/or meeting the social and economic needs of the neighbouring population. As the Jarawas constitute a very tiny social group they do not possess the necessary clout and power to influence such policies and programmes in their favour. Therefore, a mechanism of protection against such policies and processes is essential.

- The Jarawas are among the very few classical communities of foragers left in the world who are still pursuing their traditional way of life unspoilt by the processes of modernization. There is, therefore, world wide attention to protect this most precious heritage of mankind. This protection is also a matter of pride for the country as also for the other inhabitants of the islands. It would be an acid test for vindicating the policies of the Govt. towards such groups.

3. OBJECTIVES OF THE POLICY

The following are the objectives of the Policy

- To insulate/protect the Jarawa from harmful and potentially disastrous effects of sudden and multi-faceted exposure and contact with the outside world.

- To preserve the social organization, mode of subsistence, cultural identity, life style and value system of the Jarawa community against direct or indirect, intended or unintended pressures on them to conform to 'mainstream' society.

- To protect the Jarawa community from policies and programmes which may turn out to be detrimental to their survival and dignified existence.

- To reach medical help to them to prevent mortality and morbidity in case of their sudden affliction to diseases which their system is unaccustomed to.

- To conserve the ecology and envirownent of their territory and strengthen their life supporting systems in order that they could pursue their traditional mode of subsistence and way of life.

- To prevent any measure which directly or indirectly subjugates the Jarawas to the demands of the larger social aggregates or the authority structures of the Govt, pressures them to conform and lowers their self esteem and confidence.

- To ensure that policies and programmes concerning the larger population and the nation do not disturb the Jarawas in any manner or has any adverse/damaging effect on their survival with dignity.

- To ensure that situation and circumstances experienced by other hunter and food gatherer tribes, in particular Onges, are not repeated in case of the Jarawas.

- To sensitize settler communities around their habitat and other non-tribal population about the need to preserve such an ancient community as the Jarawas in its traditional form and to appreciate their unique culture and values.

4. POLICY: THE CONCEPTUAL FRAME

The Jarawas are a tiny community of less than 300 persons. Within their own society they are well-knit, cohesive and self-reliant. But their social organization is very fragile when confronted with societies built around modem technology and complex social organization. This inequality is also reflected in the thought processes and behavioural responses of the two communities. The policy to deal with the vulnerability of the Jarawas in this situation needs to be dealt around elaborate protection. This protection would encompass three aspects:

- It would secure their territory and subsistence resource base against continuing attempts at reduction of their territory and ever increasing attempts at poaching, smuggling and encroachment.

- It would insulate them to the extent possible against outside contact which threaten the autonomy of their social and cultural life

- It would put in place effective institutional arrangements so that any assault on their interests can be resisted.

The Jarawas have been afflicted with some diseases unknown to them through their contact with the outside world. Their existing knowledge and technology are not in a position to meet health hazards which can cause sudden demographic collapse. They have also acquired some harmful practices which pose health hazards or are detrimental to the pursuit of their way of life. Therefore, in some of these areas, minimum interventions may become necessary.

Both protection and intervention would call for adequate capacity and organization within Govt. to discharge this responsibility. Governance, therefore, emerges as key to pursue these objectives.

Thus the policy on the Jarawas is built around the pillars of Protection, Intervention and Governance.

PROTECTION: THE RESOURCE BASE

TERRITORY

1. Securing rights to territory	A Tribal Reserve has already been notified for exclusive use of the Jarawas through notification issued in 1956 and revised in 1979. State shall fully secure the rights of the Jarawas to this territory, their unhindered movement in it and pursuit of - their sustenance derived from its resources. It shall also create stringent legal foundations for embedding these rights.
2. Incorporating the area used for foraging outside the Reserve	It shall identify through appropriate surveys consistent with their social organization and mode of subsistence activities, and mode of movement areas outside this Reserve which the Jarawas still use for their foraging activities and other needs and shall secure their rights to such territory so that they can carry on with their traditional life style without any infringement.

3. **Demarcation of the Jarawa Reserve**	State shall ensure that the Jarawa territory is fully and effectively demarcated and cadastral maps prepared accordingly. The boundaries of the Jarawa tribal Reserve shall be depicted on the ground by erecting sufficiently high and brightly coloured pillars so that they are clearly visible to any person approaching the area as well as the enforcement agencies.
4. **No curtailment of the Reserve territory**	State shall not curtail or reduce the Jarawa Tribal Reserve. It shall not acquire any land which pertains to the territory secured for the Jarawas and central to their survival either for its own needs or for the needs of larger segments of population of Andaman islands or outside groups whether for security, development or economic growth.
5. **Removal of encroachment**	State shall identify, with the help of non-official organizations, public spirited citizens, conservation experts, social activists, areas of Jarawa Tribal Reserve which have been encroached upon. It shall remove forthwith all such encroachments and restore the land to the Jarawa Tribal Reserve. It shall also make stringent arrangements to ensure that such encroachments do not take place in future.
6. **Empowered Authority to deal with infringement of rights**	State shall constitute an authority which would have within its governing structure eminent anthropologists and other experts who have knowledge of social organization, economy and culture of the Jarwas and empathy with them. This body shall be empowered to look into complaints or instances referred to it or initiate suo-moto action on matters which allege

interference with the rights to territory or have the effect of reducing the territory, restricting their movement orinterfering with pursuit of their subsistence activities and take whatever measures necessary to protect interests of the Jarawas expeditiously and effectively.

FOOD SECURITY

7. **Mechanism for monitoring status of food resources**

State shall put in place a mechanism to estimate periodically the status of food resources the Jarawas consume and the rate of their depletion in respect of the three regions which the Jarawas inhabit. It shall also determine to what extent this resource depletion is affecting their food security and nutritional requirement and posing a threat to their survival and health. This assessment shall be used for undertaking appropriate interventions, if, when and where necessary, after adequate consultation with and consideration by experts and discussion in the public domain, as prescribed.

8. **Arrangement for meeting water stress**

State, in consultation with anthropologists, shall encourage and facilitate the process of the Jarawas taking up, in harmony with their social organization, necessary eco-friendly measures for storage of perennial sources of uncontaminated water in their area of foraging and encampment with a view to eliminating the 'water stress' experienced by them in the sununer season. It shall also help the Jarawas develop simple and locally manageable methods for making the water available in their area clean enough for drinking purposes.

9. **Natural regeneration of food resources**

The State shall pursue natural regeneration of food resources endemic to the area used by the Jarawas for their subsistence without any outside interference. It shall not introduce any species, floral or faunal to the area. Activity, if any, undertaken in the past for establishing horticultural plantations, etc. shall be discontinued.

POACHING AND SMUGGLING

10. **Safeguarding the Jarawa Reserve**

State shall rigourously safeguard the Jarawa Reserve territory against any activities, whether by locals of Andaman islands or outsiders, for occupying the land or extracting various items of forest produce, meat animals and marine resources. It shall pursue effective action against unscrupulous elements who manipulate to involve innocent Jarawas into those activities. It shall creatively engage the Jarawas in this process of protection as partner and source of valuable information and vigilant surveillance.

11. **Strengthening enforcement efforts against poaching**

State shall undertake at the earliest in-depth review of existing legal and regulatory provisions for protection of the Jarawa territory and resources and the status of their enforcement with a view to tightening efforts for stopping poaching and smuggling activities. It shall make existing laws and regulations more stringent and shall strengthen the infrastructure of enforcement machinery in different organizations with mobility and adequate resources, both financial and manpower. It shall also revamp justice delivery system to obtain expeditious and deterrent punishment to the offenders. It shall look into the existing arrangements of surveillance and shall reinforce them suitably.

12. Institutional Structure for coordination and monitoring

The task of enforcement is handled by multiple agencies, Forest, Coastguard, Defence, Police, Tribal Welfare, Fisheries, etc. and requires a great deal of co-ordination to be pursued effectively. A very high powered authority in A&N Administration headed by the Lt. Governor shall be created to effectively accomplish this task. A sharply focused monitoring mechanism shall be designed by this authority to fix responsibility of each agency to assess on a continuing basis the impact of their performance in respect of tasks assigned to it. The authority shall issue directions to enforcement agencies and undertake such other interventions as necessary to achieve the objectives outlined in this policy. Where intervention at the level of Govt. of India is required, the Lt. Governor shall take up the matter with the concerned Ministry or Organization.

It is recognized that the work relating to enforcement requires high degree of public cooperation for getting satisfactory results. The Administration shall create institutional arrangements for peoples' participation and modalities of information sharing with them. This task shall be handled with transparency to get good results.

13. Closure of ATR for traffic

Andaman Trunk Road passes contiguous to, and in some cases through, the Jarawa Tribal Reserve. This road has increased access to the Jarawas, poses the greatest threat to the Jarawas as well as THE forest that they have protected for so many years. After the Jarawas have come out of their isolation, this road has increased contact with outsiders enormously resulting in the most damaging impact on their lives. State shall, therefore, close the road to all vehicular and other traffic as per recommendations of the Shekhar Singh Committee approved by the Honourable Supreme Court and shall proceed to develop alternative means of transport for convenience of the population and the administration. This step would help in checkmating the harmful effects which the current exposure of the Jarawas has created on account of the ATR and persuade them to go back to their territory to pursue their traditional way of life unhindered by pressures to the contrary generated by it.

14. Restriction on entry in the Jarawa Reserve

State shall make stringent provisions to ensure that no person except for the Jarawas is allowed to enter the Reserve by any means unless he/she is permitted by the competent authority designated by the A&N Administration for this purpose. No such permission shall be granted unless the person is proceeding on bonafide work relating to the welfare of tribals or protection of the area.

CONCEPTUAL FRAME

15. Identity and autonomy to be maintained

State fully recognizes that contact of the Jarawas with the outside world poses serious threat to their survival which has also been borne out of the recent experience. It also shares with the perception of national and international experts that such contact would exert direct and indirect pressures on the Jarawas to conform to the norms of behaviour and values of dominant conununities around them and may result in their demographic collapse like some of the other tribes of the Andaman islands. The constitution of India and Govt. policies enunciated for the tribes from time to time have guaranteed freedom to such groups to preserve their distinct identity, cultural values, way of life, social organization, mode of subsistence and the manner of pursuit of their interests. State is, therefore, committed to preserve and protect the rights of the Jarawas in this regard and firmly believes that the future of the Jarawas is entirely for them to decide. It shall ensure that the Jarawas are allowed fullest autonomy which would enable them to choose the way they would wish to develop their relations with the rest of the world. As their social organization is inseparably linked to their physical environment and the resource base therein, they would be allowed unhindered access to resources of their necessity and maintain social and economic system they have developed'in the course of long human evolution.

16. Jarawas to be left alone to decide their future

State is deeply conscious of the vast gap that separates the Jarawas from the rest of the society in respect of mode of subsistence, social and cultural organization, value system and norms of behaviour. In the current state of their existence, therefore, they are not in a position to strike a balance between their traditional way of life and the pattern of living which the larger society surrounding them practices. The Jarawas cannot exercise a rational and informed choice about the elements of other cultures they should adopt and in the process discard some of their own. This has been demonstrated by the harmful practices on their pattern of behaviour which the recent interface of the Jarawas with the non-Jarawas has produced. State shares the view that the Jarawas have the necessary wisdom to work out what is best in their interest. But they need time free from pressures and interference to deepen their understanding of the outside world in the detached life of their traditional environment. State shall, therefore, strive to promote this process by creating objective conditions in which the Jarawas can be persuaded to go back to their life and creatively contemplate on their experience of the recent contact as also their future.

17. Need for sensitizing non-Jarawas

State is aware that the task of protecting the Jarawas cannot be accomplished without adequately sensitizing the larger population which surrounds them. It would, therefore, strive to comprehensively educate the non-Jarawa population about the need for and pride in allowing an unique group of foragers like the Jarawas to survive and grow without any interference in their way of life, social organization and system of subsistence. It would also seek their active cooperation and creatively engage them in this endeavour.

PROTECTION - INSTITUTIONAL ARRANGEMENTS
CHECKMATIONG ADVERSE PRESSURES AND DECISIONS

18. High Power Body to scrutinize projects from Jarawa angle

State appreciates that certain development, economic and security related activities intended to be taken up in the Andaman islands may have adverse impact on the Jarawas and the pursuit of their traditional way of life. State shall, therefore, set up a high powered, strong and effective body with statutory sanction. This body would be empowered to scrutinize all such projects and programmes in Andaman islands in terms of their likely impact, long-term and shortterm, on the survival of the Jarawas and autonomy to pursue their way of life and also to mobilize opinion for undertaking necessary corrective interventions. This body shall also be authorized to issue clearance in respect of such projects/programmes from the 'Jarawa' angle. Where, after consideration this body establishes/confirms that impact of such activities on the Jarawas is likely to be adverse, State shall ensure that such schemes, programmes and projects are revised, replaced or abandoned in order to accommodate concerns regarding the Jarawas.

19. Advisory Body for A&N Administration

State shall constitute a, standing body of experts not belonging to Govt. organization, who have knowledge and experience regarding tribes in the Andaman islands, desired sensitivity and possess impeccable reputation for their integrity to advise A&N Administration in matters concerning the Jarawas referred to them or initiated suo-moto to protect their interests.

20. Policy making process to be embedded in Governance This policy on the Jarawas has been made through an elaborate process which involved seeking advice of experts, subjecting such advice to a thorough discussion in the public domain and thereafter designing this policy as a transparent exercise. State agrees to follow this sequence for policy making on hunter and food gatherer tribes of A&N islands in future. Accordingly, it shall direct that this process be embedded in the structure of governance of the Island Administration. This process shall also be adopted for initiating and scrutinizing regulatory, development and welfare programmes for the Jarawas so that authentic advice concerning them is available to the Administration.

21. Non-Govt. pressure group for advocacy State would welcome emergence of any organization consisting of eminent citizens and experts who share the concern for the Jarawas as an entirely Non-govemmental Watch group for advocacy to convey frank and genuine views to Govt./Administration on matters concerning the Jarawas. It may also bring to their notice any decision/action taken in respect of them which may rum out/ has turned out to be harmful along with suggestions for corrective action. The A&N Administration shall cooperate with such a group in discharging this responsibility and furnish necessary information to it for this purpose.

22. Study on the impact of modern medicine on Jarawa Immunity System — State shall have in-depth study carried out with the help of experts from anthropology and medicine regarding the impact of modem medicine on the physiology of the Jarawas, with a view to evolving an approach to diagnosis and treatment of various diseases Jarawas suffer from which does not do any damage to their immunity system and enables them to strengthen their resistance to diseases.

23. Standardization of diagnostic methods and prescription drugs — State shall also direct experts to standardize diagnostic approach, treatment regimen and prescription of drugs in case of common pattern of diseases observed among the Jarawas so that experimentation by individual doctors and conflicting assessments among them can be avoided. Medical care records shall be mandatorily prepared in case of all the Jarawas seeking treatment.

24. Multi-therapy approach — Taking their unique situation into view, a multi-therapy (Homeopathy, Ayurveda, Ethnomedicine) approach would be tried under expert supervision to determine which system would suit the Jarawa constitution better for which complaint and would also be safer and convenient to administer in the overall interest of maintaining their sound health.

25. Consultation with experts for introducing immunization — The overall thrust of this policy is to drastically reduce the possibility of contact of Jarawas with the outside world and promote their return to their habitat and traditional way of life. State shall, therefore, undertake consultation with medical and anthropological experts about the suitability and desirability of introducing prophylactic measures, such as Universal Immunization and mass vaccination for Hepatitis-B as well as preventive measures in case of communicable diseases like Malaria, in the case of the Jarawas which are routinely administered to the target groups in the population.

26. Weaning away the Jarawas from addiction

State shall make all efforts to wean away the Jarawas from tobacco and alcohol addiction acquired by them as a result of contact with the outsiders. Suitable strategy would be evolved in consultation with experts for this purpose. It would be explored if any plant material in the Jarawa Tribal Reserve has de-addiction properties which can be used for this purpose.

27. Arrangements for medical treatment of the Jarawas

State shall ensure that for various diseases the Jarawas suffer from, the routine treatment would be given in their habitat itself and they would not be encouraged to come to the dispensary or doctors to seek it. A group of doctors would be identified who alone would be involved in treating the Jarawas with a view to developing comprehensive understanding about their health related problems and approach to their treatment. State shall organize effective mobile health teams to visit the Jarawa habitat periodically for routine health check up and medical attention. Serious cases observed during these visits would be shifted to the dispensaries and the hospitals Whenever the Jarawas need to be so hospitalized, effective arrangements shall be made to segregate them in a separate ward to protect them from the curiosity of and contact with the outsiders. During their hospital stay their cultural practices, such as those in relation to food, pattern of living, inter-personal relations, etc., would be respected except where demand of treatment itself warrants any deviation. Certain locations would be identified where dispensaries and wards exclusively catering to the Jarawas would be maintained to attend to serious cases of hospitalization and where a culturally safe and friendly environment for the Jarawas can be provided.

28. Development of ethno-medicine

State shall develop ethno-medicine of the Jarawas with a view to encouraging some degree of self-reliance among them, reducing their dependence on outside help, and for using it as the first stage of promotive and curative treatment in respect of their health related complaints of a less serious nature. It shall promote documentation of medicinal properties of forest flora and other resources used by the Jarawas and scientific validation of their potential for treatment of various diseases for this purpose. The knowledge of the Jarawas in relation to their ethno-medicine shall be protected as intellectual property so that it is not pirated and patented by any commercial organization in its name.

29. Nutritional balance through food consumption

Nutritional deficiency, if any, among the Jarawas shall be addressed by augmenting their food consumption from natural resources within their environment. The prescription of drugs as nutritional supplement would be avoided.

30. Safeguarding genetic profile of the Jarawas

State shall create a strong and effective mechanism to ensure that the confidentiality of genetic profile of the Jarawas is maintained and it is not used for commercial exploitation by pharmaceutical companies and scientific and medical research organizations. The norms of scientific and medical research would be suitably redefined and reformulated to make them more stringent in the context of their situation.

31. Longitudinal research in medicine

State shall promote longitudinal research in respect of health related problems of the Jarawas, particularly focusing on their immunity system, endemic diseases, concept of a balanced diet in their context, differential way in which their metabolism functions and reasons why their physiology does not manifest adverse clinical symptoms of various diseases associated with their food consumption pattern, such as heavy fat, lack of leafy vegetables, salt, sugar, oil and spices, etc. in their diet. The agenda of research shall be drawn up in consultation with experts. The system of medicine other than allopathy shall also be allocated areas of research taking into account their respective strengths.

COUNTERACTING HARMFUL PRACTICES

33. Weaning away Jarawas from harmful practices

Over a period of time various practices have entered the life of the Jarawas, some introduced as intervention by the Administration while others acquired through contact with outsiders which have produced adverse effects on the Jarawas. These practices include free distribution of food and other articles, use of metal and plastic containers for cooking and storage, horticultural plantation in the Reserve area, wearing of used clothes without washing, use of synthetic and cotton material for making adornments, use of inappropriate technology for resource extraction. It shall scrutinize these harmful practices and shall wean them away from them in a manner that does not hurt them and their environment. Appropriate strategy for this purpose shall be designed based on the advice of experts.

34. Developing methods of communication with the Jarawas

State shall take help of anthropologists and conununication experts to develop methods of conveying to the Jarawas the harmful effects caused by polluting agents, consumption of alien food, poisonous tubers, unclean water, intoxicants, use of garments gifted by others, pet dogs, etc. to their health and ability to forage for their survival in a manner that the community itself deliberates on these issues and takes decisions.

GOVERNANCE

35. Preparing a manual

A&N Administration shall prepare a Manual, with the help of experts duly approved by the apex Advisory body constituted to guide it, which will incorporate details of the Govt. policy on the Jarawas and the manner in which it will be implemented. It shall lay down detailed tasks for each agency, set up the structures of monitoring and specify mechanism for enforcing accountability of officials in respect of tasks assigned to them. The manual shall also indicate norms of behaviour to guide officials in their inter-face with the Jarawas.

36. Strengthening Tribal Welfare set up

A&N Administration shall create appropriate structures within its organization for ensuring that priority attention is given to the problems of the Jarawas amidst pressures of multifarious tasks it handles. The Administration shall also] undertake, with the help of Anthropological Survey of India, programmes to sensitize officials likely to come in contact with the Jarawas on how delicately they should handle matters concerning them. The set up of Tribal Welfare Deptt. would be appropriately streamlined and equipped with requisite capacity and status for this purpose so that it is in a position to command attention within the Administration in respect of problems faced by the Jarawas and matters connected to them. It shall be ensured that official heading the Dept. is selected with care, possesses necessary aptitude and commitment for this work and has a stable tenure. The deptt. shall have competent personnel with good track record, requisite sensitivity and adequate experience relevant to the work to provide assistance to senior officials in dealing with matters relating to the Jarawas.

37. Social audit of programmes taken up for the Jarawas

The State shall set up necessary arrangements to carry out, from time to time, social audit of the measures introduced for the Jarawas, both of a regulatory nature as well as those which provide certain services to them in order that critical and realistic feedback from an independent agency is available to it. The frame of this social audit shall be consistent with this policy and the methods for carrying it out shall be laid down in the manual. This social audit shall be carried out by non-official agencies which have people of high reputation and public spirit and possess necessary experience and orientation for this work.

38. Learning the Jarawa language

Officials of the A&N Administration who may be coming in contact with the Jarawas, particularly those of Health and Welfare, shall be mandated to learn their language so that they are able to communicate with them and understand their perceptions, reactions and problems.

39. Personal policy for handling the Jarawas

The stature, qualification and orientation of persons in Tribal Welfare agency, who may come in contact with the Jarawas, is very crucial as they would be the source of vital information concerning them to the Administration. Therefore, only adequately qualified, trained and sensitized anthropologists with aptitude for this work would be engaged in this task. They would be selected with care. Only a minimum number of such personnel shall be engaged. As for the personnel of other departments engaged in providing services to the Jarawas such as Health, detailed procedure shall be prescribed for their selection to ensure that they are suitable for this work and possess necessary sensitivity towards the tribe and aptitude for work concerning them.

40. Maintaining official Memory

Appropriate arrangement shall be made by A&N Administration to store and preserve all official documents and papers which relate to major decisions concerning the Jarawas so that this official memory could constitute a reference point for future decision-makers.

41. Action against abuse of rights

State is committed to safeguard, with all possible vigour, the Jarawas' right to their territory, resources for subsistence, good health and their unique way of life. It shall, therefore, sincerely and effectively implement this policy in letter and spirit so that this precious heritage of mankind is preserved. State shall, therefore, strongly deal with any abuse of their rights whether by Govt. or private agencies and shall take corrective measures most expeditiously and with the knowledge, consent and participation of the Jarawas themselves.

(CF: TS-Draft Policy on Jarawas (KBSaxena)

May 27, 2004
Submitted at the Jarawa Seminar, May 27, 2004, Port Blair

AN ALTERNATIVE FRAMEWORK FOR JARAWA POLICY

Submitted by a Group of Independent Experts & Observers

Drafted by Madhusree Mukerjee

The crisis of existence facing the Jarawa, combined with the Honourable High Court's directive to produce a thoughtful and well-considered policy for dealing with this exigency, provides an extraordinary opportunity. For the first time in India, and likely in the world, many heads-administrators, experts and concerned individuals-are coming together to think about how best to deal with a hitherto isolated tribal group, and, most important, to put a just and humane policy in place.

We hold that the premise in this discussion must always be that the best interests of the Jarawa have to be served. Lively debate exists on the means by which this might be accomplished-isolation or integration-and the present proposal does not claim to have all the answers. We take as a given, however, that the territorial rights of the Jarawa must be secured, in law and in practice, so that they have as much forest and coastline as they need to live well. Territorial and cultural integrity appears to be essential to the physical and mental health of a hunter-gatherer group. Let us not forget that thousands of years before we came, the aboriginals lived on the Andamans; their moral rights to the archipelago's resources outweigh ours.

Any final policy on the Jarawa should allow them a large measure of independence in choosing their own future. However, until a long-term vision for the Jarawa is finalized, we hold that the Jarawa need to be shielded from harmful outside influences. All dealings with the Jarawa, and indeed the other Andaman aboriginal groups, must therefore meet three criteria:

a) **Sensitivity:** All individuals dealing with the Jarawa and other Andaman and Nicobar aboriginals (including the Onge, Great Andamanese and the Shompen) must be trained and made aware of their cultural practices. These personnel must have respect for the validity of aboriginal practices as a means of survival in the island and forest enviromnent. Outsiders must not denigrate aboriginal practices or seek to impose foreign practices except for such cases as are essential for their survival.

b) Minimality: To minimize the chances of abuse, the least possible number of outsiders may deal with the Jarawa and all other aboriginal groups of the Andamans. Only the least possible number of outsiders should be allowed to enter the Jarawa reserve. Adequate care must be taken to ensure that outsiders do not transmit disease. Programs and other activity involving the aboriginals, including medical intervention, must be kept down to the absolute essentials and accomplished with minimal exposure to outside influences.

The Sentinel Islanders must be left completely alone and no attempts can be made to establish contact with them. Vigilance from a distance may be in order, however.

c) Accountability: Mechanisms must be put in place to swiftly and firmly deal with abuse of aboriginals by outsiders, especially if these outsiders are personnel who are entrusted with responsibilities regarding aboriginals. Individuals who have negative dealings with aboriginals must be suitably punished and never allowed near them again. Justice must not only be done but also be seen to be done.

With these principles in mind, we submit the following policy guidelines for dealing with the Jarawa. We further take this opportunity to suggest reform in other Andaman and Nicobar tribal regions. If this proposal passes muster, we would like to recommend in addition that a **Policy Panel** be formed to work out its detailed implementation. This Panel will preferably contain only three members: a senior member of the Andaman administration, a knowledgeable anthropologist and a senior, independent and concerned administrator as chairperson.

POLICY RECOMMENDATIONS:

1. The Honourable Supreme Court's recommendation on Inner Line regulations must be implemented on a war footing. The Andaman Islands are facing immense problems, most immediately water shortage and unemployment, because of unchecked immigration. Overpopulation impedes tribal security by increasing pressure on resources in the tribal reserves.
2. The Honourable Supreme Court's Order to close sections of the Andaman Trunk Road must be immediately implemented. In addition, the section of Jarawa forest east of the Andaman Trunk Road that was denotified in the 1970s may be restored to the Jarawa re-

serve. A suitable process for identifying this land should be initiated immediately. Increasing the territory of the Jarawa will better ensure their survival, help regenerate the forest and likely also improve the water situation on South Andaman.

3. An **Integrated Security Force** headed by the Lieutenant Governor needs to be formed to defend the Jarawa Reserve and other tribal reserves from poaching by land and sea. This Force needs to incorporate the principles of Sensitivity, Minimality and Accountability. It should include representatives from relevant departments such as Forest, Coast Guard, Defence, Police, Fisheries and others. Further, the boundaries of the Jarawa and other reserves need to be clearly demarcated. No authority can have bases within the Jarawa reserve. Strict guidelines need to be worked out on the extent to which personnel from any authority can enter the reserve in pursuit of poachers. Possibly the Jarawa themselves can assume to an extent their old task of defending their forest.

4. The administration must close legal loopholes that impede prosecution of poachers. Strict, effective penalties, including prison terms, must be introduced for poachers, for others who extract resources such as sand from the tribal reserves, and also for those having harmful dealings with the aboriginals such as offering intoxicants.

5. Strenuous efforts must be made to sensitize local populations to the rights of the Jarawas and other aboriginals, and to the dangers posed by harmful contact. Support for the Jarawa among the local population will be invaluable.

6. The AAJVS must be replaced by a new, streamlined organization that is passionately dedicated to serving the Jarawa and other aboriginal groups. For the moment let us call this organization the Andaman Adivasi Service Agency or AASA, which may be registered as a trust.

   We postulate the following structure for the AASA to incorporate the principles of sensitivity, minimality and accountability. The AASA will be run by an Executive Council of five members. The Council will have no ChairTnan but a Convener. Two of its members will be goverrunent officials, including the Lieutenant Governor, while three will be non-governmental. Council members will be required to make at least two unannounced spot checks a year of each and every tribal reserve served by AASA. In early stages, Council members will meet once in three months to resolve problems, and in later stages once in six months.

   The Executive Council will hire an Executive Officer who will be responsible for running the AASA. This Executive Officer will need to be not only sensitive but dynamic: this will not be a desk job. He or she will be in charge of hiring, training, deploying, overseeing and if necessary firing all employees. To enforce accountability it is necessary to stop not only the proliferation of personnel in the tribal reserves but also the proliferation of departments. To this end, the Executive Officer should be responsible for hiring and overseeing not only anthropologists and welfare personnel but also doctors and all other staff posted at tribal reserves.

To ensure minimality, we recommend that the Jarawa be served by three teams, one posted at Kadamtala, one at Baratang and one at Thiroor. Each team will contain a highly qualified and competent anthropologist, chosen by a nation-wide competition, who will serve as an interface between the Jarawa and the outside world. The team will also contain a highly trained and sensitized doctor. For the present moment we see no need for welfare staff serving the Jarawa. Only members of the Executive Council and Policy Panel, the Executive Officer, the resident anthropologist and the resident doctor may enter the Jarawa reserve. The staff requirements at other tribal reserves may be worked out by the Policy Panel.

7. An **Advisory Body** must be constituted with adequate expertise, including knowledgeable anthropologists, to advise the Executive Council on long-term policy regarding the Jarawa. The Advisory Body will be charged with developing a visionary and humane long-term policy regarding the Jarawa and other aboriginal groups. It will determine what the principles of Sensitivity, Minimality and Accountability mean in practice. The policy formulated by the Advisory Body will provide a framework allowing the Policy Panel, the Executive Council and the Integrated Security Force to solve day-today problems in a rational, consistent and guided manner. At present many questions remain unanswered, most importantly that of isolation versus integration. The Advisory Body is also entrusted with developing a long-term plan for research that meets the criterion of minimality but that can generate sufficient information to enable the Executive Council to formulate and revise policy periodically. The Advisory Body must within a year develop a long-term vision plan that incorporates not only questions of human rights but also the ecology and development of the Andamans as a whole. Until the Advisory Body is constituted, the Policy Panel will determine the implications of Sensitivity, Minimality and Accountability.

261

The proposal outlined above was formulated by Dr. Madhusree Mukerjee in consultation with a senior administrator who remains unnamed. It bears the consensus of a number of concerned individuals, experienced administrators and anthropologists who have looked far and wide for information and guidance relevant to the task at hand. We believe that, barring minor modifications, it will hold up to scrutiny and earnestly hope that it will be adopted as the policy toward the Jarawa and other threatened aboriginals on the Andaman and Nicobar Islands.

Samir Acharya
Society for Andaman & Nicobar Ecology (SANE),
C/o Tarang Trades, Middle Point, Port Blair - 744101.
Tel: 03192 - 232929 / 236014. Email: sane@andamanisles.com

Dr. Vishvajit Pandya
Professor, Dhirubhai Ambani Institute of Information & Communication Technology, Ahmedabad

Dr. Sita Venkateswar
Anthropologist, Massey University, New Zealand

Pankaj Sekhsaria
Kalpavriksh Environmental Action Group, Pune

Dr. Madhusree Mukerjee
Author, *The Land of naked People*, New York

Rasheed Yusoof
Vice President, Nicobar Youth Association, Nancowry

May 27, 2004
Submitted at the Jarawa Seminar, May 27, 2004, Port Blair

Acknowledgements

Fieldwork in the Andaman Islands was funded by a National Science Foundation Dissertation Improvement Grant (1991-1994), and a Graduate Research Fellowship from Rutgers University (1991). The writing of this ethnography for IWGIA was made possible by a MURF award from Massey University, which enabled me to take time off from my teaching responsibilities and complete the manuscript. I want to thank the anonymous reviewers in the IWGIA network, whose timely comments reinstated the many voices that people my ethnography. Sille Stidsen for gently steering my writing towards greater clarity. And finally, my friends and family whose support enabled me to withstand the dark moments of my research. This ethnography is dedicated to my daughter Cileme, named after the moonlight that irradiated the nights at Dugong Creek. And to my father who did not live long enough to see his daughter complete her dissertation. I can see you beaming with pride now, Appa.

264